T0313233

Gower Handbook of People in Project Management

Edited by
DENNIS LOCK
and
LINDSAY SCOTT

Routledge
Taylor & Francis Group

LONDON AND NEW YORK

First published in paperback 2024

First published 2013 by Gower Publishing

Published 2016 by Routledge
4 Park Square, Milton Park, Abingdon, Oxon OX14 4RN

and by Routledge
605 Third Avenue, New York, NY 10158

Routledge is an imprint of the Taylor & Francis Group, an informa business

Publisher's Note
The publisher has gone to great lengths to ensure the quality of this reprint but points out that
some imperfections in the original copies may be apparent.

British Library Cataloguing in Publication Data
Gower handbook of people in project management.
  1. Project management. 2. Personnel management.
  I. Handbook of people in project management II. Lock,
  Dennis. III. Scott, Lindsay.
  658.4'04-dc23

The Library of Congress has cataloged the printed edition as follows:
Gower handbook of people in project management / [edited] by Dennis Lock and
Lindsay Scott.
    pages cm
  Includes bibliographical references and index.
  ISBN 978-1-4094-3785-7 (hbk) -- ISBN 978-1-4094-3786-4 (ebk) --
  ISBN 978-1-4724-0299-8 (epub) 1. Project management. I. Lock, Dennis. II. Scott,
  Lindsay, 1974-
  HD69.P75G676 2013
  658.4'04--dc23
                                                                    2013000316

ISBN: 978-1-4094-3785-7 (hbk)
ISBN: 978-1-03-283693-5 (pbk)
ISBN: 978-1-315-58571-0 (ebk)

DOI: 10.4324/9781315585710

Contents

List of Figures

Notes on the Contributors

Alicia Arnold holds a Master of Science in Creativity, Innovation and Change Leadership from the International Center for Studies in Creativity at Buffalo State College and an MBA in marketing from Bentley University. She is a certified facilitator of the Osborn-Parnes Creative Problem Solving process and an invited presenter at the annual Creative Problem Solving Institute. Alicia has published on the topic of creativity with The National Association of Gifted Children, Businessweek and iMedia Connection. In her role as an award-winning, digital marketer she uses her passion for creativity and innovation to train teams on creativity techniques, develop breakthrough digital experiences and facilitate Creative Problem Solving (CPS) workshops for clients.

Sam Barnes ended his career as a front-end web developer to join what he calls 'the dark side of project management' and has now been working as a web project manager for almost ten years. In that time he has delivered many small, medium and large-sized digital projects that range from websites, web applications, mobile websites and native apps for clients including Dell, Oracle, BBC, Nokia, International Advertising Agency and Zebra Technologies. Sam is currently working as a web project manager at Global Personals, where he delivers projects for a global online dating and social discovery platform that serves over 14 million members (with a new member joining every four seconds). When not working in web project management, Sam writes about it on his blog at http://www.thesambarnes.com.

Jean Binder PMP, has considerable experience working in ICT, construction and R&D projects, in most of them living abroad and communicating in multicultural and multilanguage environments. He has particular experience of managing global projects, having implemented collaborative tools and techniques in a number of global organisations. The international project management framework that provides the basis for his two chapters is explained on the website www.globalprojectmanagement.org and also in his book *Global Project Management: Communication, Collaboration and Management Across Borders*, which received the Project Management Institute (PMI) David I. Cleland Project Management Literature Award (for the best project management book published in 2007).

Alfonso Bucero is founder and managing partner of BUCERO PM Consulting. Previously he managed IIL Spain and before that spent 13 years as a senior project manager at Hewlett-Packard in Madrid. Alfonso's memberships include PMI, ALI (Asociación de Licenciados, Ingenieros y Doctores en Informática), AEIPRO (IPMA member) and DINTEL's advisor. Alfonso was founder, sponsor and President of PMI's Barcelona chapter until April 2005. He was a member of the CoPAT (Congress Project Action Team) of PMI EMEA 2005 Congress in Edinburgh, 2006 PMI EMEA Congress in Madrid, and PMI EMEA Congress in Budapest. He graduated in the 'Leadership Institute Master Class

2007' on October 2007 in Atlanta (PMI Global Congress). He is an IPMA Assessor and received PMI's Distinguished Contribution Award in 2010. Alfonso has a degree in computer science engineering and at the time of writing was nearing completion of work for his doctorate in project management at the University of Zaragoza in Spain. He is a frequent international speaker and has delivered project management training and consulting services throughout the world. He has written many books and articles and is a contributing editor of PMI's *Network*.

John Cornish, a chartered marketer and Fellow of The Chartered Management Institute, enjoyed many years as a project manager in a high-tech electronics company that provided electronic equipment to defence and communications companies. John is now a director at Dorset-based Micro Planning International Ltd (MPI), responsible for sales and service across the whole of Europe. MPI offer the project planning and resource scheduling software Micro Planner X-Pert (probably the only software available that can run either activity-on-node or activity-on-arrow critical path networks). John's company also offers customer support, training on the fundamentals of project management and related consultancy work. Other MPI companies deliver Micro Planner X-Pert sales and support worldwide. John sees communication as a common thread running between his career as a project manager and chartered marketer. He believes that clear communication (combined with active listening by all concerned) is one of the key foundations for successful and rewarding projects.

Geof Cox has over 25 years of international experience as an organisation change and management development consultant as the Principal of New Directions Ltd and a partner in Learning Consortium BV. He works with public, private and not-for-profit organisations in Western, Central and Eastern Europe, USA, the Middle East, AsiaPAC and Africa. Geof has a BSSc from the Queen's University of Belfast, is a Chartered Member of the Chartered Institute of Personnel and Development and a Fellow of the Chartered Management Institute. Before establishing his own consulting business he had a successful career both as a line and HR manager with Exxon, and ran a training and video production company in Edinburgh. As a business writer and author his recent titles include *The FT Essential Guide to Negotiating*, *Getting Results Without Authority* and *Ready-Aim-Fire Problem Solving* as well as his own regular newsletter, *Cuttings*.

John Cropper has worked in the not-for-profit sector for over 20 years first with The British Council in Spain and Vietnam, and then with Oxfam (where he was Regional Programme Manager for Central America, Mexico and the Caribbean for three years and went on to manage its project management systems). He ran a global programme on gender and governance before joining LINGOs – Learning in NGOs – where he is the Director of Project Services. He is passionate about project management in NGOs and believes that can make a massive contribution to reducing poverty and suffering. John helped to develop PMDPro (a certification for NGO project managers). He helped to establish (and sits on the board of) PM4NGOs – the NGO that owns PMDPro. He is also the Vice Chair of Anti-Slavery International.

Dave Davis, PMP and PgMP is a project and programme manager and a recognised professional in leadership and project management. With over 30 years' experience as a manager, project manager, programme manager, business analyst and knowledge manager, Dave understands the challenges of being a project leader and the associated stakeholder relationships. He holds three Master's degrees including an MBA from Xavier University and the eBusiness Project Management Certificate from the University of British Columbia. He has published many articles and delivered presentations at conferences throughout Europe and North America. Dave has held many different roles within PMI including the charter sponsor for the Western Lake Erie Local Chapter, chairman of the eBusiness Special Interest Group, a contributor to PMI item writing and standards committees and most recently, he created the Leadership in Project Management Community of Practice.

Jocelyn S. Davis co-founded Nelson Hart LLC (www.nelsonhartllc.com), a woman-owned consulting firm, in 2002 and is an adjunct professor at the University of Maryland, Clark School of Engineering, Project Management Center for Excellence. Her consulting practice focuses on helping organisations in all sectors and industries to build great places to work through the application of positive psychology. She developed and teaches two innovative applied positive psychology courses: Managing Project Teams and Evolving as a PM Leader. These courses incorporate the most recent research and practice from positive psychology, the science of how people flourish. She presents to various audiences on applied positive psychology and well-being at work in the project management workplace.

Kevin Dolling is a senior consultant with the company New Habits where he operates as a coach, trainer and business consultant. Previously he worked for over 35 years in one of the world's largest financial institutions in a variety of management and consultancy roles. His final project involved taking a lead role in the creation of a corporate business school. He has extensive expertise, skills and knowledge, in the learning and development arena and has worked closely with some of the world's leading business schools (IMD, LBS, INSEAD and DUKE), commissioning customised executive leadership and management programmes for top talent populations. Kevin is committed to helping others develop both personally and professionally. He has an MBA and is professionally qualified as an ACIB. He is an NLP practitioner, MBTI (Myers-Briggs Type Indicator) practitioner, and has various psychometric accreditations. He is a member of the Association for Coaching and ANLP.

Deanne Earle helps companies to bridge the project/organisation gap and increase their project transition success rate. She established Unlike Before Ltd in 2005 and works with clients internationally on projects that trigger organisational change, particularly in complex or critical IT projects over a very wide range of industries. From a business IT background she balances a comprehensive approach with a pragmatic understanding of business drivers and financial targets and constraints. Deanne has a particular interest in emotional intelligence and understands well the project challenges of language and cultural diversity combined with geographical spread. She has written eBooks and is the force behind the popular *Change Through Action* blog. She has judged the IPMA Young Project Manager Award for two consecutive years and her White paper *Principles for Intelligent Transition* has established readership across the international project management community.

Tim Ellis is head of the Programme Management Office at Kensington and Chelsea and leads the Tri-Borough Portfolio Office – a major transformation of services across three London authorities. He also has a key role in accelerating the development of effective project and programme management (PPM) across the public sector as the Head of Profession for PPM, which is sponsored by the Local Government Association and SOLACE (the Society of Local Authority Chief Executives). Tim's other special interests include benefits realisation, senior leadership and PMOs. He co-authored the benefits guidance in the Public Sector Programme Management Approach, a Guide to Governance, *Five questions every Chief Exec should ask about change* and has also written about using communities of practice to develop project management capability. He reviewed a number of Cabinet Office Best Practice Guides and is a member of the steering group for the Association for Project Management (APM)'s PMO Special Interest Group.

Dr Steven Flannes is principal of Flannes & Associates (www.flannesandassociates.com), who provide innovative professional development services to project and programme professionals. He is co-author of *Essential People Skills for Project Managers*, a book that has been translated into Russian and Japanese. He also presents seminars on topics related to the people side of project management throughout the United States and Canada, as well as in the UK, Poland and Ukraine. Dr Flannes is experienced in operations and project management in a number of industries, which he combines with his original training as a clinical psychologist to create his special focus on the people side of project management. Dr Flannes is a regular PMI-SeminarsWorld and Global Congress presenter. His current interests are found in innovative processes and methods for maintaining high levels of project performance within demanding and changing project environments.

Joel M. Friedman is a manager with Turner & Townsend Energy. With over 20 years of professional experience, Joel is most often assigned to project controls/project service manager roles in oil and gas projects. He has provided cost, schedule and change control management services to major construction projects in the United States, across SE Asia, and in the Russian Federation. Joel places high priority on his own continuing education and professional development. In 2010–2011, Joel and Karsten Isenbeck co-authored their thesis work entitled *Eligibility Factors and Behavioral Traits of Effective Project Sponsors*. Joel's hobbies include live musical performance and digital sound recording.

Dr Paul D. Giammalvo, is Senior Technical Advisor (Project Management) to PT Mitratata Citragraha (PTMC), Jakarta, Indonesia (www.build-project-management-competency.com). He is also an adjunct professor, Project and Program Management, at the Center for Advanced Studies in Project, Program and Portfolio Management and develops and teaches graduate level curricula in asset and project management for Western Australia University, Perth. For about 20 years he has been providing project management training and consulting throughout South and Eastern Asia, the Middle East and Europe. He is also active in the Global Project Management Community, serving as an advocate for and on behalf of the global practitioner and playing an active professional role in the Association for the Advancement of Cost Engineering International, Construction Specifications Institute and the Construction Management Association of America. He also sits on the board of directors of the Global Alliance for Project Performance Standards, www.globalpmstandards.org, Sydney, Australia.

Guy Giffin is a director of Prendo Simulations Ltd (www.prendo.com). Founded in 1998, Prendo develops the world's most advanced management simulations. With a specialism in simulating the decision-making challenges associated with leading complex projects, Prendo's simulations are used at many of Europe's top business schools, including: Cranfield, HEC Paris, IESE, IMD, INSEAD, London and Saïd/Oxford. Guy has delivered hundreds of simulation workshops with many large organisations (BAE Systems, BBC, Bechtel, BT, Deloitte, EDF Energy, Goldman Sachs, IBM, Morgan Stanley, Nestlé, Oracle, PA Consulting and many others). Guy is also an Associate at the National School of Government and has worked with several government departments. Guy graduated from the University of Bristol in 1990 with a degree in Philosophy.

Paul Girling is managing director of New Habits, a company based in Sheffield in the UK. Paul has over 35 years' experience of working across the private, public and third sectors. A project manager by background, he has increasingly been involved in coaching people at all levels. Paul is the MD of New Habits Ltd. Before establishing his company he held senior project management roles in a global financial institution and a central government department. He is the author of the project game *Family Life*, published by Gower and co-author of the reframe game *How do you see this?* Significant in Paul's life was his 17 years' service with the UK voluntary organisation, the Samaritans. Those years taught him the value of empathetic listening. Now he works as a coach, consultant, project manager and trainer across the public, private and third sectors. He works successfully with people at all levels. Paul's memberships include APM, the Association for Coaching and the Association for NLP. He is a regular presenter to professional bodies, where he is known for his entertaining and provocative style.

Elisabeth Goodman is owner and principal consultant of RiverRhee Consulting, a company that helps business teams to enhance their effectiveness for greater productivity and improved team morale (http://www.riverrhee.com). She is a trainer, facilitator, one-to-one coach, speaker and writer. Previously, during over 25 years in the pharmaceutical industry she held line management and internal training and consultancy roles supporting scientific and business support teams internationally. Elisabeth has a BSc in Biochemistry and an MSc in Information Science. She is accredited in Change Management, Lean Sigma and MBTI. Elisabeth is a member of the Chartered Institute for Library and Information Professionals, and of APM.

Michael Greer, for 30 years has been helping new project managers to improve their effectiveness. Through books, articles, workshops, websites and public appearances he has tried to demystify project management and make it accessible to new and part-time project managers. Many universities have adopted his step-by-step texts. Michael trained as an instructional designer and performance analyst, and became experienced in evaluating training and skill requirements in many different industries. Using his training/performance analyst and project management background, Michael has helped to develop several project management job/competency models and career paths. His quest to simplify project management resulted in his latest book and tool collection: *The Project Management Minimalist*. Info: http://michaelgreer.biz.

Alan Harpham is a former managing director and senior consultant of Nichols Associates (now part of The Nichols Group), one of the UK's leading consultancies in project and change management. Now Alan is a management consultant focused on programme management, project management and executive coaching. He is chairman of The APM Group, chairman of Workplace Matters Hertfordshire and Bedfordshire and a previous board member of the International Center for Spirit at Work. He is also on the selection committee of the International Faith and Spirit at Work Awards. He is chairman of Cranfield University's Science & Engineering Ethics Committee and the SPD Research Ethics Committee (medical). Alan was co-owner and a founding director of P5 – the Power of Projects. He is also a former trustee of several charitable organisations including MODEM, and The Friends of the Bedford Child Development Centre. He was a founding member of the Jury for the IPMA International Project Management Awards and continued as such until 2006.

Elizabeth Harrin is director of The Otobos Group, which is a project communications consultancy that specialises in copywriting for project management firms. She has a decade of experience in financial services and health care projects. She holds a Master's degree and in addition to being a Member of the British Computer Society is a Fellow of APM. Elizabeth has led a variety of IT and process improvement projects, including e-commerce and communications developments. She is also experienced in managing business change, having spent eight years working in financial services (including two Paris-based assignments). Elizabeth is the author of several books and she also writes the award-winning blog, *A Girl's Guide to Project Management.* You can find Elizabeth online at www.GirlsGuidetoPM.com or on Twitter @pm4girls.

Peter Harrington is a senior freelance HR consultant and contractor with over 15 years' experience of working with private and public clients in many different industries including financial services, economic regulation, IT/Telecoms, business services, contact centres, central and local government departments and retail businesses. With particular interest in employee relations and employment law topics, he has delivered restructure, redundancy and acquisition projects, policy and strategic operating model development as well as pragmatic operational support and management training and coaching. A firm believer in continuous professional development, he complements his professional skills through the study of Law at the Open University.

Jon Hyde is a project and programme manager who specialises in public sector transformation. During eight years in local government, Jon has managed a diverse range of projects including the redesign of corporate websites, the roll out of new waste and recycling services, and the strategic commissioning of Built Environment Services. Jon also has a keen interest in effective portfolio management and has successfully implemented a corporate resource management process enabling improved monitoring and prioritisation of projects and programmes. He is an active member of the PPM community and regularly organises and facilitates face-to-face best practice events. Jon is also a social media enthusiast who blogs at www.publicsectorpm.com and tweets as @publicsectorpm.

Karsten Isenbeck holds an MSc in PPM, an Executive MBA and has acquired more than 15 years of PPM experience in the telecommunications industry across Europe and Asia. Karsten has achieved further credentials in electrical engineering, cost engineering as well as in project management and is working for Nokia Siemens Networks. His academic research is focused on project sponsoring in project-based organisations and its contribution to project success.

Andy Jordan is President of Roffensian Consulting Inc., where he focuses on strengthening project management environments through the development of teams and individuals. Andy is a prolific writer with over 100 published articles on a number of project management related topics, as well as an instructor and presenter on project management and leadership. Andy is driven to improve the quality of project management by providing project managers with the skills they need to become accomplished people and task leaders, as well as encouraging them to challenge accepted norms. Before starting Roffensian, Andy led business-critical strategic projects, programs and PMOs on two continents and in multiple industries. He has always concentrated on creating a 'people first' culture that allows project teams to perform at the best of their abilities.

George Jucan is a well-known and successful project management consultant, captivating speaker at public events, motivating trainer and author of high-impact project management articles. George is an experienced PMP with more than 20 years of technical and management experience in the public and private sectors. Many of his projects have won provincial and national awards and/or were profiled in specialty magazines. He is currently Executive Director, Central Region at Avalon Corporate Solutions (a Canadian company specialising in strategic and management consulting). George, a renowned expert in standards and methodologies, is chairman of the CAC/ISO/TC258, leading the Canadian representation for ISO standardisation activities in project, programme and portfolio management. He has also had leadership positions on PMI standards committees including (for example) the 4th and 5th editions of the PMBOK Guide.

Steven Lewis is a PRINCE2 practitioner, holds an Association for Project Management Professional (APMP) certificate and is a member of APM. He has held project management posts for several large international companies in a variety of industries and sectors. He has worked on many construction and fit-out projects such as Heathrow Terminal 5 and the Westfield Shopping Centre in West London. More recently he has been lead project manager on multidiscipline engineering projects in China, Saudi Arabia, Bahrain, Libya and Iran for a company specialising in the design, manufacture and installation of equipment for sea water intake filtration. Clients have included Alstom, Reliance, Babcock, China Nuclear Power Engineering Company, BAA, BT and Apple computers. Steven is currently working at Ford Motor Company as a programme management analyst for the delivery of power train manufacturing and assembly facilities. Steve is finishing an MSc in Project Management (Aberdeen) and CIMA certification. Considering himself to be still young, but now bearing the scars of project management, he is looking forward to the future opportunities and challenges the profession will bring.

Dennis Lock is a freelance writer specialising in project management. Early years as an electronic engineer were followed by management posts in industries ranging from defence electronics to heavy machine tools and mining engineering. After occasional consultancy assignments in Europe, eight more recent years were spent as an external lecturer in project management on Master's degree programmes at two British universities. Dennis is a Fellow of APM, Fellow of the Institute of Management Services and a Member of the Chartered Management Institute. He has written or edited over 60 management books, mostly for Gower. His bestseller *Project Management* has sold over 100,000 copies worldwide and is now in its 10th edition.

Donnie McNicol has extensive PM experience across multiple industries and now leads consultancy, training, facilitation and mentoring assignments for global companies and government departments. Donnie specialises in developing an organisation's project leadership capability. Widely recognised as contributing to the 'people and organisational side' of project management thinking, he is in much demand as a speaker and writer and is passionate about delivering value by incorporating the latest behavioural, cultural, human resources, project, programme and change management thinking. Donnie chaired APM's People Specific Interest Group for 10 years to 2011 and now contributes actively to a number of strategic initiatives focused on the way the profession engages with business leaders. He is also a Visiting Fellow at Kingston Business School, lecturer at other leading universities, an individual member of the Acumen7 professional network and Partner at Synatus.

Dr William A. Moylan is an assistant professor in construction management with Eastern Michigan University. 'Dr Bill' is also a professional trainer, consultant and expert witness in construction engineering and project management. He has extensive professional experience in all aspects of programme and project management, including over 12 years internationally with the Arabian American Oil Co, and, since 1983, has been involved in implementing IT. Dr Moylan has degrees from Lawrence Technological University, Massachusetts Institute of Technology and Capella University. He is active in a number of professional societies and civic activities, including the Engineering Society of Detroit, PMI, Habitat for Humanity and Toastmasters International.

Dr Judi Neal is Director of the Tyson Center for Faith and Spirituality in the Workplace at the Sam M. Walton College of Business, University of Arkansas. The Center supports research, education and business outreach for those interested in faith and spirituality in the workplace. Judi is President of Edgewalkers International, a consultancy committed to helping leaders, teams and organisations to be on their leading edge. She is the author of *Edgewalkers: People and Organizations that Take Risks, Build Bridges and Break New Ground* and *The Handbook for Faith and Spirituality in the Workplace*. She was the founder of the International Center for Spirit at Work, and a co-founder of the Management, Spirituality and Religion Interest Group at the Academy of Management. Judi has consulted to organisations such as Pfizer, Hewlett-Packard, General Electric, Jackson Newspapers, and numerous others, and has spoken about spirituality in the workplace internationally. She is considered one of the pioneers and experts in the field and has been quoted in *The Sunday Times*, *The Wall Street Journal*, *The New York Times*, *Tokyo Shimbum*, and has appeared frequently on television and radio in the US.

Dr Jason Price has almost 20 years' experience as an independent consultant in programme and project management. He has overseen the implementation of change projects alongside 'business as usual' service delivery in contact centres serving up to 4 million customers annually. Jason has been Performance and Planning manager for ANZ National Bank, Corporate Customer Relations Manager at Birmingham City Council and a customer strategy and CRM consultant at Deloitte. Jason is a Certified Management Consultant®, MSP Advanced Practitioner, PRINCE2 practitioner and APMP. He holds a PhD in Genetic Algorithms and a First Class Honours Degree in Computing Science from Aston University. He can be contacted at jason@priceperrott.com.

Penny Pullan works with people in multinational organisations who are grappling with high-risk international projects and programmes of change, often involving a complex and culturally diverse mix of stakeholders. Within this context, Penny is experienced in bringing order and clarity, giving support, and providing the tools needed to cut through the problems and deliver benefits, whilst helping the individuals involved to develop. Penny is co-author of *A Short Guide to Facilitating Risk Management* and each June hosts the Virtual Working Summit www.virtualworkingsummit.com. Clients of Penny's company Making Projects Work Ltd include Novo Nordisk, AbbVie, NFU Mutual, Quintiles, the UK Government, ESI and others from financial services, technology and pharmaceutical multinationals. Penny can be reached by email at penny@makingprojectswork.co.uk.

Joanna Reynolds is a senior consultant in the New Habits company. She has a degree in Retail Management Science. Joanna focuses on relationship management, personal development and effective communication.

Brian Richardson works with organisations and individuals to improve human performance and create lasting, successful change. For over 20 years, his study of social and organisational dynamics and his passion for a data-based, analytical approach to managing change have informed his work as a management consultant, coach, author and educator. He is the founder and CEO of Richardson Consulting Group, Inc., a professional services firm that helps organisations with strategy, implementation, business process, talent, knowledge management and enterprise learning. Leading companies such as Allstate, UnitedHealth Group, CME Group, Wells Fargo and Leo Burnett depend on Brian and his firm for fresh thinking, unbiased advice, a collaborative working style and a rigorous approach to problem solving and project execution. He has been a featured presenter at global, regional and local events for PMI, the International Society for Performance Improvement and other professional organisations.

Mark Rodgers is a principal partner of the Peak Performance Business Group. His clients achieve competition-crushing marketplace superiority, with greatly improved sales and cash flow. His coaching, speaking and consulting work attracts clients as diverse as the Harley-Davidson Motor Company, the National Association of Music Merchants and the Executive Education Program at the University of Wisconsin-Madison. An award-winning author, engaging communicator and world-class speaker, Mark has published over 100 articles, two books, and holds the coveted National Speakers' Association Certified Speaking Professional designation. Mark Rodgers lives in Milwaukee, Wisconsin, with his wife, Amy.

Dave Sawyer is a professional project manager who has worked for a department within the UK Home Office since 1995. He was involved with the delivery of 'operationally critical' technical security projects, before moving into larger IT and other projects in 2009. He is an ILM-qualified manager, a PRINCE2 practitioner and is currently studying towards an MSc in Project Management.

Lindsay Scott is a director of Arras People, a project management recruitment organisation. She is also lead committee member of the PMOSIG, a specialist group for PMO professionals. Previously, Lindsay was the Project Office Manager for Hewlett-Packard.

Ranjit Sidhu is a trainer and change management consultant with over 20 years' business experience, gained on projects spanning Europe, North America and Africa. Her work with teams across different industry sectors and cultures needed strong communication and influencing skills and this has directed her own professional development. Ranjit set up the training company ChangeQuest in 2005. She now works with organisations to help them achieve the right balance between process- and people-based skills, and so work towards excellence in the management of change. She uses innovative learning techniques to train and coach people and teams, so that they can improve their skills in project management, change management and NLP. Ranjit is an accredited trainer for the Change Management Practitioner, Agile Project Management and PRINCE2 qualifications, a coach and certified trainer of NLP and an Assessor for the APM Practitioner.

Peter Simon has over 30 years of experience as a project management consultant and practitioner across all industries and business sectors. He is a director and managing partner of Lucidus Consulting Limited; a company that specialises in 'shedding light on managed change'. Peter was Chairman of the APM's specific interest group on risk management for four years. He is a Fellow of APM, a member of the PMI, a Visiting Fellow of Cranfield University School of Management and Adjunct Professor at ESCP Business School, London.

Susan de Sousa has over 15 years' experience in the project management area, with a reputation for delivering 'impossible' projects and launching a number of 'firsts' in Europe. These include relaunching EuroMillions and creating the millionaire raffle for Camelot (the biggest UK retail launch in 2009) and delivering live TV to a mobile phone for BSkyB (first time outside South Korea), IT services platform for the launch of 3 (first videoconferencing on a mobile), the first global SMS Aggregator for O2 and Interactive TV for the BBC. Susan is site editor of MyPMExpert.com, the industry-leading project management website, is writing two books and is a highly regarded speaker and commentator at conferences and in the media.

Colin Stuart graduated in civil engineering at the University of Bristol and is a member of APM and the Workplace Consulting Organisation. From his early career designing office fit-outs Colin became increasingly aware of the impact of good design on organisational culture, well-being and a company's profitability. Colin has written articles and lectured widely on related subjects, including the need for the workplace to drive business innovation. Formerly a partner at EC Harris, Colin is now a principal of both Fastfwd

Limited and BakerStuart, specialising in workplace-driven change. Projects managed by Colin have won many prestigious awards.

Jo Ann Sweeney is a communications consultant. She helps project teams win the support of their sponsors, senior executives and end users. She specialises in helping clients develop activities that take their audiences on a journey from awareness, through understanding, to support, involvement and commitment to making the project a success. Jo Ann's projects have spanned skills development, product launches, office relocations, redundancies and redeployment, CRM rollouts, business process re-engineering, political lobbying, technology rollouts and brand makeovers for numerous corporate organisations. Jo Ann shares her knowledge and experience online through the CommsAbilities blog (www.commsabilities.com/blog.asp), Worth Working Summit (www.worthworkingsummit.com) and the Communicating Projects System (www.sweeneycomms.com/communicating-projects). She has more than 25 years' experience and is a trained journalist, chartered marketer and Fellow of the Chartered Institute of Marketing, Fellow of the Institute of Internal Communications and Member of the Institute of Directors.

Bernardo Tirado is a Six Sigma Black Belt, certified Project Management Professional, and an industrial psychologist. He is a business transformation senior executive with extensive experience in building global shared services, transforming organisations through process improvement, and developing new business capabilities. Bernardo has portfolio and programme level project management experience and (through the application of industrial psychology, Six Sigma, PRINCE2 and PMBOK methodologies) he drives profit through process. In addition to being the CEO and founder of www.TheProjectBox.us, Bernardo is an author, speaker and lead columnist for *Psychology Today*'s digital leaders.

Neil Walker is a project management professional, consultant and author. He has over 20 years' experience in leading and delivering business transformation programmes of up to $30 million; which have aligned People, Process and Technology initiatives closely with business strategy for blue-chip organisations including as ATOS, Capital One, CGI Group, Lloyds Bank, Royal Bank of Scotland. Furthermore, he has consulted (in advisory and delivery capacities) in the UK, Europe, Canada and USA in specialisations including strategic alliances, collaboration strategies, programme due diligence, delivery assurance, and turnaround of programmes and projects.

Neil is a PRINCE2 Practitioner and Managing Successful Programmes (MSP) Practitioner. He is a Fellow of the Chartered Management Institute (CMI), a Member of the Association for Project Management (APM) and a Committee Member on the APM's Programme Management SIG. He authors project management publications and blogs (www.ppmpractitioner.com). He can be contacted via www.neilwalker.net or LinkedIn (www.linkedin.com/in/neilawalker).

Dr Edward Wallington is an advocate of professional project management and business analysis in the geospatial and management information sectors. Ed is a versatile and enthusiastic project manager with a deep interest and belief in the transfer of project management theory into operational application. Ed is a member of APM, sits on regional committees and actively contributes with the aim of helping all project professionals realise their potential.

Todd Williams has for over 25 years advised top executives of manufacturing and service companies in creating leading-edge systems to improve organisational efficiency and rescue problem projects. From this experience he has developed methods for streamlining organisations and is an acknowledged expert in rescuing troubled projects from failure. He is President of eCameron, Inc. and a professional member of the National Speakers Association. He maintains a blog at http://ecaminc.com/index.php/blog that has been quoted on CIO Update, ZDNet, IT Business Edge, Center for CIO Leadership, CIO Essentials and Project Managers Planet. His book, *Rescue the Problem Project: A Complete Guide to Identifying, Preventing, and Recovering from Project Failure*, was published by AMACOM Books in 2011.

Preface

This Handbook was born in the spring of 2011, when Gower's publisher Jonathan Norman and both of us met chez Lock to discuss Jonathan's proposal that we might work together to compile a work devoted entirely to the important subject of managing people in projects. Jonathan's idea sparked something special in both of us, and we immediately set to work with vigour and enthusiasm.

This has been a true joint venture, with both of us working together with unquenchable synergy, helped by constant encouragement and support from Jonathan and from the growing group – or should we say family – of contributing writers. Lindsay's deep experience in working with project management people suggested that she should identify and invite most of our contributors and review their chapters for acceptance in the first instance. Then Dennis, editor of several management handbooks and a work-hardened writer would take over the editing, illustrations and manuscript compilation. This arrangement worked perfectly and, controlled from a simple project schedule, we completed this enjoyable project on time.

Now we have to say a word about our contributors – of which there are over 50. They have been drawn from several parts of the world and different industry sectors, and were invited to take part because of their particular reputations and skills. Of course without the willing cooperation of those contributors there would have been no Handbook. So to all our contributors, we say a big 'Thank you'.

The 63 chapters are arranged into six parts, beginning with general management and organisation, and ending with some more advanced topics. We have included a select bibliography and our index should facilitate your navigation of this substantial volume. In general, we have not attempted to cramp the style of any contributor, and readers will notice that one or two of the views expressed are a little controversial, or should we perhaps say refreshing?

Dennis Lock   Lindsay Scott
St Albans   Manchester

PART 1

Management and Organisation

1

People and Project Management

DONNIE MACNICOL

The human race has an incredible ability to innovate, adapt, change, develop and create. We do this by making change – from slow gradual change (for example by migration towards cities) through to more immediate, identifiable change (such as the development and implementation of technologies). It is these more immediate, identifiable changes that we now regard as projects, with all the defining characteristics of scope, time, cost and so on that have become so familiar to project practitioners. In consequence we have allowed these characteristics to influence the way in which we define and perceive the roles that people are given (such as project manager) and the general approach taken (for example, project management). Further distinctions have emerged around programmes and portfolios.

In spite of this progression and in particular the development of the science of project management, there has unfortunately been no significant improvement in the probability of project success. For example, in the UK public sector there has been a stream of critical reports (from sources such as the National Audit Office and Public Accounts Committee) on the failure of projects, programmes and other change initiatives. These criticisms range over many kinds of projects, from defence to IT. But, of course, project failures are not confined to the public sector. There have also been many examples of failed projects in the private sector, although these have not always been so well publicised.

Critical reports of projects often point to cultural and behavioural issues being significant factors in poor project performance, stemming from the important and constant factor present in all projects. That crucial factor is the involvement of people (which of course is the focus of this Handbook).

In the 20th century and earlier, the 'people aspect' of projects was a relative sideline for most practitioners in the project world. Although there were exceptions, the primary focus was on using the best methodology and tools to deliver success. Of course, advances in project management practice in recent years have been very important, enhanced by the rapid advance of communications and IT. But attention is turning to how people perform in projects, and how we can manage projects and programmes to improve the performance of individuals and teams. So the study of people in project management has rightly become a growing area of interest and development for the profession, as evidenced for example in training and the publication of articles in professional journals and other works such as this Handbook. However, for centuries project management in many ways defined itself by the process-driven elements, the so-called 'hard side' of project management, and it is still finding it difficult to shake off that brand.

'It's all about the people'. This, or some similar phrase, is used increasingly as those involved in the delivery of projects realise that ultimately nothing happens on a project unless it is made to happen by people (or, to put that more accurately, by each of the individuals who contribute directly or indirectly to the project). Therefore, what people do on a project, and crucially how they do it, should be the primary concern of those who manage and lead projects. An energised team can enable apparent miracles to be achieved. But without that team effectiveness, even the simplest of changes can turn into a disaster for the individuals and organisations involved.

This introductory chapter is for practitioners who wish to understand the impact of how people perceive, value and embrace what we relate to as project, programme and portfolio management. By offering a model which project practitioners can use to reflect on their own projects my aim is to help identify where insights can be found to make desired change happen more effectively – which is precisely what we are all ultimately aiming to achieve as project practitioners.

Management Challenges Specific to Projects

It is worth considering for a moment what it is about the management of people to deliver change through projects that is so much more challenging than managing people in functional or other steady state contexts.

Whether they are project or functionally based, most managers in an organisation have to deal with a high level of change. That change can be driven by different factors for each organisation, which might include for example:

- the need for constant innovation and improvement;
- increasing scrutiny of performance;
- shortening product and service life cycles, and so on.

The key distinction within projects is generally the rate of change and the complexity of relationships involved in delivery. The full range of challenges associated with managing people in projects is vast. However, I highlight in the following lists a few of the unique project complexities that we must recognise as influencing the relationships that today's project management practitioner must manage.

Organisational Context

- The need to understand many organisational models and the cultures that underlie them;
- the dynamic nature of project organisations, which can constantly change in size and shape through the typical project life cycle;
- complex nature of 'success' – defined not as a single entity but as a diverse range of transitory perceptions held by the broader stakeholder group;
- the need to have a focus on and understanding of the business context to ensure that decisions are made from the perspective of project outcome and benefits realisation;

- expectation by all those involved in the change process for high levels of openness and engagement, whether from those working directly on projects or from those who will be affected by the eventual change.

Managing Up

- Difficulty of uncovering what drives the opinions/decisions of stakeholders and discovering their relative levels of power and influence;
- need to 'sell' the vision through the stakeholders to secure the essential levels of direct and indirect support;
- recognising, valuing and marshalling the subjective views of customers and stakeholders;
- translating the 'political' into a reality – understanding and then transforming organisational strategies and expectations into not only technical but also politically feasible solutions that are supported by stakeholders.

Managing Down

- Influencing teams without traditional positional or hierarchical authority by developing and utilising stakeholder relationships;
- need to lead teams so that they become greater than the sum of their parts to offset resource shortages and can deal with the need to meet challenging objectives;
- ability to deal with high levels of uncertainty and often relentless change – which can be disconcerting and challenging for many people to deal with;
- accept and work with the inevitable resistance to change;
- ultimately the need to model constantly what you say in the behaviours you exhibit. This is a critical requirement for a leader of change.

Impact of People in Project Management

'People focused' is one of a number of terms and phrases used to describe the human aspect of project management. Alternatives include the 'soft side', 'people side', 'behavioural side' and a host of others, some less descriptive and more critical. The phrases are used without reflecting on their meaning or how they might be interpreted by others. By using these widely adopted phrases we tend to convince ourselves that we fully understand what these 'people aspects' are and how they affect project performance. But that is not yet the case. The interactions and dependencies of people in projects are only now being identified, questioned and understood. For example, how does the motivation of an individual affect the way in which he or she plans? Or, how is portfolio management accepted by an organisation in which the culture is not geared to objective decision making?

Projects, as I have said, are for and all about people. Therefore we must understand what we mean when referring to 'people' (from the individual right through all the different collective layers of teams and culture). We have to learn and understand the influence that people can have on projects, the roles inherent in the change process and how project management is defined and used.

A Model for Analysing and Improving Relationships between People and Projects

The challenge now (and one that this chapter addresses) is how do we take these people aspects and make them part of what we call the field of project management? Not a separate, stand-alone consideration, but central to how we define change, the processes we use and the roles undertaken.

To help achieve this I shall use a practical model that describes the interplay between the different *elements of project management* and the *layers of perspective* from the multiple groupings of people involved. The following explanations will make this clearer:

- *Layers*: the different layers of perspective brought by individuals, and then progressively by teams, organisations, and ultimately by the collective group that I have referred to as stakeholders. Other layers could be added but I consider these sufficient for the purpose of this model.
- *Elements*: which is a way of looking more broadly at what we define the field of project management to be in terms of the roles, the change we are looking to make and how we go about making that change.

When these layers and elements are combined, we have a model which can be used to map out the impact of people on the world of project management. First, here are the layers:

- *Individual (me)*: characteristics of the person leading to the unique way in which they perceive and interact with the world around them and the resulting impact on their behaviour towards each element.
- *Group or team (we)*: dynamics of the group or team based on the unique combination of capabilities, experiences and motivations and the way in which they interact with each project management element.
- *Organisation (us)*: the organisation and the way it relates to, values and embraces each element (in particular the executive body and organisational functions).
- *Stakeholders (them)*: capturing people and groups outside the organisation (including other professions, partners, suppliers, customers and society in general) and the way each element is regarded and valued by them.

Now, secondly, I list the *elements* that define the field of project management. For simplicity I shall refer only to projects, but the following in most cases relate also to programme and portfolio management. Here are the project management elements:

- *Roles (who)*: the roles undertaken by those involved in ensuring success of any change.
- *Processes (how)*: the processes, systems, methodologies and practices that encapsulate project, programme and portfolio management.
- *Change (what)*: the unique way we define the change through a project or programme.

	PROJECT MANAGEMENT ELEMENTS		
LAYERS OF PERSPECTIVE	**Roles (who)** *The roles undertaken by those involved in ensuring the success of any change.*	**Processes (how)** *The processes, systems, methodologies and practices that encapsulate project, programme and portfolio management.*	**Change (what)** *The unique way we define the change through a project or programme.*
Individual (me) *Characteristics of the person leading to the unique way in which they perceive and interact with the world around them and the resulting impact on their behaviour towards each element*	I value and am energetic in the role I have and support others delivering the change.	I engage positively with the processes and ways of working and support their improvement.	I am motivated by the project, believe in its success and communicate this to others.
Team (we) *Dynamics of the team based on the unique combination of capabilities, experiences and motivations, and the way in which they interact with each project management element.*	The team have clarity of purpose, work well together and are supportive of the individual roles and external teams.	The team have adopted and use the processes effectively. In turn, these support the interaction within the group.	The team have embraced the change and are fully supportive of its success.
Organisation (us) *Culture of the organisation and the way it relates to values and embraces each element (in particular the executive body and organisational functions).*	The organisation values and supports the roles associated with making the change.	The organisation endorses the processes and demonstrates that these are critical to its success.	The organisation actively supports the change being made.
Stakeholders (them) *Capturing people and groups outside the organisation (including other professions, partners, suppliers, customers and society in general) and the way each element is regarded and valued by them.*	Stakeholders perceive and value the roles and their professional standing.	Stakeholders value the processes used to deliver the change.	Stakeholders support the change being made.

Figure 1.1   A model of people in projects: Statements to consider

Source: © 2013 Team Animation Ltd. All rights reserved. Reproduced with permission.

Figure 1.1 displays the above relationships in diagrammatic form. The model can be approached and applied in multiple ways. Its primary use is to help individuals, groups or organisations to question and understand the impact caused by the interplay between each layer and the processes' roles involved. Each of these interplays can be a source of discussion and an opportunity for improvement if challenges and issues are mapped to the structure.

Practitioners will be able to identify with parts of this model. When 'people aspects' are explicitly brought into discussion, either in projects or within the profession, this often refers to the first two rows and the first column (the *individual* or *team* in terms of their *roles*).

You will probably be familiar with training, workshops or tools covering areas such as personal skills, forms of leadership, team structures and dynamics, and so on. Many chapters in this Handbook will each cover one or multiple interfaces in the model. As an example, 'project leadership' primarily focuses on the individual and the role that he or she undertakes. However, discussion on people in projects rarely extends beyond these boxes. But we need to examine broader aspects, where we can begin to gain a deeper understanding of the rich interplay between groups and organisations and what we call the 'field of project management'.

In recent years as our profession has started to gain an understanding of the way organisations relate to project management – some seem able to adapt effortlessly and adopt and sustain a project-based way of working. But others find it challenging and a continuous source of friction. In the past there has been too much of a 'one size fits all' mentality, without taking in to account the culture of the organisation and the unique context within which it finds itself. This is an emerging field of *organisational project leadership,* on which I am working with a number of business schools to develop our knowledge and thinking.

USING THE MODEL

To make the foregoing useful for practitioners, the model asks the practitioner to reflect at each point of interface between a layer and an element on a recent change in which they have been involved. These statements describe a situation between the individual, the team, the organisation or stakeholders that is likely to be positive and favourable, where each layer is positively supporting and engaging with the roles, processes and entities. The practitioner must now consider each statement and answer honestly 'yes' or 'no'.

This, therefore, has provided the project practitioner with a means for assessing her/his own situation in order to identify where action can be taken to further develop and improve the situation. As an example, people who have used this model as described have identified the following:

- The impact that their own feelings have had on not only how the project has proceeded but also ultimately on the outcome. For example, how personal fears regarding failure resulted in a downscaled (descoped) project.
- How success is viewed very differently in other people's eyes, and the lack of consideration often given to this. For instance, in one case only after the project was well under way did the true feelings of key stakeholders become evident, which resulted in considerable disruption and change.

I propose the following four-stage process as a means for using this model (Figures 1.1 and 1.2) effectively. I have included this here by prior agreement with Team Animation:

1. *Distinguish*
   Consider the context within which you work and the change you wish to consider.
2. *Assess*
   Read each statement in the model (Figure 1.1), beginning top left with 'me and my role', progressing from left to right before considering 'us and our roles' and so forth. You can either agree or disagree with each statement.
3. *Diagnose*
   Based on your responses, carry out a simple diagnosis of the situation.

   - Out of a possible 12 positive responses, how many of the statements in Figure 1.1 did you fully agree with?

- Based on this score, would you say the performance of the project is represented by this?
- If you did not fully agree with the statement ask yourself the question in Figure 1.2 and also consider the other related questions.
- From your scoring, where were most of the issues – with you, the team, the organisation or the stakeholder group?

4. *Action*

   Assess where you believe the major issues lie, using your scoring as a basis. Then identify the actions you will take.

Considering Action

Figure 1.2 includes example questions which you may wish to ask if you do not fully agree with any of the previous statements. As with any model, the myriad of possible questions for each segment has been simplified to demonstrate the key principles of the

LAYERS OF PERSPECTIVE	PROJECT MANAGEMENT ELEMENTS		
	Roles (who) *The roles undertaken by those involved in ensuring the success of any change.*	*Processes (how)* *The processes, systems, methodologies and practices that encapsulate project, programme and portfolio management.*	*Change (what)* *The unique way we define the change through a project or programme.*
Individual (me) *Characteristics of the person leading to the unique way in which they perceive and interact with the world around them and the resulting impact on their behaviour towards each element*	Is the role playing to my strengths and aspirations? If not, can I change my role or responsibilities?	What is it about the processes I use that does not energise me and what changes can be made without negatively impacting upon the performance of the project?	Which characteristics of the project are demotivating and, as it is unlikely these can be changed, how can I view the change in a different way?
Team (we) *Dynamics of the team based on the unique combination of capabilities, experiences and motivations, and the way in which they interact with each project management element.*	Why are the relationships and dynamics within the team not working?	Why is the team unable or unwilling to use the processes? What effect is this having?	Why is the team not responding positively to the goals of the project?
Organisation (us) *Culture of the organisation and the way it relates to values and embraces each element (in particular the executive body and organisational functions).*	What is it about our organisational culture or project roles that is causing resistance?	Where in the organisation do the project processes get challenged and why are these not aligned?	Who in the organisation still needs to embrace the project and why do they not value the planned change?
Stakeholders (them) *Capturing people and groups outside the organisation (including other professions, partners, suppliers, customers and society in general) and the way each element is regarded and valued by them.*	Do stakeholders value their own role, feel valued in the project, and where do they have concern about each other's involvement?	What has caused stakeholders to view the processes negatively and how could this be improved?	Why has the project not been supported by certain stakeholders and what would need to change to gain their support?

Figure 1.2   A model of people in projects: Questions to ask

Source: © 2013 Team Animation Ltd. All rights reserved. Reproduced with permission.

model. Practitioners should consider these principles and apply this thinking to their own situation.

By definition some of the aspects you may identify will be beyond most project management practitioners' direct control. Identifying underlying issues that arise from the wider context is very important, because these can directly influence the individuals and teams involved in your projects. By not considering these project and programme managers risks endless effort trying to change behaviours without ever addressing the real cause of problems. Having a simple reference framework such as this will enable you to raise concerns with senior management constructively. You will be able to deal with specific problems by relating these to both the project and the wider organisational context.

When to Use It

The core model is written for someone to use during the course of a project, which is the situation in which most people will find themselves. Here the model is commonly used as a practical diagnostic tool when a problem occurs and you wish to identify what the underlying behavioural and cultural issues may be. Once causes are understood, improvements to performance can be made.

Alternatively, the model can be used at different stages in the project life cycle. It can be used as an additional lens through which to consider:

- *Project initiation*: If the statements are considered in the future tense, then you can consider the question 'How can you prepare yourself, your team and where possible the organisation to support the change more effectively?'
- *Project Closure*: If the statements are considered in the past tense, then an assessment can be made with regards to the performance and success of the project. This is an additional lens which will help those involved to learn from the experience – something that rarely happens in any structured and value-adding way after a change.

In addition the model could be distributed among team members for them to complete independently. Then you can compare the responses. This would act as the basis for a structured and potentially challenging conversation between project teams, senior management and, possibly, your wider stakeholders.

Wider Management Perspectives

Whilst this model is written from the perspective of the project managers, it provides the opportunity to uncover relevant insights when adopted by those in other roles, as in the following examples:

Programme manager: If the procedure described above were to be completed for each project (either by the project manager or the team) then it would provide another perspective and therefore an additional source of information. When compared with project performance metrics, it would identify underlying 'people issues' that could be affecting performance.

Programme director or portfolio manager: If the model is used across the entire portfolio then there is the opportunity to understand the effect that 'people issues' are having across all projects. This additional information can be used to make decisions regarding ways of improving capability.

If the people aspects of your projects are not being actively discussed in your organisation, I would encourage every practitioner to seek out feedback and input from their managers on these areas.

Summary

It is vital for all those involved in project management to appreciate the critical part played by people in delivering the required change, or in helping other people to achieve that objective.

We must champion the role of project managers in the public eye at every occasion to demonstrate the valuable contribution our profession makes.

By applying a systematic approach to considering the different layers and elements that I have described above, a project management practitioner is equipped to navigate the complexities of people in projects. The model outlined here provides one such approach to highlight the breadth and depth of the knowledge and experience required to achieve success in the eyes of the 'many' rather than the 'few'.

Conclusion: Guidance from this Handbook

My chapter has introduced the important subject of managing people in projects. The following chapters provide a detailed and rich source of reference on this subject. The Handbook editors have arranged things so that Part 1 covers project organisation and management in general. Parts 2, 3 and 4 deal with roles and the development of individuals and teams. Human Resource Management issues and staffing are covered in Part 5, and the concluding Part 6 has some more advanced and other topics.

2 Successes and Failures of People in Projects

TODD WILLIAMS

This chapter examines research about project failure rates and focuses on those factors that are directly attributable to people. The chapter also considers what can be done to increase success. I shall discuss 'people factors' at an organisational level, at project level and within the individual practitioners themselves. Project failure rates are extraordinarily high. In some industries they are estimated at anywhere from 50 to 80 per cent (The Standish Group, 2009). Likewise, lost revenue has been estimated at a staggering $1.2 trillion annually (Betts, 2009). Whether you choose to believe these numbers or not – even halve them – they are still well outside acceptable limits.

Defining Project Success – and Some Statistics

In an attempt to improve the rate of project success, organisations such as the Project Management Institute (PMI) and the UK's former Office of Government Commerce (OGC) have published standards for managing projects. These consist of hundreds of pages of process descriptions to guide the project manager through what is or might be applicable to the project he or she is trying to run. The hope is that by following these procedures the project will avert the pitfalls that have besieged the hundreds of previous projects. But the question is, does the application of these processes improve project success? The answers are not as easy to find as you might expect.

The problem is that many factors control a project's success (size, complexity, domain, innovation and so on). Also, the judgement of project success is subjective. Looking at a project from the supplier's perspective, the project is a failure if it is significantly over budget, but the customer might be quite happy with the product received and classify the project as successful.

Likewise, a customer's failure to market their product properly does not translate into an unsuccessful project for the supplier. The organisation's perspective is critical in the definition of these terms, and terms such as success, failure, red and so on are all relative to each particular team's point of view.

However, we can generally say that a project is successful when:

1. The project delivers value to all stakeholders in the project;
2. The project maintains scope, schedule and cost within the specification, plus authorised changes.

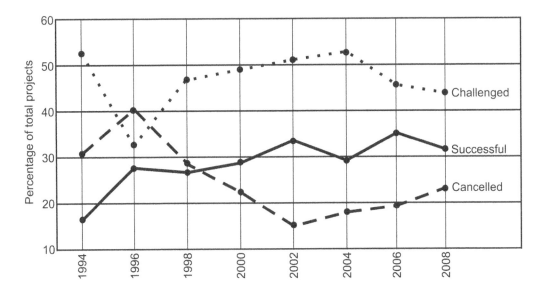

Figure 2.1   Project success and failure rates from 1994 to 2008

However, this definition simply transfers the difficulty to defining value. Value is subjective. It is far less quantitative than the famed triple constraints mentioned in item 2 on the previous page, but it is the most common measure of success. Take almost any government project that was a success on paper and ask the stakeholders if there is value in the result. The answers will span the range from 'definitely not' to 'perfect'.

The result is that we must rely on quantitative data. The only source over time has been that compiled by The Standish Group International (Johnson, 2006; The Standish Group, 2009). Plotting their Cancelled, Challenged and Successful project data provides a picture of project success rates since they began publishing data in 1994. Please refer to Figure 2.1 above.

Whether or not we are critical of these data, the importance is to focus on the trends. There is some very good news here. The 'successful' line is nicely trending upwards over time. It had a few setbacks, but it is improving, starting in the mid-teens (per cent) in 1994 increasing to the mid-thirties by 2008. In fact, it looks relatively linear (flattening a little over the last few years). The bad indication is for cancelled projects. These appear to be trending up since the 2002 survey. A closer look shows the challenged curve as a mirror image of the cancelled curve.

In Figure 2.2 I have plotted the 'challenged' to 'not cancelled' percentages and this confirms the strong correlation hinted in the previous plot. With the obvious inflection point in 2002, the logical explanation is that subsequent to the 'dot-com' bubble burst and 11 September 2001 terrorist attacks, management was no longer willing to throw good money at bad projects. It is better to cancel projects early and minimise losses. This application of good financial principles indicates improved executive skills, not project management prowess.

The reason for steady improvement in success rates is more debatable. It is nominally linear, which is contrary to the exponential growth in project management certifications noted by PMI (PMI, 2008). It does coincide with the development of new methodologies

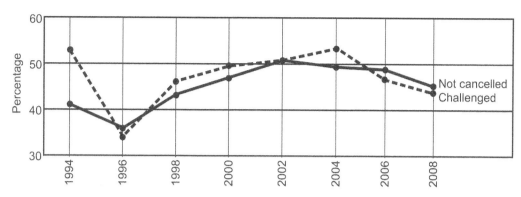

Figure 2.2   Correlation between challenged and not cancelled projects, 1994 to 2008

– moving to iterative processes and reducing the size and complexity of projects. It is widely known that smaller, less complex projects have a greater chance of success. This is the most likely reason behind the steady improvement in project success rates.

In the end, projects are getting better, not because each project is managed better, but because the organisations in which they are running are being managed better. This means organisations where people are first – not just spreadsheets and timelines.

Factors that Contribute to Project Failure

To talk about failure reasons, we need to first talk about the symptoms. Symptoms are what we associate with failures because they are what we see first. Only after an analysis can we find the actual reasons. For the sake of discussion, it is convenient to categorise symptoms into three broad groups which are: team, process and customer (please refer to Figure 2.3).

Problem area	Symptoms
Team	• Interrelationships; • Communication; • Attitude and motivation; • Management support; • Skill set.
Process	• Risk management; • Change management and scope issues; • Documentation; • Estimating and scheduling.
Customer	• Difficult, trying to get something outside the scope; • Incomplete understanding of the project (manifesting as scope issues); • Lack of project management (manifesting as scope issues).

Figure 2.3   Important symptoms of project failure

TEAM-RELATED FAILURE SYMPTOMS

Problems with teams are, by definition, problems with people including:

- communication;
- attitude;
- motivation;
- skill set;
- management support;
- interrelationships.

Dealing with these requires soft skills. Training in organisation development and leadership principles will reduce the deleterious effects.

Often though, the source of the problem lies much deeper. For instance, team members might not have the right skill set. In one case, the company policy required that all employees should be deployed on projects before contractors could be hired. This policy has excellent intentions for minimising expenses and placing employees first. However, to be effective, it needs an accompanying rule for funding the employees' continuing education on the tools needed to complete the company's 'strategic roadmap'. Without this rule well-intentioned resources are given responsibilities they might be ill-equipped to handle.

PROCESS-RELATED FAILURE SYMPTOMS

Change management and scope control, document coordination, estimating, scheduling and risk management seem relatively straightforward processes. Problems are in many cases rooted in the failure of people to implement them properly.

For instance, a common and difficult issue to identify and resolve is internal scope creep. This is where the team increases scope by suggesting features to the customer, bypassing the change management system. To correct this behaviour, the project manager must engage with the team, continuously training it on the evils of unauthorised scope expansion. What seems at first to be a process problem (poor change management processes) is rooted in the team member's inability to say 'no'. In those cases, process is of little assistance – the culture must change. Changing the culture is only accomplished by changing the attitudes and habits of the people in the culture.

CUSTOMER-RELATED FAILURE SYMPTOMS

Customer issues come in a variety of shapes and sizes, but many times the solution is training the customer in project management techniques or their product. Especially true in international projects, it might require educating the project team in the customer's culture.

The most common problem is a customer's lack of understanding of the product. Solve this by implementing a better change management process or by moving to an agile methodology. The solutions to these poor project management skills are found by educating the customer, by not using process in attempting to control them.

PROJECTS SUCCEED OR FAIL BECAUSE OF PEOPLE

In a world fixated on applying process to every problem encountered, it might sound heretical to insinuate that process is ineffective at improving projects. Of course process should have a positive effect, but that effect is overshadowed by the real problem – people. People fail to follow direction, lack leadership skills, have emotions and hold the key to success or failure. Process has its place, but that pales when compared to a well-synchronised team with the appropriate skill set and positive attitude.

People are at the root of all failures. Everything else is a symptom. If a project is over-constrained, the people who set the constraints need to correct the issue. If they do not understand the project well enough to set the constraints, or listen to the suggestions of new constraints, then they are the problem. Incorrect prioritisation, poor leadership, ineffective executive involvement – all are 'people problems'.

In truth, over-application of process masks problems with people. It creates a culture where an inanimate object (the process) shoulders the blame for failure. For example, the declaration that 'This problem is with the flow chart' not only removes the need to deal with people – it justifies their errors. People can hide behind the process ('I was just following the process') and that transfers blame to a box on a flow chart, a line in a manual, or some other non-living entity. This pleases everyone since it removes the need for direct confrontation. The need to confront human issues, personality problems, substandard skills and gross incompetence vanishes when everyone who follows the prescribed steps is considered blameless and harmless.

The human factor is sorely missing from project management and the certification processes. That's because it is difficult, if not impossible, to create tests to grade someone's interpersonal skills or leadership capabilities.

Processes and Procedures

With the industrial revolution, came the need for process. The move to high-volume manufacturing required unskilled labourers to build products rapidly and repetitively with consistent quality. Process made this possible. It is great for mechanical tasks, but is by itself an inappropriate approach to management. The emphasis of management must be on people rather than processes.

OVER-EMPHASIS ON PROCESSES

When processes are successful, the natural reaction is that we should apply them everywhere. The value of processes is that they provide a strict method of executing a set of tasks – removing the thought, ingenuity and imagination that induce variation. Sales order intake, change requests, inventory picking, time tracking and hundreds of other undertakings throughout the day have processes that we follow without question. Processes simplify our lives, so we learn to trust and rely on them.

Exceptions are usually found too late. No process is thorough enough to accommodate all possible error conditions. For example, the sales order clerk using a process that assumes rolls of wire can unwittingly misinterpret a customer's order who intended to acquire wire measured by length. This error is highlighted only when the customer requests a return authorisation for 199 x 100 metre rolls of wire. Any number of people in that order process could have questioned the quantity and averted the added expense. But more layers of process are then added, instead of improving communication or having order-takers, accounting, inventory clerks and others who must handle the material think about how each order relates to the customer.

THE EFFECT OF PROCESSES ON MANAGEMENT

Over-reliance on a process numbs people and tends to remove the need for cognitive skills. We blindly follow a process and sidestep any wrongdoing. Sadly, in some cases, even questioning a process can bring a reprimand. The organisation's culture changes to such a degree that processes actually hinder the project. People will follow a process even though they might feel it will result in a less than desirable outcome. It makes their lives easier. When problems arise from blindly following process instead of thinking, the process can be blamed.

Leading the Project

Of course processes are necessary but managing and leading people is more important. Managers in and above the project need to extract themselves from their cubicles and offices to visit the team members, experience the project, and see at first-hand how it is running – a process that has been called management by walking about. They must root out discontent, discover the reason for its existence and rectify the problem. It is essential to perform lower-level audits continuously, to ensure that people on are performing as planned.

When auditing a project, the application of processes instead of managing people is easy to identify. Simply look for the managers producing lists of completed tasks as proof that they have monitored the project:

* charter signed off;
* change management process in place;
* check risk register completed;
* check this and check that;
* check ad nauseam.

Instead of managing and leading, those managers are simply fulfilling a requirement and ticking off their checklists. Checklist managers believe that following processes supplants the need for knowledge. If this were true, managing could be reduced to a software application. To be effective, managers need to understand what their teams are producing. It requires diving down at least two layers into the group and doing spot checks throughout the team. By doing this, you will know when a process is being followed simply for process's sake.

Company Management Actions and Reactions

It happens hundreds of times a day around the world; a top executive calls an urgent executive management committee meeting. They have heard that one of the projects in the portfolio, a seemingly simple project doing a routine upgrade, is projecting a 20 per cent cost overrun and will be three months late. They are bewildered – how a project can have gone that far off track since the previous project review meeting, just a week ago? Managers scramble to get their stories straight, determine who to blame, form opinions and alibis. They pummel the project manager for failing to manage the project correctly, even though he/she has been saying the project is in trouble for months. The goal is to find someone to blame, rather than fix the problem. Seeking excuses rather than solutions.

This scenario is indicative that something has broken down in middle management. How could they fail to see the impending doom? That layer of management is supposed to monitor projects, consolidate information and provide guidance to project managers and executives. With trouble, these managers are now in a position of reacting as opposed to directing. They try to push the problem down and eventually come in to 'help' the project.

Few events strike more fear into the heart of a project manager than hearing, 'Hi, we're from management and we're here to help'. This help often takes the form of adding reports, shrinking scope and imposing time constraints rather than determining root causes. The result is a poorly developed product that remains over budget and requires excessive time and money to maintain. In the end, middle management gets credit for the rescue, the project team receives the blame, and the customer is displeased with a product having little or no value.

The problem stems from middle management's culture. They fail to report or act on actual status, which eliminates the opportunity for small mid-course corrections. In their ideal world the project will correct itself, despite the fundamental flaws in the assumptions. For them, ignorance is much easier than resetting expectations and gaining alignment.

Exacerbating this problem is a business culture that rewards the firefighter and penalises the pragmatist. An urgent rescue attempt produces immediate gratification at the cost of a robust solution, yielding only short-term benefits rather than analysing the problem logically and resolving the root causes.

In all of this, the people assigned to solve the problem – middle management – are themselves often the problem. For whatever reason (the Peter Principle, ignorance, inattention, or the desire to be a hero) middle managers generally are not monitoring projects or correcting problems when they appear. Ignorance is no excuse. Attempting to blame incomplete project reports is only admitting that the manager is failing his or her fiduciary responsibility to validate the project's progress. No matter how one looks at it, middle managers are not doing their jobs.

Everyone admires the hero who comes in to fix the problem. At least in the US, the imagery of the white-hatted cowboy riding in on a gallant steed to rescue the project by shooting all problems in one swift, albeit short-sighted, gunfight continues to capture our imagination and wonderment. As a society, we envy their capabilities.

Prioritisation of People, Procedures, and Technology

Irony abounds on how technology has supposedly made our lives simpler and less hectic. Cars are easier to maintain, instant communication has reduced our stress and technology rarely causes anxiety. However, some of us are old enough to remember the days when we could tune cars in our own garages, escape from the telephone by leaving the building, and power failures were not predecessors to panic attacks. As such, technology should not be our first line of defence or offence – it has to be regarded as a tool to be used after the right people are in place to perform the job in the most efficient manner.

Put down your cellphones, close the email, take a walk down the hall and talk to the people doing the work. One-on-one interaction (with all its body language), casual conversation (with its innocuous but vital titbits) and the ability to correct a misunderstanding quickly are at the core of communication and leadership. Doing this will identify the real status of the project, identify and help solve problems, backfill the project manager's deficiencies and quietly create success. It will lack the flash, urgency and attention of the flamboyant failure. But quiet and trustworthy success will build confidence and credibility in the manager and the leader. Success that provides value is always recognised.

At the root of organisation's problems, and manifested in project failure, is the fact that companies are tantalised by technology, processed by process and removed from their resources. This prioritisation must change. People need experience, not certifications; they must have excellent interpersonal communications, not status reports; they need to manage in the old-fashioned way, not just with checklists. The proper priority is people, then process, and, at a distant third, technology.

Improving Project Success Rates

The key to improving success – ensuring that projects produce value-laden results – is leadership. From the project manager to executive management, leadership is essential. Managers must foster individuals and teams that work autonomously, master their skills and work for a meaningful purpose.

THE ROLE OF THE EXECUTIVES

Few would question that executives are responsible for ensuring that projects are aligned with corporate strategy. They also need to ensure their initiatives continue to support those goals when business conditions change. To achieve this, executives have to be engaged with the project when it starts and monitor the project's context throughout its life. This requires more than ensuring that the project maintains its scope, schedule, and budget. Projects have to deliver *value*. Too many projects start with the inspirational support of upper management, but as each project progresses, executives disengage and are unable to see or straighten out the misalignment. This wastes company resources and hinders the company's ability to deliver.

Too often, project participants (both customers and suppliers), become enamoured of numerous non-critical features (the 'shiny ball' of new technology, or excessive process) and drift from the strategic tenets of the project. The project executives (everyone from the sponsor, portfolio managers, PMO directors, up to the CEO) need to monitor and guide projects to maintain their alignment, whilst the project manager shepherds the project within its approved scope, schedule and budget.

Executives have to focus on supplying value, for which understanding the customer's business is critical. Rather than pedantically ensuring that project charters, work breakdown structures, risk registers, and so on are all completed to some blanket standard, senior managers need to make certain that the intent and content of these artefacts indicate that the project is delivering the appropriate value. This goes far beyond the question 'Is this document complete?' The question needs to be, 'Does this document's content add value?' If the document fails to do this, the project is heading in the wrong direction. Project executives need continually to monitor value, using all means available. They must realign projects that are not providing value or cancel them.

Everything comes back to value. There is no mathematical model for it. Like beauty, the eye of the beholder plays a significant role. It is not a ratio of what should have expended on the project compared to the expectations. It is possible for a project to meet those parameters nicely but not meet the needs of the customer. Rather, value is the aggregate of the tangible and intangible, measureable and immeasurable benefits from its product.

One method to achieve this is enabling the project team to be involved with the customer at the project's initial inception – months before a project team is usually assigned. Whether internally or externally, early engagement with the customer will point out subtle distinctions in their requests that can make the difference in providing value. In many cases, the limiting factor is the project team's managers. They are either too worried about the expense of such an endeavour, or they are concerned about individuals stepping out of their roles and interacting with the customer.

Leadership and Direction

Leaders are role models for others in everything they do. They have charisma to instil faith, respect and trust. They respect others' opinions. Instead of scolding, they listen carefully and excel as coaches and advisors. Using these skills, they have developed the ability to get others to think in new ways, identifying and questioning unsupported opinion and, in its place, using evidence and reasoning. This brings a fresh approach to problem-solving in the organisation.

Leaders do not give in to all popular views or demands. They have the courage to withstand resistance against looking at ideas that are out of the mainstream – regardless of personal cost. They are adaptive and effective in rapidly changing environments. They are discerning, with an ability to discern issues, simultaneously handling a variety of problems, and making course corrections as required.

Based on a strong sense of mission, leaders are dependable, keeping their commitments and taking responsibility for their actions and their mistakes. A foundation of internal integrity guides them through what is morally and ethically correct. Superior judgement allows a leader to evaluate multiple action plans objectively using logic, analysis and comparison. They are pragmatic decision makers.

With all that is entailed in being a leader, it is easy to understand why someone would want to boil project management down to a process. Minding the scope, schedule and budget sounds quiet and peaceful, even mundane. Taking a subordinate, individual contributor role managing team members to someone else's direction, is tranquil in comparison to a leader's responsibilities. One must remember, though, there are two paths in project management – successfully managing the most difficult of projects as a leader, or following a cookbook project management style as a coordinator. To advance the project management discipline, leadership qualities are essential.

In project management, leadership is more than leading the people reporting to you. Too often, it requires leading people over whom you lack authority. The absence of hierarchical advantage is challenging but far from impossible. The key is making others feel the direction chosen is theirs. One of the best methods for doing this is to have them listen to their own story.

The Effect of a Bad Personality on the Team

Conflict resolution is a major part of recovering failing projects. The solutions range from replacing a supplier to analysing the sources of conflicts and determining a more friendly resolution. Stepping into a project with an estimate-at-completion a couple of million dollars over the budget, with everyone pointing accusing fingers and the customer screaming that the supplier is in default, replacing people can often be seen as the best option. There are times when this is true. When it is, waste no time in releasing destructive team members. The team's performance will improve, not because they are scared that they might be next to go, but rather that they are pleased to see some leadership that is stopping the insanity.

CASE EXAMPLE NO. 1

Contrary to common belief, removing problematic or high-maintenance people, even a prima donna, can have a very positive effect. At one client, nearly two-thirds of the team was going to be laid off in a workforce reduction scheduled in a few weeks. All laid-off workers would be given a severance package. However, one individual refused to do requested work and was being unprofessional, dishonest and exhibiting behaviour destructive to the team. He had been warned of his negativism and was finally recommended for termination a week before the scheduled lay-off. There was significant hesitation from company executives, especially because he was on the list for the lay-off. The issue was pushed based on the reasoning that letting him go would show the remaining team that management was intolerant of his toxic behaviour. Eventually management relented and terminated the person. After the lay-off, many of the remaining team members commented and thanked the recovery manager for showing fairness and stopping the insanity. They saw the action as positive and as a sign of being able to trust management. Sensible action and control had been applied.

Listening to Your Stakeholders

Key to listening is a desire to learn. If you are not trying to learn something from the person speaking, you are not listening. Show people that you are listening in the same way you do when you are learning – repeat what you hear, ask for clarification and take notes. Exhibiting these learning techniques as you are listening compliments the speaker. It elevates them to a teacher's role. Good leaders are learners; hence, good listeners.

Listening requires participation, not action. We need to pay attention. Unfortunately, many of us came up through the ranks of the technologist, which has conditioned us otherwise. Our lives consist of a continuous stream of puzzles to solve – subordinates presenting problems, children needing help with homework, and a myriad of gadgets to be fiddled with. We listen, dissect the problem, and take or suggest corrective action. In projects, all that is required is listening and providing guidance. Let the team create the solution.

This non-judgemental listening is the key to leading without authority. Too often, we jump to conclusions, share observations, blurt out solutions, and fail to give others time to assimilate information from our point of view. A case example will illustrate this best.

CASE EXAMPLE NO. 2

A few years ago, I was talking with a client, a manager in a successful data analysis company. He was having trouble with a custom piece of proprietary hardware for collecting data.

The first release had been a success. After a short time, however, a small company supplying one of the core components went out of business. Replacement suppliers were far more expensive. My client created a new revision by changing that component's functionality to use reprogrammable firmware to accommodate quick changes. This allowed him to contract with an individual supplier who, desperate for work, offered to supply at a low price. However, this new supplier soon found full-time employment and my client was again without support.

Then my client found that the protocol used was non-standard, unfamiliar to other suppliers. The firmware had to be rewritten. Various subcontractors were arguing that the previous vendor had designed the interfaces incorrectly. The project was stalled. My client was left with money invested in an unusable product. Insisting the problems were unavoidable and the company's strategy was prudent and financially conservative, he asked for my advice.

Building the Story for the Customer and Letting Him Come to His Own Conclusion

Back in my own office, I mulled over the options of telling my client's company that they needed to focus on gathering and analysing data, not building hardware, and that my client's pet project should be given to a company specialising in custom hardware development. After looking through my notes for each business unit's growth plan, I outlined the following agenda:

1. Summarise the information that I had gathered, asking what my client's role was in achieving his company's aggressive growth goals.
2. Determine how he was addressing the common issues that any growing company would encounter (security, cross-training, hiring new staff and so on).
3. Ask how much of his time he, as business development manager, could devote to developing business.
4. List the problems previously experienced, highlighting the time he had spent on the custom equipment versus doing business development.

I revisited my client. When I 'replayed' what I had been told, he started filling in the answers, arriving at the conclusion that they should focus on their core business of collecting and analysing data, rather than on building hardware. We never addressed the fourth item listed above; my client came to that conclusion on his own.

I could have told that company in the first meeting that product development was not their core strength, and that the business development manager's pet project of managing all the vendors was costing them dearly. But that would probably have been my last visit! As obvious as some answers seem, when situations have evolved over time the people in the middle are unable to see many of the most obvious answers. Replaying their words in a different context is the key to guiding them towards their own decision.

Difficult Decisions

The quickest way to get lost in business, in a project, or in your personal life is to be indecisive. Lack of direction increases stress and frustration. It seems natural, therefore, that teams on projects beleaguered with 'decisive-challenged' management would be excited to have the log jam broken by a dynamic, decisive leader. They are not. Cultures develop around the indecision, and people take advantage to fuel their own agendas.

REASONS WHY PEOPLE FAIL TO MAKE DECISIONS

Indecisive environments frustrate people, their morale wanes and productivity plummets. The problem must be dealt with aggressively, with a good decision process and accountable decision makers.

Educating team members on how decisions are made is the most effective method for gaining their cooperation and for removing existing subcultures and 'workarounds'. Essential for dissenters, this education is also critical to defend and correct the occasional wayward decision.

There are hundreds of reasons for reluctant decision makers, but in general they can be grouped into three broad categories:

1. individual;
2. environmental;
3. situational.

Individual Failure to Make Decisions

Some people do not have the fortitude to be decision makers. Making decisions requires taking a stand, defending the decision and, if it is incorrect, admitting the error and creating the corrective action. People who lack confidence are incapable of making and defending decisions. Those who cannot admit their mistakes are trapped in their own pride. It takes confidence, conviction and humility to be a good decision maker – key components of leadership.

Of course, there are people who are simply poor decision makers. They do not gather and analyse data objectively. Their decisions are driven by emotions rather than facts, resulting in ill-fated direction.

Environmental Factors That Affect Decision Making

Environmental factors creating a culture of indecision are the most difficult to address. Examples of people refusing to make choices until they have foolproof options, plausible deniability, or a scapegoat are commonplace. Eliminating culpability often requires referral of all decisions to a central figure or superior.

Consensus decisions slow organisations and frustrate team members. It is nearly impossible to get everyone to agree, it takes significant time and energy.

Internal people can rarely correct these problems. They are part of the culture and are blind or powerless to the issues. External consultants or new senior management well-versed in organisation development are the ones who can commonly realign organisations to a different methodology.

Situational Factors Affecting Decision Making

Situational problems arise from transient conditions. These are based on localised problems new to the organisation. Two examples are:

1. lack of problem definition;
2. poor or insufficient data.

There are many times when decisions cannot be made because the problem or the desired outcomes are poorly defined. Without understanding either of these you do not know where you are, or in which direction you are heading. Each attempt at making a decision results in identifying too many flaws. The flaws cannot be overcome because the issues are poorly defined.

Poor data usually result in bad decisions. Because almost all decisions are made on estimates, a review of the estimating processes often identifies the source of the problem. Lack of definition, inadequate understanding of problems or over-confidence can all cause bad decisions.

CASE EXAMPLE NO. 3

At times direction is set without decisions being made. That becomes obvious when an outsider examines the data. A few years ago, I was assigned to a project where the customer's documentation clearly stated that the goal was to assess the problems with an existing IT tool and 'stop the bleeding'. A tactical solution was desired because they were hesitant to invest money in something that they might well throw away in a few years.

Even though this project was listed as tactical, its budget was $1.8 million. During the previous year a similar project had been proposed with a budget of only $800,000. Further investigation uncovered statements in the original proposal documentation to the effect that 50 per cent of the existing code would be reusable. These facts seemed a little incongruous with a truly tactical project. I referred the issue to the newly assigned project sponsor. He had not been part of the original definition and he put project scope at the top of the triple constraints, which did not seem to indicate a tactical definition.

When I discussed this with the IT architect, he defined a solution that would mean moving to a completely new platform rather than modifying the existing one. By doing this, the list of activities was greatly increased and many of the new tasks lay outside the description of those that one would expect for a tactical project definition. As the team put together the final schedule, the estimated cost increased by $400,000.

Tactical	Strategic
$800,000	$1,800,000
Existing programming platform	New programming platform
Stop the bleeding	50 per cent reusable code
Priority: 1. Cost 2. Timeline 3. Scope	Priority: 1. Scope 2. Timeline 3. Cost

Figure 2.4 Comparison of conflicting decision factors in case example no. 3

I put all the data into a simple table (shown in Figure 2.4) for presentation to executive management. Within the course of a couple days, the project sponsor had an epiphany and the project was drastically scaled back. This decision to strip the project back to a tactical approach upset the team because they had been comfortable with the previous indecisiveness that would have allowed them to do as they pleased. Their angst was so bad that they had to be reassigned, and replaced by a completely new team. That caused additional start-up delays but the corporate goals were met at a difficult time when the world was going into a recession.

Team Building

The most effective tool for any project is its team. Once a team is aligned, it will have the ability to do almost anything, even including driving management. So, create a core team of open-minded members, take ownership of the project and get it moving in the right direction. Even the most ineffectual management will eventually follow. Using the following four key principles will help you to build a superlative team:

1. *The answers are in the team*: Regardless of the issues, many (if not most) of the team will know what the problems are – and know how to fix them. Strengthen every project by finding these key people and exploiting their knowledge to keep the project straight. A tight, dedicated team with near gang-member mentality is one of the most powerful and efficient tools you will find.
2. *Good teams defeat poor management*: Even mediocre teams can do amazing tasks given the right inspiration and leadership. You have to take advantage of each individual's strengths and avoid using that individual to fill an unsuitable slot. People with the wrong skills or training will struggle, get frustrated and most likely fail.
3. *Stay immersed in the team*: To keep in touch with the team and make it stronger you have to act as a peer with its members. Superiority is only on paper. Stay in touch with the day-to-day activities. Do not remain out of sight in your office or deal only with the higher executives. Become personally involved with the project requirements and even consider offloading some tasks on to yourself, if that should be necessary to avoid overloading people.

    Keep management informed – their appreciation will come with successful delivery. Executives like seeing tasks completed but can tend to forget projects when they are running well, so do not get upset if they appear to be ignoring you. The last thing you want is the CEO visiting your desk every day.

    By doing all these things you can see and feel the project move. You do not need status reports because you are there. Know the project's details and intricacies at all times. If people want details, you will be able to deliver them quickly and concisely. People will rarely question your understanding of the project.
4. *Objective facts are your friend*: This fourth principle follows from the above. People know this as knowledge is power (some also know it as data *is* power, but they fail to realise that data is the plural form of datum, so data are power). Information can certainly be powerful when it is held close, but when it is shared it becomes both powerful and friendly. Your fact-based decisions will be important in establishing you as the leader who can head your project in the right direction.

Conclusion

Projects fail for many reasons but you must learn to recognise the symptoms early. Those symptoms, often ignored, come from an organisation's idiosyncrasies or quirks. They are imbedded in its culture. Processes alone cannot deal with all the problems. Most problems boil down to the people in the project. Ineffective leadership, indecision, interpersonal challenges, supercharged egos, separate agendas – the list is long. To have successful projects you need to take the time to know, to lead and to manage the people, building them into teams that can drive the projects to success.

References and Further Reading

Betts, M. (2009), 'The no. 1 cause of IT failure: Complexity', *CIO Magazine*, December 2009. Available at: http://www.cio.com/article/511368

Johnson, J. (2006), *My Life is Failure*. Boston: The Standish Group International, p. 4.

Project Management Institute (PMI) (2008), 'Annual Report for 2008', p. 3. Available at: http://www.pmi.org/en/About-Us/~/media/PDF/Executive-Legal/PMI_AR08_FINAL_72.ashx

Project Management Institute (PMI) (2008), *Annual Report for 2008*. Newtown Square, PA: Project Management Institute, p. 3.

Row, H. (1998), 'The 9 faces of leadership', Fast Company, January 1998. Available at: http://www.fastcompany.com/magazine/13/9faces.html

The Standish Group (2009), 'Chaos Summary 2009 Report, April 2009 White Paper'. Boston: The Standish Group International Inc.

Williams, T.C. (2011), *Rescue the Problem Project: A Complete Guide to Identifying, Preventing, and Recovering from Project Failure*. New York: AMACOM.

3 *Project Life Cycles*

DENNIS LOCK

To talk about projects having life cycles suggests that they are living things. In many senses projects are. They experience conception and eventual termination. They are subject to accident, risk and even sudden death. They are dynamic and interact in diverse ways with other living creatures (usually human beings but sometimes with all manner of species from the living world). An understanding of project life cycles is necessary for all those involved with the management of projects. That need is not confined to project managers, but extends in many directions throughout the organisation, not least at the top, where strategic decisions on capital investment, staffing and facilities are made. We cannot discuss the management of people in projects comprehensively without having an awareness of project life cycle patterns.

Some Fundamental Features of Project Life Cycles

Clearly the life cycle pattern will depend to a large extent on the nature and size of project being considered. Elsewhere (Lock, 2013), I have identified four categories of project. These are generalised and subject to exceptions, but they can be summarised as:

1. Construction, including mining and quarrying. These projects are usually conducted outdoors, often at some distance from the contractor's own premises. In many cases their progress can be witnessed by the general public.
2. Manufacturing projects, which include any project to make a special item, which might be a tiny object or something as large as an ocean liner. What these projects have in common is that they can be managed within the contractor's own premises (such as a factory or a shipyard). Research and development or design projects leading to prototypes fall into this category.
3. Management projects. In companies these include changes to organisations and IT systems. Staging a dramatic performance, concert or society wedding are other examples. These projects are often focused on people and on the way in which they work or use their leisure time.
4. Projects for pure research. These are the projects carried out in experimental laboratories where no one can be sure of the results. They are difficult to project manage because there might be no plan. They are often controlled by stage gating, where funds are granted or allocated periodically, with the understanding that funding could be withdrawn at any time.

The nature of a project life cycle will depend to some extent on the category of project. For example a pure research project might have a life cycle in which the end date of the project or the directions in which the research will proceed cannot be known with any certainty at the beginning. The life cycle patterns discussed in this chapter do not take into account all the possible variations. The concern here is principally how people and life cycles interrelate.

LIFE CYCLE PATTERN FOR A SMALL PROJECT VIEWED IN DIFFERENT LEVELS OF DETAIL

By convention we describe the different parts of a life cycle as its phases, and Figure 3.1 below shows some of the ways in which people view and describe those phases. The project chosen for this first example is a manufacturing project carried out in house, for the design and manufacture of a machine that the company will use itself in the manufacture of its products. So, for this company, it is both an internal capital investment project (a management project) and a manufacturing project.

Look first at Figure 3.1(a). This is a very simplistic view of a project life cycle, but one that is commonly seen. It is fatally flawed because it misses out several important phases. Those omissions will become apparent when Figures 3.1(b) and (c) are considered.

One enormous mistake in Figure 3.1(a) is to ignore the fact that some materials, components and services will have to be purchased or otherwise obtained for the project from external sources. Project managers and their engineers sometimes seem to disparage the purchasing department and its people, even on occasion approaching suppliers directly themselves and committing their companies to purchases, without first taking commercial advice from those who are best qualified to give it. Purchasing is such an important function in most projects that it must be taken very seriously by project managers.

On some projects, bought out goods and services can account for up to 80 per cent of the total project costs (information obtained from the Chartered Institute of Purchasing and Supply). All project managers and engineers need to be aware of the importance of the purchasing function. Rules should be in place that prevent people committing their organisation to significant purchase contracts (perhaps over a specified value) without

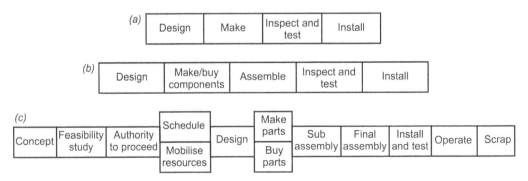

Figure 3.1   Three views of the life cycle for a manufacturing project

Note: All these views are flawed in one way or another, but the view at (c) comes closest to reality. This diagram is not drawn to a timescale.

the involvement and approval of the purchasing department. Some project organisations overcome this communication difficulty to some extent by placing one or more buyers from their purchasing department in the project team. This has the advantage that the project manager and other senior project members can have direct input to individual purchase contracts, but they have in their midst at least one person with the training and experience to ensure that serious commercial mistakes are avoided and that value will be obtained for money.

So, Figure 3.1(b) at least recognises the purchasing function. But it still tells an incomplete story. Figure 3.1(c) gets a little closer to the truth. For instance, it recognises that several life cycle phases must occur before the project is even allowed to start. Thus someone first has the idea (the concept) that a new machine is necessary in the production plant. Senior management will either refuse the suggestion out of hand or, as here, commission a feasibility study. A feasibility study can be a large project in itself for some very big capital projects, but in our example the people involved would probably be drawn from a mix of cost estimators, production engineers, design engineers and so on – not a big team by any means, but a small group with enough experience and talent to predict the financial benefits and identify some of the potential risks and problems. At this early phase it is quite possible, even usual, that no project manager will be involved or appointed. This is purely an evaluation phase. There is no project organisation.

Once senior management have given the authority to proceed, however, all that changes and a project coordinator or project manager must be nominated without delay. For this small manufacturing project a senior member of the engineering design department might take charge of the project.

Now the time has come for this company to plan for the project, attempt to schedule the human resource requirements, and then ensure that sufficient people with the appropriate skills can be made available to carry out this work (which will be additional to the company's usual manufacturing processes). At such times use can be made of temporary staff hired on hourly or weekly contracts, possibly using external employment agencies (a subject discussed briefly in Chapter 48).

The remaining phases shown in Figure 3.1(c) are self-explanatory, with a long period of successful and profitable operation of the machine envisaged once it has been manufactured and installed. But this more comprehensive life cycle diagram takes into account that the machine will eventually have to be disposed of, long after the end of the active project when the machine was first installed. In this case disposal would most probably comprise a simple scrap process, with steps taken for the recycling of materials as far as possible. But in other kinds of projects the life cycle phases for disposal at the end of the projects' useful lives can become very significant (for example in the reinstatement of land after opencast mining, quarrying or in the nuclear power industry).

There remains one important error common to all the life cycle representations in Figure 3.1. This is that in real life progress does not pass suddenly from one phase to the next at all the phase intersections. That is particularly true in the phases following authority to proceed. For example, the manufacture of parts and subassemblies might begin even though some design is still being carried out. This is not easy to show in a diagram but Dawson (2007) solves that problem neatly by drawing the various phases as overlapping ellipses. Another good way of depicting the life cycle is to draw it in the form of a Gantt chart, as in Figure 3.2 on the next page.

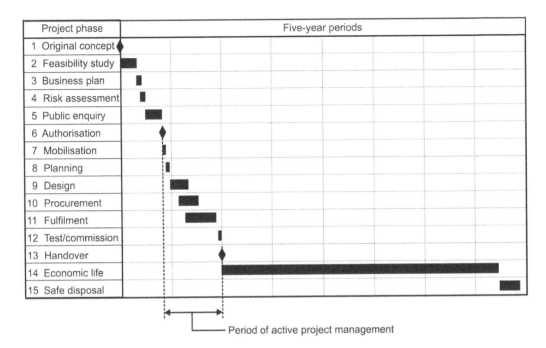

Figure 3.2   Gantt chart representation of the life cycle for a large construction project

Life Cycle Implications for People Before Project Authorisation

Figure 3.2 depicts the principal life cycle phases for a very large construction project, which might be an airport or a nuclear power generation plant. Unlike the patterns in Figure 3.1, the life cycle phases here are drawn to a timescale, which allows us to depict the overlapping phases.

CONCERNS ABOUT PEOPLE DURING THE EARLY PHASES OF LARGE INDUSTRIAL OR PUBLIC PROJECTS

News usually leaks out by some channel or other at the very early stages of public projects, when even the developers and investors have no fixed idea of how the project will turn out. This is also true of many management change projects (discussed in the following section).

In the case of large construction projects such as that depicted in Figure 3.2, a public enquiry phase is very often necessary to allow the stakeholders – all manner of people, councils and pressure groups – to express their views. For very large public projects the national government might even be involved in making final go or no-go decisions. The owner's interests will best be served at this stage if attractive and informative brochures are prepared that outline the project proposals and extol all the virtues and benefits that will accrue to the community and other stakeholders.

It is important that the project owner is adequately and robustly represented at all public and private enquiry meetings, to listen to the views of those present and answer their questions fully and as far as possible allaying any fears and resolving concerns. The line project manager might not have been appointed at this early stage, but it is common for a professional consultancy organisation to carry out the feasibility study and advise the owner in conducting the project through these early phases. That consulting organisation might or might not become the active project manager if the project is allowed to proceed.

CONCERNS ABOUT PEOPLE DURING THE PRE-AUTHORISATION PHASES OF MANAGEMENT CHANGE PROJECTS

For management change projects, general public interest will rarely be a problem, but now another issue comes into play. That is, as soon as the concept for the project has been formed and the feasibility studies begin, it always seems to happen that the staff in the organisation will suspect that a change is being proposed. Rumours spread like wildfire and, like wildfires, are difficult to extinguish. To preserve confidentiality and prevent information leaks it may be desirable to set up a temporary external office, away from the company premises (perhaps in a suitable hotel or in the offices of a consulting organisation). There the relevant managers and others conducting the feasibility study can meet, discuss the proposals freely and lay out their plans or cost schedules with less far risk of information leaks.

One example from my experience concerned the possible relocation of our company's main offices from central London to a provincial town or city. That would have meant relocating or replacing about 300 staff, many of whom were professional engineers with valuable experience and capabilities. Places investigated included Exeter, Swindon, Warwick and Newbury. In the event, Newbury was the preferred choice. After a detailed feasibility study, preparation of a proposal and even the location of a suitable construction site, the board of directors refused to allocate the considerable capital investment required and the project was abandoned.

But information about the study had leaked out. Much of that information became distorted as it was passed from person to person. Some people claimed to know where the company would be moving, even before the feasibility study had produced its recommendations. For several weeks small groups of people were to be seen standing together away from their desks, anxiously discussing their fears. Work suffered. The damage done to morale and staff motivation had been significant, with people clearly being apprehensive about their future prospects with the company.

Those difficulties could have been avoided if confidentiality had been more secure during the early project phases. That is not advocating dishonesty – just recommending no release of information before all the salient intentions have been determined. Anyone who disbelieves the power of suggestion and rumour can conduct a simple (but dangerous) experiment. Have one or two people walk through the company premises conspicuously carrying tape measures and clipboards. Then sit back and await the results. Not recommended.

Of course, as soon as the decision for any organisation change has been made, staff must be informed truthfully and fully as soon as possible. For example, if a new IT system is to be installed, it should be made clear that although people's duties might change, they can be assured of support and retraining as far as is practicable during the implementation period.

If a company is to be relocated, staff must be advised of the reasons for relocation, and reassured about the benefits that will accrue to those who move in terms of their daily lives and local amenities. For example, many people will need to know about the quality and availability of schools in the new place.

For those who decide to move with the company, reimbursement of relocation expenses should be assured. Companies can usually set up arrangements in advance with organisations such as local estate agents to give staff the opportunity of using their advice and services.

Those who choose not to relocate must be treated fairly. They must be reassured as far as possible, for example by outlining their severance or early retirement packages and by providing assistance to them in finding alternative employment.

Most importantly, consultation channels must be established between staff or their collective representatives and management. If practicable and reasonable changes to the conditions or terms are requested, they should be agreed and implemented.

Management of People in Relation to the Life Cycle Phases of a Project after Authorisation

This section considers how aspects of people management can change as a project progresses after it has been authorised to proceed and the project manager has been appointed. Here, in other words, we are considering the active stages of the project, which are sometimes collectively called project fulfilment.

PROVIDING THE HUMAN RESOURCES

Unlike routine operations in organisations such as service providers, companies that habitually undertake large projects have to plan for fluctuations in staff numbers that are associated with project life cycles. Within an individual project these staffing levels can range from near-zero personnel at project authorisation, climbing to a maximum of possibly hundreds of specialists during the peak period of activity, and then reducing back to zero when the project is finished. Of course, companies with experience of carrying out such projects often manage several projects at the same time, and are able to smooth out the worst peaks and troughs of resource requirements using well-established (but not always well-understood) project or multiproject resource scheduling methods. A project support office should have the IT facilities and competence to carry out resource scheduling, which often has to take into account predictions for future projects where the contracts have not been signed (sales opportunities). Nevertheless, most companies carrying out projects will experience and have to cater for some fluctuations in their staffing levels. It is not always possible to avoid having peaks and troughs in human resource requirements. Human resource scheduling is outlined in chapters 41 and 42.

Of course, in this section we are talking about staff who work in the home office of the company, or at least within the company organisation. For many projects, especially those in the construction industry, problems of wildly fluctuating staff number requirements for technicians, artisans and labourers are far more readily and customarily solved by adopting a contract matrix organisation, in which subcontracts are let by a managing contractor for the various specialist operations. To a large extent this relieves the managing contractor of the problem of resource scheduling, except for those who are directly employed.

Every project-based company that operates in a particular industry needs to have a core staff of people who are experienced, qualified and trained in their particular professions and skills. That way benefits the company as it gains collective experience from project to project, learning lessons, honing technical skills and judgement and giving individual people the motivating factors of relative job security and the prospect of career advancement and promotion. One solution is to employ these most valuable core staff on permanent contracts, and supplement that core from time to time using short-term or agency staff to fill occasional gaps in requirements. Thus the permanent staff can accrue experience, have possible promotion paths in their careers and accumulate pension rights with reduced fears of redundancy. Short-term contracted staff, when suitably treated, can give dedicated service to projects, working alongside their permanent colleagues and under the supervision of the relevant specialist managers.

MOTIVATIONAL CHANGES IN RELATION TO PROJECT PROGRESS

The time to begin inspiring motivation in project staff is when the project is authorised and the project manager takes command. A common way of launching a project is to invite all managers and supervisors who will eventually be working on the project to an initial meeting. This 'kick-off' meeting is not unlike the meeting that a commander will address troops before a battle. Such meetings are relatively easy to organise and can be expected to raise few difficulties, although questions cannot always be fully answered because even the project manager may not be aware of all project details when he or she is first appointed – and that early time is the best time to have the meeting. I remember one such meeting, addressed by the engineering director, in which our company had secured a big machine tool contract from (then) Rover Car Company. The contract had been signed by our parent company in the US, and we in the UK knew little about the details. Yet the engineering director was able to point out the advantages to our company and the excitement to be expected in undertaking this work. This director got the short but lively and inspiring initial meeting off to a good start by declaring 'About the only thing I can tell you about this project right now is that Rover is a darned good name for a dawg'. Humour, as on this occasion, can be a good motivator.

However, the power of a rousing kick-off meeting to motivate staff can be limited and short-lived. It is limited partly because the number of people marshalled to work on the project at the beginning will usually be low and not representative of the workforce during the peak in the active phases of the life cycle. As the project proceeds, other forms of motivation become necessary.

Demotivating factors can arise as a project proceeds. Changes in scope or design can derail a project, and every effort must be made to keep such changes to the minimum, which in turn means that project definition during the early life cycle phases has to be as accurate as possible. Project managers know that changes made late in the life cycle are liable to cost more than if the same changes had been made early, because of the need to write off wasted sunk costs and of the disruption caused to progress.

Other demotivators as the project journeys through its active phases include industrial disputes, materials shortages, technical difficulties, personal injury accidents and (for open-air projects) prolonged periods of unsuitable or bad weather. Risk management, operated by a person or people with the appropriate skills in risk assessment, should be used to foresee as many of these problems as possible, so that strategies are in place for mitigating the effects of risks.

Transfer of Responsibilities During the Project Life Cycle

Within the project organisation, it is usual for many work packages to transfer from one department to another (and thus from the responsibility of one manager to another) with the passage of time and the journey towards project completion. For example, a component of the project will begin its life under the design manager, progress into manufacture or construction under the control of a different manager, and possibly move again to become the direct and immediate responsibility of a commissioning team supervisor or manager.

Design, manufacturing, construction and supply errors can and should be dealt with using formal or informal interdepartmental communications. For the resolution of design errors or difficulties experienced in following drawings, measures such as engineering query procedures or concessions can be adopted so that problems are resolved quickly and disputes avoided. But such problems will not be resolved so readily when the responsibility for a particular work package changes from one external manager to another, which is often the case when subcontractors are used.

For example, consider a building construction project in which a number of subcontractors are involved on the site. These are all independent companies, employed and scheduled by a main contractor. The project has reached a milestone in its life cycle, when the roof and windows are in place and the dry trades are told to move in. A month later a heavy thunderstorm accompanied by torrential rain proves that the building is far from waterproof. Interior finishes being undertaken by several independent subcontractors and the electrical wiring have been damaged. Who will take responsibility for the resulting delays and who will pay for the remedial work? Thus disputes can arise between companies and their managers. Unless the contract and subcontract terms and conditions are explicit and adhered to, such disputes can stop projects in their tracks, causing all kinds of problems for the investors and the people in the project organisation.

Such difficulties associated with the transfer of work during a life cycle can occur in any project that employs subcontractors or partners. For example the Airbus A380 project, much of which was undertaken by different companies working in several nations, suffered severe delays when incompatibilities were discovered between the electrical wiring harness designs produced by some of these companies. These wiring harnesses, which in total contained some 300 miles of cabling for each aircraft, were expected to interconnect with each other to transfer power and electrical signals between major components of the aircraft. It has been widely reported that the project hit big trouble because engineers working in different companies, although they were using the same design software, were trained to use different versions of that software. There were also difficulties in transferring data between the two software versions. These problems were compounded because the incompatibilities were only discovered late in the project life cycle and first deliveries of aircraft to customers were delayed for long periods.

So any project manager must always be aware of potential difficulties when responsibilities for work packages change from one manager to another or from one company to another as the project travels through its life cycle. This advice is also to be heeded by planning engineers, because no project activity should be allowed to span two (or more) departments in a plan. That would split responsibility for completing the task between two managers and possibly more than halve the motivation and commitment of each manager. A task that progresses consecutively from the responsibility of one manager to that of another must appear in the plan as two tasks, so that each manager can be made responsible and accountable for only that part of the task over which he or she has direct control.

Difficulties Caused by Life Cycles that Do not Run to Plan

Practically every project plan will be based on the assumption that a time will come when the project is finished, all the bugs have been removed, and the end user begins to enjoy the forecast benefits. But project life cycles do not always run so smoothly. Many projects run late and some fail to produce all the expected benefits. But the worst cases of all from the people management point of view are those where the customer or investor pulls the plug, and either asks for the project to be postponed or cancelled altogether.

Projects in the defence sector are particularly at risk, because their life cycles might span the lives of several national governments, and it is not uncommon for a newly elected government to cancel a project authorised by its predecessor. There have also been many instances of projects that have been authorised and later cancelled by the same government.

Commercial customers for large projects can ask for work to be delayed or cancelled because of changes in the financial climate, or because they have unexpectedly run short of cash. For example, a Zambian copper-mining company ordered the design, delivery and installation of a new coal plant for one of its refineries from a British engineering company. During the engineering design phase the price of copper on the international market fell substantially, so that mining company's business case for the coal plant investment collapsed. Accordingly the mining company asked for further work on the project to be deferred to some later, unspecified date. So all work on the project stopped, and the design work already completed had to be mothballed. Clearly this was very disappointing and demotivating for the many engineers who had worked on the project, and the British company found it difficult to redeploy them.

So companies must always expect the unexpected. The company at most risk would be a defence contractor working on just one big project where the national government was the only customer. It is a well-known business rule that all eggs should not be put in one basket. The company best able to survive a project cancellation will be the one that has established a mixed portfolio of projects for several different customers. Then if one project should be cancelled, it should be possible to redeploy many of the staff affected on to other work. Where such redeployment is not possible, that raises once more the desirability of having a workforce that comprises a core of permanent staff, supported by short-term contract or temporary staff.

Conclusion

This chapter has described project life cycles in fairly general terms. It recognises that the course of a life cycle will depend very much on the nature of the project. Life cycle patterns are important to the way in which projects are managed and also to the way in which people perceive projects. So discussion of project life cycles cannot end with this chapter and that references to life cycles will be made in several later chapters in this book. I'm ending here with a footnote from Lindsay Scott, who reminds us that the very fact that projects have life cycles can make them attractive and stimulating for the people to work on them. Project work can be exciting because of its variety and the scope it often provides for original thought, innovation and a final sense of achievement.

References and Further Reading

Dawson, C.W. (2007), 'The project life-cycle' in Turner, R. (ed.), *Gower Handbook of Project Management*, Aldershot: Gower.

Lock, D. (2013), *Project Management*, 10th edn, Farnham: Gower.

4 *Project Sponsors*

KARSTEN ISENBECK and JOEL FRIEDMAN

This chapter is an account of the people who provide the capital or other resources for a project with the expectation of financial gain and/or other reward for their organisation. Successive sections deal with the motivations, expectations and competencies of project sponsors. In addition to relevant literature, we shall draw on the results and conclusions of our own thesis research project on project sponsor input and personal competencies.

Introduction

The PMBOK (PMI, 2008) defines a sponsor as 'the person or group that provides the financial resources, in cash or in kind, for the project'. For Patel and Morris (1999), the project sponsor is 'the owner of the project business case', and they 'represent the funder's interests'. Also, the project sponsor 'manages, administers, monitors, funds, and is responsible for the overall project delivery' (Visitask, 2011). These definitions provide a sense of how comprehensive and significant the project sponsor's role is and how instrumental that is to project success (and ultimately to organisational success).

Project sponsors may be business owners or directors, organisational executives or middle managers such as programme managers, operational managers, asset managers or cost-centre owners. The roles and responsibilities of a project sponsor are influenced by, among other things, the industry, the organisational project management culture, the project type, the project complexity and asset life cycle phases in which the project sponsor is acting. Accordingly, the project sponsor is required to have sufficient seniority to present the project to the organisation and is required to be available, provide support and make timely decisions.

Motivations and Expectations of Project Sponsors

In this section of the chapter, we touch upon some of the primary motivations of executives, managers, business owners and others for choosing to take on the challenging role of sponsoring projects. Additionally, we look into the project sponsor's base-level expectations of organisational capability and finally their views on human capital expenditure. Whilst much has been written on these subjects in general, far less has been written on these topics with respect to project sponsors.

MOTIVATION

It is commonly accepted that a project sponsor's leadership ability, and his/her associated capability to motivate others, are key to the success or failure of the project and the business plan. A topic that remains largely unexplored, however, is the project sponsor's motivations for wanting to become a project sponsor.

Many would intuitively jump to the conclusion that individuals become project sponsors for the extrinsic rewards (remuneration package and perquisites). But an MIT research study into motivation in general indicates that increased performance for increased extrinsic reward (compensation) only motivates those who do mechanical tasks (Ariely et al., 2005). The MIT study also found that for tasks which call for 'even rudimentary cognitive skill' and require some level of conceptual thinking (which certainly includes all the tasks that the project sponsor is expected to perform) a larger reward actually leads to poorer performance. Based on this and other studies with similarly documented results, Pink (2009) asserts that there is a third 'drive', additional to the biological drive and the extrinsic drive influenced by rewards and punishments, that motivates people – namely, the drive for 'autonomy, mastery and purpose'. Several of behavioural sciences' bedrock motivational theories also support Pink's conclusion (for example Maslow, and Herzberg, whose work is outlined in Chapter 31).

So whilst we believe that a sufficient, reasonable amount of extrinsic reward must be provided to entice people to take the position of project sponsor, we agree that successful project sponsors are usually self-activated, high-esteem individuals with strong intrinsic motivation. They have the 'drive' to foster a climate in which programme and project managers can perform and communicate, take responsibility for the project, identify themselves with the programme or project goals and deliver the business case benefits to the organisation.

To get a first-hand idea of what motivates a project sponsor, we polled our research test group of project sponsors on the question of 'What is your primary motivation for sponsoring projects?' We provided nine multiple choice responses for them to prioritise in response. Though our sample size was small, and therefore may not be generalisable to the population of project sponsors as a whole, the responses provide useful and personalised feedback. The top-tier responses on motivations were, in the following order:

- mastering the ability to guide/facilitate projects to success;
- enjoyment in leading people;
- making a contribution to the company.

Additionally, we asked the project sponsors to identify demotivating factors that might discourage anyone from being a project sponsor. The top two demotivations for our project sponsors were first possessing insufficient authority and, second, having insufficient organisational support to succeed in their role of enabling project success.

Concerns were raised by the project sponsors regarding potential consequences to their careers if their projects should fail. Just as sponsoring successful projects can lead to recognition, greater challenges and potentially rewards or promotions, even one failed project might damage the project sponsor's reputation and adversely impact his/her future career opportunities.

Project Sponsors' Base-level Expectations of Organisational Project Delivery Capability

According to a recent IBM study (IBM, 2010), that surveyed more than 1,500 CEOs worldwide, the CEOs noted that the world in which they operate is 'substantially more volatile, uncertain and complex' and they expect to make 'deeper business model changes to realise their strategies', to include pursuing 'more calculated risks, find new ideas and keep innovating in how they lead and communicate'. Consequently, and as business is increasingly delivered through a portfolio of projects and programmes, project sponsors become key enablers of an organisation's achievement of consistent success in line with strategic objectives. To enable consistently high performance with respect to delivering successful projects, the project sponsor would naturally look to be supported by the organisation's ability to:

- provide skilled human resources and promote their engagement and development;
- process technology;
- measure and enhance delivery capabilities;
- increase operational efficiency;
- retain and develop a talented workforce;
- maintain flexible cost structures;
- initiate and close-out projects quickly;
- establish and maintain complete work breakdown structures;
- define and tune scope and implement strict change management processes;
- promote an active risk management culture;
- analyse past situations and predict future trends;
- maintain transparency of project review processes within the organisation;
- enforce gate review approvals criteria;
- support project and programme managers in their roles and responsibilities;
- embrace ambiguity;
- improve and innovate project delivery capabilities; and, above all
- deliver the project as outlined in the business plan.

An ever more widely accepted means by which a project sponsor may express base-level expectations of an organisation's project delivery capability is through a project management maturity model. Many organisations have already implemented maturity models that assess their project management practices against standard criteria. Although as recently as 2004, there was no empirical evidence to link project management maturity level and project performance capability (Jugdev and Thomas, 2002), there were numerous '*claims* that project management maturity conferred business results' (Cooke-Davies, 2004).

In 2004, PricewaterhouseCoopers (PwC) published their landmark study 'Boosting Business Performance through Programme and Project Management: A First Global Survey on the Current State of Project Management Maturity in Organisations Across the World' (Nieto-Rodriguez and Evrard, 2004). From their study of 200 organisations with an annual turnover of USD 75 billion, this reported that among the many other benefits of attaining project management maturity there is a positive correlation between organisational maturity level and project performance. Since PwC's report was issued, many other related research studies have been conducted that confirm the positive correlation between higher organisational maturity, higher project performance and delivery capability as well as to conferred positive business benefits.

And so, in short, project sponsors may enthusiastically welcome and support the achievement of, and maintenance of, a high level of project management maturity.

Project Sponsors and Project People

No other statement more succinctly states the importance of people in project management than 'people do projects'. Dinsmore and Cooke-Davies (2006) list 'adequate resources', to include human resources, as one of six Critical Success Factors (CSFs) that support project success. Kaplan and Norton (2006) state that in the modern, global, knowledge-based business world, a company's intangible assets comprise 80 per cent of its market value. And those intangible assets include people. Human capital is the stock of competencies, knowledge and personality attributes embodied in the ability to perform labour to produce economic value. It is the attributes gained by a worker through education and experience (O'Sullivan and Sheffrin, 2003). An organisation's human capital – both generic and firm-specific – is developed through appropriate personnel sourcing and training.

Because projects are temporary endeavours, the project sponsor probably will not be responsible for managing the more long-term, strategic human capital investment for the organisation that is often based on core-versus-context and cost-benefit analysis decisions. However, with responsibility for the project's business case success, and therefore the project success, the project sponsor must ensure his/her projects are staffed with sufficient and appropriate personnel at lowest possible cost. Therefore, the project sponsor recognises an organisation's and each project's human capital investment as costly, but also as crucial to success. Associated costs include sourcing, hiring, mobilising, training and engaging the personnel that will carry the project through to success.

Whilst possibly not using the words human capital productivity and return on investment (ROI) in everyday parlance, the project sponsor obviously has a robust interest in maximising the project team's overall productivity. To this end, the project sponsor will encourage best practices of training and development, knowledge-sharing, and, if possible, transfer of personnel from project to project and back to the permanent organisation, to retain, cultivate and maximise the organisation's investment.

An IBM Institute for Business Value human resource study (IBM, 2010) further helps us to glean the project sponsor's views on human capital investment. This study was compiled from over 700 surveys of chief human resource officers (CHROs) worldwide. It indicates that whilst organisations continue to develop and deploy talent in diverse areas around the globe at an accelerated rate, the rationale behind workforce investment in recent years is changing. Unlike the former, traditional pattern of movement, in which mature market-based companies sought operational efficiency through headcount growth and associated cost savings, in emerging economies we are now seeing workforce investment moving both ways. For a variety of reasons, with minimising labour cost being just one of them, major international companies in expanding markets plan to increase their workforce presence in North America, Western Europe and other mature markets. Also driving an organisation's human capital investment are organisational opportunities to penetrate new markets worldwide and to develop new offerings and associated new markets. These trends can cause a project sponsor to respond as they support their organisation in mobilising its workforce for speed and flexibility and also in capitalising on collective organisational intelligence worldwide.

Another critical element of an organisation's human capital investment is having enough people to manage the risk of unanticipated projects and organisational events. For example, the project sponsor might receive requests for key people from other projects (either the project sponsor's own projects or from other parts of the organisation). These requests must be managed and prioritised for the greater good of the organisation's success but will be easier to manage if the organisation plans strategically for some flexibility within its human capital investment plan to respond to organisational risks.

The project sponsor might meet another hurdle when the business case for a proposed project is being developed. Although the project budget will not have been approved yet, the project sponsor will need people to support the preparation of the business plan. Appropriate investment in people will ensure that there are enough people of the right kind to develop an accurate and comprehensive project business case.

Project Sponsor Competencies

Literature on this subject highlights key areas in which project sponsors are required to be competent, as follows:

- owning, leading and being responsible for the business case, primary risk taker (APM, 2006);
- handling ambiguity especially in dealing with complex programmes and projects (Crawford et al., 2008a);
- championing the project, when the project is first conceived (PMI, 2008);
- governing the project and being a friend in high places (Dinsmore and Cooke-Davies, 2006);
- working in partnership with the project manager to achieve mutually consistent objectives (Turner, 2008);
- clearing roadblocks that appear in the path of the project manager (Kerzner and Saladis, 2009).

Individual project sponsors are required to be competent to deliver a successful project or programme. They have to realise the benefits described in the project's business plan. As we said earlier however, these competencies are multi-faceted and comprise:

- seniority in the organisation;
- applicable experiences;
- knowledge and skills;
- suitable personal attributes such as traits, behaviours and attitudes.

Crawford (2007) developed a competency model based on attribute- and performance-based competence models, dividing an individual's overall competence into three categories:

1. input competencies: knowledge, qualifications, experience and skills;
2. personal competencies: traits, behaviours, attitudes and emotions;
3. output competencies: demonstrable performance against standards.

In the following sections we review project sponsor competencies according to the above categories.

Information is available for the input and personal competencies and we were able to build on that foundation through our research. However, when it came to output competencies we found a lack of performance standards that could help us to measure the performance of project sponsors in their role. In the absence of performance standards, one might refer to the project or programme outcome that a project sponsor delivers and the degree to which it meets the criteria outlined in the business plan. However, assessing a project sponsor's performance in this manner would be difficult because:

*   project or programme success is a perception by various stakeholders throughout the asset life cycle;
*   these success criteria may cut across lines of project management success, business plan success or project success.

INPUT COMPETENCIES: KNOWLEDGE, QUALIFICATIONS, EXPERIENCE AND SKILLS

Input competencies are considered eligibility factors. If you were recruiting a project sponsor, you would wish to know that they met certain minimum criteria – quality/quantity of relevant knowledge, qualifications, experience and skill levels.

Ideally we should like to direct readers to a scientific list of minimum input competencies, complete with desirable associated quantities of each competency (such as: years of overall experience, minimum degree/credential qualifications, total number of personnel managed and so on). However, we found nothing helpful in the literature at the time of our research. So we went about searching for and investigating clues to build our own list, and then to field-test that with a real-world group of project sponsors. So we combed through the relevant literature that can refer to several academic guides on the subject.

Englund and Bucero (2006) state that the project sponsor roles undertaken during the project life cycle are that of a 'seller, coach and mentor, filter, business judge, motivator, negotiator, protector and upper management link'. They continue, 'The project sponsor is usually an upper manager who, in addition to his/her usual responsibilities, provides ongoing support to one or more specific projects'. Whilst ordinarily, the term 'roles' refers to a function or position to be assumed, we reasoned that the project sponsor would need to be experienced in these roles to be effective. We thus interpreted them to be eligibility factors that would affect a project sponsor's success.

Englund and Bucero also present a 'project sponsor behaviours mind map' that lists input competencies that can also be labelled as eligibility factors:

*   business management;
*   leadership;
*   relationship and selling;

- project management;
- consulting engagement.

These writers also provide criteria (characteristics, skills and attitudes) of successful project sponsors, to include that they:

- know the business;
- know the customer or industry;
- have a vision of the future;
- have worked at mainstream activities in the organisation;
- are knowledgeable in areas where the project team is not.

Another source for base-knowledge on input competencies of project sponsors is Pacelli (2005). His 'Top Ten Attributes of a Great Project Sponsor' include such project sponsor eligibility criteria or input competency skills as: clearly understanding the problem to be solved, ensuring that the solution fixes the problem, knowing where 'good enough' is, building the right team to solve the problem, being the advocate, coach, influencer, and battering ram and knowing, very importantly, when to 'pull the plug' on a project. The attributes that Pacelli describes are usually associated with significant experience-gained mental, and judgement, skills that are typically found in more experienced senior managers.

In summary, our literature review on input competencies revealed that successful project sponsor input competency eligibility factors include implicit and explicit knowledge, such as experience as a business person, project manager, seller, knowledge in field, appropriately educated, and being adept at mentoring and leading. This mix of eligibility attributes typically comes in a senior company manager or executive who has been through years of experience at various levels of similar projects in a similar sector.

PERSONAL COMPETENCIES: TRAITS, BEHAVIOURS, ATTITUDES AND EMOTIONS

Project Performance Assessment (Crawford and Cooke-Davies, 2011), an intensive course held in March, 2011 at the SKEMA Business School, taught that effective sponsorship depends on personal characteristics and behaviour and requires: excellent communication skills, the ability to handle ambiguity and the ability to manage self to include being adept at managing one's time and stress well. Existing literature enabled us to narrow the field to three critical personal competencies for the project sponsor:

1. self-management;
2. managing and leading others;
3. managing the business and ambiguity.

With regards to the required personal competency of self-management, motivation and time and stress management were prominent supporting traits (Englund and Bucero, 2006 and Crawford et al., 2008). Crawford et al. write that the role of the project sponsor can be stressful as it carries with it significant responsibilities and because limited time might be available to deal with issues throughout the asset planning and project implementation period. Therefore, it is important that the project sponsor is adept at managing his/her time and stress well as well as being able to maintain a positive attitude and be motivated. We find that the traits supporting self-management are:

- being able to manage stress well;
- being pressure tolerant;
- self-acceptance;
- wanting challenge;
- being enthusiastic and committed.

With regard to a project sponsor managing and leading others, the associated personal competencies are predominantly derived out of the review of the project management, leadership, asset life cycle and organisation perspectives. The three main tasks of a project sponsor are governance of the project, to be a friend in high places and to be a visible leader of change (Dinsmore and Cooke-Davies, 2006).

Throughout the asset lifecycle, we note that the roles of the project sponsor change and therefore include quite a wide range of personal competency traits. These diverse roles may include:

- communicating with stakeholders during the asset planning process;
- obtaining stakeholders' 'buy-in';
- championing the project within the organisation;
- getting applicable resources;
- communicating the objectives and goals of the project in alignment with organisation values, visions and strategies;
- authorising and enabling the project manager to execute the project;
- during project execution, coaching and supporting the project manager and being available for escalations which are beyond the authority of the project manager as well as providing timely support;
- maintaining effective relationship with stakeholders;
- continuously aligning between company and project objectives and values;
- providing direction;
- critically reviewing project progress;
- providing leadership to the project team;
- solving stakeholder conflicts and managing stakeholder satisfaction.

From the above roles, we interpret that the project sponsor is, at suitable times and situations, required to exhibit the following behavioural traits to support his/her role:

- be committed to be a change leader;
- be anticipative towards customer needs;
- be reflective on different viewpoints and collaborate with other stakeholders;
- be supportive and helpful towards the project manager;
- be able to handle conflict between competing stakeholders;
- be diplomatic;
- be able to lead and accept decision-making responsibility;
- take accountability for the project;

- empower the project manager;
- be able to negotiate with the organisation on behalf of the project.

It is worth mentioning that there are also some personal competencies or traits that will likely hinder the project sponsor in his/her various roles and thus are contra-indicated for an effective project sponsor. Being overly controlling, impulsive, neither enforcing nor permissive, neither blunt nor harsh, being unavailable, inaccessible, not showing interest in the project and not sharing information are among these.

Finally, the roles related to managing the business and ambiguity are part and parcel of the project sponsor's responsibilities as owner of the business case. Meeting these responsibilities may require the project sponsor to adopt the following roles (these can be expected to change throughout the project life cycle):

- understanding, developing and planning the business case including the associated risks;
- selling the business case to respective parties and obtaining the business case approval;
- delivering the expected benefits;
- monitoring the vital signs in changing assumptions in scope and business;
- making decisions under his/her responsibility with the required sense of urgency;
- solving stakeholder conflicts;
- managing stakeholder satisfaction with respect to the business case;
- negotiating with and convincing other stakeholders about decisions.

Consequently, the project sponsor is required to exhibit the following personal competencies or behavioural traits to optimally support him/her in the above roles: have an interest in business management, use business judgement, be analytical and have the ability to examine facts and situations logically, be optimistic about the business case, be passionate in selling the benefits of the project, be reflective on different viewpoints and collaborate with other stakeholders, take the initiative and make decisions, be trustworthy to gain continuous buy-in from respective stakeholders.

Again, we reasoned that there are some traits that would hinder a project sponsor's optimal performance in the above roles and they are:

- being blindly optimistic and neglecting the associated risk of the business;
- being defensive and not open for different viewpoints;
- being inconclusive and delaying required decisions (for example, in ambiguous situations);
- being decisive and fast but imprecise;
- exhibiting disinterest in the project and/or business case.

OUTPUT COMPETENCIES: DEMONSTRABLE PERFORMANCE AGAINST STANDARDS

Although performance standards exist for project managers, programme managers, corporate executives and many other positions, as mentioned previously, a project sponsor performance standard that would support objective evaluation has not yet been compiled and made available. However, at the time of writing GAPPS (Global Alliance for

Project Performance Standards) has begun to compile this much-needed standard. It is an exciting journey and in our opinion contributes to future project success.

Research Findings

We refer here to our thesis research paper 'Eligibility Factors and Behavioral Traits of Effective Project Sponsors', submitted in mid-2011 in partial fulfilment of our post-graduate degree requirements at SKEMA Business School. There we outlined the research methodology by which we developed an ideal project sponsor eligibility factors and behavioural trait profile, based on knowledge gained from our literature reviews and personal experience with project sponsors. We also carried out a pilot study assessment of real-life project sponsors to compare these factors and traits. That was done through close cooperation with the highly regarded behavioural trait assessment organisation Harrison Assessments (see also Chapter 26, in which Harrison Assessments' methodology is explained in some detail with respect to project managers, (ed.)).

We were intrigued by the idea of creating a baseline ideal project sponsor profile, having experienced situations in which there was no project sponsor in place to support project success, or the project sponsor was not as successful or effective as other project sponsors. Also, our literature review presented evidence that competent, accessible and involved project sponsors are necessary.

The online assessment was categorised into a series of questions related to behavioural traits, eligibility factors and demographic traits. It helped us to determine if project sponsors who perceived themselves as successful in delivering projects or programmes follow an ideal project sponsor profile. From this and earlier assessments we determined that the following traits would be essential, desired or are to be avoided:

- Essential traits (in general the higher the better the predicted performance). For example:

  - takes initiative;
  - finance/business;
  - wants challenge;
  - strategic judgement;
  - influencing;
  - analytical;
  - persistent;
  - authoritative;
  - diplomatic;
  - wants to lead;
  - enthusiastic;
  - planning.

- Desired traits (traits in which low scores can hinder performance). For example:

  - handles conflict;
  - helpful;

   – influencing;
   – optimistic;
   – pressure tolerance;
   – self-acceptance;
   – systematic;
   – warmth/empathy;
   – precise;
   – manages stress well.

- Traits to be avoided (traits in which high scores can hinder performance). For example:

   – blindly optimistic;
   – defensive;
   – dogmatic;
   – impulsive;
   – sceptical;
   – forceful;
   – harsh;
   – blunt;
   – permissive.

We also determined that the eligibility factors indicating increased likelihood of the project sponsor being more effective in his/her role were:

- higher total years of professional experience;
- greater experience in the current industry;
- greater project sponsor experience;
- greater project business/financial analysis experience;
- greater project/programme management experience;
- greater people management experience;
- higher cost budget responsibility;
- higher education level, possessing business or project management related degrees;
- higher coaching and mentoring experience;
- greater experience in managing internal and external stakeholders.

Accordingly, and in line with our vision at the start of our research, an experienced senior project sponsor exhibiting the above personal traits would be an ideal candidate for sponsoring certain type of projects.

Within the validity of our research and with regard to project management and business plan success, we found that, overall, experienced sponsors perceive themselves as more successful, particularly with those sponsoring engineering projects. Also, project sponsors exhibiting the combination of behavioural traits as defined in the ideal project sponsor profile perceive themselves as more successful.

However, we could not identify any difference in successful project output between more or less experienced project sponsors or those with more or less behavioural traits as defined in the ideal project sponsor profile.

Our key research findings also include that many project sponsor behavioural traits appear to be required only in certain situations, and so patterns of positive correlations between traits and project success did not always emerge as might have been expected. Nevertheless, our research supports that project management success and business plan success of engineering projects can be enhanced by using experienced, eligible project sponsors, who do exhibit the behavioural traits *collaborative, handles conflict* and *diplomatic*.

Owing to our small pilot study size and limited resources, we conclude that more research on the relationship between project sponsors and input and personal competencies is needed.

Conclusions

Existing literature strongly supports that effective project sponsors have a positive impact on project success. Our pilot research study also indicates this to be true for project management and business plan success of engineering projects. There is a strong statistical relationship between the ideal sponsor traits profile that was custom-generated for this pilot study through vigorous literature review, many discussions with subject matter experts and through our own interpretation of the crucial traits of successful project sponsors. Our results have been validated through indicative trends in the results of the project sponsors' own self-assessments of their success as project sponsors. The essential and desirable project sponsor traits and the traits to avoid as detailed in our original project sponsor profile are indicated to be accurate for engineering projects. Further studies are recommended, particularly to focus on the project sponsor's role in combination with other key stakeholders traits.

The available literature on the *specific* topic of eligibility and suitability traits of project sponsors and its relationship to project sponsor success is sparse. We found no similar study on project sponsor eligibility factors, behavioural traits and demographics and their relationships with project sponsor success. We hope that our research will be used to provide a bridge between the broader and deeper pools of knowledge available on eligibility and suitability traits for related job roles. That applies also to the less well researched knowledge area of project sponsor roles, activities and ideal behavioural traits.

References and Further Reading

Ariely, D., Gneezy, U., Lowenstein, G. and Mazar, N. (2005), 'Large Stakes and Big Mistakes', Federal Reserve Bank of Boston Working Paper No. 05–11, July 2005; *New York Times*, 20 November 2008.

Association for Project Management (APM) (2006), *APM Body of Knowledge*, 5th edn, Princes Risborough: APM Publications.

Brady, S. and Turner, S. (2004), 'The Proof is in the Project: Combining Personal and Team Process with CMMI Level 5', Northrop Grumman IT Presentation, 9 March 2004.

Centre for Business Practices (CBP) (2005), *Project Portfolio Management Maturity: A Benchmark of Current Business Practices*, Philadelphia, PA: CBP.

Cooke-Davies, T.J. (2004), 'Measurement of organizational maturity: What are the relevant questions about maturity and metrics for a project-based organization to ask, and what do these imply for project management research?', in *Innovations – Project Management Research*, Newtown Square, PA: Project Management Institute.

Cooke-Davies, T.J. (2005), 'The Executive Sponsor: The Hinge upon Which Organizational Project Management Maturity Turns?', paper presented at the Project Management Institute's Global Congress, Edinburgh, 24 May 2005.

Crawford, L. (2007), 'Developing individual competence', in Turner, R. (ed.), *The Gower Handbook of Project Management*, 4th edn, Aldershot: Gower.

Crawford, L.H. and Cooke-Davies, T.J. (2005), 'Project Governance: The Pivotal Role of the Executive Sponsor', PMI Global Proceedings, Toronto, Canada.

Crawford, L. and Cooke-Davies, T. (2011), 'Project Performance Assessment' (intensive course held in March, 2011), Paris: SKEMA Business School.

Crawford, L., Cooke-Davies, T., Hobbs, B., Labuschagne, L., Remington, K. and Chen, P. (2008a), *Situational Sponsorship of Project and Programmes: An Empirical Review*, Newtown Square, PA: Project Management Institute.

Crawford, L., Cooke-Davies, T., Hobbs, B., Labuschagne, L., Remington, K. and Chen, P. (2008b), 'Governance and Support in the Sponsoring of Projects and Programmes', *Project Management Journal*, Vol. 39, doi: 10.1002/pmj, S43–S55.

Dinsmore, P.C. and Cooke-Davies, T.J. (2006), *The Right Projects Done Right!*, San Francisco, CA: Jossey-Bass.

Englund, R.L. and Bucero, A. (2006), *Project Sponsorship, Achieving Management Commitment for Project Success*, San Francisco, CA: Jossey-Bass.

GAPPS (2012), See http://www.globalpmstandards.org/main/page_performanced_based_standards.html

Gibson, D.L., Goldenson, D.R. and Kost, K. (2006), 'SEI – Performance Results of CMMI®-Based Process Improvement', SEI Technical Report CMU/SEI-2006-TR-004, August, 2006.

Graham, R.J. and Englund, R.L. (1997), *Creating an Environment for Successful Projects*, San Francisco, CA: Jossey-Bass.

Hefner, R. (2007), 'Is CMMI High Maturity Worth the Investment?', Northrop Grumman Corporation.

Helm, J. and Remington, K. (2005), 'Effective project sponsorship, an evaluation of the role of the executive sponsor in complex infrastructure projects by senior project managers', *Project Management Journal*, Vol. 36, No. 3, pp. 51–61.

Herzberg, F. (1959), *The Motivation to Work*, New York: John Wiley and Sons.

IBM Institute for Business Value (2010), *Capitalizing on Complexity: Insights from the Global Chief Executive Study*, New York: IBM Corporation.

IBM Institute for Business Value Human Resource Study (2010), *Working Beyond Borders*, Dublin: IBM Corporation.

Jugdev, K. and Thomas, J. (2002), 'From Operational Process to Strategic Asset: The Evolution in a Project Management's Value in Organizations', paper presented at PMI's 33rd Annual Symposium and Conference, San Antonio, TX (3–10 October 2002).

Kaplan, R.S. and Norton, D.P. (2006), *Alignment*, Boston, MA: Harvard Business School Press.

Kerzner, H. and Saladis, F.P. (2009), *What Executives Need to Know about Project Management*, Hoboken, NJ: John Wiley and Sons, Inc.

Maslow, A. (1943), 'A theory of human motivation', *Psychological Review*, Vol. 50, Issue 4, 1943, pp. 370–96.

Müller, R. and Turner, J.R. (2010), 'Project-oriented leadership (advances in project management)', *PM World Today*, July 2010, Vol. XII, Issue VII, pp. 1–5.

Nieto-Rodriguez, A. and Evrard, D. (2004), 'Boosting business performance through programme and project management', PricewaterhouseCoopers (PwC), June 2004. Available at: http://www.pwc.com/en_BE/be/multimedia/2004-06-21-boosting-business-performance-through-programme-and-project-management-pwc-04.pdf (accessed: 17 July 2011).

Office of Government Commerce (OGC) (2009), 'Project sponsor job description'. Available at: http://www.ogc.gov.uk/User_roles_in_the_toolkit_project_sponsor.asp [Editorial comment (DL): this website no longer exists.]

O'Sullivan, A. and Sheffrin, S.M. (2003), *Economics, Principles in Action*, California: Pearson/Prentice Hall.

Pacelli, L. (2005), 'Top Ten Attributes of a Great Project Sponsor', paper presented at 2005 PMI Global Congress in Toronto.

Patel, M.B. and Morris, P.W.G. (1999), 'Centre for Research in the Management of Projects (CRMP)', 'Project Sponsor' definition retrieved from http://maxwideman.com/pmglossary/index.htm

Pink, D. (2009), *Drive*, New York: Penguin Group.

Project Management Institute (PMI) (2008), *A Guide to the Project Management Body of Knowledge (PMBOK Guide)*, 4th edn, Newtown Square, PA: Project Management Institute.

Turner, J.R. (2008), *Handbook of Project Based Management*, London: McGraw-Hill Professional.

Visitask.com (2011), 'Visitask glossary of PM terms'. Available at: http://www.visitask.com/sponsor-g.asp

5 Corporate Managers' Support for the Project Manager

DENNIS LOCK

Imagine that you are a senior manager or director of a company that carries out projects. Indeed you might be such a manager. This chapter is written as an open letter to you. For the most part it doesn't matter here what kind of projects your company is involved with.

You might never have managed a project yourself because you have reached your senior position through a career in engineering, manufacturing, logistics, marketing, finance, the law or simply through your personal talent and drive. Then you will not know, and may never need to know, the day-to-day things that your project managers do at their tactical level. Of course that is not important. You delegate all those details and must rely on your subordinates. But, you do have to be aware that strategic decisions made by you and your fellow senior managers can, at one extreme, create conditions that help your project managers to do their jobs very well. At the other extreme, neglect or bad strategic decisions can make their working lives impossible, so that your projects will fail and your company, your clients, and all the other stakeholders will suffer.

Costs and Benefits of Project Management

PROJECT MANAGEMENT AS A COST BURDEN

Unless you manage a company (such as a managing contractor) that sells project management as a service, or you can otherwise sell your project managers' time to your clients as a direct project cost, you know that every project manager you employ will add another salary to your overheads. Further, each will occupy space and use other company facilities that also have to be paid for.

On all but the smallest projects, your project managers will expect to get support from people such as planners and cost engineers, who will also do no fee-earning work and add even more costs to your overhead burden. These people might be formed into a specialist group of their own, perhaps labelled as a project support office. Then, apparently, it gets even worse than that, because project managers need help from support staff, so adding still more indirect salaries and expenses.

Additional and significant costs will be added to the project management function if your company handles several projects at the same time (a programme of projects) and you might find yourself in need of a programme director to manage the project managers. That's another layer of management.

So, at first glance, project management is not free. It comes at a cost. And an indirect cost, at that.

BENEFITS OF PROJECT MANAGEMENT

Of course you know that without project managers your projects would descend into chaos, and fail to satisfy you or your clients. So if you had someone conduct a cost-benefit analysis for you, you would want them to report that the costs invested in project and programme management will be more than recovered by preventing the costs associated with failures to deliver on time and within budget.

Now here's some good news. Companies with competent project managers typically find that there is a far greater probability that their projects will deliver their benefits on time when compared with companies where the project management function is inadequate or lacking altogether. Perhaps that is hardly surprising.

Further, every project that is finished on time will stand a far greater chance of being delivered within or below budget costs. Indeed, far from adding costs to a project, a mix of good project management and common sense can typically knock as much as 30 per cent off the direct costs of a project (when compared with similar projects conducted by the same company in the past without competent project management). Now *that* is a good return on investment.

All projects have their risks and crises, but where there is good project management those episodes are minimised. Indeed, risk forecasting and assessment is a valuable part of the duties of many project support offices. When a project is running smoothly, its technical staff spend less of their effort in fighting fires and have more time to concentrate on delivering quality. Project management therefore facilitates completion within specification.

Efficient management of any project carried out in-house is equally important but, unlike projects delivered to an external customer or client, the expectations for internal projects extend beyond completion of the initial project. For these projects there is almost always a vital implementation period, during which the project manager and all other company managers must be committed to the project and its success if the full benefits are to be realised for the company.

BENEFITS TO THE COMPANY BEYOND THE PROJECT

A company that achieves success with its projects, whether these are in-house or for external clients, can expect to gain benefits beyond those predicted for the project itself. When project management creates orderly working, without the problems of materials shortages, resource overloads, late deliveries and so on, you as a senior manager will find that your cash flow should improve, because deliveries on time mean you can call your revenues in on time. For industrial projects, your inventory turn rate should improve because work in progress will take less time and so reduce in volume.

Success spreads happiness and contentment. If project management creates a working environment where the stresses of day-to-day panics are removed, that relief of stress should permeate the whole company as people become more relaxed at work. These are not just weasel words. This is written from personal experience.

How Much Project Management Do we Need?

Clearly every project your company does needs its project manager, but how many other project management staff can you support? So, just as project costs have to be questioned and controlled, it is quite right to examine the total expense of the project management function. Ask yourself the question: 'How much should our project management activities cost as a percentage of the total costs of a typical project in our company?'

If you are consistently delivering profitable and successful projects and your project management costs are just one or two per cent of your total project costs, you are clearly getting value for money. I once headed a project management function where, by using advanced methods and competent software, our project management costs were less than one per cent of project prime costs. But I had the advantage of very supportive senior management. And, please take note, supportive senior management is the key.

GETTING VALUE FOR THE COST OF PROJECT MANAGEMENT

Some project management functions are essential, others are desirable, and still others fall into the nice-to-have but not really necessary category. Of course every facet of project management has its vociferous and dedicated advocates. But some project management activities are more necessary than others.

Much will depend on how much information you (as a senior manager) and your clients want, because compiling and reporting information for a large project can be expensive. There is much to be said for the principle of *management by exception* – which from your position as a senior manager means you should expect your project manager to report to you in detail only the things that are not running to plan or which otherwise might give cause for concern. That is often difficult to accept. You like to see well-produced graphs and pie charts showing that your projects are running to plan and budget. But those reports might cost more money to produce than you realise. And more costs in this instance usually translates to additional staff in the project support office. It is not always obvious what functions are vital to efficient project management and which functions are simply nice-to-have.

Functions Essential to Project Management

We must assume here that the role of project manager is itself essential. Just as a company organisation needs a director or manager to be responsible for every specialist function (for example, materials management, Quality, HR, IT and so on), so there has to be a person who can be held accountable for every project. A project is a living thing and like all living things it needs a parent or someone to 'own' it, to care for it from birth to maturity. So we must have project managers. Not necessarily one for each project, because there are cases where one project manager can oversee two or more small projects.

Now, as a senior manager, you have every right to question who else needs to work in the project office. You will want to justify every overhead salary.

Every project needs a schedule and detailed budgets if it is to be controlled, and those in turn require initial work breakdowns and cost estimates. Thus projects need planners and cost engineers, although for a very small project it is possible that a multi-skilled project manager can carry out these functions without assistance. For larger projects you must have at least one planner and one cost engineer. And they will form the nucleus of your project management support office.

Unless your projects are relatively simple, or in a technology over which your company has complete command, you will also need someone to predict project risks and make contingency plans for preventing or mitigating risk occurrences. That does not need to be a full-time appointment. It could be covered by someone who usually performs other duties. Once a risk register or risk log has been set up, maintaining it need not be difficult or time consuming.

If your typical project is a large one for a paying client, you can be certain that variation orders or other changes will happen. Each of those variations, although probably a nuisance, can bring in valuable additional revenue. Indeed some companies claim that they bid for their projects using a very low mark-up on prime costs and expect to make their profits by charging as much as possible for the inevitable crop of contract variations caused by the client. As each project proceeds your company will need to keep track of those changes so that you do not lose the chance to recover all those additional and valuable revenues.

So day-to-day contract administration is needed, and that can be part of the project support office's role. In general, contract administration is straightforward and inexpensive provided that records are kept of every agreed change. It does not always need a full-time appointment. The function only becomes difficult and very expensive when changes on a large contract are allowed to go unrecorded, so that a horrible clean-up operation has to take place before final invoicing can be agreed after project completion.

In one case from my experience a large London contractor was carrying out a series of office improvement projects for the company in which I worked (not, I hasten to add, as project manager). No contract administration records were kept. In today's values an amount of something like £1m was outstanding at the end of the project in respect of daywork sheets and contract variations. It took a year after project completion and the costly employment of an independent quantity surveyor to resolve the final sum. That would have been prevented by simple and inexpensive routine contract administration during the course of the project.

The case just reported was amicable but, in the sad event that legal disputes should arise, your company will need those contract administration records.

Project 'Management' Functions That Do Not Manage the Project

For statutory accounting purposes, for example when compiling tax returns or preparing company accounts, it is clearly necessary to record the costs of labour and purchases. So the accounts department has to analyse timesheets and run its payroll, bought ledgers and invoice control functions. But many projects have their own additional accounting functions, usually in a project support office, to attempt to compare costs and progress. One form of this is seen in earned value 'management'.

But consider this. Cost *reporting* is not cost *control*. That begs the question, 'What is cost control?'

From the project management point of view, the direct costs of a project (assuming that all the design people are competent) are controlled by:

1. Having good project definition in the first place;
2. Avoiding changes not requested by a paying customer;
3. Efficient purchasing and materials management (remembering that the cost of bought materials and services is as high as 80 per cent of the total cost of some projects);
4. Keeping work on progress against a practical schedule – because work that runs late will invariably overrun budget.

These, really, are the most important factors in the control of direct costs. Of course many other things can improve the performance of people working on the project and many of those things are subjects for other chapters in this Handbook.

Earned value management for a large project can be a very difficult operation to get right and can consume many hours. It might be unavoidable, for example when it is used to evaluate progress payments invoiced to a client, and that clearly impacts on credit control and cash flow. But it is nonetheless an overhead cost that adds no value to the project. It should really be called earned value *measurement*. It does have a role in assessing performance early in the project so that undesirable trends can be identified and corrected, but measurements early in a project tend to be inaccurate because they are based on insufficient data.

Your clients might expect regular cost and progress reports and, if they do, they must be given them. But remember that every time you, as a senior corporate manager, asks one of your project managers for anything other than a simple cost report from your accountants, someone in the project support office will have to prepare that report and your company, not the project client, will have to bear the report preparation cost. If you were to investigate the amount of effort needed to support investigative cost reports (such as earned value reports) you would probably be astounded, because that effort involves all the managers and supervisors working on the project – the final reports are a roll-up of all their individual reports.

So, although this chapter is really a plea for you, as a corporate manager, to support your project managers, it is right that some costs should be questioned before you sanction them.

Active Support from Senior Management for Project Management

Project managers need support in various forms from their superiors. This section discusses some of the ways in which you, as a senior manager, can help to ensure that your project management function operates efficiently and without avoidable stress.

A PROJECT ROOM

Every project manager needs access to a room where project meetings can be held. This does not necessarily have to be a room dedicated to the project because a general conference room can be used when required. But if possible a room (which does not have to be expensively decorated and fitted out) should be available that the project manager can use as a project 'war room', where plans and drawings can be pinned to walls and where ad hoc meetings of small groups or others can take place informally without ceremony to discuss project matters. Such a room can help the project to have its own identity. It can also help to create a team spirit where no team actually exists in the organisation (such as in a matrix organisation, as described in Chapter 10).

A secure project room, that can be kept locked when project staff are not in attendance is valuable for projects that have to be carried out in an atmosphere of secrecy or confidentiality. That might be required in circumstances where client confidentiality has to be preserved, for management change projects where early leakage of the work could lead to the spread of unsettling rumours, or for work carried out under The Official Secrets Act (or its equivalent in countries other than the UK).

SOFTWARE AND COMPUTING EQUIPMENT

Projects benefit from the use of purpose-designed software such as Primavera, Deltek's Open Plan and so on. Your project manager should be the best judge of which software to use. That might result in conflict with your IT manager (it happened to me once and resulted in enmity over a long period). As a senior manager you should generally support the project manager's choice, However, if you have more than one project and more than one project manager, you must ensure that they all agree on one common system – or at least on systems that are mutually compatible. Otherwise difficulties will arise, especially if multiproject scheduling across all your projects is required.

Compatibility of coding systems across your projects and your accounts department is very important and you need to ensure that your staff (especially your project managers and cost and management accountants) use codes of accounts, project cost breakdown codes and departmental codes that are compatible with each other throughout your organisation's departments and projects.

The purchase of project management software is a big investment, not particularly in terms of money, but because of the effort needed to set up the project records and maintain them. If the choice of software is wrong, the remedy can be painful and expensive. There is advice on choosing project management software in Lock (2013) on pages 285–91.

So, please take a sympathetic but careful interest in any request from a project manager for the purchase of project management software.

Computing equipment is less likely to prove a difficulty, because all or most project management software runs on Microsoft Windows and should be accommodated by your existing server and intranet. Further, specialist project management software will probably be compatible with Microsoft Office, including the ubiquitous Microsoft Project.

PROVIDING AN APPROPRIATE PROJECT ORGANISATION

The organisational structure of your company and its projects can greatly affect the way in which people in projects work and communicate. Organisation structures are discussed in Part 4 of this Handbook and those chapters should be of interest to senior managers like yourself, because organisation design is a strategic function for senior management. Project managers do not often enjoy the luxury of choosing or changing the organisation in which they are expected to work. It is usual for project managers to be appointed to project organisations that already exist and which have been established by others beyond their control – by you or your fellow senior managers. So you can help and support your project managers by listening to any difficulties they might experience that are a direct result of the organisation and communications structure in which you have placed them.

Sometimes restructuring an organisation can improve communications and motivation of all those working on projects beyond measure. However, organisational change can be disruptive to work in progress, so you will have to decide on the best timing.

It might be that the organisation pattern can be left undisturbed but you will have to change or define more specifically the relative authority and balance of power between the project managers and your functional managers. That balance of power can be a particular difficulty in matrix organisations.

Only you or other senior managers can implement such organisational changes – your project managers do not have that power and they must rely on your support.

TRAINING

Project management is still an evolving profession. Qualified project managers will be expected by their professional associations to maintain current awareness of techniques and working practices. Project managers enhance their value to your company by continuous learning, and by attending meetings where they can share experiences and learn from their peers and more senior practitioners.

Many of these meetings take place out of office hours, in your project manager's leisure time. But occasionally important seminars and international congresses are arranged by the professional project management associations and you should give sympathetic consideration to supporting time off and travel, at least for your more senior and most successful project managers.

PERSONAL SUPPORT AND ENCOURAGEMENT

Kerzner (2000) conducted a survey of some 600 American companies to investigate the process of project management implementation. Many people responded to questionnaires issued by Professor Kerzner. The results make fascinating reading. One case remains especially fixed in my mind. A very talented and competent woman spent years of her life creating an enthusiastic project management culture in the company that employed her, and everyone was benefiting from her work and inspiration. All was blown away when the company underwent several senior management changes and corporate support was withdrawn (ibid., pp. 111–14). Kerzner concluded:

Executive project sponsorship must exist and be visible so that the project-line manager interface is in balance.

But executive 'sponsorship and support' can be as simple as occasionally visiting project people in at their workplaces, taking an interest in what they do, and giving praise when a project is successful. Such praise and encouragement costs nothing. The return on this zero investment can be very valuable.

References and Further Reading

Kerzner, H. (2000), *Applied Project Management: Best Practices on Implementation*, New York: Wiley.
Lock, D. (2013), *Project Management*, 10th edn, Farnham: Gower.

6 *Project Management in the Private Sector*

SUSAN DE SOUSA

Project Management in the private sector can be a roller coaster ride. On the one hand you might find yourself involved in developing and delivering cutting edge technologies, or perhaps managing global teams of leading experts. On the other hand you will find that private sector projects often have unreasonable deadlines, tight budgets and extreme politics. Worse still, the price for failure in the private sector can be high (with project managers often being the scapegoats when things go wrong). Unlike the public sector, there is no safety net for private sector projects. Slipping deadlines and escalating budgets are simply not tolerated owing to commercial pressures (often with restricted funding). Private sector projects are always at risk of being delayed or cancelled owing to lack of resources or budget. In fact the cancellation rate of private sector projects is probably 10 times greater than in the public sector, simply because public sector projects are more often allowed to continue indefinitely. For example, in the UK the National Health Service's 'Choose and Book Programme' wasted over £12 billion but was never completed. Can you imagine that ever occurring in the private sector?

Introduction

The private sector encompasses organisations that are not fully or partially funded by taxpayers. Thus it spans an enormous breadth of industry and commerce. Here are just some examples:

- banks and other financial institutions;
- book publishers;
- civil engineering and construction;
- defence contractors;
- design agencies;
- heavy engineering and shipbuilding;
- many educational establishments;
- fashion industry;
- food retailers and supermarkets;
- gambling companies;

- hotel, catering and other service industries;
- leisure and travel;
- insurance brokers and underwriters;
- IT developers and maintenance companies;
- logistics and hauliers;
- management consultancies;
- media and advertising;
- mining and quarrying;
- pharmaceuticals;
- private healthcare;
- radio and telecommunications;
- small manufacturing enterprises;
- security services;
- veterinary products and services; and
- as advertisements tend to say, many, many more.

So the private sector covers a myriad of organisations from one-man bands to huge global conglomerates. All have their own specific needs and requirements, owing to the very different ways in which they operate. In fact the only real similarity linking private sector companies is that they always have to plan, if not for growth, at least for survival. Companies that undertake projects for others are dependent for new work not only on their reputation, but also on the economic climate. Business change projects usually have to be funded from profits, so when sales are slack or when accumulated profits are low or absent there is no pot of money to raid for projects. Thus projects in the private sector typically have to deliver more (but within smaller budgets and timeframes) than equivalent projects in the public sector.

Clearly large global companies operate on a very different scale from one-man bands, and this is reflected in the type of projects that they undertake. Unsurprisingly, multi-million budget programmes are found usually only in companies which employ at least 10,000 people. Oddly enough, at the very top end you will often find that the largest private organisations deliver projects in a manner that is more similar to the public sector than to their smaller private sector counterparts. The reason for this is that the largest private sector companies are so big that they operate in a slower, more deliberate manner. Many of them generate cash flow from products that change little over time, and they have no need to worry about new business or a lack of demand for their products. Examples include petrochemical producers and some manufacturers of household consumables. Other examples are private sector organisations with a large input from the public sector, or which were formally public sector organisations themselves.

As a result programmes and projects in the largest groups or companies tend to be highly structured, often managed following a strict project management methodology such as PRINCE2, demanding PMP-qualified managers. You will often find that project management for the smaller projects in smaller companies is done on a light-touch basis, with no established project management office. Their general rule is more likely to be 'just get it done fast'.

Organisation Structures of Private Sector Projects

Most private companies operate on a hierarchical or pyramid structure. They are organised under one leader, with a number of main board directors responsible for different areas or functions. Typically you might find the following people in a large corporate structure (which is important for any aspiring project manager to note):

- chairman;
- chief executive officer (CEO);
- chief operating officer (COO);
- chief financial officer (CFO);
- chief information officer (CIO);
- chief technology officer (CTO).

It is apparent that there is no specific senior 'C' level role for project management, even though every new product launch or upgrade is delivered as a project. Another anomaly (considering the key role which technology now plays) is that rarely is the CIO or the CTO a main board member. In most private sector organisations, these roles report into the CFO. Part of the reason for this is historical; main board members can understand CTOs (perhaps what they can't understand they prefer to ignore). CIOs are often perceived as people who overspend their budgets on technology and business change projects!

Although clearly important, I do not want to say much about project management roles, because these are well described in chapters 15 and 16. Also, chapters 9 and 10 cover the principal kinds of project organisation structures.

Senior Project Stakeholders

Most private sector projects and programmes will be initiated from one of five departments:

- marketing and sales;
- product development;
- technology;
- finance;
- operations.

Thus it is usual to expect the internal senior stakeholders to sit in one of these areas. However, whilst many projects and programmes spread across all these areas, one department will often be the key driver or source for a particular project. In that case, of course, the project manager must ensure that the senior stakeholder from that area is kept fully informed of progress and problems.

Project Management Methodology

A number of project management methods and frameworks are used within the private sector. These include PRINCE2 in the UK and PMP in the US. However, unlike the public sector, it is rare to find any methodology that is followed slavishly. In fact, most private sector organisations implement a relatively informal methodology that tries to achieve a happy medium between controlling projects and 'time to market'.

A project manager in the private sector will probably be expected to write weekly project reports detailing progress and have a high-level risk and problems log. Depending on the size and complexity of the project you should also expect to write a 'project charter' or detailed 'project initiation document' that will have to be approved and authorised before spending on the project can begin. However in most private sector organisations, there simply isn't the time to write 'project justification documents' or to run risk workshops at the outset. Also artefacts such as 'project communication plans' are usually 'nice to have' rather than a mandatory requirement.

Editorial Comment (DL)

When UK private sector companies perform projects for some public sector bodies they can be put under pressure by the customer to manage their projects according to a specific and bureaucratic methodology such as PRINCE2.

When the economy worsens there is generally less capital within the private sector for new projects. So inevitably there will be fewer new projects, but there is likely to be more pressure to deliver projects efficiently and successfully. That means exercising greater control because the private sector simply can ill afford any spending over budget. Nonetheless if you are managing a project in the private sector it is unlikely that you will have to generate the amount of paperwork endemic within the public sector. One positive outcome is that the 'lessons learned' exercise typically carried out at the end of projects will be given far more emphasis in the private sector as organisations strive to increase their efficiency and deliver more for less.

PROJECT MANAGEMENT OFFICE (PMO)

Most large companies will have a PMO to manage projects and programmes. The sheer volume of projects in the largest companies might even require several PMOs. In extremely large programmes that I have managed, each had its own dedicated PMO. The role of a PMO within the private sector is really twofold:

1. It acts as a conduit for the inception and approval of new projects;
2. It then plans, administers, monitors and controls each project through its lifecycle.

A PMO should be the nerve centre of any large project or programme. It has to keep in touch and control progress, changes or contract variations, project spending and all other aspects of the projects within its remit. In many ways the PMOs in both public and private sectors operate in a similar way. They are all responsible for managing cross-dependencies between projects, highlighting exceptions or variances, managing resource allocation and reporting overall progress to the relevant stakeholders. If there are identifiable differences for a private sector PMO compared with one in the public sector, they probably include:

- the way in which the pipeline of incoming projects is dealt with;
- continuous emphasis on controlling budgets and maximising the utilisation of resources;
- less paperwork expected from their project managers;
- less paperwork generated by the PMO – bluntly speaking senior managers are often interested only in delivery dates and budgets.

HOW THE PMO MANAGES THE PROJECT PIPELINE

In the private sector the incoming projects pipeline is managed through business cases and project justification documents. The key drivers in the approval of any private sector project are:

1. What will be the impact on the bottom line (that is, sales and revenue)?
2. Seniority and involvement of the project sponsor.

Astonishingly, a project for internal business change that aims to reduce operating costs will often take a back seat to one intended to increase revenue. That can apply even if the expected efficiency savings are the same as the forecast increased revenue. The reason is that private sector companies like to see increasing revenue and profits. That looks good in the accounts and pleases shareholders. But efficiencies in operating costs are often perceived as being possible by sacking a few people, or transferring jobs offshore, and such measures don't need expensive business change projects. We have all seen private companies make decisions to slash (say) 10 per cent of all staff across their organisation following a general directive from senior executives or the remote board of a parent company.

ROUTINE WORK OF THE PRIVATE SECTOR PMO

The two main functions of a private sector PMO are to control budgets and maximise resource utilisation.

Because funding within private sector companies is usually tight, it follows that the smaller the company, the tighter the budget is likely to be. Hence writing an exception report for budgetary reasons within the private sector is a really big deal, often with the CFO being asked for approval, even for relatively small budget increases. Thus the private sector PMO is likely to scrutinise project expenditure carefully. No one (especially the head of a PMO) wants to be the person to have to submit an exception report to a CFO for a project that they were supposed to be cost controlling.

It might be controversial to say so, but it is well known that resources in the private sector are worked significantly harder than their counterparts in the public sector. One reason is that private sector companies are less able to tolerate idle time among permanent employees. Private companies, in the UK at least, keep their permanent staffing numbers so closely under scrutiny that large projects are often resourced entirely by short-term contractors. The origins for such restrictions lie in employment legislation, which makes it difficult to dismiss permanent staff without an expensive redundancy package. There is also a need in certain key areas such as technology and business change, to use external short-term specialised resources.

Of course, one aspect of using contractors is that they are usually more expensive than permanent employees. Hence their utilisation and costs have to be strictly managed, which is where the PMO comes in as a secondary objective monitor of costs. I shall discuss the employment of contractors at greater length later, and Chapter 48 is also relevant in this context.

Support from Senior Management

Despite project management having a higher profile than ever, the level of understanding within senior management is still poor. Few understand what their responsibility as an internal project sponsor entails (I use the term internal project sponsor to distinguish this function from external sponsors such as clients and customers). This is hardly surprising since few senior management roles are advertised asking for prior experience in sponsoring projects. As such, most senior internal stakeholders simply fall into the role, which they usually consider secondary to their main work. Basically they need something delivered, whether it is a new product, an enhancement or upgrade, and they then have no choice but to be the project sponsor to ensure it is prioritised and delivered. This creates problems for project managers, who need not only to deliver their projects successfully but also to educate and convince the internal project sponsor.

Of course internal project sponsors often don't have time to get fully involved in the running of a project. They do not perceive that as their main role – they simply want projects delivered. This means that initiation processes are often rushed or completely overlooked. An example of this is that in certain industry sectors, even now, it is possible to be managing a £5 million project with no project initiation document, no risk log, and an inadequate project specification …

In certain industry sectors (for example the press, entertainment and broadcasting), time to market takes priority. Otherwise market initiative or key public deadlines might be missed. In those cases the proper processes can be seen as delaying mechanisms, and so they might be ignored. This of course creates problems. If you don't have an approved project initiation document how is it possible for everyone to understand what the project success criteria are? And without a clear risk log, is it any surprise that problems arise that no one takes responsibility for resolving?

There is more on the role of senior management in projects in Chapter 5.

Business Change Projects

Whereas most projects used to be purely technology based, many now are purely business focused. The reason for this is that private sector groups and companies are desperately trying to find efficiency savings. The best way of doing that is through one or more project processes. As a result, business change or business transformation is now the fastest growing area of project management.

So what is business change? Well many private sector companies have unsurprisingly found that when the economy shrinks, generating increased profits through increased sales is significantly harder to achieve. So another way to increase profits is by cutting existing costs. Although not all organisations realise it, intelligent people know that simply slashing random departments, wielding an indiscriminate axe and sacking employees is a sure-fire way to destroy goodwill, staff cooperation and good working practices.

Business change projects and programmes will review the way a company works, determine the areas which operate well and then devise ways in which the other departments and processes can be refined to increase efficiencies. A key part of such projects does often involve making employees redundant and closing offices, but the key goal is to do this in a way that ensures the company will operate more efficiently in future.

Whilst such projects and programmes are managed using a project management discipline, they are usually best led (or at least advised) by someone who has a sound background in either HR or management consulting in addition to competency in project management.

A new type of business change project has arisen in recent years and has now become ubiquitous. This is the offshoring project, where the company's aim is to offshore a department in totality to a third-party supplier, based abroad. The aim is to reduce costs by moving the work to a supplier who will agree to deliver that work at a lower fixed cost than currently. End users (customers) do not always take kindly when customer service departments are transferred overseas and they find themselves dealing with people who often can hardly speak English.

Offshoring projects usually involved technology teams, but have spread to all other areas of business from legal services to accounting and operations. Undertaking these projects will involve not only technology deliverables but also business change processes. As a result, a hybrid project manager who understands and can implement both technology and business process changes are required.

Sharing Best Practice

Unlike the public sector, there is little free exchange of best practices within the private sector. To do so would be to reduce one's competitive advantage and so it is rarely done. Further, whilst many companies aspire to implementing best practice, the reality is that time to market and gaining market share is paramount.

Editorial Comment (DL)

Benchmarking is an exception to this rule, although often companies will do so through a third party that allows some degree of confidentiality.

Politics

Project managers in both the public and private sectors will argue that their sector is worse for politics. However, the reality is that it depends upon the organisation, the pressures faced and the individuals involved. There are few organisations where there are no politics and many where you will encounter a frustratingly high level of politics. Worse still this rationale applies to organisations whether small or large. However, since there is significantly less job security in the private rather than public sector this tends to exacerbate the political machinations which take place.

It is often assumed that there are no politics within small companies simply because employees are too busy trying to generate business. However, that is not true. Any organisation which has more than one employee will have politics. In small companies, for example, politics will sometimes surface should one project manager level accusations of favouritism when another manager is given a particularly important project or client to work with. In larger companies such accusations of favouritism will be less likely because there will usually be more projects to share around.

Politics tends to be rife in larger organisations. Project managers will often find themselves caught up in power plays between senior executives. This particularly will impact on projects when requests for budget or resources are being considered. The reason for this is that every internal project sponsor will tend to consider their own projects to be of the highest priority. Problems will arise when a sponsor finds that his/her project has been downgraded (perhaps owing to changed priorities or a budget cutback). This can often lead to heated arguments between sponsor and project manager, and someone has to explain to the sponsor why their project has been delayed or stopped.

A further instance of politics is when projects go wrong and a 'blame game' results between various people. Again project managers will find themselves caught between warring factions and can become the scapegoats. This happens far more commonly than is assumed and is one cause of project managers getting fired.

Contractors and Outsourcing

One feature more common to private sector projects, particularly in the UK, is the widespread use of contractors. In fact on most UK projects it is common to find up to 70 per cent of resources who are contractors and amongst project managers up to 80 per cent in some cases.

One reason for this is that full-time permanent employees in management and supervisory roles are accounted for as fixed overheads. So they count in the administration costs of a company, which in turn reduces their operating profits. Using short-term contractors means that such costs are kept out of the fixed overhead costs.

Using contractors also allows companies to have a flexible resource pool. Not only can they select people with the latest or very specific experience required, but they can also take on new projects easily without affecting their routine day-to-day work. For example, one UK company increased its projects department from 50 to 500 people in over six months to deliver an enormous piece of work. On completion of that project the company was able to return painlessly to its normal departmental operating level of 50 staff, simply through using contractors.

Of course the other side of this is that often whilst the domain expertise is there, the industry experience is not. So using contracted resources can cause enormous problems in planning and budgeting, simply because no one has any clear idea of how long the work should take. Certainly it makes using development methodologies such as work breakdown structures (WBS) hard, which is probably why Agile has taken such a foothold in the UK.

One way in which private sector companies are reducing their project costs is by outsourcing work. This may involve anything from a single element of a project to the entirety of it, with the project management responsibility still retained by the client. This can create some challenges for the project sponsor or senior stakeholders. When these outworking teams are based abroad, the project manager must be aware of the different time zones involved which can make team meetings hard to organise, a different understanding of the English language and other cultural differences (see chapters 11 and 24).

The Project Manager in the Private Sector

Most business people now realise that any innovations, new products and business change are delivered through projects, and hence this is an important area to be involved in. And, with projects come project managers. However, despite this, project management is still not perceived as a route to the main board as other disciplines (like accounting or human resources, to give just two examples). That is one of the curious anomalies of project management, but as areas like business change projects expand and gain in prominence, it is likely that it will change.

One question I am frequently asked is 'How can I become a project manager?' Well the tried and tested route tends to be, being in the right place at the right time. I have known of people in call centres moving into project manager roles despite having no experience simply because the organisation needed people desperately.

However if you are not inclined to leave your career and fortune to chance, reflect that many technical project managers are former business analysts, developers or testers. In the business change area, a background in HR or finance will undoubtedly help. Previous work experience as a consultant for one of the top consultancy organisations is also becoming an important route into project management (because it is perceived that candidates will have a good foundation in the processes relevant to business change project and offshoring projects).

Many consider that achieving qualifications such as PRINCE2, PMP, MSP or an MBA will help them get into project management. Of course these are very important. But companies also want people with experience and proven track records (particularly for project management). Most of the skills required to be a successful project manager are soft skills, such as decision-making, team management, leading, negotiating and communicating. It is hard to guarantee these qualities in examination certificates or other qualifications, so having a good track record is vital. In project management there is no single degree or skill that will assure your success in becoming a project manager, unless possibly you are seeking to enter an engineering or construction discipline. In most companies it is the track record they are looking for (and at the more junior levels, the enthusiasm and passion of the person).

REMUNERATION AND WORKING LIFE

Within the private sector pay and perks can vary hugely depending upon the industry and discipline involved. Project managers with investment banks are among the most highly paid. High pay can be associated with rare and comprehensive experience in a particular skill, such as familiarity with particular software.

Project managers employed on short-term contracts can expect to earn two or three times the salary of an equivalent project manager on a company's permanent staff, but that comes with the risk of unemployment between projects. Clearly that risk is more serious for short-term projects, when long periods out of work are a greater risk. Those considerations are clearly of more concern when the economy is weak. A counter argument is that whilst contract project managers are often brought in to manage the projects and politics that no one else wants, they are often able to move around sufficiently to gain fantastic domain experience of managing a multitude of different projects in many areas.

Most project managers work normal hours until they approach the testing and launch phases of their project lifecycle. Then project managers can find themselves working 15-hour days, 7 days a week. I have known projects where the testing team were split into three teams that collectively covered 24 hours a day. Dennis Lock told me he once spent three days and nights in a manufacturing plant without going home, and without a break, just to make sure his project went on a ship that had been booked to take it to Egypt.

Whilst those occasions might not be the norm, the reality is that no matter what hours the team are working, or where they are based, the project manager is ultimately responsible. As such the role can be incredible stressful – especially when things are going wrong, and the project sponsor expects you to provide solutions not problems.

For contract project managers and even some permanent project managers the working life is more complicated because they need to go where the project work is. It is now becoming common for such project managers, especially contract project managers, to be based away from home during the week. I know of project managers who commute from the UK into mainland Europe on a weekly basis to manage projects.

Conclusion

Project management in the private sector is full of contradictions. On the one hand it can be exciting, cutting edge and empowering. On the other hand it can be frustrating, highly stressful and charged with unpleasant politics.

However, project management now has a higher profile than ever before. Whilst it can take time for senior stakeholders in some private organisations to understand what project managers do, and for effective project management processes to be implemented, there is no doubt that within the private sector project management is the place to be.

7 *People in Public Sector Projects*

JON HYDE and DAVID SAWYER

It is difficult being a project manager in the public sector. There is always the risk that one day your project is apparently doing well when suddenly a political decision cuts the budget, causing the project to be scaled down or even cancelled. Also the media are often critical of public sector projects, and when they fail the project managers get blamed. You could be made redundant and, because people believe what they read or hear in the media, you cannot easily get another job. This is of course a fairly extreme example of what it is like to be a public sector project manager, but public sector projects are vulnerable to political decisions and media scrutiny. In a failed private sector project, the circumstances are usually different because the organisation can to some extent hide mistakes from the public and shareholders and move on to the next project.

Public Sector Organisations

Most people are familiar with the different types of government in their own country. Generally, countries operate systems with a national government at the top, below which there might be regional, county, city, town and even local parish councils. Clearly working conditions and patterns vary significantly within these organisations. Because of their funding methods and the number of stakeholders involved, public sector projects are influenced by local politics, national politics and the media. Clearly there is no 'one size fits all' in the public sector. Therefore each project delivery style must fit the needs of the organisation involved.

National governments usually operate larger projects concerned with defence, infrastructure, immigration, licensing, transport, national health, utilities, taxation and others. Because of the complexity and high risk of failure, these large-scale projects need to be run using significant controls and documentation.

By contrast, local governments generally operate smaller projects, which are concerned with operations on a more local level. This is not to say that locally operated projects are not significant but their budgets, scope and exposure to risk will be far less than those undertaken at the national level. Taking transport infrastructure as an example, a national government would authorise, control and fund the construction of a major road across the country, whereas subsequent local improvements and maintenance to that highway might become the responsibility of the various local governments (councils) through whose areas the road passes.

Project management at national and local levels always involves significant skills, but applied over different areas. It is often the case that a local level project manager would be involved with all areas of the project (planning and scheduling, progress, dealing with contractors, managing budgets and risk). The greater complexity and number of dependencies in a large national project would require the project manager to act in a more managerial role (far less hands-on), with support from a sizeable project management team that might even include one or more subproject managers.

> **Editorial Comment (DL)**
>
> Unfortunately in public sector projects many strategic decisions are taken by elected politicians and councillors. These people are not usually elected for their business or commercial skills alone and many are quite ignorant of project management. Yet these same people often have considerable political power, and by means of that power introduce changes into projects or otherwise direct the project manager (interfere) in ways that will ensure project failure. Likewise, those in political power without project experience can fail to see when their project managers are underperforming. Thus an added dimension to the role of the public sector project manager is the careful management of this unique stakeholder group.

Organisation Structures of Public Sector Projects

Most large organisations are hierarchical in nature. As any organisation becomes larger, it needs to have a hierarchical structure to ensure that there is sufficient delegation of management control over tasks and employees. A suitable structure will also prevent overloading staff at the senior levels.

In every vertical hierarchy it is recognised that people also need to work and talk laterally across the structure. It can be said that although the reporting structure of an organisation might be through a hierarchical pyramid, the project deliverables cannot be achieved without cross-communication and matrix management.

Small local government organisations that are hierarchical in nature (with the classic single leader, several directors and departmental heads structure) can still operate a matrix management approach effectively. It is not uncommon for project managers to be managing staff with higher grades than themselves, and perceptions of a 'silo culture' (from which some higher government departments can suffer) do not necessarily occur.

Security and confidentiality issues are often cited as a reason for not involving all relevant parties or carrying out proper consultation – in effect building internal silos. Consider the case of the Federal Bureau of Investigation (FBI) in Holmes's article on the organisation-wide IT implementation issues (Holmes, 2005). Internal silos were created through secrecy, an 'atmosphere of distrust' and a 'culture of intimidation' – yet the organisation was able to start the steps to overcome this with strong leadership and cultural changes.

Overall, for a project manager to be successful, they need to understand the politics of the organisation and the fears, hopes and needs of the people involved – convincing everyone that the project is a good idea. Without support from the front line, the project is doomed.

Project Management Methods and Frameworks

Many public sector projects are run using a project framework. This is not peculiar to the public sector, as many large organisations use either their own or proprietary frameworks. Within the UK the Cabinet Office commonly prescribes PRINCE2 (Projects in Controlled Environments) and MSP (Managing Successful Programmes) methodologies.

The intention of using such frameworks is to improve the possibility of success by using a common standard to describe the project and the roles of the people involved. Frameworks also describe common tools and controls that aim to ensure the smooth running of the project.

Despite the claimed advantages, these frameworks are not always successful. People can be confused by frameworks or even hostile to them. They fail to understand what the framework is there for, and consequently apply it in either an overly rigid and bureaucratic way, or in a way that fails to control and govern the project sufficiently. This gives the frameworks a bad name, which they do not entirely deserve.

> *Having PRINCE2 (qualifications) doesn't make you a good project manager, but not having PRINCE2 doesn't make you a good project manager either. (Dot Tudor, author, business analyst and PRINCE2 trainer)*

SUPPORT FROM SENIOR MANAGEMENT

Senior managers often do not understand the language, terminology and concepts of the frameworks, leading to a lack of support for the project and its manager. For example, although most people understand the need to carry out a 'lessons learned' exercise at the end of the project, pressure from time and budgets often means that the 'lessons learned' investigation is one of the mostly likely tasks to be skipped. As a consequence, organisations repeat the same mistakes over and over again.

Lack of management support is often due to management not fully understanding their role on projects, as top-level political supporter for the project manager.

Project staff need time and resources to plan a project, and these will often not be available at the start, which is when they are most needed. Frameworks often direct the project manager to plan work in outline and to ensure that the concept is supported. But middle management will often keep sending such early outline documents back until they become effectively fully-costed business cases.

These simple errors often lead to massive amounts of wasted time, confusion and frustration for project managers and project team members, but they are not failings of the frameworks. They are failings of the people using them.

PROJECT SIZE AND CLASSIFICATION

Minor Projects

Minor projects are often managed in an ad hoc way from revenue budget. They are authorised and prioritised locally by middle managers and are usually carried out to achieve a locally required outcome. The problem with this approach is that there is no central oversight by a portfolio office. This can lead to variations in solutions between departments (for example where one department might have an excess of budget, whilst another is overspent). Different departments might develop competing solutions to the same problem. There will also be no facility for project support when operating in isolation, at least as far as the skills usually available in a project management office (PMO) are concerned.

In spite of these apparent disadvantages, minor projects are often quite successful, because they are relatively simple, lightweight and with few barriers on the path to successful completion (despite being well aligned with organisational priorities).

Large Public Projects

Classification of a major project varies from organisation to organisation. These projects are normally run through formal project boards, and have significant top-level support and funding from the organisation. Their impact is usually spread over several departments, which will need to have an input to most projects. Typical departments or functions involved include:

- commercial (insurance, contracts and legal);
- procurement (often associated with commercial);
- communications and IT (sometimes as separate departments);
- estates management (sometimes including local facilities management);
- finance and accounting;
- human resources management (HRM);
- project management office (PMO).

Although this ensures that the relevant people are involved in the process, it can create confusion regarding who is responsible for each function, and more importantly, who is in control.

Generally, major projects will have significant support from C-level managers. Getting the support of these managers is key to project success, as decisions made to support major projects will be reviewed and signed off by a number of heads of business areas before the project is authorised.

The main difference between minor and major projects is that minor projects are usually quite light and flexible, whereas bigger projects need significantly more funding, planning, documentation and support throughout the organisation. Without all of these things being present, the project will stall and fail.

Multi-organisation Projects

Complex issues arise when projects spread over several organisations. Even though all the organisations involved are effectively from the same 'group' of companies, each will have its own way of doing things and there can be incompatibility.

Local government is undergoing rapid transformation and many local authorities are developing services that are shared across a number of partners. For example, a number of organisations are currently working together to implement new shared electronic back-office systems, covering finance, procurement, human resources and payroll. Such projects raise interesting governance questions such as 'who is the project sponsor?' Genuine partnership working ought to facilitate the appointment of individual shared board members, project/programme managers, accountants, legal officers and so forth. However, there is usually a strong temptation in each partner organisation to retain these functions to protect their own interests, which can lead to duplication of the functions and unwieldy project teams.

Although almost all larger organisations have their own centralised PMO, many smaller organisations do not. Each organisation then runs their own PMO in a different way, with its own rules and governance structure. This has the potential to cause adverse issues when working across organisations if the particular project is not justified, aligned, or governed to the highest common standards.

SHARING BEST PRACTICE

The public sector is unique in that there is little requirement for competition between public sector organisations. This means that open and free knowledge sharing is not only possible, but is actively encouraged. Knowledge sharing is often facilitated through technology such as the Communities of Practice platform, and concepts such as volunteer-based 'unconferences' like 'govcamp' and 'teacamp', where ideas that work are shared between the sector's more innovative people. References to these methods are given at the end of this chapter.

This freedom to share and collaborate gives the public sector a big competitive advantage, and is the primary reason for the rapid spread of innovative practices across the sector. Even the most secretive of organisations still share information with each other (and with the wider sector where this is possible).

Some colleagues are still too inward looking, but that is true of all sectors. Often people do not want to change because they are scared, but those people should remember the secret of evolution: those who adapted were able to survive and those who did not became extinct.

Politics

Projects usually encounter two different types of politics. Firstly, there is the political situation that gives the organisation its strategy and authority to act. Secondly, there are the political dynamics that operate within each organisation, which are far more difficult to explain.

Politics is evident at all levels. It is one of the necessary skills of project manager to understand this and take appropriate steps to ensure successful delivery.

POLITICS AT NATIONAL GOVERNMENT LEVEL

In democratic nations it is usual for governmental policy to be linked into the ruling party's manifesto, balanced against budgets, legislation and public acceptance. A good example of this is that although there is a clear need to cut costs under austerity measures, many of the cost-saving ideas will not be acceptable to the public. Strategy is set at this level, which then trickles down to the many organisations within the sector. Many major projects and programmes have been 'culled' owing to austerity measures, and this has undoubtedly had an effect on morale, stability and capability within organisations.

Although the public are usually promised 'no cuts to front line services', most business changes will be delivered via a project, and project functions are certainly not 'front line'. PMOs become soft targets in austerity drives, sometimes viewed as an unnecessary luxury and a bureaucratic overhead. Some public sector organisations cut their PMOs (with the intention of protecting front line jobs), but it is at such times of rapid change when support from a mature PMO is most beneficial.

Changes in political party often cause an 'about-face' change in strategy. For example, left-wing parties will tend to centralise and nationalise, where a right-wing party might be more inclined to privatise. This means that initiatives such as United Kingdom ID cards, which were introduced by a Labour-led government at considerable cost were then scrapped by the following Conservative government.

POLITICS AT REGIONAL LEVELS

Each organisation sets its own internal strategy, aligned with government policy and the individual needs of its internal customers. This strategy will then be delivered locally by a variety of projects and programmes.

Programmes and major projects will usually sit at this level. These will have significant strategic support from senior management within the organisation. This portfolio of projects and programmes will normally be managed within a PMO, although it depends on the size and maturity of the organisation involved.

> *Working with councillors is interesting … they have ultimate say over whether funding is approved or not and often call the shots on matters where they are not subject matter experts. You therefore need to be very good at explaining technical matters in a non-technical way. If you don't bring councillors along with you and engage them throughout, they might one day squash your project. (JPS, a programme manager in a medium size organisation)*

The unique role of politicians in public sector projects can lead to the manifestation of 'sacred cow' projects, especially in those organisations where a weak approach to portfolio management is evident. Such projects have significant support from someone within the organisation who has power and influence, yet they are not aligned with strategy. These projects are typically started 'below the radar' and only come to the attention of other senior managers once enough momentum has been attained to make it difficult to stop the project. A robust gated approach to project initiation is required to prohibit this practice, which causes havoc in terms of resource management and delivery of the wider portfolio.

POLITICS AT THE LOCAL LEVEL

At the local level, each organisational unit sets priorities depending on their local remit. This is usually where the 'is it a project or not?' and 'should this be managed internally or corporately?' questions are introduced.

Projects initiated at this level will often have difficulty being accepted by the organisation if they need to grow or be scaled up. There are a variety of reasons for this, but if you work in this area of the business it can be very frustrating. For a small project to make it to the corporate level, it needs to have significant support from senior management in various areas of the business.

INTERNAL RESISTANCE TO CHANGE

Stakeholder 'politics' varies from people subtly undermining the project, to outright opposition and refusal to answer requests for assistance. Often, such people are acting to serve and protect their own interests rather than the best interests of the organisation. These 'hidden agendas' will often only be revealed after it is too late to prevent damage to the project, or the reputation of the organisation.

Overt resistance is easy to deal with through stakeholder management and communications. Covert resistance is more difficult to tackle, as it is often not immediately obvious where the resistance is coming from. Whenever anyone talks to me about a project I am managing I think 'What is your motive for telling me that?' This has helped to understand project political dynamics far more clearly.

So adopting a questioning nature can help with project politics, although many people might be unwilling to discuss their resistance openly because they feel it singles them out as being 'change resistant' (even though they might have good reason to question some aspect of the project). As project manager, it is a good idea to question the views or fears of the change-resistant person. You never know, such questioning might reveal that they are angry about the change because it has real flaws.

Budgetary Issues

Public sector budgets are different from private sector budgets in many respects. For example, there is usually an allocated annual budget which, within the UK is aligned with the fiscal year (which ends on 31 March). So public project costs and budgets align with financial periods as well as with work breakdown packages or delivery stages. Budgets must be often fully spent by financial year end or lost completely.

Budgets are sometimes approved and released late, forcing a narrow window in which to deliver important outcomes. Although late budget release can also occur in the private sector, in public projects late release without the ability to carry over unspent budgets from the previous year increases the risk of project stall or failure. The end-of-year cut-off can lead to poorly aligned last-minute spending decisions, which can have detrimental knock-on effects for years.

In contrast, capital projects involve large purchases (such as buildings, computer systems) where the results and benefits are typically delivered over several years. The main distinction is that when the project is signed off, a commitment is made to spend money over several years. The financial cut-off date is still the financial year end, so careful alignment of stages to reporting periods is critical.

Many projects that would previously have been capital projects are now being outsourced as services. One example is outsourcing computer systems to data centres, and then paying for them as a 'Software as a Service' (SaaS) revenue item. Because of this move from capital to revenue, the nature of project delivery is changing.

Austerity Measures

Austerity measures force many public sector organisations to scale back their portfolios of projects. Any public sector organisation with a mature portfolio approach should be able to cope with these kinds of changes. This would mean either scaling back the number of projects, or keeping the same number of projects, but downsizing them so that there are a reduced number of deliverables.

There are clearly risks for people when austerity measures are in force. Organisations might implement early retirement plans, which strip out high-level support for existing and new initiatives and can have profound effects on the way that business is done. Organisations will probably seek cost-savings within the back-office, which is exactly the area that affects project delivery. Despite organisations becoming more 'operationally focused' during times of austerity, they must understand that the services they provide, and changes to them, are still delivered through successful projects and programmes, correctly aligned to business strategy, and run with the oversight of a PMO.

There are some benefits to austerity measures. It is much easier to slim down organisations during a recession, and people who might have been operating a 'low productivity strategy' have found themselves in the firing line. Also, people who were previously self-serving have realised that they must become more open to sharing and change if they are to survive and prosper. This has led to many barriers to project success being reduced.

Use of Contractors

One issue with public sector projects is the use of private sector contractors (particularly managing contractors). During times of austerity, a skills gap emerged in some parts of the public sector when project contractor numbers were reduced. Public sector organisations had been using contractors to perform project roles, which de-risked the projects and prevented the 'brain drain' created when people are moved from their departments to project roles.

Budget cuts during the recession made it difficult or impossible to use contractors within projects, which sometimes led to a reduction in performance within the organisations whilst the internal staff coped with taking up the slack.

In other ways the reduction in the use of external consultants was very positive for the public sector because it forced organisations to empower their own staff more and rely on them for roles that previously would have been given to a contractor. This boosted the confidence, capability and performance of individual staff, and has helped to improve the overall project and portfolio management maturity and capability of the organisation.

I recently became aware of an opportunity for a project manager, where four full time contractors were being replaced by a new project management post for one person, recruited internally! I can't think of a better example of public sector project management competence. (DJM, a project manager in a large organisation)

Using main contractors and managing contractors limits an organisation's long-term project understanding, because these contractors take the knowledge away with them when they leave at the end of their contracts. This means that the knowledge has to be built up over and over again within the public organisation each time a new project is carried out.

Commercial Awareness

Many people in the public sector are passionate about public service but not quite as commercially aware about programmes and projects. Thus projects initiated at the 'organisational unit' level do not always make commercial sense and fail to provide a satisfactory return on investment.

However, commercial concerns are *not* the only drivers for public sector projects. For example, councils often need to run projects that do not offer a return on investment – they may be statutorily obliged to do the work for environmental, safety, social or other reasons. Producing a heritage strategy outlining steps to be taken to preserve the historic built environment of an area is unlikely to deliver immediate cashable savings. But it might help to ensure that the town remains prosperous and an attractive place in which to live, work and visit over the coming decades.

Within the European Union procurement for public sector contracts over a specified value are subject to tendering rules, which force public sector organisations to tender for work throughout Europe, advertising in *The European Journal*. This process is designed to provide transparency for competition and result in more cost-effective contracts. However, the process itself can extend project timescales, presenting serious challenges for time-sensitive projects.

Project Managers in the Public Sector

THE ROLE OF THE PUBLIC SECTOR PROJECT MANAGER

The role of the public sector project manager largely depends on the size and nature of the projects on which they are working. It should come as little surprise that larger, multi-agency projects will generally be managed by more experienced staff than smaller projects run by a single organisational unit.

Many project managers in small projects will multitask, working in the details of the project as well as managing the bigger picture. This is not uncommon in any project where the project manager comes from a technical background.

In the medium-sized organisation that I work for, pure project management is not an option – you've got to get stuck in and produce deliverables too. For example I'm managing the procurement and installation of a new parking system. I'm not just planning, managing risk and stakeholder engagement. I also led the business analysis, and produced the invitation to tender documentation. (JPS, a programme manager in local government)

Many public sector project managers will often get involved in project support. Writing agendas and minutes, ensuring refreshments are ordered and rooms booked are all part of the day job, as well as doing pure project management tasks, such as writing a business case or negotiating with teams, suppliers and contractors.

In larger organisations and larger projects, the complexity of the work increases, and roles will become increasingly specialised, for example as indicated below:

* business analysis;
* document librarian;
* project planning and balancing project assets;
* project administration – scheduling meetings, organising meeting support and so on;
* project communication;
* risk analysis and planning.

LACK OF EMPOWERMENT

Making progress on a public sector project is all about getting the correct people around the table and ensuring that they are empowered to make decisions on behalf of their department. The issues arise when the only person who is empowered to make decisions is the head of the department. This person will then generally either be too busy to discuss the project, or will just generally be unavailable.

The job is then delegated leaving some poor person, who will have to attend all the meetings and accept responsibility for the issues whilst having none of the authority to solve the problems. This is sometimes known as 'reverse-empowerment'; that is: they are empowered (forced) to accept responsibility, but their role does not let them fully control the outcome to the same extent.

ROUTES INTO PROJECT MANAGEMENT IN THE PUBLIC SECTOR

In business generally project management is becoming an increasingly popular career choice. For many it is a case of 'being in the right place at the right time' working within an organisation and being given a project to manage as a one-off activity. This is also true in the public sector, where project teams are drawn together from many parts of the organisation in order to deliver business benefits via a project. A 'typical' profile of a project manager recruited from within the organisation is something like this:

* experience (and contacts) within the organisation;
* proven leadership or management abilities which will allow them to fit into the project team;
* keen to progress to higher levels of management;
* able to self-motivate and work without close supervision.

The important thing to note here is that the successful candidates will already exhibit many of the soft skills, rather than the 'traditional' hard skills (such as planning, risk management or change management).

People find themselves working in projects because they want to progress or have a personal need to develop things within the organisation. This will often lead to the fledgling project manager being asked to complete a small, low-risk 'starter' project. Higher management use that as an assessment tool to decide not only whether the person can manage projects, but also if they show a desire to become a project manager in the longer term.

Once this first project has been completed, the member of staff will either go back to their original work or move on to more complex projects. This generally means that they are taking on projects with more risk, more budget, less political and stakeholder support, shorter timescales, more complexity, or multi-organisational projects.

I should also mention the importance of training and development at this point, but this subject is dealt with in later chapters.

Pay, Conditions of Service and Motivation

As a manager, it is important to understand what motivates people who work in the public sector.

Firstly, it is not all about pay. Of course money is important, but people who work in the public sector are usually drawn there because they feel a need to help others. I have spoken to countless people in the public sector about this over many years and they all share the same spirit – they want to do the right thing for the public good.

People also join the public sector because there is scope for having a 'job for life'. Some others disagree with this concept and believe that public sector workers should be on short-term contracts comparable to the private sector. The issue here is that if public sector workers lose their job security and other benefits, then the public sector has to start paying at the market rate, rather than 'up to market average'.

The general way in which salaries work in the public sector is that the top salary for a certain job within the public sector will be at the median rate for the same job in the private sector. The general idea is that job security, pensions and other benefits will make up for this reduced level of pay.

Austerity measures in recent times have led to pay cuts or freezes, which inevitably cause motivational issues. Although the primary motivation may not be money, people still need money and most people in the public sector have had their pay frozen or effectively cut during the austerity years. How does this affect people, and the ability of managers to motivate staff to 'go the extra mile'?

> *Being pay-cut demotivates even the most professional and highly self-motivated staff. Many people think, 'Why should I do more than I get paid for, if they are less well paid than they were before? (Jon, a programme manager in local government)*

Unfortunately, the public sector project manager does not have the benefit of being able to treat staff to motivational perquisites (perks) to reward them for their hard work – even when those staff have put in considerable extra effort to meet deadlines.

> *I am studying on a self-funded external course, where we undertook 'project simulation training'. Within the simulation, the staff would actually leave the project if you didn't reward them regularly for their hard work by putting on a barbeque, a staff lunch, or some other*

entertainment. I was thinking throughout the exercise 'where do we fit into this? (Dave, a project manager in a large organisation)

My view is that it is ridiculous when project managers are unable to reward their staff, showing their respect for all the efforts made. But the public sector is so afraid of criticism from the media that this opportunity to build the team and motivate people in these simple, often inexpensive, but highly effective ways is lost.

Project managers within the public sector have to think about other ways to reward effort. Aligning people with the areas that energise them, help to clear the barriers that cause frustration, challenge them and allow them the room to perform. The public sector is a great place for 'social entrepreneurs', because austerity measures are forcing public sector organisations to change rapidly so that they can continue delivering services at the required standard with less. Entrepreneurial types are flourishing under this pressure whilst the 'dead wood' is being chopped out.

Public sector employees value the working environment, where there are excellent flexible working conditions and plenty of time off. This is great for those with families, or those planning to have families in the future. But although the public sector is generally fairly 'laid-back', recent cutbacks have caused employees to panic, taking on more and more work, rather than admitting that they are operating at their full capacity.

Some end up taking work home in the evenings and at weekends in order to catch up. Of course this happens in both the public and private sectors. But this can lead to staff becoming overworked and 'burned out', and some then leave their organisations, leaving skills gaps and breaks in the business organisations. Despite the difficult financial environment, employees need to maintain a healthy lifestyle, with a good balance between work and leisure.

Conclusion

The public sector is a complex environment. It is challenging to those who attempt project delivery. There are many requirements that are not present in other sectors, and those who criticise public sector project managers should be aware that most people working in the sector are both highly professional and highly competent. Although public sector projects are a challenge, they are a rewarding challenge and that is one reason why the public sector is such a great place in which to work.

References and Further Reading

Communities of practice for public service (2011), 'Homepage'. Available at: http://www.communities.idea.gov.uk

Gershon, P. (2010), 'Tough Economic Times: Challenges & Opportunities for the Profession', Keynote Presentation: APM Conference 2010: 'Building the Future in Partnership', London, UK, 21 October 2010. Available at: http://www.youtube.com/watch?v=UXoQjhuJ8Ro (accessed October 2011).

Holmes, A. (2005), 'Why the G-Men aren't IT men', *CIO Magazine*. Available at: http://www.cio.com.au/article/5206/why_g-men_aren_t_it_men/ (accessed September 2011).

Office of Government Commerce (2007), *Managing Successful Programmes*, 3rd edn, Norwich: The Stationery Office.

Office of Government Commerce (2005), *Managing Successful Projects with PRINCE2*, 4th edn, Norwich: The Stationery Office.

Welcome to UK GovCamp (2011), 'Homepage'. Available at: http://www.ukgovcamp.com (accessed August 2011).

8 *Project Management in the Third Sector*

JOHN CROPPER

The third sector is vast. It covers everything from humanitarian response by international non-governmental organisations (iNGOs) to your local scout group – and pretty much everything else in between. In this chapter, I am going to focus mainly on international development and humanitarian response.

An Introductory Cautionary Tale

Christine's background was as a water engineer. She had arrived from Europe the day before and this was her first visit to South East Asia. All her previous experience had been in Africa, but now here was a new big emergency and experienced project managers were needed quickly. A huge number of houses had been destroyed, with many people killed and injured.

Christine was housed in a hotel used by her NGO, so getting to work was easy. She met the country director, who explained the situation. She also met the finance manager, who outlined the initial budget. The HR people sorted out her paperwork and told her which members of the team were in place and which were still being recruited.

Christine met the senior member of her team, who also spoke some English and they started working out what to do. That included writing project documentation which would be used for a funding proposal based on her experience and what the local staff told her. A visit to one of the affected areas was arranged for the next day and logistics for the trip were organised.

One week later, a lot had changed. Christine's email account was at last working in the new office and she had been added to the IT project management system. She had not been given any authorisation levels yet. Internet speed was crawling because the number of staff had trebled and other NGOs were also flying staff in. So bandwidth was a challenge, and as a senior IT person had not yet arrived, support was only possible through the very slow email service. Skype was barely functional.

There had been several coordination meetings with the UN and other NGOs. The NGOs had divided up areas to avoid duplication of effort. Logistics had done a fantastic job and supplies were arriving – so water distribution was starting up and materials for rebuilding houses and temporary shelters had been ordered. Only about half her staff had arrived and Christine was spending her time briefing them, helping them to get set up and dealing with a never-ending stream of requests for information from the media, her headquarters and the regional office – as well as from the UN and other agencies.

One month later, the funding situation had become clear. Now Christine felt she had an idea of how much money she really had at her disposal (until then, it had all been educated guesswork). She still had staff shortages. Logistics were working very hard but they had clearly never handled an emergency like this before. But, in spite of the difficulties, Christine felt that work was going well. Shelters had gone up and some reconstruction had started. She wished she knew more about the local culture but really had no time to meet staff members working on the long-term development programmes. However, she had managed similar projects many times before. She was pleased that her team understood the logical framework that she had developed in her first week and were using this as their implementation plan. (A logical framework is a tool that shows relationships between activity, outputs, outcomes and goals. It also describes indicators, means of verification and assumptions.)

But Christine was exhausted and felt that she had been firefighting constantly for the last month. Christine felt that she had coordinated through the UN and iNGO meetings, but things started to go wrong. A delegation of beneficiaries complained about the project. They had not been consulted about the design of the housing. They were grateful, but not happy with what was being done. Additionally, latrines and washing areas were being built in a way that was not culturally appropriate. Rework would be expensive and no one was clear where the money could come from. Local authorities were also upset that plans had not been shared with them. In addition, there were some real concerns about the quality of materials being supplied. The timber was of poor quality and was not seasoned. A large order had been placed. Much of the project had to be reworked at great cost.

An audit would have found no detailed project plans and a lack of shared planning. Christine had given her staff a logical framework, but that was not a project plan and there had been almost no participation. Without that participation there had been no input of essential local knowledge. Stakeholder management had been focused on only one group of stakeholders (the UN and other iNGOs), hence the problems with beneficiaries and the local authorities. Christine had worked very hard and been very busy – but she had not really managed the project. She had become involved in direct implementation, but she had not engaged sufficiently with all the important stakeholders. Given her lack of familiarity with the local culture, that was a big risk.

Nature of Third Sector Projects

International development projects can be subdivided in many ways. One of the most common ways is whether the project is operational (that is, you do it all yourself) or if you implement the project through local partner organisations (usually local NGOs or CBOs (community based organisations)).

An example of an operational project might be school building in a remote rural area of a developing country. The iNGO will have staff on the ground working with a local civil society. They establish that schools are needed and that this fits with the priorities of the iNGO itself. If there is a need but the iNGO does not work on (say) school building, then they will try and find someone who does work in this area. Staff will work with local stakeholders to ensure that a school is wanted (*needs* and *wants* are not always the same in development). Once the need is clear and stakeholders are on board, then the iNGO sets up the project. Staff needed are recruited and the project implemented largely by the iNGO itself. In some ways, this is most similar to traditional project management. Many elements are under the control of the project team.

If a project is being implemented through local partners, then the processes and the role of the project manager are quite different. The project idea might come from the iNGO staff – or a local organisation might approach the iNGO. The local organisation will have to be vetted to ensure that they have the skills and capacity to do the work and that they have similar and compatible values. It may be that the iNGO staff have to find local organisations that are able to implement the project. Stakeholder analysis will be tripartite between the local partner, communities and the iNGO staff. Relationships will have to be forged and managed throughout the project. Once everything is ready, funds are disbursed to the local partner organisation and they begin implementation. The iNGO manages the relationship and ensures that the project is being monitored, controlled and evaluated.

SOME THIRD SECTOR PROJECT CHALLENGES

Clearly the project manager in the iNGO has to manage some complex relationships. He/she has to ensure that work is being done to satisfy the objectives, but has no direct control over day-to-day implementation. At the same time, it is not (usually) a simple subcontract. The key is in the word *partnership*. The iNGO wishes to implement through a local organisation because that organisation has local knowledge, skills and – crucially – legitimacy that the iNGO does not have. Legitimacy sounds like a strange concept when related to project management. It is however critical to third sector work. No one votes for NGOs and there are no shareholders, so NGOs must ensure that their work is grounded in the needs and wishes of the communities they serve. So working through local organisations is a common way to try and ensure legitimacy. After all, how would you feel about a foreign organisation turning up and telling you how to manage your local health care?

However, local organisations may lack skills and capacity – and they almost certainly do not have project management skills. So, building up local skills will be an important element in overall project success.

Humanitarian work and especially rapid responses to conflict or natural disasters are usually operational and have a series of additional complications. Events often move very fast, information is poor and may be wrong. Staff might have been affected personally and offices or warehouses may have been destroyed.

Alternatively, the iNGO might need to get a response underway in a couple of days or even within hours of a natural disaster when they have no local office or staff in-country. For example, an earthquake happened in a residential area in a Central American capital city. One thousand people were killed and over 250,000 houses were destroyed or damaged. The iNGO had a staff of only three people in that country. Within four days, there were about 30 staff plus water and sanitation equipment to start the response.

Projects might also be massive – the second Congo war had killed approximately 5.4 million people by the end of 2008. The sheer scale can be overwhelming – a tsunami or an earthquake with an impacted population running into the millions. But, in some cases the emergency may be forgotten (see http://www.monthlydevelopments.org/article/forgotten-emergencies), or might not be media friendly.

Conflict is an additional factor – iNGOs work in war zones and that is always difficult and complex. Clearly it can often be very dangerous. Do you accept UN military logistics support? It can help ... but how will this be perceived? How does this perception change over time? Which faction supports who? How can they be convinced to allow humanitarian access? Even simple things such as gathering information can be fraught. You need to ask yourself if your conversation or questions pose a risk to the informant. Perhaps it can remind them of past traumas. It may identify them – in the eyes of some as a collaborator. Is it increasing stigma, or putting them in danger? And then stress can be a huge issue. Just how do you react when you witness murder, rape or worse and are powerless to stop it? Above all, sensitivity, acute political awareness and outstanding people management skills are a must and the cost of getting it wrong is very high. The only protection a humanitarian worker can rely on is being seen as neutral.

Yet, if the emergency is not in the news, it will almost certainly be heavily underfunded. In pretty much every case, there will need to be a substantial increase in staff numbers and this will happen very quickly – but implementation can't wait. You cannot delay distributing life-saving aid because all the staff haven't arrived, or everything isn't quite ready. So an emergency response does represent a lot of challenges to effective project management.

A FEW CASE EXAMPLES

CASE EXAMPLE NO. 1: A SUPPLY CHAIN FAILURE

Water and sanitation tubing was piled up all around a compound in El Fasher (North Darfur). It was taking up space in storerooms and even a couple of empty offices. Was the project team about to start a major project? No. Why was there so much tubing?

Logistics said the programme staff needed it. The programme staff said they had finished. No one had told logistics and logistics had not asked. Result: thousands of pounds of waste. That was made even worse because the tubing had been brought in by air freight.

CASE EXAMPLE NO. 2: OVER RELIANCE ON FRIENDSHIP

A microcredit scheme was generally working well. But there were serious problems with one organisation, whose repayment rate was below 10 per cent. Records were abysmal. Impact was non-existent.

So, what had gone wrong? Was this a surprise? Well, actually, it was not. The iNGO's team in that country had known of the problems for months. They had tried to support, held meetings, and then offered more support. They had done everything except cancel the project. Why not? They had worked well with the partner for several years but:

1. they did not analyse the partner's organisational skill base for this kind of work; and
2. they could not bring themselves to break off the long-standing good relationship.

Result: over £50,000 wasted.

CASE EXAMPLE NO. 3: INSENSITIVITY

As part of an emergency response on the Atlantic Coast of Nicaragua, the project team wanted to distribute seeds and tools to enable communities to start up their lives again following devastating floods. 'We don't fund that' came the response from their headquarters. 'We don't consider that part of the emergency'. I am not sure that the affected communities would have shared that point of view.

CASE EXAMPLE NO. 4: NEUTRALITY AS PROTECTION IN A WAR ZONE

It was a project manager's leaving party in Darfur. The army was there. So were the militias and rebels. It had been declared a neutral zone in order for the party to happen. Maybe an achievement like this is the ultimate in stakeholder management!

Funding Third Sector Projects

Funding in the third sector is always complex. Most iNGOs and local NGOs need to identify sources of funding for most, if not all work they do. Here are a few of the questions:

- Who will fund what?
- How long will it take them to disburse?
- What are the requirements?
- Will the donor fund all or only part of the work?
- If only part of the work, who will fund the rest?
- What formats does the donor use in its applications?
- What are its procurement rules?
- If two or more donors are funding one piece of work, can you use one progress and finance reporting format – or do you have to use separate formats for each funder?
- Do you wait until you know you have all the funding, or do you start work before?
- What level of security in funding do you need before you start?

These questions are indicative of how funding works for iNGO projects. Sometimes, you know there will be funding, but you don't know the amount or when the funds will become available. At other times you will not know these things.

OVERFUNDING

It is quite possible to have too much funding. That might sound strange but a 'media friendly' disaster can attract large amounts of funding. In such cases the amounts of money available might be too much for:

1. the project needs; and
2. the capability of the organisation to spend and implement.

The question might then be asked, 'Can the excess funds be diverted to another emergency project that has no funds, or a shortage of money?' Well, no they cannot because charity rules forbid this. This has another perverse impact. Some iNGOs will try to cash in where they know there will be funding, whether they have experience in the area/country/theme or not. This can and does lead to poor quality work and other iNGOs sometimes have to spend their own funds to correct poor quality work done by others. As an example, in Aceh, there were over 500 agencies working – most of whom did not have a presence in the province before the tsunami.

Some of the big NGOs keep their own emergency funds just to enable them to respond quickly. They hope to replenish these funds from donors but they cannot wait for donors to make up their minds.

Funding complexities are not linked to emergency responses. One donor took two years to finalise contractual arrangements. By that time some of the iNGO's local partners had actually closed down by the time contracts were in place.

Special Challenges for Third Sector Project Managers

Project management in development projects is immensely complex. Some of the structural complexities linked to funding and the often short timescales have already been discussed. Stakeholder management has also been mentioned but it is important to emphasise its centrality. The project needs 'buy in' at a number of different levels.

The community needing the project needs to agree to the methodology. Is this culturally appropriate? How do you convince a community run by conservative men that including girls in education is important? There will be local leaders with power. Local authorities need to agree with what the project will do and how it will be done. There may well be parts of a community that are against your project.

Development project managers must develop very clear stakeholder maps, and these can be complex. If the project is trying to change policy in some way or advocate broader change, then there will need to be an understanding of how power works at different levels. Who stands to gain? Who can help? Why should they help? Who can block change?

It is important to remember that there may well be people or organisations, which are actively opposed to a change in the status quo. They will become or remain wealthy and/ or powerful as long as the same social order persists. At the same time, other organisations could well be working in the same areas or trying to enact similar or complementary policy changes. What alliances are possible? Are there any synergies? Thus stakeholder understanding is fundamental. Without it, a project will stand a high chance of failure, which means denying poor communities the potential benefits.

At the same time, NGOs need to make sure they are tackling the root cause of a problem. They might need to use a range of tools to help analyse the situation. Again, getting the right kind of input from stakeholders is central to the accurate use of these tools.

PROJECT MANAGEMENT QUALIFICATIONS AND SKILLS

Project managers in NGOs need to have some advanced people management skills to make sure that stakeholder processes are well managed and kept alive. They have to influence, negotiate, articulate a clear vision for change, inspire, resolve conflicts and manage day-to-day planning and implementation.

The typical project manager in an NGO has probably not been recruited for project management skills. The principal recognised professional qualification is Project Management in Development (PMD) (about which I shall have more to say in the closing sections of this chapter). Before that emerged there had been no contextualised qualifications. Industry certification such as PRINCE2 or PMI is virtually unknown in these projects. What usually happens is that someone is recruited for their technical skills in whatever it is the project will be doing. Get a water expert for a water project, a gender expert for a women's empowerment project, an agriculturalist for a food security project. Project management has been treated as something that can be picked up. People work hard. They achieve some results. They get promoted and they recruit more people like themselves and the systemic weakness is perpetuated.

So if we divide NGO project management skill sets into development skills (such as poverty analysis); project management skills; and intra/interpersonal skills, we can see that the typical project manager usually has good development skills. After all, they may have lived in, worked in or be from the country and they will have a wealth of sector expertise. They need good intra/interpersonal skills, which they may or may not have. But they usually lack project management skills.

Very often, the nexus between intra/interpersonal skills and project management skills is critical. A good project manager should be able to combine project team skills (including support functions such as logistics, finance and HR) and stakeholder awareness (such as implementing partners). These must be incorporated in project management processes to ensure that plans are comprehensive and detailed. The project manager has to keep the whole team focused on the project and ensure that communications are effective and appropriate – both internally and externally. Project managers will rarely have dedicated staff, because NGO budgets do not allow for this. There may be an accountant, who spends 35 per cent of her/his time on the project. Communities may provide volunteer support. There might be one logistician covering all the projects and the project manager him/herself might cover a number of projects.

When working through implementing partners, the project manager may find that some of the people working on the project belong to one or more other organisations. Again, this emphasises the importance of teamwork and team building along with the ability to influence, motivate and inspire.

Listening is so important that it merits its own mention. To manage an international development project well, the project manager needs to be able to listen. Team members need to be encouraged to talk – and a team may be composed of several different cultures. Local partners need to be listened to carefully – they are often closest to the ground and any problems will be picked up by them first.

Donors and other stakeholders need to be listened to and their concerns understood. Some stakeholders (donors, for example) will probably not be in the same country. Above all, project beneficiaries and communities have to be listened to. They may not be accustomed to expressing their needs or opinions, but without knowing them the project could be going down the wrong track.

One group I worked with said that the NGO project manager needs to be like a rhino in ballet shoes! By this, they meant that you need to be tough to break through and get things done but at the same time nimble and fleet of foot. To this I would add the need for acute political antennae in order to sense and understand the changing power relationships that surround international development projects.

CASE EXAMPLE NO. 5

In many agricultural communities, power resides with middlemen, who purchase the food products and get them to a local market. Helping farmers to improve their position in the market may (and probably will) mean worsening the livelihoods of these middlemen. Yet these are often not wealthy people. They have managed to buy a truck and this is their livelihood. How do you get round this? If you help small producer farmers, who own land, you can help them increase revenue and/or lower costs. Yet lower costs might come at the expense of landless, migrant labour.

CASE EXAMPLE NO. 6

An iNGO had to hand back £60,000 to a donor. It had not followed the donor's procurement guidelines and obtained three quotes for corrugated iron for emergency roofing following floods in a remote area of Bangladesh. 'But there is only one supplier in that area' said the project manager. 'It was an emergency and we didn't have time to waste getting quotes from other areas of the country just to make up three quotes'. Maybe, but had a logistician been consulted at that first stage, they would have warned of the consequences – £60,000 wasted and with it, the opportunity to do £60,000 worth of work.

Summary of Project Management Standards and Practice in Third Sector Projects

Clearly project management in international development is complex and the stakes are high. Poor project management (failing to deliver on time, scope and budget) can have direct and serious consequences for people's lives. Despite this, international standards in project management have, to date, made little headway. There have been some attempts to introduce PRINCE 2 or PMP but it is difficult to find examples of successful implementation. There are several reasons behind this.

Perhaps the first of these reasons is the perception that project management is not relevant because it comes from the private sector. There is a background of perceptions like this in the third sector. The situation is starting to change but still has a long way to go.

Secondly, people sometimes feel that methodologies do not fit the development context – especially with reference to the way that funding works and with respect to the methodologies required by funding and the need to monitor and evaluate impact. There is some truth in this. But rather than viewing project management methodologies as in conflict with good development processes, it is more helpful to look at them as complementary and finding ways for them to fit together.

Finally, there are problems of access and cost. PRINCE 2 and PMP courses are expensive – too expensive for most charities. The third sector is caught in a trap. It needs better project management but cannot afford some of the existing solutions. Access is a real issue in developing countries. Most of the developing world lacks the centres needed for PMI certification or APMG certifications. No NGO should be in a position of having to divert aid money to fly staff to another country just to do a project management exam!

At present, most iNGOs use their own methodologies. These focus mostly on project design and link this to monitoring, evaluation and (especially) reporting processes. Project design is clearly important. Any third sector organisation wants to be doing the right project. Doing things right is just as important and this is where a range of problems can be seen.

This explains why there is sometimes such a lack of the availability and use of some planning tools that project managers in other sectors take for granted. It is rare to see work breakdown structures, network diagrams or similar tools being used. Indeed, most of the time, NGO staff are even unaware of their existence. Possibly as a result of this, it is common for projects to be over or under budget, late or short on scope. The sector has even developed a term: 'the no cost extension' to describe when a project has not finished on time and the iNGO requests further time but no extra funding from the donor. Clearly this is a misnomer. There is always a cost. After all, the project team isn't working for free. What happens is that the iNGO uses its own funds (usually originating in individual donations from the public) to subsidise the donor grant. In a way, poor project management means that donations from the general public to iNGOs are being used to subsidise major multilateral donors such as the European Union, USAID or DFID (the UK Government's Department for International Development).

PMD PRO

In 2007 a group of iNGOs met under the leadership of Learning in NGOs to discuss project management in the sector and the challenges described above. The outcome of this work was PMD Pro – Project Management for Development Professionals. This is an APMG-supported certification focused on international development. The manual is free and available in English, Spanish, French and Portuguese and can be accessed at www.pm4ngos.org. Exams are online at http://online.apmg-exams.com. The certification went 'live' in 2010 and since then 2,500 people have taken level one and level two has just been launched. Level three is under development at the time of writing.

The rapid uptake and interest in PMD Pro comes from its being appropriate. It is completely contextualised to international development. It is accessible online and in four languages, with more to follow. It is also affordable. The *Guide to PMD Pro* is free and certification costs between US$20 and US$120 per person. Local organisations in developing countries pay US$20 per person.

The level of interest is encouraging and shows that there is an appetite for change. In one PMD Pro course, a project manager said 'This is the first time we have been given tools to help us do our jobs. Normally we get tools that help someone else write a report'. This sums up what PMD Pro is trying to do – namely help those who do good to do it better.

Clearly, much more than certification is needed. What certification does, though, is provide a common language along with tools and techniques that can help international development organisations start to hold meaningful conversations about their projects and begin the process of improving project planning and delivery.

9 Introduction to Project Organisation Structures

DENNIS LOCK

The way in which people are organised in any kind of project will clearly influence the way that those people interact and communicate. An effective organisation will have designated lines of authority and every member of the organisation will have a clear idea of the part that he or she is expected to play to make the project a success. This is part of the management communication network that is essential if people are to be well motivated. Many different kinds of project organisations exist, although most can be identified as team, a matrix or a mix of the two (hybrid). These organisation patterns will be discussed in this chapter and the next, but first it is necessary to outline some of the theory that pertains to organisations.

Introduction to Organisation Structures

CHARTING CONVENTIONS

Organisation structures are depicted and communicated by means of charts and Figure 9.1, although very simple, contains all the elements used in conventional organisation charts (sometimes called *organigrams*).

Most aspects of the chart in Figure 9.1 are self-explanatory but the status of the secretary is not immediately obvious. This is a staff position, which means that the secretary is not contained within the vertical chains of command. There is no line authority or power attached to the job. But such jobs often carry reflected or implied status. If the secretary in this example should make some request of another member of staff, that request can be refused because technically the secretary has no authoritative power to issue commands. But no sane junior member of this organisation would want to risk upsetting this secretary by refusing to carry out a reasonable request, because by so doing that could draw down the wrath of the divisional manager. Some managers are very protective of their secretary's interests. Also, of course, this secretary can legitimately pass on a command issued by the manager to a subordinate, in that case acting as a channel of communication.

No organisation chart can accurately reflect all the ad hoc channels for communications and influences that will be formed between people during the life of the organisation. The dotted line in the example in Figure 9.1 has been put there to indicate a specified

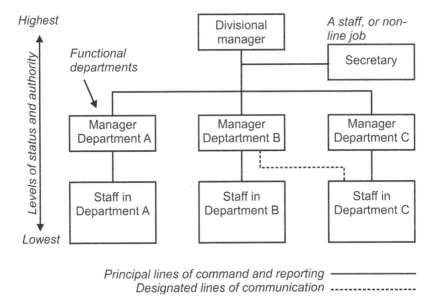

Figure 9.1   Widely accepted organisation chart conventions

chain of communication, which in this case means that a member of Department C is expected routinely to exchange information with the manager of Department B.

One generally recommended convention for company organisation charts is that the boxes should show job titles but not the individual names of the jobholders. The reason given for that is that people move in and out of jobs but the organisation by contrast remains fairly constant. But this argument is best ignored in project organisation charts, and we recommend that personal names *should* be included.

ISSUING PROJECT ORGANISATION CHARTS

One of the first steps when setting up a new project should be to produce and distribute its organisation chart. That can be part of the process of compiling a set of project procedures, which are sometimes collectively known as the *Project Handbook* or *Project Manual*. In very small projects, carried out entirely within a single company, this might not be absolutely necessary. However, in larger projects, which might involve people from several companies and other organisations, distributed organisation charts are valuable. They act as communication directories, so that people can see how other people in the organisation relate to themselves and the project.

All this may seem very straightforward and sensible, but there are often people who become upset when they see a new organisation chart. Some people will feel disappointed if the level at which they are included indicates a status lower than that which they think they actually have or deserve. A common device that attempts to overcome this problem is to include a statement declaring that levels do not necessarily indicate status (examples of this can be seen below in Figures 9.3 and 9.4). However, most people will doubt the veracity of such claims. Or in plainer language, no one will ever believe them. Even more affronted will be those people who are not shown on the chart at all, although believing in their own minds that they are sufficiently important to the project to deserve such recognition. So even the preparation and distribution of organisation charts, although necessary, can arouse unexpected discontent.

SPAN OF CONTROL AND THE WIDTH OF ORGANISATIONS

There is a wise and widely held view that no manager in an organisation should have direct control over too many people, especially when those people are in skilled jobs that are likely to require considerable individual support and guidance from that manager. The argument here is that if there are too many people reporting directly to one manager, then that manager cannot possibly devote enough care and time to support and control the work of those subordinates.

The number of people reporting directly to a manager is called that manager's *span of control*, and it is sometimes recommended that this number should never exceed five (known as the rule of five). Others advocate a rule of seven. These rules are only a general guide, and do not have to be adhered to strictly, but they do represent common sense.

The span of control can be increased somewhat without penalty if all the subordinates are relatively unskilled and are all doing identical routine jobs (for example in a call centre) because each individual is then likely to demand less of the manager's time and technical support. Technical and operational difficulties that do arise are more likely to be collective rather than individual.

An organisation in which its managers typically have wide spans of control is known as a wide organisation. Conversely, an organisation where all or most managers have small spans of control through increased delegation becomes a tall organisation, because it usually needs more levels (or layers) of management.

A wide organisation has the apparent advantage of needing fewer managers than a tall organisation because each manager is expected to manage a higher proportion of the total working staff. Managers are popularly regarded as adding considerable cost but little value to company operations. This means that a wide organisation (with fewer managers) should have lower overhead (indirect) costs than its tall organisation alternative. But that apparent reduction in overhead costs will come at the price of increased difficulties and problems in dealing with work and subordinates if the individual managers' spans of control are set too wide.

Figure 9.2, on the following page, illustrates an extreme example from my own past experience, when I was asked to investigate the number of complaints received generally about the performance of the office services department in the London headquarters of an international project engineering company. Apart from numerous general complaints about the services provided by this department, one or two serious and expensive errors had been made.

My first step in the investigation was to examine the department's organisation and, astonishingly, this revealed that the department manager had 19 staff reporting directly to him – an impossibly wide span of control. Further, that manager was expected to deal with several external service providers as well as personally being responsible for HR functions connected with the employment of contract staff overseas. Frankly, the poor man never stood a chance of running an efficient department and was severely overworked. But the blame for that bad performance had to be laid fairly and squarely at his door because it was he who had allowed this organisation to develop and persist.

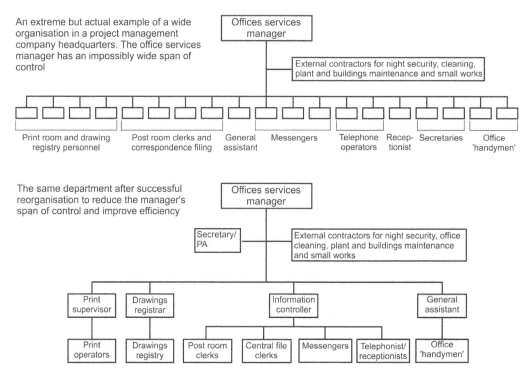

An extreme but actual example of a wide organisation in a project management company headquarters. The office services manager has an impossibly wide span of control

The same department after successful reorganisation to reduce the manager's span of control and improve efficiency

Figure 9.2   Examples of wide and narrow organisations

My recommendations led to a restructuring of the department, achieved by selecting one or two of the existing staff and promoting them to supervisory roles. This immediately increased the motivation of those promoted. Of course it also introduced another level of management, but it did not increase costs because each supervisor was a working supervisor. It was also concluded that the HR functions should be transferred to the HRM department, which was better able to cope with the workload and apply the specialist skills needed.

The department manager was replaced by promotion from within the company. Now no manager or supervisor in the department had a span of control that exceeded four subordinates.

The results of this reorganisation were immediate and dramatic. The string of complaints stopped. Everyone throughout the company (except the outgoing manager) was very satisfied with the results. Here is a case where the organisation structure and the application of proven organisation theory were directly linked with the performance of the department and its manager. None of the previous complaints could be blamed on individuals – they were simply being asked to work in an unsuitable and demotivating organisation.

So anyone who is responsible for setting up a new organisation, whatever functions it performs, needs to be aware that the organisation structure can itself have a profound effect on the people who are expected to work within it.

MANAGEMENT AUTHORITY, ACCOUNTABILITY AND RESPONSIBILITY

Imagine that you are a manager within a project to build a new road. You are allowed to make decisions on staffing and construction methods, but you did not design the road or specify its materials. Your specific task is to manage the site construction of this road. You are working to drawings and specifications prepared by others, who were never under your control.

Imagine, further, that your own job description and your designated place in the project organisation structure make it clear that you have the authority or power to engage workers or subcontractors, and to supervise all the work.

Now suppose that three months after the road has opened large cracks appear in the surface and it has to be closed for repairs. You, as manager responsible for constructing the road, are blamed, criticised and even disciplined for this failure.

If, on investigation, that failure was due to faulty workmanship carried out by those over whom you had direct control, then you can fairly be blamed. You did not ensure that every aspect of the design specification was followed correctly, as you should have done. You had the organisational authority for all the construction work and you must ultimately be held responsible for the failure.

Conversely, suppose that you had followed the drawings and specifications supplied to you exactly without error, and that the fault for the surface failure was caused by incorrect design. Now if you were to be blamed for the failure you could fairly and legally argue that the failure was caused by circumstances (the bad design) over which you had no control.

So there is an organisational theory rule which states *no manager can be held accountable for any action over which he or she has no power to control*. There can be no accountability without the corresponding power and authority.

The antithesis of this is where a manager can take some reprehensible action within his or her power without fear of retribution. That can be described as having power with no accountability – which amounts of course to dictatorship.

UNITY OF COMMAND

No person in an organisation should, if possible, be asked to report to two different managers. This has been recognised for many centuries and indeed the St James's version of the Bible contains the apposite words 'No man can serve two masters: for either he will hate the one, and love the other, or else he will hold to the one, and despise the other ...' (Matthew 6:24).

In 'management-speak' serving two masters translates into *violating the rule of unity of command*. Clearly problems can arise when a person is asked to be responsible to two different managers, particularly when both managers give conflicting instructions. For the unfortunate subordinate person this can pose a difficult problem and lead to some stress. Many years ago I was employed as a principal engineer reporting to two different managers, one of whom was divorced from the other's sister, so I write this section with some personal experience and feeling.

However, in some project organisations it is unavoidable that people might have to be responsible to two managers for different aspects of their duties. This is true in many project matrix organisations and can lead to serious rifts between the managers as well as causing demotivating stress for the subordinates. This subject, with some recommendations, will be dealt with more fully in Chapter 10.

Coordination Matrix Project Organisations

Many companies that carry out routine (non-project) operations, whether in commerce, government or manufacturing, are organised in an arrangement that is often known as a line and function organisation. This kind of organisation earns that description because a number of functional departments are linked in the organisation by lines of command. An example is shown in Figure 9.3. Such organisations are common to many companies and have existed for many, many years without any operational difficulty, at least no difficulty that can be attributed to the organisation structure.

However, when a line and function organisation is charted and analysed it is noticeable that the lines of authority and feedback all run in the vertical direction. That should not give rise to difficulties because people are able to communicate with each other across the different functions in an ad hoc way. But problems do arise when companies with line

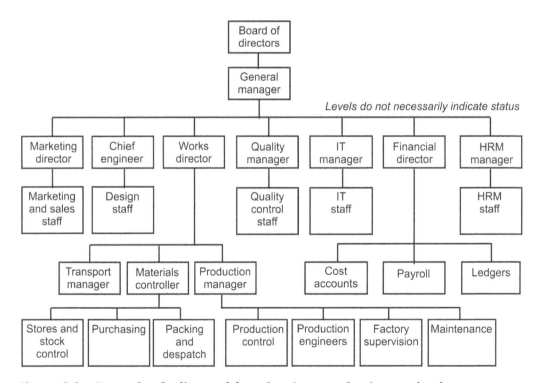

Figure 9.3   Example of a line and function (non-project) organisation

Note: This is a line and function organisation that might be suitable for a manufacturing company. Such organisations can work well for the continuous or batch manufacture of standard products. The vertical lines of command and communication are well defined. Similar organisation patterns are also seen in services industries and not-for-profit organisations. But the organisation structure shown here is not suited as it stands to the management of special projects because there is no provision for planning, coordinating and expediting the project tasks as they progress horizontally from one department to the next.

and function organisations have to deal with special, one-off projects. Projects typically progress horizontally through an organisation, and they do not usually fit well into an organisation where all the commands pass in the vertical direction. There is no manager in the system with the power to follow and control the project (or parts of the project) as it flows across the organisation. Each functional manager is responsible for a specialist department, and might manage it very well, but no one can be identified here with the authority to manage and progress the project through all it stages.

Companies that find themselves having to carry out their first project are advised to recognise this need for horizontal in additional to vertical control and appoint a person to plan and progress the project as it travels across the company organisation from one functional department to the next. The person appointed might be called a project coordinator or project manager. That person will generally have no line authority within the organisation, because all the authority in the system is still directed vertically downward by the functional managers. So the appointment should not be disruptive and no existing manager should feel aggrieved. The project coordinator is identified particularly with the project rather than with any individual function and is therefore able to plan and progress the project from start to finish holistically. It could be said that appointing the project coordinator has given the project its own identity within the company.

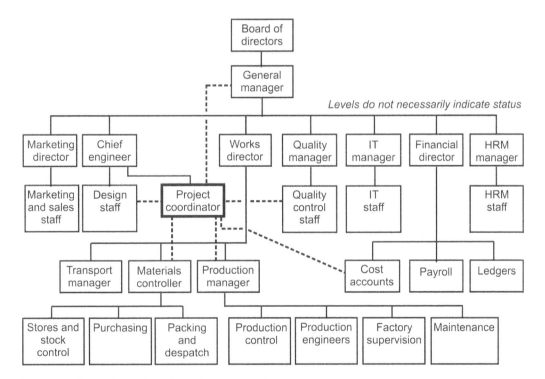

Figure 9.4   A functional matrix organisation

Note: This is the same company depicted in Figure 9.2. But here the company has undertaken a special project and, because it is set up only for routine manufacturing operations, a project coordinator has been appointed to plan the new project and monitor its progress through all departments. This is a staff position with no line authority and, as yet, there is no recognisable project team in the company.

A project coordinator occupies a staff position in the organisation because the job carries no line authority. However, as in the case of the secretary in Figure 9.1, the coordinator can usually call upon the support of a relevant functional manager, or even the general manager, in the event that one of the departments fails to perform adequately on the project.

An organisation of this kind is shown in Figure 9.4 (on the previous page), which is the same company depicted in Figure 9.3, with the only difference being the introduction of the project coordinator. In this example the project coordinator has line responsibility to the chief engineer, but is authorised to communicate independently and freely with many other managers (senior and junior) in the organisation on all matters of project planning and control. This arrangement is sometimes called a functional matrix, and it is one variation on a number of possible matrix organisation patterns where project tasks fall under the control of both a project coordinator (or manager) and the line function managers. Matrix organisations can exist in a number of different forms, and these will be discussed in Chapter 10.

Project Team Organisations

A company or other organisation established for the principal purpose of carrying out one or more projects will often set up a separate suborganisation within itself for each project. Each of these suborganisations then becomes a project team.

Unlike a functional matrix organisation (in which the project coordinator or project manager has little or no line authority) in a team all or most people working on the project come under the command of the project manager. An organisation of this kind is shown in Figure 9.5. The functions included in this example indicate that this case might be found in a project for the design and construction of a petrochemical or mining plant.

Every active person in this project reports either directly or through the chain of command to the project manager. Thus the project manager enjoys supreme authority but can also be held personally accountable for performance and the general project outcomes. This arrangement is without ambiguity. All members of the team can identify themselves directly with the project and its success or failure. Motivation stands a good chance of being high, even to the extent of enthusiasm. In other words, it is far easier to create a team spirit when the people engaged on the project are actually organised as a team.

So, why is every project not organised as a team? To understand this, at least in part, it is necessary to revisit the project life cycle. All project organisations are dynamic and change in shape and size as the project travels through time. At first the team will comprise only a few members, the pioneers of the team if you like, who set the scene and begin activities such as detailed design and planning. As the project reaches the peak of its activity clearly the team will be at its peak size, employing the largest number of people. But from then on the project team will begin to lose its members one by one until eventually there remain only one or two people to deal with post delivery problems discovered by the project's end user.

So whilst at the beginning everyone should be fired up with enthusiasm and dedicated to project success, when people begin leaving the organisation as it dwindles towards extinction, people will naturally be asking themselves the question 'What will happen to

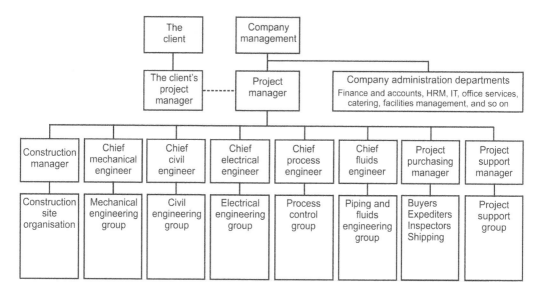

Figure 9.5   A project team organisation for a large project

Note: This example shows the organization of a project team for the design and construction of a chemical processing plant. The project manager has complete responsibility for all aspects of the project, backed by the authority of direct command. It would be usual for a petrochemical company such as this to have several such teams at any time, one for each current project and each under the command or its own project manager.

me now? Where shall I be working next month (if at all)?' Of course, in a successful and prosperous company with a full order book such difficulties are reduced because most people can expect to be transferred to other teams working on concurrent projects. Team members who are engaged on temporary agency contracts are usually able to contact their agencies to make advance arrangements for redeployment. So, unless there is a general recession in the particular industry, this disadvantage of the team organisation can usually be dealt with by a combination of forward human resource planning within the organisation and by having a workforce that is flexible in terms of numbers by adopting a suitable mix between permanent and agency staff.

One advantage of a project team is that it promotes the principle of unity of command. No person here has to face the problem of having to report to two different managers at the same time. It should be expected, therefore, that fewer internal organisational disputes will arise in a team when compared with other organisational forms.

One apparent problem with the organisation shown in Figure 9.5 is that the project manager has a fairly wide span of control. And, the project manager has to contend with a possible range of problems that might be technical, contractual, financial or to do with late progress or shortages of materials. So the project manager needs some help and support. Support must come, in a general sense, from the top down, from the corporate management. But for day-to-day assistance in dealing with operational problems and in the large amount of cost and schedule data, preparation of reports, change records, risk management and so on, here a project support office (PSO) has been set up. PSOs (sometimes less appropriately called project management offices or PMOs) are described in Chapter 16.

To resolve technical difficulties and for helping the project manager in activities such as giving final approval to drawings, a project engineer is sometimes appointed to work directly under the project manager. This is a senior role, but it usually occupies an individual staff position so that the engineer can concentrate on technical issues without the distraction of having to manage other people. For example, the project engineer might have to give final approval for the issue of specifications and drawings. This role of project engineer is not to be confused with the role of the independent engineer in a contract matrix, which will be explained in Chapter 10.

So to a large extent problems associated with the wide span of control can be mitigated by giving the project manager adequate administrative, commercial and technical support. Further it is has to be recognised that project managers in other kinds of organisations, such as all forms of the matrix, will also have wide spans of control, so this apparent difficulty is not confined to teams.

Another possible problem with teams is again connected with the project life cycle and the fact that teams are not permanent organisations. At the end of every team-based project, the team breaks up and the people are dispersed. And unfortunately, with that dispersal of people comes also the dispersal of knowledge about the particular project and some of the technical expertise that has been built up. Lessons might have been learned at the time, but the answers might not still be there in the company when a new team is set up for the next similar project. Of course much of this difficulty can be overcome be the establishment of technical databases (recorded designs and calculations are sometimes called *retained engineering*). Another good practice is for each project manager to keep a project diary of key events and meetings. Those diaries can be held on file for future reference – sometimes valuable when legal issues arise. But members of the technical functional groups in transient teams do not see a clear career path ahead within the organisation, coupled with possible promotion and continuing personal development, unlike the matrix in which the people's functional groups have lives that transcend the lives of individual projects and, from the individual's point of view, might seem to be endless and secure.

So project teams have strong advantages and are easier to manage than other organisational forms. But they also have the problems arising from their temporary nature. The following chapter will consider more permanent forms of organisations, based on matrix formations.

Further Reading

Buchanan, D. and Huczynski, A. (2010), *Organisational Behaviour*, 7th edn, Harlow: Pearson Education.

10 Managing in Matrix and More Complex Organisations

DENNIS LOCK

This is a continuation of the previous chapter, which explained some organisational principles and also described some of the advantages and disadvantages of organising projects as teams. Generally speaking, the alternative to using a team organisation is to adopt a matrix configuration. Just as a team has its advantages and disadvantages, so does a matrix. A matrix can exist in various forms, and the most common forms of these are discussed in this chapter. Also described here is a task force organisation arrangement that can be effective in management change projects (projects that are conducted within companies and other organisations that have no inbuilt project management experience, and which are intended to bring benefits to those companies through changes in the company structure or its operating systems and procedures).

Characteristics of Matrix Organisations

Functional matrix organisations were introduced in Chapter 9. A simple example for a single project in a manufacturing company was shown in Figure 9.4. That form of the matrix is sometimes called a coordinated matrix (for the obvious reason that it includes a project coordinator). It can be regarded as a temporary matrix because, when the single project has been finished, the coordinator will either leave the organisation or return to other duties and the company will continue with its routine non-project operations.

A coordinated matrix is recognised as a weak matrix, because the power of the project coordinator or manager is weak when compared with that of the functional managers. The project is not given any special priority in the organisation, at least as far as support from the organisational structure is concerned.

A more permanent form of matrix can be established when a company carries out several projects at the same time, and expects to continue to do so. An example of this, again for a manufacturing company, can be seen in Figure 10.1.

Another example of a matrix organisation for handling several concurrent projects is shown in Figure 10.2, but this one is for a company that routinely carries out construction or mining, quarrying and petrochemical projects. Although apparently complex, the example in Figure 10.2 is based on an actual case.

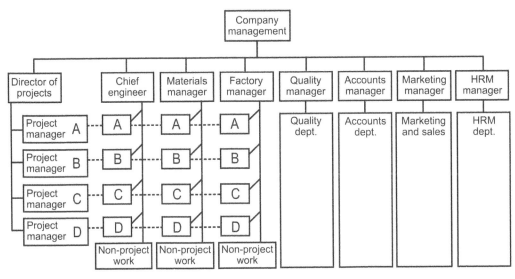

Figure 10.1 Matrix organisation for several simultaneous projects

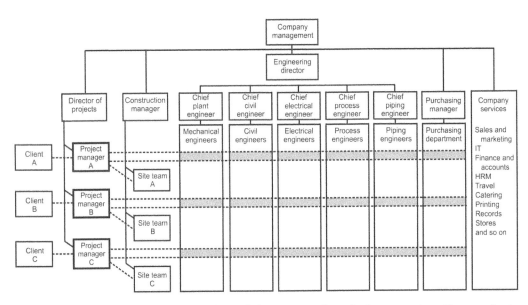

Figure 10.2 Matrix organisation for mining, petrochemical or construction projects

Note: This chart is based on an actual company organization that carried out several large simultaneous projects. It is far from ideal. There are many dual lines of command, so that a person in a functional group might have to take instruction from both their own departmental manager and a project manager. Note that general company services lie outside the projects matrix, which is customary.

Most of the discussion that follows in this section is relevant to matrix organisations for projects in any industry.

APPLYING TWO RULES OF ORGANISATION THEORY TO A TYPICAL MATRIX STRUCTURE

Project Manager's Span of Control

As with the team organisation discussed and illustrated in Chapter 9, the project manager in a matrix will usually have a wide span of control, spread over several specialist functions. Thus the project manager will need as much support as possible with routine project planning, progressing, contract administration and report preparation.

A project support office (PSO), although placing yet another manager within the span of control, will usually provide that support and relieve the project coordinator or manager of routine tasks that would otherwise dilute his or her ability to manage across the wide span. It can be assumed, therefore, that the organisations depicted in Figures 10.1 and 10.2 would have a PSO, or at least some supporting staff occupying staff roles to assist the project manager with planning, progressing and contract administration.

So when a matrix organisation is compared with the alternative of a team organisation for the same project, neither will have an advantage over the other as far as reducing the span of control is concerned.

The Rule of Unity of Command

A team organisation supports the rule of unity of command. Every senior functional manager reports directly to the project manager and no person in the organisation is expected to serve two masters.

Most matrix arrangements have exactly the opposite characteristic. Indeed, in a typical matrix, the rule of unity of command is not simply ignored – a metaphorical chainsaw slices and shreds it into unrecognisable fragments. Whereas in the team everyone should know to whom they report and can expect to receive clear day-to-day instructions and guidance, in a matrix many people will find themselves being responsible both to the project manager and to their functional manager. Therein lies a strong factor for producing damaging resentment and conflict, especially if the different managers cannot agree. Methods for overcoming these problems are outlined below.

STABILITY AND LONGEVITY OF A MATRIX ORGANISATION COMPARED WITH A PROJECT TEAM

A typical project team organisation will change in size as the project moves through its life cycle, so that before the project begins no team will exist, and the team will disperse and vanish when all the work is done. That, as explained in the previous chapter, can be a powerful demotivator that can outweigh other motivational factors associated with teams (such the promotion of a team spirit). However, another demotivator occurs when people are moved too frequently between different projects or are left idle (sitting on the bench to use a sporting analogy) and those risks can be higher with matrix organisations.

A company using several project teams can expect its organisation to be disrupted and changed as its various projects progress from beginning to end. People will have to be moved between team-based functions from time to time and the organisation will always be liable to change. If a project is postponed or cancelled, the effect can be devastating. People in general do not like change, especially when they experience disruption to their careers and working environments.

A company with a matrix organisation can overcome these difficulties to a large extent because the life of the matrix is identified with the life of the company, and not with the life of any individual project. Thus a matrix organisation is more stable than a collection of separate project teams. That is a strong reason why companies eschew the apparent simplicity and simple lines of command of team organisations and choose instead to live with the more complex command structures in the matrix. The matrix tends to act like a giant friendly sponge that can soak up new projects and squeeze out the finished or cancelled ones without changing its permanent shape.

A GENERAL NOTE FOR SENIOR MANAGERS RESPONSIBLE FOR THEIR COMPANY ORGANISATION STRUCTURE

One way to reflect on how an organisation structure can motivate or disrupt an individual is to imagine *yourself* as a person working deep inside that organisation. I recommend that any manager who is faced with strategic decisions to establish or change an organisation should take time out to do this.

So, how would a typical matrix look from the point of view of an individual working within one of its specialist functions? This might be a quite junior person, perhaps being responsible for small design tasks. But remember that the success of each project will depend to a large extent on the collective performance and motivation of all such people. I shall call this imaginary person Jo, which might be short for Joseph or Josephine.

So Jo will arrive at work every morning to carry on with the assigned task, or to accept a new task. When that task is done, a new task will replace it – not necessarily on the same project because this is a multiproject matrix organisation. As time proceeds Jo will gain experience in the chosen technical discipline. Jo's immediate colleagues will all be skilled in the same discipline and they will probably also become Jo's companions.

The manager of Jo's group or department will have attained that position through specialisation in the department's discipline and through several years' experience. Jo can go to that manager for help and technical advice whenever the task in hand proves difficult. The group remains in place from one project to the next, accumulating expertise and learning from past mistakes as time passes.

Performance assessments and salary reviews are likely to be fair, because in this stable functional group the manager knows the strengths and weaknesses of all the group members. In the longer term Jo can expect promotion within the group in line with performance and experience gained.

But Jo might experience difficulties when told to do one thing by the functional manager but is asked to do something else by the project manager. What now should this person do? To obey one manager would mean disobeying the other. So, over time, methods have been developed for adapting matrix organisations to avoid or resolve such conflicts.

Resolving Conflicting Commands in Matrix Organisations

Where commands to a subordinate originate from two different managers, and the principle of unity of command is violated, the risk of conflict can be averted if both managers always issue identical commands. Or, alternatively, those managers might be able to avoid disputes by adopting some friendly compromise, or perhaps one manager might be able to concede gracefully and allow the other manager's will to prevail. But these are often only pipe dreams and more positive steps are usually necessary to prevent or at least discourage conflict.

PRE-EMPTING POWER DISPUTES BY ISSUING PROJECT MANAGEMENT PROCEDURES

The usual way of restoring harmony in a matrix where conflict exists (although not always banishing resentment) is for senior management to arbitrate or rule to resolve disputes. Resolution of possible disputes can be pre-empted by announcing in advance which managers shall have the most power – the project managers or the functional managers. In other words, if the project and functional managers cannot agree, senior management can specify whose will should prevail.

We saw that in a coordinated matrix it was the functional managers who had the most power, because the coordinator (even if given the title of project manager) occupied a staff position and could only recommend actions and had no authority to issue commands to anyone.

Unfortunately, one weakness of organisation diagrams is that they cannot usually show which managers in a matrix have the most power and authority. So the diagrams in Figures 10.1 and 10.2 could apply equally well to any of the forms of matrix that will be described in the following sections. These difficulties can be reduced by putting relevant statements in project procedures or company procedures, or by including suitable clauses in manager's job specifications.

For example a functional manager's job specification might state that he or she has absolute responsibility for the technical content of the work in that department, whilst having to work within the timeframe and cost budgets set by the project manager. Of course job specifications are not usually worded in that way. A more practical general format is to have sections near the top of the job specification form under the separate headings 'Responsible to' and 'Responsible for'.

MATRIX ORGANISATIONS WITH DIFFERENT STRENGTHS

By convention, and also for the purposes of this chapter, a matrix is said to be *strong* when the project manager has supreme power. By contrast it is *weak* when the project manager's authority is limited to that of a coordinator. The most common variants of a matrix organisation will now be described. Remember that, owing to the deficiencies of organisation charts, both Figures 10.1 and 10.2 can be used to represent any of the following matrix forms.

Weak Matrix

A weak matrix is another name for a coordinated matrix. The project coordinator or project manager can only advise the functional managers of their project duties. Any failure by a functional manager to meet the demands of the project as requested by the coordinator will have to be resolved by another manager at a more senior level.

Balanced Matrix

In a balanced matrix the project manager and the functional managers share power and authority on a more or less equal basis. On technical issues, the functional managers could usually claim the higher authority by virtue of their specialisation and professional experience, but difficulties can arise when determining which job or which project should be given priority within each functional group.

As with a weak matrix, the successful operation of a balanced matrix depends on the goodwill and cooperation of all its managers.

Strong Matrix

Project managers in a strong matrix are given greater power than the functional managers. When disputes arise, the will of the project manager must prevail. However, it would be a very unwise project manager who attempted to overrule a functional manager on a technical issue where the functional manager has the more appropriate professional qualifications and experience to make a decision on that issue. So the project manager's power is more likely to be concentrated on work priorities, completion targets and budgets. Thus a strong matrix provides a possible solution for resolving disputes between project managers and functional managers.

There still remains the possibility, however, of conflict between different project managers within the matrix. This will happen particularly when two or more project managers disagree with each other about which of their projects has the greatest priority for using scarce resources from the functional departments. The most effective remedy for preventing this is to have a good multiproject resource scheduling system in place, operated by a project (or programme) support office. The scheduled dates in such systems must be driven by priorities measured in task float or slack, which are in turn driven by required project completion dates. That way, the allocation of resources between different tasks and different projects should be fair and not subject to personal opinions of the different project managers.

Secondment Matrix

A secondment matrix moves the balance of power so far towards the project manager that it approximates to a project team. Each functional manager will be expected to name individuals within their departments who can be assigned to the project manager for the duration of the relevant project, as and when the project manager decides they are needed. These individuals might remain located in their usual places of work but in the very strongest form of a secondment matrix they could be asked to move temporarily into an area controlled by the project manager.

Project managers are able to use the resources placed under their immediate control to work to priorities that they decide. There is reduced possibility of conflict with other project managers about task priorities because all the project managers have their resources allocated specifically to them and are thus responsible directly for allocating day-to-day tasks according to the schedule requirements.

People in a secondment matrix still have an important direct reporting link back to their functional managers for such matters as seeking help with difficult technical problems or for ensuring adherence to design standards and codes of practice relevant to each technical discipline. Each person can still expect to be given training opportunities and equitable performance reviews from the functional manager of their 'home' group.

A secondment matrix arrangement can be chosen, for example, when one or two projects claim very special high priority owing to their potential benefits or their prestige. Other projects in the same company would then remain as projects within some more balanced or weaker form of a matrix, and that would allow the organisation to continue to experience many of the advantages of a matrix.

Hybrid Organisations

Sometimes companies adopt the solution of a hybrid organisation, in which most projects are managed across a common matrix organisation, but with self-contained teams set up for certain projects when the need arises. These teams can be enclosed within the matrix. An example of a hybrid organisation is shown in Figure 10.3 on the next page, which, like other examples in this chapter is based on an actual case. This was an international mining company and the organisation also included internal specialist advisory groups (not shown in this chart) for geology, mining, metallurgy and mineral processing.

This company successfully operated a balanced matrix for almost all of its projects. However, at the time when this organisation chart was drawn, one client required the upgrading and replacement of a large electrical transformer at a copper refinery. Because most of the design of this relatively small project concerned electrical engineers, a self-contained project team was set up within the electrical engineering department. An engineer from that department became the project manager.

The same company once had to deal with a project to pump out and drain underground workings at a client's mine that had (many years before) been flooded with slurry in a tragic accident caused by the collapse of a tailings dam on the surface. When the causes for this collapse had been investigated and dealt with, the piping and fluids department became responsible for the reclamation project. A project team was set up inside that department, because most of the project was concerned with pumping and drainage operations and required specialist knowledge of the behaviour of the fluids involved.

Suppose that another client of this engineering company had required the construction of a tunnel or a bridge to connect two processing plants that were separated by a busy main road or railway line.

That project could most conveniently be handled entirely by a team set up within the civil and structural engineering department.

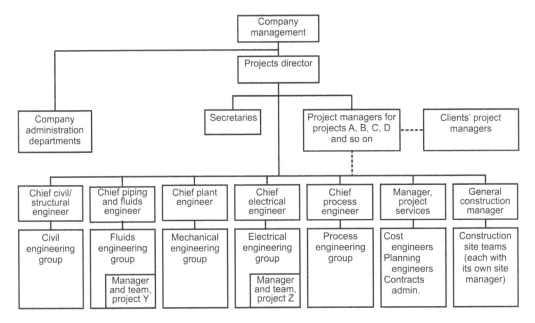

Figure 10.3 A hybrid organisation

Note: This international mining company is organised as a matrix. However, a team will be set up within the relevant department for any project that is confined to a specialist function. For example, project Y is confined to a pumping and drainage project and project Z is for the replacement of a large electrical transformer.

This was a very complex hybrid organisation, mostly operated as a matrix, but it worked well largely owing to the dedication and enthusiasm of the staff, which in turn was promoted by a company policy that respected all its staff, right down to the most junior levels, and provided generous perquisites. The founder of this company was once heard to say 'If people are prepared to make their long journeys into this city to give their time, the least we can do is treat them properly'.

Organisation of Management Change Projects

This section considers projects intended to change a company or its working procedures. Examples of such projects include a company relocation project, a new or changed IT system, an internal reorganisation or a company merger or acquisition. Changes such as these often occur in companies that run routine operations and have no inbuilt experience of managing projects. An insurance services provider has been chosen for the example in this chapter.

CONFIDENTIALITY

An important feature of management change projects is the great influence they can have on staff whose working lives will be affected in one way or another when the change is implemented. That influence is often demotivating and disruptive, because people in general do not like change. They like it even less when they first hear about a proposed change through information leaks. Those leaks sometimes distort management's intentions and can be founded on fear or prejudice rather than fact.

In the wider world of commerce, confidentiality about some changes has to be maintained for proprietary or market reasons. That would apply, for instance, in the case of proposed mergers and acquisitions. Premature leakage of information or the leakage of incorrect information can damage a company's reputation or affect dealings in its shares.

The management of information through all life cycle phases of a management change project is important. Confidentiality is usually very important when any management or internal system change is being considered, which means when the proposed project is in the early phases of its life cycle. The way in which those engaged in the project are organised can either help or hinder efforts to keep a tight hold on information management. Undoubtedly the best way to ensure confidentiality, particularly during the early project phases, is to put all those planning the project into a self-contained and secure unit. That inevitably points to the desirability of establishing a project team or task force.

ESTABLISHING A TEAM FOR A MANAGEMENT CHANGE PROJECT

External consultants are often engaged to advise companies on change projects. Those consultants might be employed on an advisory basis, or they might be given a more substantive role in planning the details of the change and managing the resulting change project. However, no management change project should be planned without investigating the existing company organisation and its operations and performance. That inevitably involves cooperation from some staff working in the organisation. Therein lies a possible source of undesirable information leaks.

CASE EXAMPLE NO. 1

Figure 10.4 shows the simplified organisation chart of a company that is about to conduct an internal management change project. Let's suppose that this company has chosen to replace its ageing IT system.

The functions shown indicate that this is a fairly small insurance services provider. It is self-contained and there are no external call centres. The company is very experienced and successful in its field of insurance. However, there is no inbuilt capability for managing a project. Fortunately, the company's managing director is aware of that deficiency. Accordingly an external consultant has been engaged to advise on the planning and conduct of the project and to give advice and direction to the member of the company's staff chosen to manage the project.

The IT manager will be well aware of the need to manage the changeover to the new system in a way that will not interrupt the company's day-to-day operations. That, for instance, will inevitably mean running the new system alongside the old for a proving period. This IT manager will play a crucial role, and will probably be chosen as the project manager.

The intentions of the managing director and other senior managers towards the project have to be safeguarded, and a steering committee has been formed for that purpose. Some or all of the departmental managers will serve on that committee, which will meet occasionally to keep an overall eye on the project's direction of travel, particularly with regard to its technical specification, budget and time schedule. The project manager cannot act in isolation, but must consult the managers of the various functional departments from time to time to ensure that their operations will be supported in all respects by the new IT system. So those managers will be seconded to the project task force as and when required or, more probably, they will send suitable delegates from their departments. However, Fowler and Lock (2006) recommend that only experts should take part in implementing management change projects, and that junior staff and trainees should learn their craft and gain their experience elsewhere, where they will not be able to cause harm to the project through their lack of expertise.

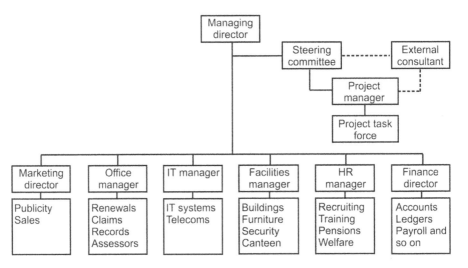

Figure 10.4 A task force organisation for a management change project

If a management change project should fail for any reason, the results not only deprive the company of the intended benefits. They can make the implementation of future change projects far more difficult because of the apathy, resentment or downright hostility caused to people who tried and failed to work within the changed procedures or organisation imposed upon them. Management change projects fall squarely within the 'must get it right first time' category. Thus, during the implementation stage of a management change project it is important to ensure that the change will be accepted by staff. Failure will mean that the expected benefits will not all be realised. That aspect of management change projects is discussed more fully in Chapter 49.

Contract Matrix Organisations

On very large projects, including those for big construction undertakings, petrochemical and mining, the project organisation can be complex because of the large number of suppliers, subcontractors and other service providers involved.

Project owners and investors will often appoint a specialist organisation to oversee or assist with the management of their project. This might be a main contractor or, in the

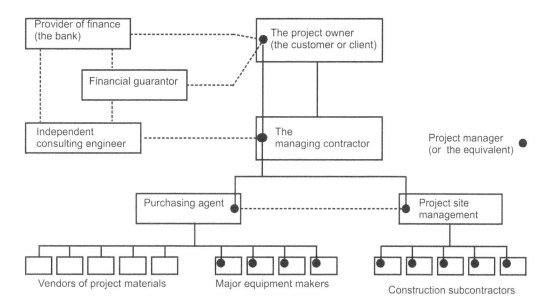

Figure 10.5 A contract matrix organisation

extreme case a managing contractor that can assume all responsibility for carrying out the project. Thus this main contractor would have the authority to hire subcontractors, purchase equipment and materials, generally supervise all the work and might also carry out detailed design. A managing contractor will employ people in its own offices to carry out supervisory tasks and manage the project, so it will have its own internal organisation as well as having to manage across the contract matrix (as this kind of organisation is sometimes called). The project owner might have its own project manager who will cooperate with a project manager employed by the main contractor. A representation of a contract matrix is shown in Figure 10.5.

The work to be performed by the suppliers of major items of equipment and some of the large subcontractors can be regarded as projects in themselves. So each of those suppliers and subcontractors will have an internal project organisation, and each of those project organisations will have its own project manager.

So in a contract matrix there can be a plethora of project managers. But the project manager with principal responsibility for successful project conclusion, and with the most authority, will usually be the one that resides in the main contractor's home office.

The funding of such large projects can become a very important factor, and one or more financial institutions (we can call those 'the bank' for simplicity) might be asked to lend or invest funds to support the project cash flow during the period before the project is completed and begins to repay its investment. But banks and other financial institutions will not usually have any people on their own staff with the expertise in the technology of the project, so they must take professional advice. That advice is often provided by a professional person or an engineering organisation that is independent of both the project owner and the main contractor. This engineering adviser is often called simply the engineer, and will usually be named in the financial contract.

The guarantor shown in Figure 10.5 is there in this example to protect the interests of the bank. For example if an overseas client should default on payments for any reason. Organisations such as the Exports Credits Guarantee Department (ECGD) in the UK or the Export-Import Bank (Ex-IM in the US) often act as guarantors in such cases.

These roles are all indicated in Figure 10.5 although, of course, with such complex and large projects there are many variations and no exact standard model.

In a contract matrix communications between people are very important. One important recommendation is that the managing contractor should publish a project manual. That, in addition to recommending or instructing the general project control procedures to be used, should include a skeleton organisation chart covering the principal players in the matrix. In particular one person or point of contact should be agreed for each suborganisation and main organisation in the matrix. Of course in a very large project there might need to be two or more designated points of contact within the same organisation, according to the aspects of the project that each is authorised to cover within the head contract and the subcontracts. A directory of these names should be distributed, preferably by including it in the project manual. Communications in the complex organisation of a project matrix can get confused and it is important to establish these points of contact and make sure that everyone who needs to communicate is aware of them.

More Complex Organisation Forms

This chapter and Chapter 9 outlined some organisational principles and have described some forms of project organisations. Chapter 11 continues with this theme, but deals with the even more complex issues of multicompany and international projects.

References and Further Reading

Buchanan, D. and Huczynski, A. (2010), *Organisational Behaviour*, 7th edn, Harlow: Pearson Education.

Fowler, A. and Lock, D. (2006), *Accelerating Business and IT Change: Transforming Project Delivery*, Aldershot: Gower.

Orridge, M. (2009), *Change Leadership*, Farnham: Gower.

11 *International Projects*

JEAN BINDER

While businesses and companies are increasingly multinational we are more frequently facing projects with participants representing various cultures, having different native languages, working in different time zones and locations. In other words, this is the world of global projects. Global projects are practically creeping into the life of companies of all sizes from small enterprises to the biggest leading players. (Kähkönen, 2010)

Introduction

International projects require specific strategies to manage global stakeholders, by understanding the differences in culture, language and time zones, and identifying how to transform these differences from challenges into opportunities. This chapter defines the main characteristics of global projects and focuses on the advantages of international teams, addressing their challenges and presenting solutions for global collaboration.

Traditional, Distributed, International and Virtual Projects

In the project management literature we can find different types of projects, when comparing the number of organisations and locations involved in their implementation. In traditional projects, a large majority of the team members are working for the same organisation and in a single location. Virtual projects involve team members working in many locations, and can also be called international projects when they include people located across country borders. Project managers may face specific challenges on virtual projects as they need to balance different interests, company cultures and working practices, and most communications occur over a distance (see Chapter 12 for more information on virtual projects).

International projects require the collaboration of people from different country cultures and languages, sometimes with the added complexity of the locations over various time zones. Global projects can be defined as a combination of virtual and international projects, which include people from different organisations working in various countries across the globe.

You can use the dimensions illustrated in Figure 11.1 to evaluate the level of complexity of your global projects. I shall now explain those dimensions.

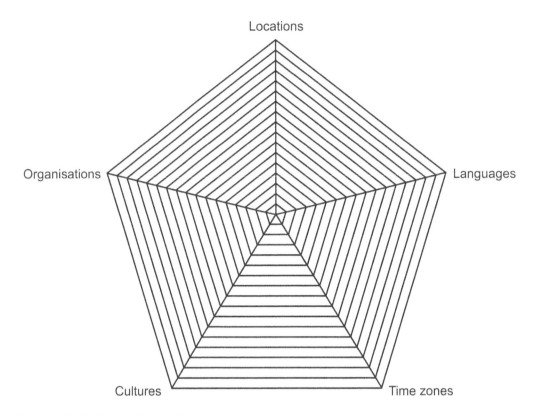

Figure 11.1 Dimensions of global projects

Number of Distant Locations

The project team can be in a single room (project war room), in different rooms or in multiple locations. When all stakeholders are in geographical locations near at hand, face-to-face meetings can be easily organised and the positive influence of body language and social interaction on the efficiency is clear. In global projects, the team members are located at least in two different countries (as illustrated in Figure 11.2). When the distance among the team members is such that travel is required for physical contact, the use of communication and collaborative tools (such as audio- and web-conferencing) becomes essential, requiring the application of specific communication strategies to ensure a high level of effectiveness. Chapter 12 is dedicated to virtual projects and the complexities of managing people in distant locations.

Number of Different Organisations

Project team members can work for a single department in one company, for multiple departments or even for multiple companies (as illustrated in Figure 11.3). Project managers must adapt their management and leadership skills to the multiple policies,

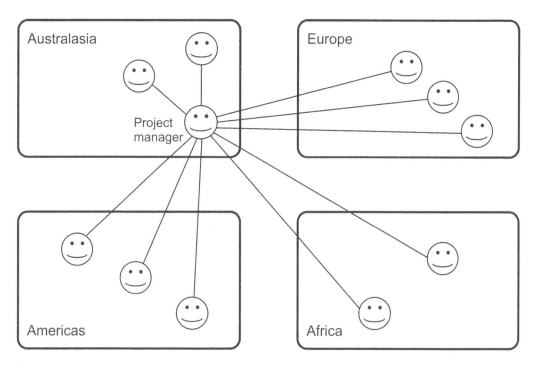

Figure 11.2 A project with team members in distant locations

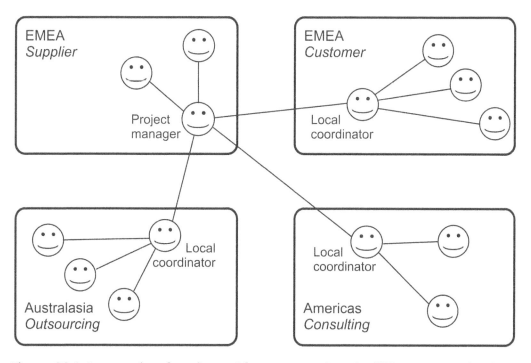

Figure 11.3 International project with team members in different organisations

procedures and organisational cultures. The complexity of commercial and contractual processes is also increased.

National Cultures

Customs and traditions of different nations and regions can add diversity to the work environment beyond the variety of organisational cultures, reducing the group thinking and improving the collective creativity. Motivation can be increased when the team prefers to work in cross-cultural environments and benefit from the rich information exchange. Nevertheless, this diversity can sometimes be the source of conflicts and misunderstandings. Project managers must apply some basic rules and practices if they want to take advantage of the cross-cultural communication and avoid its pitfalls. Chapter 24 is dedicated to the challenges and opportunities of cross-cultural encounters.

Different Languages

International companies usually establish a common language for the exchange of information, although the way people communicate is highly dependent on their own native languages. For example, if the common language is English, the effectiveness of communication by most non-English speakers will be limited by their knowledge of English expressions, vocabulary and often by their ability to make analogies and tell stories or understand jokes. On the other hand, native English speakers would need to limit their vocabulary to clear sentences and essential words, and carefully confirm the understanding of their ideas by foreign colleagues. The use of graphics and diagrams shared in online meetings (explained later in this chapter) can reduce misunderstandings and increase the commitment from international stakeholders, independently of their native language.

Time Zones

Team members are sometimes dispersed across different time zones, making it difficult (or impossible) to organise meetings in common office hours. The effect is twofold.

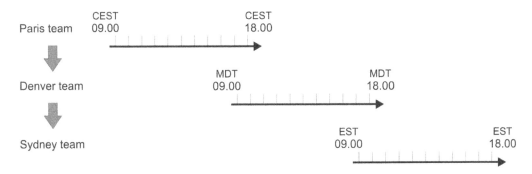

Figure 11.4 Example of 'follow-the-sun' implemented across different time zones

Programme and project managers can use the different working times to their advantage, by creating a 'follow-the-sun' implementation (as illustrated in Figure 11.4): the procedures and communication rules are defined between people in 'complementary' time zones (when there is low overlapping of working hours), reducing the duration of sequential tasks by a half or a third of the time. On the other hand, important delays can happen when the exchange of information via emails takes days or weeks to be completed, instead of a single day on a face-to-face meeting. To avoid this pitfall, the team members may need to work out of their office hours and use a smart combination of synchronous and asynchronous tools (as discussed in Chapter 12).

To Be or Not to Be ... Global?

In some situations, the geographical situation of the main customers, suppliers and partners will define that a project must be global. One example is the development of a new product by a partnership of three companies, each with a specialised laboratory in a different country. In other cases, the project scope and main deliverables may determine the need for a global project team. This can be illustrated by the deployment of a new warehouse management system that requires the transformation of buildings located around the globe. Global projects can also allow companies to unite highly specialised team members in the same project without relocating them to other countries, or to delocalise certain project work packages or tasks in order to reduce the project costs. However, there is also a cost for companies to overcome the 'large distances between team members, lengthy travel times to meetings and the inconvenience of working across time zones' (Wild et al., 2000).

Before deciding to conduct global projects, each organisation must weigh up the higher level of innovation and the cost savings offered by having human resources distributed around the globe against the challenges created by the communication across borders, and the cost of implementing processes to ensure the deliverables will be produced as expected. Every situation will bring different results to the above equation and companies can define some principles of operation to guide project managers when defining the scope, developing human resource planning and assembling the project team. One example is the creation of centres of excellence, with service level agreements specifying lead times to start activities, expected duration for common activities and the expected levels of quality. The organisation can then declare as mandatory the use of the services from these competency centres instead of developing local skills, recruiting local people or hiring third parties for specific project tasks.

When deciding to deploy a global team for important projects, organisations can evaluate the value of the main positive and negative aspects of having a global project, and then perform a cost-benefit analysis. Another alternative is to perform an evaluation of the strengths, weaknesses, opportunities and threats offered by the globally distributed team (SWOT analysis). A brainstorming session can identify the main factors applicable to each project, and the lists below can serve as a checklist to validate and complement the findings. First, here are advantages of global projects:

- access to technical experts;
- attracting the best workers, independent of location;
- environmental benefits;
- global workdays (24 hours instead of 8 hours);
- improved disaster recovery possibilities;
- increased flexibility;
- better motivation (by reducing group thinking);
- increased productivity;
- larger pool of potential job candidates;
- more accurate picture of international customers' needs;
- no need to relocate existing workers;
- proximity to customers;
- reduced labour costs;
- reduced office space requirements;
- reduced travel time and expense.

Now here are possible challenges:

- adapting the organisational culture to home working;
- adapting the organisational structure to virtual teams;
- adapting working hours to different time zones;
- building trust;
- coping with language difficulties;
- compatibility of software tools across locations and organisations;
- establishing a team identity;
- handling divergent cultural values;
- managing conflicts over distances;
- providing communication and cultural training;
- providing communication technology.

Examples of Global Projects

SOFTWARE DEVELOPMENT PROJECT

Please refer to Figure 11.5. In this example the project team members are working in four companies in different locations:

1. the software company is in London, England;
2. one development team is in Curitiba, Brazil;
3. one development teams is in Bangalore, India;
4. another development team is in Mumbai, India.

The team members speak four different native languages (English, Brazilian Portuguese, Kannada and Tamil), all with different levels of fluency in English. There are three different country cultures, and the total difference in time zones is 8h 30min. in summer (GMT-3 for Brazil and GMT+5:30 for India). In addition to the team members, there are

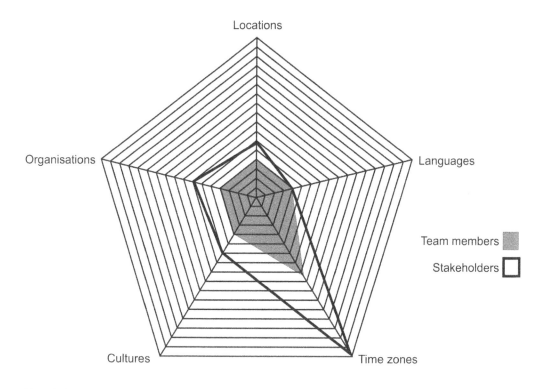

	Locations	Languages	Time zones	Cultures	Organisations
Team members	4	4	08.30	3	4
Stakeholders	7	4	17	6	7

Figure 11.5 A software development global project

stakeholders from another three locations (three pilot customers in the USA, England and Australia), elevating the number of country differences to six, and the time zone difference to 17 hours (GMT-8 for San Francisco, USA to GMT+10 for Sydney, Australia).

PHARMACEUTICAL PROJECT

In the example of Figure 11.6 the project team members for a pharmaceutical project come from a partnership of eight organisations. They are working in six locations (two laboratories in England, the main research team in France, two quality assurance teams in Germany and one specialised research team in South Africa) composed of people speaking three different native languages (English, French and German). There are four different country cultures, and the total difference in time zones is one hour in summer (GMT+1 for England and GMT+2 for the other countries). In addition to the team members, there are stakeholders from another two organisations in different locations (the European Commission in Belgium and one environmental agency in Switzerland). That raises the number of country differences to six, without changes in the number of

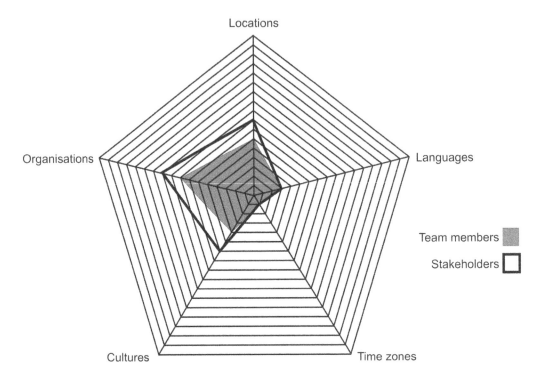

	Locations	Languages	Time zones	Cultures	Organisations
Team members	6	3	1	4	8
Stakeholders	8	3	1	6	10

Figure 11.6 A pharmaceutical global project

time zones or languages (assuming these two locations are in the French part of Belgium and Switzerland).

ORGANISATIONAL CHANGE PROJECT

An organisational change project is depicted in Figure 11.7. The project team members from two organisations (the main corporation and one consulting company) work in 14 company offices in 10 countries, speaking 8 different native languages. The total difference in time zones is 14 hours in summer (from New York, USA, to Melbourne, Australia). In this case, all the stakeholders are in the same locations as the project team members.

How to Manage Global Projects

The project management profession already has a solid foundation for processes, tools and methods. The bodies of knowledge have reached a very good level of maturity, and

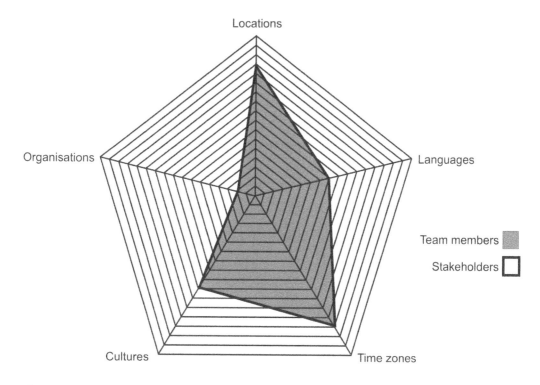

	Locations	Languages	Time zones	Cultures	Organisations
Team members	14	8	14	10	2
Stakeholders	14	8	14	10	2

Figure 11.7 An organisational change global project

most companies have adopted to some extent the principles from PMBOK®, PRINCE2 or the IPMA competence baseline. Turner (2007) consolidates these and other principles in the same reference book. Can these principles be applied to a global project? The answer is yes. All the basic project management skills taught by IPMA, PMBOK®, PRINCE2 and the *Gower Handbook of Project Management* are applied to global projects. And they are essential, as the global team will not have the opportunity to meet on a regular basis over a lunch to discuss their satisfaction level and they will not discover which tasks on the critical path are late during an informal chat at the coffee machine. Excellent project management skills are mandatory for the success of any global project, but a new set of principles is also required for successful ventures.

Many studies and textbooks cover specific practices that can increase the collaboration over a distance, helping the management of virtual and multicultural teams. Most of these practices are consolidated by the Global Project Management Framework® illustrated in Figure 11.8 (taken from Binder, 2007). This framework can be used to understand which principles apply to a particular global project when preparing the project plan and performing risk assessment. During project execution the framework is also valuable as a reference, to help the project team to communicate and collaborate effectively.

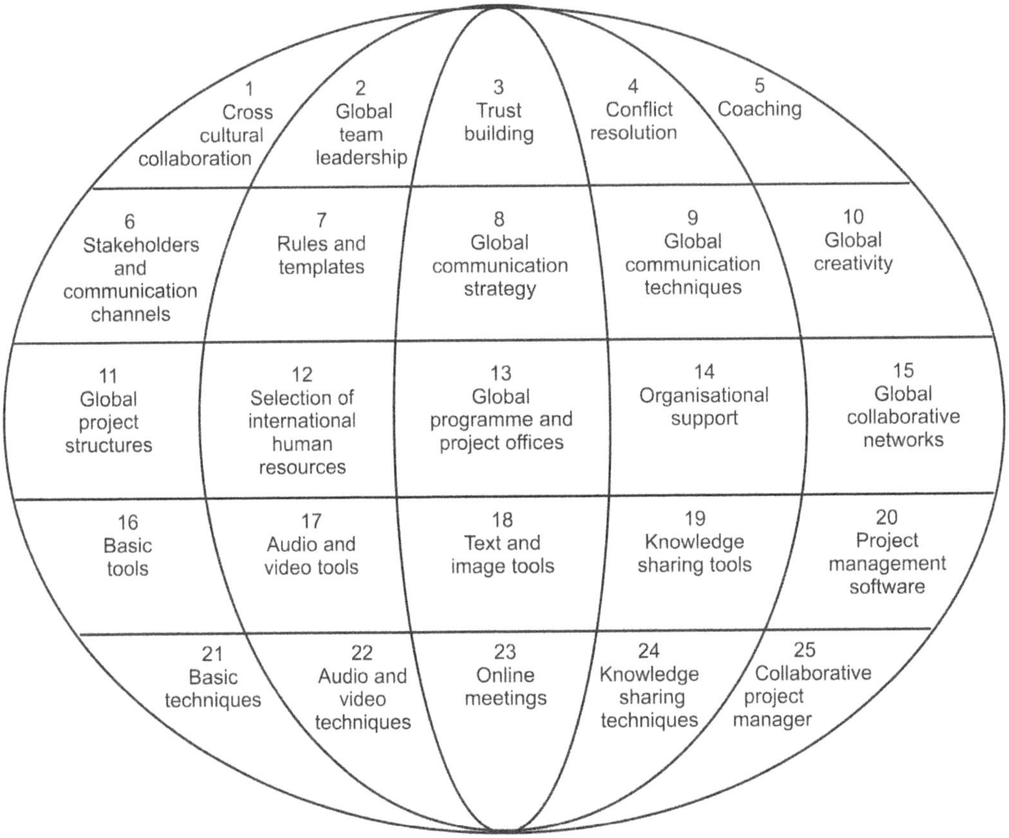

Figure 11.8 The Global Project Management Framework®

Source: From Binder (2007).

To be successful, global project management implies changes on the organisations (that need to understand the different characteristics and requirements of global projects), on the project managers' attitudes, on PMO practices and services, and on the way team members collaborate and communicate over a distance. To facilitate this process, the principles in the framework are grouped into five main categories, each representing an element from the organisation change theories: global team management, global communication, global organisations, collaborative tools and collaborative techniques. Some examples of these principles will now be provided for each category.

GLOBAL TEAM MANAGEMENT

Global project managers must have good strategies to coordinate multicultural and virtual teams, by taking into consideration the differences in culture, language skills and time zones. A good starting point is to have a solid understanding on the cultural dimensions (see Chapter 24) and different leadership theories. Using this knowledge, a trusted relationship can be developed with different stakeholders, and coaching can be a valuable tool.

Conflicting situations are inevitable. In many situations, they can bring innovation. A good project manager must be ready to resolve them and build from the differences.

Cross-cultural Collaboration

Cultural differences allow the understanding of diverse standpoints, being at the same time potential sources of innovation and reasons for conflict. Global project managers must recognise the invisible elements of the national cultures present in the project team, accepting the different mindsets and respecting them, and assigning people to the roles and activities that fit their communication style. The different cultural dimensions (explained in Chapter 24) can also be a rich source for risk identification and mitigation, when evaluated in early project stages.

Global Project Leadership

Global leaders must adapt their leadership, communication and management styles to the different cultures with which they work. They must develop an understanding of how to obtain commitment and improve the motivation level of the project team members, when having most of the meetings over a distance and outside office hours. Global leadership is built mainly on the observation of behaviours and the reactions of the team members to different situations, and on the translation of these behaviours and reactions into motivational factors.

Building Trust

Some communication channels (between team members) are more likely to require a high level of trust, when they cross country borders or involve people who have never worked together before. Project managers must identify the weak communication channels. They must actively monitor the communications and develop relationships in order to build trust. The project planning phase is often a very good opportunity to bring the team together (or around a virtual table, over web- or video-conferencing) and build trusted relationships. Those trusted relationships must last at least until the project completion and form solid links for future ventures.

Conflict Resolution

Project managers must pay special attention to the potential sources of conflict that are specific to global projects, acting as a mediator to assess the situation and resolve the conflict in the best interest of the project objectives.

Coaching

Coaching can be a powerful tool. Project managers can use it as a process, be trusted by team members, and through that can learn about their cultures. A good coaching process has a clear definition of goals, periodic reviews of the achievements, and structured agreement on the next steps.

GLOBAL COMMUNICATION

Project managers spend most of their time communicating. Collecting information from team members, compiling project status and reports, moderating planning and checkpoint meetings, distributing essential information to key stakeholders, are all part of the daily tasks in any project. Global projects bring the added challenges of distance and skewed time zones, requiring different techniques in order to excel in the same daily tasks. Add to these the multilingual and cross-cultural barriers to understanding, and the communication activities are far from simple. Global project managers must involve their team members to identify the stakeholders and the main communication channels. With this in mind, a good communication strategy must be defined, together with techniques, rules and templates to communicate and brainstorm effectively over long distances.

Stakeholders and Communication Channels

Identification, analysis and management of global stakeholders must involve the team members, who are best placed to understand and influence the interested parties on their geographical area. The project managers must lead this task, and provide coaching and support for this process to be effective. In addition, the main communication channels that span geographical and cultural borders must be identified and receive special attention.

Rules and Templates

Global project teams must agree on which communication medium suits each meeting type. They may also define templates to be deployed throughout the project, keeping in mind that the documents will be prepared and reviewed using synchronous and asynchronous electronic media.

Global Communication Strategy

The key team members should identify the types of project information, and assess the stakeholders' requirements. A good communication strategy for a global project specifies the relationship between each key stakeholder and the main information types, defining the best media and manner for the communication to take place.

Global Communication Techniques

Global project managers and project office members must master the techniques for collecting information from geographically distributed team members, exchanging project information with the main team members, and distributing project reports to key stakeholders.

Global Creativity

The uniqueness of project deliverables requires the global team members to unite their creative minds. Brainstorming sessions are widely used around whiteboards and flip charts. Global project managers must use a different set of tools and techniques to foster creative ideas and capture fuzzy knowledge in online meetings. One example is the use of mind mapping software, combined with desktop sharing tools.

GLOBAL ORGANISATIONS

When organisations start projects that span country borders, they must think about the impact on their organisational cultures and structures. The programme and project structures must be carefully designed in order to respect the geographical dispersion of the human resources, while allowing optimal communication between the team members. PMOs have a key role in interviewing the international experts and providing coaching and organisational support to the global programme managers and project managers.

Global Project Structures

International projects can obviously be structured in different ways. In centralised structures project managers communicate directly to all key team members. In distributed structures, a project coordinator is nominated to monitor the planning and execution of a group of team members in each geographical location, organisation or knowledge area.

Selection of International Human Resources

Project managers and team members must have a specific set of skills to work effectively in global projects. Global thinking, culture awareness, self-motivation and openness are examples of skills that can be required from candidates during the selection process or provided to them by training activities. Special skills must also be used to conduct interviews over distances, requiring good preparation of questions. That (along with the appropriate choice of communication technology) is the key factor for a successful selection process.

The PMO has to be Global Too

Global programme or PMOs can provide various services to improve the success rate of global projects. Knowledge management services allow standard practices during the collection and distribution of project information. Portfolio management services make sure that consistent rules are deployed across departmental and geographical borders for project selection, prioritisation and allocation of resources. Health checks, coaching and training services can help programme and project managers across the globe to use the same processes, methods and templates, and to master the communication and leadership techniques essential to international initiatives.

Organisational Support

Global organisations, alliances and partnerships must adapt their processes and policies to provide support to global project team members. Senior executives and HR departments must understand the differences across corporate and country borders, to determine which elements can influence the motivation of the international working force. Emotional Intelligence, work-life balance and international performance-appraisal systems are some examples of motivational factors that need careful evaluation.

GLOBAL COLLABORATIVE NETWORKS

Organisations are evolving from multinational enterprises to international networks, which aggregate the main suppliers, producers and customers with their subcontractors and service providers. These alliances and partnerships are often sealed around a group of programmes and projects. Senior executives must understand the different challenges faced by the global teams, in order to define collaboration strategies during early stages. Examples of these challenges are the different corporate cultures and maturity levels in project management, processes and procedures.

Collaborative Tools and Techniques

The two last categories of the Global Project Management Framework® deal with different technology areas that organisations can implement to foster collaboration on global projects.

The first steps are to evaluate the collaboration requirements, investigate different solutions to satisfy these needs, select, implement and provide basic training on collaborative tools (also described in Chapter 12). Usually this is not enough to obtain adoption of the new tools by global project managers and team members. Organisations must define collaborative techniques to make the tools known and loved by employees across the globe. When 'loved' is too strong a word, at least the project teams must see the benefits of the technologies on their daily tasks, such as:

- reduced time required to moderate meetings and prepare reports;
- fewer misunderstandings;

- electronic flows for document review and approval;
- automatic handling of basic project management and communication tasks;
- fewer and shorter business trips.

BASIC TOOLS AND TECHNIQUES

Simple tools are the foundation for collaboration across team members. We can take for granted the availability of telephones, emails and remote access to corporate systems. But are they used efficiently? Are people following simple 'etiquette' when exchanging messages? Other simple solutions might also provide a great help, such as shareable spreadsheets, websites that deal with meeting times in different time zones, and simple tools that help booking meetings between people from different companies.

Audio and Video Tools and Techniques

Audio-conferences and videoconferences are essential for any project team that is spread over different locations. The main barriers are the technical difficulties in starting the calls (particularly when connecting equipment from different companies) and the sound and video quality. To help those who arrange meetings these elements must be considered when evaluating the technical solutions and preparing training and documentation.

Text and Image Tools Used During Online Meetings

Well-established technologies allow team members to share images and improve the effectiveness of their online meetings. The routine is simple: establish (at the same time) an audio-conferencing call and a web-conferencing session, then share spreadsheets, mind mapping software or presentations. While ideas are gathered (or the project status is reviewed) the discussions are captured as they happen in a computer screen. The meeting participants can see what is being captured and react (when they disagree) or add more information. That reduces the probability of misunderstanding, and eliminates the need for late nights spent writing up minutes of the meeting. Further, there are no long delays waiting to have the draft minutes to be approved by the meeting participants.

Knowledge-Sharing Tools and Techniques

A variety of tools allow knowledge sharing, many of them coming from the open-source community. The most common for business environments are:

- Content Management Systems (CMS) that allow the publication of project news, the collaboration around documents, and the sharing of online tables to capture the risks, opportunities, issues, changes and stakeholders;
- project wikis allow the collaborative writing of project documentation and online tutorials;
- status reports can be published and reviewed by different members using blogs.

Creative project teams use these and other technologies in a variety of ways to improve the quality of asynchronous communication (mainly across different time zones) and remote collaboration.

Collaborative Project Management Software

There are technology platforms that allow project team members to create and maintain the project management plan, to monitor the execution of the deliverables, to share the project logs and to obtain approval from key stakeholders on documentation, business cases and closing reports. In global projects, the implementation of these platforms is essential for all processes that require effective collaboration across borders, such as:

* defining activities;
* identifying and analysing risks;
* monitoring progress;
* directing and controlling project work.

Summary

Global projects can bring many advantages to companies, project managers and the team members. They also raise challenges and require a different set of skills, principles and tools. Global project managers must master these collaborative tools and techniques, and take advantage of different cultures, languages, geographies, organisations and time zones.

References and Further Reading

Binder, J. (2007), *Global Project Management: Communication, Collaboration and Management Across Borders*, Aldershot: Gower.

Kähkönen, K. (2010), 'The world of global projects', in *Project Perspectives*, Nijkerk: IPMA.

Turner, R. (2007), *Gower Handbook of Project Management*, 4th edn, Aldershot: Gower.

Wild, J.J., Wild, K.L. and Han, J.C.Y. (2000), *International Business: An Integrated Approach*, Harlow: Prentice Hall.

12 *Managing People in Virtual Project Organisations*

PENNY PULLAN

This chapter focuses on those projects where the project team members and stakeholders are geographically dispersed. Project teams vary from people on separate sites of the same organisation around one country to people from many different organisations spread around the world (see Chapter 11). Whichever of these applies, the project team members do not have the same chances for interacting informally as those working in the same place. Project meetings and communication will be devoid of body language and will need to use technology instead to allow interaction between team members.

Virtual projects (Figure 12.1) have increased in number dramatically over the last decade owing to many global trends, including the following:

- the development of new technologies like VOIP (voice over Internet protocol; such as Skype), shared screens and very high quality video conferencing;

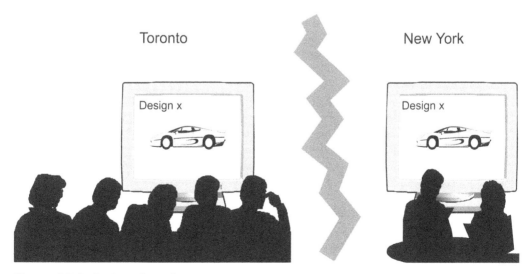

Figure 12.1 A virtual project team

- many more regional and global projects, fuelled by outsourcing and off-shoring;
- home working and telecommuting;
- climate change and more sustainable working practices;
- the global economic slowdown leading to cost-cutting of travel budgets.

Examples of Virtual Project Teams

I have worked in virtual project teams in a variety of formats, three of which I have described below. These examples are fairly typical of the diversity of such teams.

CASE EXAMPLE NO. 1: A ONE COMPANY, ONE COUNTRY VIRTUAL PROJECT TEAM

In this case, all members of the project team were located in the England. Some people were based near Leeds in the north, some in Melton Mowbray in the East Midlands and the remainder were in Slough in the south. All these project team members worked for the same company and there were clearly understood and agreed common ways of working. A strong company culture meant that each person knew what to expect from the others in their team. In addition, all project team members and their stakeholders shared the same time zone.

As the project team members were all based in the same country, they were able to meet face-to-face for a project kick-off meeting and at a few critical stages of their project. But for most of the time they worked as a virtual team. Everyone spoke English. So the only thing separating these team members was distance. I found this a very gentle introduction to virtual projects.

CASE EXAMPLE NO. 2: SEVERAL COMPANIES, GOVERNMENTS AND NON-GOVERNMENTAL ORGANISATIONS

This virtual project comprised representatives from a range of leading companies involved in the production of chocolate. They were based in the US, UK, Belgium, France and Switzerland. Additional team members included United Nations representatives based in Geneva, Switzerland. There were also government ministers from West African nations.

There were clear differences in culture between each of the commercial organisations and, to a greater extent, between those team members working in companies and those working in governments and non-governmental organisations. Time zone differences spanned up to six hours, from Switzerland to New York. The main business language used was English, although some members preferred French. This team met face-to-face twice a year for only a few hours at each time.

This project was more of a challenge and I found that it was critical to make the most of the face-to-face time by discussing the most contentious issues. The group used conference calls as their preferred technology, because mobile phones were much more reliable than the Internet in rural Africa at the time.

CASE EXAMPLE NO. 3: PROJECT TEAM MEMBERS SPREAD OVER FOUR CONTINENTS

This project involved 16 people from different companies and academic institutions. They came from all over the world – Singapore, Australia, New Zealand, the US, the UK and mainland Europe. Time zone differences spanned GMT+13 hours (New Zealand) to GMT–7 hours (the American West).

This team never met face-to-face. The biggest challenges with this project were the wide time zone differences. So same-time conversations happened very late at night for those in Europe and early in the morning for those in Singapore. This project team was made up of volunteers from around the globe and a subgroup emerged of those who were most committed to the goals of the project.

Virtual Project Teams

ADVANTAGES AND DISADVANTAGES

Some advantages and disadvantages of global projects were set out in Chapter 11. Virtual projects share many of the advantages, such as being able to use the best people regardless of their location and the reduction of travel time, expense and pollution. Unfortunately, virtual projects also share many of the challenges of global projects, particularly when it comes to trust-building, team communications and meetings. It can be particularly difficult to create a culture of openness, trust and mutual support in a virtual team. On top of this, there is the challenge of using technology, as access to technology often varies across the project team, especially across different organisations.

WHEN IT ALL GOES WRONG: SOME OF THE PRACTICAL PROBLEMS

Despite the promise of technology and huge reduction of travel costs, virtual projects are not easy to manage. I surveyed project managers across a number of industries and found a range of complaints:

- People are easily distracted in virtual meetings, by other things happening around them or by their emails (or even by Facebook).
- Quite often actions are not followed up after project meetings and they pass uncompleted until the next meeting.
- If project team members have more than one project (they usually do) their local projects tend to take preference over their virtual ones.
- It is much more difficult to get project team members to speak up about difficult or complex issues when they are a long way away, especially in team meetings. It seems to be easier for them to keep quiet. This can happen when the project manager asks a question or asks for a volunteer.
- The project manager can spend much of his/her working day (and often well into the evening in conference calls with team members.

- It can be very difficult to build up trust when people have never met in person, have never looked into each other's eyes, and have not really become personally acquainted.

So virtual projects have to be managed in a special way. For example, you cannot simply schedule an all-day project meeting based on UK time and expect your colleagues in Australia to sit at their end of the communication network when they should naturally be sound asleep in their beds. What follows is a series of pointers to help you run your virtual projects more successfully, both in their initial set up and in sustaining participation throughout their life cycles.

SETTING UP A VIRTUAL PROJECT TEAM FOR SUCCESS

As with face-to-face project teams, the initial project kick-off provides a great opportunity to set the project team up for success. During this kick-off, it is important to set a clear vision for the project and agree the goals that need to be attained. The role of each individual team member in achieving the vision and goals needs to be explained and agreed, so that everyone knows who is expected to do what. In addition, it is really important for the team to agree how they will work together: the processes they will follow and the ground rules that will govern how they interact and behave. These rules include simple but important things (like working hours) and whether or not it is acceptable to ring people before or after work. Many more complex issues will also have to be discussed, such as how decisions will be taken and how problems will be dealt with.

In a virtual team it is too easy for individual team members to lose focus on their virtual project and become involved in other things (like different projects) at their own site. After all, by being remote, a virtual project is literally 'out of sight'. So it can also be 'out of mind'. Because of this, a command and control style of leadership does not work well in a virtual environment. Instead it makes sense for the project manager to adopt a far more facilitative role, sharing leadership around the group and drawing out from people what's needed at the time. The project manager has to make sure that the project is always kept in mind.

I recommend that wherever possible a virtual project team should travel and come together for a face-to-face kick-off. Don't waste this opportunity by getting everyone to sit through presentations, but use it as a chance for people to get to know each other and to build up trust. That will pay rewards later in the project, when tough times come and challenges emerge. If some people are remote from the rest of the group and unable to travel, then treat your kick-off meeting as if it were a virtual meeting, making sure that everyone is able to take part. Without this consideration, the remote participants are likely to feel like second-class project team members.

SUSTAINING PARTICIPATION AS THE PROJECT CONTINUES

After the kick-off meeting, when team members have dispersed back to their home locations it is imperative for project success that the team members stay engaged with each other and continue to participate in the project wholeheartedly. This is particularly important in virtual projects because project team members who are 'out of sight' can also easily become 'out of mind'.

To sustain participation, plan your virtual meetings carefully. Create a level playing field for all team members so that everyone can participate easily. If you have a wide range of time zones, see that meetings times are varied, so that people take it in turns to share the pain of working during unsocial hours. For example, if you have team members who are on the other side of the world from everyone else, run some of the meetings at a time that suits them, even if that means the rest of the team are asked to stay up late or rise early. Be considerate about the technology people are asked to use. It's much easier to take a telephone conference call at 6am dressed in pyjamas than travelling to the office videoconferencing suite for a 6am meeting!

Think about how individual connections such as telephone calls between team members can keep the work progressing. This does not mean that each team member has daily interaction with every other team member. Then you would have a 'spaghetti' team with connections from everyone to everyone else, with people doing little else except actually connecting (Hall, 2007). I suggest that you consider appropriate one-to-one connections and encourage these within the team in addition to meetings.

So far, I have talked about virtual meetings and individual telephone calls. But not all interaction in virtual project teams needs to be synchronised. There are many technologies that support asynchronous interaction. See Figure 12.2 to see what you can use to support these different time/different place conversations. Social media, for example, have been used to build relationships across virtual project teams as well as to share information outside project meetings (Harrin, 2010). Figure 12.2 shows that there are many technologies available to support virtual project work and the list is growing all the time.

Same time, same place	Different time, same place
Traditional meetings	Project war rooms Shared displays
Same time, different place	**Different time, different place**
Conference calls Video conferences On line meetings Instant messenger Text messages Second life	E-mail Recordings Discussion forum Social media Blogs, Wikis, Video

Figure 12.2 The time and place grid: Populated with some of the technologies that support each quadrant

Many project managers and business leaders think that technology alone will make their virtual meetings work. However, what is more important than the technology itself is choosing and using the appropriate technology to support the work people are trying to do. Remember the choice between travelling in to use your company's top-of-the-range video suite for a 6am meeting or taking a conference call on your home telephone. Which choice would you prefer?

Virtual Project Meetings

Although social media, discussion forums and email can support some of the team's load, the most important interactions of virtual project teams are their virtual meetings. Unfortunately, these are often far from perfect, with most participants 'multitasking' on email, doing other work or even surfing the web at the same time. With these challenges pressing on each virtual meeting participant, it is crucial for the person leading virtual meetings to make them as engaging and productive as possible. This takes three stages:

1. careful preparation;
2. keeping people engaged during the meeting;
3. ensuring that agreed actions happen afterwards.

PREPARATION

Many project managers feel that a virtual meeting needs less preparation than a face-to-face meeting. After all, there is no need to set up a room with chairs, projector, flip charts and refreshments. But in reality, virtual meetings need more preparation than face-to-face meetings if you wish to command your team's full attention. Plan for the technology and test that it works beforehand. Plan also for participation and engagement. How can you do this without forgetting anything vital? I use a checklist to help make the following clear before and at the start of the meeting:

- What is the purpose of the meeting?
- What objectives need to be achieved by the end of the meeting?
- What will happen when? Have a clear, timed agenda, preferably keeping the meeting to no longer than an hour;
- Who shall do what during the meeting? Have clear roles, including facilitator, timekeeper and scribe (to take down action points, record decisions made and share these with everyone in the virtual meeting);
- What ways of working (sometimes known as ground rules) are we to follow? Examples are 'State your name before contributing' and 'Mute when not speaking if you are in a noisy environment';
- How will actions be recorded, communicated and followed up?

DURING THE MEETING

The biggest challenge during a virtual meeting will be to keep people engaged. In contrast to a face-to-face meeting, the most effective virtual meeting leader is not only a chairman, but a facilitator as well. Give up on trying to maintain control, as that is merely an illusion in a virtual meeting. After all, you cannot see who is working on their email. Instead, focus on facilitating collaboration, to engage people and work together to meet the agreed objectives. As leader, you need to draw out what's needed from the group.

One effective way of keeping people engaged is to poll the group from time to time. Let people know in advance that you will be asking them throughout the meeting for their input and views. This makes it far more likely that they will stay focused. It also means that the absence of any person who does drift away will become obvious, because they will probably ask for the question to be repeated when they hear their name.

Other ways to draw people in include using visual images in addition to audio channels. If you can, share screens, use graphics, mind-maps or visual ways of laying out information. Use stories too, as these are much more likely to be retained after the meeting than lists of facts, and also help to build more effective relationships between virtual teams (Thorpe, 2008).

A particularly effective way of using visuals to engage people is to prepare a team map, with a photograph of each team member's face placed on a map of the world showing their location. This goes some way towards fixing the problem of 'disembodied voices' by providing the context for each person and their face. That is a very powerful way of reminding people who else is present and the difference in time zones across the group.

A final suggestion for engagement during virtual meetings is to keep people occupied, not with email or other distractions, but occupied in the business of the meeting. This could be presenting, facilitating, keeping time, recording actions, noting key decisions – in fact – anything.

AFTER THE MEETING

It seems to be more difficult to get people to take action after remote meetings compared to face-to-face ones. Project team members take action as a result of the commitment that they have to the project and the rest of the project team. It is more difficult to build trust virtually. Lack of action can destroy what little trust has been built up and lead to a vicious cycle.

To help guarantee that actions are taken as intended, agree up front how actions will be documented and followed up. Run through the actions at the end of your meeting and check that everyone is clear on what they need to do and when.

It is worth checking people's intentions. How sure are you that they will carry out each action? Can you assess, on a scale of one to ten, how committed each person is? If the score is lower than ten, it might make sense to change the action slightly to make it more probable that it will be carried out. After all, an imperfect action is better than no action at all.

Make sure that action requirements are circulated immediately and that people know how their actions will be followed up. Make sure too that people know whom to contact in case they have any difficulties. It is better to know beforehand if a deadline is at risk of not being met.

Summary

Virtual projects are now a fundamental way of getting things done for many project managers. But many virtual project teams are badly set up and their virtual meetings are dismal affairs. With a little thought and preparation, project managers can set up their teams and run their virtual meetings in a way that is effective, efficient and even enjoyable.

References and Further Reading

Hall, K. (2007), *Speed Lead*, London: Nicholas Brealey Publishing.

Harrin, E. (2010), *Social Media for Project Managers*, Newtown Square, PA: Project Management Institute.

Lipnack, J. and Stamps, J. (2010), *Leading Virtual Teams*, Boston, MA: Harvard Business School Publishing.

Thorpe, S. (2008), *Enhancing the Effectiveness of Online Groups: An Investigation of Storytelling in the Facilitation of Online Groups*, Auckland: Auckland University of Technology (PhD Thesis).

13 *The Creative Organisation*

GEOF COX

A creative organisation provides a challenge (but also a real opportunity) for project management. Challenge comes because the desire for freedom to operate and pursue new ideas works against the structure and control that is inherent in project management. Opportunity to make a real contribution to creative organisations is created by providing just enough of that structure and control, so that creative ideas into practical innovations are managed but not stifled.

Innovation

All organisations will accept that they need be creative, just to survive in today's ever-changing environment – an environment that is changing faster and more radically by the year. Paradigm shifts occur with frightening regularity for anyone working in the areas of organisation strategy. But just being creative is not enough. Creativity on its own does not translate directly into survival or success. Creativity is the process that comes up with new ideas. However, a new idea is not necessarily practical, useful or profitable. In fact it is often the impractical, frivolous and outrageous ideas that generate more creative thought (as in brainstorming or lateral thinking activities). An organisation that does not have some form of critical analysis process to screen and translate the ideas into practical benefit for themselves and their customers will soon flounder. The real need for organisations is innovation – the process of applying creative ideas in a practical way to improve the organisation.

Innovation is an adaptive process, where the organisation takes on board new ideas and translates them into practical results that benefit the organisation. That means it is possible for an organisation to be innovative without being creative in its own right. It can buy in new ideas from outside (from inventors, researchers, other creative organisations, universities and consultants).

Benchmarking is a systematic way of finding and bringing in new ideas to an organisation. In that process, companies compare their operations, products and services against others in their industry in order to learn how to do things better (Codling, 1998). Some companies make benchmarking a virtue – like Procter & Gamble (P&G) – who set their sights on replacing their decades old 'not invented here' philosophy with enthusiasm for 'proudly found elsewhere'. This raised the success rate of innovation at P&G at the same time as reducing their R&D costs. With the speed of change mentioned earlier, environmental scanning and benchmarking is an essential business practice.

Benchmarking does not have to be restricted to the same industry – one major FMCG (fast moving consumer goods) organisation famously innovated its logistics by benchmarking against Federal Express (FedEx). They found that unlike FedEx, who could track the location of any package anywhere in the world in real time, they did not even know where any of their trucks were. This soon brought about rapid changes to their distribution operations that improved efficiency, cost control and customer service. Equally, any retailer who is still not addressing the opportunities for online and mobile-facilitated sales is likely to lose market share and profitability, even if there is no evidence of this in their particular sector. Looking at developments in online retailing, it is difficult to identify any product or service which cannot be sold or marketed successfully online. Organisations need to be creative and innovative in order to survive.

But even if the initial ideas come from outside, it is still essential that the organisation has a clearly defined strategy for identifying new ideas and translating them into practical innovations. This is where the organisation culture – 'the way we do things around here' – plays a vital role. Some organisations have a culture that fosters creativity and innovation, positively demanding that their staff take risks and question everything that they do.

Other organisations seem to be determined to reduce risk to zero, thus ensuring that there is no creativity. In these organisations any new idea that does emerge is quickly put down by an attitude of 'not invented here', 'it won't work in this environment', 'we've tried this before, and it didn't work', 'yes ... but' or some other killer phrase.

At the extremes, the organisation is not likely to survive in the long term. Either the organisation could stake its whole future on flights of fancy which could prove disastrous, or it makes no change and is rewarded by extinction (like the dinosaurs they have become). What is needed is some degree of balance between these two extremes.

Ready-Aim-Fire

Ready-aim-fire is a well-balanced problem-solving and decision-making process that relies on:

- following a process of gathering information and ideas (ready);
- analysing the data in order to make the best decision about the solution or strategy (aim);
- implementing that solution (fire).

Figure 13.1 shows this process graphically. Most organisations have an imbalance in this process owing to a combination of their own organisation culture and the aggregate of the personal preferences of their staff (which may in itself be due to the organisation culture, with recruitment favouring people who can 'fit in'). In order to establish a creative or innovative organisation, we have first to understand what the predominant climate and processes are in our existing organisation.

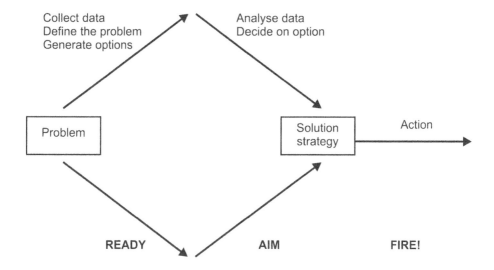

Figure 13.1 Ready-aim-fire

Ready-aim-fire started as a military analogy. You first need to know the target and have the appropriate information and resources. Then you need to take aim before going into action. Getting one of these steps wrong, or miss it out completely often has catastrophic consequences. I am not suggesting that organisations should be run on military lines, or that the military are the best role models, but there are a number of parallels and lessons that can be applied. We can use the ready-aim-fire approach to understand our own natural tendencies and then correct these to something that has creativity and innovation built in.

First we need ideas, which is the 'ready' stage. Identify what needs to be done and gather all the information and ideas available. If your organisation does not have creative people already, then look outside to benchmarking or bring in that expertise through collaboration with other creative sources. Then 'aim' – choose the best solution or strategy. Filter and analyse the ideas to come up with something that is practical and meets the organisation's objectives. This is a process of screening and building ideas into something that is workable – not a process of killing them. Now you can go into action – 'fire!'

Most organisations are imbalanced. We recruit in our own image, or the image of one or two of the organisation's more prominent opinion leaders or successes. That is to say, the organisation will tend to keep on recreating the style that made it successful. Unfortunately, as we have seen with the demise of many excellent organisations, past success is no guarantee of future success.

Fire-Fire-Fire

Organisations that are highly structured, process driven and averse to risk will focus on (and over-recruit into) the 'fire stage'. That will ensure that new ideas or ways of doing things will not be implemented because people will be too busy 'doing' to *think* about what they are doing. Even if they decide that they need to employ creative people, the incumbent management will find it difficult to identify the skills and competencies necessary for the role; and if they were by some chance lucky in recruiting someone, the existing climate of the organisation would drive out the creative person as a 'misfit' before too long.

Senior leaders do often identify this problem. They implore their employees to try something new and be unafraid of making mistakes. Allowing people to make mistakes without fear of retribution is seen to be the way to question the status quo and shake organisations into the new economic reality. Unfortunately, there is a climate of fear in many organisations that does not allow people to make mistakes (and then learn from them).

Equally damaging, is when there is no process in place to evaluate the potential of new ideas. So expensive mistakes are made and the 'new strategy' is quickly discredited. The organisation then reverts back to its norm of low risk, low innovation and resistance to change.

Being a fire-fire-fire organisation is not necessarily a bad thing. First of all it is often what is required to be done most of the time – to follow tried and tested plans and schedules and get the job done; keep the work flowing and garner the benefits of the business process design. If you are running an oil refinery, a construction site or a major factory, the last thing you want is people implementing new ideas every day. That is too risky, not just to the process itself, but also to the life and limb of its employees and the surrounding community. But such an organisation needs to be aware of the risks it takes by not having a built-in innovation culture and a process in place to overcome its imbalance.

Recognition of the implications of the imbalance can be addressed by applying project management thinking. For instance, a production team might spend 80 per cent or more of its time following the process and running the production line, dealing with business as usual. But part of their time should also be devoted to improvement (how can we do what we do better?). If this is identified as a project, it gives validity to the activity and also provides a structure that ensures the use of an approach that will overcome their cultural barriers.

A continuous improvement process ensues which identifies potential improvements, evaluates the potential of those improvements, and then puts them into practice, following the correct ready-aim-fire sequence. Because there is likely to be a low level of innate ability at the 'ready' stage (being creative) the project process will demand that some technique is adopted to force creativity into the imbalanced team. Benchmarking, brainstorming, lateral thinking and value engineering are some of those techniques.

The past master of using this approach is Toyota. Their Kaizen approach (improve business operations continuously, always driving for innovation and evolution) is adopted, copied and envied throughout the world of manufacturing. It enabled them to reduce greatly lead times and cost, whilst at the same time improving quality. This helped Toyota to become one of the ten largest companies in the world; as profitable as all the other car companies combined; and the largest car manufacturer in 2007.

Toyota harvests its own latent creativity in a systematic way, which is the benchmark for all other suggestion schemes worldwide. The Toyota Creative Idea Suggestion Scheme was 60 years old in 2011, and even with that longevity it still collects about two million ideas per year from its workforce. That is a staggering figure when compared with suggestion schemes in most other companies. Even more staggering is the participation and take-up rate: over 95 per cent of the workforce contribute suggestions. That works out to over 30 suggestions per worker per year. Further, over 90 per cent of those suggestions are implemented.

Innovation in process- and manufacturing-based industries typically follows the Toyota lead, from Total Quality Management in the 1980s (TQM), through Business Process Reengineering in the 1990s to Lean Manufacturing today. Each of these approaches uses a structured, ready-aim-fire project approach to ensure that the fire-fire-fire culture of its target adapts to benefit from innovative solutions and improvements.

Ready-Ready-Ready

At the other end of the spectrum, there is the highly creative organisation, typified by the creative agency famous for its radical ideas, or the fast-growing and quick-reacting new organisations typified by the 'dotcoms' and the Silicon Valley giants such as Google and Apple.

Creative organisations abhor bureaucracy and order. They seem to thrive on the unconventional, and in throwing away the 'normal' trappings of organisation. Offices (if they have them) are cluttered and untidy, often full of toys and distractions that help to provide a creative boost. Employees dress unconventionally, talk a different language and they are forever wanting to make changes and try out new ideas. Their approach helps them to be creative, and is tolerated by 'straighter' business people as a necessary evil (often with no understanding of how or why it works). When there is a creative department in an otherwise more traditional business (such as a research department), it will often be housed in a separate building, well away from the main organisation, seemingly so that the subversive working patterns in the department do not contaminate the rest of the organisation!

One clear implication of the imbalance of the ready-ready-ready organisation is the lack of evaluation or follow-through. They are not designed for (and their employees do not necessarily value) critical assessment or the implementation of the ideas. For a creative person, the idea itself is often the crux of the process. To develop the idea into a workable product or service requires time and effort that is not related to creating new ideas, and is therefore deemed uninteresting and not motivating. So, some great ideas are not developed and some crazy ideas are implemented that often cause the demise of the organisation concerned.

Google are an organisation that has seen phenomenal growth, not only in the use of their search engine, but also in their range of products and services on offer. Their approach is set as the norm for creative organisations. Engineers are encouraged to dream up their own projects. Project teams self-form around the best ideas. Market-based principles ensure that the best ideas receive funding. The system ensures innovation.

However, despite all of the new products and business services on offer, more than 95 per cent of Google's revenues trace back to web-based search advertising. Some of their engine room of innovative employees were even leaving to form new ventures, like Twitter. So in 2009, they applied some greater discipline to their process of evaluating and resourcing innovation, by boosting their aim and fire processes. Now, departmental heads conduct 'innovation reviews' where promising ideas are shared with Google's top leadership, helping executives focus attention and resources on promising ideas early. They are tightening up their project management to ensure that their innovation is focused and provides the highest returns. Rather than stifling creativity, project management serves to enhance it.

Ready-Fire-Aim

If ready-aim-fire is a balanced culture for organisations to aspire to, some organisations follow a different pattern in order to innovate: ready-fire-aim. Come up with an idea (ready) – try it out immediately in a low-risk or pilot project (fire) – and learn from this experiment (aim). Then learn from this experience to redesign and refine the idea, going through the ready-aim-fire process in a number of iterations until something useful is created, or the idea dies. Once again, project management plays a crucial role in managing the creative process to create successful innovation.

The innovative organisation positively demands that its employees are encouraged to experiment and make mistakes. The ready-fire-aim process is all about trying out new ideas in a small way, in a controlled situation, and learning quickly from the experience to make an adjustment and go round the cycle again. In this way losses are minimised by keeping pilot operations at a small level, and the organisation creates a culture where it is all right to test out your own ideas and make mistakes.

As we saw earlier, many Japanese companies are past masters of innovation. They collect customer information at an alarming level, and innovate at a startling rate, working to enhance current products and develop new lines through routines based on small pilot projects and customer-driven requests. But for a model of an innovation culture of ready-fire-aim in a Western company, the 3M Company stands out. The company that introduced us to the Post-It™ note. They allow their researchers and scientists to divert money from approved budgets to work on new ideas that have not been sanctioned or approved by management. That gives the researchers the freedom to pursue their own whims and fantasies and, if they come to naught, drop them before anyone is aware. From these whims and fantasies comes an occasional world-beating, innovative product, like the Post-It™ note, or the latest application for epoxy resin technology that is starting to replace carbon fibre in lightweight, durable sports equipment.

The 3M Post-It™ note took 12 years to move concept to practical innovation, and for most of that time the project had no official status or funding. It was, in the 3M terminology, a 'skunk work' – a project funded from other agreed projects, sustained through the belief of a champion. In this particular case that 'champion' was Art Fry, a researcher who had made an initial 'mistake' in the formulation of the Post-It™ glue when researching super-glue.

'Skunk working' has caught on as a concept in numerous organisations to foster creativity. Many have developed their own, unique approaches. Atlassian, a very successful Australia-based software company calls their programme FedEx Days; a 24-hour innovation immersion event that enables employees to brainstorm, prototype, and pitch their emerging innovations. (The name FedEx Day comes from the idea of delivering something overnight). Starting at 2.00 pm on a Thursday, all 4,000 employees do anything that they like, presenting their ideas in a beer and pizza event on the Friday afternoon (well, it is in Australia!). These events have developed so many software fixes, ideas for new products and innovations that they are now conducted quarterly and in every location of Atlassian worldwide. This 24-hour use of ready-fire-aim has spread to organisations like Yahoo, Symantec, Flickr, Hasbro Toy, and the Mayo Clinic. And, at the time of writing (2012), Atlassian is offering to send their own 'FedExperts' to a deserving company in order to help them conduct their own FedEx Day as part of a competition run by a leading innovation blog site.

Google have their own programme of innovation built on the skunk works model, called Innovation Time Off. Google engineers are encouraged to spend 20 per cent of their work time on projects that interest them. They do not need to get authorisation for these projects – they simply book the time to the programme. Some of Google's newer services, such as Gmail, Google News, Orkut, and AdSense originated from these personal projects and about half of all new product launches can be traced back to origins in Innovation Time Off.

Imagination, a British-based creative company, are another leading example of the creative organisation at their best. They are a mix of architects, designers, computer experts, bloggers, model builders, PR people, video producers, artists, photographers and other creative people who come together into a project team whenever and wherever they are needed. Any functional relationships are ignored. Projects they have implemented range from product and sales promotions, through theatrical productions, the design and construction of exhibitions, galleries and offices, to the concept and design for the millennium celebrations in London and New Year's Eve celebrations in Sydney, Australia.

The organisation at Imagination does not really exist, except in its flexibility. They recruit people who are good (whom they define as someone with the personal characteristics to fit into their style of work, rather than having any form of formal qualification or experience). Recruiting often happens when there is no specific job available at the time. People move around freely picking up tasks that interest them and making a difference. Imagination is in fact just a collection of creative projects. Their primary function (as the company name suggests) is to harness the imagination of 'imagineers' (as they call themselves).

By definition a creative organisation is at the leading edge, always seeking new paradigms, so it can easily lose touch with reality. Imagination keeps this tendency in check by being close to its customers – so close that imagineers are to be found in project teams that include customers as full members. They are often based in customers' premises, and their flexibility and informality allows customers to feel able to test ideas without fear of losing face or appearing naïve.

Releasing Creativity

Project-based structures like Imagination are being increasingly used to break up the bureaucratic systems that can so easily develop, even in small organisations. Instead of having a traditional hierarchy and set of reporting relationships, where the tasks are performed by people who are functional specialists, projects are established across functional lines relative to the needs for that project. So a project to design a new product would have members from research, development, production, marketing, sales and finance working together from the outset. When the project is complete, the team dissolves and the people join other projects. These new organisations are often called adaptive, as they are flexible enough to allow the form to follow the task that needs to be done. By operating this way, organisations are finding that they can not only attract and retain creative staff, but also unleash the potential creativity in all of their staff.

The key to making these structures work and making the organisation successful is involvement. That means listening to employees and customers, suppliers and partners in such a way that everyone can contribute and participate in designing systems and processes that work. Companies have been saying, for years that many of the best product ideas and innovations come from customers – not from the wizards in the research department. Yet many years on, 'listening to the customer' for many organisations still means assuming the customers' requirements and telling them what they want. It seems that less hierarchically structured organisations have a better chance of getting close to the customer and capitalising on this competitive and innovative edge.

Technology now allows project structures to operate in a virtual space with team members located in all corners of the globe, connected by a web of communications technologies and central data systems. The opportunity to involve distant contributors in real-time discussion has shortened the lead time for new product development (it has reduced the misunderstandings and delays that occurred through parts of the production cycle being located in different parts of the world). Project management facilitates that collaboration and manages the distributed tasks to ensure timely delivery.

Involvement and collaboration in creative action is facilitated by the use of other processes that can harness the potential of employees and stakeholders in large group meetings that utilise the ready-aim-fire framework. In the early 1990s, the then chief executive of General Electric (GE), Jack Welch, started to tap into the employee's brainpower by breaking down the old management style – 'taking out the boss element'. One of his weapons was called Work-Out. This is an activity that takes people from a complete department or function away from the workplace for a couple of days to identify what is going wrong in their area and come up with potential solutions. It is a problem-solving activity on a large scale over a short time period. It is not hierarchical, so it unlocks the barriers that keep staff members out of the decision-making process.

On day three the boss of the section returns (in the days when this was a total company Work-Out, with representatives from across GE, that boss was the CEO). The teams who have been working on proposals for dealing with the problems that they have identified present their ideas. The boss, on the spot, has to agree, say 'No', or ask for more information (in which case the boss must sponsor a team to do that by an agreed date).

In a normal Work-Out, the boss has to respond to over 100 proposals, allowing about one minute of thinking time for each. Typically over 90 per cent of proposals are accepted immediately. Hundreds of thousands of dollars of improvements are implemented each time a Work-Out is called – ideas and improvements that in a traditional organisation would never make it past the first-line supervisor level before someone would squash them flat.

Other technologies that encourage participation across large groups and release creativity include Open Space, Appreciative Inquiry, World Café and Future Search. These processes tap into the desire of people to contribute and – like Work-Out – significantly reduce the time frames usually associated with innovation design and implementation. By creating the conditions for effective dialogue to take place simultaneously across the whole system, these meeting processes enable rapid strategy and innovation deployment. Because the whole system is present, it is possible to gather real-time information, analyse it, create opportunities and ideas for the future, make decisions on these and plan implementation, all in the scope of two or three days. And, because everyone in the system is present in the decision-making process, there is no need for a lengthy and time-consuming cascade to 'sell' the idea to the organisation. The organisation is all present! So implementation can begin the next day.

An example of one of these processes at work can be found at IKEA, the Swedish-based furniture and household goods company. They brought together 52 people from across their organisation (including suppliers, executives, workers and customers from Sweden, Europe and North America) to redesign the supply chain for their Ektorp sofa range. The outcome of their three-day event was to double sales, increase quality, cut price by 30 per cent and cut delivery times – all without reducing profit margins or customer satisfaction.

Ready-Aim-Fire in Teams

On a smaller scale, unbalanced teams can use the ready-aim-fire process to inject creativity, ensure effective innovation and avoid the pitfalls experienced through over-enthusiastic attempts to force new ideas into projects. By assessing the team members' preferences they can identify any deficiencies in the stages and act to balance the team, using techniques to compensate for the imbalance.

So, where there is a lack of creativity (the 'ready' stage), the use of brainstorming, lateral thinking or other tools at appropriate times in the project process can ensure that new ideas are considered. If the deficit is in the 'aim' stage, the use of decision matrix or analytical criteria will help the team to make good judgements. Action plans and milestone plans will facilitate the 'fire' stage. These tools, coupled with an awareness of the need for action to correct team imbalance will help teams to cope with the reality that they are not perfectly formed.

Conclusion

The successful creative organisation is one that can innovate, because it is innovation (the translation of creative ideas into practical improvements that meet the organisation's mission) which will enable the organisation to survive and succeed. To be innovative one needs to have a source of ideas and a process for analysing and implementing those ideas. In order to analyse and implement ideas effectively, an organisation must understand its existing bias and culture. In addition it must seek to balance its natural tendency, which might be towards action for its own sake, 'paralysis of analysis', or the chaos of having too many ideas. Each of these biases is just as fatal for the organisation as the others, unless your organisation is specifically formed to exploit that strength.

A style of ready-aim-fire will give most organisations a balanced approach with which they can cope with most problems. An organisation which encourages the more innovative style of ready-fire-aim (which fosters experimentation and controlled risk taking) will be more successful in staying ahead of its competitors.

All of these approaches, coupled with the effective application and use of project management, will move pure ideas-generating organisations into innovating ones, help imbalanced organisations and teams to be more effective, and ensure that all organisations meet the demands for change and adaptation to survive and thrive.

References and Further Reading

Codling, S. (1998), *Benchmarking*, Aldershot: Gower.

Cox, G. (1988), 'The creative organization', in Lock, D. (ed.), *The Gower Handbook of Management*, 4th edn, Aldershot: Gower.

Cox, G. (2000), *Ready-Aim-Fire Problem Solving – A Strategic Approach to Innovative Decision Making*, Dublin: Oak Tree Press, available from www.newdirections.uk.com.

Cox, G. (2010), 'Getting Results Without Authority – The New Rules of Organizational Influence', www.BookShaker.com.

Huston, L. and Sakkab, N. (2006), 'Connect and develop: inside Procter & Gamble's new model for innovation', *Harvard Business Review*, Vol. 84, No. 3.

Park, R. (1999), *Value Engineering: a Plan for Invention*, Boca Raton, FL: St Lucie Press.

2 *People in and Around the Project Environment*

14 *Project Stakeholders*

GUY GIFFIN

This chapter is based partly on research that I have been conducting for more than a decade. That has included running over 250 stakeholder management workshops with senior project managers from all industry sectors, and also developing over 30 detailed stakeholder analyses of complex projects with organisations including: BAE Systems, Balfour Beatty, Bechtel, GlaxoSmithKline, Lockheed Martin, Mace, Oracle, SAP, Thames Water, Transport for London, Turner and Townsend, and Unisys. All these analyses were developed after projects had been completed and their teams had developed a profound understanding of the stakeholders. Work in this area is also informed by many leading academics with specialisms across a range of relevant disciplines, in particular: Jay Forrester, Peter Senge, Herbert Simon, Todd Jick, John Kotter, Olivier D'Herbemont and Bruno César, Deborah Ancona.

Introduction

An important characteristic of modern projects is the potentially very long list of parties that have a stake in them and that can influence their outcome. This list can include internal staff, client staff, suppliers, end users, partners, government officials, regulators, client's customers, the media, project team members, competitors, shareholders, environmental groups, local communities, trade unions and more.

Whilst historically these people and organisations have been referred to using various terms including: constituents, players, actors, interested parties or factions, the fashionable label is now 'stakeholder' and a common definition of this term is: 'anyone that can affect or be affected by the project'. Alternatively, we could just refer to them as: 'the people that count'. Occasionally, animals can also be regarded as stakeholders, but this chapter will focus primarily on the two-legged, featherless creatures that have a tendency to make our lives more complex, challenging and interesting.

Whether you are project managing a new IT system, an office relocation, a product launch or a nuclear power station, the behaviour and reactions of all the internal and external stakeholders is likely to be a key determinant of success. Hartman (2000) goes beyond that to declare that a successful project is one that makes *all its stakeholders happy*. Figuring out who all the stakeholders are is part of the challenge, and the project manager also needs to consider the stakeholders' relative importance. Whilst this is usually difficult to quantify neatly, an appreciation of who counts and who *really* counts is likely to be critical. Lock (2013) finds it convenient to classify stakeholders as primary, secondary and tertiary according to how they affect, or will be affected by, the project. Lock's work

Stakeholders	Objectives		
	Time	Cost	Specification
Project owner			
Project manager			
Bank			
Guarantor			
Statutory bodies			
Main contractor			
Subcontractors			
Suppliers			
Project workers			
General public			
Local residents			
Environmental groups			
and so on ↓	↓	↓	↓

Figure 14.1 A matrix of stakeholders' objectives

Note: This extends the concept of the triangle of objectives and allows the perceived priorities of all project stakeholders to be considered.

includes a stakeholder matrix which attempts to give more meaning to the widely used triangle of time, cost and performance objectives by asking project managers to rank those three objectives according to how they will be perceived by the different parties (see Figure 14.1).

HUMAN AND TECHNICAL CHALLENGES

Numerous project reviews point to the key reasons for project failure being connected to human factors. These include:

- poor communication between relevant parties;
- lack of consensus on objectives;
- insufficient senior management support (see Chapter 5);
- misunderstanding of requirements, difficulty overcoming resistance to change, and so on – in other words, less-than-perfect stakeholder management.

If asked what proportion of their working week is taken up dealing with human (as opposed to technical) challenges, senior project managers often respond saying: 'more than 75 per cent'. These human challenges are likely to become even more prevalent in our increasingly interconnected world, as we move further away from 'government knows best' public sectors and towards flatter and more matrixed organisations in the private sector:

Understanding physical systems is far more advanced than the understanding of social systems.
(Forrester, 1998)

ALL-ROUNDERS

In addition to needing technical, financial and commercial expertise, the twenty-first-century project manager often needs to be a politician, ambassador, promoter, consultant, listener, upward and outward communicator, diplomat, relationship manager and team leader. Whether your preferred term is 'managing', 'managing for' or 'engaging' stakeholders, the project manager's challenge of maximising support, approval and cooperation across a broad spectrum of people will always involve a range of activities: identifying, consulting, profiling, communicating, balancing interests and judging compromises, resolving conflicts, negotiating and influencing.

Often coming from specialist and technical (for example engineering) backgrounds, project managers therefore often have to make a difficult leap when moving into this 'generalist' role.

The familiar metaphor that distinguishes 'left brain' and 'right brain' activities (for example contrasting logical and creative tasks), can be applied to the range of activities and disciplines that project managers need to master. Some tasks, such as scheduling and financial modelling, require an analytical approach, but other activities (such as selecting and motivating team members) require a very different skill set. Project managers need to put both sides of the brain to work and it is therefore a rounded, 'ambidextrous' ability that is essential for managing the whole project system. In reality, the distinction between the two hemispheres of the brain is more complex than the metaphor suggests:

Attempts to decide which set of functions are segregated in which hemisphere have mainly been discarded; piece after piece of evidence suggesting that every identifiable human activity is actually served at some level by both hemispheres. (McGilchrist, 2009)

In over 250 stakeholder management education and project start-up workshops with clients primarily from the technology, defence, engineering and construction sectors, I have noted that fewer than 10 out of approximately 2,500 participants (who were typically senior project managers) had any professional or academic qualifications in psychology.

Stakeholder Management: An Integral Discipline of Project Management

Stakeholder management is not an activity to be regarded as separate from 'real' project management. It should not be outsourced or, worse still, regarded as an activity only for a public relations department. It is vital for project teams to develop continuously their understanding of the stakeholders' evolving objectives, interests, constraints and expectations (whether they are reasonable or not!), and this understanding of the stakeholders' priorities (for example customer requirements) is essential for making good decisions throughout the project lifecycle, such as decisions about the scope and success criteria, the contract strategy, scheduling, resourcing and risk management.

Stakeholder management is therefore intimately linked with all the key disciplines of project management. However, consistent with the findings that the causes of project failure usually occur in the very early stages of any project, stakeholder management is particularly important in the initial phases where the project objectives and success criteria are being established.

A SOURCE OF COMPLEXITY

Multiple stakeholders with diverging and evolving interests are a key source of complexity in any project. Some would argue that any project that involves human beings (even just one!) is bound to be complex. In addition to there simply being a long list of stakeholders, there are often numerous types of relationship *between* the stakeholders: joint venture, main contractor and subcontractor, client and supplier, and the nature of these relationships might also change over the project lifecycle: for example, partners can become competitors. An essential feature of any complex project is therefore the underlying 'social system':

- the web of interested parties;
- the subtle interplay between those parties;
- the inherent ambiguity about what information they have;
- how they actually feel about the project;
- what determines their behaviour, reactions and satisfaction levels.

Uncertainty in complex projects also stems from the fact that the stakeholders themselves will not always know their own objectives and priorities!

Defining Project Success

The importance of stakeholder management becomes even more apparent if we examine what defines ultimate project success. Traditional measures of project success have focused on the immediate time, cost and quality measures. These output measures however are not as important as the longer term *outcomes* – the benefits or value generated by the project. These outcomes can be regarded as a means to satisfy stakeholders, with the ultimate end being 'stakeholder value'.

With multiple parties involved, project success should be measured by means of an index of satisfaction across all the stakeholders, according to how satisfied and also how important they are. The project manager's mission can therefore be described as 'making the *right* stakeholders happy', which is very similar to what Hartman (2000) wrote but more achievable in practice.

Stakeholder satisfaction or 'happiness' can be indicated using a spectrum that ranges from support to opposition (Figure 14.2). But in practice it is rare for any sophisticated measure of stakeholder satisfaction ever to be quantified, which partly explains why the stakeholder dimension is not planned or resourced as deliberately and thoroughly as it should be.

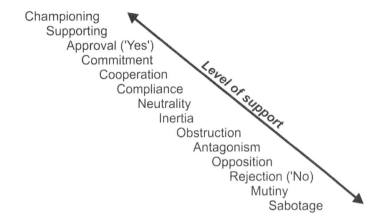

Figure 14.2 Spectrum of stakeholders' support

Inadequate Knowledge and Tools

The current line-up of tools and techniques for project stakeholder management, especially for more complex projects, is typically inadequate. The language and terminology is often naïve and ambiguous, with ill-defined and unhelpful terms such as 'soft skills' still prevailing (they occur in other chapters throughout this Handbook).

> *Stakeholder management is all too often a topic that abounds in content-free truisms, such as 'communication is key'. (Moorhouse Consulting, 2007)*

The limitations of project management textbooks and the standard methodologies are particularly noticeable in this area; there is an evident lack of clarity about what 'real' stakeholder management actually involves. Many textbooks suggest little more than the use of a simplistic 2 x 2 stakeholder analysis matrix that plots power against interest or attitude. Even the more advanced stakeholder analysis tools imply that stakeholders behave rationally. But stakeholders are (or are owned or managed by) human beings. Analysis tools do not usually detail the full range of stakeholders' motives and interests, which means the complex combination of commercial, financial, technical, political, social, historical, personal and emotional factors that will determine their attitudes and behaviour.

Based partly around my numerous and detailed studies of multiple stakeholder projects, an 'iceberg' model of stakeholder behaviour (Figure 14.3) has emerged that categorises stakeholder interests and motives into three key areas:

1. *Rational*: stakeholders do sometimes evaluate projects for good reasons, such as:

   - What return shall we get?
   - Does it help our wider corporate objectives?
   - Is it worth the investment?

2. *Social*: stakeholders' views are also determined by what other stakeholders think. Thus instead of making isolated assessments, stakeholders are influenced (for example) by their customers, their bosses, the media, and so on, and they often defer judgement to others.
3. *Personal*: stakeholders will also often react based on many things outside a purely rational calculation of whether the project makes good business sense. For example:

    *   how they are being treated;
    *   if they are being consulted;
    *   if they like the project manager;
    *   sunk costs;
    *   the impact the project might have on their personal status;
    *   and so on.

Comprehensive stakeholder analyses might accordingly contain information that is quite sensitive (perhaps including details about the stakeholders' personal agendas). Some immediate things to consider are whether this information should be recorded at all, where it is stored, for example in hard or soft copy, and with whom it is shared.

Alongside the detailed stakeholder analysis, a communication plan should also be developed that is sensitive to the stakeholders' specific areas of interest, the level of detail that they require, their language and their communication media preferences (for example email, telephone or face-to-face). The communication plan should also take into

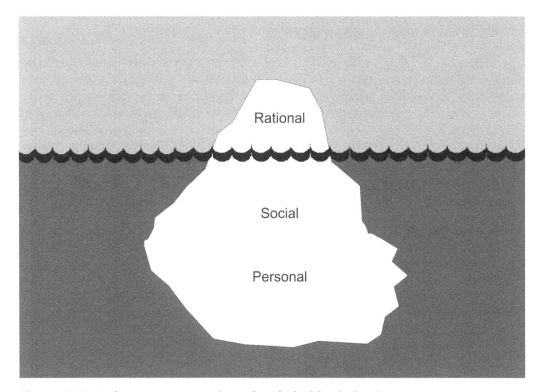

Figure 14.3 Iceberg representation of stakeholder behaviour

consideration the social networks that the stakeholders are part of, in order to exploit (for example) the influence of any allies that the project manager might have.

Developing an advanced stakeholder analysis that details a wide range of stakeholder interests relies partly on the ability to ask the right questions. This ability to ask questions illustrates the 'simple but difficult' nature of stakeholder management.

With the following consultation questions as examples, consider how simple and inexpensive it can be to gather useful information about stakeholders. But most of us (myself included!) would agree that we do not always do this effectively:

- How do you prefer to communicate?
- Which other stakeholders are you considering?
- Can you tell me anything about any of the other stakeholders?
- In which of the project outcomes are you most interested?

Science and Art

The disciplines of project management can be viewed on a continuum from objective (right and wrong answers) to subjective (no right answers). Managing the more objective aspects can be regarded as 'science', and managing the more subjective aspects as 'art'.

Stakeholder management is more art than science. Figuring out the relative importance of the stakeholders, understanding what factors really drive them, establishing how they actually feel about the project, judging the inevitable compromises that have to be

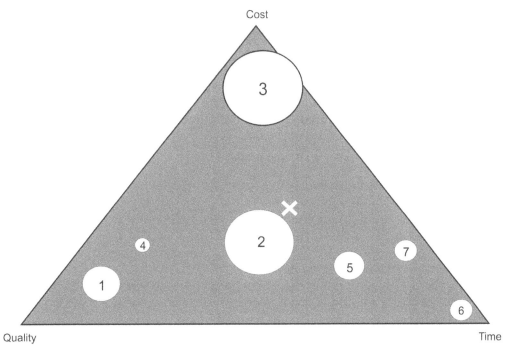

Figure 14.4 Conflicting interests of stakeholders and their centre of gravity

made across conflicting interests – these are all examples of a discipline on which the mostly 'scientific' project management methodologies and processes struggle to provide guidance.

Figure 14.4, on the previous page, is the triangle of objectives, initiated by Martin Barnes, and now familiar to all competent project managers. In my example, the diagram plots seven stakeholders, all with differing degrees of importance as depicted by the size of their circles. The positions of these circles within the triangle indicate their priorities with regard to the key project outcomes (the trade-off between time, cost and quality that are usually inevitable). The project manager is therefore being pulled in different directions. The cross in Figure 14.4 marks the 'centre of gravity' for all seven conflicting stakeholders' interests in this example, taking into consideration their positions and relative power. The position of the cross is thus intended to indicate the best compromise. However this is usually only established intuitively in the real world, with the obvious risk of misjudgement.

Planning and Modelling

Consider the depth of planning that often goes into the technical dimension of many projects. Compare that with the typical stakeholder management planning, which is often very thin, and sometimes does not exist at all. Given that the numerous indications of why projects fail are mostly connected to the 'human factors' this is perhaps not surprising. The paradox is that, typically, we plan the aspects that are least likely to cause project failure very thoroughly, but conversely we often tackle the aspects that are most likely to cause failure with an ad hoc, 'make-it-up-as-we-go-along' approach.

Engineers use increasingly sophisticated software models (for example CAD prototypes) in order to understand and optimise designs for the physical dimensions of their products. Architects use software to create building designs that take into account the movement of occupants, for example in escaping safely from emergencies such as fires. With a similar logic, a new approach to modelling the stakeholder dimension of complex projects is emerging that combines detailed stakeholder analyses (that *do* model the full range of motives and interests) with other models of the key project variables (such as scope options and business outcomes).

Concluding Case Example

In 2011, my company was part of a team (led by a well-known business school) that conducted a research project for one of Europe's largest national postal operators on 'sustainable urban logistics (UL)'. The research was supported by a grant to the business school from the postal operator's group company.

UL is critical to support the movement of goods between suppliers and retail stores, and for deliveries from businesses to households. The UL sector has grown considerably in the past decade, partly because of e-commerce. At the same time, increasing congestion on city streets and increasing pollution from (for example) carbon dioxide, mono-nitrogen oxides and particulate matter are concerns directly connected to UL.

Various options were available for dealing with these concerns, for example through better urban planning and the use of less polluting vehicles for local transport and deliveries. There was also a long list of stakeholders with varied interests involved. The Sustainable Urban Logistics Project was set up to explore the alternatives for structuring UL systems for major metropolitan areas over the next decade.

We developed a detailed analysis of the relevant variables in order to help decide how to integrate sustainability factors (concerning carbon dioxide and other emissions, noise, congestion, respiratory illnesses and so on) into the design of UL service offerings, and for developing an effective stakeholder management approach during the design and roll-out of new UL services.

Our analysis included models of the *objective* parameters (such as the various distribution options and their corresponding impacts) and also the *subjective* factors (like the wide range of stakeholder interests, priorities and potential reactions). Combining these two models provided profound insight into the project design by giving an opportunity to analyse, test and see not only the objective impacts (such as projected costs and pollution levels) but also the subjective impacts (like stakeholder reactions) of the numerous potential specifications.

The modelling approach outlined above is evolving to give project managers much greater understanding of the stakeholder dynamics of their projects. It will also provide more opportunities to test plans and strategies in safe environments, thus enabling a method that is much more rigorous than the current, mostly ad hoc or intuitive, methods.

However, not every aspect of stakeholder behaviour in complex projects can be modelled.

Managing stakeholders is also about day-to-day relationship building. That will always remain an art, relying on interpersonal skills, charm and having a sense of humour.

References and Further Reading

Forrester, J. (1998), 'Designing the Future', internal paper presented at the University of Seville, 15 December 1998.

Hartman, F.T. (2000), *Don't Park Your Brain Outside*, Newtown Square, PA: Project Management Institute.

Lock, D. (2013), *Project Management*, 10th edn, Farnham: Gower.

McGilchrist, I. (2009), *The Master and His Emissary*, New Haven, CT: Yale University Press.

Moorhouse Consulting (2007), 'Beyond Conventional Stakeholder Management', White Paper. Available at: http://www.moorhouseconsulting.com/news-and-views/publications-and-articles/beyond-conventional-stakeholder-management

15 *People in Senior Project Roles*

GEORGE JUCAN

This is the first of two chapters in which I shall describe the roles of people in projects. This chapter will concentrate on those who perform senior or delivery roles, and Chapter 16 will be more concerned with people in supporting roles.

Introduction

It has been said that management is the art of getting results through people. That is as true in project management as in any other form of management. The success of a project does not depend only on its methodologies, processes, techniques, equipment or other tools. Projects are done by people. The team members from the project manager downwards will make or break the project. Equipment, tools or processes can only help people to achieve their objectives easier or faster. Good people with bad tools will still get the job done, but it will take a miracle for unqualified people to reach success, even using the best tools available.

The focus and reliance on people is a direct result of the unique characteristic of projects. It is comparatively easy to train people to produce high-quality work when the tasks are highly repetitive and governed by defined processes, methods and equipment. Projects are different. In projects people rely on their ability to be innovative, to be creative and to work outside their 'comfort zone' to perform unusual activities. They are expected to create a new product or outcome. They might still use familiar tools and techniques, but the application of these must be adapted to the circumstances of each project. Thus highly qualified people with the appropriate experience are in extreme demand in order to ensure project success. Such people are often hard to find, and they can come at a significant cost.

STANDARDISATION OF JOB TITLES

The high cost and low availability of top people can have a direct impact on how those people are assigned to project work. The organisational structure of a project also has a direct impact on a person's assignment to executing one project, multiple projects or a combination of project and non-project work. The traditional full-time assignment of a person to a single project is losing ground every day to more dynamic arrangements. Now some people are required to divide their attention between executing on a daily (or

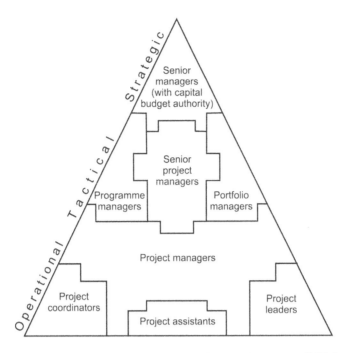

Figure 15.1 Common project management roles and responsibilities

even hourly) basis between different assignments. This dynamic state can wreak havoc with job titles.

A glance through the job postings will reveal a variety of titles and descriptions. Often the same title will have totally different responsibilities in different organisations. Conversely, jobs requiring similar responsibilities and duties can carry different titles.

In the absence of a recognised standard, companies have developed their own career frameworks and job descriptions. Furthermore, there are many executives (and even project managers) who consider that project roles are specific to each company and that no standards exist. However, the same was once said about project management itself, but now we have widely accepted standards for project management terms (such as those defined by the Project Management Institute in its *Project Management Book of Knowledge*). Now these standards are extending also to portfolios and programmes.

Before describing each role in this and the next chapter I must first define the governance framework in which the roles operate. Figure 15.1 includes the roles of people who spend all or most of their time in the management of projects or multiple projects. Chapter 16 describes supporting roles.

Project Management Roles at the Governance Level

EXECUTIVE SPONSOR

The project, programme or portfolio sponsor is the highest executive authority directly involved in the project initiative. Regardless of whether the project is carried out internally or performed for a paying customer, the executive sponsor is the ultimate decision maker and has the ultimate responsibility for the alignment of project outcomes. In many cases, especially within government, the executive sponsor is supported by a steering committee.

Chapter 4 dealt with the role of project sponsor in detail, so I need write no more on that subject here.

PORTFOLIO MANAGER

The portfolio manager has the most strategic exposure in the world of project delivery. If organisational middle management is considered to be the link between senior executives and the company's operations as far as the line of command goes, the portfolio manager is the link between the executive vision and the activities necessary to enhance operational capacity.

A portfolio manager is responsible for a group of projects, programmes and possible also other work.

All those things are not necessarily interdependent or directly related, but they generally support the common strategic objectives. This is a high-level tactical position, which quite often allows the portfolio manager to be involved in strategic decisions as an advisor to the executives.

A typical portfolio's components are large projects, programmes and supporting activities, each coordinated by a project, programme or operational manager. Thus the portfolio manager has limited exposure to each component's details. This role regards the portfolio components in their entirety, being mostly concerned with their business performance analysis. It is the portfolio manager who has principal authority for authorising (or rejecting) the initiation of each component. That authority also includes making go or no-go decisions for continuance at predefined stage gates. The role is responsible for the efficient distribution of an organisation's resources over all projects to achieve maximum results in terms of strategic achievements.

Programme, project or organisational managers reporting to the portfolio manager are responsible for each endeavour included in the portfolio. However, with the exception of government departments and *Fortune* 100 companies, in most cases programmes tend to have life cycles of their own and a portfolio will usually include only projects and supporting activities.

Smaller organisations might decide to run all their projects as part of a single portfolio to enable better comparative benefits analysis and efficient allocation of resources to achieve various organisational objectives. Large organisations will typically run several portfolios, each one coordinated by a senior executive, which enables the portfolio manager to act as an advisor in strategic decisions. In very large organisations and governments, a portfolio manager might only have responsibility for a subset of the organisation's projects and their alignment to organisational strategic objectives.

Typical duties and responsibilities of a portfolio manager would be:

- strategic management of portfolio components (projects and programmes);
- assessment and monitoring of business and financial performance;
- authorisation and management of portfolio components' relationships and dependencies, as well as overall integration and resolution of difficulties;

- ensuring distribution of organisational resources between components;
- possibly interacting with senior managers, executives, and major stakeholders to establish strategic plans and objectives for the organisation;
- where there is no project management support office, possible responsibility for the organisation-wide integration of consistent project management methodologies and terminology.

Typical authority levels for the portfolio manager would include:

- able to coordinate project, programme and line managers within the portfolio area;
- has autonomy with portfolio limits, reporting to an executive committee;
- can negotiate project initiation, based on performance and resources;
- can institute adequate controls for underlying programmes and projects;
- can propose enhancements to portfolio management methodology/framework.

Typical competencies and experience for a portfolio manager include:

- project, programme and portfolio management methodology and framework experience;
- business acumen with strong strategic visioning and tactical planning;
- objective decision-making ability, based on strategic objectives priority, business performance analysis and resource availability;
- specialised training for the selection and coordination of multiple initiatives;
- strong communicating, negotiating and influencing capabilities;
- on average 15–20 years of project/programme/portfolio management experience;
- in almost every case the portfolio manager has a PMP or equivalent designation.

PROGRAMME MANAGER

A programme manager is assigned to coordinate a number of related projects (and sometimes other operational work) that are directed towards the same business objectives and have significant interdependencies or relationships. On occasions the programme manager may have some involvement at strategic level, but this is mostly a tactical role that will normally report to a senior organisational manager or an executive. It will usually subordinate a number of senior project managers, project managers and, sometimes, organisational managers responsible for programme components.

Specialised programme management training and a PMP or equivalent certification are considered by most organisations as mandatory requirements to be effective in this role.

A programme manager is the natural extension of a senior project manager, joining back the two directions seen for senior project managers who have to coordinate complex projects with subprojects and guide other project managers. If the subprojects are now full projects targeted to deliver the same business objective (or related business objectives) the programme manager will not only guide but will actually manage/coordinate the project managers leading those projects.

Instead of focusing on task relationships the programme manager will analyse cross-project interdependencies to avoid potential impacts and identify optimisations with regards to the overall scope, schedule and resources utilisation.

A programme manager needs to demonstrate not only solid project/programme management knowledge, but also the ability to understand the business objectives that programme has to achieve, and the alignment of those objectives within the overall organisational strategy. Whilst still being a very tactical role, the programme manager may occasionally have some involvement at strategic level. In most cases the programme manager will report to and/or have access to an organisation's executive management, so the communication abilities must shift from project to business level to be successful.

Typical duties and responsibilities of the programme manager include:

- ensuring alignment of subordinated projects with business objectives;
- prioritisation and assignment of shared resources to programme components;
- assessment and monitoring of projects' business and financial performance;
- monitoring programme components' relationships and dependencies, as well as overall integration and the resolution of problems;
- coordinating the project managers who deliver individual projects within the programme – they are directly responsible to the programme manager for the execution of their projects as part of the programme;
- usually responsible for stakeholder management, particularly stakeholders outside the organisation.

Typical authority levels for the programme manager include:

- works with constituent project managers to monitor cost, schedule and technical performance of component projects and operations, whilst working to ensure the ultimate success of the programme;
- has autonomy within the programme boundaries, under the guidance of an organisational executive or portfolio manager;
- negotiates scope and schedule adjustments within the reporting structure;
- determining and coordinating the sharing of resources among their constituent projects for the overall benefit of the programme;
- process and methodological tailoring to better fit the programme's particularities.

Typical competencies and experience for the programme manager are:

- expert knowledge of project and programme management methodology, tools and techniques;
- strong tactical planning and leadership skills;
- strong communication, negotiation and conflict resolution capabilities;
- advanced understanding of corporate environment and objectives;
- on average 11–15 years of experience managing projects and/or programmes.

PROJECT DIRECTOR

The role of project director is often encountered in organisations that have no project management office (PMO) as a substitute for the coordination activity usually exercised by the PMO. In most cases, the project director coordinates a number of projects (and their corresponding project managers), usually acting on behalf of an executive or project sponsor. In such cases the project director is almost equivalent with a portfolio manager and requires significant project management knowledge.

However, in other cases the project director is a representative of the client or user community group, representing a single point of contact between an external or internal supplier and the business community that will benefit from the project delivery. In such cases the project director typically requires only business skills, especially revolving around feasibility and cost efficiency. Extensive project management expertise is not always required. Typical duties and responsibilities of a project director are as follows:

- project initiation and strategic project alignment;
- guidance, mentoring and/or coordinating project managers;
- ensuring alignment with business objectives and needs;
- improving processes and methodology.

Typical authority levels for the project director are:

- coordination of one or more projects from a strategic perspective;
- ensuring stakeholders expectations' management, including contractual negotiations and performance;
- can propose changes to the management framework of the initiative.

Typical competencies and experience for the project director include:

- demonstrated understanding of organisational environment and projects' alignment to corporate objectives;
- advanced leadership skills;
- advanced general management skills;
- advanced communicating, negotiating and conflict resolution capabilities.

Project Management Roles at the Operational Level

In the first part of the twentieth century the title 'project manager' was good enough to describe most people who led projects. Later different titles emerged, such as project leader, project coordinator and so on. But each title might mean something completely different depending upon the organisation in which it was used. A classic example is the title project leader, which in some organisations carries the authority of a project director. However, workforce mobility in recent years has meant that job-seekers and organisations need some standardisation of job titles, giving a common understanding of duties and appropriate qualifications. This common perspective has been followed as far as possible in the remainder of this chapter.

SENIOR PROJECT MANAGER

A senior project manager has a demonstrated ability to manage complex projects efficiently, based on sound methodological knowledge as well as 'people skills'. Typically holding a PMP or equivalent designation, a senior project manager is able to understand cross-project interdependencies, identify gaps or overlaps and negotiate scope adjustments not only with the corresponding project managers but also with executives and sponsors. With a solid understanding and practical experience of formal methodologies, a senior project manager usually has the ability to adjust predefined processes to the project needs realistically. These capabilities make senior project managers perfect candidates to be part of PMOs and for providing guidance and mentoring to other project managers.

A senior project manager usually has about 10 years' experience, manages complex projects (not just large projects). This might be independently or as part of a portfolio or programme. In such cases they usually have project assistants, or they might delegate subprojects to other project managers, coordinators or leaders.

Under the general direction of either a portfolio or a programme manager, a senior project manager leads strategic projects from original concept through to final implementation, often involving considerable resources and complex cross-functional integration. In smaller companies they could report directly to a senior organisational manager or even a senior executive, but most often they report to a departmental manager, a PMO manager or a portfolio/programme manager.

A senior project manager will have significant experience of interacting horizontally with many functional groups throughout the organisation. That enables a perspective that is not obvious in the traditional hierarchical model.

This role manages complex projects based on sound methodological knowledge and requires advanced people skills. It seeks the project's alignment to business needs (even beyond chartered scope statement) and realistically adjusts predefined organisational processes and policies. Also, it is expected that the senior executives will rely heavily on the senior project manager's understanding of the project's alignment to business needs and organisational relationships. The executives might also seek advice from the senior project manager regarding tactical decisions and even organisational strategy.

In summary, the typical duties and responsibilities of a senior project manager include:

- often involved in project initiation and strategic project alignment;
- interfaces with all areas affected by the project, including end users, partners and suppliers;
- guides, mentors and/or performs project planning for all knowledge areas;
- takes corrective actions as required to deliver complete scope, at the desired quality, on time and within budget;
- ensures adherence to quality standards and reviews project deliverables;
- process and methodology improvement.

Typical authority level for the senior project manager includes or allows:

- manages end-to-end strategic projects, large in scope, budget and team;
- may communicate directly with senior executives;
- reports to an organisational manager or to a programme or portfolio manager;
- coordinates project leaders or project coordinators assigned to deliver subprojects of a complex project managed by the senior project manager;
- can propose changes to the project management methodology, framework and best practices.

Typical competencies and experience required for the senior project manager are:

- expert knowledge of project management methodology (typically at PMP standard);
- advanced leadership and general management skills;
- advanced communication, negotiation and conflict resolution capabilities;
- understanding of organisational environment and project's alignment to corporate objectives;
- effective problem-solving and decision-making skills.

PROJECT MANAGER

A project manager typically acts at the operational level, directly managing project teams. Preferably holding a professional certification, a project manager has good command of the processes, tools and techniques required to manage most projects, independent or within programmes or portfolios. However, for complex projects usually acts under the guidance of a senior project manager and may subordinate project coordinators or leaders. In the ideal situation a project manager would report to a mid-level organisational manager who has line authority over most people that one would find in a typical project team.

Editor's Comment (DL)

The term project manager is often also used for the person in sole charge of a very large and complex project, indicating some confusion with the term senior project manager as described above. This illustrates forcibly the point that all these role titles vary considerably depending upon the particular industry or organisation in which they are used.

Typically working under the guidance of a portfolio, programme or senior project manager, the project manager is able to lead and manage multiple projects or a large project. Even if the ideal result of getting everything done on time, within budget and to specification might sometimes be out of reach, a competent project manager will have the tools, knowledge and experience to drive the project as far as possible towards that ideal.

With an overall perspective of all project management knowledge areas, the project manager should be able to demonstrate both the 'hard' methodological skills and the 'soft' skills required for project success. An effective project manager knows how to choose and use the appropriate technique or behaviour required to maximise the project benefits.

In most cases, a project manager can persuade or negotiate with internal and external project stakeholders to achieve the desired results, and should only need occasional support from the reporting organisational manager or executive. Large and complex projects might require support from a project assistant, or delegation of some duties to project leaders or coordinators.

By accumulating experience and formalising their knowledge (usually evidenced through a professional designation such as PMP), the project manager can expect to become a senior project manager, programme manager or portfolio manager.

Typical duties and responsibilities of a project manager include:

- assembling the project team;
- assigning individual responsibilities within the team;
- responsibility for estimating, planning and scheduling project tasks;
- estimating the total resources necessary for timely project completion;
- managing, monitoring and reporting progress;
- taking corrective action where necessary to keep the project on track;
- ensuring effective communication with internal and external stakeholders;
- maintaining a project diary, recording principal events and problems;
- from project records and experience, ensuring improved performance for future projects as a result of lessons learned.

Typical authority levels for a project manager might include:

- can manage end-to-end tactical projects of various sizes;
- has authority over the project team (if there is a project charter, authority levels should define those);
- reports to a project executive, sponsor, or other mid to senior manager;
- has autonomy within project boundaries;
- can negotiate scope, resources and schedule changes with stakeholders.

Typical competencies and experience for a project manager are:

- in-depth knowledge of project management methodology, tools and techniques;
- leadership and general management skills;
- stakeholder communication, negotiation, influencing, persuasion and so on;
- consistent professional behaviour in all activities;
- typically three to five years' project management experience;
- might need occasional guidance from a senior project manager, programme manager, portfolio manager or functional area manager.

JUNIOR PROJECT MANAGER

A junior project manager is either a recent project management graduate or postgraduate, or a technical or administrative person who was assigned to manage a small project (or part of a larger project). In most cases a junior project manager has formal project management training, but not extensive experience. Some junior project managers work independently on small projects and a well-established junior project manager might handle autonomously all aspects of a small project over its entire life cycle, usually under the guidance of a more senior project manager.

Whatever the responsibilities, the junior project manager must be familiar with project scope and objectives, the project schedule, and the roles of the other team members. Whilst typically having the required knowledge for a project manager, a junior project manager must enhance performance and personal capabilities to become self-sufficient. In most cases junior project managers will continue on a self-improvement path, with the objective of becoming an autonomous project manager. However, in some cases 'accidental' junior project managers return to their previous duties as soon as their assignment is complete.

Typical duties and responsibilities of a junior project manager might include:

- performing overall project planning based on predefined objectives;
- collecting estimates and preparing resource schedules;
- monitoring task execution and progress, probably under guidance of a more senior manager;
- drafting consolidated status reports to stakeholders;
- taking corrective actions as required to keep the project on track, or reporting shortfalls to senior managers to obtain such actions.

Typical authority level for a junior project manager might be:

- reports to a project executive or sponsor, normally at mid-management level;
- has autonomy over a small project team within specified boundaries;
- can negotiate (under guidance) scope, resources and schedule changes with stakeholders;
- can assign tasks to team members and manage their work;
- is allowed to implement corrective actions for small project deviations.

Typical competencies and experience for a junior project manager are:

- good knowledge of project management principles;
- good working knowledge of project scheduling and monitoring tools;
- understanding of quality and cost control processes;
- able to negotiate and resolve minor problems and conflicts with stakeholders;
- good communication skills for interaction with team members;
- will most likely have up to three years' experience in projects.

PROJECT LEADER

Project leaders often evolve from technical or team leaders who have become recognised experts in their field. This role is sometimes known as project engineer, which is seen (for example) in some mining and petrochemical projects.

Team members look up to the project leader for technical guidance and direction. They are also ready to accept estimating and scheduling direction owing to the trust they have earned for their technical capabilities. Usually without project or management training, the project leader is supervised and guided by a project manager or other organisational manager.

The project leader is most of the time an expert in the project technical arena but might have no formal project management training. By having participated in many projects in the same technological area, the project leader will have acquired good judgement in the techniques of estimating, scheduling and job performance assessment. On the other hand, a project leader might not be proficient in non-technical tasks like communication or risk management.

Without guidance from a project or organisational manager, a project leader might deliver good products but would be less likely to achieve project success owing to being unfamiliar with client requirements and other stakeholders' expectations. If not supervised by a project manager scope creep or 'gold-plating' could occur.

Very often project leaders enjoy their hands-on activity and will usually favour an organisational management path over a switch towards project management. Whatever the case, the areas that will mostly need development are people skills, such as managing team members and interacting with non-technical stakeholders.

Typical duties and responsibilities of a project leader include:

- participation in project planning and estimating;
- coordinating and monitoring task execution and progress;
- providing consolidated status reports to the project manager;
- providing technical support to team members;
- advising the project manager on risks and other issues that could affect the project adversely.

Typical authority levels for a project leader might be:

- operates under the supervision of a project or organisational manager;
- has autonomy in managing end-to-end subprojects or small projects;
- has authority to assign tasks to team members and require progress reports;
- can implement corrective actions for small project deviations.

Typical competencies and experience for a project leader include:

- has attained expert level in the relevant project technical area;
- has a general understanding of project management principles;
- can estimate times and costs for project tasks;
- has the ability to organise work for self and others;
- has basic leadership and general management skills;
- has the basic communication and negotiation capabilities that one would expect from the leader of a technical group.

PROJECT COORDINATOR

A project coordinator will typically handle day-to-day activities of subprojects or simple independent projects under the direct supervision of a project or organisational manager. This is usually a person with proven organising skills and understanding of main project management processes, even if (in many cases) there has been no formal training in the area. The role usually evolves from a project assistant, but it could also originate from a lateral move from a business area, end user or even a trained office clerk.

As the project coordinator might not have the technical expertise to estimate or truly understand the task interdependencies, the project team members mostly work independently, with the coordinator acting in a facilitating and reporting capacity. The project coordinator will monitor task execution (start, progress and completion) and update corresponding documents, maintain and issue change logs (change registers) and organise project meetings and their associated tasks (see Chapter 34 for the conduct of meetings).

The project coordinator who wishes to advance towards a project manager role will typically need to acquire leadership and stakeholder management skills.

Typical duties and responsibilities of a project coordinator will include:

- monitoring task execution (start, progress and completion);
- updating project documents such as progress schedules and change logs, issue logs, expenses and so on;
- organising project meetings, including preparation and distribution of materials as well as recording the minutes and following up on action items;
- assisting the project or organisational manager in the coordination of day-to-day activities;
- understand and perform some control functions as assigned by the project manager;
- maintaining, and sometimes developing, the project schedule.

Typical authority level for a project coordinator:

- operates under the supervision of a project or organisational manager;
- has autonomy in progressing end-to-end subprojects or small projects;
- can require progress reports and other relevant project information;
- can implement corrective actions for small project deviations.

Typical competencies and experience levels for a project coordinator:

- knowledge of project management concepts and techniques;
- good knowledge of information-gathering techniques, procedures and practices;
- ability to coordinate project activities within assigned responsibilities;
- effective oral and written communication skills with people at all organisational levels;
- ability to cope with several tasks simultaneously according to their priorities.

Conclusion

The roles described in this chapter are not exhaustive. They are based on research indicating the current state and trends observed in most companies. I have outlined the more senior roles that operate in many project organisations. Although I have described these as typical, as I indicated in my introduction there is no standardisation of job titles throughout all the different industries and organisations that conduct projects. However, I have provided a good general coverage of typical project management roles (whatever their actual job titles might be in practice). This subject continues in the following chapter.

16 *People in Supporting Roles*

GEORGE JUCAN

This chapter continues on from Chapter 15 to describe people involved in project work. Here I focus on those who support project management, but are typically not dedicated to any single initiative.

Introduction

Many supporting roles in projects are typically found in a project management office (PMO) – sometimes named a programme or portfolio management office. Regardless of the PMO type, these roles have at least a supporting function to provide projects with the specialised expertise needed for particular activities. This expertise can be in different areas, from advice in implementing the project management methodology, to executing some specialised tasks, such as scheduling or implementing cost control.

Other people who have a portion of their time assigned to projects can be found in departments such as finance, human resources, procurement and so on. Small simple projects may be able to contain all potential issues within the project boundaries. However, for large or complex projects, it is quite common for some activities to be 'outsourced' to other organisational departments. A traditional example is procurement, where the project manager would define the needs but the actual acquisition is handled by a specialised department. The same applies to recruitment, and so on.

The remainder of this chapter will describe common roles encountered in most organisations. I have to acknowledge these might have other titles specific to the industrial domain of the project. In some organisations there might even be shared resource roles not described here.

PMO Roles

One of the most important functions of a PMO is to provide a human resource pool of project management professionals that can be rapidly deployed to assist or even perform project activities. For the PMO to be able to fulfil this function it must have available the mix of skills and expertise appropriate for the type of projects executed by the organisation. As mentioned above, some of these skills might only be needed by individual projects for a limited amount of time, so pooling them within the PMO allows the organisation flexibility to balance the project needs and the resource availability.

Whilst some PMOs include project managers in their staff, once any of these are assigned to a project they usually fulfil that role for the entire project duration. As such they are in fact fulfilling the project manager's role described in the previous chapter.

In this chapter I shall focus on other PMO roles that support the project managers in their activity, such as project schedulers, planners and controllers. These are project personnel with advanced technical skills in specialised areas. Some other supporting roles also help the project managers by freeing their time from administrative tasks, information collection, report generation, storing and classifying project documents and so on.

Outsourcing the 'science' part of project management to specialists allows the project manager to focus more on stakeholder management, communication, achieving the project objectives and other 'soft' activities.

PMO MANAGER

A typical PMO manager has the knowledge of a senior project manager, but on day-to-day duties acts mostly as a line manager. The PMO manager provides leadership, organisation and coordination to PMO staff during their activities (either within the PMO or on projects supported by the PMO).

Combining organisational and project management knowledge, PMO managers ensure development, application and advancement of project management principles, methodology and framework throughout the enterprise. They promote and support the continuous improvement of project management related processes and manage the change introduced by such improvements.

The PMO manager's role also includes enabling and maintaining a uniform approach to project management across the organisation, ensuring that all projects administered by the PMO adhere to the methodology, standards and best practices for project management. The PMO manager will assign appropriate resources to each project to perform, coordinate or monitor the project's activities from a project management perspective.

The PMO manager's duties may vary depending on the type of PMO (supportive, controlling and so on), but they will typically include:

- managing the members of the PMO, providing leadership, coordination and management to PMO activities;
- ensuring a uniform approach across an organisation of project related control/analysis/reporting processes;
- acting as a change agent for continuous improvement by advocating the adoption of project management capabilities enrichment;
- ensuring that PMO staff and the project managers leading projects receive appropriate guidance, mentoring and coaching to apply current methodology and standards and continue to develop their personal capabilities;
- negotiating with executives the application of project management in the organisation, and the role and responsibilities of the PMO;
- participating in organisational process improvement, either as advisor or as decision maker.

Typical levels of authority for the manager of a PMO would include:

- time and activities assignment of PMO members;
- overseeing enterprise project management strategy, processes, training, communication and so on, as well as the development and enhancement of required processes, templates and tools;
- endorsing or approving project initiations;
- approving changes to the project management methodology and best practices;
- approving methodology adjustments for specific projects.

For successful performance of duties, the competencies of a PMO manager would include:

- organisational management abilities as for any line manager;
- advanced knowledge of project management standards, methodologies, tools and techniques;
- ability to manage, coach, mentor, train other staff, including project managers;
- advanced communication skills in negotiation, influencing, persuasion and so on.

PROJECT METHODOLOGIST

Some organisations create their project management methodology through a collective effort of PMO members (or of the entire project management body coordinated by the PMO). However, if the required skill set is not present in the organisation, or the project management community is not cohesive enough (for example, PMO), some organisations rely on dedicated full-time employees or external consultants to create and maintain a methodological approach to project management.

The project methodologist is usually a project manager with proven knowledge of standards and methodologies applicable in the area of activity. The methodologist should also have a good understanding of the organisation's particularities to be able to customise a proven standard (such as PMBOK) or acquired methodology to the specific needs of that organisation. On rare occasions the project methodologist will be required to write an entire custom-made methodology specific for that organisation.

In some organisations, the project methodologist is known as 'subject matter expert in project management, which mercifully shortens to SME PM. The SME PM will have advanced overall project management knowledge and demonstrated expertise in one or more specialised areas, such as cost control, scheduling, risk or quality. The typical duties of a project methodologist include:

- developing and implementing project management standards, methodologies, frameworks and processes;
- recommending and implementing enhancements to tools and templates to increase efficiency within the PMO;
- providing guidance and mentoring to project managers regarding the application of methodology for individual projects;
- assessing and approving requests for customisation of the methodology or exemption from mandatory processes for a specific project;
- participating in organisational process improvement.

The project methodologist typically has the authority to:

- oversee the development, improvement and application of project management methodology, processes and so on, as well as the development and enhancement of required processes, templates and tools;
- approve changes to the project management methodology, framework or best practices;
- approve methodology adjustments for specific projects.

The competencies required from a project methodologist include:

- advanced knowledge of project management standards, methodologies, tools and techniques;
- analytical and problem-solving skills;
- advanced oral and written communication capabilities;
- understanding organisational strategic directions and project management's contribution to organisational strategy;
- advanced education (degree or certification) in project management;
- prior experience in hands-on management of projects;
- ability to coach, mentor and train other project managers.

RELATIONSHIPS MANAGER

PMOs in medium and large organisations often have a dedicated person acting as relationships manager (also known as business client manager or account manager – not to be confused with the sales function that also carries the title account manager). This role manages the overall relationship between the PMO and the business lines initiating projects, as well as the project teams delivering them.

The relationship manager is a value added partner to the project teams who takes over a significant portion of stakeholder management activities. Having a relationship with both the business client and delivery team, this person acts as an independent advisor, providing objective insight, identifying potential risks and response strategies, identifying and managing problems and so on. When conflict arises, the relationship manager acts as a negotiator between the two parties, facilitating constructive resolutions that move the project forward whilst aligning with the business needs and objectives.

This job typically includes the following responsibilities:

- serving as main contact point within the PMO for both business clients and delivery teams, balancing delivery needs with the strategic organisational goals;
- helping project teams to identify issues, escalate when needed and manage the issue resolution process until achieving an acceptable solution;
- monitoring project status to anticipate potential problems;
- providing feedback on best practices, communication processes and engagement models;
- promoting the adoption of project management standards and best practices as defined by the PMO;
- communicating regularly with both business clients and delivery teams using a variety of written and oral delivery channels.

In most cases the relationships manager does not have significant authority over the business line or the delivery teams. However, the role might have some decision power on:

- escalating issues and managing the resolution process to an outcome acceptable for both parties;
- the negotiation or arbitration of conflicts between business client and delivery team.

Being a very complex role, a relationships manager would require a varied set of competencies such as:

- understanding the business needs and incorporating them correctly in business cases to support decision-making processes for the initiation and prioritisation of projects;
- experience with project management methodologies, frameworks and processes;
- experience with the organisation's project delivery process;
- developing and managing business relationships at all levels;
- experience with the project governance structure;
- proven executive ability to balance efficiency and effectiveness;
- excellent communication skills, written, presentation and oral negotiation skills.

RESOURCE MANAGER

The role of resource manager is usually found in medium and large organisations that use a matrix reporting structure. The resource manager is responsible for the development, implementation and ongoing management of resource planning practices and processes, in order to ensure that current and planned projects are staffed with the necessary resources at the time they are needed. As the success of many projects depends on having the right resources available, the resource manager has to balance the projects' human resources requirements with the organisational need that scarce or key resources are utilised as efficiently as possible.

The resource manager will work with the other PMO members, with the project executives and with functional managers to develop and implement appropriate resource management methods and processes, and also to develop and maintain a long resource management plan that will not only satisfy immediate requirements but also forecast future needs and prevent resource shortfalls. The resource manager will also monitor the actual utilisation of shared resources, report trends in resources usage and adjust the plan as needed.

The typical responsibilities of a resource manager include:

- defining and managing the processes, tools and techniques necessary to identify, analyse, track, manage and resolve human resource issues that impact the projects;
- participating in the definition and implementation of PM methodologies from resource management perspective;
- interacting with the project and functional managers across the organisation to establish common practices in assignment and management of shared resources;
- negotiating the assignment of resources to resolve immediate project needs, and plans to fulfil future human resource needs for upcoming projects.

A resource manager's role could vary from negotiator to decision maker, so the corresponding authority will typically include:

- defining, improving and implementing the resource management process;
- managing the assignment of scarce human resources to multiple projects, in collaboration with the functional managers to whom these resources report;
- defining future human resource needs and coordinating with procurement areas to provision necessary resources;
- resolving or escalating issues related to the sharing of resources across multiple projects.

The competencies usually required for a resource manager are:

- general human resources management domain area knowledge;
- good understanding of organisation's standards and processes applicable to delivering projects;
- some audit and analysis experience, especially with regards to project governance, estimating, performance monitoring and so on.

PROJECT ESTIMATOR

A project estimator, as a specialist within the PMO, is assigned to projects to either create their initial estimates or to review the estimates put forth by the project. Under the direction and with support from the project manager, the project estimator will collect all required inputs and apply suitable methods to produce adequate task estimates.

In recent years, specialised project estimators have become more common in service delivery organisations where most contracts are obtained through bidding. In such organisations the project estimator is involved from the initial phases of each project, working with the sales group and/or the client to understand the project requirements, participating in solution definition and providing accurate estimates for the work involved. Sometimes this role is titled project cost estimator, but even when so it still has responsibilities in estimating the work and materials for each task before assessing the expected cost, so it is essentially the same role as described above. The main responsibilities of a project estimator are:

- work with assigned projects to gather detailed information regarding the project scope, assist with clarifying scope of work and create the task estimates and cost baseline for the project;
- participate in the preparation of the initialisation documents (project charter for internal projects or bid response for contracts);
- prepare and maintain historical records of workload and cost elements, such as wages and unit rates, direct and indirect field costs and overhead, material price lists, equipment, delivery times and so on;
- monitor actual cost data and their variances from baseline estimates, analyse those variances and trends to improve future estimates;
- evaluate scope changes for their impact on baseline estimates;
- define and improve estimating processes, procedures, databases and toolsets.

The project estimator's authority is quite limited, and usually only includes:

- defining, recommending and sometimes approving the estimating methodology and toolsets to be used by an organisation;
- certifying the baseline estimates as accurate, based on the collected information and organisational context.

The competencies usually required from a project estimator are:

- knowledge of estimating techniques and methods, as well as supporting disciplines such as statistics and forecasting, cost management and control, procurement;
- an appropriate level of experience in the industry domain to understand the scope of work of the projects being estimated;
- education and training in project management, or previous experience as a project manager;
- ability to interface and communicate effectively with others;
- strong analytical skills, with attention to quality and detail.

PROJECT PLANNER/SCHEDULER

The role of project planner is generally fulfilled by an expert in the area of scheduling who is either lent to projects to create their baseline schedule with the guidance of the project manager, or works with the multiple project managers to review and advise them related to their corresponding project schedules. In some cases the project planner will also have responsibilities in monitoring and controlling the schedule accomplishment and alerting the project manager about potential deviations from baseline.

The project planner interacts with the project manager, stakeholders and team to gather information required from a scheduling perspective, such as task effort and duration estimates, mandatory task dependencies as well as specific preferences for activity sequencing and so on. Based on this information the project planner will sequence the activities to optimise the path of a project through its entire life cycle from start to delivery.

Throughout the project execution the project planner may be assigned to identify potential impacts on the schedule baseline and approved milestones, as well as assessing the deviations and impacts on critical path(s), critical activities and float statistics.

Typical responsibilities of this role are:

- advise management, project managers and key stakeholders regarding scheduling concepts, theory and alternative approaches to scheduling activities in order to optimise project delivery;
- liaise, consult and negotiate with the project manager(s), stakeholders and team members in relation to scheduling project activities;
- recognise and analyse conflicting requirements and make recommendations for project adjustments to create an efficient schedule;
- produce various representations of the project schedule to suit different audiences;
- monitor schedule progress and archive actual schedule achievements to improve future estimates in similar conditions;

- evaluate schedule impacts arising from change requests or variations from baseline and provide advice on scheduling alternatives to implement corrective actions.

Typically a project planner has authority over:

- establishing project schedule and timelines in agreement with the project manager;
- analysing the validity of schedules submitted by project teams, or by outside parties contributing to the project;
- monitoring actual job progress and reporting progress and variations from the plan;
- forecasting the impacts of variations or proposed changes on schedule baseline;
- recommending policy or procedural revisions that will improve the scheduling process.

The project planner is normally expected to have the following competencies:

- understanding of project methodologies (for example, PMBOK and PRINCE2) with particular emphasis on scheduling processes, tools and techniques;
- understanding the business context of the project to identify dependencies between activities;
- knowledge of multiple analysis techniques, particularly in the area of schedule development and variations identification and assessment;
- being detail oriented and highly organised to ensure correctness and completeness of the schedule baseline;
- having excellent communication skills for working with multiple stakeholders and prioritising requests.

PROJECT CONTROLLER

The project controller role is typically found in medium and large corporations running a significant part of their activity as projects. This role is responsible for the monitoring and control functions of one or more projects, typically in the schedule and cost areas. These functions usually include monitoring the project schedule and schedule changes, as well as actual cost data collection and monitoring against budget baseline. On some occasions it also involves monitoring schedule float and critical path, work hours actually performed and resources load. The project controller might also assist management with identifying trends and forecasting budget requirements.

The project controller is typically responsible for the accuracy of project cost reports, resources load, and milestones information. Sometimes they also validate the other control mechanisms used by the project, such as issues log, action log, change logs and risk register.

A part of the role of a project controller is to ensure accuracy and completeness of actual data; it may also have the function to maintain a central repository of information to be used by future projects to improve estimating accuracy. In such cases the project controller will assist in establishing and improving project control and reporting methodology based on trends observed during the analysis of actual performance. The typical responsibilities of a project controller are:

- collect, analyse and interpret performance data;
- monitor task execution and progress;
- provide consolidated status reports to the PM;
- escalate to the PM risks and issues with potential significant impact.

Whilst in some organisations the project controller may have specific authorities, in general these are limited to:

- activating work under the supervision of a project manager;
- defining and improving the collection, processing, reporting and approval processes of performance data.

The project controller will not usually have line authority over project staff. The project controller is a specialist working in a specific area, and thus the required competencies are typically focused on:

- having formal training in project management principles and methodology, as well as in specific areas (mostly scheduling, cost and risks);
- advanced knowledge of project scheduling and monitoring tools;
- advanced financial skills, especially in preparation of cost performance reports and periodic financial statements;
- understanding of quality and cost control processes;
- demonstrated analytical ability;
- experience in summarising results and producing management reports.

PROJECT ADMINISTRATOR

A project assistant or administrator is usually regarded as a secretary or office clerk, performing routine tasks assigned by the project manager. If suitably trained, a project assistant could perform some project management tasks such as updating the schedule, monitoring people's availability, centralising and monitoring costs and so on.

After accumulating enough experience (based on the project manager's assessment) this position usually evolves into a project coordinator's role, is assigned subprojects and, later on, to independent small projects. Less often, a project assistant could transcend into a project specialist position such as schedule controller, cost controller and so on.

The typical responsibilities of a project administrator have some variations based on organisational context, but they generally include:

- collecting and archiving project forms (NDAs, copyright, technical set-up and so on);
- collecting and centralising regular status reports, time sheets, expenses and so on and distributing information as described in communication plans;
- scheduling and sometimes coordinating meetings, recording minutes and action items, and following up on action items to monitor process;
- assisting with the preparation and maintenance of project documents (for example, issue log and change requests), presentations and so on;
- maintaining the project documents repository, organising relevant specifications, notes, minutes and so on;

- sometimes involved in project accounting support, most likely for medium to large size projects;
- other project administration tasks.

The authority of a project administrator is derived from the project manager. As such it varies not only between organisations, but even between projects within the same organisation. Authority characteristics typically include:

- always under the guidance and supervision of the project manager;
- can initiate recurring tasks or predefined repetitive activities (such as calls for status reports, timesheets or expenses and following up on action items);
- within limits, can decide on timing and location of meetings to best fit the project and individual participant's schedule;
- can initiate and monitor project activities under instructions from project manager.
- Similar to other administrative positions, the project administrator requires at minimum the following competencies:
- general exposure to project management principles;
- understanding of financial management and reporting basics;
- organised, detail oriented and efficient in prioritising tasks;
- good oral, written and electronic communication skills for interaction with team members;
- able to follow instructions well, but also able to take the initiative when required;
- typically requires at minimum a high-school diploma or equivalent.

Organisation Roles

The previous section described people acting in supporting roles for projects, but typically shared between multiple projects. There are also resources that are normally part of operational activities that occasionally play a role in projects.

Subject matter experts (SMEs) are an important organisational resource contributing to one or more projects under execution at the same time. Because of their in-depth knowledge of the corresponding domain, line of business representatives are indispensable for normal operations as well as for any project touching the business area. Both routine operations and projects need SMEs to be successful, so SMEs have to share a portion of their time for each initiative.

Other organisational resources occasionally used within projects are procurement, training and quality assurance. These are typically organised as separate departments and most of their activity is focused on operational activities. They have involvement in projects only when needed. In each department there might be many roles that interact with projects, I am not proposing to analyse each one in detail. Rather, I shall describe within each a representative project role within each function.

SME

SMEs, also known as domain experts, are individuals who have in-depth knowledge of a business area and are able to provide the details needed by the project team. Their normal duties may be in the actual domain (for example, engineers or accountants), or in managing or in observing the business domain (such as business/process/systems analysts).

If the project sponsor owns the requirements process, the SMEs provide the content to explain clearly the scope items. They create and manage changes to one or more requirement specification documents. SMEs are expected to provide input to the project in the form of work recommendations, but they also have the responsibility of reviewing the deliverables of the team on behalf of the project sponsor.

The responsibilities of SMEs vary greatly between organisations, business lines and projects. Some of their typical responsibilities are:

- collecting requirements from other users, resolving conflicts between proposed requirements and describing them in formal documents;
- evaluating the impact of proposed requirements changes on users and business processes;
- specifying user acceptance criteria to be used in evaluating the project deliverables;
- ensuring that the organisation is ready to realise the desired business benefits once the project deliverables are transferred to the executing organisation.

For the same considerations described above the authority of SMEs in projects is extremely diverse, but it typically includes:

- reviewing and signing off requirements, process flows, gaps and design documents;
- participating in defining implementation priorities and making change decisions;
- performing deliverables validation and being accountable for final acceptance;
- becoming a champion and contact point for using the project's deliverables in achieving desired objectives.

The competencies required for SMEs are specific for their domain area and therefore not detailed herein.

PROCUREMENT

This category encompasses multiple roles in the area of procurement and contracting, such as procurement specialist, purchasing officer, purchasing agent, contract administrator and subcontract liaison. In many organisations the procurement function is centralised, and specialist groups execute procurement processes for service, supplies and facilities management contracts. These groups provide advice, management and coordination of procurement related activities within the organisation.

A procurement officer utilises the resources list and specifications provided by project managers and will perform a market assessment, locate vendors and negotiate contracts to obtain the best possible products or services that meet the needs at the best possible price. During project execution the procurement officer works with vendors to ensure delivery as scheduled, liaises with vendors for any problems that may occur and ensures that vendors are paid at the right time. The procurement officer's role has various responsibilities based on the actual organisation and job function. As it relates to projects, the main activities include:

- managing the tender lists and obtaining tenders from potential vendors;
- coordinating the appraisal and evaluation of bids on the basis of predefined criteria;
- negotiating with suppliers for best purchasing package in terms of quality, price, term, delivery and service;
- ensuring execution of all necessary purchases according to the relevant contracts;
- coordinating with the project team and suppliers to resolve potential problems;
- documenting procurement activities, procedures and decisions and making improvement recommendations as appropriate.

The most usual authorities of a procurement officer in a project context are:

- conducting meetings to identify purchasing requirements;
- deciding the most appropriate procurement strategy;
- managing the tendering, selection and contract negotiation processes;
- placing or approving purchase orders based on contractual agreements;
- authorising payments to suppliers for correctly fulfilled purchase orders.

To support project activities effectively, the procurement officer needs competencies such as:

- formal education in procurement activities and some knowledge of project management practices;
- ability to communicate at a senior level and to contribute proactively and positively in a team environment;
- able to think creatively and develop innovative strategies based on a good knowledge of procurement rules and policies;
- a high level of verbal and written communication skills to communicate complex contractual matters in a logical, clear and concise manner.

TRAINING

The training departments are responsible for continuous capabilities improvement of individuals and teams, responding to organisational business needs. Specific duties of training staff include designing the educational curriculum, preparation of instructional materials for training and facilitation of training courses both live and online.

The training manager will normally consult with organisational management to identify training needs not only to respond to current skill gaps but also to build competencies that will support the strategic direction of the organisation. Based on the organisation's needs and research on supporting behavioural and knowledge objectives, the training department designs an appropriate curriculum that includes a set of training materials targeted to ensure that staff gain and develop the skills they need to carry out their jobs effectively. People working in training departments are typically responsible for:

- designing training materials to cover both the organisation's current and future needs;
- organising and managing the various training programmes within an organisation;
- delivery of a variety of training courses as included in the training curriculum.

The authorities of a training manager are typically limited to:

- defining the overall training plan;
- managing a training budget;
- producing materials for in-house training;
- assessing the success of both individual training and the overall curriculum for continuous improvement.

Being a complex role with interactions practically with the entire organisation, the competencies listed below as being common for trainers are just a starting point:

- one-on-one and group presentation and facilitation skills, with ability to encourage and motivate people on an improvement path;
- excellent verbal and written communication skills, with particular focus on conflict resolution and negotiating;
- strong interpersonal skills and relationship building, with sensitivity for cultural differences;
- understanding of the organisation's business, policies and practices;
- analysis, research and problem-solving skills.

QUALITY ASSURANCE

The quality assurance roles vary greatly by the type of industry, but they also have several common elements that are similar in every organisation. These can be summarised by the responsibility to develop and enforce quality management policies, procedures and systems to eliminate or at least significantly reduce the number and severity of defects for deliverables.

A quality assurance specialist reviews and participates in the clarification of business requirements, and sometime even participates in initial consultations with the client for the purpose of understanding the project scope. The testing plan or quality specification is created based on the parameters outlined during the client consultations to ensure conformance to requirements. Testing metrics are recorded and monitored to track the outcomes of the testing process and progress towards the desired level of quality for project deliverables. The typical responsibilities of a quality assurance specialist are to:

- review and improve the current policies, processes and quality standards;
- develop and coordinate test plans, ensuring that plans are complete and will completely validate the deliverables;
- lead or perform software quality assurance activities according to the test plan;
- determine and document any areas that might need improvement;
- review and validate the effectiveness of the modifications made;
- maintain product consistency throughout each product cycle, to include all stages through quality checkpoints and testing.

Within projects, the quality assurance specialist usually has the authority to:

- decide the quality assurance processes and procedures that will be used to validate the deliverables;
- approve the deliverables' advancement through quality checkpoints as defined in the approved test plan;
- approve the deliverables' release to the client based on successful test results;
- evaluate disadvantages of the process and suggest solution improvements including (but not limited to) changing processes, products or quality assurance standards, where warranted.

Quality managers must ideally possess qualities such as:

- knowledge of tools, concepts and methodologies of quality management, including all relevant ISO quality and performance standards;
- experience with implementation and administration of quality assurance metrics, such as defect profiles and performance to entry/exit criteria;
- effective communication and report writing skills;
- analytical skills and advanced problem-solving capabilities.

Conclusion

This chapter described organisational roles or people who would normally dedicate all or a part of their time to working in one or more projects. These are generally highly specialised resources in short supply in the organisation. They are thus too expensive to be dedicated to a single project (where they may not have 100 per cent utilisation), so they are usually shared resources.

Depending on the complexity of the organisation and on the industrial area of activity there will be project roles in addition to those listed here, such as engineers, architects, knowledge managers, surveyors and so on.

A project's success relies significantly on the collaboration between dedicated and shared resources, and their ability to work as a single team despite the diverse nature, perspective and priorities derived from their level of involvement. Therefore one of the most important duties of the project manager is to enable, influence and support a cohesive team contributing towards the same goal regardless of any such differences. That is not an easy task, but it is one of the most rewarding when successful.

17 *The Project Office Environment*

DENNIS LOCK

This is the first of three chapters in which the physical working environment of project workers is considered. In this chapter the concern is with those who work in offices, with particular attention to the project management function for a medium to large size project.

Management Responsibility for the Office Environment

Ultimately, of course, office working conditions are the responsibility of senior management. It is they who set the accommodation budgets, approve designs and decide the location of office buildings. In all but the smallest of companies, day-to-day responsibility for setting up and maintaining office accommodation will usually be assigned to an administration manager or facilities manager. With few exceptions administration and facilities managers do not report to project managers.

There are exceptions to most rules. I can think of two for this reporting rule. One is for construction or other outdoor projects where the part of the project management function will be given office accommodation in a temporary building, such as a hut or one or more Portakabins. Another exception would be a joint venture project, for which a limited liability company might be established and housed entirely in its own premises – in which case that joint venture company's CEO will effectively also be the overall project manager. But for most projects, project managers and their team members will be asked to work in offices that are provided for them and managed by others.

Every project manager cannot help being aware that the performance of those who carry out project tasks will be affected either advantageously or detrimentally by their working environment and the office equipment provided for them. An inappropriate office layout can hinder good interpersonal communications. Malfunctioning equipment, poor lighting, inadequate ventilation, unreliable telephone systems, difficult access to an efficient photocopier or printer can all disrupt and delay work. Even a broken or dirty vending machine can divert the attention of people from their project duties, cause general discontent and add indirectly to project costs and delays.

So it is for project managers' best interests, and in the interests of their projects, that they should support observations (usually a euphemism for complaints) from their staff concerning any shortcoming in the office environment. Sometimes, perhaps in older buildings, allowance has to be made for conditions that are less than perfect. But remedies that *can* be made *should* be made.

RESPONSIBILITY FOR ALLOCATING OFFICE SPACE

Most project managers would be delighted to be asked how much space they need for their team. More usually they will simply be told 'You can put your people in there'. It often happens that the team cannot all be accommodated in one area, or on one floor level, or even (as has been my experience) in the same building. In one case our project teams were in London but our purchasing department was 50 miles away.

There is often great difficulty in planning and organising space in a projects-orientated organisation that habitually handles several projects simultaneously. Staffing numbers for individual projects change frequently as they travel through their life cycles. Project organisations are dynamic, and thus so are their office space needs. To be practical, therefore, the office planner has to regard the total office accommodation for a portfolio or programme of projects. Depending on the company organisation structure and titles given to its managers, that means it would be the programme director or projects director who would be more directly concerned with agreeing the allocation of space between projects.

Legislation

In developed countries legislation will be in place that is designed to protect workers, both from the physical aspect of their working environment and in connection with their health and wellbeing. In the UK the principal relevant legislation for office environments is embodied in the Offices, Shops and Railway Premises Act, 1963 and the Health and Safety at Work Act, 1974, together with subsequent amendments.

There are also many supplementary regulations, some of which are less relevant here because they deal with matters such as hazardous substances that are more applicable to manual workers or to those directly responsible for maintenance of the premises.

In the UK, penalties attach to those responsible who are in breach of the law. In many cases the conditions stipulated by the Offices, Shops and Railway Premises Act are minimum standards, and it will often be in the best interests of office workers and their productivity to provide working conditions that exceed them.

The Health and Safety Executive (HSE) publishes a wide range of leaflets that can either be bought from HSE Books or (more conveniently) downloaded free at http://www. hse.gov.uk/pubns. That website will guide you to the catalogue of all HSE publications.

Regulations will also cover fire precautions. These include ensuring that fire extinguishers or fire extinguishing systems are provided and regularly checked and maintained. In the UK companies are expected to keep log books to record these regular inspections. Particularly important in fire regulations is that everyone has access to a means of escape, and that usually means that stairwells and corridors have to be kept clear of obstructions and combustible matter, and protected from smoke by doors that can withstand fire for a specified period (usually one hour). Such doors must not be wedged open, although arrangements can be made for them to be held open on magnetic catches that automatically release and allow the doors to close if the fire detection systems are activated.

Elevators may not be used for escape, because people could get trapped in them. Maybe I'm getting into a little too much detail here, but fire precautions are clearly extremely important and must be enforced. For example some office workers will wedge doors open or stack things in corridors if they are not watched.

Planning the Office Layout

The first requirement in planning office space is to know how many people are going to occupy the office space and what kind of accommodation each person will need.

HOW MANY PEOPLE NEED TO BE ACCOMMODATED?

Strictly we should be considering how many people need to be accommodated simultaneously, because in any company some people will always be absent from their desks at any given time. That is particularly true of commissioning engineers and others (such as sales engineers) who are often working on clients' premises or making sales visits. Such itinerant people could be asked to share working spaces: for example it might be possible to allocate three workstations or desks to five commissioning engineers.

For current estimates and predictions of staffing in the immediate future, the numbers must come from the project resource estimates, coupled with a study of organisation charts and so on to identify the unscheduled overhead and administrative support staff.

Every prudent company should have its forward plans, perhaps extending for five years into the future and updated annually. An essential ingredient of those plans will be the staffing predictions, a subject that is touched upon in Chapter 42.

If your company is successful and expanding, it will be necessary to plan for space for the future additional staff and equipment. That might mean planning to occupy more premises. But if there is sufficient spare space in the existing offices that issue should be easier to manage. One rule here is to designate any space destined for future expansion, cordon it off, and leave it empty. Unlike a farmer's set-aside field you will get no compensation, but unless you forbid any occupation at all you will discover inevitably that your existing workforce will find some way of moving into the beckoning unoccupied areas and spread themselves.

OPEN-PLAN OR CLOSED OFFICES?

People like to have their own enclosed offices. It gives them a feeling of authority and status. They will argue, if challenged, that they need an office for holding meetings with their subordinates or visitors. But do they all need individual offices all the time? Enclosed offices are wasteful of floor space, cause ventilation and air-conditioning problems, increase the cost of services such as fire detection systems and, most important of all, can impede natural and vital interpersonal communications. So consideration should be given to providing spare offices that can be easily reserved and used for an hour or so by individuals whenever their need arises.

Open-plan offices are the most efficient users of space and are the easiest to ventilate or air condition. They also provide the quickest means of escape in a fire. Provided that people are placed in groups according to their functions, they allow for easy communications. But fully open-plan offices do not always provide *good* communications because of the many visual and aural distractions.

Visual distractions can be reduced by the use of portable screens with a height of about one metre or slightly more. Acoustic screens, sound-absorbing ceilings and furnishings greatly reduce noise levels. Printers and other office equipment are generally far quieter than the typewriters and printers that once existed, so are now less likely to cause irritation. General conversation and movement are more likely to be the principal distracting factors.

However, it is well known that an open office that is deathly silent brings its own problems because confidential conversation is impossible – a word spoken at one end of the office can be heard clearly at the other. Also, anyone who has ever worked in an anechoic chamber will know just how unsettling complete silence can be. So architects and planners sometimes allow for the injection of a small amount of white noise (noise that covers the entire audio frequency spectrum) into the office space. Air-conditioning systems sometimes produce sufficient low-level noise by themselves.

People need a sense of belonging and the comfort of a nest or home, a space that they can call their own in the office. That can usually be provided in an open-plan office simply and relatively cheaply by arranging desks, bookcases and portable screens to form personal cells. When individuals sit at their desks, they can then have a degree of privacy.

POSSIBLE LAYOUT CONFIGURATIONS

There are many ways in which people, furniture, equipment and partitions can be arranged. But here are six principal traditional possibilities:

1. Put as many people as possible in individual private offices.
2. Put as many people as possible in private offices, but have them sharing (say two to each office).
3. Have most people distributed over a large office floor, but separate them with fixed partitions that are something like two metres tall (not reaching the ceiling and allowing air to flow above).
4. Provide furniture that has its own raised screens or shelving attached, so that people sit at work stations that surround them on two or three sides (these are sometimes called carrels).
5. Have people distributed over the office floor in a non-geometrical arrangement, with free-standing screens and plants to give them some feeling of privacy or a space that they can own. This is sometimes called landscaping, or open-space planning. The concept was introduced and perfected by the German company Bürolandschaft over 50 years ago.
6. Set desks out in a grid pattern in an open-plan arrangement. This harks back to Victorian times but the arrangement is still sometimes seen, for example in some call centres.

Principal characteristics	Enclosed offices (private)	Enclosed offices (shared)	Fixed half-height partitions	Work stations (carrels)	Open space (landscape)	Open plan (grid layout)
Privacy for the individual	●●●●	●●	●●	●●●	●●●	●
Freedom from distraction	●●●●	●	●●	●●●	●●●	●●
Ease of personal communication	●	●●	●●●	●●	●●●●	●●●●
Flexibility to change	●	●	●●	●●	●●●●	●●●
Ease of supervision	●	●●	●●	●	●●●	●●●●
Economic space utilisation	●	●●	●●	●●●	●●●●	●●●●

Best: ●●●●   Worst: ●

Figure 17.1 Comparison of some possible office layouts

Figure 17.1 tabulates and compares some of the advantages and disadvantages of the above arrangements. But one also needs to ask the question 'How pleasant or unpleasant will the occupants perceive their work environment?' All these can be motivating or demotivating factors. Clearly one needs to avoid the unfriendly, regimented look of the open-plan. However, open space is a different story and can provide pleasant working surroundings whilst still allowing efficient and flexible use of the accommodation.

PREPARING A SPACE REQUIREMENTS SCHEDULE

Most space planners will need to be given a list not only of the number of people to be housed, but also of the way in which that number breaks down into the different grades or job specialisations. Someone senior has to make (or agree) a decision that sets out how much space each person in each staff grade should be allocated as a minimum. Space requirements are not always based on grade or status, because some office workers will need more equipment than others and that will determine their minimum space needs. But it is usually possible to compile a schedule that lists the various staff grades to be employed down one column, with an adjoining column setting out the individual space allowance for each individual within each of those grades.

DISTRIBUTION OF PEOPLE THROUGHOUT THE LAYOUT

Ideally layouts should be arranged so that people are distributed throughout the office area according to their communication patterns. Those expected to communicate most often with each other should not be placed too far apart. Much of this will depend on the type of organisation chosen (team, matrix or hybrid, as described in chapters 9 and 10).

With a matrix organisation, the specialist functional groups have more permanence than those specialisations would have in a pure project team, so the office layout would probably be arranged to accommodate each specialist group together, along with its specialist manager. Matrix organisations are easier to manage than team organisations when planning space, because the organisation is more stable and less likely to change as projects move through the company.

It is possible to carry out a study to determine the lengths of the physical communication paths between different people and marry that to the number of times people communicate with each other. This has been done by methods as simple as hammering pins into a board, with the board representing the office space and each pin representing a person or group of people. Communication channels are represented by pieces of string tied between the relevant pins and a string diagram results.

More flexible and practical solutions rely on charting methods, for example with lines ruled to represent the communication channels on drawn plans of proposed layouts. In many, if not most cases, simple common sense will provide the answers.

KNOWING HOW MUCH SPACE IS AVAILABLE

Office space is still often quoted in square feet in many countries, but whether square feet or square metres are used the office planner will need to know several things about that space. One vital thing is to know whether the space available is the gross or the net area. The gross area will include space for corridors, walkways, stairwells and so forth. Even a stated net area must be examined to ensure that space is allowed for such things as photocopiers, vending machines and designated walkways. What the office planner is really interested in is the *net useable space*.

PLANNING AIDS

An architect's or surveyor's plans of the areas to be occupied is essential. These should be obtained as a master drawing (or master file in the CAD system) for each floor or major area. Each master drawing should show the positions of windows, fixed internal walls, doors, supporting columns (what a nuisance they can sometimes be – they always seem to be in the most awkward spots!) and so on. The master for each floor level can be used over and over again for different purposes – furniture layouts, cabling diagrams and so forth can be overlaid upon the masters.

The planner has the choice of using cardboard cut-out templates to represent the various desks and other pieces of equipment, or using a suitable computer drawing application.

A Suggested Office Layout for the Project Management Function

For the core project team, which might comprise a project manager, the project management office (PMO) and associated secretaries or clerical staff, it makes sense to arrange the accommodation in a cluster. One such arrangement is shown in Figure 17.2.

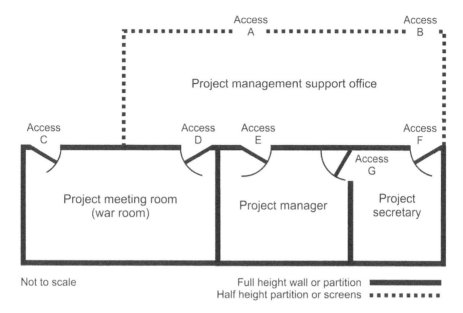

Figure 17.2 Possible office layout for a project management function

This example would be suitable for one fairly large project or where the manager and the control team handle a succession of smaller projects. There are a number of points to note about this layout.

OFFICE ARRANGEMENT FOR THE PROJECT MANAGER

The project manager has a private office, but its door (Access E in Figure 17.2) allows easy access to the project management office (PMO) and the wider world. The door can be locked for private interviews (perhaps when counselling a member of staff) but should normally be unlocked during office hours.

The project manager's secretary in this case has a private office because secretaries often have to handle or prepare documents or hold conversations that must be kept confidential. Other secretaries and clerical staff can be housed with the PMO.

The project manager must regard having a private office as a privilege, and not as a barrier to other project staff on the project team. Remember that project managers will motivate others best if they adopt a 'management by walking about' policy. The following case example is from my own experience and, I assure you, is true in every respect.

CASE EXAMPLE NO. 1: A CAUTIONARY TALE

A director of projects was accommodated in an office arrangement like that shown for the project manager and secretary in Figure 17.2 except that there was no adjoining PMO. Both offices were beautifully furnished with personally chosen reproduction antique furniture.

In this case the door at Access E was always locked. Anyone wishing to see the project director had first to negotiate Access F, then face the secretary, and then pass through Access G into the inner sanctum. Too often staff were greeted by the secretary with a message that amounted to 'access denied'.

From the open-plan offices immediately outside it was not possible to see whether the project director was at home or away. Indeed he was rarely seen. Those open-plan offices housed about 50 highly skilled designers, working on several large capital projects. The designers resented the fact that the project director took no personal interest in them, never stepped out of his office to talk about their work or give them any encouragement.

Thus a rumour grew that there was no project director. He was a myth and did not exist. There was only an empty office guarded by the secretary. Although amusing in retrospect, there was hostility behind that rumour and it became a powerful demotivator. And the office layout had much to do with that.

PMO

Typical functions of a PMO include cost estimating and cost control, planning and scheduling, contract administration, risk management, change control, progress monitoring and reporting and so forth. It is usually convenient for these functions to be within easy reach of the project manager, and the arrangement in Figure 17.2 would allow for that.

Note that the project support staff are shown partitioned off in their own enclosure, but those partitions are not full height and there are no doors – only gaps in the partitions. This illustrates a general point about office planning, which is that local government planning authorities can frown upon full-height partitions with enclosing doors here because then the project manager's office and the secretary's office would both become 'rooms within rooms'. Apart from problems with ventilation, rooms within rooms are considered a hazard because they increase the chances of people being trapped in the event an emergency.

PROJECT MEETING ROOM

Project people need ready access to a room where they can hold meetings and put out schedules, drawings and other documents (perhaps displayed on walls). These meetings will sometimes be formal and at other times informal. They might be regular meetings, one-off diary events or ad hoc meetings called on the spur of the moment.

Ideally the project meeting room should be regarded as a kind of club room or war room for the project team. The room should be provided with locking doors, so that confidential plans and schedules can be left out pinned to walls when the room is vacated (say for luncheon breaks or even overnight). This room can become the physical heart of the project management function. It should be located as near to the project manager and the PMO as possible.

The meeting room needs to be furnished with a long table so that large documents can be laid flat for everyone to gather round and examine. For schedules that need to be displayed semi-permanently, one tip is to fix a painted flat mild steel strip along one wall, so magnets can be used to support long documents (a fridge magnet kind of arrangement that I have seen used with great success).

Whatever communications equipment is necessary in the meeting room should be for the benefit of those present at project meetings rather than for those intent on interrupting the proceedings. For example, telephones should not be listed in directories and should be set for outgoing calls only.

The Visual Environment

APPEARANCE AND DÉCOR

Of course the layout is only part of the office design. When given the opportunity, designing the furnishings and décor can be a creative and rewarding task.

Carpets using artificial fibres are hard wearing, usually non-slip, and relatively cheap and easy to clean. They are preferable to hard surfaces for many reasons. However, they can become charged with static electricity in dry conditions, so the office humidity will have to be controlled unless people start getting irritating shocks from door handles or, worse, computing equipment is compromised.

I have worked in a company where the occupiers of individual offices were allowed to choose their own colour schemes, and this led to some bizarre combinations (my own office walls were a bright mustard yellow, which produced dramatic effects when they caught the afternoon sun).

The most pleasant (and also very practical) colour schemes for floors, walls and furnishings use coordinated browns and mid greens. These are the colours of nature and of humankind's early existence, and it seems that we are still programmed to prefer those.

One of the most attractive suites of offices I ever knew was finished in different but coordinated warm shades of brown (except for the white ceilings) and that created a cosy atmosphere that all the staff appreciated. Yes, that was indeed a really happy place in which to work, and that kind of satisfaction can only increase motivation and productivity.

LIGHTING

Light has several qualities that must be taken into account for office work. Not everyone agrees on the amount of light that should be provided, but there is no doubt that illumination should be:

- distributed as evenly as possible (for example avoiding dark walls or ceilings);
- associated with the above, avoiding shadows (for example behind supporting columns);
- diffused so that there is no glare, either from the luminaires or from objects in the office;
- constant (without flicker);
- of sufficient intensity for the work being performed;
- with a colour value that approximates to white light (daylight) as nearly as possible.

With energy conservation in mind, it is important that as much of the electrical energy required for lighting is converted into light rather than heat, and for that purpose fluorescent lamps are indicated for general lighting in offices (other forms of low-energy luminaires are available for industrial premises). Desk lamps using white light-emitting diodes (LEDs) are very efficient for highlighting task areas where very fine detail has to be observed.

Lighting Intensity

Illumination intensity is measured in lux. One lux is a light intensity of one lumen evenly distributed over an area of one square metre. It is usual to take the measurement on a flat desktop.

General standards for office lighting are usually in the range of about 800 to 1,000 lux. Where people are working on art layouts or designs using drawing boards, or doing other work that requires close attention to detail levels above 1,000 lux might be preferable.

I knew of one American company where the design offices were illuminated at a massive 2,000 lux, because the company directors understood that their engineers were expected to work to very fine design limits on complicated drawings. I spent some time in those offices and found them to be free from glare, not uncomfortably bright, and very pleasant places in which to exist and work. The luminaires were twin-tube fluorescent fittings mounted flush in a suspended ceiling, with polished 'egg-crate' diffusers to prevent glare, which has always been my own preferred method of general office lighting. At 2,000 lux, most of the ceiling space was taken up with the light fittings.

So common sense would say, illuminate your offices at 800 or 1,000 lux, but downgrade that to 500 lux for areas such corridors.

In meeting rooms it is useful to be able to draw dark opaque curtains across windows and fit dimmers to the artificial lights when projectors are to be used. However, most modern projectors – even portable ones – have been improved to the extent that they can operate in normal lighting conditions.

None of this takes into account the effect of natural light from windows, but of course natural light is not available in all seasons at all times of the working day or in offices with large floor areas. Some offices make allowance for light coming through windows by arranging their lights to be switchable in banks, so that luminaires nearest to the windows can be dimmed or switched off, either manually or automatically, when sunlight allows.

The design for lighting a new office will be based on the rated outputs of the luminaires. And herein lies another factor to be taken into account, which is that the output of fluorescent tubes falls off significantly during their life, with much of that deterioration happening relatively early. So architects should pitch their design standard somewhat higher than the required operating level to allow for the initial fall-off in performance of the luminaires. The facilities manager would probably be advised to operate a planned maintenance system in which fluorescent tubes are replaced at intervals (possibly annually) so that efficiency is maintained at reasonable levels and failures are avoided. Nothing irritates people as much as a failed tube that is constantly flashing on and off.

One danger to be avoided is to have sharp changes in illumination between the offices and non-working areas such as corridors and staircases. Eyes take time to adjust to different lighting levels, and although the illumination in transit areas is not required for work, safety becomes a consideration. Switches for such areas, especially staircases, are best placed in a central control room or some other place not accessible to general staff. I once had to have all the staircase lighting switches in a large London office building removed to a remote location because our energy-conscious managing director was in the habit of switching the lights off every time he used the stairs. There were no windows on those dark stairwells and safety arguments must clearly override energy-saving considerations.

Some offices have energy-saving measures that rely on movement sensors. After a preset period with no detectable movement in the office, the lights automatically switch off. Clearly the sensitivity of such systems is important. I once had the misfortune to be lecturing in a new university building in a seminar room with no outside windows where the lights kept switching off and plunging us all into pitch-black darkness at irregular intervals, irrespective of movement in the room.

Emergency Lighting

In most countries regulations will exist that call for the installation and regular maintenance of emergency lighting. These lights need only provide a level of illumination for a sufficient time that will allow the office occupants to make their way to the nearest fire exit should a fire start and the mains electricity supply fail. Emergency lights work from batteries that receive a constant charge from the mains supply and they operate automatically when there is a power cut (but not when the lights are switched off in the normal course of the day).

One risk with emergency lighting (as with many other office services) is neglect and poor maintenance. The lights work fine when they are first installed but unless they are regularly maintained will not operate in an emergency because their integral rechargeable batteries have come to the ends of their lives. So periodical testing is recommended, with the results kept in a fire precautions log book.

The Climatic Environment

HEATING, VENTILATION AND AIR CONDITIONING

Adequate ventilation is necessary to remove excess carbon dioxide and other vapours, such as the chemical emissions from new furnishings like carpets (which have been known to make people feel unwell).

People generate considerable heat (perhaps 100W per person) and that heat has to be dissipated. When lighting is provided at high intensity, even so-called low-energy luminaires will collectively emit considerable heat. In cold winter conditions that can be fine, but on hot summer days the air conditioning has to be designed accordingly if the offices are not to become unduly warm.

People's perception of an ideal temperature in offices will vary. Most people in the relatively sedentary work of offices should expect to exist in an ambient temperature between 21 and 23 degrees Celsius. In older buildings or where the air-conditioning equipment is barely adequate temperatures can be allowed to fall below those limits, but 18 degrees should be regarded as the minimum (and at that level you can expect complaints). In hot summer weather there is no upper legal limit in the UK but clearly all possible measures (such as the provision of fans) should be taken for employees' comfort where air conditioning is inadequate or absent.

Obviously the best choice is for air conditioning or climate control, in which the air is replaced continuously by a system of fans, ducting, humidifiers and heat exchangers. If poorly maintained or installed, such systems can cause downdrafts that will give people aches and pains, or be noisy. Of course full air conditioning is not always possible in some older buildings.

It is important for ventilation and air-conditioning systems to be given regular maintenance and periodical cleaning or sterilisation. There is a risk of harmful bacteria build-up if too much dirt is allowed to accumulate in hidden places.

A build-up of the very dangerous legionella bacterium can build up in air-conditioning systems that use water-cooling towers, and indeed that danger is also present in any water system (especially in infrequently used shower heads and taps). Cases of infection (legionnaires disease) are relatively rare, but they are very serious (often fatal) when they do occur. Even passers-by in the street can be affected by droplets from water-cooling towers mounted on roofs. Office occupants need not be unduly alarmed, but they do deserve the assurance that air-conditioning and other water-containing systems are regularly serviced by competent maintenance engineers.

Catering for the Needs of the Individual

The study of the interaction between people and their immediate work is called ergonomics. Most reasonably priced office furniture will have sufficient adjustment between the chair and the desktop height for individuals to make themselves comfortable. Backrests are also usually adjustable.

However, some people have special needs. For example those with short legs should be provided with footrests, if they cannot plant their feet firmly on the floor when working. Sympathetic consideration should always be given to any person who has some physical disability, one of the most common being back pain. Requests for suitably designed seating should not be ignored.

It is now generally acknowledged that use of computer screens does not by itself cause permanent eye damage, but people should be allowed breaks to give their eyes a rest from time to time. The screens should not be placed facing windows or lights that could reflect and cause glare.

Repetitive strain injury (RSI) is common among people who use keyboards (or perform any other routine manual operation continuously and repetitively) for long periods. Wrist supports are known to ease this problem. Again, people should be allowed to take short breaks.

Some office managers like uniformity and 'neatness' in a large office, but I take the view that some individuality should be allowed. Clearly risqué calendars are not desirable and should be banned, but if someone wishes to have a family portrait or a picture of a loved one displayed on their desk it would be petty and unfair to disallow that. Some people also like to have screensavers showing personal pictures. Why not? After all, an average office worker spends a good proportion of their waking day at their desk, so if they want to make it a little home from home, my view is, let them. But everything within reason, of course.

Conclusion

As a project manager you might not have direct responsibility for arranging and maintaining the office environment for your project team. But you should be aware that office conditions are great demotivators when things go wrong. Conversely, support your team in getting for them the best possible office environment, and you will be rewarded by increased motivation, better communications and enhanced productivity for your project.

References and Further Reading

Health and Safety Executive, (2006), *Working with VDUs*, HSE reference ING136, rev. 3, HSE Books. Available at: http://www.hse.gov.ik/pubns/indg36.pdf

HMSO (1963), *Offices, Shops and Railway Premises Act 1963*, London: Her Majesty's Stationery Office.

HMSO (1971), *Fire Precautions Act 1971*, London: Her Majesty's Stationery Office.

HMSO (1974), *Health and Safety at Work Act 1974*, London: Her Majesty's Stationery Office.

Warner, M. (1998), 'Facilities management', ch. 57 in Lock, D. (ed.), *The Gower Handbook of Management*, 4th edn, Aldershot: Gower.

18 *The Construction Working Environment*

STEVE LEWIS

Construction projects are perhaps the most typical type of project. They exhibit the factors that make up the popular definition of 'a project' so well that they are frequently used as examples in educational texts on project management. Indeed, modern project management owes much of its current thinking and best practice to tools, techniques and methods developed in the construction industry. Construction projects however are notably different from projects undertaken in other sectors and have certain characteristics, especially with respect to the physical working environment. Anyone new to working on construction projects should immediately be aware of this important difference.

Introduction

I must start this chapter by discussing some important factors in the context of people management. These factors deserve consideration when planning a construction project because they will influence the path to project success. The following factors are particularly relevant to construction projects:

- project location;
- physical environment;
- employee well-being;
- motivation;
- working conditions and health and safety requirements.

I shall discuss these topics (with some case examples) in the context of improving quality and the prospect of project success,

Project success is usually determined by comparing the outcomes against the intended budget, the time taken, and the quality of the delivered project. Setting out the project success criteria at the very beginning of the project is critical in gaining consensus from all the stakeholders. For our interests, I shall be looking at success from the perspective of the project manager and those working on a construction project site. More specifically, I shall be considering what can be done to increase the chances of delivering a successful construction project, with particular regard to the physical environment.

Geographic Location and Human Resource Availability

An almost unique phenomenon of construction projects is that the asset being built will have a fixed geographical location, usually at some distance from the project company's headquarters. That produces a requirement for workers to travel to the location wherever it may be, rather than being able to move the project or parts of it to where the best or most suitably qualified workers can be found.

For example a bridge, highway, airport, oil refinery and so on will require people, whether they are managers or artisans, to travel to the project site. Other projects can be managed inside enclosed factories or offices or even over virtual organisations where people work remotely and separately. There are exceptions, for example where some parts of a construction project are prefabricated off site and transported to the site for assembly. However, most, if not all, construction work must take place at (or very close to) the project's final location.

This can present challenges in finding appropriately qualified and skilled people locally to work on the project. That difficulty can be compounded on certain government construction projects where the geographic location is chosen on the basis that the investment would aid local area regeneration. Thus the demographic profile near the project location will not always contain the skills necessary to support the project. In those circumstances, if the duration and value of the project allows, training of local people can be considered.

These factors apply to projects undertaken nationally and internationally. For example it is not uncommon for engineering companies to insist that their products are installed and commissioned by their own staff no matter where in the world they are sold. The most important reason for that is that the project contractor cannot guarantee that the client's own local resources will be sufficiently qualified to install and commission the equipment to the standard necessary for validating guarantees and warranties.

Clearly the typical construction project will therefore require some workers who are unavailable locally (particularly those with specialist skills) to commute perhaps considerable distances. They might even have to live away from home for long periods. This can apply whether they are in management positions and office based, or to tradespeople doing the physical work in both permanent and contract positions. Whatever the case, the additional stress caused by travel and living in temporary accommodation can have an adverse effect on people's motivation and performance.

From the perspective of someone who is considering working on a construction project, the geographical location, travel and accommodation concerns are clearly important, but there is little that can be done once the project is under way. Time spent investigating the site location and working conditions before agreeing to a contract is seldom wasted.

The project manager responsible for employing staff on any contract basis (permanent, fixed term, temporary or subcontract) has a duty of care under the Health and Safety at Work Act to provide minimum standards with regard to the working environment. I shall discuss this in more detail later.

Also, consideration has to be given to providing a physical environment that supports individual and team productivity. But, if you are a contractor employing site staff you might well be wondering, why should I provide (and more importantly pay) for anything more than the bare minimum? Surely if project staff have agreed to the terms of the contract and they don't like it they can go elsewhere. Whilst that is true, if they do decide to leave you could find that finding replacements for unhappy subcontractors and people, possibly at short notice, is costly and will have an adverse effect on project quality. In fact it is generally accepted that the cost of 'churn' can be as high as 8 to 10 times the relevant portion of contract value when you combine all associated costs such as:

- contract cancellation penalties;
- initial recruitment costs;
- replacement recruitment costs;
- reduction in motivation and performance of other staff (who have had to work harder to compensate for the vacant positions).

It is also possible in extreme circumstances for a construction project to develop a reputation for being an unpleasant place in which to work, so that people are repelled from working there altogether. Clearly that will make replacements even harder to find.

A further and more potentially significant impact comes from the reduction in quality suffered as a result of a high labour turnover. It is no secret that those working on a project who are unhappy with working conditions will undoubtedly not give their best, and they might fail to perform to the required standard. In a construction project some of these people will be in a position to affect the quality of the finished product directly. Further, their lack of motivation can spread through the site workforce like a contagion.

CASE EXAMPLE NO. 1

The principal contractor on a high-end residential construction project in a prestigious London borough was temporarily failing to provide satisfactory welfare facilities for the site-based workers, whereas staff in the site office had been well catered for. The resulting effect on the attitudes of tradespeople and their workmanship was appalling. Mechanical, electrical and plumbing services were regularly broken or damaged. They were not installed to the required standards and in some cases finished works were deliberately vandalised.

EXCEEDING MINIMUM STANDARDS

It is much better to invest in providing support in the physical environment at a level above that required by health and safety laws and regulations. That will help to ensure your project staff are kept content and willing to perform as expected. In this way you could be saving money on costly reworks. You could generate a culture of exceeding performance expectations. The important point is that the physical environment of the construction site needs to support the people working in it, especially those who are travelling from far and wide to get there. That will increase the chances of project success.

CASE EXAMPLE NO. 2: TWO EXAMPLES

The Heathrow Terminal 5 project was pioneering in its approach to the level and quantity of facilities provided for all project personnel, regardless of employment type. It raised the standard for traditional construction projects. In recognition of the risk that the project was going to need considerable resources which could not possibly be supported by local population alone, arrangements were made for temporary caravan site facilities. Thus the project would be better able to attract people from far and wide. This is not a novel concept in itself – highways projects have been doing that for decades. However, the Heathrow project did not stop there. Local vacant housing was also bought to provide cheap accommodation. This, combined with the quality of the facility (and the fact that it provided an alternative to expensive local hotel or bed and breakfast accommodation) helped to ensure that the project attracted the right people. Perhaps even more importantly, the measures helped the project to retain those right people. Other facilities that exceeded the minimum requirements were:

- secure on-site parking;
- free bus service;
- good canteen;
- clean welfare facilities with showers;
- ATM machines;
- rooms for prayer and worship.

All this contributed to a project that was a resounding success in terms of meeting quality and health and safety obligations.

In stark contrast to the Heathrow project there was a residential building project in London which provided only the bare minimum of facilities for its workers. The only facilities available for 100 people were:

- a single source of hot and cold water;
- a woefully inadequate number of lockers;
- only two Portaloos;
- no parking.

As you can imagine the project suffered from poor quality workmanship and a high rate of churn. These two factors created a vicious circle that caused the problems to grow and made recovery of the project next to impossible.

Environmental Psychology in Construction

It's not a recent discovery that our physical work environment has an effect on the way we conduct ourselves and how well we perform in society as well as at work. Evidence as early as the 1960s proved the existence of 'sick building syndrome'. Things such as lighting, high noise levels and poor air quality led to absenteeism caused by stress. The typical construction project site presents the worst of all these negative factors and more. Further, the temporary nature of a site limits what can be done to reduce unwanted environmental factors cost effectively. Some of these adverse factors include:

- exposure to the environment: wind, rain, heat, cold, dust and noise;
- handling hazardous chemicals, tools and equipment;
- slips, trips and falls;

- handling of heavy or awkward materials;
- working at height;
- working in confined spaces;
- constant danger of physical harm.

These are just some of the risks that exist in construction projects. Indeed, when you look in detail at a construction site it is surprising that anyone would want to work there at all.

Clearly all these travel, risk and living factors can have possible negative motivation effects, and that can directly affect the quality of a project. Thus investment into construction site welfare should be seen as an important issue. Whether that investment is actually made will depend heavily on the project value and contract type and duration, but it is well worth carrying out the relevant cost/benefit appraisal.

Employee Well-being, Motivation and Working Conditions

Motivation in the context of management is a complex subject that could fill several volumes. It is also discussed in several chapters in this book (for example in chapters 31 and 33). However, it is necessary to discuss motivation briefly in order to illustrate the points that I make.

MOTIVATIONAL THEORY

Several theories on motivation are in use today, including for example the work of Hertzberg (two-factor theory), Maslow (hierarchy of needs) and Alderfer (ERG (Existence, Relatedness and Growth) theory).

The basic premise of Maslow and Alderfer is that people seek first to satisfy certain fundamental needs (survival for example) as far as they can. When their most basic survival needs are assured, they aspire to higher things and move up to a new motivational level in the quest to satisfy their next level of need. They might eventually reach the topmost motivational level, where self-actualisation through growth and advancement becomes the target of their energies. (Whether or not self-actualisation can ever be gained or sustained however, is another debate. I've never met anyone who has claimed to be self-actualised, at least not on a construction site.)

A theme common to all motivational theories is that they identify those needs related to the physical environment as fundamental human needs. That means, if these basic needs are not met, needs that come higher up the hierarchy of needs cannot be met (or if the basic needs are not met a person might be motivated by other needs). For example, if a person were to start working on a construction project and found that physiological needs were not being reasonably met, he/she might be motivated to remove themselves from the situation by leaving the project – with the associated negative connotations that brings. We can therefore deduce easily that the physical environment is an important consideration in motivational theory. It can be considered a success factor when considering construction projects.

Health and Safety Requirements

If there is only one thing to remember regarding health and safety in construction, please remember this – it is very important, and will continue to become even more so.

Owing to the large number of health and safety regulations and laws in use around the world the subject cannot be covered comprehensively here. But I can make those who have not worked in construction before aware of health and safety in general and introduce some of the more important concepts.

HEALTH AND SAFETY QUALIFICATIONS

In the UK at least the last 20 years has seen the importance of health and safety come to the forefront of the construction industry. It has even spawned an industry of its own, staffed by health and safety consultants, inspectors and legislators. Anyone working in a managerial or trade capacity on a construction site is now required to have minimum qualifications just to get on site, with further, site-specific training required once there.

Although there are minimum legal requirements, each site and principal contractor will specify which qualifications they require for site access. Unfortunately however, alignment between the governing bodies is poor. So certain contractors in different continents and countries will prefer some qualifications over others and might fail to recognise the relevance of one qualification over another. So when seeking to obtain health and safety qualifications it is important to check the level of recognition given by the area of construction you wish to move into. Here is a small selection of possible qualifications and awarding bodies:

- The Construction Skills Certification Scheme (CSCS);
- Site Manager Safety Training Scheme (SMSTS);
- Site Supervisor Safety Training Scheme (SSSTS);
- Plant Manager Safety Training Scheme (PMSTS);
- Client Contractor National Safety Group for the Engineering Construction Industry (CCNSG);
- The National Examination Board in Occupational Safety and Health Awards, Certificates, and Diplomas (NEBOSH);
- Institution of Occupational Safety and Health (IOSH);
- British Safety Council Certificates and Diplomas (BSC);
- City and Guilds level NVQs.

HEALTH AND SAFETY AND THE LAW

There is an enormous body of law regulating health and safety at work. The primary legislation underpinning it all in the UK is the Health and Safety at Work Act 1974, which imposes a host of duties on employers, the self-employed, controllers of premises, manufacturers, suppliers and employees. Detailed regulations, many based on EU Directives, cover health and safety in the workplace, work equipment, manual handling, personal protective equipment, noise, substances hazardous to health and so on.

Enforcement of health and safety law in the UK is through the Health and Safety Executive (HSE), whose inspectors have significant powers. They can instigate prosecution through the criminal courts. Who is responsible for breaches of the legislation will depend on the terms of the particular piece of legislation. It could be the company, but can be extended also to individuals within the company who occupy a particular position of responsibility (not necessarily just the company directors, but managers too). Clearly this is important as it is no longer possible for anyone to 'hide behind the company' when an incident is being investigated. If charges are brought, the law can make individuals personally liable.

The civil law recognises certain obligations, other than contractual obligations, not to cause unjustifiable harm to other persons or their interests. There may be an obligation to compensate persons so harmed. One of the most common types of action in this branch of the law is an action based on negligence. To succeed in an action for negligence, it has to be shown that:

- there was a duty of care;
- that the duty of care was breached;
- the loss was caused by the breach of duty.

Professional persons whose expert opinion is relied on in a particular matter will normally owe a duty of reasonable care towards those who foreseeably rely on their opinion. Some statutes impose strict liability (where negligence does not have to be proved) and a civil remedy might be available under the statute.

MORAL AND ETHICAL CONSIDERATIONS IN GENERAL

At this point I would like to take a brief sidestep away from health and safety and talk about moral and ethical considerations in their widest sense for construction projects. In this wider context, ethics, stakeholder management, corporate social responsibility (CSR) and welfare are all intertwined. This can present difficulties for the management on a construction project.

I have already mentioned the internal aspects of CSR and the importance of providing adequate welfare facilities and working conditions on site. But what if the corporate strategy of the principal contractor takes a short-term view and is driven only by the need to increase profits? This is not uncommon – after all the business of business is *business*, especially where companies have shareholders expecting a return on their investment. This short-term outlook can restrict the view held by the project managers. That, and the pursuit of project success under pressure to perform, can cloud the judgement of a project team.

However, whatever one's motives and spiritual standpoint, moral and ethical issues undoubtedly deserve consideration for construction project success, as the following case study will illustrate.

CASE EXAMPLE NO. 3

A classic example of a failure to pay attention to consider moral and ethical principles occurred during the decommissioning of an oil platform. The management of this project were aware of its unpopularity in the public domain owing to its alleged impact on the environment. However, the managers failed to include suitable stakeholder management in their planning. That resulted in an underestimation of the power and influence that environmental conservation groups could wield. Such was the power and influence of these groups that eventually the managers of the decommissioning project were forced to replan the endeavour completely. That caused great financial expense, not to mention the cost in terms of public relations.

Clearly the lesson here is to ensure that the needs of those affected by the project are considered and planned for. Failure to do that can cost more than the relevant mitigating action. Yet there is also a wider issue to consider. If the organisation had in place a CSR strategy from which the project team could take guidance, would they have experienced the same outcome?

The moral and ethical difficulties for managers on a construction site do not stop there. Owing to the temporary and relatively short-term nature of projects (and especially construction projects) it is difficult to espouse moral and ethical values when the vast majority of the people working on the project and in a position to enact those values will be gone at the end. They are unlikely to be affected by the outcomes and they can have only a short-term view of the economic gain.

MORAL AND ETHICAL CONSIDERATIONS IN HEALTH AND SAFETY

Notwithstanding the legal and financial ramifications of health and safety, there are moral and ethical considerations to be taken into account. As a manager on a construction site who is in a position to affect the outcome of adherence to health and safety policy, ask yourself: 'Would I want a preventable death or life-changing injury weighing on my conscience for the rest of my life?' If you are a normal person, undoubtedly the answer must be a most definite 'No'.

Fortunately decisions on whether or not to invest in safety equipment or to adhere to health and safety regulations have largely been taken out of principal contractors' hands. However, there are still a few smaller construction projects where contractors will bend rules and exploit loopholes if they think that will save them money. My firm advice here is that clients for construction projects should not engage contractors with a poor health and safety record, and main contractors, in addition to examining their own health and safety practices, should similarly be scrupulous when overseeing subcontractors.

Whatever health and safety measures are put in place and enforced, it remains a fact that construction sites are dangerous places. Even with the regulations and legislation that exist to try and minimise the risk, accidents (fatal or otherwise) unfortunately still happen.

CASE EXAMPLE NO. 4: TWO EXAMPLES

Dennis Lock told me that he was part of a small examination board for a group of MBA students. They were all mature part-time students with senior positions in their working lives. Each student was delivering the required five minute oral presentation summarising his or her final assignment report. One had written an excellent assignment paper and his oral presentation was going very well until he reached the words 'We only lost three people killed on that project'. Dennis was suitably horrified and lost no time in saying so. However, the student remained unmoved, declaring that the industry norm is one corpse for every mile of tunnel, and this had been a 20-mile job.

Whilst smaller, lower value projects can be identified as potentially risky, it is clearly the much larger projects or super projects that are statistically more likely to have a fatality. This was recognised by managers on the Heathrow Terminal 5 project, where statistics based on past trends indicated that the project would cause 11 fatal accidents. That prediction was clearly bad and unacceptable. So the project employed considerable resources (far beyond the accepted norm) to reduce the risks. Although still tragic and unacceptable, the number of fatalities was reduced from the predicted 11 to 2.

BEST PRACTICE

In the UK the former Office of Government Commerce (OGC) cited commitment to excellence in health and safety performance as a critical success factor in construction projects. The OGC published a series of documents called *Excellence in Construction*, in which the following were listed as essential processes:

- risk and value management;
- integrating the project team;
- procurement strategy;
- whole-life costing;
- performance measurement;
- design quality and, of specific relevance here;
- health and safety aspects and sustainability.

CONSTRUCTION DESIGN AND MANAGEMENT REGULATIONS

Although specific to the UK (and technically to Europe, but in other forms) the Construction Design and Management Regulations (CDM) have to be mentioned. These regulations mean that anybody working on a construction project may have certain duties placed upon them – so clearly people need to be aware of their obligations in this respect.

I must refer here to the CDM European Directive of 24 June 1992 on the implementation of minimum safety and health requirements at temporary or mobile construction sites (eighth individual directive within the meaning of Article 16 (1) of Directive 89/391/EEC). This directive places specific legal responsibility on European construction designers to consider health and safety for the whole life cycle of the structure. Within the UK, this has been principally enacted via the Construction (Design and Management) Regulations 2007.

CDM 2007 places legal duties on virtually everyone involved in construction work. Those with legal duties are commonly known as 'duty-holders'. Again, the scope of the regulations prevents them from being discussed in any detail here, but the following list indicates how broadly the responsibilities are spread:

- clients;
- CDM coordinators;
- designers;
- principal contractors;
- contractors;
- workers.

As you can see if you are involved in a construction project you *will* have a level of responsibility and should arm yourself with the correct information to ensure you are not unwittingly non-compliant and left open to being held accountable or more importantly liable at law.

Responsibilities

I would like to end the chapter by talking a little about the level of responsibility a project manager working on certain construction projects may have. The outcome of some projects, and the environment in which they are undertaken are potentially very dangerous, both to those working on them and to those affected by their intended use. Examples of such projects include:

- defence projects for the construction of weapons and armed vehicles;
- construction and engineering projects in the nuclear and oil and gas industries;
- mining and quarrying;
- demolition projects.

Conversely, some projects provide enormous benefits to individuals and whole communities. Here the responsibility to deliver the project is intensified by the positive life-changing effect the benefits have on people's lives. Examples include:

- construction of schools and hospitals in deprived areas of the world;
- relief projects undertaken as a result of disasters;
- regeneration projects to improve the prospects of entire towns.

In order to be successful, project managers need to manage how these responsibilities are likely to affect them. In the case of health and safety, as previously mentioned, whilst everyone has a duty to look after the well-being of everybody else, the project manager has particular legal, moral and ethical obligations. How would you feel if a member of your construction team lost their sight or became permanently unable to walk because of something you had done or not done, or a decision you had taken? The construction project manager carries this level of responsibility. In order to make sure that serious incidents are avoided, you have to plan, organise, monitor and control accordingly. In other words, you have to be an effective project manager.

When considering defence projects, it is a fact that you are involved in producing something that may well one day be involved directly or indirectly in injuring or killing other human beings. How a project manager reconciles the moral and ethical aspects of that with his/her self is very personal and largely outside the scope of this book.

At the other end of the spectrum there are projects for the construction of things which offer hope and great joy to the users. In this situation, whilst using the eventual satisfaction that comes with knowing you have done something good as a motivating force, it is important to remember that projects still require a project manager to balance the constraints and deliver to satisfy a business case. That is not to say all projects are expected to provide a return on their investment, but even non-profit projects have to be completed within their budget to be considered successful.

Concluding Summary

Here are some concluding thoughts to remember:

- Success factors are those things that, if present, although not guaranteeing project success, will have a positive influence on the overall success of the project.
- Critical success factors are those things that, if not present, will cause the project to fail.
- Construction sites, even if managed well, are often unpleasant and dangerous places.
- Construction projects usually have a fixed geographical location. That can cause difficulties in obtaining workpeople owing to local demographics. The alternative means asking people to life on site or travel. If adequate consideration to the physical environment is not given, high labour turnover (churn) and reduced amount and quality of work can be expected.
- Motivational theories suggest that physiological needs are fundamental to achieving a well-motivated workforce. Thus, investment in the physical environment at a construction site will motivate the workforce and potentially yield a benefit, as well as being morally and ethically the right thing to do.
- Health and safety in construction is important – and will continue to become more so.
- Health and safety qualifications of one sort or another will be required to gain access to a construction site. You need to familiarise yourself with these requirements and note that some qualifications do not have an equal level of recognition across international borders.
- In the UK the Health and Safety at Work Act places a responsibility on almost everyone to accept a duty of care on a construction site. Where this duty of care is proven to have been neglected, individuals can be held accountable. So you need to check your status and ensure you comply with the regulations and legislation to protect yourself and (more importantly) others.
- The HSE provides most of the information you need on their website.
- Specific courses on health and safety are readily available from hundreds of course providers. Ignorance cannot be used as an excuse for health and safety failure.
- Health and safety is everyone's responsibility. Don't put yourself in a situation where morals and ethics are called in to question and loss of a life or avoidable injury rests on your conscience.

References and Further Reading

Cooper, D. (2004), *Improving People Performance in Construction*, Aldershot: Gower.

Health and Safety at Work Act 1974, London: The Stationery Office.

Health and Safety Executive: comprehensive information at www.hse.gov.uk

Lock, D. (2004), *Project Management in Construction*, Aldershot: Gower.

Thorpe, T. and Sumner, P. (2004), *Quality Management in Construction*, Aldershot: Gower.

19 *The Workplace of the Future*

COLIN STUART

The world has always changed, however the pace of change seems to be accelerating. New advances in IT are changing the way we work and our relationship with the office. This has the potential to drive fundamental and profound changes to society, and the way in which we work and manage people.

Introduction

Modern organisations are under more pressure than ever to keep ahead of, or even up with, the competition. Recent difficulties in the global economy have increased that pressure. Increased globalisation has opened up new markets for us, but in turn has led to increased international competition. The rise of the BRIC economies (Brazil, Russia, India and China) is changing the balance of power between the East and West, between the old and new economic powerhouses.

The design of offices and the way they are utilised has not really changed fundamentally for over 100 years. Recent technological advances have been used to squeeze more efficiency out of our office space but that will only give increasingly smaller returns and eventually impact on morale and productivity. To adapt to the pressures and drivers that the business world faces and to stay competitive in the global market, we need a paradigm shift in the way we work and the way in which we interact with each other at work. We must connect up our two most important and costly assets – our staff and our real estate – to add value to, and enhance each other.

The key is to unlock the human capital value inherent in the organisation. Human capital is the knowledge and capabilities of the workforce; often only tapped in an unplanned and erratic way and often only by those individuals within the organisation who actively network and exchange knowledge. It is a significant area of untapped potential within individual organisations and the economy as a whole. Designing office facilities with the primary intent of unlocking the value of this human capital will have a marked effect on the 'bottom line' (Vischer, 2012).

To accomplish this, our use of, and interaction with, the workplace needs to evolve. As Barak Obama said, 'work is something you do, not somewhere you go'. We need to view our work as a series of activities, interactions and outputs that we need to accomplish and we need to choose the most appropriate and conducive space to perform each task. Ultimately we have to change our attachment to the lumps of wood we use to keep our computer, pens and paper off the floor. We must stop seeing these as our own personal possessions but instead regard them as tools to be used to accomplish certain tasks during our day, along with a number of other 'work settings' or locations for other tasks.

During the last 10 years, emerging technologies have allowed us to re-evaluate our relationship with the workplace. Jobs are no longer seen as a job for life. There is increasing mobility within and between workspaces. Advances in computer hardware and software have allowed us to connect with each other and interact as never before.

As project managers and real estate professionals, we and our clients will all be affected by the changing landscape of work. Whether leading remote multidisciplinary teams or actively involved in projects ourselves, we can take advantage of new technologies and innovations in the world of work to our benefit. Further, we can lead this change in working practices, to open our organisations and our clients' eyes to what is possible – to the step change that is possible in the office, in work and in corporate culture. Benefits to the individual employee are significant, the benefits to the team as a whole are even greater, but more significantly the financial benefits are impossible to ignore. We can redesign our facilities and workspaces to act as a catalyst for driving cultural change throughout the organisation.

This chapter begins by describing the evolution of the modern office workplace. I shall explore the factors driving and enabling the change in the way we work and examine what we can do to drive and manage that change and thus unlock the organisation's human capital value. I shall also explore what the future workplace could look like and how it can benefit us and our projects.

Darwinism and the Evolution of the Office

To understand how the modern office has evolved and the pressures it is under to evolve further, we need to look back through history. From our early beginnings as simple single-celled organisms life has evolved and adapted to changing conditions in the environment. Early hominids came down from the trees, stood on two legs and adapted to the new environment. *Homo sapiens* evolved, discovered fire and started early agrarian civilisations. Those species not able to evolve and adapt successfully to the changing environment like the Neanderthals became extinct. As early technology advanced, so our culture changed and adapted. The cultures that were able to develop new ideas and technologies and adapt to make best use of them came to prominence. Embracing new discoveries (such as the wheel) helped early empires to develop and reign supreme until the next empire with its superior technology or evolved structure came along. Society evolved with the evolving technology.

It can be argued that the first 'office' was founded by the Romans. In fact the word office itself derives from the Latin *officium*. The Roman Empire demanded tax instead of military service from the regions they conquered. To manage this, Roman governors had an administrative staff to levy tributes, establishing a civil service and bookkeeping function. This was driven by the need to administer and control, hence the office evolved as an administrative function of the state.

The Middle Ages saw the emergence of the mediaeval chancery, a development of the Roman administrative office as a place for the drawing up of government letters, proclamations and copying of laws on to parchment. Through the Renaissance the office

Figure 19.1 'Moving again: I've just finished redecorating'
Source: © 2011 Bud Goldston-Browning and Colin Stuart.

continued as a manifestation of the power of the state, and a centralised or administrative function. A notable example is the Palazzio Uffizi, built to house the Florentine magistrates. Technological and societal advances such as the printing press and the rise of mercantilism saw power move to the merchant lords, with their business centred around a multifunctional commercial building. The clerical office for the business was often housed alongside warehousing and retail space.

The industrial revolution saw the first modern commercial offices appear. The evolution of telegraph and telephone meant administrative functions could be centralised away from production facilities and could be located where the workforce were more literate and within easy reach of transport hubs. Further technological advances increased the pace of the centralisation of commercial offices. Technologies such as steel-framed buildings and lifts allowed for high-rise buildings centred in commercial districts, giving birth to the modern central business districts as we know them.

The principles of the modern workplace were established by Fredrick W. Taylor (see Chapter 31). He applied scientific measurement of productivity in the workplace to improve efficiency. Tasks were analysed and split into repetitive acts. This led to a production line arrangement which Frank and Lillian Gilbreth saw could be applied equally to the office as well as the factory floor. It manifested itself as a series of regimented spaces with workers in rows in large rooms, facilitating close supervision. The most obvious example would be the typing pool. Other early influencers include Frank Lloyd Wright (1867–1959). With a focus on the individual, he designed residential buildings with large open-plan spaces, simple clean geometry and large low windows to make the inside space an extension of the outside. His designs and the Taylorist principles of efficiency were developed and used in commercial buildings by leading architects and designers of the early twentieth century, such as Mies Van Der Rohe, Le Corbusier and other architects from the Bauhaus school. They laid the foundations of the modern commercial office buildings, with large areas of glass and open-plan floors.

Technological advances in the 1940s and 1950s helped make the office even more efficient and regimented. Air conditioning and the invention of the suspended ceiling allowed the building of large deep efficient open-floor plates. The 1950s also saw the rise of a new movement in architecture, driven by Europe's predominantly socialist values at time, the Bürolandschaft ('office landscape') movement. Those designs were more focused large open-plan spaces subtly subdivided into varied arrangements and landscapes which allowed for greater communication. The Bürolandschaft was ahead of its time, and the more humanistic and worker-centric principles they established were soon eroded. The good intentions regarding the soft low subdivision of space evolved into the dreaded office cubicle, driven by a greater number of middle managers wanting recognition and more than just a desk. The egalitarian principles of Bürolandschaft were further rejected during the 1960s and 1970s, when offices were increasingly designed as cellular spaces with long corridors, typically supporting the hierarchical nature of the corporate culture.

This trend was halted in the early 1990s. Among other notable examples Frank Duffy's groundbreaking books on 'new ways of working' (Duffy, 1992) and the research undertaken by Gavin Turner and Jeremy Myserson (Turner and Myserson, 1998) showed the potential that a modern people-centric-designed office could achieve and was seen as the blueprint for the future. Open-plan working and the inherent breaking down of the physical barriers within the office began to be more widely accepted, with its improved collaboration and connectivity between staff and between managers and staff.

Technological advances in networking with the advent of Wi-Fi, roaming profiles, virtual private networks and portable laptops increased worker mobility, allowed more effective hot-desking within the office environment and facilitated home working on a corporate scale. A number of companies started to implement flexible working environments within their offices, moving to completely open-plan environments and utilising hot-desking and hoteling to create exciting office landscapes with maximum flexibility.

This brave new world of user-centric offices seems to take a few steps forwards only to see several steps be taken backwards. With a few notable exceptions such as Google or Microsoft's facility in Schipol, the trend after the millennium has been to focus on the workplace as a cost that can and must be reduced to improve operating margins. The new technologies have been harnessed to reduce the desk footprint and maximise desk sharing. On the whole lip service has been paid to the introduction of other work settings (such as breakout space, collaboration areas and quiet booths) with these often being seen as overflow space for when the desk areas are at capacity. Home working is on the increase but again driven largely by the desire to reduce office costs rather than a step to empower the individual and unlock the value in the organisation's human capital (Myerson, Bichard and Erlich, 2010).

But is increasing efficiency a long-term answer? With the efficiencies within the current model of the office almost at a maximum, where do we go from here? In trying to be even more efficient we could damage productivity, creativity and culture. Morale will suffer and absenteeism and attrition rates could increase. Taylorism has run its course and a new model is required.

Figure 19.2 'You think we've had it bad …'

Source: © 2011 Bud Goldston-Browning and Colin Stuart.

The Perfect Storm

The global workforce is also changing. Here in the UK almost 50 per cent of our workforce can be classed as knowledge workers. They are the foundation of the UK service-based economy. But are workplaces designed and based on Taylorist principles developed 120 years ago relevant for the modern knowledge worker, enabled as they are with all the latest mobile technology?

To maximise their potential and productivity knowledge workers need to collaborate, to share knowledge and spark innovation. It is often in the chance encounter rather than the formal meeting that new ideas are created and new products developed. Companies that use their workplaces to encourage this sort of interactivity are the ones most likely to succeed in the highly charged competitive corporate world.

Studies have shown a high degree of correlation between the level of interaction between staff and the development and speed to market of new products. Viagra is a case in point, a drug developed by Pfizer to treat angina that had some interesting side effects on the test subjects. Those side effects, as the story goes, were discussed by chance by two colleagues from totally separate divisions of the company, one in heart research and the other on the sexual health side. Within a year they were undertaking field trials for its use in erectile dysfunction. Through a casual meeting between colleagues, one of the biggest selling drugs of all time was born.

Interaction between staff, especially those 'knowledge workers', is therefore key. However, knowledge workers, as well as benefiting from interaction with their colleagues, also need quieter environments to develop that knowledge in isolation, to read or write that important report. Modern open-plan offices are often noisy environments and, although encouraging more collaboration and interaction, are not conducive to more quiet contemplative work.

We also need to factor in the changing demographics of the workplace. Generation Y (often also called the 'Millennials', the generation born from the 1980s to the millennium) have entered the workplace and Generation Z (those born since the millennium – the 'iGeneration') are not far behind. These people are very highly IT literate – having grown up in a world of Facebook®, Flickr® and instant messaging, even email seems archaic to them.

The new generation have also been trained by our education system to be output driven and flexible about where and when they work. If you consider an 11-year-old on his/her first day of secondary school, they have to get themselves to the right classroom, with the right books and the right homework done on the right day. So very quickly they learn to organise themselves and be results driven. This training to be flexible and output driven continues into sixth form college, with the teenagers trusted to turn up when they have lectures. At university it reaches its extreme – does the tutor care if the essay is completed at midnight or midday, in the library or lying on the student's bed? No, providing it is handed in on time and is of good enough quality. So what do we do with all these highly independent, motivated, output driven, flexible products of our education system when they enter the workforce – we chain them to desks from 9.00 to 17.30 and force them to conform to our ways of working! We knock all the flexibility out of them. Why are we not adapting to bring the best out of them, providing them with the right IT systems, the right workplace and managing them in the right way to nurture these skills to our companies' advantage?

A growing awareness of environmental issues is starting to make us question the ethics of millions of people commuting to central locations every day. Increasing work

Figure 19.3 The perfect storm
Source: © 2011 Bud Goldston-Browning and Colin Stuart.

pressures (caused in part by our new technology and the pace of work/life) are increasing stress levels, which in turn are not helped by the morning commute. The negative effect on morale caused is leading to levels of attrition and absenteeism which are impacting on the bottom line. Research has proven that staff who are unhappy with their job are absent more often (Nelson and Quick, 2008). The psychological rationale is that individuals will withdraw from dissatisfying working conditions. Research by PricewaterhouseCoopers estimates that UK employees are taking off 10 unauthorised days per year and that this is costing UK business payroll £32 billion (PricewaterhouseCoopers).

It is not difficult from these studies to assume that improvements in the workplace (leading to improved morale and job satisfaction combined with an adoption of more flexible working patterns) will not only reduce absenteeism due to dissatisfaction with the workplace but also absence caused by clashes between work and family life and lead to a drop in attrition levels. Typically the effect of losing a valued employee is equivalent to a year's salary, once you have taken into account all the direct and indirect costs, disruption to others, and the loss of goodwill (Stuart, 2012). With UK absenteeism running at between 5 and 10 per cent and attrition levels anything up to 25 per cent even small changes can have a big impact on the company's bottom line.

The current pressures on our working lives will necessitate a revaluation of how we work. As mentioned earlier, this is being enabled by the new and emerging technologies. Social networking sites such as Facebook were until recently viewed as a threat to productivity, with many companies blocking its use, but social networking is now making its way into the corporate mainstream. Sites such as Huddle are bringing social networking into the workplace in a legitimate, planned and controllable way, enabling communication, file sharing and community-wide discussions. The use of 'to desktop' videoconferencing utilising Skype, Lync or other platforms will very shortly be widespread.

Cloud computing is enabling effective, secure and easy access to files, software and systems as well as improving resiliency and removing the need for the owned data-centre infrastructure. Online file sharing started to become widespread via systems such as Dropbox. However, MS Sharepoint is steadily becoming adopted as the versatile, configurable corporate platform.

Countrywide wireless connectivity became a reality with the 3G networks, although the download speeds are still limiting and coverage is patchy. 4G promises to give high bandwidth, high-speed connectivity, which combined with the adoption of cloud computing will enable the workforce to work wherever and whenever. In the meantime, there has been a significant rise in the number of wireless hotspots accessible to members of the public from coffee bars to railway stations. The use of these locations as additional local office space has become known as 'third place' working and instead of paying annual rent you can now effectively buy your office space 'by the cup'.

This has created a perfect storm, in which the economic climate, the ageing demographic, the new iGeneration and the changing demands on the workplace are combining with the enablers of new technology to allow us to make this fundamental step change. The focus is moving on to the individual worker and empowering that individual to work in the most effective way. In broader terms, that will unlock the value in the human capital of the workforce, beginning a new era in the way we work.

Organisations with visionary chief executives and boards are leading the way, prepared to experiment with new working models, to take risks and invest in innovative workspace. The vast majority of organisations, however, are in a dilemma. They often recognise the need to change, to innovate, to maintain competitive advantage or improve value and service but cannot justify the funding to invest in a new working environment to facilitate this, especially in economically challenging times. Others are afraid of failure, they do not fully believe that the working environment can act as a catalyst for cultural change or deliver value to the bottom line. They see and admire the market-leading few who have radically changed their cultures but feel it is not for them, that they are somehow not worthy or different. This is often due to the failure to fully understand and define the benefits case for a change to the organisational structure, the working environment, and the impact that using these to drive change in employee behaviours will have on the bottom line.

The Paradigm Shift

So what must organisations do to continue to improve, to deliver increased shareholder value year on year? For the vast majority of organisations their human capital (the inherent knowledge in their employees and value in their social networks) is their most valuable and important asset (Vischer, 2012). It is this focus of the value in each employee and the design of the organisational structure, its culture workplace and supporting environment to maximise each employee's potential that will lead to the revolution in the way we work.

But how is the human capital value unlocked? Change to the workplace if undertaken with the right focus on ultimate goals can lead to fundamental changes to corporate culture and staff behaviours. Changing the culture of an organisation and the corresponding changes to staff behaviours are the key to delivering increased value. But how do we set our goals? An organisation's culture can broadly be measured using four traits (Cameron and Quinn, 2006):

- clan (a friendly mentoring culture);
- adhocracy (a dynamic, entrepreneurial and creative culture);
- market (a results-orientated competitive culture);
- hierarchy (a formalised, structured and controlling place to work).

Mapping where an organisation currently sits with respect to the above against where they want to be gives a blueprint for the ultimate culture that the workplace is trying to create. This blueprint can be further refined and developed into a benefits case using a series of measures to track the value created and targets set, often in terms of direct financial impact. Using this blueprint and maintaining a focus on the end game, the space subsequently designed and delivered, along with a structured training and change programme, can and will deliver change in employee behaviours and corporate culture. This in turn acts to unlock human capital value and positively impacts on the organisation's bottom line or delivery of service to its external stakeholders.

Ideally an organisation needs to link its physical environment with its organisational objectives, so that the workspace is viewed as a resource to support human capital. The workplace needs to be seen as an investment to unlock the value of this capital and to maximise its growth. Measuring the impact that unlocking human capital value has to an organisation's bottom line gives us a framework within which we can prioritise investment of financial capital to areas with the greatest impact on the bottom line.

We need to redefine the corporate working model, not just the workspace. To be effective the model we need should link the organisation's objectives with the desired culture, staff behaviours, organisational structure, IT platform and ultimately the workplace itself. We need what is sometimes referred to as an 'agile working' model, which defines our new operating environment against three parameters:

- people (our culture and behaviours);
- process (our organisation, processes and functions);
- place (our physical and virtual environment).

There are several different agile working models being rolled out in leading organisations that we don't have the time to look into in depth. However, one of note is known as a 'Results Orientated Working Environment' (ROWE). Developed by Cali Ressley and Jody Thompson for Best Buy in the US, ROWE is a management strategy and operating model focused on employee outputs only. It is not just working from home or flexible hours (flexitime) but a complete strategy to shift emphasis on to employee management, motivation, reward and the outputs achieved. It is focused on employee productivity – not in a closely measured Taylorist way – but one in which employees are empowered, given choice and rewarded by results. Results have been very impressive. Those allowed to choose when and where they work have shown significant gains in morale, reductions in absenteeism and staff turnover. The ultimate result has been improved productivity and profits. Although perhaps a significant step for most organisations to take, it is a model worth reviewing when undertaking any workplace-driven change programme.

Every organisation is different, and every organisation will change. It is important that the model is designed for the particular organisation and reviewed as the organisation develops. In designing a new model, it is important not only to keep a focus on the desired culture but also to ensure that you do not dilute the essence and values of the company. When introducing any form of flexible working allowing employees to work away from their team's core location (whether within a building or in other remote locations) it is vital to ensure that the team's connectivity and collaboration is enhanced – not diluted.

A complete IT solution needs to be implemented that not only maintains or enhances productivity in terms of quick and easy access to shared files and software, but which also provides a tool for keeping people keep in touch with one another.

This sort of environment is becoming known as 'jelly bean working', after the green/red 'jelly bean' that software such as Skype, Lync and others use to show when a user is online and available, busy or offline. The use of jelly beans allows colleagues to be conscious of their colleagues online, to see when they are available and to communicate with them effectively. Use of these sorts of software package, along with effective file sharing and remote access software will allow for effective remote collaboration. When implementing an agile working environment, it is important to provide staff and managers with training as part of a structured change programme – not just in using the new software itself but in how to communicate and stay in contact with one another. The software can also help people manage their own time and focus on outputs and how to manage their subordinates (which is discussed in Chapter 30).

As project managers, in addition to managing the change itself we need to be advising the board or leadership team about which workplace model is best for the organisation in the next phase of its evolution. Every organisation is different and is often changing and evolving at some pace. One size definitely does not fit all organisations, all departments or even individuals within departments. We need to be challenging our colleagues or clients during the briefing process to be looking ahead to the future and design the workplace for what we want to become in terms of culture, work styles and organisational structure. We also need to be asking the difficult questions, often acting as the 'critical friend'.

In defining our new model and then developing the various aspects of that model and the implementation programme, we need first to set our parameters. It is important that we analyse the nature of the tasks and outputs the organisation is undertaking. Only with a good understanding of what we do can we hope to design a working model that will support this effectively. Using techniques such as 'activity analysis' we can analyse in detail what the various staff members do, how much time is spent on each activity and where that activity is currently undertaken. We need to look at how staff and teams currently interact in delivering their outputs, and the times of day when that interaction occurs. This, combined with other surveys, provides an excellent data set to help define our model and our brief.

Establishing a business case with full 'buy-in' from the leadership team is vital. The more time and effort devoted to getting a robust business case in place with a correspondingly detailed brief, the less opportunity there will be for it to be challenged and the lower likelihood there will be of significant change during the project. In broad terms, a workplace-driven cultural and organisational change programme can have a number of qualitative benefits from improved staff work/life balance, increased staff satisfaction and morale through to better customer perception, improved speed to market and improved customer service. However, it is ultimately the quantitative impact on the bottom line that counts.

Most financial directors have not attained their current positions by taking unnecessary risks. Most will agree that a new value-focused workplace will deliver benefits to the company, but for funding to be unlocked the benefits need to be compelling and quantified. It has become increasingly popular to measure benefit not just by the traditional financial bottom line, but also by its ethical and environmental performance. That is commonly known as the 'Triple Bottom Line' (Elkington, 1998). However, for most organisations it is still important that the financial return is viable. We need to establish a series of credible measures that can be used to create a benefits case and model the financial impact of a new facilities management and workplace model.

These measures can be used to assess the success of the project and can also be used to test the benefits of any suggested change to the programme – does it ultimately contribute to delivery of the benefits case? Any business case for workplace-driven change can have a clear measurable benefits case and quantifiable financial targets as follows (Stuart, 2012):

1. Reduced operating expenses – reductions in real estate footprint and support costs;
2. Improved productivity – this can be sometimes hard to quantify, but depending upon the organisation, can be measured in billable hours, calls made per day, outputs per period or profit margin improvement;

3. Reduced absenteeism and staff attrition – directly measurable by most HR departments and quantifiable from the payroll.

Once we have designed our initial agile working model, developed our benefits and business case and received senior management buy-in, we need to develop an overall change programme to deliver the benefits case. It is outside the scope of this chapter to go into any depth on this. However, as project managers and real estate professionals we need to be driving and managing this change, to deliver the best results to our companies and clients. I use the Managing Successful Programmes (MSP) methodology myself. The new workplace will become the underlying catalyst for this change and is an excellent way to get a break in people's mindsets. However, it is important use a broad programme management approach to the delivery of the workplace and allied change programme.

Investment in the IT infrastructure and software will also be required. It will often be a significant investment, so early engagement with the in-house IT team is vital. Without the tools to work in an agile manner, communicate and collaborate, any new working environment (however well designed) will never be effective and old habits will inevitably creep back in.

Management of your stakeholders is key to delivery of the cultural change aspects of the programme. You will need close liaison with your colleagues in the HR and organisational development departments. A robust and extensive communication and engagement plan (often with a very clear project brand) to involve all stakeholders and make them feel that their voices have been heard is vital to overcome the natural resistance to change. It is important where practical to involve your stakeholder groups in the development of the model to generate a sense of ownership.

Alongside this, a training and mentoring programme should be implemented to train staff in how to work in the new environment effectively and also to train managers in how to manage a remote team. It is often not the staff who have the greatest anxieties but their managers, who are afraid that they will still have to deliver the same targets from a team which they can't see every minute of the day. There are e-learning training packages available that have extensive modules for both managers and staff that can be deployed quickly and cheaply in support of the change programme.

The Future?

I said earlier that the modern workplace was created during the technological advances of the industrial revolution, but, that it has remained largely unchanged for over 100 years. We are now facing another period of significant change in technology – one that could lead to a similar change in society and the way we work.

It is time the workplace took another step forward. So we are at a crossroads in terms of the workplace. A perfect storm is building, driven by new and emerging technologies and whipped up further by changing workplace demographics and the different attitudes and inherent skills of the new generation entering the workforce. The office as we know it is in danger of being swept away.

We need to harness the energy, flexibility and enthusiasm of the new generation by providing a working environment that truly empowers and supports them. We need to provide work settings and a working environment that supports knowledge workers and allows for both the development and sharing of knowledge. We need to manage our staff in a more flexible way, trusting them to manage their own time and to choose the most appropriate and effective time, place and manner in which they produce their outputs.

But what could that environment be? Current technology allows us to work effectively anywhere, staying in touch with our colleagues, collaborating and communicating with them even though they might be at opposite ends of the globe. We should be striving to minimise the overbearing nature of the office, giving our staff choice of timing, location and work setting.

In the short term we need to wean ourselves off our dependence upon desks, to break that mental link of 'I am working therefore I need to work at a desk'. We need to design our working environments to provide a choice of sufficient work settings which support the various activities that our staff will be undertaking. We need to balance the ratio of the different spaces so that it reflects the relative amounts of time spent on the various tasks. We need to improve mobility, to get our staff interacting, collaborating and sharing, but also developing knowledge where and when appropriate. We need to provide the right IT systems to support that environment, but most important of all we need to develop the right corporate culture to support this new operating model, through planned organisational change and training for staff and managers.

I can foresee a time very soon, when corporations become largely virtual from a real estate perspective. Staff could be predominately home working, working on client sites or commuting to local hubs within a few miles of home. Meeting facilities will be rented when and where required. The hubs will potentially be shared with other corporations who are all paying a rate per head or per usage to provide their staff with access to a business lounge with a number of different work settings and facilities.

Team meetings will be held by videoconference with potentially each team member in a different location. 'Jelly bean' software will allow team members to stay in close communication, to interact, collaborate, share ideas and work together. Staff will be measured on their outputs and trusted to manage their own work time, improving their work-life balance. A number of these business lounges have already sprung up in major locations, predominately focused on the smaller entrepreneur with no fixed abode. It will not be long before major corporations start using them extensively and significantly reducing their real estate. A number of organisations (such as banks) have large distributed estates with under-used facilities in key locations crying out to be turned into shared facilities. How long will it be before we see a business hub on every high street and every street corner?

To conclude, we are at a major point in the evolution of the world of work. If we don't evolve we shall become extinct. We as project managers need to be leading the way in that evolution.

Acknowledgements

Thank you to Bud Goldston-Banning for use of his cartoons and to Tsunami-Axis Ltd for allowing Bud to contribute to this chapter. The illustrations in this chapter and their captions are copyright Bud Goldston-Banning and Colin Stuart 2011, with all rights reserved and no unauthorised reproduction permitted.

References and Further Reading

Cameron, K. and Quinn, R. (2006), *Diagnosing and Changing Organizational Culture*, San Francisco, CA: Jossey-Bass.

Duffy, F. (1992), *The Changing Workplace*, London: Phaidon Press.

Elkington, J. (1998), *Cannibals with Forks: The Triple Bottom Line of 21st Century Business*, Oxford: Capstone.

Myerson, J. (2012). 'Workplace redesign to support the "front-end" of innovation', in Alexander, K. and Price, I. (eds), *Managing Organizational Ecologies* (ch. 4), New York: Routledge.

Myerson, J., Bichard, J-A. and Erlich, A. (2010), *New Demographics, New Workspace*, Farnham: Gower.

Nelson, D. and Quick, J. (2008), *Understanding Organizational Behavior*, Mason, OH: Thomson.

PricewaterhouseCoopers (n.d.), 'Absenteeism costing UK business'. Available at: http://www.ukmediacentre.pwc.com [accessed August 29, 2011].

Stuart, C. (2012), 'Value rhetoric and cost reality', in Alexander, K. and Price, I. (eds), *Managing Organizational Ecologies* (ch. 11), New York: Routledge.

Turner, G. and Myserson, J. (1998), *New Workspace, New Culture*, Aldershot: Gower.

Vischer, J. (2012), 'Managing facilities for human capital value', in Alexander, K. and Price, I. (eds), *Managing Organizational Ecologies* (ch. 3), New York: Routledge.

3 Improving Project Teams and Their People

20 *Identifying and Building Key Relationships*

NEIL WALKER

It is acknowledged that project management is not so much about managing projects as managing people. The more effective a project manager is at managing the intricate relationships with the people involved in the project, the higher the rate of success that project manager will achieve. Irrespective of how meticulously a project is planned, the degree of painstaking dedication to perfect deliverables, the unfaltering commitment to best practice project management methods and processes, the agility of the project team to perform and deliver; it is routinely the *people factor* that derails the potential for project success. When it comes to projects, managing people is a foremost challenge.

Introduction

Managing people generally begins with obtaining the right people, with the right skills (with the proper tools), in the right quantity and at the right time. It also means ensuring that these people know what is expected of them, what needs to be done, by when and how it should be done. Additionally managing people means motivating, coaching, leading and getting these people to buy in to the project (ideally getting them to take ownership of the project).

In a project team, a project manager has authority and can direct and drive activities. But clearly the project manager must adopt a different approach over the wider network of people who contribute to project success. He/she has to develop and sustain working relationships that will allow practical cooperation over the project life cycle. So, the project manager has to become an enabler.

The Challenge of Relationship Management

Relationships are generally understood to be the state of affairs existing between people having associations or dealings. For a project manager, relationships are a set of connections and interactions with individuals or groups to facilitate the project during its life cycle. This is irrespective of whether these people or groups are directly or indirectly affected by the project outcome.

People are individual, eccentric and finicky. Each person is as idiosyncratic as the next and no two people are the same. Each person has different motivations, largely dependent on their culture and life experiences. So understanding people can give a project manager useful information on how to structure engagement more effectively.

Project success or failure always depends partly on the effectiveness (or ineffectiveness) of key relationships during the project life cycle. Project managers have to develop numerous relationships and a broad range of alliances with individuals and groups. Each of these relationships will begin differently and have its own degree of complexity, with different expectations and end goals. Also, these expectations can change as the project progresses.

Most people underestimate the myriad of relationships that transpire during the life of a project. The number of relationships that emerge at the start of the project has a tendency to swell as the project evolves. The challenge is to identify and engage these relationships early. Each project is unique, and one tends to find previously unidentified groups or individuals that 'creep out of the woodwork' as the project progresses and end up becoming a risk to the project.

Failing to identify a relationship early in the project, or allowing an existing relationship to deteriorate, will cause the project manager unnecessary confrontation and anxiety. It will necessitate the project manager taking prompt remedial action in order to avoid the relationship becoming a problem.

CASE EXAMPLE NO. 1

I ran a complex 'politically sensitive' project for a UK retail bank in 2002, working with senior management from the outset. The project sponsor identified 15 groups that needed to participate in the project. For the project 'kick-off' key representatives from these groups were invited to meet at the bank's London headquarters.

On the morning of the meeting, the project sponsor and I were stunned to discover over 40 uninvited delegates, representing 33 additional business areas, departments and subsidiary companies. These extra people all insisted on participating. Obviously word had spread. It became apparent that this extended group was very passionate about the project. So non-participation in the project was out of the question.

During the life cycle of this project there were over 60 internal groups who actively participated in the project. Each of those groups had several key representatives. Managing the multitude of internal and external relationships became a full-time role.

Why Relationships Require Active Management

Why can't relationships between people in projects just evolve in their own way? Well, we might equally ask why plan a project, why manage it? Experience teaches us that planning gives focus, helps to drive delivery and enables progress to be tracked. What level of success might we expect if we just let the project happen and evolve in its own way with no direction or leadership? Would it get delivered? It might happen, but not within a realistic timescale. The lack of focus and drive would result in either no delivery or very late delivery.

Relationships need similar attention. A valuable working relationship is dynamic, continually developing and growing – building on what transpired earlier to become mutually beneficial. Positive relationships are necessary to achieve the outcomes of the project. Without continuous attention relationships may become stagnant, easily manifesting into unreceptive behaviours and difficulties. Left unchecked these may fester into a spiral of decline and opposition. Often when a relationship has degraded this far it can turn out to be confrontational. Once the relationship has declined into this negative state turning it around is an endeavour, not an undertaking for the faint-hearted.

I often refer to a garden analogy when I explain the need to manage relationships in projects. Project relationships are like gardens. In a garden, you spend considerable time, cultivating the ground, sowing seeds, watering, feeding, weeding and nurturing. If neglected the plants will soon be overrun by weeds and eventually perish. Regular attention will help to ensure the garden remains lush.

Project relationships need to be planned, have objectives and be actively managed. The project manager must lead these relationship activities proactively. Where appropriate, others in the project environment, such as the sponsor or programme manager, must be used to ensure that relationship efforts are sustained.

The project manager must be attentive and responsive, aware of changing needs, wants and desires of the individual or group. That has to be maintained throughout the project. Eventually the project manager will acquire a good grasp of the prevailing mood of a relationship and be able to predict issues and opportunities. This will come with experience. When a project manager has built effective working relationships, communication across the project seems to work effortlessly.

What does it mean for the individual or group in a well-managed relationship? Individuals or groups in a well-managed relationship will be satisfied with the type of interaction and the level of communications between the parties. Their level of satisfaction will typically make them committed, allied and engaged. They are more likely to contribute proactively and have these contributions acknowledged. Their needs and expectations are taken into consideration. Their idiosyncrasies and unique methods will be accommodated.

Under such productive relationships, the individuals or groups will do more to support the project manager and the project. For example, when the inevitable project challenge arises it will be resolved more quickly and be addressed with less resistance from the parties involved.

So, when it comes to managing a successful project, project relationships take on considerable significance. Success is governed by the constant support of the groups or individuals. As a project manager it is imperative that you facilitate and nurture this support, and at the same time deter or countering any opposition. As the diversity of relationships accumulates, it will be necessary to give them more thought, dedicate more effort and allocate more of your valuable time. But in order to manage the various relationships, it is first necessary to identify them.

Identifying Project Relationships within the Organisation

Projects would be less of a challenge, perhaps even straightforward, if it were feasible to discriminate between the participants – not in a harsh sense, but being meticulous when choosing them. An analogy here is when the manager of a professional sports team carefully selects particular team members from a pool of resources to optimise overall team performance on match day. The manager's sole aim is optimising the team's success rate against known variables (expert opinion on the opposing team). The manager has an ongoing engagement with their team, understanding each team member's talents. By selecting the best permutation of high performers and specialists to engage the opposing team efficiently, the team manager builds what they believe to be the team with the best possible chance of success.

Every project manager aims to emulate a successful sports team and achieve such triumphant outcomes – exercising his/her own talent alongside a team of hand-picked, highly motivated performers, all driven on uniting to deliver a successful project. But, of course, in the real world, this is unlikely to happen. Project organisations typically result in an incongruent set of people being assembled to work together. Also, numerous external influences can play havoc on the selection process. The project manager is often happy just to have a full complement of people. In most organisations, the project manager is bestowed with those people who are available. He/she must then shape these people into an effective team, building effective relationships with the members as they progress.

Identifying Stakeholders

The perceptions and expectations of key stakeholders determine the overall success of the project, so how the project manager interacts with stakeholders is also essential to success. When it comes to stakeholders outside the project team, the project manager has even less power and control. So judgement, influence and 'people skills' are the only possible tools. Knowing who the stakeholders are is essential; otherwise how can engagement begin? So, the project manager must identify the stakeholders at the beginning of the project, and then monitor stakeholder changes throughout the life of the project.

Some stakeholders must be 'managed' by specialist units. For example, managing a project that may get public attention can result in all communications being vetted by (or initiated through) a specialist media or PR department or agency.

Stakeholders have a widespread and often changeable influence on the project and its outcome. This influence results in numerous demands, needs, concerns and expectations that they want fulfilling or at least addressed, to their satisfaction, by the project during the life cycle and by its outcome. Typically many of these demands conflict with one another; it's the project manager's task to balance the needs of the stakeholders, if possible getting stakeholders to align their expectations with one another.

Ultimately, a project manager's goal is to gain stakeholder support for the project. This means effective engagement with the stakeholders, managing the project relationships between the project and the stakeholders, and even between the stakeholders themselves. Therefore identifying who these key stakeholders are becomes an important early step towards attaining project success.

Inexperienced project managers are inclined to underestimate the effort required to identify stakeholders (and deal with them). At first, it does appear to be comparatively easy, but once the obvious stakeholders are identified, the remaining stakeholders are somewhat more difficult to pinpoint.

The consequences of not identifying and engaging stakeholders early on in the project can be disastrous. A neglected key stakeholder might have requirements that need to be part of the project. Excluding these requirements at the start can result in changes later in the project (when the stakeholder is eventually identified and the late engagement with the stakeholder starts). Late changes are always more expensive and disruptive than changes identified nearer the project start. Neglected stakeholders will not be happy if they feel that they have been disregarded and could become troublesome and demanding.

So, clearly it is necessary to identify all the stakeholders from the start of the project and to keep abreast of changes within the stakeholder community as the project progresses.

PRACTICAL STEPS FOR IDENTIFYING STAKEHOLDERS

Typically the key stakeholders on a project will include the project manager, project team members, project sponsor and customer (or customer representative). Other types of projects may additionally have citizens, politicians, functional heads, senior management, users, suppliers and contractors. Each stakeholder will have different needs, requirements and expectations. I have found that a systematic approach works best when identifying the stakeholders on a particular project.

The place to start is the early project documentation, which can include the following:

- proposal;
- feasibility study;
- impact assessment study;
- consultation processes;
- documents that facilitated the project (project charter, business case);
- related programme evaluations, high-level business requirements.

Historic records, such as past stakeholder information and consultations, lessons learned, and policies and procedures for identifying stakeholders can also be helpful. Particularly useful are the distribution lists and signature pages of these documents, along with deliverables and dependency sections. This search can identify stakeholders or business units that are typically forgotten.

Organisation charts can be used to ascertain key functional areas, subsidiaries and so on. Project portfolio diagrams might identify key areas and programmes, and related projects which may have interdependencies with the project.

So you can analyse this material to find key stakeholders and the project's sphere of influence (the project's primary purpose, planned outcomes, related areas or projects, potentially cumulative impacts or predicted related developments). Running through the various items of project-related collateral provides an essential first attempt at identifying stakeholders. It is useful to ask oneself the following questions:

- Are there any gaps in the understanding?
- What knowledge is needed to fill the gaps?
- Who can provide this information?

From all this information, the project manager can start to construct a list of stakeholder groups and individuals. The project sponsor and core project team should be engaged to add their insight, running through the findings to date and identifying any gaps. During these sessions, be sure to identify and document relevant information regarding the stakeholders. The level of detail is dependent on the project manager's needs, but it is essential that all stakeholders are identified, including their interests, involvements, impact and potential influences (especially negative) on the project.

Checklist

The following checklist should be useful for identifying stakeholders. The list should be tailored appropriately for the project.

- Who is funding or paying for the project?
- Who is approving the project?
- Who is contributing to the project?
- Who is designing, building, testing or implementing the project?
- Who will operate, support, maintain, market, sell and use project deliverables or the outcome of the project?
- Who needs to know about the project?
- Who will be affected by the success or failure of the project?
- Is there any financial, legal or regulatory impact or other compliance? If so, who should be represented?
- Who has a stake (positive or negative) in the critical issues addressed by the project?
- Who is most affected by the problems or issues being addressed by the project? Who is concerned? Who may have different views? Who are the key players?
- What problems have been identified during the project and who is best able to help resolve them?
- Is there a person in the area/department who could 'champion' the project?
- Is every affected area, department or business unit represented?

Stakeholder Register

At the end of the analysis you should have a detailed list itemising who is relevant to the project. On occasion stakeholders – even key stakeholders such as the project sponsor – will change throughout the project's life cycle. This is particularly prevalent in larger projects of long duration. Some project managers follow the PMI PMBOK guidance and document stakeholders in a stakeholders' register.

Stakeholder Analysis

Following the identification process, the project manager should construct a detailed 'stakeholder needs' analysis. Intended to document and map out who the stakeholders are, this is an essential stage in developing a strategy for engaging with stakeholders.

In a nutshell, the stakeholder analysis identifies key issues for each stakeholder and the action planned to resolve conflicts or maximise opportunities. The items should include known or potential stakeholder interests, impact of change, issues and concerns, importance and influence, and attitude. Other factors that may be covered are explicit expectations/requirements, stakeholder objectives, stakeholder conflicts, risks and opportunities for synergies. Identifying and capturing these components at an early stage allows for early analysis on how to manage the stakeholders. Figure 20.1 illustrates a typical format for tabulating the results.

Stakeholder's name	Position	Area of interest	Impact of the project on the stakeholder	Potential issues and concerns	Stakeholder's importance and influence on the project	Attitude

Figure 20.1 Stakeholder analysis page headings

Engaging with Stakeholders

When the stakeholders have been identified, analysed and profiled, the project manager must engage with them effectively. Having the right people involved in the project at the right times makes a project run much more smoothly. So it is important to take time to build on those relationships.

Commonly project managers will have limited time to give every stakeholder an equal amount of attention. As some stakeholders are more critical than others to the success of the project then clearly these stakeholders must be prioritised. I have often use 'Pareto's Principle', the 80–20 Rule, in prioritising stakeholder activities. The principle is based on the opinion that 20 per cent of some input is responsible for 80 per cent of the output (explained in more detail in Chapter 31). Experience with stakeholders has shown that 20 per cent of the stakeholders often account for 80 per cent of the activities (impact, influence, challenges and so on). (Obviously these are generalisations and each project would need to be assessed individually.) On this basis a project manager could prioritise the key 20 per cent of stakeholders and focus time accordingly.

The project manager must prioritise his/her efforts with the help of a 'power/interest matrix' (Figure 20.2). This quadrant-based matrix is used to determine the type of relationship each stakeholder requires and how the different stakeholders should be managed. It classifies stakeholders in relation to the power that they hold and their anticipated interest in the project. Each identified stakeholder should be mapped on to the matrix, positioned in the relevant quadrant according to the level of power and level of interest, as follows:

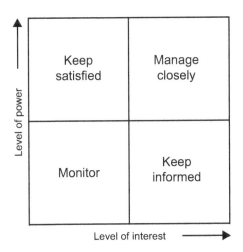

Figure 20.2 Stakeholder power/interest matrix

Stakeholders with low power and low interest fall into the 'monitor' quadrant. Although the project manager will need to monitor these stakeholders, time investment should be minimal.

Stakeholders with low power and high interest fall into 'keep informed' quadrant. These stakeholders require more attention because some could influence the more powerful stakeholders. They have high interest in the project and its outcomes, but have limited means to influence things directly. Often these stakeholders prove to be valuable allies in supporting important decisions. The project manager will need to keep them informed about the issues in which they are interested.

Stakeholders with high power and low interest fall into 'keep satisfied' quadrant. This group can prove challenging. They behave passively for much of the time, showing little or no interest in the project. However, when they react to something, they can exert enormous impact on the project. The project manager will need to keep a close eye on these stakeholders to analyse their intentions and reactions. Interactions and communication must be maintained at a level which keeps them informed (especially about the issues in which they are interested).

Stakeholders who have high power and high interest fall into 'manage closely' quadrant. These key stakeholders clearly require the most time and attention. They can ensure project failure if they are not managed properly. It might be necessary to adapt the type of relationship with each stakeholder to ensure their particular relationship requirements are met.

Using the stakeholder mappings the project manager can channel time and energy on the stakeholders that have the most power and interest in project success. Keep the following questions in mind when dealing with stakeholders, 'Who needs to be informed of what, and when?' and 'Who needs to be consulted about what, and when?'

But I have to add a note of caution. Just like the stakeholder analysis, this process is very subjective and can be prone to error. Continuous examination of how things are working with the stakeholders should help reveal any errors.

Building and Maintaining Relationships

Relationship building, in the context of a management role is an acknowledged competency. The American Management Association defines this competency as 'being skilled at detecting and interpreting subtle clues, often non-verbal, about others' feelings and concerns. People with this competency display empathy and sensitivity to the needs and concerns of others and support others when they are facing difficult tasks. When you have this competency, you enjoy dealing with people and working with people of diverse styles and backgrounds.

Relationship building is a vital factor in managing performance and delivering results. Fundamentally it is the ability to work openly with others, closely coupled to the abilities of listening, questioning, building rapport and emotional intelligence. The project manager must lead and influence others and build effective relationships in order to manage change and conflict. This typically entails:

• anticipating needs (such as sharing information before it's requested);

- active engagement (reaching out to advance communications);
- being openly communicative and building connections and networks.

Building effective relationships requires steady truthful communication, whether that is communicating good news or bad news. Getting to know the stakeholders and taking an interest in what is important to them will help to enhance the engagement. Aiming to establish a sustained connection that makes each stakeholder feel valued may eventually lead to 'loyalty'.

WHY BUILD RELATIONSHIPS WITH THE STAKEHOLDERS?

Projects face many complex challenges in the process of delivering expected outcomes. Project managers are unable to solve these in isolation, and must work in partnership with the project team and others, both within their organisation and outside. Such complex challenges require a coordinated effort, with the project manager, project team and multiple stakeholders collaborating and contributing to deliver innovative and viable solutions.

Projects are deemed successful when they deliver appropriate value to the key project stakeholders. To discover the expectations of these people or groups, clearly the project manager must engage and build relationships with them. Engaging in a collaborative relationship with stakeholders can help steer projects to avoid or minimise risk and create opportunities. This benefits the project manager.

Stakeholder engagement is the foundation of relationship management with stakeholders. If done well, it enhances ties with stakeholders; helps propel the project forward, and will deliver planned outcomes. Of all the tasks involved in project managing, stakeholder engagement is usually the most challenging and one of the most critical activities. The project manager rarely has the power to compel activities of all stakeholders, so there can be great disparity between what individuals promise to do and what actually happens in practice. Occasionally the effort pays off and yields a 'champion' to serve as an advocate for the project.

The purpose of engaging stakeholders is threefold, as follows:

1. To make them aware of the project, from why it is starting, why it is important, what role they are expected to perform, the benefits they may expect from their involvement and so on.
2. Discovering what they are expecting of the project, what they need and how they want to be communicated with.
3. It affords an opportunity to inspire and motivate stakeholders' active support and involvement.

The goal in engaging with the stakeholders is to build firm working relationships with them. Relationships are built on trust. Stakeholders need to know that you can follow through on any deliverable or promise – that you have their best interests at heart. Gaining stakeholders' confidence and trust in you and your project team is key to developing good stakeholder relationships.

ESTABLISHING A RELATIONSHIP: INITIAL CONSULTATION

The aim is creating the right first impression and maintaining it in the long term. For the first meeting, it is better to meet individually with a stakeholder. Face-to-face is best, although a telephone can still be valuable.

- Prepare for the relationship. Stakeholder engagement begins with consideration of who the stakeholders are, their interests, their perspectives and so on.
- Use the information captured in the stakeholder analysis to get to understand your stakeholder.
- Think about who else needs to be involved or consulted.
- Put an agenda together to outline the topics and purpose. Obtaining unambiguous answers for these questions will save time and help set expectations.
- Arrange a consultation with the stakeholder. The consultation is a two-way process. It is the first opportunity for you to learn first-hand, providing valuable information, clarification of issues and so forth. This meeting is the first opportunity to engage and will be the foundation of the relationship, it is important to get it right, so plan accordingly. Active listening will help avoid misunderstandings and mistakes.
- Aim to reach an initial agreement. During the initial consultation aim to get an understanding of your stakeholder's perspectives. At the same time outline the project's perspective. Identify common ground. Clarify roles and responsibilities. Aim to agree joint objectives and set SMART (specific, measurable, agreed upon, realistic and time-based) objectives.
- Agree the method and frequency of communications. Making the effort to have a regular personal, face-to-face contact with each stakeholder will benefit in building the relationship.
- Adopt an effective approach used by external consultants. Consultants come in and need to hit the ground running, so developing a stronger working relationship with the key stakeholder is a vital activity. Consultants endeavour to speed up this process by engaging informally, with the aim to get to know people better (a brief conversation in a corridor, informal meeting over a coffee and so on).
- Build the relationship with communication, trust and transparency. The aim is to develop and sustain a mutual connection. This way the relationship will be nourished and maintained.

Communication is the key factor in developing and sustaining a relationship with stakeholders. For it to develop there needs to be constant interaction between people. That interaction needs to be appropriate, timely and effective.

Trust and respect are critical aspects in a relationship. Trust is the foundation of every relationship; it is not easily given and not easily earned. Trust is destroyed easily, such as a promise or an expectation that is not fulfilled, or a deliverable that is expected is not carried out.

Ensure that you adopt appropriate levels of transparency with the stakeholders. Being open and honest, making information accessible to impacted stakeholders is essential in building and maintaining the relationship. Don't make assumptions; ask stakeholders what information they need, when they need it and how it should be delivered. Respect is also a fundamental aspect of relationships. Respect means understanding the other person's attitudes, values, views and beliefs.

Once a relationship with a stakeholder is broken, fixing it can be difficult, and more challenging than establishing it in the first place. It is better to maintain durable ties through diplomacy.

Often the relationship with the stakeholder will undergo some level of conflict. Unfortunately during the course of a project there will be the inevitable challenges that strain the relationships. In order to keep the relationship intact the project manager must maintain a diplomatic perspective regardless of the situation.

CONTINUOUS IMPROVEMENT TO MAINTAIN THE RELATIONSHIP

What a project manager must do ideally is keep the demands of each stakeholder balanced with the needs of the project and those of the other stakeholders, facilitating stakeholder engagement to ensure relationships are maintained and buy in continues for the project.

Typically with so many stakeholders to deal with, the project manager must prioritise when and where attention is needed. In order to do this the project manager assesses the state of stakeholder relationships to identify where attention is required to strengthen the relationship. This is a continuous process, covering the entire life cycle of the project.

When assessing the state of the relationship between a project and a stakeholder, the project manager must look at both the relationship with each stakeholder and between the stakeholders. Often the project manager's relationship with the stakeholder is sound but relationships between key stakeholders are strained – in these situations it is unlikely that any intervention from the project manager would improve the situation. However, such cases may require a modification in the way the project manager deals with these stakeholders.

Assessing the state of a relationship tends to be done by soliciting feedback or by performing an informal survey of the stakeholders, to discern how weak or strong the relationship is. By measuring the strength of stakeholder perceptions, one is able to gauge the strength of a particular relationship. Performing this activity across the stakeholder community will enable the project manager to identify the weaker relationships and focus efforts or take remedial action to get it back on track.

The key element towards building and maintaining stakeholder relationships is effective communications. Stakeholder relationships are continuously cultivated through enriching the project's communication efforts, these communications efforts are targeted to the specific requirements of each stakeholder.

Arrival of New Stakeholders

The arrival of a new stakeholder raises the possibility of clashes of interest. This often provides the project manager with a dilemma of how to (or how not to) satisfy the new stakeholder's needs, whilst avoiding conflict with the present stakeholders. Ideally, a fine balance could be achieved to satisfy all stakeholders whilst obtaining the project's objectives.

However, certain stakeholders may have completely conflicting expectations, demands and measures of success. In such cases it may be prudent to perform an impact assessment on other stakeholders and on the project. Occasionally the only resolution is to escalate the issue to the project sponsor.

Conclusion

Project managers must identify stakeholders early in the project and ensure that each stakeholder is engaged effectively in order to obtain a positive impact from their participation. Each of these stakeholders has a different perspective and motivation for participating in the project. Their expectations are diverse and seldom align, certainly at the outset of the project.

Actively engaging the key stakeholders to build and maintain relationships will require good communication and proactive involvement in the project. The goal in engaging with the stakeholders is to build and maintain firm working relationships to achieve positive influence and outcomes. But each stakeholder is unique. Individual demands and expectations may well conflict with other stakeholders. The project manager must adapt each engagement accordingly, because with stakeholder relationships there is no 'one approach fits all'.

As the stakeholder environment evolves over time the project manager must become familiar with each new stakeholder. Inevitably this requires continuous attention to build and maintain stakeholder relationships.

The project manager must act as both driver and enabler in the traditional role of managing and driving the project delivery to satisfy agreed scope, schedule and budget. But the project manager needs to do more in the complementing role of enabler. Developing, sustaining and enhancing relationships with the network of project stakeholders to facilitate, coordinate, align and harness their individual energy for the benefit of the project.

21 *Creating and Changing a Project Team*

ANDY JORDAN

This chapter will examine the variables that need to be considered in building a project team. It will also consider decisions for making changes to the team and will explore the impact that changes can have and examine ways for overcoming any negative effects.

Introduction

Here are three questions for consideration:

1. What makes a strong project team?
2. How can we ensure that the groups we assemble and assign to a project will quickly develop into a high-performing team?
3. How do we help that team through the inevitable changes that will occur during the project?

When it works, the project team is an extremely complex 'ecosystem' that is constantly evolving and adapting to its environment. It might simply be a group of individuals, but the collective team organisation is so much more than that. It's the cohesive unit that can achieve the seemingly impossible whilst growing ever stronger. Yet it is also extremely fragile – make one change and the whole entity suffers, requiring an extended period in which to recover (if, indeed, recovery is possible at all).

We must also recognise that there are project teams that do not function well, some of which will never grow and develop no matter how well they are nurtured. They always seem to be a collection of disparate parts that do not fit together properly, that seem to work against one another, so that with them nothing seems possible.

Building a Team

Suppose that we start with the apparently obvious beginning, which is building the team. But that isn't the true beginning. Before we can build a successful team we need to plan for it; we shouldn't start by procuring resources, posting job advertisements and so on. Instead we should understand our resourcing needs and how best to meet those needs with a group of complementary resources that will be able to work together to achieve the project's goals. That means considering a number of different aspects that will impact upon our team selection decisions.

All of these considerations are related to one another, and cannot simply be considered in isolation. This is a complex set of variables that needs to be balanced if we are to build the foundations of a strong team. The variables include:

- *Internal versus external* – Are we going to use only existing resources or are we going to bring people in from outside? This decision may be taken for us – the budget might not allow for any additional hiring, but in some cases external resources will be available and can make or break the project. If we are going to bring people in from outside then we also need to consider whether we are going to hire additional employees, bring temporary contractors on board or partner with a third party organisation that specialises in the areas we need.
- *Skills and experience versus personality and fit* – It's tempting to try and bring all of the 'experts' together on our project so that each work package has the best possible person responsible for it. The problem with that approach is that it makes no allowance for how well those people will be able to work together. If the best minds on the planet are busy arguing with their colleagues on how to do the work, then they aren't helping the project to succeed. Of course the counter argument is also true – you can't have a group of people who get along with one another really well if they don't have the skills necessary for the work.
- *Experience versus enthusiasm* – Building on the previous item, there are dangers in bringing a group of highly experienced resources together without balancing them with some less experienced, more enthusiastic people who can bring a fresh perspective and a willingness to challenge and question the status quo. Of course if you have too many people like that then you don't have sufficient experience to make the right decisions.
- *Skill level* – Not all tasks on our project will need highly skilled people. Assigning highly skilled individuals to menial tasks will disillusion them, cost the project more than is necessary and prevent those people from being available to other projects within the organisation. On the other hand, if you don't have someone skilled enough for the tasks, then those tasks will take longer and work may not be produced to a high enough standard.

This argument could be continued, but clearly this is difficult. When we start building the project team and put names against roles, we have to consider all of those variables in order to try and ensure that we get the right balance. In some cases we may have no choice – there may only be one person available who meets the skills criteria, so we have to accept the experience, personality traits and so on that they bring with them (assuming that we can't spend time searching outside the organisation for someone 'better').

In other areas we may have a choice of people who meet the skills requirements of the project role and we can consider the people who will fit best with the rest of the team, the ones who will gain from the opportunity and be more valuable to the organisation in the future. As project managers we need to balance all the variables if we are to bring together a group of people who can evolve into a high-performing team. This means being prepared to compromise where necessary in order to make the overall team stronger –

assigning someone to the team who has fewer skills and less experience because they are a better 'fit' for the group of people that make up the project team for example.

We also have to recognise that we cannot create a team ourselves. All we can do is bring a group of people together; they have to make the conscious decision to work together as a team for the benefit of the project. This can be tough to achieve. Opposites only attract in clichés and if you have people with different working styles, attitudes, personalities and so on, there can be some initial resistance to working together. A successful team needs to be able to put its differences aside and focus on what the group has in common, leveraging those commonalities and strengthening the bonds between the team members.

Bruce Tuckman introduced his model of group development in 1965 and it is still the standard that we use today (Tuckman, 1965). He proposed that a team goes through four distinct stages of development – forming, storming, norming and performing, as they develop those commonalities and bonds. I shall refer to those as we look at developing the team.

Developing the Team

Team development takes time. We cannot mandate a high-performing team in a week just because that's what the schedule requires. People need to figure out for themselves how to work with their colleagues, and that requires building a comfort level around them, understanding personalities, working styles, personal motivators and so forth. Project managers need to allow for this process to take place on the project. We won't have a period in the schedule for nothing but 'team building', but we shall recognise that productivity will be lower in the early stages as people get to know one another and develop working relationships. We have to allow more time for tasks to be completed in these early days and weeks. This is typical of the 'forming' phase identified by Tuckman.

Project managers also need to ensure that they are doing all that they can to help the team development process. Involving everyone in the kick-off meetings, having them work on common objectives, and facilitating communication and collaboration, will all help the individuals to understand how their colleagues work and will begin the process of evolving a group of people into a single cohesive unit – a team.

Even a task as simple as creating a project name or logo can be beneficial. That might sound silly, but it can force the group to focus on a common goal and create a common identity that they can relate to. It starts to make the project something tangible and real, and it gives the group a sense of ownership of that project.

As with any other group of people, project team members need to find their place in the team hierarchy. Are they 'leaders' or 'followers'? Who can they trust and who are they wary of? What agendas do other people have and which of those agendas run counter to their own agenda? This isn't malicious or even necessarily conscious; it's just part of getting to know the people that they are working with and establishing their role as a part of that team. Until each team member establishes and becomes comfortable with this they will feel uneasy and will spend more time focused on ensuring that their own needs are met and less time focusing on the needs of the project. This is typical of the 'storming' stage that Tuckman identified, and it can be a potentially dangerous time. We cannot avoid having teams go through this process, but as project managers we need to ensure that the team is able to move past this.

By selecting team members with complementary styles and personalities we can minimise the severity and impact of any conflict, but people still need to learn how to work together. Friction is inevitable during that process. Our focus needs to be on helping the team to move past this phase as quickly as possible to the point where the team is working together for the good of the project. This means:

- Providing continued areas of focus – Involving the team in project-related tasks – the work breakdown structure, risk identification exercises and so forth will provide them with a common area of focus and will immediately help them to move beyond individual differences and focus on the shared goal of completing the work.
- Ensuring that disagreements remain objective – You don't want a team that is always in agreement, because that will not always lead to the best solutions. You need team members to discuss options, debate alternatives and so on because ultimately that leads to an improved outcome. As a project manager you need to encourage these debates, but ensure that they remain focused on the project challenges and do not become subjective arguments based on personal bias and positioning.
- Dealing with conflict – As project managers we have a unique position on an initiative – we are part of the team, but distinctly removed from the other team members because of the particular role that we play. We need to establish our own position with the team and ensure that we have built credibility and respect with our colleagues. Dealing with the conflicts that will inevitably arise will go a long way towards achieving that goal. We need to ensure that we remain objective and avoid taking sides, but we cannot allow conflict to fester because that would have the potential to destroy the team. That means bringing the issue back to the project challenges and away from personal disagreements.

As people become more involved in the project work and more familiar with their colleagues the relationships between individuals will strengthen and team members will become more engaged in the collective team. People learn that they can disagree with their colleagues without damaging relationships. People will learn to read the signs when someone is having a bad day, feeling stressed and overworked, and so on. This is Tuckman's 'norming' stage. It is indeed exactly that – finding a normal level at which to relate to people and to focus on goals.

This is a natural part of getting to know people and we can all relate to it from our own lives. Just as importantly, we as project managers get to the same point with the team (collectively and individually), recognising when people are having problems, learning how people like to work and so forth.

As people feel more comfortable with the team and their place in it we will see an increase in productivity and an improved sense of energy and engagement from the team. This is often the point when project managers make the fatal mistake of thinking that team development is completed. Teams need to continue to develop or they will stagnate and decline, and whilst they will naturally tend to evolve together without as much support from the project manager, the project manager still needs to be conscious of any disagreements that develop and manage them carefully to avoid damaging the overall environment. This 'performing' phase is where we get to the point of high productivity and high effectiveness. Not every team will get here, but those that do will be able to achieve greatness.

It is also important to recognise that there is no ceiling on performance. A team can continue to improve its effectiveness throughout the project, with individual team members driving one another to achieve ever greater performance. Too many project managers strive to bring their teams to a 'plateau' of performance and keep them there, accepting the team's productivity as 'good enough'.

Changing a Team

It may be a cliché, but the statement that 'the only constant is change' is true. Most projects will be subject to some kind of change in the team during their life. This may be the result of a change in one of the project constraints (people are added, removed or swapped owing to budget, time or scope changes) or it could be the result of a team member leaving and having to be replaced. From a management standpoint there are two elements to a change in the team:

1. the decision to make the change;
2. the management of the impact.

In all cases both of these elements have to be considered. Even if a team member made the decision to resign to take advantage of another opportunity we need to consider whether there are issues with the project and/or the team that led the individual to reach that decision.

When we make a more conscious decision to change the team we are effectively conducting a cost-benefit analysis. Every change has a cost associated with it beyond the obvious financial cost, even if the only change is the addition of resources. The overall productivity of the team will suffer as the new team members are incorporated into the group and new working relationships are formed and developed.

As a result, we need to be confident that the net gain is positive, and that the advantage will be significant enough to warrant the impact on the team. When we are simply adding new resources that should be an easy case to prove – once the team has adjusted to the new team member(s) the productivity gains from more people being involved should be obvious.

The situation is complicated by the likelihood that there will be a trade-off on the project constraints. The timeline might well have shortened, for example. But this will still be the easiest decision for a project manager and stakeholders to make.

When we make a decision to replace one individual with another, the cost-benefit equation could be more difficult. Even if we are replacing a less skilled, less experienced or less motivated team member with a highly skilled enthusiastic replacement, there will still be some productivity impact that needs to be overcome, and the improved productivity that the new resource brings might not be needed for long enough to overcome the productivity deficit that will be incurred by making the change.

In this situation we need to look for opportunities to strengthen the overall team performance by making one or two changes – improving everyone's productivity by changing one or two components – taking the team to a whole new level if you like.

Consider the example of a Premiership football team. Suppose that the team manager replaces one of the players through a transfer process with the intention of strengthening the squad. This isn't just about upgrading one position. Rather it's about making the people around that player perform at a higher level, improving the 'chemistry in the dressing room' and so forth. That's exactly what a project manager and the stakeholders should be trying to achieve when making a change to the project team – strengthening the whole with just one or two key changes.

We need to be sensitive to the fact that we are dealing with individuals and their feelings. If we make a change on our project then we are having an impact on people's careers. A resource who is reassigned to another project may take with them the reputation that they 'weren't good enough' to cope with their former project and that can make it difficult for them to be accepted into new initiatives. At a more extreme level, there may not be another project for them to move to and they may have to leave the organisation entirely.

In the vast majority of circumstances we should try and take steps to correct the issues with any team member in order to avoid the need to remove them from the project. There will be exceptions (inappropriate behaviour, serious breach of contract and so on) that will demand immediate removal, but those are rare cases. If we are able to upgrade the performance of our existing team then we shall avoid some of the productivity losses incurred by making a change.

At the risk of oversimplifying things slightly, we deal with two types of inadequate performance on our teams which are:

1. a shortfall in ability;
2. a shortfall in attitude.

If the problematic team member is lacking in the skills and experience needed for their role, but is a generally solid part of the team, then training and support may be all that is needed to improve that person's productivity. Certainly the first step should be to attempt to lift the performance whilst keeping him/her on the team. The fact that the person is a solid team member will mean that removal and replacement with someone new must have a negative effect on that person's colleagues. This might require some compromise, such as allowing the person additional time for tasks, reallocating some work to colleagues and so forth. But this can be seen as a longer-term investment – taking a short-term 'productivity hit' in order to provide a future key contributor with some additional experience.

If the issue is not one of skills or ability but rather is an attitudinal one, then the approach may be slightly different. We should still attempt to correct the behaviour and turn the team member into a valuable contributor, but we need to be sensitive that a bad attitude may already be having a negative impact on team productivity and that 'addition by subtraction' can occur (which means that the overall team productivity improves when the problematic member is removed, even if he or she is not replaced by another immediately). In this situation we are less tolerant of issues and need to see a rapid turnaround in attitude before the team member is branded as a 'problem'. As project managers we need to be direct and prescriptive with people in this situation. We need to clearly establish what standard of behaviour is expected, and what the consequences will be if that standard is not met.

As we have discussed, project managers face a balancing act when making a decision to change team members. Weighing up the costs and the benefits, and key stakeholders' interests also need to be part of the decision-making process. By far the biggest mistake that project managers and other stakeholders make in this area is a failure to act quickly and decisively. We should always try to deal with performance issues by upgrading skills and/or changing attitude, but we also cannot delay in making the change if it is the right thing to do – that would just delay the inevitable and cause the team to deal with the issues for an extended period.

Policies at each organisation will dictate some of the mechanics of making the change, especially if it results in the individual leaving the organisation, but the message needs to be delivered in an objective, unemotional way. The person who is being told that they are no longer part of the team is likely to be shocked and upset. You need to ensure that they clearly understand what is happening, why it is happening and that there is no opportunity to negotiate or change the decision. This is not being heartless. It is ensuring that the conversation remains objective.

Once the change is made, the project manager will face some of the biggest challenges. Remaining team members are likely to be surprised and potentially upset by the change, and they will need time to come to terms with what has happened. As project managers we need to ensure that the team is advised of the change as soon as possible, but we also need to recognise that there are limitations on what can be achieved at this point. Initially we should concentrate simply on the delivery of the news. That alone will need to be understood and processed by the remaining team members and that will take time. People might feel guilty for having criticised the person who left. They could have conflicting emotions or even be concerned that they could be next. Whatever they feel, they need to process those feelings and find a new 'level' within the team.

Thinking back to Tuckman's group development model, we should be prepared for the team to take some steps backward. This will show itself through a drop in productivity during the first few days following the announcement. People could act differently, be short tempered or lack focus – which is all part of coming to terms with what has happened. The project manager needs to provide time and space for the team to spend time together, focusing simply on helping one another through the change, and concentrating on strengthening the bonds of their team. This may sound melodramatic, but in some ways it is no different to the stages of grief that people go through. The 'loss' may not be as severe, but the emotions are just as real for people. Even if the change was a result of a colleague obtaining a new job, many of these emotions may still be felt, and could remain hidden if the person who is leaving is working through a notice period.

Individuals will come to terms with what has happened at different rates. As project managers we need to be prepared for many questions as the information is digested and the impact is assessed. We need to ensure that we provide answers that are as honest and open as possible – we must demonstrate that we are worthy of the team's trust.

As people come to terms with what has happened and demonstrate a readiness to refocus on work, we need to provide them with tasks upon which to concentrate as quickly as possible. This will help the team to pull together around the project work and provide a common goal for people to work towards. The first people who are able to concentrate on their deliverables again will provide some subconscious peer pressure on their colleagues and the remainder of the team will probably soon follow (although productivity may still be adversely affected for a while).

If a replacement resource is to join the team then it's important to bring them on board as swiftly as possible to provide continuity to the work and to minimise the continued disruption to the team. The addition of a new team member will again have an impact on team performance and we don't want that to happen after the team has just recovered their productivity from the departure of their former colleague.

Whenever a new person is added there is the risk of a 'them and us' mindset on the team. Existing team members draw together and see the new team member as a potential threat. From a practical sense there is the concern that working relationships and practices will have to change to accommodate the new colleague, and from an emotional sense there may be an unwillingness for an 'outsider' to come into the team.

In addition, there may be anger or resentment from people who did not want to see the previous team member leave. They project their anger and frustration at the new team member and do not give them a chance to become a valued team member.

As project managers we also need to ensure that we coach the new resource. They need to understand the situation that they are coming in to and recognise that they may not be immediately welcomed by everyone. They need to understand that this is not a reflection upon them, but rather the result of the circumstances that have led to their joining the team. The new person needs to ensure that they avoid inflaming the situation by comparing themselves to the person from whom they are taking over, or by criticising that person's work.

Whilst this isn't the same situation as the team development discussed at the start of this chapter, many of the same processes need to occur if the team is going to come back together as a cohesive unit with the new member. The team will still go through a form of forming, storming, norming and performing as the new team member is integrated. It will probably be a quicker and easier transition, but we need to allow the team time to accept and incorporate the new person – bringing them up to speed on the way in which the team operates, familiarising them on routine issues such as where documents are stored, when team meetings occur and so on. A group event, such as a team lunch, to welcome the new team member can help and will provide everyone with a 'bonus' as a result of the addition to the team.

From a practical sense, we need to recognise that team effectiveness will take a temporary step back as the team moves through Tuckman's model and the new person integrates with the people, the processes and the work packages. But we also need to recognise the opportunity that the change introduces.

A challenge such as a team change can often create stronger bonds than those which previously existed. The project manager who helps a team to come to terms with the change, provides the time for people to adjust, and creates the environment where that adjustment can happen in a non-threatening way will probably find that the overall performance has been lifted to a higher level than before the change. The performing stage ends up reaching a higher level of productivity than before. And that was the whole point of making the change in the first place.

References and Further Reading

Belbin, R.M. (2003), *Management Teams: Why They Succeed or Fail*, 2nd edn, Oxford: Elsevier Butterworth-Heinemann.

Tuckman, B.W. (1965), 'Developmental sequence in small groups', *Psychological Bulletin*, 63(6), 384–99.

22 *Building Relationships through Influencing*

MARK RODGERS

Project management is often one of the most challenging positions in an organisation. Whatever the industry, project managers are usually responsible for achieving 'mission-critical' deliverables. They have to navigate the complex world of organisational politics, survive cut-throat competition for resources, and coordinate the efforts of many people and organisations. Often they are given precious little authority. When they are successful, project managers are considered to be just doing their job. But if they fail, the blame will fall squarely on their shoulders. Clearly the role of project manager is not for the timid. Many factors go into the make-up of a successful project manager but a key element is the ability to build relationships so that the project aims can be accomplished. That requires understanding the influence terrain.

The Intellect of Influence

Attempts to define aspects of organisational life in terms as amorphous as 'relationships' and 'influence' can get messy. But I can offer some parameters to help guide you through this chapter.

Relationships can be described as positive (for good) or negative. Of course there are also cases where no relationship has been built up.

Influence can be defined as: *the capacity to be a compelling force which produces effects on the opinions, actions and behaviour of others.* Think of this as your professional and personal credibility, your organisational political capital, your corporate 'sway'.

The objective is to understand how you, as a project manager, can develop and use your influence to improve you relationships, as follows:

- optimise your existing positive relationships;
- repair your negative relationships;
- create positive relationships where none previously existed.

Although these actions may not seem simple, the process can be simplified. To do that means using an idea called 'enlightened self-interest'.

The concept of enlightened self-interest was described by the nineteenth-century French economist and social observer Alexis de Tocqueville in his landmark work, *Democracy in America* (volume 1 of which was published in 1835, followed by volume 2 in 1840). He observed that Americans work together to further the interests of a group, which thereby furthers the interests of individuals to do what is right (it could be argued that navigating away from this idea is what led to the American and subsequently the global economic crises of 2008 and beyond).

The idea here is to do things that are:

- positive and right (meaning both ethical and profitable) for your organisation;
- positive for you (leading to increased income and professional status) and;
- positive for the larger whole in which you operate (your industry and your community).

Self-interest can be good but enlightened self-interest is great. If you want to get more people to say, 'Yes' to you and your offers, then you should appeal to their enlightened self-interest.

True Project Leadership

It is important to define true project leadership (or any leadership for that matter). True leadership is none of the following:

- psychological manipulation;
- using bribes or trickery to get what you want;
- using self-serving flattery or being a 'yes' person;
- agreeing with superiors regardless of direction (Revamp the entire organisation, overnight? Yes, we can!).

Although there have been many definitions of 'leadership' proffered throughout the ages, the one upon which I rely is simple and effective. It is:

True leadership is when people follow you because they want to, and not because they have to.

When you conduct yourself so that people *want* to help it may be for many reasons. It might be because people genuinely understand the objectives, or the larger role of the project, see the benefit for themselves, or because they are fulfilling their component of a reciprocal exchange. Or it could be a combination of these. In any event, the important result is the same: commitment. People perform well because they want to and not because they have to.

Your path to this organisational nirvana can be hastened by understanding the human tendency towards a concept called reciprocity: we want to repay others in kind. If you help me with a report, I'll want to help you. If you provide resources on a task force, I'll be more likely to provide the same for you. It has been said there is not one human society on the planet which does not teach its members the concept of reciprocity. When you can intelligently don the yoke of service, you can be significantly advantaged in your journey towards building relationships through influence.

So now we know something about building relationships through influence. Now we must identify the various routes to success (power sources). We shall then build our engine of influence (intellectual horsepower). After a few quick 'rules of the road', we shall create a navigation system so that we never get lost in the organisational morass. But no discussion on building project management relationships would be complete without a review of the typical routes to power in an organisation, their tendency towards compliance and commitment and the possible risks of resistance.

Typical Routes to Power

Sociologists, French and Raven (1959) articulated power categories towards the end of the 1950s. My views build on those ideas to explore the various positions of power available to a project manager.

REWARD

Reward is when you have the ability to give your project team members something in exchange for their efforts. The most common example is an increase in compensation or a bonus. But there are many other intangibles (often not considered) that could be even more powerful than monetary compensation. Many studies cite money as important, but not the most important factor driving human performance (see, for example, Chapter 33 on motivational methods). Other ways that a project manager can build relationships and reap rewards include:

- providing an unexpected service or favour;
- giving information first;
- demonstrating trust (for example by full delegation, and not micromanaging);
- showing cooperation;
- mentoring someone to improve their skills;
- honestly complimenting someone's work;
- really listening to what someone has to say;
- being positive and energetic;
- recognising people's efforts openly;
- if possible, allowing flexible working times;
- giving people your full and complete attention (not, for example, checking your emails or doing other distracting tasks whilst you are conversing with them).

PUNISHMENT

If the rewards of the previous section represented the carrot, punishment is the 'stick' component of working relationships. This means withholding something desirable, or imposing something undesirable on a person. Often such actions are obvious, but sometimes they are not. They can be intentional or unintentional. The astute project manager will be 'tuned-in' to the nuances of the project team, to avoid inflicting unintentional punishment. Unintentional punishment is a constant risk that has to be avoided. Here are just two examples:

- allocating a role to someone that they dislike (such as expecting someone to address a meeting who is uncomfortable in front of an audience);

- pairing two people to work together on a project task, even though their personalities clash.

On occasion punishment is intentional. Because of the lack of direct authority this most often arises in cases where tasks have been left incomplete, so that now more accountability is required. Daily progress reports, or updating the public project calendar are some of the roles that team members often find punishing. Of course, there is always the dreaded action of bringing an underperforming team member's manager into the loop; communicating however subtly that his/her person isn't doing their share of the work.

The challenge with relying on this particular factor is that getting the project team member's commitment is doubtful, and their resistance will be sky high. You might well get the person to comply, but you will have created an adversary instead of the ally that you needed.

POSITIONAL POWER

Positional Power of Status

Another power source is positional. This is when the organisational influence is bestowed on the person, not so much because of their professional or personal traits but rather as a result of the particular office or title in the organisation. This is perhaps the weakest of all power propositions, and the most fleeting. Rarely will people be committed to a weak or incompetent person, even if their title is something like senior manager or chief engineer. Resistance will be high. No one likes it when people rely on their position and although compliance might be gained, it will be reluctant.

Positional Power of Experts

The positional power of an expert is quite a different story from power through organisational status. When you can demonstrate relevant expert knowledge or competence you will stand a good chance of gaining respect and cooperation. That can extend beyond your own organisation and across different functions. Your recommendations are more likely to be taken seriously. You might even be asked to speak to others at meetings, review findings and publish what you know.

Positional power is terrific, because people have a tendency to defer to experts. If an expert says something, we are very often moved to take that advice or recommendation. Cialdini (2009) calls this the principle of authority. As a project manager, if you have a particular level of expertise about a particular topic you will be well served. Your specialism might be in electronics, advanced construction methods, social media, search engine optimisation, reinsurance underwriting or any of an infinite number of topics. You will occupy an 'expert' power position from which you will very likely get the commitment of others working with you (either from deference to your accomplishments or because you clearly know what you are talking about). Compliance here is almost assured. There might be some resistance but here it could be described as *possible*, not *probable*.

Referent Power

Referent power, although listed last here, is actually the closest to my definition of leadership (having people follow you because they want to and not because they have to). This is the power bestowed upon someone because they are respected in the organisation. It has been described as, 'the ability to influence based on the respect, loyalty, admiration, affection or simply the desire to gain the approval of this person'.

Although this is the most productive and efficacious of all the power positions, it is clearly not the easiest to attain. It requires that you don the yoke of service and really work for others. Showing acceptance, acting supportively, making sacrifices and being credible and competent are all parts contributing to your journey towards referent power.

This is the optimum power position for a project manager, with maximum possibility of compliance and commitment and least risk of resistance. This is not easy to achieve but I shall outline key ways to develop just these necessary traits as we go through the rest of this chapter.

In reality though, the effective and influential project manager may, at any time, use any of these power positions (and you may even develop variations of your own). It depends on the project. Factors such as time, budget, market opportunity and so forth will all come into play. Just as you would not use a spreadsheet to create slides, your effective use of a 'power' position can help your relationships and your organisational influence.

Building the Engine of Influence

Understanding the sources of power and their availability to you as 'influence options' creates the foundation to understanding how you can wield the power of influence intelligently. Now that you have the road map, you'll need a vehicle with the power to traverse those curvy and sometimes uphill roads. What you should take into consideration is how to build your intellectual horsepower.

People will tend to spend time with (and thus build relationships with) those who can improve their condition. If as a result of spending time with you they know more about a particular subject, or are able to see situations (project, business conditions, people and so on) in a new or different light, that will attract people to you. The more people you can help, the better your organisation and your projects will become, and not unimportantly, the more people will think of you.

This is not to say you should be pompous or arrogant. Instead you need to be informed, educated and able to transfer your knowledge and skill to others. When you do, those interacting with you become improved. As they improve they will think better of you, because it was you who helped. So how can you build intellectual horsepower? You start by looking through the prism of time and perspective.

PRISM OF YOUR PERSPECTIVE

Your project knowledge (or any knowledge for that matter) can span a continuum from general, through more focused, to fairly specific. Then you can analyse things from a historical perspective or a contemporary perspective (or more simply, past and present).

And of course, when possible, include a qualitative as well as a quantitative perspective. Consider:

- What do you know generally about the historical state of your industry?
- How about your company?
- How about the previous attempts at similar projects?

This is then a historical perspective of things which can help. For example, in the early 1900s there were hundreds of manufacturers of motorcycles. They were used primarily as utility vehicles. Harley-Davidson, was one of many players, not even necessarily well known, looking for ways to expand their business. So they came out with a variety of different products, diverging from their primary focus (heavyweight motorcycles) to things as varied as lightweight motorcycles, golf carts and even snowmobiles.

How can a historical perspective help? Although it cannot predict the future, it can give you an indication of how people might behave. Technologies change rapidly and drastically, but people do not. George Santayana (1905–06) stated, 'Those who cannot remember the past, are condemned to repeat it'. It is important to know the lessons of history and then adjust to fit contemporary circumstances. Then you can apply these three categories of inquiry to your present-day situation.

- What is the current state of your industry?
- How about your company?
- How about your projects?

By blending your historical perspectives with your present-day observations you will be more able to provide guidance and insights to others. For example, now there are really only a handful of motorcycle manufacturers on the planet. Motorcycles are no longer used mainly in utilitarian ways, but rather now for pleasure, thrill seeking and personal expression. And today many motorcycle manufactures, including Harley-Davidson, are looking to expand their customer base. Will they resort to manufacturing golf carts?

Most people however, do not do the intellectual 'lifting' in order to have these sorts of perspectives. Just imagine what you might be able to add to the organisational discussion of things if in fact you did.

MINE YOUR EXPERIENCE

Many people go through their existence in a fairly unconscious manner. If you want to build the intellectual horsepower necessary to be more successful in your relationships and your attempts at influencing, a more cognisant approach may help. Throughout your workday and week, dozens and dozens of situations present themselves to you and you respond to them. The result is then one of the following:

- what you hoped for;
- not what you hoped for;
- something else.

These are learning opportunities. They should not be squandered. Few project managers have the discipline to do what I am now about to suggest, but those that do will find themselves standing in the company of the best of the best.

For a six-month period, at the end of each day, you should capture three successes from that day. Perhaps you were able to get a low-performing project team member to commit to submitting work on time. You might have effectively negotiated the sharing of a needed IT resource with another project manager. Or you presented an idea to a senior vice president and they gave you the go ahead to proceed. These experiences will do several things for you:

- Like a well-worn trail through a mountain pass, this will give you the guidance necessary to navigate similar situations in the future.
- Reviewing these successes will give you the confidence to keep moving, growing and trying new techniques.
- Reviewing your successes will give you the resilience to bounce back when you are not successful.

Important research from world-renowned psychologist Martin Seligman suggests that people who do this experience mood elevation similar to those who take anti-depressant medication. We all experience setbacks from time to time and this technique can help you work through them.

The other benefit of this conscious approach to recording your successes is that you will build a catalogue of experiences that you can relate to others, helping to overcome future difficulties. Without being arrogant in an 'I know everything manner', you will be able to say with some confidence 'When we faced something like this before, we tried this and it worked. Do you think it might work for us now? This of course, leads us to the next component of building your intellectual horsepower, which is your use of language.

SUPERCHARGE YOUR LANGUAGE

The words you choose, and the phrases you use have a powerful effect – consciously and subconsciously – on the person or group with whom you are communicating. If you really want to start building your 'organisational horsepower' you need to be able to grab people's attention, you need to be able to persuade them, you need to be able to get them to think in new ways.

Do you want to become more influential with others? One way is to develop your use of adjectives. Of course these are the parts of speech which modify nouns. When in meetings or conversations, an apt descriptor of something will make your conversations more interesting and probably more accurate.

For example, consider the following bland statement: 'The vendor has created a good design'. Try instead, 'The vendor has created an elegant design'. Or, provided the design really is good, instead of 'elegant' you could use 'complete', 'comprehensive', 'intuitive' or perhaps even 'inspired'.

Here's another example. You could say 'the project's budget is insufficient'. But you might also try 'this project's budget is 'inadequate', or 'woefully deficient' or even 'pathetic'.

You don't want to speak in hyperbole, but well-chosen adjectives can make you a dramatically more persuasive project manager. People will be more interested in what you have to say if you are more precise in your descriptions and more interesting in both your spoken and written communication.

ANSWER THE QUESTION 'WHY ARE WE DOING THIS?'

Points of justification are another mainstay of creating your influence horsepower. Far too few project managers use them. This really means talking about the ultimate result, or the purpose of your efforts. 'By completing this project, our business unit will generate the revenue necessary to pass our competitors in the marketplace'. Or 'By completing this project, we shall be able to bring our products from concept to completion more quickly'.

The problem for many is that during a project, when things start to go awry, we have a tendency to get caught up in the minutiae. We talk about why a particular work breakdown structure won't work, or we argue the merits of some parallel path. It's as if we have a microscopic view of a grain of sand and it looks like an impassable boulder. Rather, if we bring the perspective back to why your organisation or business unit is engaged in the project (to increase profitability, decrease time to market, and keep everyone employed!) then the issues can be seen more accurately like grains of sand on the beach that can easily be crossed.

METAPHOR AND ANALOGY

Although there are innumerable language skills you could use to build relationships through influence, I shall end this section on supercharging your language with this final thought.

> To be more engaging in your communication efforts, try using more descriptive language.

A metaphor is a figure of speech in which a word or phrase that ordinarily designates one thing is used to designate another, making an implicit comparison. For example:

- This product is the heart and soul of this company.
- This project is a diamond in the rough.
- There has been an explosion of interest in this project.

You can also supercharge your influence efforts through the use of analogy. An analogy is drawing a comparison with something in order to show some similarities and make your point with more interest. For example:

- Using a parallel path method here in our project will be like launching a fighter jet off an aircraft carrier.
- We are planning to navigate the next series of project tasks as smoothly as Tiger Woods swings his driver.
- The result of this project will be a product so interesting that it will be like the *Mona Lisa* of our product range.

EXPERT SPEAK

If you're the project manager you should automatically be bestowed with a certain level of expertise relevant to the project or initiative. You can exploit that position of expertise and authority. If you want more people to take your direction, try using terms like, 'recommend', 'suggest' or 'advise'. For example:

- Knowing what we do about the situation, I would *recommend* that we take the following actions.
- Because of various conditions happening in our organisation and the marketplace, here are the three actions, I would *suggest* we take.
- There have been some timeline developments. Here are some changes to the work breakdown structure I would *advise* that we consider.

When your language is interesting, vivid and compelling you will be better able to make your points, get more attention and improve your contribution to your projects and your co-workers; essential elements to building superior relationships.

Rules of the Relationship Road

To recapitulate, we know our intended destination (building relationships through influence), we know some routes to success (power sources), and now we've built our engine of influence (intellectual horsepower). Before we fire up that engine and start driving towards project management success we have to understand a few quick rules of the relationship road.

USE SELF-DEPRECATING HUMOUR

Do you want people to think better of you? Admit your foibles in an interesting and humorous way. No one likes to be made fun of, but we all enjoy a meeting leader or manager who doesn't take themselves so seriously that they can't laugh at themselves. We all make decisions which, after the fact, seem blindingly obvious and silly. We have all been in social situations where we've said or done the wrong thing. We've all had a project not go exactly as planned (has any ever gone *exactly* as planned?!) When you recognise these times publically and humorously, your project stakeholders (either consciously or subconsciously) might think, 'Here's a person I can work with!'.

Self-deprecating humour also helps to create your project team culture, which encourages:

- open exchanges ('Hey we can talk about this stuff!');
- risk taking ('Everyone makes a mistake once in a while and that's okay'); and
- a learning organisation ('Here's what we *should* have done').

Some hardened business people might look at suggestions like these and scoff. But my suggestion is not mere food for thought. It is powerful relationship-building advice. Ignore it at your career's peril.

DRESS WELL

For you to be 'of influence' in your organisation you do need to be respected, and of course, all of the advice given thus far will point you in that direction. But here's another tip that, far too often, project managers ignore. If you want more people to follow your direction, think well of you and want to build relationships with you, you need to dress well and have high quality accessories (pen, watch, shoes, planner and briefcase).

Numerous studies reinforce this claim. The physician phenomenon of 'white coat' syndrome proves the effect of dress on biological responses (for some, when someone wearing a white coat enters the room their heart rate goes up). For others the response is psychological. In one study, a person wearing street clothes gave passers-by a specific direction (put change in a parking meter) and not one person followed the direction. When the same person was dressed in what appeared to be a law enforcement uniform, everyone did as asked.

Another study used walking against a traffic light as the evidential case. When the leader wore working man's attire, no one followed him across the intersection. When the same person dressed in a three-piece suit, people followed him across the street like the pied piper.

This is not to say you should show up wearing evening dress to your project management meetings. Rather, calibrate to your organisation's dress code, and dress one notch above it. If your organisation dress norm is casual, you wear smart casual. If it's business casual, you go to formal business clothing. This will contribute to creating your influential image in your organisation.

INVERSE CORRELATION OF INTEREST

If you want others to find you more interesting (and therefore want to spend time with you and do things for and with you), you have to be more interested in them. Instead of talking about yourself and your experiences, talk about them and their insights. When you do, they will find you fascinating. That is an interesting component of the human condition.

RELATIONSHIP NAVIGATION

So now, how can we build more and better relationships? How can we develop or repair damaged ones? You can achieve these ends by understanding the two simple plans with which all relationships reside. You are either known or unknown to key stakeholders in your projects. You either have low credibility or high credibility (let's dispense with any notions of *average* credibility; we don't have space in this chapter to attack self-worth issues!).

The quadrant diagram in Figure 22.1 will help you understand how you might respond in any given situation. Use the relationship quadrant to act as your navigation system to assess where you reside professionally with a particular team member or stakeholder. Then use it as a guide regarding how to proceed with the relationship. This systematic approach to credibility and influence can speed your development and your success.

	Low credibility	High credibility
Known	*Known/low credibility* • Rebuild relationship; • Apologize for past mistakes; • Move slowly, start small; • Keep your promises at all costs; • Communicate well and often.	*Known/high credibility* • Previous experience with positive results; • Trust in your performance; • They request advice; • Never take advantage of this position (easy to lose it); • Keep expectations reasonable.
Unknown	*Unknown/low credibility* • Build a relationship; • Find reasons for you to interact; • What does the other person value? • How do they process information? • Provide third-party backup for your insights; • Bring outstanding value; • Do high quality work.	*Unknown/high credibility* • Solid reputation; • 'Word of mouth' interest; • Need to deliver on expectations; • Perception must match reality to maintain credibility.

Figure 22.1 Relationship quadrant

Influencing Upward

I shall end this chapter by taking on a topic which always garners interest: executive influence. How can you be thought of credibly by senior managers in both your organisation and perhaps in client organisations? A few knowledge areas and questions to ask yourself follow.

Know Your Company

Do you understand the organisation and the political terrain? Can you articulate the company's strategic position? What are the company's goals and objectives? What performance measures are used? How does your department fit in? Who are the key decision makers? Where does the power lie?

Know Yourself

Evaluate yourself, including your strengths, weaknesses, interpersonal skills and credibility. Can you read a group of managers and know what they are thinking and feeling? Are you 'quick on your feet' and able to change tactics if needed? Can you manage your emotions when necessary? Do you have credibility with the right people? What do you want from your boss? Are your goals realistic?

Know Your Senior Managers

What are your manager's information needs? What time pressures are they facing? What are your manager's priorities and plans? What is his/her history with the organisation? What is his/her current level of power and credibility?

Acting as a Peer in Your Group

And finally, you need to comport yourself as a peer. Perhaps not in pay grade, but in your ability to understand business, the political climate and what's required to get results. Not some hat-in-hand subordinate. And stifle the urge to be a sycophant. When you can intelligently, respectfully and coherently present a contrarian point of view, that's what makes you credible with senior managers.

Conclusion

To build relationships you must conduct yourself so that others follow you because they want to and not because they have to. You need to realise that there are at least five routes to power in any given situation and the more you understand that and can use them well, the better off you'll be. It's imperative for you to build your intellectual horsepower, using your perspective, your experience, your language and your presence. In short, when it comes to building relationships through influence, it's your performance that matters.

References and Further Reading

Cialdini, R.B. (2009), *Influence: Science and Practice*, 5th edn, New York: Pearson Education.
de Tocqueville, A. (1899), *Democracy in America*, University of Virginia: American Studies Programs. Available at: http://xroads.virginia.edu/~HYPER/DETOC/toc_indx.html [accessed 6 March 2012].
French, J.R.P. and Raven, B. (1959), 'The bases of social power', in Cartwright, D. and Zander, A., *Group Dynamics*, New York: Harper & Row.
Santayana, G. (1905–06), *Life in Reason*, Vol.1 *Reason in Common Sense*, Champaign, IL: Project Gutenberg. Available at: http://www.gutenberg.org/files/15000/15000-h/15000-h.htm [accessed 6 March 2012].

23 *Managing Conflict in Projects*

FRED MURRAY-WEBSTER with PETER SIMON

This chapter explains the principles of conflict management, helped by some well-known models and enhanced with practitioner coaching points. We aim to improve your understanding of conflict management, explain how this is different from conflict resolution, and list the things you can do to improve your ability to deal with conflict in a multitude of project situations.

Introduction

Conflict is inevitable, and most people learn how to deal with it in life, at least to some degree. So what is different about managing conflict in projects?

In our personal lives, we have a choice about whether to engage with the person or group with which we are in conflict and we can choose how to behave. We are serving our own objectives, and can act accordingly. In our professional lives, we represent our organisation, so we must disregard our personal views and act in the best interests of the project. Conflicts about requirements, resources, progress and success are common in projects. Conflicts with sponsors, team members and stakeholders must be resolved in a way that protects the project and preserves relationships.

Project managers cannot avoid conflict. Yet many practitioners lack confidence in their ability to turn conflict into opportunity for the team, for the project and to ensure wider organisational effectiveness. In this chapter we describe some conflict management approaches. Then we shall suggest a multilevel structure to describe conflict management competency in your project team and wider organisation.

Conflict or Opportunity?

Dictionary definitions of the word conflict reflect the 'struggle' and 'clash' between opposing forces. All conflicts have the potential to become negative, debilitating, relationship-destroying occurrences. Research into conflict and peace studies assumes that whilst conflicts are the expression of opposing interests, and are characteristic and endemic of modern society, the conflict is resolved when some mutually compatible set of actions is worked out (Nicholson, 1992).

We usually perceive conflict from a negative standpoint, focusing on the struggle rather than on a beneficial outcome. But another perspective is to think of conflict as being neither positive nor negative, but natural and therefore neutral. In other words, conflict can result in good or bad outcomes. This view can be compared with ways of thinking about risk (neither good nor bad in itself but with the potential for a positive or negative impact on objectives). Thinking about conflict in projects as natural and inevitable helps us to think more neutrally about what would be a good outcome in a particular situation. That can allow us to move on in the best way to achieve objectives and create an environment where progress is swift and effective.

Conflict management here is the ability of one individual to deal with day-to-day problems in a project. A project manager can do well if the conflict opportunities for project improvement are fully realised, with negative conflicts causing minimal damage to the objectives.

Project management requires active conflict management. The project manager has to focus on the project deliverables and cannot spend inappropriate amounts of time or money trying to make everyone happy. So there will be residual conflict and some stakeholders might be less happy than others. The ability to make good judgements about how much time and effort to invest in trying to resolve a conflict is a key skill. The best project managers have an extremely flexible and situational approach.

In the following sections we explain how a flexible and situational approach can be achieved followed by some thoughts about overcoming natural preferences, and dealing with those stakeholders who do not see the situation in the same way as you. But first we need to think about how a situation could be perceived as representing a conflict in the first place, and how we can make sense of different perceptions. What we currently 'see'

Figure 23.1 What do you see?

Note: This drawing by W. E. Hill appeared in 1888. People interpret the image in different ways, as explained in the text.

in our mind's eye is *our* reality – *our* perception based on historic and current information. When we are faced with a project problem, we have at our disposal our own view and the views of the other stakeholders. These views may all be different.

Here is an example to illustrate how people can have different views, developed from a common set of facts or image. You might be familiar with the perceptual illusion in Figure 23.1 in which the brain can switch between seeing a young lady and an old lady. This picture was popularised by the British cartoonist W.E. Hill in 1888. Individuals who look at this picture see a variety of images. Some see nothing at all, just frustrating confusion. Some see a young lady; others see an old lady. Among many other things, people have seen a black lizard climbing up a rock, a golden eagle's head, an old man reclining in a chair whilst smoking a pipe, a black-bodied bird pecking food off the ground, a ship going into a harbour and a map of a familiar coastline. The only solid fact is that there is black ink on a white background (or is it white ink on a black background?). Everything else is shaped and explained by the individual's perception.

Accepting that every individual makes sense of the same situation from their own perspective is fundamental to managing conflict. We have used this 'young lady/old lady' exercise with groups for more than 20 years. It helped us to allow project managers to achieve what can be an 'Ah Ha!' moment. That is the point in time when we see what the other party sees. It does not mean that we have to agree with their view and lose our own (different) perspective.

Basic Concepts

Acknowledging that people have different perspectives is one of the building blocks of conflict management competency in projects. This can be extended by thinking of the saying first attributed to St Francis of Assisi and popularised by Covey (1989), 'Seek first to understand, then to be understood'.

It is a powerful step to see and hear first the other party's perception and needs, because that usually allows them to express any emotion first. You then have the opportunity to respond in a way that builds rapport. This can also set the pattern of behaviour for them to listen and understand your perception and needs. The 'ball' is now moving in a positive and constructive manner.

This approach allows another fundamental point to be addressed, namely that *behaviour breeds behaviour*. Thus it is difficult for anyone to be cross or aggressive with someone who is displaying tolerance and empathy.

Managing conflict in a way that protects project objectives implies that it also needs to be managed in a way that protects relationships with key stakeholders. That requires an understanding of stakeholder perceptions and expressed needs. If you understand these needs and can listen and respond empathetically to them (even if you don't agree) you will be in a powerful position to choose an approach that you deem best for your project.

This positive series of events is shown in the upper half of Figure 23.2. The opposite (and perhaps more instinctive, more negative) series of events is shown in the lower half of the diagram. Instead of 'seeking first to understand' when faced with conflict we often do not demonstrate any emotional control. Instead we react with behaviours that are

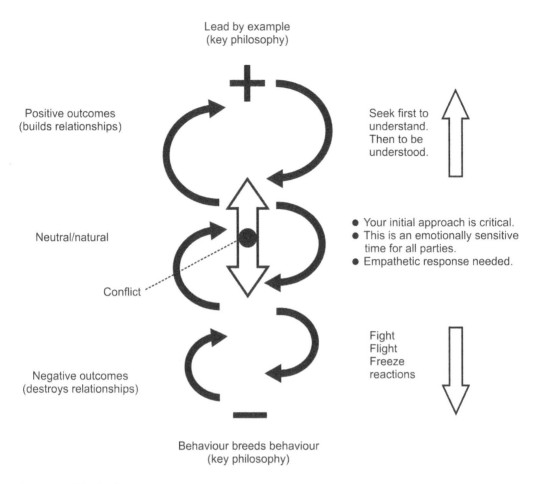

Lead by example
(key philosophy)

Positive outcomes
(builds relationships)

Seek first to
understand.
Then to be
understood.

Neutral/natural

● Your initial approach is critical.
● This is an emotionally sensitive
time for all parties.
● Empathetic response needed.

Conflict

Fight
Flight
Freeze
reactions

Negative outcomes
(destroys relationships)

Behaviour breeds behaviour
(key philosophy)

Figure 23.2 Basic concepts

more akin to a basic fight, flight or freeze response. This is much more likely to damage stakeholder relationships and project success.

Your behaviour will affect the direction that conflict takes. Choosing an appropriate behaviour is therefore key. You will never get it right every time, but the more flexible your choice of behavioural approaches the better. Other parties clearly have an equally important role to play, but *behaviour does breed behaviour*. Being armed with a perspective on the conflict that takes into consideration your own and other stakeholders' thoughts and attitudes will enable you to consider how to manage the situation most appropriately.

There are undoubtedly times where it is best not to try to find a resolution to a conflict – it can sometime be better to 'lose the battle in an attempt to win the war'. At other times it might be appropriate to 'force' your own objectives, overriding the other party's wants and needs. It is widely accepted that a situational approach to managing project conflicts is needed, as suggested by models like the Thomas-Kilmann Conflict Mode instrument that we describe below.

Choice of Conflict Response

In conflicts there are rarely any clear rights or wrongs. In some ways a project manager has to behave like an actor and choose a conflict management style appropriate to the case. This might be different from your natural choice, or indeed different from what you believe is the appropriate (or even ethical) approach according to your own value system. Your approach might even result in a short-term negative outcome, which in many ways contradicts the ideal of holistic conflict management. However, in the long term you are responsible for project outcomes and maybe even benefit realisation. So you must bear that in mind when choosing your approach.

There are many conflict management models and associated diagnostic tools but the best known is the Thomas-Kilmann model (TKI) first published in 1974 (Thomas and Kilmann, 2007). This model suggests that basic behaviours are exhibited when managing conflict and that these are related to:

- the degree to which we desire to assert our own needs (the vertical axis in Figure 23.3); and
- the degree to which we desire to cooperate with the other parties' needs (horizontal axis in Figure 23.3).

Thomas and Kilmann call the five positions shown on the grid in Figure 23.3 'conflict handling modes'. These can also be interpreted as conflict management styles, given that we all have individual preferences according to our personalities. But we can choose to override those tendencies and adopt a style that responds most appropriately to a specific situation. Each of these behaviours or conflict management styles can be explained as follows.

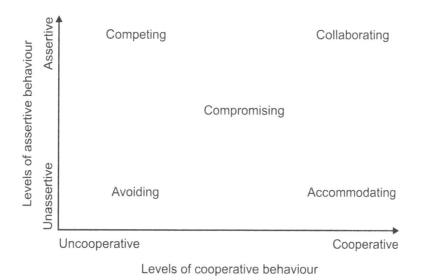

Figure 23.3 The five basic behaviours, modes or conflict management styles that underpin the Thomas-Kilmann Conflict Mode instrument

Competing is assertive and non-cooperative, often called a power-orientated mode. When competing, an individual pursues his/her own concerns at the other's expense, using whatever power that seems appropriate to win. It is an 'I win you lose' approach. The guiding behaviour of assertiveness should be to stand up for your position and needs but without denying those of the other party. Say what you want to say honestly and without degrading the other party. As a project manager there will be many occasion when you need to compete, for example when you know you are right, when losing would undermine your authority, or when you need a quick decision.

Accommodating is unassertive and cooperative. It is the opposite of competing. When accommodating, an individual neglects his/her own concerns to satisfy the concerns of the other party. This can be seen as an 'I lose, you win' approach. When used tactically this can be seen as a 'lose the battle to win the war' tactic. Alternatively you might choose to use accommodating when you know that the other party is correct or it is very important to the other party that their solution is accepted.

Collaborating is both assertive and cooperative. In this approach you are working with the other party to find a solution that fully satisfies everyone concerned. The ultimate goal is an 'I win you win' solution. Within a project, particular care must be taken to avoid spending too much time trying to please everyone. So collaboration has to be used selectively. It should be used when anything but 'win-win' would seriously jeopardise project success. The collaborating style is the only one that is truly focused on trying to 'resolve' the conflict, rather than manage it.

Compromising is the intermediate position between assertiveness and cooperativeness; you are trying to find a mutually acceptable expedient solution that partially satisfies both parties. This approach can be seen as the 'half win – half win' or the 'half lose – half lose' approach (depending on your outlook). It seeks the middle ground. You have to be flexible on your perceived needs. Overuse of compromise in project management can mean that nobody is totally happy, even if the project gets finished on time. After a compromise it is wise to be prepared for possible future (negative) consequences.

Avoiding is unassertive and uncooperative. When avoiding, an individual does not immediately pursue his/her own concerns or those of the other person. The individual does not deal with the conflict. This approach can be described as 'I lose – you lose'. However there are situations where avoiding in the short term (provided you have a valid reason for doing so) will benefit your project. Examples include times when you have more important things to do, when emotions are running high or you are totally unprepared for the required discussion.

The inventory that supports the TKI is designed to help you to know your personal preferred response (the approach that comes most naturally to you) and therefore your areas of weakness (the approaches that you tend not to use naturally). This knowledge of yourself is perhaps the first stage in becoming skilled in managing conflict. As Socrates (469–399 BC) reportedly said 'Know thyself to be wise'. Once you have taken the first step to becoming a reflective practitioner (capable of analysing your own behaviour when interacting with stakeholders) perhaps your next stage will be to observe and privately reflect back on how others see you.

Wha the gift that God would gee us... to see ourselves as others see us. (Robert Burns 1759–96)

BEHAVIOURS BEYOND THE THOMAS-KILMANN MODEL

Once you have grasped the principles of the original TKI it is helpful to consider the unacceptable areas of behaviour that can be observed. These unacceptable behaviours could be said to lie outside the normal and reasonable assertiveness/cooperative spectrum. Figure 23.4 indicates four unacceptable behaviours that can surround the five Thomas-Kilmann conflict modes. Each of these can be explained as follows.

Aggression – This behaviour is present when an individual, team and/or organisation forcibly stand up for their rights whilst totally denying the rights of any other party. This could colloquially be called bullying. It does not necessarily mean physical violence. Aggression can be disguised in the subtle use of language, change of voice or emphasis on specific words.

Desertion – This behaviour is displayed when individuals fail in their duty of care to themselves and others in carrying out their professional responsibilities (towards their organisation, or their team or even their customers). An example of this would be a person openly denies that there is a conflict, when other parties want to fight. *Avoiding* suggests that you will return to the matter later, *desertion* means you will never return.

Submission – This is when individuals totally give up their right, without voicing their needs at all. This could be seen as just saying 'Yes' with no discussion. Alternatively, if you are asked to jump you just say 'How high?'

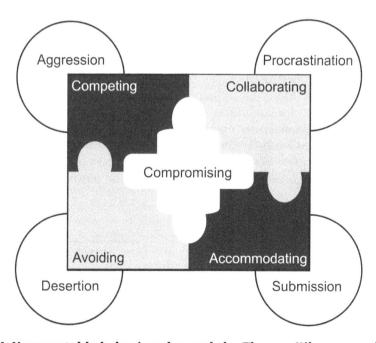

Figure 23.4 Unacceptable behaviour beyond the Thomas-Kilmann model

Procrastination – This can occur when an individual focuses all her/his effort into addressing the root cause of a problem whilst seeking a total resolution for all parties involved in the project. This can lead to a disproportionate amount of time and effort being spent, with inappropriately small benefit to the project. Judging how much time should be spent is difficult but sometimes it is too easy to keep talking whilst getting nowhere.

Supporting Conflict Management Skills

After reading so far, let's assume that you have a good understanding of the principles of and what it means to adopt a particular conflict management style (win-win, win-lose, lose-win, lose-lose, half win-half win/half lose-half lose). Now you can start to develop your skills in order to achieve what you want. Part of this understanding will include fully appreciating the advantages and disadvantages of your choice, and its potential impact on the project.

There are many things you can do to improve your conflict management skills by adapting your behaviour to suit the situation. These are described in the following sections.

ASSERTIVENESS

We explained earlier that there will be occasions when you need to be assertive (with assertiveness defined as standing up for your rights without violating the rights of other parties). There are three identifiable levels of assertion. These are illustrated in Figure 23.5 and explained below.

Level 1: Empathetic Assertion

Empathetic assertion is best used where an individual, team or organisation is in an emotionally sensitive position. Whilst being sensitive and caring towards the individual, there still remains a need for you to state your rights.

For example, a small family-run engineering company that is providing components for your project are three weeks behind schedule. This is mainly because their managing director died suddenly a few weeks ago. Your company sent directors to the funeral and conveyed appropriate condolences to the family and the business. But you now need

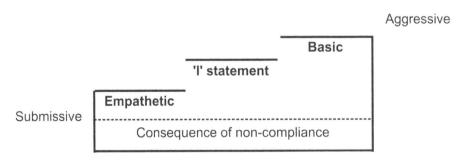

Figure 23.5 Levels of assertive behaviour

to discuss the failure to supply with the supplier's new managing director (a son of the deceased man).

An empathetic assertive statement might be: 'Whilst we fully understand what a difficult time this is for you personally, your family and your company, we need to discuss a problem with you. The component design phase is three weeks behind schedule. We know you are aware that your component plays a critical part in our project. Please update us about what you and your colleagues intend to do to bring the plan back to the original timeline. Please take some time to work out what you can do and then let me have your written answer by close of business tomorrow'.

Level 2: 'I' Statement Assertion

'I' statement assertion is perhaps most often the appropriate approach. It is done by first describing the action or problem that is causing the difficulty, then your response (how it makes you feel emotionally) and finally your preferred outcome (how you would like it to be going forward). By presenting the information in this way you give the other party an opportunity to consider their action and be aware of how you are affected. It also gives them an opportunity to reframe their words or modify their actions. You would normally delay stating the consequences that might arise should the issue not be resolved. This will allow the other party to respond to your statement. If there is no response or an unfavourable response, you can then use the option of stating what the consequences will be if the behaviour is repeated (but only do that if you are prepared to pursue those consequences).

For example, on day 16 of a 120-day project, a colleague has failed to release the six members of their team to carry out 40 hours of work (per person) on your project. You are now 12 man-hours behind with another 228 man-hours exposed if an immediate fix cannot be found. Your response, using an 'I' statement might be: 'When senior colleagues fail to release their staff to carry out essential work as agreed in the project plan, I feel let down and disappointed that you have not taken the time to communicate your staffing difficulty with me before today's deadline. I would prefer you to communicate your difficulty to me now and I shall do my best to understand, help and agree a resolution with you. However, if I cannot help the only option left to me will be to raise this situation as a project issue and take it to my sponsor to be resolved at steering group level'.

Level 3: Basic Assertion

Basic assertion is a direct instruction (last resort) given by a person who is authorised to give the direction. Suppose, for example that an organisation was contracted to deliver a product by a specified date and they indicated that owing to other business demands the item would be late. It would be reasonable for the project manager to give a direct instruction to the appropriate person within the supplier organisation to deliver on time according to the agreed contract. The project manager would explain that failure to do so would lead to implementation of the contingency plan (to get the product from another provider, activate the penalty clause in the contract). There would also be the potential future consequence of lost business for the supplier. Of course, this is only a good thing to do if you really have a contingency plan in place, and the supplier is not of strategic importance to your organisation for the future.

An appropriate statement would be 'We both have clear evidence that you are failing to meet your obligations under our agreement. In order to avoid me recommending to my sponsor initiating contractual or legal options, I need to hear from you with a new and final solution to the current problem by email or telephone within the next four hours'.

HARNESSING COOPERATIVE POWER

Having the ability to harness your energy and power with the energy and power of the other party and direct the forces towards a positive outcome can help in reaching your desired outcome. Developing this idea, we use a model developed by Cornelius and Faire (2006). They build from the power triangle (from transactional analysis) towards what they call a discovery circle.

The opposing behaviours of the power triangle (Figure 23.6) can be seen in conflicts. They are destructive in nature, because the individuals' roles often lead them to perpetuate the conflict. Often the original issues are often never dealt with, as the conflict caused by the behaviour of all involved parties becomes the main problem.

Persecuting
I'm OK.
You're not OK.

Rescuing
I'm OK.
You're not OK.

Playing victim
I'm not OK. You're OK.

Figure 23.6 Power triangle (negative behaviour roles)

There are many true victims of conflict in this world but this is not what the power triangle is about. The concept of 'playing victim' here relates to manipulative behaviour used in a calculated way to win, or at least to reduce the negative effect, by using the energy of the rescuer to fight for you. You probably know how a bully behaves. It has probably been done to you, and you might possibly have done it to others. Most of us like to come to the rescue (hero). It gives us power over the victim and legitimises our attack on the persecutor. Playing victim (poor me) is when you manipulate the other parties to resolve the conflict in your favour, by playing one off against the other.

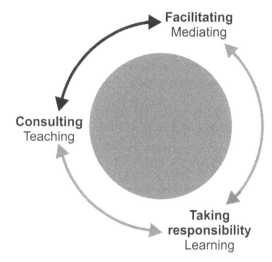

Figure 23.7 The discovery circle (positive behavioural roles)

Consider these behaviours as a basis for changing to an alternative behavioural approach, as shown in Figure 23.7.

- Instead of persecuting, take a consultative approach, by seeking out the needs, concerns and expectations of others, whilst then educating them on your needs, concerns and expectations.
- Instead of rescuing, facilitate a discussion about the problem to uncover the root cause of the conflict. Mediate if both the other parties feel that you are the right person to do it.
- Instead of playing victim, take responsibility for your destiny. Assert yourself and your views in a polite and well-constructed manner.

CASE EXAMPLE NO. 1

Consider the following scenario. You are managing a fixed-price contract with an important new client. The sales representative won this business against competitors by driving a very hard bargain. The contracted delivery time is six months.

After two months your project is two weeks behind schedule, but costs are on track to make the projected 20 per cent margin. You are working closely with the engineers to recover lost time, although your senior engineer thinks that the salespeople were optimistic in their promises to the client. You have just returned to the office from a meeting where the client gave you a hard time for non-performance so far. You have to resolve the conflict with the client and your internal colleagues in engineering and sales.

In dealing with this conflict, do you adopt the role of the 'persecutor' (blaming the sales representative for agreeing the original contract)? Or would it be better to adopt the role as 'victim' (poor project manager being squeezed by the client, the engineering team and sales team all at once)? Or, as another option, would it be best to be the friendly 'rescuer' (trying to stop the sales and engineering teams battling with one another)?

Put in these terms we are sure most people reading this would deny that they would ever adopt any of these three potentially dysfunctional roles. Yet we know we all do from time to time. But worse still is the tendency of some project managers who (from our experience) abdicate their responsibility for resolving the conflict. They, instead, would escalate the problem by referring it to the sponsor or some other senior manager for resolution.

The skilled conflict resolver knows how to be 'hard on the issue yet soft on the person' – to focus on finding a way forward without placing blame – but also avoiding taking all the problems on their own shoulders. Key skills are:

- being assertive (neither aggressive nor passive);
- having the facilitation skills to find common ground;
- being willing to resolve the underlying tensions.

Doing this typically requires us to manage our emotions. Emotional intelligence is a generic term to describe the thinking that influences our behaviour when we interact with others. Goleman (1995) introduced the basic principles. The concept of emotional intelligence begins with you as an individual being conscious (self-aware) of how your emotional state affects your behaviour, before, during and after dealing with a conflict. This in turn will have an impact on your ability to self-manage (to regulate your behaviour) whilst at the same time affecting the behaviour of others (awareness of others). This can be shown as in Figure 23.8. You can read more about emotional intelligence in Chapter 53.

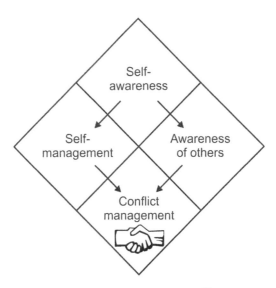

Figure 23.8 Emotional intelligence input to conflict management

Managing Conflict through Mediation

In some ancient civilisations when two or more members of the tribe were in disagreement (conflict), they would take their problem to the village elders. The disputing parties and the elders listened to each other; in particular the elders heard not only the words that were spoken, but they also observed everyone's body language. The elders then discussed the merits of both parties' positions in the conflict and where possible a judgement or award was given. If this was not possible the elders would aim to reach agreement through mediation. That would be accepted by both parties as the most effective way forward.

That ancient process should be the basis of all conflict management. Listen, observe, discuss and then make a judgement to resolve the conflict.

Mediation is a voluntary process during which the parties to a dispute meet first separately, and then together, with an independent third party (the mediator). The mediator designs and conducts a process which enables them to explore and decide how the conflict can be resolved. In the UK the Arbitration and Conciliatory Service (ACAS) is renowned for performing this role, particularly in disputes between employers and trades unions.

It is rare in project management that you would have the time to carry out a full mediation process using a professional mediator. However, if conflicts reach a level where they could have a significant impact upon your project you might choose to become a mediator. That will require you to focus on the mediation process and remain non-judgemental about the people, whilst never suggesting a solution to their problem. This creates an environment where the responsibility for resolving the conflict is left with the parties involved. What actually happens at all mediation stages depends on the people, the issues and the situation.

A simple, four-stage mediation process can be summarised as open, establish, move, and close, as follows:

1. *Open* – Create the appropriate environment for a meeting. Define the role of the mediator. Agree the behaviour required of all the participants during the process.
2. *Establish* – Each person describes the problem or problems (sources of conflict) as they perceive them and how they feel. Their detailed needs and concerns should then be recorded and any misperceptions clarified. It is important to check to ensure that all parties hear everything and are therefore aware of all the key points.
3. *Move* – Try to find areas of agreement. Generate and note options. Allow the parties to negotiate between each other. Use private meetings that will allow parties to consider and clarify where they are and where they might be able to move (given that doing nothing would seriously damage or stop the project). The need for a quick solution could lead to compromise on behalf of one or more parties (rather that achieving a collaborative outcome).
4. *Close* – Draft a contract of agreement acceptable to all parties. Agree to review and acknowledge progress.

If the agreement reached changes any condition of the project it is essential that actions resulting from this mediation process are administered using the relevant change control or configuration management procedure as part of document control. As mediator, it is your responsibility to help and guide all the parties involved through the agreed four-step process – not to fix it for them.

Controlling Yourself

For some individuals a first step in conflict management is to gather control of their own thinking. This sounds easy but many people find themselves physically and mentally off-balance when initially confronted with a conflict.

For some individuals it can help to develop the ability to centre one's self by drawing on approaches from martial arts. The following example draws on learning from the Japanese martial art of Aikido (Morihei Uyshiba) – 'the way'. Here is the procedure:

Stand or sit upright with your feet positioned a shoulder's width apart and breathe in a controlled manner to balance your body posture. You must think about your 'hara' which is the centre of your being (a point two inches below your bellybutton and midway between the front and back of your body).

When you are physically balanced and are breathing in a controlled and relaxed manner you can release your thinking mind. Then by focusing your physical and mental energy on the problem in hand use the energy of the other person and work with that to manage the conflict. 'Flow with' rather than 'fight against'.

Conflict Sites in Projects

CONFLICT WITH THE PROJECT STEERING GROUP

As a project manager you should not find it necessary to deal with conflict with an individual from the steering group or the group as a whole. At this senior level that responsibility lies with the project sponsor. In some cases problems or conflicts that you cannot resolve will be escalated to the project sponsor for resolution with the steering group.

CONFLICT WITH THE PROJECT SPONSOR

Clearly the relationship that a project manager has with the project sponsor is a key element of project success. As project manager you must put every single effort into understanding the preferred, conflict-related behaviour of your sponsor. This will include analysing their conflict management approach and monitoring their standing within your business. It is your role in the first instance to support fully your sponsor in the role of financial risk taker.

Developing the capability to know where and when to assert yourself with your sponsor (depending on the particular conflict) is essential to your successful delivery. If your sponsor makes an unreasonable request of you or your team, you need to consider your position and use appropriate assertive behaviour. This is sometimes called 'managing up' and refers to your ability to manage conflicts with senior stakeholders to suit your needs.

Conflicts with the project sponsor can arise over the release of funds, unrealistic deadlines, availability of resources or changing priorities. These all have to be resolved to deliver the project.

CONFLICT WITH THE END USER

Any conflict with the end user must be dealt with at the earliest possible opportunity. Avoidance or delay will ensure that the conflict will soon become serious. So the sooner the conflict is dealt with the sooner you can get that end user on your side to ensure that the end product of the project is fit for purpose.

One of the signatures on the final handover document will be that of a senior end user. This is the main reasoning for having end users involved throughout the definition and implementation phases of the project. It is also part of quality management. This ensures that any difference of opinion on the suitability of the end deliverables will be brought to the project manager's attention as early as possible.

Conflicts with the end user may arise from a disagreement on requirements (such as what will be included and what will not). Other conflicts could come from the type of solution chosen and its operability or maintainability.

CONFLICT WITH YOUR TEAM MEMBERS

It is important at this point to remember that project managers who work in a matrix organisation will not have line management control over their team members. Conflict and stress are almost inevitable in matrix organisations (Chapter 10). In a matrix organisation the project manager has to be a motivator, encouraging the organisation's members to overcome their problems.

In any project organisation (team or matrix) the project manager should have a unique relationship with each member. A key responsibility is to develop and enable the organisation's members to manage problems within their specific area on a day-to-day basis. That will minimise the manager's problems.

Conflicts with team members can arise over things like their ability to do the work or their liking or not for the assigned tasks. Also, where the project manager is not their line manager conflict will almost certainly occur between their project work and any business-as-usual (BAU) responsibilities.

CONFLICT WITH SUPPLIERS

Conflict with suppliers can arise from a multitude of areas, including (for example) the amounts and timing of progress payments, and changes to the order or contract. Thus a conflict resolution/mediation clause should be in the contract. Great care needs to be taken when drafting contracts and expert advice should always be taken and followed. The more time and effort that goes into the drafting, the less confusion and conflict there will be between all parties involved. These steps should minimise any need to resort to the courts to resolve conflict.

CONFLICT WITH ROUTINE FUNCTIONAL DEPARTMENTS

Whilst you are focused on your project objectives it is always good practice to keep one eye on what's happening in the operational side of your business. A significant number of key project resources can sometimes come from non-project departments (also known as BAU departments). So you might possibly have to manage conflict with operational managers.

Maturity in Project Conflict Management

We know that conflict may arise with many different stakeholders. An appropriate situational response to conflict is needed, but an appropriate response can only be made when there is a good understanding of the problem and enough rapport to find a way through that preserves relationships for the future.

Our work with organisations has led us to suggest that there are levels of conflict management maturity that can be useful in identifying whether there are generic training needs for organisational managers, or needs for coaching for particular people. The next section pulls together the insights from the chapter so far into a short description of levels of maturity.

Conflict management is the responsibility of each individual within the organisation. Directors and senior management in general have the ultimate responsibility to set the standard for conflict management. We know that behaviour breeds behaviour and therefore if project managers and other staff are subjected to bullying or coercive behaviour from senior colleagues, then it will be no surprise that they run their projects from a similar standpoint. The 'tone from the top' matters in the context and culture for appropriate conflict management for the project.

CONFLICT MANAGEMENT MATURITY IN YOUR OWN ORGANISATION

Consider your organisation, reflect carefully and decide which of the following maturity levels applies.

Level 1: Oblivious

- *Attitude* – the individuals of the organisation believe that it's a win-lose world. Individuals instinctively adopt a defensive or aggressive posture.
- *Ability* – individuals fight for what they think is right on every occasion and individuals support a blame culture. Individuals use many skills to ingratiate themselves with those in power. Individuals manipulate the truth to their best advantage.
- *Approach* – there are no processes in place to provide any alternative to this adversarial win-lose justice. Processes are in place (some partly hidden) to control the use of power.

Level 2: Semi-conscious

- *Attitude* – there is a clear failure to display the positive state of mind that produces willingness to resolve everyday workplace conflicts.
- *Ability* – a few individuals demonstrate some of the key tools that are part of the project conflict management toolbox.

- *Approach* – processes are being put in place to offer an alternative to the use of an adversarial process for dealing with conflict.

Level 3: Conscious

- *Attitude* – most individuals are aware of the possibility that managing conflict does not require a 'fight'.
- *Ability* – some individuals are conversant with the main aspects of the conflict management process. Some might have undergone development in conflict management related subjects like assertiveness, negotiation and mediation skills.
- *Approach* – a basic process exists that allows conflict to be managed without immediately adopting a 'fight' approach.

Level 4: Enabling

- *Attitude* – many leaders in the organisation take a very positive view towards conflict management and confront bullies and apathetic behaviour appropriately.
- *Ability* – many individuals are conversant with the main aspects of the conflict management process. They may have undergone development in conflict management related subjects such as assertiveness, negotiation and mediation skills.
- *Approach* – the organisation has policies, processes and procedures in place to educate staff and customers as to how conflict management will be achieved.

Level 5: Cultivated

- *Attitude* – most people positively embrace the processes and philosophy of conflict management.
- *Ability* – all managers are trained and practised in conflict management skills and in the management of the process. A small number of key personnel are trained and practised and qualified at an advance/professional level of project conflict management.
- *Approach* – a fully integrated and accessible system exists which is being used. Audits provide information for all concerned. Continuous improvement models allowed from the positive growth in this area.

Level 6: Habitual

- *Attitude* – the project conflict management process and human wisdom levels are accelerating at a natural speed, not hindered by financial time limitations. The value of the time and effort is measured 'to be worth its weight in gold'.
- *Ability* – all personnel are undergoing a personal development plan focused on project conflict management. Before selection to serve in any key role within the organisation

individuals must demonstrate an inherent conflict management approach, which is flexible across all issues.

- *Approach* – conflict management processes are self-generating, modifying and regulating.

Conclusion

When managing conflict within a project environment you inevitably will not keep all of the people happy all of the time. The balance that the project manager is encouraged to keep will definitely leave some stakeholders disappointed, perhaps annoyed and in some cases even angry.

Conflict is rarely about who is right and who is wrong. It is about appreciating people's different perceptions and valuing those differences to develop a creative response so that you can move forward to deliver your project. The following summary lists the key concepts and philosophies of conflict management in projects:

- handle conflict early;
- really listen to the other side;
- say what the problem is for you;
- be hard on the problem;
- be soft on the person;
- explore needs before solutions;
- look for answers together;
- build in wins for everyone.

References and Further Reading

Covey, S. (1989), *The Seven Habits of Highly Effective People*, New York: Simon & Schuster.

Cornelius, H. and Faire, S. (2006), *Everyone Can Win: Responding to Conflict*, 2nd edn, Sydney: Simon & Schuster.

Goleman, D. (1995), *Emotional Intelligence*, New York: Bantam Books.

Nicholson, M. (1992), *Rationality and the Analysis of International Conflict*, Cambridge: Cambridge University Press.

Thomas, K.W. and Kilmann, R.H. (2007), *Thomas-Kilmann Conflict Mode Instrument*, Mountain View, CA: Xicom (subsidiary of CPP Inc.).

24 *Cross-cultural Relationships*

JEAN BINDER

We need a certain amount of humility and a sense of humour to discover cultures other than our own; a readiness to enter a room in the dark and stumble over unfamiliar furniture until the pain in our shins reminds us where things are. (Trompenaars and Hampden-Turner, 2005)

This chapter focuses on national cultures, not corporate cultures – on people, not organisations. Here I shall propose a definition of culture applied to project environments, review the cultural dimensions and their implications for international projects, discuss the danger of generalisations and the benefits of multicultural teams, and conclude by proposing a simple framework for effective cross-cultural project management.

Defining Culture

Consider the following definitions:

- 'Culture ... is the collective programming of the mind which distinguishes the members of one group or category of people from another. ... The "mind" stands for the head, heart and hands – that is, for thinking, feeling, and acting, with consequences for beliefs, attitudes and skills. ... Culture in this sense includes values: systems of values are a core element of culture' (Hofstede, 2001).
- 'Our own culture is like water to a fish. It sustains us. We live and breathe through it' (Trompenaars and Hampden-Turner, 2005).
- 'Culture is a fuzzy set of attitudes, beliefs, behavioural norms, and basic assumptions and values that are shared by a group of people, and that influence each member's behaviour and his/her interpretations of the "meaning" of other people's behaviour' (Spencer-Oatey, 2000, cited in Dahl, 2004).

As I wrote in Chapter 11, global project teams can only communicate and collaborate effectively after understanding the differences in culture, language and time zones, and identifying how to transform those differences from challenges into opportunities. One of the main challenges of team management across the globe is that most concepts and practices are dependent on the different personalities and cultures involved (Binder, 2007).

Many modern studies have analysed and defined the challenges of cross-cultural management, most of them based on Geert Hofstede's and Fons Trompenaars's and Charles Hampden-Turner's cultural dimensions. Their two theories were built around extensive surveys of managers who worked in different countries. Hofstede's research covered one big multinational company (IBM). Trompenaars and Hampden-Turner looked instead at managers working in different companies in different nations.

Project managers must understand human nature and personalities in order to be able to select team members, assign correct roles and responsibilities, and perform stakeholder analysis. In addition to this, global project managers need to recognise how the different attitudes, beliefs, behavioural norms, basic assumptions and values can affect collaboration among team members – people who come from many different countries. We have to learn how to adapt our leadership style to all the different cultures involved in our global projects.

Culture and Project Management

Culture is often represented as icebergs (with their hidden and visible features) or as onions (representing the different layers or levels of depth of cultural manifestations). According to Hofstede (2001), the visible layers (also called practices) are manifested by:

- symbols (words, gestures, pictures and objects);
- heroes (real or imaginary persons serving as models of good behaviour);
- rituals (collective activities with no practical purpose, but which are essential to keep the individual bound within the norms of the collectivity.

Significant cultural differences occur even between nations that share a common language (think of the UK, the US, Canada and Australasia for example).

You can observe cultural differences when you visit other countries and when you receive foreign visitors. However, only people inside those cultures can easily capture their real meaning. So, if you find yourself asked to manage projects that cross national (and cultural) boundaries, you must make an effort to:

- discover the meanings of different symbols used by local people, in order to respect and follow their basic instructions. In project management, the symbols can translate into the specialised terms, techniques and diagrams;
- know their local heroes, to understand the role models of behaviour. The organisational heroes can be the people who advance quickly in their career, employees receiving management awards or popular team members;
- understand and respect the rituals, which in business are often present in the way people organise or attend meetings, in local practices for celebrating success, in negotiation processes and by the demonstration of power when attending or rejecting meeting invitations.

Hofstede (2001) suggested that the 'invisible' core of culture is formed by the values, which broadly represent tendencies and preferences over different aspects of social or professional life. The following are examples of values that may affect global projects, as they differ depending on the geographical location of team members:

- Is it polite to decline meetings because they occur during your lunch hour?
- Conversely, is it acceptable to book regular meetings during the lunch hour?
- Is it acceptable to organise a meeting starting at 6pm on a summer Friday afternoon?
- Is it acceptable to ask your project team to cancel their summer holidays to finish an overdue task?
- Are project managers more effective when they use their formal power (their hierarchical position) or their expert power (based on their competences)?
- What is the preferred leadership style for project managers, in each part of the project life cycle?
- How important is the performance of the team members, when compared to the way they respect and relate to their colleagues?

THE CULTURAL DIMENSIONS DEFINED BY HOFSTEDE

It is very important to understand what types of differences you can come across when working on global projects. The existing cultural studies identify and measure the relation of cultural aspects among various cultures, classifying them under distinct dimensions. The following classification summarises the dimensions defined by Hofstede (2001).

Power Distance

This dimension reflects how individuals from different cultures handle the fact that people are unequal, and how the project stakeholders are likely to be involved in the decision-making process. For a more detailed definition of power distance index, search at http://www.clearlycultural.com.

Here is an example. Some team members coming from countries with larger power distance rates may find it more difficult to disagree with their project managers in front of other people when compared with individuals from countries that have smaller power distance rates.

In order to discover whether or not this general rule is applicable to your project team members, you can organise some one-to-one sessions with different individuals to validate their thoughts and compare them with the opinions they give (or do not give) during team meetings. You can then reduce this power barrier by organising 'round-table' discussions, asking all team members to give their opinions on key project decisions. When some of them give short affirmative or neutral answers, you can stimulate their thinking by raising questions that allow them to voice their opinions without a feeling of agreement or disagreement. One such line of questioning might run as follows:

- Have you seen a similar event in a previous project?
- How was that handled?
- Do you think we could have the same approach in this project?

INDIVIDUALISM AND COLLECTIVISM

This dimension classifies countries according to the relationship between individuals and societies, the extent of group cohesiveness, the importance of participating in a social group and the values attached to working conditions and ambitions. Generally, team members with individualist mindsets praise self-determination, are fond of having sufficient time for their personal lives, enjoy freedom in selecting the way they will execute the tasks assigned to them, and thrive on challenging activities and competitive environments. Work tends to be performed better when the project objectives coincide with the team member's personal interests. The business aspect of the relationship between the workers and the project organisation is often prominent.

By contrast, the collective will of a group or organisation can determine the behaviour of team members from collectivist cultures, who are likely to give more importance to improving their skills, using their abilities and having good physical working conditions. A higher degree of achievement occurs when the project objective and strategies coincide with the interests of the groups represented by these stakeholders, who will probably see their relationship with the project manager on moral terms.

Masculinity and Femininity

Using Hofstede's terminology, in the more masculine countries the degree of gender differentiation is high. Individuals tend to associate men with control, power and material ambition, and women with modesty, tenderness and focus on quality of life. The ideals are economic growth, progress, material success and performance. In the more feminine societies, the level of discrimination and the differentiation between genders tends to be low. Individuals are likely to treat men and women equally, and value the quality of life, human contact and caring for others.

Female project managers from feminine countries may need to be patient and assertive to overcome perceptions of the stakeholders from masculine countries. Male project managers from masculine countries must show modesty, humility and competency to win the confidence of team members located in feminine countries. Global project managers may need to encourage and support female team members from masculine countries to contribute and express their viewpoint actively.

Uncertainty Avoidance

This dimension reflects the resistance to change and the attitude to taking risks of individuals from different countries. As most projects are elements of change and involve risks, the stakeholder analysis and management activities can certainly be more complete and effective when the national differences are taken into account.

Individuals from countries with stronger uncertainty avoidance indexes are more inclined to avoid risks, enjoy working with tight rules and control systems and resist innovation. Team members are likely to enjoy tasks requiring precision, punctuality and hard work and feel more comfortable with detailed planning and more short-term feedback. Stakeholders from countries with weaker uncertainty avoidance indexes enjoy innovation, accept higher risk levels and are comfortable with open-ended learning situations. The team members tend to resist stress better and accept work packages with lower levels of definition.

Having a good mix of people from different countries in the project team allows the organiser of a brainstorming exercise to identify how to win over the resistance and obtain buy-in from different types of stakeholders. The understanding that team members might have different tolerance levels for ambiguity or uncertainty will help you to determine the level of detail required for the rules, conventions and standards in your project (as well as the level of definition of the work packages that will be assigned to team members from different cultures).

Long-term Orientation

The fifth dimension from Hofstede opposes long-term to short-term aspects of Confucian thinking. People from long-term oriented cultures tend to give high importance to values such as:

- persistence when results are slow;
- thrift;
- savings;
- having a sense of shame.

Stakeholders from these countries are more likely to support entrepreneurial activity and stimulate investments.

Individuals from short-term oriented cultures may aim to achieve quick results and give more attention to personal stability, protecting their reputation and respect for tradition. These stakeholders would like to see more frequent progress reports that clearly show:

- benefits already achieved;
- short-term targets to be accomplished before the next reporting cycle.

CULTURAL DIMENSIONS FROM TROMPENAARS AND HAMPDEN-TURNER

Trompenaars and Hampden-Turner defined a different set of dimensions during their cross-cultural studies. These can be an alternative or a complement to Hofstede's dimensions. The following classification shows the main dimensions defined by Trompenaars and Hampden-Turner (2005) and summarised by Trompenaars and Woolliams (2003). The comparisons with Hofstede's dimensions will help you to understand the extent to which the two models can be used to complement each other.

Universalism versus Particularism

The first dimension defines how people judge the behaviours of their colleagues. People from universalistic cultures focus more on rules, are more precise when defining contracts and tend to define global standards for company policies and human resources practices. Within more particularistic national cultures, the focus is more on the relationships; contracts can be adapted to satisfy new requirements in specific situations and local variations of company and human resources policies are created to adapt to different requirements.

Project and programme managers from universalistic countries will prefer to define a clear set of standards for practices, processes and templates across different countries and companies before starting to work together. Conversely, the more particularistic will favour the establishment of generic rules and concentrate on the deliverables, caring less if each project manager uses a different set of practices.

Individualism and Communitarianism

This dimension is similar to the 'individualism and collectivism' presented by Hofstede. It classifies countries according to the balance between the individual and group interests. Generally, team members with individualist mindsets see the improvements to their groups as the means to achieve their own objectives. By contrast, the team members from communitarian cultures see the improvements to individual capacities as a step towards the group's prosperity.

Stakeholders from individualistic countries are inclined to accept that one representative makes a choice on behalf of a team or group. They will also be keen to use voting to take important team decisions without losing time. The drawback is that the stakeholders who do not understand the rationale – or who simply don't agree with it – might ignore the group decision, or start lobbying to change it. This can increase the total time taken to implement the actions decided (thus delaying the project).

Decision-making processes take much longer in more communitarian cultures. The stakeholders from these countries will prefer to have a group of representatives for each party, who deliberate until a consensus is reached. The decision is likely to be followed by all participants, as they all know the reasons for it. As a consequence, the time to correct problems created by dissidents will be reduced.

Achievement versus Ascription

This dimension, presented in Trompenaars's and Hampden-Turner's studies, is very similar to Hofstede's power distance concept. People from achievement-oriented countries respect their colleagues based on previous achievements and the demonstration of knowledge. They show their job titles only when relevant. On the other hand, people from ascription-oriented cultures use their titles extensively and usually respect their superiors in hierarchy.

If you and most of your project team members are from achievement-oriented countries, and a group of people is located in one or more ascription-oriented countries, the role of the local managers will have a special importance. You might need to involve the functional managers in project review meetings and keep them copied in most email communication. The team members are not likely to take important decisions before consulting their managers.

In opposite situations, project managers from ascription-oriented countries need to understand that their team members from achievement-oriented countries will prefer to be consulted instead of being given instructions. They can also have a high degree of independence from their managers when making decisions in their areas of specialisation.

Neutral versus Affective

According to Trompenaars and Hampden-Turner, people from neutral cultures admire cool and self-possessed conducts and control their feelings (but these can suddenly explode during stressful periods). When working with stakeholders from neutral countries you might consider avoiding warm, expressive or enthusiastic behaviours. Instead prepare beforehand, concentrate on the topics being discussed and look carefully for small cues showing whether the person is angry or pleased.

People from cultures high on affectivity use all forms of gesturing, smiling and body language to voice their feelings openly. They prefer heated, vital and animated expressions. To improve the collaboration of stakeholders from affective countries you might need to:

- avoid detached, ambiguous and cool behaviour;
- appreciate good work in previous projects;
- tolerate excess of emotionality;
- evaluate the real contents of messages received beyond the colourful adjectives and superlatives.

Specific versus Diffuse

Trompenaars and Hampden-Turner researched differences in how people engage colleagues in specific or multiple areas of their lives, classifying the results into two groups.

People from more specific-oriented cultures tend to keep private and business agendas separate, having a completely different relation of authority in each social group. Team members might have more authority (depending on their experience and knowledge level) when meeting their functional managers at non-professional events. They are usually precise, transparent and direct, preferring meetings with precise agendas and detailed plans.

In diffuse-oriented countries, the authority level at work can reflect into social areas. Employees can adopt a subordinated attitude when meeting their managers outside office hours. Stakeholders from these cultures will tend to be ambiguous, evasive and act indirectly. They feel more comfortable with free-form meetings and work packages defined in less detail, allowing them to exercise personal judgement and creativity.

Human-nature Relationship (Internal versus External Control)

Trompenaars and Hampden-Turner show how people from different countries relate to their natural environment and changes. Global project stakeholders from internal-oriented cultures may show a more dominant attitude, focus on their own functions and groups and be uncomfortable with change. Nationals from internal-control countries (for example, Venezuela and China) are less likely to believe they are in control of their own fate than people from external-control countries (like Norway, Israel and Uruguay).

Stakeholders from external-oriented cultures are generally more flexible and willing to compromise. They value harmony and focus on their colleagues. They tend to be more comfortable with change.

Human-time Relationship

Similarly to Hofstede's long-term orientation, Trompenaars and Hampden-Turner identified that different cultures assign diverse meanings to the past, present and future.

People in past-oriented cultures tend to show respect for ancestors and older people and frequently put things in a traditional or historic context. They can usually be motivated by reviewing previous success stories as a preparation for project planning sessions.

People in present-oriented cultures enjoy the activities of the moment and present relationships, tend to be less motivated for planning sessions and might show resistance to following detailed plans.

People from future-oriented cultures enjoy discussing prospects, potentials and future achievement. They tend to participate actively in the planning sessions.

A second division of country cultures is based on the time orientation, in which *sequential cultures* drive people to do one activity at a time and to follow plans and schedules strictly. People from *synchronic cultures* can do work in parallel, and follow schedules and agendas loosely, taking the priorities of individual tasks being performed as a dominant factor.

The Impact of the Dimensions on Global Project Management

Before using the dimensions described above, please make sure you understand the following considerations:

- The dimensions assess the structure of each national culture's business communities. They are not intended to be guidelines for tourists and are not concerned with personality.
- The dimensions only give an illustration of the kind of issues you might face when working with people from various national-value systems. They cannot be used to predict a person's effectiveness in another culture.
- These dimensions reflect general standpoints from national cultures. They do not take into account other distinctions such as gender, generation, social class, education or organisation. Trompenaars's and Hampden-Turner's longitudinal research also reveals shifts and convergences in many cultures over the last 20 years, with consequent changes in the dimension scores.

Global project managers can consider these dimensions when assigning roles and responsibilities to team members from different country cultures, and when forming working groups. During the project execution activities, these differences are potential sources of conflict that can engender advantages to the project and reduce group thinking when correctly managed.

The models from Hofstede and Trompenaars and Hampden-Turner provide a valuable framework that allows us to begin to understand the relevance of culture in business. Ultimately, it is not about simply understanding differences, but how differences can be both connected and harnessed through reconciliation (as described in Trompenaars's and Hampden-Turner's more recent publications).

In addition, intercultural awareness sessions and cross-cultural team-building exercises are powerful tools during project initiation workshops and kick-off meetings, well worth the investment for global projects with a high level of cultural complexity. You can evaluate this complexity by considering the different project locations and their positions in the cultural dimension classifications.

CASE EXAMPLE NO. 1: A REAL-LIFE EXPERIENCE

The level of information exchange required on a project can vary depending on the cultural patterns of the stakeholders. In one real-life example the project implementation would affect the availability of computer systems in various factories across the world. Early approval was required from six country representatives. In the first project phase, an overall description of the activity was distributed by email and the electronic approval was requested using an automated change configuration tool.

Country number one's representative called the project manager on the same day, used the opportunity of the telephone call to have a long discussion, and then promised quick approval (which happened three days later).

Country number two's representative called the project manager, spent a short time in informal discussions, and then discussed the activity at a detailed level. After receiving explanations about the risk assessment, and understanding the contingency measures, the activity was approved on the same day.

Country number three's representative sent the project manager a lengthy email, with copies to two senior managers and the project sponsor. The email explained tersely that more details were needed. So the project manager was forced to:

- Organise an immediate audio-conference, to review the detailed project plan, all the risk responses and to introduce the project team members who were coordinating and executing the critical activities;
- Write precise meeting minutes to capture all the points discussed;
- Reply to the original email, with a copy to everyone who had received it. These replies had to include a link to the meeting minutes. These email responses had to be left on file in case more information had to be communicated.

After one week, the electronic approval was provided from this third country, without any informal telephone call or email. But the remaining three country representatives had not replied.

The project manager called the representative of country number four, who told the project manager that approval would not be forthcoming without a detailed level of information. So the information was sent. Four days later, the representative gave the electronic approval, and forwarded an email which revealed a long thread of internal reviewers who had participated in an internal meeting. During that meeting the reviewers had discussed the activity and validated all its details.

When the representative of country number five was called by the project manager, the response was an email received only five minutes later which gave approval. This representative apologised for the delay, blaming the excessive number of previous emails.

Emails were sent to the representative of country number six, but no reply was received until three weeks after. The representative provided the approval without any question or request for details.

The project manager considered all these behaviours and reviewed the project communications plan for the second phase of this project. This second phase would also need approval from the same six country representatives. As a result, when the email was sent to invite this second-phase approval it contained the following information:

- Two paragraphs that described briefly the planned activities, risks involved and response strategies;
- A link to the project plan, detailed risk analysis and the roles and responsibilities matrix;
- A final paragraph inviting all six representatives to an information session conducted by audio- and web-conferencing. This would allow more detailed discussion of the activities. It was suggested to the representatives that they might wish to invite all colleagues who would be involved in the approval process.

The country managers (senior to the representatives) were included in the distribution list of this email, and they were asked to take action in case their subordinates should be unavailable at the time of the virtual meeting. The email produced the following results.

1. The first two representatives called back on the same day for informal discussions. They gave quick approval and declined the invitation to a virtual meeting because they were satisfied with the level of detail given in the email.
2. The third and fourth representatives did participate in the virtual meeting, with their colleagues. They gave approval after one week.
3. The fifth and sixth representatives answered the email within one week. They apologised for not taking part in the virtual meeting, and for their delay in replying. However, they gave positive feedback on the information contained in the project manager's email and approved the change.

The project manager's revised approach was part of this project's lessons-learned experience, and the same procedure was followed successfully for subsequent projects. Those involved different representatives from the original six countries.

The main conclusion from this experience is that the adoption of a holistic approach to communication, providing different levels of information to various stakeholders from distinct cultural backgrounds, can improve understanding and reduce conflicts.

Avoiding Generalisations

Most of the studies available on cultural differences reflect general observations and research on the national cultural level. You can use them as a basis for understanding the most likely behaviour of your colleagues and team members from a specific country. They can also help you to accept certain attitudes and discuss them with other team members to resolve conflicts. However, you need to make sure that the global team members will use this knowledge to understand and accept the cultural differences, whilst avoiding negative generalisations and stereotyping.

Stereotyping is an exaggerated and limited view of the average group behaviour under the cultural lenses of the observer, taking a few examples of cultural encounters – or the information from the cultural dimensions – as the only reference. You will also find different behaviours when working with a team of people from the same country, as the values and norms discussed in the cultural dimensions are not only dependent on the nationality of team members. In your life, you can be part of different cultural groups, accumulating experiences that help make you unique. Some examples of characteristics that define your cultural groups can be:

- the region (inside the country) where you live;
- your ethnic origin;
- your religion;
- your language;
- your gender;
- your age or generation;
- your education level;
- the industry you work in;
- your company;
- your job function.

Perhaps the most important lesson for global project managers is the openness they should have in relation to the cultural dimensions. Take this example: Hofstede (2001) evaluated the relationship between the power distance dimension (PDI) and planning and control systems, concluding that, 'Lower-PDI control systems place more trust in subordinates; in higher-PDI cultures such trust is lacking'.

CASE EXAMPLE NO. 2

Hofstede identified that Malaysia is higher than Austria in power distance. The wrong usage of this information is to relax on project control when dealing with activities performed by Austrian members, and adopt a directive approach to the Malaysians. The preferred approach is:

- Start using the same processes and management style for all team members – you can control the activities of the Austrian and Malaysian team members with the same frequency and using the same processes.
- Observe the different reactions and behaviours under the lenses of the cultural dimensions. Note whether or not team members are performing their activities on

time, verifying the work executed. Identify if the Austrian team members really have less need for control than the Malaysians. This will not show a weakness from either team, but will simply indicate different behaviour.

- Be ready for surprises. In many cases, the team members are well adapted to the company cultures, and will react in a way different from that which you expect. The Malaysian team members might in fact work independently, with a reduced need for control.
- Adapt your style to the differences. If you notice that the team members from Malaysia require a more directive approach for control, you can organise a weekly meeting to follow their activities in more detail, whilst reviewing the overall project status together with the Austrians in a separate fortnightly meeting.

Building on the Richness of a Multicultural Team: Crossvergence and Hybridisation

Global project managers can use originality to deviate from general norms and obtain competitive advantage, improving the likelihood of project success. An interesting concept from recent research is 'crossvergence', which according to Jacob (2005) is, 'all about fusing together management practices of two or more cultures, so that a practice relevant to a heterogeneous culture can be assembled'. Global teams can provide all elements for an effective fusion of different project management practices: people from various country and company cultures, enriched by different experiences and management theories, implemented by a team in different countries, with a wealthy mix of skills and beliefs.

Hybridisation is another concept on multicultural management, which can be defined as the use of a common body of knowledge, enhanced with selective parts of successful practices from the countries where the project is being implemented, or from the team members' original culture.

When starting a global project in a new country, or when new project team members have a cultural origin that you have never experienced before, the cultural dimensions (presented earlier in this chapter) can be a first source of reference to understand their general mindset, and the cultural patterns likely to be found in their culture.

A second step is to read different sources of information on the country, not only to show the team members that you care for their culture, but to really understand how they live, think and what the main sources of cultural and economic richness are.

The third step (certainly the most important) is to pay attention to the behaviour of the team members, to understand their values during informal conversations and to show respect for these values, whilst letting them know your own opinion, the project communication standards and the important norms that must be followed for them to be accepted by the other team members (Connaughton and Daly, 2004).

The development of these skills is not a simple task, and can only be achieved after some years of experience in multicultural teams. To reduce the time to master these skills, and improve the likelihood of success in your first global project, you can attend 'soft skills' training sessions and request coaching from more experienced global project managers.

Fisher and Fisher (2001) suggest that a good training plan will also include language lessons (for people in frequent contact with a foreign language), technical training (when there are different levels of understanding on technical disciplines that can create conflicts or risks to the collaboration) and cross-cultural training (when team members and key stakeholders come from different cultural backgrounds and there are many differences in the cultural dimensions explained earlier in this chapter).

Conclusion

Global project managers must understand the definitions, dimensions and implications of culture on project management, in order to respect and use the cultural differences across various countries, improving project innovation and teamwork. The dimensions from Trompenaars and Hampden-Turner and Hofstede can be used as a starting point, but the real experience of the global project team is a rich resource to be evaluated, documented and discussed. To conclude, here is a five-step framework for effective cross-cultural development:

1. Reflect upon how the definition of culture applies to project management. Discover the different project management symbols, the local heroes and the business rituals.
2. Learn the different types of culture: the cultural differences that exist across countries, but which are also influenced by a diversity of age, gender, regions, religions and many other types of social groups. Consider the dimensions presented in this chapter as a starting point from which to build your own cross-cultural knowledge.
3. Understand the cultural differences. Use the cultural dimensions to know what differences to expect between people from different cultures. Employ a team-building exercise to identify how your team and colleagues view these differences.
4. Respect the cultural differences. Keep the differences in mind when confronted with opposite views of the world. You must accept them and show respect for the different standpoints.
5. Vive la difference. Enjoy the richness of a multicultural team. Remember that you can build on the differences to identify and mitigate risks, to find alternative approaches and achieve the project objectives in better ways and increase the level of innovation and quality of your project deliverables.

References and Further Reading

Binder, J. (2007), *Global Project Management: Communication, Collaboration and Management Across Borders*, Aldershot: Gower.

Connaughton, S.L. and Daly, J.A. (2004), 'Long distance leadership: Communicative strategies for leading virtual teams', in Pauleen, D.J. (ed.), *Virtual Teams: Projects, Protocols and Processes*, Hershey, PA: Idea Group Publishing.

Dahl, S. (2004), 'Intercultural Research: The Current State of Knowledge' in Middlesex University Discussion Paper No. 26. Available at: http://papers.ssrn.com/sol3/papers.cfm?abstract_id= 658202

Fisher K. and Fisher M. (2001), *The Distance Manager*, New York: McGraw-Hill.

Hofstede, G. (2001), *Culture's Consequences: Comparing Values, Behaviors, Institutions and Organizations Across Nations*, 2nd edn, London: Sage.

Jacob, N. (2005), 'Cross-cultural investigations: Emerging concepts', *Journal of Organizational Change Management*, 18(5), 514–28. Available at: http://www.emeraldinsight.com/Insight/viewContentItem.do?contentType=Article&hdAction=lnkpdf&contentId=1515000&dType=SUB

Trompenaars, F. and Hampden-Turner, C. (2005), *Riding the Waves of Culture: Understanding Cultural Diversity in Business*, London: Nicholas Brealey.

Trompenaars, F. and Woolliams, P. (2003), *Business across Cultures*, Oxford: Capstone Publishing Ltd.

25 *Project Communications*

JO ANN SWEENEY

Project communication within and outside the project team is all about changing attitudes and perceptions; moving people from being negative to being positive and believing that our project is good for them. This means moving people along a continuum – firstly creating awareness, then building their interest, creating a desire to be involved and finally having them participate. We move people from one end of the continuum where they know little or nothing about our project to the other end where they willingly embrace the project and all its intended consequences.

Communicating Project Information

Creating awareness. Our initial aim is to make our target audiences aware of our project – who is involved, why it is being introduced, when it will be starting, where it will be rolled out and how they will be affected.

Building interest – Then our aim is to build their interest – by explaining the benefits for them, their teams and their customers. How will this change make it easier for them to do their jobs effectively? How will it speed up or simplify processes? How will it improve the systems they currently use? How do the benefits of changing outweigh the effort and personal costs involved?

Desire and action – We want to change audience perceptions so that they believe our project is good for them, their colleagues and customers – so that they want to be involved. When we have done that our final aim is to persuade them to take action – to become involved and committed.

Two-way conversations – Communicating projects is about content-rich conversations. That means both sides listening to each other – not just one-way traffic where one side does all the talking. It's also about more than project data. People have to be personally involved; they want content that relates to them and to which they can relate. This means tailoring content to their needs rather than presenting it from the project manager's perspective. It's about putting ourselves in the shoes of our audiences.

Developing Personal Communication Skills

I am occasionally asked the question 'Are people born as communicators or can the skills be learned and developed over time?' Both can be true. Some of us communicate easily, whilst others have to make an effort to see things from perspectives different from their own. Developing these skills should be regarded as a continuum rather than an either-or situation. So we must know where we are on the continuum and decide where we want to be. The starting point is about seeing people and the role they play in the team as being as important as the team's tasks and objectives. When we have this mindset we are willing to put significant chunks of our time and energy into encouraging people as well as into tasks.

Valuing individuals for who they are is also important. People who like other people, who respect and value them, are easily recognisable. Their attitudes show in the way they interact with others, both in conversation and in their actions.

Dealing with people is a critical factor in project management. Those who do not naturally have the necessary skills can – and must – develop them. But communication skills are not something you can learn overnight. You cannot open a book and learn them. Listening, understanding, collaborating and other communication skills are built through practice. The more we practise the more competent we become, especially if we have someone more experienced to guide us. Learning to communicate involves trial and error. If you work at it and practise you can develop a strong communication skills set.

Top Communication Skills for Project Managers

I once asked project managers from many countries what communication skills they thought they needed to lead their teams. I have since tested their views against those of people attending my communicating projects workshops. The following five factors came top:

1. active listening;
2. building relationships based on trust;
3. setting clear priorities;
4. enabling collaboration;
5. conveying vision.

ACTIVE LISTENING

Active listening means listening to others and understanding the meaning behind their words. We must not interrupt or let our minds wander. We must ask questions to check understanding and observe non-verbal signals. The benefits include getting people to speak freely (open up). Then many misunderstandings and conflicts can be resolved.

At its heart the secret of active listening is to remove the focus from ourselves and put it on other people. When we listen we hear their interests and concerns and begin to understand how these affect their attitudes and behaviour. The better we listen the more we hear and understand.

Reading non-verbal signals (facial expressions, body language and tone of voice) is part of active listening. Does the other person look bored or nervous? Are they fiddling with their hands? Do they keep checking the time?

Active listening means paying full attention to what the other person is saying, rather than planning what we will say when they finish talking. That requires self-discipline. We have to keep our own emotions in check and not take things personally.

When people speak we are continually analysing what they are saying. We are asking ourselves whether their words reflect what they really feel or think, and whether there is anything left unsaid. We spot their key points and reflect on those to check our understanding.

We need to listen so we can understand requirements, especially with stakeholders. This should happen throughout the project, not just at the beginning.

Not everyone is good at articulating what they think and feel. Some people take time to think about things, they may get tongue-tied, or use abstract words that have multiple meanings. Using open-ended questions will help you make sense of their confusion.

The intentional use of silence is a very powerful listening tool. Most people are uncomfortable with silence. Rather than let a pause continue, your opposite number will speak into the gap and reveal more than they intended about what they are thinking and feeling.

BUILDING RELATIONSHIPS BASED ON TRUST AND RESPECT

Trust and respect are the cornerstones of personal relationships. They are earned (not a right) and come from experience of our honesty, integrity and expertise. Trust provides the underlying emotional glue that ensures team members keep their promises to each other, share knowledge and complete their tasks within time and specification.

Mick Cope (2003) says there are five key trust attributes among teams and organisations. The initial letters of these attributes spell out T-R-U-S-T, as follows:

- **T**ruthfulness – the opposite of secrets and lies. Ask yourself if team members freely reveal what they think and feel, or if they repress their fears and failings. Can you rely on what they say, or do they withhold bad news until the last minute?
- **R**esponsiveness – our openness with each other and our willingness to share ideas and information freely. It's the next step on from listening and understanding and is how we reveal that we are interested in others and willing to include their relevant views and experiences.
- **U**niformity – the level of consistency, predictability and reliability in a relationship. When we are our words and behaviours are consistent and synchronised, others come to depend on us. They know we will not keep changing our minds, or make promises until we know we can deliver.
- **S**afety – loyalty and our willingness to protect, support and encourage each other, including when we make mistakes. This could be safety in the physical environment, but is more likely to be about our emotional and social environments. Another way to think about safety is to ask ourselves how people feel when they are around us. Do they feel good about themselves, or do they cloak themselves in protective armour so that we cannot hurt them?
- **T**rained – this is about knowledge, skills and competence rather than qualifications. As project leaders we need the abilities and experience to provide wise counsel to team members when they face challenges. And they need to recognise these attributes in us.

SETTING CLEAR PRIORITIES

Project managers are like conductors, choreographers and air traffic controllers. They provide the big picture, ensuring everyone is united behind the common goal. They bring team members in on cue and create a harmonious whole from quite different skills and personalities. The key to this is communicating goals, plans and priorities clearly for the team and making clear what is expected of each person to achieve these.

Explaining Content and Context

Content is the what, who, when, where and how of any project; the nuts and bolts detail that tells team members how what they do fits into the overall project.

Context is the bigger picture for both the project and for individual team members. It explains the difference we expect the content to make to people and to the organisation.

Clear, specific deadlines and quality standards help team members focus on key activities and differentiate between things that are urgent and those that are important. Our tendency is to do first those activities that are quick and easy, but often it is the more complex, time-consuming activities that make a greater impact on project success.

It is too easy to assume that we have explained things clearly and that team members understand both what we mean and what we are asking of them. Asking them to confirm their understanding will show whether or not they have listened and heard what you have said.

Effective project managers are also interested in what people think about the team's goals and objectives, even when these are set in stone. Giving team members the chance to voice their views and listening to what they say shows that you care about them. It may be that you can feed their views up the organisation, or it may be that helping them understand other perspectives will increase their commitment to the goals.

ENABLING COLLABORATION

In a collaborative environment team members support and encourage each other rather than focusing solely on their own tasks and responsibilities. They are willing to cooperate and share information, ideas and assets to help each other. Five tips follow for developing a collaborative team culture.

Tip 1: Look to Yourself First

Collaboration is a mindset. People who like people – who like relating to others – are good at helping their team members to share and support each other. For project managers this translates into thinking about the way you relate to your team members. Ask yourself how much time you spend with them, whether you are willing to collaborate and if they recognise this.

Tip 2: Model Collaborative Behaviour

Collaboration starts with modelling the behaviours you want your team members to show. You can begin by increasing the amount of information you share, asking their advice, encouraging them to contribute ideas and raise concerns, recognising their contributions and including them in the rewards of success.

Tip 3: Create Respect for Diversity

Good project managers build teams that are balanced, not just in knowledge and expertise, but also in cultural understanding, perceptions, attitudes and probably gender, age and ethnicity as well. They include within the team people who are different from themselves as well as those with whom they get on with naturally. They also help team members to value their different contributions, and to understand and respect each other.

Tip 4: Reward Accountability

Collaboration includes clarity as an essential element, with team members having clear expectations of each other that link to both the project goals and business needs. Each person has responsibility for an aspect of the project that leads to overall success. They can see that it is in their interests to collaborate because team success requires each individual member to do their own bit well.

Tip 5: Make Time to Socialise

Collaboration includes friendship; where team members are willing to share some of their lives outside work, talking about families, hobbies and the other personal things. In doing so they become real to each other, not just two-dimensional characters whom they forget about as soon as they leave the office.

CONVEYING THE ORGANISATION'S VISION

One of my favourite sources of leadership advice is Olivier (2001). He says:

> Vision is like a breath of fresh air, it gives energy … the fundamental ability of an inspirational leader is to change the energy in those around them. And one of the most effective ways of doing this is to have and hold a vision that means something to those who will have to put it into action.

A clear vision helps team members focus on the big picture of why their organisation has invested in the project alongside the more prosaic milestones, targets and deliverables. Vision creates the sense of urgency, of purpose, that motivates people. It is also the rudder that keeps a project on course to the business need, as the team moves through the process of identifying, testing and implementing solutions.

As project managers, we need to convey the link between our project and the organisation so that we can show we are delivering value. Here are six easy-to-implement steps:

1. *Keep it clear and simple*: so that people understand exactly what the vision is and how it relates to them and what they do. Explain the vision from memory if possible, in words that make sense to you and your team. Then people will remember.

2. *Personal commitment*: as team leader you must be committed to the vision. People will spot the inconsistency if you do not believe what you are saying. They will judge your commitment through both your words and actions. If both support the vision they will believe you.

3. *Build consent*: personal commitment also extends to individual team members, with each person making an emotional commitment to play their part in delivering the vision. Before they can do that they need to understand how their role and objectives relate to what the vision expects of them.

4. *Repetition*: people need to hear the same ideas repeatedly so that they can sink in and be remembered. Repeating the vision happens at two levels. On one level it is using metaphors, analogies and examples to help people understand the big picture. On the other level it means continually mentioning how the vision relates to what people and the team are doing. Kotter (1996) wrote 'these brief mentions can add up to a massive amount of useful communication, which is generally what is needed to win over both hearts and minds'.

5. *Participation*: sharing the vision means more than persuading people to get on board the 'vision bus'. It means giving people space and time to help shape the vision to create a sense of team ownership. This is also about allowing people to ask questions, propose new ideas, think through the implications and be creative.

Communications with Stakeholders

Keeping different audiences up to date with what is happening in your project takes time, effort and budget. How can you be sure it is worthwhile? When thinking about this it is easy to focus on outputs – how many reports you have produced, or presentations you have given. Partly this is because such things are easy 'boxes to tick'. But they do not deal with the more fundamental question of why you are communicating with your different audiences; what you are trying to achieve and the result that you want. There are four overarching reasons for telling people about your project:

1. *knowledge*: you want them to know more than they currently do;
2. *attitude*: you want them to feel more positive;
3. *support*: you want them to say positive things about your project in public;
4. *involvement*: you want them to get involved in some way.

You will probably have different aims for each of your audiences. For instance, you will want end users to be involved, executives to be supportive and middle managers to be positive. There is no right and wrong – each project is different. What is consistent though is that this is a spectrum with 'knows nothing' at one end and 'fully involved' at the other.

Identifying your Target Audiences

When you communicate your project you should not send the same information and the same amount of data to everyone. Some people will be more interested in your project and others will have more influence over how successful you are. If you send everyone the same content some will get too much and others will not get enough. Also you will probably be putting more time and money into communicating than necessary. Typically there are at least three key audience groupings for projects, which are sponsors, senior executives and end users.

Sponsors are often senior directors and other board members. They are most interested in how your project reflects their performance – the things for which they are held accountable by the board of directors, shareholders and financial institutions. This means they do want to hear:

- regular progress updates;
- how your project links to the organisation's business plan;
- issues you are facing and any concerns you have;
- ways they can support you that will make a difference.

Ask for their views as well. They can probably see the big picture better than you can. They know what else is going on in your unit, your organisation and your industry. They can see synergies and potential areas of conflict.

By senior executives I mean those people responsible for functions with significant budgets. If your project is one for internal change, the senior executives will probably include managers of the units to which your end users belong, and they can use their wider visibility to influence the attitudes and motivations of the end users. As far as each internal change project is concerned, senior executives are usually most interested in:

- expected project benefits;
- the delivery time for those benefits;
- risk of project failure, and the associated consequences;
- the impact on the organisation's motivation and productivity during implementation; progress during all stages, particularly during implementation;
- any issues and concerns you have;
- how you want them to be practically involved.

Understanding Sponsors' Perspectives

Winning the support of sponsors involves putting ourselves in their shoes and seeing our project from their perspectives. When we learn how to do this we develop continuing relationships based on respect and trust. Here are some keys to help you as you develop such relationships.

- *Understand who your sponsor is*: Before we can build a relationship with another person we need to know who they are – not just the obvious but also what they think and feel, their passions and idiosyncrasies.
- *Uncover what they are interested in*: When sponsors can clearly see the links between their priorities and your project they will be supportive.
- *Relate to their view of the world*: We each of us look at the world through a tunnel constructed from our experiences and mindset. What we seldom realise is that each

person's tunnel is slightly different and none of us sees the world in exactly the same way.

- *Identify shadow issues*: This is about the extent to which unacknowledged attitudes and behaviours will affect support from your sponsor. Surface issues are those things they are willing to tell you about. Shadow issues are things they do not discuss or manage openly. Usually there are good cultural and political reasons why these issues are hidden and trying to force them into the open can make people defensive. The trick is to learn to recognise the shadow issues and manage them without shining a spotlight on them.
- *Balance their needs*: Cope (2003) writes:

> *Consulting projects often fail because all the needs of the various stakeholders are not taken into consideration. This puts the whole project out of alignment because one group's needs are given priority over those of another. Like a three-legged stool, the consultancy process must always be in balance and the needs of the client, consultant [project manager] and end user understood and maintained. All have deep motivational needs and if one is left partially dissatisfied, the project is likely to hit problems.*

Cope is one of my favourite project management writers.

Providing Opportunities for Senior Executives to Get Involved

As project managers we cannot expect our sponsor and the managers above us to be deeply interested in our projects. We have to win their support. The best way to do that is by communication. My experience is that support for projects within companies is a top-down chain reaction. The higher up support starts, the greater the support at the bottom of the organisation. For me this means five things:

1. *Maintaining interest*: Regular communications tailored to the needs of senior executives will keep them interested in your project from initial planning to well after rollout as you take the outputs into 'business as usual'.
2. *Getting support when you need it*: Senior executives who understand the value of your project to themselves and the organisation will give practical support when you hit problems and resistance. When you cry 'Help!' you will get it.
3. *Acting as advocates*: One great value of a supportive sponsor and senior executives is that they can act as advocates for your project with other key people – especially people with whom you cannot otherwise communicate easily (such as the CEO).
4. *Feedback*: When you and your project team have trust-based relationships with your sponsor, they will be more likely to let you know about other director's concerns regarding your project. You cannot disprove or resolve such concerns if you do not know about them.
5. *Highlighting critical success factors*: Senior executives can give you early warning of strategic decisions that could affect your project. Now you can plan a response rather than being taken by surprise.

OVERCOMING RESISTANCE FROM THE END USERS OF CHANGE PROJECTS

Communicating with internal end users is particularly important for driving change projects through until their predicted benefits are achieved. End users for these projects are interested (often concerned) about the impact on them in their jobs. The need to know why they should change the way they work. They will ask what (if any) benefits they can expect personally.

Some end users will have seen many changes in their working lives that have not delivered lasting benefits or have failed disastrously. They will be sceptical until you demonstrate that you are listening and understand their interests and concerns.

Without support from end users any change project will fail, if not immediately then in the longer term. Why? Because ultimately projects are about changing the way end users do their jobs. If they refuse to change the project cannot deliver.

Resistance might indicate that you have not paid enough attention to the 'people side' of the project. In rolling out your project you are effectively asking people to change the ways in which they work and relate to each other. That is much to ask of anyone. Most likely the end users are happy with the way they are currently working, believe they are doing a good job, and think they are contributing to the company's success.

You are asking people to step out of their comfort zones. They will need good reasons to do that. You have to point out that the change is in the best interests of their customers and colleagues. Above all, you must convince them that the change is also in their own interests. When you understand the emotions and fears behind resistance you can develop effective strategies that persuade them to become supportive. Those strategies always involve communications.

Minimising the Risks for End users

It is the perception of risk (not objective measurement) that will determine how end users respond to change. The advantages of a well-managed change project should far outweigh the risks, but our end users cannot always see that. Even when they can, they might not believe they are going to be better off themselves. Yet again, communications are crucial. You need to persuade end users about the benefits of change on two levels – *logical* (cognitive) and *emotional*. Then they will understand and believe that your project is good for them, their colleagues and customers.

Creating a Desire for Change

Change cannot be forced or imposed successfully. Instead people have to be persuaded to the point where they will associate the change with some guarantee that benefits will result for them. For project managers this translates into a series of communication activities. First they must tell end users about the change. Then they have to explain the rationale, list the benefits, and then persuade end users to view the change positively so that they will willingly embrace the new way of working. Chapters 10 and 11 in Fowler and Lock (2006) give practical advice on how to do that.

The Project Communications Route Map

When it comes to planning the communication aspects of any project, I believe in keeping it simple. It might be only a list of things to do and key messages that you wish to get across to people. That would qualify as a plan (even though it might seem too simple) provided it is clearly linked to the project's aims and outcomes.

More likely you will need something a little more detailed. Most project managers find they need at least a schedule of activities that clarifies:

- the objectives of each activity;
- key audiences in order of priority;
- which communication channel to use;
- production and delivery timescales;
- monitoring mechanisms;
- the name of the person responsible for each activity.

In the remainder of this chapter I shall develop a two-part project communications route map, comprising a framework for communication activities and a practical schedule of activities. I can identify the following points or steps in creating the framework for communication activities:

1. SWOT (strengths, weaknesses, opportunities and threats) analysis to understand the difference communication makes to your project's success;
2. Prioritised list of your key audiences, including the journey on which you want to take them;
3. Overarching communication objectives linked to the commercial aims of your project and key audiences;
4. Key themes that guide communication activities and motivate audiences to respond;
5. Key messages that give context to activities;
6. Calendar of activities for your project and organisation;
7. Balanced portfolio of communication channels;
8. Allocated communication responsibilities among your team members;
9. Matrix of mechanisms to monitor the effectiveness of activities.

Stocktakes are worthwhile throughout the project life cycle. Each time that means looking at what we are doing and how our audiences feel. Three questions require answers, which are:

1. How effective are our existing communications activities?
2. What do our key stakeholders think and feel about our project?
3. How can we improve activities so stakeholders are more positive?

You might know the answers to these questions already or just need someone else to prompt you to draw them out of your subconscious mind.

If you are new to the project or organisation you may need to conduct an audit. Your audit can be formal, structured and rigorous, or an informal listening exercise. Either is fine as a starting point for planning communication activities.

Quantitative audits are the factual evaluations of what you do and how well you do it. During this audit you look at what has actually happened to date, how people find out about your project, what channels work best, how much time activities take to create and manage, what you should continue doing, what to stop and what to do differently.

Qualitative audits examine what your audiences think and feel about your project. They identify how familiar they are with your aims and activities and how positive they are towards the changes you are introducing.

Professional communicators use six principal methods for gathering information about what is happening in reality and how audiences feel:

1. Questionnaires and surveys, by telephone or online sampling;
2. Face-to-face or telephone interviews for a more probing first-hand feel;
3. Focus groups where small groups of people meet to talk among themselves, led by a facilitator;
4. Observing people to see if what they do is the same as what they say they do;
5. Personal logs where people observe themselves and keep a diary;
6. Interrogation of existing databases and records.

Prioritising Key Audiences

You need to work out who your key audiences are. Then you can identify groups that need many detailed briefings and those that need to receive some, but less detailed information. The best way to do this is to brainstorm to identify all your potential audiences and then prioritise them according to their influence on the success of your project, as well as how much effect the project will have on them.

Clarifying Communication Objectives

When authorising projects, executives are often committing their company to significant capital expenditure and taking experienced employees away from their usual revenue-earning activities. They will only do this if they believe there are clear commercial benefits for the organisation. As project managers we need to understand what these commercial expectations for our project are. Then we can then use communication activities to show we are meeting those expectations.

We also need to understand the specific change our project is expected to deliver. Mick Cope's five-rung change ladder is particularly helpful for this (Cope, 2003):

1. Assets: These are the tools, plant, equipment and so on used to deliver a product or service.
2. Blueprint: This comprises the systems, applications, processes, procedures, plans and strategies.
3. Capability: The skills, knowledge, experiences and aptitude of people in our team or organisation.
4. Desire: The motivations that drive people to take action and embrace change.

5. Ethos: This is the core reason why an organisation or team exists. For individuals it's our fundamental beliefs and attitudes. For instance the sports teams we support, the reasons we give to charity and why we do more than is required of us at work.

Projects deliver lasting change when we move people to the top of the ladder. If we do not change their motivations and attitudes they will revert to their old ways of working when the project ends. They might even pay lip service to change during project rollout.

Key Themes that Guide Activities

Themes are overarching statements that permeate all communication activities relating to our project. They are usually corporate and help explain to audiences the main focus of our project. The principal reason for having key themes is to create clarity and consistency in your project. They give consistency to communication activities, especially when many people are involved and are managing diverse activities.

Themes also help team members stay focused on the key reasons your organisation is putting resources into your project. It's easy when we get into the detail of a project to forget the bigger picture and become fixated on the assets and blueprints we are rolling out. Themes help prevent this happening.

The following is an example from a project in which I was involved. It shows how themes should be specific to the overall project. You will notice that themes are emotive as well as factual, because most audiences respond to appeals to their emotions more readily than they respond to facts.

'Customer Relationship Management (CRM) Programme'

- Customers expect us to know all about their interactions with our company when we meet them or speak with them on the telephone.
- Sharing your customer details with others helps the whole team to understand and meet the customer's needs.
- Our CRM system gives you the big picture of all your customers' dealings with our company, helping you to understand and meet their needs.

Chip and Dan Heath (2010) give some useful pointers for creating themes:

- You've got to change the person's situation.
- What looks like a people problem is often a situation problem. For anything to change people have to start acting differently. For a person's behaviour to change we've got to influence their environment as well as their hearts and minds.
- Appeal to the elephant and its rider. For individuals and organisations, our emotional side is like an elephant and our rational side is its rider. Both have strengths and weaknesses that are opposites. In change the rider provides planning and direction, whilst the elephant provides energy and drive. If we want change to happen we need to appeal to both. Themes help us understand how to do this.

- Create many small changes. Usually in change we are tinkering with behaviours that have become automatic. These take a far greater amount of mental energy to change. Asking people to take small steps one at a time – steps that they believe they have the energy to take – overcomes their blocks.
- Provide clarity of information. What looks like resistance is often lack of clarity. Our audiences don't understand what we are asking them to do or how to do what we are asking. To convince them that it is possible to make the change we should find compelling examples that are real and tangible – examples that also appeal to our audiences' emotions.
- Provide crystal-clear direction. Clear direction ensures people know exactly what they need to do. Understanding the behaviour that you are trying to change – what needs to happen for them to do what you want them to do – means you will be clearer in your instructions.

KEY MESSAGES THAT GIVE CONTEXT

Key messages are the themes of particular communication activities. They provide a framework that ensures activities meet the rational needs of the project and also the emotional needs of our audiences. If people remember only one thing after each activity; our messages are that thing.

Key messages help us to identify specific changes in attitudes and behaviours that we want, before we begin creating content for activities. This ensures activities that link to each other and the overall project aims.

They also help project content creators to understand the aims behind the content they are creating. Plus they remind content creators that content should be people-centric, positive, encouraging and motivating.

Examples of Key Messages

Compare these with the key theme examples given above. They are from the same 'CRM Programme'.

- Our new system is robust and will not compromise your customer data.
- It's easy to load your client data into the system and it won't take too much of your time.
- Having all our European customer data in one place will give us a much broader and more detailed understanding of clients' needs and expectations.
- CRM helps us identify timely solutions in a complex, changing and cost-sensitive European health care environment.

Tips for Creating Key Messages

In formulating messages we need to solve four problems:

1. What to say (message content): This is all about how to appeal to our audience to produce the response we want. There are three choices:

    - rational appeal to their self interest;
    - emotional appeal that stirs up negative feelings such as shame, fear and guilt, or positive feelings such as humour, pride or loyalty;
    - moral appeal directed at their sense of what is right and proper.

    Messages should not:

    - be too divergent from what they currently believe, because they will not change their belief;
    - restate what the audience already believes, because they will not pay attention.

2. How to say it logically (message structure): With structure you have the following choices to consider:

    - will you draw a conclusion for the audience or leave it to them to make up their own minds (depends on their level of intelligence)?
    - will you present both sides of the argument or just one side (depends on level of education, knowledge and whether they are opposed or supportive)?
    - in which order will you present the for and against arguments (positive view first or last)?

3. How to say it symbolically (message format): This determines the visual and aural appeal. Your choices are:

    - in print and online (headlines, subheadings, body text, illustrations and colour);
    - in person (body language, speech rate, facial expressions, physical appearance and emotions);
    - audio-visual (music, words, images, voice qualities and vocalisations).

4. Message source: Messages delivered by sources that are considered attractive by audiences have higher attention and recall. The three factors that underlie credibility of sources are their perceived expertise, their perceived trustworthiness and their likeability.

CALENDAR OF ACTIVITIES

Production and distribution timescales for communication activities should be linked to the project's milestones, as well as to other events and activities taking place in your organisation that target your audiences or will have an impact on them.

A calendar of activities (possibly on an Excel spreadsheet) is one great way of keeping the project team and your sponsor up to date with planned activities. If you are familiar with project planning methods you might prefer a Gantt chart.

You can include project activities, communication activities and other activities happening in the company. This calendar should be continually updated so it remains useful.

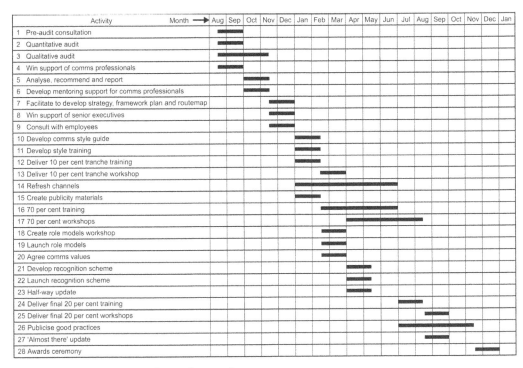

Figure 25.1 Example of a culture change programme

It is good to schedule communication regularly and sequentially. For projects lasting less than a year, allocate activities to weekly or fortnightly time slots. For longer-term projects it is good to allocate activities to four- or six-week time slots. An example, in Gantt chart form, is shown in Figure 25.1.

Creating a Balanced Portfolio of Communication Channels

To communicate effectively we need what professionals call a balanced portfolio of communications channels. This just means that we have a variety of channels that work

Print channels	Face-to-face events	Online channels	Multimedia channels
Background briefings	Celebrations	Blogs	Audio streaming
Brochures	Conferences	Broadcast emails	Business radio
Case studies	Demonstrations	Extranets/shared	Business television
Guides	Exhibitions	workspaces	Compact discs
Leaflets and pamphlets	Meetings	Ezines	Conference calls
Letters	Networking	Forums	Podcasting
Magazines	One-to-one briefings	Intranet	Teleseminars
Media packs	Presentations	Social networking	Text messaging
Newsletters	Receptions	(Twitter and so on)	Video streaming
Posters	Seminars	Website	Videos and DVDs
Reports	Site visits	Wikis	Webinars
White papers	Workshops		

Figure 25.2 Examples of communication channels for projects

both for our audiences and also for our team and our organisation. This mix of channels should balance cost, production timescales and speed of distribution to reach each of our audiences in the most effective manner. Figure 25.2 includes lists of the most commonly available channels.

PRINT CHANNELS

Print is a cost-effective way of disseminating information to many people. You can give just highlights or cover a subject in depth. Audiences can read articles at their leisure and keep for reference.

Most print channels have long production schedules, typically three to four weeks for design and print after the text has been approved. If there are too many changes, checkers and approvers can throw the schedule. Limited space means that writing has to be concise (but with no detail missed). Concise writing will help to keep readers interested.

FACE-TO-FACE CHANNELS

Events for two or more people allow our audiences to meet and interact with us and with each other. They allow us to give the same message to everyone at the same time. We can go into detail, see how they respond, deal with concerns and issues and ask questions and obtain their feedback.

Events can be costly in terms of venue, hospitality and travel, particularly because they take people away from their day-to-day work. Also, events take time and effort to organise. Get the details wrong and the event can have a negative impact on our audiences, rather than the positive impact we planned.

ONLINE CHANNELS

Online channels allow audiences to watch or read at a time that suits them, no matter where they are in the world. Online is usually a cost-effective way of reaching mass audiences. Most people are now positive towards receiving information in this way because they perceive they have control over when and where they access it.

Drawbacks are that it is often difficult to tell if audiences are accessing information, as most analytics provide basic information. It is also difficult to tell what impact content has had on audiences. Security is becoming a bigger problem as people hijack control of online from the organisation. Navigation is also crucial to allow audiences to find your content easily.

MULTIMEDIA CHANNELS

Multimedia channels are wonderful for engaging and entertaining people. Your recipients are more likely to stop and pay attention when you present messages this way. It's also great for simulating face-to-face communication when speakers can't be present in person.

These channels are usually expensive and time consuming to produce. Often they also require specialist applications or skills that you may have to look for externally.

Allocating Responsibilities among Team Members

Now you are ready to allocate key responsibilities to ensure that each communication activity happens and meets the objectives you have set for it. Most of the activities you implement will have four components:

1. Planning and management oversight;
2. Creating the content;
3. Production and distribution;
4. Monitoring and measurement.

Consider tasks and responsibilities for the six communication tools you are most likely to use in project management, which are:

1. Generating news

    - Media relations: contact with editors and journalists to agree stories;
    - Copywriting: researching, writing and clearing copy;
    - Printed information: deciding content, allocating copywriting, proofreading, liaising with designer and printer;
    - Distribution: delivering the publication to your audiences.

2. Speeches

    - Account management: support to speakers;
    - Copywriting: speech and slide pack;
    - Public speaking: delivering the presentation to an audience;
    - Events: logistics – venue, hospitality, agenda, technology, speakers and so forth;
    - Management: so that everything runs smoothly on the day;
    - Post-event: evaluation, report and recommendations.

3. Audio-visual

    - Creative: deciding all the elements;
    - Production: recording and filming;
    - Distribution: getting to the audience.

4. Digital and social media

    - Editing: deciding content, allocating copywriting, proofreading, and overseeing webmaster;
    - Copywriting: creating the content:
    - Webmaster: managing the technical elements.

Matrix of Monitoring Mechanisms

Monitoring lets communicators demonstrate to their sponsor and senior executives that they are delivering value to their organisation in addition to achieving their project objectives.

So what should you monitor? There are five essential areas:

1. Whether you have achieved your objectives for communication activities.
2. How well you have managed the activities.
3. Levels of awareness and understanding.
4. Changes in perceptions and satisfaction among your key audiences.
5. Cost effectiveness and value for money.

Measurement needs to be quick and easy. There isn't the time for in-depth, objective assessment and it's not necessary. Much of the time we can use measurement mechanisms from other aspects of our project; for instance registration of interest, process maps agreed and signed off, number of issues raised and number of pilot users. If these mechanisms are not available or relevant, you will need to develop specific mechanisms for measuring communication activities. Here are some examples:

• feedback questionnaire;
• focus groups;
• website page hits;
• how much read – all, most, some, none?
• recall of key details;
• increase in participation;
• level of interaction;
• number of attendees.

These mechanisms can be put into a four-quadrant matrix. Consider each mechanism from the perspective of how easy it is to use for your team members. You have four choices:

1. face-to-face + quick and easy;
2. face-to-face + time consuming;
3. written/online + quick and easy;
4. written/online + time consuming.

CREATING A PRACTICAL SCHEDULE OF ACTIVITIES

Your schedule will need to show clearly what is going to happen and when, as well as who is responsible for each of the elements. The easiest way to schedule communication activities is with an Excel spreadsheet. All you need is a column for each of the elements – activity, target audience, objective, timing, responsibilities, channel and measurement. Then allocate a row for each activity. Figure 25.3 is a segment of such a schedule.

You have to know the specific audience grouping or groupings who are your primary target for each activity (you can also have secondary audiences). Next you must develop

Activity	Target audience	Objective	Timing	Channel	Responsibilities	Measurement
Listening	Sponsor	Understand why involved and the concerns	April	Breakfast meeting	Date in diary - AB Attend - EF	Attendance Analyse notes taken
Explanation	Board directors	Build knowledge of the project	April/May	Presentation at board meeting	Content - EF Present - sponsor	Questions asked Follow-up
Workshop	Executives of business units affected by the project	Build knowledge of the project	May	Half-day interactive workshop	Invitations - AB Content - CD Present - EF	Attendance Participation Feedback
Briefing	End users in business units	Create awareness of the project	May	Presentation pack	Content - CD Distribution - AB Deliver - unit heads	Awareness survey
News story	All employees	Create awareness of the project	June/July	Staff magazine or intranet	Contact editor - CD Interviewee - EF	Unnecessary
Sharing concerns/ listening	Executives of business units affected by the project	Gain support for the project	August	Half-day open forum	Invitations - AB Content - CD Present - EF	Attendance Consensus Support promised

Figure 25.3 Segment from a schedule of project communication activities

specific and measurable objectives for each activity. This means setting a hard measure that determines how much awareness, understanding, support, involvement or commitment the audience has at the end of the activity. You must establish the timetabling production and distribution for each activity, setting time deadlines. You must allocate responsibility to people who can ensure that each activity happens.

Another question to answer is 'Who is responsible for the key areas of production and distribution?' You can have different people for each key area. You will have to select the communication channel (or channels) for each activity. This can include the print, face-to-face, online or multimedia channel to be used, perhaps including the name of a publication or event at which you will present. Finally, you must have some means of measuring the results from each activity, to determine how well (or how badly) your communication objectives have been achieved.

Summary

I began this chapter with my top five communication skills for project managers, explaining how to apply them and the difference they can make to project success. Next, I plotted the communications journey on which stakeholders should be taken, first to build their awareness, then helping them to feel more positive before asking for their specific help and involvement. I encouraged you to focus communication efforts on the three stakeholder groups who can have most influence over the success of your project, and who are most likely to be affected by the project outcome. Finally, we progressed through nine steps required to create an effective communications framework, together with practical activities you can undertake with your available resources.

References and Further Reading

Cope, M. (2003), *The Seven C's of Consulting*, Harlow: Prentice Hall.

Fowler, A. and Lock, D. (2006), *Accelerating Business and IT Change: Accelerating Project Delivery*, Aldershot: Gower.

Heath, C. and Heath, D. (2010), *Switch: How to Change Things When Change is Hard*, London: Random House.

Kotler, P. (1988), *Marketing Management: Analysis, Planning, Implementation and Control*, 6th edn, Englewood Cliffs, NJ: Prentice-Hall International.

Kotter, J.P. (1996), *Leading Change*, Boston, MA: Harvard Business School Press.

Olivier, R. (2001), *Inspirational Leadership*, London: Spiro Press.

Pink, D.H. (2009), *Drive: The Surprising Truth About What Motivates Us*, Edinburgh: Canongate Books.

Quirke, B. (1996), *Communicating Corporate Change*, Maidenhead: McGraw-Hill.

Shone, A. and Parry, B. (2004), *Successful Event Management*, London: Thomson Learning.

Sweeney, J.A. (2011), 'Write for your reader'. See www.sweeneycomms.com

Sweeney, J.A. (2011), 'Communicating projects system'. See www.sweeneycomms.com/communicating-projects/

26 *Behavioural Traits*

A RESEARCH PAPER BY DR PAUL GIAMMALVO

Given the observation that some people are just naturally 'good' at managing projects and are able to deliver 'successful' projects consistently, and given further that no obvious educational, certification, age, sex or any other demographics differentiate them, the research question that resulted in this chapter is whether there are any behavioural attributes which can serve to predict with any accuracy who is likely to be a 'natural' project manager. This chapter explores a pilot research project that was carried out to see if the behavioural profiles of successful project managers could be created (proved). The research then examined whether a behavioural profile was a reliable predictor of who would likely be a good or successful project manager. The paper concludes that, whilst there is anecdotal evidence to support such a claim, further research is necessary to help validate by adjusting the behavioural profile. The behavioural profile method used the Harrison Assessment Instrument.

Introduction

Have you ever noticed that some people are just 'naturally' good project managers? That some people, when given a project, seem to be able quickly to define what needs to be done, find the right people, then organise, delegate, lead and motivate the team to complete the project? And have you also noticed that in doing all this they seem to make it look easy?

In over 40 years as a practitioner, I saw enough examples of these 'natural' project managers to rouse my curiosity. I wanted to explore whether or not they had anything in common. Simple observation and reflection made it clear that no single factor such as gender, age, education, ethnicity, religion, formal training or job title was the differentiator. So what was? Given such broad diversity, it became obvious that this had to do more with their personalities – that there must be some behavioural traits that differentiated those who were 'naturals' from those who had to work harder to become successful.

Initially, I turned to the work of Max Wideman,[1] who had done some research using Myers-Briggs. However, that proved to be too generic, with the initial research indicating that there were 'naturally successful' project managers coming from each of the 16 Myers-Briggs types. This meant that we needed a finer measure – an instrument that went deeper than Myers-Briggs.

---

1   Wideman, R. Max. See http://www.maxwideman.com/papers/profiles/myersbriggs.htm [accessed 29 August 2011].

Methodology

Looking for something more granular than Myers-Briggs, I investigated Caliper (which measures some 23 variables) and Hay McBer (which measures 6 leadership variables over 4 dimensions, yielding 24 possible combinations). Again, preliminary research (unpublished) indicated that a much more detailed instrument was necessary to be able to determine which, if any, behavioural traits were common to all naturally successful project managers. My quest for something more granular finally turned up Dr Dan Harrison, and his Harrison Assessments (HA).[2] Unlike Myers-Briggs,[3] Kiersey,[4] Caliper or Hay McBer, the HA instrument measures some 155 different behavioural traits. Furthermore, the HA instrument offers two very important advantages:

1. HA has a feature that measures the *consistency* of the responses that provides an accurate measure of how truthful the respondent is being, or whether they are trying to 'game the system'. Gaming the system means using the rules, policies and procedures of a system against itself for purposes beyond that for which the rules were intended.[5]
2. Instead of using bipolar scales, HA uses a paradox matrix, which combines two bipolar scales to produce an X-Y coordinate chart (see Figure 26.1). This particular paradox matrix measures an aggressive or dynamic trait against a passive or gentle trait.

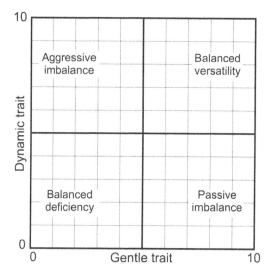

Figure 26.1 This illustrates the Harrison paradox between dynamic and gentle traits

Note: See Appendix 1 of Harrison Assessment Report of 'Peter Sample', page 6 of 22.
Source: Harrison Assessments International Ltd.

2   See http://www.harrisonassessments.com/ [accessed 9 April 2009].
3   See http://www.personalitypathways.com/ [accessed 9 April 2009].
4   See http://www.keirsey.com/ [accessed 9 April 2009].
5   See http://www.wikitruth.info/index.php?title=Gaming_the_system [accessed 9 April 2009].

The HA instrument measures 12 of these paired paradoxes. This produces a much more detailed view of the individual who is being assessed in the behavioural profile of 'project manager'.

Having found what I was looking for, I approached Dr Harrison who suggested I contact his regional representative and master distributor, John Suermondt. John, who is now living in Perth, Australia, has more than 20 years of global experience in behavioural assessment using HA.

All the participants in the pilot study came from people in the various in-house classes that I teach for our Fortune 500 clients. These classes included:

- The Project Management Institute (PMI) Project Management Professional (PMP) certification exam;
- The Association for the Advancement of Cost Engineering's (AACE) Certified Cost Consultant/Certified Cost Engineer (CCC/E) examination preparation course;
- My graduate level university classes at ESC Lille Masters of Science in Project Management;
- The University of Western Australia's masters degree in Energy Systems, or Petrochemical Engineering.

A pilot group of 28 practitioners were selected who were deemed to be 'successful' project managers. For this description of 'successful', these individuals had to satisfy three conditions:

- They had to be active in the position of 'project manager' in their company;
- They had to have demonstrated to me in the classroom environment that they had exceptional leadership skills (which meant being in the top five per cent of their class);
- They had to have at least five years of working experience as a project manager.

This initial pilot study group comprised 28 people. They were divided equally between men and women (14 of each) but were otherwise diverse, as follows:

- nine were Asian (32 per cent of the group);
- six were North American (21 per cent);
- five were from Australia or New Zealand (18 per cent);
- five were European including Eastern Europe, Northern Africa and Turkey (18 per cent);
- three were from Central or South America (11 per cent).

Analysing the group by the industries they represented gave the following results:

- nine were from oil, gas or mining (32 per cent of the group):
- nine were from telecommunications or IT (32 per cent);
- five were from HRM, sales or marketing (18 per cent);
- three were international development (11 per cent);
- two were from finance (7 per cent).

Findings

Based on the initial pilot study, the research indicated that there are seven traits which, when combined with the other attributes, are reliable predictors of 'success' as a project manager.

The illustrations used in this paper came from the top-scoring individual from the initial pilot study. He has been named Peter Sample to protect his identity. He scored 96 per cent. He also scored 90 per cent on his 'consistency' score, which indicated that he was honest in his answers and did not try to game the system. This consistency (or perhaps we might say integrity) score has proven to be an interesting side finding, given that those who scored low in their consistency also had a tendency not to be very good project managers.

It was interesting to note that top-scoring Peter is an underground mining superintendent from a major gold mine in Indonesia who has adapted project management methodologies for use in an operational environment. This exemplifies the application of Bloom/Anderson and Krathwols's higher order cognitive skills of analysis, evaluation and synthesis.[6] We believe that to be essential for project managers, given the unique and ever-changing realities of project management.

The illustrations that follow in the remainder of this paper show what went into making the overall score, as shown in Figure 26.2. They have been redrawn in monochrome and slightly simplified for the purposes of clear reproduction this Handbook.

Figure 26.3 shows the essential traits (in order of importance) or *core* attributes that were reliable predictors of success in the customised template of project manager. That is, *all* of the 28 people in the pilot study scored high in these traits. The shaded area within each box (green or red in the originals) indicates the *probable* impact on performance of the candidate's tendencies (their score) for that trait. To clarify further on these seven traits:

1. Takes initiative: *'The tendency to perceive what is necessary to be accomplished and proceed on one's own'*. All 28 people scored 'substantial' or 'strong' for this attribute. Thus they are all self-starters.
2. Enthusiastic: *'The tendency to be eager and excited toward one's own goals'*. Again all 28 people scored 'substantial' or 'strong' for this attribute. Thus these people are able to motivate and energise those around them.

Overall Percentage of Requirements Met = 96%

Figure 26.2 Overall results for Peter Sample (detail)

Note: See Appendix 1 of Harrison Assessment Report of 'Peter Sample', page 1 of 22.

Source: Harrison Assessments International Ltd.

---

6   Atherton, J.S. (2011), 'Learning and teaching: Bloom's taxonomy' [Online]. Available at: http://www.learning andteaching.info/learning/bloomtax.htm [accessed 29 August 2011].

Peter Sample Behavioral Assessment Score = 96%
(percentage of behavioral suitability requirements met)
Peter's suitability is ideal

Essential traits for this position (in order of importance)

	Trait score	Negative Impact				Red Green		Positive Impact			
		Very strong	Strong	Substantial	Moderate	Slight	No impact	Slight	Moderate	Substantial	Strong	Very strong
Takes initiative	10.0											
Enthusiastic	9.9											
Finance/business	10.0											
Wants to lead	8.0											
Analytical	6.8											
Handles autonomy	9.2											
Wants challenge	7.3											

Figure 26.3 Essential traits for success as a project manager

Note: See Appendix 1 Harrison Assessment Report of 'Peter Sample', pages 1 and 2 of 22.

Source: Harrison Assessments International Ltd.

3. Finance/Business: *'The interest in commerce or fiscal management'*. Again, all 28 scored very high in this attribute. They had a 'natural head' for business.
4. Wants to lead: *'The desire to be in a position to direct or guide others'*. So much for project management being the 'accidental profession'.
5. Analytical: *'The tendency to logically examine facts and situations (not necessarily analytical ability)'*. The people did not succumb to 'paralysis by analysis'. They were able to gather enough facts to make sound business and technical decisions, but did not agonise over making those decisions.
6. Handles autonomy: *'The tendency to have the motivation and self-reliance necessary for a significant amount of independence from immediate supervision (does not indicate the necessary job related knowledge)'*. These people did not have to be told what to do or when to do it. Not only did they take initiative, and were enthusiastic, but they were able to work out what needed to be done and when.
7. Wants challenge: *'The willingness to attempt difficult tasks or goals'*. This group tended to be impatient and easily bored. They wanted to attempt difficult tasks.

The definitions in italics above are verbatim quotations of those used by HA.

The second grouping of traits in this customised position template of project manager is called *desirable traits* (see Figure 26.4). As with the essential traits, these are listed in descending order of importance. So if a person scored low, it would detract from their overall suitability score. Put another way, it was not important for them to have scored high in these traits, but rather that they did not score low, since that could have a potential negative impact on the overall probability of their being successful as project managers.

As noted previously, research showed that scoring high (that is, to the right) was not important for these desirable traits. But if the candidate did score low (to the left),

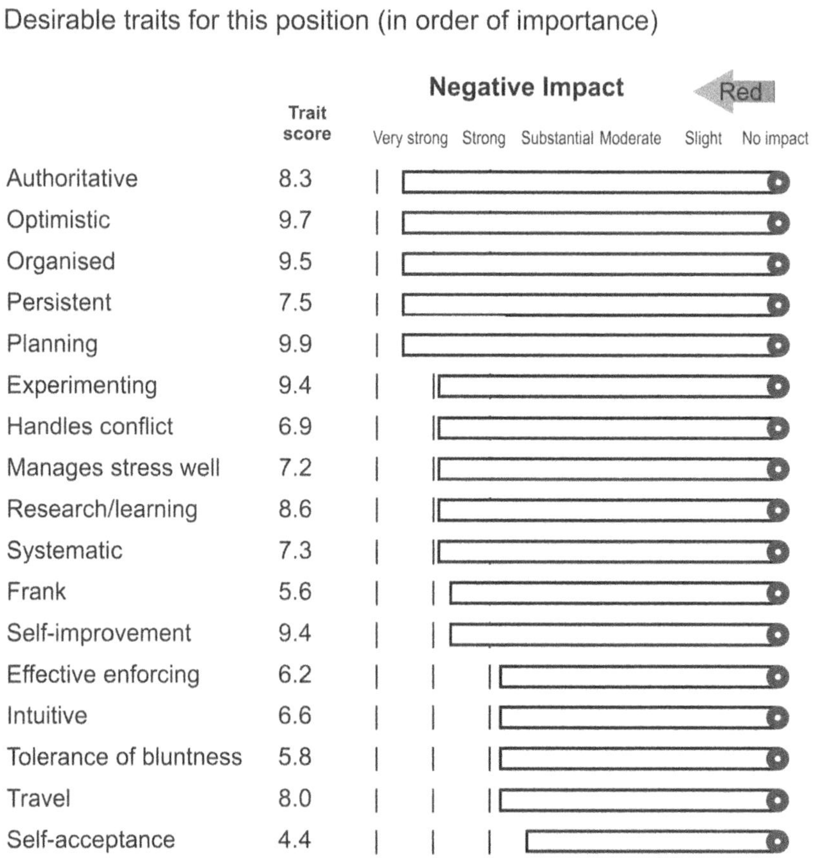

Desirable traits for this position (in order of importance)

Figure 26.4 Example of desirable traits assessment score
Note: See Appendix 1 Harrison Assessment Report of 'Peter Sample', pages 2–4 of 22.
Source: Harrison Assessments International Ltd.

indicating a potential negative impact that would lower their overall suitability for project management. As in the essential traits, the box to the left/right of each trait indicates the *potential* negative/positive impact of that trait on performance.

This part of the research proved to be very interesting because, when we first started out, we expected that organising, planning, handling conflict, managing stress and a systematic approach would be the top-ranked predictors. But our initial research showed otherwise.

Then we identified another set of attributes described as: *traits to avoid* (see Figure 26.5). These are 'killers'. If a person had a high score, indicating to the left on any of these, it would be unlikely that they would succeed as project managers at all. A person who scores even moderately-to-strongly to the left is unlikely to succeed as a project manager. Whilst these traits are fairly obvious, and would probably be unacceptable to anyone working in a management position, the primary impact would be to lower the overall score.

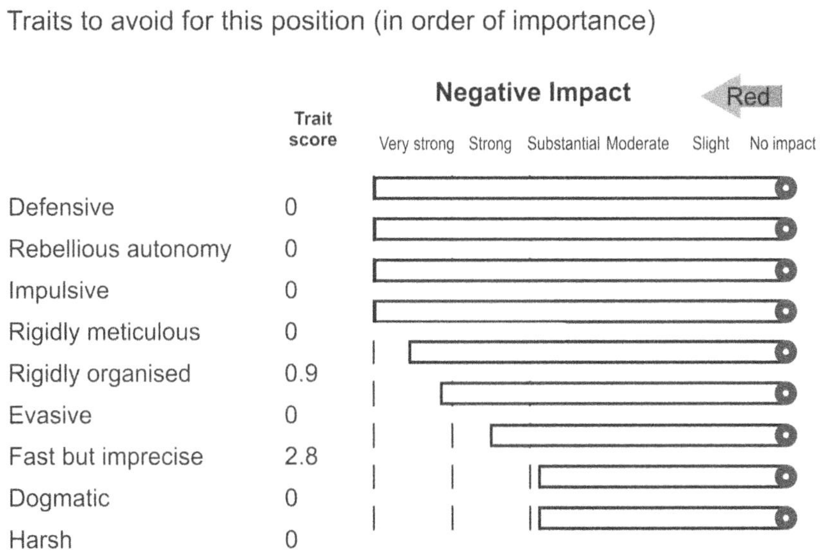

Traits to avoid for this position (in order of importance)

Figure 26.5 Example of killer attributes assessment score

Note: See Appendix 1 Harrison Assessment Report of 'Peter Sample', pages 4–5 of 22.

Source: Harrison Assessments International Ltd.

Using the Behavioural Profiles in Practice

There are many reasons to justify the use of the results or outputs from assessing our employees or potential employees against the HA Project Management Template.

Reason 1: To Screen People Being Considered for Hiring by Our Organisation as Project Managers

Examination-based credentials and certifications, although prolific, are not reliable predictors of whether any individual has what it takes to be 'successful', especially in a new or different environment. The HA Project Management Template will help corroborate claims that the person is or is not 'successful' as a project manager. (After all, who would ever give a bad reference?)

Reason 2: To Screen Those Currently Working in Our Organisations to See if There Are Any with Unrealised Potential to Become Project Managers – This Might Avoid Hiring New Employees.

We had an example from a leading telecommunications client who has a policy of only selecting or promoting engineers to the position of project manager. Yet after having worked for several years with one of their HR people, we became convinced *she* would make an exceptionally good project manager. We convinced her boss to put her in our training course. Not only did she graduate top in the class, but she went on to enjoy several years' success in that organisation as a project manager, until company policy dictated that she could no longer be promoted because she didn't have an engineering degree. So she left the company and went to a competitor, where she is enjoying considerable success and the respect and remuneration that comes with it.

Reason 3: To Help Us Intervene to Make Our Current Employees Become 'Better' Project Managers

Based on the concept of 'better the devil you know than the potential devil you don't know' it might well be more advisable to develop the people currently in your organisation than try to hire people from outside. The challenge we face is that unlike learning to use the tools and techniques, achieving behavioural changes takes a long time. Simply having people attend courses (without a robust career path development programme in place that measures and rewards behavioural changes) means that any intervention is likely to fail.

Reason 4: To Help Us Select Those in Our Organisation Who Might Get Full or better Use of Project Management-related Training and Certifications

One of the reasons we found ourselves doing this research is because, as trainers, we were getting frustrated with people in our training courses who were not getting the full value of the experiential-based training we offer. Because our training is relatively expensive, we did not want our clients sending us people who were unlikely to benefit from our experiential-based programme and project management training.

From Theory to Reality

Since development of the initial behavioural profile we have tested it out on two ASEAN-based telecommunications companies. One of these was a large Telco services provider (owner organisation) from which some 100 participants were selected for participation in a newly formed PMO team. The other company was a large global telephone and Internet equipment manufacturer/installer (contractor). Some 140 of its subjects were selected to receive advanced project and programme management training.

Non-disclosure agreements (NDAs) prevent us from sharing the specific details. However, in both cases, those who scored high on the Harrison Project Manager Profile tended to perform high in the subsequent experiential-based project management training. Conversely, those who scored lower tended to do less well in the training environment than those who scored higher. However, in neither case study was any follow-up research done to see if those same people went on to become 'successful' or 'less successful' project managers after the training.

An interesting side note was that there was a favourable correlation between the *consistency* scores and those who succeeded in our programme. The more self-integrity or

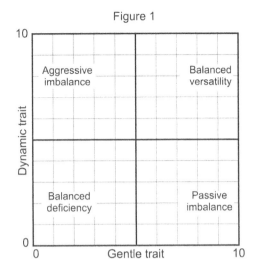
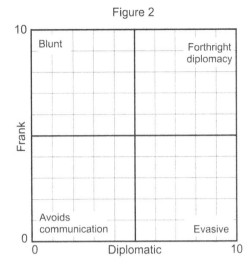

Figure 26.6 Scoring conventions

Note: See Appendix 1 Harrison Assessment Report of 'Peter Sample', page 6 of 22. These are Figures 1 and 2 from the HA report for Peter Sample (redrawn).

Source: Harrison Assessments International Ltd.

more genuine the participants were in their answers, the more likely they were to succeed in an experiential-based project and programme management training course.

That brings up the second and perhaps more relevant, yet challenging application. Please consider:

1. most organisations do not have the luxury of being able to hire project management specialists, but have to select them from within their existing pool of possible or potential project managers;
2. the top-scoring candidates, having been recognised as naturally good project managers, have probably already been assigned.

So, if the top scorers have already been assigned, can we use the results of the HA to improve or raise the effectiveness of those who score somewhere in the middle? So here we are not talking about the people who scored in the top 20 per cent, but those who scored in the range of 60 to 80 per cent (say).

Enter once again the Harrison paradox matrix. In addition to assessing individuals against a specific behavioural profile, the HA instrument also evaluates candidates against a preset 3 x 4 matrix of attributes generally recognised to be positive or desirable to have. This is shown in Figure 26.7 but first view the two figures in Figure 26.6. The left-hand figure illustrates the principle, whilst the right-hand figure is a sample from the 3 x 4 group.

In each case the ideal score falls in the upper right-hand quadrant, which represents a clear balance between the 'gentle' traits shown on the *x* or horizontal axis and the dynamic or aggressive traits, shown on the vertical or *y* axis.

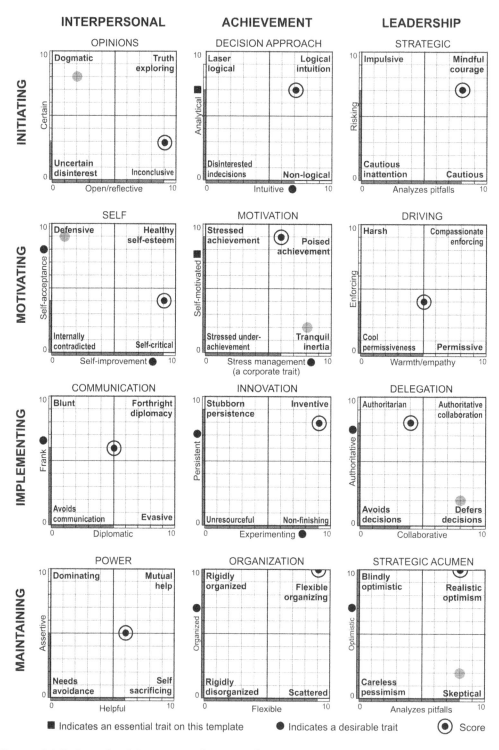

Figure 26.7 Standard 3 x 4 paradox matrix

Note: See Appendix 1 Harrison Assessment Report of 'Peter Sample', page 8 of 22.

Source: Monochrome adaptation of an original kindly supplied by Harrison Assessments International Ltd.

Any score in the upper right-hand quadrant is known as 'balanced versatility' and represents the desired or ideal behavioural profile. Conversely, any score in the lower left-hand quadrant represents weakness in both the dynamic and the gentle traits, which is known as a 'balanced deficiency', meaning that this individual is weak in both the dynamic and the passive or gentle traits and needs the appropriate training to help build confidence.

If we look at the upper left-hand quadrant, we see an example of a person with an aggressive imbalance, meaning they are good on the dynamic trait, but weak in the passive trait. The exact opposite applies to the lower right quadrant, where we have a passive imbalance – which is fine on the passive trait but needs to be balanced by more strength in the dynamic trait.

As we can see in Figure 26.7, the HA paradox report shows the dynamic relationships of the pairs of traits for each of the 12 paradox pairs. The column titles *interpersonal*, *achievement* and *leadership* are broad subject categories.

The row titles *initiate, motivate, implementing* and *maintaining* are progressive stages of action. For example, the 'innovation paradox' is the *implementing* stage of the achievement column:

- initiate – not only the ability to initiate projects, but also self and others;
- motivate – again not only the ability to motivate self, but also others;
- implementing – which is the ability to get things done, not only through your own efforts, but those of others as well;
- maintaining – the ability to persevere and show stability over time, neither wildly optimistic nor easily discouraged.

Together, these 12 paradoxes provide insight into the behavioural changes that this particular project manager would have to make to raise his/her score higher and, implicitly, become an even better, more effective project manager in the process.

Figure 26.7 shows that even though Peter scored 96 overall in his suitability as a project manager, and scored in or near the balanced versatility quadrant in many of the 12 paradox comparisons, there are still character weaknesses that he could address to make him an even better project manager.

Figure 26.8 gives some examples of how to interpret the results by showing what kinds of improvements this individual could undertake as part of his career path development plan. We have to bear in mind that behavioural changes are amongst some of the most difficult to undertake and that unlike taking a three- or five-day course, behavioural changes take place over extended periods of time. That time is usually at least one year, but it is more likely that several years will elapse before any meaningful improvements show.

Using several selected examples, we can see that Peter scored very well against the project manager profile (with a score of 96), and even scored in or close to the balanced versatility quadrant in many of the 12 paradoxes. Yet despite this high score we can see (for example) that under his *opinions*, at the intersection of *initiating* and *interpersonal*, if he were to learn to become more assertive in expressing his opinions, becoming more confident without diminishing his openness or reflectivity, he could move from being in the passive imbalance quadrant (lower right) to the balanced versatility quadrant.

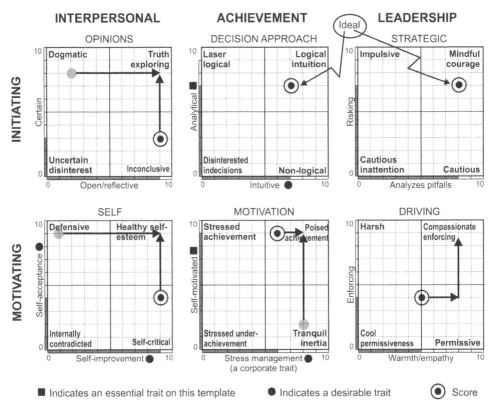

Figure 26.8 Showing interventions which could be considered by this individual

Note: See Appendix 1 Harrison Assessment Report of 'Peter Sample', page 8 of 22.

Source: Harrison Assessments International Ltd.

The same holds true for Peter's self image, located at the intersection of *initiating* and *interpersonal* and his motivation, located at the intersection of *achievement* and *motivating*. At the intersection of *leadership* and *motivation*, we find one of the few examples where he is weak in both the dynamic and gentle traits. He is not as strong at enforcing as he could be, but at the same time, he does not have sufficient warmth and empathy for others necessary to move him from being borderline balanced deficiency into the balanced versatility quadrant. So in this example, Peter would have to work on becoming stricter in enforcing the use of the tools and techniques or the procedures associated with project management, whilst at the same time, demonstrating more empathy for those on his project team.

As can be appreciated from looking at Figures 26.7 and 26.8, 'training' someone to become more willing to take risks, or to becoming more confident in their opinions, warmer or more empathetic or stricter about enforcement is not something that can be achieved by taking a three-day course. It can only happen over time. That is one argument for accepting that whilst there are unquestionably 'natural' project managers, most of us have taken years to develop not only the skills necessary, but also the confidence in which tools/techniques to use under which circumstances. Such competencies only come with time and experience. However, once a practitioner knows and understands these weaknesses not only can they work on improving them over time, but by taking the same assessment several times over an extended period it is possible to measure improvements in behavioural changes.

Conclusions

From an academic perspective this initial research has been validated under less than perfect conditions. It provides anecdotal, but no empirical evidence that:

1. individuals who score high (80 per cent or more) on the HA instrument against the project manager profile tend to perform better than those who do not, under classroom-simulated project conditions;
2. individuals who score lower (below 80 per cent) on the HA instrument against the project manager profile tend to perform less well than those who score higher (again under classroom-simulated project conditions).

Further research is necessary to see if:

1. the observations made during the classroom performance hold true outside the simulated project environment;
2. those who score high in the *desirable* traits but low in the *essential* traits and neutral in the *negative* traits were average project managers;
3. those who scored high in the *negative* traits consistently made poor project managers.

I can explain the need for this further research in another way. It appears as though individuals who score no 'lows' in a combination of the essential, desirable and negative traits appear to be 'natural' project managers. But how well or how poorly do those who score low on any or all of the traits perform as project managers?

Acknowledgements

The editors and I are indebted to John Suermondt, Master Distributor for HA for his assistance in providing the *Behavioral Impact Graph* report for Peter Sample dated 2005 and other related material.

The editors note that the graphs and diagrams in the original report were larger and in colour. The smaller-scale examples in this paper are extracts (details) from the originals and have been redrawn in monochrome for clarity in these book pages: thus they do not fully reflect the presentation impact and quality of the originals.

Those wishing to inquire more about the Harrison methodology, see the full HA Report of Peter Sample, or take part in one of their programmes should contact John Suermondt, who is Master Distributor for HA and Principal Director, AusIndo Ventures Ltd, Perth, Australia. John can be reached at john@harrisonassessments.com

27 *Ethics in Project Management*

WILLIAM A. MOYLAN

Project management discipline must include consideration of ethical considerations in satisfying the needs of all project stakeholders. The policies of leaders are only as good as their actions. Astute project managers serve as role models through their own ethical behaviour and personal involvement with their team members in the processes of planning, execution and control. As role models in setting ethical behaviour, project managers can reinforce the organisation's values and expectations whilst building leadership, commitment and enthusiasm throughout the organisation.

Project-driven organisations must articulate a general strategy for ethical leadership and a series of implementation tactics for the project manager to follow in creating solutions where everyone wins. This chapter considers three principal topics:

1. an understanding of the ethical basis for project-driven organisations;
2. suggested methods for implementing ethics into professional project management;
3. a model for assessing ethical project leadership.

In addition, a review of professional codes of ethics for project leaders and a case study on the application of management ethics in construction projects are included.

Ethical Base for Project-driven Organisations

The two key themes that provide the basis of ethical project leadership are:

1. self-interest and good ethics generally coincide;
2. the stakeholder model of business.

A brief summary of each business ethics theme follows.

SELF-INTEREST AND GOOD ETHICS

The assertion that 'self-interest and good ethics generally coincide' (Beauchamp and Bowie, 2001) has grounding in both various ethical theories and refutation by others.

Ethical theories that support this premise include common morality theories, cultural relativism, rights theories, virtue ethics and possibly, Kantian ethics and the feminist theories and ethics of care law. These theories are altruistic in nature. Asserting a selfless concern to put others' interests over one's own, and subjugating one's own needs and interests to those of the group is common morality theory. Cultural relativism and rights theories support the axiom. Focusing on individual rights in concert with those of the larger group or culture, prudence dictates one's human dignity and personal rights secured through proper moral behaviour. The virtue ethics theory based on the virtues of one's personal character supports the positive ethics portion if the individual desires to be virtuous as to trustworthy, loyal and conscientious (ibid.).

Ethical theories that refute this axiom of 'self-interest as good ethics' include the theories of ethical and psychological egoism and utilitarian theories. The selfishness of egotism, in both ethical conduct and psychological motivations, violates the self-interest in good ethics since the reactions and feelings of others are important. The utilitarian theory premise that considers the consequences of the actions done for the greatest good for the majority confounds the self-interest in ethical actions that may adversely affect a minority faction.

Prudence shows the axiom as plausible based on both virtue ethics and common morality theory. Asserting a selfless concern to put others' interests over one's own needs and subjugating one's interests to those of the group is a viable premise. In addition, cultural relativism and rights theories both support this axiom, as it focuses on individual rights in concert with those of the larger group or culture. Human dignity and personal rights are endurable through the proper mix of moral behaviour and personal character. The positive individual desire to be virtuous as to trustworthiness, loyalty and conscientiousness is a sustainable human imperative. Moreover, a self-imposed obligation (that is: self-interest) to hold one to the highest ethical levels (good ethics) is a flexible standard. Common morality theories hold that strong moral demands may override when circumstances dictate prudent action to the contrary (ibid.).

STAKEHOLDER MODEL OF BUSINESS

The classical theory postulated by Milton Friedman (1970) considers the stockholders as the owners and does not recognise the other stakeholder parties as legitimate entities. Friedman claims the primary purpose of the public corporation as maximising the wealth the sole rightful owners of the firm – the stockholders. In Friedman's terms, increasing profits made payable to the owner-stockholders is the only social responsibility of business. Anything else, Friedman considers as the 'unadulterated socialism' of anarchistic nihilists bent on destroying the free-enterprise system, democracy and western civilisation.

This argument clashes with the purpose of the corporation vis-à-vis the stakeholders' needs that distinguish the parties in the model including:

- owners as financiers and stockholders;
- management as agents;
- the company's employees;
- suppliers;
- customers;
- the local community.

Freeman (1994) counters the Friedman argument with a stakeholder model that considers the needs of the owners, management, employees, suppliers, customers and the local community all as legitimate heirs in moulding the broader purpose modern corporation. This stakeholder theory allows the stockholders a legitimate yet focused privilege, based on their ability to readily enter and exit the arrangement via the stock market. The enabling terms of corporate governance, external costing and contractual relationships, agency and continuance, equitably address the needs of the other parties to the corporation without damaging their situation, responsibilities and legitimate rights.

These two axioms of 'self-interest as good ethics' and the stakeholder model of business form the basis to implement ethics into professional project management, as discussed in the next section.

Infusing Ethics into Professional Project Management

Extended enterprises turn to project management as an effective approach to deliver successfully programmes that would otherwise overextend the capabilities and capacities of their functional organisation. In turn, a new set of conflicts, intergroup relations and ethical considerations specific to temporary project teams arise that differ from the stable organisation (Kloppenborg and Opfer, 2002).

Project-performing organisations making a substantial commitment of time and resources in order to achieve the appropriate level of maturity in project management must define the organisational needs for ethical leadership along with the profit and performance criteria (Pennypacker and Grant, 2003). To implement project management successfully the enterprise must treat ethical project management as a priority. This paradigm for ethical project leadership includes infusing ethics into the professional discipline, team building, proper executive sponsorship and stakeholder analysis.

Project management as a profession has received considerable recent attention. Management guru Tom Peters (1997) identifies 'projects is life' as one of the five essential attributes of the new American professional, suggesting that organisations transform everything into scintillating projects. Although Peters sees nirvana in the profession of project management as the career choice of the new millennium, the current research does not totally support this hypothesis (Kloppenborg and Opfer, 2002). Project management struggles in developing a true sense of professional community when the critical organisational dynamics that are essential to develop the behaviours and cultural aspects of a true profession are lacking. The profession of project management has established a recognised body of knowledge, standards, and certification and education programmes. However, project management has not established itself as a professional community in which its members share a sense of identity, the bond of a common culture, and an ethical rigour (Wang, 2002). Many consider project management as an accidental profession, with the common occurrence of the project manager who possesses little formal authority and functions outside the traditional organisation hierarchy. A common occurrence for the novice project manager is finding he or she has inadequate training for the task, since most management development deals with preparing one for the organisation's functional management and operational staff positions (Pinto and Kharbanda, 1995).

The professionals who populate the project organisation will influence the organisational behaviour of the particular business unit and the supporting project management office. To gain value from the discipline of project management, the business enterprise must organise itself for projects executed by teams (Cleland, 1996; Frame, 1995 and Verma, 1995). The social group of project professionals built around 'what one does', as opposed to the 'where one sits' found in the traditional hierarchical-based functional organisation, must include a model for professional ethical behaviour. Building strong project teams with the proper ethical focus is essential for managing projects within an organisation (Kloppenborg and Opfer, 2002).

Ethics in Team Building

Cleland (1996), one of the gurus of project management, coined the term 'teamocracy' to describe the use of teams in organisations. The team (as the building block of the networked enterprise) displaces the traditional bureaucratic hierarchy of successive levels of pyramided authority. In a teamocracy, the teams form the lattice network of cross-functional/cross-organisational projects that integrate the activities of the work groups and reflect their empowerment, dedication, trust, loyalty and commitment.

Teams are an effective approach to both meeting the needs of organisation in terms of satisfying operational needs and expectations, whilst successfully completing the project scope per cost budget, performance and on time. Moreover, membership on teams is a prime source of improved personal job satisfaction and morale (ibid.). From an enterprise perspective, teams are effective at eliminating redundant layers of management and gaining productive efficiencies by getting more done with fewer resources in a shorter length of time.

Differences exist in the dynamic/project versus stable/operational environment, geographically dispersed project teams. Their use of new electronic technologies to manage themselves still values trust as the prime rubric for evaluating their leaders (Adams and Adams, 1997). The global competitiveness of international firms, rooted in project teams, requires high trust among all participants, continual and open sharing of information, and clear organisation structures on member roles and responsibilities. It is essential for teams to receive the proper direction and support from their management in order for them to succeed. Unfortunately, a common problem of project teams is the lack of support they receive from their executives (a topic mentioned in Chapter 5). The 'selling' of project management to them by the responsible project managers is a very big issue in gaining the necessary support for the project teams.

Executive Support for Ethical Project Management

Gaining cooperation on projects requires both project managers and senior executives to agree on the value of project management. However, in the 'selling' of project management to senior level executives by project managers there is a fundamental difference between the ways project managers promote and think about project management techniques and the executives' needs and thinking.

The project managers tend to focus on the tactical benefits of project management, for example, effective tools and techniques, scheduling and delivery methods and tested methodologies. Further, project managers also consider project management as an essential way of doing their work and a life philosophy. Conversely, executives generally think more strategically, by considering the value to the organisation and the benefits of a new initiative to their own personal growth. The inevitable disconnect between the executives and the project managers seeking their support is due to their convergent reasoning styles and a misalignment between the 'buyers and sellers' concerning the values of the discipline of project management.

Herein lies the dilemma of defining what ethical project management is. A severe crisis in the organisation normally triggers the acquisition of project management as the organisational solution. Overcoming the value credibility gap between the practitioners and their executives as to their understanding of project management is rarely a strategic decision in an organisation. Rather, project managers appear 'accidentally', in response to a crisis with no time or resources to consider the ethical basis of their actions (Thomas et al., 2001). With such lacklustre support from executives, communicating both the urgency and ethical basis of the team's mission is imperative.

Although gaining support for project management is important, the major ethical issues that occur in the workplace and on projects centre on the due process of employee concerns versus the legitimate company expectations of employee due diligence. Such ethical issues include the rights of employees in cases of 'employment at will' situations, the rights of personal privacy versus the employer's right to know, and the duty of loyalty and trust. The privacy issues include the employer's rights to subject candidates and employees to drug testing, genetic screening, electronic performance monitoring (EPM) and restrictions on fraternisation with other employees. Concerning the duty of the employee to exhibit loyalty and trust to their employer touches on the conflict of performing illegal activities or other work duties, which the employee considers wrong and the possible 'whistle blowing' on such activities.

The recurring ethical theme that seems to run through these situations of employee rights versus employer responsibilities is the need for respect by both parties of the other. A 'David versus Goliath' scenario exists with the individual contending with the employer for legitimate and proper treatment, including respect, fair remuneration and the rights of communal association. This notion conspires with the corporate desire for a workforce that is dedicated, focused, dutiful and content with being subjugated, and employees willing to be subjected to management's whims for increased production, control and manacle power. As noted by Wade and Airitam (2002), 'Despite the codes of ethics, the ethics programs and the special departments – corporations don't make the ultimate decisions about ethics. Ethical choices are made by individuals'. The challenge is for executives, management and employees to act ethically as individuals, treating each other with respect, dignity and empathy for their respective positions.

Ethical Analysis of Stakeholders' Needs

Stakeholder analysis requires understanding of the broader strategic goals of the enterprise, as developed in a project portfolio of all of the enterprise's programmes. Project portfolio management requires a highly networked organisation with well-defined decision-making structures and transparent communications channels for partner networking that focus on individual projects as solutions to business opportunities. Moreover, this stakeholder-focused approach requires companies to manage the interaction across boundaries between the portfolio and its projects, between single projects, between different portfolios, and between different corporations in business networks (Artto et al., 2002). To manage properly the project portfolio requires the project management office to address stakeholder needs and expectations, gain a proper understanding with executives on the value of project management, and properly develop and analyse the project portfolio. The complexity of gaining the cooperation of all stakeholders is inherent to managing the project portfolio.

The project stakeholders form an interrelated set of obligations and responsibilities to the corporation, which produce a mutual set of tensions, interrelated responsibilities and potential conflicts between each group (Greenwood, 2002). By reframing the competing forces, each project stakeholder assumes a duty to each other stakeholder and to themselves to pursue long-term goals, whilst concurrently conducting themselves in an ethical manner that promotes the goodwill of the other participants. Shareholders, desiring maximisation of profits, have a shared stewardship to provide capital or other valued input to the organisation. In return for a proportioned ownership position in the company, shareholders receive weighted voting rights, the fair distribution of profits and an ease of liquidating their proceeds.

Project managers are obligated to conduct project activities appropriately and ethically to ensure the best business decisions abide by pre-established ground rules. The project execution ground rules are set according to the principles of entry and exit, governance, externalities, contracting costs, agency and immorality.

The members of the project team require adequate security and remuneration in return for working diligently and showing loyalty. The contract between management and the employees expects sound work ethics and working a full day, doing their best to produce a product or sell a service.

Suppliers are obligated to furnish quality raw materials at a price level that allows the corporation to operate profitability in creating quality products. In return, the client firm is loyal to its suppliers and pays fair amounts for the material furnished, whilst considering the cost of materials in a constant flux based on how well the products are selling.

Considering a broader context of project stakeholder, the local communities have the ability to impose laws, taxes, penalties or a cooperative withdrawal of support from the corporation that makes business unprofitable or impossible. The corporation is expected to operate in a socially responsible manner and donate money to community charities. The citizens of the community have an obligation to shop at the corporations that contribute to the good of the community. Customers exchange resources for the firm's products and product benefits as the firm provides high quality and safe products, friendly to the environment. With all of these considerations, the success of the corporation and the project depends on how well the stakeholder groups work together for the common good.

Implementing project management requires infusing professional ethics as an essential part of the corporate and project culture. An assessment of the requisite ethical conscientiousness and social responsibility of the project managers is the result of the model, discussed in the next section.

A Model for Ethical Project Leadership

The proposed paradigm for ethical project leadership uses the *facilitating idealist* model of an effective steward leader. This leadership paradigm requires the project manager to perform a 'technical audit' of their conformance to the values of their organisation, followed by a stakeholder-based 'perceptual audit' on critical decisions. The model assumes that an effective corporate and professional culture for project management success requires the project manager to take a proactive, preventive approach to improvement, rather than following a reactive, punitive routine to addressing project issues and solving problems. The following sections discuss each topic in detail.

SELF-AUDIT OF ETHICAL CONFORMANCE

After the first task of defining reality, the role of the leader is to lead by example. Since project managers are adept at comparing actual results to requirements, the project manager should assess their own conformance to their organisation's values and ethics. This project leadership 'technical audit' would first review and set the limits of each guiding principle or organisation value. Using recent decisions as test specimens, the project manager performs a self-assessment of their decisions to determine their level of conforming to the stated values. This self-audit focuses on the circumstances surrounding the decision-making process. The process analyses each decision to determine if it meets the 'letter of the law' and 'satisfying the spirit' of the value. Besides conformance, the project manager determines if a different decision would have conformed better.

An analytical method to assess the relative ethical position of the project manager's decisions considers their concerns for people and organisations. The scale covers positions from 'ethically detrimental' on one end to 'ethically virtuous' on the other with a neutral position in the centre (Caldwell, et al., 2002) This self-audit of ethical conformance will yield insights on patterns, root causes and processes that should change to ensure future compliance (Hopen, 2003). The next step is to do a stakeholder-based 'perceptual audit' on the project manager's ethical behaviour.

STAKEHOLDER PERCEPTUAL AUDIT

In the next step of the model assessment, the project manager interviews a cross section of her or his key stakeholders to determine their perception of the project manager's ethical decision-making capability. This stakeholder-based 'perceptual audit' would examine the same critical decisions made by the project manager to determine how others view the project manager's conformance to the corporate values. Regardless of the project manager's self-assessment score, the perceptions of others will be most instructive in determining the project manager's level of ethical behaviour and compliance to the values of the organisation.

Analysis of the stakeholder perceptual audit guides the project manager on the necessary improvements to their decision-making and leadership skills. Since a project manager's policies are only as good as their actions, leading by ethical example is the most profound manner of implementing ethical project leadership in the organisation. Instead of a heroic style, an engaging management showing concern, involvement and endearment with one's followers is the appropriate leadership model. A method of appraising the project manager's engaging style could use a grid of 'values consistency' versus 'stakeholder responsiveness' as the grading rubric (Begley and Boyd, 2003).

Professional Codes of Ethics for Project Leaders

A normative organisation establishes a set of rules (the 'norms') for its members to follow. These norms set the requirements for joining the group (initiation) and for staying a member in good standing (membership). Breaking the rules will risk reprimand, punishment, banishment or expulsion from the group depending on the severity of the infraction. Toe the line (comply with the norms) and one gets to stay a member (involvement).

Examples of normative organisations include professional societies, bowling leagues, the military, university fraternities and high schools run by the Jesuits. These organisations' membership rules (codes of ethical conduct) might seem arcane and/or absurd to the outsider; the better to adapt the member to the group.

TWO ENDS OF THE PROFESSIONAL SOCIETY SPECTRUM

In the US, professional societies span the gamut from the American Medical Association to the American Management Association. The American Medical Association comprises an esteemed professional society of medical physicians focused on establishing the norms for the highest level of patient care and healing. Doctors of medicine, who have taken the Hippocratic oath as they entered their profession, are held in the highest esteem by society for whom their patients owe their health, well-being and possibly their lives. Not to say that some physicians may have pursued the profession of medicine for the fortune and fame, society is indebted to them for their ethical conduct and professionalism.

On the other hand, members of the American Management Association enjoy discounts on professional development courses and reference books; can attend informative presentations and fun parties; have access to networking opportunities with other members; and feel connected to a bigger group than just the duller individuals they contend with at their boring jobs and daily life routines. Some management professionals may pursue their work with totally altruistic motives to improve society and the betterment of mankind, but business is about making money.

PROFESSIONAL SOCIETIES FOR ETHICAL PROJECT MANAGEMENT

Is *project management ethics* an oxymoron, like *jumbo shrimp, airline cuisine, civil servant,* or *moral majority*? Two global professional societies focused on promoting the profession of project management may beg to differ. These professional organisations are the Project Management Institute (PMI) and the International Project Management Association (IPMA). Both of these organisations have deliberated upon the appropriate code of ethics and professional conduct for project management professionals. Further information on the codes of ethics for project managers of PMI and IPMA can be found respectively at the following:

- http://www.pmi.org/About-Us/Ethics.aspx
- http://www.ipma.ch/Documents/IPMANewsletterQ12008.pdf

THE IMPORTANCE OF THE CODES OF ETHICS

As already noted, project management struggles in developing a true sense of professional community. A 'Code of Ethics and Professional Conduct' is one of the critical organisational dynamics that is essential to develop the behaviours and cultural aspects of a true profession, which had been lacking.

The profession of project management has established a recognised body of knowledge, standards, and certification and education programmes. Although it might be considered restrictive and outmoded, an established code of ethics is essential for project managers to establish their work as professional. Internally within their professional community, the members (project managers) who adhere faithfully to their code of ethics will begin to share a sense of identity and the bond of a common culture (Wang, 2002).

The project manager who complies openly with a code of ethics will help dispel the characterisation of project management as the 'accidental' profession. Likewise, the project manager who possesses little formal authority and functions outside the traditional organisation hierarchy will begin to earn rightful professional respect and esteem. Organisations which consider project management as a profession will see it in their self-interest to develop professionally their novice project managers and reward their progression with life-long learning and professional development opportunities. The social group processes of cognition, comparison and motivation as commonly applied within the operational setting will begin to blend with the project team setting. For example, conflict within the project team will be recognised as progress (Pinto and Kharbanda, 1995).

Ethics in Construction Projects

The construction of a facility involves a series of projects, from the initial conception, development of the design to meet the owner's intentions, procurement of materials and services, all stages of construction, commissioning, handover and then operation and maintenance. A future phase (project) will be final decommissioning of the facility. This series of integrated projects, which make up the entire construction facility programme, are both 'brain-based' (mental effort) and 'brawn-based' (physical effort) involving multiple stakeholders over relatively short time periods. Opportunity for ethical misconduct is endemic throughout the construction process.

The construction industry is keen on developing and maintaining a high degree of professional ethics in the variety of business dealings between all the players involved (owners, architects, engineers, constructors and so on). This includes (but is not limited to) bidding and award scenarios, in meeting contractual obligations and in resolving disputes (Rooley, 2001a and 2001b) – for which values-based leadership (VBL) concepts would clarify issues for the stakeholders.

Comprehensive research studies by Morris (2000) and Moylan (2005) on the applicability of VBL concepts, values and skills on different types of construction projects showed the values to all stakeholders of construction professionals conducting themselves ethically. In addition, this interest in improved professionalism in construction (a VBL concept) extends to developing ethics education in the construction education programmes at the college level (Killingsworth, 1992 and Robertson, 1987).

Looking internationally, a philosophical study by Uff (2003) on the European construction market concluded positively the practicality and suitability of a separate, multidisciplinary ethic in the field of construction law. This study considered professional ethics to have an increasingly important role in the execution of the construction process. A proper consideration of ethics in construction serves both the public interest and the professionals involved, and is essential to solving many of the key problems plaguing the construction industry.

Industry trade groups in the US, such as the Associated General Contractors (AGC), and professional associations, like the American Institute of Constructors (AIC), actively participate in ethics in construction programmes for their memberships (Gonchar, 2003). These construction ethics programmes mirror the tenets of VBL, including stressing the need for shared business and ethical values, integrity in the bidding and contracting processes, common understanding of industry professional practice, partnering, balancing of risks with financial rewards and the building of long-term trusting relationships.

Moreover, an ethical leadership approach melds with the 'integrity chain' of James (2002) that links integrity in the process, trust amongst the members, repeat business based on satisfactory performance and quality, and a profitable relationship for each the parties. Although technical knowledge and management expertise is important, it is essential for construction managers to exhibit the innate ability to interact effectively with people to execute the project (Rubin et al., 2002). These values-based ethical leadership traits of trust, integrity and people-orientation are critical to success in the construction industry. Ethical missteps on construction projects are most frequent in the bidding cycle.

SOME HURDLES FOR ETHICS IN CONSTRUCTION BIDDING

Anyone who is familiar with the construction industry's bidding process knows that 'Who you know' is often more important than 'What you know' for a bidder, regardless of the estimated proposal costs. Reality is that construction is a highly fractionated industry of speciality companies – people who work on temporary projects and deliver services based on short-term contracts and brief partnerships. Owner, architect, engineer and contractor each represent separate interests with diverse professional values, particularly during the bidding process. Project participants often have goals that are at variance to those of the project stakeholders.

A clear understanding of the motives of project participants is necessary to establish an appropriate business ethic and professional conduct in construction bidding. The following passages reflect the views of two well-known business gurus, Friedman and Freeman.

Sole Goal: Stockholders' Profits or Wider Stakeholders' Interests?

Milton Friedman (1970) holds the purist's view supporting the 'stockholders as owners' argument: the primary purpose of a public corporation is to maximise the wealth for the sole rightful owners of the firm – the stockholders. Here, in short, increasing profits for the owner-stockholders is the only social responsibility of business. Anything less than this is 'unadulterated socialism' of anarchistic nihilists bent on destroying the free-enterprise system, democracy and western civilisation.

Friedman's extreme argument clashes with the purpose of the corporation from the stakeholders' viewpoint and from Freeman (1994), who believed that the ethical model for a corporation must include not only the needs of the owners as financiers and stockholders, but also the goals of management, company employees, suppliers, customers and the local community.

The inclusion of the wider body of stakeholders in the corporation's obligations and responsibilities creates more potential conflicts and tensions among project participants. In this tension, or competition between forces, all stakeholders assume a duty to one another and to themselves to pursue long-term goals – not just stockholder profit – whilst at the same time acting in an ethical professional manner that promotes the goodwill of all the participants.

Friedman and Freeman's economic views are used as a grading rubric in assessing the ethics of construction delivery methods, especially competitive bidding schemes, the effects on the parties involved and ways to improve the long-term results. On the one hand, we have Friedman upholding profit for owner/stockholder as the main objective, by demanding the lowest price and shortest project schedule. After all, it is the stockholders' capital that finances construction projects. On the other hand (Freedman's), a competitive bidding and trading arena for construction services ensures the needs of all the corporation's shareholders whilst maximising the return on investment and long-term goals.

A successful contractor is someone who can build a quality facility according to the design within budget and on time; contractors who cannot compete under these terms will fail. Competitive bidding guarantees a fair profit for the risks assumed by the selected general contractor, in comparison to proposals submitted by competing bidders, and the owner is assured of paying a competitive price for the project. To Friedman this process is an excellent example of the capitalist system at work: benefiting all concerned, especially the corporate stockholders.

Competitive Bidding: Maximising Return in Shared Profit

For Freeman, the bidding process requires a series of specific safeguards to maintain ethical integrity in construction bidding. Friedman states that, for any request for proposal, the market for construction contracting must be truly competitive: open to all interested and responsible bidders who possess the requisite technical expertise, financial capacity and management skills. Interested bidders must furthermore be responsive to the terms and conditions of the tender, cooperate during all phases of a project with the owner representatives, design architects and engineers. In this way, the owner obtains a quality facility, built on schedule and within budget.

Each project participant has important responsibilities in this project delivery process: owners must commit the necessary time and resources to project definition and actualisation; the engineer/architect must produce an efficient design that meets the owner's mandate and is constructible using conventional technologies; and the contractor/supplier must be responsible, competent and cooperate fully with the owner representatives.

Freeman's premise is that this harmonious working relationship among facility owner, engineer, architect and contractor further benefits the eventual facility tenants – building occupants who enjoy a suitable environ in bringing goods and services to the marketplace. In this scenario, a well-designed and built facility not only allows the corporation to perform its mission to generate revenue and eventually shared profits with the stockholders, but also benefits the local community.

Bid Shopping, Rigging and Reverse-auction Bidding

Deemed unethical by both Friedman and Freeman are the practices of bid shopping and rigging, albeit for different reasons. By unfairly sharing information relevant to a contractor's bid details with unauthorised parties, a bid-shopping scheme essentially destroys the integrity of the competitive bidding system. True competitive bidding requires submittal of a lump sum bid price for a fixed design, with the contractor's 'methods and means' remaining strictly confidential. Sharing of a contractor's proposal, the contractor's intellectual property, without just compensation for proposal efforts, is destabilising to the free marketplace and ethical business practice.

Bid rigging is also equally repulsive to both Friedman and Freeman. Friedman claims that bid-shopping practice (wherein the contractor is not fairly compensated for its proposal efforts) adversely affects the bidding company's owners and stockholders. Non-payment for services rendered is heresy to sound economic theory. At the same time, bid shopping unfairly rewards the owner whilst unjustly compensating one bidder over another – without paying for the development of shared proposal data. Bid sharing undermines professional integrity and breaks the bonds of trust among the various stakeholders in the execution of the work. Likewise, bid-rigging schemes conducted by an unscrupulous group of conspiring contractors redirect funds that should rightly be paid to stockholders as dividends by artificially inflating construction costs.

In the Freeman thesis, bid-rigging schemes are unethical practices that unfairly favour the supplier stakeholder and harm the facility owner stakeholder. Like bid shopping, bid rigging unfairly rewards one segment of the project stakeholder triad, in this case the contractor/supplier (who receives inflated profits for services) and unjustly penalises the owner with unnecessarily high project costs. Again, the integrity of the system is undermined and the bonds of trust between the stakeholders are broken.

Reverse-auction bidding is considered very detrimental to the general contractors, speciality-trade contractors, and the competitive bidding arena. Contractors are forced into this scenario via the Internet; it begins with a target price set by the owner, after which bidding contractors post proposals to a central website. Impelling contractors to perform bidding online without just compensation for direct costs, overhead and profit potential, is condemned as unethical and poor business conduct by Friedman.

Freeman describes reverse bidding in more simple terms: the owner benefits at the construction contractor community's (supplier stakeholder's) expense.

In one instance, an industry group representing mechanical contractors (who were being forced into a reverse-auction bidding situation by a national merchandise retailer) effectively challenged this process. After repeated requests by the mechanical contractors association asking that the owner's contracting officer cease reverse-auction request for bids, the association petitioned the merchandiser's corporate board as 'concerned stockholders' representing the substantial pension funds of the mechanical tradesmen. The merchandise retailer owner quickly relented. This situation involved the effective use of both economists' rationales: establishing stockholders as the legitimate owners of the corporation as well as insisting on a balanced scorecard for all stakeholders involved, including stockholders, management and suppliers.

REWARDING ETHICAL CONDUCT IN THE CONSTRUCTION INDUSTRY

One way to reward ethical conduct in the construction industry is to establish an 'integrity chain' as the true path to long-term profitability (James, 2002). The first link in the chain is a competitive bidding system based on integrity in a fair process respecting the rights of each stakeholder, including the facility owner; engineer; architect; constructors; subcontractors and material suppliers. Project stakeholders cannot resort to 'robbing Peter to pay Paul' tactics.

The system's integrity builds a foundation of trust among all project team members and the external community. A sound construction industry for the long term can only be based on trust in business relationships and on ethically executed project management. Trusting, ethical relationships between all project stakeholders reward successful team members for projects built on time, within budget, according to design specifications and guarantees repeat business. Repeat business in the construction industry is the key to legitimate profitability and satisfying the needs of all stakeholders.

Editorial Comment (DL)

In the EU higher value public sector contracts are subject to the Public Sector and Utilities Directives, designed to ensure transparency and fair competition in bidding.

Conclusions

The ethical base for project-driven organisations rests on the themes of enlightened self-interest and servant-style leadership to satisfy the needs of all stakeholders. Implementing solid project management in an organisation requires infusing ethics into the project manager toolkit of professionalism, team building, executive support and stakeholder needs analysis.

The *facilitating idealist* model of an effective steward leader requires the project manager to perform a 'technical audit' of conformance to organisational values, followed by a stakeholder-based 'perceptual audit' on critical decisions. The model assumes that an effective corporate and professional culture for project management success requires the project manager to take a proactive, preventive approach to improvement, rather than following a reactive, punitive routine to addressing project issues and solving problems. The ethical project manager values substance and serving the stakeholders over self-serving aggrandisement.

References and Further Reading

Adams, J.R. and Adams, L.L. (1997), 'The virtual project manager: Managing tomorrow's team today', *PM Network*, 28(1), 25–32.

Artto, K.A., Dietrich, D.H. and Ikonen, T. (2002), 'Industry Models of Project Portfolio Management and their Development', paper presented at Project Management Institute Research Conference, July 2002, Seattle, WA.

Axelrod, R. (1997), *The Complexity of Cooperation: Agent-based Models of Competition and Collaboration*, Princeton, NJ: Princeton University Press.

Beau, D. and Buckley, M.R. (2001), 'The hypothesized relationship between accountability and ethical behaviour', *Journal of Business Ethics*, 34(1), 57–73.

Beauchamp, T.L. and Bowie, N.E. (eds), (2001), *Ethical Theory and Business*, 6th edn, Upper Saddle River, NJ: Prentice Hall.

Begley, T.M. and Boyd, D.P. (2003), 'The need for a corporate global mind-set', *Sloan Management Review*, 44(2), 25–32.

Caldwell, C., Bischoff, S.J. and Karri, R. (2002), 'The four umpires: A paradigm for ethical leadership', *Journal of Business Ethics*, 36, 153–63.

Cleland, D.I. (1996), *Strategic Management of Teams*, New York: John Wiley & Sons.

Frame, J.D. (1995), *Managing Projects in Organizations*, San Francisco, CA: Jossey-Bass.

Freeman, R.E. (1994), 'The politics of stakeholder theory', *Business Ethics Quarterly*, 4, 409–21.

Friedman, M. (1970), 'The social responsibility of business is to increase its profits', *New York Times Magazine*, 13 September 1970.

Gonchar, J. (2003), 'Courses are expanding to meet gradually growing gains: But states requirements may not be serving the best interests of engineers and the public', *Engineering News-Record*, 27 October. Available at: http://enr.construction.com/archive/features/education/ [accessed 1 April 2004].

Greenwood, M.R. (2002), 'Ethics and HRM: A review and conceptual analysis', *Journal of Business Ethics*, 36, 261–78.

Hopen, D. (2003), 'What's happening to leadership in America?', *Quality Digest*, 22(11), 62.

James, R.E. (2002), *The Integrity Chain: The Link to Profitability in Construction*, Raleigh, NC: FMI Corporation.

Killingsworth, R. (1992), 'Integrating Ethics into Construction Curricula', *ASC Proceedings of the 28th Annual Conference*, April 1992, Auburn, AL.

Kloppenborg, T.J. and Opfer, W.A. (2002), 'The current state of project management research: Trends, interpretations, and predictions', *Project Management Journal*, 33(2), 5–18.

Mintzberg, H., Simons, R. and Basu, K. (2002), 'Beyond selfishness', *Sloan Management Review*, 44(1), 67–74.

Morris, J.L. (2000), 'Values-based leadership skills, values, and concepts', (Doctoral dissertation, Capella University, 2000), *Dissertation Abstracts International*, DAI- A 61/10, p. 4082, April 2001, (UMI No. 9991684).

Moylan, W.A. (2005), 'Building ethics in construction partnerships: An analysis of values-based leadership', (Doctoral dissertation, Capella University), *Dissertation Abstracts International*, DAI-A66/03, p. 1075, September 2005, (UMI No. AAT 3168176).

Pennypacker, J.S. and Grant, K.P. (2003). 'Project management maturity: An industry benchmark', *Project Management Journal*, 34(1), 4–11.

Peters, T. (1997), *The Circle of Innovation*, New York: Alfred A. Knopf.

Pinto, J.K. and Kharbanda, O.P. (1995), 'Lessons for the accidental profession', *Business Horizons*, March–April 1995, 25–35.

Robertson, H.D. (1987), 'Developing Ethics Education in the Construction Education Program', *ASC Proceedings of the 23rd Annual Conference*, April 1987, West Lafayette, IN.

Rooley, R. (2001a), 'Professional codes of conduct and the law'. Available at: http://www.hpac.com/member/archive/0108law.htm [accessed 8 March 2004].

Rooley, R. (2001b), 'Ethics in construction and arbitration: Professional codes of conduct and the law', *Heating, Piping, Air Conditioning*, 73(8), 72–5. Available at: http://www.hpac.com/member/archive/0108law.htm [accessed 8 March 2004].

Rosen, R., Digh, P., Singer, M. and Phillips, C. (2000), *Global Literacies: Lessons on Business Leadership and Natural Cultures*, New York: Simon & Schuster.

Rubin, D.K., Buckner Powers, M., Tulacz, G., Winston, S. and Krizan, W.G. (2002), 'Leaders come in all shapes and sizes but the great ones focus on people', *Engineering News-Record*, 2 December. Available at: http://enr.construciton.com/archieve/features/bizlabor/ [accessed 1 April 2004].

Schein, E. (1997), *Organizational Culture and Leadership*, 2nd edn, San Francisco, CA: Jossey-Bass.

Senge, P.M. (1992), 'Mental models: Putting strategic ideas into practice', *Planning Review*, 20(2), 4–12.

Senge, P.M., Kleiner, A., Roberts, C., Ross, R.B. and Smith, B.J. (1994), *The Fifth Discipline Fieldbook*, New York: Doubleday.

Thomas, J., Delisle, C.L., Jugdev, K. and Buckle, P. (2001), 'Selling Project Management to Senior Executives: Preliminary Phase II Findings', paper presented at a Project Management Institute Symposium, Nashville, TN.

Uff, J. (2003), 'Duties at the Legal Fringe: Ethics in Construction Law', public lecture delivered at The Great Hall, King's College London 19 June 2003, London: Society of Construction Law.

Verma, V.K. (1995), *The Human Aspects of project Management, vol. 1, Organizing Projects for Success*, Newtown Square, PA: Project Management Institute.

Wade, E. and Airitam, S. (2002), *Ethics 4 Everyone: The Handbook for Integrity-based Business Practices*, Dallas, TX: Performance Systems Corp.

Wang, X. (2002), 'Developing a true sense of professional community: An important matter for the project management professionalism', *Project Management Journal*, 33(1), 5–11.

28 *Leadership*

ALFONSO BUCERO

The most appropriate definition of a leader is someone who has followers. Leaders might or might not have any formal authority. They are highly visible. They set examples. Leadership is not rank, privileges or money, it is responsibility. Every project manager needs to be a leader. So this chapter is intended to provide you some ideas and best practices to help you to develop your own leadership skills.

Historical Background

The search for the characteristics or traits of leaders has been going on for centuries. History's greatest philosophical writings from Plato to Plutarch have explored the question 'What qualities distinguish an individual as a leader?' Underlying this search was the early recognition of the importance of leadership, together with the assumption that leadership is rooted in the characteristics that certain individuals possess. This idea that leadership is based on individual attributes is known as the 'trait theory of leadership'.

The trait theory was explored at length in a number of works in the nineteenth century. The general evidence suggested that people who are leaders in one situation may not necessarily be leaders in other situations (Stogdill, 1948). Additionally, during the 1980s statistical advances allowed researchers to conduct meta-analyses, in which they could quantitatively analyse and summarise the findings from a wide array of studies.

The situational leadership model proposed by Hersey and Blanchard (2007) suggests four leadership styles and four levels of follower-development. For effectiveness, the model posits that the leadership style must match the appropriate level of follower-development. In this model, leadership behaviour becomes a function not only of the characteristics of the leader, but of the characteristics of followers as well.

Functional leadership theory (Hackman and Walton, 1986; McGrath, 1962) is a particularly useful theory for addressing specific leader behaviours expected to contribute to organisational or unit effectiveness. This theory argues that the leader's main job is to see that whatever is necessary for group needs is done. Thus a leader can be said to have done their job well when they have contributed to group effectiveness and cohesion.

The transformational leader (Burns, 1978) motivates his/her team to be effective and efficient. Communication is the base for goal achievement, focusing the group on the final desired outcome or goal attainment. This leader is highly visible and uses chain of command to get the job done. Transformational leaders focus on the big picture, so they need to be surrounded by people who can take care of the details. The leader is always looking for ideas that move the organisation to reach the corporate vision.

Leadership Attitude

Leadership can be perceived as a particularly emotion-laden process, with emotions entwined with the social influence process. In an organisation, the leader's reaction has some effects on his/her group. These effects can be described in three levels:

1. *The mood of individual group members*: Group members with leaders in a positive mood experience more positive mood than group members who have leaders in a negative mood. The leaders transmit their moods to other group members through the mechanism of emotional contagion.
2. *The affective tone of the group*: Group affective tone represents the consistent or homogeneous affective reactions within a group. Group affective tone is an aggregate of the moods of the individual members of the group and refers to mood at the group level of analysis. Groups with leaders in a positive mood have a more positive affective tone than do groups with leaders in a negative mood.
3. *Group processes (such as coordination, effort expenditure and task strategy)*: Public expressions of mood have an impact on how group members think and act. When people experience and express a mood, they send signals to others. Leaders signal their goals, intentions and attitudes through their expressions of moods. Beyond the leader's mood, the leader's behaviour is a source for positive and negative employee emotions at work. The leader creates situations and events that lead to emotional responses. Certain leader behaviours displayed during interactions with their employees are the sources of these affective events. Leaders shape workplace affective events.

Leadership Styles

Leadership style refers to a leader's behaviour. It is the result of the philosophy, personality and experience of the leader. Here are the most commonly recognised styles:

- *Autocratic or authoritarian style*: Under the autocratic leadership style, all decision making powers are centralised in the leader, as with dictators. Leaders do not entertain any suggestions or initiatives from subordinates. The autocratic management has been successful as it provides strong motivation to the manager. It permits quick decision making, as only one person decides for the whole group and keeps each decision to him/herself until he/she feels it needs to be shared with the rest of the group.
- *Participative or democratic style*: The democratic leadership style favours decision making by the group. Such a leader gives instructions after consulting the group. They can win the cooperation of their group and can motivate them effectively and positively. The decisions of the democratic leader are not unilateral as with the autocrat because they arise from consultation with the group members and participation by them.
- *Laissez-faire or free-rein style*: A free-rein leader does not lead, but leaves the group entirely to itself. Such a leader allows maximum freedom to subordinates; they are given a free hand in deciding their own policies and methods. Different situations call for different leadership styles. In an emergency when there is little time to converge on an agreement and where a designated authority has significantly more experience or expertise than the rest of the team, an autocratic leadership style may be most

effective; however, in a highly motivated and aligned team with a homogeneous level of expertise, a more democratic or laissez-faire style may be more effective.

- *Toxic leadership*: A toxic leader is someone who has responsibility over a group of people or an organisation, and who abuses the leader-follower relationship by leaving the group or organisation in a worse-off condition than when he/she first found them.

Leading Yourself

If you want to lead people you need to lead yourself first. I have seen some project managers who want to be followed, but are not able to lead themselves first. The key to leading yourself well is to learn self-management. I have observed that many people put too much emphasis on decision making and too little on decision managing. As a result, they lack focus, discipline, intentionality and purpose.

Successful people make right decisions early and manage those decisions daily. Some people think that self-leadership is about making good decisions every day, when the reality is that we need to make a few critical decisions in major areas of life and then manage those decisions day to day.

Here is a classic example. Have you made a New Year's resolution to exercise? You probably already believe that exercise is important. Making a decision to do it is not hard, but managing that decision and following through is much more difficult. Let us say, for example, that you sign up for a health club membership during the first week of January. When you sign on, you are excited. But the first time you show up at the gym, there is a mob of people. There are so many cars that police are directing traffic. You drive around for fifteen minutes, and finally find a parking place four blocks away. But that is all right; you are there for exercise anyway. So you walk to the gym.

Then when you get inside the building, you even have to wait to get into the locker room to change. But you still believe that is all right. You want to get into shape. This is going to be great. You continue to think that until you finally get changed only to find that all the machines are being used. Once again you have to wait. Finally, you get on a machine. It is not the one you really wanted, but you take it and you exercise for twenty minutes. When you see the line for the shower, you decide to skip it, take your clothes and go home to change. On your way out, you see the manager of the club, and you decide to complain about the crowds. She says:

> *Don't worry about it. Come back in three weeks, and you can have the closest parking place and your choice of machines. Because by then, 98 per cent of the people who signed up will have dropped out!*

It is one thing to decide to exercise. It is quite another actually to follow through with it. As everyone else drops out, you have to decide whether you will quit like everyone else or if you will stick with it. That takes self-management.

Nothing will make a better impression on your leader than your ability to manage yourself. If your leader must continually expend energy managing you, then you will be perceived as someone who drains time and energy. If you manage yourself well, however, your leader will see you as someone who maximises opportunities and leverages personal strengths. But the question is: what does a leader need to self-manage?

To gain credibility with your leader and others, focus on taking care of business in the areas outlined below.

MANAGING YOUR EMOTIONS

A study revealed that people with emotional problems are 144 per cent more likely to have automobile accidents than those who do not have such problems. The same study evidently found that one out of five victims of fatal accidents had been in a quarrel with another person in the six hours preceding the accident (Maxwell, 2006).

It is important for everybody to manage emotions. Nobody likes to spend time around an emotional time bomb that may 'go off' at any moment. But it is especially critical for leaders to control their emotions because whatever they do affects many other people.

Good leaders know when to display emotions and when to delay them. Sometimes they show them so that their people can feel what they are feeling. It stirs them up. Is that manipulative? I do not think so, as long as the leaders are doing it for the good of the team and not for their own gain. Because leaders see more and ahead of others, they often experience the emotions first. By letting the team know what you are feeling, you are helping them to see what you are seeing.

At other times leaders have held their feelings in check. When I say that leaders should delay their emotions, I am not suggesting that they deny them or bury them. The bottom line in managing your emotions is that you should put others, not yourself, first in how to handle and process them. Whether you delay or display your emotions should not be for your own gratification. Ask yourself, what does the team need? What will make me feel better?

MANAGING YOUR TIME

Time management issues are especially tough for people in the middle layers of management. Leaders at the top can delegate. Workers at the bottom often punch a time clock. They get paid an hourly wage, and they do what they can whilst they are on the clock. Middle leaders, meanwhile, feel the tension challenge, and they are encouraged, and are often expected, to put in long hours to get their work done.

Time is valuable. Until you value yourself, you will not value your time. Until you value your time, you will not do anything with it. Instead of thinking about what you do and what you buy in terms of money, instead think about them in terms of time. What is worth spending your life on? Seeing your work in that light just may change the way you manage your time.

MANAGING YOUR PRIORITIES

In some companies, project managers have no choice in managing priorities because of the 'multi-hat' challenge. But at the same time, the old proverb is true: if you chase two rabbits, both will escape.

What is a leader in the middle to do? Since you are not the top leader, you do not have control over your list of responsibilities or your schedule. You must still try to get yourself to the point where you can manage your priorities and focus your time as follows:

- Spend 80 per cent of your time on the work where you are strongest;
- Spend 15 per cent of your time on work from which you are learning;
- Spend the remaining 5 per cent on other necessary areas.

Clearly this might be difficult to achieve, but it is a good mix to strive for. If you have people working for you, give them the things to do that you are not good at, but which they can do better. Or if possible, trade some duties with colleagues so that each of you is working within your strengths. Remember, a way to move up from the middle is to shift gradually from generalist to specialist, from someone who does many things well to someone who focuses on a few things done exceptionally well. The secret to making such a shift is often discipline.

Be ruthless in your judgement of what you should not do. Just because you like doing something does not mean it should stay on your to-do list. If it is a strength, do it. If it helps you grow, do it. If your leader says you must handle it personally, do it. Anything else is a candidate for your 'stop doing' list.

MANAGING YOUR ENERGY

Some people have to ration their energy so that they do not run out. Up until a few years ago, I was not one of those people. When people asked me how I got so much done, my answer was always, 'High energy, low IQ'. From the time I was a child, I was always on the go. I was six years old before I realised my name was not 'Settle Down'.

Now that I am older, I do have to pay attention to my energy level. Here is one of my strategies for managing my energy. When I look at my calendar every morning, I ask myself, 'What is today's main event?' That is the one thing to which I cannot afford to give anything less than my best. That one thing can be for my family, my subordinates, a friend, my publisher, the sponsor of a speaking engagement or my writing time. I always make sure I have the energy to do it with focus and excellence.

Even people with high energy can have that energy sucked right out of them under difficult circumstances. I have observed that leaders in the middle of an organisation often have to deal with 'the ABC energy-drain', which is explained as follows:

- **A**ctivity without direction – doing things that do not seem to matter;
- **B**urden without action – not being able to do things that really matter;
- **C**onflict without resolution – not being able to deal with what does matter.

If you find that you are in an organisation where you often must deal with these ABCs, then you will have to work extra hard to manage your energy well. Either that or you need to look for a new place to work!

MANAGE YOUR THINKING

Being too busy is the greatest enemy of good thinking. Middle leaders are usually the busiest people in an organisation. If you find that the pace of life is too demanding for you to stop and think during your workday, then get into the habit of jotting down the three or four things that need good mental processing or planning that you cannot stop to think about. Then set aside some time later, when you will be able to give those items some good 'think time'. That may be 30 minutes at home the same day, or you might want to keep a running list for a whole week and then take a couple of hours during your weekend. But do not let the list get so long that it disheartens or intimidates you.

DELEGATING

Although a project manager cannot delegate everything in a project, delegating can make a project manager's complete life easier. But many are hesitant to pass on responsibilities. For example, many organisations have a low project management maturity level, and management focus is on project results – not on project control. Many project managers do not have enough authority and so they also perform a technical role at the same time as trying to manage their projects. Many people have been promoted from technical positions to project management positions. As individual contributors they were not used to practising delegation. They did their technical tasks and just followed the project plan, but they did not delegate. They did not feel comfortable delegating because they were not confident with their people, and nobody explained to them why and how to do it.

To be able to delegate you need to be conscious that you have a team – that you have people who can help you to achieve project success. You will know that you cannot achieve project success alone – you need people. It would be very helpful to be trained how to delegate. Here are some reasons (or even excuses) why people do not delegate:

- It's faster to do the job myself.
- I am concerned about lack of control.
- I like to keep busy and make my own decisions.
- People are already too busy.
- A mistake by a team member could be costly for my project.
- Team members lack the overall knowledge that many decisions require.

Many project managers are responsible for more than one project and they also have to juggle a mix between technical and project management tasks. So all the above answers can make sense, but the real reason for failure to delegate often comes down to deep insecurity. This self-defeating attitude influences how you accept and recognise the performance of those who work under you. Do not think of delegating as doing the other person a favour.

Delegating some of your authority only makes your work easier. You will have more time to manage your project, monitor team members and handle conflicts. Your organisation will benefit too, as output goes up and project work is completed more efficiently. To delegate effectively, follow the following four steps:

Step one – Outline the purpose and importance of the project. Do not expect team members to ask enough questions to define the project.

Step two – Give your delegates the necessary authority. Make sure each team member has the power needed to complete the task. Otherwise, requests to others for help and information might be ignored because they do not come directly from you.

Step three – Delegate for results. Set standards and make sure team members know they will be held accountable. When a problem arises, use it as a chance to show your subordinate how to handle it.

Step four – Review and follow up. Setting deadlines and enforcing them will establish commitment.

To make sure you delegate each task to the appropriate person, consider the following factors:

- Friction: disagreement between you and the person taking the assignment can be healthy while the assignment is being made. It only becomes a problem if it extends into the execution stage.
- Track record: match the task to the person. Past performance is significant only as it relates to the job you are delegating.
- Location: do not delegate only because someone is close by, not busy, or convenient to use.
- Organisation level: if you want to delegate a job to someone several levels down in the organisation, first confer with his or her supervisors and explain the situation.
- Compatibility: ideally, the styles of both people involved will be complementary.

Communication is the key to delegation. Without communication, assignments are blurred, deadlines are vague and results are predictably poor. If you want your team to excel as they take on added duties, talk to them, recognise them and reward them.

Leading Upwards

Project managers with the ability to communicate well, especially when addressing executives and project sponsors, always have an advantage. This is especially useful when dealing with executives who believe they do not need to know much about projects or the project management process because, 'That's the project manager's responsibility'.

It is generally the case that project managers take great care of the projects they manage, whilst executives and senior managers take care of business results and monitor overall business success. But when each wants to be understood by the other, they need to speak the language the other group understands. Managers, in general, do not care about technical terms – they take care about results, objectives and return on investment. It is difficult to put yourself in the shoes of your boss, and it is also difficult for your boss to understand your problems as a project manager.

Several years ago I worked in Spain for one of the largest multinational companies in the world. I managed an external customer project with a €10 million budget, 150 workers and four subcontractors. During the project's two-and-a-half-year duration, my senior manager visited the customer only once, and whilst I met with him monthly, our project status reviews never lasted more than ten minutes. In all, this manager expressed very little interest regarding the problems I found managing the project.

This type of counterproductive behaviour is starting to change in the south of Europe. As project management awareness grows in organisations, executives are coming to understand the importance and necessity of planning before implementing activities. And who knows more about people, organisational abilities and what it takes to implement a project than a project manager?

Executives need project managers to implement strategy. Project managers can align themselves with executives by finding and focusing on these commonalities:

- Ultimately, project managers and executives share the same organisational objectives because they work for the same company.
- Because more than 75 per cent of business activities can be classified as projects, project managers and executives arguably have the same impact on business operations and results.
- The experiences and education of project managers give a company a competitive advantage. Wise executives find ways to utilise the experiences of the individuals in their organisation to gain an upper hand.
- Executives and project managers both must learn to navigate political climates successfully to ensure results.

Even with these similarities, executives know only one part of the story. They miss a great deal of insight that comes from dealing with the customer, which is something project managers do much of the time. So many organisations tend to focus on project manager development as it correlates to improving project results. But what about educating the executives? There is value in teaching an executive about a project's mission, implications and desired effects, because that can result in more clearly defined roles and better relationships between the executive and the project manager.

Unfortunately, project managers often talk to their upper managers only when they run into problems. Executives do not speak enough with project managers because they perceive them simply as the 'doers'. In this paradigm, opportunities to act as partners are lost, and many organisations fail to grasp multiple opportunities to become more profitable and successful through project management practices.

Project Management Charisma

In my experience as a project manager, I am aware of the huge importance of people who attract others. They have something that is called 'charisma'. Most people think of charisma as something mystical, almost indefinable. They think it is a quality that comes at birth or not at all. But that is not necessarily true. Charisma, plainly stated, is the ability to draw people to you. You need to be the kind of person who attracts others, personifying the following pointers.

1. Love Life

People enjoy project managers who enjoy life. Think of the people you want to spend time with. How would you describe them? Grumpy? Bitter? Depressed? Of course not. They are celebrators, not complainers. They are passionate about life. If you want to attract people, you need to be like the people you enjoy being with. When you set yourself on fire, people love to come and see you burn.

2. Put a '10' on Every Team Member's Head

One of the best things you can do for people, which also might attract them to you, is to expect the best of them. When rating others on a scale of one to ten, putting a '10' on everyone's head helps them to think more highly of themselves. At the same time, it also helps you.

3. Give People Hope

Hope is the greatest of all possessions. If you can be the person who bestows that gift on others, they will be attracted to you, and they will be forever grateful.

4. Share Yourself

People love leaders who share themselves and their life journeys. As you lead people, give of yourself. Share wisdom, resources and even special occasions. I find that is one of our most favourite things to do. Put a personal touch in the stories and examples you tell others. For example, I went to an annual dancing festival in Tenerife. It was something I had wanted to do for years, and when I was finally able to work it into my schedule, my wife and I took one leader of my staff with his girlfriend. We had a wonderful time, and more important, I was able to add value to their lives by spending special time with them.

ROADBLOCKS AND CLEARWAYS TO THE CREATION OF CHARISMA

When it comes to charisma, the bottom line is other mindedness. Leaders who think about others and their concerns before thinking of themselves exhibit charisma. How would you rate yourself when it comes to charisma? Are other people naturally attracted to you? Are you well liked? If not, you may possess one of these roadblocks to charisma:

- Pride: nobody wants to follow a leader who thinks he is better than everyone else.
- Insecurity: if you are uncomfortable with whom you are, others will be too.
- Moodiness: if people never know what to expect from you, they stop expecting anything.
- Perfectionism: people respect the desire for excellence but dread totally unrealistic expectations.
- Cynicism: people do not want to be rained on by someone who sees a cloud around every silver lining.

If you can stay away from these qualities, you can cultivate charisma. To focus on improving charisma, here are some clearways for you to follow:

- Change your focus: When talking with other people, how much of your conversation is concentrated on yourself? Be more focused on others.
- Play the first impression game: The next time you meet someone for the first time, try your best to make a good impression. Learn the person's name. Focus on his or her interests. Be positive, and treat that person as a '10'. If you can do this for a day, you can do it every day. That will increase your charisma overnight.
- Share yourself: Make it your long-term goal to share your resources with others. Think about how you can add value to five people in your life this year. Provide resources to help them grow personally and professionally, and share your personal journey with them.

Effective Leaders – Based on the Results of a Seminar

The setting for this section is a seminar that was held on 'Management, Leadership, and Team Building in the Project Environment'. Delegates were asked to share their experiences about one or more leadership qualities that they have admired in a leader. That leader could be themselves, a manager they have worked with, a public figure, someone they have studied or anyone else.

Instructions to the delegates were to write an essay identifying the admired quality in the chosen leader, explain how that quality became manifest or implemented, describe the impact it had on the writer and then share their experiences with the other delegates. This activity was intended to encourage delegates to reflect on influential people in their lives, share the multitude of ways in which we lead each other, and practise storytelling as a leadership tool. This reflective exercise highlighted what the delegates learned from their own as well as from other people's experiences.

The collective results should now help us to appreciate dramatically how each of us is influenced by others in various ways. By comparing the results from all these essays, it becomes possible to extrapolate from these experiences to indicate how we can influence and lead others ourselves. The remainder of this section outlines the results, expressed in terms of project organisations.

LISTENING TO YOUR PEOPLE

All good leaders listen to their people. To foster involvement in team members, listen to them constantly. This can be done informally at a coffee break or formally at a planned project meeting. Listening is such a routine project activity that few people think of developing the skill. Yet when you really know how to listen, you increase your ability to acquire and retain knowledge. Listening also helps you to understand and influence team members and other stakeholders.

There are cultural differences that affect effective listening. Listening means different things to different people. The same statement can mean different things to the same person in different situations. I have observed the following different listening behaviours:

- *Hearing*: they hear your comments but they are not processing anything in their brains; then they forget the message.
- *Information gathering*: they are just collecting information but not listening.

- *Cynical listening*: they seem to be listening to you, they nod, but they are not actually listening.
- *Offensive listening*: they are not focused on your talk, they do not look at you, or they are doing other things whilst listening (for instance working on their computer or answering a telephone call).
- *Polite listening*: people who take care of formal manners and act politely.
- *Active listening*: they paraphrase and validate what they have understood about your talk.

Listening is hard work. Unlike hearing, listening demands total concentration. It is an active search for meaning, whilst hearing is passive. Try to listen with the following questions in mind:

- What is the speaker saying?
- What does it mean?
- How does it relate to what was said before?
- What point is the speaker trying to make?
- How can I use the information the speaker is giving me?
- Does it make sense?
- Am I getting the whole story?
- Are the points being supported?
- How does this relate to what I already know?

Also ask questions – especially clarifying questions. Words have definitions, but their full meaning comes from the person who is speaking. To understand that full meaning you might have to help the speaker by following up with questions. Maintaining eye contact and an appropriate nod or two also help to let the speaker know that you are listening.

Paraphrase when you want to make sure you have understood, when you are not sure you have caught the meaning, and before you agree or disagree. Paraphrasing is also useful when dealing with people who repeat themselves – it assures them they have communicated their ideas to you.

Cultural Differences

In reply to a question about whether project managers should consider listening as a priority some cultural differences emerged from which it was apparent that professionals have to take different approaches depending on the circumstances. For instance, Spanish people look directly into the face of the person talking to them. Conversely, people in Asian countries often consider it offensive to look directly into the eyes of the person talking to them. However, all agreed that listening is a priority. In cross-cultural exchanges:

1. Pay attention to the person and the message.
2. Create rapport.
3. Share meaning.

Listen better to project stakeholders, and you will learn more about your project.

COURAGE MAKES THE DIFFERENCE

You can lose money, you can lose allies along your projects, but if you lose your courage you lose everything. Without courage, there can be no hope. Professionals are inspired by leaders who take the initiative and who risk personal safety for the sake of a cause. Only those project managers who act boldly in times of crisis and change are willingly followed.

Complete project managers need courage to manage and overcome project obstacles and issues. Great courage, strength of character and commitment are required to survive in the project management field worldwide. This is not the time for the timid. Leaders need to summon their will if they are to mobilise the personal and organisational resources to triumph against the odds. They need boldness to communicate reality honestly to project team members.

A critical success factor in being courageous is human freedom. Most admired leaders (Martin Luther King, Gandhi and Mother Teresa) have given others their freedom. People revere those who have the courage to give up their own liberty so that others can be free. We, as project professionals, often talk about the courage of our convictions, meaning that we are willing to stand up for what we believe.

We need to believe in our projects. Otherwise we will not be able to transmit positivism and passion to team members and other stakeholders. But perhaps the courage of conviction can be better understood as the willingness to risk surrendering our freedom for our beliefs. It would seem that the truest measure of commitment to common vision and values is the amount of freedom we are willing to risk.

European project managers carry the 'flag of courage' as our symbol. There are more and more global multicultural projects in Europe. Project team members can come from different European countries like the UK, Netherlands, France, Italy, Spain, Portugal, Germany or wherever, so the project leader needs to have courage when managing people from different cultures and behaviours and to take action to achieve project objectives.

One delegate to the seminar wrote in his essay: 'The project manager must spend a lot of time understanding and listening to their team members. He or she must spend time with them. Courage consumes a lot of energy; empower your people and charge your batteries through them'.

BALANCING HOPE AND WORK

Surrendering freedom is relative, of course. In times of trouble, you not only discover what you truly believe but whether or not you can act on your beliefs. And your team is observing your reactions in those cases. You need to lead by example.

Whatever you hope for – freedom, project success, quality, career path progress – you have to work for it. And the more hope you have, the more work you put in it to get what you want. That is because courage and actions are connected. That is what it means to surrender your freedom. If you hope more than you work, you (and your team members) are likely to be disappointed. And your credibility is likely to suffer.

But what about balance? Do complete project leaders have balance in their lives? Certainly they do. And balance is relative. None of us can determine if another's life is out of balance without knowing the weights and measures in that person's life. If a leader, for example, loads up one side of the scale with a ton of hope, the only way his or her life will be in balance is to load the other with a ton of work. Anything less would surely bring disappointment.

However, if a leader has only an ounce of hope and loads the scale with a ton of work, the scale is out of balance. The secret is not to overload the scale on either end. When hope and work, challenge and skill are in equilibrium, that is when you experience optimal performance.

People with high hope are not blind to the realities of the present. If something is not working or if current methods are not effective, they do not ignore it, cross their fingers or simply redouble their efforts. They assess the situation and find new ways to reach the goals. And if the destination begins to recede rather than appear closer, people with hope reset their goals.

Changing the strategy or aiming for another target is not defeatism. In fact, if a project leader persists in a strategy that does not work or stubbornly pursues one that is blocked, project team members can become frustrated and depressed, leading them to feel defeated rather than victorious. It is better to find a new path or decide on a different destination. Then once that end is reached, set a new, more challenging objective.

Credibility is not always strengthened by continuing to do what you said you would do if that way is not working. Admitting that you are wrong and finding a better course of action is a far more courageous and credible path to take. Courage is also required to push back when sponsors impose unreasonable schedule, scope or budget constraints. Without the courage up front to constructively resist and to negotiate with due diligence, project managers set themselves up for failure.

DEVELOPING RELATIONSHIPS

All good project leadership is based on relationships. People will not go along with you if they cannot get along with you. The key to developing chemistry with leaders is to develop relationships with them. If you can learn to adapt to your boss's personality whilst still being yourself and maintaining your integrity, you will be able to lead up.

In response to the question asked at the seminar, 'Was the chemistry between your project team, your executives and yourself working properly throughout your projects?', one delegate gave the following answer:

I believe this can be achieved dealing with people as human beings, not only as employees. Being confident, respectful, sincere, creating a team spirit in the project, clarifying the common objective. These attitudes should generate enthusiasm itself.

The job of a complete project manager, as a leader, is to connect with the people being led. In an ideal world, that is the way it should be. The reality is that some leaders do little to connect with the people they lead.

As a project leader, take it upon yourself to connect not only with the people you lead, but also with the person who leads you (your manager, your project sponsor). If you want to lead up, you need to take the responsibility to connect up.

Personal, Practical Advice

People can usually trace their successes and failures to the relationships in their lives. The same is true when it comes to leadership. I shall now list some practices that I find extremely valid in running projects within organisations.

LISTEN TO YOUR LEADER'S HEARTBEAT

Try to understand what makes your leader 'tick'. That might mean paying attention in informal settings, such as during hallway conversations, at lunch, or in the informal meeting that often occurs before or after a scheduled meeting. If you know your leader well and feel the relationship is solid, you may be more direct and ask questions about what really matters to him or her on an emotional level. If you are not sure what to look for, focus on these three areas:

1. What makes them laugh? This is very important.
2. What makes them cry? This is what touches a person's heart at a deep emotional level.
3. What makes them sing?

These are the things that bring deep fulfilment. All people have dreams, issues or causes that connect with them. Those things are like the keys to their lives. From your own point of view, are you aware of the things that touch you on a deep emotional level? What are the signs that they 'connect' for you? Do you see those signs in your leader? Look for them, and you will likely find them.

KNOW YOUR LEADER'S PRIORITIES

The priorities of leaders are what they have to do. This is more than just to-do lists. All leaders have duties that they must complete if they are not to fail in fulfilling their responsibility. It is the shortlist that your boss's boss would say is do-or-die for that position. Make it your goal to learn what those priorities are. The better acquainted you are with those duties or objectives, the better you will understand and communicate with your leader.

CATCH YOUR LEADER'S ENTHUSIASM

It is much easier to work with someone when you share enthusiasm. If you can catch your leader's enthusiasm, it will have a similarly energising effect. And it will create a bond between you and your leader. If you can share in that enthusiasm, you will pass it on because you will not be able to contain it.

SUPPORT YOUR LEADER'S VISION

When top leaders hear others articulate the vision they have cast for the organisation, their hearts sing. This feeling is very rewarding. It represents a kind of *tipping point*, to use the words of author Malcolm Gladwell (Gladwell, 2000). It indicates a level of ownership by others in the organisation that bodes well for the fulfilment of the vision. Leaders in the middle of the organisation who are champions for the vision become elevated in the estimation of a top leader. They 'get it'. They are 'on board'. And they have great value.

Never underestimate the power of a verbal endorsement of the vision by a person with influence. As a leader in the middle, if you are unsure about the vision of your leader talk to that person. Ask questions. Once you think you understand it, quote it back to your leader in situations where it is appropriate to make sure you are in alignment. If you get it right, you will be able to see the reaction in your leader's face. Then start passing it on to the people in your sphere of influence. That will be good for the organisation, your people, your leader and you. Promote your leader's dreams, and that leader will promote you.

CONNECT WITH YOUR LEADER'S INTERESTS

One of the keys to building *relational chemistry* is knowing and connecting with the interests of your leader. It is important to know enough about your leader to be able to relate to them as an individual beyond the job. If your boss is a golfer, you might want to take up the game, or at least learn some things about it. If they collect rare books or porcelain, then spend some time on the Internet finding out about these hobbies. Just learn enough to relate to your boss and talk intelligently about the subject.

UNDERSTAND YOUR LEADER'S PERSONALITY

Two staff members were discussing the president of their company, and one of them said, 'You know, you cannot help liking the guy'. The other replied, 'Yes, if you do not, he fires you'.

Leaders are used to having others accommodate their personalities. As you lead down from the middle of the organisation, do you not expect others to conform to your personality? I do not mean that in an unreasonable or spiteful way (so that you would fire someone who did not like you, as in the joke). If you are simply being yourself, you expect the people who work for you to work with you. But when you are trying to lead up, you are the one who must conform to your leader's personality. It is a rare great leader who conforms down to the people who work for him or her.

It is wise to understand your leader's style and how your personality styles interact. Most of the time, personality opposites get along well as long as their values and goals are similar. Trouble can come when people with similar personality types come together. If you find that your personality is similar to your boss's, then remember that you are the one who has to be flexible. That can be a challenge if yours is not a flexible personality type.

EARN YOUR LEADER'S TRUST

When you take time to invest in relational chemistry with your leader, the eventual result will be trust, in other words, relational currency. When you do things that add to the relationship, you increase the change in your pocket. When you do negative things, you spend that change. If you keep 'dropping the ball', professionally or personally, you harm the relationship, and you can eventually spend all the change and bankrupt the relationship.

LEARN TO WORK WITH YOUR LEADER'S WEAKNESSES

You cannot build a positive relationship with your boss if you secretly disrespect them because of their weaknesses. Since everybody has blind spots and weak areas, why not learn to work with them? Try to focus on the positives, and work around the negatives. To do anything else will only hurt you.

Concluding Summary

The professional project manager needs to be both a leader and manager. This requires placing a priority on understanding and listening to people. Lead by example. Demonstrate a positive attitude. Cultivate relationships up, across and down the organisation.

Identify leadership qualities that have made a difference in your life – people who have influenced you. Study what they did. Be the 'teachable' student who continuously learns and applies a flexible approach to leadership.

Know yourself, believe in yourself, take care of yourself first, and then take care of others. Follow a proactive model of professional development.

References and Further Reading

Bucero, A. (2010), *Today is a Good Day! Attitudes for Achieving Project Success*, Ontario: Multi Media Publications.

Burns, J.M. (1978), *Leadership*, New York: Harper & Row.

Gladwell, M. (2000), *The Tipping Point: How Little Things Can Make a Big Difference*, London: Little, Brown and Company.

Hackman, J.R. and Walton, R.E. (1986), 'Leading groups in organizations', in P.S. Goodman (ed.), *Designing Effective Work Groups*, San Francisco, CA: Jossey-Bass, 72–119.

Hersey, P. and Blanchard, K.H. (2007), *Management of Organizational Behaviour*, 9th edn, Englewood Cliffs, NJ: Prentice-Hall.

Maxwell, J.C. (2006), *The 360° Leader with Workbook*, Nashville, TN: Thomas Nelson Publishers.

McGrath, J.E. (1962), *Leadership Behavior: Some Requirements for Leadership Training*, Washington, DC: US Civil Service Commission.

Stogdill, R.M. (1948), 'Personal factors associated with leadership: A survey of the literature', *Journal of Psychology*, 25, 35–71.

29 *Conducting One's Self in Project Management*

DENNIS LOCK

Many chapters in this Handbook deal with psychological and motivational issues and they inevitably refer to the research of psychologists and management theorists. In this chapter I want to talk more about managing one's self in an organisation, based largely on my own experiences. There is always a danger of boring everyone to distraction when talking about one's self. Every worst piece of writing or talk begins with 'I', whereas of course one should focus instead on the reader or the audience. So I shall mix personal advice with illustrative anecdotes. My purpose is to share some of the lessons I have learned in the context of how one should behave when given the privilege of managing other people.

Knowing your Organisational Environment

This section is concerned with those of you who are beginning work in a new organisation. You might be fresh from business school, or you could be taking up an appointment as a more experienced new starter. If you are a new recruit, joining an establishment that has any credentials at all, your introductory period should include an induction process of some kind. I know of one organisation in the UK that sent its new senior staff to the US headquarters for three to six months, just so that they would absorb the corporate culture and become familiar with the standards expected throughout the group. Most induction processes are of course far more modest.

In a typical induction programme you can expect to be told mundane facts about such things as car parking, hours of work, catering facilities, health and safety responsibilities and what to do in the event of a fire. All very important in their various ways. You will be probably also be taken on a conducted tour of the organisation and its facilities. During that tour, you might be introduced to many people. Too many to remember immediately possibly, but you *must* remember the key people because as you develop in your role as project manager some of those people will depend on you and, conversely, you will need their cooperation as your project develops,

If possible, obtain a company organisation chart. In some companies these are out of date or simply do not exist. If that is the case, ask questions, note the answers and then draw your own chart. As far as possible you must learn the important roles that exist, how they are related and the names of all the significant jobholders. You must get some idea of the vertical and horizontal organisation. You have to determine from the beginning where you are going to fit into that organisation. You need to know your powers and the limits of your authority in relation to the company's line management structure. In a typical pyramid hierarchy, looking at the organisation chart and running your eyes up and down the lines of command that intersect your own position will give you most of the answers. There will undoubtedly be others in the company who have no line authority over you but whose status or influence demands that you treat them with special respect. These can include specialists such as a company solicitor and managers in functions like HRM, finance and procurement. Failure to understand at least these essential management characteristics from the start can lead you astray and cause you to make mistakes that will give offence in some cases and could even damage your future.

You also have to discover as early as you can what the culture of your organisation is and what protocols are in place. If your company is part of a group of companies, you must also research where your company sits in the scheme of things and how all the different companies in the group trade with each other. Your company might have especially valued clients or customers, and it could be useful to know who they are.

Learning About Your Project

PROJECT SPECIFICATION

Once you have recovered from the gratifying news that you have a new project to manage you must clearly discover all you can about the project itself. That might mean asking many questions. So many questions, that perhaps you should prepare a checklist. In the previous section you were learning about people in the company organisation but now you will be dealing with technical issues and numbers. You must absorb all the facts that together make up the project definition. Make certain you are given enough information. You really need to be armed with a full project specification from the beginning.

In some companies a project charter is prepared as part of the authorisation process, and you should find much of what you need to know in that document. I have known companies that prepare an internal project contract in addition to the project charter. This has nothing to do with an external client or customer but is (I think rather confusingly) an internal contract between the project manager and the company. Other companies use simpler methods, such as a project initiation document (PID), a project authorisation procedure or a works order form. It all depends on the type of project and your company's preferences. What is important is that your project authorisation documents include or are accompanied by a technical and commercial specification that sets out all the things your project will be expected to achieve – in other words – your project deliverables. These are the project results for which you are going to bear ultimate responsibility.

If you are going to manage an internal business change project, you need to be assured that you have all the important facts from the business case that caused this project to be approved in the first place (and you to be appointed). If the project is for an external customer, you must study the sales order and your customer's specification so that you learn exactly what the customer expects to receive.

UNDERSTANDING YOUR PROJECT ORGANISATION STRUCTURE

Once you know something about your new project, the voyage of discovery is by no means over. Now you must look inwardly to the way in which your project people are (or will be) organised. In many cases the manager is appointed to a project organisation that already exists and you will have no initial authority to change the way in which people are organised. Whether that is the case, or you are more fortunate in being able to ask for the kind of organisation you would prefer, you need to have some idea of organisational theory. You have to know something about the different project organisations that are possible, and then identify the pattern of the organisation that is actually being placed under you – reading chapters 9 and 10 could prove helpful in that respect.

Your future conduct as project manager and your level of authority and freedom to act will depend to a great extent on how your project is organised. If you realise that your project is organised as a functional matrix, your academic training (if you had any) should tell you that:

- You will only be able to get things done if the functional managers (over whom you can have no authority) agree to collaborate with you and support your project activities. Those functional managers will have to allow their staff to work on your project and accept your directions as to which tasks they shall perform. In other words, you must depend on others for your project resources. So clearly you will have to cultivate the friendship of all those functional managers. Without their cooperation, you and your project will struggle or fail.
- You have to be ready to get things you need done by exercising persuasion, because in a matrix organisation you will not have supreme line authority. Instead you will be burdened with management by consensus.
- You have to be aware that conflict of interests, possibly leading to actual hostility, are more likely to be found in a matrix organisation than in a team.

If you find that you have been placed in charge of a project that is organised as a team over which you are to enjoy sole command, then you should know the following facts:

- You should count yourself fortunate. Managing a dedicated team or task force gives you freedom of command and, if the project proves successful, you can soak up the praise and rewards at the end.
- Many lines of communication in a team are shorter and more direct. You can get results faster.
- As autonomous team leader you will be able to issue direct commands and, provided that you have not asked for the impossible, you should expect that your commands will result in the actions that you want from the members of your team.
- The corollary is that with supreme power comes sole personal responsibility. When things go wrong, the leader takes the ultimate blame. So being team leader is not all milk and honey.

Whatever the organisation, every project manager has to work with some people and other organisations over which he or she has no authority. These can include other managers and specialists within your company, outside organisations, regulatory bodies, local and national government departments, subcontractors and other stakeholders. Now there's a very important word – *stakeholders*.

KNOW YOUR PROJECT'S STAKEHOLDERS

Every project has stakeholders. A stakeholder is any person or organisation who can affect a project or be affected by it. On a large project there might be hundreds – even thousands of stakeholders. Clearly you cannot know every one of these personally but not all of them will carry equal weight or have great influence. You can make your life easier by recognising that it is possible to sort stakeholders into categories, only some of whom will need to command your full attention. You should be able to group your stakeholders under the headings *primary*, *secondary*, *tertiary* and so on, depending on how greatly they will affect, or be affected by, your project.

So at first you need to know who your primary stakeholders are. These will certainly include the project sponsor, who will most likely be a senior manager within your company if the project is for an internal business change. If your project is for an external customer, then that customer is paying, and is therefore almost certainly the most important sponsor and stakeholder. You must identify each stakeholder by finding the name, address and contact details of the individual or (if the stakeholder is an organisation) the principal representative with whom you will have to deal. In some companies all those contact details will be entered in a specific project manual, which I regard as very good practice.

In some large projects there might be several very important stakeholders, including investment banks, large contractors, public authorities and so on. You have to arrange to meet these people as soon as you can, introduce yourself and sow the seeds for future good personal relationships.

In projects with significant public exposure you might also have to deal with environmental groups, local authorities and members of the public. You could even have to attend or arrange one or more public meetings where you will have to make the case for going ahead with your project.

No one involved in managing projects can fail to have heard of the triangle of objectives, which was first introduced by Dr Martin Barnes. This triangle summarises the deliverables that can spell success or failure of a project under the three headings of cost, time and performance. Later versions of the triangle assign different names to these deliverables, but the general concept remains the same. Individual stakeholders can place their own different emphasis on these deliverables. It is even possible to draw a matrix on which you, as project manager, can record the different stakeholders' interests. There is an example in Chapter 14 (Figure 14.1) where you can read more about the various groups of project stakeholders.

Kick-starting Your Project

So far I have been considering organisational factors. You are beginning to establish your internal and external communications frameworks. Now it's time to look inwardly at the project itself.

Undoubtedly the best way in which to start a new project is to have a kick-off meeting. Ideally that should be initiated and chaired by a manager who is senior to you.

For an internal change project the project sponsor might chair the meeting. Otherwise, a director of projects, a programme manager or some other senior person (depending on the organisation) can open the meeting. All senior people who will be involved in your project tasks should be invited.

The kick-off meeting has several purposes, all of which are designed to help you get your project started as well as possible. The principal purposes are to:

- announce the project and explain its purpose;
- introduce you to other relevant managers and key people as the project manager;
- for an external project, give everyone some information about the customer;
- outline the project deliverables (especially scope, specification, timescale and budget);
- answer general questions about the project and remove any initial doubts or unknown quantities;
- breathe fire into the project and motivate all those who are going to take part.

When the project kick-off meeting ends and its members disperse, you should have been given a personal kick-start too. A well conducted kick-off meeting can generate enthusiasm and excitement. You must strive not to lose that momentum as your project continues its journey through its life cycle.

IMPORTANCE OF YOUR PROJECT MANAGEMENT OFFICE (PMO)

I am assuming that your project organisation has a PMO. If not you must establish one immediately. But by that I do not mean attempting to recruit many people to staff a large office. It all depends on the size of your project and what its budget will stand. Remember that a PMO is usually an overhead expense and returns no direct value for its cost (or, put another way, it adds cost without value). Of course it will give you essential support and, by improving project control, should save costs elsewhere.

For a small project your PMO might even comprise only one person (but that would have to be a versatile, multiskilled person). Your PMO has to include the essential functions of planning and cost reporting, change control and (if there is an external customer) contract administration. Some PMOs also administer a risk log and some form of earned value measurement. Your PMO is going to be your right arm, and your first task is to ensure that they plan your project so that its tasks can be allocated according to their priorities.

If I say much more here I shall be starting to write another textbook on project management, but I emphasise that you will need help, whether from a PMO or from a competent individual, to schedule and monitor your project. Notice I did not include 'control' in there, because control will be your job.

KNOWING OR ALLOCATING RESPONSIBILITIES

When you know something about the organisation and everything possible about your new project, you have to combine that knowledge and decide, in outline, *who* will be responsible for *what* as your project proceeds. By that I most certainly do not mean listing all the detailed tasks and attempting to allocate them to individuals – that is a far more detailed process that must happen later when your PMO has planned and scheduled your project in detail, That detailed process will need work-to lists from a suitable software package and is a project management function outside the scope of this chapter (or indeed this book).

Here I am talking far more broadly about allocating or acknowledging general responsibilities of key members in the internal and external project organisation. Clearly these people will include some who work under you, but you must also learn of the responsibilities to be borne by others outside your control. For example, your customer might have responsibility for finally approving critical design features, or even authorising release of funds for a few major purchases from third-party suppliers.

Fortunately there is a very simple tool that you can use, both as a checklist and as a place in which to record your findings. That tool is a responsibility matrix, an example of which is given in Figure 29.1. The matrix shown is designed for a construction project, but can easily be modified by choosing the responsibilities and people to suit any kind of project. This simple tool requires little explanation except to point out a few guiding principles:

1. No single responsibility should be split between two or more people if that can be avoided. That will prevent possible disputes or misunderstandings later.
2. Where two or more people will be jointly responsible, try to ensure that one has primary responsibility, and the other secondary responsibility.
3. A responsibility matrix can also be used to show people who will have no responsibility but who 'need to know'.

Task type:	The client	Project manager	Project engineer	Purchasing mngr	Drawing office	Construction mngr	Planning engineer	Cost engineer	Project accountant	and so on
Make designs		✚		●						
Approve designs	●	■	✚							
Purchase enquiries		■	✚	●						
Purchase orders	■	■	✚	●						
Planning	■	■	✚	✚	✚	✚	●	✚		
Cost control		●		✚		✚		✚		
Progress reports		●	✚	✚	✚	✚	✚			
Cost reports		●		✚		✚		✚	✚	
and so on										

● Principal responsibility (only one per task)
✚ Secondary responsibility
■ Must be consulted

Figure 29.1 Linear responsibility matrix

Establishing Relationships

Getting to know you, Getting to know all about you.
Getting to like you, Getting to hope you like me. (From The King and I, *Rogers and Hammerstein).*

Clearly you have to get to know the people in your organisation who are going to perform the many detailed project tasks and give you their loyal support. You have to make a good first impression on them all, because first impressions are important and get remembered. If you have already studied your organisation and learned people's names and what they do, you will be off to a good start.

Chapter 58 ends with a section based on the acronym RESPECT (relationships, empathy, sincerity, principles, empowerment, compassion and trust). Mutual respect between managers and their subordinates is clearly very important, so you have to do everything you can from the start to gain the respect of your colleagues. If you have a good track record and are known as a successful project manager, this task will be relatively easy. If not you must earn respect. I can give a few hints here that might speed the process.

Communicate well. If you ask someone to perform a task, make certain that they know what is required. Invite them to ask questions. If you intimidate them they might be afraid to ask key questions.

Communicating also means *listening*. You might need to heed advice from juniors, because some of them might have more experience of the company and its practices than you and they might remember past mistakes and so prevent you from walking into traps. On that issue, I'm definitely speaking from personal experience.

Try not to boast, but let your reputation speak for itself. But of course if your superiors openly heap praise upon you, then blush, appear modest and be grateful.

If the project domain is not in your own area of technical expertise, some of your subordinates could perceive that as a weakness and you might be at an initial disadvantage. So try to be confident (but never arrogant) and make the most of your other attributes and general project management experience and skills.

Show that you are a good and fair decision maker. Listen to arguments (both sides if there is a disagreement). If necessary say that you will need time to make a decision, but keep that time short.

When you do make a decision, be prepared to give your reasons. If you cannot make a decision easily, do not be too proud to seek advice from your superiors.

Be supportive and sympathetic to people personally. When individuals or groups of your staff are distressed for any reason, remember that the Samaritans achieve their results above all by listening. You will find that if one or more members of your staff occasionally become overwrought for any reason, just inviting them into your office and allowing them to pour out their troubles and unburden themselves will often see the problem vanish. More than once I invited someone into my office who was flushed and almost in tears (usually through pressure of work), but I had to do nothing except listen sympathetically to their problems and watch the distress drain from their face as they told their story.

Of course you will respect cultural differences and not allow yourself to be prejudiced in any way by people's race, religion, age or gender and you will support anyone who is subjected to victimisation for any reason. Sometimes you might have to show tolerance or be prepared to make provisions and allowances for people, for example if you have a handicapped person in your team you will often be able to take some simple action that will make their life easier and help them to perform their role better. Conducting yourself as a competent, decisive but compassionate and listening manager will not only earn you respect – you will discover that people actually get to like you and will put themselves out and go the extra mile when needed.

After respect and getting people to like you comes loyalty and trust. The more people respect and like you, the more loyal they will become. You too have to be loyal, to all those around you and especially to your employer.

Much of this is common sense. In fact most of project management is just common sense and logical reasoning. Respect is something that should grow as people get to know you and your management style as time passes. But do you know what your management style is? That leads to the next section.

Management Style

The development of management theory has one thing in common with the fashion industry, namely that *this* year's topic of discussion can be *next* year's history. However the behavioural theorists (discussed in Chapter 31 and many other places in this Handbook), have added greatly to our understanding of management. Here I want to give just a few examples of different management styles. You might wish to consider which of these apply to you.

MANAGEMENT BY OBJECTIVES

This management style is explained in Chapter 31. All I need to say here is that, crudely put, it comprises setting quantifiable targets and measuring how well people perform. Well, as a project manager you set objectives whenever you give someone a task. So, undoubtedly, management by objectives will be part of your management style. In recent years some people have heaped scorn on target setting as a means for achieving results. We all have to agree that setting targets alone will not guarantee success. So this management style has to be used along with others that give individuals support and encouragement towards meeting the goals you set them.

MANAGEMENT BY THE SEAT OF THE PANTS

This style of management derives its name from riding a horse or flying a plane. It refers to a kind of control that is based on instinctive feelings of whether or not things are going in the right direction. Although there are a few individuals who possess this ability in project management, most of us do not. Therefore we must rely on more formal methods.

MANAGEMENT BY WALKING ABOUT

There is no complex theory behind this style of management. All it means is making the effort to walk about and visit people who are working on your project. It might mean more than walking if some of your project workers are in different locations or even overseas. But people will respond well if they have your personal message that they and their work are appreciated. A word of encouragement costs little but the return on investment can be enormous. Conversely, ignoring people and their efforts on your project is a great demotivator. Not many projects can be managed effectively by sitting all day behind a desk.

MANAGEMENT BY SURPRISE

Management by surprise can happen in any command system where work instructions are issued without corresponding monitoring or feedback of results. In management by surprise a manager issues work to a person or group, waits, and is surprised when the completed work does not get done.

MANAGEMENT BY EXCEPTION

It has been said that a successful manager can be seen asleep or reading a newspaper because he/she knows that everything is running smoothly. Exceptions are things that do not go according to plan. Exceptions might be divergences from schedule or budget. Or they might be unexpected technical setbacks. Cost and management accountants call their exceptions *variances*. Exceptions or variances can apply to advantageous differences from plan but, for control purposes, it is the negative exceptions and potential failures that should command your attention.

Management by exception means concentrating your efforts on the bad variances or exceptions. If something is running five per cent below its budget, that's fine, leave it alone, don't tell me about it. But if another job is running late or over budget, concentrate on that and put it right. Similarly, if all jobs except one are running on time, it's that one late job that has to be examined and expedited.

Exceptions are also important when you are asked to make cost and progress reports. You have to highlight things that are not going to plan (and if possible, say what will be done to correct the problem). Exception reporting requires you to be open and honest, which might mean giving your project sponsor and other stakeholders early warning of difficulties, unless you know for certain that you can overcome the difficulty.

The Commercial Aspects of Your Project

Too many project managers (and project management texts) ignore the commercial side of project management (things such as conditions of contract, purchasing, risk insurance and so on). You, of course, are too sensible to make that mistake. These commercial aspects might be especially complex and important if the project is for an external customer. For example, your project contract might set out terms of payment, in which you should expect to receive payment from the customer in stages, with each payment being dependent upon progress or achievement of a particular milestone. If your project runs late, your claims for payment will also have to be delayed. Delayed revenues will impact negatively on your company's cash flow, and as project manager you could have to take the blame and provide the excuses.

Purchasing is very important in some projects, where it is essential to get goods and services delivered efficiently without wasting money. I was told by the Chartered Institute of Purchasing and Supply that purchased goods and services can account for up to 80 per cent of the total direct costs of some projects. I have also seen profits eaten away because contractual disputes continued long after project completion, with lawyers and court proceedings eroding what had been healthy profits.

You need to make sure that you and those working for you respect commercial managers in your company and cooperate with them. For example, stamp heavily on any design engineer who commits your company to the purchase of goods and services from any supplier without first getting advice and authorisation from your company's purchasing manager.

If you have a risk manager, or at least someone responsible for a risk log, in your project organisation, you can be sure that they will have read at least one good textbook on project risk management. But too often all suggested countermeasures ignore the fact that it is possible to insure against some risks. Some insurance measures might be required in your project's terms of contract with the customer. National governments impose obligations on employers to insure against liability to employees for injury and so forth.

So, however glamorous and exciting your new project happens to be, never neglect the comparatively boring and routine commercial issues.

Project Methodology

Managing your new project will require a mix of management skills and methods that together will become your operating methodology. That mix can change with time. In some organisations you will be expected to use a methodology that already exists (it might be enshrined in a set of company operating procedures). If you have a sensible methodology, managing your project will be made easier. But the imposition of an inappropriate methodology can make your life a misery. There are some ready-made methodologies such as PRINCE2, or the guidance in PMI's Body of Knowledge. However, you have to be aware that:

- all these methodologies were put together by some kind of committee (and in the case of PRINCE2 that was a UK government sponsored committee);
- every methodology has its good and its bad aspects;
- there is no one-size-fits-all solution.

You might be so unfortunate as to have to follow a prescribed methodology that is in some way deficient in common sense or is otherwise inappropriate for your project. You will be very disadvantaged if that is the case. If you are new to project management, that's going to be tough for you. However, if you have a strong background of project success, you will probably be listened to when you complain and ask to be allowed to use your own preferred methods.

Every methodology is a mix of techniques (such as critical path planning, risk management, earned value measurement) plus recommended organisation structure roles, reporting and control methods and so on. As you develop experience, and provided you have the twin gifts of logic and common sense, you will be able to choose and use the best from existing techniques and guidelines, reject those that are inappropriate for your circumstances and (here's the exciting bit) develop new techniques of your own. You might then become a specialist in one area of project management, but you will need support and even inspiration from your superiors.

So my advice is to look at the methodologies available to you, read what others think about them, identify and use the best aspects but do not slavishly follow bad practice. Every project is unique, and you will do best if you can tailor the available methods to suit your own project and organisation. That selectivity extends to choosing and using appropriate project management software and the most popular programs are far from being the best.

This is a huge subject that causes much heated argument. You will have to pick your way through the minefield using common sense and good judgement.

CASE EXAMPLE NO. 1: ADAPTING EXISTING METHODS TO SUIT A PARTICULAR PROBLEM

I'll finish this section with an example of how an established method can be adapted to suit a particular case. I was once called in to rescue a project from potential disaster. I suppose that made me a hero project manager (see Andy Jordan's excellent Chapter 57 on that topic).

The project had no plan, had three separate product streams, and the only concrete fact was that everything had to be ready in four months' time so that prototype products could be exhibited at a forthcoming trade show in central London. The products were all connected with medical instrumentation and hospital theatre equipment.

This was not a case where the methodology was wrong. There simply was no methodology at all. The project had not even been recognised as a project. We clearly needed a schedule for the work remaining, but no one could even tell me the current status in any detail. So I conducted a brainstorming meeting to draw a critical path network for all the work remaining. 'So what?' I can read in your minds, 'that's standard methodology'. Well, your thoughts are not quite accurate in this case because:

- no one except for myself in that meeting had any expertise in critical path planning;
- no one could tell me the current state of progress;
- no one could list the tasks remaining or their interdependencies or their expected durations.

So I had to find a new method. I began by drawing the exhibition opening day as the last project milestone at the right-hand side of a large whiteboard. Then I had to ask a series of probing questions. After some prompting from me the dialogue went something like this, with the answers (A) coming from different people:

DL: 'Imagine that you are on your exhibition stand just before the doors open. What is the last thing you would need to do?'
A: 'Dust everything and make sure all the leaflets are laid out'.
DL: 'And before that?'
A: 'Unpack the products and display them'.

> DL: 'And before that?'
> A: 'Deliver the products'.
> DL: 'And before that?'
> A: 'Pack the products'.
> DL: 'And before that?'
>
> Now I got separate replies, one for each product, for the activity of final inspection and testing.
>
> So my backward network diagram began to branch. As each answer to every subsequent question was received I wrote the corresponding activity on the whiteboard, still working from right to left. So a network logic diagram appeared as the dialogue continued until it petered out in a number of start dangles at the left-hand side.
>
> Amazingly, although I was the only person present with any project planning experience, we had just produced a logic diagram for the whole exhibition project. Even more satisfyingly, all of us could now see exactly where we were in terms of current progress. The next step was to agree estimates of the duration of every task on the plan. Then the meeting dispersed and it was left to me, overnight, to carry out time analysis and prepare a work-to list for each manager or supervisor.
>
> Now our exhibition project had a plan and all tasks had known priorities. If a task should slip, that would become obvious and we could take steps to bring work back into line. So we had retrieved order from chaos. This was a jointly owned solution that had everyone on board and committed to the plan.
>
> Of course the exhibition was a success. That success came about partly because everyone who mattered had contributed. But the rescue began by adapting an existing methodology to suit our own purpose.

Temptations

BRIBERY, CORRUPTION AND THEFT

You will probably be given discretionary power to authorise claims for expenses and purchases, but almost certainly you will be bound by financial limits. As time passes and mutual trust between yourself and your company grows you should expect those limits to increase. But internal auditors will always be interested in how much financial freedom each manager is given. Here's what happened in my case when I worked in a subsidiary company of British Petroleum (BP). One day some BP auditors descended upon us and engaged our managing director in a series of questions. The dialogue concerning me (which I was told about afterwards) went as follows:

> Auditor: 'Who is responsible for authorising purchase orders?'
> MD: 'Dennis Lock'.
> Auditor: 'What are Lock's financial limits of authority?'
> MD: 'He has no upper limit'.

Auditor: 'Who authorises payment of suppliers' invoices?'
MD: 'Dennis Lock'.
Auditor: 'Up to what financial limit?'
MD: 'He has no limit'.

The auditors were shocked. In theory I could order anything I wanted for my personal use, approve the supplier's invoice and the company would pay for it. Of course that never happened because I occupied and respected a position of trust.

Most managers will be subjected to temptation by being offered gifts or hospitality. In moderation, that's fine. But there are limits. I once told a building contractor that I would be out of the office for a couple of days on leave. 'Going somewhere nice?' they asked. 'No, just doing some work on my roof' was my answer. 'Oh we can send a couple of people out to do that for you' was their response, which of course I declined politely. I have been told of people being offered gifts worth far more, even a house in one case, but none of those managers were so silly as even to contemplate acceptance.

Common sense tells us never to accept any gift or offer of hospitality that would cause us to treat an outside supplier or contractor preferentially. A small gift is one thing but beyond that lies a world of possible bribery and corruption. You must always be able to criticise an outside supplier or terminate an unsatisfactory contract without hesitation.

Theft from your employer or from a colleague has to be dealt with promptly and severely (but of course I'm not talking about paper clips or pencils). Although I have had many cases of theft brought to my notice, almost all were committed by walk-in intruders. Modern security systems can deter intruders but criminals will often find ways in which to circumvent these. On the only occasion when I was asked by a police officer what should happen to a member of our staff who had been stopped in the street carrying goods stolen from my employer I unhesitatingly said 'Charge him'. The policeman replied 'Oh thank you sir. If only everyone took your attitude'. The culprit was dismissed the following day and was eventually put on probation. He also threatened to invite his chums to knife me, which was a little unsettling and I definitely watched my back when walking to and from my train station.

SEX AT YOUR WORKPLACE

Now I am sure I have your interest. A report by Alyson Shontell (2010) bears the title '15% of women have slept with their bosses – and 37% of them got promoted'. When people work together some will inevitably form social relationships. That of course is to be encouraged. But it sometimes leads to people having affairs. I am not going to moralise, which would be straying into the territory of Chapter 62. But as a responsible and caring manager you do need to be aware of possible difficulties that might arise between members of your workforce.

People often form very close bonds simply because they spend long hours working together. As a manager you might even come to realise that others in your organisation are attracted to you sexually by virtue of your apparent power, influence and (possibly) wealth. Also, you might observe that people are flirting with each other during their working hours. All these things are part of human nature and (within bounds) add to life's enjoyment. But when things go too far, careers and families can be destroyed.

Some companies have a culture that derives from their founders or current senior managers, where employees are expected to conduct themselves with especially strict morality and dignity. Woe betide anyone working for them who falls foul of their code.

At the beginning of this chapter I promised you some anecdotes. Here are three true cases.

Case 1 – In a small factory there was a production office in which a young attractive female clerk sat at a desk opposite another clerk who was male and at least twice her age. He was a chain smoker with poor teeth, badly shaven, shabbily dressed and untidy. A greater contrast between two people could hardly be imagined. One Monday morning their two desks were unoccupied and we discovered that this unlikely couple had eloped together over the weekend. That left the company with two immediate vacancies and a sudden severe work overload in the production office. So never be surprised by what might happen.

Case 2 – I walked into my London office and was followed in there by a woman whom I hardly knew.

Without even giving me time to reach my desk she blurted out 'How's about you and me having an affair Dennis?' Apocalyptic visions of an abrupt end to my career and marriage flashed before my eyes in a moment of stark terror. But I managed to dredge up the apparently nonchalant reply 'I can't really say that I have given the matter a great deal of thought'. So the lady left, without feeling insulted and I breathed a big sigh of relief. No harm done, career and marriage safe. But this extraordinary case illustrates some of the perils associated with status and power.

Case 3 – A member of my department complained to me that he was being sexually harassed by a female member of staff. I strongly suspected that he had encouraged her, but I dutifully referred his complaint to HRM. The unhelpful advice I got from the HR manager was 'Tell him that is not a tax-deductible benefit'.

Case 3 was of course potentially serious and any form of harassment in a project team has to be stamped out. In some cases you will be the only person to whom the victim can turn for effective support, and my advice is that you take every complaint very seriously. Make it clear that you have sympathy for the victim, and then seek advice from HRM. I hope that your HRM department will take the complaint more seriously than the flippant HRM manager in my case (who incidentally was later asked to leave the company for a variety of other reasons).

Managing Stress and Your Personal Health

ACUTE AND TEMPORARY STRESS

Most management jobs involve stress, which sometimes goes with excitement and drive. Stress is fine in small doses. It could be said that there is no success without stress. Stress only does serious damage to your health when it becomes chronic and continuous. Stress is often linked to phases in the project life cycle. If you are able to recognise that, you will be able to look ahead and know that some causes of stress are temporary and will eventually disappear. So no need for despair there.

Some stress can even be enjoyable. Most project managers accept that their position of responsibility will cause them to work during unsocial hours from time to time. From my own career I remember having to remain at work for three days and nights without a break just to ensure that a project was shipped on time.

Many years later I was duty manager on 24-hour call for a 37,000 sq ft office building in central London, which resulted in occasional call-outs at night from my St Albans home. On one of those occasions (the last night of a Christmas holiday) I had just retired to bed with a bad cold after a hot bath and soothing drink when my bedside telephone delivered an urgent message. It was snowing hard outside. I drove nearly 20 miles along icy but deserted roads to the offices and was able to take action that allowed everyone to return to work normally the next day, preventing one day's idle time for hundreds of staff. And, in spite of my interrupted night and illness I was there early to welcome staff, explain the emergency and ensure that everything went as smoothly as possible for them. Of course that was stressful, but it was also satisfying and exciting. And the stress was short-lived and I enjoyed the resulting praise. The point here is that my stress was temporary and I soon got over it.

CHRONIC STRESS

Suppose that the following story represents a typical day in your office. You constantly have a queue of people asking questions and your emails are too numerous even to contemplate. Whilst you are trying to deal with those problems, your telephone rings and presents you with yet another problem. Then you get a call to go and see your boss immediately. That kind of existence leads to chronic stress and can cause you to stop functioning rationally, eventually leading to a possible breakdown. So what can you do in those circumstances?

Provided you are not a one-man band, your recourse is to delegate some of your duties. You might be able to do that by looking down into your organisation and picking one or more individuals whom you could promote. They can still be working supervisors, but you will be able to delegate work or problems to them.

Have a look at your organisation and count how many people report directly to you. If the number is more than (say) five, your span of control might be too wide (for more on span of control see Chapter 31 and Graicunas (1937)). I once took over a failing department from a manager who had 19 people reporting directly to him, with no management structure whatsoever. The poor fellow did not stand a chance and was out of his depth. Worse, complaints were constantly being made about his department and some serious mistakes were made. My first act on taking over was to appoint two supervisors from those 19 people. I was very careful to choose people who performed well and who were popular with their colleagues. Then I had an efficient and manageable department.

Your Career

Too many years ago loyalty to one's employer was seen as paramount to career progression. But in modern times, mergers, acquisitions and company failures have changed most of that. The business world carries risk and uncertainty and is dynamic. The same applies to government organisations. So wherever you work, you must reflect from time to time about your position in your company and your career. Ask yourself some questions.

- Are you being suitably rewarded?
- Is your employer prosperous or do you work for a company that is in any kind of financial stress that could put your future at risk?
- Have you been unfairly overlooked for promotion more than once?
- Were you given inadequate recognition for a major project success?
- Are you continuing to develop in your career and are you given the management support essential to managing your projects?
- Are you respected and placed in a position of trust with freedom to make important decisions?
- Do you like your boss, and does he/she inspire you with ideas or relate experiences that enrich your own fund of knowledge?
- Are you happy in your job?

In other words, are you in the right job? Provided that your age, health, family and the economic climate allow, you must always be prepared to seek another post if you feel that would be the only way to advance you career.

References and Further Reading

Graicunas, V.A. (1937), 'Span of control', in Gulick, L. and Urwick, L. (eds), *Papers of the Science of Administration*, New York: Institute of Public Administration.

Gurek, B.A. (1985), *Sex and the Workplace*, San Francisco, CA: Jossey-Bass.

Lock, D. (2013), *Project Management*, 10th edn, Farnham: Gower.

Melhuish, A. (1992), 'Executive health', in Lock, D. (ed.), *Handbook of Management*, 3rd edn, Aldershot: Gower.

PMI (2008), *A Guide to the Project Management Body of Knowledge (PMBOK® Guide)*, 4th edn, Newtown Square, PA: Project Management Institute.

Shontell, A. (2010), '15% of women have slept with their bosses – and 37% of them got promoted for it', in *Business Insider*. Available at: http://www.businessinsider.com/sex-is-killing-the-workplace-2010-8 [accessed 8 May 2012].

30 *Managing Daily Routines: A Day in the Life of a Project Manager*

SAM BARNES

Editorial Comment (DL/LS)

We hope you will enjoy reading this chapter on personal efficiency as much as we did. The format differs slightly from other chapters in this Handbook, so a word of explanation from us will help you to navigate this entertaining text. After his novel introduction, the author presents his chapter in the form of a personal project manager's diary that includes comments and practical advice to project managers about managing their daily routine. Sam works in the web development industry, so some of his advice is particularly relevant to those who work in that industry sector.

Introduction

Other chapters in this Handbook deal with managing individuals or attempting to improve team performance. But what about our own performance, from day to day, from hour to hour and from minute to minute? Team efficiency begins with the project manager. This chapter is about how we, as professional managers, should conduct our own daily routine so that our employers, our subordinates and all our other stakeholders get the best possible use of our time.

REVERIE

It's nine o'clock in the morning. Walking into the office, I'm pleased to notice that all the people working on the single project which I'm currently managing are already at their desks. They have their heads down, are clearly focused, and are obviously working hard and productively. I approach my own desk and see that someone has already made me a coffee. I sit down and look forward to my day.

After firing up my machine I find that I still have Inbox Zero from the previous day and so swiftly move on to check my project budget and schedule. As expected, we are within budget and on schedule. I walk around asking my team how they are doing, and they all smile and respond positively. I let my manager know that all is well. The morning passes quickly and pleasantly. I decide it's time for lunch.

After dining well at a local restaurant I answer a few emails, spend time working on internal processes and end the day happy to see that we are still on schedule and everyone has completed their timesheets accurately.

I pack up and leave for home with a spring in my step. My project management duties for the day are done. As I'm walking through the office heading for the exit I hear a very faint beeping sound and feel a tapping sensation on my head. Then – I wake up!

REALITY

My alarm is screeching at me like a banshee from hell and my cat is punching my face repeatedly to let me know it's feeding time. Cruel reality has struck. It would appear that my actual day of project management is just about to begin. The question is: will it go as smoothly as it did in my dream? If at this point you are not knowingly smirking, you are probably not a project manager.

One Day in the Life of a Project Manager

09:00 – THE RED PILL

It's nine o'clock in the morning. I'm a project manager running 12 separate web development projects for a company that runs a global platform, has over 14 million members, with a new member joining every four seconds.

My projects are all in different stages of their life cycles. Some are just starting, most are in development and one is due for launch today. These projects cover a variety of areas, including new member features on both desktop and mobile platforms, system performance, API development, financial security and even the brand-new company website. In total I have around 20 people to manage directly today, plus one agency and the opinions of 100 other people at the company.

When I arrive at my desk there is no coffee. I note that one of my key team members is not yet at his desk. The office cleaners did not empty my waste bin. This is no dream. It's reality and time to start another day.

09:05 – THE USUAL SUSPECTS

Fuelled by my breakfast banana and coffee (which I had to make myself) I open up the usual suspects on my machine. These include my to-do list, email client, team schedule, timesheets, instant messenger and our group chat software. Note that first item 'to-do list'. Every person in any office has one thing in common – their own personal to-do list. I must now take time out from my diary and explain more about personal to-do lists and how I use my own list to good effect.

To-do Lists

Everyone has their own to-do list. But the arrangement and effectiveness of those lists varies considerably from one person to another. Whilst many will try and enforce their own methods to keep track of their tasks, the truth is that there is no one best individual method. The right way is any way that works for you and enables you to keep on top of your workload.

However, putting this valid but clichéd answer aside, I must confess that when I see people maintaining to-do lists by using hundreds of Post-It notes randomly stuck on and around their desks, or simply scribbling on a notepad, I secretly want to sit them down and explain about these new things called computers and the Internet. I fantasise and need to explain how much more quickly these inventions allow us to capture and update actions; how resistant these tools are to illegible scribbles, the lack of any sense of priority, misplaced items and over-zealous office cleaners. I want to enthuse about the amount of time that can be saved by 'going digital'. But usually I'll just smile. Now here I have my chance.

Long ago, when I retired from digital production and joined the dark side of project management, one of the first things to hit me was the change in pace, context switching and sheer amount of things with which I had to cope and master. For several months I struggled to find a way to keep track of everything. That was before a mentor introduced me to GTD. After that, order emerged from the chaos that had been my world. GTD is short for the 'Getting Things Done' methodology created by David Allen (2001). There are several applications available on the Internet that you can use for compiling and managing to-do lists and some of these are available online free of charge. My own choice is a browser-based tool that allows me to manage my workload using a very basic interpretation of GTD. You can find a list of similar tools by searching for GTD online. Wikipedia gives some lists.

The full GTD methodology contains enough processes to fill several large books, but I use a super slimmed-down version that follows just three basic principles:

1. My to-do list is broken down into the three following categories:

    – next action
    – waiting for …
    – some day.

2. I have a self-imposed militant daily 'Inbox Zero' regime.
3. I adhere to the GTD rule that if something will take no longer than two minutes, I don't capture it as an action but just do it immediately.

What all this actually translates into is that every time I get an email, take a phone call or have a meeting I assess what my personal actions should be. Then I add these to my 'next actions' list. Of course I must also add the date on or before which I need to do each action. Once an action has been captured from an email in this way and transferred to my next actions list (which, of course, is a digital file), I transfer that email from my inbox to an organised folder for the relevant project.

If I am waiting for someone to get back to me or finish something, I'll have that in my 'waiting for' list, also with a date.

All those things that I should probably do some day, but are low priority (such as some internal work) will go into my 'some day' list. These low-priority items carry no date.

So, what is the result of using this GTD process? It means that at any given time I have no emails waiting in my inbox because all have been received, scanned and their actions captured. Every email is stored away in its project file. Now I have one to-do list that I can access quickly from anywhere and from any device.

Now that my readily accessible to-do list is prioritised, I can find clearly and quickly those actions which I have to do next. I also know who needs to get back to me in order to move all of my projects forward. Using the dates, my list self-organises itself into priority order, telling me what I need to do today and who I need to chase today for their actions or answers.

The main point of GTD is to be highly organised and reduce your stress levels. This is achieved by making sure you're not trying to retain any actions in your memory, but instead processing everything in one single place – which means you can go home each evening safe in the knowledge that you've missed nothing. Clearly that is far preferable to having notes written on scraps of paper. Can you really imagine that any large project (the 2012 Olympic Games for example) was managed using thousands of Post-It notes stuck all over a desk?

Whenever I explain this approach to anyone, it always strikes me how convoluted and time consuming it sounds and I do concede that in the beginning it takes quite a bit of getting used to and requires some discipline. But once it becomes second nature it takes absolutely no time at all, is incredibly efficient and can earn you a tenacious reputation for never letting any actions slip. Indeed, as my colleagues will testify, I like to tell people 'Once you go on my list, you don't come off it until you've completed your task'.

One Day in the Life of a Project Manager: Resumed

09:10 – TIME TO START ANNOYING PEOPLE

Until now the project teams have not heard a peep from me, but now it's time to start annoying them. A quick scan of my 'waiting for' list shows one item with a big red label saying 'Overdue by 1 day'. The head of user experience (UX) was meant to review some wireframes and provide feedback. I find my original email to him, hit 'reply' and explain politely that I need this feedback today – or we'll be behind schedule.

Also in my waiting list I can see that one of my own 'next actions' today is to provide the CEO with a website analytics report. This is something I added as a next action a month ago, but was unable to do until today owing to relevant report dates. I quickly run the report and send it to him. I tick this next action and cause it to vanish from my 'next actions' list, but I immediately add a new 'waiting for' action which says that the CEO needs to provide feedback on this report in a couple of days.

Now I check my calendar. I see that I have a meeting at 10am. I must get my project teams moving for the day before then. Glancing at today in the team schedule I remind myself briefly of who should be doing what, and mentally prioritise who I need to see first (which happens to be the team working on today's project launch).

09:15 – HURRICANE PROJECT MANAGER

I'm 15 minutes into my working day. For those not in project management, what happens next always seems to happen a little too early. But for a project manager with responsibility for multiple projects and teams this is the way it must be.

I walk around the department rounding up those on the launch project and usher them to the quality assurance (QA) area. Some grab their coffees, some a form of breakfast, one takes a last memorising glance at the article he was reading (which had nothing to do with our work). I round up one latecomer as he walks in though the office door, as I explain 'Sorry, it's launch day, we're having a catch-up, NOW!'

I begin by summarising where we are on this project, stressing the fact that we have to launch today. I explain that in order to do this we must go through a deployment to the staging environment, perform a round of testing (fixing any problems along the way), followed by a final deployment to production and another test. This process involves the lead developer, UX, QA and technical operations teams.

I set out the timeline that I want and the project needs. This involves passing all stage testing by lunchtime. So politely, but firmly, I ask everyone to hold off from disappearing to lunch until we hit this key point. Now I act dumb and don't react to the few who give each other sneaky glances as if to say 'Who does this guy think he is?' I could react, but that would only irritate and antagonise people at the time when I need them most. What I shall do however is to keep a close eye on them as it gets nearer lunchtime, using my project manager's metaphorical periscope – we see everything.

I pass over to the team asking if anyone has any concerns about the plan for the day and they discuss a few areas, but overall we sound good. I finish by asking everyone to let me know if anyone else requests their time today, in which case 'Send them to me!' For the next seven hours, I am the gatekeeper to this team. Try to steal them at your peril!

09:30–09:55 – GETTING EVERYBODY MOVING

For the next 25 minutes I hold several different project team catch-ups that all have the same format and aim (our position regarding the schedule and budget, plus any other news I have on the projects). I ask each team member 'How did yesterday go?', 'What are you aiming to achieve today' and 'Is anything currently blocking you that I can help with?'

Today I have four projects in their development (production) phase. Another two projects are in their technical specification phase. This is where I've already written the business case, high-level brief and functional requirements (what each project is expected to achieve) and received management sign-off. Today I want the UX and development teams on these projects to complete the technical specifications (setting out the how the solutions will be achieved along with time estimates). In my own experience at least, my involvement as project manager is at least as high in the beginning or end phases (see Figure 30.1).

Non-project managers would be surprised at just how many people you can set off on a full day of work in a relatively short amount of time. But as well as making sure you're on top of everything, one aim of the quick daily catch-up is just to get everyone focused and moving. However, it's crucial to recognise that a daily catch-up meeting is not always needed and can sometimes even be counter-productive. Only a naive project manager blindly follows a project management methodology to the letter – no matter what. Wise ones know when to break the rules.

I have a meeting in five minutes' time. That allows me just enough time to add the actions I picked up from my daily catch-ups to my 'next actions' list, grab a second coffee (which once again I have to get for myself).

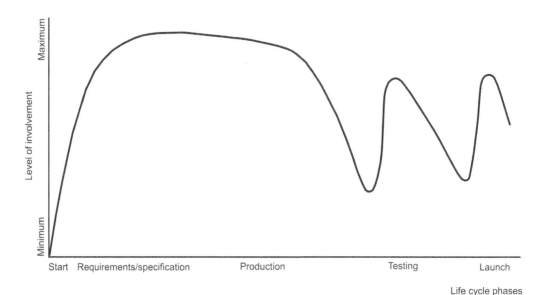

Figure 30.1 Level of this author's involvement as project manager over the life cycle of a single project

10:00 – MEETING THE BOSS

Clutching my latest printed reports and iPad I head to my manager's office with my fellow project managers. We spend the time going through the status of each project in progress and the schedule for the week. We each have a few people who are not yet fully utilised on some days, so we discuss tasks for them. We also have two people away sick today, and that is putting two project timelines in jeopardy.

Together we resolve these scheduling issues. Then we are each pressed to commit to deadlines for completing certain aspects of our work. These include:

- specifications finished and ready for sign-off;
- kick-off meetings;
- gaining clarification on various questions of scope from heads of department and the CEO;
- completing financial and admin-related tasks that are crucial to the company's finance department and end-of-year reporting.

Glancing quickly at my iPad and my to-do list I can see two items relating to my boss in my 'waiting for' list. Although I was expecting email replies back to these questions, I use this opportunity and ask for answers there and then. I get the answers that I needed and now I tick them off my list.

The boss also informs us of a few business-critical tasks that will need to be completed this week and several projects that need to be started. He knows we are busy. But as all good project managers are aware, there's always a way to fit in those business-critical tasks, even when that might seem impossible. As I said, there's always a way – but the skills of the project manager are needed to find that way.

10:30 – SMALL TASKS TIME

Getting back to my desk, I know that I have 30 minutes before my next meeting. So it's time to get some work done. I start by quickly scanning through my mails and pinging off a few replies, I check yesterday's timesheets to see if anyone incorrectly logged time under the wrong project which, of course, they did. I make corrections and send off a quick message asking them to log their times correctly today. Most people will respond positively to a polite respectful request rather than a tirade – that might seem obvious, but too many middle managers just don't appreciate this.

I move on to some other tasks such as:

- closing off projects with all relevant documentation and reporting;
- booking meetings with department managers to discuss requirements for several projects at their early stages of requirements gathering;
- talking to colleagues in different departments about questions they've asked me;
- chasing the lead architect for some feedback on how I intend to run a project and who I want to be involved;
- reviewing and replying to items logged in our internal ticketing system (both platform new feature requests and reported bugs). Incidentally, I have my own views about how to deal with bug reports, but they are outside the scope of this chapter.

Having launched a project last week, I send our business intelligence manager an email to ask for the latest results on that project, and then book a retrospective meeting (post-mortem) with the project team. This is where we'll review how the project went, the good, the bad and ultimately what lessons we learned.

It's important always to review how projects went, but it's even more important that any post-mortem results in distinct actions with somebody assigned who will help future projects. Post-mortem meetings where everyone pats each other on the back or tries to blame everyone else are pointless if there are no clear resulting actions. The real focus should be on trying to replicate the parts that went well, perhaps by revising the project life cycle process to incorporate, or taking clear steps to ensure what went wrong doesn't happen again.

As a project manager, if you come out of a post-mortem with no actions written down for which someone is now responsible, I believe you have not done your job in that meeting. You simply had the meeting to tick boxes, which is very naughty indeed!

11:00 – PROJECT KICK-OFF MEETING

Kick-off meetings can take many forms depending on your type of business. As all project managers know, when one project is closed off another will begin (unless you have the misfortune to work in a commercial company where the order book is empty). Now it's time for my next project kick-off meeting.

Best practice is to always follow up every kick-off meeting with a documented summary of the key points and get an informal nod from everyone involved. This ensures that everyone's expectations are aligned. That is the best possible foundation for a happy project. To get back to my kick-off meeting in particular, the whole team is attending plus my manager.

Everyone has a copy of the latest version of the specification document. I sent that out to everyone a few days ago so they could read through it. I start by quickly running through the team set-up, explaining who will be leading the project from a production perspective.

I run through the business case put forward for this project, which sets out what are we trying to achieve as a business by undertaking this project, including the commercial as well as the technical arguments. I believe that project managers should ensure wherever possible that their teams always have a strong commercial understanding of their projects, not just the technical aspects. Too often project managers believe their project teams have no little interest in the business side of things, but in most cases they are wrong. The only result of hiding commercial details is to isolate teams from the rest of the business and limit the possible solutions the team may come up with. In other words, if you tell creative or technical people what solution to deliver, they'll deliver exactly that and no more. But if you can explain the desired commercial or strategic aims, they might well have some of their own ideas that will deliver the same or better results in a more efficient and elegant way – not to mention the positive effect on morale.

Once I've run through the business case I proceed with the functional requirements. Then it's time to invite discussion. This is when everyone on the project has a chance to ask questions or put forward ideas. I try to answer any questions thrown at me and make sure to note down any that I can't, promising to find out the answer and get back to them. It's never wrong to admit that you don't know an answer to a question, as long as you commit to finding out the answer and delivering it. I'll also make a note of any areas of concern that the team has and anything at all that could affect the project (from new ideas to possible risks).

I conclude the kick-off meeting by defining the next steps, which for this project require the team to begin work now on the technical specification. I tell them that I expect to see the completed specification within one week and ask how they feel about this deadline. Everyone think that's reasonable. I utter the words 'Ok, let's crack on' and everyone leaves the room.

You can read more about the conduct of kick-off meetings in Chapter 34.

11:30 – PROJECT SPECIFICATION, BUDGET AND SCHEDULE SUBMISSION

With many small tasks out of the way I decide to dedicate the next 30 minutes to a single project that is with me to move forward. The development, UX and QA teams have finished their technical specification parts of the project, along with time estimates.

Now it's over to me to ensure that it's solid, wrap it up, put a bow on it and get it approved so that we can make a start on it. I have to review everything that's been added to make sure all functional requirements have been dealt with, ensure the risk register is complete, see that all tasks have been estimated and all questions and comments have been resolved, in-scope and out of scope areas clearly defined.

Having considered all that I need to for this project, I create a complete breakdown of the project tasks and estimates and fill in the all important final number that translates to a cost. I tick off the task to 'Compile the specification, estimate and schedule for project X and submit for approval' on my next action list and add an item to my 'waiting for' list to get feedback or approval on this from management.

A Note About Project Estimates and Budgets

The only estimates which the teams have added are for their specific tasks. In the project management land of dreams simply totalling these numbers would result in the project budget. However, that is far from reality. The reality is that a project manager must at this point bring all of his/her experience into play, including some seasoned psychic crystal ball powers, in order to create a realistic budget that will cater for a variety of project factors including:

- project complexity;
- skill and experience level of the team;
- size of the team and the number of departments involved;
- whether the solution is similar to a previous one or venturing into unknown territory;
- history of estimation accuracy from those on this project team;
- stakeholders involved and how they tend to behave on projects;
- project management time needed;
- third party services needed;
- number of development, test-and-deploy cycles (if using a phased release approach);
- contingency allowances;
- a million other factors.

12:15 – CHECKING UP ON THE PROJECT LAUNCH

Throughout the whole morning, whilst doing everything else I've had one eye and one ear on the team responsible for today's project launch. My aim to have all testing wrapped up by lunchtime is of course still my target.

They've been busy deploying to staging and running through the QA test plans. My heart has skipped a few beats as I heard various expletives from both QA and developer. There have been problems – there always are – but it's better to expect them than to be surprised by them. Even NASA famously expects to have 'a glitch on every mission'.

Periodically I've asked various team members how it's going and received a myriad of responses, but generally we seem to be okay.

I spy one team member making all the signs that he's about to head off for lunch and have to stop him until I'm sure we're on target. This is never a nice thing to do but it is sometimes necessary to be the bad guy or the 'company man'. I grab the hungry person and usher the team over to one desk for a quick status report.

The report I get is that testing is almost complete, but probably won't be finished by 12:30. I say that it would make all our lives better if we get it done before lunch. The hungry people look slightly disheartened but everyone agrees and continues with haste.

By 12:45 I get the final nod from the lead QA engineer that all testing has now been completed with all reported issues marked as resolved on retest. Hurrah!

I thank the team for sticking around to get the job done and tell people I'll see them in an hour to start the project launch. I send a quick email to the stakeholders informing them we're ready to 'make it go live' after lunch and just need final approval to do so. I get a prompt positive response.

Now we can all eat.

14:00 – PROJECT LAUNCH

With everyone back from lunch I give the nod to launch the project and the team gets to work.

Days before this point I had been doing work that the production team rarely see, preparing the business for the launch. This essentially means constant communication to the other parts of the business that need to know what the new project is, how it will affect them and making sure they have time to prepare anything they need to in time for launch (anything from user guides for their respective teams, to email campaigns informing our users what the new feature is and how to use it). These things take time and coordination, and 'coordination' is every project manager's middle name, alongside 'leader', 'control freak' and 'potential scapegoat'.

If I've done my job well the business will have known for weeks, if not months, that we're going live today and I just walk around letting everyone know.

The person at the end of the line hits the final button and we go live. Before announcing it to the business, the whole team (including myself) start testing the feature in the live environment. But after five minutes no one can break it and everyone starts to relax slightly. We look golden, but I can't relax just yet.

I let the whole business know we're live and the marketing department say they're ready to send out a campaign tomorrow. Why not right now you may ask? Well because that's just asking for trouble and the marketing manager is wise enough to know, where possible, that it's best to wait a certain amount of time to allow for any problems to be reported before the fanfare. After all, we are a professional outfit. But it's just not possible to test something as well with a project team of five as well as it is with 14 million users in a few hours. It there are any problems, they will find them.

Now that we're live I create a quick 'next action' on my to-do list to check with the reporting team on key metrics tomorrow – both core business metrics and numbers specifically relating to this project. These points are aligned to the success criteria, and we have to check whether the project is affecting any core numbers positively or negatively, and whether the project is changing the specific numbers as we expected.

But for now I'm a happy project manager and tomorrow I'll formally close the project down. So now I take some time to prepare the appropriate documentation.

15:00 – TIME TO DO EVERYTHING ELSE

For the next two hours I perform a plethora of tasks. The one thing a project manager must be good at is multitasking. I always find that when a project manager lists out in detail what they've done in any given day to someone not in project management it results in a widening of the eyes. This is often because people working on the production side of projects naturally develop an insular view on what a project manager does; I know because I used to be on that side of the fence.

A good project manager handles not only the big things like launches, but also the little jobs that go unnoticed to most people. Those small tasks can make a huge difference to a business and would certainly be missed if they were suddenly removed. I'm about to do some of these things with the next few hours of my day, examples of which are:

- project update meeting with other departments to let them know about upcoming, in progress and soon-to-launch projects;
- work with the finance department to ensure all of the time logged last month is correctly categorised so that the business is capitalising as much as possible;
- look at the entire project schedule for the next few months with my fellow project managers to identify potential bottlenecks or gaps and decide how best to deal with them;
- sign off people's holidays;
- create monthly timesheet reports for all time logged;
- prepare slides for the next company meeting, where each department gives a summary of the previous month's work and results;
- write weekly management reports that give project status snapshots for the executive management team and board of directors;
- write up project retrospectives and distribute these across the team;
- create all documents and online elements required to make a project live;
- review and update project progress tools such as Gantt charts or Kanban boards;
- provide support to junior project managers;
- answer the daily barrage of questions from your own and other departments (in person, by mail, instant message or chat room);
- attend a meeting with the CEO and my boss to get the initial brief on a brand-new project idea;
- deal with all purchase orders, order forms and invoices from external suppliers;
- communication with those external suppliers;
- chase up people on non-project specific actions assigned to them, such as those derived from retrospective meetings;
- write user guides for the more complicated features delivered as part of projects;
- update the historical project analysis documents with previously launched project data;
- revise the specification document template so that it's easier to work with for all involved;
- discussing the latest designs, wireframes or prototypes that the UX team have produced to ensure they're aligned with the project's overall scope;
- negotiate with stakeholders over scope changes, document those approved and update schedules, budgets and communicate to the project team.

Those who manage projects know that the tasks listed above and described elsewhere in this chapter are what we do each day. To any non-project manager this probably seems like quite a lot. It might not seem exciting, but it is important and a skill in itself to be able to manage all these tasks well.

17.00 – TRACKING TODAY AND PREPARING FOR TOMORROW

At the end of every day I like to follow the same routine. I'll start by making sure my own timesheets are complete, after all there's nothing worse than berating someone for forgetting to complete their timesheet only for you to be caught doing the same. Part of being a project manager is to set an example.

I'll then move onto a review of my inbox, always making sure that I end the day with Inbox Zero, followed by a review of my to-do list, updating everything as necessary so that when I get in the next day, all I need to concern myself with are the things that are tagged overdue or today.

If I have any meetings first thing in the morning I'll prepare for those by either printing out what I need to take or just reading through anything I need to.

Not needing to run around in the morning is a blessing for project managers whose mornings are often already busy enough. In general, I aim to leave the office without any loose ends or the need to rush around in the morning.

17:30 – TIME FOR HOME

For the purposes of this chapter I'm going to say that at this time it's time to pack up my things and head home.

I would place a large bet that most people reading this will be chuckling and thinking 'I wish' at the thought of leaving bang on time, but I genuinely believe that if any employee is regularly having to work extra hours, then it's often a sign that they either need help or are simply too stretched, as opposed to just being incredibly dedicated. Please don't walk past such people. Identify those who might need help, be nice and go and have a quick friendly chat with them, perhaps you can help them. A disgruntled or burned out employee is no good to anyone. As a project manager (whether it says so in your official job description or not) I believe it's part of your remit to keep an eye on your colleagues' well-being.

Of course I do my fair share of late ones. This goes with the job. There are also the odd late night or weekend work sessions, where you make a point of telling everyone how productive you are as if this is some kind of revelation (of course I do this too) but right now, and to leave it on a happy note, I'm leaving the office, tired but safe in the knowledge I did my job well today.

My day of project management is now over, it's time to get home and feed my violent cat.

References and Further Reading

Allen, D. (2001), *Getting Things Done*, London: Piatkus Books Ltd.

Blanchard, K. and Johnson, S. (1983), *The One Minute Manager*, London: HarperCollins.

Taylor. P. (2009), *The Lazy Project Manager: How to be Twice as Productive and Still Leave the Office Early*, Oxford: Infinite Ideas.

31 *Management Theorists of the Twentieth Century*

DENNIS LOCK

This chapter lists some of the many observers and scholars whose work over the last century has affected our thinking about managing people who work in industry and in projects. The key word here is *people*, to accord with the subject of this Handbook. Thus I have generally excluded the many industrialists, engineers, inventors, scheduling experts and entrepreneurs who, although their names might be remembered in connection with great products, projects and other achievements, have been concerned more with *things* than with *people*.

Introduction

Over the thousands of years of recorded human history there has been no shortage of people offering advice on how we should behave in our working and family lives. It is not entirely by accident that people of most religious faiths work for six days in each week and reserve the seventh for their Sabbath day of rest and prayer. If only it were the same day of each week for all faiths we would be spared some communication problems in international projects, but that's another story.

Here we must at least mention and pay brief tribute to those who, although not in any sense management theorists, have through their active or passive endeavours greatly improved the way in which people are treated politically, socially and at work. Many even gave their lives in their pursuit for justice. The Tolpuddle Martyrs, the suffragette movement, Martin Luther King, Nelson Mandela are just a few of the hundreds of people who have influenced our attitudes to, and treatment of other people. Their influence has greatly improved the way in which people in the civilised world (including project managers) interact with workers and other stakeholders regardless of their race, religion, sex or political persuasion. However, in this chapter I am considering specifically those theorists who have studied people from the particular aspect of managing them at work.

So one question facing me when I wrote this chapter was where should I begin? The Greek philosophers? The Romans? Macchiavelli or more modern times? Clearly I had to set practical limits. So I have chosen to begin with the early twentieth century, when there was an explosion of interest in studying people at work, particularly in the US. At the beginning of this period the emphasis was more on productivity and manufacturing efficiency than on consideration for the well-being of the people who were being observed, although there were exceptions.

Pareto: An Early Economist with an Interest in Demographics

Vilfredo Frederico Pareto (1848–1923) was an Italian whose wide interests embraced civil engineering, politics, economic and sociology. During his later life he lived and lectured on economics in Switzerland. His study of official Italian statistics led him to the discovery that 80 per cent of the nation's wealth (measured by land) was owned by only 20 per cent of the population. He argued that this ratio could be applied to many other situations, particularly relating to social issues such as class and politics. Thus the sharing of political power through democracy did not fit his theories because he believed more in the totalitarian state, with an elite top layer (Mussolini was greatly influenced by Pareto's observations).

For us in management, the 80/20 ratio of distribution has become known and widely used as Pareto's Law or the Pareto Principle, in which 80 per cent of any 'population' can be regarded as the 'insignificant many', whilst the remaining 20 per cent holds the 'significant few'. This is also known as the 80/20 rule. One application is in inventory control, where it can be assumed with some confidence that 80 per cent of the items held in stock by quantity represent only 20 per cent of the total inventory value (and conversely 80 per cent of the total inventory value is represented by only 20 per cent of number of items in stock).

The 80/20 rule has many other applications for modern management (for example in salary distribution over an organisation) and suggests that, for the most efficient control effect, management attention should always be directed at the significant few items rather than the insignificant many. That, of course, is somewhat similar to the practice of management by exception.

The First Industrial Observers

In the first years of the twentieth century most of the work done by management theorists was directed at increasing production, particularly in machine shops and assembly bays. Time and motion study became the vogue, and earned distrust from the workers because their interests were often seen as secondary to those of industry and company profits. From closely watching how people performed their jobs, with clipboards and stopwatches as their principal tools, these observers developed standard times (often measured only in seconds) that people were expected to achieve during their daily work. Those who managed to do better than the standards were deemed worthy to be paid a bonus in addition to their hourly wages, so creating a supposed incentive to work harder and faster,

Frederick Winslow Taylor (1856–1915) was foremost in this group. He was president of the American Society of Mechanical Engineers but he always appeared to attract controversy and dissent. He studied not only the productivity of people in precise detail (time and motion study), but also speeds at which machines were able to cut metal. He had the concept of finding the optimum working practice, which he called 'the one best way' (Kanigel, 1997). Taylor and his authoritarian methods caused unrest and distrust among workers, who (with justification) saw Taylor's motives aimed solely at increasing output and company profits with too little regard for their welfare or opinions. However, his influence was substantial and international and he has been called 'the father of scientific management'.

Henry Gantt (1861–1919) was an American mechanical engineer who worked with Taylor at Midvale Steel and Bethlehem Steel, where Taylor was particularly interested in the most efficient 'feeds and speeds' of machine tools. Gantt was particularly fond of using charts in many forms to help him, factory managers and supervisors to understand better how operations were being performed against targets. Of course it was he who was responsible for the now ubiquitous bar chart (Gantt chart) that is used by project managers to display their schedules.

An Increasing Interest in People Rather than Tasks

THE GILBRETHS

Frank Gilbreth (1868–1924) worked with his wife Lillian (1878–1972) and they (like Taylor) were also Americans interested in increasing efficiency of production. Frank began as a contractor in the building industry, and found himself examining ways of not only increasing output in bricklaying but also making the job easier for the workmen. So unlike Taylor he was interested not only in increasing output but also in making the work easier. The Gilbreths founded their own management consultancy (surely one of the first?) and studied working methods in both manual and clerical occupations. Frank even studied and improved the way in which surgeons and nurses worked together in surgical operating theatres.

Frank served during the First World War, during which his skills were used in teaching troops how to dismantle and reassemble small arms in battlefield conditions. In civilian life he was particularly interested in observing, timing and even filming the motions of workers. He identified 17 basic human motions (such as 'grasp' and 'hold') which he called 'therbligs' (an approximate reverse spelling of his own name). So any work could be described, analysed and timed in terms of a combination of the therbligs involved. He divided his therbligs into two groups, which he called effective and ineffective (today we might say those tasks that add value for cost, and those which add cost without adding value). For example, 'assemble' is an effective therblig but 'avoidable delay' is ineffective.

The Gilbreths showed more concern for the whole person than just the stopwatch timing of operations practised by Taylor. One has to admire Lillian particularly for her achievements (including high academic awards) in a world where prejudice against women at work was the norm.

MARY PARKER FOLLETT

Mary Parker Follett (1868–1933) was another of those rare women to achieve distinction in a man's world. She suffered from cruel discrimination just because of her sex (a famous university reportedly refused to award her doctorate degree simply because she was a woman). However she later achieved recognition to the extent that she even became a consultant to President Theodore Roosevelt on organisational management issues in government departments. She was a sociologist and management consultant, so her studies were far removed from mechanistic work study. Her concern was organisational theory and the behaviour of people in organisations (including matrix structures). Although she was yet another American, her influence spread to Europe and she lectured in Britain. She was clearly a remarkably tenacious and talented woman whose work influenced many later theorists. Where Taylor has become known as the 'father of scientific management', Mary Parker Follet is acknowledged by some as its mother.

ELTON MAYO

Elton Mayo (1880–1949) was born in Australia and began his career as an academic at the University of Queensland. However, he moved to America, eventually to work at Harvard. So he became yet another person involved in the advance of management theory in America. Mayo is now remembered particularly for his observations of workers at the Hawthorne Plant of the Western Electric Company, near Chicago in a series of experiments conducted around 1930.

One of his most famous experiments was an extended series of observations of workers in a relay assembly room (for those who are not technically minded, relays are electrical switching devices). All or most of these workers were women. Their output was measured by the numbers of relays which they managed to assemble within each measurement timeframe. Mayo and his assistants made several incremental changes to the working conditions, such as lighting levels, timing of rest breaks and the payments of incentives. He invited (and got) cooperation from the women by asking for their suggestions.

Analysis of the results showed that productivity increased even when changes (such as lighting levels) were reversed. This has since led to recognition of the phenomenon known as the Hawthorne Effect, which indicates empirically that there can be a positive result in people's performance simply because they are being observed and consulted.

Greater Interest in Personality and Self-motivation

MASLOW AND HIS HIERARCHY OF NEEDS

One person who was concerned particularly with what motivates people was Abraham Maslow (1908–1970). He identified a 'hierarchy of needs' that motivate different people's

Figure 31.1 A very basic display of Maslow's hierarchy of needs

actions (Maslow, 1954). This hierarchy has been represented diagrammatically in a number of forms, but the classic version is shown, greatly simplified, in Figure 31.1.

At the most basic part of the hierarchy lie those needs that are associated with life and our very survival. These are the physiological needs that include the clean air that we need to breathe, food, water and so on.

At the next, second level up come more needs that are also fairly basic, associated with safety and security. This means not only physical safety, but also economic security, such as having some savings to act as a cushion against expenditure, job security and the promise of a pension in later life. These needs are clearly strong motivators, or put another way, issues that can cause anxiety and worry if their provision is threatened.

Moving further up the pyramid of needs brings us to the belonging needs, which include the need for friendship generally, and for family love. This clearly has relevance in projects in melding teams together. We probably can all think of a few exceptions, people we have known who do not seem to have these needs.

At the fourth level in the hierarchy come the esteem needs. These needs drive our ambition to succeed and earn self-esteem. Writers love the self-esteem that comes from seeing their work published, irrespective of the financial rewards – trust me on this one.

The highest level of needs, which Maslow called self-actualisation needs, are more esoteric and difficult to define. They can be quite different according to the abilities, morality and personality of the individual. These needs generally (but not always) only come into play when all or most of the lower needs have been satisfied. Many exceptions are evident throughout history and religion where people deprived of more basic needs still strive to satisfy these higher needs. Thus self-actualisation needs differ very much according to the circumstances and personality of the individual. They can be summarised as striving by the individual for self-improvement to attain the highest level of fulfilment, performance or moral conduct.

Maslow went far beyond the simple summaries presented here and the subject is complex. Not only does the balance of these needs vary from one person to another, but they also change throughout the life of the individual. To complicate things further, these needs can also be applied to groups of people who share common circumstances.

HERZBERG'S MOTIVATIONAL THEORIES

Frederick Herzberg (1923–2000) was another American psychologist who specialised in motivational factors. Hertzberg's outcome has been called the dual structure theory because (unlike Maslow) he chose to display his factors not in a hierarchy, but in two different sets. He labelled these 'motivator factors' and 'hygiene factors' (Figure 31.2). He also gave the hygiene factors the alternative names 'maintenance factors' or 'environmental factors'.

He arrived at his lists after interviewing about 200 engineers and accountants. This choice of subjects led to subsequent criticism that he studied only professional workers, but that should not concern us because most of the workers on projects are professionals of one kind or another.

Herzberg considered both sets of factors from several viewpoints. He found that the motivational factors could result in causing the individual's satisfaction in varying

Motivators	Hygiene factors

Sense of achievement
Recognition
The work itself
Responsibility
Status
Promotion opportunities
Personal growth
	Pay and benefits
	Technical supervision
	Company policy and administration
	Interpersonal relationships with
	    subordinates, peers and
	    supervisors
	Job security
	Working conditions
	Personal life

Figure 31.2   Human motivational and job satisfaction factors according to Herzberg

degrees, and at the lowest level (when the motivators were absent) no satisfaction at all. However, their absence would not cause dissatisfaction. They are all true motivators, particularly associated with the work.

The absence of a hygiene factor could cause dissatisfaction. However, by themselves the hygiene factors are not motivators and neither do they cause satisfaction. They are connected more with the working environment. One interesting point is that pay is included among the hygiene factors, so Hertzberg found that by itself it is not a motivator.

MCGREGOR'S THEORY X AND THEORY Y

Douglas McGregor (1906–1964) was an American theorist and lecturer who was interested in what motivates people at work. He described two different kinds of people, at extreme ends of a personality scale. At one end of this scale lies the person whose personality and behaviour can usually be expected to fit Theory X, whilst at the other is the individual who satisfies Theory Y. These theories are described through the eyes of a notional manager, and the personality and motivation of the manager is a reflection of his perception of the subordinate. This should become clearer in the following explanation.

In Theory X the subject person is seen as being lazy and lacking in initiative. This person will avoid work if possible and must be driven with force or threats of punishment to perform as required. The person has little ambition, but Maslow's need for security is high. There have been managers who attribute all or most of their subordinates with these characteristics, and this leads them to adopt an authoritarian management style. We might call them bullies now.

The person who exactly fits Theory Y loves work, is regarded as ambitious, has great initiative and will solve problems without direction. The Theory Y manager, who credits subordinates with these personal qualities, will treat them accordingly, leading to a participative management style.

Of course these styles are two extremes, and in practice people can behave or hold beliefs that can lie along a continuum between them. Further, managers' perceptions of subordinates can change or be influenced by outside factors from one day to another.

There is a very practical account of these theories and their application online at http://www.businessballs.com.

THE BLAKE AND MOUTON MANAGERIAL GRID

Some management theorists have always had a particular fondness for grids, in which various properties are displayed in four (or occasionally more) divisions of a square.

Marketing people will all be very familiar with SWOT analysis, where market **S**trengths, **W**eaknesses, **O**pportunities and **T**hreats are displayed, often in grid quadrants, to assist their strategy and decision making.

Every competent project manager should be familiar with the grid used to describe and display the significance or ranking of project risks. This grid, in its simplest form categorises each risk as:

- high impact/high probability of occurrence (the most severe form of risk);
- high impact/low probability;
- low impact/high probability;
- the least serious case of low impact/low probability.

However, here we are concerned principally with people, and the grid that stands head and shoulders above the rest in this context is Blake and Mouton's managerial grid.

Robert Blake (1918–2004) and Jane Mouton (1930–1987) were interested particularly in leadership styles and during consultancy work developed their managerial grid (Blake and Mouton, 1964). The concept is that a person's style of leadership can be represented by placing a cross at an appropriate spot on the grid. The process is similar to specifying the location of a place on a map or atlas by giving the map coordinates. The managerial grid has obvious uses for consultants or others who need to compare or assess different managers working in an organisation. It could also be used as a tool in counselling a manager to improve leadership style.

The grid is shown in various guises but Figure 31.3 is an edited version of that which is commonly seen. It is convenient for a moment to talk about the grid as if it were a

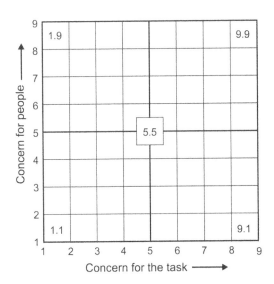

Figure 31.3 Blake and Mouton's managerial grid of leadership styles

graph with x and y axes. All the scaling is linear. The y axis represents the manager's concern for people, with the lowest point at position 1 and the highest at 9. The x axis is used to measure the manager's interest in accomplishing the project or task, again with 9 being the greatest value.

So a manager considered or observed to have the highest regard for people on a project team coupled with the maximum desire to get the job done would be placed in the 9.9 square on the grid. This person would be regarded as exhibiting the style of a good, rounded team leader.

A manager whose mark belongs in the bottom right-hand corner, at position 9.1, would be said to have a 'produce-or-perish' style in which the task is always given highest priority, pretty well regardless of consideration for the people involved.

A person seen as someone with a high regard for people, but with the minimum intention of forcing the pace of the task would score 1.9. This is the 'country club style' manager. The manager respects the team members and trusts that they will do a good job.

A weak manager in every sense is the person who fails to lead and has little regard for either the task or the people involved. The score achieved by this manager at the extreme worst would be 1.1, and the style (if there could be said to be any style at all) is called 'impoverished'.

Henri Fayol

Henri Fayol (1841–1925) appears to have been ahead of his time in management theory. Born in Turkey, he spent most of his life in France. He was a mining engineer before becoming a management theorist. Unlike other theorists, he offers direct, specific advice, much of which still has great practical force for project managers (and managers generally) today. Although he published his work in 1916, his book was written in French, which might explain why it did not get the international exposure and recognition it deserved until the English edition appeared much later in 1949 (Fayol, 1949).

Fayol identified the following five primary management functions:

1. Planning;
2. Organising;
3. Commanding;
4. Coordinating;
5. Controlling.

Although one can argue that the last three of these functions are not mutually exclusive, and we would now include the most important function of all, which is communicating, it has to be recognised that Fayol's five functions bear some resemblance to the steps needed to manage a modern project. But Fayol went much farther. He listed 14 principles of management, many of which we now take for granted:

1. *Specialisation of labour* – In short this means matching a person's skills to each task, which also allows better opportunity for skills to be developed through experience and practice.
2. *Authority* – A manager's right to issue orders and expect them to be obeyed.

3. *Discipline* – This relates to respect for the organisation and its rules.
4. *Unity of command* – Each worker should report to only one boss. Not easy in a project matrix, but an ideal arrangement nonetheless.
5. *Unity of direction* – This requires that there should be one objective, with one plan, controlled by one manager. Might not always be possible in today's workplace, but it's a good principle.
6. *Subordination of individual interests* – The interests of the organisation take precedence over those of individual people or groups. Not popular with the trades unions, I suspect.
7. *Remuneration* – Fair pay.
8. *Centralisation* – This relates to the point in the organisation where decisions are made. Fayol thought there should be a balance between centralised and subordinates' decisions. I suppose we might call this a form of participative management.
9. *Scalar chain* – Today we would call this the line of command. Commands are sent down the lines and the managers expect to get feedback through the same communication channels on the results.
10. *Order* – All materials and people have their designated location. One might say a place for everything and everything in its place.
11. *Equity* – Fair treatment for people.
12. *Personnel tenure* – The idea that employees can look forward to a secure future in the organisation as a reward for good work. If only …
13. *Initiative* – Described here as the ability to form a plan and then make it happen.
14. *Esprit de corps* – Good harmony and relationships throughout the organisation.

Spanners

I have taken a small liberty with the title of this section, which summarises briefly two theorists who were interested in theories containing the word 'span'.

THE MANAGER'S SPAN OF CONTROL ACCORDING TO GRAICUNAS

V.A. Graicunas was born in Chicago in 1898, where he studied and graduated. He remained a US citizen all his life but his working years were spent in different countries in Europe. His activities during the Second World War are not public knowledge but might have led to his death in tragic circumstances in Moscow in 1947 as a victim of the cold war. He was greatly respected by other prominent theorists such as Lyndall Urwick, who helped publicise his work (Graicunas, 1937).

Graicunas was interested in organisation structures, and particularly in the number of people that any particular manager had as direct subordinates (which he called the manager's span of control). As soon as the number of these subordinates grew beyond two, Graicunas observed that control and communication became more difficult because the number of direct lines, indirect lines and more complex lines of communication increased exponentially as the span of control widened. This has since led to something called the 'rule of five' by some managers and others accept as the 'rule of seven', where the number is sometimes regarded as the maximum practical span of control. I have applied this theory myself when restructuring my own department and that case is described in Chapter 9. At that time I knew the rule, but did not know its source. Now I am wiser, and we should all be very grateful to Graicunas for his contribution to the theory of organisations.

ELLIOTT JAQUES AND HIS TIME SPAN OF DISCRETION

Elliott Jaques (1917–2003) was born and studied medicine and psychology in Canada. In the 1940s he moved to the UK, where he spent the remainder of his life. He is remembered partly for his work for Glacier Metal and the Metal Box Company. Although it is claimed that his work on organisational development remains influential, he is not prominent in the literature. He is credited with coining the term mid-life crisis, but I wonder how many people know that?

My interest in Jaques lies in his theory of the time span of discretion. Put simply this says that, other things being equal, a person's remuneration should be proportionate to the time intervening between the making of decisions expected in the role and the time when the impact of those decisions is typically realised or seen.

Put more simply, if a managing director makes a strategic decision affecting the company, it might be months or years before anyone can say that the decision was wise or unwise. On the other hand, if a cook in the restaurant of that same company makes a decision to add salt to a meal and gets it wrong, it will only be a matter of hours before the mistake is realised by the unsatisfied diners. So the CEO is worth a higher salary than the cook.

An engineer who makes a design error in a drawing could expect that several weeks or months would pass before the error is discovered in the factory or assembly process. However, if a factory worker drills a large hole in the wrong place and ruins the workpiece, the result of the wrong decision is immediately apparent.

Theoretically the time span of discretion could be used to compare and help grade the remunerative value of a number of jobs in an organisation. But the theory has to be applied with a great deal of caution. Once, when I was a management student and the time span of discretion was explained to us by an enthusiastic lecturer, I asked how it would apply to airline pilots. The embarrassment of that lecturer was apparent for all to see and for weeks afterwards, whenever we met face to face, he would mutter 'airline pilots' under his breath.

Nonetheless, it has to be seen that the time span of discretion theory can have value as part of deciding salary structures in some cases. But it can only ever be one component of that process.

Peter Drucker, John Humble and Management by Objectives

Peter Drucker (1909–2005) was an Austrian who, four years after moving to Britain in 1933 to escape Nazi Germany spent the remainder of his long life working in the US, later to achieve much fame as a management guru. He described the concept of management by objectives (MbO) in a book that covered wider areas of management (Drucker, 1954). John Humble (1926–2011), who was at one time a director of British management consultants Urwick Orr and Partners Limited, did much to introduce it to companies in the UK. I have a personal interest because I was involved peripherally in MbO in three ways:

1. As a junior manager for Honeywell Controls in the 1960s, where MbO was introduced informally with some success.
2. As a more senior manager working in a London company that attempted unsuccessfully to implement MbO in its complete form. That attempt failed when the company reorganised and thus destroyed the structure upon which MbO was being overlaid.
3. As editor of a book to which John Humble contributed, which led to my realisation that he was a very courteous man, enthusiastic and dedicated to his work (Humble, 1972).

In its fullest and purest form, MbO begins at the top of the organisation when the CEO or other senior manager defines or redefines the corporate objectives. One requirement of MbO is that every objective shall be quantified in some way, so that any change in performance over time can be measured quantitatively. Then, going down through the hierarchy the objectives of every manager and supervisor are evaluated and again quantified. This is a participative process, in which one-to-one manager/subordinate discussions take place so that objectives are not forced upon people, but are mutually agreed.

After a certain time, which might be several months, the company will arrive at the situation where the organisation is overlaid with these objectives, with the ideal case being that the sum of all the individual objectives will match the corporate objectives. This process can involve making certain that every relevant post has its job description checked and, where necessary, updated.

Once the framework of objectives has been established, managers are expected to be aware of them, strive to meet them, and thus improve their performance. At suitable intervals (typically every three months) the one-to-one meetings are repeated and the results assessed.

This is an iterative process that continues indefinitely, and one expects to see both individual and corporate performance improve as a result. However, in its most formal guise, the system can break down if the organisation is changed substantially. Used sensibly and informally, it forces communication between managers and their subordinates and can help greatly to improve personal and corporate performance.

I have repeated these accounts in different words in Chapter 38, in connection with developing competency.

The Quality Gurus

I don't want to go into too much detail about the work of the quality gurus in the last half of the twentieth century because most of their work was concerned with such things as statistical process analysis and total quality control – things and processes rather than people. Outstanding among these gurus were Crosby (1926–2001), Juran (1904–2008) and active into his nineties, and Deming (1900–1993). Those of us who drive automobiles today and take their reliability for granted owe much to the teachings of these quality gurus. I have omitted some other prominent names because they were more involved with process than with people. What these three named quality gurus have done is to shift the emphasis for achieving quality from only designers, quality control inspectors and checkers towards creating a quality culture throughout whole organisations. So everyone within a factory or project organisation of any mind has some personal responsibility for the quality of the product. Without the work of these quality gurus it is doubtful that we would have the effective range of ISO quality and environmental standards as we know them internationally today.

Conclusion

In this chapter I have concentrated on the theorists who worked earlier in the twentieth century. Some of their work has been supplanted by new theories or questioned by their successors but in general the early theorists were pioneers who laid the foundations for much of what takes place in management today. The early theorists tended to concentrate on the mechanics of production, but as time advanced the focus became more concentrated on people – how we think – how we are motivated – how we communicate and how we should be organised. Many new theorists have entered the field since and much of their work is described in other chapters throughout this Handbook. You will find many of their names in the index, and that will direct you to chapters where you can read more about their work and contribution to management thinking.

References and Further Reading

Blake, R. and Mouton, J. (1964), *The Managerial Grid: The Key to Leadership Excellence*, Houston, TX: Gulf Publishing Co.

Cirillo, R. (1978), *The Economics of Vilfredo Pareto*, Totowa, NJ: Frank Cass & Co.

Crosby, P.B. (1979), *Quality is Free: the Art of Making Quality Certain*, New York: McGraw-Hill.

Deming, W.E. (1986), *Out of the Crisis*, Cambridge, MA: MIT Press.

Drucker, P.F. (1954), *The Practice of Management*, New York: Harper & Row.

Fayol, H. (1949), *General and Industrial Administration*, London: Pitman. This is an English translation of the French edition, published in 1916.

Follett, M.P. (1949), *Freedom and Coordination*, London: Management Publications Trust.

Graicunas, V.A. (1937), 'Span of control', in Gulick, L. and Urwick, L. (eds), *Papers of the Science of Administration*, New York: Institute of Public Administration.

Handy, C. (1976), *Understanding Organizations*, Harmondsworth: Penguin.

Humble, J.W. (1972), 'Management by objectives', ch. 4 in *Director's Guide to Management Techniques*, 2nd edn, Lock, D. (ed.), London: Gower Press.

Humble, J.W. (1973), *How to Manage by Objectives*, New York: AMACOM.

Juran, J. and Godfrey, A.B. (eds) (1999), *Juran's Quality Handbook*, 5th edn, New York: McGraw-Hill.

Kanigel, R. (1997), *The One Best Way: Frederick Winslow Taylor and the Enigma of Efficiency*, London: Little, Brown and Co.

Macchiavelli, N. (1532), *The Prince*, modern English translation, by George Bull, (1961), London: Penguin.

Maslow, A. (1954), *Motivation and Personality*, New York: Harper & Row.

Mayo, G.E. (1933), *The Human Problems of an Industrial Civilization*, Boston, MA: Harvard Business School.

Mintzberg, H. (1973), *The Nature of Managerial Work*, New York: Harper & Row.

Peters, T. and Waterman, R.H. Jnr (1982), *In Search of Excellence*, New York: Harper & Row.

Sadler, P. (1998), 'Principles of management', ch.1 in Lock, D. (ed.), *Handbook of Management*, 4th edn, Aldershot: Gower.

32 *Team Development*

ELISABETH GOODMAN

All project teams, whether they are short- or long-lived, go through several stages of development, very much like those experienced by more permanent organisational teams. Although teams can reach high performance at some point in their lives, it is probably in the interest of all concerned (given the usual expectation that they will need to deliver to very tight timelines) that these stages of development should be accomplished as quickly, painlessly and effectively as possible. That is the subject of this chapter.

Introduction

This chapter draws on concepts and approaches described in this book and elsewhere, as well as on my own experience of working with project and organisational teams, to help team leaders and members understand the different stages of team development. Following from that, I describe how to accelerate the transition to achieve high performance as quickly as possible. The chapter also describes the different preferences and behaviours that team members might display, and how to draw on these differences for the benefit of the team and its work. The chapter ends by describing well-established learning techniques for using the knowledge and experience of individuals within and outside the team in team development.

Stages of Team Development

Tuckman and Jensen (1977) described four stages of team development, which are:

1. Forming;
2. Storming;
3. Norming;
4. Performing.

Stott and Walker (1995) offer a different, more bluntly worded alternative version that also gives some indication of what might be happening at each stage. Their stage sequence is:

1. Polite niceties;
2. Politicking;
3. Achieving;
4. Competence.

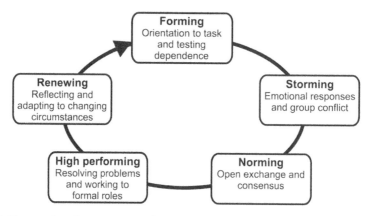

Figure 32.1 Team development cycle

My version of the team development sequence is shown in Figure 32.1, including five stages:

1. Forming – when team members are finding out about the overall goals and objectives and their roles within these.
2. Storming – when people's personalities and the dynamics of the relationships between them start to emerge, with the added influence of any worries and concerns.
3. Norming – the point at which the team is able to have open conversations, and settles into its pattern of work and relationships.
4. High performing – this is the stage when individual strengths really come to the fore, with plenty of energy, creativity, goodwill and a real sense of achievement. Now the team should be at its ideal stage, even to the extent that the collective team strength amounts to more than the sum of its parts.
5. Renewing – the time when the project team is coming to an end or transforming into a new team, ready for the next challenge.

The fifth (renewing) stage could also intervene at any point during a project team's life if it has to undergo a significant change in its goals, its membership or any other occurrence that affects its roles and relationships.

Although some project teams might continue working together through successive projects, the assumption in this chapter is that each project starts with a new team. Even when a team has become well established, adding only one new person can change the team dynamic, so that the team development cycle is either set back or restarted.

Accelerating the Transition to High Project Team Performance

Project managers clearly have a key role to play (and personal interest) in helping their teams get to high performance as quickly and painlessly as possible. Although, the ideal result would be to attain high performance from the start of the project, realistically some interaction must take place before this can happen. Figure 32.2 illustrates my own experience of how the different stages of team development typically correspond with

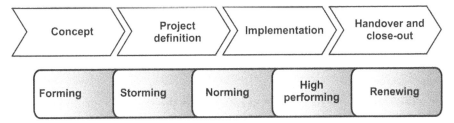

Figure 32.2 The stages of team development aligned to the project life cycle

the project life cycle (assuming here, of course, that the team actually does achieve the high-performing stage).

Blanchard et al. (2005) describe the behaviours that a leader might adopt in different situations. These can be translated to a project leader's role at each stage of team development. There are also other things that a project leader could usefully do to help each stage develop fully, and so pave the way for the next one.

TEAM LEADER BEHAVIOURS

Directive Behaviour

During the forming stage, team members expect to get clear information from the project leader on the goals of the project and on their roles. Team charters can be very useful here to help team members understand where they fit in. A face-to-face start-up meeting, with visible input from the team's sponsors, and some form of team-building exercise will also enable the forming stage to take place more fully and quickly. An external facilitator, experienced in team building, could be very helpful at this point.

Supportive Behaviour

During the storming phase, team members tend to worry about their positions within the team, and whether their views and ideas will be heard. Project leaders will do well at this stage to:

- devote personal time to individual members;
- give team members tasks that will foster interactions between them;
- steer discussions during team meetings to allow sufficient time and space for every team member to voice their ideas and opinions, whilst still maintaining focus on the way forward.

Participative Behaviour

Once the team has reached the norming stage, the leader will be expected to participate actively in the exchange of ideas and information alongside the team members. He/she may also have a specific role to play in achieving some of the team's tasks.

Delegatory Behaviour and Stakeholder Focus

At the high-performing stage, team members should be well immersed in their individual roles and the project plan should be in full swing. Now the project deliverables begin to emerge.

Clearly the team leader has to stay in touch with the stakeholders, to keep them well informed on progress and to check their requirements on a continuous basis. Checking is a key role for the team leader, who may need to delegate other responsibilities to ensure that sufficient time is available for doing this. Indeed some of the team members may be seeking (and welcoming) additional ways in which they could support the team and its leader.

Directive and Coaching Behaviour

When the project comes to its end, assuming that the team did achieve the high-performing stage, there will be strong bonds and a sense of personal achievement. So people will naturally feel a sense of loss with the cessation of the team. A good project team leader will guide the team through this stage to ensure that all the loose ends are tied, and to help the members through the transition to what they will do next. This should leave each team member feeling strong and ready for the next, renewing, stage.

Preferences and Behaviours of Individual Team Members

We all have our own way of viewing and interacting with the world and with each other. These individualities will affect the dynamics within a project team, and the team's interactions with the stakeholders. This will be seen, for example, in how people communicate, how they collect and process information, how they make decisions, how they respond to change and ambiguity and so on. It will also influence the roles that team members will naturally gravitate towards during their time in the team.

This chapter concentrates on the Myers-Briggs Type Indicator (MBTI) and the Belbin team roles as two well-established approaches for helping team leaders and members understand each other's preferences and behaviours within a project team (Myers and Briggs, 2000; Belbin, 2003). These methods are summarised in Figure 32.3.

Myers-Briggs type indicator

Extravert-introvert	Intuition-sensing	Thinking-feeling	Judging-perceiving

Belbin

Plant	Resource investigator	Contributor	Coordinator	Shaper	Monitor evaluator	Teamworker	Implementer	Completer finisher	Specialist

Figure 32.3 Two different approaches to describing personal preferences and behaviours

THE MBTI

The MBTI is based on the work of Katharine Briggs and Isobel Myers. They adapted the original work of the Swiss psychologist Carl Jung to describe preferred ways of behaviour that are intrinsic to our personalities. We will each have a set of preferences drawn from each of the four pairs (or dichotomies) in Figure 32.3 that reflect us in our most natural condition and make up our individual personality type. There are 16 possible different permutations of these 'types'. However, all of us can and will learn to behave in ways that are different to our preferences, so that people with the same 'type' profile will behave differently in different situations.

There is always a risk, when using approaches such as MBTI, of putting people into 'boxes' or stereotypes and expecting them to behave consistently in a certain way. Organisations such as OPP train people to be qualified to administer the MBTI questionnaire and work with clients in its interpretation, to avoid stereotyping and provide guidance in the ethical use of this tool. The website for OPP can be found at http://www.opp.eu. They strongly advise that this method should not be used for recruitment, or performance reviews, and that individuals have the discretion to share or not share their MBTI profiles with colleagues, managers or prospective employers. A brief description of each of the preference pairs follows.

Extravert–Introvert

The words *extravert* and *introvert* are used in the MBTI context to describe how we prefer to renew our energy and focus our attention. People with an extravert preference will tend to renew their energy, work out their problems, and learn new things through their interaction with other people and their involvement in a wide breadth of interests. People with an introvert preference will tend to do all these things through more individual reflection, and a smaller range of more in-depth interests. As with all preferences, people will display both types of behaviour at some time or other, but one type of behaviour will come more naturally to them.

Intuition–Sensing

Intuition–sensing preferences deal with how we take in and communicate information. Those with an intuition preference, when taking in information or communicating it to others, will tend to focus on the 'bigger picture' and its interpretation. They will take a more forward-looking stance and explore what might be. Those with a sensing preference will focus on the detail, and on the present situation, or on what they have learned from experience. They will communicate this greater level of detail to others.

Thinking–Feeling

Again, we will all display both of these preferences, but one will come to the forefront when dealing with problems. Those with a thinking preference will tend to focus on how to resolve the problem, on facts and data, on cause and effect and on the logic of a situation.

People with a feeling preference will empathise more with what someone is experiencing in relation to a problem. They will be concerned about personal values and will tend to look for common ground and for ways to create harmony.

Judging–Perceiving

Judging–perceiving complete the list of MBTI preferences. They are concerned with how people deal with their outside world, with decision making and with meeting deadlines.

Those with a judging preference will like things to be ordered, to make decisions as quickly as possible and to have clearly articulated steps for reaching a deadline.

People with a perceiving preference will want to keep things open, so that they can explore possibilities. They will also want decisions made and deadlines achieved, but may want to reach these in a more fluid way.

Drawing on MBTI Differences in a Positive Way for the Team and its Work

Recognising that team members are likely to have different preferred ways of behaving is an important insight for a project team leader. The leader might choose to complete the MBTI questionnaire and have a workshop as part of the team's start-up activities. That can explore and understand people's different personality types, and study how they can use each other's strengths. Figure 32.4 is my very personal view of how the

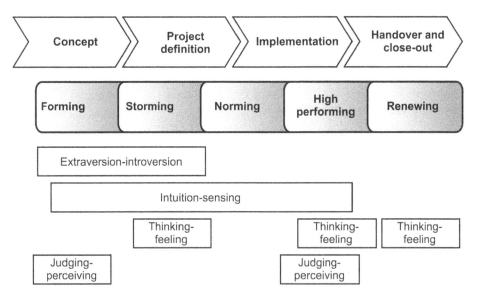

Figure 32.4 Stage when awareness of MBTI preferences will particularly assist team development

different MBTI preference dichotomies might come into play at the different stages of team development.

Appreciating people's extravert–introvert differences will help the project leader and the team members to ensure that they allow those with an introvert preference the time and space to express their opinions and ideas (when they might be less quick to come forward than those with an extravert preference). Also, the project leader and team members will need to give those with an extravert preference the opportunity to discuss their opinions and ideas at greater length than those with an introvert preference might have a tendency to do.

It will be important to identify these patterns of behaviour during the early stages of the project team's life, although they will continue to play a role during the whole of the project. I have seen that without this approach there can be a risk of misjudging those with an introvert preference as being unwilling to fully participate in the team. Also, those with an extravert preference might mistakenly be considered as being too domineering – whereas both types may simply want to contribute in the best way that they can.

The intuition–sensing dichotomy will help the team in its fact finding, planning and communications. Those with an intuition preference may find it easier to speak in terms of the team's goals and vision, and to shape the project plan and communications to stakeholders accordingly. These will be important strengths at the start of the project and during implementation. Those with a sensing preference may find it easier to seek out and present supporting facts and data: information that will be particularly important at the definition stage of the project life cycle.

The natural ability of those with a sensing preference to focus on a greater level of detail will also be useful when communicating with stakeholders who themselves have this preference. Part of a team's stakeholder management should therefore be to understand their stakeholders' preferred level of detail, and to determine how best to use team members' preferences in stakeholder communications.

The thinking–feeling preferences will play an important role at any time that the team is working through personal, relationship or task-based problems. Personal or relationship problems will be most evident during the storming and renewing stages although they could arise at any time. Task-based problems are likely to be most acute during implementation. By ensuring that the views of people with each preference are expressed in turn, the project leader and team members will be able to optimise the discussion and ultimate resolution of the problem.

The thinking–feeling dichotomy can also have an important role to play in stakeholder communication associated with change management. It will help the team ensure that they deal with what stakeholders need to hear from both perspectives.

As the judging–perceiving dichotomy is particularly important for planning, and for making decisions, appreciation of the differences will be especially important during the definition of the project and during its implementation. Balancing input from people with either of these two preferences will help the team to achieve its goals in a timely way, whilst not closing down its exploration of options too quickly.

Finally, awareness and appreciation of the differences in and strengths of team members' MBTI preferences will accentuate the team's overall emotional intelligence – something that must surely also contribute to its ability to reach the high-performing stage.

Belbin Roles in a Project Team

The Belbin team roles were developed by Dr Meredith Belbin and his research team at the Henley Management College in the 1970s. They discovered that the success or failure of a team could be linked to various behavioural clusters, which they defined as individual team roles. Each team role is associated with a particular way of behaving, contributing and interrelating with the other members of the team. A balanced team needs to have a good mix of each team role, and not too many of any particular one.

Belbin (2003) describes the Belbin team roles, but they are summarised here for the reader's convenience, along with my suggestions (by no means definitive) for when they might have the greatest part to play in the project team's life.

The Plant

The plant is invaluable for the team's creativity, innovation and problem resolution. Such people tend to be highly creative and will often find unconventional ways of solving problems. The plant's creativity will be especially useful at the point when the project has moved into identifying and implementing its solutions. This is also when the team should be in high-performing mode. However, a lower level of creativity may be helpful at all stages of the project.

Resource Investigators

Resource investigators have a strong outward focus, both in finding out what competitors are doing, and in assessing the viability of the team's ideas in the outside world. The resource investigator will be bringing external insights at the point when the team is defining what it will do. This might be despite any storming that is going on, but it may also contribute to the churn of discussion about the team's way forward. Their external perspective will of course also be needed as the team plans for project implementation.

Coordinators

Coordinators help the team to focus on its objectives and involve all members through discussion and delegation of work. The coordinator's relationship-building, involvement and delegation skills are going to be needed throughout the project team's life, because these focus on both the behaviours and the tasks of the team.

Shapers

Shapers will challenge the team and ensure that it keeps focus and momentum against its goals. The shaper will therefore support the team as it goes through the storming phase of team development, and as it defines its role and carries out implementation.

Monitor–Evaluator

The monitor–evaluator keeps an eye on the team's logic and helps it to assess options and make decisions objectively. The monitor–evaluator comes to the fore in the most active and productive phases of the team's life (definition and implementation), being essentially concerned with the tasks that the team needs to deliver. This role is most likely to find its niche when the team is in the norming and high-performing stages.

Teamworker

Teamworkers foster relationships within the team and will look out for what work needs to be done and how they can help complete it on behalf of the team. The teamworker, like the coordinator, will be active throughout the whole life of the team, focusing as he/she does on behavioural and task-related aspects and on how to help actively with these.

Implementer

Implementers consider how the work of the team can be achieved in as practical and efficient a way as possible. The implementer is important in the development of the team's project plan during the definition phase of the project, and in the implementation phase to monitor and advise on progress.

Completer–Finisher

Completer–finishers are the quality 'gurus' of a team. They look at how the completed work can be polished and finished to the highest possible standard. Completer–finishers will be at their most productive once the team starts producing tangible outputs, and they could also help the team to define the success criteria (or the benefits realisation framework and metrics) at the definition stage of the project.

Specialist

The specialist has in-depth knowledge of a key area with which the team is concerned. The specialist could give valuable input at any stage of the team's work: not only in providing ideas but also in helping to build the knowledge base going forward. That will be discussed in the following section on learning techniques.

Figure 32.5 represents my view of the stages of the project life cycle and team development at which each team role might have the most significant part to play. Again this is by no means a definitive representation.

As with MBTI, it will be useful to identify people's preferred roles during the team start-up phase, thereby also allowing enough time, if necessary, to adjust the mix of team roles represented. Individuals can find out about their most natural role by completing

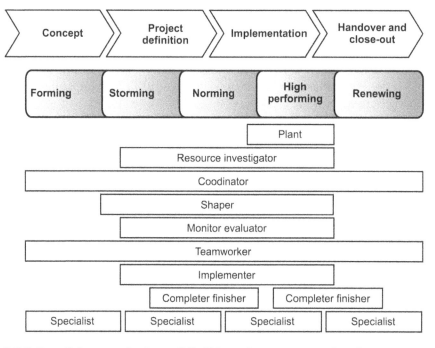

Figure 32.5 Possible correlation of Belbin roles to team development and the project life cycle

a questionnaire. This and the associated report are available from the Belbin Associates website at http://www.belbin.com/rte.asp?id=8.

Learning Techniques

Although we all learn and share our knowledge and experience during our work with each other, it tends to be in a fairly ad hoc way, whereas there are some well structured techniques to help teams do this more effectively as illustrated in Figure 32.6.

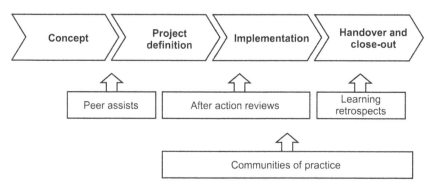

Figure 32.6 Learning techniques for supporting team development shown in their time relationship with the project life cycle

Peer Assists

'Peer assists' consist of inviting help or advice from people, so that teams can learn from the experience of others at the start of the project. This process consists of inviting people with relevant experience of the work that the project team is undertaking to share information on:

- their insights;
- best practices;
- risk identification, avoidance or mitigation.

The discussion is usually fairly formally structured, allowing time for the project team to articulate their questions and for the guest experts to formulate and share their replies. Peer assists are usefully carried out during the start-up phase of a project.

After Action Reviews

'After action reviews' are a useful approach to adopt at the point when the project team is starting to achieve significant milestones (most probably during the definition and implementation project stages). After action reviews can be included as regular agenda items in team meetings, or in specially set-up debriefs after significant milestones. They usually consist of internal team discussions but can involve stakeholders external to the team. They typically address a formal set of questions such as:

- What was meant to happen?
- What actually happened?
- What went well?
- What could we have done differently?
- What have we learned?
- How and with whom will we share these lessons to ensure that we derive the fullest value from them?

Learning Retrospects

A 'learning retrospect' is a lengthier version of an after action review. Although project team members typically find it difficult to take the time to do these, they are an invaluable part of the close-out process and can provide emotional support to the renewing stage of team development. One way to perform learning retrospects is to carry out a face-to-face workshop where the original project plan has been mapped out in advance on brown paper, and annotated with any changes to the plan. During the workshop, team members can use Post-It notes to add comments on what went particularly well at the various stages, and what could have been done differently. These visual aids can then act as a backdrop for discussing what the team has learned, and what it wishes to share and with whom as a result of these lessons.

Communities of Practice

'Communities of practice' are a method of sharing learning and knowledge that can begin during the active stages of the project, and continue beyond it with members of operational teams who are using or supporting the outcomes of the project. They tend to consist of informal networks of people, drawn non-hierarchically from across the organisation, but with a common passion or interest in increasing their knowledge and expertise in a particular area of practice.

ENDNOTE TO LEARNING TECHNIQUES

All of the learning techniques listed above rely on an active sharing of knowledge and experience – between those who have something to share and those with an interest in learning from others. Some common barriers to the success of these learning techniques include:

- Capturing and burying information in a physical form that no one chooses to, or is easily able to, access (the 'black hole');
- An unwillingness to find the time, make a priority of, or just simply to share or learn from others;
- The lack of an established way of working to share with, and learn from others.

There is a lot more that the reader can discover about these and other learning techniques, for instance through Collison and Parcell (2004).

Conclusion

Hopefully the reader (whether a team member or a team leader) will have reached this point in the chapter with at least one or two new insights and approaches to help them in getting their team to a high-performing status more quickly, painlessly and effectively than they have done before. These insights and approaches should include one or more of the options to:

- Take a more objective view of the stages of a team's development and of what can be done to enhance its effectiveness;
- Appreciate the differences and strengths that will exist in team members' preferred ways of behaving, of preferred team roles, and of how to better understand and make use of these;
- Be aware of learning techniques that could be used to enhance a team's sharing and acquisition of knowledge and experience, and of how to apply these.

References and Further Reading

Belbin, R.M. (2003), *Management Teams: Why They Succeed or Fail*, 2nd edn, Oxford: Elsevier Butterworth-Heinemann.

Blanchard, K., Fowler, S. and Hawkins, L. (2005), *Self Leadership and the One Minute Manager: Increasing Effectiveness Through Situational Self Leadership*, New York: William Morrow and Co.

Collison, C. and Parcell, G. (2004), *Learning to Fly: Practical Knowledge Management from Leading and Learning Organizations*, 2nd edn, Chichester: Capstone.

Hirsh, E., Hirsh, K.W. and Krebs Hirsh, S. (2003), *Introduction to Type and Teams*, 2nd edn, Mountain View, CA: CPP.

Myers, I. and Briggs, K. (2000), *Introduction to Type*, 6th edn, Oxford: CPP.

Reid, T. (2008), 'Managing teams, the reality of life', ch. 34 in Turner, R. (ed.), *The Gower Handbook of Project Management*, Aldershot: Gower.

Stott, K. and Walker, A. (1995), *Teams, Teamwork and Teambuilding. The Manager's Complete Guide to Teams in Organizations*, Englewood Cliffs, NJ: Prentice-Hall.

Tucker, J. (2008), *Introduction to Type and Project Management*, Mountain View, CA: CPP

Tuckman, B. and Jensen, M. (1977) 'Stages of small group development revisited', *Group and Organizational Studies*, 419–27.

33 Motivating People in Projects

BERNADO TIRADO

In order to motivate the members of a team one first has to learn something about the personality of each person. This chapter begins by identifying four factors that are important in this profiling process. I shall then consider some of the available motivational theories and discuss how they might be used, according to the identified profile of each team member.

Profiling Team Members

Many motivational theories have been developed over the years. Some of these are described in other chapters, including Chapter 31. They offer a range of tools that leaders can use. But the manager must have the ability to determine a personality profile of each person, so that he or she can choose and use the motivational tool that would be most effective for that person. Leaders either use their instincts to decide which motivational concept works best, or they might simply use trial and error.

Profiling is an important process because it enables the leader to understand the types of intrinsic and extrinsic factors that can be the most effective motivators for each team member. I shall consider four factors that are fundamental to this process. These are:

1. self-awareness;
2. baselining;
3. kinesics;
4. birth order.

SELF-AWARENESS

Within 30 seconds of meeting someone new, we've made an unconscious judgement of that individual. We do that because it is part of human nature to categorise individuals. That makes it easier for most of us to decide how to interact with the other person. However, such 30-second assessments can be inaccurate and thus dangerous. We are associating good and bad experiences with an individual whom we've never met before and, as a result, we might easily make false judgements based only upon our prejudices.

To combat these unconscious prejudices, one needs to think back to one's childhood. It sounds odd but most of our formative prejudices in adult life come from our childhood experiences. For example, when a boy falls down, scrapes his knee, and starts to cry, the father or mother would typically say 'Now, now, you're a big boy and boys don't cry'. If the child had been a little girl, the mother or father would be more likely to say 'It's okay, let it out'. So (generalising) boys are conditioned to not express emotion whereas girls are encouraged to express emotion; hence, why Men are from Mars and Women are from Venus.

The point I'm making here is that cultural and family norms govern how we behave and perceive the world. To profile someone, one must know what these governing factors are, and be aware of them when making judgements. Once this self-awareness has been established baselining can begin.

BASELINING

A baseline is a standard behaviour pattern relative to the individual. This is sometimes referred to as a norm or *norm baseline*. When a person gets upset or flustered, the individual will exhibit an elevated behaviour pattern known as a *stress baseline*. These baselines remain consistent throughout the exhibited behaviour. Once these baselines have been established, one can identify behavioural variations known as hotspots (Figure 33.1). Hotspots give interviewers cues as to when to ask probing questions.

Of course one must never assume that one behavioural deviation by itself automatically means deception. It just means that one needs to ask more questions to understand the root cause of that deviation. Questioning becomes especially important when you see or hear a cluster.

A cluster is a pattern where one sees or hears three deviations or more happening at the same time. These might include body language shifts, micro-expression leaks and speech deviations. Mainly used by law-enforcement officers to interview suspects, these techniques allow us to open our thought processes to observe behaviour that we would not otherwise see or hear. They also allow us an opportunity to apply the appropriate motivational theory to an individual.

Suppose, for instance, that you ask Sara 'What do you think of your project manager Bob?' and she replies 'Oooh, he's great' whilst rolling her eyes. One might assume that Sara is being dishonest and concealing her true feelings about Bob. But instead of using our innate logic to explain her facial expression, we can apply our new knowledge on baselining and ask ourselves, 'Why did Sara roll her eyes?' instead of taking what she said at face value.

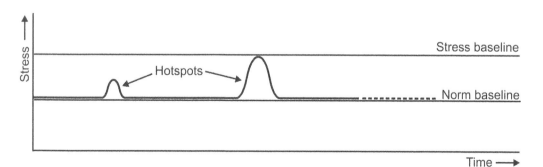

Figure 33.1 Stress hotspots

So in that case we would need to ask a follow-up question, which could be as simple as, 'Really?' That might provoke the following unexpected response from Sara: 'Absolutely! When you asked me about Bob, you reminded me that I have not finished a job he asked me to do last week'. So Sara's facial expression had nothing to do with her personal opinion about Bob. Instead it had to do with suddenly remembering something that she had forgotten to do for him.

In dialogue, we naturally tend to have multiple thoughts whilst listening. These thoughts could result in facial expressions that have nothing to do with the dialogue at hand. So the lesson here is not to put too much weight on one behavioural deviation.

KINESICS

Kinesics is the study of non-verbal communications. In the 1960s, Dr Albert Mehrabian (Mehrabian, 1971) developed a communication model known as the 7 – 38 – 55 per cent rule. His research (which is constantly contested by scholars) found that we absorb information through:

- words (7 per cent);
- tone of voice (38 per cent);
- non-verbal signals such as facial expression and body language (55 per cent).

When motivating individuals, we may need to consider the non-verbal cues happening during or outside meetings. These cues come in the forms of body language, micro-expressions, and paralinguistics (the way in which the words are spoken). Two examples of body language cues one should look out for when conversing with team members are the so-called 'belly button rule' and 'power gestures'.

The belly button rule is intended to gauge the person's interest or intent by the position of the person's belly button in relation to the other person. If two people stand facing each other, that indicates that they are interested in what each other is saying. If the two people are standing at an angle to each other (so that their belly buttons are not exactly facing) their interest in each other is less. This snippet of information will help you to understand if the person is engaged or disengaged in your conversation.

One of the strongest examples of a power gesture is the so-called superman pose. Here the person has a confident facial expression, and stands facing full on with feet planted astride and hands on hips.

Observing behaviour in the workplace provides a project leader with data for understanding further the factors that would motivate the team member.

BIRTH ORDER

Another data point is birth order, which I shall cover in more detail in Chapter 52. Research shows that birth order has a lot of influence on how we behave in the workplace. Whether we like it or not, we unconsciously create a family environment at work. Sometimes it resembles our personal family dynamic and sometimes it resembles the ideal family dynamic that we never had.

Having the ability to predict someone's birth order provides you with a competitive advantage in understanding how to work with that individual. For example, first-born tend to be governed by punctuality, structure and power. Last-born are more comfortable with ambiguity and tend to 'go with the flow'. Neither of these is good or bad but the knowledge will allow you to know how to best approach each individual at work.

Overall, whether we have siblings or not, the dynamics we experience as a child tend to manifest themselves in the workplace. Many studies have shown that people would prefer to make less money and work with people they like, as opposed to making more money and working with people they dislike.

Having discussed and gained some understanding of what to look out for in individuals, it is time to consider some motivational theories.

Motivational Theories

Management scientists have defined motivation as the process of exciting, directing and maintaining behaviour towards a goal. Motivation is highly complex because people are motivated by many factors, which can result in conflicts.

For example, a factory worker might be motivated to make a positive impression on their supervisor by doing a good job, but at the same time they might also be motivated to maintain friendly relations with their co-workers by not making them look bad. This example has to do with job performance, and indeed, motivation is a key determinant of performance. However, it is important to note that motivation is *not* synonymous with performance.

MASLOW'S HIERARCHY OF NEEDS

This subject was introduced in Chapter 31. Maslow's need hierarchy is based on fulfilment of five different types of needs, which are:

1. physiological needs (the lowest-order needs), which involve satisfying biological drives such as the need for air, food, water and shelter;
2. safety or security needs, concerned with the need to operate in an environment that is physically and psychologically safe, secure and free from threats of harm;
3. social needs, which include chiefly the need to be liked and accepted by others;
4. self-esteem needs; the need to achieve success and have others recognise our accomplishments;
5. self-actualisation needs, which refer to the individual working to become all that he or she is capable of being.

These five needs, which are illustrated a little later in Figure 33.2, can only be activated in the order listed above. Thus the theory suggests that people are motivated to work because they first have to meet their most basic survival needs for food, water and shelter. When those needs have been taken care of, the person is motivated to satisfy the next layer of needs, which are the safety and security needs; and so on, ascending the sequence from one to five.

Maslow's theory gives excellent guidance on workers' needs relevant to their motivation. Many organisations have taken actions directly suggested by the theory and have realised success.

EQUITY THEORY: THE IMPORTANCE OF BEING FAIR

Organisational theorists have been actively interested in the difficult task of explaining exactly what constitutes fairness on the job, and how people respond when they believe they have been unfairly treated. This is now known as the science of 'equity theory'.

Equity theory (Adams, 1965) proposes that people are motivated to maintain fair, equitable relationships between themselves and others. By contrast, we must avoid those relationships that are unfair or inequitable. To make equity judgements, people compare themselves to others by focusing on two variables which are:

1. outcomes (for example pay and prestige);
2. inputs (for example time worked and units produced).

People make equity judgements by comparing their own outcome/input ratios to the outcome/input ratios of others. It is important to note that equity theory deals with outcomes and inputs as they are perceived by people. So these are not necessarily objective standards or measurements.

A person who perceives inequity will become demotivated and disengaged. To create a balance to this inequity, the individual would lower their inputs – meaning that they would not work as hard (resulting in late completion of tasks). But if people can change their perception, and come to regard inequitable situations as equitable, they will be relieved from their feelings of guilt and anger. Those negative moods will then be transformed into feelings of satisfaction.

EXPECTANCY THEORY

Expectancy theory is based on the premise of 'believing you can get what you want' (House, 1996). People also are motivated by the belief that they can expect to achieve certain desired rewards by working hard to attain them.

This is one of the basic ideas behind the popularity of pay systems known as pay-for-performance plans, which establish formal links between job performance and rewards. However, a survey found that only 25 per cent of employees see a clear link between good job performance and their pay increases.

Expectancy theory claims that people will be motivated to exert effort on the job when they believe that doing so will help them to achieve the things they want. It views motivation as the result of three different types of beliefs that people have. These are:

1. *Expectancy* – the belief that one's effort will affect performance. Sometimes people believe that putting forth a great deal of effort will help them to get a lot accomplished. But in other cases, people do not expect that their efforts will have a great effect on how well they do.
2. *Instrumentality* – the belief that one's performance will be rewarded. Even if an employee performs at a high level, his or her motivation might suffer if that performance is not appropriately rewarded. In other words, performance is not perceived as instrumental in bringing about rewards.

3. *Valence* – the perceived value of the expected rewards. Valence is not just a matter of the amount of reward received, but it is also about what that reward means to the person who receives it.

As project leaders, we need always to ensure a direct correlation between an action and the rewards associated with accomplishing that action.

For example, suppose that you hold a competition amongst your team, encouraging individuals to come up with the best idea, stating that you will provide a reward for the winner. So clearly the team member who wins that contest will be expecting that reward. But there have been many past instances where the leader in such cases was merely giving lip service and no rewards were given. Under those circumstances it is not surprising that the team will become demotivated, because the action and its result do not match.

SETTING TARGETS

Taking aim at performance targets (goal setting) can lead to marked improvements in performance. It has been found that improvements result when the goals are set with three conditions. The goals should be:

1. specific;
2. difficult but acceptable to achieve (challenging);
3. accompanied by feedback on the results.

Setting Specific Goals

People perform better when they are asked to meet specific high-performance goals than when they are directed simply to 'do your best', or when no goal at all is assigned. Where possible the goals should be quantified, so that performance against them can be more easily compared.

When people are faced with challenging goals they are motivated to try to meet them not only to fulfil management's expectations, but also to convince themselves that they have performed well.

Setting Difficult but Acceptable Goals

People will work hard to reach challenging goals so long as these are within the limits of their capability. When goals become too difficult, performance suffers because people reject the goals as unrealistic and unattainable. Specific goals are most effective if they are set neither too low nor too high.

Feedback on Performance

Although it might seem obvious that feedback on performance is essential, in practice it is not given as often as one might expect. It has been found that feedback and goal setting can dramatically increase group effectiveness. Group feedback improved performance approximately 50 per cent over the baseline level. Adding group goal setting improved it by 75 per cent. Clearly the combination of goal setting and feedback help raise the effectiveness of group performance.

In connection with target setting generally, see also the section on management by objectives in Chapter 31.

Applying Motivational Theories

I have now explained how to profile a team member and I have outlined the motivational theories. Now it is time to consider how all this applies to managing projects.

The pyramid in the centre of Figure 33.2 (Maslow's hierarchy of needs) helps to answer the question 'How is motivation affected by basic human needs?'

In essence, people work to live. To survive, humans need the basic essentials, most of which are made possible with money. Concurrently, people want to feel emotionally and physically safe in their work environment. These two fundamental stages of Maslow's hierarchy of needs motivate people to work. If they are compromised, a project manager may face challenges when trying to motivate team members. For example, if one team member is aggressive towards another team member, the one who is being bullied will disengage. As a leader, it would be the project manager's job to step in and work on building a safe environment for the person being bullied.

As project leaders, very often the people in our teams are assigned to us only for the duration of our project and we might have no direct say in how much each team member gets paid. But we need to understand that pay is not the only motivator, and indeed it is not usually the principal one. Project managers need to understand, through relationship building, team members tend to work and perform because they see that as their career. So projects can be affected by many basic human needs.

On the left of each hierarchy level in Figure 33.2 you will find statements expanding Maslow's stated needs. These are the things that people seek. Each hierarchy level must be

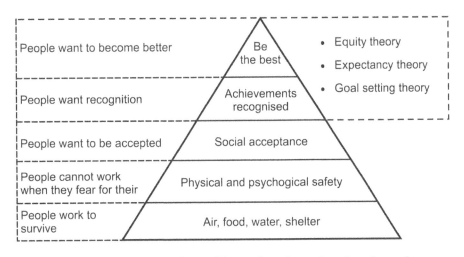

Figure 33.2 Understanding Maslow's hierarchy of motivational needs

continuously maintained or the pyramid will not be complete. Most people will get to the 'social acceptance' level but, above that level, differences will emerge in how individuals perceive work.

To the right of the pyramid you will find the three theories listed that I discussed above. Each theory provides project managers with motivational insights that can be used according to the individual team member's disposition.

Suppose I begin with perceived fairness (the equity theory). Many times we have encountered individuals where we ask ourselves 'How did that person get that job? Clearly, he or she is not qualified'. Or we might work with a peer whom we believe is the boss's favourite. We form the conclusion that he or she can never do wrong. These perceptions feed into how we believe our immediate leaders treat us compared to others.

This concept is also true for us as project leaders. When a person feels that a leader is favouring one individual over another, or believes that they could do a better job than the project leader, that individual will disengage.

It is, therefore, important that a project leader should monitor how they treat their team members. The tricky part is that it's all about perception. If a team member feels that they are being treated differently compared to a peer for one reason or another, that team member will begin to disengage or will find ways to feel fairness.

CASE EXAMPLE NO. 1

Jane is a project leader, and she is implementing a new technology project in her organisation. She has assigned to her a team of six subject-matter experts. Bob, a change management specialist, and Sarah, a communications expert, have also been provided to work with Jane. Over the weeks, Bob feels left out because Jane is never reaching out to him and when she does, she's ordering him what to do rather than seeking his expert opinion.

When they do meet, Sarah is there and it appears that change management and communications discussions have already happened between Jane and Sarah – leaving Bob to wonder why is he there at all.

But Bob is a non-confrontational type of person and, instead of voicing his concerns, he simply puts Jane's requests at the bottom of his priority list. To feel fairness, Bob has unconsciously undermined Jane's ability to do her job because he perceived he was not adding any value in Jane's eyes.

To minimise perceived unfairness, Jane should meet with Bob and Sarah to set expectations on how she works.

What Bob did not know, was that Jane did not have confidence in Sarah's ability to do her job and, as such, spent more time with her. Jane believed that Bob was experienced enough, and that he would be able to get the job done with his eyes closed.

This sounds like a complete misunderstanding, and for the most part it is. However, perception is *not* always reality. Understanding how people perceive fairness is critical to how leaders work with team members and drive their motivation.

CASE EXAMPLE NO. 2

Here is a different case. At times people have a sense of entitlement (expectancy theory). What project leaders need to consider is why? Why do people believe they should get what they want? Of course, getting what you want (if deserved) is not a bad thing and I ask that you keep that in mind.

Some people who work hard expect to achieve a certain status, accomplishment or reward. Project team members are typically assigned or volunteered by their leaders for one reason or another. If they do not want to be working with you, that already puts you at a disadvantage.

During relationship building, it is important to work out what type of reward is expected (for example, project experience, a 'Thank you' letter, a competition reward and so forth).

Frederick is leading a newly formed technology team with no experience in process efficiency. He works in a corporate culture that thrives on competition. As a team-building exercise, Frederick decides to hold a competition within the team. The individual who comes up with the best cost-savings idea will win a prize. But Frederick does not say what that prize will be.

After a few weeks, the team presented their ideas and it turns out that this team, with little or no process efficiency experience, generated ideas worth approximately three million US dollars in cost savings. A winner was named but no prize was given.

Most of the team were indifferent about the fact that no prize was given. But other members felt deceived and started to disengage.

The expectancy theory provides project leaders with a simple concept around 'leaders must walk the talk' or 'do what you said you were going to do'.

CASE EXAMPLE NO. 3

Another extreme example has more to do with individual agendas around progressing. Some individuals, who are driven by power and status, would thrive on ensuring that some projects succeed or, in some instances, fail. The 'success' individuals might be closely tied to the project sponsor. Others might associate themselves with someone powerful in the organisation that would prefer that the project fail. Project leaders need to be very wary of these individuals because their project could be comprised as a political piece on a large chessboard.

To neutralise or manage this situation, the project leader needs to be aware of the sphere of influence that the particular project team member has and develop a strategy to ensure the individual only gets information as appropriate, or arrange the relationship to have the project stand out (in a good way) to senior leadership.

Conclusion

Project managers need to make time within their project plan to get to know as many of the team members as possible. By doing so, they will learn about each individual's 'What's in it for me?' (WIIFM) and other motivational and personality factors.

Studies have shown that high-performing teams function best with specific goals or targets (goal-setting theory). For this reason, many companies use specific, measurable, attainable, relevant and time-bound goals. This has been called SMART management, but those who use it should be aware that the SMART acronym is a Trade Mark of Francis Hartman Holdings Limited (Hartman, 2000). However, goal setting is an important motivator, irrespective of the goals chosen. Short time-frame goals enable the project team to have a sense of accomplishment even if a project is cancelled or fails. Out of all the theories listed, goal setting enables team members to focus on tangible results, and it holds each team member accountable for the success or failure of the project.

References and Further Reading

Adams, J.S. (1965), 'Inequity in social exchange', in *Advances in Experimental Social Psychology*, Vol. 2, New York: Academic Press, 267–99.

Greenberg, J. (1999), *Managing Behaviour in Organizations*, 2nd edn, Upper Saddle River, NJ: Prentice-Hall.

Hartman, F.T. (2000), *Don't Park Your Brain Outside*, Newtown Square, PA: Project Management Institute.

House, R.J. (1996), 'Path-goal theory of leadership: Lessons, legacy, and a reformulated theory', *Leadership Quarterly*, 7(3), 323–52.

Maslow, A.H. (1970), *Motivation and Personality*, 2nd edn, New York: Harper & Row.

Mehrabian, A. (1971), *Silent Messages: Implicit Communication of Emotions and Attitudes*, Belmont, CA: Wadsworth Publishing Company.

34 *Conduct of Meetings*

DENNIS LOCK

All who are concerned with projects will know that much time (often too much time) can be taken up by meetings. This chapter begins with some generalisations about the administration of meetings, and then moves on to consider meetings that have particular applications in project management. It is assumed here that the meetings described take place in a shared physical environment, such as a conference room or hall. There is always the possibility, of course, of conducting meetings by video link, if one or more delegates would find it difficult or inconvenient to be present physically in the meeting room; but that subject is discussed in Chapter 12 in the context of the virtual organisation.

Administration of Meetings

MAKING THE ARRANGEMENTS

The organiser should ensure that, as far as possible within the organisation's available accommodation and resources, an environment is provided for the delegates that will allow discussion in reasonable comfort and without distraction or interruption from external sources. The meeting organiser might not necessarily be the chairman. For example, in some meetings the delegates elect the chairman. Here is a short checklist of factors to be considered when a meeting is planned:

- Have the delegates been given an agenda well in advance, so that they know the purpose of the meeting and can come properly prepared and equipped?
- Has a check been made to discover whether the proposed venue and time will be suitable for all the delegates?
- Has a meeting room of suitable size been reserved?
- Will there be enough seats for everyone?
- Are appropriate audio-visual aids in place and functioning?
- Are the communications facilities such that they can be used where necessary for the purposes of the meeting yet will not cause distractions (for example by having incoming telephone messages intercepted)?
- Is there adequate ventilation or air conditioning?
- Are arrangements in place to greet visitors and conduct them with courtesy to the meeting room?
- If the meeting is expected to be a long one, have refreshments been arranged?

Of course emergency meetings or informal meetings sometimes have to be called in projects at short notice where there might not be time to fulfil all the steps listed in the above checklist.

Meetings should not be timed to start too early in the day if that would cause inconvenience to visiting delegates (especially those from a project client). Overnight accommodation might have to be arranged for delegates travelling long distances.

Some argue that meetings should be scheduled for mid- to late afternoon, so that there is an incentive to get proceedings over and done with as quickly as possible. On the other hand, people tend to be more alert early in the day, and more creative and collective brainpower is likely to be available then to deal with any difficult problems or to achieve creativity. The organiser will have to decide which option is best for the particular occasion and the types of people expected to attend.

The following quotation from Scott Belsky is interesting in this context of timing:

> *Most impromptu meetings that are called to quickly catch up on a project or discuss problems can happen in 10 minutes or less. However, when they are scheduled in formal calendar programs, they tend to be set in 30 or 60 minute increments. Why? Just because it is the default calendar setting. Ideally, meetings should just have a start time and end as quickly as they can.*[1]

GENERAL CONDUCT OF MEETINGS

The chairman is principally responsible for the conduct of meetings, which is of course stating the obvious.

Project meetings, especially progress meetings, often become sidetracked by technical issues that are best resolved outside the meeting. Such issues can be very time consuming. They tend to involve only two or three of the delegates, so that the remainder of the people in the room become bored and feel that their time is being wasted. An efficient chairman will not allow such distractions, but will keep the meeting on course according to its published agenda.

Other distractions that can disrupt proceedings or cause irritation include such inconsiderate actions as the use of mobile telephones. The chairman should ask that these, along with other portable electronic devices such as laptop computers, should be switched off and kept out of sight, at least whilst the meeting is in active session and debate.

Arguments in meetings can provoke creative discussion and may not be undesirable, but they must be resolved before the meeting ends so that people do not leave feeling resentment or dissatisfaction. The chairman has a duty to uncover the facts which underlie any interdepartmental or interfunctional problems, not so much to apportion blame as to ensure their resolution and the continued progress of the project.

The chairman's role does not end when the discussions are over and all decisions have been reached. Good practice is for the chairman to run back through the events of the meeting, summarise the discussions that have taken place, and ensure that everyone agrees with the conclusions that have been reached. Some of those conclusions will often result in actions being requested of delegates, and it is important that those delegates understand and agree to those actions and accept them as a personal commitment.

---

1   See http://the99percent.com/tips/5798/Meet-Until-Youre-Weak-in-the-Knees

When a meeting breaks up, it will have been successful only if all the members feel that they have achieved some purpose and that actions have been agreed that will benefit the project. Apart from the usual courtesy of thanking the delegates for attending, the chairman can also ask them generally if they thought the meeting had been worthwhile and had achieved its purpose. Meetings can be very productive when they are efficiently managed, but they can be damaging to morale and waste time if the delegates depart feeling that nothing of use has been achieved. The last thing one needs to hear from departing delegates is 'Well, that was a complete waste of time'.

ISSUING THE MINUTES

The minutes and any resulting action requests must be issued without delay so that they do not become outdated by further events before distribution. Minutes should be clearly and concisely written, combining brevity with clarity, accuracy and careful layout, so that each action demanded can be seen to stand out from the page. Minutes that are too verbose might not even be read by everyone. Short, pointed statements of fact are all that is needed.

No ambiguity must be allowed after any statement as to who is directly responsible for taking action. Every person listed for taking action must receive a copy of the minutes (an obvious point that is sometimes overlooked, especially when action is directed to someone who did not attend the meeting). Times must be stated with precision. Expressions such as 'by the end of next week' or 'towards the end of the month' should be avoided in favour of actual dates.

A SIMPLE MEETINGS CONTROL PROCEDURE

Trevor Bentley (1976) described a simple form and procedure which still remains very effective for the management of meetings. The form shown in Figure 34.1 on the next page is closely adapted from the one designed by Bentley. This is how it works.

The person calling the meeting (usually the chairman) fills in the agenda on a form and lists all those invited to attend, after telephoning as many of them as possible to check that the proposed time and place will be convenient. (A client of mine where I introduced this system found it more convenient to use a separate form for each item on the agenda.) Copies of the form are distributed to all the delegates, preferably at least a week in advance of the meeting.

When the meeting takes place, the chairman uses his or her copy of the form to record the proceedings. The first action is to tick or encircle the names of those who actually turn up. Then the chairman notes the decisions made and actions agreed as the meeting progresses.

Just before the meeting breaks up, the chairman's copy of the form, now complete with all its annotations, is photocopied. All members of the meeting are given a copy as they leave. Thus instant issue of the minutes is achieved. All the decisions taken and actions are recorded exactly as they were agreed during the meeting, fresh in people's minds. No one can claim that the minutes have been fudged after the meeting to distort the agreements reached.

Bentley originally recommended that a copy of the annotated control form should be sent to the chairman's immediate superior after each meeting. Then, if any meeting

Lindlox Projects Ltd
Meeting notification

Date, time and place	Meeting/project reference

To attend:

Agenda:

Decisions:

Action required:	By whom:	By when:

Figure 34.1 A combined form for the agenda and minutes of a meeting
Note: Based on an original idea by Trevor Bentley.

should fail to result in positive decisions or actions, the chairman would be expected to explain why the meeting had been called and what purpose it had served. An interesting idea, but perhaps too provocative?

Purposes of Project Meetings

There are clearly many reasons for meetings but this chapter focuses on those most commonly encountered in project management. These project meetings are intended to:

- Inform (in which case they often become presentations). In projects these include kick-off meetings at the beginning of a new project. In management change projects they also include meetings where the proposed changes are announced and explained to the staff. Public enquiry meetings, although on a larger scale, also fall into this category in many respects.
- Facilitate or find solutions through collective brainpower. In projects these include meetings for finding solutions to difficult technical problems, or for procedures such as value engineering. But the most common project management application is in mapping out the project process when the project network diagram is drawn.
- Consider proposed changes. Many companies set up a change board or change committee for this purpose. These meetings are not discussed here but change procedures are explained in detail in Chapter 25 of Lock (2013).
- Review progress.

PROJECT KICK-OFF MEETINGS

Whether or not a project has a general gathering in the form of a kick-off meeting depends to a large extent on the kind of project, and whether or not it is to be conducted in the open or with a blanket of confidentiality. Here we take the case of a project that has been sold to an external customer, where the project organisation is about to be set up. The purpose of the kick-off meeting in such circumstances is often to introduce the project manager and the functional managers to each other, and to outline the purposes and scope of the project. Another very important purpose is to fire everyone up with enthusiasm for the project.

It is recommended that, at least when the meeting begins, a member of the organisation's senior management should open the proceedings and introduce the project manager, as well as outlining the advantages and importance of the new project to the company.

Kick-off meetings often fall loosely into the 'presentation' class of meeting, accompanied by slides projected on to a screen. Microsoft PowerPoint is the universal tool for this purpose, but so many times one sees the opportunity missed to make the most of this presentation tool, only to be faced with a series of boring bullet-point lists. PowerPoint gives the presenter the opportunity to use colour, animation, pictures and sounds and these can greatly enhance the audience's experience, capturing their attention. But some people recommend that no more than about six slides should be presented, so as to keep within people's attention span. The expression 'death by PowerPoint' has been used to describe the over-use of this tool.

People should leave the kick-off meeting impatient to start work on the project. This is an important opportunity for setting a project off on the right foot.

PROJECT PLANNING MEETINGS

In the ideal planning meeting, the heads of the functions that will take part in the project (or their fully-empowered delegates) should be present. The project manager will often hand the meeting over to an experienced planning engineer (who will ideally be a member of the project support office).

An initial planning meeting has much in common with a brainstorming meeting, where a group of people assemble and throw all kinds of ideas into the air, and have them recorded on flipcharts. The meeting chairman is in effect a facilitator, who encourages people to produce as many ideas as they can and then analyses the results, so that the cream of the ideas become adopted.

In project planning, the planning engineer becomes the facilitator, drawing out the ideas for how the project will proceed and, instead of writing them as flipchart lists, puts them into a critical path network sketch. An experienced planner, even for projects where he or she has no technical knowledge, can ask questions that will tease out tasks that would otherwise be forgotten.

Don't you have to paint this panel before it can be used?

How confident are you that this software will work first time? Would you not have to run it in parallel with the old software before making the changeover?

Would you not have to wait for this concrete to cure before you can build this wall?

When the network diagram has been sketched to represent the project process, those present can be asked to estimate task durations and resource requirements. Having the people present who will later be responsible for managing those tasks is important because in making their estimates they also accept their subsequent commitment to the tasks.

PROGRESS MEETINGS

Any project manager worthy of the title will want to make certain that whenever possible his or her tactics are preventative rather than curative. If a special meeting can be successful in resolving problems, why not pre-empt trouble by having regular progress meetings, with senior representatives of all departments present?

Regular progress meetings provide a suitable forum where essential two-way communication can take place between planners, managers and other project participants. The main purposes of progress meetings emerge as a means of keeping a periodic check on the project progress, and the making of any consequential decisions to implement corrective action if programme slippages occur or appear likely to occur.

There are certain dangers associated with the mismanagement of progress meetings. For instance, it often happens that lengthy discussions arise between two specialists on technical issues that should be resolved outside the meeting. Such discussions can bore the other members of the meeting, waste their scarce and expensive time, and cause rapid loss of interest in the proceedings. Although it is never possible to divorce technical considerations from progress topics, design meetings and progress meetings are basically different functions which should be kept apart. Discussions should be kept to key progress topics, with irrelevancies swept aside.

The principle of management by exception is important to save time at progress meetings. This means that time is not wasted in discussing tasks that are on plan. Instead the meeting should concentrate on tasks that are either late, over budget or otherwise at risk of falling outside the plan.

The frequency with which meetings are held must depend to a large extent on the nature of the project, the size and geographical spread of its organisation, and its overall timescale. On projects of short duration, and with much detail to be considered, there may be a good case for holding progress meetings frequently, say once a week, on an informal basis at supervisor level. For other projects, monthly meetings may be adequate. Meetings at relatively junior level can be backed up by less frequent meetings held at more senior level.

Project review meetings, which can cover the financial prospects as well as simple progress, can also be arranged. For some capital projects most senior managers might wish to drop in on the proceedings. The customer might also wish to attend or be represented.

Meetings held more frequently than necessary create apathy or hostility. Supervisors and managers are usually busy people whose time should not be wasted.

A CASE EXAMPLE OF PROGRESS MEETINGS BECOMING UNNECESSARY

The above account of progress meetings adheres to the conventional view that progress meetings are an accepted way of project life. Here is some food for less conventional thought.

A heavy-engineering company had long been accustomed to holding progress meetings. Depending on the particular project manager, these were held either at regular intervals or randomly whenever things looked like going badly adrift (most readers will have encountered such 'firefighting' meetings).

Meetings typically resulted in a set of excuses from participants as to why actions requested of them at previous meetings had been carried out late, ineffectually or not at all. Each meeting would end with a new set of promises, ready to fuel a fresh collection of excuses at the next meeting. This is not to say that the company's overall record was particularly bad, but there was considerable room for improvement and too much time was being wasted at meetings and too many promises were being made and broken.

Senior company management supported a study which led to the establishment of a small project support office. The engineers in this office used critical path networks and the computer produced detailed work-to lists, which were filtered and sorted using work breakdown structure (WBS) and organisational breakdown structure (OBS) codes so that managers received schedules that pertained only to the tasks within their functional departments.

Two progress engineers from the project support office followed up all tasks, using the work-to lists. They knew which jobs should be in progress at any time, the scheduled start and finish dates for those jobs, how many people should be working on each task, how many people should be working in total on each project at any time and the amount of remaining float available for every task.

If a critical or near-critical task seemed to be in danger of running late, steps were taken to bring it back into time (by working overtime during evenings and weekends if necessary). All the managers and workers cooperated well, and they experienced a new sense of order in their working lives.

After several months under this new system it dawned on all the functional managers that they were no longer being asked to attend progress meetings. Except for kick-off meetings at the introduction of new projects, progress meetings had become unnecessary.

MEETINGS TO INFORM PEOPLE ABOUT THE PROPOSED OUTCOME OF A PROJECT

It sometimes happens that a meeting has to be called to advise non-project members (stakeholders) about a proposed project. Although this might be necessary for various occasions, we can identify two main categories of such meetings.

Sometimes, early in the life cycle of a large public project, one or more consultative meetings have to be arranged to which members of the general public are invited, along with civic dignitaries and all other kinds of interested parties. That might be part of a lengthy public enquiry into the project. Such meetings fall into two parts, which are first a presentation of the facts of the proposed project, followed by a question and answer session during which representatives of the project management or investment team listen to questions or statements from those present.

Another kind of presentation meeting is seen when a management change project is nearing its conclusion and the time comes to announce the changes to all the staff whose working lives will be affected by changes in procedures or the organisation. Very often people become concerned for the security of their jobs, worry about their status under the changed regime, or have doubts about their ability to master the new challenges presented to them.

Although these two kinds of meetings take place at opposite ends of the project life cycle and are very different in scale, they have some similarities and have two requirements in common.

The first requirement is that the project management team must be fully prepared. They need to have 'done their homework' and have all the facts of the project available. A good presentation, showing the project in its most attractive aspects, makes a good start. The reasons for the project and the advantages for the community or the organisation must be presented in the most attractive light. For public projects models and plans should be placed on public display for perhaps a week before the meeting takes place, so that people can familiarise themselves with the proposals and come to the meeting prepared.

The second essential factor for both public meetings and in-house meetings is that the project management team must anticipate the questions that will be asked and be ready to answer them as fully and truthfully as possible. The audience, whether public or in-house, must be given the feeling that they are (as far as is practicable) being consulted. They must feel that their questions and apprehensions are being taken seriously. They need reassurance that any fears they might have about the project are either groundless, or will be taken into account.

So, the overriding piece of advice here is 'be prepared'.

References and Further Reading

Bentley, T. (1976), *Information, Communications and the Paperwork Explosion*, Maidenhead: McGraw-Hill.

Lock, D. (2013), *Project Management*, 10th edn, Farnham: Gower.

Roberts-Phelps, G. (2001), *50 Ways to Liven up your Meetings*, Aldershot: Gower.

Streibel, B.J. (2007), *Plan and Conduct Effective Meetings*, New York: McGraw-Hill.

Developing the Individual

35 *Learning and Training: Part 1*

DAVE DAVIS

There is a difference between learning and training. Learning involves increasing both the amount of data in a person's memory and the ability to retrieve this data in a specific context. Training, on the other hand, is the ability to control an individual's behaviour based on response to a situation.

Learning and Wisdom

As people achieve higher levels of leadership responsibility, effectiveness is less a matter of knowledge and more a matter of influence. Leaders grow through using wisdom. That wisdom is achieved by increasing the data in their brains through:

- learning;
- categorising the data into various intelligences;
- and finally training their behaviour to select the correct approach for a given situation.

As indicated by Figure 35.1, knowledge is the result of being able to build on data, putting it into a proper context and then turning that information into knowledge. Wisdom is a leader's ability to be able to question knowledge and then apply it for optimum results.

Here is a brief case example to illustrate the concept of a leader using wisdom to resolve a situation. There was a television commercial in the US several years ago in which a leader was observing the work habits of the office staff. When this leader noticed that most staff preferred using a certain brand of computer over another; he was able to relate that behaviour to a context of productivity and preference. This led to the knowledge that users preferred this brand of computer to the other. A technical person told the leader that the despised machines had more memory, more processor power, and more disk space and therefore must have been superior. However, this clearly was not the case. The leader queried this knowledge and retrieved it to make the observation that perhaps there was something beyond the technology that caused people to use the apparently inferior machine. Clearly that machine was a better fit for the office needs. The leader applied wisdom against the data and made a conclusion. The conclusion was that the technical specification was only a portion of the entire productivity equation. That ability to put information into your brain and use it to build knowledge is an example of learning. Figure 35.1 illustrates the process.

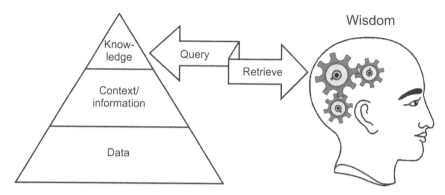

Figure 35.1 From data to wisdom

Wisdom involves more than just the ability to query knowledge and bring it into your brain. Wisdom involves a multitude of soft skills including knowing how to explain the observation, when to share the observation and finally to obtain feedback on the wisdom. So leadership training needs to involve the soft skills associated with obtaining data and assimilating data in order to communicate wisdom. This chapter will investigate how to help leaders gain the ability to influence wisdom and other soft skills.

Training and Intelligence

Traditionally, training has focused on building the knowledge of an individual. However, the trend is changing from memorising knowledge to application of knowledge and soft skills in order to provide a higher level of assimilation for the trainee. Moore (2006) discusses how training is more than just learning the technical aspects of a job – it involves understanding the 'customer experience' and how to provide excellent customer service. When describing the training experience Moore states: 'Starbucks focuses much of its store-level barista training programs on teaching employees to deliver not ordinary customer service but legendary customer service. However, Starbucks doesn't rely totally on bulky and verbose training manuals to teach baristas how to 'deliver legendary customer service'. Instead, Starbucks instils two customer-service-focused mantras in the hearts and minds of every barista:

1. Just say 'Yes';
2. Connect, discover, respond.

Leadership training has an even greater emphasis on defining the experience and less on the technical tools required to perform a transformation.

INTELLIGENCE

Education is no substitute for intelligence. (Frank Herbert)

Training has migrated from the activity of acquiring knowledge to the activity of growing the ability to utilise wisdom as an influencing behaviour. Applying this concept requires understanding of how the human being is able to take different data, wrap it around a context, build the knowledge, assimilate the knowledge and apply into a specific situation. Intelligence defines this capacity for internally converting external stimuli into knowledge, behaviour or means of interacting with other stimuli. For many years the psychology world focused primarily on intellectual intelligence as a means to measure how 'smart' a person was in relation to others, which means that determination of intelligence does not involve solving a numerical formula. On the other hand, determination of intelligence quotient (IQ) does involve a mathematical equation (IQ = 100MA/CA, where MA is mental age and CA is chronological age).

What if we looked at intelligence in areas other than intellectual capability? If we consider data sources to be contained in many different types of packages, such as people's behaviour, musical notes or spatial relationships, we begin to realise that there are many different levels of intelligence. More succinctly, the brain is able to process many different types of data and has a different capacity for different data types. Thus enters the term *emotional intelligence* (EI). EI is one term given to the concept that there are many distinct types of intelligence an individual possesses for processing data (see Chapter 53 for more on EI).

Gardner (1983) lists seven distinct types of intelligence as follows:

1. *Logical/mathematical* – probably the closest to the traditional idea of intelligence, manifested by a facility for science, puzzles, mathematics, estimating and planning.
2. *Linguistic* – manifested by the ability to acquire language and fluency in discussion. People with high linguistic intelligence enjoy lively debate, writing letters, books, poetry and verse, and filling out forms.
3. *Spatial* – the ability to map or picture the environment mentally, a process or a concept. Spatially intelligent people can easily visualise and manipulate shapes, are highly observant, have a good sense of direction, can easily follow diagrams and assemble furniture or other do-it-yourself projects.
4. *Musical* – musically intelligent people have the facility for creating, remembering or replaying tunes or the playing of an instrument, but can associate those tunes with other facts as a learning or memorisation tool.
5. *Body-kinaesthetic* – those with high kinaesthetic intelligence are well coordinated, work well with their hands, and are high-energy on-the-go people who learn through example and hands-on experience (trial and error). Associated professions would be as diverse as athletes, typists, carpenters and dancers.
6. *Interpersonal* – the facility for understanding and cooperating with other people, to notice and appreciate what affects others; sensitivity. They are good listeners and group leaders and participants; social butterflies; nurturers. Highly interpersonally intelligent people make excellent teachers, nurses, salesmen, politicians and diplomats.
7. *Intrapersonal* – the facility for looking within oneself, of understanding one's own emotions and motivations. Highly intrapersonally intelligent people do not make quick, rash decisions and often enjoy solitary pursuits and hobbies. They often keep a journal and diary.

Gardner seeks to disprove the notion that intelligence in a human being can be completely measured by common standardised tests like the IQ test. In his own words, 'the score of intelligence tests does predict one's ability to handle school subjects though it foretells little of success in later life'.

The term *emotional quotient*, or EQ, would be used to measure these seven intelligences within a person and their capacity to work within each one. The interpersonal and intrapersonal intelligences focus heavily on understanding people and are the foundation of many leadership models including the *motivational value skills* (MVS).

Whilst these models focus primarily on human intelligence and EI, there is a theory that intelligence needs to focus on a scale larger than just the human being's internal capacity to process data. It should relate to an individual's capacity to assimilate data and apply it to a specific life situation. Beyond intellectual intelligence and EI, the concept of managerial intelligence is based on work by Stemberg (1997). The management intelligence model focuses on being able to relate EI and ethical practices, with business intelligence, functional intelligence and technical intelligence. This holistic view does include the subsets of EI and IQ, but is noteworthy due to its specific capability to assimilate business principles with human principles.

Managerial intelligence differs from general intelligence as it is primarily focused on the domain of business, or in other words the ability to create a product or deliver a service that provides added value for the shareholders. To remain consistent with other intelligence models, the concept of *managerial quotient*, or MQ, would be able to measure the capacity an individual would have to handle the application of people and data to business.

There are many theories of intelligence and their associated quotients but I shall restrict myself in this chapter to IQ, EQ and MQ because these are more directly related to improving leadership in business.

The effective manager, and leader, must have more than just data intelligence and ability to retrieve data. The most effective manager must have a mixture of IQ, EQ and MQ with the ability to apply that mix at the proper time with the appropriate level of detail. The professional employment agency CareerBuilders conducted a survey asking executives which intelligence is most sought after when hiring new executives or promoting from within. The breakdown of the results was as follows showed the following weightings:

IQ, 26 per cent;
EQ, 36 per cent;
MQ, 38 per cent.

The same survey mentions how executives value EI over IQ. For workers being considered for a promotion, the high EI candidate will beat the high IQ candidate 75 per cent of the time. Why does do these data matter? Simply put, rules for leadership have changed over the last few years and leaders must adapt to remain effective.

Learning for Leadership

The following emotional skills are associated with building leadership capabilities.

1. Intrapersonal

    a) self-regard;
    b) emotional self-awareness;
    c) assertiveness;
    d) independence;
    e) self-actualisation.

2. Interpersonal

    a) empathy;
    b) social responsibility;
    c) interpersonal relationships.

3. Stress management
    a) stress tolerance;
    b) impulse control.

4. Adaptability

    a) reality testing;
    b) flexibility;
    c) problem solving.

5. General mood

    a) optimism;
    b) happiness.

6. Positive impression
7. Inconsistency index

There are many assessment tools available on the Internet to help an individual determine their training needs for improving each skill. Effective twenty-first century leaders will have a grasp of their personal intelligence inventories and seek to improve understanding of their personal capabilities. Learning leadership is a combination of learning about yourself, learning how others perceive you and improving your emotional skills.

The leader is not expected to become a different person in order to achieve a position of importance. Instead, the expectation is to grow to a more emotionally intelligent individual that influences the behaviour of team members. This growth is a lifelong journey; don't expect leaders to be able to master all dimensions of EI and emotional skills at once. Superhuman efforts are not required to make meaningful change. Rather, the leader should take careful stock of their current goals, their organisational culture and the feedback they receive from others. With this information, they can identify the two dimensions that they most need to work on right now. The goal is to lead like *you*, only better!

Cognitive Response

Leadership rests not only upon ability, not only upon capacity; having the capacity to lead is not enough. The leader must be willing to use it. His leadership is then based on truth and character. There must be truth in the purpose and willpower in the character. (Vince Lombardi)

Leadership is about inspiring people to achieve a common goal, it is not a popularity contest, nor a 'how to win friends and influence people' mindset. It is the ability to make difficult decisions and providing purpose for team members. The true leader will do that instinctively, without having to consult notes or Google searches to find the appropriate response to each situation. For that kind of response you need to train your brain – so that you utilise your skills and knowledge without having to go into the deeper recesses of your knowledge.

There is ongoing controversy on whether or not leadership is a natural ability, or if an individual can be made a leader through schooling. If leadership is a behaviour, then leaders can be made. An individual's cognitive behaviour to react in a certain leadership way to a situation can be taught so that it becomes their dominant personality trait. This leadership behaviour needs to be reinforced with every life experience in order for it to move to a cognitive or subconscious level of reaction.

Although my premise is that leadership training can change behaviour at a cognitive level, it is a great deal easier to define that behaviour based on an individual's DNA. This DNA, which includes their hardware learning styles, intellectual capacity and ability to store and retrieve knowledge, is the foundation of how a leader's cognitive ability is formed. By increasing each of these components, an individual's leadership capability increases and their cognitive capacity expands. If an individual is able to maximise their intellectual capacity to process information in a multitude of types (IQ, EQ and MQ), then they are better able to learn the behaviour of a leader. By mastering this behaviour, a leader constantly grows in their ability to demonstrate wisdom and influence the behaviour of others.

Learning and Learning Curves

Everyone knows what a curve is, until he has studied enough mathematics to become confused through the countless number of possible exceptions. (Felix Kline)

People learn at different rates based on the subject matter that is being studied, the atmosphere in which one is studying and whether they are studying to master a skill or just adding data to their memory storage. The rate at which an individual learns is referred to as a learning curve.

A learning curve is a concept used to measure how quickly a skill can be mastered. Usually shown as a simple graph, a learning curve often depicts the combination of the time it takes to learn a new idea or skill set, combined with the rate at which mastery is achieved. Figure 35.2 demonstrates this concept.

Learning curves are often used to measure an individual's progress against an average. A steep curve means there is a large gain of knowledge in the early stages, displayed on the usual graph as a steep incline at the beginning that gradually tapers out. Chess,

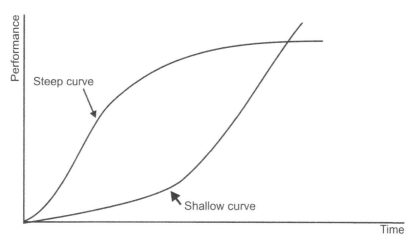

Figure 35.2 Learning curves

for instance, might be considered a game with a steep learning curve, for whilst the rules are simple and quickly learned, mastery over the game may take years. The term is also sometimes used to describe a particularly difficult or arduous skill to learn, as steep slopes are presumably harder to climb. The shallow line represents a gradual learning, for example: an initial set of rules is learned and then these rules are built upon over time. The overall learning will eventually get to the same point (a level of knowledge over time) but the path to get there differs. Steepness of the curve is analogous to the ability to store information and master an associated skill.

The beginning of this chapter discussed learning as a means of putting data into your brain and being able to structure the data into useable pieces of knowledge, it discussed the ability to query that knowledge and bring back an answer as a distinct step. But not all knowledge is equal. Figure 35.3 shows that there are different levels, or depth of knowledge, that go from a level of shallow knowledge to episodic knowledge. Learning plays an important role in an individual's depth of knowledge, by adding more facts and examples to the information in the mind, and organising it in different patterns, the learner has increased their ability to store and retrieve information.

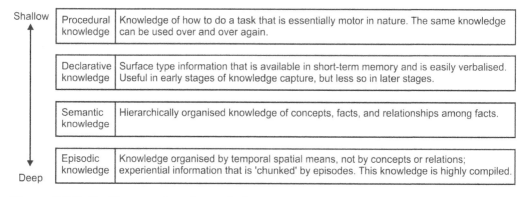

Figure 35.3 Shallow to deep knowledge

Skill is a slightly higher level than learning. A skill is the ability to use your knowledge to have your body perform a specific action to complete a task. This can be a skill to utilise a tool or machine such as pounding a nail with a hammer or being able translate a thought into an SQL query to get data from a database. Even answering a question involves a skill – when asked the question, you query your memory for the answer and then your body translates that memory into the proper words to answer the question. A person's ability to perform a skill can be improved and demonstrated through mastery.

Wisdom usually combines both knowledge and skill. Consider the skill of tightening a screw with a screwdriver. An individual has a great deal of knowledge in order to know that the screw is the proper equipment to use in order to connect two pieces of material. Based on the type of screw (cross head or slotted) the person will use their knowledge, and wisdom, to select the proper screwdriver for the task. The person will then use his/her skills to insert the screwdriver into the screw and turning clockwise with the proper pressure to drive it home.

Behavioural modification or cognitive learning is a completely different type of learning. Rather than adding knowledge to your memory, the learning is training on how to behave based on the situation. This cognitive learning requires a constant series of rewards and punishment. The concept is that when acceptable behaviour is demonstrated, the learner is rewarded (like treats for a dog that sits on command). An example of the punishment alternative for undesired behaviour would be a fine for speeding on the highway. These actions and responses take time, so a leader's cognitive learning can take an extended period of time. As will be discussed later, each individual has a style that best meets their ability to learn knowledge and train their cognitive responses.

Another factor that contributes to an individual's overall acceleration on a learning curve is the result of timing. As I wrote above, the rules of chess might be easily learned, but mastery of chess might take many years. The same is true with a leader's emotional skills and cognitive behaviours. Change is generally dependent on timing,

Blanchard (2009) provides an example that training needs to have the proper preparation and introduced at the appropriate time. He writes:

> Experience has shown that most organizations jump into change leadership strategy much too soon. In many cases, executives announce the change and try to get people into training as soon as possible. Unfortunately, people's information and personal concerns have not been addressed, so the results of the training are less than optimal. Also, training often is delivered before all the kinks are worked out, contingencies are planned for, help desks are created, or systems are aligned. Finally, early training usually fails because it's 'one size fits all'. After the learning's from pilots and experiments are culled and the right infrastructure is in place, training for the change should be done in as individualized a way as possible. Ideally, a training strategy for each individual should be delivered at just the right time.

An individual's learning curve is just that – individual. The shape of the curve is not as important as the individual's ability to move upward along the curve. The upward movement demonstrates an increase of knowledge over time. The curve can also be applied to learning a skill and its associated mastery.

Knowing Yourself

Understand your staff, clients and prospects by understanding yourself in terms of your personality and your personal communications style. When you understand yourself you will understand what is going on around you. (Wendy Evans)

Self-understanding is fundamental to success. It requires an honesty which acknowledges our imperfections and an understanding that we have developed definite preferences and prejudices about life. Having imperfections, preferences and prejudices is all part of being human. But it is the failure to recognise the influence they have on our everyday decisions and actions which hinders our progress.

Our imperfections, preferences and prejudices govern our behaviour whether we are aware of them or not. If we are not aware of them we remain under their control as we can do nothing to control them or counteract them. Self-aware people, who at least are able to name their imperfections if not overcome them, have more control over their lives as they understand the way they naturally prefer to respond. Before they respond or react they can decide if that is an appropriate response and, if need be, choose to modify their behaviour. A leader's personal learning styles, motivational values system, body language, speech inflection and level of enthusiasm, whilst natural to them, might alienate others. Once a leader learns how to understand themselves, they have the tools to understand other people and inspire them to behave in accordance with their goals and objectives.

KNOW YOUR PREFERRED NEURO LINGUISTIC PROGRAMMING (NLP) LEARNING STYLE

Just as people have different ways of querying and retrieving knowledge, and subsequently apply wisdom, people have different ways of getting data into their brain and organising the data into information. So as part of learning to be a better leader and understanding yourself, you must understand your appropriate learning style. Many psychologists believe that there are as many subconscious and cognitive factors involved in learning (inward creation of knowledge from shallow to deep), as there are in behaviour (outward action based on knowledge retrieval and application). The science of understanding how we process data from outside our self into our self is known as NLP and that subject is discussed at greater length in Chapter 50. One subset of NLP is the theory that people have four different profiles of learning and, like the concept of behaviour, one profile dominates the others. These are the four identified learning styles:

- visual: learning by seeing something;
- auditory: learning by hearing something;
- kinaesthetic/tactile: learning by feeling, touching, from a hands-on experience;
- internal dialogue or auditory digital: person learns by reading, research and e-learning. Very astute at using social media.

Visual

A visual learner associates best with pictures, drawings, diagrams and other things that are seen. Some good learning traits for visual learners include:

- Write things down. Take notes in class to help you remember things better and for use in studying for tests. Compare your notes with those of a friend who is a good note taker.
- Use a highlighter for main ideas and important facts in your textbook or notes.
- Preview a chapter before reading it by looking at the titles, introduction, subtopics, key terms and conclusion/summary.
- Pay attention to graphs, pictures and charts.

Learning from a lecture is not easy for visual learners. When listening to a lecture, always look at the speaker to help you maintain your attention. Summarise important concepts but don't try to write verbatim what they are saying. Sit close to the front of the room and away from distractions such as your close friends, doors or windows. Practice visualising or picturing important information. Use flashcards to help you isolate and mentally 'see' facts and their chronological or sequential order.

Auditory

Auditory learners learn best by hearing or listening. They prefer talking about a situation. They express emotions verbally; enjoy listening, but cannot wait to talk. They like hearing themselves and others talk and they learn best through verbal instruction. They study well when they have a friend to discuss material with. An auditory person would learn about the D-Day invasion in the Second World War by listening to audio tapes of the event. Some good learning traits for auditory learners include:

- Tape-record classroom lectures and class notes. Summarising is especially helpful.
- Listen to books on CD or interviews on the radio to enhance knowledge exposure.
- When preparing for a test, tape-record review sheets and important notes and listen to the tape several times.
- Write vocabulary words on index cards with definitions on the back. Review them by reading words aloud, repeating the definition and then checking to see if you are correct.
- Verbalise things you want to remember such as dates, key terms, quotes and important events.
- Read aloud whenever possible.

If you can verbalise the information, you increase the probability of understanding it. Have a study partner ask you questions and vice versa. Verbally review facts and terms which must be memorised.

Kinaesthetic/Tactile

Kinaesthetic/tactile learners learn best by doing. They need direct involvement. They fidget when reading and are not avid readers. They remember best what is done, not what is seen or heard. They express emotions physically by jumping and gesturing. They do not listen well. They try things out by touching, feeling and manipulating. They need frequent breaks when studying. A kinaesthetic/tactile person would learn by dramatising, or acting out a scene. Some good learning tips for these people include:

- Whilst in class, experiment with ways of moving without disturbing the class. For example, cross your legs and bounce your foot that is off the floor, roll a pencil between your fingers, squeeze a large eraser or doodle on a piece of paper.
- Write vocabulary words or terms on an index card and walk around whilst reviewing or reciting them.
- Try to act out words or events with simple gestures which will aid your recall (such as smiling at the word 'amiable' or making a tight fist for the word 'penurious' or 'miserly'.
- Whenever possible, use graphic note-taking methods such as mapping, concept trees or time lines.
- Use a highlighter pen for main ideas and important facts in your textbook or notes.
- Try studying in different positions; like lying on your back or stomach and change position frequently.
- Take frequent, short breaks and do something that involves light activity such as getting a drink of water.
- Try writing key terms in the air with your finger or on a smooth surface or in the carpet.
- Whenever possible, experiment and 'do' your assignments, experiments and projects in an active way. For example, make drawings of key events.

Internal Dialogue or Auditory Digital

Internal dialogue or auditory digital learners learn best by reflecting, summarising or transposing into multimedia. They enjoy reflecting on thoughts and making mental models of complex concepts. They are meticulous at tracking and recording experiences and like to use social media. They memorise lists, procedures and processes. Some good learning traits for internal dialogue learners include:

- Listening to podcasts or video webcasts: things that can be started and stopped using a computer media player.
- Creating study cards in a spreadsheet or developing online quizzes.
- Liking information mapped into a logical flow or other means that demonstrates sequence and relationships.
- They love lists.
- Like to read and will seek out extended information on a specific topic.
- Talking inwardly to themselves, often using facts, figures and other logic.
- Making plans as a matter of course.

DETERMINING ONE'S PERSONAL LEARNING STYLE

Most people learn from a combination of these learning styles, but more strongly lean towards one style in particular.

One way to determine an individual's preferred learning style is through a questionnaire-led survey. A typical learning style survey consists of situational statements and a preference scale. Individuals completing the questionnaire are asked to choose or rate how they prefer to deal with a situation. Based on responses to the scenarios, points are added up to determine which sensory learning method the individual tends to use most often.

As with all models, there are many variations, and this NLP model is no exception. Some studies associate learning styles with intelligence types, and assume that our capacity to acquire knowledge aligns with our capacity to process information. Utilising the intelligence model would accommodate a person's monolithic style and address whether they like to learn in groups in a higher social setting (intrapersonal) or prefer learning on their own in a solitary setting (interpersonal). Again, these are models, and you are free to pick and choose what best applies to you, but the concept of knowing yourself and how you learn, should be a critical factor in determining which type of learning and training you wish to pursue.

Mindset for Training

Education is the kindling of a flame, not the filling of a vessel. (Socrates)

The most important aspect of education, learning, training, or whatever term you wish to use, is the mental state of mind that the learner brings to the experience. If the individual is not open to learning new things, then they will most likely fail as a leader. Learning involves much more than acquiring knowledge, it is the application of that knowledge and being able to adapt to changing circumstances that define a distinguished leader. If you think you already know everything there is to know about leadership, then this chapter will serve no purpose for you. However, if you believe that leading includes constant acquisition of knowledge and training the cognitive self to be able to best respond to various scenarios, then you are on the path to greater learning.

MOVING TRAINED REACTION TO COGNITIVE LEVEL

A person always doing his or her best becomes a natural leader, just by example. (Joe DiMaggio)

The ultimate goal of leadership training is to move the best practices and ability to work with people into a person's cognitive thinking. It becomes natural. Continuous improvement is an example of being a natural leader, you keep learning, do your best, fail, learn from the failure, reflect on what happened, observe people and talk with people. And your behaviour is such that you are able to do this without thinking.

Nelson Mandela is a great example of a great man who learned to be a leader. He started at a low level on the social ladder and most likely had a pretty low self-esteem. Yet he retained his equilibrium. Always able to see the good as well as the bad, he could describe the dirt-floored hut he inhabited in the black township of Alexandra without rancour. Crime, filth and poverty were endemic in his neighbourhood, but he found the precarious life there 'exhilarating'. He focused on its liveliness and his neighbours' resourcefulness. Neither weak nor naïve, he truly believed that by remaining optimistic and expecting people to do the right thing, they often surprised him by doing just that. The positive attitude and faith that informed Mandela's character would see him through the great hardships of his life.

MORAL COMPASS

In summary, the best guide for your own leadership training journey is listening to your moral compass – that internal direction set by your personal values, your EI and your wisdom in order to do the right thing. Most leaders don't fail because of lack of EI; they succeed or fail because of an issue related to character. Irwin (2009) discusses four reasons why most leaders fail, as follows:

1. *Character trumps competence* – Whilst being good at what we do is essential, more people fail because of some issue related to character. Many of those I studied were ultimately fired not because of a lack of competence but rather a failure of character. I don't mean character in the sense of being dishonest and defrauding the organisation. Rather, the absence of one or more of four dimensions of character is clearly tied to derailment: authenticity, self-management, humility and courage. The full expression of the dark side of these qualities nearly always dooms us.
2. *Arrogance is the mother of all derailers* – Arrogance takes many forms. The most rudimentary is the self-centred focus that fosters a belief that I am central to the viability of the organisation, the church, the ministry, the department or the team. A dismissiveness of others' contributions is inevitable.
3. *Lack of self/other awareness is a common denominator of all derailments* – A failure of self-management and the imperceptive, ill-conceived, impulsive or volatile actions that follow are certain derailers. Leaders who eschew corrective feedback become 'truth-starved'.
4. W*e are always who we are … especially under stress* – Stress brings out what's inside us. If you don't think you have a dark side to your character, then you probably haven't been under enough stress! Wise leaders manage their stress levels and mitigate its pernicious impact on our behaviour.

Derailment is not inevitable, but without attention to development, it is probable. Derailment is a process that proceeds in predictable stages. Ignoring the early warning signs puts us in great peril. Effective leaders must set direction, gain alignment among diverse constituencies, risk change, build high-performing teams, achieve results, go the extra mile and endure ungodly stress. However, to be enthusiastically followed, leaders must also be guided by an inner compass that fosters trust on the part of their followers and includes continuous growth in all matters of knowledge and intelligence – continually learning and trying. Success is guided by an internal compass and that compass is character. When character is seriously compromised, derailment often follows.

References and Further Reading

Arbinger Institute (2010), *Leadership and Self-Deception: Getting out of the Box*, San Francisco, CA: Berrett-Koehler, 137–8.

Blanchard, K. (2009), *Leading at a Higher Level, Revised and Expanded Edition*, Upper Saddle River, NJ: Pearson Education.

Blanchard, K. and Barrett, C. (2010), *Lead with LUV: A Different Way to Create Real Success*, Upper Saddle River, NJ: Pearson Education.

Dulewicz, C., Young, M. and Dulewicz, V. (2005), 'The relevance of emotional intelligence for leadership performance', *Journal of General Management*, 30(3), 71–87.

Gardner, H. (1983), *Frames of Mind*, New York: Basic Books.

Goldsmith, M. and Reiter, M. (2007), *What Got You Here Won't Get You There: How Successful People Become Even More Successful*, New York: Hyperion.

Irwin, T. (2009), *Derailed: Five Lessons Learned From Catastrophic Failures of Leadership*, Nashville, TN: Thomas Nelson.

Lennick, D., Kiel, F., Huntsman, J.M. and Parker, J.F. (2011), *Essential Lessons on Leadership*, (Collection), (Kindle Locations 308–309), Pearson Education (US), Kindle Edition.

Moore, J. (2006), *Tribal Knowledge: Business Wisdom Brewed from the Grounds of Starbucks Corporate Culture*, Kaplan, Kindle Edition, 86–7.

New Word City (2010), *Nelson Mandela's Leadership Lessons* (Kindle Locations 90–92), Pearson Education (US), Kindle Edition.

Stemberg, R.J. (1997), 'Managerial intelligence: Why IQ isn't enough', *Journal of Management*, June 1997, 23(3), 475–93.

Swenson, R. (2004), *Margin: Restoring Emotional, Physical, Financial, and Time Reserves to Overloaded Lives*, Colorado Springs, CO: NavPress.

Terez, T. (2009), 'Better Workplace Now', Tom Terez Workplace Solutions, Inc. Available at: http://www.betterworkplacenow.com

Walsh, B. (2011), *VAK Self-Audit: Visual, Auditory, and Kinesthetic Communication and Learning Styles* (Kindle Locations 17–19), Victoria, Canada: Walsh Seminars Ltd.

36 *Learning and Training: Part 2*

DAVE DAVIS

Chapter 35 focused on the importance of learning and training methods for a leader. This chapter describes some of the different methods or opportunities for learning. Coaching and mentoring are clearly part of learning and training, but I shall not describe these here because they are discussed fully in Chapter 40.

Knowledge, Skills and Abilities

> *If money is your hope for independence you will never have it. The only real security that a man will have in this world is a reserve of knowledge, experience, and ability. (Henry Ford)*

KSA is an abbreviation for knowledge, skills and abilities, a series of narrative statements that are required when applying for federal government jobs in the US. KSAs are used along with resumés to help select the best applicants. KSAs necessary for the successful performance of a position are contained on each job vacancy announcement. KSAs are an effective means of categorising the capability of an individual. They emphasise previous accomplishments. The following definitions are a précis of those used by the US Department of Veterans Affairs.

Knowledge – an organised body of information, usually factual or procedural in nature. For example, having knowledge of human resources rules and regulations could be used as a KSA for an HR specialist position.

Skill – the proficient manual, verbal or mental manipulation of data or things. For example, having skill with operating personal computers could be used as a KSA when applying for an office automation position. Respondents would be asked to explain the computers and software programs they had used at work.

Ability – the power or capacity to perform an activity or task. For example, having the ability to use a variety of laboratory instruments could be used towards obtaining a position as a laboratory technician. Applicants would be asked to describe the types of laboratory instruments and equipment they had used, the types of assignments completed using that equipment, and the impact of using the equipment on their work environment.

Soft skill	Definition
Thinking	The process of using one's mind to consider or reason about something. Thinking results in a variety of ideas that contain actions needed to reach a desired outcome. One of the challenges is to agree on what the different types of thinking are, with some models having three types but others up to 15 types. These types could include critical thinking, creative thinking, strategic thinking and many others. The training challenge results from the circumstances of the particular case, or in other words the problem that causes thinking exercises to happen. Whilst it is relatively easy to teach the mechanics of thinking, teaching how to pattern-match or think critically involves a deep understanding of a particular domain of knowledge.
Decision-making	Makes sound, well-informed and objective decisions. Perceives the impact and implications of decisions. Commits to action, even in uncertain situations, to accomplish organisational goals. Causes change.
Interpersonal skills	Shows understanding, friendliness, courtesy, tact, empathy, concern and politeness to others. Develops and maintains effective relationships with others. Might include dealing effectively with individuals who are difficult, hostile or distressed. Relates well to people from varied backgrounds and situations. Is sensitive to cultural diversity, race, gender, disabilities and other individual differences.
Problem-solving	Identifies problems. Determines the accuracy and relevance of information. Uses sound judgement to generate and evaluate alternative solutions and to make recommendations.
Communicating	Expresses information (such as ideas or facts) effectively to individuals or groups, taking into account the audience and the nature of the information (for example, whether the information is sensitive, technical or controversial). Makes clear and convincing oral presentations. Listens to others. Picks up non-verbal cues and responds appropriately.
Teamwork and collaboration	Inspires, motivates and guides others towards accomplishing goals. Consistently develops and sustains cooperative working relationships. Encourages and facilitates cooperation within the organisation and with customer groups. Fosters commitment, team spirit, pride and trust. Develops leadership in others through coaching, mentoring, rewarding and guiding employees.

Figure 36.1 Some soft skills that might feature in a KSA list

KSAs are effective tools for summarising your current skill set and for identifying gaps where you might seek additional training. One of the benefits of the KSA model is that it accommodates both hard skills and soft skills, with hard skills being the technical and mechanical ability to perform a task, whilst soft skills represent your people skills in order to get individuals to work as a team. There is a cliché that soft skills are the hard skills to master, and that is because they do not have immediately observable results. Soft skills involve human emotion and logic and represent factors that distinguish quality leaders from standard leaders. Figure 36.1 above is a sample of some KSA soft skills with their associated definitions.

Facilitated versus Solitary Training

For the purpose of this chapter, training is defined as a pre-planned set of objectives with structured content and exercises to reinforce the concept being taught. There are many different opportunities for a leader to obtain training to learn new skills, enhance existing skills or practise for mastery. These opportunities can be offered through professional organisations, universities, online business training, books and computer-based education. In selecting training opportunities, the individual must first define a topic they wish to be trained on, and then the delivery method that is being used to provide the training.

There are primarily two types of training delivery as follows:

1. *Facilitated training* involves a person, or team of people, to guide the learning experience. In facilitated training, the instructor guides the learning topics and flow of the course. The instructor determines what lessons are being covered, facilitates discussion and provides feedback. Facilitated training often involves a classroom and with a timetable for classes. There can also be a predefined schedule for tests and assignments. Trainee assessment is provided by the instructor and is often based on a combination of testing and class involvement.
2. *Solitary training* involves an individual self-guided experience. In solitary training, the individual guides the learning topics and the course of the flow. Trainees determine the sequence of lessons and can perform class work whenever they want to. There is no interactivity with instructors or other students and limited opportunity to ask specific questions or participate in active discussions. Trainee assessment is provided via self-directed testing and survey. It has no feedback from a facilitator. Reading a book, attending an online webinar, listening to podcasts or watching instructional videos are all forms of solitary learning. Some webinars do allow for student questions, but they are rarely specific or structured. Many of these training opportunities are customer education pieces designed to sell a product or service.

Distance learning is a hybrid of facilitated and solitary training. Many universities and private firms offer such training as an option to have some guided lesson exposure, but giving the student the flexibility of deciding when and where to study. These opportunities have an online facilitator who can guide moderated discussion, give feedback and provide assignments that can utilise work experience.

Figure 36.2, on the next page, compares facilitated and solitary training delivery as these apply to certain learning characteristics. Remember that an individual's learning style is going to be the principal criterion for determining the best delivery method.

Training ultimately is a means of providing knowledge improvements to an individual and perhaps maximising intelligence to process information more efficiently. However, training cannot be used for ethical behaviour of an individual. Lennick et al. (2011) discusses the fact that training does force ethical behaviour:

> *Ethics are standards of conduct that we ought to follow. There is some overlap of the two, but virtuous behaviour usually is left to individual discretion. All the professional training in the world does not guarantee moral leadership. Unlike laws, virtue cannot be politically mandated, let alone enforced by bureaucrats, but that doesn't stop them from trying. Congress considered the corporate world today so challenged when it comes to ethics that it enacted the Sarbanes-Oxley Act in an attempt to regain credibility for the marketplace. Ultimately, though, respect, civility, and integrity will return only upon the individual-by-individual return of values.*

The ultimate challenge in training leadership is not just providing opportunities to improve knowledge, but to programme a leader to use ethical discretion in all activities.

Characteristic	Facilitated training	Solitary training
Ability to do coursework at one's own time.	Limited. Classes are usually scheduled at set times with attendance required. The facilitator might provide homework that can be completed by the trainee at any time during the day.	High. There are no structured classes and thus no specific time commitments. Many solitary classes might require indication of completion (such as completing an on-line test by a set date) but the training can be taken at any time the learner wishes.
Ability to review material.	This is dependent upon the individual's notes and class material. Class materials can be read at any time.	Very flexible. This is good for digital learners. The individual can retake lessons, listen to podcasts or watch video casts over and over again.
Interaction with other students	Very high. A class is led by a trained instructor who can elicit experience from all class members. Good for people with high intrapersonal emotional intelligence tendency.	Limited. Many solitary classes allow no opportunity to discuss curriculum with other students.
Specific questions relating the material to one's own situation	Very high. The classroom environment encourages discussion that can bring real world cases into a controlled learning environment. The instructor also has the ability to supplement answers at a whiteboard and can draw logic flows and sketches.	Limited or non-existent. If the solitary training is a self-paced transfer course, then the knowledge flows only one way, from the instructor to the student. Distance learning classes do allow for specific questions, but often lack the benefit of real-time interaction. Questions are posed and answered through discussion forums, with limited capability to supplement the responses with visuals such as sketches or flowcharts.
Feedback	High. The instructor and other students provide feedback continuously during the life of the course.	Low. Usually feedback is limited to grading an answer to a question with a right or wrong indicator. Limited ability to ask questions as to why that result was obtained.

Figure 36.2 Facilitated and solitary training compared

Training Techniques

Being ignorant is not so much a shame, as being unwilling to learn. (Benjamin Franklin)

This section will look at different techniques that are used to facilitate learning. Many training curriculums discuss various techniques and by understanding what the technique is, the individual can align his/her learning style with the technique for maximum benefit.

BRAINSTORMING

Brainstorming asks that people free their minds to come up with ideas and thoughts that can at first seem to be a bit crazy. The hope is that some of these ideas can be crafted into original, creative solutions to the problem that you are trying to solve, whilst others can spark still more ideas. This approach aims to free people's minds from preconceptions and jolt them out of their normal ways of thinking. The excellent website www.mindtools.com gives valuable advice on many aspects of brainstorming. Brainstorming is also described elsewhere in this Handbook (for example in Chapter 34) but I shall comment further here.

In group brainstorming bad behaviour can creep into a session and people start to criticise ideas. A person might fear ridicule that an idea is too dramatic, and 'boss approval' becomes evident. Also, people can pay too much attention to other ideas and then become 'blocked' from coming up with their own. The final challenge with group brainstorming is avoiding 'group think' in which the brainstorming starts to become a justification exercise for a popular idea.

Whilst brainstorming sounds like a completely facilitated exercise, there is much benefit to be gained from individual or solitary brainstorming. Individual brainstorming tends to produce a wider range of idea topics than group brainstorming. You are less likely to 'piggyback' on other people's ideas and do not have to concern yourself with other people's egos, opinions or retaliation. Individual brainstorming gives you a better chance to explore the idea that is inhibited in groups. And finally, you do not have to wait your turn and have someone else stop speaking before you contribute your idea.

THE SARAH MODEL

Another useful training technique involves understanding the ability of people to adapt to change. The way change is introduced and the project leader's support and empathy are critical to its success. The initials SARAH stand for shock, anger, rejection, acceptance and hope, which are sequential stages that have been observed in people's reactions to imposed change. This is all relevant to the process for managing change, and that is dealt with more fully in Chapter 49. However, now the tables are turned and instead of learning and being trained for leadership, the project manager is expected to train others to accept change.

ACTION LEARNING

Action Learning is a facilitated method of learning on-the-job developed by Professor Reg. Revans. The unique and surprising characteristic of Action Learning is that it is not learning on one's own job, but through a process of temporarily swapping people between different jobs. So the learning experience is from doing someone else's job. You can read more about Action Learning in Chapter 38.

BUSINESS GAMES

Business games or simulations have been described as 'dynamic, ongoing subsets of real life'. In a business game, the players manage a hypothetical business situation with a defined set of rules that may or may not be revealed to all players before the start of the game. The game will be structured with the intention of reflecting the inherent risk and chaos associated with implementing change and leading a group of people. In the game, a problem is defined and as the players attempt to solve the problem, various events happen that can alter the plans or extend certain deliverables. The players have to make decisions subject to rules, and receive feedback concerning the results of their decisions.

Decision results can then be used as the basis for the next round of the game, and more decisions are made. The game progresses through several rounds with the final score being determined by the goals achieved. Games can be all inclusive or small teams can be formed to compete against each other.

Games are often computerised, which allows for the introduction of random reactions to decisions made by the players. Many games are currently in existence, from general 'top management' games to those concerned with only a particular business function such as production or inventory management. The benefit of the games for the leader is that leadership skills must be practised to get all members of the team to align to the strategies and embrace the decisions made based on the randomly changing conditions. Although the topics vary widely, there are seven areas seen as the domain in which business games are effective:

- decision-making skills;
- planning and forecasting skills;
- recognition of the interrelations and interdependencies in business firms;
- high participant interest and motivation;
- knowledge of facts and use of specific techniques;
- interpersonal skills;
- organising ability.

Business games are seen as being effective by many university and industrial practitioners in a number of important areas, and the level of support for these beliefs is quite substantial. But the effectiveness of a game is in direct proportion to the interest of the leader. Games have the potential to decline into a level of silliness if strict adherence to the rules and the process are not followed.

Learning opportunities that use games align well with kinaesthetic/tactile and digital learners. The idea of being a role player and having influence on outcomes is attractive to spatial thinkers and to those with data-driven emotional intelligence tendencies. For a leader it delivers important learning regarding the need to being able to explain decisions and comprehend that everything does not always go as planned.

There are times when circumstances outside anyone's control affect results, and team members are looking for leaders to get things back on track. The leader is also exposed to the truth that if you tell people to do something they can't do, or if you don't give them the proper tools or training, or if people don't understand why they should do something, they simply will not do it. Put that into the context of a distributed workforce spread all over the country, it is hard to make people do things they don't want to do.

If you want to implement something swiftly and successfully, you need to understand what people can do, you need to give them the tools and training to do it, and you need to tell them why they should do it. In the end, people must want to do it. This requires a leader whom people trust and respect.

T-GROUPS

A T-group (sometimes also referred to as a training group or sensitivity-training group, human relations training group or encounter group) is a form of group psychotherapy where participants learn about themselves through their interaction with each other. They can use group discussions, critical thinking skills, problem solving and role play to gain insights into themselves, others and how people interact. They are a training opportunity for improved understanding of an individual's interpersonal and intrapersonal emotion intelligence.

A T-group meeting is very open ended and usually has no defined agenda or explicit learning objective. Instead, it depends on a facilitator harnessing the energy of the team and channelling emotional reactions as they arise in participant interactions. An individual's statement may be decomposed into anterior motives and unintended interpretations and the participants learn to accept that an individual's learning style, emotional intelligence and mindset are powerful factors in communication.

The behaviours expressed in this type of learning border on the area of dangerous. As people are expected to reveal more and more about themselves, it is possible that drama can overtake the results. Extreme T-sessions might last for a weekend or more, with people sleeping, eating and talking in a confined area. There is a tendency to focus on negativity and emotive anger as a means of understanding yourself. The facilitator has to be highly effective at downplaying resentment and encouraging understanding and facilitation.

Editorial Comment (DL)

I once attended a weekend T-group as a participant and suffered no ill effects. However, I learned from our facilitator that there have been sessions that lasted for over a week. Those longer sessions bring natural leaders to the fore, which is useful information for the sponsoring employers. But the effects on the weaker participants could sometimes be disastrous, leading to mental breakdown and even suicidal tendencies.

Learning opportunities that use T-groups align well with kinaesthetic/tactile learners. The exercise requires a deep dive into an individual's emotional intelligence and the associated flaws inherent in everybody. This may not be a good model to use with subordinates as there is the possibility that unintended consequences could result from revealing too much about your opinions and beliefs. It is best to do as a retreat with people in similar positions in other organisations as it aligns with the US army idea that knowing yourself is the first step in leadership.

WORLD CAFÉ

The World Café is a structured approach to facilitating large group discussions and generating understanding. World Café is based on five principles that are the foundation of every discussion. A World Café can be face-to-face or virtual. Whilst the context, numbers, purpose, location and other circumstances can change with each event, the following are constant.

1. Setting: A special environment is created with small groups gathered at tables. There can be many tables at the café, but only four people are seated at one table at one time. Each table might have flowers, bread and butter, crayons, paper and so forth, but one item is designated as a 'talking stick'. The person holding the stick gets the floor.
2. Welcome and introduction: Each café has a host who sets the tone for the event. The host begins with a welcome and introduction to the protocol of the café, café etiquette and setting the context.

3. Small group rounds: The process begins with the first of three or more 20-minute rounds of conversation for the small group seated around a table. At the end of the 20 minutes, each member of the group moves to a different table. They may or may not choose to leave one person as the 'table host' for the next round, who welcomes the next group and briefly fills them in on what happened in the previous round.
4. Questions: Each round is prefaced with a question designed for the specific context and desired purpose of the session. The same questions can be used for more than one round, or they can be built upon each other to focus the conversation or guide its direction.
5. Harvest: After the small groups (and/or in between rounds, as desired), individuals are invited to share insights or other results from their conversations with the rest of the large group. These results are reflected visually in a variety of ways, most often using graphic recorders in the front of the room.

This technique was developed in the mid-1990s and has created quite a following in the Internet age. The World Café organisation has a website (see http://www.theworldcafe. com) which provides many tools and other information about the concept and its history.

Learning opportunities that use the World Café model align well with auditory and visual learners. This is a highly energised environment that focuses on creative thinking and application of knowledge. The topics can delve into the deepest levels of thinking and knowledge and challenge the participant to express abstract thoughts, ideas and beliefs in an understandable manner. It is a wonder technique to help a leader learn how to communicate vision.

MASTERY AND CONTINUOUS LEARNING

One can have no smaller or greater mastery than mastery of oneself. (Leonardo da Vinci)

The deepest level of knowledge is analogous with mastery of the facts and rules of a particular topic. Mastery means that you as an individual have achieved an extremely deep level of knowledge and are giving back to humanity what you have learned. Mastery represents a long continuous learning experience that incorporates many hours of study and learning. But mastery is not static – it is constantly being tweaked and maintained for comparison with knowledge and the latest trends and circumstances of modern life.

Obtaining mastery is not an accidental occurrence and takes many hours of effort. Several well-known authors, including Malcolm Gladwell, have stated that it takes a minimum of 5,000 hours to achieve mastery – and that is just the beginning. Mastery includes not just the deep knowledge, but the ability to communicate to others how that knowledge applies in society. But once mastery is earned, it has to be maintained.

Maintaining Mastery

One of the important aspects of mastery is maintenance. Staying in alignment requires regular tune-ups to monitor and prevent damaging effects of moral viruses and destructive emotions. But most important, alignment depends on continuously developing our moral and emotional competence. Maintenance is a series of continuous learning. Today's leader is always trying to learn more, implement their seven types of intelligence to their maximum efficiency, and increasing skills and knowledge to achieve the maximum benefit.

A leader must be constantly seeking training opportunities and reflect on all experiences to increase their learning.

Personal Margins

Swenson (2004) introduces the concept of margin and how important it is to the success of an individual. In general, Swenson's margin is the gap between you living your life as a spiritual person and your life running you as a slave of the modern world. Swenson defines the difference between having a margin and being marginless as follows:

> *The conditions of modern-day living devour margin. If you are homeless, we send you to a shelter. If you are penniless, we offer you food stamps. If you are breathless, we connect you to oxygen. But if you are marginless, we give you yet one more thing to do. Marginless is being thirty minutes late to the doctor's office because you were twenty minutes late getting out of the bank because you were ten minutes late dropping the kids off at school because the car ran out of gas two blocks from the gas station-and you forgot your wallet. Margin, on the other hand, is having breath left at the top of the staircase, money left at the end of the month, and sanity left at the end of adolescence.*

Leaders must learn to have control of the margins in their lives and to define themselves as much by what they do, as what they don't do.

References and Further Reading

Lennick, D., Kiel, F., Huntsman, J.M. and Parker, J.F. (2011), *Essential Lessons on Leadership*, (Collection), (Kindle Locations 308–309), Pearson Education (US), Kindle Edition.

Swenson, R. (2004), *Margin: Restoring Emotional, Physical, Financial, and Time Reserves to Overloaded Lives*, Colorado Springs, CO: NavPress.

See http://www.mindtools.com/brainstm.html

See http://www.newyorker.com/reporting/2012/01/30/120130fa_fact_lehrer

See http://www.techrepublic.com/blog/tech-manager/soft-skills-in-high-demand-in-a-high-tech-world/6881

See http://www.va.gov/jobs/hiring/apply/ksa.asp

37 *Self-development*

EDWARD WALLINGTON

This chapter outlines what self-development is, why it is important, how to approach it to maximise benefits and discusses the potential return on investment (ROI) of self-development.

Introduction

If you are not going forwards, you are either standing still, going sideways or going backwards – is this a position you want to be in?

Project management professionals, by the nature of their work, are regularly at the forefront of developments, pushing boundaries, exploring and using new approaches. Given this, is it possible to 'stand still' with little or no training, out-of-date knowledge or training that occurred 'many years ago'? Many would argue that as professionals, project managers need to ensure a continuous programme of self-evaluation and self-improvement, which allows enhanced and efficient working, and adaption to current and emerging challenges, whether these are well-defined projects, or ones with a high degree of uncertainty or complexity.

It has been recognised that little formal training in project management goes on for most people involved in managing projects, so the emphasis here is on self-help (Harland, 1989). Although stated a few years ago, this statement is still largely relevant. There has been an increase over the last 10 years of qualifications provided by project management associations and training companies, but it is variable as to how many project managers continue training and development beyond the initial 'basic training'.

The importance of self-development is highlighted by two of the largest professional project management organisations:

Andrew Bragg, Chief Executive of the Association for Project Management (APM), commented in a personal communication that:

> *APM considers continuing professional development (CPD) to be one of the hallmarks of the true professional. Adopting a structured approach to CPD is key to keeping up to date in a rapidly changing environment, allowing professionals to match development opportunities and needs effectively, and so exercise personal responsibility for their career. CPD is simply the professional's way of working.*

In another personal communication, Chris Field, President of PMI's UK Chapter, said that:

Given the cut and thrust of the day job, it's all too easy to neglect your own professional development, but do so at your peril. Increasingly in today's competitive environment it's vital to ensure you keep your skills contemporary and consistent with the demands of the job. Given the advent of new trends in project management those who invest in their own professional development are well placed to succeed in their future careers.

Definition of Self-development

The term self-development can mean different things to different people, and there are a number of different terms which are often used interchangeably. Many people refer to 'self-development', 'self-improvement', 'CPD' and 'continuous or life-long learning'. No matter which term you adopt and use, they all refer to the ongoing development of skills, knowledge and experience – whether this applies to your professional career or to personal interests.

It is fairly common to hear comments along the lines of 'I don't need to learn any more', 'I cannot see benefit in attending another course, I did one five years ago' or 'the business cannot afford to invest in staff attending yet another course'. These comments may stem from individual or organisational experience of courses previously undertaken, from a misunderstanding of what operating as a professional is about, or because of funding cutbacks in difficult economic conditions. The continuous need for self-development needs to be recognised, particularly by each individual.

As a project management professional, one needs to take personal responsibility for your continuing learning and development to develop talents and to be able to realise your full potential. It is not simply a case of sitting back and waiting for the organisation to train you. It is true that some organisations invest in staff training and organisational development, but more often than not these are not tailored to the individual. The organisation might, for example, bring in a training company to roll out the latest 'project management essentials' course and then leave it at that – you have been trained, now get on with it. Self-development is even more relevant for independent project managers who need to put aside time (usually unpaid) to focus on self-development activities.

Self-development is an essential tool that allows professionals to learn continuously and develop knowledge, behaviours and skills. The key element here is that it should be self-led, and you should not rely on or be led by your organisation and its desire to impart skills as part of a framework – that is important, but not the only development route.

Megginson and Whitaker (2007) sum up CPD with a number of key principles, as follows:

- Professional development is a continuous process that applies throughout a practitioner's working life;
- Individuals are responsible for controlling and managing their own development;
- Individuals should decide for themselves their learning needs and how to fulfil them;
- Learning targets should be clearly articulated and should reflect the needs of the employers and clients as well as the practitioner's individual goals;

- Learning is most effective when it is acknowledged as an integral part of all work activity rather than an additional burden.

As a professional person, taking an active interest in, control of, and responsibility for, your own learning and development is crucial. Self-development contributes to your ability and effectiveness through a continuous process of reflection and learning, to make sure you are informed of the latest project management methodologies and how to adopt new techniques to support project delivery.

Self-development is based around a structured approach to self- evaluation, learning and reassessment, to enable improvements to your knowledge, skills and understanding, supported by practical experience and application to increase competence and capability. This provides a framework for continued learning and development to ensure you are up to date with current practices to help you achieve project success. This is not about one big front-loaded effort, it is about a gradual development of abilities, and the accrual of benefits over time – it is a continuous process.

Self-development is not just about learning theory. It is important to translate new knowledge into the operational environment and use what has been learned. To realise the benefits of self-development, we need to embed learning through application. If we don't use something we have just learned, we will soon forget it.

An essential element of self-development is the ability to assess current skill and knowledge levels. It is important to stand still and have time to reflect – but stand still too long, and the opportunity will be gone.

Importance of Self-development

As project professionals we have responsibilities. We need to ensure we are working to a high quality standard, informed by skills, expertise and experience. This is supported within an ethical and duty of care framework of doing our best for our employer, our clients, the project management community, and ultimately ensuring we are delivering to the best of our abilities. This is furthered by our interest in projects and our desire to help ensure projects succeed and see that benefits are realised. This is why I am always astonished when I hear people question the benefits and importance of self-development.

I believe that continuous self-development is critical. The need to be able to demonstrate continuous learning and application of the theory is essential for any professional, in any business domain. We need to maintain our project management understanding, develop new skills, and ensure we are best placed to tackle increasingly complex projects. Do you have the correct skills and information to be able to deliver a quality of service, be able to maintain expertise and be able to manage yourself and your team? On the one hand, the competence of the project manager is in itself a factor in successful delivery of projects and on the other hand, the project manager needs to have competence in those areas that have the most impact on successful outcomes (Crawford, 2000). It is important to focus not only on the technical skills, but also the soft skills, such as communication and leadership. Projects are about people, and will not deliver unless you have the appropriate skill set and breadth of knowledge to be able to operate in a changing environment. Good project managers have a lot of skills already but self-development is about learning to use different skills in different situations (Obeng, 2011).

The need for CPD arises because security for individuals no longer lies in the job or organisation we work for, but in the skills, knowledge and experience that we have within ourselves (Megginson and Whitaker, 2007). Project management professionals need to be continuously improving and adapting so as to best deliver projects – simply relying on a course we did 10 years ago is no longer good enough. There is a need to undertake objective assessment of one's own capabilities, and apply corrective actions to improve areas of weakness and enhance strengths. Continuing your education is proof of your involvement in your own future (Taylor, 2011). It is an investment you make in yourself and helps you become more creative in tackling new challenges. Beyond giving you the skills to perform, it reinforces your professional credibility and shows that you are making an investment in yourself. This is important in today's market place (working independently or employed) where there is a need to demonstrate CPD showing dedication to your project management profession, as well as your sector of work and your career (Wallington, 2011) and helps ensure your employability.

Employability is partly about marketing yourself, and having a personal brand which clearly shows that your are competent, confident and professional is essential – either to mark your status within an organisation which allows you to advance your career, or to make you more attractive to potential employers. As a minimum, you need to be able to show that you are abreast of your peers. Ideally you should stand out. The ability to demonstrate ownership of your continuing development is a powerful asset that will strengthen your professional credibility and prepare you for greater responsibilities and rewards. Self-development should be seen as a competitive necessity by project managers, their employers and even their clients. If you are not continuously developing in your career, you are going backwards, and with the need for ever greater professionalism in project management that's likely to result in failed projects for a project manager (Taylor, 2011a).Through self-development opportunities we can also help to reinforce our CVs, and have a bank of examples that we can draw on when required, either as case studies when 'selling' project management, or as a range of scenarios when at interview, be this for your next career move or your next project.

As part of your professional standing you are likely to be a member of a project management organisation (again demonstrating your commitment to advancement for yourself and support of the project management community/profession). It is highly likely that as part of this membership you are required to demonstrate and maintain an obligation to self-development and to accrue a certain number of CPD points/hours per year. This will be particularly important when you apply for higher levels of membership. The higher membership levels further demonstrate your abilities, experience and status within the community, and ultimately ranks you in the workforce, and can accelerate your career development.

Undertaking self-development has even more benefits. It makes our working lives more interesting and enjoyable and increases job satisfaction. It is very easy to become 'stuck in a rut' and end up undertaking the same tasks and roles regularly. I would argue that this is not why we became project management professionals – we like the challenges and excitement of new projects and the new benefits we are enabling. As demonstrated in Mazlow's hierarchy of needs (described in Chapter 31), the self-actualisation level of needs pertains to a person attaining their full potential. We have an inbuilt desire for personal growth and fulfilment and the experiences that this brings, and we should harness and enable this through self-development.

As project managers we are expected to deliver ever-changing and more complex projects. How can we possibly be expected to achieve if we do not continuously change and adapt ourselves accordingly?

How to Approach Self-development

Self-development should be approached in a structured manner, building on existing knowledge, experience and activities. To be of benefit, your development should be a logical series of undertakings that enable you to reach a desired objective and to realise the benefits of this. Much in the same way as you would approach a project, you do not just 'dive in'. Instead, you plan.

Self-development isn't hard, but to be effective and provide benefits you do need to focus, set aside time, and take it seriously and be committed to the long term. It is not a case of just doing self-development once and then you're done, it is an iterative process of gradual development, review and realignment of new objectives. There are a number of approaches which you could take, either 'big bang' in a course lasting one or two weeks, or in small incremental steps (which may be more achievable and more valuable for quick application to project work). Employed project professionals could aim to integrate self-development opportunities in daily work or allocated slots during the week.

Contract and independent project personnel might not want (or be able) to use time during their working week. They have a good opportunity for self-development during breaks in contracts or when searching for their next role. This 'down time' could be used more productively to maintain and increase skills in support of the next role and to demonstrate to potential employers your commitment to development and progression.

Self-development means seeking and using feedback, setting development goals, engaging in developmental activities, and tracking progress on one's own (London and Smither, 1999). Essentially, we are assessing:

- Where am I now?
- Where do I want to be?
- How do I get there?

Then comes a review at the end. The process is similar to how we approach projects. It is worth recognising that self-development does not have to be a big investment of time or funding. Development opportunities span a wide range of activities, and could be just an hour a week, part of your current role or attending a short course. At the other end of the scale it could mean studying for a degree. You need to tailor your development to how you work and how you learn best. This will be different for every person, and at different stages in our careers. Doing a little often can provide big benefits, and such learning can be applied in the workplace for immediate effect.

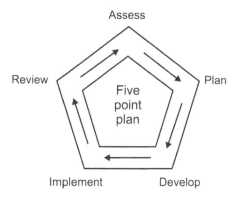

Figure 37.1 Five-point development plan

A Five-point Plan for Self-development

There are five steps in what I have termed the self-development five-point plan (see Figure 37.1). These are:

- assess;
- plan;
- develop;
- implement;
- review.

Five-point Plan Step 1: Assess

Before you can begin, what are you looking to achieve? Are you expecting to develop to support a current role, your next role or a career move to a different sector? Or are you seeking to improve for personal interest and enjoyment? It is important to keep a focus on what your immediate needs are, but more importantly to look at the longer term and think strategically about your aims and career goals – where are you going and what will you require to take you there and when you get there. So before you can begin to assess what learning to undertake, you need to decide why you are undertaking it. Examples include:

- remaining competent and capable in your current role;
- keeping up to date with project management developments, new techniques or new technology;
- to learn a new skill to facilitate promotion or to secure a new role;
- to enable a change of business domain, for example are you looking to move from an educational background into the finance sector?

You need to assess current skills, knowledge and experience (technical, soft skills and wider domain awareness). Looking at current and future needs, the aim is to identify strengths, and look to maintain and enhance these, and to identify areas of weakness which can be developed. You need to be brutally honest with yourself – you are the one who stands to benefit.

There is a wide range of tools and approaches for assessing skill levels and areas for development/improvement which could be used. These can include self-evaluation or peer and colleague feedback (360 degree feedback). Professional bodies might provide simple tools to help you evaluate yourself against knowledge and competency frameworks. Looking at job advertisements can highlight particular skill sets that employers are seeking.

No matter how you approach your self-assessment, it can be distilled down to: what am I good at and what am I not so good at, or what do I know and what do I not know? This will then highlight the areas for maintenance, improvement and development.

Five-point Plan Step 2: Plan

The next stage is to plan your development of the skills/experience gaps identified. This will include prioritisation, setting learning objectives, identifying learning activities and target dates for completion.

One suggestion during planning is to make sure that the objectives and activities are SMART – **S**pecific, **M**easurable, **A**ttainable, **R**elevant and **T**imely. It is often advisable to approach in small incremental steps as opposed to one large 'big bang' effort. Do not overcommit yourself and try to achieve too much in a given timescale. A good timescale is a 12-month cycle, or you might have a certain time frame in mind (such as a change of role within the next two months for example). You need to remember that you will probably be working at the same time, as well as having personal and family commitments, so be sensible when considering how much time you can spare each week.

An individual learning plan can then be created which itemises the plan and enables progress to be measured. A simple plan might have columns for:

* each objective (such as 'learn more about earned value');
* the activity you will undertake to meet each objective (such as ask a colleague, a one-day course, a one-hour webinar or read a book);
* a date for achieving each objective;
* criteria for checking you have met your objective (for example ability to apply earned value to my next project or to communicate the approach to your project team).

Five-point Plan Step 3: Develop

When you have assessed and planned, it is time to act. That clearly means undertaking the learning activities indentified in your plan.

Five-point Plan Step 4: Implement

The implementation stage is where you receive the benefits of your new learning. You will have learned the theory. Now you can implement and try out your new skills and knowledge. This has two advantages:

1. It helps to reinforce what you have learned (maybe via an examination or through trying something out in a project).
2. You can begin to realise benefits from your learning (for example, implementing a new team communication approach will provide quick results and early feedback).

Five-point Plan Step 5: Review

Perhaps the most important and final stage of self-development is reviewing your activities and knowledge. At the end of any learning experience we need to reflect. We must take stock of what has happened, evaluate where we are now and decide where we go from here (Minton, 1997). There are several aspects to this. At the high level, has your plan worked? Have you achieved your objectives and learning activities? You need to build in regular checkpoints (perhaps every three months) to ensure you are keeping on track. Does it appear you are trying to take on too much or not enough? Have your circumstances changed and do you need to reprioritise your learning objectives?

At the end of each learning activity it is important to review what you have learned. Did this activity meet your objective, expectations and learning criteria? If not, why not, and how would you do it differently in the future? Were there any new development opportunities you identified during your planned learning?

Taking time to consider and reflect on what has been undertaken is essential, and in itself is a valuable self-development activity. It also gives the opportunity to celebrate what you have learned and achieved, and aids self-motivation if you feel you are making progress.

Following the review of your learning activities, the outcomes can be fed back into a reassessment of where you are, your current skills, future requirements and so on. This should result in updating your self-development plan and so the process continues.

Self-development Log

It is important to keep a record of your self-development as a demonstrable asset. Maintain a log of your learning and outcomes, along with any certificates or other evidence that you might receive along the way. This will provide a source of reference when you assess your requirements, undertake reviews and plan future learning activities. As well as providing a useful personal resource, a learning log provides evidence that you have been undertaking self-development and continuous learning. Evidence will probably be required if you are a member of a professional body or seeking higher membership status.

More importantly, the log acts as a personal 'lessons learned' document for future reference (for example for applying learning to projects). It also acts as a reference point when undertaking performance reviews (for example, where you can demonstrate the activities you have been undertaking to achieve your development requirements, and to help the organisation support your continuing development by identifying future development areas). A self-development log is also a good reference document for completing job application forms or updating your CV, because all your development activities will be listed.

Formal activities	Self-directed activities
Undergraduate and post graduate degree courses. Professional qualifications (such as APM, PRINCE2, PMP). Undertaking research. Self-study courses. Writing articles, books and so on. Delivering training. Attending courses. Distance or on-line learning.	Reading a book, academic journal or professional magazine. Reading blogs, websites or other use of social media. Undertaking some voluntary work. Reviewing books or articles.
Professional activities	**Work-based activities**
Supervising some research. Organising or delivering a course. Lecturing or teaching. Being an assessor, coach or mentor. Involvement in a professional body. Being a subject matter expert. Participating in a committee or group. Attending an event, seminar, webinar or conference. Networking. Contributing to discussion forums. Presenting at a conference or event.	Discussions with colleagues. Mentoring and learning from others. Delivering a presentation. Coaching others. Work shadowing. Secondments or representation at meetings. Supervising students, staff, others. Visits to other companies or departments and feeding back. Doing your job, with lessons learned. Work shadowing. Expanding your role, or involvement in aspects outside your core role.

Figure 37.2 Summary of development opportunities and activities

Self-development Options

Self-development can take a range of forms, and these can be tailored to individual circumstances and learning styles. Any relevant learning activity can be used, as long as it is structured and has clear learning objectives, or is an activity with the potential to provide a measureable learning objective.

The table in Figure 37.2 provides a summary of potential learning activities, but this is by no means exhaustive. The activities include formal, informal, directed and self-directed learning, and I suggest that the optimum approach is a blended combination of many of these. There is certainly no common solution, or a specific combination that 'works the best'. The beauty of continuing education is that you can choose to improve your skills in a number of different and interesting ways (Taylor, 2011). This is all down to your personal choice and your experiences (based on trying different approaches to see what best suits your needs).

When looking at potential activities, consider your learning style. Do you like reading theory books before you consider best ways to implement? Or are you a hands-on learner who learns best by undertaking a task? When looking at activities, bear in mind your learning objectives, the time available, and what combination of one or more activities will deliver the success criteria for the learning you want to undertake. Do not always take the easiest option. Challenge yourself, at least occasionally – that is how we usually learn best.

It is worth remembering that a learning opportunity is not purely about you learning something directly, such as undertaking a course. You can also realise development opportunities by imparting your knowledge to others (for example in mentoring, leading a course or chairing a meeting). You will certainly gain from such experiences. There is an old saying that goes along the lines of 'you don't really know something until you try to teach it', so there is a good chance to test yourself, whilst at the same time helping someone else.

It is often considered that a self-development activity is going to cost money. It is true that some activities will incur expense (for example a five-day course or a degree), but the vast majority of opportunities will be low cost or free of charge (such as reading, work-based activities or attending a seminar or webinar). Do not let the concerns about cost put you off; undertake your assessment and planning and at that stage assess which learning activities are most appropriate for you, with cost being just one element of consideration.

ROI

The ROI of self-development (or essentially why bother, what are the benefits?) has hopefully been highlighted throughout this chapter; however a short summary here is useful. ROI can be assessed at a number of levels, from the individual to the entire organisation.

People undertake self-development for a number of reasons that are not always directly linked to financial gain. For example, there is the desire to make better decisions, deliver better projects and avoid spending time reinventing techniques and processes that already exist. For many, having the appropriate skill set and experience to be able to secure a new job is motivation and self-satisfaction, and must be a good demonstration of ROI for the effort.

The 'flip side' is maintaining job security. That, for me, and I suspect for a number of others, is the motivation for not falling into a dull routine. Project management by its nature is exciting and ever changing, and project professionals need to ensure they react to these changes, whilst at the same time keeping the motivation high by keeping the job interesting.

From an organisational perspective, staff development will ultimately affect project success through better trained and more capable staff, with knock-on effects in increased efficiency, productivity and therefore the bottom line or profit. Successful projects equate to financial success and repeat business (Taylor, 2011a), which is always a good motivator to support continuous learning opportunities for staff. For example one organisation has seen significant financial benefits through project management staff competency, assessment and improvement, with a critical success factor of reducing the number of failed projects, and reducing the severity of those that do fail. Based on those results, that organisation now invests approximately £12,000 per project manager annually in training and CPD (Taylor, 2011b).

Organisations investing in and supporting staff self-development also benefit from attracting the best staff and retaining them for longer. This also helps with succession planning and maintaining the project management resource pool. Organisations can then focus on continuous improvement of products, services and organisational processes (Cleland and Ireland, 2007).

Conclusion

Clearly organisations cannot assume that immediate benefits will be reaped simply because an employee has undertaken a project management course. They need to support their team members' self-development continuously and recognise that this is a key element in organisational development strategy.

Without self-development you cannot evolve or stay abreast of current best practice. You have to ensure that you are constantly challenging yourself to enhance your strengths and correct any weakness. Ultimately it is your responsibility to recognise the need for self-development and appreciate the rewards that this can bring. Different people will approach their self-development in their individual ways. But even if you can spare only an hour or two each month, that will be valuable and you should not miss any such opportunity.

References and Further Reading

Cleland, D.I. and Ireland, L.R. (2007), *Project Management, Strategic Design and Implementation*, 5th edn, New York: McGraw-Hill Professional.

Crawford, L. (2000), 'Profiling the Competent Project Manager', in *Project Management Research at the Turn of the Millennium: Proceedings of PMI Research Conference*, 21–24 June, 2000, Paris, France. Sylva, NC: Project Management Institute, 3–15.

Harland, R.E.W. (1989), 'Training project managers in the UK', *Project Management*, 4, November 1989, 197–8.

London, M. and Smither, J.W. (1999), 'Empowered self-development and continuous learning', *Human Resource Management*, Spring 1999, 38(1), 3–15.

Megginson, D. and Whitaker, V. (2007), *Continuing Professional Development*, London: The Chartered Institute of Personnel and Development.

Minton, D. (1997), *Teaching Skills in Further & Adult Education*, 2nd edn, London: City & Guilds and Thompson learning.

Obeng, E. (2011), 'Meet the new world', in *Project*, Association for Project Management, Issue 242, October 2011, 12–15.

Taylor, P. (2011), 'Education, education, education, but how?', *Project Manager Today*, September 2011, 40.

Taylor, R. (2011a), 'Personal Communication of Russel Taylor', Projects Director at Roke Manor Research.

Taylor, R. (2011b), 'Sound investment', in *Project*, Association for Project Management, Issue 243, November 2011, 30–31.

Wallington, E.D. (2011), 'Opinion piece: Without the desire to learn and improve, we run the risk of trying to find 'square peg' solutions to ever-more complex problems', in *Project*, Association for Project Management, Issue 240, July 2011, 8–9.

38 *Developing Competency*

DENNIS LOCK and JOHN CORNISH

This chapter is about the process of developing members of the project organisation to the point where they become capable of performing their roles to the best mutual benefit of themselves and the organisation. If you are an employer who has just engaged a new member of your project workforce, you will know that it will probably be some time before that person gains enough experience of projects in general and your organisation in particular to develop their full potential. If, on the other hand you are that new staff member, unless you are particularly arrogant you will know that you need time before becoming fully useful to your employer, and you might even feel intimidated or eclipsed by the talent demonstrated by your peers.

So this chapter is about the period in the typical project member's working life when he or she has to develop competency for fulfilling a new or changed role. We have to exclude from the discussion in this chapter the 'interim project managers' described in Chapter 48 and the 'hero project managers' of Chapter 57 because those people have, through their exceptional talents and experience, already developed and demonstrated universal competency of a very high order.

The Nature of Competency

GENERAL CONSIDERATIONS

Many personal attributes, such as height, weight, gender and so on are easy to describe by simple measurement or observation. Other personal qualities like intelligence, leadership, innovation, aptitude, attitude, reactions to various stimuli and so on might be a little more difficult to define, but tests can be used to assess them. All these characteristics are inherent and most change only slowly throughout a person's life. Competence is altogether different. It is neither an absolute personal quality nor a constant characteristic. It has to be learned. Although competence will always be dependent upon relevant personal attributes, in projects it is mostly acquired through experience and training,

Assessment of a person's competence must always be qualified by answering the associated question 'Competence for what?' A person who is brilliant in one role might be totally useless in another. Someone who is very capable when managing a planning meeting and producing the optimum project schedule might be totally out of their depth when placed in the position of having to manage people to carry out the tasks in that schedule. So competence is not a personal quality that can be discussed or assessed without also considering the role that the person is expected to perform. It is a complex mix of aptitude, attitude, training, experience and other personal abilities, all relative to the job requirements.

STANDARDS FOR MEASURING COMPETENCE IN PROJECT MANAGEMENT

Much work has been done internationally to develop a standard for defining competence in projects, particularly with reference to the functions that might be found in a project management office (PMO) or more generally in project management. Various professional associations have examined this question and their conclusions are embodied in their requirements for membership, or for the certified qualifications that they originate and oversee.

Of great significance to project management competence is the work done by GAPPS, which is the Global Alliance for Project Performance Standards. This is an international committee. A detailed and well-produced document detailing their recommendations is available on the Internet (GAPPS, 2007).

With special relevance to the work of a project support office or PMO is the *Crawford-Ishikura Factor Table for Evaluating Roles* which mercifully abbreviates to the acronym CIFTER (pronounced 'sifter'). An excellent introduction to this method has been written by William R. Duncan (Duncan, 2006).

However, these standards all apply particularly to the project management or project support functions, and in this chapter we must not forget the many other people who work in projects, such as the specialist technical members of the organisation. Projects clearly depend on the general competence of *all* who work in the project organisation – not just those in the PMO.

Developing Competency within a Defined Role

In projects, as in many other enterprises, assessing competence has to begin by judging a person's ability to perform against a particular job specification. Given the appropriate starting qualifications (which might be a combination of academic and industry-specific certification plus relevant experience) an employer should be able to expect that a new recruit will develop competence to perform well in the new role in an acceptably short period of time as experience is gained and training is provided. Some of that learning process is the core subject of this chapter.

There are, however, complications in the development process. Development of competence within a defined role can be expected to follow a learning curve, such as that illustrated in Figure 38.1.

The first person accredited with the concept of a learning curve (or experience curve) was German psychologist Hermann Ebbinghaus (1850–1909). Earliest experiments were in word recognition but the initial application in industry was in manufacturing, where observations showed that the expenditure in time or money per unit of production decreased by a fixed proportion every time the quantity of production was doubled. Mathematical expressions were developed to quantify the results, but we can avoid these here.

This repetitive doubling is an exponential function that is easier to express graphically, especially if we use a logarithmic x axis, as in Figure 38.1 (which has the effect of straightening the plotted curves). Our graph is illustrative of the principle but

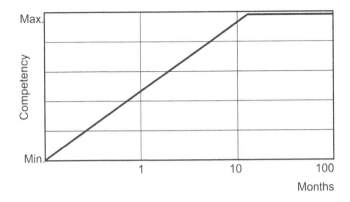

Figure 38.1 Example of a learning curve towards competency

clearly cannot show absolute values, because these will depend on the specific task and the proficiency of the individual. Note that *minimum* competency on the *y* axis does not necessarily mean *zero* competency.

However, all this assumes there will be no change in the job. But of course roles in projects *do* change, either when different projects come along, or when people are asked to perform new jobs or are promoted. Clearly a person who has learned to become competent in one role will need time to adapt and become competent once more when presented with a new challenge. Figure 38.2, again using only patterns with no absolute values, shows what might happen to a person's learning curves and job competence as a result of two promotions during a long career with one employer.

In this example, it can be seen that the person under observation had to undergo new learning after the first promotion, but soon became fully competent once more. However, after the second promotion, learning in the new role was not so successful and the person did not have the ability (or was not motivated) to become competent to perform at the more senior level. This is an illustration of the Peter Principle (Peter and Hull, 1969), which says, somewhat tongue-in-cheek, that 'in a hierarchy every employee tends to

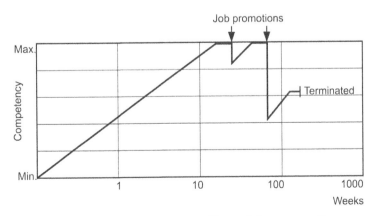

Figure 38.2 A competency learning curve affected by promotions

rise to his level of incompetence'. For our purposes, this simply reinforces the fact that competency is always relevant to the role that the individual is expected to perform.

Counter to the Peter Principle is what happens to employees when, through no fault of their own, their project role becomes diminished and the demands made on their competency are reduced. For example, during an economic recession or following a company reorganisation the position of an individual might change as the employer, anxious not to dismiss someone who has proved valuable in the past, retains that individual in a less senior and less demanding role in the hope that better times are just around the corner. But the employee will most likely be demotivated and disappointed with the new unchallenging work (perhaps accompanied by downgraded status). That can result in a deterioration in performance and, ultimately, in a gradual deterioration of competence and value to the organisation.

The Employer's Role in Developing Competency

INDUCTION TRAINING

The employer can clearly do much to help or hinder the process of learning towards competency. For every newcomer to the organisation the starting point is usually a period of induction training. All except the very smallest companies will probably have a well prepared and regularly used standard programme for induction.

It often happens that several recruits join on or about the same date, and in those cases the induction training will include some 'classroom' sessions to familiarise people with the organisation, its culture and its products. A tour of the premises will invariably follow, during which the trainees meet key members of the organisation with whom they will later come into contact in the course of their work. Larger companies often produce introductory literature, perhaps in the shape of a 'welcome aboard' booklet that both gives encouragement to each newcomer and also spells out some disciplinary rules.

In some companies induction training is very informal, perhaps consisting only of a conducted tour of the premises. At the other extreme, one heavy-engineering projects company ensured that every new senior member of its UK engineering design department was given several months' work experience (on-the-job training) in the company's larger and longer-established US headquarters before being allowed to perform design work on projects back in the UK. Much clearly depends on the complexity of the project's technology, and the desire of the company to instil a feeling of company culture in the individual.

Whatever the nature of the induction training, it will form part of a general training and experience mix that puts the newcomer on a theoretical platform from which the learning curve for the new role begins. In other words, induction training and other specially designed initial training provided by the employer can give competency development a jump start.

TRAINING TO IMPROVE COMPETENCY DURING AND AFTER THE INITIAL LEARNING PERIOD

Opportunities for training to improve a person's competence are not usually confined to the early days of an appointment but continue throughout the individual's career. At first this might be on-the-job training, learning from one's immediate superiors and peers. However, there will always be the opportunity to attend seminars and other events, such as those organised by the person's relevant professional association. Sometimes these involve absence from the place of work during working hours, perhaps for one day, but sometimes for a little longer. Employers must, of course, assess the potential benefits of such events (clearly not all have equal merit) but, where justified, they should be prepared to grant leave of absence, pay fees and reimburse reasonable expenses.

Intelligent employers will know that even if a particular seminar does not live up to its published expectations, individuals almost always learn (enhance their general competency) through discussing experiences and problems with people from other organisations whom they would not otherwise have met.

Project management is still a relatively new profession and is still undergoing development, with different facets being given new or enhanced emphasis as various enthusiasts and experts step in and make their voices heard. The core technology of the project organisation will also be developing, sometimes at a rate so alarming that the technology existing when a project begins will be obsolete by the time it is delivered. Keeping up with all these developments is part of the process of maintaining and improving competency.

RESPONSE TO MISTAKES MADE BY THE INDIVIDUAL

It has often been said that the only people who never make mistakes are those who do little or nothing. Most people make mistakes. And here we include everyone working on the project, whether in the PMO or working on project tasks. No one is perfect – how often does even the most brilliant student achieve 100 per cent in a final examination? Indeed in one university from my lecturing experience (DL) the Microsoft Excel spreadsheets that recorded students' examination marks had only two columns in the marks field, so no one could ever be given a score of more than 99 per cent.

Many mistakes go undiscovered and are corrected by the culprit before they surface to become apparent to others. Strictly speaking, any mistake, however trivial, is to some extent a failure in competency but of course common sense will determine the reaction by the individual and, if the mistake becomes apparent, by that person's superior. A competent and conscientious worker who makes a mistake will automatically learn to be more careful in future, perhaps by conducting self-imposed checks and reviews. But how should a manager react when a subordinate fails to produce perfect work or makes an incorrect decision?

Much must depend on the individual employee's record, contrition and honesty in describing what went wrong. The reasons behind the mistake are clearly also critical here. There might have been exceptional conditions, such as having to work extended hours, poor environment and so on. The consequences of the mistake are also important. A good manager will take all these facts into consideration. Applying disciplinary procedures to a person with a good work record can be counterproductive. Learning from mistakes is often part of the process of gaining competency.

So an appropriate course of action is to begin by discussing with the employee the reasons for the error. If the mistake was a genuine one-off lapse, and the employee is sufficiently conscientious and contrite, a reprimand might be unnecessary. Guilt and remorse will then take over as the potent medicine. But should an underlying weakness in the competency of the worker, or inexcusable carelessness become apparent, then a range of options is open, ranging from retraining, a job transfer, demotion or in the hopeless case, dismissal.

'To err is human, to forgive divine' (Alexander Pope, 1688–1744, *An Essay on Criticism*). From a management perspective, the appropriate response to mistakes is to try not to let anger rule the mind, but to apply reason and be scrupulously fair to the person who has been proven to be less than perfect, but only human.

Assessing and Improving Competency after the Initial Learning Period

Competency in a role has to be assessed by measuring results, or in other words how well the person performs in the role. Most employers do this by means of performance assessments (often known as performance appraisals) which might be conducted annually (perhaps with a salary review in mind), six-monthly or even quarterly. Performance appraisals should go hand-in-hand with guidance and other measures that attempt to improve performance (and thus competency). Performance and competency in a job are closely related but not identical. A person might be fully competent to do a job, but through bad attitude or for other reasons might not be performing at full potential.

Appraisals are dealt with more comprehensively in Chapter 46, and we provide only a summary here in the context of competency development.

AN INFORMAL SYSTEM OF OBJECTIVES AND PERFORMANCE APPRAISALS

A few years ago it was the fashion in some companies to set up a formal Management by Objectives (MbO) system, in which the organisation's objectives were first defined, and then spread down throughout the organisation so that each department (and its manager) had its own selected portion of the overall company's objectives assigned to it.

Thus a pyramid of objectives was formed, with the organisation (and the CEO) at the apex and all the contributing objectives set out hierarchically in layers below, assigned to the relevant managers down through the lines of command. The principal progenitor of the process in the UK was the late John Humble, and it was first promoted in the UK by management consultants Urwick Orr and Partners towards the end of the 1960s. The process could prove too formal and too inflexible to adapt to company changes. It might take a year to set such a system up, at considerable expense, only to see it all destroyed in a few days if the company underwent even a fairly minor reorganisation or some other change.

However, the underlying principle of setting mutually agreed objectives and measuring performance against them remains sound in many applications and works well at the individual manager–subordinate interface. The rules can be very simple. Every person in the organisation is invited to agree with his or her superior a few significant job-related objectives that are easy to quantify and measure. For a project manager, for example, one objective might be to improve progress so that 10 per cent more tasks are achieved on plan (perhaps allowing more stage claim payments from clients to be made on schedule, thus improving the organisation's cash flow).

Managers must interview each of their subordinates after the lapse of a few months to assess performance against the individually agreed objectives. If any shortcomings are detected, training or other measures can be put in hand to create improvement. If the subordinate's competence is proved to be on target, then the manager can discuss whether or not the objectives might be set a little higher for the next period. Of course, even senior managers must also agree their own objectives with their superiors and be assessed.

The objectives can be agreed (and we stress the word *agreed*) either to correct an identified weakness in performance, or to help the person under observation to become more competent in preparation for undertaking increased responsibilities in the future. The entire process should contribute towards achieving the expected strategic development of the company. It can also help to develop better communications between managers and their subordinates because it forces them to spend some time together in one-to-one meetings. The scheme should always be seen and promoted as a means of constructive discussion and communication rather than a disciplinary process.

In the wider context, of course, project management itself is a matter of setting and achieving objectives. The specification, schedule and budget are clearly all objectives.

A MORE GENERAL APPROACH TO REGULAR PERFORMANCE APPRAISALS

Most companies carry out performance appraisals in one guise or another, often aimed not only at improving an individual's performance but also to give some guidance to the employer when the time comes to review salaries. It is usually claimed by employers that performance appraisals and salary reviews are entirely separate activities, but some correlation between the two processes cannot be avoided and the people under review will be difficult to convince otherwise.

In the usual kind of performance appraisals there might be no quantifiable objectives against which to measure performance, so the process becomes qualitative rather than quantitative. Reviews are most commonly carried out annually, unless the individual under scrutiny has been found to be seriously underperforming, in which case more frequent and urgent reviews will be indicated.

A combined checklist and score sheet can help to oil the wheels of the process and ensure that all staff are assessed on a similar basis. We have included an example of such a sheet in Figure 38.3 on the next page. The contents of this form are fully self-explanatory and need no further description here.

The Individual's Role in Developing Competency

In times of economic crisis and market depression, individuals will generally have reduced choice in the jobs open to them. However, each individual must have some kind of plan, informal or formal, for career development and that must go in step with first becoming competent in the current role. That means developing one's skills through learning, which usually means learning from others in the organisation. At first this will involve learning from one's colleagues, which is a form of on-the-job training (which has been crudely referred to in some manual jobs as learning by 'sitting next to Nellie').

Personal attributes	?
Knowledge of work: familiarity with individual tasks and tasks performed by the business unit	
Energy level: energy exhibited satisfies job requirements?	
Ability to work under pressure: Ability to maintain control when the pressure is high	
Decision-making ability: willingness to make decisions and the quality of judgements made	
Creativity: able to find innovative and appropriate solutions to problems	
Communication - written: ability to write accurate, thorough and legible reports	
Communication - oral: accurate, persuasive, likeable	
Risk-taking: ability to accept calculated risk in the pursuit of goals and new methods	
Initiative: ability to think and act without the need for frequent direction from superiors	

Performing or managing tasks	?
Technology: understands the technical principles pertinent to the job	
Planning: quality of planning (relative to the person's status and job requirements)	
Performance against objectives - 1: time and the plan	
Performance against objectives - 2: cost and the budget	
Performance against objectives - 3: quality of work and the specification	

Working with subordinates	?
Delegation: ability to delegate without losing sight of control	
Listening: ability to receive and consider information from others and make informed decisions	
Informing: ability to describe task needs or other project information to others	
Motivational leadership: ability to motivate people successfully to achieve their given tasks	
Inspirational leadership: ability to inspire subordinates with a positive vision of the future	

Working with others	?
Peers: ability to cooperate with, influence, and gain respect of peers.	
Teamwork: active contributor toward accomplishment of joint goals.	
Teamwork: encouraging trust, openness and responsibility	
Externally: works effectively with clients, suppliers, government agencies and others	

Scores: 5 = outstanding; 4 = above average; 3 = acceptable; 2 = needs improvement; 1 = unsatisfactory

Figure 38.3 An example of a formalised checklist for use in performance appraisals

Valuable learning can also come from subordinates, even from those at the most junior level. Listening to them can sometimes reveal past errors and prevent one's-self from repeating them. Pride can be the enemy here. One must never be too aloof to listen to advice from subordinates, although of course skill and judgement is needed in deciding whether or not to act upon that advice.

A more serious aspect of introspection comes from asking oneself 'Am I learning from my superiors in this organisation?' There are various possible causes for a deficiency here. These can include one of the following:

- promotion of one's self to a more senior role;
- company reorganisation;
- unfair promotion of a colleague so that he or she becomes one's new but less-than-competent superior;
- starting a new job in a company where the job description in the recruitment campaign was hyped up, so that the responsibilities and challenges are far less than promised.

One's boss should ideally also be one's mentor. Of course the subordinate should always attempt to act and make decisions without unnecessary referral up the line of command, but there will always be times when the support and guidance of a superior manager can make life easier and, at the same time, improve one's own learning experience and competency. One of us (DL) has always followed the principle that if, in the course of time, learning from one's job and superiors has ceased, the time has come to explore fresh more challenging (and more rewarding) opportunities in another organisation.

It is assumed here that the individual is a member of an appropriate professional organisation. If the individual lacks sufficient academic qualifications and experience, he or she can always join a professional association or institution at student level and progress from there. Such membership greatly broadens the level of experience possible because one can meet others in the same profession from different organisations at seminars, exhibitions and other external events. Subject to some care in maintaining the employer's professional confidence, much can be learned by discussing the successes and mistakes made by others in similar roles.

Membership of one of the respected professional associations, such as the APM or PMI gives the individual access to various tools against which competency can be gauged. For example the entry requirements for different professional levels of membership or the syllabus for an examination can be used as starting-point checklists from which the individual can develop at least some knowledge of those aspects of project management in which competency will be needed should he or she advance to a more rewarding and more senior role.

Action Learning as a Competency Development Technique

Action Learning is well named. This subject is touched upon in Chapter 42, in the context of people temporarily changing roles so that they could act as understudies should key members of the project organisation be absent for any reason. However, in its full glory, Action Learning consists of deliberately taking people from different jobs, even from different industries, and interchanging their roles (usually at managerial level) for a prescribed period. Thus a project manager from an oil company might be asked to work in a bank, the bank manager could be catapulted into a managerial role in an electronics company, and the electronics manager on one astounding Monday morning will be expected to show up to replace the project manager in the oil company. Such interchanges are, of course temporary and last only as long as the predetermined training period (which might be 12 weeks). This all requires considerable organisation and the unfettered cooperation of all the host companies. The process has to be controlled and moderated by one or more skilled observers.

When successful, the process broadens the outlook and experience of each participant, brings fresh ideas from untrammelled minds to each organisation, and results in general permanent enrichment and, of course, thus improves competency of the individuals and of the organisations.

The undoubted specialist of Action Leaning in the UK is Professor Reg. Revans (see Casey and Pearce (1977) and Revans (2011)).

A PERSONAL CASE EXAMPLE OF ACTION LEARNING

Of course Action Learning is a brave step for any individual or organisation to take, but in its reduced version within the same organisation much benefit can be gained. Here is one example from my own early experience (DL).

I was working as projects coordinator in a division of an international company when I was seconded temporarily to work in the company's accounts department, reporting to the chief accountant instead of to the engineering director. In those early years my previous background had only been in electronics engineering and light manufacturing, and I knew nothing about cost accounting.

For 12 weeks I worked in various parts of the accounts department including bought and sold ledgers, and management cost accounting. This was all with a view to my setting up within the accounts department a system for project cost control that could be aligned with project work breakdown and cost breakdown structures. When I returned to my former role as projects coordinator the company benefited from the new systems, and I had gained an invaluable insight into the way in which an accounts department operated. Communication on project data between the project staff and the accounts department improved dramatically. I have been grateful for that experience ever since, and it certainly increased my own competency in project management.

Conclusion

Competency means the ability of a person to perform according to the requirements of the project, the organisation and the project sponsors or investors. Competency is a personal attribute that can be developed through training, experience and learning. It is not an absolute quantity, but must always be considered in relation to the expected role.

When considering competency in the management of people in projects, this should not be limited to those working in the project management function such as in a PMO. It has to exist also in all others who work in the project organisation (who must contribute in some way to the success of the project).

The competency of an individual can be assessed and developed to some extent through performance appraisals and the associated practices of mentoring and further training. People also have considerable personal responsibility for developing their competence through career choice and career planning.

There is a notional limit to the level of competence that any particular individual can attain but competence development can be accelerated by training or by techniques such as Action Learning, which demand active support and encouragement from the employer.

References and Further Reading

Casey, D. and Pearce, D. (1977), *More Than Management Development: Action Learning at GEC*, Farnborough: Gower.

Duncan, W.R. (2006), 'Sifting with the SIFTER', available at http://www.asapm.org/asapmag/articles/cifter.pdf

GAPPS (2007), 'A Framework for Performance Based Competency Standards for Global Level 1 and 2 Project Managers', Global Alliance for Project Performance Standards, available at http://www.globalpmstandards.org

Peter, L.J. and Hull, R. (1969), *The Peter Principle: Why Things Always Go Wrong*, New York: William Morrow and Company.

Revans, R. (2011), *The ABC of Action Learning*, Farnham: Gower.

39 *Developing Project Management Capability*

TIM ELLIS

This chapter explores how communities of practice (CoPs), forums and formal/informal networks can operate to help organisations and individual practitioners develop their project management capability. I shall explain how these groups can be set up and I shall describe the form and structure they should take and their benefits.

Introduction

> *Communities of practice are groups of people who share a concern or a passion for something they do, and learn how to do it better as they interact regularly. (Etienne Wenger)*

The traditional route to developing and demonstrating project management capability is through formal training and accreditation. However, it is now clearly demonstrated in the field of learning and knowledge management that most development of capability does not take place in the classroom or in front of a textbook. Rather our capability (and mastery of a subject) develops through the practice of doing the job and learning from our colleagues.

Have you learned more about the software on your PC from training courses and manuals or by asking for help from the people around you? Have you picked up useful tips or been prevented from making mistakes by watching others? When we learn from others in these ways we are benefiting from a 'community of practice'.

The concept of CoPs recognises this reality about the way our capability develops and seeks to capitalise on it. CoPs consciously encourage and strengthen peer-to-peer learning. The concept should not be seen as technical or different from the kind of collaborative activity in which we naturally plan and engage. Rather it is about a more conscious and planned approach to this activity and a focus on how to maximise the learning that can result. Of course formal training is important, but CoP learning can be blended with it.

Figure 39.1 lists some of the activities that might be carried out by a CoP, according to Wenger (2006).

Problem solving	'Can we work on this design and brainstorm some ideas. I'm stuck.'
Requests for information	'Where can I find the code to connect to the server?'
Seeking experience	'Has anyone dealt with a customer in this situation?'
Reusing assets	'I have a proposal for a local area network which I wrote for a client last year. I can send it to you, and you can easily tweak it for this new client.'
Coordination and synergy	'Can be combine our purchases of solvent to achieve bulk discounts?'
Discussing developments	'What do you think of the new CAD system? Does it really help?'
Documentation projects	'We have faced this problem five times now. Let us write it down once and for all.'
Visits	'Can we come and see your after-school program? We need to establish one in our city.'
Mapping knowledge and identifying gaps	'Who knows what, and what are we missing? What other groups should we connect with?'

Figure 39.1 Typical activities that can be carried out according to Wenger

CoP Forms and Approaches

A CoP can exist in many forms. These can include:

- a virtual group whose members never or rarely meet (such as in a multinational corporation or a nationwide interest group);
- face-to-face interactions between individuals in a single organisation in one location;
- a single functional group across multiple organisations (project managers, for example);
- a multifunctional group within a single organisation (for example, those involved in change within an organisation which could include service managers, support functions and project managers);
- it could be focused on a subject or content (for example climate change);
- it could relate to a process (for example change management).

There might be different subgroups within a community who will engage in CoPs in quite different ways. Some might not even be aware that they are members of the community but find themselves invited to particular events. For example, the members of a finance function might be invited to a presentation by an external expert in benefits realisation, or to a discussion on tracking project costs.

Role of a CoP Facilitator

In addition to a shared concern or passion, an effective CoP is often distinguished by the presence of one or more facilitators. A facilitator considers the needs of the group and its requirements for developing capability. She/he ensures that the group is more than the sum of its parts. Here are some of the functions or roles that a facilitator can play:

- consider the purpose and goals of the community;
- stimulate interactions between the members;
- act as a moderator;
- translate complex or specialist terminology to make discussions accessible;
- establish a tone and culture;
- ensure that requests from members are met;
- monitor and evaluate patterns of activity and engagement to understand how individuals are using the community (which in turn identifies the typical content and can encourage discussions to develop).

WHAT MAKES A GOOD FACILITATOR AND WHY WOULD ANYONE WANT TO BE ONE?

Facilitators need a passion and degree of understanding for the subject matter. They need to spot opportunities and find ways to motivate others to contribute. For example, they might post a polemical, thought-provoking or topical discussion on an online forum. Or the facilitator could encourage a contribution from an individual whose views on a particular subject would be of value. 'Back-channelling' phoning or emailing someone offline to encourage participation from selected individuals is a key approach – the 'pump priming' of many successful debates.

In a face-to-face forum, inviting a speaker who can engage the audience and inspire and inform the discussion can be crucial. By keeping the needs of the community in mind the facilitator may be able to add considerable value with small slivers of time alongside the day job. A facilitator also needs to act as a 'host' modelling behaviour and setting the tone or culture of the community. In an online community rapid responses, even if they are of the 'Great question, my organisation is struggling with that too' variety, encourage posting and an informal tone usually encourages participation.

The facilitator does not need to be an expert although expertise can help. Indeed, being a facilitator can give a relatively inexperienced person exposure to experts in the field. It can also give the facilitator the opportunity to build a strong network of contacts and raise their individual profile and status. Whilst expertise is optional there is a definite benefit in having someone with excellent communication and 'people skills' – most importantly someone who is prepared to commit time and effort to the role because that really will come through in the vibrancy of the community.

To end this section, here's what one community facilitator had to say:

> As a facilitator I've had a lot of satisfaction from supporting the development of project management capability. I have also learned a great deal because I keep up to date with everything that is going on and have built a really strong set of relationships – not just with my peers but also with some of the leading experts in the field. This has definitely enhanced my CV and I'd like my next job to move my career more into the field of social media and knowledge management.

Case Examples Both Within and Across Organisations

CASE EXAMPLE NO. 1: A FACE-TO-FACE COMMUNITY

An organisation wanted to strengthen the delivery of projects and programmes. It established a post to explore whether and how this might be done. There was considerable scepticism and a lack of understanding of project and programme management. A stakeholder analysis identified key roles and individuals who needed to understand how programme and project management could help them to meet the challenges they were facing and enable them to play their roles effectively. There were three groups of stakeholders, plus the executive team:

1. project and programme managers (and those who might later take on these roles);
2. key support functions (such as finance, audit, procurement and HRM);
3. managers whose services would be involved in projects and programmes.

All these stakeholder groups were important. There was a need to build a shared understanding and commitment and ultimately a demand for professional project management, showing that key individuals saw it is as something that would help them to deliver their responsibilities.

Quarterly meetings of all three stakeholder groups were convened. Activities included:

- talks by experts from similar organisations who were further ahead on the journey;
- workshops to establish a shared understanding of issues;
- training seminars for developing a shared understanding of key project and programme management principles.

There were targeted activities for subgroups within this whole community. For example, an in-house accredited course in programme management was run for those who needed practitioner skills. The group of staff who completed this course built strong relationships, which led to mutual peer support and adoption of the best practice. They also began to develop a sense of professional identity as programme managers and became a nucleus around which best practice could develop.

A specific presentation on benefits realisation was made to the finance community and a small group of service managers who were particularly interested or committed.

Two particularly important learning events were held for more senior staff. A two-day business change manager course was held for senior managers. A session was also held for the executive team, helping them to develop their understanding of:

- their individual roles as sponsors (or senior responsible owners) of particular initiatives;
- their collective role as the sponsoring group for all the major change programmes.

The period of intensive development of the CoP continued for around eighteen months. Significant understanding had been achieved and the organisation formed a project management office (PMO).

Investing the time in developing capability pays off and cannot be avoided. People can't 'buy in' to things they don't understand and until they have been enabled to understand in a way that fits in with their busy schedules.

Here are the comments of a programme manager and participating community member.

> *Previous attempts to introduce best practice approaches had not gone well. Templates and guidance were cooked up corporately and then launched. But there was very little buy in. Often the products simply were not relevant to the requirements of actually running a project or programme in an 'immature' programme and project management (PPM) environment and the culture of the organisation did not support an enforced approach. Through the community approach we worked with the PMO. Actually they understood how we were working and what we were trying to do. As programme managers we agreed that we would agree a common approach to planning, reporting, risk management and so forth, and the PMO acted as facilitator and developer. For the first time we have really useful tools and feel as if the PMO understands how to add value.*

CASE EXAMPLE NO. 2: AN ONLINE COMMUNITY

Within the public sector, some practitioners identified a need to network together to share best practice experience. They had some face-to-face meetings, but these proved expensive in time and travel and could only be held infrequently. So they decided to form an online CoP using social media. Volunteer facilitators were identified from across the UK. They received a one-day training course in knowledge management and, through regular monthly telephone conferences, planned and promoted activity on the CoP and ensured that all the members were welcomed and encouraged to participate. Some of the principal activities of this CoP are tabled in Figure 39.2.

'Hot seats' with national experts	Chances for community members to ask experts for their views on key topics over a four- or five-day period.
Themes	Focus on themes of particular interest to members (for example, benefits realisation or assurance). The facilitators work to ensure a range of postings and ideally arrange a supporting face-to-face meeting.
Article of the month	Sources from the wider project management world. Often focused on subjects of most concern.
Links to key websites and resources	A magnet feature, attracting a range of key links.
Jobs	Another magnet feature. Free advertising of relevant jobs.
Documents, toolkits and presentations	Intellectual capital that can save thousands of hours and millions of pounds if accessed by the right people at the right time.
Forums, threads and discussions	Informal meetings of the on-line community giving members opportunities to ask their peers about work and work problems.
Surveys and polls blogs	These are used to elicit understanding of members' views, and also as a feedback mechanism to determine priority areas for activity.
Newsletters and alerts	Effective ways of summarising activity so that the community understands what is going on and interacts with it. The community in Case Study 2 experienced a 70 per cent 'spike' after each monthly newsletter.

Figure 39.2 Key activities of a CoP in the public sector (Case Study 2)

Here are the (slightly edited) comments of two participants. From the head of a portfolio office:

> *When I was appointed to a new role with the task of improving PPM in my organisation one of the first things I did was to read the PPM CoP. It helped me to understand the different approaches that were being taken across the sector, and where the examples of best practice were. I used the CoP to contact and meet some key individuals, who saved me a lot of time in sharing lessons learned. I used their guidance to develop our organisation's approach to project management. I was so impressed from what I learned from the CoP that I became part of the core team and developed a PPM CoP within my own organisation. Three years on, this learning and sharing continues both online and face-to-face. It is invaluable in improving our organisation's maturity in PPM.*

From another head of a portfolio office, who was also a facilitator:

> *Just after taking up the role of project manager for a project that had to be closed, a colleague recommended I look at the UK PPM CoP. This was one of the best discoveries of my career. Suddenly I found an amazing amount of information, help and support that I'd never known was out there. One of my best strengths is networking, so you can imagine how the community supported my preferred modus operandi. Following the successful closure of that project, my new task was to set up a PMO for my employer and establish an in-house tailored approach to PRINCE2. There was no way I could have done this as quickly (and with the confidence that I was using today's best practice) unless I had been part of the CoP. The wealth of experience residing in its members is vast. The ease of posting questions, discussing topics with others, finding what you need to adapt to your own ends makes the whole concept dynamic and a truly living community. I could not have done my job in the last two years without its existence. I'm now in the process of creating an internal community which is part of this wider one. I hope that this will not only enable our own staff to use it as a new tool, but that they will also be able to see the breadth of knowledge in the UK that is now being successfully shared. Now it's time for me to give something back to the community by sharing more of my own experiences. Becoming one of the facilitators will also help me develop my own skill set in yet another direction.*

Checklist: Three Questions to Ensure That Your CoP is Fully Effective

WHO?

- Do you know who the customers are? Is there a product they want?
- Are you clear who needs the community?
- Do they recognise that need? If not you will have a challenge to get things started and face-to-face engagement might be needed before you can consider online communication.

Remember to segment your members and approach them in different ways. They may have very different interests, needs and tolerances. Senior managers will not usually be engaged by an in-depth technical discussion – in fact this could be very counterproductive and with few exceptions will be less likely to find the time to engage online.

Find out what people want. Best of all; develop the community in collaboration with the members. This has a close relationship with stakeholder identification, analysis and engagement – especially in a CoP within a single organisation. Indeed, a CoP may provide a framework and a set of opportunities or reasons for engaging with stakeholders in a positive and productive way. Of course, content is key. If you cannot generate anything to offer people will not engage.

Think about who you let in. A closed community with approved members can promote trust, a focused set of interests and reduce irrelevant discussions. It can also prevent the use of the community as a sales opportunity.

On the other hand, open membership can encourage all enthusiasts, including those you didn't know about – or even suspect existed – to join in. So they might create a greater diversity of views and altogether new ways of thinking about problems.

A seminal moment in developing the concept of CoPs came from the petroleum industry. It became apparent that solutions to problems of drilling into deep-sea rock structures were being developed at coffee breaks, where scientists from different disciplines shared expertise rather than in the laboratories where they worked within the confines of one discipline. So whilst CoPs are all about engagement and involvement of the members, the way in which you label the community and determine its parameters can define and can limit its conversations. Is your community a 'PPM community', or a 'change', 'transformation' or 'innovation' community?

A slow start in a community could indicate that it is not needed or the time is not right. Many communities have a life cycle. When they have done their job it is important to recognise that and move on. Even apart from what the RSPCA might say, there's no point in flogging a dead horse.

Finally, reverting to the question 'who?' Make sure you have active and committed facilitators as discussed above.

HOW?

Here my question is about ethos and culture. Are you willing to give it all away and do people want to join in? Is there an ethos of sharing?

Enough members of a CoP need to put something into the pot and share their thoughts and materials. An underlying set of attitudes, values and behaviours needs to be in place. A CoP requires effort and a generous, collaborative and trusting approach. The belief that if you give away your knowledge and intellectual capital it will come back to you with interest is important – but not always correct. If the environment is competitive or adversarial a CoP approach will struggle. In the private sector, cross-organisation communities will be more challenging if there is direct competition.

Also, ensure that participation is wanted. A compulsory CoP will not work. You have to focus on the willing enthusiasts and not those most difficult to convince. Go with the energy.

CoPs are all about engaging people. You need a welcoming environment, which usually means a relatively informal group. One online community learned that a warm, personal welcome message to new members had a huge impact on their subsequent engagement.

WHY?

Think about the reasons why people might engage and what motivates them. Keen and knowledge-hungry people need the right content and responses. If this is provided they are likely to come. You might end up with many attendees.

Online you could get the unkindly named 'lurkers'. These are people who are listening or reading but not participating. In fact, for online communities it is not unusual to find that only 5 per cent of members contribute. But apparently passive recipients might benefit considerably and share what they learn from the community in other ways. However, converting this interest into active participation will benefit everyone.

In an online community do not underestimate the challenge of making the first posting. This might be a combination of not being sure about how the technology works or simply the unnerving experience of posting your first thoughts. Such 'shyness' can be worse if the community is large or the discussions are dominated by 'experts'. When that is the case the basic questions, bringing answers that are of use to most people, can feel silly. Overcoming these initial hurdles takes effort and input. You might need to find ways to show people how to use the technology and encourage people to post. You should reassure them that there is no such thing as a silly question.

In a face-to-face community within an organisation the challenge is to think about the requirements of individuals and set up forums (such as workshops) where these can be met. Bringing staff together from different disciplines (for example, finance, procurement and PPM) or from different levels of the hierarchy in a setting where they have different sorts of conversations can be powerful in unlocking potential collaboration and illuminating divergent underlying drivers or perspectives.

The more experienced have less to benefit from receiving, so it is important to think about what might motivate them to participate and engage. Never underestimate how much people enjoy helping others and sharing their knowledge. Also remember the power of recognition and acknowledgment. To be conferred expert status or a platform can be psychologically rewarding and also improve one's marketability. It can pay dividends to invest time ensuring that individuals are recognised, thanked and rewarded.

In an online community it is important to consider whether face-to-face events or telephone contacts over the phone can be arranged. These can be used to generate connections and also content (for example posting the notes of a meeting online).

How Individuals and Organisations Benefit from CoPs

A CoP can help an organisation pass a 'tipping point' in terms of its understanding of PPM. By drawing key individuals into a collaborative, learning environment we can understand perspectives and foster the development of key relationships and alliances.

This may never be achieved through classroom training especially where this is focused only on those in the 'doing' role of project managers and not on the key role that leaders must play as sponsors of change. A CoP can support formal learning. A 'light bulb' moment in a project management training course can be hard to translate into reality, especially in an organisation where the development of PPM is at a low level of maturity.

This is what one head of a centre of excellence had to say:

> *The organisation sent hundreds of people on project management training – both in-house introductions and more expensive accreditation courses. The courses were highly rated but we were not seeing a return on this investment through a strong improvement in our projects. We followed up those who had been trained a few months later. We found that whilst the courses were valued, as managers and other colleagues did not understand or support a best practice*

approach, the initial enthusiasm of those who had been trained was quickly lost and they began to forget what they had learned. Through a CoP approach we brought some of these project managers together. They were able to support one another by sharing experiences, helping them to realise that they were not isolated and reminding them and reinforcing what they had learned. We also encouraged peer-to-peer mentoring. This has also helped us to develop recommendations and to develop the understanding and capabilities of those in managerial roles.

CoPs can be more cost effective than training courses. If the organising is done well there is less need for trainers, because the community members 'train' one another. Internal speakers in a CoP bring a shared understanding of the organisational context 'how things really work' – something that an external trainer cannot usually do.

CoPs can also be highly cost effective in sharing intellectual capital which may be worth hundreds of thousands of pounds. Consultancies make their margins by developing intellectual capital and then selling it many times. If the members of a community can share this intellectual capital, significant costs can be avoided. Hundreds of thousands (if not millions) of pounds of intellectual property can be shared. Further value can be gained through collaborative action.

A capability improvement programme in a local government organisation developed a best practice PPM approach collaboratively. This would previously have cost tens of thousands of pounds for an individual organisation to produce in isolation. Now it was produced once and shared many times, avoiding millions of pounds of expenditure.

Networked communities are also speedy and effective ways of spreading best practice. Are you more likely to take practice recommended by a peer whom you know, respect and trust than to take the time to read glossy marketing literature? Viral marketing recognises this potential to accelerate knowledge transfer through communities and connections.

As well as avoiding costs through the 're-invention' of the wheel, CoPs can prevent mistakes (and the costs they create) by sharing 'lessons learned' and by taking advice from peers based on experience. This is even harder to quantify but nonetheless very valuable.

CoPs can be enjoyable, as well as being an effective way to work. That is particularly the case where PPM practitioners are isolated. Having links with their peers, who recognise the same issues and face similar challenges, can provide valuable support.

Acknowledgements

Local Government Association Knowledge Management Team.
London Boroughs of Hackney and Sutton.
Hampshire Fire and Rescue Service.
Royal Borough of Kensington and Chelsea.
Norfolk County Council.

References and Further Reading

Wenger, E. (1998), *Communities of Practice: Learning, Meaning, and Identity*, New York: Cambridge University Press.

Wenger, E. (2001), 'Supporting communities of practice: A survey of community-oriented technologies', self-published report. Available at: www.ewenger.com/tech

Wenger, E. (2004), 'Knowledge management is a donut: Shaping your knowledge strategy with communities of practice', *Ivey Business Journal*, January 2004.

Wenger, E. (2004), 'Learning for a small planet: A research agenda'. Available at: www.ewenger.com/research

Wenger, E. (2006), *Source Communities of Practice: A Brief Introduction*, (self-published). Available at: www.ewwenger.com/pub/index.htm

Wenger, E and Snyder, W. (2000), 'Communities of practice: the organizational frontier', *Harvard Business Review*, January–February 2000, 139–45.

Wenger, E., McDermott, R. and Snyder, W. (2002), *Cultivating Communities of Practice: A Guide to Managing Knowledge*, Cambridge, MA: Harvard Business School Press.

40 *Coaching and Mentoring*

KEVIN DOLLING and PAUL GIRLING

Project management is acknowledged often to be a demanding and complex role. How do we learn to do such difficult stuff or deal with the inevitable problems? Or, of more immediate interest to individuals, where can we turn to get direction or help, or to find answers to questions that appear to be unanswerable? People are more complex than any project or process or technology. After all, we are the product of millions of years of evolution. Each individual is unique. So clearly a one-size-fits-all approach to solving project management difficulties cannot work.

In our company ('new habits') we recognise that there is lots of training and many qualifications available for project managers. But it is probably fair to say that many of us still develop our competence through experience (both good and bad). Whilst we can learn hard lessons though our bad experiences, mistakes can be costly.

So how valuable would it be, when faced with tough, sensitive or complex questions and decisions, to have someone to turn to for guidance, advice and support? And, to be able to do that at the time when you most need it? Someone who either knows the answer or, far better, could ask the right questions to help you free up your thinking and allow you to find your own way forward? Some sort of 'coach' or 'mentor' maybe? Would that in any way make a difference to the projects you deliver? But who and where are these people, these coachers and mentors? In this chapter we shall explore these topics, and draw on the experience of my company's 'coachees', hopefully to encourage you to investigate for yourself.

Origins of Coaching and Mentoring

Wise men learn by other men's mistakes, fools by their own. (Proverb)

The first use of the term 'coach' to mean an instructor or trainer came around 1830. It was Oxford University slang for a tutor who 'carries' a student through an examination.

The origins of 'mentor' were around 1750 (online *Etymology Dictionary*). It meant 'wise adviser' and came from Mentor, the adviser of the young Telemachus in Homer's *Odyssey*. It has come to mean 'an experienced and trusted adviser' (the online *Oxford English Dictionary*).

Coaching and mentoring have been part of the work environment from the times of apprenticeships in guilds. However, coaching and mentoring in business is relatively new, but has had a rapid rise in recent years.

Coutu (2009) describes the changing face of coaching. Ten years ago US companies engaged a coach to deal with 'toxic' behaviour at the top of the organisation. But now the aim of most coaching is to develop the capabilities of high-potential performers. In fact, Coutu describes having a coach as 'like having a badge of honour'.

Coaching and mentoring are powerful tools. So how can we start using them?

How About an 'ology?

Hell, there are no rules here – we're trying to accomplish something. (Thomas A. Edison)

Project management abounds with methodologies. Here are some examples from the many:

- Event chain methodology;
- Rapid unified process (RUP);
- PRINCE2;
- Process-based management;
- SCRUM (an agile project management method).

We are also surrounded by a plethora of special techniques, including:

- communication planning;
- cost-benefit analysis;
- earned value analysis;
- critical path analysis;
- risk analysis;
- investment analysis;
- stakeholder management;
- value benefit analysis.

So surely there must be at least one process for coaching and mentoring? Well, yes, there are many. We shall describe the most common coaching model, which is GROW.

THE GROW COACHING MODEL

Decide which is the line of conduct that presents the fewest drawbacks and then follow it out as being the best one, because one never finds anything perfectly pure and unmixed, or exempt from danger. (Niccolo Machiavelli)

The GROW model was developed in the UK in the 1980s and is now the most widely used coaching tool. It is commonly used by line managers to coach team members. GROW is likely to be attractive to a process-based mentor or coach because it is a four-stage problem-solving model. Whitmore (2007) sets out these stages:

- **G**oal, which is what the coachee wants to achieve;
- **R**eality, the current situation;

- **O**ptions, generate as many alternatives as possible;
- **W**ill, convert the discussion into a decision(s).

Supporters say that GROW provides a practical framework for helping coachees to set goals and move towards them. It can be used by anyone, is easily understood, straightforward to apply and very thorough.

However, Clutterbuck (2010) is concerned that process-based coaching can become mechanistic, manipulated to the coach's agenda, focused on defining goals too early and can lead to a rigidity of thinking.

My concern is that a project manager might not have a problem requiring a goal but may have an opportunity or a problem, or could just need thinking space.

Definitions of Coaching and Mentoring

You don't have to be a 'person of influence' to be influential. In fact, the most influential people in my life are probably not even aware of the things they've taught me. (Scott Adams)

There are many definitions of coaching. Academia is full of them. They tend to revolve around two key concepts:

- improving performance through learning;
- behavioural change (to enhance performance).

Bluckert (2006) pulls the key elements together in his definition:

Coaching is the facilitation of learning and development with the purpose of improving performance and enhancing effective action, goal achievement and personal satisfaction. It invariably involves growth and change, whether that is perspective, attitude or behaviour.

Again, there are many definitions of mentoring. But we like this explanation of the mentor role from a NASA program:

A mentor is an experienced individual that serves as a trusted counsellor, loyal adviser and coach who helps and guides another individual's development. The mentor is a confidant who provides perspective, helps the candidate reflect on the competencies they are developing, and provides open, candid feedback. Mentors have a unique opportunity to serve as a 'sounding board' for the candidate on issues and challenges they may not share with individuals within their own organization. Mentors are people who are interested in and willing to help others. (NASA FIRST Mentoring Program Handbook)

There is a lot in common between these two descriptions, including the notions of 'facilitation' and 'development'. But perhaps the most important phrase is '… people who are interested in and willing to help others'. Later in this chapter we shall suggest that mentoring and coaching, as they tend to be described, fall towards opposite poles of a continuum of styles.

We (and our company) believe there is another important component, and that is 'choice'. So coaching and mentoring are also about helping an individual identify his/her choices.

Another possible difference between coaching and mentoring is that the individual may have less opportunity to exercise his/her own choices in a mentoring relationship, because mentoring is likely to be more directive, whereas a coaching relationship will lean towards being non-directive.

Editorial Comment (DL)

People do not all agree on these definitions. For example, Clutterbuck and Sweeney (1998) transpose these definitions of coaching and mentoring.

Does it actually matter whether you have the title of coach or mentor (or coachee or mentee) for that matter? We believe it's not about the titles but more importantly about the quality of the relationship between the two people involved. At 'new habits' we tend not to talk about coaching or mentoring an individual (which implies doing something to someone). We 'work with' or 'support' an individual. We like to establish a relationship of equals. So, in the remainder of this chapter, we shall use the term 'supporter' (for the coach or mentor) and individual (for the coachee or mentee).

This is not an academic paper and we do not want to get hung-up on semantics, so we propose the following definition for coaching and mentoring:

> Supporting an individual to identify their options and choices for growth. Growth may be through new knowledge, awareness or change.

The emphasis here is *why* one is coaching/mentoring – not how one does it.

RECAPITULATION

So a project manager can experience particular pressures and a supporter can help him/her to identify options for dealing with them. After all, support is common in the wider business community. All this requires is '... *people who are interested in and willing to help others'*. But can we achieve this if a 'process' is not necessarily the answer? Individuals with whom our company has worked have variously described being supported as:

- a training and development tool, tailored to the need of the individual;
- a continuous process, giving the individual continuous development;
- a way of balancing and managing my work life and home life;
- learning the techniques to enhance personal development;
- opportunity to think, explore situations and prepare for change. Opens my mind to different views;
- help for dealing with specific situations, difficulties and dilemmas.

Supportive Environment

If you can't have empathy and have effective relationships, then no matter how smart you are, you are not going to get very far. (Daniel Goleman)

Having a supportive environment is key to growth. It is the role of the supporter to create a safe environment and promote a trusting and respectful relationship.

The supportive environment is a safe haven. In many ways it is almost the opposite of the project manager's normal visible, dynamic, complex environment. We can learn about supportive environments from organisations and other support services who create a private, calm, safe place where people are given time and space to discuss and explore difficulties and problems freely. A good example of this in the UK is the Samaritans. Empathetic listening is core to the practice of such organisations. It is immensely powerful. So if it can help an individual find the resources to carry on when all has seemed hopeless, just think what it could do for a project manager faced with a problem on the project.

THE DYNAMICS OF SUPPORT

Our company has found in our role as supporters that success hinges on two sets of dynamics, which are:

1. the quality of the relationship;
2. the quality of conversation.

Quality of the Relationship

Trust is the lubrication that makes it possible for organizations to work. (Warren G. Bennis)

Both participants in a coaching or mentoring relationship must invest emotionally to enable the individual to grow. This can be represented by the four-box emotional investment model in Figure 40.1.

For the individual, this means committing to the process and his/her own development. To benefit, the person must be open to exploring his/her situation and options, and also be open to being challenged. Normally, this commitment grows as trust is established between both parties.

Rarely, we have encountered individuals who have been 'strongly recommended' or sent to us for coaching. They could be underperformers for whom coaching is the last attempt to improve performance. This is not ideal because being in the 'last chance saloon' puts the individual (and potentially the supporter) under great pressure to succeed.

The supporter must similarly be committed – but not just in terms of time and energy. This is demonstrated by showing belief in the individual's commitment and in their potential for almost limitless growth.

Gallwey (2000) sheds light on this in his simple, yet powerful, formula for an individual's performance:

$$\text{Performance} = \text{Potential} - \text{Interference.}$$

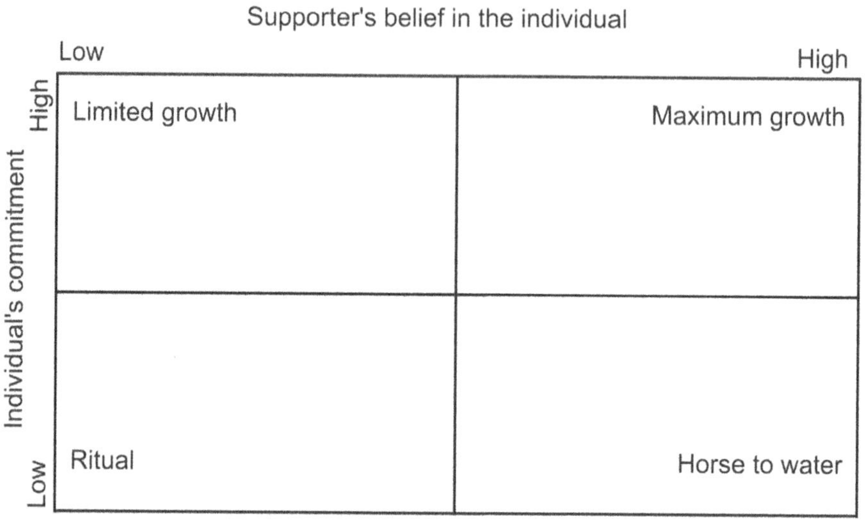

Supporter's belief in the individual

Figure 40.1 Emotional investment model

This means that the level of achievement in an undertaking (for example, playing tennis, giving a presentation or supporting an individual) is their total potential minus interference. Gallwey says that interference comes from within the individual. This includes their limiting beliefs, risk aversion, conditioning and so on. We prefer to take this further to include the external environment, including for example the organisational culture.

To encourage growth, it is essential that the supporter demonstrates belief that the individual has great (even limitless) potential. So when we look at our emotional investment model (Figure 40.1):

- maximum growth results requires high commitment by the individual, together with high belief by the supporter in the individual's commitment and potential for growth;
- limited growth will come from a relationship between a highly committed individual and a supporter who does not believe in the individual's potential and/or commitment;
- 'horse to water' (you can take a horse to the water but can't make it drink) is the situation where the supporter believes in the individual but the individual is not committed to the relationship. This is likely to be frustrating for the supporter and a waste of time for the individual;
- 'ritual' describes the relationship where neither party invests much emotionally. Both will simply be going through the motions and wasting time.

The following repercussions can be expected from not operating in the top right box (maximum growth):

- the support process could be discredited because it does not yield the desired results;
- time, resources and energy are wasted;
- the potential of individuals is not realised;
- the development opportunities are missed for supporters.

Quality of Conversation

The greatest compliment that was ever paid me was when someone asked me what I thought, and attended to my answer. (Henry David Thoreau)

This 'quality of conversation' dynamic is dependent on the supporter. It can be represented by another four-box model which is shown in Figure 40.2. The two dimensions relate to the supporter's position and the style that he/she adopts. The result is the impact on the conversation in terms of breadth of perspective or view and the type of outcome for the individual.

SUPPORTER'S POSITION

On the supporter impact model (Figure 40.2) we have called the two ends of the spectrum for the supporter's position informal/outside the organisation and formal/inside the organisation. These are simplifications that include several factors which are not shown separately, namely:

- Source of the supporter – whether the supporter is from the individual's organisation or is external. Here we suggest that being from within the same organisation is formal, whilst being external is towards the informal end of the scale. Our company has operated in both capacities and discovered that individuals have found external supporters particularly helpful. However, independence does not mean ignorance,

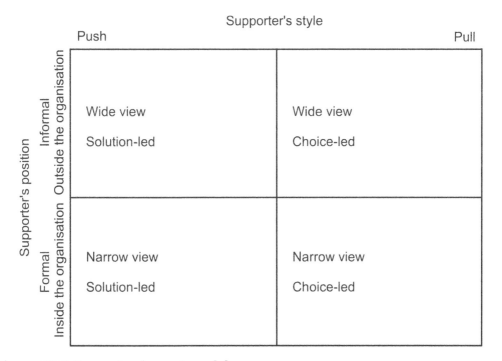

Figure 40.2 Supporter impact model

because our experience has shown that a supporter with an appreciation of the business and the organisational culture can help the quality of the conversation.

- Position of the supporter – whether the supporter is the individual's line manager? This takes the issue of internal versus external supporter a stage further. We argue that line managers can struggle with this 'role'. It is too easy for them to see the right answer (or what they think is the right answer). Also, there is often pressure for a quick resolution. This pressure can be transferred to the individual, limiting exploration and forcing them to accept the first solution. The supportive approach takes time and effort, so pressure for an outcome will be counterproductive. The supportive environment should be non-judgemental but a line manager might carry preconceptions or knowledge about the individual that could lead to prejudgement of the individual or the outcome. That, again, will be counterproductive.

- Supporter experience – whether the supporter needs to be more experienced than the individual in the field of work (project management). This consideration is a bit more 'swings-and-roundabouts'. If the individual is seeking information and guidance then clearly a more experienced project manager could be an effective source. However, our experience suggests that an individual rarely seeks just information and guidance. Instead they often need thinking space and a sounding board. In this case, we argue that 'naivety' of the specialist area can be an advantage because the supporter's 'simple' questions can encourage wider exploration of the issues and options. Individuals with whom we have worked have commented favourably as follows:

  - 'Value of talking to an independent third party'.
  - 'An opportunity to think and talk outside the working environment in confidence'.
  - 'Gives me freedom to express my thoughts'.
  - 'Explore my thoughts and ideas and self with someone who is non-judgemental, confidential and unbiased'.
  - 'Having someone who is truly objective and supportive who needs nothing from me other than my time'.

SUPPORTER'S STYLES

All our knowledge has its origins in our perceptions. (Leonardo da Vinci)

The table in Figure 40.3 is a simplification of Downey's spectrum (2003). It shows a range of possible supporting styles. We can look at the poles as being directive (push) and non-directive (pull).

The 'push' approach is where the supporter takes full responsibility for solving an individual's difficulty or problem. This is likely to be through a directive technique. It could, for example, be telling a project manager what course of action to take.

The 'pull' end of the spectrum is where the supporter helps the individual to explore a problem using non-directive techniques (such as deep listening, in which all the supporter's senses are engaged in understanding the individual and helping him/her to work out their own way forward).

There is a graduation of possible techniques between push and pull. These range from offering guidance through giving constructive feedback through to open questions and summarising understanding. Clearly, a supporter will not be limited to one extreme from

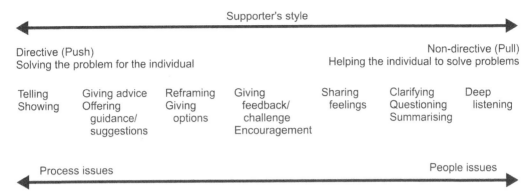

Figure 40.3 Supporter's style model

the possible range of techniques but our experience shows that we are likely to have a natural preference for one side of the spectrum over the other. We must now explain how such a preference might come about.

STYLE PREFERENCES

There are several factors that influence our preferred style. We shall mention three here:

1. The supporting skills and attributes we possess will have a major impact – whether we have the broad range required to operate across the style spectrum. The 'pull' style requires a range of subtle skills and special attributes. If you don't possess these then you may be locked into the push style. After all as Abraham Maslow put it: 'If you only have a hammer, you tend to see every problem as a nail'.
2. As we remarked above: does the supporter have more experience than the individual? The push approach is likely to be more natural for the supporter with greater knowledge or experience than the individual. Conversely, the pull approach is likely to be easier to adopt for the supporter with less knowledge or experience of the work area.
3. The third factor we must mention is the issue of time constraints. Will these (whether real or imposed) significantly affect the choice of style adopted? It's fair to say that push can be quicker than pull by virtue of its direct approach.

APPROPRIATE STYLES

The quality of the outcome is clearly dependent on the supporter's style and the nature of the individual's difficulty or problem. The project manager who goes to his/her supporter for guidance on process or technique (like stakeholder mapping, for example) might just require an explanation and an example to follow. So in that case push could be suitable.

However, the project manager who has concerns about how to gain commitment from a major stakeholder is unlikely to benefit from clear instruction. This individual will need an opportunity to bring out and explore the issues, before seeking options to engage the stakeholder. After all, there could be a great deal at stake. In essence, we are suggesting that when the individual's work involves relationships, adopt the pull option.

This is likely to be most of the time. After all, projects are rife with politics – and politics often require subtlety.

The pull approach is often described as Socratic. Socrates said, '*I can't teach anyone anything; I can only make them think*'. There is an apocryphal tale of Socrates and one of his students. The student asked him, 'Master, why, when I ask you a question, do you always answer me with a question?' Socrates replied, 'Do I?' Socrates knew a lot more than we do, but we can only commend this view. It is empowering to work out one's own way forward. Also, people often need support, not because they don't know the answer (we all know much more than we realise) but, because they just need a different perspective.

The pull approach requires investment of time and effort and significant skill. Pushing, on the other hand, requires less from the supporter and can appear to be a quick win. So push can be expedient. But pull contributes to sustainable growth and a productive quality relationship.

Individuals with whom we have worked have commented about the supporter's style as follows:

- 'It's about learning rather than being taught'.
- 'Facilitated reflective session, where you are encouraged to explore different option/ approaches, whilst being supported'.
- 'Teases out my own ideas', 'Gives me an opportunity to reach my own conclusions'.
- 'Allows individuals to come up with their own solutions and identify their own way forward'.
- 'Having my problems played back to me always makes them seem easier to fix'.
- 'A positive experience with someone independent who can bring a new perspective on challenges'.

Returning to the supporter impact model (Figure 40.2), the four boxes can be summarised as:

- Wide view and choice-led: the supporter is independent enabling him/her to take a wider perspective than those within the organisation. It adopts a pull style which involves greater exploration of issues and choices.
- Wide view and solution-led: the supporter is independent, enabling him/her to take a wider perspective. However, the push approach restricts exploration and the solution will come from the supporter, not from the individual.
- Narrow view and choice-led: the supporter is from within the organisation and could even be the individual's line manager, meaning that his/her perspective is probably limited. However, the pull approach leads to broad exploration of issues and choices.
- Narrow view and solution-led: the supporter is from within the organisation and adopts a push approach. That means the range of exploration will be limited and the solution will come from the supporter.

So support is not just a process; it is providing a safe environment based on empathy. Both parties must invest emotionally in the relationship – the individual by committing to their development and the supporter by believing in the potential of the individual. Supportive conversations are dependent on the supporter being from the appropriate background and adopting the appropriate style.

Key Skills and Qualities for a Supporter

Give people enough guidance to make the decisions you want them to make. Don't tell them what to do, but encourage them to do what is best. (Jimmy Johnson)

If support is not simply following a process; what is it? It has been described as 'a way of being'. This sounds a bit vague. So we must list what we believe an effective supporter needs in terms of skills and qualities.

KEY SKILLS

The key skills for an effective supporter are as follows:

- ability to build rapport, to help the individual be at ease and create trust;
- effective listening and questioning, to help the individual to explore issues and options;
- summarising and clarifying. Ability to clarify one's own understanding, showing the participant that you have been listening and are able to offer another perspective;
- ability to provide constructive feedback and to share your views about the individual (for example their progress, their options and so on);
- challenge sensitively, which will encourage the individual to review his/her thoughts, feelings or beliefs and to consider alternatives;
- prompting insight, to offer your perspective or alternative interpretation;
- sharing personal reflections – sharing your own thoughts and feelings about how the individual is behaving during the conversation;
- encouraging – positively reinforcing the individual's commitment to explore and grow.

THE KEY QUALITIES

The following is a list of the key attributes or qualities that we believe are needed by a good supporter:

- trustworthy and confidential;
- demonstrating belief in the individual;
- understanding and empathetic;
- non-judgemental;
- patience;
- approachable;
- honesty and integrity;
- insightful.

In our view, skills are competences that are learned (and may become second nature). They are controlled by the head.

Attributes, on the other hand, are manifestations of our hearts. They are inherent in us and are an expression of our values. To repeat the earlier NASA view:

Mentors are people who are interested in and willing to help others.

If you are interested and willing, that's all right. But never pretend, because that can do more harm than good.

RESPECT IN THE SUPPORTER/INDIVIDUAL RELATIONSHIP

I speak to everyone in the same way, whether he is the garbage man or the president of the university. (Albert Einstein)

We said earlier that supporting is not something you do to someone but is a relationship of equals. In fact, both parties have a responsibility to treat each other with mutual respect. We like to think of it in terms of the acronym RESPECT, which is core to 'humanability®' (which we outline in Chapter 58):

- **R**elationships – building and maintaining reciprocal relationships;
- **E**mpathy – putting oneself in the shoes of another, appreciating their feelings;
- **S**incerity – being honest with self and others;
- **P**rinciples – operating by one's principles or moral code;
- **E**mpowerment – empowering self and others to grow;
- **C**ompassion – dealing with others compassionately, with care;
- **T**rust –showing trust in others and building trust.

SO WHO SUPPORTS WHOM?

There is a drawback with assigning labels to the participants in the relationship because it can imply an unnecessary formality. Does there need to be a mentor and mentee or a coach and coachee? We like to promote a supporting culture – the practice of quality conversations between colleagues, where sometimes you are the supporter and other times you are supported. Here an individual can take an issue to a colleague and receive an empathetic ear.

WHERE HAS THE STORY GOT TO?

Project managers can have particular pressures, and having support to explore problems and choices can be invaluable. It doesn't matter whether we call that person a coach or mentor – it's how and why they do it that's important. It is a relationship of equals, where both parties engage emotionally and *respect*. Support requires both the head and heart. Having said all that; is it worth it?

Does the Business Case for Coaching and Mentoring Stack Up?

Everything that can be counted does not necessarily count; everything that counts cannot necessarily be counted. (Albert Einstein)

Project managers worth their salt will want to know the cost-benefit analysis of support. Support comes with the tangible cost of time. A supportive conversation could last anything from a few minutes to a few hours. This must be multiplied by two because there are two participants who have taken time from the project and other responsibilities. There are intangible costs too, which include:

- effort – a supportive conversation can be mentally and emotionally demanding; it requires significant work from both parties;
- skills – supporting requires many skills that that must be learned;
- discomfort – the conversation may take either or both parties outside of their comfort zone (as we mentioned above).

We have not yet researched the tangible benefits of supportive conversations, but we suggest that the time invested would be repaid manifold. We would expect the individual to develop and use his/her hard and soft skills more effectively and develop better strategies for tackling issues and opportunities that arise. There are also intangible benefits, as follows:

- Supporter skills – the skills that the supporter acquires are valuable in any relationship, for example with team members, clients, suppliers and all stakeholders.
- Relationship – the supporter/individual relationship is sustainable. It will be a basis of reciprocity (refer to humanability® in Chapter 58).
- Investment in the individual – project managers who have been supported feel valued and show increased loyalty.
- Satisfaction – supporting can generate great job satisfaction. It is an expression of our ethics of care and reason.
- Culture – support can become part of an organisation's culture. A supportive culture promotes high levels of collaboration, knowledge sharing and best practice.

It is up to you to weigh the costs and the benefits. But what have you got to lose by giving it a go? After all, individuals who have been supported by our company tell us that they have benefited in the following ways:

- 'Increased confidence, heightened self-awareness and perception as part of continual improvement'.
- 'I see the value in myself and others'.
- 'Helps me understand others, transforming my working relationships'.
- 'An understanding of why I behave, react and interact the way I do'.
- 'Gives me a clearer view of what I need to do, making me feel calmer and in control'.
- 'Skills for adapting my own management style and gaining a considered approach to my work'.
- '... enabled me to get the right results in the best possible way'.

Summary: A Chemistry Lesson

The most effective way to achieve right relations with any living thing is to look for the best in it, and then help that best into the fullest expression. (Allen J. Boone)

Coutu (2009) surveyed coaches about the value of coaching. She identified the two most important factors in a successful coaching relationship as: actively engaged coachees who are ready to learn and good chemistry between the coachee and coach. We believe that quality conversations in a quality relationship provide the environment for that chemistry. In fact the supporter could be regarded as the catalyst for change in the individual.

So we want to offer you this chemistry equation:

$$R + C = E + A$$

where:

R = quality Relationship
C = quality Conversation
E = Exploration
A = Awareness (of choice).

Here is a final word – if you must have a process. The essence of support is to be genuinely interested in people's growth and development – including your own! But if you feel the need for a process, we offer you our seven-point process for supporting another person:

1. Open your ears – so open your mind and your heart;
2. Face away from the clock and hide your watch;
3. Listen;
4. Listen some more;
5. If in doubt, say nothing;
6. Ask an open question;
7. Go to step 1.

After all, it could be *you* on the receiving end.

References and Further Reading

Bluckert, P. (2006), *Psychological Dimensions of Executive Coaching*, Maidenhead: McGraw-Hill.

Clutterbuck, D. (2010), 'Coaching reflection: The liberated coach, coaching', *An International Journal of Theory and Practice*, 3(1), 73–81.

Clutterbuck, D. and Sweeney, J. (1998), 'Coaching and mentoring', in Lock, D. (ed.), *The Gower Handbook of Management*, 4th edn, Aldershot: Gower.

Coutu, D. (2009), 'Survey realities of executive coaching', *Harvard Business Review*, 2009.

Downey, M. (2003), *Effective Coaching: Lessons from the Coach's Coach*, London: Texere Publishing.

Gallwey, W.T. (2000), *The Inner Game of Work: Focus, Learning, Pleasure, and Mobility in the Workplace*, New York: Random House.

Whitmore, J. (2007), *Coaching for Performance – GROWing People, Performance and Purpose*, London: Nicholas Brealey.

Project Staffing and HRM Issues

CHAPTER

41 *Scheduling People for a Single Project*

DENNIS LOCK

Resource scheduling is apparently a complex subject because it has to deal with a large number of variables. But if this is approached like a mathematical problem in which the variables are solved one by one, the process becomes relatively simple. However, it does require suitable software and it must be carried out by someone with appropriate skills and training. The most suitable place in which to establish this function will usually be in a project or programme support office. This chapter considers scheduling resources for a single project. The more complete picture, taking in all corporate resources, is dealt with in Chapter 42.

Making a Start

The scheduler has to assemble some basic data and make several assumptions before a sensible schedule can be made. The principal objective is to plan the deployment of people on the project over its active life cycle in such a way that their time is used to best purpose so that the project is finished on time. An ideal schedule will avoid impossible work overloads, yet prevent periods when people are idle. It has to be recognised that this ideal might not always be possible. Resource scheduling often involves making compromises. Remember too, that all resource scheduling is based on estimated data and can never be an exact science.

Some of the factors governing project resource scheduling for a single skill type are shown in Figure 41.1. These problems will apparently be multiplied in a typical projects company by the fact that more than one kind of resource has to be scheduled, but that difficulty disappears in practice when a computer is used. There might also be several other projects in progress, but taking that further step up into multiproject or programme scheduling will be held over until the next chapter.

Resource scheduling used to be carried out by a dedicated planner spending many hours with an adjustable wall board on which project tasks were represented by horizontal strips. This, in effect, was an adjustable Gantt chart, where the strips representing the tasks could be moved back or forwards sideways to delay or accelerate the start of the tasks. The aim was always to achieve the smoothest possible use of resources. The number of each resource required in each day (or week) was found simply by counting the number of strips occurring in each period column. Task strips could be coloured to

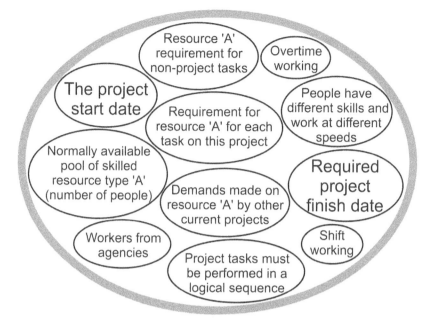

Figure 41.1 Problems of resource scheduling in a nutshell

represent different resource types. When a task required more than one unit of a resource (more than one person working on the task) that could be depicted simply by placing the appropriate number of strips on the chart in parallel or by writing the relevant number on the strip. That method has long since been superseded but a mental picture of one of those charts can still help people to understand the principles of resource scheduling. Now more powerful and (crucially) far more flexible computer applications can do the work, saving much time and no longer causing the eyestrain and sore fingers that used to afflict planners struggling with all those coloured strips.

It is important to use competent software, remembering that the most popular project management software on the market might not be the best software for serious project scheduling. There is detailed advice on choosing project management software for this purpose in Chapter 18 of Lock (2013).

Which Project Resources Need to Be Scheduled?

The question about which resources need to be scheduled begs another question, and that is which resources *can* be scheduled? Because this Handbook is concerned with people, the answer to this question in our context is any resource that can be:

1. identified by a type or name (such as programmer, systems engineer, design engineer, electrician and so on) and;
2. quantified in simple numerical units (which in this case means identifying a number of people of the particular skill).

The same project management software that schedules people can also schedule quantities of other resources, such as materials and (with particular expertise) cash flows. One resource that is difficult to schedule using project management software is project accommodation and storage space, because that involves three-dimensional shapes. However, in this Handbook we are concerned only with people, who are of course the most valuable project resource.

By no means does every resource need to be scheduled. Suppose, for example, that a software company employs 10 people who spend all their project time designing applications and writing code. Suppose also that an additional 5 people are employed to check the work of those 10 programmers and run performance tests on the software. The resource scheduler does not need to use the computer to discover that one checker will be required for every two programmers on any typical project. Further, if the workload pattern of the programmers is smoothed to avoid idle times and overloads, then the work that they produce will be fed to the checkers at an even rate. So the checkers do not need to be scheduled by the computer – their requirements simple follow on from those of the programmers. Similar arguments apply to any resource that supports another, such as electrician's assistants, design checkers, paint shop operators, manufacturing inspectors and so on.

Although modern software can usually schedule well over 100 different resource types, my experience has shown it is necessary to identify the key resources and then schedule only those. In one very successful case it was necessary to schedule only 6 different resource skills to obtain good schedules for all the direct workers in a company of about 600 people.

Clearly many indirect staff (including managers) do not need to be scheduled, because their project duties are continuous. Likewise, it is not usually necessary to schedule people who provide a general service to projects, such as the people within the project management office, purchasing department and so on. This is not to say that the resource requirement for all these support people can be ignored. But the numbers of people needed in those roles is simply a matter of allocating them as a proportion of the key people who *are* scheduled. However, if the same project management software is being used also to schedule project cash inflows, outflows or (more cleverly) net flows, then any skills that are not included in the scheduling database must be allowed for.

Setting up the Resource Files and Entering the Scheduling Data

It will be necessary to set up a separate file in the computer for each resource skill to be scheduled. Competent software (not all software is competent in this respect) will require the following data to be entered for each skill.

- Resource name (for example, systems engineers);
- A short code to identify the resource (often one or two alpha characters);
- A level of availability for the resource (the number of people that can be allocated to project tasks);
- The start date from when the resource will become available;
- A finish date after which the available number of resource will change;
- A cost rate for the resource (if required), best expressed as a rate per day.

It is usually possible to specify different availability levels for future periods, so that planned recruitments or dismissals can be taken into account.

Some software will allow each resource type to be allocated to its own calendar, which is useful if shift working, six- or seven-day weeks or any other unusual work patterns are envisaged that will be applicable only to that resource. But the preferable option is usually not to specify a calendar for the *resource*, but to allow each *task* to be associated with a specified calendar (which will take out public holidays and so on). In practice this is not as complicated as it sounds, because the computer will usually allocate tasks to a default calendar for the project unless the scheduler determines otherwise.

TASK DATA

Much of the task data to be entered will be familiar to anyone who regularly plans projects using critical path analysis. The minimum requirement is usually:

- task number;
- task description;
- numbers of either immediately preceding tasks or immediately succeeding tasks (which defines the network logic);
- estimated task duration (preferably expressed in days).

If shift working is to be involved, or if different calendars are otherwise required, then additionally the relevant calendar number must also be given for each task. Otherwise tasks will take the default calendar.

For many tasks that will be the only data to be specified. But for every task that is expected to use *scheduled* resources, the following additional data must be given:

- the resource code;
- the resource quantity (preferably as the number of people required per day);

Some tasks might require more than one resource type and quantity to be specified.

SPLITTABLE AND NON-SPLITTABLE TASKS

Resource scheduling can theoretically mean that a non-critical task can be planned to stop temporarily and restart later to release its resources for work on a critical task. Many people would argue that interrupting any task for such reasons could lead to discontent from those working on the task, and might increase the chance of mistakes or poor workmanship standards. Good software will allow the scheduler to specify any task that can be split to improve the smooth allocation of resources, but the default condition of all software will ensure that tasks are non-splittable unless they are declared otherwise. I do not recommend splitting tasks.

RATE-CONSTANT AND NON-RATE-CONSTANT RESOURCE USE

The simplest and recommended way in which to view the use of a resource for any particular task is to assume that the same quantity of resource will be required

(a) Rate-constant

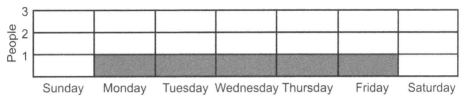

(b) Non rate-constant

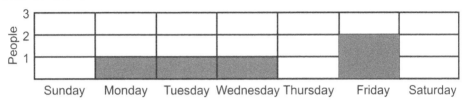

Figure 41.2 Rate-constant and non-rate-constant resource usage for a project task

Note: Although non-rate constant patterns might occur in a project, in practice it is not usually necessary to specify them in the database because the variations tend to cancel out over the large number of tasks that take place concurrently.

uniformly from the start to the end of the task. That is called *rate-constant* resource use. In practice there will often be tasks that require different levels of a resource on different days for a task (Figure 41.2 shows a simple example). Some advanced software allows such patterns to be specified. However, that level of planning detail is an unnecessary complication because in a typical project there will be many tasks running together using the same resource type, and any variations in one task will be cancelled out in the total resource usage pattern. Further, it is very difficult to see non-rate-constant patterns in the database once the input has been made and the data become invisible and lost to view. So my firm recommendation is to keep it simple and stick to rate-constant usage.

SPECIFYING THE AVAILABILITY LEVEL OF A PARTICULAR SKILL

Suppose there is a group of 20 designers available in a department. The first inclination of the scheduler might be to declare in the computer input data that 20 designers are available for project work. However, at any given time one can be sure that some of those designers will not be able to work on projects. Reasons for this non-availability include:

- absence through annual leave or any other form of leave;
- sickness;
- time out for training or attendance of seminars, exhibitions and so on;
- rectification work left over from previous tasks;
- ad hoc tasks, such as answering queries from other departments or from customers;
- giving support to sales staff in the preparation of new sales proposals; and so on.

Rather than attempt the impossible process of scheduling these miscellaneous drains on availability, all that is necessary is to deduct a proportion of the total workforce from the declared availability level. Start by allowing 15 per cent for all non-project distractions. So if there are 20 designers employed in a group, 'tell' the computer that you have 17. You will always be able to adjust this proportion later, as experience is gained.

Establishing Priorities

Modern resource scheduling requires in the first instance that a detailed critical path network exists for the project. By 'detailed' is meant that the network should not allow any task to move consecutively from the control of one manager or supervisor to another – in other words a new task must be created whenever responsibility for carrying out a task changes from one department (or manager) to another. Thus no task can have two different people responsible for it, and that usually means (conveniently) that no task will undergo a change in the type of resource needed to carry it out as the task progresses.

TASK PRIORITIES

When the computer has finished time analysis of the network, the database will hold the following time-related information for each task:

* duration;
* earliest possible start date;
* latest possible start date;
* earliest possible finish date;
* latest possible finish date;
* free float;
* total float.

Competent software will allow the scheduler to specify priority rules for allocating resources to tasks, and the most convenient rule to choose is to give priority to tasks with least total float. In fact, this becomes a little more complicated because, if the computer delays any task until resources become available, some of the total float in the network will be used up and we get another quantity for each task, which is called *remaining float*. This is important information for anyone with the responsibility for progressing project work but by no means all software has the capability to report it.

PRIORITY RULES FOR THE PROJECT

If there are insufficient resources to carry out all tasks within their available float, something has to give. Either the project date will have to be extended or more resources must be found. So, before the resource calculation, the scheduler will have to instruct the computer to carry out either a *time-limited* or a *resource-limited* schedule computation. These concepts are illustrated in Figure 41.3, which shows usage patterns for just one resource type in a small imaginary project.

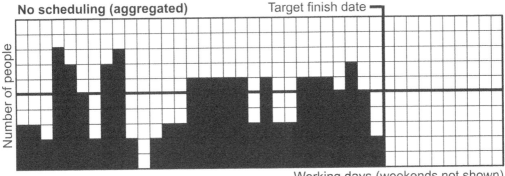

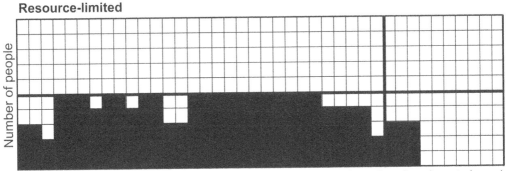

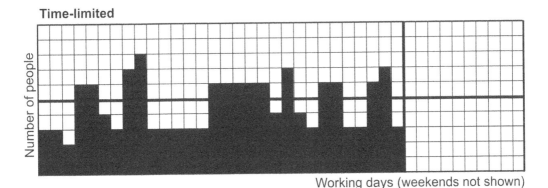

Figure 41.3 Effects of different project priority rules on resource usage patterns

Note: The patterns shown here are for typical for a single resource in a small project.

When the resource-limited rule is applied, the computer is not able to exceed the available resource levels at any time. If the resources are not available in sufficient amounts, the inevitable consequence is that the computer must schedule some tasks beyond their critical dates, and the project will be scheduled to finish late. Tasks that are scheduled later than their latest permissible dates derived from time analysis then acquire negative float (another important quantity that some software appears to be unable to report).

If the time-limited rule is used, the computer will produce a schedule that satisfies the required (target) project completion date, even though that might mean showing resource usage levels that are above those available. So resource overloads are forecast even before the project has begun. Because time is usually a critical performance factor in project management, the project manager will want to do everything possible to find the additional resources needed to bring the schedule back within the desired time frame. And the way to do that is clearly to plan for bringing in additional resources, which in project management software terms are called *threshold resources*.

Threshold Resources

Again, as in so much of resource scheduling, we have identified a feature that is not possessed by all software. With the appropriate software however, the project scheduler is able to specify a higher level of resource availability that the computer can call upon if (but only if) resource limitations would otherwise cause the project to be scheduled late.

Threshold resources can be obtained by taking a number of actions. Working overtime is one possibility, but that must be discouraged. Overtime working should never be planned into a schedule for several reasons. People who work long hours too frequently will become tired, their work efficiency will drop, and after a time they will produce no more work in their extended hours than they previously produced in normal hours. But overtime is a valuable reserve for those (hopefully rare) occasions when things do go seriously wrong. I once supervised a small group of volunteers who worked continuously without sleep for three days and nights to get hospital project components ready in time for space reserved on a ship that was sailing at the end of the week. A more effective source of threshold resources is likely to be short-term hires, usually from an agency (see Chapter 48).

When costs are being scheduled along with human resources it will be necessary for the scheduler to specify a cost rate (typically per day) for the threshold resources. This will usually be higher than the rate for normal resource levels.

Of course one advantage of resource scheduling, in addition to achieving relatively stable levels of resource deployment on tasks, is to give the project company adequate notice that additional workers will be needed. That enables forward planning to obtain those additional staff, from whatever source is most appropriate.

Using the Resource Schedules

All project managers will be familiar with the work schedules produced by project management software when resources are not considered. Typical column headings for tabular reports would be arranged, from left to right, as follows:

* task ID;
* task description;
* estimated duration;
* earliest start;
* latest start;

- earliest finish;
- latest finish;
- free float;
- total float.

All such reports, by the use of departmental codes as filters, should be edited so that each manager gets a list of only those tasks for which he or she is responsible. Sorting those tasks into date order (usually by earliest start) makes the lists more convenient and they are often called 'work-to' or 'work-to-do' lists. Many managers are content to work from such lists and take their chance on resource availability, but that clearly should not be the preferred option.

After resource scheduling, three additional and most important components are substituted in the 'work-to' reports, which are:

- scheduled start;
- scheduled finish;
- remaining float.

Now each manager has recommended 'scheduled' dates which, if adhered to, will ensure that resources are used in line with their availability. An example of a tabular work-to list is shown in Figure 41.4. Of course, the software will also be able to produce graphics, often in attractive colours, and even with 3D effects for usage histograms in some cases. But tabular reports are to be preferred because they provide data that do not have to be read off scales.

Task ID	Task description	Dur (days)	Earliest start	Schedule start	Schedule finish	Latest finish	Rem. float	Resources
1012	Design transfer layout	12	22Feb14	22Feb14	09Mar14	22Mar14	9	1 DE
1004	Design bore head layout	15	22Feb14	22Feb14	12Mar14	25Mar14	9	1 DE
1015	Design fixture layout	15	22Feb14	03Mar14	23Mar14	23Mar14	0	1 DE
1017	Design turnover layout	8	10Mar14	10Mar14	19Mar14	01Apr14	9	1 DE
1520	Review transfer design	1	10Mar14	10Mar14	10Mar14	26Mar14	12	-
1024	Review bore head layout	2	15Mar14	15Mar14	16Mar14	29Mar14	9	-
1032	Review turnover design	1	22Mar14	22Mar14	22Mar14	02Apr14	9	-

Figure 41.4 A convenient format for a departmental project schedule after resource levelling

TREATING PEOPLE AS NUMBERS

So far in this chapter, people of a particular skill (resource) have been lumped together and described by simple numerical quantities. We have discussed people as numbers which, to some extent is thinking of them as commodities, all identical, like cans of beans. But of course people are not identical. For example, I knew of a case in a small construction company where Paul had a fear of heights, and could not be allocated tasks that meant climbing tall ladders (and so he became known as Bungalow Paul). The manager of any functional group will know the different personal traits and skills of those in that group.

Mary might be better suited to perform one project task than Mark, but on other tasks that apparently require the same resource skill, Mark might be better suited.

So when the time comes to allocate tasks to people, they can no longer be considered as numbers (as they were when the resource schedules were calculated). Only the department manager has the personal knowledge of people with the group. The final step in resource allocation must be left to the departmental managers and supervisors. But they can work with the assurance that the tasks required from their departments are being scheduled at a rate that is consistent with the total resource availability.

Some project management software will allow individual names to be declared as resources. Even people's annual leave dates can be entered. But when projects with a duration of many months or several years are being scheduled that is hardly practicable – indeed it becomes absurd. People come and go from work groups for a variety of reasons as time passes.

So resource scheduling should never be expected to remove the responsibility for allocating tasks to individual people from the functional managers. Resource scheduling must be regarded as a tool that helps managers to do their job, reduces the risk of overloads and idle time, but leaves managers free to exercise their skill and judgement in allocating jobs to the people they know.

Conclusion

Many project managers go through their working lives without using resource scheduling, preferring instead to try and start every task at its earliest possible time, accepting the difficulties and panics that this approach often causes. This chapter has shown that resource scheduling is not something to be feared and is not magic. It does, however mean making judgements and compromises and should never be regarded as an exact science. It cannot be precise because all project schedules are based on estimates. However, given good software (such as Primavera, 4c Systems, or Micro Planner X-Pert) and the intelligent use of data, highly practicable schedules can be produced. The project support office is the ideal home for the process. Many non-expert people will attempt to persuade the planner that every last second of every person needs to be entered into the scheduling data. That way lies the path to failure. Resource scheduling requires a common sense approach, often making assumptions and compromises that seem surprising – even reckless. But if the process is not kept within rational bounds things will become truly impossible when the step into full multiproject and corporate scheduling is taken. That further important step is described in the following chapter.

References and Further Reading

Lock, D. (2013), *Project Management*, 10th edn, Farnham: Gower.

42 Resource Planning for People in a Projects Company

DENNIS LOCK

The previous chapter discussed the process of scheduling people for a single project. This chapter takes the process forward into the wider procedures for scheduling a programme of projects (multiproject scheduling), and then looks forward to planning a company's human resource levels in the longer term.

Scheduling People for all Current Projects

To be able to carry out multiproject scheduling, the project manager or scheduler has first to be entirely conversant with scheduling resources for a single project. Thus, either the reader should be familiar with project resource scheduling or the previous chapter should be read first.

The step up from single-project scheduling to full multiproject scheduling is not difficult, and should be fairly painless. The same principles apply broadly in both cases and, as for the single project, it is necessary to exercise much common sense and avoid unnecessary detail. Again it must always be borne in mind that scheduling is not an exact science and, indeed, all the data are eventually traceable back to estimates and decisions that might be flawed.

To some extent the decisions and judgement required from schedulers for full multiproject planning are more straightforward than those needed for single projects. Now the planner does not have to make any mental provision for the demands on common resources of projects that are not in the scheduling mix, because the power of the computer will be harnessed for that job.

As with single-project scheduling it will probably be necessary to schedule only a chosen few key people skills and then ensure that people working with the associated supporting skills are kept available in the proportions that the organisation's experience has shown to be necessary.

It must be assumed that a suitable computer system is available, with software that is capable of doing the job. The same software that can schedule a single project will usually be suitable also for scheduling multiple projects, bearing in mind that the most popular general project management software will probably not be the appropriate tool for the purpose. When choosing software, the same rules apply as for scheduling single projects. There is a detailed checklist and advice on that subject in Chapter 20 of Lock (2013).

For multiproject scheduling it is even more important that the process is managed within a project support office and that access to the system to add new projects or change its operating rules is restricted to those with the relevant training and experience. People made responsible for this kind of scheduling require special aptitudes, which include a high intelligence quotient and the ability to disregard unnecessary detail and see through to the essentials. Otherwise the organisation will fall into the trap of trying to schedule people's times in units of hours, when the task estimates have been made in days or weeks, and of attempting to schedule every last Tom, Dick and Harriet in the organisation for years ahead. People outside the project support office will often try to argue for every half hour or every person to be scheduled which, for a company-wide schedule covering perhaps five years is plainly ridiculous. The task of keeping the schedule simple and practicable will be difficult at first, but the scheduler(s) must be resolute if the system is not to choke on its own data.

As more and more data are entered into the computer a virtual model of the company's project resources deployment is created. Although the process is simply a matter of using common sense and making intelligent decisions about which resources to schedule, it needs only one inexpert change to the system parameters to corrupt the database and wreck the model. Recovery from such a disaster can be very difficult and time consuming. Prevention is inestimably better than cure in this case. So access to the model's operating parameters must be restricted to the professional schedulers in the project support office.

IDENTIFYING THE SEPARATE PROJECTS

In some computer applications the total multiproject schedule is known as the project, and all the individual projects in the programme are then called subprojects. However, here in this chapter we can refer to the collective schedule as the multiproject schedule or programme, so that all the individual projects still stand on their own as projects.

The company's name can often be given as the title for the entire programme. Every project within the programme must be given both an identifier and a title (which the project management and cost accounting procedures would require in any case). The software should allow the project cost code, as it appears in all other company documents, to be used as the identifier for each separate project. Good software will allow the relevant cost codes from the work breakdown structure for each project to be built into all the task identifiers in the network diagram, and that can be extremely useful when sorting and filtering reports for all kinds of management purposes.

ALLOCATING PRIORITIES TO PROJECTS

Every project should, of course, have its own target start and finish dates. For projects being conducted for external customers, the target finish dates will most probably be the same dates as the contracts' required delivery dates. Some project managers prefer to set their scheduled target dates a week or two earlier than the dates promised to customers, to provide a safety margin or buffer zone.

Every individual project within the programme must have its own critical path network and all the network data will therefore exist in the database. So, among other things, all tasks across all the projects will have their total float, free float and remaining float identified and available in the database. Thus, even though there might be many projects in the scheduling mix, perhaps even with tens of thousands of tasks in the database, every individual task across all those projects has its priority (and the urgency of its claim for finite human resources) determined ultimately by the target completion date for its particular project. The process is completely automatic and far, far easier to manage than it sounds here. Although the process is very complex, often involving tens of thousands of tasks and a great amount of data, it is very simple from the scheduler's point of view because the computer takes care of the mass of detailed calculations.

There is, however, often one serious flaw in this utopian picture. And that flaw comes from potential interference from senior managers. Senior managers often have preferred customers and clients, perhaps because of the prestige and market importance of those companies, or simply through personal friendships with their counterparts in the client companies. It often happens that senior managers will ask the individual project managers or the project support office to report progress on their favoured projects (no serious harm in that). But they might go on to ask that those projects be given special priority (plenty of potential harm there). Such interference can be irritating at best, and damaging and disruptive at worst. Senior managers must be persuaded to allow the computer to take the strain and schedule resources so that, unless there are really exceptional circumstances, *all* projects – not just a favoured few – are planned to run on time. The project support office must work hard to convince senior managers that it is best to drive priorities from agreed target completion dates without interference and rely on the system to produce schedules that are fair to all. This is a question of everyone gaining confidence and giving credibility to the process and its resulting schedules.

However, if there happens to be a genuine reason for giving one project special priority over all the others, that can be arranged simply by giving it a slightly advanced target completion date.

Frequency of Schedule Updating

The work-to lists that emerge from a multiproject schedule will be the tools from which departmental and group managers issue project tasks to individuals under their control. It should be mentioned here that getting those line managers to accept the schedules as their working tools is not always easy and (especially when the scheduling system is new) some managers will attempt to time the allocation of work according to their own preferences, so damaging the efficacy of the scheduling process.

Progress data for updating the schedule will usually come into the project support office according to the communications established between the project support office and the line managers. Any responsible person in the organisation should be allowed direct access to the model to report progress (reporting tasks as started or finished, or revising the estimated time-to-completion for a task). However, repeating my earlier advice, beyond reporting progress no individual outside the project support office should be allowed direct access to the scheduling system's operating parameters or core data, to prevent the risk of corrupting the virtual model.

Some organisations update their schedules in line with reported progress at regular intervals, which might be every two weeks or every four weeks. Whether or not the schedule needs updating must be a decision for the project support office. There is a good argument for only updating a schedule and reissuing the departmental work-to lists when it threatens to become unworkable owing to too many delayed tasks, a change in the organisation (even an outbreak of flu can disrupt a programme) or the introduction of a new project.

What-if? Testing

The multiproject model is an ideal place in which to test the possible effects of injecting a new project into the existing programme and the changed requirements for human resources. In theory, one simply runs the model again with the new project added to all the existing projects. This usually has to be done twice, once using the resource-limited rule and once in the time-limited mode. Then one can observe the increased levels of total human resources required for the company or, alternatively, note the delaying effect of the new project on the scheduled completion dates of the current projects using the existing resources. Of course, it's never quite that simple.

One apparent snag with testing possible new projects is that it will be most unlikely that any critical path network will exist in detail for those projects. However, that is not really important for what-if? testing. All that is necessary is to produce a skeleton network for each possible new project. The skeleton need contain only a few bones – just enough summary tasks to ensure that the outline resource usages fall in their appropriate time periods in relation to the projects' starts and finishes.

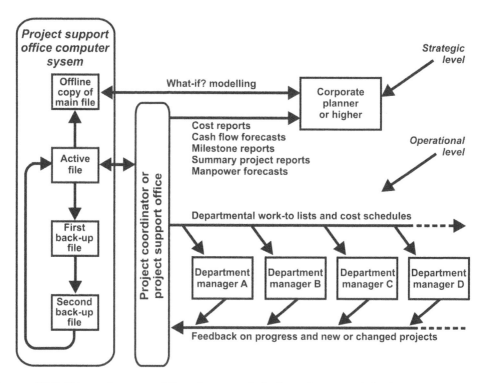

Figure 42.1 Managing a multiproject model of projects and their resources

Another potential and more serious problem with what-if? testing is that after each test, when the trial project has been removed, restoration of the schedule to its exact former state might not be possible. Line managers will not appreciate having their work-to lists replaced and changed for no good reason.

The only way to achieve safe what-if? testing is to copy and paste a duplicate of the working schedule into a file that is entirely separate from the active model. Then that separate file can be used as the experimental database. Anyone outside the secure boundaries of the project support office may be allowed to 'play' with the duplicate in the knowledge that the original is protected and safe from corruption.

The usual method of keeping secure daily back-up files is recommended. Although setting up a multiproject schedule should be straightforward to the experienced scheduler, it requires careful and dedicated adherence to prescribed routines. The concept of secure management of the working schedule, whilst allowing access for progress reporting and what-if? testing, is shown in Figure 42.1.

Contribution of the Multiproject Schedule to Corporate Human Resource Planning

The kinds of schedules that we have considered so far are intended primarily to ensure that projects can proceed through their life cycles avoiding late completion and without causing undue overloads or idle periods for the available human resources. Before moving on to consider all corporate human resources over the longer term, people should be aware that there is one very useful report that can be obtained when the appropriate project management software is used. This is a day-by-day forecast of the resources needed for all the projects in the multiproject mix. Figure 42.2 shows the ideal format for such a report for one company department. All the data in this figure are imaginary, but the format is based very closely on schedules produced for real projects in my experience. The software used in the original example for this case is available as 4c, from 4c Systems Limited, a UK company that can trace its pedigree and its software back to the 1970s.

In practice the length of reports like that in Figure 42.2 can be extended out in time as far as predictions allow – until the last task in the last project has been finished. The project manager and other company managers can scan down the columns to obtain the most accurate forecasts possible of how many people in each reported department will be required for project work.

Where the report shows negative numbers of free people, this is the result of running the schedule under the time-limited rule, so that projects are scheduled to complete on time even where this means exceeding the resource levels declared as available. For management purposes these results give advance warning of the need to hire additional people, either as permanent staff or from an agency.

Looking further down the resource usage columns will inevitably reveal the time when scheduled resource usage falls away. In one such case under my control, I was asked in April by my managing director, 'Dennis, when shall we be able to begin our next big project?' (We had a customer intending to sign a new valuable contract.) My answer was 'Fourth of October'. That date not only fell in line with the resources

Date	Senior designers			Detailers/checkers			Cost	Cum. cost
	Avail.	Usage	Free	Avail.	Usage	Free		
05Jan15	11	9	2	16	16		4,360	4,360
06Jan15	11	9	2	16	16		4,360	8,720
07Jan15	11	9	2	16	16		4,360	13,080
08Jan15	11	11		16	16		4,760	17,840
09Jan15	11	11		16	16		4,760	22,600
12Jan15	11	11		16	18	-2	5,080	27,680
13Jan15	11	11		16	18	-2	5,080	32,760
14Jan15	11	11		16	18	-2	5,080	37,840
15Jan15	11	10	1	16	18	-2	4,560	42,400
16Jan15	11	10	1	16	18	-2	4,560	46,960
19Jan15	11	11		16	18	-2	5,080	52,040
20Jan15	11	11		16	16		4,760	56,800
21Jan15	11	11		16	16		4,760	61,560
22Jan15	11	11		16	16		4,760	66,320
23Jan15	11	11		16	16		4,760	71,080
26Jan15	11	12	-1	16	17	-1	5,120	76,200
27Jan15	11	12	-1	16	17	-1	5,120	81,320
28Jan15	11	11		16	17	-1	4,920	86,240
29Jan15	11	11		16	17	-1	4,920	91,160
30Jan15	11	11		16	17	-1	4,920	96,080
02Feb15	11	11		18	16	2	4,760	100,840
03Feb15	11	10	1	18	16	2	4,560	105,400
04Feb15	11	10	1	18	16	2	4,560	109,960
05Feb15	11	10	1	18	18		4,880	114,840
06Feb15	11	8	3	18	18		4,480	119,320
09Feb15	11	8	3	18	18		4,480	123,800
10Feb15	11	8	3	18	18		4,480	128,280
11Feb15	11	7	4	18	15	3	3,800	132,080
12Feb15	11	7	4	18	15	3	3,800	135,880

Lynlox Projects Ltd   Report date 31 Nov 2014

Resource schedule, all projects   Design department

Figure 42.2 Report format for departmental resources after multiproject scheduling

available, but also fortunately suited the customer's own schedules. The new project actually did begin at the beginning of October because all the schedules were very practicable and progress control was continuous and effective. The costs reported by the same project management system in that company fell within 5 per cent of those estimated completely independently by the company's cost estimating department. Such accurate results can come with experience, a good project support office, the use of common sense and competent software. Even though most of the data are based on estimates and the resources actually being scheduled might be only the few core skills, the large volume of data in the typical system will tend to cancel out the inaccuracies and simplifications.

Extending Human Resource Planning beyond Existing Projects

First, a recapitulation. In Chapter 41, scheduling to match people and tasks in a single project was discussed. The step up to full multi-resource scheduling of all active projects has been described in preceding sections of this current chapter. The next and final step forward in the scheduling process is to look at the wider implications of future project work for the numbers of people in the organisation over the longer term. This requires not only that active projects are scheduled, but also that possible future projects are considered and entered into the calculations. So our process has moved from single-project scheduling, through multiproject or programme resource scheduling to looking at the entire portfolio of actual and possible projects.

Clearly the further we look into the future, the less accurate the data become. Estimating accuracy will most likely move from fairly confident, through approximate to speculative. This is usually no longer a scheduling process that can be confined within a project support office. It must involve also the marketing and sales organisation, and (where such exists) the strategic planning function. The views of economists on the probable future direction and growth of the relevant market might also be invaluable, although it is well known that economists are prone to disagree with each other.

This forecasting process carries far higher risks of inaccuracies than planning for existing projects because so many future events and trends are unpredictable. Outside factors such as government policies, mergers and acquisitions, market shifts and so on all play their part. In some countries natural disasters occur at frequent but irregular intervals, making planning even more difficult.

SALES FORECASTS AND PROJECT PORTFOLIOS

Clearly long-term sales forecasts are an important ingredient for long-range planning. Sales people do tend to be optimists, but their predictions clearly have to be taken into account as part of the longer-range resource planning process. Although it might be relatively simple to construct a skeleton plan and resource schedule for each new project opportunity, it has to be accepted that many of those opportunities will either pass to competitors or the projects will never go ahead. Against that argument, some projects might arise at short notice that the sales people had not foreseen (for example, satisfied customers sometimes return with urgent requests for new work).

A method used in many companies to attempt a realistic forecast of future project work is to ask the sales department to list all the desirable projects that they foresee as possibly becoming firm orders over as long a period as is considered practicable. In some companies the nature of the projects might allow this period to be five years. The next step is to assign to each of those projects a probability factor ranging from 1 per cent (for no chance of gaining the order) to something over 90 per cent (for certain). It is unwise to allocate 100 per cent probability to any project where the contract has not been signed.

It has further to be recognised that not every project opportunity will be seen by senior management as a viable or desirable opportunity. So another element of doubt is introduced because not all future project opportunities will be acceptable to the company. This is part of the portfolio management process. Factors such as the historical records of customers and clients for paying on time, their solvency, their country of origin, and other sundry matters can decide whether or not entering into those contracts with those companies will be viewed as acceptable at corporate level.

Thus a composite work level forecast, in terms of people of all the different skills, can be assembled based on:

1. Remaining work for projects that are in progress.
2. Known work for projects that have just been contracted for or which are certain to become live.
3. A composite estimate of future resource needs based on a statistical analysis of sales forecasts for the foreseeable future.
4. Longer-term forecasts based on the predictions of the economists and market advisers according to their views on the future market opportunities.
5. The decisions of corporate management on additions to the projects portfolio.

So, using all these data and predictions, the company can produce forecasts of its future resource needs that, in the immediate future will be accurate and based on data from the multiproject schedule from the project support office, but (unsurprisingly) in the longer term will become less accurate the farther into the future one looks.

CORE COMPETENCIES AND MINIMUM LEVELS

It is clear from the foregoing that forward resource planning for projects is a very inexact business, prone to surprises both pleasant and unpleasant.

A sensible approach is to plan to maintain staff in the organisation on permanent contracts at levels that will ensure sufficient availability of people in each core competency to support guaranteed future project work.

If the more optimistic forecasts of future work do materialise, the additional staff requirements can be sourced using agency staff, along the lines discussed in Chapter 48. When trends and forecasts indicate steady and continuing growth, the ratio of permanent staff to agency workers can be increased.

RARE SKILLS

Future resource planning does, of course, extend far beyond just considering particular group skills. People are not uniform commodities that can be quantified in the same way as cans of beans. All have their individual skills, personalities and competencies. That becomes particularly apparent when considering the future staffing of key roles that are represented by perhaps only one or two people in the organisation.

This tends to become more of an issue the farther up the management hierarchy one looks, but it is not only a matter of seniority. A person in the project support office who has learned through experience and aptitude to become expert in using the equipment and methods specific to that role is someone who would, without taking precautions, become impossible to replace or augment at short notice.

The stage provides a good analogy here. Consider an opera house putting on a live performance that is fully booked. If one of the chorus should fall ill or miss a train, their absence would probably go unnoticed. But what happens when the lead singer has laryngitis? The show must go on. So step forward the understudy! The understudy must have adequate competence – an audience that has paid to hear *Madame Butterfly* should not expect to be fobbed off with a caterpillar. And that is the vital clue in how to plan future key skilled resources in a projects company where the future work forecasts and staffing are unpredictable.

In other words, every core role in a projects company should have at least one understudy. This is usually brought about by having people nominated as relief workers for the key roles. Each of these understudy workers can spend some time being transferred to work alongside the key performer so that in the event of an emergency the understudy can step into the key performer's shoes and take over. This is a kind of *action learning* in miniature. (Action learning is a management development method that involves managers exchanging their quite different jobs under supervision for a prescribed period under the guidance of a facilitator. The guru and foremost exponent of this is Professor Reg. Revans (Revans 2011).) This understudy training process provides for back-up in the case of emergencies but it can also greatly enhance the work experience and the motivation of those who are asked temporarily to swap roles.

Not often talked about, but relevant here, is the subject of key person insurance. Named people within the organisation can be part of an insurance policy that offers financial compensation should the company's profits suffer as a result of accident or other reason why a nominated key person is unable to fulfil the expected role. Whilst key person insurance can, to some extent, repair financial damage to the projects company, it cannot put the project back on track and satisfy the customer.

Conclusion

Planning for future human resource requirements is a very inexact process, yet it has to be done to the organisation's best endeavours, if only because staffing an organisation cannot be achieved at short notice. The process for a projects company begins with scheduling current projects, but has to be extended to include the full possible portfolio of future projects. A project support office will be the best centre for that scheduling but when full corporate resources are to be considered other experts must be brought into the process. They can include market researchers, strategic (long term) planners, economists and the sales organisation. Many external factors over which the organisation has no control mean that human resource forecasts are subject to many risks and inaccuracies. A sensible approach is often to plan for a complement of permanent staff to cover core competencies and have plans available for hiring from agencies to cover overloads. All prudent organisations will back up their key staff availability by providing in-house training to other staff who will be able to step into the key roles as understudies if necessary.

References and Further Reading

Lock, D. (2013), *Project Management*, 10th edn, Farnham: Gower.
Revans, R. (2011), *The ABC of Action Learning*, Farnham: Gower.

43 *Recruitment*

LINDSAY SCOTT

Clearly no project can be completed without people. Further, no project can be completed successfully without the *right* people. Every organisation has at some time in its existence the need to recruit those people. Thus the subject of this chapter is especially important within the scope of this Handbook. Of course recruitment is a two-way process. That presented me with a slight dilemma on whether to write this chapter from the viewpoint of the potential hirer or to give advice to candidates. In the event, I have chosen to describe the process as dispassionately as possible, but where necessary my emphasis has been from the hiring manager's point of view.

Introduction

Recruitment for project management is very much the same as for other business sectors. The objective is to find the right person at the right time with the requisite blend of education, skills, experience and personality for the job. Success is achieved by focusing on key areas relevant to the vacancy – factors such as education, training, skills, competence, experience, qualifications and other things that make one candidate stand out from the others. This chapter follows the five generally recognised recruitment stages (shown graphically in Figure 43.1).

Recruitment is not a task to be undertaken lightly, because so much depends on its outcome. Project management recruitment is a blend of art and science, not without problems. As the hiring line manager you have to give recruitment activities priority. It is difficult to continue with your day job and stay committed and enthused about bringing new people into the organisation. So your workload will inevitably increase

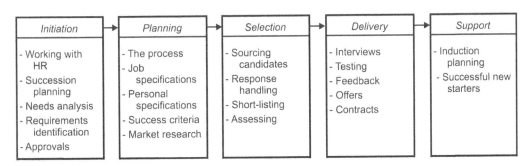

Initiation	Planning	Selection	Delivery	Support
- Working with HR - Succession planning - Needs analysis - Requirements identification - Approvals	- The process - Job specifications - Personal specifications - Success criteria - Market research	- Sourcing candidates - Response handling - Short-listing - Assessing	- Interviews - Testing - Feedback - Offers - Contracts	- Induction planning - Successful new starters

Figure 43.1 Recruitment life cycle

for a short time whilst you review CVs, attend interviews and give careful thought to selection. Get it wrong, and you will have incompetent or disillusioned new staff, whom you will either have to improve or remove. Introducing an inappropriate person into an existing group can demotivate that group, damage your project and give you more headaches. Recruitment can be costly in terms of fees paid to advertisers and agencies and in the time taken up in interviews and all the other recruitment processes. Hire the wrong person, and you might even end up having to make redundancy payments when parting company is the only remaining option.

Project Recruitment Stage 1: Initiation

When a new project member is needed, the temptation is often to jump into the process of creating a job specification and then advertise the vacancy as a matter of urgency. So line managers must listen to the advice of their HR department and follow the appropriate recruitment stages under their guidance. Of course, I am assuming here that the vacancy or vacancies have budget authorisation from senior management – if not you are in a whole heap of trouble.

WORKING WITH THE HR DEPARTMENT

It is in the project manager's interests to understand how the HR department functions on recruitment matters and exactly how they can help bring about a successful hire. As part of that understanding, it is also important to know how far you can operate outside the procedures. Many unsuccessful recruitment campaigns fail because the line manager is operating outside the rules. Indeed one of the most common reasons why a recruitment process fails is because of an inadequate approval process – or the line manager just decided to do it him/herself because the correct process was too lengthy or bureaucratic. Success depends on finding the balance between what the HR department can do and what the line manager is prepared to do to ensure the right person is brought on board.

The HR department is there to support best practice in areas such as employment law, employment contracts, brand management and the processes outlined in this chapter. They are also there to help in subsequent training, staff development and succession planning. One thing that can never be underestimated is the time and effort needed for a recruitment campaign. This can range from a matter of days for immediate contract hires to several months for a specialist permanent employee (I knew a case that took 11 months).

All HR departments get mixed reviews. For hiring managers, the HR department will be their strongest ally in engaging a new person, but only if the rules of engagement are known and negotiated up front. Understanding the organisation's hiring procedure is important, but knowing which parts of the process are flexible is even more so, as the following case illustrates.

CASE EXAMPLE NO. 1

This case happened in a government organisation needing a temporary project manager. Recruitment started with a job description and person specification drawn up and assessed by a committee. After that assessment, the line manager felt that the committee had not graded the job correctly and time was required to rectify it. The job was advertised for three weeks. Applications then had to be reviewed. It proved impossible to get the temporary project manager engaged in time. Clearly the ponderous recruitment process for a permanent resource did not work for temporary resources and greater flexibility was needed.

SUCCESSION PLANNING

There may be no need to look outside the organisation for a new appointment. HR departments will insist that current employees are considered for new posts. That brings both advantages and disadvantages:

- Advantages: current experience in the organisation, no (or very low) associated costs and benefits for morale.
- Disadvantages: no fresh perspective or infusion of new blood, the skills required may be too specialised, so that all internal applicants must be rejected (which can be bad for morale).

Succession planning or 'managing the talent pipeline' is the key to ensuring that an organisation can quickly and successfully fill vacancies, especially in top positions like project management (Rothwell, 2001). Succession planning focuses on current employees, and examines what is required to increase their 'promotability' within the organisation at the appropriate time.

CASE EXAMPLE NO. 2

BAE Systems is a global defence and security company with approximately 100,000 employees worldwide, 6,000 of whom are project managers. To ensure that the organisation had enough experienced people to manage its many programmes and projects, BAE Systems introduced a scheme to meet those needs. It set up a 'project control academy'.

In addition to succession planning for existing staff, the academy would also target school leavers who were not destined to continue their education at university level (BAE Systems already had a programme for graduates). BAE Systems would initially target school leavers who were close to BAE System's main office and other facilities.

Prior analysis gave interesting results *'whilst it takes 5–10 years to develop a competent project manager, it still takes 3–5 years to develop a competent project controller'*. This academy initiative would ensure a steady stream ('talent pipeline') of project controllers to meet BAE System's future needs. Clearly BAE System's Project Control Foundation Scheme (PCFS) is a long-term investment in talent for BAE Systems and its employees – a programme combining on-the-job training with academic study.

NEEDS ANALYSIS

Needs analysis starts by asking 'Why is there a vacancy?' In projects it is often the case that the organisation is in need of a specialised resource. Or there might simply be too few people to work on committed projects. But occasionally there is no real vacancy to fill – it could be just an inexperienced project manager who has failed to plan and resource the project correctly. Or, it could be a very experienced project manager with empire-building delusions of grandeur.

The hiring/line manager must establish the business case for hiring before approaching the HR department. Without a clear business and project need for additional project resources, the approval might (and should) be blocked by senior management.

REQUIREMENTS IDENTIFICATION

Requirements for a new job should be set out in a requirements identification document. Most organisations use these, and they might even have pro forma templates available. The chances are that you could be required to hire a new type of resource or just want to ensure that a job specification matches your own exacting standards. In those cases the requirements identification part of the recruitment process gives the opportunity to define the role and the kind of person needed for it. A format is shown in Figure 43.2.

Identification area	Response
Role summary and objectives	- Summary or outline of what the job is - Main objectives of the roles
Position within the organisation	- Who the role reports to - Are there any subordinates? - Include an organisation chart
Key accountabilities	- List of all the main accountabilities of the role - Break down the percentage time of each
Knowledge required	- Specific knowledge required for the role (project management, technical, domain) - Minimum experience required to carry out the role
Experience required	- Specific experience required (project size, complexity and team size)
Qualifications required	- Professional accreditations plus specific training - Minimum level of qualifications
Capabilities and attitude	- Behavioural characteristics of the role - Behavioural characteristics required
Network/contacts	- What working relationships will be required (clients, suppliers, management, peers and so on)
Specific project management requirements	- Areas of importance for special mention. For example, leadership, budget responsibility, commercial responsibilities and so on
Impact	- Impact of the role withing the organisation - Long and short-term impact

Figure 43.2 Requirements identification checklist

Initiated by the immediate hirer (for example, the project manager), this tells the HR department formally what is required.

The requirements identification form captures all the key criteria, roles and responsibilities, the behavioural characteristics, position in the organisation and impact of the hire. Job hire specifics may also be added to the form. For example, is it a permanent or contract hire? How long is the contract resource required for? What job grade level is this position?

This is a crucial step, forming a baseline in the recruitment process. It tells all parties clearly what is needed. It also forms the basis for a job specification that will be unique for the vacancy rather than relying on old templates.

APPROVALS

Skipping the approvals part of the recruitment process can be damaging for the hirer and ultimately for the organisation. Consider the case where a hiring manager sets about the recruitment process by contacting a number of recruitment agencies directly, with a request for a contract project manager. The recruitment agencies duly provide a shortlist of suitable candidates within three days and the hiring manager chooses four people to interview. Following the interviews, all four candidates wait, and continue to wait, and wait, for feedback on their interview performance.

Then the hiring manager cannot be contacted via telephone or email. He/she has apparently vanished. None of the four candidates ever receives any further news. In fact the manager had no authority to recruit in the first place, and has been reprimanded for this direct approach, which ignored the HR department and senior management approval.

A parallel analogy is when project engineers approach suppliers direct, and commit their organisations to purchase contracts for goods and services without going through the formal purchase order procedure.

Now consider the effect on those four unfortunate candidates. They had their hopes raised and their time taken by interviews. What do you think they would tell you and the world at large about their experiences of that organisation? When applicants have bad recruitment experiences they will tell other people in other organisations. Statistically each time someone experiences bad service they will tell 8 to 16 people about their problems. With expanding social networks these numbers can increase dramatically into thousands (Blackshaw, 2008). That is a sobering thought and not something the recruiter's PR people would welcome.

Project Recruitment Stage 2: Planning the Process

It is common to underestimate the time needed for recruitment. However, shorter recruitment times can be achieved using a plan that makes all the elements visible up front and recognises their logical sequence. Figure 43.3 shows the recruitment process in its entirety and the tasks typically necessary for a successful outcome.

Multiple tasks can be done simultaneously rather than sequentially. For example, writing the job advertisement and the interview questions can be done at the beginning rather than rushing to write the interview questions just before the first candidate steps over the interview room threshold.

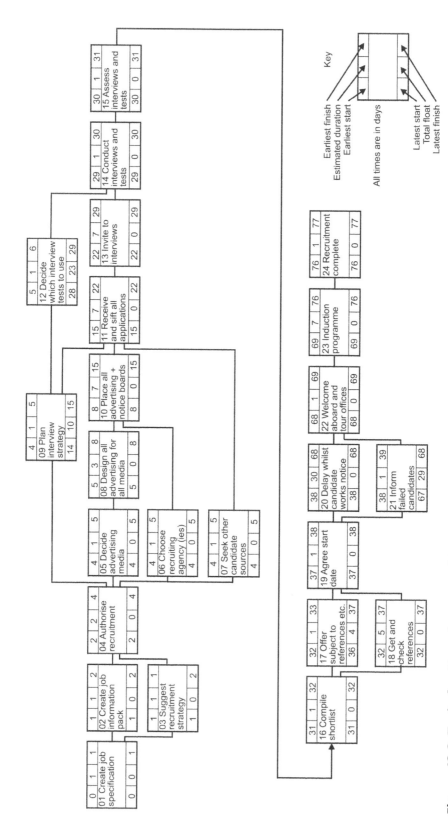

Figure 43.3 Typical pattern for a recruitment programme

The plan recognises that the interview process is a small project in itself, beginning with the specification and authorisation and ending with a successful new starter. A network diagram, such as that in Figure 43.3, not only communicates the recruitment process but can also be used to indicate from the offset who will be responsible for what.

JOB SPECIFICATION

The job specification derives most of its input from the requirements identification document described earlier and, indeed, many people regard the two as the same. However, the job specification is more than a description of the job because it also covers the skills, knowledge, experience, abilities and characteristics of the person required to do the job. Figure 43.4 shows a specification for a project office manager. Job specifications might be more detailed than this example but the main elements include:

- where the job is located;
- who the person will report to;
- how many subordinates the person will have;
- a brief job summary;
- key accountabilities;
- knowledge and experience required;
- capability and aptitude required.

Yates (2005) gives three key focus areas when constructing these specifications. These are:

- skills;
- professional and educational experience;
- the job's benchmarks (accountabilities).

Skills are 'learned professional behaviours' and include such things as communication, time management, team participation and behavioural skills like persistence, confidence and integrity. For educational experience a distinction has to be made between education that is essential for the position and that which is desirable or 'nice to have'.

Yates also draws attention to the 'manageability' of the person required. That is defined as the ability to work either independently or in a team, avoidance of emotional involvement in work interactions, and the capacity to respond productively to criticism.

Finally, Yates highlights something that is often overlooked in specifications, which is *the cultural fit*. Each organisation looks for someone who is qualified, motivated and manageable. They must also look for people who are going to fit within their organisation's culture and way of getting things done. The personal part of the job specification allows us to concentrate on the 'softer skills'. Project practitioners usually find no difficulty in creating the key accountabilities or describing the tasks required to be performed in a role, but creating a meaningful person specification can be somewhat more difficult. There are three models:

- Seven Point Plan (Rodger, 1952);
- Five-Fold Grading System (Munro Fraser, 1950);
- Eleven Point Plan (Proctor, 1987).

Job specification
Project office manager

Department: IT
Responsible to: Head of IT
Responsible for: Project office coordinators (5), project administrators (2).
Location: Holborn office

Job summary:

Manage the IT project office, ensuring that the project management and monitoring procedures are implemented and maintained across the IT project portfolio.

Key accountabilities:

* Run and maintain the project office organization.
* Ensure the agreed project management methods, standards and processes are maintained throughout the lifecycle of initiatives in the IT project portfolio.
* Manage the project office team on a day-to-day basis.
* Assist the project managers in the production and maintenance of project plans.
* Assist the project managers in facilitating project progress.
* Project management skills and knowledge transfer to project resources.
* Ensure the production of all reports and produce project summary reports.
* Implement appropriate configuration management procedures.
* Assure systems for recording project costs.
* Manage project administration procedures in accordance with agreed methodology.
* Advise and assist project team members in the application of project procedures, disciplines and recording and reporting standards.
* Facilitate effective communication mechanisms between the teams.
* Provide direction, performance appraisals and other HR duties for the project office team.
* Undertake any other project management tasks as requested by the head of IT.

Personal specification

Knowledge and experience:

* Knowledge and experience of managing a project office (using PRINCE2 methodology would be an advantage).
* Experience of managing a project office team.
* Knowledge and experience of facilitating project management skills transfer.
* High degree of computer literacy, including good working knowledge of MS Office.
* Knowledge of MS Project would be an advantage.
* Experience of setting up and maintaining project office processes and procedures.
* Previous experience of working on IT related projects.
* Previous experience of working with senior managers.
* Experience of presenting information in document form.

Capabilities and aptitudes

* Positive attitude to working in a changing environment.
* Organizational and leadership skills.
* Ability to analyse and present information clearly and concisely.
* Strong interpersonal and communications skills, oral and written.
* Good judgement, self-motivating and persuasive.
* Able to work unsupervised and as part of a team.
* Able to work confidently with senior managers.
* Able to establish priorities and meet deadlines whilst preserving the high level of accuracy and confidentiality needed.

Figure 43.4 Example of a job specification

Impact on others: Physical make up, appearance, speech, manner, authoritative, public speaker, cooperative.	Physical make up: Health, appearance, bearing, active, fit, gravitas. seniority, social.	Motivation and commitment: Job satisfaction, professional interests, PM CPD, motivation of self, team.
		Qualifications: Minimum qualifications required, accreditations, professional training.
	Attainments: Education, experience, qualifications, accreditations, professional training.	
Acquired qualifications: Education, vocational training, work experience, on-the-job experience, degree level, CPD.		Experience: Relevant and related experience, sector, projects, team size, complexity.
	General intelligence: Initiative, problem solving, creativity, innovative, reasoning.	Skills and proficiencies: Specific skills required, methodology, project type, leadership.
		Aptitudes: Become proficient at a task, numerical, verbal, reasoning, decisions.
Innate abilities: Quickness of comprehension, aptitude for learning, report writing, succinct, PC skills.	Special aptitudes: Manual/mechanical dexterity, facility in the use of words/figures, special talents.	
		Intelligence/mental capacity: Initiative, Problem solving, creativity, innovative.
	Interest: Intellectual, practical, constructional, subject matter expert, industry knowledge.	Personality: Character traits, introvert, extrovert, influencer, leader, methodical.
Motivation: Individual goals, success rates, determination, motivation of self and others, ambition, track record.		Interest and personal achievements: What the role requires, interest in sector, working with public.
		Ambitions: Ambition levels, career climber, board level, steady, leader.
	Disposition acceptability: Personality, temperament, character, influence over others, dependability, accountable.	Health and physical make up: Ability to keep the pace, stamina, active, fitness, stress.
Adjustment: Emotional stability, stress management, working with others, relationship builder, stakeholder management.	Circumstances: Special demands of the job, client sites, working abroad, work from home.	Circumstances: Job requirements. travel, work from home, unsocial hours.
Fraser's five-fold grading system (1950)	Rodger's seven point plan (1952)	Proctor's eleven point plan (1987)

Figure 43.5 Three models for writing person specifications

Each of these models provides categories which can be included in the person specification part of the job description (Figure 43.5).

For a project office manager the person specification would include (for example) relationship building, communication styles and intelligence (including numerical and analytical skills). The job specification brings together all the requirements for the vacancy. Once recruitment has been successful, the specification can be used in appraisals and performance reviews.

SUCCESS CRITERIA

The job description lists the criteria for the person we are we seeking to recruit. If we are really lucky we might receive an application for the job where the applicant satisfies all the conditions. In reality we are never that lucky and chances are we will have a number of less-than-perfect applicants to compare.

Now we need to think about success criteria. In other words, how shall we know when we have the right person? We shall be setting success criteria at different stages of the recruitment process (for example, when we review applicants' CVs how shall we select the people to interview? At the interview stage, how shall we choose the person to whom we make an offer?).

It is useful to rank all the criteria for the job in order of importance, with the most critical factor at the top of the list.

Stating a success criterion not only allows you to stay focused when all the applications come in, it also serves as a way to ensure fairness (see Chapter 44 on legal issues and best practice with regard to recruitment). If all the applications are viewed and assessed in accordance with the set criteria there is less room for subjective views and opinions. This is especially important when there is more than one reviewer in the process.

MARKET RESEARCH

How much are we going to pay the successful applicant and what other perks might he/she expect? To answer those questions we have to be careful first to understand our existing salary structure because if we pitch our bid too high, a successful applicant paid substantially more than his/her peers will cause justifiable jealousy. And it's useless to argue that salaries are confidential because people always find such things out. Pitch our offer too low, and we shall fail to attract the right person. So we need to do some research, both within and outside our own organisation.

Understanding the market rates for a position can be done by searching online for similar roles currently being advertised. Finding up to five or more will give us a median around which to work. The HR department can help here through their benchmarking research.

The HR department should also be able to find where prospective applicants are likely to be working now. Gaining an insight into who your competitors are in the job market will mean that you can improve your market edge by discovering their recruitment strategies. Find out where they advertise, how their advertisements are presented, and what rates and other incentives they offer.

Project Recruitment Stage 3: Selection

SOURCING CANDIDATES

As a hirer you have a number of resources for attracting applicants. Some methods will be better than others, for example:

- high or low cost;
- quality of applicants attracted;
- quick turnaround or time consuming.

You might opt to carry out all the publicity yourself, outsource it to a professional agency or do both.

Advertising

Before advertising, you must write the advertising copy, for which the principal source will be the job specification. Regardless of which method you choose and the medium in which the advert will feature, your copy must be written for maximum effect. Printed media (newspapers, journals, industry magazines and so on.) will need professional design and contacts within the advertising fraternity to secure the best deals. Owing to the costs, time involved and advances in online media, many organisations have turned away from the traditional modes of classified ads. Online media such as job boards, Internet microsites and social networking have led to cheaper, faster, wider-reaching recruitment campaign options. But all these options still need a job advertisement. Depending on where you choose to advertise the copy may have to change to reach the target audience. Consider the two advertisements shown in Figures 43.6 and 43.7 on the following pages.

Figure 43.6 is an example of an advertisement you may find on a online network such as Facebook™. It is shown at approximately actual size and it is apparent that only the barest of amount of information can be given. But the advertisement will show up on a user's profile page if they have shared details about their chosen profession.

Now compare with Figure 43.7 which shows a more typical online job advertisement layout. The title of the role is prominent, as is the location and salary on offer. The advertisement uses the term 'project office' a number of times to help attract applicants who are searching for project office positions. The advertisement also includes just enough details about the position to let the reader make informed decision about whether this job will be suitable for them. Giving instructions about what you would like the applicant to do next is one of the most important aspects of the advertisement (visit a website, send a CV and covering note and so on). Finally including details about the company is considered to be good form because some will not have heard about this organisation before.

Once the advertisements have been created we can choose where to place them to attract the best the market has to offer. Figure 43.8 shows my selection of the top five options, I recommend using more than one of these options to achieve greater market exposure.

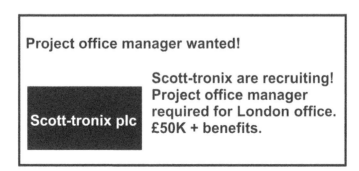

Figure 43.6 Social network job advertisement (shown actual size)

Scott-tronix plc

Project Office Manager - London - Circa £50K + benefits

Looking for a project office role in a progressive and innovative company? This could be for you!

Managing the IT project office and up to seven PMO analysts and coordinators, this Project Office Manager position is a key appointment within Scott-tronix plc. You will provide project office and implementation support for key IT projects within the portfolio - ensuring implementation of project management methods, standards and processes to support our entire project delivery lifecycle.

Key responsibilities

- Maintain agreed project management methods, standards and processes throughout the lifecycle of initiatives in the IT project portfolio.
- Manage the project office team on a day-to-day basis.
- Assist the project managers in the production and maintenance of project plans.
- Assist the project managers in facilitating project progress.
- Project management skills and knowledge transfer to project resources.
- Ensure the timely production of all reports and produce project summary reports.
- Advise and assist project team members in the application of project procedures, disciplines and recording and reporting standards.
- Facilitate effective communication mechanisms between the teams.
- Provide direction, performance appraisals and other HR duties for the project office team.

Knowledge and experience

- Knowledge and experience of managing a project office (using PRINCE2 methodology would be an advantage).
- Experience of managing a project office team.
- High degree of computer literacy, including a good working knowledge of the MS Office suite.
- Knowledge of MS Project would be an advantage.
- Experience of setting up and maintaining project office processes and procedures.

Location: Holborn (Zone 1).

Closing date: 21/09/2019

To learn more about this position and to apply please visit http://www.scottronix.com/careers

About us

Scott-tronix plc is a brand leader in mobile technologies and associated consumer products. Formed in 1986 and headquartered in London, UK, we now have 16,000 employees in 25 countries. We specialize in next generation communications and advanced innovative solutions for consumers and business.

Figure 43.7 Typical online job advertisement

Option	Advantages	Disadvantages
Internal systems - own company website - notice boards.	- low cost - low workload - quick response.	- less diversity in applicants - not applicable to short or fixed-term contracts - scarcer skills and knowledge than available from external applicants.
Online media - job boards - social networks - microsites.	- relatively cheap - focused on the project management or industry sector - good for brand awareness - quick response.	- time consuming dealing with large number of applicants - dramatic variation in quality of applicants - building online networks is time consuming.
Offline media - classified newspaper adverts - trade journals - magazines.	- focused on the project management or industry sector - good for brand awareness - good for mass recruitment and ongoing campaigns - suitable for senior roles (executives).	- slow turnround time - quickly out of date - not wide-reaching - prolongs the recruitment campaign.
Networking - events - exhibitions - job fairs - open days.	- good for selected roles (graduates) - good for mass recruitment and ongoing campaigns, - good for getting instant feedback from applicants.	- higher costs - dependent on timing of events - time consuming - heavy on resources.
Recruitment specialists - specialist recruitment agencies - headhunters.	- specialist areas - knowledge and market insight - quick turnround.	- possibly expensive - quality of agencies and applicants can vary drastically.

Figure 43.8 Options for attracting job applicants

CASE EXAMPLE NO. 3

A large UK employer needed to fill a number of project management positions. Because of many different level vacancies spread over five locations, the company first created a microsite (a subsection of their own website), listing all the available vacancies in detail.

This microsite address would then be used in all forms of advertising ensuring that each applicant would apply through this central point. The microsite was also used to inform applicants about what they could expect in working for the organisation giving overviews of the different departments where project managers were required and information on relocating and the local surrounding areas.

The microsite carried the same design and branding as all the other advertisements. Adverts were placed in all the major newspapers, local press (relevant to particular vacancies) and professional and trade-related journals.

The company hosted job fairs in the key locations, followed by events at local universities to help attract applicants for the support roles. Several recruitment agencies around the country were brought on board to launch local and national campaigning. Finally online job boards, pay-per-click advertising and social networks were used to attract web-proficient applicants.

This costly but well-executed campaign lasted for six months, but it ensured that no one with project management experience and in the market for a new role could fail to notice that this company was hiring. Those who had not seen the campaign were probably told about it from their own network connections in project management. This recruitment campaign was everywhere. That's publicity!

RESPONSE HANDLING

Response handling has to be considered before the responses start coming in and, depending on the publicity channels used, those responses might come from several different sources. Now we need to decide who will be responsible for acknowledging applications and what expectations will be presented to each applicant. It's important that all candidates are treated professionally, equally and with respect. One of the most common causes for complaint in a recruitment campaign is that applicants get no reply to their applications.

'Candidate experience' is one of the buzz phrases heard from HR departments, who should be keen to ensure that no applicant has a bad experience with their organisation. Considerate response handling takes time and effort, so it should be planned into the recruitment campaign from the start.

Will you elect to respond to each and every applicant, thanking them for their time, and letting them know when they can expect to hear the outcome to their application? Will you notify all those applicants who were not successful this time and the reasons why? Although the HR department might be responsible for this part of the process, communicating the timescales and the selection criteria to which you (as hiring manager) are working is crucial to this working partnership.

Another common complaint in this part of the process is timing. At the beginning there is normally a deadline date set for all applicants. Suppose this is two weeks. Organisations that choose to conduct their recruitment campaign in a strictly sequential fashion (post advert, wait two weeks for the deadline and then start reviewing CVs) will lose the best candidates. Why? Because good people get snapped up quickly. They won't wait for weeks wondering whether you want to interview them. The trick is to shortlist against your selection criteria as soon as the applications come in. You don't need to wait for comparisons against other applicants at this stage. You just need to tell those who look promising that you want to interview them. Keeping candidates 'warm' will ensure that they remain interested.

SHORTLISTING

Before we shortlist, we need to take care of the longlist. That will include all applications received from all sources. Reducing the longlist in the first instance can be done quickly. This will depend on three things – how long the list is, how ruthless you are and how tight your selection criteria are. If your vacancy is for a specialist role with few applicants, you can get straight to work on your shortlist. If you are ruthless you might want exclude people who did not follow the application process correctly. For example they:

- did not supply a covering letter;

- failed to provide answers to particular questions you set;
- left serious spelling mistakes or unexplained gaps in their CV;
- did not satisfy selection criteria for education levels or accreditations;
- had an inadequate level of experience.

I must repeat the importance of fairness and impartiality in the shortlisting process. Applications should be reviewed against the set selection criteria. This process risks being subjective, so it is useful to attempt to quantify it by applying logic and a scoring system. Different people in the hiring organisation will have different knowledge and experience of recruiting project management staff. How can we be sure that the HR department (who traditionally do the initial shortlisting) will not exclude someone that the hiring manager would regard as excellent?

Using a Scoring System

A simple scoring system is shown in Figure 43.9. I have listed some desirable criteria in the left-hand column and each item has been given a scoring weight between 1 and 10 (with 10 being the most important). The other columns have been allocated to individual applicants (named from A to K). The chart shows the scores achieved by each applicant for each of the selection criteria before and after applying the appropriate weighting

REQUIREMENTS		CANDIDATES' SCORES (O = original score, F = score after factoring by the relevant weighting)																				
Item	Weight 1>10	A		B		C		D		E		F		G		H		I		J		K	
		O	F	O	F	O	F	O	F	O	F	O	F	O	F	O	F	O	F	O	F	O	F
University degree	10	10	100	0	0	0	0	9	90	10	100	10	100	10	100	10	100	10	100	10	100	10	100
PRINCE2	8	8	64	10	80	9	72	9	72	9	72	10	80	9	72	10	80	9	72	9	72	9	72
Project office experience	10	2	20	6	60	10	100	10	100	4	40	2	20	8	80	10	100	4	40	2	20	6	60
Line mgmt experience	9	5	45	10	90	10	90	10	90	0	0	0	0	5	45	10	90	5	45	5	45	5	45
IT projects environment	9	10	90	5	45	5	45	10	90	5	45	5	45	10	90	5	45	10	90	10	90	10	90
Project planning	8	0	0	10	80	10	80	5	40	5	40	0	0	5	40	10	80	0	0	0	0	10	80
Project mgmt best practice	9	0	0	8	72	10	90	10	90	4	36	2	18	10	90	8	72	2	18	2	18	8	72
Reporting experience	9	10	90	10	90	10	90	10	90	5	45	10	90	10	90	10	90	10	90	10	90	10	90
TOTAL SCORE		409		517		567		662		378		353		607		657		455		435		609	

Figure 43.9 Scoring method to help shortlisting

factor. An unweighted score of 10 indicates that the condition is well met or exceeded. These scores have to be based on the evidence of applicants' CVs and covering letters. Candidates D, G, H and K have scored well and would probably survive the initial round of shortlisting.

The attributes listed in Figure 43.9 are of course not applicable to all jobs. A company in heavy engineering, mining or construction might list different attributes from those shown here. Also the weightings given to attributes would vary from one vacancy to another (clearly experience would be weighted high for a senior position but low when recruiting an apprentice or trainee). There might be special considerations that need to be taken into account, such as willingness to travel. All hirers have their preferences and many jobs have their special requirements. But the framework of Figure 43.9 can be used universally provided that the attributes and their weightings are chosen sensibly.

CV Quality

The procedures described here highlight the relevance of CVs when shortlisting for interview. However, a problem with every resumé is that its writer cannot know for certain what will impress its readers. So it is tempting for candidates to include everything done in a long career in the hope that this 'scattergun' approach will pay off (even if a 10-page document results).

I have reviewed countless project management CVs over 10 years in my recruitment agency business and I know what works well for project management. Often when an advertisement for a project manager is posted we get a good idea what the selection criteria might be. The advertisement will cover required experience, project management competencies needed and a general sense of the seniority of the position. But most project management candidates fail to focus on this information and simply submit their standard photocopied resumé without editing or changing it to suit the particular vacancy. They do not mention relevant business cases, scope management, schedule or risk management (perhaps taking for granted that every project manager's job would include all of these things).

Too many resumés are written using terminology and a general approach that does not match the advertisement. Instead people quote acronyms or terms used in their current organisation. Where a position calls for 'excellent leadership skills', the resumé will probably be full of technical project management skills, but fail to mention relationships, stakeholder management, influence and team management experience. So, each resumé must be relevant and written for the job advertised.

Project Recruitment Stage 4: Delivery

INTERVIEWS: PLANNING THE STRATEGY

It is good practice to start planning interview strategy early, along with the specification and advertisements. Getting a head start on planning the type of interviews to conduct, arranging the logistics and selecting assessment methods are all part of the strategy. The easiest part of the process is setting the dates and locations for the interviews. You also need to consider how many interview stages will take place. For junior contract positions this might be one interview (perhaps just by telephone). Permanent positions could need two or even more stages.

Calling candidates back for more than two interviews can make them question your organisation's competence and decisiveness in choosing who to appoint. Too many years ago to admit, Dennis Lock spent a whole day being interviewed and tested for an aerospace job, but received a fresh invitation for interview weeks later because the company had no record of the first day's results. Interviewing is a two-way process and not only will candidates expect to impress you, but you will want to show them an organisation that is well run and attractive to work in.

You need to choose who will conduct the interviews. The line manager will typically conduct the first interview, either alone or with others. Those others could include an HR representative, another team member or a senior manager. If a subsequent interview is needed, the candidate would probably be quizzed by at least one senior member of the organisation.

INTERVIEWING METHODS

It is worth looking at the latest research in interviewing methods. Huffcutt (2010) is one source. He lists seven principles:

1. acknowledge the inherent difficulty of making judgements from an interview;
2. know as little about the candidate as possible;
3. avoid poor questions (interviewers are encouraged to ask questions about knowledge, skills, abilities and other characteristics);
4. structure the interview (and standardise questions for easier comparison of all the candidates);
5. avoid making judgements early in the interview;
6. watch for applicant performance effects (tactics used by candidates to create a good impression);
7. look for multiple sources of evidence (evidence that will confirm an applicant's claims).

Structuring interviews, using good judgement, looking for the real evidence, being aware of your own behaviour and influence are all areas to consider and improve on when interviewing. The biggest problem to avoid is bias and this is illustrated perfectly by Gladwell (2000). It reminds us that many interviewers are not trained to conduct structured interviews – perhaps this should be mandatory if we are to pick out the people who will perform well in the job.

INTERVIEW QUESTIONS

There are three popular types of interviewing within project management:

1. traditional approach of asking questions based on the applicant's CV;
2. competency-based interviews;
3. scenario-based questioning.

Scenario questions allow interviewers to choose situations closely aligned with the vacancy. This has become increasingly popular as a means for understanding and testing a project manager's skills and competence levels. A project-based hypothetical situation or scenario is presented in the question and the interviewee's answers must draw on a combination of theoretical and practical experience to demonstrate his/her capability. Examples include:

- Two of your team members do not work well together and are disrupting the rest of the team. What steps would you take to overcome this?
- One of your main stakeholders has started going directly to your sponsor when problems crop up on the project. How would you regain control?

I asked several people for their favourite questions when interviewing for project manager vacancies. Here is a selection from their replies:

- How would you rescue a failing project?
- If we appoint you, what will you do during your first 90 days here?
- What do you think is the most important project management document, and why?
- When did you last learn something significantly new about project management? This question seeks to learn how interested the candidate is about his/her chosen profession and self-development.
- Your choice is either to deliver one project on time or keep a senior stakeholder on another project happy. What would you do? This is a great question for gaining an insight into the candidate's decision-making process.

INTERVIEWS: TESTING AND ASSESSMENT

Formal testing and assessment can be used, especially for project manager vacancies. These tend to be favoured by larger organisations, but of course they take time. I have seen this played out as an advantage for smaller businesses when recruiting project managers because not only is their hiring time shorter but also, if given the choice, who among us would opt for facing a barrage of tests and assessments!

Three forms of testing and assessment feature most in the recruitment of project managers. These are:

- verbal and numerical reasoning tests;
- presentations;
- assessment centres.

Verbal and Numerical Reasoning Tests

Verbal and numerical reasoning tests are the most popular tests for project management candidates and both are chosen owing to their possible similarities to project management tasks.

Numerical reasoning tests cover a multitude of mathematical-based tests. These include basic functions like multiplication, percentages and fractions alongside data interpretation. A typical test will last for 45 to 60 minutes and will be designed to be impossible to complete in the time allowed (in an attempt to eliminate the need to race through the test rather than concentrate on getting the answers right).

It is recommended that candidates take practice tests before the real test to familiarise themselves with the process. Free tests are available from the most well-known providers. Visit for example SHL at www.SHL.com. Test results are a great way for organisations to differentiate between candidates, either as part of their first interview or following subsequent interviews.

Presentations

In many ways presentations have become useful in helping interviewers take scenario-based questioning to the next level. Rather than just posing a question during the interview, many organisations are opting to use case studies and presentations to learn more about the interviewee's capabilities. There are two different approaches.

In one approach each interviewee is asked to prepare a presentation based on a case study (documentation and instructions given a few days before the interview). Presentations usually last about ten minutes, with an extra five minutes allowed for questions afterwards. In-tray exercises are a popular form of case study. Examples that work well include fictitious project plans or status reports, with problems that the fictional project manager needs to deal with. Another example is a new project brief that requires a step-by-step guide to what should happen next.

The second approach is giving the interviewee no prior notice about the presentation. The interviewee will be asked to attend an interview which is scheduled to take two to three hours. Other interviewees will also be invited to attend the organisation at the same time. Whilst one candidate is facing his/her face-to-face interview, other candidates will be given other tasks to do, such as testing or preparing a presentation.

These interview structures are demanding but tend to be enjoyed by both interviewers and interviewees for a number of reasons. Generally this approach gives both parties a greater mutual insight into how they like to operate.

Assessment Centres

Assessment centres (ACs) take testing to the next level and tend to be used by larger organisations when they have multiple project management positions to fill. Invariably there is a higher cost involved in choosing to conduct an AC but organisations believe that an AC is a good predictor of performance in the job. The AC 'is a standardised evaluation of behaviour based on inputs from multiple assessment methods' (International Taskforce, 2009). A job analysis or competency framework is used to identify 'dimensions' or competencies for project management candidates. Examples would include methods such as planning, change management and reporting. Behavioural competencies like leadership, team management, conflict resolution and influencing would also be chosen, based on the hiring organisation's best interpretation of the project manager's role in their business.

Multiple assessment methods are then chosen based on 'simulations of job-relevant situations' (Thornton, 2011). ACs tend to use methods which 'stimulate the most challenging situations a worker might face' (Jackson et al., 2011). In project management AC methods can include:

- in-tray exercises;
- case studies;
- group decision making;
- group competition;
- role-playing interviews and presentations.

Within each exercise the participants are observed by an assessor. A final score (an overall assessment rating or OAR) is given for each participant's performance.

An interesting observation from project management ACs is the assessment of leadership. Project manager positions are intrinsically leadership orientated. So in AC exercises where leadership is being observed there is often a great jostling of position between participants. Then other competencies or behaviours will also be assessed simultaneously, such as empathy, flexibility, developing people and influence.

There are many other assessment possibilities, some mentioned in other chapters, and I had space to list only a few here.

FEEDBACK TO INTERVIEWEES

There has been a marked increase in the number of job-seekers who ask for feedback. Only a small number of organisations include feedback as part of the recruitment process, and that often leads to job-seekers hearing nothing at all. Krause (2011) gives figures for feedback to candidates following the AC at just 7 per cent in South Africa, 25 per cent in the USA and 50 per cent in Western organisations. From the organisation's point of view there is reluctance because it is deemed to be difficult or could even leave the organisation open to litigation. But job-seekers perceive such organisations to be lazy, disorganised or too scared.

A project management community in a particular area or technical domain operates in a small space when seeking to attract present and future talent. Candidates should be treated with a courtesy that leaves them with a good impression of the organisation, regardless of whether they got the job or not. If you fail in this respect, be aware that bad customer service is remembered and talked about much more than the good experiences.

Because project management is a professional career, its candidates look for constructive feedback that will help them better prepare for future interviews. These people usually take their careers seriously, want to make a good impression and above all else prepare well for their interviews. Most professional workers receive constructive feedback in their working lives through appraisals and reviews. Feedback after interviews is similar and should be treated in the same way.

Feedback should be given as soon as possible, either at the end of the interview or within 24 hours. Verbal feedback is preferable because it allows dialogue, whereas written feedback can be open to misinterpretation. It is always good practice to provide context, such as how many applicants there were, the number shortlisted, and so on. A great opening question when giving feedback is, 'What did you think about your performance in the interview?' This works for candidates likely to receive an offer and those who didn't make the grade. Interviewees will often be self-aware of areas of the interview that went badly for them.

Positive feedback should be given first (what you liked about the candidate's experience, skills and so on). Then comes critical or constructive feedback. The skill here is to concentrate on where the person did not meet the selection criteria. Keep feedback to the competencies and behaviours exhibited, and avoid any feelings or impressions of the candidate's personality. Try to pick out two or three key points and offer suggestions for improvement if you feel knowledgeable and empowered to do so. Finish up by asking if there are any questions. Most candidates at this stage will just thank you for your time and the opportunity to interview in the first place.

Successful candidates are just as keen to hear feedback on why the organisation has chosen them. Be prepared with your feedback when you call to make an offer.

MAKING AN OFFER

In the most straightforward of recruitment cases making a job offer is an easy and pleasant part of the recruitment process, which can seem to make it all worthwhile. The offer can be made in writing or verbally in the first case, and here I consider first the verbal approach. An offer is usually made subject to satisfactory references. If the offer is verbally accepted, a formal offer comprising the details of the position and contract of employment will be sent to the candidate. A start date is agreed, references checked, documentation signed and returned. Everyone can now start planning for the new starter to come on board.

When the offer process is less straightforward we can expect negotiation to take place. A counter-offer might be made. Other complications are unsatisfactory references, or an indecisive candidate who is contemplating one or more other job offers. Of course the candidate might simply refuse the offer.

Negotiations on job offers for project management professionals are not uncommon. After all, it is in their nature! Indeed many organisations welcome negotiation as long as it is reasonable and not greedy and too far from the original advertised salary and package on offer.

Counter-offers can be used by candidates to gain advantageous influence with their current employer. This is the tactic of having an offer on the table for a new job and using this to extract an increase in salary, perks or even promotion in the existing job. But that can backfire. Often this will mean stalling on accepting a new job offer and organisations in such cases will often withdraw offers. It can be a risky game for an applicant to play as it often leaves their current employer questioning loyalty and integrity.

Reference checking is still an area of contention, especially as many HR policies on references advocate giving scant detail about their employees (just confirming the dates of employment and job title in many cases). This is useful for checking that a candidate did actually work where they said they did but does not clarify character or work experience. Often character references will be carried out more informally, with previous line managers being prepared to bend the HR rules.

Checking qualifications and professional accreditations is relatively straightforward through the education system and/or professional bodies, especially for project management-related credentials. Security clearance is needed for defence, police and some areas of the public sector like central government. Criminal record (DBS) checks might be needed for project managers working with the young and vulnerable. Detailed financial/credit checks have been mandatory for work within banking and areas of finance for a number of years.

There has been an increase in multiple offers for talented candidates during the recent economic period. Candidates interview at different organisations, spreading their bets until they find a good opportunity that is worth leaving the security of a current job. The 'war for talent' (Michaels et al., 2001), as organisations face competition in attracting and retaining the best staff, is seen in the project management field. This continues even though the job market has become flooded with project managers, which in theory should allow organisations to pick and choose (in effect a buyer's market). But of course not all project professionals are equal; only a relatively small number are well trained, have the right level of experience and the requisite behavioural skills to be classed as talented and in demand.

Project Recruitment Stage 5: Support

INDUCTION PLANNING

Induction or 'on-boarding' planning is a standard HR-led practice designed to assimilate the new starter into the organisation quickly. The focus is on increasing 'competence' and 'engagement' of the new employee into the organisation. On-boarding actually begins at the start of the recruitment process (Glennon, 2010), yet most organisations tend to think about induction only at the first day of work.

The on-boarding period should last until the new employee feels sufficiently engaged with the organisation and is deemed to be competent in their new position. Research in 2004 from SHL showed that new employees take a number of months to become competent at their job. Across countries this time varied: in Sweden it was 10.1 months, in the US 7.8 months, in Australia and UK 7 months and India 6.6 months. There is limited research on the numbers of employees who leave their new job within the first year yet Sindell and Sindell (2006) estimate that 25 per cent of employees are fired within the first 90 days of employment whilst SHL (2004) give ranges across countries within 12 months as Sweden 8 per cent, the US 13 per cent, Australia 14 per cent, UK 12 per cent and India 17 per cent. Clearly there is a business impact in ensuring new employees are engaged quickly and performing well.

On-boarding at a basic level is educating the new employee on organisational procedures like health and safety in the workplace, orientation in the organisation, employee benefits and terms and conditions of employment. The real work of on-boarding and the work that will improve engagement and competent starts when the new employee is introduced to the department or project team to begin work.

There are two main areas of focus when on-boarding new project employees. Learning and integrating with the 'social norms' (Glennon, 2010) of the organisation's culture is one and understanding how 'projects get done around here' is the other.

Glennon describes the 'social norms' as, for example, how the employees work – collaboratively or autonomously – how decisions are made, how new ideas are shared and so on.

The project or programme management office (PMO) is ideally placed to support the process of on-boarding project managers into the project organisation. Many PMOs take responsibility for induction programmes. These typically include a timetable of activities, events, meetings, training, introductions to the wider project management community and of course ongoing support as the new project manager finds his/her feet. Practical support from the PMO includes:

- the induction manual (a guide to the project management method, tools, processes and templates);
- access to intranet for resources;
- orientation guides such as organisation charts, telephone lists, roles and responsibilities;
- administration procedures (claiming expenses, booking meeting rooms and so on);
- basic information such as car parking and catering arrangements and fire drill;
- training on the basics of telephony, IT and business conduct.

The PMO becomes a vital lifeline and support for the critical initial period of employment for project managers, enabling them to understand how the organisation works and what standards of work are expected. Continuous engagement with the new starter during the first formative months will help to ensure that the new hire is successful.

References and Further Reading

Blackshaw, P. (2008), *Satisfied Customers Tell Three Friends, Angry Customers Tell 3,000: Running a Business in Today's Consumer-Driven World*, New York: Doubleday.

Gladwell, M. (2000), 'The new-boy network – what do job interviews really tell us?', *The New Yorker*, 29 May 2000. Available at: www.gladwell.com/pdf/newboy.pdf [accessed 30 September 2011].

Glennon, R. (2010), 'On-boarding for organizational growth'. Available at: http://central.shl.com/SiteCollectionDocuments/White%20Papers,%20Guidelines%20and%20Other/White%20Papers/Onboarding%20For%20Organisational%20Growth.pdf [accessed 1 February 2012].

Huffcutt, A. (2010), 'From science to practice: Seven principles for conducting employment interviews', *Applied H.R.M. Research*, 12(1), 121–36.

International Taskforce on Assessment Center Guidelines (2009), 'Guidelines and ethical considerations for assessment center operations', *International Journal of Selection and Assessment*, 17, 24–253.

Jackson, D., Ahmad, M.H., Grace, G. and Yoon, J. (2011), 'An alternative take on AC research and practice: Task-based assessment centers', in N. Povah and G.C. Thornton (eds), *Assessment Centres and Global Talent Management*, Farnham: Gower, 163–71.

Krause, D.E. (2011), 'Assessment center practices in South Africa, Western Europe and North America', in N. Povah and G.C. Thornton (eds), *Assessment Centres and Global Talent Management*, Farnham: Gower, 351–61.

Michaels, E., Handfield-Jones, H. and Axelrod, B. (2001), *The War for Talent*, Boston, MA: Harvard Business School Publishing.

Munro Fraser, J. (1950), *A Handbook of Employment Interviewing*, London: Macdonald & Evans.

Proctor, R. (1987), 'Recruiting staff', in A. Vaughan (ed.), *International Reader in the Management of Library, Information and Archive Services*, Paris: UNESCO.

Rodger, A. (1952), *The Seven Point Plan*, London: National Institute of Industrial Psychology.

Rothwell, W.J. (2001), *Effective Succession Planning*, AMACON.

Scott, L. (2011), 'The modern project management apprenticeship', ArrasPeople.co.uk Project Management blog. Available at: http://www.arraspeople.co.uk/camel-blog/projectmanagement/the-modern-project-management-apprenticeship/ [accessed 15 September 2011].

Interview with Don Hazeldine of BAE Systems – Project Control Foundation Scheme.

SHL and Future Foundation (2004), *Getting the Edge in the New People Economy*, London: Future Foundation.

Sindell, M. and Sindell, T. (2006), *Sink or Swim*, Avon, MA: Adams Media.

Thornton, G.C. (2011), 'Fifty years on: The ongoing reciprocal impact of science and practice on the assessment center method', in N. Povah and G.C. Thornton (eds), *Assessment Centres and Global Talent Management*, Farnham: Gower, 163–71.

Yates, M. (2005), *Hiring the Best*, Avon, MA: Adams Media.

44 *Legal Issues*

PETER HARRINGTON

Project managers worldwide are often faced with many challenges and legal disputes, typically concerning contracts between companies. However, because this Handbook is about people in projects, this chapter concentrates on legal issues that might face a project manager involved in the employment of people at home or overseas.

Legal Issues in General and Internationally

Legal issues surrounding recruitment and the employment of staff can be particularly daunting for a 'non-people' manager, especially if that manager is operating in a global environment, where projects can touch or be carried out in different territories or across different legal jurisdictions. The nature, scope and influence of labour laws will need to be determined in the various places and even if jurisdiction is at first not seen to be a major issue (for example where employees are based offshore or with no fixed place of work), it might be necessary to determine whether employees are able to bring claims in the courts, appeal to tribunals or other legal forums, or otherwise rely on certain rights in what might be considered the home country of the employee or company.

Even if local laws do not apply or are different from the manager's regular rules and conventions, it will be important for managers to be aware of local sensitivities, regulations or social policies. For example, in the US employment is mostly undertaken with an 'at will' attitude, whereas EU employment policy is on a much more social basis with additional protection afforded to employees and workers in many areas.

In the EU, directives are passed at European level and must be implemented in domestic law. Thus many protections and case law are effectively standard across the EU. However, it is possible when enacted at country level that additional levels of protection are implemented above and beyond those required to execute the EU directive.

Obligations or commitments to potential employees do not begin at the date of the commencement of the contract and end the day the employment contract is terminated. Many duties can begin from the moment a manager considers hiring someone to undertake a particular task. Responsibilities can last (whether by contract or by statute) for many months or even years after employment has ended.

All legal topics here are described in a generic way and will often follow best practice, even if this area is not highly legislated for in a particular jurisdiction.

EXPERT ADVICE

Legislation and case law is constantly evolving. So managers and organisations must seek appropriate indemnified, professional advice tailored to their specific circumstances, the particular legislative environment and in relation to any specific issues, individuals or programmes.

To ensure compliance with local legislation, managers should ensure that experts are engaged to reduce the risk of falling foul of employment legislation. In most organisations it will probably be necessary to speak with the HR department, who will be able to advise on the necessary requirements for operating within the country (or countries) of the project or task in advance of project start-up and the engagement of people.

If the HR department does not have the necessary expertise it should be able to appoint one or more suitable advisers. Where convenient, it can be prudent to ensure that the HR 'business partner' is engaged as part of the project team. Then that partner can provide strategic and ad hoc advice to the project process as required or be in a position to keep an operational link with the workforce experts. This might perhaps be part of HR shared services and with trades unions, so minimising disruption in project implementation.

If there is no established HR department, managers may need to engage with lawyers, consultants or other advisers directly. Recommendations should first be sought on the suitability of potential firms *before* they are engaged to advise on matters of employment regulations, commitments and obligations.

Discrimination

Discrimination in employment can take many forms. These might be on the grounds of sex/gender and gender identity, age, religion or belief, marital status, sexual orientation and disability. These are sometimes called 'protected characteristics' because for social policy reasons in many countries discrimination on any of these grounds is outlawed. Thus potential and actual employees are protected from discrimination in employment situations on each or any combination of these grounds. In the EU and the US discrimination is not only outlawed in employment but also more widely in society (for example in relation to the provision of, or access to services).

Regardless as to whether these characteristics are protected in any area in which the project operates, there is considerable benefit in having a diverse workforce that reflects society at large and in ensuring that the different views, needs and experiences are used for the benefit of the project and organisation generally. Narrow views or prejudices of the capabilities of people who are different from us or our social group are most likely to be wrong and outdated. For example, assumptions about what a person with disabilities is capable of can very often be very different from the actual capability of that individual. Failure to recognise this can not only be very hurtful and restricting for the person but it also collectively holds back a section of society which has the potential to contribute positively to the project or project programme. All this is relevant to the wider economy. Open and fair competition when filling roles or recruiting and promoting staff is vital.

In cases of discrimination, it is not only the organisation that can be open to legal challenge. Individuals can be cited in legal cases, pursued and awards made personally against them. Additionally organisations can be held vicariously liable for the actions of their workers.

Thus it is important for organisations to ensure they have robust anti-discriminatory policies and training to rebut or mitigate accusations of 'institutional discrimination'. Organisations should also make sure that all complaints of discrimination are fully investigated, dealt with and the results recorded. Lack of investigation or appropriate internal sanction can reinforce poor behaviours, attitudes and mindsets. Managers and leaders should underpin a non-discriminatory workplace by role-modelling appropriate conduct to ensure that others know that these types of stereotypical viewpoints will not be tolerated.

It is also important to appreciate that discrimination does not just happen during the employment life cycle. Very often potential candidates could make challenges before employment, during recruitment or even before a job is advertised. Writing a job description in a certain way or planning a particular recruitment campaign poorly could give rise to a dispute, so it is vital that managers consider the consequences of their actions at all times.

TYPES OF DISCRIMINATION

Direct and Indirect Discrimination

Discrimination can occur in one of two ways: *direct* and *indirect*. Direct discrimination occurs when a particular method, criterion or assumption directly affects a particular group of people. For example, advertising a particular role as 'for men only' or not recruiting a certain person because he or she is gay or practises a certain religion would be directly discriminatory.

Indirect discrimination is where a certain criterion in recruitment adversely affects a particular group of people and (because very often it is not blatant or obvious) can be missed as potential discrimination and leave the project or manager open to risk. An example of indirect discrimination would be allowing a role to be offered on a full-time basis without considering part-time engagement for no good reason. This would adversely affect women (because more women than men work part-time, meaning that fewer women could potentially apply for the role or be appointed).

Gender Discrimination

Discrimination on the basis of gender or gender identity happens when a discriminatory act is carried out on the basis of a person's gender – or the gender that the person identifies with (for example, transsexuals).

Discrimination protection extends to both sexes. It is particularly important to ensure that women who are pregnant, or who are on or returning from maternity leave are treated appropriately. It is not acceptable (or legal) to refuse employment to a woman because she is pregnant or likely to take maternity leave in the future. It is beyond the scope of this section to discuss this area in greater detail but it is important to ensure that women are treated appropriately. Projects can present their own difficulties in this area, where roles and responsibilities change through the project life cycle. Also, a project might end before the end of a woman's period of maternity leave, so that the question of what happens when she returns to the non-existent job has to be planned for. If managers are in doubt about their responsibilities then they should seek advice from their HR department or adviser.

Disability Discrimination

In the UK, a disability is defined as a condition that is long term (generally considered to be lasting more than 12 months or until the end of life if shorter) and has a substantial effect on the ability to carry out day-to-day tasks (not just work tasks but also general activities such as feeding oneself or brushing one's hair). It includes both physical and mental conditions – not just 'seen' disabilities such as someone using a wheelchair, for example.

There is or should be a requirement to make *reasonable adjustments* to mitigate the effect of the disability in work settings. This might involve making changes in the workplace to facilitate access for a person with a physical disability. Examples are:

- installing wheelchair ramps;
- arranging interviews (and subsequent work) on the ground floor;
- allowing a sign-language interpreter;
- using a hearing loop to assist people with a hearing disability;
- permitting a candidate more time to complete recruitment tests if the person has dyslexia.

The requirement to make reasonable adjustments, although qualified, persists through the recruitment process and (should the candidate be appointed) to enable them access (not necessarily in a physical sense) to work.

Age Discrimination

Discrimination on the basis of age is where a discriminatory act is carried in the form of refusing employment to someone younger or older than a preferred age range – for example advertising for 'under 25s only' or 'must have ten years' experience'.

Discrimination can also occur through the recruitment process because of false, preconceived ideas about what a person of a certain age might or might not be like. Examples are:

- employing a younger person because there is a belief he or she is more energetic or has more ambition;
- employing an older person because they are perceived to be more 'steady' or take fewer days' absence.

Religion or Belief Discrimination

A discriminatory act on the basis of someone's religion or belief can take the form of not employing someone because they hold certain beliefs or is a member of, or practises, a certain religion. For example, discrimination would occur if the best candidate for a job was not appointed because they were Jewish.

Sexual Orientation Discrimination

Discrimination on the grounds of someone's sexual orientation can occur not only when a person is actually gay, bisexual or lesbian but also on any perception that a person might or might not have a particular sexual orientation. For example, if there are rumours that a person is gay when he or she is in fact straight and that person is not appointed or promoted because of those rumours, then the person could potentially bring a claim.

Equal Opportunities

As well as ensuring that any project or recruitment activity is run in a non-discriminatory way, equal opportunities should be actively promoted by any organisation. Most businesses and organisations will want to ensure that they have a very clear public statement on their equal opportunities policy, not only to meet legislative requirements but also to demonstrate to their employees and to potential applicants that the organisation appoints and promotes people on merit. In other words, no personal characteristic is considered more or less favourably owing purely to prejudice.

There are many other ways for organisations to demonstrate their commitment to equal opportunities in employment. One scheme is the UK 'two ticks' scheme, which guarantees interviews for people with disabilities if they meet minimum criteria for the role. The Stonewall workplace equality index, which is run not only in the UK but has a global best practice section, also yields important engagement indicators for potential employees.

Businesses may choose to gather and record information about their candidates and employees to measure the diversity of their workforce. Positive measures can be taken to encourage employees and potential employees who are members of particular groups that are under-represented in that organisation to apply for roles or promotion.

Positive action is sometimes confused with positive discrimination. The latter would mean employing someone only because they come from an under-represented group, regardless as to whether or not they have the right and relevant skills and qualifications. Positive discrimination is unlawful because discrimination is not permitted at any point.

Some actions managers can consider legally to promote the concept of positive action and encourage job applications from sectors of society that are under-represented include:

- using media outlets to advertise where there is a higher penetration/awareness in the particular sector, for example, ethnic newspapers, magazines and websites about disability or sexual orientation issues;
- using employment agencies where under-represented groups have population concentrations, so that the organisation reflects the wider local population demographics;
- positive encouragement, training or mentoring/coaching for promotion for employees who lack particular expertise because of their background, but show potential;

- recruitment and training schemes for school leavers, such as apprenticeships;
- retraining for older workers.

Positive action is not about giving more favourable treatment to particular groups in the recruitment process. Selection for recruitment or promotion should always be solely on the basis of competency for the role being advertised.

Job Descriptions, Sifting and Interviewing

Many adverse issues in employment and recruitment occur because agreed procedures are not followed. If the organisation has a procedure, managers should follow it – courts generally take a dim view of organisations that publish one thing but actually do something different.

The process that managers follow in recruitment should ensure that risk of challenge is minimised. Throughout the sift and interview, records should be kept to provide evidence of the process and the decisions made. These records may form the basis of any defence and might have to be produced as evidence in court, so they should be compiled appropriately and in line with relevant data protection and processing laws.

Job descriptions, person specifications and job profiles are important tools in the recruitment process and should ensure that the process and appointment is fair and legal. Job descriptions must accurately and fully describe the purpose of the role (not the person!) and the tasks to be undertaken, including the expected outputs (deliverables). Describing the role's responsibilities well will ensure that the recruiting manager and potential applicants are clear about the level and scope of the role being advertised.

The person specification should be clear on the skills, qualification, experience and competence of the desired candidates. In some organisations, a job description and person specification will be combined into a job profile, although the terminology is very often interchangeable.

Hopefully, following a period of advertising or instructing agencies or head-hunters to source candidates, a manager will have a good selection of candidates for potential interview. If not done already by an agency, it will be necessary to sift the applications received to narrow the field of candidates (shortlist) to remove those clearly unsuitable and provide a manageable number for interview.

Having a good job description and person specification will ensure that the recruiter can take an objective view on the suitability of the candidates, either through a yes/no appraisal of suitability against the criteria in the person specification or a more sophisticated system of scoring competence by applying a range, for example giving a score (possibly weighted) on whether the candidate is unsuitable, probably suitable, suitable or highly suitable.

Pre-employment Checks, Right to Work and Visas

Most organisations will want to carry out some degree of pre-employment checks before appointing a person into a role, or at least make an offer that is subject to satisfactory checks received. This could include references from previous employers, checking qualifications, background checks for roles that involve access to sensitive information, credit checks if the role involves the handling of money or financial services/regulation or criminal record checks if the role involves close contact with vulnerable people or children or jobs in the police or legal profession.

All countries in the world will have specific rules determining who may or may not have the right of abode and the right to work in that territory. The exact nature of these restrictions for work will be complex and require specific advice tailored to the individual based on their own nationality, length of stay and immigration status. Countries will publish requirements for workers in their jurisdiction (even if they are not going to be wholly resident).

Visa agents may also be able to provide advice for visitors and workers. Sometimes visas may not be required for short stays, for example for attendance at short business meetings. But for longer stays visas or work permits might be needed.

Organisations should satisfy themselves of a person's right to work. In some countries there is a legal obligation to keep records of a person's right to work in that country through nationality, immigration or work visa. That diligence is exercised in the recruitment process. An organisation can incur substantial fines for failing to perform these duties.

It will also be necessary for organisations to be aware of workers' personal circumstances and local customs or laws. For example, in some countries homosexual acts are illegal and can carry substantial penalties or at the very least deportation of foreign nationals, so this may cause difficulties if organisations are deploying their resources globally and a homosexual person has a civil partnership and the partner is travelling with the worker. It is important to highlight these types of risks or cultural sensitivities well ahead of time to give individuals time to decide whether it may or may not be appropriate for them to travel to those countries and also to minimise the risk to the project or task. If necessary it may be prudent to make any recruitment/job offers that require work permits or visas conditional on these being obtained and the person legally being able to undertake that role.

Contractual Status

When is an employee not an employee? This might seem on the face of it to be a fairly simple question but a person's contractual status and the way the individual behaves under a contract can determine whether that person can argue employment status and then be able to claim benefits or protection afforded to employees in that company. People may well desire to describe themselves as self-employed to enjoy various tax benefits or status. But they may be more likely to argue that they are employees if there are disagreements during the assignment or at the end of contracts when there might be a desire to take advantage of severance or lay-off/redundancy packages.

Generally a good starting point is to ensure that a contract is actually in place. If organisations employ directly there will be a clear contract of employment and that will indicate that the person is an employee. The definition of a 'worker' can be defined by legislation, particularly in relation to EU directives. Broadly, 'workers' are defined much more loosely than just having a contract for employment or services and will probably include most people working in an organisation, including some self-employed people, casual and seasonal staff.

So, when might the self-employed workers, casual and seasonal staff be considered employees? Courts have considered this over time and by and large they have come to the conclusion that if it looks like an employee, acts like an employee and smells like an employee then it is an employee!

The implication for managers is that courts will look beyond what the contract actually says (even if it is clear and explicit) and consider how the person behaves and is managed under that contract. Therefore if someone is genuinely self-employed, they should behave and be treated accordingly and not as a regular employee. That includes not inviting them to staff events, excluding them from staff activities such as engagement surveys or performance management processes or participating in staff reward schemes.

Many managers and organisations will want to be inclusive and engaging with their temporary and contractor resources but must appreciate the difficulties that occur by blurring the lines around who is or isn't an employee. Issues can arise in the treatment of casual, temporary or seasonal staff where employment patterns become regular or where temporary, short-term contracts turn into longer-term assignments lasting many years that completely negate the purpose of hiring someone on a temporary or casual contract. Then the worker may automatically acquire employment rights or protection simply because of the regular nature of their work or length of time engaged in that organisation.

Managers should therefore ensure that people resources are contracted appropriately for the needs identified and are allocated accordingly, with contracts being regularly reviewed and if necessary terminated before obligations arise. Managers must ensure that there is sufficient break between contracts if the same person is engaged on a number of assignments, because short periods may become joined over time, thereby giving the individual unexpected privileges or rights. The key is to ensure that resources are contracted in the most relevant way at the point of recruitment so that issues do not arise out of the blue later. For example, only employ temporary workers if the work is short term and time-bound – if it is open-ended or over an extended period then more permanent resources might be appropriate (and less costly in the longer term).

Contracts

The exact requirements for completing a well-drafted, valid contract will depend on the laws, jurisprudence and courts governing the contract. Contracts should be confirmed in writing so that both sides are clear on the obligations and commitments each has entered into. However, contracts can also be made verbally, so managers should ensure they do not inadvertently agree to something in discussions that cannot be delivered or which commit the organisation adversely.

The general characteristics of an employment contract will be remuneration in the form of a salary paid periodically (normally weekly, 4-weekly or monthly) in return for work between certain hours for a set number of hours. The contract will also more often than not detail:

- specific company rules, guidance and policies that employees will need to be aware of and abide by through express or implied terms;

- notice periods required by the employee and employer to terminate the contract;
- benefits or non-financial remuneration;
- holiday entitlement and time-off periods.

Sometimes the additional information may be non-contractual, so they could be found in a statement of terms and conditions provided separately from the contract, or in a printed online handbook.

There are many types of employment contract that can be used to commit staff to a project or organisation, these include:

- *Permanent or enduring* contract – no fixed end date and probably the most commonly used in an employment setting;
- *Temporary, seasonal or fixed-term* contract – a fixed end date contracting an employee for a certain period with a determined end date or variable end date based on completion of a task, project or return of another employee, if it is a maternity cover, for example;
- *Casual* contract – generally no obligation to offer or accept work, with no fixed hours, work pattern or end date.

Other methods of contracting staff include self-employed contractors, directly or through a third-party, agency staff and independent consultants.

Equal Pay

The concept of equal pay for equal work links with other forms of anti-discrimination in employment. It has particular associations with gender discrimination, where traditionally (and sometimes currently, despite legislation) women have been paid less than men for equal value work. However, organisations will want to ensure a fair reward system across all roles and levels regardless of gender and ensure that work of equal value is rewarded uniformly to ensure even-handedness and equality. This not only minimises challenges but could improve staff morale and engagement, and thus organisational effectiveness.

Many organisations will utilise their job evaluation process to analyse roles objectively and to benchmark their roles internally and externally. Managers should ensure that new roles or roles that have significantly changed are evaluated in this way if appropriate in their organisation.

Minimum Wage and Maximum Working Hours

Some countries have regulations set by government or some other body that stipulate a minimum wage which must be offered to all workers by age, type of contract or industry sector. The rates stipulated as a minimum wage will be reviewed regularly to ensure they are in line with general economic conditions, inflation and so on.

There may also be a non-mandatory *living wage* in areas of high cost of living such as in cities like London. This living wage will be higher to reflect the increased costs of housing, food and travel. Businesses may be encouraged to offer this higher living wage rather than the mandatory minimum wage for general society benefits.

Maximum working hours legislation will stipulate the maximum number of hours a person may work in a day, week or other set period before they are entitled to a break or rest period and when they can start working again. These rules might differ depending on a person's age, industry and time the person works. For example, regulations for night workers may differ from day workers. Safety-critical jobs may have more breaks than regular jobs. The rationale behind regulations is to ensure worker health and safety and to promote a healthy working environment. Under certain circumstances, derogations can be made by individuals to opt out of the regulations.

Trades Unions and Right of Representation

The right of freedom of association and to join (or not to) join a trades union is a basic right in many countries. Some jurisdictions will seek to minimise the power or influence of labour or trades unions. Others will see benefits associated with:

- engagement in consultation;
- working in partnership with employee representatives;
- setting up works councils or consultation forums where business decisions affecting staff can be discussed, consulted upon or negotiated.

A union will want to protect and advance the interests of its members in the workplace, discussing concerns that affect staff and promoting health and safety in work.

Some organisations may recognise unions or works councils for the purposes of collective or group consultation, negotiation and bargaining. They can then choose to use these forums to avoid or settle disputes. Where discussions result in the organisation changing terms and conditions of employment (including pay), these changes will apply to the whole – employee population which the union/works council is recognised as representing – even those who are not union members themselves.

Developing good relationships with representatives is an essential skill of a good 'people manager'. Larger businesses might employ industrial relations experts to manage and structure this relationship and reduce the risk of disruptive disputes and industrial action.

Union members or representatives may be protected from action or victimisation against them for being members of a union, for taking part in official action, or for undertaking union duties.

Remedies

What if it all goes wrong? Despite the best efforts of people managers and HR, some problems will not be possible to resolve at a local level. In these circumstances, staff should be encouraged to use all internal methods of dispute resolution, which will normally involve a meeting and a senior manager making a decision on the merits of the case put forward. This might be a grievance procedure or a separate procedure specifically designed to deal with particular issues such as bullying or harassment.

Once internal avenues are exhausted and the employee still does not believe their concerns have been addressed then they may decide to issue proceedings or a lawsuit in the relevant court, tribunal or department specifically set up to deal with employment cases. A judge or panel of adjudicators will then decide on the case and what remedy might be appropriate to resolve the case. This might involve compensation, reinstatement or re-engagement or a combination of these. Damages may also be awarded in some cases.

Sometimes cases can be resolved through mediation or arbitration without resorting to legal action, which can often be costly, stressful and uncertain to achieve a desired outcome. In the UK the Advisory, Conciliation and Arbitration Service organisation ACAS is widely respected for its arbitration work.

References and Further Reading

There are many free, reputable resources available on the Internet relating to employment guidelines in different countries. Some are listed below.

Advisory, Conciliation and Arbitration Service (ACAS) (UK) – see www.acas.org.uk/
Australian Government, Employment and Workplace – see http://australia.gov.au/topics/employment-and-workplace
Singapore Ministry of Manpower – see http://www.mom.gov.sg/Pages/default.aspx
Directgov.uk – UK public services in one place – see http://www.direct.gov.uk/en/Employment/index.htm
United States Department of Labor – see http://www.dol.gov/elaws/elg/

Many commercial organisations and law firms also have free and chargeable resources available.

45 *Pay and Rewards for Project Management Work*

LINDSAY SCOTT

Not many professions can boast a salary range from £20,000 to over £200,000. That makes a discussion of pay and rewards for project management practitioners particularly challenging. However, in this chapter I shall attempt to cover the complete remuneration package, which includes financial rewards such as base pay and bonuses, holidays, pension provisions and fringe benefits. I shall summarise some recent research conducted into the project management profession and indicate how pay and rewards are determined by individual experience and competence; the organisational hierarchy and expectations of the project management role.

Studies into how Pay is Determined

There have been numerous research papers and academic studies into pay and rewards in the workplace. It makes sense to set the scene for project management compensation by reviewing just a few of those which have a strong bearing on project management workers.

Fundamentally, pay is the reward given to an employee for his/her labour, productive output or actual effort into producing goods or services (Bryson, 2006). The precise payment will differ amongst workers and could include holiday pay, pension payments and other fringe benefits like health insurance and car allowances. Payments will also differ owing to obvious factors like the type of work involved, the experience and skills levels of the worker, sector and tenure. Variations in payments are also set by organisations simply as a matter of choice (for example by creating salary bands for job families or role groupings).

Research into the links between compensation and employee performance, motivation and attitudes also gives an insight into how pay is determined. Being paid well alone does not guarantee good performance, Gardner et al. (2004) looked at the motivational effects of pay levels on performance and found that 'Organisational Based Self-Esteem (OBSE)' was the main factor in providing a positive effect on performance levels. OBSE is described as, 'an employee's self-perceived value as a member of a specific organisation' and when an employee is paid well their OBSE increases. When we feel valued *and* are paid well our performance levels will increase. Interestingly workers who are considered to have high self-esteem are, 'strongly task-motivated, less distracted by adverse role conditions and more persistent when dealing with obstacles'. That sounds like the beginnings of a job description for a project manager.

The social exchange theory (Blau, 1964) sets the basic premise that the more inducements (in the form of pay) that an organisation provides to an employee, the more that employee will reciprocate by performing at higher levels.

The equity theory (Adams, 1963) takes reciprocation further and also helps to explain why pay and conditions alone do not determine motivation and increased performance from workers. The equity theory focuses on fairness and reciprocity, specifically that an employee's perception of their input and effort into their work and the resulting rewards are similar to other workers both inside and outside their organisation. Brown et al. (2008) also found that pay satisfaction and a worker's general well-being are 'highly correlated with perceptions of their pay relative to their peers'. We can be highly paid for the work we do, but if the pay is not the same or higher than our peers a decrease in performance can follow.

'Efficiency wages' is often seen with professional workers. This means in effect that the organisation pays above the market rate (or next best alternative offer for a worker) in compensation. Efficiency wages can act as a motivator for workers to carry on performing well, because they fear that if they lose their job they would find it difficult to find work at a comparable level (known as the Shirking Model, Shapiro and Stiglitz (1984)). Efficiency wages can also attract a higher calibre of worker, or workers from competitors (known as the Adverse Selection Model, Guasch and Weiss (1980)).

Erez et al. (2001) proposed a reflection theory of compensation which looked at how pay is meaningful to workers and how pay affects and motivates them. It is called the reflection theory because pay only really becomes meaningful when it is linked to an employee's self-identity in the workplace. This reflection is what employees consider important in their work and Thierry proposes four ways in which pay can have meaning for an employee: motivational (instrumentality); relative position (feedback and status); control (autonomy); and spending (what can be purchased with pay). See Figure 45.1.

Meaning	Description
Motivational	Pay is considered as a means of achieving important goals and is seen as a personal achievement. (It allows a certain level of lifestyle, or prominence and visibility in the organisation).
Relative position	The pay system used provides feedback to the employee about his/her performance in relation to others in the organisation. (It signifies status compared with others in the same group. It also links to goal-setting theories in performance appraisals).
Control	Pay mirrors the 'rate of dependence' of an employee's job level within an organisation: the 'power position'. (That is, the level of authority, level of upward influence in the organisation, management of others, autonomy and self-regulation of performance levels in the job).
Spending	Pay is meaningful when it affects what an employee chooses to spend his/her wages on. (That is, the capability to buy whatever goods or services are needed to achieve a level of material well-being).

Figure 45.1 Reflection theory: The four meanings of pay

The theories of pay setting lead us to examine what actually constitutes pay in the work environment.

Remuneration

Remuneration is the total compensation a worker receives in exchange for performance in a job. Types of compensation could include:

- base pay;
- benefits;
- incentives;
- overtime.

BASE PAY

Base pay for job roles in organisations is the foundation block for compensation systems. Job analysis, pay structures and job evaluations enable pay levels to be set depending on the main functions of job. I look at project management base pay in further detail later in the chapter.

BENEFITS

In addition to base pay most employees can expect additional benefits (deferred payments). Generally there are four different types of benefits: core, flexi, voluntary and salary sacrifice (see Figure 45.2).

Core benefits (benefits which all employees within an organisation receive) could include pensions, health insurance, sick leave and holidays.

Flexi benefits are benefits which employees can choose depending on their own situation. For example, employees might trade income protection insurance for additional holidays, or a company car for a car allowance payment.

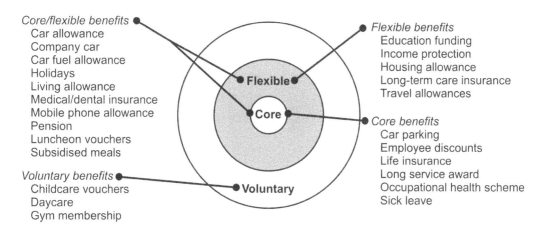

Core/flexible benefits
  Car allowance
  Company car
  Car fuel allowance
  Holidays
  Living allowance
  Medical/dental insurance
  Mobile phone allowance
  Pension
  Luncheon vouchers
  Subsidised meals

Flexible benefits
  Education funding
  Income protection
  Housing allowance
  Long-term care insurance
  Travel allowances

Core benefits
  Car parking
  Employee discounts
  Life insurance
  Long service award
  Occupational health scheme
  Sick leave

Voluntary benefits
  Childcare vouchers
  Daycare
  Gym membership

Figure 45.2 Types of employee benefits

Voluntary benefits are benefits where the organisation has agreed with suppliers to offer discounts to their employees. Employees pay for the benefits from their base salary – for example, childcare vouchers or gym membership.

Salary sacrifice benefits occur where employees agree to give up part of their base salary in exchange for some benefit in kind from the employing organisation. Salary sacrificing schemes are becoming an increasingly popular way to subsidise pensions.

Recent research by Arras People (2012) with over 1,500 project management practitioners has shown that the larger the base salary, the greater additional rewards in the form of benefits can be expected. Contributory pensions were the most popular benefit, followed by health care related benefits, mobile phone allowances and life insurance. Project management practitioners working within the public sector can expect to receive a funded pension provision but typically their additional benefits were minimal when compared with the private sector.

Perquisites (commonly known as perks) are employee benefits provided by an organisation on a more discretionary basis. These perks can often distinguish one organisation from another in terms of how well they look after their employees. Luncheon allowances, first-class travel, shopping vouchers, free tickets to major sporting events, gala balls and birthday gifts are just some additional benefits to performing the role in some organisations.

INCENTIVES

Part of an organisation's compensation system can include incentives for staff. Here I include variable pay components such as bonuses and commissions. Incentives are used in a number of ways with the intention of increasing worker performance. Incentives can help an organisation to set employee or team work goals, influence worker behaviour, increase motivation levels and reward exemplary work. Incentives fall into two categories: financial and non-financial.

Financial incentives can vary from individual incentives such as cash bonuses, stock options and salary increments through to rewards such as paid-for study or free gym membership. Group financial incentives can also be used, such as team performance bonuses, profit-related pay, and gainsharing where group performance is rewarded.

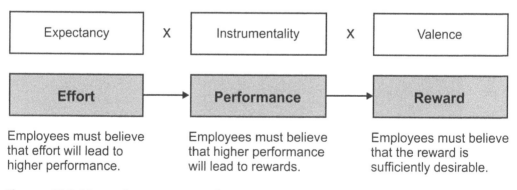

Figure 45.3 Vroom's expectancy theory

Non-financial incentives can be wider ranging such as VIP parking, professional membership fees, additional holidays, awards for achievements, flexible working options or inclusion on specific advanced management programmes.

Incentive programmes only work when they are devised, constructed and rolled out in accordance with the level of worker in the organisation and the role they perform. Vroom's (1964) expectancy theory shows that in its simplest terms for incentives to work (to increase performance and motivation in a worker or group of workers) employees must believe that increased effort on their part will lead to rewards that they deem to be desirable. If any of the three components shown in Figure 45.3 are considered to be weak, the incentive plan will fail.

In a 2005 research paper by Raduescu and Heales, incentives were specifically looked at within the information systems (IS) industry and the project management environment. Incentives for successful project outcomes (like early project completion; high-quality work and less costly completions) all sound straightforward in theory. In practice project-based incentives were not used often enough. Although the research sample was relatively small (500 professionals at management level in IS, just 57 projects used incentives), where incentives had been used there was a 100 per cent success rate in those projects. Project managers felt that the whole team should be incentivised; that incentives should be introduced at milestones and project completion, and that there was a marked improvement in the quality and speed of delivery. The research also concluded that for the incentives to work the project managers would have to show strong leadership and provide mentoring and motivation for their teams in order to reach the goals.

One particular type of incentive scheme normally found in a sales-based environment is that of at-risk pay. The Raduescu and Heales research wanted to see if project managers would be prepared to put a specified percentage of their base salary at risk against a more than double compensating reward if their projects met certain objectives. For example, would a project manager be willing to take a 10 per cent reduction in pay if that meant he/she were able to see a 20 per cent return as a reward for project success? Just over one quarter of those questioned were not prepared to make this gamble, but almost half would consider a reduction of between 1 and 10 per cent.

OVERTIME

Overtime has become an accepted part of the job for many white collar professional managerial posts and project management is no exception. Generally overtime is deemed to be the hours worked over and above the contracted hours stated in the employment contract. Within the UK, the contract should state the organisation's policy on overtime although there is no legal requirement to pay overtime or to state at what rate. The Working Time Directive mandates that an employee should not regularly work more than 48 hours in a week, but senior managers and professional workers can opt out of this Directive if they wish. In the US an exempt employee, normally a salaried employee at a managerial level is not entitled to overtime. Even contractors, self-employed or otherwise, often receive no pay for overtime hours because they are normally contracted on a rate per day.

The twenty-first-century office has accepted the unpaid overtime state of play and project managers, like other managers, can often expect no immediate remuneration for their extra work. A project manager however may influence the ability to reward the team with a completion bonus in recognition of the long nights and weekends worked by the team. Project managers can also influence the opportunity to provide time off in lieu (TOIL) for team members and indeed for themselves.

Most professional workers see unpaid overtime as a quid pro quo and take the opportunity to redress the work/life balance when the project eases up or is completed.

Factors Affecting Base Pay

Having looked at the remuneration, the types of compensation a project manager could expect to receive in his/her job, I now want to look at the base salary in more detail. Here I shall cover the factors that affect wage levels, including:

- the individual – the role he or she performs, skills and experience, status, qualifications and age;
- organisational factors – such as team size, span of control and degree of budget responsibility;
- the economy and the marketplace.

THE INDIVIDUAL

The Role

Project roles are discussed in some detail in chapters 15 and 16. Generally, of course, the more responsibility a project practitioner has, the higher the salary he or she can command. Four relevant factors here are for the individual:

- project complexity;
- level of risk;
- organisational span of control;
- level of budget responsibility.

Clearly as practitioners progress in their careers from managing simple projects through to higher positions (such as managing complex programmes of multiple projects) their salary levels will increase.

Research (Arras People, 2012) across the main roles of project manager, programme manager and project management office (PMO) manager showed a very wide span of pay, as shown in Figure 45.4. Data collected for 2012 show the following average annual salaries:

- programme managers £58,788;
- project managers £43,762;
- project consultants £67,237;
- PMO managers £57,560.

Incremental increases in line with increasing responsibility can also be seen in a PMI project management salary survey. Compared with the role with the lowest salary

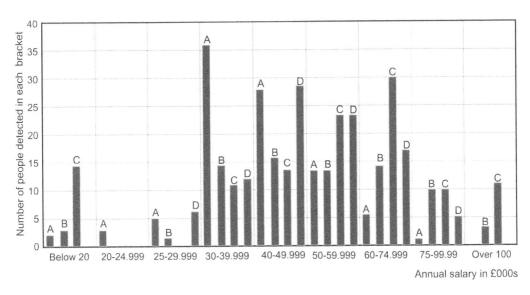

Key: A = project manager; B = project consultant; C =programme manager; D = PMO manager

Figure 45.4 Annual salary diversity across different project management roles

(project manager) the highest paid role (head of project management) receives 75 per cent more.

Experience and Skills

As a project practitioner becomes more experienced within the role it stands to reason that the earning potential increases. Organisations see experience and skills as the dominant factor when choosing to employ project practitioners (Arras People, 2012). That ranks higher than personality, domain experience, professional accreditations and education. To offer higher rates of pay, organisations look for project managers who have 'been there and done it before' to minimise the risk on their investment. The project management industry also sees pockets of skills shortages which drive up pay levels.

The PMI survey also highlighted technique experience as a differentiator in salary levels. Examples such as agile, extreme project management, project portfolio, and interactive project management give an insight into the types of techniques or specialism that practitioners can choose to work within. Smart project practitioners are able to maximise their earning potentials by actively seeking out opportunities where skills shortages exist and exploiting them.

Job Status

Earning levels for project management practitioners also depend largely on their work status (whether working in a permanent position for one organisation or preferring the contractor/self-employed route).

Contracting can be a lucrative mode of operation for a project manager, with the rates of pay being on average within the range of £350–650 per day. Variations are seen for variables such as work sector, years of experience and the actual project management role performed.

Contracting as a project practitioner is not without its difficulties and those can have an impact on earning levels. In 2012 Arras People reported in the UK that contractors had been facing a tough time, with rates of pay moving downwards coupled with a reduction of available contracts over the year (Arras People, 2012). This has been a trend since 2008 owing to depressed economies in the UK and overseas. The same Arras People report has shown a trend for project practitioners who have recently been made redundant to opt for the contracting route. Rather than this becoming a new way of life in the long term, evidence suggests that these new contractors are looking for any port in a storm until the economic outlook improves.

Qualifications

In 2011, Arras People used data from 1,500 project management practitioners to see if there was any correlation between qualifications and remuneration in the UK (Arras People, 2011). 27.2 per cent of respondents had no PPM qualifications and the research tackled the question, 'Does this affect the salary and day rates achieved compared to those who have invested their time and money in qualifications?' According to Figure 45.5, the answer is 'Yes!' For salaried practitioners, those with qualifications are on the whole distributed at higher levels of remuneration across the £35K to £70K salary bands. 33 per cent of those indicating no accreditation were earning below the £35K level and those trading on experience alone still managed to earn more at the £70K+ levels.

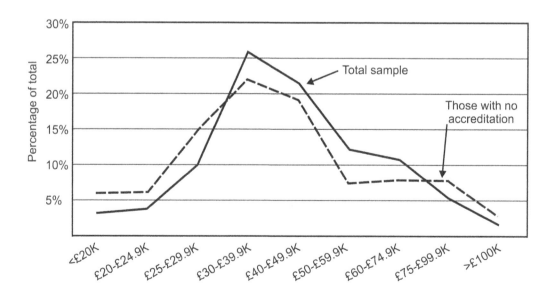

Figure 45.5 Annual salary for all programme and project managers compared against those with no accreditation

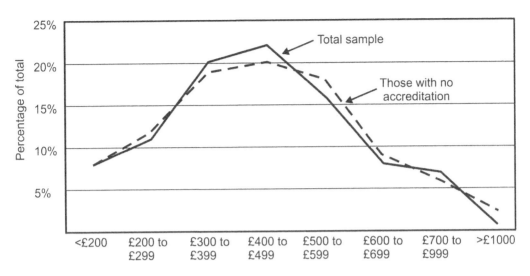

Figure 45.6 Day rate payments for all programme and project managers compared against those with no accreditation

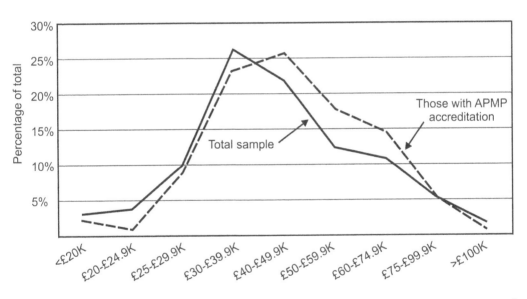

Figure 45.7 Annual salary for all programme and project managers compared against those who also have APMP accreditation

The position is not as clear cut when it comes to those earning a living as a contractor (Figure 45.6). Here the qualified practitioners fare better in the £250 to £550 per day range, although unqualified people still appear to be unhindered through the £550 to £750 per day range. Above this day rate the overall distribution is even, although it would appear that those with qualifications are being valued.

The research also looked at the salary levels relevant to the type of qualification. PRINCE2 (a popular qualification in the UK) had a positive impact on the salary level but the difference was small, indicating that PRINCE2 has become a 'me too' qualification for project managers in the UK. However, with the Association for Project Management's APMP qualification there was a significant upwards shift into higher levels of remuneration with the average salary moving by £10K (Figure 45.7).

In the PMI research from 2011, the results for their PMP qualification were similar for some nations. New Zealand, Belgium, the US and Canada all reported a significant salary increase of over 10 per cent for those with the qualification against those without. Of the nations paying the highest salaries, Switzerland, could account for a mere 3.5 per cent difference between those with and without the PMP qualification.

The research showed that for qualifications to make such an impact on salary levels, the length of time and experience levels that a practitioner has achieved also plays a big part.

Age

Research (Arras People, 2012) has shown that as project practitioners increase in age, their salary levels will also increase (Figure 45.8). This is the case only for practitioners who have continuously worked in the project management field for some time (over 10 years), which indicates that experience levels must also have increased with age. Whilst this is to be expected, the same research also revealed that as project practitioners become older they are more likely to opt for a better work/life balance (which affects their salary levels). Older practitioners have more choice and flexibility about how and where they choose to work, for example by choosing part-time hours or working in the third sector.

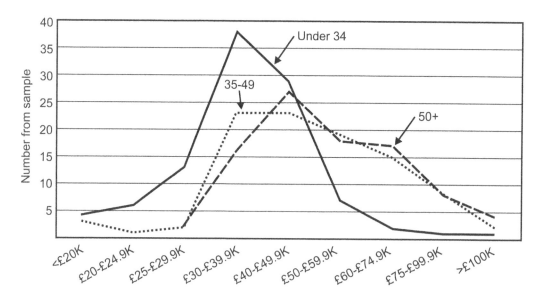

Figure 45.8 Annual salary for all programme and project managers ranked by age group

Older practitioners are also at a disadvantage when it comes to unemployment. The older the practitioner, the longer they are likely to be out of work, affecting their salary levels towards the end of their careers when ideally they should be maximising their earning potential.

Gender

The ratio of men and women working within the UK project management industry has been consistent over the last seven years at 75:25 (Arras People, 2006–2012). Internationally most male: female ratios currently sit at 80:20 (PMI Survey, 2011). However, there are some notable exceptions. In the US the number of women working as project managers is slightly higher (37 women for every 63 men). But in Saudi Arabia there are 99 men for every woman.

In 2009 (Arras People, 2009) it was clearly reported that a gender pay gap did exist in project management, with more male project managers earning salaries in the higher salary bands whilst more women earned salaries in the lower bands. The role of gender in pay and rewards however is not simple to unravel. Salary levels within project management specific to gender are shown to depend on years of tenure, the age of the practitioner, the length of experience in the job and the industry sector.

A 1993 research paper (Baroudi and Igbaria, 1993) specific to those working within the IT sector showed that again women were under-represented in the higher wage categories and found that males tended to be older, had worked longer and had more experience in the role. This was also seen in the 2008 report from Arras People, with 72 per cent of male project managers having 10 years or more experience compared to just 47 per cent of female counterparts (Arras People, 2008).

In the same research paper by Baroudi and Igbaria, one particular gender-specific wage difference is relevant to the project management industry. Women do work in male-dominated positions like project management but they tend to climb the career ladder more successfully in female-dominated industries like health care, education and personnel-related industries (which tend to pay less than 'large, private, productive, profitable, capital intensive corporations').

In 2009 (Arras People, 2009) there were two gender-specific conditions which affected salary levels for female project managers. The first of these conditions was the career break for child rearing. The second was the need for flexibility in working hours and location to allow women to carry out the primary carer role.

LOCATION

Location can play a huge part in the salary levels a project practitioner can expect to achieve. National variations, as highlighted in the PMI annual salary survey for 2011, can be as much as $130,000 a year.

Within the UK, further differences in salaries can also be seen across regions, with the highest salaries in London. Owing to the higher cost of living in popular urban areas like London and the South East, project practitioners will command higher salaries and often receive additional benefits to assist with the costs of living in these areas (see Figure 45.9).

Top 10 countries for highest salaries	10 countries with the lowest salary levels
Switzerland: $160K	China: $23K
Australia: $139K	Taiwan: $29K
Germany: $110K	Nigeria: $29K
Netherlands: $109K	India: $31K
Belgium: $108K	Peru: $34K
United States: $105K	Malaysia: $39K
Irish Republic: $101K	Mexico: $42K
Canada: $98K	Columbia: $49K
United Kingdom: $96K	South Korea: $56K
New Zealand: $91K	Saudi Arabia: $63K

Figure 45.9 Average salary levels for project practitioners in different countries

Top 10 countries	Top industry sector	Middle industry sector	Bottom industry sector
Switzerland	Insurance	Food and beverages	Telecommunications
Australia	Resources (like mining)	Utilities	Financial services
Germany	Healthcare	Financial services	Engineering
Netherlands	Resources	Financial services	Telecommunicaitons
Belgium	Pharmaceuticals	Consulting	Manufacturing
United States	Consulting	Resources	Pharmaceuticals
Irish Republic	Utilities	Financial services	Consulting
Canada	Resources	Consulting	Real estate
United kingdom	Resources	Consulting	Financial services
New Zealand	Consulting	Financial services	Telecommunications

Figure 45.10   Highest salary levels for countries and industry sectors

INDUSTRY SECTOR

Maximising a project practitioner's earning potential will depend heavily upon the industry sector within which he or she works, combined with other factors like the location of the organisation and current economic and market conditions. Taking a deeper look at the PMI's annual salary survey for 2011 and the countries which saw the highest project management salaries, the top three industry sectors which commanded the highest salaries are highlighted in Figure 45.10.

ORGANISATIONAL FACTORS

Organisational factors that impact the accountabilities and responsibilities of a project practitioner also have a bearing on the salary levels. PMI's 2011 salary survey showed the differences in wage levels dependant on the project team size commanded by the project manager. In Hong Kong a project manager with fewer than five team members on average earns $60,000. With more than 20 team members this rises to $105,381, an increase of 76 per cent. By contrast, team size numbers have little or no bearing for Saudi Arabian, Nigerian and Mexican project practitioners.

The same PMI report also looked at the salary levels for project practitioners in relation to the size of project budget for which they were responsible. Nigerian project practitioners could see a 116 per cent increase in their salary levels when their managed budgets increased from less than $100K to over $10 million. Once again, the Saudi Arabian project managers could only expect a small increase of 10 per cent across the same bandings.

The Economy and the Marketplace

The basic rule of economics in relation to supply and demand is played out in the project management marketplace, with buyers' markets and sellers' markets. In expanding markets, where a shortage of experienced and qualified project managers exists, not only do we see a fight for talent amongst organisations – we also see project practitioners in a sellers' market. In a sellers' market (with more buyers than sellers) higher rates or remuneration can be commanded owing to the excess of demand over supply. In contracting markets, in its simplest terms, the reverse is true. More sellers are available (which causes an excess of supply, so that rates stabilise or are driven down).

Within the project management industry there are buyers' and sellers' markets in operation across all industries at any one time. With cutbacks in sectors such as construction, health care and defence since 2008, project managers with specific skills and experience in these areas have felt the effects of the buyers' market. With many more project managers being available for work with skills specific to these industries, the marketplace becomes flooded with available resources.

In a contracting economy, many organisations when considering remuneration packages or looking for new project management hires, perceive the market to be a buyers' market and set their rates and salaries accordingly. Often this means a reduction in rates on those offered previously when the marketplace was in balance.

Interestingly, since 2008 when the markets began to contract and the recession started in the UK, a true buyers' market has not fully emerged in the UK. Organisations have found it difficult to attract the right level of talented project managers to their businesses. Although there might be a surplus of project managers available, they are not necessarily the right ones for these organisations. Many highly talented and in-demand project managers have been retained by employers or have decided to sit tight for a while until the economy improves before seeking to move on to pastures new. This strangulation of supply, combined with the perception of high unemployment, has created a false buyers' market – where remuneration and rates offered by organisations are just not enticing enough or worth the risk of people changing jobs (people know that it could be a case of last in, first out if their new employer were to run into trouble).

Looking to the future of the project management industry, the supply and demand of qualified and experienced project practitioners will be affected further by changes in business and an increased focus on project management as an essential business skill.

In a 2010 PMI paper, *The Power of Project Management*, written to appeal to educational establishments interested in developing project management courses, emphasis is placed on the increasing need for project management skills within businesses coupled with the growing skills gap of those required to deliver projects. The lack of investment in bringing on new and emerging talent, together with the 'baby boomer' generation that is now approaching retirement age, has created a perfect storm. As demand continues to increase in the developed market along with the gathering pace in emerging economies, we shall soon see demand (and thus salaries) surge internationally.

References and Further Reading

Adams, J.S. (1963), 'Toward an understanding of inequity', *Journal of Abnormal and Social Psychology*, 67: 422–436.

Arras People (2006), *Project Management Benchmark Report*, 1st edn, Manchester: Arras People.

Arras People (2007), *Project Management Benchmark Report*, 2nd edn, Manchester: Arras People.

Arras People (2008), *Project Management Benchmark Report*, 3rd edn, Manchester: Arras People.

Arras People (2009), *Project Management Benchmark Report*, 4th edn, Manchester: Arras People.

Arras People (2010), *Project Management Benchmark Report*, 5th edn, Manchester: Arras People.

Arras People (2011), *Project Management Benchmark Report*, 6th edn, Manchester: Arras People.

Arras People (2012), *Project Management Benchmark Report*, 7th edn, Manchester: Arras People.

Baroudi, J. and Igbaria, M. (1993), 'An Examination of Gender Effects on the Career Success of Information Systems Employees', Center for Digital Economic Research, Stern School of Business, Working Paper IS-93-17.

Blau, P.M. (1964), *Exchange and Power in Social Life*, New York: John Wiley.

Brown, G., Gardner, J., Oswald, A. and Jing, Q. (2008), 'Does wage rank affect employees' wellbeing?', *Industrial Relations*, 47, 355–89.

Bryson, A. and Forth, J. (2006), 'The theory and practice of pay setting', Manpower Human Resources Lab Discussion Paper, 1, Manpower Human Resources Lab, London School of Economics and Political Science, London, UK.

Erez, M., Kleinbeck, U. and Thierry, H. (2001), 'The reflection theory of compensation', *Work Motivation in the Context of a Globalizing Economy*, Hillsdale, NJ: Lawrence Erlbaum Associates Inc.

Gardner, D.G. and Pierce, J.L. (2004), 'Self-esteem within the work and organizational context: A review of the organization-based self-esteem literature', *Journal of Management*, 30(5), 591–622.

Guasch, J.L. and Weiss, A. (1980), 'Adverse selection by markets and the advantage of being late', *The Quarterly Journal of Economics*, 94(3), 453–66.

Project Management Institute (2010), 'The Power of Project Management', White paper, Newtown Square, PA: Project Management Institute.

Project Management Institute (2011), *Project Management Salary Survey*, 7th edn, Newtown Square, PA: Project Management Institute.

Raduescu, C.O. and Heales, J. (2005), 'Incentives and their Effects on Information Systems Project', in D. Bartmann, F. Rajola, J. Kallinikos, D. Avison, R. Winter, P. Ein-Dor, J. Becker, F. Bodendorf and C. Weinhardt, *Proceedings of the 13th European Conference on Information Systems*, Regensburg, Germany, (471–83), 26–28 May 2005.

Shapiro, C. and Stiglitz, J.E. (1984), 'Equilibrium unemployment as a worker discipline device', *The American Economic Review*, 74(3) 433–44.

Vroom, V. (1964), *Work and Motivation*, New York: Wiley.

46 *Performance Appraisals*

DENNIS LOCK and LINDSAY SCOTT

Those of us who have worked overseas will know that in some cultures there is a tendency to lack patience with underperformers, so that dismissal and replacement is seen as the first choice, with little regard for employee appraisal, counselling and improvement. Clearly we do not need to discuss that 'hiring and firing' culture here, but instead should always be looking at ways of working together with our employees so that they can develop in their jobs, with employers and employees collaborating in a partnership for mutual benefit. Performance appraisals should be part of that development process. The most important aim of formal appraisals is to seek to improve the performance of every individual. By continually improving the performance of individuals, the collective performance of the organisation should also improve. In other words the human capital of the company will be enhanced.

Performance Appraisals: Formal and Informal

As managers, we should be observing the performance of our subordinates continually. So we come to learn the abilities, weaknesses and idiosyncrasies of those who report to us. In an organisational hierarchy this observation takes place, either consciously or unconsciously, at every level. It happens, between senior managers, supervisors and juniors. By offering advice and answering questions, every manager is helping subordinates and at the same time gaining some idea of their competence, which is a kind of informal appraisal. Also, in discussions about work and people between managers at different levels, the names of those who are performing particularly well will probably come up in discussion, as will also the identities of those who are seen to be underperforming.

So there is a continual informal element to all performance appraisals, and the motivation and effectiveness of all project staff should thus undergo natural enhancement in the course of the daily routine. For those who appear to be underperforming, the enlightened manager will attempt to discover the cause and find a remedy without waiting for a formal performance appraisal.

Much depends on the organisational span of control that each manager has. A manager with 20 people to control directly will clearly have less time for informal appraisals at the individual level than a manager with just two or three people as direct subordinates. So performance appraisal cannot really be separated from the question of organisation structure, and senior managers should always ensure that the span of control of individual managers is not too wide (not more than about five people to each group leader, supervisor or manager would be a good working number).

So in the course of these informal appraisals, managers can develop friendly relationships (but of course avoiding favouritism) that will encourage managers to bestow praise where deserved, and criticism where that is appropriate. At these informal levels, people should be encouraged to be open and not reticent about coming forward with problems that could affect their work and performance.

The formal performance appraisal can be a source of dread for managers and employees alike, especially where criticism has to be meted out. Whilst the forward-looking development aspects of the appraisal should be welcome, it is the review of past performance that sometimes causes difficulties or even resentment. In part this can be due to the process an organisation chooses to adopt for performance appraisals and the subsequent behaviours that it encourages amongst managers and employees.

Project managers may be responsible for conducting performance appraisals for employees who report directly to them in their team. However, in a matrix organisation project managers might not have line authority over everyone working on their project, so might be required to provide some feedback to functional managers (in other words, to those who *do* have line authority).

Of course, we must not forget that, as project managers, we shall probably also be subject to performance appraisals ourselves.

Types of Performance Appraisals

Performance *appraisals* are part of the wider remit of performance *management*. Performance management takes place all the time (whether consciously or not) when a manager allocates tasks and then sets out to ensure that they are performed as required. Performance management is more 'of the moment', seeking to get results. Performance appraisals have a retrospective element, looking back on what has (or has not) been achieved by personal effort, usually with the goal of improving performance for the future.

In this chapter we are concerned with appraisals that take place in a structured way, throughout all or part of the hierarchy. They are usually conducted with the specific aim of improving each person's general performance. Here is a short selection of some well-established and more recent methods:

- Management by Objectives (MbO). This system was promoted by UK management consultants Urwick Orr in the 1960s and 1970s. A manager and employee agree specific objectives and performance is reviewed periodically based on the success or failure to meet those objectives.
- 360 degree, multi-sourced feedback, gained anonymously from an employee's 'circle of influence' (Edwards and Ewen, 1996). Feedback will be received from an employee's subordinates, peers, managers, customers and suppliers.
- Forced ranking. Managers make comparisons between employees and rank them from best to worst performers. This is often deemed to be a controversial approach (Grote, 2005).
- Peer review/crowdsourced or peer-to-peer unsolicited recognition and feedback (Mosley, 2012). This taps into the social networking generation, with the ability to

solicit real-time feedback or praise from colleagues (rather than the retrospective feedback which is characteristic of other appraisal methods).

Appraisal Frequency

Most companies will conduct periodical performance reviews, with the interviews being arranged at all manager/subordinate interface levels in the hierarchy. Such reviews are often held annually and they might be associated with salary reviews (whether or not that is acknowledged). Many companies will claim that performance reviews have no connection with annual salary reviews. However, any person undergoing a performance appraisal will inevitably think that the results will affect their eventual salary progression. If possible, performance appraisals *should* be kept separate from salary reviews (Armstrong, 2010).

Some companies conduct their performance appraisals annually. More frequent appraisals are sometimes appropriate, for example when:

- the company is undertaking a programme of MbO;
- when the performance of an individual has been criticised for being below the standard expected, or below that of other members of the team, so that the individual has been asked to demonstrate some improvement over a short period.

MbO programmes are a special case, where specific, quantified targets are set and mutually agreed between staff at each management interface level. In those cases three-monthly intervals are often appropriate, because that interval allows each person to perform and be measured against the mutually agreed specific objectives. Manager and subordinate can then agree and set new objectives for the forthcoming period, so that the cycle repeats itself. Such objectives should always be quantifiable, and should contribute either to the overall project or corporate objectives. Then the individual, the job and the company can all potentially benefit collectively.

MbO-driven performance appraisals have been criticised and mooted as out-of-date for twenty-first-century businesses. Coens and Jenkins (2000) outline the failures of MbO as a motivator for employees, with many organisations dropping MbO in the 1990s but failing to drop performance appraisals with it. Performance appraisals, instead of motivating people, drive feelings of distrust amongst employees. Coens and Jenkins even go as far as to say, 'while performance appraisals may have been intended to weed out poor performers they actually insulted everyone across the board'.

When specifically working within a project environment, performance ratings and feedback need to be collected continually, because performance appraisal life cycles and many project life cycles do not run together in synchronisation (Scott and Einstein, 2001). Within the course of a year employees could have been working on multiple projects with multiple teams. The project manager often logs feedback on her/his project team as part of the project closure process in readiness for requests from functional managers when it is time to schedule performance appraisals. Crowdsourced feedback seems ideally suited for the project environment, with team members encouraged to recognise and highlight good work by their peers throughout the project life cycle.

Preparation and Planning

With a traditional appraisal approach, where feedback is solicited before an appraisal meeting with an employee, prior planning has to take place. It is considered good practice to allow an employee to see feedback and a partially completed performance appraisal form before formally meeting for the review. Armstrong (2010) believes that to make a review meeting more productive and less stressful for an employee, sharing feedback beforehand allows them to take on board the feedback they have received. The employee has time to reflect and to prepare their own responses in a considered manner, rather than feeling they have been put on the spot.

THE MEETING TIME AND PLACE

The manager should strive to create a cooperative atmosphere for the review, where the employee is put at ease and encouraged to talk freely.

If the manager's office has a round table with chairs, that can be used. Otherwise a meeting room with those facilities should be reserved. The room should be free from interruptions, either from people in person or from telephones. If the manager is using a pro forma (such as that shown in Figure 46.1) then the employee should be able to watch the entries being made so that there is no hidden agenda.

A busy manager will want to schedule appraisal sessions, allocating people to set times and dates. However, people should be asked if those times and dates will be convenient and, where reasonable, people should be allowed to choose alternative times. After all, even junior employees have their work commitments when interruption might be inconvenient or even delay a vital project task. If the time and date is mutually agreed, that approach will help to set the scene for openness and cooperation.

STRUCTURE

It is best if performance appraisals can be structured, with the same pattern applied as far as possible for all staff. It is often feasible, and should be attempted, to assess each person in terms of the contribution they are making to the progress of the current project, past project work within the review period and also over the longer term to the prosperity of the company. Clearly this company aspect will assume more relevance for more senior people in the organisation.

Performance appraisals are usually conducted on a one-to-one basis, with no one else present. However, in some cases it could be appropriate to have a member from HR present.

A structured appraisal will usually begin with the manager greeting the subordinate with a handshake and a friendly smile. Then it is important to let the employee have his/her say about any issues that they might have about any aspect of the company or the work environment. It is recommended that managers use 'active listening' and should not be talking for more than 25 per cent of the time (Arthur, 2007). Any feedback already relayed before the review meeting can obviously be discussed now. One aspect of this feedback could be to stimulate a 'stop, start, continue' conversation. In other words, which areas of work should the employee stop doing, start doing and continue doing?

Now the employee has the opportunity to tell the manager of any special personal achievements that they think deserve praise or recognition. Managers might sometimes be pleasantly surprised at what has been achieved. Hidden talents of the employees could

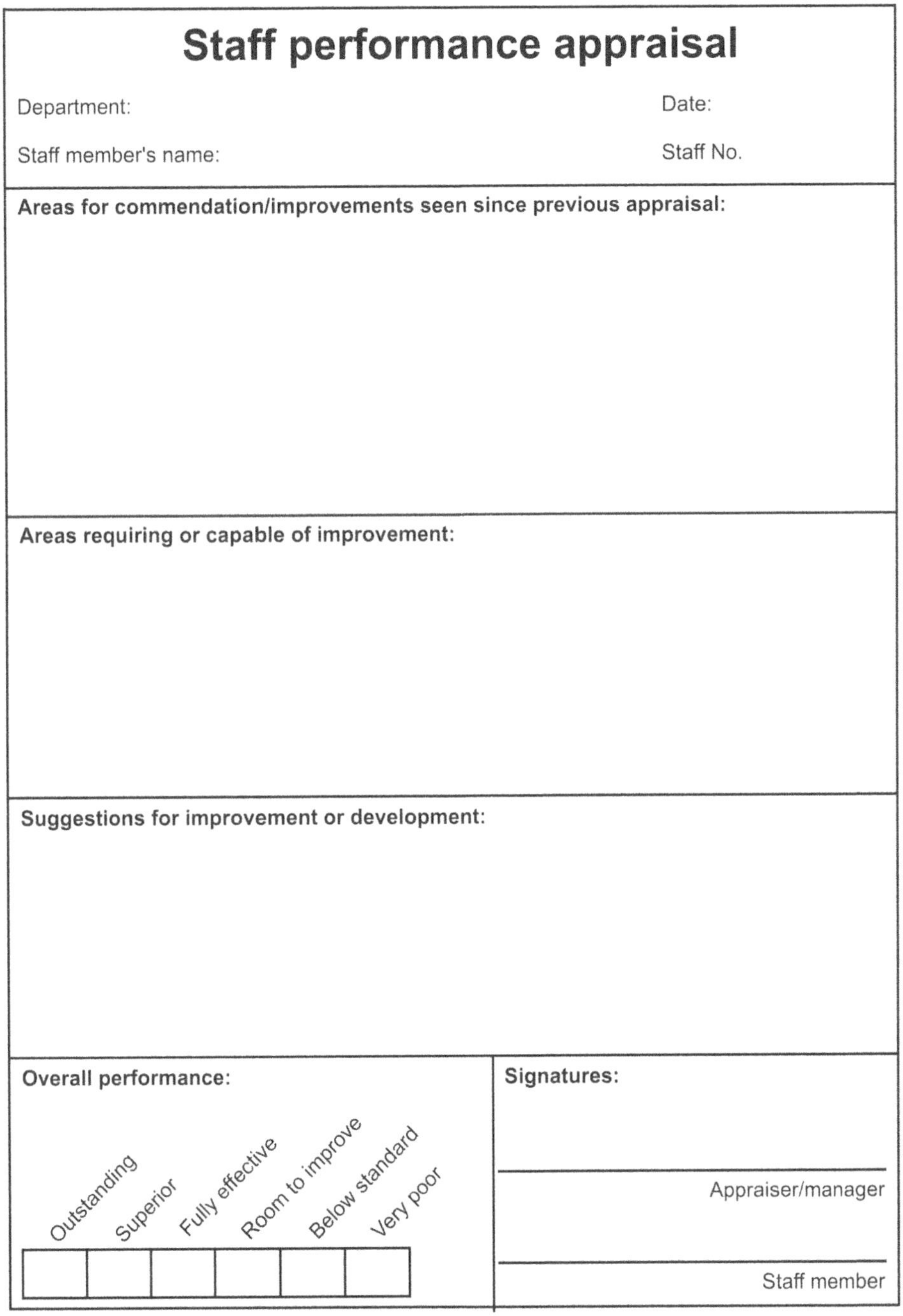

Staff performance appraisal

Department: Date:

Staff member's name: Staff No.

Areas for commendation/improvements seen since previous appraisal:

Areas requiring or capable of improvement:

Suggestions for improvement or development:

Overall performance: **Signatures:**

Outstanding	Superior	Fully effective	Room to improve	Below standard	Very poor

_____
                                   Appraiser/manager

_____
                                      Staff member

Figure 46.1 Combined performance appraisal checklist and record

Effect	Description
Halo	Allowing an employee's top attribute to colour the whole review.
Horns	Letting one disagreeable quality influence opinion.
Sunflower	Giving your team better scores to make you look like a better leader.
Leniency/harshness	Being too tolerant or too severe.
Central tendency	To avoid favouritism, everyone receives middling scores.
Sugar-coating	Not documenting the full scope of concerns raised.
Recency	Only considering recent failures or accomplishments.
Personal bias	Giving a good review to people who are most like you.
Attribution bias	Ascribing good work to factors outside the employee's control but blaming them unfairly for poor results.

Figure 46.2 Common errors in performance reviews identified by Armstrong (2010)

be revealed that could otherwise have gone unremarked. The employee's enthusiasm and motivation should shine through at this stage.

One attribute managers should also be wary of is 'overconfidence bias'. Many of us have a tendency to think we are better than we actually are. Feedback which supports accomplishments should be sought out.

One unpleasant task of the manager is to point out shortcomings or actual mistakes. Genuine mistakes should never be punished, provided that the culprit recognises the shortcoming and is willing where practicable to take steps to correct poor performance and prevent a recurrence. Everyone should be allowed at least one mistake provided there was underlying good intent. But a succession of careless mistakes is different and must clearly be dealt with.

It is useful for the manager to have a checklist in the shape of a pro forma, so that every individual being appraised can to some extent be assessed using the same parameters. Such a checklist will help to promote even-handedness as well as saving the busy manager's time. A suggestion for such a pro forma is given in Figure 46.1.

Apart from job performance, attributes such as punctuality, ability to cooperate with colleagues, motivation, enthusiasm, personal drive and ambition and loyalty to the organisation can all be assessed. Armstrong (2010) highlights common mistakes that managers make during performance reviews, specifically in relation to the judgements that are made either from feedback or the manager's own perceptions of the employee. These are summarised in Figure 46.2.

A performance review gives the opportunity for goal-setting and discovering individual development needs. Suggestions for improving performance should be followed up in a constructive way. That could lead to the manager recommending coaching, mentoring, training or some other form of skills development. The employee might also have views about possible further training or development that would require a contribution of some kind from the company. If necessary a special supplementary performance review meeting can be held after an appropriate interval for investigation.

It is important that the person being appraised leaves the meeting with a positive outlook, encouraged by the manager. A session where nothing but blame and criticism is heaped upon an individual will have them leaving the meeting not only feeling downhearted or even angry, but sharing those demotivating thoughts with colleagues. So an appraisal meeting should always be ended on a positive note.

Special Circumstances for Project Managers in Performance Reviews

Project managers can be somewhat special when their performance is up for review because they often have many objectives to fulfil in their roles within and beyond the organisation. A project manager interacts with many different colleagues, stakeholders and customers. That creates multiple potential feedback sources. Also, a project manager might have been responsible for several projects during a review period, and there could have been a mix of successes and failures among them.

Those reviewing the performance of project managers have to ensure that they are assessed not only on their *project* objectives and metrics (factors such as schedule, budget and project quality) but also on their performance as managers of people. The communication and HR management aspects of a project manager's role are deemed by some to be the most important metrics when assessing performance (Marius, 2009), ranking above areas such as cost, risk and time management. Research by Chen and Lee (2007) reinforces the view that leadership has special significance (revealing the capability of making decisions and giving or seeking information as most important leadership attributes for project managers).

A project manager's performance appraisal should preferably also include activities that he/she performs outside the immediate or current project environment. Examples are improving good general practice in project management for the good of the organisation, and work carried out in coaching and mentoring.

Project managers often have to rely on many people outside their direct control for success and they have no chance of checking every detail of the work performed. For example, the project manager who shipped two prefabricated, fully equipped operating theatres for installation in a hospital in far away Sweden could not be blamed for the fiasco that erupted when, in the presence of the local press and civic dignitaries it was discovered that main structural frames would not fit together because the factory (a department well outside the project manager's control) had shipped the wrong components.

References and Further Reading

Armstrong, S. (2010), *The Essential Performance Review Handbook*, Franklin Lakes, NJ: The Career Press.

Arthur, D. (2007), *The First-Time Manager's Guide to Performance Appraisals*, New York: AMACOM.

Coens, T. and Jenkins, M. (2000), *Abolishing Performance Appraisals*, San Francisco, CA: Berrett-Koehler.

Edwards, M.R. and Ewen, A.J. (1996), *360 Degree Feedback: The Powerful New Model for Employee Assessment and Performance Improvement*, New York: AMACOM.

Grote, D. (2005), *Forced Ranking: Making Performance Management Work*, Boston, MA: Harvard Business Review Press.

Marius, T.C. (2009), *The Performance of a Project Manager*, Vol. 8, University Iasi: Faculty of Economics and Business Administration.

Mosley, E. (2012), 'Crowdsource your performance reviews', *Harvard Business Review*, 15 June. Available at: http://blogs.hbr.org/cs/2012/06/crowdsource_your_performance_r.html [accessed 1 September 2012].

Scott, S.G. and Einstein, W.O. (2001), 'Strategic performance appraisal in team based organizations: One size does not fit all', *Academy of Management Executive*, 15(2), 107.

Sherman Garr, S. (2011), *Performance Management Framework – Evolving Performance Management to Fit the Modern Workforce*, Oakland, CA: Bersin & Associates.

Sheu Hua Chen, S.H. and Lee, H.T. (2007), 'Performance evaluation model for project managers using managerial practices', *International Journal of Project Management*, 25(6), 543–51.

47 *Employment Termination: Letting People Go*

LINDSAY SCOTT

The old concept of a 'job for life' is no longer applicable in today's corporate world. Job security is threatened increasingly by factors such as the economy; how the economy affects the particular industry sector and organisation; the skill level of the individual worker and whether those skills are in demand by the marketplace. For the project manager, job security, one could argue, is automatically decreased owing to the very nature of projects – temporary, transient and time-bound. A project manager's current job may not be for life but project management skills and good project managers remain in demand across multiple sectors.

Introduction

In this chapter I shall consider those times when termination is indicated for a project manager or other project worker for one of the following reasons:

1. unacceptable performance;
2. gross misconduct;
3. redundancy;
4. constructive dismissal;
5. unfair dismissal;
6. discrimination.

The Individual's Reaction to Being Told

Although some reasons for employment termination are easily understood, when an individual receives the news that they are going to lose their job a whole range of emotions and feelings start. The initial news is just the beginning. In some cases, employment termination is seen as a turning point for a project manager – the opportunity to find a new and exciting challenge.

In other cases, probably in most cases, the news is not welcomed at all and for those individuals it has been likened to the grieving process following the death of a loved one. The psychiatrist Elisabeth Kübler-Ross, who was particularly interested in 'near death' studies, proposed a five-stage cycle in her book *On Death and Dying* (Kübler-Ross, 1969).

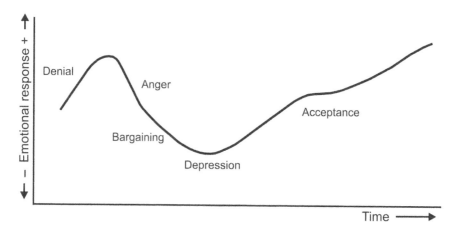

Figure 47.1 The five steps of grief according to the Kübler-Ross model

Her model (Figure 47.1) has subsequently been used in relation to job loss. It charts the five stages from the initial moment of job loss:

1. Denial: believing that the organisation might change its mind, or might have mixed the person's name up with someone else's. In this stage the individual experiences shock and might also withdraw from normal situations (home life and so forth);
2. Anger: the person becomes outraged at the organisation and how they have been treated – even targeting individuals within the organisation. Anger could also spill over to their personal life;
3. Bargaining: the individual starts to make bargains with themselves (and even with the organisation). This period is focused on the past and is full of 'what-ifs', 'if-onlys' and self-blame. 'If only I was better at my job ...';
4. Depression: this stage in the cycle moves to the present day where acute feelings such as despair, uselessness or worthlessness surface;
5. Acceptance: accepting the loss, being more hopeful, ready to accept that a change has occurred that will give new opportunities.

The total cycle of the model and time at each stage can vary in length from individual to individual. When conducting unemployment support services for project managers in the UK in 2009–2010, I saw individuals at different parts of this process. Some were still very angry with their previous employers some six months later whilst others were ready to move on, excited at the prospect of finding new opportunities. The same cycle and impact on an individual can occur regardless of the situation or circumstance in which an employee loses their job.

Unacceptable Performance

All project managers will undoubtedly experience performance issues with project team members at some points in their careers. Some project managers might experience difficulties in their own careers that will be considered as unacceptable performance, leading to dismissal from the organisation. Sandler and Keefe (2007) stated that employees often have performance issues in the following nine critical areas:

1. showing up for work on time prepared to work;
2. not completing tasks and goals on time, missing deadlines;
3. disorganised and inefficient work;
4. building and maintaining skills;
5. information security – misuse of company data;
6. harassment;
7. legal matters – including criminal acts, dishonesty and so on;
8. drug or alcohol abuse;
9. discrimination.

Experienced project managers are skilled at dealing with poor performance (most of which fall into categories 1–4 above), taking action to ensure the rest of the team are not affected and the project remains on course to deliver successfully. An informal chat with the individual might be all it takes to get things back on track. Reassessing the resource requirement and the skill set of the individual with a view to providing additional training or support might be required. When time is crucial and opportunities for training are scarce, mentoring or peer pairing might provide a solution.

When the underperformance is serious enough and becomes wholly unacceptable, not just within the project but also for the organisation, a more formal approach is necessary. Dealing with this level of unacceptable performance requires additional support for the project manager from experienced HRM or legal professionals. Project managers should always inform those departments and take their advice.

Procedures for dismissing an individual from an organisation will depend on the employment laws where the organisation operates. For instance, within the UK the Employment Act 2002 sets out disciplinary and grievance procedures (ACAS, 2003), which are used by employers and workers. The procedures cover dismissals arising from unacceptable performance and misconduct. The project manager may be involved in this process owing to his/her close working relationship with a team member. This involvement might include presence at formal meetings, where documented evidence will be required. Alternatively the project manager might be required to work closely with the nominated manager without attending meetings. The process for dealing with unacceptable performance follows a prescribed sequence of steps:

1. *Informal action*: discuss the performance shortcomings with the team member and agree corrective courses of action.
2. *Written warning*: if performance does not improve to acceptable requirements, send the employee a letter defining the underperformance (what the employee has done and why it is unacceptable). Then proceed to the next step.
3. *Hold a meeting*: arrange a meeting with the employee and the appropriate manager(s). The employee has the right to be accompanied at the meeting and to receive in advance any documentation that will be used in the meeting. This meeting allows all the evidence to be shared and gives the employee the opportunity to answer the case.
4. *Actions after the meeting*: the employer decides whether further disciplinary action is necessary. Where no further action is necessary the employee is informed of the

outcome. If further action is necessary, it is considered best practice to progress to the next step 'short-term objectives'.

5.   *Short-term objectives*: now the process has become formal. Short-term objectives are a written instruction which sets out the following:
   -   the performance issue;
   -   the improvement required;
   -   the time when the improvement is required by;
   -   the date when the outcomes will be reviewed and also what support the employer will give during this period. The employee must be made aware that this is the first stage of a formal procedure and that failure to comply could result in a final warning and dismissal. If improvements are made from this first formal action, notes are maintained on the employee's record for a specific period of time (for example, six months) and performance is monitored and reviewed during that time.

6.   *Final written warning*: if performance does not improve following a period of short-term objectives, the employee is issued with a final written warning (following a further meeting to discuss the lack of progress so far). The letter gives the employee one final chance to improve and warns that if improvements are not made the next stage will be dismissal. If improvements are made, the warning letter remains on the employee's record for a set period (for example, 12 months) for monitoring and review.

7.   *Dismissal*: Other options are available before dismissal from the organisation is considered. These include demotion, transfer or reduction in seniority/pay. If no other option is to be considered the employee is informed by letter, stating the reasons for dismissal, the date of employment termination, details about the notice period and also rights to appeal.

This comprehensive process within UK law is not the standard for other countries. For instance, in most US states the 'employment-at-will doctrine allows for the dismissal of workers for any reason, or for no reason at all' (Leviter and Muller, 2007) but there is protection against termination due to discrimination.

   Owing to the nature of projects and the need for temporary resources on a project team, the project manager has some degree of flexibility when it comes to dealing with unacceptable performance. Contract and temporary staff can be hired – and fired – quickly and without the need for protracted procedures to be followed. There will normally be a notice period that must be honoured (paid in lieu) but the underperforming contract employee can be removed and dismissed from the project that very day.

CASE EXAMPLE NO. 1

Dismissals based on unacceptable performance can be a long and time-consuming process for managers. RJR manages a team of six in a large IT organisation in the UK. He noticed that the level of output for one member of the team (let's call him Jason) seemed to be dropping. Jason performed his tasks, but did so in a lacklustre and mediocre way. Jason seemed to 'not be firing on all cylinders'. Fortnightly one-to-one meetings were regularly held, so RJR set about preparing for the next informal conversation with Jason. He wanted to understand if there were any underlying issues, perhaps outside work, that might be affecting his work.

The meeting started with RJR telling Jason what had been noticed about his performance, going on to ask if there was anything he would like to talk about. The response was immediately defensive, Jason telling RJR to mind his own business. The team member was adamant that there was nothing to discuss. He felt victimised and asked RJR to 'prove it'.

For a relatively new manager, preparing for conversations like this can be difficult. Working through likely scenarios and how the discussion will go can only prepare you so far. Sometimes the responses can come as a total surprise (to both the employee and the manager!). In this case RJR decided to let the situation cool, ended the meeting and set another for two days' time.

RJR sought advice from HRM. He used that department to learn more about the policy for performance management issues and used his own manager as a sounding board to provide further advice on carrying out the next steps.

The second meeting was still an 'informal meeting'. This time RJR clearly set out the performance issues and calmly addressed the accusations of victimisation by providing clear evidence of the issues. It also became very clear that the employee's negative attitude also had to be addressed. The outcome was an 'informal warning' and the instigation of a six-week period of performance management. This performance management process included giving Jason some reasonable objectives. So some tasks were set with time estimates, and RJR monitored the employee as well as seeking feedback from other colleagues on how Jason was doing.

Jason's grievances were public knowledge and the team's initial reaction was to defend their colleague against RJR and the accusations. On reflection, RJR admits that being the manager of a team can be a lonely place when you have to make difficult decisions. Neglecting to take direct action against underperformance makes the situation far worse for everyone in the long run.

A performance review was scheduled after the six-week performance management period. This review was carried out by RJR and a senior manager. It had a formal agenda, starting with the evidence laid out of the continued performance and attitude issues. Jason was asked to respond but he chose to explode with anger and verbally abuse both managers. Clearly the outcomes were becoming more extreme. The review outcome was the first official warning in the form of a letter. Jason was given a further eight weeks of monitoring and review, with the objective that there had to be tangible and sustained improvements during that time.

Throughout the process, RJR's emotions included:

- doubt: as a manager did I get my facts right before approaching Jason to talk about performance issues?
- shock: that the reaction from the employee could be so extreme;
- annoyance: that the process was distracting, and affecting the rest of the team;
- frustration: the process was taking so long.

In this case the performance management process for the employee was brought to a swift end when the organisation announced there would be redundancies across the organisation. The team had to be reduced by one member. RJR was advised to take the most obvious option and select the underperforming team member.

> Looking back at that time RJR, reflected that the remaining team (although upset that Jason had been given a redundancy package) were happy to get on with the tasks in hand and improved their performance levels.

Gross Misconduct

Employment termination for gross misconduct can be a swift and decisive end to an employee's career within the organisation. Acts of gross misconduct are serious breaches of an employment contract and can include:

- fraud;
- dishonesty;
- acts of violence;
- impropriety or immoral conduct detrimental to, and inconsistent with, the organisation's business;
- unauthorised possession of company property or unauthorised use of company stationery;
- conduct of a criminal, dishonest or immoral nature inside or outside working hours which is detrimental to and inconsistent with the company's business affairs;
- disorderly conduct which is detrimental to and inconsistent with the company business;
- use of abusive or threatening language;
- refusal to obey a reasonable instruction from a superior;
- duplication of or unauthorised possession of keys or security cards or similar material belonging to the company;
- being under the influence of drugs (other than medically prescribed drugs) or alcohol during working hours or overtime hours or when otherwise engaged on company business;
- falsification of any documents or material, including misleading completion of the company's self-certification form;
- causing deliberate damage to any property belonging to the company or any employee of the company;
- disclosure of confidential information to an unauthorised party;
- unauthorised, illegal or fraudulent use of software and the company's IT systems;
- sexual or racial harassment of colleagues.

Part of all project managers' responsibilities to themselves and to their team members is to ensure that their working environment is safe, free from hazards and in compliance with all national and local laws. When a project manager has team members who have a blatant disregard for their colleagues, company property, or even for themselves, swift action needs to be taken.

In the UK, the disciplinary and grievance procedures already mentioned in this chapter are also used for dismissal by gross misconduct. The process recommends that once an employer considers an employee to be guilty of gross misconduct there should be immediate short-term suspension from the organisation until the facts are established. It is important that the employee is aware that this step is not considered to be disciplinary action at this stage. Best practice indicates that the employee should be given a disciplinary meeting in order to state their case. Following this meeting, if the decision is made to uphold the gross misconduct claim the employee can be dismissed at once.

Disciplinary and grievance procedures are often noted in the contract of employment that each individual signs when starting employment.

Individual organisations may have their own approaches to dealing with gross misconduct dismissals. These can include dismissal without pay and other claims, to such things as outstanding holiday allowance.

CASE EXAMPLE NO. 2

Project managers leading teams of diverse individuals clearly have to be ever watchful of how the working relationships form and develop between team members. RAB is a manager of IT projects in Mexico. In a large system development project made up of multiple work-streams, he was responsible for the team of programmers. This team comprised a small pool of junior men and women working alongside a male senior programmer.

A few weeks later RAB was told that the women were unhappy with the senior programmer. RAB interviewed the women and they complained that they had been subjected to sexually expletive language and sexual advances, with the additional menace of being told not to say anything or they would lose their jobs. RAB was unsure about the legal implications of the situation and was hesitant about the next steps without taking formal advice. He spoke directly to his line manager and then consulted the HRM department.

Once the process for dealing with such a complaint was clear, RAB arranged a meeting with the senior programmer. The facts were clearly explained, the legal implications conveyed and the offender was informed of the final decision to be taken – which was instant dismissal. The programmer was given an opportunity to clarify his story but he decided to remain silent. RAB brought the meeting to a close and referred the case and all his paperwork to the HRM department to complete the process.

RAB then had to inform the remaining team that the programmer had been withdrawn from the project. He chose not to elaborate beyond 'there had been complaints' in order to keep the team focused and motivated. Upon reflection, RAB felt disappointed that he had not been aware of the problem until it had started to affect the project. He learned from that experience and now makes sure that he has regular meetings with the entire project team to observe how interpersonal relationships develop. He has also become more responsive to the small signals that arise in casual conversations.

CASE EXAMPLE NO. 3

Not many project managers would expect their day-to-day work to include uncovering criminal activity. WCS is a senior project manager overseeing construction projects in Africa. Two members of one of his project teams found that working on a construction site presented 'opportunities' which proved to be too tempting. As a result materials began going missing from the site. Also there was a phantom worker on the payroll who did not exist.

WCS was able to pick up these discrepancies by studying the weekly materials requirements estimates and from financial reporting on the payroll. Perhaps unorthodox in his approach, WCS turned detective and planted a casual worker among the team, who was able to confirm his fears. The two culprits were identified and promptly dismissed. In addition, the criminal acts (theft and fraud) were deemed serious enough to notify the police. The miscreants were subsequently arrested and charged. The court awarded the company restitution.

WCS maintains that it was the effective monitoring and evaluation procedures in his project that allowed him to spot and locate the discrepancies.

Redundancy

I have to begin this section with a note on the meaning of redundancy. Although a person might talk about having been made redundant, to be precise it is the job that has become redundant, not the individual. If an individual can be persuaded to believe this, some of the damage to his/her self-esteem can be avoided.

Dismissal through redundancy can take many different forms. In project management it could mean the redundancy of one employee or all the project team. In extreme cases it can mean the loss of all jobs when a company is closed down (for whatever reason).

National and local laws in relation to redundancies differ considerably. Within the UK, for example, the government has to be informed if more than 20 people will be made redundant within a 90-day period (ACAS, 2010). Within the US there is no specific law in place to cover redundancies and there are no requirements to pay severance pay (US Department of Labor, 2011). In Australia (Australian Government Ombudsman, 2010) redundancy pay applies to employees who have completed one or more years of service.

Regardless of individual laws it is agreed that redundancies within an organisation are periods of change that produce great stress and anxiety. The key to working through this period as painlessly as possible is, as in so many other things, good communication.

Redundancy announcements from the organisation are usually followed by a consultation phase (dependent on national and local laws). The consultation phase is designed to bring together employers and employees to discuss the issues facing the organisation and the possibility of offering alternative solutions to redundancies. Communication between the parties can go some way to placating the fear and stress that some employees feel on hearing that they could lose their jobs. The consultation period will also include discussions about the amount of redundancy payment available for those who will be dismissed.

When the consultation period is over, if there is no alternative to redundancies the organisation makes the decision to proceed. The options include compulsory redundancy or voluntary redundancy.

COMPULSORY REDUNDANCY

Compulsory redundancies are those where the organisation decides which employees will face redundancy and ultimately leave the organisation. There is a procedure to be followed that is intended to ensure openness and fairness. Clearly the selection process (deciding who should go and who should stay) is important. In the UK the selection process (ACAS, 2010) includes as basic criteria:

- skills and experiences;
- standards of work;
- attendance and disciplinary records.

ACAS recommends that flexibility, adaptability and an employee's approach to work should also be included in these criteria.

A company that has to reduce its number of project managers can be expected to prefer keeping its most successful managers. The redundancy selection criteria could include:

- project management skill levels (through competency assessments or skills-gap analysis);
- training and accreditations;
- previous success stories and track record;
- previous performance reviews;
- feedback from line managers, peers and customers;
- contributions to the profession, or advancement of project management in the organisation.

Each of these selection criteria has to be applied fairly to everyone who has the same role and level of seniority. Thus (for example) project managers should not be compared with programme managers; nor should junior project managers be compared with more senior project managers.

VOLUNTARY REDUNDANCY

For some organisations, the consultation period outcome may be the decision to move forward with voluntary redundancies. The organisation gives employees the choice to take redundancy based on all the information provided during the consultation phase. This route is more favourable for organisations in the sense that it can be less demoralising on staff than enforcing compulsory redundancies. Employees might also be incentivised to consider the option when employers produce a more favourable redundancy package for volunteers.

Voluntary redundancies can be counterproductive because they can result in an organisation losing their most experienced staff. Worse, those staff will tend to have the highest severance packages owing to their seniority and length of service. To manage that issue, an organisation will draw up a list of all those who volunteered for redundancy, but makes its own choices from the list. This in turn presents further issues when those volunteers who were not selected are left feeling disgruntled or bitter about the decision.

Redundancies never feel like a win-win situation. For those employees facing dismissal through compulsory redundancy, the experience can be a long and stressful time. Some organisations take steps to minimise distress and disruption by offering 'outplacement services' which are designed to help the employee mentally and physically prepare for leaving the organisation. These services offer counselling and coaching alongside practical considerations like CV writing and how to apply for new jobs.

The redundancy period not only affects those selected or at risk from dismissal, but also those employees who remain and consider themselves to be. Noer (1993) introduced the term 'survivor syndrome' which proposes that those employees who survive a redundancy period are often worse off than those who leave. Employees facing redundancy are offered severance packages, relocation to other offices, outplacement support and counselling whilst the remaining employees receive little or no support.

A further study from Cranfield University, UK (Sahdev and Vinnicombe, 1998) showed that the remaining employees felt 'cheated of an opportunity to start a new career or pursue other interests' when thinking about the employees who had left with severance packages. The remaining employees also felt 'they had lost the old, original organisation they had joined and hence there was a sense of isolation and low morale; this was accompanied by increase in workload and uncertainty'.

CASE EXAMPLE NO. 4

Project managers can be asked to provide information on team members during a redundancy period. This is logical because through past project work each project manager should have a good grasp of the skills and experience levels of their team members. Managing a team through a redundancy period can be tough enough when morale is taking a battering but a project manager is also at risk.

BRD worked as a project manager on IT systems implementation projects in the UK. He found that project team redundancy announcements were only the beginning of a long process that ended with his own redundancy.

One of the organisation's largest customers was experiencing financial difficulties which led to a current project being axed at its delivery stage. BRD's project team was working on a final phase for additional functionality alongside a third party. Following the decision to end the project, the project team was notified that there were to be compulsory redundancies.

There were no options for the project team to be deployed elsewhere within the organisation although BRD was informed that his role would be safe for another 12 months. BRD continued to manage the team as the project was winding down.

There were mixed emotions in the team. Some felt anger, others despair and in some cases there was a real sense of wanting to do something proactive like finding out if there were positions available with their third-party supplier. Further anguish was felt by the team in the way the HRM department was handling the process. There was deemed to be a lack of consultation with employees. The consensus formed that, by making piecemeal redundancies, the organisation was avoiding the formal declaration that they were duty bound to report to the UK government when more than 20 people are made redundant at any one time.

Some errors in the consultation process meant that the HRM department had to backtrack quickly on their notification to BRD that his position was safe. He received the call one morning, four weeks after the initial announcements, that he too would be terminated in three months.

CASE EXAMPLE NO. 5

Compulsory redundancies are usually the only option when an organisation is facing financial ruin (one exception being a company rescue by merger or takeover). In the short term a project manager faces day-to-day battles as the project team continues to reduce in size. In the longer term it might be considered better to walk away from the organisation before experiencing the bitter end.

FLR is an IT project manager in software development in the US. His account of employment in the final months of an organisation highlights how extreme some environments can be and just how some employees cope when faced with redundancy. Business was affected when the one major customer experienced financial difficulties. All current and future spending was frozen at once, which had an immediate impact on FLR's organisation. Around 75 per cent of revenues had been coming from this single, failed customer.

Panic ensued, with the organisation trying to create new markets and land new business. When business continued to fail, senior management championed new development, looking for the next big revenue generator, rather than focusing on retaining the customers they still had.

Things went from bad to worse. Creditors were turning up at the office or telephoning demanding to be paid; lawsuits were threatened. Employees of course were aware of the difficulties the company was facing but there was no communication from management. That left the employees to fill in the information gaps. There had been previous lay-offs in the company and many employees were used to that happening. This time employees were guessing what the problems were, even sharing a joke or two about it. FLR described the atmosphere as being 'like a pressure cooker' with employees' inappropriate behaviour such as shouting and yelling from senior managers. Employees were pushed to work harder under extreme time constraints. Worried for their jobs if they didn't comply, they were working 12-hour days and weekends.

When the redundancies were finally due to be announced, the HR director told FLR the names of those chosen for redundancy. FLR rounded up the selected employees in a conference room away from other employees. The HR director then called the room and, through a loudspeaker telephone delivered the stark announcement 'Everyone in this room is no longer employed by the company. Your jobs have been eliminated. If you have any further questions, call me'.

FLR said, 'We put those people through the ringer, making them sacrifice their families and personal welfare, after allowing them to think there was some chance their efforts might help them keep their jobs'.

FLR quit that organisation a few weeks later, when it became apparent that more redundancies would happen and yet the remaining employees were expected to carry on delivering projects with just skeleton resources. FLR reflected that remaining within the organisation after the redundancies carried all the hallmarks of the 'survivor syndrome' and he was just relieved to get out and move on. FLR is now working in an environment that he describes as 'more sane'.

CASE EXAMPLE NO. 6

The threat of redundancy can be an emotional time not just for you but also for your loved ones, it can seem like the end of the world; but it also can be seen as a great opportunity that kicks you into doing something that you had previously only ever imagined or talked about.

VAL was a project manager within a worldwide manufacturing organisation who opted for voluntary redundancy after 10 years within the company. The organisation had strategically planned for downsizing its workforce some years before with the proviso that the numbers would be reduced naturally through retirements, hiring freezes and outsourcing. But a few years later they began making much larger redundancies than planned and closed some manufacturing plants.

The changes were swift. The 45-strong project management team was informed that there would be only 20 vacancies available in the new structure. VAL found himself at a real career crossroad. Taking the decision to accept the voluntary redundancy option came after much reflection about not only what did he want next in his career but also thinking about the realities of staying with the company. 'Organisationally there were a number of issues that I had been debating over the past few years that the restructuring forced me into addressing'. The company culture had changed over the years and there were doubts about continuing support for the project management function. Project management roles had started to be outsourced and there was no obvious career path for project management following the restructuring. VAL sensed that further redundancies would follow as the trend continued towards outsourcing as a strategy to deal with projects.

The voluntary redundancy process was straightforward. The employees were able to elect a representative who provided an influential role in negotiating terms for areas such as a training budget. In addition to the usual outplacement services of CV writing and interview preparation courses there were individual training funds which could be used for project management courses and accreditations.

VAL's redundancy package was generous giving him enough time to take personal time out yet there were further concerns that he needed to make clear in his mind. Would he go back into a permanent role or should he seek some contract work? Would his project management experience to date be considered as 'proper project management' that matched what the marketplace was looking for? How much could he earn? What did he need to be marketable?

Although I enjoyed the time out I had I do not realise that there is a cost. The longer you are out of the work loop, the more your confidence about eventually finding a job shrinks and your paranoia about what jobs you can do does grow. And there would be times when my partner was more confident that I could do an advertised job than I thought I could.

VAL learned some valuable lessons from his experiences and advises:

- If you are affected by redundancy, do not take that as a personal criticism of you or your work. It is usually a purely business decision driven by a revenue or cost-saving target.
- Try and be logical about the situation. In some respects the tools and techniques that you use in your day-to-day project management can help. Once there is talk about redundancies you need to assess the risk and your response to that risk.

- Update and maintain your resumé regularly. It is easy to forget achievements and details about the projects you have worked on.
- If you are with a company for a long period of time there is less emphasis on industry qualifications as you are already there doing the job. But, whether facing redundancy or not, you should never overlook the importance of project management certification. Take time to keep up with the project management industry outside your organisation.
- After redundancy, take job searching seriously. It takes time and self-discipline to find the ideal role. It is a full-time exercise.
- It helps to share your thoughts and feelings with friends and family during the redundancy period.
- Remember this is *your* life. You can only live it once and it is a life that is too short for you to become stuck in a situation where you are not happy.

Constructive Dismissal

Having to resign from your job owing to the unacceptable behaviour of your organisation is 'constructive dismissal'. Typical cases include a breach of employment contract by the employer for example not being paid, being demoted for no reason, changing working conditions without consent and bullying or harassment. In these cases all reasonable attempts will have been made to deal with the problem and the employee will not have accepted these changes. The end result is that the employee will be forced to leave because of the breach (or after a series of incidents which amount to a serious breach).

Unfair Dismissal

'Unfair dismissal' is closely linked to 'constructive dismissal'. Employees who leave employment owing to constructive dismissal have in effect been forced to resign. Law courts both in the UK and US can rule that in a situation where an employee has been forced to resign this is in effect 'unfair' on that employee.

An ex-employee in the UK with at least one year's service has an automatic right to bring a complaint against the former employer in a tribunal. This action is taken if the ex-employee wants to pursue reinstatement (getting their old job back), engagement (getting a new job with the same employer) or compensation. The decision to take action is not one that should be taken lightly.

CASE EXAMPLE NO. 7

OLM was a project manager for a public sector organisation in the UK. He reports his experience of constructive dismissal and the tribunal process as 'very hard work, very stressful and whilst gaining some financial recompense I did not get my day in court'. This is his story.

OLM had recently joined a new organisation following a long career within another area of the civil service. Almost at once there were organisational and project problems which had to be dealt with including:

- retirement of the senior project manager;
- project understaffing;
- accusations of unacceptable behaviour in the project team;
- cancellations on project go-live dates.

The difficulties were further compounded by serious breaches of health and safety and working conditions for the project team, coupled with inaction and a lack of accountability from senior management. OLM was acting in the best interests of his team in ensuring the working conditions problem was reported yet conditions deteriorated.

Months later with conditions still intolerable, OLM was called into a meeting with superiors to discuss project progress. Project start-up had finally happened after two previous attempts that were aborted owing to organisational and technical errors. At this meeting OLM was informed that his line manager would be replaced and that he also had one month to increase his performance levels. By contrast, at the same time he also received notification that he had passed his probation period successfully and should look forward to setting targets for the following performance year.

Only a few weeks later OLM was called into another meeting to hear that he was being dismissed because of 'poor performance'. He was told to collect his belongings and leave the building. A letter would be sent detailing the next steps of a dismissal hearing.

OLM says:

> As a project manager I was used to being in control of situations and being able to put into action plans to overcome any difficulties that I might experience, in this case I was powerless as I had very little idea of what was happening. This of course made me more angry and frustrated and also led to my seeking advice from my doctor about managing stress.

OLM was allowed by law to take a representative to the dismissal hearing. But all his choices were blocked by the organisation because they were existing employees. The organisation felt they might be needed to defend the organisation should the process end with a tribunal in the future. Thus OLM attended the dismissal hearing alone. He was informed of the 'performance issues' and left one hour later with his dismissal upheld.

Taking the decision to the next stage (the tribunal) meant that OLM had to engage legal advice. It would be a process that lasted 12 months. In order to prepare for the court date, OLM was given a full list of the alleged performance problems on which the organisation had based their decision. For each issue OLM could have a right to reply, stating his version of events. OLM says that 'A point worth remembering about tribunals is that it is not your word against theirs, witnesses are also called'. OLM had little choice in who to call on for witnesses and was grateful for team members. 'I cannot imagine the difficult situation it must have put these people in and can only admire their bravery and determination to speak out against their employer'.

As the tribunal date approached it was clear that many of the allegations of 'poor performance' were unfounded. Speaking out against serious health and safety breaches had clearly upset management within the organisation. OLM's case for unfair dismissal never reached court; the organisation settled three days before the hearing was due.

OLM reflects:

I had to take a very long hard look at myself and ask truthfully if I felt that I was at fault and that my actions had led to my dismissal. That's difficult and stressful. However it is a kind of cleansing process which allows you to draw a line and start to move on. The tribunal process allowed me to see many things that I would not have been allowed to see had I just walked away. In my heart of hearts I still do not know why I was dismissed, but I do know it was not for 'poor performance'.

Discrimination and Harassment

Every employee has the basic right to conduct their work free of discrimination or harassment from management and co-workers. An employee cannot be discriminated against because of:

- gender;
- race;
- ethnic background;
- disability;
- sexual orientation;
- nationality/national origin;
- religious beliefs;
- political opinion;
- pregnancy;
- age.

There are two types of discrimination, 'direct' and 'indirect'. The International Labour Organization (2011) describes these as:

- Direct discrimination is when rules, practices and policies exclude or give preference to certain individuals because they belong to a certain group, for example in job advertisements where it is indicated that only men should apply.
- Indirect discrimination is when apparently neutral norms and practices have a disproportionate and unjustifiable effect on one or more identifiable groups. For example, requiring applicants to be of a certain height, which could disproportionately exclude women and members of some ethnic groups.

In the developed world, where discrimination laws and policies have been in place for decades, there is still cause for concern. In times of prolonged global and financial problems, antidiscrimination becomes less of a focus for organisations and discrimination cases increase.

Professionals within the project management field are less likely to fall victim to harassment and discrimination in the workplace. The highest number of cases affects low-skilled workers, immigrants, older and younger workers. That said, no one is really immune from the possibility that it could happen to them.

Arras People's reports captured ageism and gender related discrimination as the most common forms (Arras People, 2006–2011). In relation to ageism there were concerns from both older and younger project managers. In the older age groups, there was an increase in worries related to finding new work for those over 50 years old, especially when trying to move from one sector into another. With the younger project managers notably it was the perception that as a younger project manager you had to work twice as hard to gain recognition and promotion to positions with more responsibility and challenge.

In 2008 Arras People reported that 34 per cent of women project managers claimed that gender issues had affected their career, compared with 6 per cent of males (Arras People, 2008). Women in project management 'still dominate the lower-paid bands as either contractors or employees, and are more likely to be in project support roles than leading the field'. Whilst most women reported that they work in a discrimination-free workplace, instances of grievances included:

- 'I am convinced that a number of roles have gone to less qualified men where I have not been shortlisted because of fit with the organisation – totally unable to prove anything of course'.
- 'In certain corporate cultures it is still harder for a woman to gain the respect of the team. They will challenge you harder than they would a male manager'.

Gender discrimination works both ways and is not considered to be a women-only issue. Respondents – both male and female – demonstrated that through comments such as 'males can be seen as overcommitted in their approach whereas woman will be seen as focused for the same behaviour' and 'the drive to recruit more females meant positive discrimination against males even if males were better qualified'.

Whilst these are all examples of gender and age concerns that a project manager might encounter, only the most serious cases lead to employment termination. Termination by discrimination is often treated as constructive dismissal – where an employee is forced to resign owing to unacceptable behaviour and culture of the organisation. It is when the employee takes the matter to a tribunal appeal that the real facts emerge.

Conclusion

Project managers can find themselves managing an employment termination process as a leader of a project team, or they might become involved in the process themselves. None of us really knows how we might feel if placed under threat of redundancy, or expected to work in an intolerable environment.

The case examples in this chapter show that the right information is crucial to enabling an individual to feel some kind of control in what is generally an uncontrollable situation. Understanding the employment contract, the organisation's policies and procedures on termination and the local employment laws have helped these project managers navigate through testing times in their careers.

References and Further Reading

ACAS (2003), *Disciplinary and Grievance Procedures*, London: HMSO. Available at: http://www.acas. org.uk/media/pdf/9/5/CP01_1.pdf

ACAS (2010), 'Redundancy handling'. Available at:
http://www.acas.org.uk/CHttpHandler.ashx?id=877&p=0 [accessed 3 October 2011].

Arras People (2006), *Project Management Benchmark Report*, 1st edn, Manchester: Arras People.

Arras People (2007), *Project Management Benchmark Report*, 2nd edn, Manchester: Arras People.

Arras People (2008), *Project Management Benchmark Report*, 3rd edn, Manchester: Arras People.

Arras People (2009), *Project Management Benchmark Report*, 4th edn, Manchester: Arras People.

Arras People (2010), *Project Management Benchmark Report*, 5th edn, Manchester: Arras People.

Arras People (2011), *Project Management Benchmark Report*, 6th edn, Manchester: Arras People. Available at: http://www.arraspeople.co.uk/project-and-programme-management-resources/the-project-management-benchmark-report-from-arras-people-2011/benchmark-report-archives/

Australian Government Ombudsman (2010), 'National Employment Standards (NES)'. Available at: http://www.fairwork.gov.au/employment/national-employment-standards/pages/default.aspx

International Labour Organization (2011), 'Equality at work: The continuing challenge – Global Report under the follow-up to the ILO Declaration on Fundamental Principles and Rights at Work', presented at the International Labour Conference, April 2011. Available at: http://www.ilo.org/wcmsp5/groups/public/---ed_norm/---relconf/documents/meeting document/wcms_154779.pdf

Kübler-Ross, E. (1969), *On Death and Dying*, London: Routledge.

Leviter, L. and Muller, A. (2007), 'Termination of employment', USA International Labour Organization. Available at:
http://www.ilo.org/public/english/dialogue/ifpdial/info/termination/countries/usa.htm

Noer, D.M. (1993), *Healing the Wounds – Overcoming the Trauma of Layoffs and Revitalising Downsized Organizations*, San Francisco, CA: Jossey-Bass.

Sahdev, K. and Vinnicombe, S. (1998), 'Downsizing and survivor syndrome: A study of HR's perceptions of survivor's responses', Cranfield, Cranfield School of Management. Available at: https://dspace.lib.cranfield.ac.uk/retrieve/483/coareport9108.pdf

Sandler, C. and Keefe, J. (2007), *Fails to Meet Expectations*, Avon, MA: Adams Media.

US Department of Labor (2011), 'The Fair Labor Standards Act of 1938 (FLSA)'. Available at: http://www.dol.gov/compliance/laws/comp-flsa.htm

48 Advice for Project Managers on the Employment of Supplementary (Temporary) Workers

DENNIS LOCK and LINDSAY SCOTT

Practically all managers, whether they work in projects or not, are familiar with the practice of hiring additional workers from external organisations. Temporary arrangements usually work well to cover secretarial and clerical work overloads, for example when permanent staff are absent owing to vacations, special leave or sickness. The durations of such engagements can range from a few days to many months. If a temporary worker fails to please, or alternatively does not feel comfortable in the job, the relevant agency should be able to make a change at short notice, certainly within one week. Some project vacancies can also be filled by temporary staff relatively easily and successfully, for example in well-defined project management roles. These jobs require special skills, but those skills are usually transferable from one company to another. However, some project work, especially concerning innovative design, managing a business transformation programme or managing a portfolio office, differs considerably from one company to another and that can raise doubts and difficulties when that creative work has to be entrusted to people who are not permanent employees of the project company.

Fluctuating Staff Levels for Project-based Companies

Most companies experience fluctuations in their staff level requirements. In some service industries these can be seasonal and predictable. Companies that carry out projects are more likely than other companies to experience fluctuating workloads that are not seasonable and easily predictable, but which vary as their various projects progress through their life cycles.

Resource scheduling can do much to smooth out the day-to-day peaks and troughs and maintain constant requirements but some company departments will find that their requirements for highly skilled staff can vary considerably and unavoidably over longer periods. This is more likely to be a problem in companies that handle a few concurrent

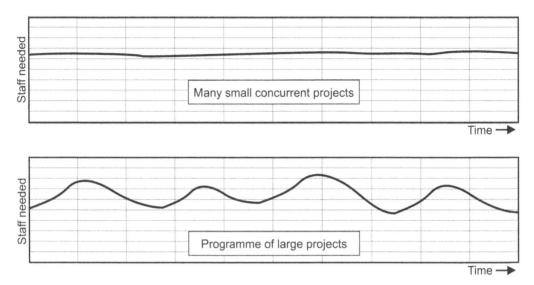

Figure 48.1 Staffing Requirements for Two Different Project Companies

Note: The company in the upper diagram regularly carries out a number of fairly small projects. The company in the lower diagram carries out a smaller number of projects but these are larger and longer-term ventures.

or consecutive large projects than in a company that customarily has a larger number of small projects in progress. In the latter case it is more probable that the peaks and troughs in workloads for individual projects will balance out when the total programme of projects is considered. Figure 48.1 illustrates this, where the graph in each case might be for one particular skill, or for the total project staff.

Companies can overcome the problem of fluctuating workloads to a considerable extent by maintaining a core of permanent staff, and supplementing these people from time to time by hiring additional staff on a temporary basis (usually from agencies) either to work in-house or from home.

The advantages of using agency staff are clear. The project company's temporary employment contracts are made with the agencies, and the temporary workers are employed by those agencies. There are other types of temporary workers (contractors, for example) where the project company's temporary employment contracts are still made with the agencies but a contract is then made between the agency and the contractor's legal entity (the limited liability company). So the project company can, within reason, expand or contract its staff numbers without penalty. The agency workers expect to move from one company to another because that is the way of life they have chosen. They are thus less likely to be demotivated when the project company has to release them.

Note, the contractual arrangements made for temporary workers largely depend on the country or local laws in place. Project managers are advised to use their human resources department to ensure that local employment laws and legislation are adhered to.

The project company will probably have concerns about maintaining the quality and innovation of its technical specifications and designs. Temporary workers might not identify with the established culture of the project company. There could also be problems with intellectual property or business confidentiality. Some project companies spend considerable time and money on induction courses for their new recruits, and temporary workers cannot usually be put through that process.

Case Examples

We now present four case examples. The first two cases illustrate how two different companies used temporary agency staff for project work. Agencies in these two cases are defined as supplying specialist staff for industries such as manufacturing and engineering, where the staff might be supplied to work either on the project company's site or from the agencies' own offices.

Cases 3 and 4 show how a project company can use agencies and external consultancies to provide effective 'body shopping' solutions to periods of peak demand in projects and also using more experienced agency workers as interim managers.

CASE EXAMPLE NO. 1

The company in this case had a permanent staff of about 250 people, mostly very experienced and well-qualified engineers and designers. At least as many people were employed on short-term contracts through external agencies.

Temporary staff worked alongside their permanent colleagues in the same offices. There was no shortage of accommodation at these staff levels. For work purposes, temporary staff were treated on a day-to-day basis just as if they were permanent staff. To the casual observer, permanent and temporary staff were indistinguishable. Cooperation between permanent and agency staff was very good. All enjoyed company amenities such as the staff restaurant and social events. But the temporary staff members were not paid for absences, and were of course not able to join the company's retirement pension scheme.

Because the temporary staff worked in the company's own offices, their work was supervised directly by the company's functional managers. To clients, the work delivered on their projects was just as good as if it had been performed by the company's permanent staff.

If the workload increased significantly for a new long-term project that could not be accommodated within the existing premises, additional premises were hired for the duration of the project. A mix of agency and permanent staff were moved into the temporary accommodation. No work was carried out externally in the offices of agencies. So the project company retained direct supervision of all its design work and the quality of the work remained high.

Projects in this company tended to have long life cycles. The project workload was supplemented by service contracts with one or two major clients for the resolution of technical problems. These service contracts required the same staff who worked on projects, so they provided a stabilising base that helped to smooth the workload. So the workload did not fluctuate greatly in the short term and resembled the pattern shown in the upper half of Figure 48.1. However, work in the longer term was subject very much to world commodity

---

prices, and when those prices dropped there was reduced demand for new projects. In the worst case existing projects could be interrupted or even cancelled.

Project work eventually fell away owing to political decisions by a foreign government and through a fall in world commodity prices. A steady decline in staff requirements was inevitable. But the company was able to retain its loyal permanent staff members for a relatively long time and reduce its liability for making severance payments considerably because so many of its staff were on temporary agency contracts.

CASE EXAMPLE NO. 2

This case is outlined here because it is a good example of how to use external agency staff to best advantage when the project company's workload fluctuates considerably.

A company in the business of designing and making very heavy special-purpose machines had a project portfolio that produced fluctuating workloads, very similar to the manner shown in the bottom half of Figure 48.1. This company had almost no spare accommodation within its own premises to accommodate agency staff.

The normal professional permanent staff complement in the engineering design department was approximately 50, in a company with a total workforce of about 600. When project design work reached its highest peaks, the engineering design staff complement could rise as high as 150. Thus this company could at some times require as many as 100 temporary staff, mostly working externally in the agencies' own offices. These were all highly skilled engineers and designers. More than one agency was involved. Thus problems of quality assurance, progressing and budgetary control arose.

All work was planned using critical path networks, and these were processed together using full multiproject resource scheduling. All priorities were driven by the required project delivery dates, so that each task had scheduled start and finish dates calculated by the computer to achieve those dates. The schedules were run using the time-limited rule, which meant that additional agency resources were hired when that was necessary to keep the projects on schedule. Thus all resource overloads were met using agency staff (mostly working in external offices).

The numbers of staff within each skill required to offset these overloads could be found from the computer reports for up to a year in advance. So there was plenty of time in which to find suitable agencies and to discuss requirements, cost rates and working arrangements with them. All agencies were visited to inspect their premises and working conditions before entering into contracts.

The project company's small project management office (PMO) included a liaison engineer whose job was to visit the external agencies at frequent intervals, to deliver new work, to check on the work in progress and to answer any technical questions on the spot.

CASE EXAMPLE NO. 3

This case highlights the advantages of recruiting multiple temporary project workers within an organisation which delivers programmes and projects on behalf of its clients, as a professional consultancy. This organisation often had demanding and fluctuating resource requirements throughout the entire portfolio of work. There was a need to balance this organisation's own workforce to ensure that their time was not spent 'on the bench'. This company used 'on the bench' to describe time when project workers were not assigned to any project, so that their time was not being utilised and could not be billed to a client (so that it became an overhead cost). In other companies this would be called 'idle time' or 'waiting time'. However, there had to be enough available resource for periods of peak demand.

A resource management centre was established, which monitored the availability of project workers throughout the organisation and also provided a current list of all the available skills and specialisms that these workers possessed. The centre was managed by two permanent members of staff. When a new project was being initiated, or when existing projects were experiencing resource difficulties, this resource centre was the project manager's first port of call.

Where resources were unavailable, the resource management centre called on its list of preferred recruitment agency suppliers and submitted job specifications for the resources needed. Roles frequently needed in the organisation included programme managers, project managers, project support people, business analysts and technical consultants. The recruitment agencies would then submit a shortlist of potential candidates and the organisation would interview and make selected hires for deployment on the relevant project. In periods of peak demand, the temporary worker requirement was as a much as a third of the organisation's total size.

When the number of temporary workers required increased, the organisation looked for other avenues to be able to sustain the levels of resources required. A partnership was made with an external consultancy organisation that specialised in a very similar field to the project company. The external consultancy was able to guarantee to supply experienced and skilled resources with immediate availability as and when required. The body shopping of resources, where the external consultancy contracted out their skilled workers on a short-term basis to the project company, was deemed to be a much more cost-effective solution than agreeing individual terms with multiple recruitment agencies.

CASE EXAMPLE NO. 4

This case highlights the solutions available when a company needs to take on a highly experienced project worker for a high profile or specialised role where none already exists in the organisation.

The company, a marketing and sales organisation, was looking to undertake a significant change programme which would dramatically change its product lines, channels to market and internal processes and procedures. The vacant position required someone who would form part of the organisation's board and be responsible for the entire change initiative across all areas of the company. Such a person did not exist in the company and it was felt that approaching the usual recruitment agencies to hire this individual would be too high risk – this change programme would determine the future for this organisation and failure was not an option.

The organisation decided to appoint an interim manager for the position. Interim managers are considered to be senior executives who have a good track record in specific businesses or areas like project management and change management. Interim managers are used by organisations to meet specific objectives within set time frames. Often interim managers are considered to be overqualified and experienced for the posts they undertake but in this case the positive impact made within days of the appointment gave the board the reassurances they needed. The interim manager took the title of Programme Manager and delivered the changes through a business transformation programme incorporating all the departments of the organisation. The change was successfully delivered eight months later and the interim manager was then released from the contract.

Agency Charges

Agency charges are either based on hourly or day rates. The rates payable are often negotiated individually with each agency and can vary considerably from one agency to another. An agency that quotes a relatively high rate need not necessarily be excluded, provided that its other requirements (especially its reputation for quality) are satisfactory.

Many organisations opt for a preferred supplier list (PSL), which will feature a number of agencies all working at the same rate. Alternatively they might appoint just one recruitment agency to provide a 'recruitment process outsourcing' (RPO) service which, in effect, means that a single recruitment agency will provide the recruitment assistance needed for the whole organisation at very competitive rates.

The relationship between the agency and the organisation is actively managed through formal Service Level Agreements (SLAs) or Key Performance Indicators (KPIs) to ensure that the quality of the recruitment processes and subsequent hires made remain at a high level. Regular reporting on KPIs can help maintain an effective working relationship. Typical KPIs include:

- ratio of hires to personal resumés submitted;
- ratio of interviews to hires;
- time to fill vacancies.

Although the project company will have a budget for every temporary worker it needs, these budgets are often driven by market forces beyond the company's control. Factors include the availability of certain key skill sets, competing requirements from other organisations in the same sector, and recessionary and economic effects in local markets. Whilst the agency rate will be fixed and agreed up front, the rate for each worker will be agreed on a case-by-case basis.

Consideration must also be given to the inclusion of payable expenses to the agency worker. In some incidences reasonable expenses can be expected on top of the agreed hourly or daily rate of pay. Reasonable expenses could include travel costs over and above those costs incurred travelling between home and the main office of work (travel to client sites for example); meals with the client or hotel costs incurred whilst visiting clients. Steps should be taken at the point of contract negotiation to confirm what the reasonable expenses are likely to be in the course of the worker's role and an agreement made to suit all parties.

Accelerated Induction Processes

In some manufacturing and engineering organisations, design work subcontracted to external offices might be of a senior nature, requiring that the agencies' senior design engineers have a good working knowledge of the project company's standards and design practices. For example, permanent staff employed by one company would undergo an induction programme, sometimes involving a few months spent in the offices of the company's parent company in the US. That was clearly not possible for agency staff for many reasons, not least of which would be the unproductive time and cost involved. This problem was overcome very successfully as follows.

Whenever a work package from the WBS for each project was selected for allocation to one of the external agencies, a senior engineer from the external agency would be asked to work in the project company's offices under the direct supervision of the senior project engineers to produce the overall layout drawing for the chosen work package. This process might take two months, during which the agency engineer would acquire a good knowledge of the project company's design practices and standards. When the layout design was completed and checked, the agency engineer returned to the external agency office and supervised a small group of more junior agency engineers for the completion of detailing, checking and preparation of bills of materials.

Thus, in other words, parcels of work from the WBS were issued to the external offices. The conceptual design and layout was carried out by senior engineers who, although employed by the external agency, had received sufficient on-the-job training in the project company's main offices.

In other industries, the induction process can be managed more quickly and easily where the project company has a PMO or similar function. The PMO is then responsible for ensuring that all project workers within the organisation (permanent and temporary) are familiar with the company's approach to project management and have access to the right tools and information about project processes.

Time Sheets and Invoices

The time spent by each worker on each project task is normally recorded on weekly time sheets. Each worker's time sheet must be approved by the appointed manager before being submitted to the relevant agency to generate billing and payment.

Temporary contracts will invariably state that payment for work cannot be released by the company without a signed time sheet.

In manufacturing and engineering industries, the time sheet data from temporary workers can be just as important for historical records as the times recorded by permanent staff. All times should be recorded against job numbers derived from the relevant project WBS. The hourly times recorded not only support budgeting and invoice control, but can also be entered into the company's project information system. These records can have many uses, whether as part of the earned value measurement system or other budgetary procedures for the current project, or to provide a valuable estimate base for future projects.

Conclusions

All companies working on projects will experience fluctuating workloads according to project life cycles, and those fluctuations can be managed to a large extent by employing workers through agencies and consultancies. The following pieces of advice emerge from the cases outlined above:

1. External agencies can provide a valuable resource when staffing or accommodation problems limit the amount of work that can be done in-house.
2. There are a number of options available to bring in additional temporary workers, depending on the industry sector, local conditions and international employment laws.
3. The project company will need to ensure that the workers from external agencies can work to the required project standards. That can be achieved by identifying senior staff within each agency to work for a short time in the project company's offices under the supervision of the project company's own senior staff or by providing introducing an appropriate induction process.
4. The hourly rates quoted between different agencies can vary considerably but this is not always reflected in the *total* amounts invoiced for work packages of equivalent size and complexity.
5. All agency staff should be asked to submit time sheet information in the same way as the project company's permanent staff.
6. The project company should ideally appoint a permanent member of staff to manage the organisation's resource requirements, including providing a main point of contact for all recruitment activity with external agencies and consultancies (a role that can be contained within a PMO).

If the agency options are managed with common sense and sensitivity, there is no reason why the quality of work produced by their workers should not be equally as good as that produced in-house.

More Specialised Topics

49 *Managing the People Side of Change*

BRIAN RICHARDSON

Early in my career, the senior technical manager on a large, international IT project said to me, in a moment of frustration, 'This project would be so easy without all the people issues!' This manager was responsible for hundreds of technical requirements, multiple system releases and dozens of interfacing systems. The technical, 'hard' aspects of the project were complex and difficult, yet he viewed these as straightforward in comparison to the 'soft' people issues. I have found this to be true over and over again in many years of managing projects. The 'soft' stuff is the hard stuff when it comes to projects and change. So my chapter takes a systematic approach and discusses how to apply key scientific and business insights when managing the people side of business change projects.

Introduction

Research confirms that many projects fail because people are not adequately considered. Projects and programmes struggle or fail owing to individual, organisational and cultural factors that are not adequately understood, planned for, managed or addressed. As a result, the target stakeholders are unable or unwilling to embrace and sustain change. Understanding and managing these factors and the complex interactions among them requires a blend of analytical rigour, interpersonal awareness and execution discipline. This chapter discusses four key topics in relation to change management success:

1. the value of change management;
2. overcoming resistance to change;
3. a framework for change;
4. managing change through the project management life cycle.

The Value of Change Management

Multiple studies across project types, cultures and geographies have found that 50–80 per cent of projects fail to achieve the objectives of schedule, budget and performance (I am lumping quality and scope in with performance here). Consequently they also fail to achieve their promised return on investment (ROI). One study conducted by IBM spanned 15 countries and 21 industries. It found that 41 per cent of projects were unsuccessful in meeting their objectives (IBM Global Services, 2008). IBM found that the most significant challenges were people-oriented, as follows:

- changing mindsets and attitudes (58 per cent);
- corporate culture (49 per cent);
- underestimating project complexity (35 per cent).

These were more significant than non-people related factors such as:

- lack of resources (33 per cent);
- change of process (15 per cent);
- technology barriers (8 per cent).

The top performing 20 per cent of organisations in the study reported an 80 per cent success rate, nearly double the average. By contrast, the bottom performing 20 per cent of organisations were successful only 8 per cent of the time. The same study found that the primary success factors for successful projects were heavily weighted towards 'soft', 'people-oriented' factors such as:

- top management sponsorship (92 per cent);
- employee involvement (72 per cent);
- honest and timely communication (70 per cent);
- a corporate culture that motivates and promotes change (65 per cent);
- change agents (pioneers of change) (55 per cent);
- change supported by culture (48 per cent).

Another study (McKinsey, 2002) looked at project ROI for 40 organisations and found an overall 42 per cent success rate in meeting or exceeding ROI targets. The McKinsey study also found a strong correlation between the level of ROI achieved and the quality of change management at the senior, middle manager and front-line employee levels of the organisation. Organisations that excelled at all three levels delivered, on average, 143 per cent of the expected ROI. In contrast, organisations that struggled at all three levels achieved an average of only 35 per cent ROI.

These and other studies indicate that good change management practice almost doubles project delivery success and triples ROI. If change management effectiveness correlates strongly to project success, project and programme managers with a better mastery of the skills and process of change management will be more successful and deliver better business results.

Overcoming Resistance to Change

RESISTANCE TO CHANGE

Resistance to change is much-studied and written about in business literature. It is a fact of life for every project. Most conclude that resistance to change is:

- natural;
- unavoidable;
- predictable;
- manageable.

Resistance is natural, unavoidable and predictable because it is a fact of human nature. The human species is naturally curious and eager to learn, but is also wary of change. This is an essential survival instinct. Our success and the success of those around us depends on assessing new things in our environment, understanding what they are, what they mean and how they can help us or harm us. In a hunter-gatherer society, people are rightly suspicious of a new tribe or a new food source for fear of being killed or poisoned. In corporate life, people are rightly suspicious of organisation change or process reengineering for fear of being downsized or having their jobs made more difficult for no good reason.

Project managers should expect resistance to change from every stakeholder at every stage of the project. Accepting that resistance to change cannot be avoided prompts us to prepare and plan for it. In so doing, we are better able to manage resistance throughout the project life cycle, just as we manage scope, schedule, quality, cost, risk and business benefits. As project managers, expecting resistance to change and having a desire to understand and deal with it is the first step to greater project delivery success and ROI. We need next to understand resistance to change on a deeper level, how to diagnose the nature of resistance, and how to deal with it in a systematic way.

Individual Capacity for Change

Resistance to change indicates a deficiency in the capacity to change. The individual capacity to change is based on two factors, competence and motivation (Connor, 1992, p. 127):

Competence is having the requisite knowledge and skills to accept and adopt the change. It comprises:

- *Knowledge*: command of facts, information and insight. For example, knowing the steps in a new sales process.
- *Skills*: ability to apply knowledge to perform tasks. For example, being able to perform the steps in the new sales process, applying knowledge about customer needs.
- *Aptitude*: the physical and mental capacity to acquire new knowledge and skills. Individuals have a level of aptitude for learning new sports, concepts, technical skills, interpersonal skills and so on. A salesperson with experience in many organisations and many sales processes may have a higher aptitude to learn a new sales process than someone with less experience.

Motivation is the individual's drive to accept and adopt the change. It is composed of:

- *Attitudes*: positive or negative views of a person, thing or event. For example, some individuals enjoy and readily adopt new technology that would intimidate others.

- *Goals*: results that a person is attempting to achieve. Individuals have personal goals related to development, career advancement and fulfilment. Any change introduced will be perceived and evaluated by the extent to which it helps or hinders these personal goals.
- *Critical behaviours*: observable actions that contribute to success. Individuals differ in the extent to which they demonstrate behaviours that may be critical to success such as detail-orientation, initiative, teamwork and resilience. For example, a change that requires a high degree of teamwork will be more difficult for those who prefer working alone.

Deficiencies in either competence or motivation will affect how quickly individuals embrace and adopt change. To illustrate the difference, consider the following two examples:

Case 1: Eric, a new project manager at a large company is eager to participate in the launch of a 'Project Management Community of Practice' to codify and promote good project management practices within the company. He believes in the value and importance of sharing knowledge, but he lacks the background and skills necessary to write articles on project management topics or to answer questions from others with confidence.

Case 2: Erin works in the same company as Eric but she is a more experienced project manager. For example, she is able to write articles on a range of topics and answer many questions with a high degree of confidence. But Erin sees no good reason or opportunity to do so, given her many other responsibilities.

Both Eric and Erin are limited in their *capacity to change*, but the nature of their limitations is fundamentally different. For Eric, his high motivation is constrained by his limited competence. Erin's high competence is constrained by her low motivation. In other words, Eric is willing, but not able, and Erin is able, but not willing.

Distinguishing between motivation and competence issues is important because the nature of the resistance requires different responses. In the examples above, training can redress Eric's skill deficiency, but would have little to no impact on Erin's motivational deficiency. Making answering questions and publishing articles an explicit performance expectation would affect Erin's motivation, yet that would not deal with Eric's lack of background and skills.

Motivation Matters More Than Competence

Motivation is instinctive, powerful and difficult to alter. Individuals with an innate positive bias towards a change will look for opportunities to learn about, support and implement the change. Motivated individuals will even convince others of the need to change and overcome significant obstacles in order to make the change successful. In the example we can imagine Eric seeking out training and information to build his skills, but it is difficult to imagine Erin taking the initiative to adjust her own motivation.

More dramatic examples of the power of motivation are mass political movements such as the rejection of Communism in Eastern Europe in the late 1980s and early 1990s and the Arab Spring of 2011. Individuals advocating change spontaneously organised to challenge and eventually overthrow long-entrenched regimes; overcoming deficiencies in political power, military strength and financial resources to do so. Their high levels of motivation enabled them to be both relentless and resilient in the face of violent opposition. They acquired the knowledge, skills and resources they needed to achieve goals, but would never have done so without an overwhelming commitment to the need for change.

No matter what the stakes are, motivation matters because enthusiastic, motivated proponents of a change create energy, recruit others, provide constructive feedback and freely devote time and effort to supporting the change. On the other hand motivated resisters of change actively discourage others, create obstacles, raise objections and use their power to stifle progress. Motivation creates change capacity as well as the energy to expand capacity, whilst competence affects capacity alone.

Imagine an equation for change capacity. We might propose the following:

$$\text{change capacity} = \text{competence} \times \text{motivation}$$

But that treats both elements as equal contributors. However, motivation has to be regarded as a kind of force multiplier, and the following equation is closer to reality:

$$\text{change capacity} = \text{competence} \times \text{motivation}^2$$

The Language of Resistance

Distinguishing between motivation and competence issues requires diagnostic tools and skills. Formal measurement methods exist, but on a day-to-day, interaction-to-interaction basis, the most important foundational skill for project managers engaged in creating change is *listening*. By paying close attention to the language that stakeholders use when they express their attitude towards the project or the change, we can gain insight into the nature of the resistance. Stakeholder language gives us important clues we can use to determine whether resistance is rooted in a competence deficiency or a motivation deficiency.

For example, when stakeholders talk about time, priority and necessity, they are discussing their level of motivation. When they exhibit defensiveness, indifference, passive aggressiveness or open hostility towards the change, they indicate insufficient motivation. When stakeholders talk about ability, understanding, knowledge, information and clarity, they are indicating their level of competence. When their questions centre around how they are expected to participate or what they are expected to do, they are demonstrating that they are motivated to change, but need more knowledge, skills or aptitude to improve their competence. Figure 49.1 provides some guidance on how to use stakeholder feedback to identify resistance as either motivation-related or competence-related.

Whilst Figure 49.1 provides some guidance and direction on diagnosing resistance, it is not a simple formula of inputs and outputs. Stakeholders often express resistance

Component	Sample feedback
Motivation	This change is a low **priority** This change is not **necessary** This is not the right **time** This change is not a good use of my **time** I do not know **why** we are doing this I'm not sure we are **solving the real problem** This change is not **practical** Providing alternative solutions (have you considered . . .?) Second-hand feedback (Are you aware that . . . I'm hearing that . . .) Asking for justification or data (Where are the data to prove that? Anger Silence Defensiveness Repeating questions or explanations
Competence	I don't **understand** I am not **clear** on . . . I don't **know** what to do next I don't **know** how this affects me **When** is this happening? **How** will this be implemented? **What** is the plan for . . .? I need more **information** about . . .

Figure 49.1 Stakeholder language diagnostics

indirectly, and/or have deficiencies in both areas. In addition, stakeholders often mask deficiencies in motivation because they feel compelled to demonstrate public support for the change. They may raise a series of objections that are competence-related, but the frequency, force and/or tone of those objections indicates that their motivation to change is lacking. To be more effective in diagnosing and dealing with resistance to change, as project managers we can practise some simple, yet effective steps:

1. Meet resistance with acceptance and acknowledgement. Assume that all stakeholders, including project sponsors, will demonstrate resistance to change at various stages of the project. Acknowledge and accept that resistance is natural and unavoidable, and engage stakeholders in open, honest dialogue about it. It is frustrating when stakeholders verbalise or demonstrate support for a change/project, then later express doubts or objections. However, this is more typical than not, and a response that starts with acceptance and acknowledgement of resistance opens the possibility of dialogue. When we dismiss or minimise objections, or offer solutions before fully exploring the problem and the underlying cause, we risk increasing resistance. Resistance becomes the focus of the interaction, and creating change becomes secondary.
2. Give stakeholders every opportunity to take ownership and control the way they adopt change. Often, they can solve their own problems and deal with their own sources of resistance, or else tell us what they need. Rather than attempt to answer

every objection and solve every issue on their behalf, engage them in creating the solution. We are all more attached to our own ideas and choices than those given to us from someone else. Consider the following examples of a dialogue between a stakeholder (SH) and the project manager (PM).

Example 1

SH: 'This project sounds like a good idea, but we have so much going on right now. I really don't have the time to focus on it'.

PM: 'This is a high priority for Sponsor X, and she expects you to participate. We really need your help to meet our deadline'.

The SH is expressing resistance based on not having time to participate, which indicates a motivation issue. The PM responds by telling the SH that he has little choice, and that the sponsor, who is of higher rank in the organisation, requires their participation. This carries with it a veiled threat of punishment or consequence if the SH does not comply. This puts the SH in a defensive position, which will probably have the unintended consequence of further reducing their motivation and intensifying their resistance. The SH might continue to object, or ask their direct supervisor to escalate the issue and shield them from punishment. Even if they accept that they have no real choice but to say yes, they may accept the responsibility but miss deadlines, or do the minimum possible amount or quality of work, or look for the first opportunity to say 'No' later. In any case, the resistance either persists or is temporarily overcome, but is never explored or dealt with.

Example 2

This is an alternative scenario for the same characters in Example 1. In this case the PM could take a different approach, accept that resistance to change is part of the process, engage in further dialogue to understand the source of the issue, and give the SH an opportunity to take ownership and control of the solution. Here's the dialogue:

SH: 'This project sounds like a good idea, but we have so much going on right now. I really don't have time to focus on it'.

PM: 'I understand you are very busy. Sponsor X asked me to reach out to you to for help, but it sounds as if you have a lot going on right now. What would you suggest?'

SH: 'Well, Sponsor X has me working on four other projects right now, and two of them are due next week. What is your deadline? How much time do you need from me?'

PM: 'Our deadline is in eight weeks and we were looking for your feedback in the next four weeks, but I don't know if that's practical given your workload. I estimate it will take four hours of your time to review our design, fill out the feedback form, and attend a meeting to review requirements'.

SH: 'Four weeks from now? I'll have time to put a few hours towards this after next week. Can you send me your documentation, then set up time to discuss after next week?'

In this dialogue, the PM acknowledged and validated the objection, but then asked the SH for suggestions. Notice they also invoked the sponsor's name, without an explicit directive or threat. This reinforces the priority, but does not back the SH into a corner. By then asking the SH for a solution, instead of telling them this is a higher priority than their other work, or that there is a consequence of not participating, it allows the SH to develop a solution that they own and can commit to. The SH then starts to ask questions about deadlines and how much time was required, which are competence issues. In this example, a tough motivation issue became a straightforward competence issue because the PM listened, acknowledged and validated the resistance, and gave control to the SH to come up with the solution.

Even as we apply these principles to our day-to-day interactions with SHs, we shall still encounter resistance that is not easy to overcome. Not every interaction will be successful in diagnosing and solving resistance right away, but applying this approach over time leads to better results more often than not.

INTERNAL AND EXTERNAL MOTIVATION

As motivation issues are more important and difficult to deal with than competence issues, PMs should also understand the types of motivation on a more granular level, including intrinsic and extrinsic motivation and the relationship to competence. Research on human motivation (Ryan and Deci, 2000, p. 54) has delineated a basic distinction between *intrinsic motivation*, which is doing something because it is inherently interesting or enjoyable, and *extrinsic motivation*, which is doing something because it leads to a desired result. Decades of studies have shown that people with intrinsic motivation perform better for longer periods of time than those with extrinsic motivation.

Studies have further demonstrated that different types of extrinsic motivation have varying impacts on performance. For both intrinsic and extrinsic motivation, the underlying basic human needs that drive the level of motivation and performance are:

1. *Autonomy*: control over one's mind and actions;
2. *Competence*: the need to develop new knowledge, skills and abilities;
3. *Relatedness*: the need to be connected to the individuals, groups, leaders or cultures connected to a goal.

The extent to which these needs are met affects the individual's level of interest and effort, as well as their ability to learn and to cope with setbacks. Some additional insights from this research are:

1. Competence is best acquired by self-determined effort. Even where individuals value learning a task or skill, their motivation and performance declines if they feel they are being compelled or manipulated.

2. Intrinsic motivation only occurs for activities that hold inherent interest for the individual, however, external motivation can produce similar levels of interest, enjoyment and competence when the activity is:
    a) self-directed;
    b) consistent with internal goals and values;
    c) valued by others to whom they are connected or would like to be connected (family, group, society).
3. Negative motivators degrade motivation. Deadlines, directives, threats, negative consequences, pressure to compete and guilt all diminish motivation, even when they temporarily improve effort. When these methods are used, individuals tend to have lower interest, are more likely to blame others for a negative outcome, and are less able to recover from setbacks.
4. Extrinsic rewards diminish motivation and performance. Tangible rewards, like paying for performance, focus the reason for performance on external values and goals. Higher performance is achieved when the task is aligned to internal goals and values.

We can apply these insights to develop change strategies that enhance motivation, such as cultivating strong sponsorship, coaching and self-directed learning. We can also avoid strategies that tend to degrade motivation such as coercion, compliance directives and, in many cases, financial incentives.

A Framework for Change

Individual motivation and competence are not static and do not exist in a vacuum; they are influenced by a number of dynamic factors present in the surrounding organisation or environment. These factors form a complex system, depicted in Figure 49.2 on the next page. The change management framework shown in Figure 49.2 (Richardson Consulting Group, 2006–2012) illustrates the connection between individual factors (motivation and competence) and external factors (leadership, organisation, business process and culture).

Each factor is further elaborated into components. This framework, like any framework, is a simplification of a complex reality. It is intended to make a very complex system of interrelated, interdependent components easier to understand. In so doing, we are able to use this framework in two distinct ways:

1. As a *diagnostic tool* to relate individual competence and motivation issues to a larger context.
2. As a *solution framework* to design and implement effective change strategies to influence competence and motivation.

For example, on one project users of a new online reference system reported that they found the online tool easy to use. However, many of them still relied on paper-based binders because they regarded the binders as more reliable and up to date. We *diagnosed* the resistance as being more motivation-related because they knew how to use the new tool, but viewed the binder system as better able to meet their needs. Further investigation revealed that the old update *process* and *communication* had not changed to fit the new tool. The online tool was being updated just-in-time, but users were not being notified,

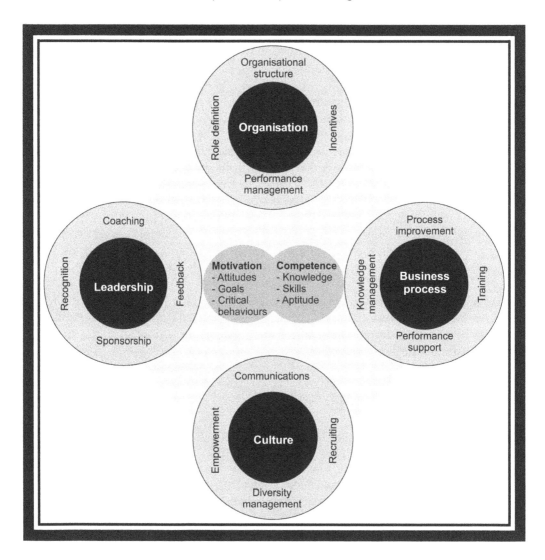

Figure 49.2 Richardson Consulting Group change management services
Source: © 2006 Richardson Consulting Group.

whilst the paper-based updates were still going out to users via email. They were printing the updates and placing them in their binders as they always had and, because they were not receiving notification of changes to the online tool, they assumed that the paper updates were more reliable and current.

The *solution* was to change the process so that the email *communication* included links to the updated sections of the online tool. Users were able to see that the updates to the online tool had already been completed, and that they would be able to trust the information. In a short time most users abandoned their paper-based binders, viewing them as redundant and unnecessary.

This dual use as diagnostic and solution framework means the elements and their components are both areas of *inquiry* during change assessment and areas of *intervention* that can be planned, managed and executed as part of a change management plan. A *change assessment* looks at the strengths and weaknesses of the current state for each element and component. The *change plan* details the target interventions and timing as well as the resources required. The change plan is integrated into the overall project/programme plan. The assessment and planning considerations are summarised in Figure 49.3.

Component	Change assessment considerations	Change planning considerations
Motivation		
Attitudes	- Degree to which change is viewed as threat to community - Level of organic support or resistance	- Description of target attitudes - Approach to be used to achieve the target attitudes
Goals	- Priority of the change - Degree to which the change aligns or conflicts with existing goals and aspirations	- Align change and design messaging with individual goals - Approach and resources to align individual goals with the change
Critical behaviours	- Existing behaviours which align to, or conflict with the change	- Target behaviours - Approach to be used to achieve the target behaviours
Competence		
Knowledge	- Personal understanding of the change - Personal understanding of the change's impact	- Knowledge requirements - Approach and resources to build and reinforce required knowledge
Skills	- Capacity to carry out the roles and tasks required by the change	- Target skills required by the change - Approach and resources to build and reinforce required skills
Aptitudes	- Ability to acquire knowledge and skills required to adopt the change - Identification of stakeholder groups with aptitude deficits	- Mitigation for at-risk groups - Approach and resources to expand and remedy aptitudes
Leadership		
Coaching	- Formal and informal methods to improve skills and behaviours via inquiry, reflection, and discussion, both individual and team - Existing relationships, methods and resources	- Coaching methods and relationships - Approach and resources to design, build and implement target coaching interventions.
Feedback	- Formal and informal methods to provide feedback to individuals as follows: 1. 360 feedback; 2. manager-employee 3. peer-peer; 4; automated - Existing methods, relationships and resources	- Feedback methods, relationships and resources required - Approach and resources to design, build and implement target feedback
Sponsorship	- Champions, advocates and supporters of the change - Breadth of sponsorship v breadth of change impact - Risks associated with sponsorship	- Sponsorship requirements - Mitigation for sponsorship risks - Approach and resources to build and sustain required sponsorship
Recognition	- Systems and processes to recognize positive behaviour and contribution: manager-employee; employee-manager; peer-peer - Existing recognition programmes and methods	- Target recognition - Approach and resources to recognize positive behaviour and contribution

Figure 49.3 Richardson Consulting Group change management assessment and planning considerations

Component	Change assessment considerations	Change planning considerations
Organisation		
Role definition	- Jobs and roles affected by the change - Existing jobs and role definitions - Accuracy of role definitions - Process and resources to add or change roles	- New and modified jobs and roles required - Approach and resources to design, build and implement target jobs and roles
Organisation structure	- How jobs and roles relate to one another - Formal structures that support or inhibit the change - Informal structures that support or inhibit the change - Structures affected by the change - Process and resources to modify organisation structure	- New and modified formal and informal structures required by the change - Approach and resources to design, build and implement target structure
Performance management	- Performance criteria and standards - Process to measure and manage performance - Process and resources to modify performance criteria and standards	- New and modified performance criteria and standards required by the change - Approach and resources to design, build and implement target performance management
Incentives	- How performance is rewarded in both monetary and non-monetary terms - Current incentives that support or run counter to behaviours expected from change - Process and resources to modify incentives	- New and modified incentives to support the change - Approach and resources to design and implement target incentives
Process		
Process improvement	- Processes affected by the change - Processes that support or inhibit the change - Process and resources to change business process to improve effectiveness and/or efficiency	- New and modified processes required by the change - Approach and resources to design, build and implement target processes
Training	- Learning interventions to impart new or improved skills - Existing training affected by the change - Process and resources to create or modify training	- New and modified training required by the change - Approach and resource to design, build and implement training
Performance support	- On-the-job task support tools such as job aids or online reference - Existing performance support tools affected by the change - Process and resources to create of change performance support	- New and modified performance support tools required by the change - Approach and resources to design, build and implement target performance support
Knowledge management	- Strategies, systems and practices to acquire, develop, retain and distribute knowledge and insights - Existing strategies, systems and practices affected by the change - Existing strategies, systems and practices that support of inhibit the change	- New and modified strategies, systems and practices required to support the change - Approach and resources to design, build and implement target knowledge management

Figure 49.3 Continued

All aspects of the framework are interconnected, interdependent and dynamic. As a system, each of the external factors (leadership, organisation, business process and culture) affects both the individual factors (competence and motivation) as well as the other external factors.

Component	Change assessment considerations	Change planning considerations
Culture		
Training	- Learning interventions to impart new or improved skills - Existing training affected by the change - Process and resources to modify training	- New and modified training required by the change - Approach and resources to design, build and implement training
Performance support	- On-the-job support tools such as job aids or online reference - Existing performance support tools affected by the change - Process and resources to create of change performance support	- New and modified performance support tools required by the change - Approach and resources to design, build and implement target performance support
Knowledge management	- Strategies, systems and practices to acquire, develop, retain and distribute knowledge and insights - Existing strategies, systems and practices affected by the change - Existing strategies, systems and practices that support or inhibit the change	- New and modified strategies, systems and practices required to support the change - Approach and resources to design, build and implement target knowledge management

Figure 49.3 Continued

As an example, a new senior leader in a traditionally command-and-control culture may model and expect more open, inclusive and collaborative behaviours, which will change the culture over time. As the change takes hold, the organisation structure, roles, process and performance expectations, and business processes will also adapt to incorporate these behaviours. Individuals who are unable or unwilling to adapt will leave the organisation, and individuals predisposed to the new culture will be attracted to it, further strengthening the cultural change.

Changes that may have been very easy to implement in the old culture, such as policy and procedure changes requiring only cascading communication and training, may require a more robust approach in an organisation where change invites constant questioning, collaboration and discussion. Changes that would have been difficult or impossible to implement in the old culture, such as team-based sales and service, might now find more natural, organic support. Whilst the relationship between the factors and elements is fluid, the framework provides a way to view and deal with them systematically to ensure that important areas are considered.

Managing Change through the Project Management Life Cycle

In order for PMs to apply individual listening skills and the framework for change, they need to understand how the process of change relates to the project management life cycle. Harvard Professor John Kotter has proposed an 8-step programme for implementing change that has been widely embraced and adopted. In the 2005 field guide based on this programme, Dan Cohen (Cohen, 2005) describes the process of change as follows:

Creating the climate for change:

1. *Increase urgency* – change leaders build a sense of urgency, increase energy and motivation. To do this they reduce the fear, anger and complacency that may be associated with the change.
2. *Build guiding teams* – mobilise leaders who are focused, committed and enthusiastic because they have a deep understanding of the need for change, model the 'right' behaviour, and hold themselves and others accountable for results.
3. *Get the vision right* – create a clear, inspiring, compelling, achievable, actionable picture of the future. The vision must articulate the required behaviours in the future state so that change strategies and metrics can be created to support the vision.

Engaging and enabling the whole organisation:

4. *Communicate for buy-in* – change leaders must deliver honest, clear, concise messages about the change in order to build and sustain trust, support and commitment.
5. *Enable Action* – change leaders must remove obstacles to achieving the vision and align new processes and programmes to the future state.
6. *Create short-term wins* – leaders sustain energy and urgency by achieving visible, meaningful improvements to demonstrate progress towards the vision.

Implementing and sustaining the change:

7. *Don't let up* – leaders monitor and measure progress, continue to ensure accountability for results, and do not declare premature victory.
8. *Make it stick* – leaders recognise, reward and model the new behaviour in order to embed it into the organisation and culture.

Like the project management life cycle, this process is iterative and can be applied at any point in a project. It is flexible and dynamic in that, whilst the steps build upon one another, they can be done out of sequence or in parallel to fit a specific situation. Some PMs have argued to me that they believe this model applies only to 'organisation change' projects, and can be safely ignored for other types of projects such as IT or marketing. But the research demonstrates, and my own experience confirms, that most projects would benefit from incorporating these activities. Some specific deliverables intended to deal with the 'people aspect' of change that are applicable to most projects are:

- *SH analysis* – identifies key SHs, the change impact, their criticality to the change effort, their current and required level of commitment to the change.
- *Change readiness assessment* – identifies the organisational readiness to accept and support the change. This is administered at the beginning of the effort to establish a baseline and then re-administered at regular intervals to measure progress and identify problems.
- *Change management plan* – the schedule of change interventions required to achieve urgency, commitment and readiness. This is incorporated into the overall project/ programme plan.

- *Measurement plan* – the plan to measure urgency, commitment, readiness and business results.
- *Communication and involvement plan* – the component of the change management plan that addresses SH communication and involvement.
- *Implementation checklist* – a set of criteria that must be satisfied for an implementation to be successful.
- *Roles and responsibilities* – a list of roles and responsibilities to create and sustain the change.
- *Change summary* – a component of project/programme close-out that details the measurable achievements and lessons learned of the change effort.

Figure 49.4 depicts the Kotter process and above deliverables within the project management life cycle.

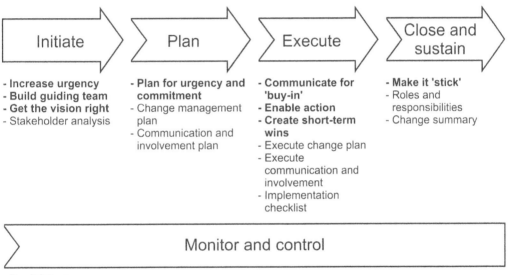

Figure 49.4 Change management activities and deliverables within a project life cycle

INITIATION

In addition to taking steps to deliver a unique product or service, a project has to deliver a sense of urgency and commitment on the part of SHs. Whether the SHs' role is to contribute to the design and delivery of the product/service, or to accept and adopt it once it is delivered, the SHs need motivation to do so. They also need competence, so that they have the knowledge and skills they need to change. Taken together, these ensure that SHs are ready, willing and able to change.

During the initiation and planning phases of the project or programme, it is best practice to assign dedicated resources to the change effort, including a professional change manager. I've seen many projects where the change management responsibility falls to the PM, or where the project counts on SHs to change themselves. Neither of these approaches is as effective as assigning a dedicated professional change manager.

Like project management, change management is a professional discipline with proven processes and methods. Whilst professional PMs are skilled in tools and techniques to deliver against scope, budget and timeline to achieve business benefits, professional change managers are skilled in tools and techniques to deliver urgency, commitment and readiness to maximise business benefits.

Even for projects where the change manager's role is part-time, assigning a dedicated change manager to the project team ensures focus on change issues. The change manager can apply consistent practices and improve the likelihood of long-term, sustained success. In the initiation and planning phase, the change manager will work with SHs to:

1. Build guiding team(s). Many projects establish steering committees that receive regular status updates, provide input and provide resources. Guiding teams extend beyond the typical steering committee role to become motivated, active agents for change who are involved, committed, engaged and accountable. They are responsible to set the vision and create a sense of urgency.
2. Establish vision for the change. The vision needs to be clear, compelling and inspiring to anchor people to the end state for the change.
3. Create a sense of urgency. In order to overcome resistance, SHs need to have a sense of urgency about the change.
4. Assess initial individual and organisational readiness. The change manager conducts an initial readiness assessment to identify potential change barriers and enablers. The initial assessment establishes a baseline for the effort. Subsequent assessments can be compared against the initial assessment to measure progress.

The Richardson Consulting Group (RCG) change management framework is used as a diagnostic in this phase to filter and interpret the assessment results. The change manager and guiding team(s) identify and diagnose both challenges and opportunities related to competence and motivation, as well as the external factors (organisation, business process, culture and leadership).

CHANGE READINESS ASSESSMENT

Depending on the complexity and degree of change, conducting the initial readiness assessment may be as simple as asking SH representatives and the project team to identify potential barriers and enablers to the change. Or it could involve multiple SH interviews, focus groups, surveys or other analysis tasks to assess attitudes towards the change and to answer questions such as:

- What benefits to the organisation are expected from the project/programme?
- What individual benefits are expected for members of each of the target SH groups?
- What attitudes, aptitudes, skills and behaviours exist to support the change?
- What attitudes, aptitudes, skills and behaviours exist that resist the change?

- To what extent is the change perceived to align with existing intrinsic motivators such as attitudes, values and goals, and critical behaviours?
- To what extent is the change perceived to align with existing external motivators such as incentives, performance expectations, social expectations and leadership expectations?

Choosing the assessment methods requires balancing the cost of measurement against the reliability of the data. Some of the more common measurement methods include interviews, focus groups, surveys, observation, analysis of existing data and gathering new data. Figure 49.5 summarises the advantages and disadvantages in terms of cost and reliability:

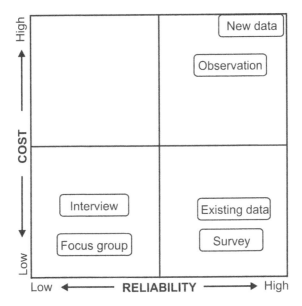

Figure 49.5 Cost vs reliability of assessment methods

Using the RCG change management framework, change managers, PMs and guiding teams can filter the assessment results to identify barriers and enablers to change. The assessment should answer questions such as:

- What aspects of the organisation culture support or inhibit the change?
- What aspects of the organisation structure support or inhibit the change?
- What existing elements or infrastructure within the organisation might inhibit or help accelerate the change?
- What is the current breadth and depth of sponsorship within the organisation?

For example, a customer-centric culture may enable implementation of a new customer service process if the benefits to the customer are clear and well understood, yet the sensitivity to impact on the customer will be high. This sensitivity may be a source of resistance that demands detailed information on how the change will be implemented and the customer experience at each step.

An honest, early assessment of the sponsorship for the change is crucial. Weak sponsorship indicates a lack of urgency, and represents a significant risk to success of the project/programme. Whether the root cause is insufficient benefits, weak messaging, or competing, higher-priority change initiatives, the project/programme team should look at all available options to address the issue. Options may include cancelling the change, deferring the change, redesigning the change initiative to achieve more benefits and sponsorship, recruiting new sponsors or enhancing communication to gain more support.

PLAN

As part of the analysis of the initial assessment results, project/programme risks will be identified, and changes may be required to the project charter and/or project plans. The change manager works with the guiding team(s) to create a change management plan that specifies the tasks and deliverables required to build and maintain urgency, energy and motivation and to achieve SH commitment and readiness. Multiple research studies and experience suggest that a guideline for most projects is to allocate 10–11 per cent of the project budget for change management activities, including:

- sponsorship;
- communication and involvement;
- training;
- organisation design;
- culture;
- process design activities.

A higher level of investment might be required for high-risk, high-complexity projects. For most projects, a lower level of investment introduces a risk of lower ROI or project failure. Given this low level of investment relative to the total project budget, and the high level of ROI associated with investing in change management, adhering to this guideline during the plan phase serves as a useful baseline.

The RCG change management framework can be applied during assessment and planning (see Figure 49.4 on page 635). Figure 49.6 depicts how to use the framework to identify interventions based on feedback gathered by the assessment:

CHANGE PLANNING

Benefits realisation is at the heart of change management, both for the individual and for the sponsoring organisation. Attending to the people side of change helps ensure that the expected benefits become reality. A key component of the planning phase is to develop a communication and involvement plan that frames the change in a way that engages SHs and personalises the meaning of the change. Many change efforts define benefits to the organisation such as cost savings or revenue growth and assume these will be persuasive to everyone in the organisation. Individuals are interested in benefits

Component	Feedback	Interventions
Motivation	This change is a low priority This change is not necessary This is not the right time This change is not a good use of my time I do not know why we are doing this I'm not sure we are solving the real problem This change is not practical Have you considered . . . Are you aware that . . . I'm hearing that . . . Where are the data to prove that? Anger Silence Defensiveness Repeating questions or explanations	**Organisation** • Incentives • Performance management • Role definition **Leadership** • Coaching • Feedback • Sponsorship • Recognition **Culture** • Communication • Empowerment • Recruiting • Diversity management
Competence	I don't understand I am not clear on . . . I don't know what to do next I don't know how this affects me When is this happening? How will this be implemented? What is the plan for . . .? I need more information about . . .	**Organisation** • Organization structure **Business process** • Process improvement • Training • Performance support • Knowledge management **Leadership** • Coaching • Feedback **Culture** • Communication

Figure 49.6 Richardson Consulting Group change management intervention planning

for the organisation, but need to understand the change also in terms of personal impact and personal cost/benefit in order to contextualise, internalise and commit to the effort.

Benefits can also affect society, customers, SHs and working teams. But because change happens at the individual level, the most important benefits are defined and articulated in individual terms – that is – 'What's in it for me (WIIFM)?'

In addition to benefits, WIIFM messages can also articulate the cost of not changing. Research has demonstrated that we are more motivated by fear of loss than by the promise of gain (De Martino et al., 2006). In one experiment, subjects were given an initial sum of money, then given an option to keep a portion of the funds, or gamble the entire amount with an equal chance of retaining or losing the entire amount. When the choice was framed in terms of the amount retained, subjects were risk (change)-averse. When it was framed in terms of the amount lost, they tended to be risk (change)-seeking. Even though the amounts and options were exactly the same, when the choice was framed in terms of loss, people were much more motivated to change. For our purposes, we can apply this insight to include messaging about the costs of not changing as well as the benefits of adopting the change. Some of the most common messages about the benefits of the future state and the costs of maintaining the status quo are:

- easy/difficult to learn;
- easy/difficult to use;
- fun/boring;
- engaging/distracting;
- satisfying/disappointing;
- cheap/expensive;
- fast/slow;
- high/low quality;
- save/waste money;
- save/waste time;
- save/waste effort;
- recognition/criticism;
- gain/lose status;
- gain/lose authority;

A mix of both gain and loss messaging improves communication effectiveness. For example, if we are deploying a new IT system, we can use a combination of cost messaging and benefits messaging such as:

> *Costs*: users report the current system is difficult to master and difficult to navigate, wasting considerable time and effort. A new system is needed to solve this problem.

> *Benefits*: the new system will be easy to learn and easy to use, saving you time and effort.

Where there is resistance to change, it is an indication that the benefits are perceived as insufficient, or the costs of the status quo are not very high. SHs may not be aware of benefits, may not believe the benefits apply to them, or may believe there is no/low cost of maintaining the status quo. Some strategies to overcome resistance include:

- Communicate the benefits of change and the costs of the status quo clearly and consistently to correct the perception of the change (if the perception is incorrect).
- Redesign the change to deliver more benefits, or increase the cost of the status quo (if the perception is correct).
- Bundle less beneficial changes with more beneficial changes. For example users might have anxiety around a change to the organisation structure, but if that roll-out is bundled with more flexible work arrangements (flexible hours, work from home options), they may be more receptive.
- Give SHs control of the pace of change. For example, when deploying a new process, give people the option to continue using the old process in parallel for a period of time until they are comfortable with the new process.

These are all positive strategies designed to increase motivation. However, many projects rely heavily or exclusively on strategies that carry significant risks of decreasing motivation:

- Create incentives. The cost of incentives must be considered as well as their durability. Incentives also carry a risk of reducing motivation and creating unintended consequences.
- Compel the change by forcing people to adopt it. This strategy carries a high risk of increasing resistance, and/or creating a high cost of continued enforcement. Increasing the pressure to change often creates the unintended effect of increasing the strength of the resistance. Until the ultimate sources of resistance are understood and addressed, coercive solutions are both temporary and expensive.

To the largest extent possible, the change plan should emphasise individual choice, engagement and benefits. It should avoid incentives and compulsion. This maximises the levels of urgency and commitment, and minimises the risks of unintended consequences and increased resistance.

EXECUTION

Once the plan is established, execution begins. The goals of this phase are to achieve the desired level of SH urgency, commitment and readiness. Change management activities take place throughout the project life cycle and extend beyond the implementation date(s). The guiding team(s) have a key role in execution, building and sustaining urgency and motivation.

The guiding team(s) and the project team(s) also have constant interaction with all levels of SHs who provide direct or second-hand feedback regarding the change. Both the guiding team and the project team should be alert to both positive and negative feedback and work with the project and change manager(s) to assess the feedback and determine whether or not action is required:

- Are certain groups or individuals enthusiastic about the change? If so, what reasons and benefits do they cite? Is there a way to recruit these groups and individuals to help design, test, promote and support the change?
- Are certain groups or individuals openly negative about the change? If so, what reasons do they cite? Do the reasons cited indicate a deficiency in competence, motivation or both? Is there a way to recruit these groups to help design, test, promote and support the change?

The most vocal proponents and opponents of the change are a valuable source of information on how to improve the design and implement the change, because they exhibit a sense of urgency. Proponents can provide perspective on individual-level benefits, input on the design of the change and are good candidates to be early pilot participants, champions or mentors. Vocal critics are also valuable as they articulate concerns and objections likely held by others who are less vocal. The fact that they are vocal indicates that they are motivated and engaged. Critics whose concerns are listened to and addressed can channel that motivation to become powerful advocates for the change. Even if they are not entirely won over, engaging critics in a direct and honest dialogue ensures their input is heard and steps are taken to improve the design and implementation of the change to the largest extent possible. The change manager, PM, guiding team(s) and project team can use the RCG change management framework to filter positive and negative feedback, diagnose issues and develop responses.

An additional task is to create and execute an implementation checklist to document verifiable, measurable criteria for readiness. These criteria include completion of key activities, like delivering communications and training, identifying roles and responsibilities, as well as achieving measurable targets for urgency, readiness and commitment.

MONITOR AND CONTROL

The goals of the monitor and control phase are to:

- monitor SH urgency, commitment and readiness;
- convert SH expectations to measurable goals;
- detect and address resistance;
- measure and manage goal achievement.

This starts concurrently with the 'Initiate' and 'Plan' phases and with the creation of the measurement plan. This measurement plan encompasses the commitment and readiness targets, as well as the SH expectations. To create this plan, the change manager should:

1. Baseline the readiness assessment, set targets for readiness and then take periodic assessments to measure against the baseline and the targets.
2. Document and prioritise SH expectations, and convert these to measurable goals. For example, stakeholders may expect a new process to be 'efficient' and 'effective'. The guiding team should determine how to verify that the process is 'efficient' and 'effective', what the targets should be, how to collect the data and who will conduct the analysis.
3. Measure against the readiness targets and goals on a regular basis throughout the project.
4. Use the RCG change management framework to evaluate feedback and data in context, identify competence and motivation measures, and conduct root cause analysis. For example, readiness assessment data may indicate that people do not believe the change will have a positive impact on their jobs, when the intent is to have a large, positive impact on those jobs. Using the framework as a diagnostic, we can ask if this is a competence or a motivation issue (or both), and what the root cause(s) might be. The jobs may not yet be designed with the change in mind (role definition), the communication to the audience may be lacking or ineffective (communication) or a sponsor may not be fulfilling their responsibility to build urgency and commitment (sponsorship). Once we settle on a diagnosis, we can use the framework to develop corrective actions such as better communication, training, or coaching of the sponsor.

CLOSE AND SUSTAIN

The goals of the close and sustain phase are to:

- establish long-term change ownership;
- document outstanding readiness and commitment issues and next steps;
- report goal achievement;
- document lessons learned and best practices.

Project resources need to be released at the end of the project in order to allow them to move on to other initiatives. The traditional project management 'close' phase accomplishes this, but change needs to be sustained on a long-term basis. Therefore the conditions to sustain the change must also be met in this phase, which is why we refer to it as *close and sustain*.

Clear roles and responsibilities for sustaining the change and achieving the long-term success of the project or programme will be defined during the course of the change effort, and should be verified as part of implementation. During the project close-out process, the change management aspects are incorporated into the project close activities and deliverables. Planned versus actual urgency, commitment and readiness should be documented, along with any outstanding issues or risks, with clear ownership for next steps. Lessons learned and best practices for managing change should be documented to benefit future projects.

The change manager, guiding team(s) and project team can apply the RCG change management framework to evaluate data in context, assess any remaining competence or motivation issues, and determine appropriate interventions to sustain the effort.

Conclusion

Managing the people side of change is difficult and challenging for PMs and project teams, yet success in managing the people side of change is critical to project success. Organisations that excel in this area deliver better against time, budget, scope and ROI than organisations which do not. As PMs we should recognise the value of change management, apply insights into human motivation to overcome resistance, and dedicate resources to change management activities throughout the project life cycle. By applying a systematic approach to managing the people side of change, we decrease project/programme risk, improve delivery success and multiply ROI.

References and Further Reading

Cohen, D.S. (2005), *The Heart of Change Field Guide: Tools and Tactics for Leading Change in Your Organization*, Boston, MA: Harvard Business School Publishing.

Connor, D. (1992), *Managing at the Speed of Change: How Resilient Managers Succeed and Prosper Where Others Fail*, New York, NY: Villard Books.

De Martino, B., Kumaran, D., Seymour, B. and Dolan, R.J. (2006), 'Frames, biases, and rational decision-making in the human brain', *Science*, 313(5787) 684–7. Available at: http://www.ncbi.nlm.nih.gov/pmc/articles/PMC2631940/ [accessed 18 April 2012].

IBM Global Services (2008), 'Making change work'. Available at: http://www-935.ibm.com/services/us/gbs/bus/html/gbs-making-change-work.html [accessed 1 July 2011].

McKinsey (2002), 'Helping employees embrace change', *McKinsey Quarterly*.

PMI (2008), *A Guide to the Project Management Body of Knowledge (PMBOK® Guide)*, 4th edn, Newtown Square, PA: Project Management Institute.

Richardson Consulting Group, Inc. (2006–2012), 'Richardson Consulting Group Change Management Framework'. Available at: http://www.richardsonconsultinggroup.com/business-communication-planning.php [accessed 1 July 2011].

Ryan, R.M. and Deci, E.L. (2000), 'Intrinsic and extrinsic motivations: Classic definitions and new directions', *Contemporary Educational Psychology*, 25, 54–67. Available at: http://mmrg.pbworks.com/f/Ryan,+Deci+00.pdf [accessed 4 April 2012].

50 *Neuro Linguistic Programming*

RANJIT SIDHU

As a project manager, you probably already use Neuro Linguistic Programming (NLP). Indeed if you have little positional power, you will have to rely on your communication and influencing skills to get things done. There is a difference though between the skills we use instinctively and those over which we have full control. This chapter will help you to learn how NLP contributes positively to communication and influencing, so that you will be able to develop an invaluable toolkit – one that will help you get the very best results across all your projects. These concepts will help you to identify the everyday communication patterns used by you and those around you. The perspectives of others will become easier for you to understand and your skills in gentle influencing and negotiating should be greatly enhanced.

Introduction and Definition

Neuro Linguistic Programming is a composite name derived from neuro (pertaining to the brain), linguistic (to do with language and communication) and programming (which in this case refers to the structures or patterns of behaviour that we use). In more colloquial terms it is the study of what makes people 'tick'.

NLP as we know it today began with the work of Richard Bandler and John Grinder in the 1970s (Bandler and Grinder, 1979). They were psychology and linguistics scholars who observed exceptional people in action, studied what they were doing, and identified what worked best. Research was influenced by earlier scholars such as Korzybski (1921), Chomsky (1957 and 1968) and Bateson (1972). The methodology created by Bandler and Grinder can be learned by anyone to improve their personal and professional effectiveness and NLP has become an important part of management training programmes.

Well-formed Outcomes

It is natural for project managers to focus on goals and on what has to be achieved or delivered. In NLP, we talk about 'well-formed outcomes'. Much has been written about the importance of stating project objectives clearly, but NLP takes this further and highlights the importance of visualising what success will look like. How will you know you have reached your goal? Mastering the skill of creating well-formed outcomes is a way of ensuring that goals are effective and achievable and that you have fully explored their wider consequences.

In his research into the sources of motivation, neuro psychologist Mark Solms (1996) suggests that the process of creating well-formed outcomes stimulates the human reticular activating system (RAS) which is responsible for increased motivation to organise thoughts and activity towards meeting that goal. This is clearly a very logical approach. The more clearly the outcomes can be defined, the more information is fed to the brain, which means the brain will be better able to notice the things that will help you to achieve those outcomes. All project management bodies of knowledge highlight the importance of clarifying project goals, but the NLP approach offers us something extra.

SIMPLE STEPS TOWARDS WELL-FORMED OUTCOMES

Here are six steps towards achieving well-formed outcomes.

1. State positive outcomes:
    This means that each outcome is directed towards something you want rather than away from something you wish to avoid. This will help to keep your focus and energy on moving towards the goal.
2. Consider the evidence:
    Focus on the desired outcomes or customers' success criteria, and constantly assess the evidence as to whether these are being achieved. How will you know you are on track for each outcome? What will you see, hear and feel? Can you describe success specifically, from all angles and from all stakeholders' perspectives? Not only will this make it easier to know when you have finished, but it also means you will more easily be able to assess whether you are on track.
3. Review issues of control:
    Is the task you are taking on within the project manager's and project team's control? Teams need to set the outcomes for their own areas, helping them to feel empowered and motivated.
4. Check resources:
    Ask what is needed to achieve each outcome and whether it is worth it. If the outcome is too big, it will need to be broken down into more suitable chunks. If the risks involved are too great, then revisit the outcome. In helping to set their outcomes, team members should identify any additional support they may need.
5. Consider the consequences:
    If the initial outcome is achieved, what will be the wider benefit and consequences, for you, the team members and the organisation? Do the consequences fit with the strategy and core values of the company? What else could happen as a result of this outcome and is there anything good about the present situation that could be lost?
6. Plan and take action:
    All project managers know that a required outcome usually requires the manager to plan some action. But the process might have to be repeated more than once before arriving at a compelling outcome to which people feel committed.

Activity Suggestion

Use the six steps outlined above as a checklist the next time you need to set a piece of work. Or use them to check how well your project has been defined.

Systems Thinking

NLP is very much about the interrelationship of things. None of us exists in isolation; we are all functioning within wider systems, organisations or divisions, project teams or departments. NLP encourages us to consider the effect of everything we do with respect to the wider system.

The relevance of this is highlighted by the 'butterfly effect' from chaos theory (Lorenz, 1972), which suggests that the smallest change like a butterfly flapping its wings on one side of the world could cause a hailstorm on the opposite side of the world. This is more relevant to today's project managers than at any time in the past because of the complex environments in which we now operate.

Systems thinking is thinking in loops rather than in a linear fashion (Figure 50.1). When one part of the system changes there is a ripple effect on the other parts, as a result of which, the other parts change and the ripple cycle continues, impacting the original part and so on.

Think about feeling thirsty. Your body lets you know. So you drink. You only know how much to drink because your body indicates when you no longer feel thirsty. This is a feedback loop. Becoming more aware of these and noticing feedback from everything we say and do is a critical message from NLP that can make an immediate impact on our success.

A conversation is a prime example. You think of what to say, and then you say it. The other person listens, which affects their thoughts and feelings, and they reply. You perceive their response and react with your own thoughts and feelings. The outcome of the conversation will be very different if you fail to notice and respond to the feedback you are getting.

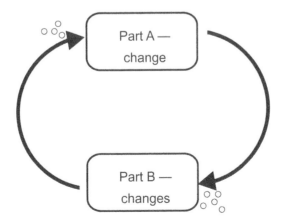

Figure 50.1 Systems thinking involves continuous feedback loops

When you send out a project progress update, some people might say they have received the email and seen the update, but they might not understand the full impact of the changes and just how much they will be expected to do further into the project. Project managers need to think about ways to ensure that the feedback loop is complete, for example by asking specific questions, or by providing additional forums where more interaction and dialogue can take place.

Activity Suggestion

Review your communication plans and think about where it would be useful to introduce more feedback loops.

Filters and Interpretation

We are bombarded continuously with information and we take this in with our senses through which we see, hear, touch, smell and taste. Our brains have to try and make sense of this information, but we can only take in a limited amount in each moment. This idea was outlined by George Miller in his classic paper *The Magic Number Seven, Plus or Minus Two* (Miller, 1956). He conducted research into how many bits of data people can process at any given time and concluded that it was 7 ± 2 bits of information. To avoid being overwhelmed, we have to filter the information coming in.

For each of us, our personal filters are based on our previous experiences, memories, values, beliefs, the assumptions that we hold and the culture in which we have been brought up. We should be aware that our filters cause information to be deleted, distorted and generalised, and that other people have different filters and are likely to end up with a different interpretation of the same situation. This is a bit like creating a map. We cannot include every aspect of detail on a map, yet maps are invaluable in helping us find our way around.

Awareness of the three following main filters can make a huge difference to project managers:

1. *Deletion* – This prevents us from being overwhelmed by every element of detail or from being distracted.
2. *Generalisations* – These are useful for the same reason as deletions. They save time by using rules from a single example and applying these to a much wider group.
3. *Distortions* – We tend to think that some things are more significant than others. In some cases this can lead us to exaggerate their importance, making something seem better or worse than it really is.

Filtering creates our own 'mental model' of the world (Craik, 1943) As a result of filtering we create our own ideas and perception of reality. This is why, for example, two people emerging from a cinema find when they discuss the film afterwards that they each remember different points. In the same way, people might interpret the conclusions from a meeting in different ways. Hence it is necessary to check their understanding and provide clear action points.

Being able to work with a variety of different perspectives is a critical project management skill. It helps to avoid the many conflicts that can occur when different perceptions are not respected.

If you feel that someone is behaving in an irrational way, step back and consider what their perspective might be. What filters are they running? There might be more logic than you initially appreciated behind their behaviour. Take time to understand their reasoning and motivation, and resist trying to convince them that you are right by pressing your own point of view.

Activity Suggestion

Reflect on the filters that your team might be running on your project. Are they holding any unhelpful views about the customer or the level of support they get from other areas?

Communication

In a conversation, there are clearly two sets of filters in operation. The information being shared is being filtered (deleted, distorted and generalised) in unique ways by each person in the conversation. No wonder communication is so easy to get wrong! In fact it is surprising that we ever manage to communicate successfully. But we know that communication is critical to pulling teams and stakeholders together to work towards common goals. NLP can give us the tools we need to do this successfully.

When we consider the meaning of communication, we tend to think of how we articulate our own thoughts and feelings. When we consider 'good' communication, we think of ways to articulate our thoughts more clearly and more precisely. A key principle of NLP is that communication is a loop and 'the meaning of communication is the response that you get'. This reminds us that communication has to involve at least two people, and the essence of communication is the response from your audience. If you talk to a wall, are you communicating? Or is this meaningless because you get no response?

Communication occurs when you perceive the response of another and react to that. You have to pay attention to the person receiving your message to know how best to respond. The meaning of communication is the response that results.

Of course we communicate in other ways than with our words. The tone of our voice, our posture, gestures and expressions, all communicate an enormous amount to anyone tuned in to these. Social psychologist Michael Argyle (Argyle et al., 1970) proposed that 55 per cent of the meaning of a message can be inferred by observing the physiology of another person, 38 per cent of the meaning can be inferred from the voice qualities we notice and only 7 per cent from the words that are used. Mehrabian's better-known research (Mehrabian, 1971) supported these findings. So it is not just what we say, but the way we say it, that makes the difference. Actors know this well. For example, they can express the word 'no' in many different ways, using different tonality and body language.

Watzlawick (1967) suggested that 'we cannot not communicate'. He stresses that everything we do conveys some message, even if we say nothing and stay as still as possible.

Activity Suggestion

Next time you are sitting in a meeting, consider what you are communicating.

Questions of Language and Precision

We communicate using language, with which we attempt to convey the thoughts that we hold in our heads. The problem is that language is limited and can never fully describe the whole picture.

Imagine you are trying to describe the view over the Serengeti as the sun rises. You may say that it is just breathtaking, but these words do not come even close to the sights, sounds and feelings that go with the full sensory experience.

It does not help that we think much faster than we can speak. We sometimes experience an overwhelming sense of frustration that language is simply inadequate. We might say 'It left me speechless', expressing the sensation that words could not possibly describe the experience. Language cannot do justice to the speed and range of our thinking, but it is what we have to express ourselves. Language can only express the very tip of the iceberg. The rest of the iceberg is what lies unseen beneath the surface, which represents the whole of your experience.

Chomsky (1957) suggested that language comprises two parts: 'surface structure' (which includes everything we say both to ourselves and to other people) and 'deep structure' (which covers the underlying meaning of what we say, including what we do not express or maybe even consciously know). The 'deep structure' is the way we represent our experience in our own minds.

Good communicators are able to explore the 'deep structure' – the unsaid elements of communication – the experience that goes beyond the words. They can draw out what a person means, and then express their own ideas in words they know the other person will understand. Paying attention to the language someone is using gives us clues as to how the person is thinking, and what they have filtered out or assumed.

Project managers regularly have to make decisions without the luxury of ample time to gather all the information needed. Asking precision questions enables us to gather information effectively and clarify meaning precisely. It helps to unravel the processes that have taken place as people convert their experiences in 'deep structure' to the words they then use to describe them. In this way we can identify the limits buried within the words that people say, and open up choices that would otherwise remain invisible and unsaid.

By asking the right questions at the right time we can start to fill in some of the missing pieces of information and gain a fuller understanding, making more sense of the communication. This is critical to gaining a shared view of project goals to avoid the misunderstandings that so typically cause problems and to getting better results faster.

CASE EXAMPLE NO. 1

Here is an example of a case where precision questions would have been useful. I was in a meeting, and people were talking about general issues within the department when one of the managers made the statement, 'There is not enough communication going on here'.

There were nods in agreement from around the table with other managers confirming, 'Yes, we need to do something about that'. There was even an action point raised for the manager of the department.

I could not help wondering just *what* that manager was going to do about it. What did they mean by 'communication'? Who exactly was not communicating? What information was it that was not being communicated? If something changed, how would they measure what 'enough' communication would be?

When we hear vague language, our immediate response is to fill in the missing pieces of information ourselves with what we think the meaning should be. It's like getting some pieces of the jigsaw puzzle and then completing the puzzle to make the picture in our own minds. We quickly jump to conclusions and start thinking about a solution that is wholly based on our own assumptions. The key to overcoming this is 'to get out of your own way' first. Stop yourself from completing the puzzle. Ask the questions with a really open mind and then complete the jigsaw puzzle with the information that you are given.

Examples of distortions

'The users are very resistant to this change'.	What leads you to believe that? How specifically do you know? What do you base that on?
'They do not respond to my emails, so they are not interested'	How does their not responding to my emails mean that they are not interested?
'There is no collaboration at all'.	Who should be collaborating, and how?

Examples of generalisations

'We always do it this way'.	Absolutely always? Are there any exceptions? What would happen if we did not do it this way?
'I can't tell them'.	What concerns you about telling them?
'I just couldn't say no to their request'.	What prevents you from saying 'No'? Just suppose you did, what would that mean?

Examples of deletions

'Mistakes have been made'.	What mistakes, exactly?
'The meeting went badly'.	What are you comparing that with? Badly in what way?
'They have got better over time'.	Better in what way?

Figure 50.2 Questions for surfacing filtered information

Figure 50.2 shows a list of statements which reflect different patterns of filtering. Alongside these are precision questions which are aimed at recovering the missing information. However, here is a word of caution. When asking these kinds of questions, we need to do it with rapport and in a considered way. Think about what the purpose is behind each question. What information will it unravel and how will that be helpful?

Activity Suggestion

Note that as well as using precision questions with other people, they work equally well with yourself. Test your own assumptions, to help you clarify your own thoughts on an issue.

Thinking Styles

We have said that much of our success as project managers depends on our ability to understand the perspectives of others – our teams, customers, sponsors and all our stakeholders – and to communicate with them in a way that makes sense for them. To do this it is useful to understand their thinking styles.

Consider the mix of people in your teams and how they interact during meetings. Perhaps you have some members who like to talk through all their ideas and discuss them at length. There may be others who want to be able to grasp the situation quickly and get a 'gut feeling' for the way forward without examining detail.

Just as we experience the world outside us by using our senses to see, hear, feel, smell and taste, we use the same senses to store our thoughts. When we are thinking we are making mental pictures. We recall sounds and experience the feelings in the same way. Just think for a moment about a can of fizzy drink being poured into a glass with ice. As you think about it, can you visualise a picture? Can you hear the sound it makes as the can is opened and the drink is poured over the ice? Can you get a sensation of what that would taste like and how it makes you feel? You get the idea.

When we are thinking, the three main senses used are visual, auditory and kinaesthetic (which represent seeing, hearing and feeling or touch). Obviously there are exceptions; for instance, if you are a wine taster your taste buds and sense of smell are going to be very finely tuned to make more distinctions. But for most of us, visual, auditory and kinaesthetic are the main senses and people tend to prefer one or two of these. People express their thoughts using language, so someone's style of language tends to provide vital clues as to their thinking style, as follows:

Visual:
- I get the picture;
- that is a lot clearer now;
- I see what you mean.

Auditory:
- that rings a bell;
- it sounds okay to me;
- I hear what you're saying.

Kinaesthetic:
- that feels right now;
- we need to get a grip;
- let's touch base.

By picking up on the language people are using, we can use similar language ourselves to strengthen our connection with them. If you communicate with someone by matching their thinking style, it helps to build a bridge between you and them. When we recognise that we have been communicating well with someone, we often say 'We were speaking the same language'. Well, that is exactly what is happening. It is important to realise that a person doesn't just use only one pattern all the time; it will vary depending on the situation and the context. The important thing for project managers is to develop flexibility in language and learn to listen to the language of others, so that when responding to your team members and stakeholders you can match their language.

Paying attention to language also gives us clues about how people process information. For example, when you ask 'How was your journey to work this morning?' do you get a fairly succinct answer, or lots and lots of detail? If you know your sponsor prefers to have lots of detail, then they will only be satisfied if you provide that level of information yourself.

Activity Suggestion

Next time you are having a conversation with someone, listen out for the words they use and note if there is a preference for one style more than others. Practise matching the styles of others. You can also record interviews on the television, play them back and listen for patterns.

Reframing

Putting a frame around something draws our attention to it. Setting a project objective and identifying the scope puts a frame around what the team needs to focus on. Putting a frame around something is also how we give meaning to it – it is where the frame is placed that defines the meaning.

Take a look at the pictures of fish in Figure 50.3. Changing the frame changes the meaning; it shows a different perspective and gives a different meaning to the situation. Being able to do this helps with solving problems, making decisions and resolving conflicts so you have more choice and flexibility. Daily examples of reframing are phrases such as:

- Looking at it another way;
- Let's think about it differently;
- Let's turn it on its head;
- Out of the box thinking.

One way of reframing, is to broaden the context. For example, consider an occasion when a risk is being assessed. In isolation, each risk may not seem to pose too big a threat on a

Picture 1

Picture 2

Figure 50.3 Picture frames

project, but if it is considered alongside other risks, the cumulative effect could be enough to trigger a review of whether the project should continue.

Another example is that if the team is too focused on problems and their causes, the same content can be reframed to encourage them to think about outcomes and solutions. Changing the frame in this way helps to move things forward. It is a little like choosing which way to walk down a road: if we walk one way, we shall see one view, but if we walk the other way, we shall see something quite different. It's the same road and both views are equally true. But we can choose which way to go.

Multiple Perspectives

Project managers are often required to make difficult decisions and help resolve tough issues. Being able to take a balanced view and remain objective under pressure is a necessary skill and very much a part of the role.

When thinking about your own approach to dealing with difficult situations, consider these three different perspectives:

1. Your own point of view as project manager;
2. The other person's point of view;
3. The 'fly on the wall' overview perspective (that is, being independent and impartial).

This is a great approach for developing a balanced viewpoint and dealing with situations in an objective way. The following steps will help you work with these three different perspectives.

Step 1: Put yourself in the first of the above positions – this is about looking at the situation from your own perspective. What do you feel about the situation? What is important to you? What do you want?

Step 2: Put yourself in the second position – step completely into the other person's shoes. You may find it helpful to move physically to a different place or sit in another chair. Act as if you are role playing and you are being the stakeholder. Really experience the situation from their perspective. See things as they do. Hear what they hear and feel what it is like to be them. As the stakeholder, what is important? What do you need?

Step 3: Move your position again. Shift to a different spot, a bit further away. This time, it is as if you are a 'fly on the wall' or a completely independent person who has just walked in and just happens to be witnessing an interaction between these two people. It is as if you are completely detached and have no personal involvement in the situation. What do you notice about the other two positions? What is going on?

Step 4: Go back to the first position and reflect on the situation, taking into account any insights you have gathered along the way.

Activity Suggestion

Next time you find yourself thinking about how to deal with a challenging interaction (such as a difficult stakeholder) try the above four steps as part of your preparation before meeting with them.

Rapport

Communicating in such a way that we can influence people is a vital skill for project managers. Being able to exchange information and resolve problems effectively saves much time and avoids many problems on projects.

Rapport is the way in which we relate to others to create a climate of trust and understanding. In many cases, an element of rapport is there naturally – it feels effortless, and you do not have to try. In these cases there is a relaxed exchange of ideas and discussion and things tend to move along quite well. If you look around at people talking and interacting, you can usually tell those who are in rapport. They tend to mirror and match each other with their posture and gestures. It is almost as if they are engaged in a dance.

Equally, it is easy to spot people who are not in rapport. There is a mismatch in their body language and gestures. Where rapport is not present naturally or there is not enough of it, then we need to put some effort in to build it and create relationships of mutual respect and influence.

It is easy to end up spending more time with people 'like us', people whom you find easy to get on with, but as project managers you need to be able to communicate with everyone, including all the stakeholders – even the ones you might find difficult. Investing time in establishing and building relationships with your clients, your teams and other stakeholders is just as important for the success of your projects as ensuring that they are well planned. To build rapport, you need to:

- Listen to people and show a genuine interest in them;
- Put yourself in their position and be curious about seeing things from their perspective.

You do not need to be their best friend or agree with them, but you can show that you respect their point of view. This mindset will go a long way to helping you to develop rapport with people. A lot of this you will be doing already. Finding things in common to talk about, whether it is the weather or traffic on the motorway, are also ways of establishing rapport. Other factors you can consider are to match the other person's:

- postures and gestures;
- rhythm of movement and energy levels;
- voice tonality and pace;
- language patterns and the words which they emphasise.

Doing this with sensitivity and respect helps to establish a solid foundation for effective communication to take place. So often, we put a lot of thought into the words we speak but overlook what the rest of our body is communicating – even over the telephone. To achieve rapport and earn trust, our words and every aspect of our manner, need to work in harmony to convey a consistent message.

Activity Suggestion

When you are interacting with other people, notice when you feel in rapport and when you do not. What are you doing when it works and what is missing when it doesn't? What can you do to establish rapport more easily?

Putting it all Together

Having read about some of the key aspects of NLP, now consider how they can work together (Figure 50.4). To conclude this chapter, here is a case example.

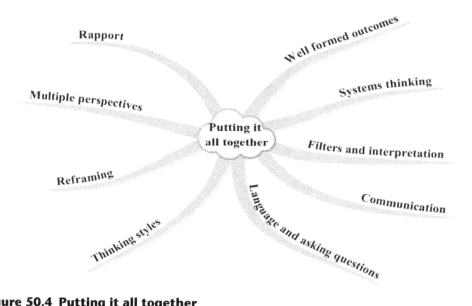

Figure 50.4 Putting it all together

CASE EXAMPLE NO. 2

The Difficulty

Jim, a project manager, walks into a meeting with the project's main supplier. The day has already been stressful. Even though it was a lovely sunny day, there is much to discuss in a stuffy conference room. Jim confidently expects the supplier's account manager to report that the first deliverable is ready for testing, and at least then they can get on with this part of the project.

But when Jim walks into the conference room he immediately notices that the supplier's account manager is not present but has sent a stranger as her deputy. This does not bode well with the project manager who wonders what is going on, and why his company is not considered important any more.

The first item on the agenda is the supplier's deliverable. The deputy starts to make what sound like excuses about not having the deliverable ready. This triggers several thoughts in Jim's mind:

- Perhaps failure is why the account manager is not present and has sent a deputy;
- The supplier is incompetent, failing to deliver anything at all;
- How am I going to explain this to my superiors?
- What is everyone else on and outside the project going to think?
- What impressions will this give of me as a competent project manager?

Jim feels angry, stressed and frustrated. He cannot think clearly. The day is going from bad to worse.

But it did not have to go like that.

The NLP Solution

Figure 50.5 highlights some of the things that Jim could have done to achieve a very different and more positive outcome from the meeting. Using these NLP tools, this is how Jim's meeting could have turned out:

We pick up this case again from the point where Jim walks into the meeting and notices that the supplier's account manager is not there. Jim reflects upon his internal thoughts and takes a deep breath, a reminder to 'pause for thought' for a moment and not jump to conclusions, but to remain open minded.

The first item on the agenda is about the supplier's deliverable. The supplier's deputy starts to explain the situation, that there is a delay as there has been a technical hitch. Jim asks the deputy to explain the situation more fully and listens carefully. This encourages the deputy to elaborate on the problems and explain all the options that they have considered to resolve the delays.

Now Jim and the deputy discuss alternatives and agree together what the next steps will be, what the impact is on the plan, and how they can work together to minimise this impact. Jim is not badly stressed and feels that the meeting has been very productive. Both parties have a better understanding of each other's circumstances and priorities.

That is a very sound way in which to move forward.

Example of areas to be considered	Aspects of NLP that can be helpful
Preparation for the meeting.	Use the steps for *well-formed outcomes* to prepare for the meeting.
The day has already been stressful.	*Reframing:* it's good to have the project manager position and the responsibility which comes with that. Some of the problems which have occurred offer a challenge and opportunity to get different team members working together. Focus on the outcomes. *Systems thinking:* in the wider context, a lot of things are going well, both at work and outside work.
Walks into the office and notices that it's not the usual account manager.	*Filters and interpretation:* it does not have to mean bad news. Keep an open mind and become curious instead. Here is an opportunity to use rapport skills, to establish a connection quickly.
A project deliverable is not ready.	*Use precision questions:* to get more specific information and understand the situation from the perspective of the other people. *Multiple perspectives:* consider these and the wider context. Continue to maintain *rapport,* listening for the *language* patterns and thinking styles used, as well as non-verbal behaviour. Get one's own point across. Remember the *communication* loop and get feedback to ensure that your point is being understood. Consider using steps from well-formed outcomes to agree actions to take the project forward.

Figure 50.5 An application of NLP methods

References and Further Reading

Argyle, M., Salter, V., Nicholson, H., Williams, M. and Burgess, P. (1970), 'The communication of inferior and superior attitudes by verbal and non-verbal signals', *British Journal of Social and Clinical Psychology*, 9(3), 222–31.

Bandler, R. and Grinder, J. (1979), *Frogs into Princes: Neuro Linguistic Programming*, Moab, UT: Real People Press.

Bateson, G. (1972), *Steps to an Ecology of Mind: Collected Essays in Anthropology, Psychiatry, Evolution, and Epistemology*, Chicago, IL: University Of Chicago Press.

Chomsky, N. (1957), *Syntactic Structures*, The Hague: Mouton & Co.

Chomsky, N. (1968), *Language and Mind*, New York: Harcourt Brace & World, Inc.

Covey, S. (1989), *The Seven Habits of Highly Effective People*, New York: Simon & Schuster.

Craik, K. (1943), *The Nature of Explanation*, Cambridge: Cambridge University Press.

Korzybski, A. (1921), *Manhood of Humanity: the Science and Art of Human Engineering*, New York: E. P. Dutton & Company.

Lorenz, E. (1972), 'Predictability: Does the Flap of a Butterfly's Wings in Brazil Set Off a Tornado in Texas?', 139th meeting of the American Association for the Advancement of Science.

Mehrabian, A. (1971), *Silent Messages: Implicit Communication of Emotions and Attitudes*, Belmont, CA: Wadsworth Publishing Company.

Miller, G.A. (1956), 'The magic number seven, plus or minus two', *Psychological Review*, Princeton University's Department of Psychology.

Senge, P. (1990), *The Fifth Discipline: The Art & Practice of the Learning Organization*, New York: Doubleday.

Solms, M. (1996), 'Towards an anatomy of the unconscious', *Journal of Clinical Psychoanalysis*, 5, 331–67.

Watzlawick, P. (1967), *Pragmatics of Human Communication*, New York: W. W. Norton & Company.

51 *Positive Psychology*

JOCELYN S. DAVIS

Editorial Comment (DL/LS)

This chapter describes a teaching regime in use at the Project Management Center for Excellence (UMD PM Center) at the Clark School of Engineering at the University of Maryland. It will be of particular value to others considering designing or improving courses relevant to people managing teams in projects.

Project management is continually evolving. This evolution is described, for example in Morris (1994) and Shenhar and Dvir (2004). Each change is supposed to bring advancement in project management practices and greater reliability and professionalism. Yet projects continue to fail. We believe that the next developmental stage for project management is to focus on the needs of the people who are carrying out the project. In order to take that step, education for project management (PM) professionals must help project managers to understand the people they manage, in all their diversity and complexity. There is a growing body of research in psychology and management sciences to support developing that understanding for PM professionals thereby moving this knowledge from the universities and colleges to common practice in the workplace.

Introduction

This chapter reports work that we are doing at the Project Management Center for Excellence (UMD PM Center) at the Clark School of Engineering at the University of Maryland, where we have developed an innovative response to the evolving needs of PM professionals. We have developed two graduate courses which are based on *applied positive psychology*. This work was initiated by John H. Cable, the director of the UMD Center and me (his consulting partner).

Our first course was introduced in the autumn of 2004 and has been offered in the autumn and spring semesters each year since then. The first course is required for all master's and doctoral level students. Entitled *Managing Project Teams for Sustainable Competitive Advantage*, the course focuses on developing self-awareness, learning management skills, and understanding how to create and sustain workplaces where individuals flourish and organisations thrive.

Our second course, *Evolving as a PM Leader*, is an elective which considers leadership theory and practice. Students develop their own philosophy of leadership, assess where they are as PM leaders, their vision as a PM leader, and a professional and personal development plan to become the PM leader they choose to be.

This chapter will focus on the challenges faced by PM professionals, our response using applied positive psychology to enhance project outcomes, our approach to teaching applied positive psychology to graduate engineers, the innovative teaching model at the Center, the content of the *Managing Teams* course, and our thoughts for further development of PM education.

The Challenge

Some project teams respond to the challenges of complex projects and changing environments with resilience and innovation, whilst other project teams may start strong but then diminish in productivity and fail.

As described throughout this Handbook, much of the difference is directly attributable to practices related to the management of the people involved in project execution. Some project managers seem to know instinctively how to organise groups to be effective, how to motivate people and how to deal successfully with the inevitable changes, conflicts and ethical questions. But many others rose into PM based solely on their technological and domain expertise, without any particular knowledge about how to manage people. Closing this knowledge gap is critical to successful project delivery.

In the UMD PM Center we believe that professional project managers should have domain-specific knowledge, PM knowledge, and expertise in how to create a work environment where teams are able to do their best work.

This is based on the fundamental belief that project managers can learn people management skills. Contrary to popular belief, people skills are not inborn personality traits that people either have or do not have. With appropriate knowledge and effective practice, people *can* learn these skills (Whetten and Cameron, 2011). The skills may be complex, but one skill supports another. They can be combined with project domain knowledge to enhance the ability of our graduate PM students to manage today's complex and challenging projects to successful conclusion.

Our Response to the Challenge: Using Positive Psychology as the Foundation

Our relevant courses at the UMD PM Center are:

- Managing Project Teams, Building and Maintaining Competitive Advantage (Managing Teams course) and;
- Evolving as a PM Leader.

The first of these is required and the second is an elective. This chapter will focus on the *Managing Project Teams* course.

PM, a nascent profession in the 1960s, is now central to organisations' execution of their strategic plans. Despite this rise in strategic importance, PM has continued to report relatively high failure rates in meeting the traditional triple constraints of scope, schedule and budget, not to mention client expectations. The addition of other criteria such as sustainability only complicates successful delivery. The PM profession has advanced, as reported by Shenhar and Dvir (2004), through several developmental stages:

- 1960s: scheduling;
- 1970s: teamwork;
- 1980s: risk and uncertainty;
- 1990s: simultaneity;
- 2000s: adaptation, strategic globalisation and maturity models.

We believe that the next critical stage of development for PM is *people management*. We are not alone in this belief. The triple bottom line (3BL) (Savitz and Weber, 2006) involves thinking about organisational outcomes not only in terms of profit (financial capital or return-on-investment), but also *planet* (natural capital or the organisation's impact on the environment), and *people* (social capital or the organisation's impact on people – stakeholders, employees, customers, communities, suppliers and even competitors).

We also believe that the next frontier for PM will be a more effective focus on the needs of the people who are carrying out the project. In order to take that step, education for PM professionals must help people understand themselves and the people they manage, in all their diversity and complexity. There is a growing body of research in psychology and management sciences to support that understanding. We have relied substantially on the science known as *applied positive psychology* to complement and enhance traditional management practices relative to people on projects.

ACADEMIC FOUNDATION OF COURSES.

The UMD PM Center courses build on empirical research from the fields of positive psychology (Peterson and Seligman, 2004; Snyder et al., 2011; and Linley and Joseph, 2004), Positive Organizational Behaviour (POB) (Luthans et al., 2007), Positive Leadership (Cameron, 2008), and Positive Organizational Scholarship (POS) (Cameron and Spreitzer, 2011). These fields study the conditions that support people and organisations being strong, resilient and productive. We call the goals of these practices 'positive workplaces', that is, workplaces where individuals flourish and organisations thrive (Davis and Cable, 2006).

Positive psychology as a term of art was coined in 1999 by Martin E. P. Seligman when he was president of the American Psychological Association (APA). After the Second World War, research funding in psychology, at least in the US, was directed primarily to the relief of psychological suffering. Seligman wanted to supplement psychology as usual (a deficit reduction or medical model) by initiating a complementary emphasis on the conditions under which people flourish. This area was not new, having been addressed in religious and philosophic texts across many cultures, ancient and modern. Seligman strove to refocus the discussion in the science of psychology, as he stated eloquently in a frequently viewed TED talk (Seligman, 2004), psychology should be just as concerned with:

- strength as with weakness;
- building the best things in life as repairing the worst;

- making the lives of normal people fulfilling and with nurturing high talent as with fixing pathology.

These goals resonated with the dilemma often observed by managers that they spend a disproportionate time on anticipating, intervening and correcting poor performance. In a practical sense, incorporating applied positive psychology into PM education and practice involves being just as interested in what already works well and finding ways to get more from it as figuring out what's problematic and how to fix it. Further, as described by Spreitzer and Sonenshein (2003, 2004), correcting weaknesses moves capability from 'weak' to 'not weak' – it does not, and will not, move capability from weak to strong. The concept of managing to encourage positive deviance (Spreitzer and Sonenshein, 2003, 2004) is central to our UMD PM Center courses.

Like psychology in general, positive psychology is an empirical discipline that tests hypotheses empirically to inform practice. Many of our ideas about what may be helpful in the workplace are common sense, but others are common mistakes. By relying on empirical research, we are able to sort the wheat from the chaff. Over the course of the semester, our students read works by the major contributors to the field, not so that they know where important ideas come from, but they also learn some of the people to watch as knowledge in the field expands. This supports our students' continuous learning in the field and their ongoing development in practice of empirically-informed practices.

A related field at the intersection of psychology and management science, POB is 'the study and application of positively oriented human resource strengths and psychological capacities that can be measured, developed, and effectively managed for performance improvement in today's workplace' (Luthans, 2002, 59). The psychological capacities contemplated for POB must have the following characteristics:

- they must be theory and research based;
- valid and reliable measures exist;
- they are state-like and can be developed through interventions;
- they impact work performance positively (Luthans, 2002; Luthans et al., 2007).

So far, the research on POB has yielded four qualities that meet these criteria: self-efficacy, optimism, hope and resilience (psychological capital). One of the goals of our curriculum is to ensure that students know these concepts thoroughly, including both the business value and the numerous interventions that can build these qualities in workplace settings.

POS is 'the study of that which is positive, flourishing, and life-giving in organizations', (Cameron and Caza, 2004, 731). Thus the focus on individual flourishing is expanded to take in the qualities that cause organisations to thrive, including the interpersonal dynamics that lead to *positive deviance*, defined by Spreitzer and Sonenshein (2003, 209) as 'intentional behaviors that depart from the norms of a referent group in honorable ways'. Just as positive psychology rebalances the study of individuals, POS rebalances the study of organisations, expanding the existing focus on eliminating non-standard performance to include also fostering non-standard performance in the positive direction. By teaching the concept of positive deviance, we open up discussions of ways that organisations can go beyond what is considered normal towards exceptional performance.

The newest research, even well-tested practical research, is slow to reach practitioners and often arrives in a few simple applications taught for immediate use without their research underpinnings making them appear to be management fads. We believe that to be truly useful, applications need to be taught within the context of the original research so that practitioners are able to expand the application in the field to meet current circumstances; an application taught without this is a tool with minimal flexibility. To go beyond management fads, our courses at the UMD PM Center are aimed at the 'sweet spot' between research and practice. We help students understand the importance of empirical research as a foundation for management excellence. We teach many models, always with the caveat that models are valuable only insofar as they are both research-based and practically useful. We help students to assimilate durable and creative new ways of thinking about people at work. We also help students practice evaluating the claims of emerging research, so that they can be informed consumers of advances in the field that occur after they leave our class.

The 'People Portfolio'

Our interdisciplinary courses focus on PM practices that lead to individual flourishing, highly productive workplaces and effective leadership. Students are learning to manage the *people portfolio*. As illustrated in Figure 51.1, the courses focus on practices that create an environment where people feel committed to the work, respond resiliently to work

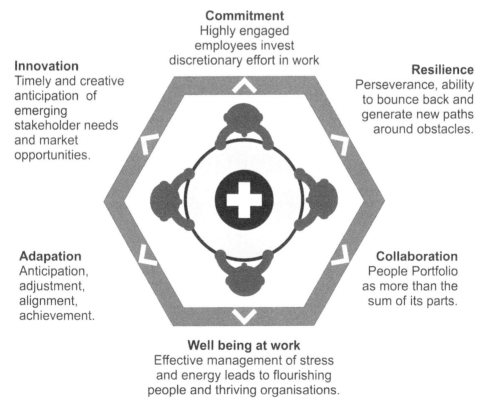

Commitment
Highly engaged
employees invest
discretionary effort in work

Innovation
Timely and creative
anticipation of
emerging
stakeholder needs
and market
opportunities.

Resilience
Perseverance, ability
to bounce back and
generate new paths
around obstacles.

Adapation
Anticipation,
adjustment,
alignment,
achievement.

Collaboration
People Portfolio
as more than the
sum of its parts.

Well being at work
Effective management of stress
and energy leads to flourishing
people and thriving organisations.

Figure 51.1 Managing the people portfolio

challenges, collaborate to get the work done, manage stress and physiological well-being so that they have high levels of energy to invest in work, adapt to changing requirements as projects evolve, and innovate effectively both at the macro-level with new invention and at the micro-level with more effective day-to-day project execution. These are all requirements of our rapidly changing PM world.

We think of PM as an incubator for organisational change. Projects by definition are:

- time-limited;
- not routine work;
- of strategic importance to the sponsoring organisation;
- managed with high performance standards with respect to scope, schedule and budget.

Tools and techniques learned on one project, if successful, are then taken to the next project as teams form, disband and reform over time.

THE BUSINESS CASE IN BRIEF

Global employment trends indicate that there will be critical shortfalls of qualified technical professionals over the next several decades. This critical shortfall is the result of changes in immigration laws in the US, enhanced opportunities for technical professionals in their own countries, and the impact of retirement (albeit delayed by the global recession) of the 'baby boomers'. Some people estimate the total reduction in people available to work in the US at nearly 30 million. Fundamental changes in the nature of the employer/employee contract (from employment for life with one employer to the current generation's new employer every two to three years) are creating the need for employers to be competitive – to become and to remain employers of choice. Whether they are government organisations, non-profits, large corporations, or small businesses, workplaces of the twenty-first century face the following challenges:

- significant fundamental changes are in motion globally that impact how we work;
- the speed at which new information is generated and then becomes obsolete is accelerating. It is estimated that what a college freshmen learns will be obsolete before they graduate;
- globalisation of work now requires 24/7 connectivity as well as adaptability to work effectively with an increasingly diverse workplace, separated by language, culture and time zones and unified by shared economic interests;
- the rate of technological change is now so fast that we are trying to prepare students for careers that don't yet exist.

As economies in developed countries move from heavy reliance on production or manufacturing to service and knowledge-based industries, the management paradigm has to change to be effective. The earliest theories of management assumed that people were lazy or incompetent or both (requiring active surveillance and discipline to be productive). People were assumed to be motivated solely by their pay cheque and the only valuable awards were assumed to be monetary (Deci and Ryan, 1985; Pink, 2009). Individuals were imperfect, but perfectible; any person with sufficient training, monetary incentives and aggressive goal setting and performance management could do any job. The usual standards of civility were for personal social engagements but not essential to the workplace. Incivility, depersonalisation and emotional disregard were acceptable tools to get the work done. Organisations measured and rewarded output without regard to how it was produced.

Recent economic pressures exacerbated an existing trend to demand continuously that people do more with less, assuming that there is no upper limit to either the amount of work people can produce under threat of job loss or the amount of stress they can endure and still be productive. Our most critical competitive resource (our people) was assumed to be infinitely adaptable to increasingly demanding circumstances at work. The costs of these practices are substantial, as follows:

- Turnover: people leave *managers* more than they leave *companies*. Turnover is very costly. Estimates range from 6 months' salary for hourly workers to 18 months' salary for managers.
- Bullying: workers who are subjected to workplace bullying tend to decrease in self-confidence, efficiency and effectiveness (Namie, 2003).
- Absenteeism increases when people are either disengaged from work or unduly stressed to the point of physical and mental illness.
- Multitasking and continuous partial attention. People who feel pressed to do *more* with *less* tend to try to do multiple tasks at once. Research showed that people who multitask frequently get less done and at lower quality levels (Ophir et al., 2009).
- Theft and sabotage: people who don't feel valued at work are more inclined to 'get back' at their organisations.
- Lack of safety leading to low levels of resilience to change and innovation.
- Negative emotional tone. Negative emotional responses to workplace and other stresses are normal. When strongly outweighing the positive emotional responses in the workplace, negative emotions actually diminish people's ability to think creatively, engage within a diverse workforce, be resilient in the face of setbacks or change (Fredrickson, 1998; Fredrickson and Losada, 2005).

Gallup and other researchers on employee engagement have found that a focus on strengths-based management, coupled with employee engagement efforts results in a substantial reduction of actively disengaged employees. Actively disengaged employees are estimated to cost the US economy nearly 10 per cent of GDP annually (Gallup, 2006, 2009).

More recent research in well-being at the nation-state level (New Economics Foundation, 2008) and the concept of work engagement (Bakker and Leiter, 2010) has provided an overarching model for thinking about people at work and under what conditions they thrive.

Overview of the *Managing Teams* Course

In response to the changing needs of the project manager to be better able to manage the most complex asset on any project (it's the people) we developed the *Managing Teams* course in 2004. This course was designed to be positive, psychology-based and focused on applications. The core content and our approach to the course itself are discussed below.

First, we believed that to be a great manager you have to first be able to manage yourself. Self-management capability comes from self-knowledge. *Know Yourself/Know Others* is the first content section and is about 30 per cent of the course time. This is based on one of the major class themes – excellent managers have to know themselves first, understand their own core qualities and quirks, and be able to manage themselves before they can become effective managers of other people.

Each of our semesters begins with the students sharing a best-self introduction (Seligman, 2004). These introductions are contrasted with the more standard introduction common in the workplace which offers name, profession, home town, degree and the likes. Each student is asked to tell a brief, true story about themselves being, not doing, their best. Stories are quite varied and students sometimes choose the least disclosing story they can offer and meet the requirement for an introduction. We then have the class do strengths-spotting (Linley et al., 2010) and then ask how those strengths might contribute to project success.

SELF-AWARENESS THROUGH SELF-ASSESSMENT

People are the most complex resource deployed on any project. They are complicated individually and team complexity is exponential.

Over time we have developed a portfolio of well-validated self-assessments to help the students get to know themselves. This is partially accomplished by completing and debriefing self-assessments and partially, and perhaps more powerfully, by providing the students with a structured time for deep self-reflection through our self-assessment workbook titled *Know Yourself, Know Others* which we developed to help students document and process the self-assessment information.

SELF-ASSESSMENT PORTFOLIO

Our self-assessment portfolio is drawn from positive psychology, general psychology and other sources. We use trait-based assessments, trait-state assessments, and state assessments to help the students understand themselves in terms of stable, somewhat malleable and highly changeable characteristics. Our self-assessment portfolio includes the items shown in Figure 51.2 on the page opposite. Selected self-assessments used in our course are discussed briefly below.

Personality and Temperament

Some suggest that differences in personality type are the root cause of the most workplace conflicts. Understanding personality and being able to work successfully with differences in the workplace is central to healthy, productive work and workplace interactions. The MBTI (Myers-Briggs Type Indicator) is the most frequently used, non-diagnostic psychological assessment. It describes how people gather data, make decisions, generate energy and orient themselves to the outside world.

Assesses	Self-assessment	Notes and references
Personality and temperament	MBTI personality type indicator	One of the most frequently used non-clinical personality type indicators. See Chapter 32. See also www.myersbriggs.org
Strengths	VIA survey of character strengths and virtues	Developed by Peterson and Seligman (2004) See www.authentichappiness.com
	Realize2	Developed by Alex Linley, Centre of Applied Positive Psychology, Warwick, UK. See www.cappeu.com
Positive psychology	Optimism	See www.authentichappiness.com
	Positive relationships	See www.authentichappiness.com
	Work/life questionnaire (job/career/calling)	See www.authentichappiness.com
	Psychological capital	Luthans, Youssef and Avolio (2006)
	Good life survey	See www.authentichappiness.com
Management skills	Personal assessment of management skills	Whetten and Cameron (2011)
	Time management	Whetten and Cameron (2011)
Analytical skills	Problem solving, creativity and innovation	Whetten and Cameron (2011)
Change orientation	Locus of control	Whetten and Cameron (2011)
	Tolerance of ambiguity	Whetten and Cameron (2011)
Psychology	Core self-evaluation scale	Whetten and Cameron (2011)
	Social readjustment scale (stress assessment)	Whetten and Cameron (2011)
	Stress management assessment	Chapter 61 and Whetten and Cameron (2011)
	Emotional intelligence	Chapter 53 and Whetten and Cameron (2011)
Well-being at work	Well-being at work	www.nef-consulting.co.uk and www.well-beingatwork.net

Figure 51.2 Self-assessment portfolio

Strengths

The business value of strengths-focused management is substantial. We utilise two strengths assessments.

The first, the Values in Action Inventory of Character Strengths, was developed by Peterson and Seligman (2004). This strengths assessment focuses on 24 ubiquitous character strengths which were derived from the study of written moral and religious traditions across the world and across history (Peterson and Seligman, 2004). These 24 strengths are readily recognised by all students and help establish bonds early in class. By definition, these strengths are who you are at your best and are relatively stable or trait-like over time.

The second strengths assessment we use is the Realize2 developed by Alex Linley et al. (2010) of the Centre for Applied Positive Psychology, Warwick in the UK. We believe this assessment tool is particularly innovative. It includes 60 strengths, divided into five families (Being, Motivating, Communicating, Relating and Thinking), and categorised for reporting and analysis into four categories based upon frequency of use, impact of use on energy, and skill in use. The resulting matrix of strengths reports realised strengths, unrealised strengths, learned behaviours and weaknesses. This assessment considers strengths deployment at work as dynamic in response to workplace requirements and how they are approached by the individual.

Management Skills

For the personal assessment of management skills (PAMS) our primary textbook is Whetten and Cameron (2011), which presents a comprehensive assessment of management skills that closely parallels positive psychology applied in the workplace. We ask students to take this self-assessment prior to the beginning of the course and at the end of the course to measure their progress. Additionally, we ask the students to carefully analyse their results at the start of the course to focus their efforts on their individual developmental needs. For many of our students, the results from this self-assessment are less favourable than they anticipated and it is a forcing function for taking on the challenging personal work of becoming a great PM.

Psychological Capital

Psychological capital (Luthans et al., 2007) is optimism, resilience, self-efficacy and hope. By definition, psychological capital levels are related to positive organisational outcomes and are subject to improvement through proven low-cost interventions. Optimism allows us to interpret work events in a manner that supports positive next steps; hope allows us to step back from obstacles and redesign our approaches to be successful; resilience allows us to persevere in the face of major change, positive or negative and self-efficacy provides the confidence for us to take action within our sphere of subject matter expertise. Each of these qualities has clear benefits within the project environment (ibid.).

Change Orientation

Within the Whetten and Cameron (2011) textbook are two other self-assessments that we use in our course:

- tolerance of ambiguity;
- locus of control.

These two describe orientation to change, with locus of control describing whether there is an internal or external locus of control and tolerance of ambiguity describing one's ability to act without complete data or in the face of relatively undefined goals of conditions.

We believe that this combination of self-assessments assist our students in beginning to define the types of projects at which they are more likely to feel most comfortable and excel. Those with a lower level of tolerance of ambiguity and a more external locus of control may find, for example, that they are more likely to be successful in projects that are more routine, have clear precedents upon which to rely, have clear scope, and minimal requirement for innovation. By learning this about themselves, we anticipate that our graduates will be better able to effectively staff project teams.

Social Readjustment Scale (Stress) and Coping Skills

Workers subjected to unending stress become less healthy, less efficient, and eventually burn out (Whetten and Cameron, 2011). Stress contributes to 'an estimated $200 billion per year in absenteeism, lower productivity, staff turnover, workers' compensation, medical insurance and other stress-related expenses' (Maxon, 1999).

Moving from 'Me' to 'We'

After laying the groundwork with self-knowledge through self-assessment and reflection, we then move into building high-performance teams (Fredrickson and Losada, 2005), employee engagement (MacLeod and Clarke, 2009) and work engagement (Bakker and Leiter, 2010) and communications.

Employee and Work Engagement

Engagement as a course subject covers multiple meanings of the word. We include employee engagement (an employee's emotional attachment to their colleagues, their work and their workplace, which correlates with increased discretionary effort) as defined and researched by the Gallup Organization (Gallup, 2006, 2009). The Gallup model for employee engagement has significant overlap with self-determination theory (Deci and Ryan, 1985), which we outlined earlier.

Combining efforts to enhance employee engagement with strengths-based management results in reducing the percentage of the workforce that is actively disengaged. And, as Seligman reports (2004a) happiness at its most durable – the engaged life (strengths at work) and meaningful life (strengths in service of a cause greater than yourself) – is strengths-dependent. Clearly, helping students learn to work from their strengths and to recognise and deploy strengths in others has a favourable organisational impact.

WELL-BEING AT WORK

We have most recently added a well-being at work model to the course. This model when mapped to our existing course content has proven to be an overarching model for a positive workplace. Developed by the New Economics Foundation following research reported in the National Accounts of Well-Being (New Economics Foundation, 2009), this model of well-being at work is comprehensive and based on leading-edge research in the field of well-being. The dynamic model assesses four meta-domains which are each divided into four domains (New Economics Foundation, 2012).

OTHER COURSE MODULES

The remaining lectures in our *Managing Teams* course are briefly described below.

Planning and Measuring Our Performance

Goal setting and performance management are the next area of our course content. Goal setting at its best is a collaborative process that dynamically matches the individual to the task to optimise use of strengths and to manage or minimise weaknesses.

Optimising Our Performance

Motivation theory, successful change, effective conflict and setting the stage for creativity are our next topical areas. Motivation theory is an untapped PM tool, now made popular in the trade publication, *Drive,* by Daniel Pink (2009).

Building On Success

Knowing that the emerging work environment requires rapid learning and development in the face of uncertainty, we have recently added appreciative inquiry to our *Managing Teams* course to help project managers make the shift from problem-solving to solution-finding.

Living Our Values

Originally, this section was about business ethics. We helped the students to develop their personal values statements and create their personal vision statements. We have since incorporated values-based behaviour as an extension of this values definition content.

Teaching Protocol

Today's projects often involve new invention and working on the edges of what's known. In order for people to become top-notch performers, they have to be willing to try things that they have not done before, sometimes to fall short, and to learn from that experience. Therefore, we have modelled our classroom experience on that process, separating educational assignments from evaluative assignments.

We are experimenting with shifting the classroom work towards more applications, discussions and exploration whilst shifting the out-of-class work towards basic content understanding. To that end, we have initiated weekly quizzes on the required readings;

these fall due prior to the related lecture. The quizzes are evaluative, meaning that they are intended to assess mastery of the material. Each class begins with a review of the quizzes, where the students support the review of the correct answers rather than relying solely upon the instructor.

Educational assignments, which may be resubmitted based on instructor feedback for the ultimate grade, include weekly short essays that focus on applying the lecture's content to real-world situations designed to help students move from lower-order thinking skills to higher-order thinking skills meaning that the students can actually use the knowledge attained in new and different ways (Forehand, 2011).

We demonstrate this cycle with all written assignments. First, we give honest and often critical feedback, describing what might make a better submission. Then we give students a chance to redo the work so that they can respond to our feedback. The final grade is given for the resubmitted assignment.

Thus we model the ideas that we discuss in the class on growth mindsets, goals and feedback. This includes having faith that they want to do well and can do well, once they understand what is required. It includes the provision of feedback that is specific, timely and leaves the correction to the student. One student commented after he'd finished revising his self-assessment workbook that he learned as much in the revision stage as he worked through instructor comments as he did writing it initially, and the revision stage took much less time. Many students have reported an increase in self-efficacy from being allowed to respond to appropriate feedback.

Each of these topics is supported by a Socratic lecture style that involves the students. Many of the students are part-time, studying whilst they work in professional jobs. Even the full-time students have generally returned to school after a few years of professional work experience. We have had a number of naval officers given a year to complete the PM degree, civil, mechanical and systems engineers earning the PM degree to augment their existing careers, and even a few executives who have managed large groups working on multiple projects. Therefore we are aware that there is significant experience in the room of both good and bad management practices in action. We tell our own stories to prime the pump, and then invite students to contribute their stories to augment their own learning and the learning of their peers.

Of course, there is never adequate time in class to hear from every student about every topic. To give students an additional opportunity to reflect on the intersection of what they're learning with what they have already experienced and to apply the topics in their work lives, we assign pearl-diving assignments for most topics. In these short essays, students may be asked to reflect on past experience, showing how they might interpret it differently based on what they're learning. Others are asked to try something and then observe what happens.

We believe this process enhances the learning opportunity for the students by giving them the opportunity to directly and consistently engage in a dialogue with the instructor through these assignments.

CSIKSZENTMIHALYI'S CONCEPT OF FLOW

The experience of attaining the dynamic balance of skills and challenge and being one with the experience is presented in our course (Csikszentmihalyi, 1997 and 2008). We use this work to help PM students understand how to build skills, relieve anxiety and reduce boredom for themselves and their team members. We recently expanded our course content to include work engagement, which combines flow or absorption with dedication and vigour (Bakker and Leiter, 2010). We have found the work engagement model to be better for the PM students as it incorporates health and vitality and work conditions conducive to concentration and skill development. Careful consideration of the work engagement research has led us to a further expansion of our course content to include well-being at work explicitly.

Impact

Students tend to enter the class sceptical of the class material and doubtful about their own abilities to manage people. But generally they don't leave that way. Here are some of their observations at the end of the semester:

- 'The pearl-diving assignments give us a chance to reflect on the topics and make a personal connection with the course content'.
- 'The ability to resubmit changed the focus from earning high grades to mastering the material'.
- 'Through the self-assessments, I've got to know myself better'.
- 'I've gained tools to manage myself better, and thus become a better manager of other people'.
- 'I had encountered some of these topics before, somewhat peripherally in other classes and workplace trainings. This class pulled these ideas together into a coherent and structured picture'.

We think of PM as an incubator for organisational change. Projects are by definition time-limited in duration; they are not routine work; they are of strategic importance to the sponsoring organisation; and, they are managed with high performance standards with respect to scope, schedule and budget. Tools and techniques learned on one project, if successful, are then taken to the next project as teams form, disband and reform in the PM cycle.

Over the last seven years, more than 700 students have gone through our classes on their way to PM degrees. Think of that as an injection of 700 people with heightened self-awareness and the fundamentals of management skills into the world of work.

References and Further Reading

Amabile, T.M. and Kramer, S. (2011), *The Progress Principle: Using Small Wins to Ignite Joy, Engagement, and Creativity at Work*, Boston, MA: Harvard Business School Publishing.

Bakker, A.B. and Leiter, M.P. (eds) (2010), *Work Engagement: a Handbook of Essential Theory and Research*, New York: Psychology Press.

Britton, K.H. (2008), 'Increasing job satisfaction: Coaching with evidence-based interventions', *Coaching: An International Journal of Theory, Research and Practice*, 2(1), 176–85.

Cameron, K. (2008), *Positive Leadership: Strategies for Extraordinary Performance*, San Francisco, CA: Berrett-Koehler.

Cameron, K. and Caza, A. (2004), 'Contributions to the discipline of positive organizational scholarship', *American Behavioral Scientist*, 47(6), 731–9. Available at: http://webuser.bus.umich. edu/cameronk/PDFs/POS/ABS%20-%20INTRODUCTORY%20ARTICLE%20-%20REVISED.pdf [accessed 22 May 2012].

Cameron, K. and Spreitzer, G. (2011), *The Oxford Handbook of Positive Organizational Scholarship*, New York: Oxford University Press.

Cameron, K., Dutton, J.E. and Quinn, R.E. (2003), *Positive Organizational Scholarship: Foundations of a New Discipline*, San Francisco, CA: Berrett-Koehler.

Csikszentmihalyi, M. (1997), *Finding Flow: The Psychology of Engagement with Everyday Life*, New York: Basic Books.

Csikszentmihalyi, M. (2008), *Flow: The Psychology of Optimal Experience*, New York: HarperCollins.

Davis, J.S. (2010), 'Building the positive workplace: A preliminary report from the field', in P.A. Linley, S. Harrington, and N. Garcea, *Oxford Handbook of Positive Psychology and Work*, New York: Oxford University Press.

Davis, J.S. and Cable, J.H. (2006), 'Positive Workplace: Enhancing Individual and Team Productivity', paper presented at the Project Management Institute Global Congress. Available at: http://tinyurl. com/DavisCable [accessed 22 May 2012].

Deci, E.L. and Ryan, R.M. (1985), *Intrinsic Motivation and Self-determination in Human Behavior*, New York: Plenum.

Dutton, J.E. (2003), *Energize Your Workplace: How To Create and Sustain High-Quality Connections at Work*, San Francisco, CA: Jossey-Bass.

Forehand, M. (2011), 'Bloom's taxonomy'. Available at: http://projects.coe.uga.edu/epltt/index. php?title=Bloom%27s_Taxonomy [accessed 4 October 2012].

Fredrickson, B. (1998), 'What good are positive emotions?', *Review of General Psychology*, 2, 300–319.

Fredrickson, B.L. and Losada, M.F. (2005), 'Positive affect and the complex dynamics of human flourishing', *American Psychologist*, 60, 678–86.

Gable, S., Gonzaga, G. and Strachman, A. (2006), 'Will you be there for me when things go right? Supportive responses to positive event disclosures', *Journal of Personality and Social Psychology*, 91(5), 904–17.

Gagne, M. and Deci, E. (2005), 'Self-determination theory and work motivation', *Journal of Organizational Behavior*, I, 26, 331–62.

Gallup, Inc. (2006, 2009), 'Q12Meta-Analysis: The Relationship Between Engagement at Work and Organizational Outcomes', White paper. Available at: http://www.gallup.com/strategic consulting/126806/Q12-Meta-Analysis.aspx [accessed 5 October 2012].

Hsieh, T. (2010), *Delivering Happiness*, New York: Business Plus.

Linley, A.P. and Joseph, S. (2004), *Positive Psychology in Practice*, Hoboken, NJ: John Wiley & Sons.

Linley, A., Willars, J., Deiner, R., Garcea, N. and Stairs, M. (2010), *The Strengths Book: Be Confident, Be Successful and Enjoy Better Relationships by Realising the Best of You*, Coventry: CAPP Press.

Loehr, J.E. and Schwartz, T. (2003), *The Power of Full Engagement: Managing Energy, Not Time, is the Key to High Performance and Personal Renewal*, New York: Free Press.

Luthans, F. (2002), 'Positive organizational behavior: Developing and managing psychological Strengths', *Academy of Management Executive*, 16(1), 57–72.

Luthans, F., Youssef, C. and Avolio, B. (2007), *Psychological Capital: Developing the Human Competitive Edge*, New York: Oxford University Press.

MacLeod, D. and Clarke, N. (2009), 'Engaging for Success: Enhancing Performance Through Employee Engagement', a report to the UK Government. Available at: http://www.berr.gov.uk/ files/file52215.pdf [accessed 1 October 2009].

Maxon, R. (1999), 'Stress in the workplace: a costly epidemic'. Available at: http://www.fdu.edu/newspubs/magazine/99su/stress.html [accessed 12 September 2009].

Morris, P. (1994), *The Management of Projects*, London: Thomas Telford.

Namie, G. (2003), 'Workplace bullying: escalated incivility', *Ivey Business Journal Online*, Article # 9B03TF09. Available at: http://www.iveybusinessjournal.com/view_article.asp?intArticle_ID=449 [accessed 15 October 2009].

New Economics Foundation (2008), 'Five ways to well-being'. Available at: http://www.nef-consulting.co.uk/ [accessed 13 January 2012].

New Economics Foundation (2009), 'National accounts of well-being: bringing real wealth into the Balance Sheet'. Available at: http://www.nationalaccountsofwellbeing.org/learn/download-report.html [accessed 16 June 2010].

New Economics Foundation (2012), 'Happiness at work survey'. Available at: http://www.nef-consulting.co.uk/ [accessed 13 January 2012].

Ophir, E., Nass, C. and Wagner, A.D. (2009), 'Cognitive Control in Media Multitaskers', *Proceedings of the National Academy of Science*, 6(37), 15583–7.

Peterson, C. and Seligman, M.E.P. (2004), *Character Strengths and Virtues: A Handbook and Classification*, New York: Oxford University Press.

Pink, D.H. (2009), *Drive: the Surprising Truth About What Motivates Us*, New York: Riverhead Books.

Savitz, A.W. and Weber, K. (2006), *The Triple Bottom Line: How Today's Best-Run Companies Are Achieving Economic, Social, and Environmental Success: And How You Can Too*, San Francisco, CA: Jossey-Bass.

Schat, A.C.H., Frone, M.R. and Kelloway, E.K. (2006), 'Prevalence of workplace aggression in the US workforce: Findings from a national study', in E.K. Kelloway, J. Barling and J.J. Hurrell (eds), *Handbook of Workplace Violence*, Thousand Oaks, CA: Sage, 47–89.

Schneider, B., Macey, W., Barbera, K.M. and Young, S. (2009), *Employee Engagement: Tools for Analysis, Practice, and Competitive Advantage*, Oxford: Blackwell Publishers.

Seligman, M.E. (1994), *What You Can Change And What You Can't: The Complete Guide To Successful Self-Improvement*, New York: Knopf.

Seligman, M.E. (2004a), *Authentic Happiness: Using the New Positive Psychology to Realize Your Potential for Lasting Fulfillment*, New York: Free Press.

Seligman, M.E. (2004b), 'Martin Seligman on Positive Psychology', TED talk. Available at: http://www.ted.com/talks/martin_seligman_on_the_state_of_psychology.html [accessed 22 May June 2012].

Shenhar, A.J. and Dvir, D. (2004), 'Project Management Evolution: Past History and Future Research', presented in London, 2004, PMI Research Conference.

Snyder, C.R., Lopez, S.J. and Pedrotti, J.T. (2011), *Positive Psychology: The Scientific and Practical Explorations of Human Strengths*, Thousand Oaks, CA: Sage.

Spreitzer, G. and Sonenshein, S. (2003), 'Positive deviance and extraordinary organizing', in K.S. Cameron, K.S, Dutton, J.E. and Quinn, R.E. (eds), *Positive Organizational Scholarship: Foundations of a New Discipline*, San Francisco, CA: Berrett-Koehler.

Spreitzer, G. and Sonenshein, S. (2004), 'Toward the construct definition of positive deviance', *American Behavioral Scientist*, 47(6), 828–47.

Whetten, D. and Cameron, K. (2011), *Developing Management Skills with MyManagementLab: Global Edition*, 8th edn, Harlow: Pearson Education.

Workplace Bullying Institute (2010). 'Results of the 2010 and 2007 workplace bullying surveys'. Available at: http://www.workplacebullying.org/wbiresearch/2010-wbi-national-survey/ [accessed 22 May 2012].

52 *Industrial Psychology*

BERNARDO TIRADO

Industrial psychology (also known as social-organisational psychology) is the study of people in the workplace. The earliest attempts to study behaviour in organisations came out of a desire by industrial efficiency experts to improve work productivity, and some of their work is outlined in Chapter 31. In this chapter I shall discuss some of those theories in greater detail. Understanding the dynamics of behaviour in organisations is essential to achieving personal success as a project manager. Principles of organisational behaviour are involved in making people both productive and happy in their jobs. We cannot rely on common sense when it comes to understanding behaviour in organisations accurately. To provide you with an industrial psychology perspective, I have divided this chapter into four modules, which are:

1. personality types;
2. attitudes towards work;
3. power and leadership;
4. group dynamics.

Personality Types

Projects require project managers to interact with multiple types of personalities. Knowing an individual's personality type will enable a project manager to develop the best approach in assigning tasks to keep team members motivated. There are five dimensions of personality that project managers should know about:

1. emotional disposition;
2. competitiveness;
3. attitude;
4. self-esteem;
5. motivation.

Emotional Disposition

Emotional disposition refers to the mood we have at work. For instance, a person's mood may shift from good to bad because they are not content with what the leader said to them.

People who are high in the trait of *positive affectivity* tend to have an overall sense of well-being, see people and things in a positive light and tend to experience positive emotional states. By contrast, those high in the trait of *negative affectivity* tend to hold negative views of themselves and others, interpret ambiguous situations negatively and experience negative emotional states

Competitiveness

When it comes to competitiveness, individuals classified as having a 'Type A' personality do not always perform better than people with a 'Type B' personality?

Individuals categorised as Type A show high levels of competitiveness, irritability and time urgency (they are always in a hurry). In addition, they demonstrate certain stylistic patterns, such as loud and exaggerated speech, and have a tendency to respond quickly in many contexts (for example, during conversations they often begin speaking before others are through).

Individuals classified as Type B show the opposite pattern; they are much calmer and relaxed. Although Type A people excel on tasks involving time pressure or solitary work, Type B people have the advantage when it comes to tasks involving complex judgements and accuracy, as opposed to speed.

Attitude

Attitude is the third personality dimension that's important. There are times when we 'psych' ourselves out of succeeding because we are not confident about our ability to perform a task. This attitude has to do with self-efficacy, which has been found to be a good predictor of people's success with jobs and an important aspect of personality. Attitude relates to a person's view on a task.

Self-esteem

Self-esteem is about the individual's disposition and perspective of themselves. People high in self-esteem evaluate themselves favourably, believing they possess many desirable traits and qualities. In contrast, people low in self-esteem evaluate themselves unfavourably, believing that they are lacking in important respects and that they have characteristics that others consider unappealing. Research has shown that the lower an employee's self-esteem, the less likely he or she is to take any active steps to solve problems confronted on the job. As a result, their performance tends to suffer.

By contrast, employees with high levels of self-esteem are more inclined to attempt actively to acquire the resources needed to cope with work problems and use their skills and abilities to their fullest extent. When that happens, higher performance results.

Motivation

Achievement motivation, also known as the need for achievement, has to do with an individual's desire to excel. People high in achievement motivation may be characterised as having a highly task-oriented outlook. They are more concerned with getting things done than they are with having good relationships with others. They also tend to seek tasks that are moderately difficult and challenging.

By contrast, people who are low on achievement motivation very much prefer either extremely easy or extremely difficult tasks. If the task is easy, success is practically guaranteed. If the task is impossibly difficult, there is an excuse for failure and external sources can be blamed.

Applying the Five Dimensions of Personality to Project Management

Now that you're familiar with the five dimensions of personality, below is a case example of how to apply this knowledge to your project.

CASE EXAMPLE NO. 1: LEADING A CROSS-FUNCTIONAL TEAM

You have recently been asked to lead a team of subject matter experts to implement an enterprise-wide system. These individuals have varying levels of tenure and seniority. You are conducting the kick-off meeting and this is the first time the team members are meeting each other and you. Based on what you understand about the five dimensions of personality, make mental notes for each of the team members. You might find the checklist in Figure 52.1 to be a helpful guide.

Emotional disposition:→	Positive affectivity ☐	☐	Negative affectivity:
Competitiveness:→	Type 'A' ☐	☐	Type 'B'
Attitude:→	High self-efficacy ☐	☐	Low self-efficacy
Self-esteem:→	High self-esteem ☐	☐	Low self-esteem:
Motivation:→	High need to achieve ☐	☐	Low need to achieve

Figure 52.1 Checklist for the five dimensions of personality

Suppose that you make the following notes. You would have to make them mentally, of course.

Mental notes for Bob: negative affectivity; Type A; low self-efficacy; high self-esteem; high need for achievement.

Mental notes for Sarah: positive affectivity; Type B; high self-efficacy; low self-esteem; low need for achievement.

Mental notes for Jack: positive affectivity; Type A; high self-efficacy; high self-esteem; high need for achievement.

> Mental notes for Samantha: negative affectivity; Type B; low self-efficacy; low self-esteem and low need for achievement.
>
> Now that you've made some mental notes about your team members, how would you divide work packages amongst this group or whom would you pair up to work together?
>
> First, separate out work packages based on time sensitivity and complexity. If work packages require time and patience, then either Sarah or Samantha would be a perfect candidate owing to their Type B personalities. Research shows that Type Bs are more attuned to taking time for accuracy versus Type As' desire for speed.
>
> If you were looking to pair two individuals to work together, Bob and Jack would not make a good pairing. Why? Well, they are both Type A, have a high self-esteem and have a high need for achievement. Although both would get the job done, they will be debating and colliding every step of the way.

ANOTHER METHOD

Once your team is established, another assessment tool that can be used is Myers-Briggs. The Myers-Briggs Type Indicator (MBTI) test is a psychometric questionnaire designed to measure psychological preferences in how people perceive the world and make decisions (MBTI is a registered name). It is a tool that has been used by many large organisations to help individuals know their working preference. According to the Center for Applications of Psychological Type (CPP), approximately two million people a year take the MBTI test and it is the most widely used personality inventory in history. The test puts individuals into 16 categories as illustrated in Figure 52.2 opposite.

Having insight into each individual's preferences will allow you to think about how to manage the individual or how the individuals within your team will work with each other. For example, knowing that someone's preference is to be the 'Supervisor' (ESTJ), you would want to assign a sub-team allowing the individual to fulfil their leadership need. Or if you have a 'Teacher' (ENFJ), you can delegate tasks that have to do with marketing, teaching or educating non-project team members about your project.

By using Myers-Briggs you will be able to determine your team member's personality and work on techniques to achieve a united front of working together efficiently and effectively. It can also help you understand and leverage your own strengths to motivate and create a cohesive work environment.

Attitude Towards Work

The reason why we go to work every day (besides the pay) is because we either like the people we work with, we enjoy the job we do or we like the company we're associated with. If you don't fall into either of these categories then, you're most likely looking for another job or are completely miserable in the one you're in at the moment. Attitude towards work consists of three components:

1. Evaluative – you either like or dislike a particular person, thing or event;
2. Cognitive – your beliefs;
3. Behavioural – predisposition to act a certain way.

Although attitudes towards work are not perfect predictors of behaviour, they do provide a baseline to understand how a person feels about the work they are doing.

Many times, project managers inherit individuals to work with them on projects. Assessing and understanding an individual's attitude towards work would help the project manager determine the best method to motivate their team members.

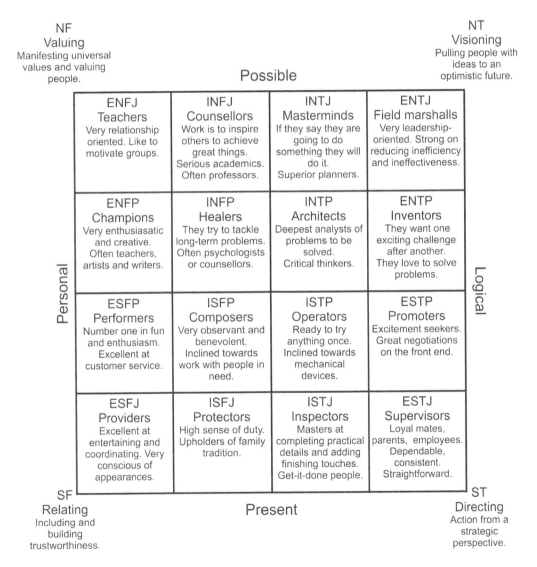

Figure 52.2 A Myers-Briggs table

Note: This table provides an insight into how work packages might be assigned based on personality disposition.

Job satisfaction is the number one reason why people stay in their current roles. Managing a project team is no different. The project manager sets the tone and direction of how the team members would be enriched by their experience of working in the team that you lead.

Before I cover some of those areas, I need to cover some job satisfaction fundamentals that all project managers should know. Although there are many different approaches to understanding job satisfaction, two particular methods stand out as providing our best insight into this very important attitude. These are:

1. The two-factor theory of job satisfaction;
2. Value theory.

Frederick Herzberg (the two-factor theory) conducted a study where he assembled a group of accountants and engineers and asked them to recall incidents that made them feel satisfied and dissatisfied with their jobs. Herzberg found that satisfaction and dissatisfaction stemmed from two different sources, motivator and hygiene factors (Herzberg, 1964).

He found that motivators are associated with personal satisfaction from aspects of their jobs that had to do with the work itself or with the outcomes directly resulting from it, such as promotion, recognition and achievement.

Hygiene factors are associated with the conditions surrounding the job, such as pay, relationships with others and work conditions.

Herzberg conceived satisfaction and dissatisfaction as two separate independent variables. Research has shown that dissatisfaction is greater under conditions that are highly overcrowded, dark, noisy, have extreme temperatures and poor air quality. There is more on Herzberg and this subject in Chapter 31.

The value theory argues that almost any factor can be a source of job satisfaction as long as it is something that people value. The less people have of some aspect of the job (for example, pay or learning opportunities) relative to the amount they want, the more dissatisfied they will be. Thus, value theory focuses on discrepancies between what people have and what they want: the greater those discrepancies, the more dissatisfied they will be.

Knowing these theories helps project managers to assess the best way to increase job satisfaction for project team members. To increase engagement and job satisfaction amongst project team members, the following need to be in place:

1. Reward and recognition (for example, a thank you note, coffee and cakes and so forth).
2. Team members believe that their project manager is competent, they are treated with respect and believe that their project manager has their best interests in mind.
3. The project manager enables team members to participate freely in the decision-making process.
4. The project manager assigns tasks that match and fulfil individuals' job interests.

Power and Authority

Industrial psychologists tell us that power and authority play a significant role on being an effective leader. There are five bases of power that exist in building work relationships:

1. Legitimate (or positional) power. This is the power that someone has because others recognise and accept his or her authority such as a teacher, police officer or boss.
2. Referent power. The power someone has simply because he or she is liked and respected.
3. Expert power. The power derived from the skills or expertise you possess.
4. Reward power. Associated with positions that come with the power to control the rewards others receive.
5. Coercive power. This results from the capacity to control punishment.

Out of these five bases of power, expert power is the most applicable to project managers. For example, if you are a project manager specialising in outsourcing, systems implementation, construction and so on, it means that your expertise allows you to be seen as an expert in those areas.

Why is this important? Many project managers do not get a proper introduction to the team by the project sponsor. Instead, people are told by their immediate leaders that they've been selected to be a part of a cross-functional team. Then they are informed that you will be holding a kick-off meeting – and off we all go.

That lack of an introduction to the team by the project sponsor already puts the project manager at a disadvantage. It's important to have the sponsor or someone senior to kick off the meeting because that will signal the importance of the project to the team members. It will also give an opportunity for the project manager to be introduced to the team by the sponsor (or senior manager), who can explain why that project manager was chosen.

This approach is simple but effective. It's so important that I shall repeat it. If you are chosen as project manager, get the sponsor or senior manager to do two things at the kick-off meeting:

1. Announce the project and stress its importance.
2. State why you were the person chosen to lead the team.

That will get you off to a flying start. After that, it's up to you. If you do not get that support, then people will tend to ask themselves 'If this project is so important, why don't we ever see the senior managers or hear from the sponsor'?

Leadership

Equally important to power and authority is leadership. From the trait leadership approach (are leaders born?) to contingency theories of leadership effectiveness, the most currently used is situational leadership.

Developed by leadership theorists, Paul Hersey and Ken Blanchard (2007), situational leadership refers to choosing the leadership style appropriate to a given situation. The theory is based on two dimensions: supportive behaviour and directive behaviour. The concept helps project managers to adapt their leadership style based on individual needs.

Figure 52.3 illustrates four different situations, each associated with the most effective leadership style that should be used.

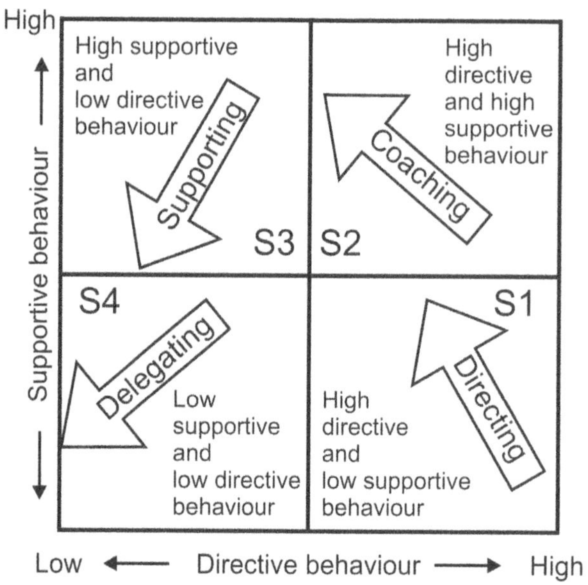

Figure 52.3 Situation leadership: The four leadership styles

Starting at the lower right-hand quadrant, S1, individuals are unable and unwilling to take responsibility for their actions; they are not motivated and do not possess the appropriate skills to perform adequately. Leaders would need to spend more time, provide specific instructions and be directive as to how to complete the tasks. This could be a case where a person is learning on the job where, because he or she is new to the task, they have become frustrated and demotivated because they do not possess the skills to complete the task.

Moving up to the upper right corner, S2, are individuals who lack the skill but have the will. Leaders are very directive and supportive, to make up for each individual's lack of ability. This approach is coupled with being supportive and helping the people to cooperate and do what the leader is asking of them.

On the upper left corner, S3, individuals need very little guidance regarding how to do their jobs, but need considerable emotional hand-holding and support to motivate them. A participating style of leadership works well in such situations because it allows individuals to share their experience whilst enhancing their desire to perform.

Finally, at the lower left corner, S4, individuals are both willing and able to do the job. The project manager can delegate all the responsibility to them for making and implementing their own decisions.

Group Dynamics

Social scientists have formally defined a group as a collection of two or more interacting individuals with a stable pattern of relationships between them who share common goals and who perceive themselves as being a group. Groups can be formal or informal.

Formal groups are those which are created by the organisation and are initially designed to direct members towards some organisational goal. In other words, formal social groups are mandated by the organisation. For example, project teams are formal groups because they are mobilised to meet a particular objective.

Informal groups develop naturally among an organisation's workforce without any direction from the management of the organisation within which they operate. One key factor in the formation of informal groups is a common interest shared by its members. These groups are not mandatory and individuals participate in them voluntarily. One example would be an employee networking group.

To understand group dynamics it is necessary to consider the way in which groups influence individuals and, conversely, the way in which groups are influenced by individuals. Three areas to consider are:

1. Group norms;
2. Social facilitation;
3. Social loafing.

These technical terms are not as complicated as they sound but some explanation is necessary here.

GROUP NORMS

Group norms together comprise a consciously or unconsciously agreed-upon set of rules that guides the behaviour of group members. Norms differ from organisational policies in that they are informal and unwritten. Norms can be subtle and group members may not even be aware that they are operating.

Norms develop due to precedents set over time. For example, behaviours emerging from an initial team meeting will usually predetermine a standard for how that group operates in subsequent meetings. For instance, over time people will tend to sit in the same seat. If a meeting is allowed to start five or ten minutes late, people will get the impression it is all right to be late in future meetings. In other words, a norm has been established.

People draw from their previous experiences to guide their behaviours in new situations, which means that norms also develop because of carry-overs from other situations. For example, if you move from one department to another, you might find that your new department has a 'sink-or-swim' norm similar to that which existed in your previous group. This particular case is more in tune with organisational norms.

SOCIAL FACILITATION

Social facilitation is the enhancement or impairment of an individual's performance that results from the presence of others. For example, it is noticed that people perform better in the presence of others than when alone. Conversely, the opposite might be true so that sometimes they are observed to perform better alone than when in the presence of others.

Management scientists have found that this matter boils down to several basic psychological processes. It is the result of a heightened emotional state that people experience when in the presence of others. For instance, you might be in a sporting team of some kind. Your group might want you to kick a ball into a net or run faster to take the baton in a relay race. So individuals would be stimulated to excel or fail based on the role they have in the team. It's the same in project teams.

Social facilitation happens because the individual has a fear of being evaluated or judged by one or more other people. It's like the first day of school where we were anxious to fit in and be liked.

SOCIAL LOAFING

Social loafing occurs when several individuals contribute to the same task. The more people who work on the task, the less each individual's contribution tends to be. As a result, the more people who might contribute to a group's project, the less pressure each person faces to perform well.

For example, if you go through a revolving door and you know that there are others going through the door ahead of you and/or behind you, the energy exerted to move the revolving door decreases because each individual is thinking that the other will push the door.

Another example, that could have serious consequences, is when a fire breaks out in a building occupied by several people. When social loafing occurs, each person might think that someone else has called the emergency services, when in fact no one has. Thus the responsibility for doing a job or even performing a simple action is diffused over several people. Hence, each group member feels less responsible for behaving appropriately – and social loafing occurs.

Social loafing can happen when people feel that they can get away with 'taking it easy' under conditions in which each individual's contributions cannot be determined. So one possible antidote is to make each performer identifiable.

Another way to overcome social loafing is to make work tasks more important and interesting. Research has revealed that people are unlikely to go along for a free ride when the task they are performing is believed to be vital to the organisation.

It also has been suggested that managers should reward individuals for contributing to their group's performance – that is, encourage their interest in their group performance.

Yet another mechanism for overcoming social loafing is to use punishment threats. To the extent that performance decrements may be controlled by threatening to punish the individuals slacking off, such as putting them on a performance plan or advising their immediate leader of the performance issues.

Now that you have an understanding of how individuals contribute to groups, I shall focus on how groups contribute to individual performance.

The Influence of Groups on Individual Performance

You may have heard the terms 'forming, storming, norming, performing and adjourning' the first four of which occur in other chapters in this Handbook. These are the five stages of group development identified by Dr Bruce Tuckman (Tuckman, 1965). Each stage reflects how individual behaviour evolves as a group matures (Figure 52.4).

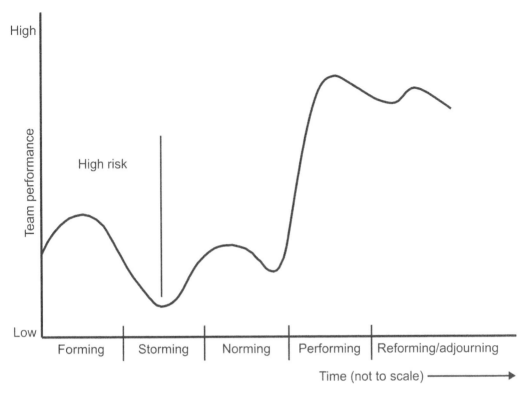

Figure 52.4 Tuckman's five stages of team development

TUCKMAN'S STAGE 1: FORMING

Individual behaviour is driven by the desire to be accepted by team members. As a result, the individual tries to avoid controversy or conflict at this stage.

Individuals focus on team structure, raising such questions as: 'How often will the team meet?', 'Who is going to do what?', 'Shall I like this group?', 'Is this project manager going to be a good leader?' and so on.

Individuals are also gathering information and impressions about each other during the first few meetings. Consider this stage as the 'honeymoon period' where everyone gets along well with each other and any kind of conflict is typically avoided.

TUCKMAN'S STAGE 2: STORMING

Now the honeymoon period is over. Important issues start to surface at this stage, and minor confrontations can arise. This stage sets the tone as to how the group will either work or not work through the forthcoming project tasks and problems. Such issues may relate to the work of the group itself, or to roles and responsibilities within the group. Depending on the organisational culture and/or individual disposition, any conflict could be suppressed and become an undercurrent that could compromise the project. Individuals will eventually seek structural clarity and look for rules that will prevent future conflicts.

TUCKMAN'S STAGE 3: NORMING

The 'rules of engagement' are established in this stage. This is when individuals determine the best way to work with each other. But if all the difficulties of Stage 2 have not been resolved, disgruntled team members might unconsciously undermine the project.

Having worked through any difficulties, team members begin to understand each other better and can appreciate each other's skills and experiences. The group starts to get into a rhythm and cohesiveness will grow between team members.

TUCKMAN'S STAGE 4: PERFORMING

By the time this stage is reached, everyone knows each other well enough to be able to work together. Sufficient trust exists between people to allow independent activity. Roles and responsibilities change according to need in an almost seamless way.

Group identity, loyalty and morale are all high, and everyone is equally task-oriented and people-oriented. This high degree of comfort means that all the energy of the group can be directed towards the work in hand.

TUCKMAN'S STAGE 5: ADJOURNING

The fifth stage is focused on disengagement once a project is complete. Since individuals tend to be proud of project accomplishments and the experiences with the group, some group members will feel a sense of loss.

Many times this stage fosters long-term professional relationships after the group has disbanded. Typically a smaller subgroup of individuals set up recurring events (for example, luncheons, dinners and so forth) to remain connected.

SUMMARISING THE FIVE STAGES

Now you have a sense of what happens during each of Tuckman's stages. The biggest risk areas that I have found for project managers occur within the forming and storming stage (see Figure 52.4). It is within these stages that individuals start to develop their perception of the project manager's superior or inferior leadership.

If an inferior perception is built about a project manager's leadership, the team will unconsciously look to someone else within the group to lead them (even if that individual has not been formally assigned).

The Work of Kevin Leman

Most industrial psychologists are found in either HRM or consulting. Marrying industrial psychology and project management has been my focus over the last 16 years or so. What is different and valuable to project managers is knowing how to apply much of the research and knowledge to leading teams.

For example, consider our understanding of birth order. Research shows that birth order has much influence on how we behave in the workplace. Whether we like it or not, we unconsciously create a family environment at work. Sometimes that resembles our personal family dynamic and sometimes it resembles the ideal family dynamic that we never had.

I study people in the workplace and have come across many individuals that fall into the typical scenario of first-, middle-, and last-born children. However, I wanted to gain a deeper understanding of the science behind birth order.

Dr Kevin Leman (2009) has spent over thirty-five years as a psychologist studying birth order and is the world-renowned expert on this topic. His book provided insights into how one can predict an individual's birth order.

Having the ability to predict someone's birth order provides you with a competitive advantage in understanding how to work with the individual. For example, first-born tend to be governed by punctuality, structure and power; whereas last-born are more comfortable with ambiguity and tend to 'go with the flow'. Neither is good nor bad, but this knowledge helps you to know how to best approach each individual at work.

The following will provide you with an overview of how your birth order affects you at work. For further information on birth order, I highly encourage you to read Leman's book (ibid.). It's easy to read and doesn't follow the traditional academic writing style.

First-born (Or an Only Child)

First-born people are perfectionists, reliable, conscientious, list-makers, well organised, natural leaders, critical and serious. These qualities are typically attributed to mother or father unconsciously placing the first-born into a leader role by saying, 'You're a big boy now and you have to look out for your younger brother' (just as my mother used to say to me).

Conversely, only-children are very thorough, deliberate, self-motivated, positive thinkers, fearful and cautious. Only-children never have to compete with siblings for personal attention, which makes them more confident and articulate. However, they struggle with the concept or imagination of having brothers or sisters, and that can result in them being self-centred.

In the workplace, first-born and only-children have strength in being known as straight thinkers, organised and goal setters.

The Middle Child

A middle child tends to be a mediator, diplomatic, one who avoids conflict, loyal to peers, has many friends and independent.

At work, they are skilled at mediating disputes, willing to work things out and can be trusted with sensitive information.

The Last-born Child

Typically last-born people are manipulative, charming, blame others, attention seekers, natural salespeople, engaging, affectionate and so forth.

In the workplace, they are able to read others well and know how to work one-on-one successfully or in small groups. They are caring, always wanting to help and are easy to talk to.

Conclusion

Most of what I have just shared really depends on the family unit. Dr Leman explains that if siblings are born five or more years apart, the first-born status gets recycled. In part, that has to do with the number of years the parents had to take care of a newborn.

Leman further explained that first-born characteristics may be suppressed if a first-born has a first-born mother and father. As a result, the first-born may rebel and act like a last-born and then the last-born might take on the first-born characteristics.

Overall, whether we have siblings or not, the dynamics that we experience as children tend to manifest themselves in the workplace. Many studies have shown that people would prefer to make less money and work with people they like rather than make more money and work with people they dislike.

Understanding people in the workplace will provide project managers with a competitive advantage on how to drive successful projects and have the most attractive projects assigned to them.

References and Further Reading

Hersey, P.H. and Blanchard, K.H. (2007), *Management of Organizational Behaviour*, 9th edn, Englewood Cliffs, NJ: Prentice-Hall.

Herzberg, F. (1964), 'The motivation-hygiene concept and problems of manpower', *Personnel Administration*, January–February 1964, 3–7.

Leman, K. (2009), *The Birth Order Book*, 2nd edn, Ada, MI: Revell.

Mayo, G.E. (1933), *The Human Problems of an Industrial Civilization*, Boston, MA: Harvard Business School.

Myers, I.B. (1962), *Manual: The Myers-Briggs Type Indicator*, Princeton, NJ: Educational Testing Services.

Riggio, R.E. (2007), *Introduction to Industrial/Organizational Psychology*, 5th edn, Englewood Cliffs, NJ: Prentice-Hall.

Staw, B.M. (1991), *Psychological Dimensions of Organizational Behaviour*, 2nd edn, Englewood Cliffs, NJ: Prentice-Hall.

Tuckman, B. (1965), 'Developmental sequence in small groups', *Psychological Bulletin*, 63(6), 384–99.

53 *Emotional Intelligence in Project Management*

DEANNE EARLE

In all projects, whatever their size, nature and duration, the 'hard skills' of their project managers will help those managers to 'hit the ground running', whether they kick a project off from its start or come in further along the track. Well-developed hard skills include planning, tracking, controlling and reporting, and these are clearly essential as part of the drive for project success. But hard skills alone are not enough. Whatever form a project takes there will always be *people* involved and where there are people there are *emotions*. Emotions influence people's actions, their behaviours and their responses to the emotions of others. So welcome to the world of 'emotional intelligence'. I am confident that you will you will find this chapter informative and discover new insights you that can apply straight away.

Introduction

Emotions cannot be managed with hard skills. For those we need to engage our soft skills. Without soft skills project management has a significantly reduced chance of success. Soft skills are not new and there is no magic about them. Here are some familiar examples:
    The ability to:

- give constructive feedback;
- display active listening techniques;
- engage with and motivate others;
- make bad news palatable;
- maintain motivation and momentum during times of change.

These are all skills associated with good management and effective leadership, yet they are difficult to teach in a classroom. More often than not we learn and practise soft skills through our experiences.

   I once had overall delivery responsibility for the software development division of an IT solutions and services company. This team had joined the company through an acquisition. There were about 25 of them, all young, enthusiastic and hard working people with high intelligence quotients (IQs). They had huge potential – yet they were struggling to adjust and contribute fully in their new environment. I could see what was happening (as I have done so many times since). You will have seen it too. It happens whenever things change.

Change is always happening (hence the paradoxical expression 'change is constant'). But people have a natural resistance to change. What my team had always known (and were previously comfortable with) had gone. They were being challenged to improve their performance, but at the same time were placed within an unfamiliar operating model. They needed help to shift their thinking. That takes patience and time. But we do not always have much time. We have to keep things moving because business never stops, timelines are not open ended and budgets do not get replenished automatically. Even though hard skills were important in this case it was the soft skills that were critical for the team.

During that time I learned how emotions affect us. We would have called it 'people management skills' then but that description does not really go far enough. Now we call it 'emotional intelligence', which is often abbreviated to EI. EI is the soft skill that underpins all others.

To give some background to this subject, this chapter first summarises the evolution of EI and names some of the principal theorists. The chapter will continue by exploring how EI is used and how it can benefit project management. The examples described here are based on real cases and I am sure that you will be able to draw parallels with your own experiences.

The Evolution of EI as a Recognised Subject for Study

EI refers to the following attributes (Goleman, 1998):

- the capacity for recognising our own feelings and those of others;
- for motivating ourselves;
- for managing emotions well in ourselves and in our relationships.

In 1990 Peter Salovey and John D. Mayer (two psychologists) proposed a comprehensive theory and it is they who are credited with coining the term EI (Salovey and Mayer, 1990). Daniel Goleman became aware of Salovey and Mayer's work in the early 1990s and went on to write *Emotional Intelligence* in 1995 followed by *Working with Emotional Intelligence* in 1998. He had previously worked as a science journalist for the *New York Times* reporting on the brain and behavioural sciences. In his 1998 book he writes about how he adapted Salovey and Mayer's model to include the following five basic emotional and social competencies:

1. Self-awareness: knowing what we are feeling in the moment, and using those preferences to guide our decision making; having a realistic assessment of our own abilities and a well-grounded sense of self-confidence.
2. Self-regulation: handling our emotions so that they facilitate rather than interfere with the task at hand; being conscientious and delaying gratification to pursue goals; recovering well from emotional distress.
3. Motivation: using our deepest preferences to move and guide us towards our goals, to help us take the initiative and strive to improve, and to persevere in the face of setbacks and frustrations.

4. Empathy: sensing what people are feeling, being able to take their perspective, and cultivating rapport and attunement with a broad diversity of people.
5. Social skills: handling emotions in relationships well and accurately reading social situations and networks; interacting smoothly; using these skills to persuade and lead, negotiate and settle disputes, for cooperation and teamwork.

Reading Goleman's definitions helps us to appreciate where EI 'sits' and the difference it makes to how we and others work. If we can understand the competencies we can quickly see how EI can, and does, lead to better work – and ultimately to improved business performance.

But although Salovey and Mayer coined the term EI, and Daniel Goleman wrote about it, that was not really where it all started. Is EI really a new skill we should all hurry up and learn? No, not really. In fact it's been around for a long time, most predominantly in the US. More recently EI has been gathering attention in the business and education sectors around the world. Now a Google search on the term 'emotional intelligence' returns millions of results. To keep things simple, Figure 53.1 provides a snapshot of the most commonly attributed influencers of EI evolution over the past 70 years or so.

EI is being recognised as essential to management and business success, to the extent that educational institutions are incorporating it into their syllabuses. It also now forms a key part of many MBA programmes. The Weatherhead School of Management, a private business school of Case Western Reserve University in Cleveland, Ohio, was particularly influential in this early on. They developed an innovative course after acting on feedback from MBA students (who had criticised them because their courses focused too much on cognitive capabilities).

The Consortium for Research on Emotional Intelligence in Organisations has more on this subject together with a wealth of other information on the history of and research into EI. The Consortium can be reached at www.eiconsortium.org.

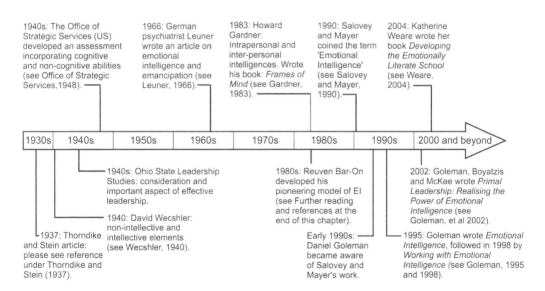

Figure 53.1 A brief chronology of emotional intelligence research and theory

Some Definitions and Comparisons

EI AND EMOTIONAL QUOTIENT (EQ)

Now we have some understanding of what EI is, at this point we need to recapitulate and review what EI is not.

The abbreviation EI is often interchanged with EQ. However the two are quite different. Quotients are *measurements*. So whereas EI is the *capacity* or *ability* to understand emotions, EQ is the *measurement* of that ability. To calculate someone's EQ they have to be tested. Testing gives a tangible measurement from which an assessment of their EI level can be made.

EI AND IQ

EI is not the same as IQ. IQ is the measurement of a person's intellect. IQ is *cognitive* whereas EI is *non-cognitive*; so these are hard versus soft skills. Whilst a person might have a high IQ, there is no rule that says they will have a high EQ or well-developed EI. In fact they might be EQ deficient because their education and training has focused on IQ only. People with incredibly high IQs are sometimes overlooked for more senior roles purely because their underdeveloped EI affects their ability to get things done through productive relationships.

EI COMPARED WITH OTHER CONCEPTS

Without much difficulty we can find elements of EI in many leadership and management concepts and methodologies. If we scratch the surface slightly the interconnections are easily recognisable. This is because soft skills underpin all management principles whether they're used together or applied independently of each other. For example:

NLP – Neuro Linguistic Programming

NLP is very relevant to EI because of the help it provides in personal and interpersonal relations. NLP is discussed in Chapter 50.

Maslow's Hierarchy of Needs

In Maslow's hierarchy of needs (Maslow, 1954), we can be fairly certain that those at the top of the pyramid will have a high EI and those at the bottom struggling with basic life needs will have a lower EI. Those in any of the pyramid's three middle sections will have differing areas showing up for EI development as they move up the pyramid.

Stephen Covey's 7 or 8 Habits

There is a strong presence of EI throughout Covey's 7 habits (Covey, 2004a). Covey's 8th habit (Covey, 2004b) deals with personal fulfilment and helping others to achieve the same. People with this habit would have well-developed EI and sit comfortably at the top of Maslow's pyramid.

Other Concepts or Soft Skills Relevant to EI

Other concepts or soft skills relevant to EI include:

- Ethical business and socially responsible leadership (see Chapter 27);
- Compassion and humanity: EI helps people appreciate and develop connections between self, others, the purpose and meaning of life and so on;
- Empathy and active listening: this is the subject of Chapter 55.

Whatever the concept or methodology, most of those involving communications (Chapter 25) and behaviour (Chapter 26) become more powerful and meaningful when related to EI.

Investing in and Developing EI

Before investing in anything you need a baseline. Measuring from a known datum point makes it easier to calculate the return on investment. So how can you find out your EI baseline to ensure that you invest wisely? There are a number of assessment tools already available. Some like the Jung Typology Test, more commonly known as Myers-Briggs, have been used by companies around the globe for many years. See Chapter 32 for more on Myers-Briggs.

Assessments like Myers-Briggs were created primarily for personality typing leaving EI adrift. But that does not mean they are irrelevant when measuring EI. Actually they can help to focus EI investment, so long as the results are interpreted appropriately with that purpose in mind.

Another assessment method is Anthony Mersino's 'Emotional Intelligence Mini-Assessment' (Mersino, 2007). This is a quick self-test of 20 questions where people answer either 'Yes' or 'No'. The sum of the 'No' answers categorises them into one of four levels. Even though this is fairly simple, it does give a person an overview of their EI development, albeit without pretending to be all inclusive or trying to determine any precise level of EI.

And again the EI Consortium is a good point of reference here, listing a number of tests and assessments. Whilst they do not go as far as endorsing any particular one on the list of tests, it does give people a good basis from which to start searching for a tool that will work for them (the web link for these details is: http://www.eiconsortium.org/measures/measures.html).

Investing in EI is not solely a financial matter. There also needs to be an investment of time. Time enables us to practise EI and as we practise we learn from each situation what our position is on the EI continuum. Knowing this helps us take corrective action if we do fail or 'lose it'. Known as an amygdala hijack, we can all 'lose it' and we've all witnessed others do the same too. (The amygdala is part of the human brain that is involved with our emotions.)

Emotionally
intelligent

Emotionally
unintelligent

Figure 53.2 Asking 'Where am I on the EI continuum?'

Consider the project manager who is being challenged by their customer about testing. No matter what the project manager said, the customer was not interested. With one side closed off to any discussion and the other indignant, EI had vanished. Shouting ensued and both people were at the emotionally unintelligent end of the EI continuum. The person who learned more and went on to develop their EI capability was the one who quickly recognised their imbalance and made the necessary adjustments to the way they managed that kind of situation. In project management we must always be ready to ask ourselves: Where am I (or they) on the EI continuum (Figure 53.2)?

With the number of certified project managers continuing to increase we need to question if they are being given all the tools they need for project management in the real world. Most project management education and training continues to be cognitive, taught in classroom-like situations, with an examination or other assessment at the end. But if, as the research suggests, IQ or cognitive abilities account for only 20–30 per cent of success (even that's generous) then project managers cannot rely on hard skills alone or this method of learning. With objective eyes it is easy to see in any project or organisation that those people who are most effective, liked and respected are those with well-developed EI skills. There is also plenty of evidence to show that the further up the career ladder you go, the more important EI becomes. This is because at the higher levels in many projects you will be more effective by how you are 'being' than what you are 'doing'.

'Being' is all about how we are and far less about what we do. It's about behaviours, tone of voice, integrity, the attention we give whilst someone else speaks (active listening), and our use of language whether it be spoken or body language. 'Being' can be difficult for project managers because they deal with facts and data, make decisions, work to deadlines and help, sometimes drive, others to do the same. The focus is control; controlling timelines, scope, budgets, situations and people. Control is all well and good but there needs to be a balance and it's EI that provides it. Too much control is damaging. People feel constrained, unable to contribute, quickly become disillusioned, demotivated and negative. Too much EI is equally damaging as it may be viewed as weak, result in 'analysis paralysis' and seriously delay decision making.

As I began working with the new team I knew I had some of the emotional and social competencies that make up 'Goleman's five' (see above). Some were definitely more developed than others and some were non-existent. I could handle my emotions, was conscientious and pursued my goals with a vengeance. Self-motivation was a non-issue, with empathy and social skills coming to the fore as I got to know my team as

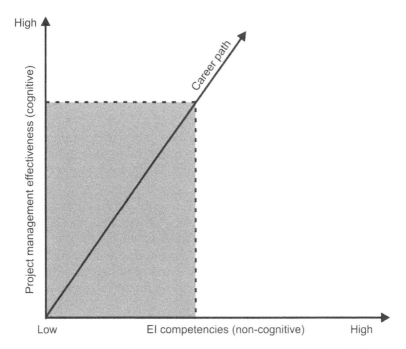

Figure 53.3 Hard (cognitive) skills versus soft (non-cognitive) skills
Source: Adapted from Burmesch, 2010.

individuals. What I did not fully understand was how to develop further what I already had and how to fill in the missing bits. This is what annual reviews and training/develop project management plans are designed to deal with, but soft skills do not always fall into nice neat training buckets. And because our career paths are not linear, we do not all learn at the same pace or by the same methods. It is natural that we acquire or develop skills at different rates over time. The shaded box in Figure 53.3 represents this variation in learning. It shows that at any point in time in their career, people will have higher levels of hard (cognitive) skills than soft (non-cognitive) skills.

Mayer et al. concluded through their research that, regardless of the rate of development, EI skills progress naturally through four different stages. They've called it the four-branch model (Mayer et al., 2004). The stages are listed below.

Stage 1: Perceive emotion – This is the ability to recognise or see emotion in another person through their body language or facial expressions. Without this ability understanding is impossible. For example, a project coordinator insists everything is under control yet his/her facial expressions and body language do not bear that out.

Stage 2: Use emotion to facilitate thought – Emotions, how we feel about something, along with knowledge from past experiences helps us prioritise our thinking. For example, a so-called 'urgent' issue might not have the highest priority, but it could be preferable to deal with it quickly (oil the squeaky wheel) and so reduce the chance of escalation leading to a much bigger problem.

Stage 3: Understand emotions – Any emotion that we observe can be triggered for a variety of reasons. We must interpret the trigger behind that emotion and think what it might mean. For example: if the project sponsor appears to be annoyed and snaps at you, it could be because of a surprise budget overspend, because they damaged their car that morning, or because they have to cancel their holiday. Remember it is not always about you.

Stage 4: Manage emotions – How we regulate and respond appropriately to our own emotions and how we respond to the emotions of others are all important. For example: shouting at the project sponsor in reply to his/her outburst is purely reactive when we have no idea what caused the annoyance.

The natural progression from one branch to another, and the sequence of these branches, helps us see to what extent they are integrated into our own personality. How do you learn these four stages and further develop your own EI competencies? Often the best and most effective way to learn something new is to do it on the job. EI is no exception and the following options are available to everyone, regardless of their position or seniority:

- Find a mentor. This is a simple and effective way of learning. Identify and approach someone you trust and respect, whose abilities you admire and respond to. It's not necessary to act alone or reinvent the wheel when you can learn from someone else's experiences.
- Work with a coach. This is generally shorter term and more structured than mentoring. It is not necessary that the coach has experience of the person's job. Meetings are more structured and formal, and the focus is on specific development areas/issues.
- Experimentation (trial and error). Apply those new skills to your own working style and personality. Make adjustments as you go along until you are comfortable with what works for you. Over time things will become so integrated that they will happen unconsciously.
- Read. There are now many books on the subject of EI as well as leadership books that incorporate many aspects of EI.
- Shared experiences. Talk to others face-to-face, through forums or social networking. Share ideas and experiences and pick up new methods or concepts to try.

Developing EI competencies means developing people who:

- know how and when to express emotions;
- have an increased awareness of the impact of their emotions on others, which helps them to exercise self-control;
- can further develop their intuition in order to tune in to, appreciate and understand other people's emotions;
- are more likely to be intrinsically motivated, think with both head and heart, and trust those all-important 'gut instincts';
- have the ability to adapt responses and approaches to different situations.

Use and Benefits of EI

Now more than ever we understand that to achieve anything in project management we are dependent on people. People *are* projects. Whilst there are some who continue to survive against the odds, there is a definite opportunity to increase business value with EI. As every person has their own connected web of complex systems it is the manager's job to make it all coalesce. This is especially important in project management, because projects are temporary and each one is unique. EI helps project managers to build on their standard project management competencies so they are better able to cope:

- when their power and authority is limited;
- with the challenges associated with global projects and their inevitable diversity of language and culture;
- with others' expectations that they will be 'on' for their project all day and every day, particularly when a project crosses time zones, continents and hemispheres.

As projects shift ever further away from traditional teams towards remote working, with people involved from different cultures spread geographically, the greatest benefits will be derived from EI-competent project managers. This is because they can keep disruptive emotions and impulses in check. Take my earlier example of the indignant project manager and the disinterested customer. Language and cultural differences added to the challenge yet the project manager could have recognised earlier that the customer's body language did not match what they were saying. It would have helped the project manager to prioritise any attempt to convince the customer and quickly work out that the customer was not actually interested in discussing the testing process at all. The reason they were challenging the project manager was simply to reinforce their presumed position of power in front of other customer representatives and vendors.

With geographically spread teams the principles are the same, although some soft skills deployed must be heightened over others. Active listening is one of those skills, and particularly necessary when project management is done through virtual means, such as email, conference calls or net-meetings. To perceive emotion over the telephone the project manager has to tune in to what is *not* being said as much as what is. In these situations project managers must also use their EI competencies in other ways. They cannot operate with a silo mentality and have to work harder to build trust. If the geographically spread team believes that the project manager embodies EI competencies rather than just espousing them, it will be inspired and have the confidence to get things done.

My software team were all based at the same office but spent large amounts of time working at customer locations around the city. By using a logical and pragmatic approach I got to know my role and team. Actively listening to my manager and watching his body language helped me ask pertinent questions and uncover the direction the company wanted the team to move in. Openly communicating my plan to the team established a mutually understood platform from which we could all move forward. Then by actively listening to each team member they quickly understood that I was human and would do what I could where it made sense (and where authority and strategy permitted). Where possible I was empathetic. Where that was not possible, I was sympathetic.

The benefits were huge. EI helped to create a genuinely open environment where relationships based on trust were developed, and that resulted in a culture of mutual respect. We all knew where we stood. The attitude of the team shifted, with many barriers between individuals and expertise disappearing. They started sharing ideas, respecting each other and they became a group of self-motivated high-performers. Because someone had bothered to find out about them they felt valued, became more confident in their abilities and secure in the knowledge that if they asked for help they would get it.

The projects the team delivered somehow seemed easier and less stressful. They were definitely of higher quality. After that the team did not really need much managing. They were confident in themselves and their colleagues, and earned the respect of other departments. They were able to recognise situations earlier and provide assistance and direction. They were learning how and when to balance individual needs against project and business drivers, and they were making more informed decisions. And the biggest benefit overall? Everyone increased their own EI levels. And that contributed to higher productivity, increased profits and repeat business.

In project management the simplest yet most effective way to help people share issues or problems and in turn develop their own EI is to say: 'I can't manage what I don't know, so if you tell me I can help you, but if you don't I can't'. With that approach not only do people benefit, but the organisation does too.

EI helps project managers to look outside their 'personal box' to appreciate the wholeness of an organisation, a project's place in it and the potential of its people. Then the organisation achieves increased productivity, higher profits and contented customers. Other benefits are increased sales, better recruiting and staff retention, and more effective leadership.

Conclusion: The Future of EI

A survey published in August 2011 by the US online job site 'CareerBuilder' showed some results about how employers are valuing EI over IQ (for those who are interested, the web link is http://www.careerbuilder.com/share/aboutus/pressreleasesdetail.aspx?id=pr652&s d=8/18/2011&ed=8/18/2099&siteid=cbpr&sc_cmp1=cb_pr652_).

Key statistics from this survey were:

- 34 per cent of hiring managers said they are now placing greater emphasis on EI when hiring and promoting employees post-recession;
- 71 per cent said they value EI in an employee more than IQ;
- 59 per cent of employers would not hire someone who has a high IQ but low EI;
- 75 per cent are more likely to promote an employee with a high EI over one with a high IQ.

If my recent discussion with the director of a specialist UK project management recruitment company is anything to go by, these statistics do not reflect what is happening in the UK. In response to my questions her assessment revealed that UK hiring requirements put the ratio of hard skills (standard project management knowledge and industry experience) to soft skills (primarily those involved in managing a team and stakeholders) skills as high as 75:25. This was a surprise to me as I expected it to be the opposite but it seems that UK companies continue to be risk averse, believing that technical knowledge and previous experience in their sector will increase the chances of project success. Even for senior roles where it may be acknowledged that soft skills are higher, current demand suggests that a person lacking direct industry or project type experience and qualifications could be overlooked during recruitment.

However, my informant also said that regardless of the project or seniority, EI will become increasingly important as the need for more team-based collaboration across organisations, countries and cultures continues to rise. Her company is constantly educating clients about the benefits of excellent soft skills because the fact that someone can create a Gantt chart will not necessarily save a project. If the US survey results are anything to go by it should not be too much longer before UK employers realise the business benefits associated with project management delivered by EI-competent project managers.

As we saw earlier in this chapter, the Weatherhead School of Management EI is also influencing learning (see page 693). Not only what people are taught but also through changes to the way in which they are taught. In education as in business, if we value different ways of being bright we shall give people with different thoughts and ideas room to evolve and an even greater chance of fulfilling their potential. Focus will then be on the extent to which emotional competence can be developed not just the teaching of EI concepts.

EI is not the next big thing, a buzz-word, a craze or a bandwagon for consulting firms and training companies to jump on whilst they wait for the next wave to roll in. It is not to be confused with sympathy, implied agreement or taking sides. It is real and needs to be taken seriously. The survey of US employers has made that very clear. EI is a critical aspect of project management particularly for project managers who wish to deliver hugely successful projects with significant added value to the business. Clever project managers will review their EI strengths and weaknesses, and then work hard at developing those areas that will make them outstanding and highly sought after. Through that investment their teams will flourish, and managing people will not be quite such the headache it was.

References and Further Reading

Bar-On, R. Visit his personal website for information about the Bar-On model of EI. Available at: http://www.reuvenbaron.org/bar-on-model

Burmesch, B. (2010), 'Emotional Intelligence (EI) – A Critical Skill in Project Management', presentation given at the conference *Secrets of Success in Project Management*, July 2010, Platteville, WI, University of Wisconsin.

Covey. S.R. (2004a), *The 7 Habits of Highly Effective People*, 2nd edn, London: Simon & Schuster.

Covey, S.R. (2004b), *The 8th Habit: From Effectiveness to Greatness*, London: Simon & Schuster.

Deutschendorf, H. (2009), *The Other Kind of Smart: Simple Ways to Boost Your Emotional Intelligence for Greater Personal Effectiveness and Success*, New York: AMACOM.

Gardner, H. (1983), *Frames of Mind*, New York: Basic Books.

Goleman, D. (1995), *Emotional Intelligence*, New York: Bantam Books.

Goleman, D. (1998), *Working with Emotional Intelligence*, New York: Bantam Books.

Goleman, D., Boyatzis. R. and McKee, A. (2002), *Primal Leadership: Realizing the Power of Emotional Intelligence*, Boston, MA: Harvard Business School.

Leuner, B. (1966), 'Emotional intelligence and emancipation', *Praxis der Kinderpsychologie und Kinderpsychatrie*, 15, 193–203.

Maslow, A. (1954), *Motivation and Personality*, New York: Harper & Row.

Mayer, J.D., Salovey, P. and Caruso, D.R. (2004), 'Emotional intelligence: Theory, findings and implications', *Psychological Inquiry*, 15(3), 197–215.

Mersino, A. (2007), *Emotional Intelligence for Project managers: The People Skills You Need to Achieve Outstanding Results*, New York: AMACOM.

Salovey, P. and Mayer, J. (1990), 'Emotional intelligence', *Imagination, Cognition and Personality*, 9(3), 185–211.

Thorndike, R.L. and Stein, S. (1937), 'An evaluation of the attempts to measure social intelligence', *Psychological Bulletin*, 34, 275–84.

Weare, K. (2004), *Developing the Emotionally Literate School*, London: Paul Chapman (Sage).

Wechsler, D. (1940), 'Nonintellective factors in general intelligence', *Psychological Bulletin*, 37, 444–5.

54 *Managing Social Communications*

ELIZABETH HARRIN

We've all seen business stakeholders on their smartphones in meetings or sponsors who whip out their iPads in project board meetings. But is this really productive? And do project managers need to be in on it too? This chapter explores what social communications are and how project managers can tap into social communications to improve collaboration on their projects.

Introducing Social Communications

Human beings are sociable creatures, and we've been finding ways to interact with each other for thousands of years. In that respect, social communications are not new. However, the tools available in the twenty-first century make a big difference to the way in which we can communicate and collaborate with others. Social communications are exactly that – communicating and collaborating with purpose. In a work environment it's not about sharing funny pictures of cats or telling the world what you had for lunch. It's about using web-enabled technology to get things done more effectively, tapping into the way people are running their lives outside of your project team.

STRATEGY FIRST

Social communications is a generic term given to using modern technology and tools to connect, communicate and collaborate with others in your project environment. There are formal and informal channels that you can adopt on your project but the most important thing is to remember that it does not matter which software products you use. At the time of writing, the micro-blogging site Twitter and the social network Facebook are still going strong, and photo-sharing site Pinterest is a new player.

Ultimately, for project management professionals, it's about doing things the way that other people are doing them and are comfortable with. A project manager who insists on monthly status updates using a complicated slide template is not going to be popular with stakeholders who can get real-time information displayed clearly on their smartphone screens on any other topic *except* your project.

But by the time you pick this book off the shelf in years to come, these tools could easily have been replaced by other brand names. It is the strategy that sits behind the products that is important for your project. For example, if your aim on the project is to capture all the relevant information in one logical place, a wiki would be a good choice. Simple to set up and easy to customise, wikis enable anyone to edit structured web pages and create links between pages. This means that you can navigate through the knowledge gained about your project, jumping from page to page following information strands that are relevant to you at that moment.

If your aim is to produce a continuous flow of project news to be read by other people in the company, or interested external stakeholders, a blog would be a suitable channel. Blogs are made up of articles that generally appear in chronological order, so they read like an online journal. They are a great way to tell the story of your project, and they allow you to embed photos, audio and videos as well.

To give an example, a collaboration tool would meet the strategic need to get a virtual team working effectively together across distance and time zones. The functionality of collaboration tools tends to include ways for team members to share and annotate documents, hold online discussions synchronously or asynchronously, track progress against tasks and ask questions. Those, and many other features, are aimed at making it easier to work together.

There isn't space here to go into every type of tool and see how it can benefit the project manager, but the most important message is to be strategy-driven – not tool-driven. Don't adopt a social communications product because it seems like the right thing to do: make sure you really are addressing a project management need.

The Social Project Manager

Social communications have a number of benefits and enhanced communication with stakeholders is top of the list. You can use your social communications strategy to identify and map stakeholders. Your chosen tools enable the project team to engage with stakeholders in a way that suits their preferences.

Web-enabled technologies make it easier for your project communications to reach a wider audience. Where the strategy is to communicate – and not collaborate – with stakeholders (for example, members of the public during a public sector or third-sector project), social communications enable you to reach a wider group. Whether you limit the readership of your project blog to your company's employees, or share short status updates with the world on your favourite social networking site, the reach of your project communications now goes far beyond an email distribution list or a printed project newsletter.

Social communications are also convenient, especially when working with virtual teams. Many tools are designed to be accessed 'on the go' from multiple devices such as smartphones or tablets. Tapping into the mobility that these products offer means that you can communicate with your team, wherever they happen to be. This can improve collaboration because it is easy to stay in touch this way, and when working practices are easy, people are more likely to adopt them.

However, the most important thing for the connected project manager to do is to ensure that there are benefits in working this way. If you cannot identify benefits to the project and to your team, then don't adopt social communications technology. An example would be a small agile team, all based in the same location and working closely on a software release. A collaboration tool would not provide any benefit over and above the daily face-to-face cooperation from which the team benefits. However, if the team needed a knowledge repository, a wiki would be a good addition to their toolset.

Social collaboration tools are not necessarily appropriate for all teams and all projects, so weigh up the benefits before making the decision to adopt them.

Challenges of Social Communications

Whilst the connected project manager can gain many benefits from using social communications tools, there are also challenges to be overcome. This section discusses several of the major issues and considers ways for dealing with them appropriately. You will, of course, have to adapt your management of these challenges to suit your own environment, your team, your senior executives and also the tools you wish to adopt.

THE CULT OF PERSONALITY

In one of my books (Harrin, 2010) I talk about the seven Cs of social media:

- community;
- collaboration;
- communication;
- constraints;
- connectivity;
- channels;
- content.

Now I'd like to add another 'C' to that list, which is *character*. Social communications work because people want to connect to other people. Your blog posts, status updates, discussions and commentary should come from you as an individual, not on behalf of a nameless project team. The most engaging online networks are those that encourage individuals to act and collaborate as individuals, with all the knowledge and skills that they have to share. In other words, if you try to anonymise everything and create generic accounts that don't link back to an individual project team member, you will lose some of the power of a social network.

It is important to make it as easy and pleasurable as possible for people to interact with each other through a mediated community. If you do not have engagement, you don't have a community. If your aim is to increase communication and collaboration on projects, then you need members of the social communications network to want to be there, collaborating with their colleagues.

A virtual team in particular needs to feel that a mediated community offers them a shared sense of place, somewhere that the team can work together as individuals and as a productive team. Too much chit-chat about the weekend's television highlights will not define the space as a valued work environment. Too little, and the team loses the sense of community and trust. Trust comes from sharing small confidences, so encourage some water-cooler conversation through your social communications tools: it will build relationships between team members more quickly.

Personality also comes into play when looking to gain 'buy-in' for your social communications initiative. As with any project to introduce new technology, your new tools need to be championed by someone – a project management office (PMO) director, a senior project manager or anyone else in the organisation who can clearly see the value of introducing a new way of working. In the absence of someone to fulfil this role, you will find your project struggling. And you should consider the introduction and adoption of social communications tools as a project, with all the associated change management that goes alongside changing ways of working.

Without a clear sponsor, your social communications project will struggle. Resistance to change is common in organisations and you may find it difficult to find a volunteer who can act in this role. Executive resistance is one of the challenges of adopting social communications that the connected project manager has to overcome.

MEASURING SUCCESS

One of the big challenges when adopting a social communications tool is knowing whether or not that decision was successful. How will you know if your social communications tool is improving the way in which project team members communicate and collaborate with each other?

Social communications tools have the capacity to track a variety of metrics that you can use to measure success. There are a number of ways of measuring the success of tool deployment including:

- Subscribers: how many people have subscribed to project alerts?
- Hit counts: how many visitors are viewing your social communications tool? Where are they from and how often do they come back?
- Journeys: what are people looking at when they come to the tool?
- Engagement: how much project chatter is going on? Is the site well used by the people who need to use it for their day jobs?
- Efficiency: are collaborative tasks now done in a timelier manner?

Unfortunately it is difficult to track some of these, especially targets around efficiency. If you didn't have benchmarked numbers before your social communications tool was implemented, you'll have nothing to compare your new efficiency levels to. Also be wary about seeing high numbers as a mark of success. The fact that 80 per cent of your company is looking at your project wiki could be a good thing – but if the 20 per cent of employees who are not looking at it are your target stakeholder group then the tool is not meeting its objectives. Define metrics that are meaningful to you and your project before you start so that you have something tangible to show 'success'.

Another option is to decide *not* to measure the return on investment or performance against success criteria. Research by Watson Wyatt (2009–2010) shows that only 16 per cent of companies have tools in place to measure the effectiveness of their social communications projects. As many project managers do not measure the effectiveness of meetings, conference calls or other traditional project communication and collaboration methods, you could opt to measure benefits and success only anecdotally, instead of through a structured programme of success criteria.

MANAGING PROJECT RISK

The security of project information is probably the largest concern for many executives, especially if you choose to adopt cloud-based technologies that store project data outside the organisation and enable it to be accessed from anywhere. Whatever solution you adopt, you must ensure that it has adequate security and authentication protocols for your needs. You will also want to carry out some awareness training so that users know what is and is not appropriate to share on the forum.

This is particularly relevant if you are sharing information with third parties. You may choose a tool that allows you successfully to ring-fence content that your partners can see, so reducing the implications for privacy. Social communications tools with few or no privacy settings can be perfectly adequate, but you must ensure that you know who is using the tool, so that sensitive project data is kept secure.

The final risk of social communications is that it moves everything to an online space, whether your company hosts a product or you use a cloud-based provider to store your project data. You have to ensure that whatever solution you adopt has adequate back-up and recovery options in case the worst happens. This is the reason why it is essential to involve your corporate IT department.

Corporate IT teams can also help you establish whether your chosen social communications tool has an audit trail – and how you can best access this within the legal boundaries of monitoring an employee's work. Audit trails are useful for finding out who was the last person to log in, use a document, comment in a discussion, amend the wiki and so on. In a straightforward project environment you should not need to use the audit trail information but in certain circumstances (such as dealing with a disgruntled employee) it may become necessary to track who has used the tool.

The final project risk I want to discuss here is that of overload. Social communications do not replace 'offline' communications. The connected project manager will still have to prepare written board reports, use emails, produce presentations and everything else he or she did before. Today, social communications rarely replace the need for project managers to communicate through other mechanisms. As a result, it is possible to feel overloaded by the volume of discussion happening in social communications tools. This additional channel requires constant attention, and it can feel like you are losing control.

There are a number of solutions for dealing with this including using aggregation tools (where they exist) to consolidate feeds from multiple channels into one location for you to review at your leisure. However, the easiest way to deal with overload is to ignore it. Switch off the feeds and stop following the discussions. It may feel as if you are losing your grip on the detail of the project, but unless you were a particularly command-and-control style project manager you never had this grip anyway. Social communications tools make discussions visible that would have previously happened over email between team members or on the phone. You would not monitor your team members' phone conversations, so don't expect to need to monitor everything on the tool. You can train your team to flag important items to you, or implement a categorisation system so that you only have to read items tagged with particular words.

MANAGING PERSONAL RISK

Managing personal risk is less of an issue at work, and more of a potential problem if you choose to use social communications tools outside the workplace (for example, for career progression and networking). Many social project managers choose to display their personal profiles on professional networking sites, or to extend their personal social networks to work colleagues. This can be a straightforward and positive way of keeping in touch with colleagues, and is now so commonplace that project managers without a presence online can be at a disadvantage when it comes to finding out about job or training opportunities.

However, social project managers need to remember that the Internet has a long memory. If you choose to post personal information about yourself online, your employer could see it. That includes holiday photos, comments about your workplace and colleagues and the jokes you choose to share with your network. For the main part, professional project managers should have nothing to fear from sharing a bit of their personality with their contacts online. But you need to know where to draw the line, and that line is usually at the point where you wouldn't mind if your manager saw the information. If you would not share it with your boss, don't share it online.

This issue is also a concern on corporate social networks where project team members can provide their own profile information. In your profile and in your communications with your team members, make sure that you act professionally and respectfully at all times, as you would with face-to-face communication. The next section looks at social communications policies which aim to codify how to appropriately behave when using social communications tools at work.

Social Communications Policies

Once you have decided to embark on a social communications initiative, it is essential to set some guidelines for your team. You may find that your company already has corporate policies around the use of social media tools and that these can be adapted for the use of social communications solutions on projects. If no such guidelines exist, ask your PMO for assistance in producing them, or simply draw up a brief document yourself on which you and your project team can agree. Search the Internet for examples of social media policies: many companies are happy to share their policies and have posted them publicly online, so there is no need to start from scratch.

An alternative to a social communications policy is to build the relevant guidelines into existing corporate policies. Many companies have a suite of human resource policies relating to appropriate behaviour, and you could ask for these to be updated to include online behaviour as well.

Social communications policies should include:

- standards for online behaviour such as the official position on suitable language and any links to codes of conduct;
- privacy/data security/confidentiality guidelines to protect project and personal information;
- guidelines around the use of individual or generic logins;

- guidelines for mentioning other staff members or company business outside the project;
- details about the appropriate use of the company or project logo;
- clarity around the fact that the individual represents both the project and the company when operating on internal and external sites;
- a statement around using good judgement and common sense when posting to social communications tools.

Your social communications policy should be incorporated into the project governance framework and communications plan. You will want to include the use of your social communications tools in your communication plan as well.

Monitor the adherence to your policy as you monitor other elements of your project and team performance. If you find that there are some elements which are not working, take the opportunity to amend the policy until it provides a suitable backbone for your social communications activity on the project.

Moving Forward with Social Communications

Social communications form a large part of life outside the office, and the connected project manager needs to incorporate those ways of out-of-the-office communications into working practices today. Many stakeholders already use publicly available, consumer-led social communications tools to manage their personal networks. In our drive to be easy to do business with, it is essential that project managers adopt relevant tools to ensure that the gap between home and office ways of working is not extreme to the point where stakeholders choose not to work with us.

The connected project manager can incorporate social communications in project reporting, for example by making the report available in multiple formats and accessible through multiple channels. Reports can also include multimedia elements, such as video, audio and photographs. This can be particularly useful if your project is constructing something tangible, such as a building.

Social communications tools also enable you to personalise the users' experience through content filters and dashboards, so once a product is in place on the project, embedded and operational, you can look to adapt it further to ensure each stakeholder receives the relevant information in a format that suits them best. Content filters, such as behavioural-based advertising, are already in use on consumer-led websites, and whilst there is some discussion that marks these as intrusive it is likely that we will see more movement towards personalisation in both consumer and corporate social communications tools.

There has also recently been a rise in the number of training companies incorporating digital learning into their offerings. Project managers and PMO teams are likely to see more and more of this – training courses being offered with digital material instead of printed textbooks, and incorporating online discussion forums and podcasts (online radio shows) to continue the learning after a classroom event.

These types of learning can spill over into the project environment. The connected project manager can incorporate social communications channels and digital media as part of a structured change management approach for projects. This could include, for example, using podcasts and video to train staff on the deliverables of the project, such as new software.

PLANNING FOR ACCESSIBILITY

Disability discrimination laws, regulations and guidelines are different in every country. However, it is clear that as workforces are becoming more diverse, it is important to ensure that the tools you use for project management are suitable for everyone to use. This is even more necessary if your project is delivering services to the general public and you have chosen to build in social communications as part of your wider community communications plan.

Consider the needs of all your users when adopting social communications tools, and if for any reason you have chosen to build these products in-house with the help of your IT team, get some advice about how to make them accessible for everyone. As this area develops, we will see the user interfaces and mobility options for tools increase. This is good for all members of the workforce and community – good, accessible design benefits everyone.

PLANNING FOR INTEROPERABILITY

At the time of writing, interoperability between social communications tools is in its infancy. Many of the more established products that are aimed at a consumer audience have the ability to link to other products, but normally to provide add-on services (such as being able to post photographs from one social media network to another). There is a growing interest in dashboard products that allow you to manage multiple accounts from a single platform: these are particularly useful for business users, but again are mostly aimed at consumer end users, not a corporate market.

So, for the social project manager there are a number of tools to choose from to enhance communication and collaboration in the enterprise, but a limited number of ways to join these up and present a single view to the project team and stakeholders. This situation is likely to get better with time, but at present, the end result is that project managers and their teams will probably have to use a number of tools, or to limit themselves to perhaps one that does not quite fulfil all their needs.

PLANNING FOR NETWORKS

The social project manager spends more time than ever before creating, building, planning and managing networks. There is no doubt an overhead that comes with adopting social communications tools, because the stakeholder communities are as yet not prepared to move away from the traditional communication and collaboration channels (and perhaps never will). As a result, there is a continuing responsibility to link online and offline communities to ensure that each network has the same amount of project information and the same opportunity to collaborate. Balancing the complex, in-person links of a face-to-face network with that of an online, virtual, community is a skill that the social project manager has to excel at.

It is hard to predict future trends in a world that is constantly changing. There are new social communications tools released regularly, aimed at both consumers and business users. However, one thing is certain, social communications are here to stay. Regardless of the tools, platforms, data input methods or storage locales, we shall be using social communications in the workplace and in our personal lives for years to come.

References and Further Reading

Harrin, E. (2010), *Social Media for Project Managers*, Newtown Square PA: Project Management Institute.

Watson Wyatt (2009–2010), 'Communication ROI study report'. Available at: http://www. towerswatson.com/research/670

55 *Empathy in Project Management*

GEOFF CRANE

As an introduction to this chapter on empathy in project management, I would like to tell you a story about what happened to me a little earlier in my career.

Introduction

A few years ago I took a job as a programme manager for a big Asian bank. This position oversaw well over 90 ongoing projects each month, most of which were based around an innovative enterprise trading platform. I had sponsors and stakeholders across the entire breadth of the corporate investment-banking arm of the company. I had considerable previous experience on the technology end of trading, so I was very familiar with my stakeholders' needs but I had never managed a platform as complex and chimerical as that currently under my purview.

One day I asked the man who had hired me away from another bank, 'Why me? Why would you pick me when I have no experience with this platform, and have never managed a portfolio of this size? Surely there were better candidates?' To this day I'm going to believe his reply was a compliment. He said, 'Geoff, you know some people, they bring impeccable organisational skills to their job'. I smiled tentatively. 'And some', he went on, 'bring outstanding domain expertise to work. Some people even have extraordinary technical prowess. You, I'm sorry to say, don't have any of those things'.

My jaw hit the floor. 'But', the man continued, 'you get people to work together unlike anyone I've ever met. We are in sore need of that around here'.

After I had picked my bruised ego up off the floor, I left to consider his words. On meeting with my primary stakeholders, I saw that the operation I'd inherited was in a terrible state. Project objectives were poorly defined, short-term projects were rarely delivered within agreed service levels and the general attitude was that my people were unskilled and unhelpful.

So I looked at the people I had on my staff. From outward appearances, my team had all the requisite skills, was highly trained and took care of all the right relationships. As an outsider looking in, it seemed all the correct pieces were in place. So why were my stakeholders so dissatisfied?

The answer was not hard to find. When I met with my people, every last one of them had a protectionist attitude towards their work. They took ownership of the tasks assigned to them, but not the inputs. When I asked them who defined the parameters of their work inputs, the answer was usually, 'My input is someone else's output. It's not my responsibility'.

If you have ever managed enterprise-level projects, you know that this attitude will not succeed. Changes made to one area of an enterprise backbone will have ripple effects that spread throughout the system. If each person in the organisation fails to maintain a high-level view of his or her work, the result will be anarchy.

Clearly, the problem which faced me appeared to be behavioural. I would not be able to solve this with traditional project management techniques. Something more fundamental would be required – something that spoke to the base attitudes of my staff (and later to my stakeholders, whom I discovered were equally culpable). But how could I find a solution when I had yet to understand the details of the problem?

For this, I relied on the one management skill I possess that I did not learn in a classroom. A skill I've been cultivating and refining throughout my entire life. I'm talking about empathy.

Understanding Empathy: A Definition

What is empathy? The Merriam-Webster online dictionary defines it as 'the action of understanding, being aware of, being sensitive to, and vicariously experiencing the feelings, thoughts and experiences of another of either the past or present, without having the feelings, thoughts, and experience fully communicated in an objectively explicit manner; *also*: the capacity for this'. Whew, that's a mouthful. Putting the definition a simpler way, empathy is the ability of a person to place themselves into the shoes of another.

But if we allow that to be the end of the definition, the concept of empathy appears nothing more than a notion to help children socialise in the playground. It's very nice, but quite irrelevant in the professional world. To find its place in a project management context, we really need to elaborate on this definition further.

Before I continue, I want to point out that because an empathic relationship is composed of two parties, discussing empathy can become a little confusing. For the purposes of this chapter, I shall use the terms, 'empathiser' or 'listener' to describe the party who is attempting to empathise, and 'speaker' to describe the party who is communicating their emotion.

Empathy is a process that facilitates the flow of emotional information in such a way that the receiver can recognise, appraise and respond to it. For our purposes, this definition sheds a little more clarity on the concept: *empathy is a form of communication*. Since roughly 80 per cent of a project manager's job is communication, the development of empathic skills is critical.

When we think of communication in project management, some of us are reminded of PMI Knowledge Area No.10, which is communications management. We think of status updates and Gantt charts. We think of stakeholder identification and information distribution processes. It's all very cold and clinical. Partially because we project managers are conditioned to speak in the language of analytics, we often overlook the emotional undercurrents that flow through our projects like water. When presented with emotional information during a status review, a typical project manager's response is, 'let's just stick to the facts'.

But emotions are facts too, as discussed in Chapter 53. They are powerful and undeniable. More importantly, people sometimes act on their emotions in unpredictable ways. If left unchecked, these actions may have adverse effects on work in progress. A project manager who refuses to manage emotional information effectively exposes the project to risk.

It's important here to note a marked difference between empathy and sympathy. If a project manager merely acknowledges another's emotions, but makes no attempt to connect with the person they're speaking with, they may be demonstrating sympathy. Sympathy is detached. It's something you may feel towards someone you don't know, like when you drive by a funeral in progress and see a bereaved family from your car window. You may feel compassion *for* the family, but may have no reason to attempt to experience their pain.

Empathy is different. Note that the dictionary definition requires the empathiser to 'vicariously experience the feelings ...' of another. This means that to empathise effectively, the person in question must consciously put their own feelings and beliefs on hold, and temporarily switch places with the other person. The first person does this in order to see the world through the second person's eyes. A simple representation of this is given in Figure 55.1.

In some cases, and under the right circumstances, this is not a difficult task. If you ever had a close friend experience a personal tragedy, their pain likely became your pain to a certain degree. Because of your friendship, you shared a bond. That bond became a conduit for some of your friend's emotions to pass through to you. When people speak of empathy, they often use the term in a context of difficult emotions.

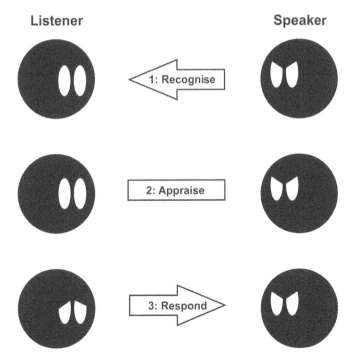

Figure 55.1 Stages of empathic communication

But not all emotion is painful, nor are all circumstances debilitating. I have noticed in my career a direct relationship between instances of overt empathic expression and the emotional tension of a given situation. That is, the more emotionally expressive a person is about a problem, the more likely people around him or her will be to empathise with their position. Unfortunately, the opposite is also true. Sometimes people fail to show their emotions overtly, perhaps because they feel their circumstances don't warrant it, or because they feel vulnerable publically expressing emotion. In these instances, I have observed that others around them tend to turn a blind eye to the emotions that may be expressing themselves in quieter ways. Herein lies a terrible problem when it comes to getting work done.

You have probably heard the expression 'project management is about people'. New project managers sometimes have a hard time understanding this concept because so much of what they learn as students focuses on analytics and methodologies. Despite all the tools and methods available to project managers to help manage their triple constraint, project managers are wholly dependent on the whims of the people whose work they shape. If they choose to ignore, incorrectly adapt or otherwise fail to follow the prescribed tools and methods, the project may only succeed in spite of itself.

Understanding Empathy: A Deconstruction

Now that we've discussed what empathy is (a form of communication), and what it isn't (sympathy), our next step should be to break it down into its component parts. Research by Stiff et al. (1987) found that empathy is composed of three dimensions. The first, they call 'perspective taking'. This refers to the ability of an individual to assume temporarily another's point of view.

PERSPECTIVE TAKING

Perspective taking is the first step in developing an empathic connection with another person. Sometimes this process begins almost automatically, such as when we see someone we know in tears. When that happens, it's common for us to say, 'what's the matter?' in an attempt to understand the other's position.

If the empathiser takes perspective correctly, then as the details unfold, he or she will be able to appreciate the story from the crying person's point of view. They will understand the reasons for the tears. One example of perspective taking might be, 'Sally is sad because she's lost the tickets she bought her husband for his birthday'. It's important to note, however, that effective perspective taking remains free of evaluation. Using the above example, if the empathiser thought inwardly 'Sally is sad because she's lost the tickets she bought her husband for his birthday ... and that's stupid', the occasion for empathy is closed. The evaluative component closes the door to further empathic involvement.

Taking perspective doesn't require any emotional investment on the part of the empathiser. For that reason, some might say that this is the easiest of the three dimensions to perform. Sometimes, though, perspective taking can be a bit more difficult. Without a stimulus as visible as tears, there may be no outward indicators to suggest that an empathic connection might be needed. In these cases, we have to work harder to take perspective by temporarily setting aside our own viewpoints to consider those of the other person.

EMOTIONAL CONTAGION

The second empathic dimension is called 'emotional contagion'. This means that the empathising individual experiences an emotional response 'parallel to, and as a result of, observing another person's actual or anticipated display of emotion' (ibid.). That is, when we see someone in tears, we feel sad ourselves. When we witness someone happy and excited, we take on a similar emotion. This dimension is crucial to effective empathising because without it, we cannot share the experience of the other person. If we can't access the other's feelings within ourselves, we cannot appreciate their emotional state.

Part of emotional contagion happens automatically in response to another's emotional expression. Wicker et al. (2003) discovered that when a subject witnesses a facial expression in another person, the part of the brain that corresponds to the witnessed emotion fires. Sometimes subjects had a tendency to automatically imitate the facial expressions they observed. Levenson et al. (1990) found that when people make certain faces, the new muscular configurations elicit the emotions demonstrated in the face they're making. So there is a limited physiological basis for emotional contagion. When you see someone make a face that demonstrates surprise, for example, you might unconsciously make a surprised face yourself. The act of shaping your face in this manner would give you your own primitive version of surprise (see Figure 55.2). All of this happens without a word having been spoken.

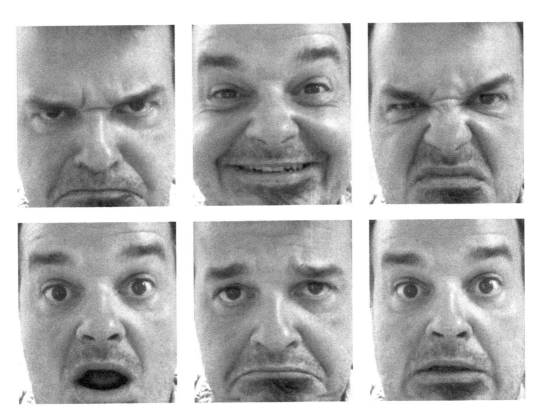

Figure 55.2 Facial expressions of emotion

Dialogue, however, is generally required to hone the emotional contagion into a more specific feeling. Again, this is something we tend to do automatically, although our reasons here have more to do with cultural conditioning than anything physiological. 'What do you have to be so happy about?' you might ask a smiling person without thinking. Or 'why the long face?' Unless we consciously choose to ignore the visceral reaction we get from seeing another's expression, we'll often give in to the urge to find out what lies behind the externally presented emotion.

This is where we find out the details of the emotion our counterpart feels, which may give rise to a similar reaction in ourselves. For example, if you find out that the person you're speaking with was unfairly treated at the bank, you may feel a similar, rising sense of injustice as the story unfolds. The essence of emotional contagion lies in these details.

EMPATHIC CONCERN

The third and final dimension of empathy is called 'empathic concern'. This concept is a bit more complicated in that it's made up of two primary components. Empathic concern requires:

1. a general concern and regard for the welfare of others and;
2. the stipulation that the [emotion] is *not* parallel to that of the target person (Stiff et al., 1987).

The second component means that to feel empathic concern, one must set aside the emotion they experienced through emotional contagion, and feel something else in response. Empathic concern requires the individual to care, yet still maintain a sense of self.

This is the toughest part for most people. Empathic concern requires a certain level of emotional maturity and strong self-awareness. This sounds somewhat ironic – why would we need to understand ourselves when, in an empathetic context, we need to understand other people? The answer is fairly simple. Self-awareness comes most easily from hard experience, which in turn provides context. Until we find ourselves in a given situation, we cannot know how we would respond. The further away a potential scenario lies from our own experience, the less able we are to evaluate it.

This fact was driven home to me during my research. I had occasion to speak with a teacher who discovered one of his students had been sexually assaulted. He was able to feel horror at her plight and recognise that her suffering must have been terrible, but he was unable to empathise. In his words, 'all I could think to do was teach her how to multiply fractions'. He said he felt overwhelming impotence. He wanted to be able to do something for her that would 'fix it', but her trauma was so far removed from his experience, he could not take the final step to empathy.

The Johari Window

The relationship between self-awareness and empathy can be demonstrated using a model called the Johari Window (Stiff et al., 1987) which is introduced in Figure 55.3. Imagine a box that contains absolutely everything there is to know about you. Inside the box are all of the things you like and don't like, all of the ways you respond to stimuli

Figure 55.3 The Johari Window components

Note: This model deconstructs everything there is to know about you and breaks it into sections.

around you, all your wishes and all of your secrets. Some of the things in this box you will already know about yourself, and some things you won't (yet). We could demonstrate this by splitting the box in two parts.

We can also look at the box in a different way. There will be some things inside that other people already know about you and some things other people don't know about you. We can divide the box a bit differently to show this relationship. When you put it all together, this box that contains everything there is to know about you can be broken into four parts.

Part 1 contains all the information that you know about yourself and other people also know about you. We can call this 'open'.

Part 2 would contain information that you do not already know about yourself, but of which other people are aware. This part would be 'blind'.

Part 3 would contain your secrets – the things about yourself that you know, but that other people don't. This is your 'hidden'.

Part 4: nobody at all knows what's in Part 4. It's 'unknown'.

These separations make up the default Johari Window, as shown in Figure 55.4.

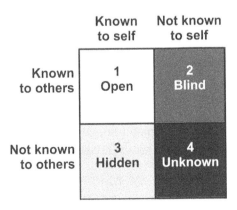

Figure 55.4 The Johari Window

Note: A model showing the relationship between empathy and self-awareness.

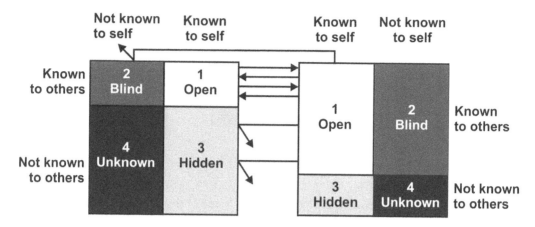

Figure 55.5 A Johari Window demonstration

Note: Successful empathetic pathways require shared ground.

Source: Adapted from Chapter 6, 'Understanding Interpersonal Relationships' in Adler, et al., (2008), *Understanding Human Communication*, Toronto, Oxford, p. 237.

Things get complicated when we stop to realise that our respective selves are not so easily symmetrical as the default Johari Window suggests. For example, one person may have a very small open pane and a very large hidden pane. Another may have a huge unknown pane and also be quite blind. If two people are to have a chance at forging an empathic connection, there must be some level of overlap between the open areas of both parties.

As you can see in Figure 55.5, if one person attempts to pass emotional information from their open area to a non-open area in another person, that communication will fail. This was the case with the aforementioned teacher, who, despite wanting to empathise with his student, lacked the experience to be able to do so. There are methods for overcoming this difficulty, which I shall discuss later, but for now, suffice it to say that for someone to feel empathic concern for another, a personal awareness of the emotion in question must make its way to the open area of their Johari Window.

Empathy requires all three dimensions (perspective taking, emotional contagion and empathic concern) to function. If one is missing, then the empathic connection fails. Think of the manager who walks around asking people 'how's your family?', but without a trace of genuine interest. The words are there, but nobody's fooled.

Given the above, how are these empathic dimensions relevant in a project management context? Consider for a moment a stakeholder who is resistant to a change request. As a project manager, your concern is about getting the change approved, so that your project can move on. Your stakeholder does not care about what you want. He or she does not care about your processes, or your approach. Their concern is whatever problem they see with the change request, which they may or may not articulate to you.

In such a situation, you have many different options available to you. You could get the other stakeholders to gang up on them and try to bully them into changing their position. You could try to force the issue yourself and exert whatever authority you feel you have. You could even proceed with the change request anyway and ask for forgiveness later. None of these approaches will ensure any degree of success, and worse, you could create problems for yourself later on in the project (especially if the stakeholder in question has both high interest and influence). Looking at the situation through the dimensions of empathy, there could be other alternatives.

The Behavioural Change Stairway Model (BCSM)

In response to growing instances of terrorism and the resulting demand for hostage negotiation, the United States' Federal Bureau of Investigation needed to find a way to influence the behaviour of hostage-takers. They recognised that terrorists could not be coerced through conventional methods without seriously risking the lives of hostages. And so they developed the BCSM as shown in Figure 55.6 The intent of this model is to get a terrorist to willingly perform whatever tasks the negotiator asks of them. This could include releasing hostages, reducing demands or even giving themselves up to authorities without incident.

The BCSM is important for our purposes because it gives us a model to see precisely how empathy fits into a project manager's arsenal. It is a precursor that leads directly to the behavioural changes he or she may wish to elicit in stakeholders, vendors or project team members. With this in mind, we should explore the model's different stages.

Stage 1: Active listening – Before the project manager can climb the BCSM and drive the behaviour changes they're seeking in others, they must first hear and understand the positions of their counterparts. Active listening is a collection of techniques used by therapists and counsellors to build therapeutic relationships with their clients. These will be covered in detail later in this chapter.

Stage 2: Empathy – Here the concepts discussed above show themselves. Empathy is a natural by-product of active listening. If the first stage has been successful, the listener should have received a perspective of the speaker's situation, should have experienced some form of emotional contagion and should also be able to demonstrate empathic concern whilst maintaining their individual sense of self. Once this has been achieved, the listener can move on to take real action.

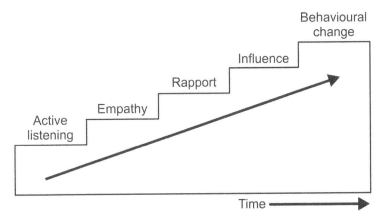

Figure 55.6 The behavioural change stairway model
Source: Adapted from Vecchi et al. (2005).

Stage 3: Rapport – The first two stages of the BCSM are more about the listener developing an understanding of the speaker's emotional circumstances. To begin to drive behavioural change, we need to get to the point where we can start to exert some influence. This third stage is where we plant those seeds. Rapport between both parties develops through the display of empathy. During this phase, the listener can begin to build themes with the speaker in ways that shed new light on the situation which elicited the emotional response. The listener can reframe problems to present them in a different light and offer plausible, desirable outcomes.

Stage 4: Influence – By this point in the BCSM, both parties have established a relationship. Because of this, the speaker would be open to suggestions from the listener. The most important aspect of this stage is that the listener has broken through important barriers and has earned the speaker's respect.

Stage 5: Behavioural change – This is the final stage. Once the previous steps have been successfully climbed, both parties have arrived at a place where real change can occur. Both a positive relationship and mutual respect are in place. At this point, the listener can suggest the desired course of action and, if things have gone well, the speaker will follow it. If the listener moved too quickly through the stages, and the speaker is not ready, both parties will have to take a few steps back and try again.

Probably the greatest benefit of the BCSM is that it results in *willing* behavioural changes in the target person. No coercion is necessary for the project manager to achieve the end he or she aspired to at the beginning of the process. That makes this an incredibly powerful tool.

Developing Empathy: Active Listening Techniques

Earlier I mentioned that emotional knowledge must reside in the open area of the Johari Window for empathy to work. If that knowledge has not already been acquired through experience, the empathiser must move it there through alternative means. This happens in baby steps, and it's done through a conscious and deliberate attempt to understand another person. We accomplish this through active listening, which is the first step on the BCSM. The following are the listening techniques (also see Figure 55.7).

Mirroring

Mirroring is a technique where you repeat the last words of the person you're speaking with. For example, if a stakeholder says to you, 'I'm tired of having these processes jammed down my throat', you could respond, 'You feel these processes are being jammed down your throat?' A response of this nature shows that you're listening, first of all, but it also opens the way for further dialogue. 'Yes', they may reply, to which you can prompt them for further details. This is of particular importance when trying to get to the bottom of a problem you don't yet understand. Remember that people may not always be forthcoming with the reasons behind their emotions. Until you have these, you're in no position to determine a course of action.

Core active listening skills

1 Mirroring
        a. The 'gist'
        b. Last few words

2 Paraphrasing
        a. Put meaning into your own words

3 Emotional labelling
        a. Identify the feeling
        b. 'You sound . . .'
        c. 'You seem . . .'
        d. 'I hear . . .'

4 Summarising
        a. Restating the content and emotions of a person's story
        b. Combining the information obtained during paraphrasing and emotional labelling

Supplemental active listening skills

5 Effective pauses
        a. Silence
        b. Used immediately before or after saying something meaningful

6 Minimal encouragers
        a. Indicates your presence and attention to the subject
        b. 'Uh-huh,. . . yes . . . right . . . okay'

7 'I' messages
        a. 'When you say . . . I feel . . .'

8 Open-ended questions
        a. 'What . . .?'
        b. 'When . . .?'
        c. 'Tell me more . . .'
        d. 'I'd like to hear more . . .'

Figure 55.7 Core and supplemental active listening skills
Source: Adapted from Vecchi et al. (2005).

Another benefit of mirroring is that it's non-confrontational. If discussions are tenuous or the mindset of the person you're speaking with is not yet known, showing any kind of judgement could be damaging to your purposes. Mirroring helps to keep your presence neutral, and also demonstrates that you are, indeed, listening.

Paraphrasing

Paraphrasing is an important active listening technique where you rephrase what you heard to clarify whether or not your understanding was correct. I am often mocked for this because so many of my sentences during project discussions begin with 'what I'm hearing is ...'. I do this so often that my colleagues say it back to me when I order a sandwich.

This technique, however, is very effective at getting to the heart of an issue. Roughly 80 per cent of a project manager's job is communication. If the project manager incorrectly relays any piece of information, others may take action on a misunderstanding. That could be very damaging to the project and result in a substantial amount of rework. By paraphrasing what you've heard, you confirm to your speaker that you've understood them. If you haven't, you've gained an opportunity for clarification.

Before you can connect empathically to the person with whom you are working, you need to identify their emotion correctly. Remember that the emotional responses evoked by a set of circumstances are unique to each person. There may be other factors of which you are unaware, which could be affecting the other person's emotional experience.

One effective method to assess another person's feelings is to use *emotional labelling*. Given a project team member who is showing signs of throwing in the towel on a particularly onerous task, you may say, 'You seem to be frustrated by this job – as if you want to give up'. On the one hand, the team member might agree with you, in which case you will be free to pursue a line of questioning that leads to a task-related problem. On the other hand, you could find that the team member raises another, completely unrelated issue which requires resolution. Either way, your next course of action will become clearer.

Summarising

Summarising is another core active listening skill. Here, the listener restates the content and emotions of the story they've just heard, combining it with other details they've picked up along the way. This activity might sound similar to paraphrasing in that the listener is restating the story in his/her own words, but there are a couple of important differences.

Whilst paraphrasing may be an attempt at clarification, the act of summarising intends to weed out extraneous details of the story and condense it into its purest form. Good summaries show the speaker that you are listening and also produce useful results which one may want to return to during later stages of the BCSM.

Effective Pauses

Effective pauses are excellent for extracting information to inform the connection you are trying to establish. People seem to have a built-in need to fill gaps in a conversation with dialogue. If you feel you are honing in on a hidden problem or feeling that the person you're working with may be loath to discuss, you may wish to keep quiet deliberately when it's your turn to speak. Sometimes the resulting conversation that rushes in to fill the space can be quite illuminating.

Using silence effectively takes some practice because the timing is very important. Staying quiet at the wrong time could cause the other person to become sceptical of you, or simply wonder why you are not talking. When used properly, however, a well-timed pause can elicit excellent information.

Minimal Encouragers

Minimal encouragers form another technique that helps your counterpart to know that you are listening. These are short sounds and gestures that encourage dialogue. They can include a nodding of the head, motioning with the eyes and hands, or saying 'uh-huh, yep, sure'. They're meant to keep your counterpart talking and show them that you're listening. Use minimal encouragers judiciously. They are facilitators. They should not be expressed so frequently that your speaker thinks you've actually tuned out.

'I' Messages

Careful pronoun use is particularly important. Statements that begin with 'you' can seem accusatory. Statements that begin with 'I' tend to be more neutral and are generally more accurate and less presumptive. These *'I' messages* help to put you on the same level as the other person. One of the challenges project managers face is that team members or vendors might feel hesitant to express themselves honestly, or face consequences. By appealing to them as a peer rather than as an authority figure, you create a platform of trust.

'I feel frustrated that we haven't signed off on these requirements yet', you might say when speaking with a business analyst who does not appear to be getting the job done. Note that there's no judgement in that statement, only an expression of emotion (and possibly a sense of urgency).

'I feel uncomfortable when you yell at me, because I don't understand the reason', you may say to a stakeholder who's coming down on you for reasons you have yet to ascertain. 'I' messages are not judgements. They are factual statements that help you connect with others.

Open-ended Questions

Open-ended questions are useful for clarifying information when you need to understand someone's intent. Many people find these challenging because they feel that exposing their ignorance to a stakeholder or vendor reflects poorly on them. However, since the goal of a project manager must always be to uncover the truth, open-ended questions can do just that.

'I'm sorry, but I didn't understand you – could you please explain that further?' may be something you could ask. The goal of the question is to keep the other person talking, so that meaning becomes clear. 'How do you feel about that?' or 'Can you tell me more?' would be other examples. This line of questioning need not be specific – it only needs to pertain to what you've heard so far.

Asking open-ended questions contrasts with asking someone 'why' questions, which sound like judgements and suggest you might not agree with the other person. 'Why' questions are confrontational and could indicate that you have not been listening. Open-ended questions, on the other hand, simply indicate that you don't yet have a complete picture.

It is worth pointing out that research by the Center for Creative Leadership demonstrates a positive correlation between empathy and job performance. In a study of over 6,700 leaders in 38 countries, they discovered universally that 'empathic emotion as rated from the leader's subordinates positively predicts job performance ratings from the leader's boss' (Stiff et al., 1987).

I believe that these results stem not from the practice of empathy directly, but rather from the results that empathic practice engenders. Empathic people are better able to form relationships, influence work and align different groups of people. The practice of empathy leads to specific, desirable behaviour changes.

Conclusion

Do you remember that story I told you at the beginning about the enterprise trading platform I managed? Well, instead of interfering in day-to-day work, I spent my first several months following the very steps I've outlined in this chapter. I followed the BCSM with my project teams, my stakeholders and my vendors. Once I understood the complete picture, I successfully changed *everybody's* behaviour to align with my programme vision. It was a tremendous amount of work but after six months my biggest client paid my managing director the best compliment ever. She told him, 'Geoff did what three vice presidents before him could not. He got those people to work together'.

References and Further Reading

Adler, R.B., Rodman, G. and Sevigny, A. (2008), 'Understanding interpersonal relationships', in *Understanding Human Communication*, Toronto: Oxford University Press.

Gentry, W.A., Weber, T.J. and Sadri, G. (2007), 'Empathy in the Workplace: A Tool for Effective Leadership', white paper based on poster session presented at the Society of Industrial Organisational Psychology Conference, New York, New York. Available at: http://www.ccl.org/leadership/pdf/research/EmpathyInTheWorkplace.pdf [accessed 4 September 2011].

Levenson, R.W., Ekman, P. and Friesen W.V. (1990), 'Voluntary facial action generates emotion-specific autonomic nervous system activity', *Psychophysiology*, 27(4), 363–84.

Stiff, J.B., Dillard, J.P., Somera, B., Kim, H. and Sleight, C. (1987), 'Empathy, Communication, and Prosocial Behavior', paper presented at the Annual Meeting of the Speech Communication Association (73rd, Boston, MA). Available at: http://www.eric.ed.gov/PDFS/ED294266.pdf [accessed 4 September 2011].

Vecchi, G.M., Van Hasselt, V.B. and Romano, S.J. (2005), 'Crisis (hostage) negotiation: Current strategies and issues in high-risk conflict resolution', *Aggression and Violent Behavior*, 10, 533–51. Available at: http://www.eisf.eu/resources/library/hostage_negotiation.pdf [accessed 4 September 2011].

Wicker, B., Keysers, C., Plailly, J., Royet, J-P., Gallese, V. and Rizzolatti, G. (2003), 'Both of us disgusted in my insula: The common neural basis of seeing and feeling disgust', *Neuron*, 40, 655–64. Available at: http://www2.unipr.it/~gallese/Wickeretal2003.pdf [accessed 4 September 2011].

56 *Creativity*

ALICIA ARNOLD

The conference room was abuzz with project managers gathering for creativity training. Once everyone was seated, we began with introductions. The first project manager spoke. With her head hung low, she shared her name and quietly added, 'And, I... I'm not creative'.

Introduction

Some say perception is reality. If you do not view yourself as creative, then chances are you will not behave creatively. Given the speed of change, complexity and uncertainty in business, the ability to take risks, to find new ideas and to innovate, is crucial to an organisation's success (IBM, 2010; Thomas and Mengel, 2008). The need for creative leadership spans all industries and disciplines. However, project management often sits at the precipice of success or failure. The challenge for project management is perplexing. Even though there is a growing emphasis on project management training, on standards and on certification, 'projects continue to fail at an alarming rate' (Thomas and Mengel, 2008).

The dilemma is two-fold. On the one hand, complexity demands that project managers must be 'both technically and socially competent to develop teams that can work dynamically and creatively toward objectives in changing environments across organizational functional lines' (Thamhain, 2004a, 2004b). Yet, on the other hand, 'Project management methods are well established, built around clearly specified output, accepted procedures, and structured operations' (Ekvall, 1997). According to Singh and Singh (2002), in order to succeed in an environment of increasing complexity, project managers need 'to pay greater attention to the non-linear and subtle influences in their planning and management and shift away from the primal importance they grant to quantitative analysis and project controls'.

When it comes to project management, it might be worth comparing the words 'manager' and 'leader'. With the changing dynamics of business, organisations may be expecting more leadership rather than management. In a well-regarded Harvard Business Review essay, Zaleznik (1977) compared and contrasted management and leadership. Zaleznik found the greatest differences in personality, attitudes towards goals, conceptions of work, relations with others and sense of self (see Figure 56.1).

Similarly, Murray (2010) defined the job of a manager as 'planning, organising, and coordinating', and the job of a leader as 'inspiring and motivating'. Continuing along these lines, Martin and Ernst (2005) stated, 'by their nature, complex challenges

Characteristic	Manager	Leader
Personality	- rationality and control	- challenges the status quo
Attitudes towards goals	- reactive - responds to ideas	- is proactive - shapes ideas
Conceptions of work	- enables process - limits choices - avoids risk	- develops fresh approaches - opens new options - seeks risk
Relationships	- low emotional involvement	- high emotional involvement
Sense of self	- belongs to an organisation	- works at an organisation

Figure 56.1 Managers and leaders compared

require new knowledge, resources, and perspectives found outside current organizational capacity. As such, these challenges create new demands for leadership'.

Perhaps, the time has come for project management to add a new tool to the toolbox – creative leadership. In an IBM (2010) Global CEO Study, researchers conducted over 1,500 face-to-face interviews with executives in 60 countries and 33 industries. Their study identified creativity as 'the single most important leadership competency' for the future. More than integrity, influence, openness or dedication, *creativity* was cited as the leadership quality most required for navigating complexity.

Specific to project management, Thomas and Mengel's (2008) research verified the need for building creativity skills. They discovered that:

> *highly adaptive and responsive systems with a large number of independent yet interacting agents call for new leadership approaches beyond the control-room metaphor of management and for an education of the understanding and creative facilitation of change.*

The good news is creative leadership can be taught. And, just as people can learn how to develop a project plan, they can also learn how to be creative. The Greek philosopher Plato believed creativity was a gift from the gods and that people were either born creative or not born creative (Runco, 2007). But scientific research debunks this theory. As humans, we are innately creative and we can learn how to reach our creative potential. Therefore, over time, the prevailing question has evolved from, 'Are you creative?' to 'How are you creative?'

In this chapter I shall explore what creativity is, where creativity comes from, how to identify creative strengths and how to lead creatively.

Definition of Creativity: Some Myths Dispelled

The scientific study of creativity is only 50 years old. Advances in technology and what we understand about brain functions will change our knowledge and beliefs. But we have already learned quite a bit. Researchers have been able to study creativity-related cognitive processes using methods such as electroencephalography (EEG), positron emission tomography (PET), and functional magnetic resonance imaging (FMRI). In their research Sawyer (2011) and Dietrich (2006) found that much of what we thought we knew about creativity is inaccurate. In the remainder of this section I shall list some of these inaccuracies.

CREATIVITY PERCEIVED AS DIVERGENT THINKING

Most people believe creativity is about the generation of ideas or divergent thinking. This is not true. Guilford (1962) was clear to identify convergent thinking, or the ability to judge and identify the most promising solutions, as important to creativity. Therefore, creativity is not just about coming up with ideas, but includes the ability to synthesise them as well. This is illustrated in the following discussion about brainstorming.

Brainstorming

Is there a right way to brainstorm? The answer is 'Yes'. Here are some tips:

1. *Appoint a skilled facilitator* – This person will be responsible for controlling the tone and rhythm of the brainstorming session. He/she will work with the key parties before the brainstorming session to identify and distil the essence of the problem. The facilitator will help to identify the key artefacts, or data, to bring to the brainstorming session so that everyone in the room starts out with sufficient context and background. A trained facilitator can also help level the playing field between extroverted personalities and introverted personalities. By 'reading the room' and alternating between individual and group activities – and by speaking out loud or working quietly, the facilitator can create a suitable environment for everyone.
2. *Clarify the problem* – The importance of clarifying the problem cannot be overstated. Many times when brainstorming goes awry it is due to poorly constructed problem statements. In order to brainstorm, it is most productive to articulate clearly the problem you are trying to solve. This helps focus the brainstorming session and prevent ideas that are all over the map. Whilst some people think that coming up with ideas is the most helpful when solving the problem, it is really the other way around. Coming up with clearly articulated problems helps generate better ideas.
3. *Diverge ideas* – Diverging involves thinking up ideas whilst converging involves choosing those that are most promising. During the diverging stage all ideas should be put on the table, and it is important for everyone to listen carefully to one another and to build upon one another's ideas. Ideas usually start out as kernels of poorly formed thoughts. Through true listening, fledgling ideas can be strengthened.
4. *Converge ideas* – A very common mistake in brainstorming is diverging without converging. When divergence is complete, it will be time to converge. Divergence and convergence should never happen simultaneously (that is, thinking up ideas and discarding them at the same time). This is for practical reasons, as well as to drive action. By first diverging, and then converging, the brainstorming team will have a better shot at creating robust solutions and identifying actionable next steps.

Though well-read publications claim brainstorming is dead (Bronson and Merryman, 2010), the articles misinterpret Alex Osborn's concept of brainstorming. Osborn (1963), who coined the term brainstorming, described the mind as,

> *mainly two-fold: (1) a judicial mind which analyses, compares and chooses, (2) a creative mind which visualizes, foresees, and generates ideas. These two minds work best together. Judgment keeps imagination on the track. Imagination not only opens ways to action, but also can enlighten judgment.*

Clearly, Osborn's definition of brainstorming includes both divergent and convergent thinking. Unfortunately, over the years brainstorming has been misconstrued as the one-sided generation of ideas.

THE RIGHT-HAND SIDE OF THE BRAIN PERCEIVED AS THE ORIGINATOR OF CREATIVITY

General convention held that creativity is a right-brain activity but in fact the entire brain becomes active when engaged in creative tasks. The question is not whether you are left-brained or right-brained, or if either the left or the right brain is active during creativity-related processes, but which specific brain areas display statistically differential activity (Sawyer, 2011). Creativity is less about which side of the brain is used, but how quickly information passes across the two hemispheres (Bruer, 1999).

CREATIVITY SEEN AS A MYSTERIOUS PHENOMENON

Although creativity has an aura of mystique, studies have found that when people are creative they use the same parts of their brains as with everyday tasks. In essence, creativity is part of how a normal brain operates (Boden, 1998; Ward et al., 1999; Weisberg, 1993). The challenge is that the multifaceted and intricate nature of creativity makes it difficult to fully understand the construct. With advances in technology, we are just beginning to scratch the surface of understanding.

Definition of Creativity

Now that we have debunked some of the more prevalent creativity myths, I can turn to the definition of creativity. The standard definition of creativity is attributed to Sternberg and Lubart (1999) who cited creativity as 'novelty that is useful'. In this definition, novelty referred to newness, originality and a fresh approach; whilst originality referred to serving a purpose and having value (Mumford, 2003). Rhodes (1961) elaborated on the multifaceted nature of creativity by defining creativity as a complex interdisciplinary construct. These constructs, otherwise known as the four Ps of creativity, comprise:

- people (personality);
- products (outputs);
- process (sequence of tasks);
- press (environmental setting).

By looking at creativity through the lens of the four Ps we can isolate each construct, assess performance and work towards improving areas of weakness.

Where Does Creativity Come from?

Studies confirm that the brain's prefrontal cortex is critical to creative thinking. Although it is not the only part of the brain responsible for creative thinking, the prefrontal cortex plays a big role (Sawyer, 2011). When comparing creativity in children to creativity in adults, children tend to exhibit creativity that is more random or free flow. This is due, in part, to the development of the prefrontal lobe. Since the prefrontal lobe does not fully develop until a person is in his or her twenties, creativity in children is often less directed.

The prefrontal lobe is also the first part of the brain to deteriorate. This might shed a light on why some research finds that creativity declines with age. Most of our brain cells were formed before birth, but most of the connections between the cells were made during infancy and early childhood. This means that early experiences and interactions with the environment play a strong role in brain development. As a baby learns, cells connect to one another forming patterns. By the age of three, a child's brain has formed about 1,000 trillion connections – about twice as many as adults have. A child's brain gets rid of extra connections; so that by the age of 11, the brain becomes more efficient (Sawyer, 2011; Marcus, 1999). The more a circuit is used, the stronger it gets.

By the time we enter the working world, our brain circuits have become accustomed to connecting in certain ways. These time-tested connections create well-worn pathways. Thus a project manager's role becomes both more challenging and more important. With the world growing more and more complex, it is no longer feasible to use the methods of doing business used by past generations. Project managers have to find multiple solutions to problems. This need to innovate and come up with new products, services and modes of business, requires project managers to become adept at leading through change. Given the well-worn neural pathways, helping team members to tap into creativity and think differently is crucial to success.

ASSOCIATIVE THINKING

From time to time I test out new creativity techniques on my children before I use them in a business setting. It is a great way to work out any kinks. It is also a great source of learning for the children. I find that if I am able to explain a creativity technique to a very young child, then it is easy enough for an adult.

Each of us has a preferred method for interacting with information and processing it. In thinking about visual learners, auditory learners and kinaesthetic learners (those who learn by physical activity), I devised a creativity technique that tapped into a variety of learning styles. For the test run of this creativity technique, I played a song (auditory) on the computer. As the song played and the graphics danced around the screen (visual), I invited the children to keep the beat by tapping their fingers (kinaesthetic). Then, I asked them to come up with as many ideas as they could for what the images on the screen might be. They started out with literal ideas like, 'purple moving around the screen' and 'colours running'. Then they gradually worked their way up to more unique ideas. The highlight of our experiment was when my three-year-old said, 'Mommy, it looks like a merry-go-round going upstairs'. At that moment, my heart sang out, 'Eureka, it works!'

When I use this creativity technique in business settings, I ask participants to:

- consider the challenge they are looking to solve;
- listen to the music;
- watch the images;
- tap along;
- write down all the ideas that come to mind for solving their challenge.

Whilst this technique of associative thinking increases the quantity and quality of ideas, it also highlights how children sometimes have an easier time stretching for unique ideas than adults. Practising this technique will help re-map and build new connections in your mind. In case you are curious, the science behind changing the human brain as a result of one's experience is called neuroplasticity.

How to Identify Creative Strengths

Whilst Runco (2007) identified that there is no single personality trait, nor one personality type for creativity, there are a number of personality characteristics that come together to identify highly creative individuals. Selby et al. (2005) found that,

> lists of creative personality characteristics abound. Many of these lists overlap, whilst others offer unique examples ... no one person can be expected to exhibit all of the characteristics that appear in the literature, nor will an individual who exhibits one or more of these characteristics necessarily exhibit that one or those characteristics all of the time.

With that said, Davis (1986) reviewed numerous research studies and found a multitude of personality traits for highly creative individuals including: being curious, energetic, experimenting, independent, industrious, flexible, open minded, original, playful, perceptive, persevering, questioning, risk taking, self-aware and sensitive. Outside of personality, a more comprehensive way to identify creative strengths is to look at creative style.

Creative style 'identifies differences in the ways people approach problems they encounter in their environments' (Selby et al., 2005). By looking at creative style, researchers are able to determine 'how' or 'in what way' individuals are creative. As Selby et al. (2005) found, by 'identifying the ways individuals prefer to process information, generate new ideas, test them, and put them into practice', one can identify an individual's creativity preference. To follow, I shall take a look at two assessments of creative style. First I shall review the Myers-Briggs Type Indicator (MBTI), then I shall discuss FourSight (more information about these assessments can be found at http://myersbriggs.org and http://FourSightonline.com).

MBTI

The MBTI is based on Carl Jung's research on personality types. In his findings, Jung put forth four dichotomies, which are listed and explained by Nix and Stone (2010) as follows:

- extraversion or introversion – looking at where people focus their energy. Extraverts focus their energy on the 'outer world' around them whereas introverts focus energy on their 'inner world'.
- sensing or intuition – which looks at perception. Individuals with sensing preferences tend to focus on facts and what can be perceived using the five senses, whereas individuals with intuitive preferences look at possibilities that 'were worked outside of the conscious mind'.
- thinking or feeling – this focuses on how an individual makes judgement. Individuals with a thinking preference base conclusions on logical knowledge whilst individuals with a feeling preference bring in 'personal and social experiences and values'.
- judging or perceiving – individuals with a judging preference prefer decisiveness and closure whilst those with a perceiving preference enjoy flexibility and spontaneity.

Using these four dichotomies, Katharine Briggs and Isabel Briggs Myers developed the MBTI to sort individuals within the sixteen possible personality types shown in Figure 56.2.

ISTJ Introvert/sensing/ thinking/judging.	ISFJ Introvert/sensing/ feeling/judging.	INFJ Introvert/intuitive/ feeling/judging.	INTJ Introvert/intuitive/ thinking/judging.
ISTP Introvert/sensing/ thinking/perceiving.	ISFP Introvert/sensing/ feeling/perceiving.	INFP Introvert/intuitive/ feeling/perceiving.	INTP Introvert/intuitive/ thinking/perceiving.
ESTJ Extrovert/sensing/ thinking/judging.	ESFJ Extrovert/sensing/ feeling/judging.	ENFJ Extrovert/intuitive/ feeling/judging.	ENTJ Extrovert/intuitive/ thinking/judging.
ESTP Extrovert/sensing/ thinking/perceiving.	ESFP Extrovert/sensing/ feeling/perceiving.	ENFP Extrovert/intuitive/ feeling/perceiving.	ENTP Extrovert/intuitive/ thinking/perceiving.

Figure 56.2 16 MBTI personality types

Building further upon the MBTI body of research, Killen and Williams (2009) investigated the link between the 16 MBTI types and innovation. In this context innovation is defined as a 'process that requires different strengths during different phases'. Killen and Williams reported that the second and fourth letters of a person's MBTI type had 'a significant bearing on that person's approach to innovation'. These innovation attitudes, or combinations, include SJ, SP, NP and NJ, as outlined below.

NP People: Different Ideas

People with NP preferences are drawn to ideas that no one else has thought of or implemented. They are attracted to the prospect of doing things that do not appeal to others. The innovation challenge for NPs is recognising that solutions are useful when they are implemented – not when they are discovered.

NJ People: Adopting Ideas

Those with NJ preferences collect and connect ideas from a wide range of settings. They like to adopt the innovation and original ideas of others. The innovation challenge for NJs is to learn to explain their ideas so that everyone gets the full picture.

SP People: Refining Ideas

People with SP preferences like to draw on previous ideas that fit well with their current situation. They adapt to their current activities rather than change them dramatically. The innovation challenge for SPs is to recognise that it is impossible to know everything in advance, requiring them to take what might feel like a leap of faith.

SJ People: Efficiency Ideas

Individuals with SJ preferences are naturally on the lookout for incremental changes that improve their effectiveness and efficiency. They want to find the best way to do what they are doing. The innovation challenge for SJs is being patient when generating ideas and delaying judgement on what will work.

Acknowledgement

Principal reference source for the above section can be found at: http://www.psychometrics. com/en-us/articles/type-and-innovation.htm
Please note there is more on Myers-Briggs in chapters 32 and 52.

FOURSIGHT

No, this heading is not a spelling error, but is the name of an analytical tool similar to the MBTI. FourSight also assesses creative style. According to Puccio et al. (2002), the assessment is 'designed to help individuals and teams understand how they approach solving problems through creative thinking'. FourSight identifies natural tendencies and strengths during the creative process and gives individuals or teams a way to identify circumstances where they might encounter challenges. Puccio et al. (2004) wrote:

> The essential theoretical underpinning to FourSight is that the creative process involves a series of distinct mental operations that can be described via the CPS (creative problem solving) model, and that people possess different degrees of preference for these mental operations.

In looking at ways to use creative preferences to build innovation teams DeCusatis (2008) found that, 'while the creative process is universal, each step requires unique mental skills, and most individuals prefer some skills above others. Such biases show up as strong points and potential blind spots when solving problems'. This is where FourSight can help. The FourSight assessment identifies an individual's preference or preferences. These preferences include:

- *clarifier* (preference for clarifying or asking questions);
- *ideator* (preference for coming up with ideas);
- *developer* (preference for working with ideas to turn them into solutions);
- *implementer* (preference for implementing, or getting things done).

A project manager can demonstrate creative leadership by orchestrating a team's FourSight preferences. This approach is summarised in Figure 56.3.

FourSight preference	Description
Clarify the situation	- Clarifying a situation means bringing a problem, challenge or opportunity to its most granular level. - Clarification requires data gathering, understanding the context of a situation and asking many questions. - Clarifying a situation can be time-intensive because it requires a significant level of detail to ensure that there are no lingering assumptions which could derail potential solutions.
Generate ideas	- Generating ideas (or 'fluid ideating') requires divergent thinking. - Divergent thinking is about looking at the 'big picture' and playing with potentially abstract concepts that stretch the imagination. - 'Ideation' requires a more intuitive approach, whereas clarifying is most effective when using concrete thinking.
Develop a solution	- Developing a promising idea or series of ideas into a workable solution is about giving ideas the support needed to stand on their own. - Developing a solution includes comparing and analysing several noteworthy ideas in order to prioritise and strengthen one or more of them, and then planning for their implementation. - Developing a solution is about shaping raw ideas into a workable solution. - Successful solution development also requires a contextual understanding of the environment, such as identifying stakeholders who will either assist or resist solution implementation. It also means taking action to amplify support and mitigate opposition.

Implement a plan	- Implementing is clearly putting the plan into action.
	- Whilst *developing* a plan details things that need to happen if an idea is to solve a problem, *implementing* the plan is about giving structure to the idea in order for it to become a reality.
	- Being able to implement a solution successfully needs persistence and determination.
	- Because implementation generally requires engaging a variety of stakeholders, implementation lends itself to re-iterating the breakthrough thinking process:
	  - Is the solution workable?
	  - Are we solving the right problem?
	  - What to we need to rethink?
	  - Who do we need on board to support this effort?

Figure 56.3 FourSight preferences

Source: DeCusatis, 2008.

When it comes to project management, knowing your own and your team's preferences can help with collaboration and with determining an individual's best fit for the innovation process or creative problem-solving task. According to Killen and Williams (2009), different innovation attitudes are best matched with different phases of innovation as follows:

- SJs prefer the 'deliver' phase;
- SPs prefer the 'define' phase;
- NJs prefer the 'decide' phase;
- NPs prefer the 'discover' phase.

Similarly, FourSight finds that:

- clarifiers prefer problem identification;
- ideators prefer idea generation;
- developers prefer solution development;
- implementers prefer implementation.[1]

There are no right or wrong innovation attitudes or preferences but each offers something of value during the creative process. As team leaders, project managers are crucial in helping each 'type' reach his/her potential in order to unlock creativity and work towards creating better ways of forming, growing and sustaining teams of innovators (DeCusatis, 2008).

How to Lead a Creative Team

When it comes to working in an environment of complexity and change, Jaafari (2003) cited Geyser's (1998) research identifying four types of people:

1. those who thrive on change;
2. those who abstain from change;
3. those who resist change;
4. those who are oblivious to change, but manage to cope with it.

According to Jaafari (2003), project managers must be able to assess and manage these four different reactions to change. Harris (2009) found that:

> to be creative means releasing talent and imagination. It also means the ability to take risks and, in some cases, necessitates standing outside the usual or accepted frames of reference. Creative people push the boundaries; they seek new ways of seeing, interpreting, understanding and questioning.

When it comes to leadership, leaders of creative efforts exhibit particular attributes when it comes to what they do and how they think.

---

1   Source: Puccio et al., 2004

Practice	Description
Model the way	- Sets a good example for what she/he believes in. - Clarifies and shares values. - Builds agreement around common principles and ideals. - Puts forth relentless effort, steadfastness, competence and attention to detail.
Inspire a shared vision	- Shares visions and dreams of what could be for the organisation. - Has the ability to make something extraordinary happen. - Enlists others in a common vision. - Breathes life into the hopes and dreams of others. - Inspires others through her/his enthusiasm.
Challenge the process	- Seeks to change the status quo; to challenge the process. - Adopts a pioneering attitude. - Listens more than tells. - Looks outside of self and the organisation for new ideas. - Creates a climate for experimentation. - Takes risks (tries, fails, learns).
Enable others to act	- Builds teams based on solid trust and strong relationships. - Fosters collaboration. - Makes it possible for others to do good work.
Encourage the heart	- Demonstrates genuine acts of caring. - Recognises contributions. - Shows appreciation. - Builds a strong sense of collective identity and community spirit.

Figure 56.4 Five practices of exemplary leadership

In studying leaders personal-best leadership experiences, Kouzes and Posner (2007) found 'five practices of exemplary leadership', which I have shown in Figure 56.4.

For project management to lead within escalating business complexity means exploiting creative leadership skills. Where leadership is primarily concerned with influence and change, creative leaders must understand how to influence upwards, downwards and laterally within an organisation in order to release and capitalise on the talent of their teams (Harris, 2009). Importantly, Harris (2009) found, 'This cannot be done in a manipulative way, as creativity can only really flourish where the formal leadership authentically and genuinely reflects a desire for the many rather than the few to excel'. The following sections provide food for thought, creativity tools and techniques to help build creative leadership skills.

USING CREATIVE LEADERSHIP TO CHANGE A SITUATION

When our prehistoric ancestors sensed change they saw two options – fight or flight. For those of us who tap into creativity, there is a third option, which is to use our natural creative abilities to change the situation. So we can apply the following strategy at the workplace:

- Set clear goals. Think about what you are trying to achieve and then keep sight of that.

- Experiment and prototype. Try experimenting with different concepts, different behaviours and by collaborating with different people. Take a look around and survey what works. Are there particular norms or ways of doing things that seem to be effective? Consider your findings and prototype solutions.
- Create win-win situations. List your helpers or people who can assist you in reaching your goal. Now, think about what motivates each of these people. Finding a way to tie your goal to something that motivates your co-workers will create momentum.

FAILURE CAN LEAD TO INNOVATION

My young sons covered a table with paper airplanes. One was orange and looked different from the rest. I asked about this orange airplane. One son frowned and confessed, 'It was a mistake. I couldn't figure out how to make it correctly and it turned out like this'. Then, his frown turned into a smile and he continued, 'But, then I looked at it and really liked it'. From there, he shared all of the features of his new design with me, including boosters to make the plane fly faster, the unique design of the wings and how particular folds helped the plane glide better.

With this thought in mind, I considered the many failures that became successes. We all know about the story of 3M and Post-Its, but did you know that:

- PEZ was introduced in Austria as an after-smoking mint. Luckily, the inventors realised PEZ was better as a children's candy.
- Jacuzzi tubs were invented in the 1950s for arthritis sufferers. It was not until the company positioned Jacuzzis as a luxury item that they found success.
- Viagra was brought to market to relieve high blood pressure. Although it failed for that purpose, it opened up an entirely new, now well-known, pharmaceutical application.

When staring failure in the face, it might be good to take a second glance. You never know when a slight change in positioning, target market or unintended consequence might open up a whole new category.

FOSTERING CREATIVITY IN THE WORKPLACE

Fostering a creative environment in the workplace is rather like nurturing a garden. Just like our prized plants, creativity in the workplace requires care and feeding. Researchers Amabile et al. (1996) identified six stimulants for fostering creativity in the workplace and two obstacles, as follows:

Stimulants for creativity:
- *Organisational encouragement*: an environment that encourages risk taking and idea generation.
- *Supervisory encouragement*: managers who set clear goals, model creative behaviour and value individual contributions.
- *Supportive work groups*: teams of diverse people who communicate well, trust one another, strive to make one another's work better, and are open to new ideas.
- *Freedom*: autonomy to control what work gets done and how to do it.
- *Sufficient resources*: the right balance of resources and enough of them.

- *Challenging work*: work that is intellectually challenging and important to the organisation.

Obstacles to creativity:
- *Organisational impediments*: internal strife including politics, harsh criticism, destructive competition and engineering desire to stick with the status quo.
- *Workload pressure*: unrealistic time constraints.

Assessing the workplace against these criteria can help to identify areas where companies are doing well and areas with problems.

SELF-COACHING YOURSELF TO CREATIVITY

Emotions play a big role in creativity. Keeping a positive mindset helps to unlock creative energies. Whilst some tension always exists with creative endeavours, too much stress becomes unproductive. Understanding why you are feeling stressed is the first step to self-coaching yourself to creativity. Stress is sometimes due to our values being out of synchronisation with what we are experiencing. The more congruent our values are with the situation we are in, the more energy we will have. When we lose energy, it is typically because we are operating outside our values. Here are four sequential steps that can help you to identify your values:

- *Step 1*: Sketch a timeline of your life including your childhood, teens, 20s, 30s and so on.
- *Step 2*: Fill in your timeline by adding key peaks and valleys – the positive, and not so positive, experiences that have shaped who you are.
- *Step 3*: Detail the people, places, emotions and things that stand out about these experiences.
- *Step 4*: Once you've filled in your timeline, take a step back and ask yourself what was important about each experience. Why was it important?

This learning will shed light on your values. With this learning in hand, consider your situation and identify what's working and what's not working. From here you will be better equipped to make the choices and take the actions towards aligning closer to your values.

EVALUATING CREATIVE WORK

Evaluating creative work is often very subjective, but I can suggest a few questions for taking the subjectivity out of the evaluation. If the creative work that you are evaluating falls short on any of the following questions, don't throw it away but instead take the time to identify what can be improved. So, ask the questions listed below:

Does the Creative Work Answer the Problem You Set Out to Solve?

There are endless ways to express something creatively. Whilst many people judge creative work based on personal tastes and preferences, one way to remove some of the subjectivity is to evaluate the creative work based on how well it answers the problem you set out to solve. Regardless of whether you prefer the font, headlines or imagery, take a step back and ask yourself, 'Does this solve the problem?'

Is the Style of the Creative Work Well Suited For the Audience?

Once you have answered whether the creative work solves your problem, the next step is to look at the element of style. But here's the catch. Don't look at it from the point of view of an audience of one. Rather, evaluate the style of the creative product based on its intended audience. A good way of figuring out how well the creative product fits with the audience is to hold a focus group, or to question members of the intended audience informally. Whilst you might not personally prefer bold colours and loud music, these work for a teenage audience.

Is There Something Unique and Memorable About the Creative Work?

Take a step back and evaluate the distinctiveness of the creative work. One of the reasons you set out to do something creative was to stand out from the crowd. Don't stop now, evaluate how unique and memorable the creative work is.

FIVE WAYS TO GET OUT OF A CREATIVE SLUMP

From time to time everyone gets into a creative slump. What's a person to do? Here are a few tricks you can try:

1. Collaborate with inspiring people. Robinson and Aronica (2009) talked about 'finding your tribe'. A tribe is a group of people who inspire you and push you to become better at your craft. Tapping into your tribe when you are in a creative slump can help to get your creative juices flowing.
2. Change your scenery. Stepping out into nature can help with creativity. Sometimes being confined inside, or in the mundane setting of an office can zap your energy. Take a moment to grab some fresh air and people watch.
3. Make use of your creative energy when you have it. Sometimes creativity comes in fits and starts. When you are feeling particularly creative, be sure to keep a list of all of your ideas. Then, when you feel a creative slump coming on, refer to this list for a kick start.
4. Pick up a new book, watch an interesting video or listen to great music. Sometimes when looking for inspiration you can find it in a great book or an interesting video. Head to the library or find a cosy nook at the bookstore. If you are online, try watching a video or listening to music. A unique spin on a video, movie or music might be all you need to get your creativity going.
5. Step away. If all else fails, step away from your problem and sleep on it. Sometimes all you need is a breather to give life to a creative idea. The art of incubation can help connect unconscious associations into new and novel ideas. Have you ever come up with a brilliant idea after sleeping on it or whilst in the shower? These 'Aha!' moments might be a result of stepping away and incubating.

Concluding Observations

At the start of this chapter, creativity was defined within the construct of the four Ps (people, product, process and press). In reviewing Kouzes and Posner's (2007) five practices of exemplary leadership, the four Ps are evident. Creative leadership is a selfless act. In essence, creative leadership can be seen as a form of 'servant leadership' where the main leadership task is to connect different people, ideas and ways of thinking. It is leadership that develops the capabilities and capacities of all those within the organisation so that creativity, wherever it occurs, on whatever scale, can be captured, supported and enhanced' (Harris, 2009). Creative leadership is a skill that can be learned. As a discipline, project management holds the ability to help navigate the ever-changing and complex business environment by inspiring hearts and minds. The possibilities for developing novel solutions to business challenges are limitless. Tapping into the four Ps and creative leadership can help project managers unleash human potential. I shall conclude with some case examples.

HOW RIGHT TURNS SAVED UPS $3 MILLION

A few years ago, the logistics company UPS was facing pressures to cut costs. UPS also had an environmental stewardship policy. In thinking about how to solve their budget challenge, UPS put two seemingly unconnected ideas together. After analysing driving routes and realising that left turns resulted in wasting fuel whilst waiting in traffic, UPS rearranged their routes so that drivers turned right 90 per cent of the time. Some drivers were sceptical. Christopher Broder, a driver for 25 years was willing to give the right-turn policy a try, but in the same breath asked, 'Am I going to be driving in a circle all day?' Well, this story has a fairy-tale ending. The creative right-turn policy had a big impact. In 2007 alone, right turns helped UPS to:

- shave nearly 30 million miles off already streamlined delivery routes;
- save 3 million gallons of fuel;
- reduce CO_2 emissions by 32,000 metric tonnes – the equivalent of removing 5,300 passenger cars from the road for an entire year.

Simplicity is at the core of this novel solution. Nowadays, when so many people turn to complex technical solutions to solve problems, the right-turn programme serves as a reminder that human ingenuity and a dash of creativity can bring about fascinating innovations.

PANERA BREAD'S INNOVATIVE WAY FOR HELPING TO FIGHT HUNGER

The other day my eldest son asked, 'What happens if you go to a restaurant and eat, but don't have enough money to pay?' A common answer is, 'you will wash dishes'. But, the real answer depends on where you are dining. If you happen to be at Panera Bread Co's non-profit St Louis location, you would pay what you could. The restaurant helps feed the needy and also raises money for charitable work. The retail location began in 2010 to test the 'community kitchens' concept where businesses operate partly as charities.

In case you are wondering if this concept works, it does! Panera is planning to open one community kitchen store every three months. Paying what you can works out to 60 per cent of people choosing to pay the retail price, 20 per cent choosing to pay more, and 20 per cent paying less. The net result yields about $3,000 to $4,000 a month to be used for training at-risk youths.

HOSPITALS TURN TO CREATIVITY AND INNOVATION TO DELIVER BETTER HEALTH CARE

Though this might be counter to how many people view productivity, in order to improve patient safety whilst being squeezed by health care reform, Bassett Healthcare Network gave leaders and staff paid sabbatical days (Bush, 2011).

What does paid time off have to do with delivering better health care? Well, Bassett Healthcare Network recognised that doing more with less requires creativity and innovation. Sabbatical days allowed leaders and staff the time to think up and pursue new ideas. This time away from the 'daily grind' and pressures of meeting financial performance goals and providing better services paved the way to thinking differently about the challenges that plague the health care industry.

As you can imagine, implementing sabbatical days and focusing on creativity and innovation requires a cultural shift. Within any established organisation there is always resistance to change. Some of the ways Basset Healthcare Network helps to build a culture of creativity and innovation in addition to their policy of paid sabbatical days include:

- *Exposing hospital executives to the front lines of hospital care* – Think of this as out of the board room and into patient rooms. This practice is resulting in bringing together the executive staff with the front-line staff.
- *Embracing the notion that good ideas come from everywhere* – An expectation is that employees regularly reflect on questions like, 'Can an employee two steps lower on the organisational chart ask a question that challenges the firmly held opinion of a leader?'
- *Encouraging discussion rather than giving and taking orders.*
- *Setting aside a budget for implementing new ideas.*

Although some of these policies might seem like no-brainers to those who are not in health care, the established ways of the health care system are deeply embedded within the people, processes, policies and culture. Inviting change also means inviting fear.

When summing up the challenges faced with embracing creativity and innovation the vice president of nursing and patient care services said, 'They're afraid'. Change can indeed be scary for many people. Creativity and innovation do not come easily within established businesses and institutions. A focus on the people side of the equation and the culture of the organisation can help to improve success.

References and Further Reading

Amabile, T.M., Conti, R., Coon, H., Lazenby, J. and Herron, M. (1996), 'Assessing the work environment for creativity', *Academy of Management Journal*, 39(5), 1154–84.

Boden, M.A. (1998), 'Creativity and artificial intelligence', *Artificial Intelligence*, 103, 347–56.

Bronson, P. and Merryman, A. (2010), 'The creativity crisis', *Newsweek*, 156(3), 44.

Bruer, J.T. (1999), 'In search of … brain based education', *Phi Delta Kappan*, 80(9), 648–54.

Bush, H. (2011), 'In an era of doing more with less, executives nurture creativity', *Hospitals and Health Networks*. Available at: http://www.hhnmag.com/hhnmag/HHNDaily/HHNDailyDisplay. dhtml?id=4400001030

Byrne, C.L., Mumford, M.D., Barrett, J.D. and Vessey, W.B. (2009), 'Examining the leaders of creative efforts: What do they do, and what do they think about?', *Creativity and Innovation Management*, 18(4), 256.

Davis, G.A. (1986), *Creativity is Forever*, 2nd edn, Dubuque, IA: Kendall-Hunt.

DeCusatis, C. (2008), 'Creating, growing and sustaining efficient innovation teams', *Creativity and Innovation Management*, 17, 155–64.

Dietrich, A. (2006), 'Who's afraid of a cognitive neuroscience of creativity?', *Methods*, 42, 22–7.

Ekvall, G. (1997), 'Organizational conditions and levels of creativity', *Creativity and Innovation Management*, 6(4), 195–205.

Guilford, J.P. (1962), 'Potentiality for Creativity and its Measurement', *Proceedings of the 1962 Invitational Conference on Testing Problems*, Princeton, NJ: Educational Testing Service, 31–9.

Harris, A. (2009), 'Creative leadership: Developing future leaders', *British Educational Leadership, Management and Administration Society* (BELMAS), 23(1), 9–11.

IBM (2010), *Capitalizing on Complexity: Insights from the Global Chief Executive Officer Study*, New York: IBM Corporation.

Jaafari, A. (2003), 'Project management in the age of complexity and change', *Project Management Journal*, 34(4), 47–57.

Jung, C.G. (1959), *The Basic Writings of C. G. Jung*, New York: The Modern Library.

Killen, D. and Williams, G. (2009), *Introduction to Type and Innovation*, Mountainview, CA: CPP, Inc.

Kouzes, J.M. and Posner, B.Z. (2007), *The Leadership Challenge*, San Francisco, CA: Jossey-Bass.

Marcus, D.L. (1999), 'How children learn', *U.S. News and World Report*, 10(127), 44–51.

Martin, A. and Ernst, C. (2005), 'Leadership, learning, and human resource management: Exploring leadership in times of paradox and complexity', *Corporate Governance*, 5(3), 2005, 82–94.

Mumford, M.D. (2003), 'Where have we been, where are we going? Taking stock in creativity research', *Creativity Research Journal*, 15, 107–20.

Murray, A. (2010), *The Wall Street Journal Essential Guide to Management: Lasting Lessons from the Best Leadership Minds of our Times*, New York: Harper Collins.

Nix, A.A. and Stone, R.B. (2010), 'The Search for Innovation Styles', *Proceedings of the ASME 2010 International Design Engineering Technical Conferences and Computers and Information*, in *Engineering Conference IDETC/CIE* 2010, 15–18 August 2010, Montreal, Quebec, Canada.

Osborn, A.F. (1963), *Applied imagination*, 3rd edn, New York: Charles Scribner's Sons.

Puccio, G.J., Miller, B. and Thurber, S. (2002), *FourSight Your Thinking Profile: A Tool for Innovation*, Evanston, IL: Thinc Communications.

Puccio, G.J., Wheeler, R.A. and Cassandro, V.J. (2004), 'Reactions to creative problem solving training: Does cognitive style make a difference?', *Journal of Creative Behavior*, 38(3), 192–216.

Rhodes, M. (1961), 'An analysis of creativity', *Phi Delta Kappan*, 42, 305–10.

Robinson, K. and Aronica, L. (2009), *The Element: How Finding your Passion Changes Everything*, New York: Penguin Group.

Runco, M.A. (2007), *Creativity Theories and Themes: Research, Development and Practice*, San Diego, CA: Elsevier.

Sawyer, K. (2011), 'The cognitive neuroscience of creativity: A critical review', *Creativity Research Journal*, 23(2), 137–54.

Selby, E.C., Shaw, E.J. and Houtz, J.C. (2005), 'The creative personality', *Gifted Child Quarterly*, Fall 2005, 49(4), 300–14.

Singh H, and Singh A. (2002), 'Principles of complexity and chaos theory in project execution: a new approach to management cost engineering', *Journal of Cost Engineering*, 44(12), 23–32.

Sternberg, R.J. and Lubart, T.I. (1999), 'The concept of creativity: Prospects and paradigms', in R.J. Sternberg (ed.), *Handbook of Creativity*, Cambridge: Cambridge University Press, 3–15.

Thamhain H.J. (2004a), 'Linkages of project environment to performance: Lessons for team leaderships', *International Journal of Project Management 2004*, 22(7), 533–44.

Thamhain H.J. (2004b), 'Team leadership effectiveness in technology-based project environments', *Project Management Journal 2004*, 35(4), 35–46.

Thomas, J. and Mengel, B. (2008), 'Preparing project managers to deal with complexity – Advanced project management education', *International Journal of Project Management*, 26, 304–15.

Ward, T.B., Smith, S.M. and Finke, R.A. (1999), 'Creative cognition', in R.J. Sternberg (ed.), *Handbook of Creativity*, Cambridge: Cambridge University Press, 189–212.

Weisberg, R.W. (1993), *Creativity: Beyond the Myth of Genius*, New York: Freeman.

Zaleznik, A. (1977), 'Managers and leaders: Are they different?', *Harvard Business Review*, 55, 67–78.

57 *The Hero Project Managers*

ANDY JORDAN

We've all come across them in our careers. You see them walking down the corridor and whisper to your colleague about them in hushed tones. You expect them to disappear into the broom cupboard and emerge seconds later wearing a cape and a one-piece Lycra suit. These are the *hero project managers* (PMs), that small and elite group which is parachuted into troubled projects to rescue things and deliver a seemingly lost project on time, on scope, on budget and on quality. Clearly the world is a better place because of these exceptionally gifted men and women.

But wait a minute: let's roll back to that bit where these hero PMs are parachuted in to the project to leap tall obstacles in a single bound. Why do we need these people in the first place? If we are doing a good job of managing our projects, then surely things should never get to the point where we need hero PMs? We should have processes and tools in place to provide early warnings when things begin to go wrong. Then surely we could take corrective action to avoid the melodrama of having to 'call in the doctor' to save the lives of our projects? This chapter investigates how projects can deteriorate to the point of needing a 'hero', what makes a good hero PM and what organisations can do to render them unnecessary.

Introducing the Hero PMs

Hero PMs are especially gifted and experienced people who are asked to rescue projects from apparently irrecoverable situations. They may be saving their own projects, but more usually they are asked to step in as replacement PMs when things are looking lost. The interim manager described in Case Four in Chapter 48 was a good example of a hero PM. Hero PMs are typically seen as the last hope to deliver ailing projects on time, scope, budget and quality (or at least as close to those objectives as possible).

Every hero PM has to 'hit the ground running' and will be expected to add value on day one, and thenceforth constantly deliver improvements to get the project back on track. Hero PMs need to build relationships rapidly with the project team, understand what needs to be done and motivate their resources to achieve it. They may need to spend some time understanding exactly where the project currently stands if the status reporting and project schedule are not providing a clear or accurate picture (or if the reality is very different from what has been reported to stakeholders to this point). They will have to compromise in the way that the project is executed in order to try and deliver results – effectively cutting corners and assuming additional risk to try and accelerate real progress.

Hero PMs are usually experienced PMs who know which risks can be taken and which need to be avoided. They understand the implications of their shortcuts and aggressively manage the project to deal with problems immediately and decisively. They have to be fearless, being ruthlessly decisive and never second-guessing themselves. They must be able to command the respect of their team so that they can turn a group of demoralised individuals into a team of overachievers who can not only rescue the project but also redeem their own reputations and self-confidence.

On the face of it all this seems incredible. Here is a group of 'super PMs' who step in to deal with the 'problem projects' that an organisation always seems to be dealing with. Who would not want to be able to call on one or two of these people when things get tough? It's an executive's dream to be able to light up the sky with a special sign and have a larger-than-life PM standing in their doorway.

But is this really an acceptable situation? What's really happening here is a failure of in-house project execution – clearly something has gone badly wrong with any project that requires outside resources to step in and try to save the situation.

Factors Leading to the Need for a Hero PM

How can a project can deteriorate to the point of needing a hero PM? Here is an indication that the project plan and the project reality have become seriously misaligned. That, in turn, implies that one or more of the following situations has occurred:

1. Bad planning – inaccurate effort estimates, inappropriate resource allocation, missed work items and so on;
2. Bad project management – failure to recognise problems that were occurring, failure to take timely corrective action, failure to identify slippages, lack of change management, masking of the true situation and so on;
3. Bad stakeholder/sponsor leadership – failure to approve recommended corrective actions, failure to deliver on approved actions, unrealistic constraints and so on.

All of these are serious issues, but they are not going to result in the need for a hero PM immediately, there has to be another factor as well, which is *time*. Even the most serious problem is unlikely to result in complete catastrophe immediately – it's the failure to take the appropriate corrective actions in time that will seal the project's fate.

Consider one of the examples above. Suppose that a project is suffering from bad planning estimates and that these bad estimates occur throughout the entire plan. A PM should be able to identify this problem as soon as he or she sees that the actual figures are at a considerable variance from the plan. They conduct the analysis, establish that the estimates are flawed and then look at all of the other estimates to see whether the problem exists elsewhere.

Once they have established that the problem is widespread they can advise stakeholders, re-estimate the work and establish a more realistic project schedule. There may still be some difficult discussions with stakeholders about the project constraints, but there is as yet no apparent need for a hero PM to be dropped into the project.

However, what often happens is an attempt to 'cover up' the problem. The PM (or sponsor) will try to implement their own plan to recover the situation, whilst still reporting the project as 'on track' so that they are not seen as having made a mistake. They work with their team leaders to arrange for overtime, look for ways to move people around to preserve the schedule, identify tasks that can be skipped or cut short, and so on, in the hope that the situation can be resolved within the team.

Of course things rarely work out that way; it's far more common for things to get worse. That provides even more incentive for PMs to try and recover things themselves – otherwise not only will they have to admit to the original problem, but also to their failure to deal with it. Within a very short time the project moves seriously off track, to the point where it is too late to recover using conventional approaches – cue the hero PM. We've all seen these projects. They are the ones that suddenly go from 'on target' to three months late in the status summary. Typically cost performance against budget will track the same pattern.

A More Detailed Description of a Typical Hero PM and the Job Requirements

I touched on the characteristics of a hero PM earlier. Now it's time to examine the special talents of hero PMs in a little more detail.

First, consider the situation in which these heroic people find themselves. They are stepping in to a project part way through, knowing full well that the project is headed for impending doom. They are either replacing the unsuccessful PM or they are being asked to work alongside the original PM – someone who has been at least partly responsible for the current situation, and is very likely to be both demoralised and potentially resentful of the hero PM coming in to take over.

In addition the project team will probably have extremely low morale. No one wants to be associated with failure, and team members will be concerned that the project's problems reflect on themselves. They may well be 'burned out' from trying to recover the project from its difficulties, and resent the fact that they are now being asked to accept more changes and try again to deliver an 'impossible' project.

Clearly this is not the ideal situation for anyone to step into, let alone an individual who is expected to provide salvation. It's easy to understand why these men and women are considered to be heroes. To be successful they obviously need to be skilled PMs, but more importantly, they also need to be skilled people leaders. Let's look at their skill sets in more detail.

ANALYSING AND UNDERSTANDING

The first thing that the hero PM needs to do is understand exactly what the situation is that they are stepping in to. This means undertaking an analysis of the project to establish:

- current status (which is not necessarily the same as what is indicated by the status reports);
- the issues that the project is facing together with the root causes of those issues;

- the actions that have been taken to try and recover from the situation and the outcome of those efforts;
- the variances between the current state and the project goals (cost and schedule);
- what can be achieved within the current confines of budget, scope, schedule and quality;
- the additional budget and/or schedule required to deliver the full scope and quality or the reduction in scope and/or quality required to stay within current budget and schedule-time analysis.

The last item in the above list in particular is likely to involve a number of reiterative analyses and discussions with stakeholders about different scenarios in order to develop the most acceptable (or the least unacceptable) outcome.

The hero PM also needs to understand how the recognition that the project needs rescuing will impact upon stakeholders, and in particular the PM's management of those stakeholders. The stakeholders will have expectations around the project, either consciously set by the original PM or through a lack of management of expectations on their part. All of those expectations must now be reviewed, and either revalidated or changed.

This might all be a fairly straightforward process. If some of the major stakeholders were responsible for calling in the hero PM, then there will already be a recognition that things needed to change. However, that might also result in those stakeholders thinking that *they* can control the project because the new PM is 'theirs'. On the other hand, the stakeholders may be taken by surprise by the sudden change of PM and the circumstances that led to it. That could be as a result of one or more of the following:

- a lack of information (leading to incorrect assumptions);
- a lack of understanding of how bad things were;
- over-optimistic or actually misleading status reports from the original PM.

The hero PM must analyse all of these stakeholder positions, expectations and agendas and ensure that their incorrect assumptions are rapidly corrected. As they move through the following steps they need to consider the stakeholders constantly, ensure that realistic expectations are set and that the stakeholders themselves are actively managed. Even hero PMs cannot remove individual stakeholder bias or personal agendas, but they can ensure that they understand them and manage accordingly.

Of course, this analysis cannot happen in isolation. The project is in serious trouble and actions need to be taken immediately to try and recover it. As a result the analysis must be conducted in parallel with the actions described below, with adjustments to those steps being made based on the outcome of the analysis. From this it will become apparent that we need to add expert multitasking to the hero PM's skill set!

BUILDING PRODUCTIVE RELATIONSHIPS

No matter how good the hero PM is, they are not going to be able to turn the project around on their own. They need to work through the project team, and that can pose a significant challenge. Whenever there is a change within a team it takes time for that team to find a new 'normal' working relationship. The team has to adjust to its new member so that it can accept them into the team and so on. When the change is the PM, that is likely to be even more dramatic and disruptive. Indeed it can result in a tendency for team performance to drop as everyone becomes more focused on establishing their own position in the changed team.

The hero PM needs to focus quickly on each team member (both as individuals and as a group) as well as on the tasks that need to be completed. Team members must understand that the best way to demonstrate their value is to concentrate on the work and start delivering on the tasks that will ultimately result in project success. This can be much harder than it sounds – especially since the team is the same group of people who were responsible for the project when all of the past problems occurred.

The hero PM must focus also on creating a positive environment where the team (individually and as a group) feel comfortable. They cannot be allowed to feel as though the causes of the project's problems are still being held over them. They have to be convinced that the 'hero' is bringing a fresh start where everyone has a new chance to demonstrate their abilities. The hero PM cannot ignore any people-related problems that have occurred to this point, but he or she needs to ensure that those issues are managed within a new positive and forward-looking environment.

For example, if a team member is not pulling their weight and their deliverables are slipping, then the hero PM needs to manage them aggressively to meet deadlines on the tasks to which they are now assigned with, as far as possible, no reference to what has happened in the past and how that may have impacted upon the project. The new process is simply about getting each assigned task completed by the deadline date.

Another point of focus for the hero PM is the collective morale of the team and of each individual within it. We can all think back to projects where things have not been going well, and that is never a pleasant experience. The team will most likely have been working long hours (especially in attempting to catch up on the schedule). Its members will be feeling down because of the unresolved problems, and frustrated that things are not improving. There might be individuals who are starting to 'point fingers' or remove themselves from any responsibility and there will certainly be a sense of 'what's the point?' for the future of the project.

Whilst the hero PM will bring a fresh approach to the project there is no getting away from the fact that the team will have to continue to work hard, and that means they need to place all their trust and loyalty in the new PM. Here the analogy of a military leader is a good one. If the leader stands at the back and instructs the team where to go, then the individuals will be unlikely to give their all. On the other hand, if the leader stands at the head of the team with an attitude of 'come on, follow me, let's get this done' (that is, leading from the front) then the team will be fired up with courage and enthusiasm, and will thus be far more inclined to follow the leader.

Clearly all this means that the team believes in its new PM, and that in turn means open and frequent communication, engaging the team in determining the actions to be taken (covered in more detail below) and frequent positive reinforcement.

The project solution might involve bringing additional resources into the project, but this is not automatically a good thing. Not only will new people cause additional disruption to the team dynamics, they can cause separate cliques of 'old' team and 'new' team, and working 'flat out' may not help – not every problem can be solved by 'throwing people at it'.

Editorial Comment (DL)

Additional resources might be considered undesirable or unauthorised because of budget constraints but very often the additional cost will be offset by the cost advantages of recovering the original schedule. Always remember that time is money.

BEING DECISIVE

Hero PMs do not enjoy the luxury of being able to take time to consider all options before taking action. When the project is in trouble it is not going to get better by doing nothing. That said, it obviously can get worse if one does the wrong things.

One of the first tasks that the hero PM needs to do is ensure that the team is making progress on tasks that are going to add value to the project. This action might be limited at this point because the PM has had no chance to conduct the analysis recommended above in the 'Analysing and Understanding' section but there will still be some items that can move forward. The hero PM will focus on work that is critical to the project's outcome – items that cannot be modified or removed if the project is ultimately to be considered a success.

Ideally the problem project will have been accurately defined from the start, possibly by a project charter, and certainly by a scope statement, requirements documents and other notes to specify all the project deliverables. If not, that will be a failure of the project management system and the hero PM will have to work with the sponsor, customer and other key stakeholders to establish those 'must haves'.

As the analysis proceeds, so more courses of action will become clear and the hero PM will need to move resources around to ensure that the focus is always on the critical tasks (the tasks that are going to contribute most to achieving the end goals). This requires decisiveness, even if there is a general lack of confidence in the course of action being pursued. That does not mean work for the sake of work – it means approving the work that will add the best value based on the information currently available. As the hero PM learns more about the project's situation, or as stakeholders make decisions around mutually acceptable compromises, then those decisions need to be revisited and adjusted if necessary.

It should be apparent from all this why the strong relationships described above are important. Resources are going to be moved between different tasks more frequently as the effort is diverted to where it is most needed. The people involved need to be able to trust their new PM to be making the right decisions.

The situation described here is by no means as chaotic as it might sound. The hero PM should always be focused on developing a clear and complete picture as soon as possible, but also needs to make progress from the beginning, in parallel with the process of analysis and understanding.

As soon as the PM has gained a clear picture of the current project state, and the stakeholders have agreed on the areas (if any) where compromises can be made (cost *versus* quality *versus* delivery date *versus* scope) they need to work with key team members to develop a realistic plan to achieve a successful project. Team members might be reluctant to commit themselves to change because of their earlier experiences, especially if incorrect estimates were part of the problem. So the hero PM needs to lead this process (and here again good relationships are vital). However, it is also important that the team members have 'bought into' the plan – the hero PM cannot force it upon them.

ACCEPTING AND MANAGING RISK

No matter how engaged the team is, or how accommodating stakeholders have been in freeing up the budget, reducing scope or pushing out deadlines, execution of the revised plan is going to be difficult. The project had already reached an unacceptable point when the hero PM was brought in and for things to improve rapid progress is now necessary.

As a result the organisation is usually going to have to accept that the project will incur more risk than was previously considered acceptable. One of the major skills that sets hero PMs apart is their ability to handle risk. Hero PMs must:

- be comfortable when managing initiatives where risks are higher than normal;
- be able to remain calm and objective when significant risks become realities;
- accept that in these less-than-ideal circumstances risk management plans may be less thorough than usual, resulting in a greater degree of residual risk;
- be prepared to introduce controlled risk to the project in order to save time and/or money.

In a 'normal' project, all risks are reviewed in advance and, for the significant risks, appropriate actions are taken to manage the likelihood and impact of those risks as part of a wider and ongoing risk management strategy. At its most simple level this is an investment of time, effort and (potentially) money in order to minimise the possible negative impact (or maximise the potential positive impact) in the future.

Hero PMs will not have as many resources to invest in this preventative approach, so more risks will have to be accepted as they stand. Thus only the most significant risks will get active management. However, that does not mean that all these risks are ignored. Unmanaged risks require more attention, not less. The hero PM needs to ensure that these risks are being monitored for warning signs that they are becoming real so that swift and decisive actions can be taken to try and eliminate any negative project impact.

Of course, with less active management of risks then more of them will actually materialise, so contingencies are an important consideration for the hero PM. Here too, the options are limited and compromises will be necessary. The PM will need to work closely with the project stakeholders to determine what the response strategies will be if risks do become reality. In some cases the realisation of key risks may result in the project simply being unable to meet its goals and objectives. Stakeholders will have to accept that risk related costs will increase – it's unavoidable, and cannot be eliminated just by a refusal to set aside a budget for it! Additionally, whilst some trade-offs between cost and budget are possible, the risk costs should anticipate both financial and schedule impacts.

Perhaps the hardest part of risk management for hero PMs is the recognition that their own activities and decisions will tend to introduce risk into the project – effectively trading accelerated progress towards project goals for increased risk.

For example, an organisation's project processes, tools, templates and so on are all designed to provide a standardised approach to project management that is well proven and maximises the chances for success. However, these processes all take time and effort to execute and the hero PM may not have that time and effort available. They need to be prepared to trade the 'best' or the 'right' way of doing things for the 'only remaining' way that will give them any chance of delivering against the objectives.

This can be a tough step for PMs to take – processes are the cornerstone of project management and it feels wrong to abandon them. Additionally, failure to follow process may well be the reason why the project got into trouble in the first place, so continuing along that path seems like a recipe for disaster.

This is why hero PMs must be experienced PMs. They need the experience to determine where corners can be cut and where the processes have to be followed 'to the letter'.

Even where processes are not followed precisely, they are not entirely abandoned. For example, the project might not provide formal weekly status reporting, but the PM may well chair daily 'scrums' with key team members to ensure that no tasks are being held up, all resources are working on assigned tasks, no adverse issues are arising and so on.

Eliminating Hero PMs

By definition a hero is someone who goes to extraordinary lengths to achieve a goal. Heroes go far beyond what anyone has any right to expect, indeed far beyond anything that can be sustained for any length of time. This is why so many heroes have unfortunately to be recognised posthumously (hopefully not literally in the case of project management). Although their lives might not be at risk, hero PMs can easily become burned out and demoralised, and may well look for other opportunities in organisations where they can have a more 'normal' project management career.

In organisations with hero PMs there can also be a tendency to set unreasonable goals. Sponsors demand unrealistic delivery dates, budgets and scopes because they know that a particular PM with an appropriate reputation can most likely deliver when faced with these challenges.

Whilst hero PMs can be the salvation of an individual initiative, the focus of an organisation has to be on eliminating the need for the role in the first place – to improve the way in which projects are executed to ensure that no project ever reaches the point of needing its hero. Heroic project management is effectively a trade-off, sacrificing the long-term health of the project resource pool for the sake of progress on a specific initiative. If this becomes normal behaviour then the organisation will see a significant drop in its project execution capability over the longer term.

All this requires a very honest analysis of failed projects – and a project that requires a hero PM is a failed one even if the goals and objectives are ultimately achieved by the hero PM's efforts. There needs to be an understanding of the root causes of the adverse issues – not just the visible symptoms but also of the underlying problems that must be dealt with in order to prevent recurrence. These may be process-related or people-related (or some combination of both) but it is important to understand and deal with these issues as soon as possible to prevent them from recurring.

This careful consideration will depend on who is doing the problem analysis. There can be an assumption that the original PM acted perfectly but was dragged down by inappropriate, outdated, incomplete and/or ineffective processes. Alternatively there might be an assumption that the processes are perfect and all of the problems lay with the original PM's inability to follow the specified processes or a lack of project management skills. In truth, it is unlikely that either of these situations will be true. Processes need to evolve continuously to remain as effective as possible in supporting the changing needs of the organisation's project portfolio. Over time major overhauls will be necessary to respond to evolving project management approaches, changing technology, changes in working arrangements and so on.

Not all PMs are created equal. There may well be situations where additional training is required, formal performance management needs to be implemented or the type of project assigned to the individual PM needs to be reconsidered.

Consideration must also be given to ensure that there is not an overreaction. Sometimes projects just go wrong through no fault of the processes or the PM. Bad things happen to good projects!

Ultimately the organisation needs to ensure that its project execution approach is built to maximise the likelihood of success, as follows:

- effective processes consistently applied with checkpoints and gateways at key points;
- consistent compliance with process and tool requirements;
- an environment of trust and openness where PMs can accurately report project status without fear of reprisals;
- recognition by stakeholders that projects require budgets (financial and schedule) for risk management and contingency;
- understanding that demanding a project be completed by a certain date, for a certain budget, with a specified scope and quality level does not in itself make it possible – these triple constraints are not optional.

Conclusion

Hero PMs might be the worst thing that has ever happened to project management! These PMs, with their almost superhuman abilities to rescue success from the jaws of complete disaster, allow organisations to think that it's all right to allow projects to 'go off the rails'. Hero PMs become an almost normal part of the way that projects are managed, and that is an extremely risky attitude that will ultimately fail when the last PM hero quits and goes to a competitor who has an effective project execution approach that eliminates the need for heroes in the first place.

Hero PMs are bad for projects in general – they send a message that it's not serious to have a project that has completely lost its way because someone can always be called in to come along and rescue it.

Hero PMs are bad for PMs – because they can remove the pressure to perform well. If generally tolerated, they allow substandard performance to become the norm because someone else can always come along to clear up the mess.

Hero PMs are bad for organisations – because they can mask inherent problems in the way that projects are executed by the organisation.

Hero PMs are bad for the hero PMs themselves – they demand excessive amounts of effort in extremely stressful situations and cannot be maintained for extended periods of time.

If an organisation is faced with a situation where it is relying on a hero PM, then it should be grateful that he or she is available, and then do everything possible to ensure that they are never needed again.

58 *Human Traits and Behaviours in Project Management*

KEVIN DOLLING, PAUL GIRLING and JOANNA REYNOLDS

This chapter is about what our company ('new habits') calls Humanability®. Everyone knows about project failure. Reasons often cited include lack of user involvement, unrealistic timescales, poor requirements definition, scope creep, having no clear sponsor or champion and many others. However, we believe that projects and change initiatives do not generally fail for technical reasons. They might fail for procedural reasons, but mostly they fail for human reasons. These can include political struggles and power games, lack of 'buy-in' (from a whole assortment of stakeholders), poor motivation, not understanding what others want and focusing on the wrong things. So unsuccessful project managers probably focus on the wrong things. But on what should they focus? We want to share our company's views with you. Our aim is to provoke you to question your own practice and behaviour.

Economic Environment

A downturned economic environment makes things even tougher for a project manager. It creates pressure. The recession (current at the time of writing) means that investment is cut back savagely. Therefore funding for projects is scarce. Added to this, there is a feeling of doom. All we get is bad news and self-fulfilling pessimism.

Managers appear to be scared of failure. They take refuge in the left side of their brains (the logical, safe-keeping side) rather than engaging the right side (the creative, emotional, fun-seeking side). This is expressed in micromanagement and tight control causing people to play it safe – keeping their heads down and following rules.

However, measuring, taking apart, quantifying and analysing doesn't necessarily mean making things clearer and more effective. The constant pressure of knowing you might have to justify, in minute detail, every decision you make, hampers performance. So what gets measured gets done. In micromanagement there is no space left for inspiration, entrepreneurism and creativity.

Allowing Individual Freedom

CASE EXAMPLE NO. 1

Annette Simmons (2006) tells a story about a family wedding that an engineer attended when he was aged 16. That wedding was the last time this engineer saw his two uncles at the same time. His favourite uncle (Henry) was a prominent lawyer. His other uncle (Horace) was considered crazy. Horace always wore purple trainers and would sometimes deliver shocking statements like 'Helen is a bitch', which everyone knew to be true but no one else was game to say. He loved his Uncle Horace best because he wasn't afraid of anything or anyone. He seemed more alive than all the sane people. But Uncle Horace had not always been 'crazy'.

Both Horace and Henry had been brilliant as young men and were given excellent educational opportunities. By the age of 18 Horace had graduated from Harvard with a degree in psychology. Henry studied law and did well, but Horace was considered the brilliant one. Despite the brilliance, or because of it, during the 1950s Horace was diagnosed with 'brain fever'. He might have been depressed, neurotic or eccentric – no one could remember. They just knew that his behaviour seemed strange to the family.

In the 1950s the cure for 'brain fever' was a lobotomy. Uncle Horace was admitted to hospital and part of his brain was removed – along with his brilliance. His brilliance was destroyed.

One of the morals of the story is that sometimes, when we don't understand something we try to take it apart, piece by piece. But in that process we destroy it.

Some people may 'wear purple trainers' and be exceptional at what they do but we have no idea how they get the results that they get. Don't destroy their brilliance by trying to measure it or quantifying it, with rigorous measurable outcomes. Just be happy they are in the team, being uniquely brilliant.

CAN YOU LET YOUR PEOPLE WEAR PURPLE TRAINERS?

The problem is that 'working to rule' is inflexible. It creates what we call 'jobsworths'. These are people who cannot venture into different ways of achieving results. In an environment that requires creativity and inspiration, 'working to rule' prevents people from being their best.

This is strange because whenever we give presentations to professional associations we ask 'What is your organisation's best asset?' The response is always overwhelmingly 'Our people'. Yet people can be treated like machines. Or they are treated even worse than machines, because machines have maintenance schedules, experts to keep them functioning and repair them when needed. People are more adaptable and versatile than any machine, but many are neglected or even abused. Yet they still deliver results. This is clearly not the way to get the best out of people. How much better could they deliver if they were 'maintained'?

In fact, rigid compliance to rules turns people into machines. As we shall mention later, adults don't like rules. So we rebel against them.

It can be argued though that good project management uses rules by setting clear, quantifiable targets. This sounds good in theory, after all, *'What gets measured, gets done'* (which has been attributed to Peter Drucker, Tom Peters, Edwards Deming, Lord Kelvin among others). But the issue here is that we can end up by being obsessed with quantification. We create a 'tick-box mentality'. As a frustrated employee at Ford put it,

> *The bean counter wants to know all along the way how much is this, how much is that – and even before you get the genesis of the thing organised, they want to know the exact cost of each part. And you can't think that way, so what you do is lie, fake, hide things behind the blackboard [...] they can always prove they are right. They've got it on paper. They are right, but they are wrong. (John Kay, 2011)*

Which of us has not felt the pressure to record the required metrics so that we can get on with the real job?

Constraint from Imposed Methodologies and Targets

At the risk of being strung up by many members of the project management community, we would like to consider PRINCE2 and other project methodologies. There has been a vast amount of money 'invested' in them, both in their development and in training practitioners. Our concern is that they focus on *processes* to follow and not on *people*. Such methods are based on the ethic of obedience. That means having rules to follow (which we shall come to later). It is argued, by experienced practitioners, that one should employ one's judgement to adapt the method to fit the needs of the project. However, you can only tailor and adapt when you have experience. It's a classic 'chicken and egg' dilemma. Further, methods are based on the premise that you require structure and quantified targets. We think the issue is well stated in this piece found on the Internet:

> *The idea you can specify everything up front, execute the project in pre-defined phases, base your testing on your specification etc. etc. is all very persuasive. If however, you start to feel it's a little unreal – not the way the World works, don't worry. It's not you that's got the wrong end of the stick.*

Another Internet contributor was more caustic:

> *The most massive IT cock-ups in the UK are usually PRINCE structured, so you might say it is good for raising project costs one-hundredfold.*

Dennis Lock told me that he finds PRINCE2 to be prescriptive and bureaucratic (he facetiously calls it POUNCE – projects overspent in uncontrolled environments).

SILOS

In practice, management driven by rigid objectives can be like putting blinkers on people, creating silos so that they cannot or will not see outside their immediate area of responsibility. It can lead to suboptimisation, where one group might appear to function well but actually affects others negatively and does not contribute effectively to the overall goal. This silo mentality reduces *trust*, which is an essential ingredient in getting the best out of people. According to Lencioni (2006):

> Silos are ... the barriers that exist between departments within an organization, causing people who are supposed to be on the same team to work against one another.

Silos occur because there is no compelling reason to work together. So people focus on their tactical work, assuming they are working in the best interest of the organisation. But they see colleagues elsewhere going in different tactical directions. This lack of common purpose can be destructive:

> And then the worst thing possible happens – they actually start working against those colleagues on purpose!

Whereas, all they need is a common goal to create collaboration. What do we want?

Fulfilment

If we accept that rule-driven, micromanagement does not get the best out of us, what *will* get the best out of us? The answer is 'fulfilment'.

Aristotle (384–322 BC) described the concept 'eudemonia' – happiness or flourishing (fulfilment). His ethical system has influenced thinking for the last 2,000 years. Now we recognise a difference between happiness and eudemonia. Psychologist Daniel Nettle (2005) suggests three senses of happiness, as follows:

1. The lowest level of happiness is the momentary feeling that makes us happy – the joy of sex, the pleasure of a beautiful sunset.
2. The intermediate level is a state of mind not a physical response. For example, a sense of satisfaction and well-being.
3. Eudemonia is the highest level – a sense of quality of life, of flourishing, of fulfilling one's potential.

We have found from our research and experience as coaches that people are fulfilled by the following factors:

- Achievement – overcoming challenge and achieving a result. This can bring a sense of growth. It can be at work or in one's private life.
- Freedom – having time to do what one wants; not being encumbered; being able to choose one's path.
- Close relationship(s) (giving and receiving love from a partner, children and/or friends).
- Sense of belonging to a team. Again, this can be at work or in one's private life.
- Sense of contribution – making a difference to others or for a cause (voluntary work, for example).

So fulfilment is not bought and cannot be quantified. Albert Einstein reportedly had a sign on his office wall that stated:

Not everything that counts can be counted, and not everything that can be counted counts.

Cricketer Ed Smith (2008) puts seeking to fulfil potential (personal growth) and winning (achievement) into perspective as follows:

I am not saying that personal development is more important than winning ... enjoying the journey of self-discovery, by removing some of the pressure and angst associated with winning at all costs, is one way of helping you to win more often.

FLOW AND INNER GAME

Fulfilment or flourishing does not mean soft-pedalling. In fact, it can mean just the opposite. Psychologist Mihalyi Csikszentmihalyi (2008) describes what people experience in demanding activities as 'flow'. It is 'the sense of effortless action they feel tends to occur when a person's skills are fully involved in overcoming a challenge that is just about manageable'.

We can experience flow in our work lives. For example, an engaging presenter may 'lose' themselves when in full 'flow'. We often lose sense of time in flow. In neuro linguistic programming, this experience is often described as being 'in the zone'.

A coachee of our company (we prefer 'coachee' to 'trainee' in this context) who was a professional rugby player, told us that his best performance in games happened when he didn't think about it. It came instinctively.

Flow experiences contribute to our fulfilment and long-term well-being. We think that flow corresponds to Timothy Gallwey's performance model set out in The Inner Game of Work (2000) and his other Inner Game books. As well as being successful in business, Gallwey was a tennis coach, which is where the model has its roots. He proposed that we have two inner selves:

- inner-self one, which is protective and seeks to get us to do things properly (according to the rules);
- inner-self two, which is our creative, natural self with vast potential.

Gallwey expresses the relationship between these with the equation:

$$\text{Performance} = \text{Potential} - \text{Interference}$$

Our performance is equal to our potential (what inner-self two could achieve) minus the interference (doubts and negative thoughts) that our safe-keeping inner-self one generates. We cannot switch off inner-self one but we can distract him/her. So when we are in 'flow' we are working close to potential because inner-self one is distracted.

EXTERNAL INTERFERENCE

Whilst Gallwey's model (2000) identifies interference as being internal, we extend the model to the interference imposed by the behaviour, rules, constraints and culture of the workplace. This means that micromanagement does not enhance performance but diminishes it.

So when we tackle a challenge, it can lead to flow. Overcoming challenges can bring fulfilment; as can freedom to be oneself, having close relationships and a sense of belonging. We desire fulfilment but do we get it at work? The important questions are:

- What would it be like to get fulfilment at work?
- And if we did, what would our contribution be like?
- Wrong focus – just what is failure?

Project Success or Failure

Project success is normally defined objectively in terms of quantified costs and benefits. Classically this means: the required outputs are delivered on or under budget and on or under timescale. In other words, the business case has been met. The corollary is that if the business case has not been met, then the project is a failure.

However, are success and failure that simple? Kay (2011) suggests that pursuing quantified goals is artificial and too rigid. He argues that the sorts of models and projections upon which a business case is based are inadequate and too simplistic because the business environment is too uncertain for us to forecast the future. In times of national and international economic turmoil, such as exist as we write this, who can reliably predict financially 12 months ahead?

The business environment is complex. Many factors are involved so we simplify them. We make assumptions and restrict the business model by eliminating 'unimportant' factors. So the model becomes too simplistic.

FRANKLIN'S RULE AND FRANKLIN'S GAMBIT

The response of other parties (individuals, departments, organisations and cultures), cannot be predicted accurately. So our knowledge of the business environment is incomplete. Indeed there is so much that we don't know that the 'unknowns' may well outweigh what we profess to know. And, of course, the business environment is constantly changing.

Nonetheless, project managers would still argue the case for objectivity. John Kay (2011) illustrates this desire in relation to Benjamin Franklin who set out his rule for an objective decision making in a letter to the English chemist Joseph Priestley. This (Franklin's rule) reads as follows:

> Divide half a sheet of paper ... into two columns; writing over the one Pro, and over the other Con. Then ... I put down under the different heads short hints of the different motives, that at different times occur to me for or against the measure.

> When I have got ... one view, I endeavour to estimate the respective weights ... I have found great advantage for this ... moral or prudential algebra.

In principle, organisations follow formal processes that resemble moral algebra (Franklin's rule), when making decisions, for example appointing to a job or choosing between options in a project.

However, Franklin knew that moral algebra is not how people and organisations really make decisions. He later went on to describe what became known as Franklin's gambit, which reads as follows:

> so convenient a thing is it to be a reasonable creature, since it enables one to find or make a reason for everything one had a mind to do.

So in fact, moral algebra is really just a justification for a decision that has already been made. The interview report or the option appraisal usually follows Franklin's gambit rather than Franklin's rule.

Do you know of any project manager who has skewed a business case to justify a preferred option (theirs or that of a powerful sponsor)?

Quantified objectives are not as powerful a motivator as having a sense of purpose. Patrick Lencioni (2006) describes this well:

> resist the temptation to say, 'Revenue is all that matters, because …' Even the most driven employees … will not be as motivated for hitting the numbers if they don't understand how they fit into the bigger picture.

Branson (2007), when people ask him what business they should pursue, writes:

> When people ask me … I always tell them … have a passion for what you do, for the moment it becomes all about the money is the moment you will cease to go forward.

This applies equally well to project management. It is not enough simply to chase quantified targets.

On which of the following two projects would you wish to work?

- Project 1 – to deliver a mortgage processing system, within a total budget that must not exceed £2.5m and to be fully implemented in 15 months; or
- Project 2 – to produce a simple, timely and accurate home-buying service that will satisfy both customers and operators.

PROJECT SUCCESS IS SUBJECTIVE?

A special interest group of the APM developed a presentation called 'Project Success is Subjective?' The premise is that for project managers to be successful they must focus on managing stakeholder perceptions. This is because projects are complex owing to the sheer number of people involved. Also, except for identical twins, no two people are alike. We each judge success by our own subjective criteria and our perceptions can change over time. So the accepted measure of success (meeting the business case) is inadequate.

Consider a construction project. It began with a forecast completion time of six years and a budget of $7m. It actually took 16 years, and the final cost was $102m. So it was finished 10 years late and cost more than 14 times the original budget. Was it a success? Using traditional measures, it was clearly a failure. However the Sydney Opera House is a great outcome – Australians love it. It was made a UNESCO World Heritage Site on 28 June 2007. The architect, Jørn Utzon, received the Pritzker Prize, architecture's highest honour, in 2003, with the citation:

> There is no doubt that the Sydney Opera House is his masterpiece. It is one of the great iconic buildings of the 20th century, an image of great beauty that has become known throughout the world – a symbol for not only a city, but a whole country and continent.

A further topic in the APM group's presentation is project managers' responses when relationships become complex and stakeholders express dissatisfaction with a project. Typically a project manager will seek a simple process-based solution, which does not deal with the core issue of a dysfunctional relationship. We observe this in relationship management workshops where project managers discuss processes and cite and impose rules rather than listen to, and engage with, customers, suppliers and other stakeholders. A more useful strategy might be to agree boundaries and give the freedom to explore options for dealing with the issues.

RECAPITULATION: THE STORY SO FAR

- Projects fail because of people issues.
- The challenging economic climate puts greater pressure on project managers to deliver results.
- But are they chasing the wrong targets? The pursuit of quantification can be counterproductive and the predictive models we use are inherently flawed.

Whilst we all espouse that people are our best asset, there is a prevailing JFDI (the polite version of which is 'just focus and do it') culture. Nonetheless we all desire fulfilment and are highly productive when we work in an environment that helps deliver it.

Ethics and Decision Making in Project Management

We believe there are two keys to successful project management:

- making the right decisions;
- showing respect to all stakeholders.

Project management (like all management) hinges on sound judgement in making decisions. We suggested earlier that 'objective' decision making is flawed because we claim to use Franklin's rule or something similar but more often than not we use Franklin's gambit to justify a decision that has already been made. So what are the alternative methods?

Luke Rhinehart (1971) offered a decision-making method in *The Dice Man*, where the main character changed his approach to life by making all of his major choices based on a dice roll. '*And so you, my friends, when you've picked up a pencil and written a list of options and rolled the dice ...'*. However, this method has its drawbacks, as he went on to say, *'you may be disappointed'*. Again, it smacks of Franklin's gambit. So how about ethical decision making instead?

Perhaps we should stop here and introduce a definition of ethics. Here's what *Chambers 21st Century Dictionary* says:

> ethics (plural noun): *rules or principles of behaviour.*

In the context of project management we prefer to put the emphasis on 'principles' rather than 'rules', since we do not believe that ethics is a process or an audit procedure. Our personal ethics matures as we go through life. Here we draw on Roger Steare (2009). In his excellent book he describes the following stages in ethical development.

STAGES IN ETHICAL OR MORAL DEVELOPMENT ACCORDING TO STEARE

The first stage in our moral development is the 'ethic of ego'. It is an internal driver of behaviour that manifests itself in our early years. Its purpose is survival so it causes us to be greedy, fearful and self-centred. It can be summarised as *'what's right is what's best for me'*.

Do we ever lose this powerful, physiological driver of behaviour? Probably not; just consider the origins of the banking crisis – greedy, undisciplined bankers. The question is 'should we still let it drive us?' What about the project manager who can see nothing but his/her project?

The second stage of development is our first moral conscience, the 'ethic of obedience' or rule compliance. It is an external driver of behaviour because it develops as we begin to understand instructions from our parents. It is based upon being aware that the consequences of our choices are reward or punishment. We learn this aspect of moral conscience when we are about four to five years old. This can be summarised as *'what's right is following orders'*. It can be argued that rules are for children and that we rebel against rules as we get older. (Remember your teen years!) We are more likely to comply though, if we are consulted on and agree on the rules.

John Kay (2011) uses the analogy of chess to illustrate the true importance of rules. For most of us, chess is a complex, strategic game. Novice chess players often lose because they make mistakes by forgetting or not applying the basic rules. But novices can often lose because they *do* apply the basic rules. Gary Kasparov and other grandmasters are experts not only at applying the rules, where they make few mistakes; they also understand when to break the rules.

Studies on paramedic experts show that the general public did not value them for following procedure but valued their confidence, decisiveness and results (or outcomes).

Skilled practitioners use pattern recognition (rather than calculations), successive limited comparison, make an assessment and, if evidence seems inconsistent, they adopt an alternative. This is what Kay (2011) calls an oblique approach.

When asked, most successful businessmen will describe their achievements (outcomes), or they might describe their general approach. But they cannot explain their detailed steps.

So a novice is consciously competent and will follow the rules, whilst experts who have been trained to hone their skills will be unconsciously competent. In other words, expert skill will be second nature. Experts can do without the rules.

Richard Branson (2007) uses an interesting analogy when describing the types of people he wants in his organisation.

Don't lead sheep, herd cats. It's easy to herd sheep, but impossible to lead them from the front. Cats, on the other hand, are independent and intelligent and those are the kind of people we want … employ thinkers, not yes men.

As project managers, do you want team of cats or a herd of sheep? Returning to Steare's ethical development stages, we come to the third stage. Our third ethical stage develops when we are young adults. It is the 'ethic of care' or social conscience and relates to the moral values of humility, love and fairness. It is an interactive driver of behaviour based on 'give-and-take' within relationships. This ethic builds community integrity, for example in families, neighbourhoods and, in the context of project management, in the workplace. It can be summarised as *'what's right is what's best for all of us'*.

An expression of the ethic of care is reciprocity. Our company often illustrates this by asking our coachees two questions. First we ask them to list people, from within and outside their organisations, from whom they can ask favours and expect support. We then ask our coachees to list the people, again from within and outside their organisations, who come to them for favours. Not surprisingly, for each individual, the same people tend to be found in both lists. This is *reciprocity,* which is expressed in two ethical 'rules'.

1. Golden rule: 'One should treat others as one would like others to treat oneself'. For example, the commandment 'Love thy neighbour as yourself' (Leviticus 19:18). The 'golden rule' has its roots in a wide range of world cultures (including ancient Babylon, Egypt, Persia, India, Greece, Judea and China) and religions (including Jewish, Christian, Hinduism, Buddhism, Taoism and Zoroastrianism). It is the basis for today's concept of human rights, where each individual treats all people with consideration, not just members of his/her group.
2. Silver rule, written by Confucius (551–479 BC): 'One should not treat others in ways that one would not like to be treated', for example, 'Do no harm' (Hippocratic oath).

Reciprocity is the basis of sustainable relationships. Effective project management is built on sustainable relationships, where bartering and trading are based on mutual trust. Richard Branson (2007) sums up the ethic of care well in his book *Screw it, Let's do it*:

Change the world, even in a small way. Make a difference and help others. Do no harm.

Always think what you can do to help.

Steare's fourth and final listed stage of development is the 'ethic of reason' or principled conscience which we reach in our early sixties. Aristotle is recognised as the founder of this school of ethics. This internal driver of behaviour comes from deep inside. It helps us to decide what's right by acting in accordance with our values and principles, such as fairness, courage and kindness. We display integrity when we live by our principles. It's our moral DNA. It can be summarised as *'what's right is what I/we judge is right'*.

However, principles can conflict. For example, we may have the values of 'truth' and 'loyalty' but what do we do if we know that a member of our family has committed a crime? Or our principles of determination and fairness can be in conflict; how does the conscientious, determined project manager act with team members who do not put in the same hours because of their domestic circumstances?

DOING THE RIGHT THING

So ethics is 'doing the right thing'. It isn't adopting just one of the ethical stages. Steare (2009) offers a framework for making choices or decisions that incorporates all three stages. The framework helps us to deal with the contradictions and ambiguities we can face. It is summarised by the acronym RIGHT, as follows:

Rules – This relates to the ethic of obedience; for example, is there legislation, policy or a code of conduct that prescribes what should or should not happen?

Integrity – How do the options align with my core integrity? This relates to the ethic of reason; what do my wisdom, self-discipline and sense of fairness tell me? How does this align with my principles and values?

Good – What good will come of the decision? This relates to the ethic of care, the golden rule; what benefit does the outcome bring to whom?

Harm – What possible harm will come from the decision? This also relates to the ethic of care, the silver rule; what harm or cost will the outcome bring to whom?

Truth – What if the truth should come out? This relates to both the ethics of care and reason. It is a powerful final question to ask ourselves, 'Could I sleep at night?'

Lessons from Carers

In our company we have been fortunate to work with informal carers in workshops, such as assertiveness and effective communications. An informal carer is a person who looks after another person. That might be an aged parent, a spouse, a son or daughter and so on. These carers are called 'informal' because they do not get paid for their efforts. Along with many others, we believe that the UK's six million carers are undervalued by society. They are exceptional people. One common feature we have observed is their capacity to fight for the rights of their cared-for individuals (often at a high cost to themselves). Carers demonstrate the following traits:

- belief in the vast potential of each person;
- focus on what a person can do (not what they can't do);
- encouragement and support for the individual (in fact, they often show good coaching skills);
- investment in and empowerment of the individual;
- desire to challenge limits imposed on a cared-for individual.

Overall they treat their cared-for people with respect and fight for other people to do likewise. Carers and their cared-for also demonstrate that each of us can tap into a vast well of determination, resilience and inner-strength. They illustrate our belief that 'we are all very resourceful'. In respect of Gallwey's (2000) formula (performance = potential – interference) carers help their cared-for to overcome both external and internal interference to strive to fulfil their potential.

What does this mean for project managers? How would it be, to be a project manager whose team members are pushing to fulfil their potential? And how would it be to work with or for a project manager who believed in you, listened to and encouraged you, helped you to grow your abilities and confidence, empowered you and fought for you? What would that do for your performance and what would you give in return? What would it be like to be the customer of a project manager with those values?

At 'new habits' we like to use the acronym RESPECT to identify the people traits that (project) managers need to be effective:

Relationships – building and maintaining reciprocal relationships.

Empathy – putting oneself in the shoes of another, appreciating their feelings.

Sincerity – being honest with self and others.

Principles – operating by one's principle or moral code.

Empowerment – empowering self and others to grow.

Compassion – dealing with others compassionately, with care.

Trust – show trust in others and build trust.

Conclusion: Humanability®

We like to sum up the essential message in this chapter as Humanability® – a belief in oneself and others. It encompasses:

- human ability: people have immense potential. We can be like carers and see people's ability not their disability;
- humanity: the quality of being humane; showing benevolence;
- humility: the quality of not being too proud about yourself, recognising collective effort of other people.

SUMMARISING OUR CHOICES

Relationships with Stakeholders

- expedient or sustainable? Go for the short-term, immediate needs or develop long-term reciprocal relationships?

- competitive or collaborative: pursue our own needs, ignoring others' needs – or look for joint solutions?
- approach to issues: rules or people; impose processes and rules or listen and engage with stakeholders?

Process or Creativity

- follow set ways or look for creative solutions?

Managing the Team

- command or empowerment: inflexible management (JFDI) or trust and empower;
- use or value; team members are resources or team members are people with great potential.

Your Impact on the Team

- demotivate or motivate;
- oppress team members or get the best out of team members;
- dissatisfaction or fulfilment: fail to meet people's needs or help people get fulfilment at work.

Therefore choose what is right and show respect.

References and Further Reading

Branson, R. (2007), *Screw It, Let's Do It: Lessons in Life and Business*, London: Virgin Books.

Csikszentmihalyi, M. (2008), *Flow: Tthe Psychology of Optimal Experience*, New York: HarperCollins.

Gallwey, W.T. (2000), *The Inner Game of Work: Focus, Learning, Pleasure, and Mobility in the Workplace*, New York: Random House.

Kay, J.A. (2011), *Obliquity: Why Our Goals Are Best Achieved Indirectly*, London: Profile Books.

Lencioni, P. (2006), *Silos, Politics and Turf Wars: A Leadership Fable About Destroying the Barriers That Turn Colleagues Into Competitors*, San Francisco, CA: Jossey-Bass.

Leviticus 19:18, *The Holy Bible*, King James Version (1769 Oxford 'Authorized Version').

Nettle, D. (2005), *Happiness – The Science Behind Your Smile*, Oxford: Oxford University Press.

Rhinehart, L. (Cockcroft, G.) (1971), *The Dice Man*, London: Talmy, Franklin Ltd.

Simmons, A. (2006), *The Story Factor: Inspiration, Influence, and Persuasion through the Art of Storytelling*, Cambridge, MA: Basic Books.

Smith, E. (2008), *What Sport Tells Us about Life*, London: Penguin.

Steare, R. (2009), *Ethicability: How to Decide What's Right and Find the Courage to Do it*, 3rd edn, London: Roger Steare Consulting Limited.

59 *Career Paths in Project Management*

JASON PRICE

Whether you are new to project management, or a seasoned professional looking for ways to develop junior staff and your organisation's culture, this chapter provides some thoughts to stimulate individual development planning. Other chapters discuss aspects of the project team, such as its behavioural traits and structures. Here in this chapter, I shall draw these concepts together into a 'road map' for a rewarding career.

Professionalism and Project Management

Is project management perceived as a professional skill? It is worth dealing with some of the perceptions that might lie behind this question.

Consider a scene from the deservedly popular television series *The Apprentice*. A rich and successful businessman leans over a table, stabs a finger at one candidate and regardless of that person's background declares, 'You're the project manager on this task'.

At a stroke, the ultimate power of a job title provides the chosen candidate with supreme authority to make random and autocratic decisions. Over the next hour, we witness the sentence 'I'm the project manager' being wielded as justification for bludgeoning a dysfunctional team into action, in the same way that a lion motivates a gazelle towards its destruction. In the real world the case where a senior manager assigns the latest high-profile challenge to a 'rising star', based on their reputation for 'getting things done quickly without all the paperwork', is not uncommon.

Once, in a personal discussion, an internal change manager and project sponsor told me 'We don't have time for planning, we just have to get on with it' and 'There hasn't been time built into the project for testing, so we'll just have to do our best at 'go-live''. That manager was responsible for a multimillion dollar business change project affecting millions of customers.

The 'rising star' is sometimes scheduled to attend the next in-house project management skills course, usually timed to take place well after the essential planning stage has finished. And that assumes the training is not cancelled altogether owing to the inevitable time pressures that result from poor project planning! It is this kind of reality that emerges from a flawed assumption by decision makers that project management is merely a job title that can be assigned to anyone; rather than a professional skill. There is much evidence that this assumption is held worldwide.

CONSEQUENCES OF INADEQUATE PROFESSIONAL CAPABILITY

High-profile enquiry reports often highlight the lack of basic skills in career project management as causal links for project failure. For example:

- 'The Auditor-General found there was no project plan current during development of Edge and no formal development methodology' (O'Neill, 2005).
- Edward Leigh, chairman of the UK House of Commons Public Accounts Committee, called the National Offender Management Service (NOMS) project a 'spectacular failure' and a 'masterclass in sloppy project management'... He added: 'All of this mess could have been avoided if good practice in project management had been followed' (Ford, 2009).

The cost of such failures is immense, estimated in 2004 across 214 European IT projects alone to be €142 billion (McManus and Wood-Harper, 2007). The need for professional skills in project management is well proven.

PROFESSIONALISM AS A ROUTE TO REDUCING PROJECT FAILURE RISK

Failures in project management skills appear high on the list of evidence presented by academic research into the early warning signs of impending project failure (Kappelman et al., 2006).

One day, you might be unlucky enough to find yourself encountering a well-meaning, but ill-informed, senior decision maker who (in an attempt to defy the laws of probability) believes their project will still succeed without the 'overhead' of project management. You should now have some evidence to challenge that view (although you could still have much convincing to do). Given sufficient courage you might ask this manager if, in the event that they were unfortunate enough to need serious surgery, they would choose to put their fate in the hands of a consultant surgeon or pick the nearest medical student.

Having explained our *raison d'être* as skilled professionals in project management, it is possible to examine the exciting opportunities this rewarding career path can provide.

Skills Underpinning a Project Management Career Path

A career in project management presents people with a wide range of opportunities to fulfil their potential to a personal level and at a pace of their choosing. The breadth and depth of experience, skills and technical knowledge available offers the individual a choice of excitement, challenge or stability in a career path tailored to their personal aspirations and ability.

Whether you're a career ladder climber destined for the boardroom, or looking for a regular routine job supporting work around your family life, there is space for you as a project management professional. Before discussing any specific roles, I must outline some of the generic skills and competencies needed to underpin a project management career.

At the start of one's career, the dizzy heights of the portfolio director's chair can seem like the summit of Everest as viewed from the lowest base camp. The aspiring Edmund

Hillary will need experience, judgement, determination, resilience, adaptability and the support of an outstanding team to survive the journey and get there.

In the spirit of good project management, we need to take a 'product-based planning' approach and look down from the summit at the route up. What are the skills and competencies likely to be required to fulfil this career climb to the top? Typically, these fall into three categories (expanded in Figure 59.1):

1. technical skills;
2. managerial skills;
3. interpersonal skills.

Existing literature reports a clear link between successful project outcomes and the presence of these skills in project professionals. Thus the competent general management and leadership texts on these topics are directly relevant to those of us who are interested in project management. Equally this demonstrates the value of project management as a discipline for those studying general management and leadership. The opportunity to avoid becoming the 'well-meaning, but ill-informed senior decision maker' thus presents itself.

TECHNICAL COMPETENCIES

The technical list in Figure 59.1 identifies the mechanics associated with effective implementation of project methodologies as, for example, those found within good practice guides such as the Association for Project Management Body of Knowledge (APM, 2008). Whatever the methodology chosen for a project, achieving improved project performance in organisations has been linked to the adoption of common project management frameworks of reference (Eskerod and Riis, 2009).

Domain knowledge, at the head of the list, means experience in the field in which a particular project is being carried out. This area is open to debate, with different

Technical	Managerial	Interpersonal
• business analysis • change control • configuration management • contract management • domain knowledge • estimating • facilitation skills • financial management • meetings management • project planning • report writing • requirements definition • resource scheduling • risk management • vendor management • workshop design and delivery	• communicating skills • decision making • delegating skills • HR management • organisation skills • presentation skills • problem solving and analysis • self-organisation • staff development • stakeholder management • team building • time management	• conflict management • dealing with difficult people • empathy • emotional intelligence • influencing • integrity and honesty • motivational leadership • negotiating skills • relationship building • resilience and adaptability

Figure 59.1 Skills and competencies required (and acquired) in a project management career

viewpoints as to whether one needs domain expertise to deliver projects successfully. For example, could an IT-trained project manager deliver in a construction environment without any construction knowledge?

From observation, the sales pitches of many management consultancies and independent contractors are based largely on this principle, namely that generic project management skills are transferable without the need for specific domain expertise. This ability to apply proven project management techniques in a new domain arguably provides opportunity for personal growth – a basis for project management as a career independent of domain. Of course there are risks in that approach.

Adequate Domain Knowledge and the Dangers of 'Relative Expertise'

Generic project management in a new domain places greater reliance on domain expertise within the team, and the managerial ability to motivate, lead and inspire. This requires the qualities listed in the other areas of Figure 59.1. It also risks overconfidence leading to disaster. At this point, it is relevant to explore some of the findings of human psychology.

Pierce and Cheney (2008, pp. 259–65) discuss the concept of 'generalised obedience'. This refers to the general tendency shown by people to follow instructions given to them by those in positions of authority. It arises from the societal structures in which we all grow up. The experiments of psychologists such as Milgram (1974) demonstrate this concept starkly, even to a degree where individuals overcome their own moral objections in highly extreme circumstances of human suffering. Generalised obedience, as a basic tenet of human behaviour, has implications for the need for appropriate experience in project managers.

When a project situation arises in which this behavioural trait is combined with insufficient actual experience (in project management or domain knowledge), the risk posed to a project by the adage 'a little learning is a dangerous thing' becomes of great relevance (attr. Alexander Pope, 1688–1744). I have formalised this in my 'Price's laws of relative expertise', as follows:

1. In any given situation the individual with the greatest degree of domain knowledge is the relative expert amongst their peers in that situation.
2. An individual's ability to present themselves as the relative expert in a group is not necessarily related to the actual degree of domain knowledge that they possess.
3. The human tendency towards 'generalised obedience' (to authority) presents a risk in situations where a relative expert's perceived ability falls below the minimum required standard.

When unrestrained by a self-awareness of the limits of personal domain knowledge, or unchallenged by someone with more substantive experience, a risk exists that the confidence gained from being a 'relative expert' could lead a project along a dangerous path towards failure. I can illustrate this with an extreme screenplay scenario (similar to the case of the medical student doing advanced surgery on your manager mentioned at the beginning of this chapter).

You are flying home from holiday when the pilots are all incapacitated with food poisoning. 'Is there a pilot on board?' asks the cabin crew. A confident person proclaims 'I'm world champion on the Microsoft Flight Simulator and I've got a 100 per cent safe landing record on the Boeing 737'. At this point, unless someone who has actually flown intervenes, the once-confident person recognises that Microsoft Flight Simulator is not landing a real 737 in a crosswind. You have just experienced someone demonstrating all three laws of relative expertise. Now is a good time to order another gin and tonic and find your life jacket.

Back in the real world, it is thus essential that a project professional with limited domain expertise recognises the risks associated with 'relative expertise' (in themselves and others). An overconfident project manager can soon apply the laws of relative expertise to create a project disaster. Too often, generalised obedience means that nobody will stop them.

Project management professionals who are not technical experts must therefore apply a generous helping of managerial and interpersonal skills to ensure that the whole project team's experience is fully utilised. That means listening to team members who do have the relevant experience and competency.

ACQUIRING TECHNICAL COMPETENCIES AS A CAREER PATH ASPIRATION

The remainder of Figure 59.1's technical competency list looks past the importance of domain knowledge into core project management skills. The competent project professional should be looking to identify the roles, industry sectors, project and business opportunities that will allow them to gain experience in each of these competency areas as part of their career journey.

In some cases a particular skill might involve learning a concept (such as planning to define and structure deliverables into a coherent and achievable series of tasks). It could involve a specific methodology, for example product-based planning. Generally, one should focus on ensuring the concepts are in place before turning to different methods of delivery, although there is no reason why the two cannot be learned together.

But the aspiring project professional should be aware of the limits of their knowledge and ensure that the laws of relative expertise are taken into account. They must seek advice elsewhere if they lack specific skills on a particular project assignment.

MANAGERIAL COMPETENCIES

The managerial competencies in Figure 59.1 distinguish between the procedural and interpersonal skills associated with leadership. Management theorists (for example Thomas, 2004; Pettinger, 2002, p. 469) discuss such differences at length. Both skill sets contribute to career path planning, but the differences between the two should be understood.

Generally speaking, Figure 59.1 lists skills associated with organising and managing oneself and others as managerial competencies. Skills such as presentation, stakeholder management and communication have elements of a technical nature, but are also considered as managerial competencies here because this is where they are most frequently applied in project management.

INTERPERSONAL COMPETENCIES

The human skills associated with working with others are recognised as being at the core of management and leadership development (see for example Pettinger, 2002, pp. 466–491). Of course interpersonal skills are not solely the preserve of the successful project management professional but they are clearly very important for the project team and at all levels of career path planning. Managers who already have these interpersonal skills in abundance from other experience can choose to develop their project management capability by developing technical skills – and learning how to apply their interpersonal skills in the new environment of project management.

Research has identified the way in which interpersonal skills listed have contributed to project success:

- *Influencing skills* – motivating the team by providing greater work challenges has a beneficial effect on project staff and overall project performance, whereas authority-based influence has been shown to have a negative impact (Thamhain and Gemmill, 1974).
- *Emotional intelligence* – managerial competency (see the previous topic) and emotional intelligence as examples of leadership qualities were shown by Geoghegan and Dulewicz (2008) to have a specific link to the achievement of successful outcomes by project managers. Clarke (2010) has shown that emotional intelligence measures and empathy are related to the project manager's effectiveness in managing conflict and teamwork.
- *Personal resilience* – not everything goes well in a project environment. The ability to learn lessons from failures is directly related to the individual's ability to manage their negative emotional reactions (Shepherd and Cardon, 2009). Managing our own reactions when difficulties arise is an essential prerequisite to gaining positive benefits from learning – and is another recognised quality of effective leadership (Thomas, 2004, p. 128).
- *Motivational leadership* – Schmid and Adams (2008) reflect the views of current thinking in their survey of 115 certified project managers, identifying motivation and communication skills by the project manager (particularly at the start of a project) as a crucial factor in project success. Thal and Bedingfield's (2010) study applied psychological research, as set out in Costa and McCrae's (1992) 'Big 5' characteristics of personality. Their observations of 34 project managers at the US Department of Defense found the positive predictors of a project manager's success to be *conscientiousness* (the degree of organisation, persistence and motivation in goal-directed behaviour) and *openness* (the active seeking of experience for its own sake; tolerating and exploring the unfamiliar).

SUMMARY OF THE EFFECT OF SKILLS AND COMPETENCIES ON THE CAREER PATH

The skills and competencies in Figure 59.1 form the foundation for considering specific career paths. They provide guidance on:

1. the three competency groupings relevant to project management careers;

2. an informal 'checklist' of the capabilities required, allowing individuals to assess their personal strengths and weaknesses;
3. the importance of domain knowledge in an effective project team – and the skills required of managerial and interpersonal competency where domain knowledge is not a strong point;
4. the human psychology and behaviours inherent in us all. If unchecked, these can lead to Price's laws of relative expertise increasing the risks of project failure owing to a lack of leadership and managerial competency;
5. the evidence from the literature of links between generic management skills, leadership competencies and project success.

I now want to focus on applying this knowledge as we look at:

- how each career path or role can help us build the required skills;
- how far along the career path we would like, as individuals, to progress;
- how to build a personal plan for our own careers in project management.

Navigating the Career Path

Chapters 15 and 16 discussed project roles at senior and supporting levels. Other chapters provide a general discussion on psychology, skills and competencies plus possible training and qualifications. A career path for project management draws these elements together, looking at the dependencies between them and the implications for personal career planning.

Just as the underlying skills and competencies of project management split into three areas, there are three main routes to a career in project management. These are:

1. the *technical route*, based on specific domain expertise;
2. the *managerial* route, based on business and people skills;
3. the *support route*, based on experience and techniques in project delivery.

Description of these routes will lead inevitably to some generalisation of roles. However, the routes broadly summarise the entry points into a project management career, regardless of project domain.

Before mapping out your own personal career road map, it is sensible to spend some time thinking about where you are starting from, where your strengths and development areas lie and how far you would like to progress. This will help you to identify the most likely entry route, based on your skills, aptitudes and desires. Questions to ask yourself might include:

- Which skills and competencies do I already have?
- Which skills and competencies do I most need to work on?
- Which entry route suits my experience and background, giving me the best chance as I start and develop my career?
- What are my career aspirations? Do I want to progress up the project management hierarchy or find a niche at a certain level?

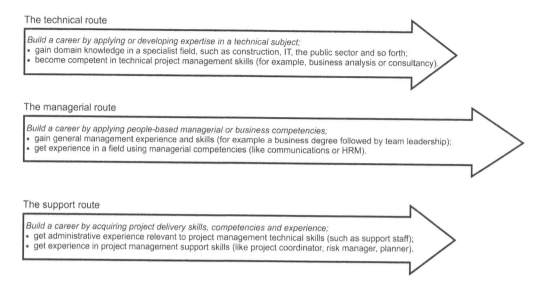

The technical route

Build a career by applying or developing expertise in a technical subject;
- gain domain knowledge in a specialist field, such as construction, IT, the public sector and so forth;
- become competent in technical project management skills (for example, business analysis or consultancy).

The managerial route

Build a career by applying people-based managerial or business competencies;
- gain general management experience and skills (for example a business degree followed by team leadership);
- get experience in a field using managerial competencies (like communications or HRM).

The support route

Build a career by acquiring project delivery skills, competencies and experience;
- get administrative experience relevant to project management technical skills (such as support staff);
- get experience in project management support skills (like project coordinator, risk manager, planner).

Figure 59.2 Characteristics of the three main routes to a project management career

- Am I looking to gain qualifications and accreditation, whether for career progression or personal achievement reasons?

To help with these considerations, Figure 59.2 provides a broad outline of the three career path routes, with some illustrative examples.

CAREER PROGRESSION WITHIN AND ACROSS THE ROUTES INTO PROJECT MANAGEMENT

Many people have highly successful careers in project management as specialists or support professionals, choosing to progress no further up the hierarchy. Success in project management is an individual choice and does not mean that one has to ascend to the mountain summit as a portfolio director or head of programme management. Success includes becoming genuinely competent at your chosen peak level. It means establishing competency through the right balance of skills and experience (not just reading some books so that you can 'say the words').

Thus the choice of career path is a most important complement to the training and accreditation options, enabling the essential hands-on experience on which meaningful accreditation depends.

The Managerial Career Path: A Special Case

The managerial route is something of an exception, in that it cannot be avoided by those who choose to progress up the career hierarchy. If your objective is to climb the rankings, there will come a time when you can progress no further until you have developed some proficiency in the interpersonal and managerial skills. The sharp-eyed reader will have spotted that this is signified in Figure 59.2, where the managerial arrow is longer than the other two routes. But individuals who have followed the managerial route as their natural starting point are likely to find themselves reaching a plateau of career progression if they do not spend sufficient time gaining more than a passing acquaintance with the competencies in the technical and support routes. These are key points to understand before all the pieces of the career jigsaw can be put together.

Now it is time to take a look in more depth at the kinds of roles offered by each route and the way in which training, accreditation and experience combine to form a career path.

THE ROLE OF EXPERIENCE AND TRAINING IN CAREER PROGRESSION

The laws of relative expertise mean that someone can bluff their way through career stages. However, for those seeking true professionalism, a blended approach to training and experience is by far the most robust way to plan a sound career progression. That is illustrated in Figure 59.3.

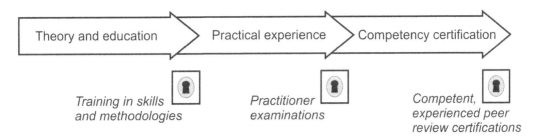

Figure 59.3 The links between training, experience, competence and accreditation

The foundation for gaining experience comes from having appropriate theoretical training, taught in a manner that relates to a specific personal need. This training must happen at the right time, which means *before* having to perform to satisfy that personal need. This is a basic point worth hammering home repeatedly because this common sense view does not appear to be universally held in all organisations.

Some managers seem to believe that staff should be able to absorb knowledge magically (and without making any mistakes) in areas they've never been shown before. These managers should be referred to Bunch (2007) for a myriad of references to research that show 'a strong link between the credibility of training and demonstrable training effectiveness'. Bunch also gives a good discussion on how training failure is linked to organisational culture. These same errant managers might also be interested in findings that identified insufficient training as early warning signs for IT project failures (Kappelman et al., 2006).

Failure of managerial common sense here is undoubtedly linked to the increased manifestation of Murphy's Law (if things can go wrong, they will). This has a nasty habit of derailing projects, leading to a poorer return on investment than would ever have been the case from the cost of an appropriate training investment.

Reinforcing training with practical experience is essential in all three career routes, regardless of the level of advancement. The reasons for this include:

- human beings, like all animals, learn by trial and error and it requires us to see, imitate and experience to achieve learning (Pierce and Cheney, 2008, p. 15, p. 256);
- we acquire interpersonal skills in the process of applying theory in practice, widening our general skills;
- career progression is enhanced by additional credentials and 'real world' experience of applying tools, techniques and skills in a particular sector;
- personal experience enhances trial and error learning, providing a wider base of experience for application in practitioner accreditations;
- personal confidence, interpersonal relationships and continuing professional development opportunities are encountered, extending individual experience.

PROFESSIONAL ACCREDITATIONS: BADGES TO COLLECT OR COMPETENCY ASSESSMENTS?

Figure 59.3 links experience to different types of professional accreditation. This is worth discussing, as it relates both to the point made in the previous section and to the worrying tendency among some to mistake 'credential shopping' for a valid demonstration of professional competence. It is professional experience gained from a career path that demonstrates whether the certificates held are worth the paper they're printed on.

A mini-industry exists around the 'handy hint' guides that support the 'fast track' project manager who has chosen to collect qualifications as quickly as possible. Contrast that with the individual who has used accreditation to support their understanding of the *why and how* behind the core concepts of project management. Then we see a difference between the wisdom of knowing how to apply their knowledge of methodology '*x*', rather than merely the deployment of a kitbag of paperwork templates. Figure 59.3 makes the point that it is not the qualification alone that demonstrates competence, but the manner in which it has been obtained and applied.

Basic training provides essential knowledge. Experience allows this to be developed, leading to *understanding*. A practitioner-level qualification validates this real, applied understanding, whilst further experience allows higher standards of certified accreditation based on peer review. This approach lets the individual demonstrate judgement and application in extending their skills into new areas.

The result is a higher quality of learning for the individual, a general raising of standards and faith in the value of accreditations. Most importantly, it leads to better project outcomes, achieved by experienced individuals who minimise risk by demonstrating their competence. Not a bad club in which to enjoy membership!

THE CAREER PROGRESSION HIERARCHY

I have described how training and experience are a good grounding for a chosen career path. Now I want to describe the roles found in each route. Clearly I cannot cover all circumstances because job titles and duties differ greatly between organisations. However, Figure 59.4 illustrates typical roles found in each of the three career progression paths. I shall look in general terms at how these different roles provide opportunities to develop the skills and competencies listed earlier in Figure 59.1. I shall also extend that into the natural career hierarchy that exists between the various roles.

Support Roles

Support roles provide tremendous opportunities for people to develop a solid foundation in the technical skills listed in Figure 59.1. In many cases roles such as project coordinator, administrator or assistant give an oversight into the entire process of running a project or programme. With specific career paths available in areas like a project management office, a broad base of general experience can be built that stands an individual in good stead throughout their career.

More specialism is also available, with many support roles being responsible for tools such as risk and issue registers, reporting, configuration and library management. Roles such as communications, change assistants and project planners provide opportunities to deepen skills in a specific technical area.

Support roles also provide a natural platform for developing interpersonal skills and competencies, through their widespread communication with members across the project team and at all levels in the hierarchy.

Whilst some might argue that many support roles are at the more mundane, administrative end of a project, there is the obvious riposte on two fronts:

1. They teach the essential skills and competencies that underpin many of the technical project management elements required for leadership. The importance of knowing why and how to deliver core project activity is critical to future leadership success.
2. Senior programme or project managers frequently tell you how a highly competent project assistant has 'saved their bacon' on a regular basis. It is the support team's proficiency in the basic tools that provides the 'oil between the gears' of highly complex, multi-stream projects.

Highly talented support staff are worth their weight in gold, whereas poorly skilled support teams can drag your programme into an administrative quagmire of inefficiency. Effective support staff provide the life-blood of a project or programme and this is a point never to be forgotten – whatever the level of project management to which you aspire.

Technical Roles

The technical roles box in Figure 59.4 might seem light on job titles, but 'subject matter expert' covers a multitude of industry-specific job titles. For the purposes of this discussion, there is a fine distinction between some support and technical roles. Looking back at the rationale for our definitions, roles such as business analyst or change management analyst provide a greater depth of domain knowledge, exposing the individual to the more specialist skills and competencies listed in the technical box of Figure 59.1. It is in these kinds of roles that more domain-specific techniques, such as business analysis,

Support roles	Technical roles	Managerial roles

• project coordinator
• project assistant
• risk analyst
• communications assistant
• project administrator
• project librarian
• project planner
• project HR/resource manager
	• business analyst
	• change management analyst
	• subject matter expert
	• business change manager/
	  change manager
		• work package/work stream
		  leader
		• assistant project manager
		• project manager
		• senior project manager
		• programme manager
		• PMO manager
		• portfolio manager
		• programme director
		• head of unit
		• general manager
		• senior executive/director

Figure 59.4 Typical roles within the three career routes

financial management, project accounting, procurement and contract management can be developed.

Other areas of domain expertise are dependent upon the field in which the project or programme is operating. This gives a whole range of technical specialisms on which entire careers can be built, such as software development, hardware design and network engineering in the IT industry. Similarly, construction, public sector vocations and virtually any other industry that one can name will have their own technical specialisms required within a project. Domain professional expertise plays a significant part in the technical route into a project management career path for many people.

There is widespread opportunity to develop both interpersonal and managerial skills in the technical route, as soon as one gains opportunities to take responsibility for other team members. This provides a natural stepping stone into the managerial route for those interested in following that path.

Managerial Roles

The managerial career route includes many of the higher-level leadership roles, reinforcing the point that progression at this level requires candidates to have aptitude and ability in the broad range of skills shown in Figure 59.1

Typical roles provide a natural career hierarchy in which individuals can develop their skills in management and leadership. By taking responsibility for a particular technical deliverable or work package, the opportunity to develop managerial skills and be accountable for the results of a team emerges. Thus transition from a technical specialist or support career path into a managerial career path can be achieved by developing leadership skills to complement a technical base.

In all three routes – managerial, technical and support – there is a wide range of accreditations that support career progression. These include trade qualifications (for example chartered engineering status or competence in the Business Analysis Body of Knowledge) or a technical product certification, such as Microsoft Certified Systems Engineer (MCSE).

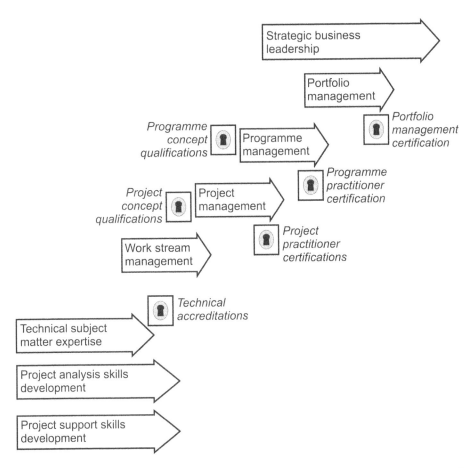

Figure 59.5 The career hierarchy of skills, project leadership and accreditations

The Hierarchy of Career Progression

Figure 59.5 provides the final piece to complete the career path jigsaw. This illustrates the points already made, showing the support, technical and managerial routes against the relative hierarchy of career progression. The diagram shows the essential foundations that the technical and support routes provide to more advanced managerial careers.

For those choosing a career path within support or technical roles, it is the progression to work stream/work package management that marks the boundary with the managerial route. Thenceforth, development in the interpersonal and leadership competencies becomes a prerequisite for further success and advancement.

Figure 59.5 also illustrates how qualifications and accreditations support advancement through the career path. This shows how my earlier discussion around the acquisition of 'concept' qualifications at the start of a role, backed by subsequent experience, provides practitioner validation on the way up the hierarchy.

Whilst there is no explicit bar to stepping over a particular role on your route, the transition from work stream – to project – to programme – to portfolio is a natural progression. Experience in each preceding role will inevitably make you more competent at each new rung of the career ladder.

STRATEGIC BUSINESS LEADERSHIP: TOP OF THE TREE?

Now, here's a debate undoubtedly held at every water cooler on the face of the planet – just how much experience does one's boss really have! Figure 59.5 appears to indicate that a good understanding of project management is a prerequisite to taking on decision-making business roles in a leadership environment. As I have shown in earlier discussions, belief in project management is not (unfortunately) a prerequisite for attaining a leadership role in business.

Senior business leaders must have an immense wealth of interpersonal and leadership skills for them to have attained their positions. For such individuals reading this who have no project management experience, this chapter highlights the value that such experience can add to your own career, and to the careers of your subordinates.

This does not mean you have to drop to the bottom of the chain and work your way back up to become proficient at project management. However, in your role as a project sponsor or a business champion of projects (discussed in chapters 4 and 5), you will need to have a good understanding of how project management helps your business perform and why it is a valuable and necessary career route for your staff.

For those reading who may already be following a project management career path and are focused on senior business leadership, this chapter gives a view of how your background will add value to future decision making when you do make it to the boardroom table.

Preparing Your Personal Career Plan

For this exercise you will need to have Figures 59.1, 59.2, 59.4 and 59.5 at close hand.

Using the information in this book to suit your own circumstances, write down your answers to the following questions:

1. Where am I now in my career and where do I want to be?
2. Which skills and competencies in Figure 59.1 correspond to my own personal strengths and weaknesses (list in two columns)?
3. Which skills and competencies do I need (or want) to develop?
4. Which of the career routes in Figure 59.2 is the most natural fit to my skills and experience? Which most reflects my ultimate career ambition?
5. Which types of role in Figure 59.5 most represent (a) my current level of experience; and (b) the areas most likely to give me the development experience I need (after listing them, sort them into a suitable sequence)?
6. Where in the hierarchy of Figure 59.5 is my chosen career goal?

Now, to break all this information down into a series of manageable steps, write down answers to the following, for each of the roles you listed when answering question 5:

• Which skills and competencies do I need to develop at each step?

- Which roles/industry sectors/geographies are likely to help me gain the experience I need to be promoted to the next level?
- What relevant training shall I need to build my skills in each new role?
- What professional accreditations should I seek to achieve in each role when I apply my training in practice, and what experience do I need to gain?

Now for a cross check. Ensure that you are clear on your (current) ultimate career goal and the position from which you are starting. You should now have the basis of a career path that covers (in this order):

1. the skills and competencies that are your greatest strengths today;
2. the skills and competencies you most want, and need, to develop;
3. the roles in the three career streams that link to your development needs;
4. an 'order of battle' for progressing through the role hierarchy;
5. an understanding of the training, experience and accreditations that will support you in the journey (giving self-assurance and independent evidence of your professional competence).

Congratulations on a well-structured career plan. Now go out there and show them how it's done properly.

Acknowledgements

I acknowledge with much gratitude assistance by way of discussion and reviews in the preparation of this chapter from Dr Catherine Haddon, Miss Emma Rogers, Miss Kate Symons and Mr Mark Plant. They all gave their opinions and time freely and without hesitation.

References and Further Reading

Association for Project Management (2008), *APM Body of Knowledge*, 5th edn, High Wycombe: APM Publications.

Bunch, K.J. (2007), 'Training failure as a consequence of organizational culture', *Human Resource Development Review*, 6(2), 142–63.

Clarke, N. (2010), 'Emotional intelligence and its relationship to transformational leadership and key project manager competences', *Project Management Journal*, 41(2), 5–20.

Costa, P.T. Jr and McCrae, R.R. (1992), *Revised NEO Personality Inventory (NEO-PI-R) and NEO Five-Factor Inventory (NEO-FFI) Professional Manual*, Odessa, FL: Psychological Assessment Resources.

Eskerod, P. and Riis, E. (2009), 'Value creation by building an intraorganizational common frame of reference concerning project management', *Project Management Journal*, 40(3), 6–13.

Ford, R. (2009), 'Spectacular IT failure costs taxpayer millions', *The Sunday Times*, 12 March 2009.

Geoghegan, L. and Dulewicz, V. (2008), 'Do project managers' leadership competencies contribute to project success?', *Project Management Journal*, 39(4), 58–67.

Kappelman, L.A., McKeeman, R. and Zhang, L. (2006), 'Early warning signs of IT project failure: The dominant dozen', *Information Systems Management*, 23(4), 31–36.

McManus, J. and Wood-Harper, T. (2007), 'Understanding the sources of information systems project failure', *Management Services*, 1–6.

Milgram, S. (1963), 'Behavioral study of obedience', *Journal of Abnormal Psychology*, 67, (1963), 371–8.

Milgram, S. (1974), *Obedience to Authority: An Experimental View*, London: Harper Collins.

O'Neill, R. (2005), 'Verdict on a $64m project failure', *Sydney Morning Herald*, 15 April 2005. Available at: http://www.smh.com.au/news/Breaking/Verdict-on-a-64m-project-failure/2005/04/15/1113509904098.html

Pettinger, R. (2002), *Introduction to Management*, New York: Palgrave.

Pierce, W.D. and Cheney, C.D. (2008), *Behavioural Analysis and Learning*, 4th edn, New York: Psychology Press.

Schmid, B. and Adams, J. (2008), 'Motivation in project management: The project manager's perspective', *Project Management Journal*, 39(2), 60–71.

Shepherd, D.A. and Cardon, M.S. (2009), 'Negative emotional reactions to project failure and the self-compassion to learn from the experience', *Journal of Management Studies*, 46(6), 923–49.

Thal, A.E. Jr and Bedingfield, J.D. (2010), 'Successful project managers: An exploratory study into the impact of personality', *Technology Analysis & Strategic Management*, 22(2), 243–59.

Thamhain, H.J. and Gemmill, G.R. (1974), 'Influence styles of project managers: Some project performance correlates', in M.A. Rahim, R.T. Golembiewski and K.D. Mackenzie (eds), *Academy of Management Journal*, 17(2), 216–24.

Thomas, N. (2004), *The John Adair Handbook of Management and Leadership*, London: Thorogood.

60 Project Management Certification: Taking Charge Locally

MICHAEL GREER

Editorial Comment (DL/LS)

The views expressed in this chapter are entirely those of the author. Clearly neither we nor the publishers can possibly agree with all the comments and advice given. However, there is plenty of good food for thought here. The author makes a convincing case for the fact that some staff selection procedures will cause applicants to be rejected, even though they might be perfectly qualified through their reputation, experience and track record to fill the vacancies on offer. The only thing that these failed applicants do not possess is accredited certification.

Introduction

No one can make you feel inferior without your consent. (Eleanor Roosevelt)

During the course of this chapter I shall try to answer three questions:

1. How does competence differ from certification?
2. Instead of jumping through some artificial hoops erected by one or another certifying organisation, why should I not simply bestow upon myself my own, unique project management (PM) certification based on my experiences and my track record?
3. How can I easily construct a 'do-it-yourself' PM certification so that it is a completely credible, detailed, accurate and defensible representation of all the PM skills I possess?

Competence v. Certification

I am going to begin with a couple of examples that illustrate how competence operates in the real world. Then I shall show how certifications are often applied (and sometimes misapplied) to measure and validate competence.

ALMOST EVERYONE IS COMPETENT AT SOME LEVEL

Imagine you are shipwrecked on an island. You need shelter from the sun, wind and prowling night creatures. You find a few tools and materials in the ship's wreckage. You cobble together a rough shelter that meets your simple needs. You survive.

Now imagine that you are the head of a pioneer family, heading out into vast unexplored regions of a new land. You will be taking along some livestock and seeds for crops. Before you leave civilisation, you assemble a few sturdy tools and materials to help you set up your homestead. After months of travel, alone in a strange land, you work with your family to build a small farm that provides shelter for yourselves and your livestock, as well as crude, but efficient, facilities to store your harvest and tools. You survive.

Now let your imagination 'fast-forward' for a couple of decades. Imagine that other people have arrived nearby. Your little pioneer family has acquired some friendly neighbours. Over time a small settlement has evolved, complete with merchants, a bank, craftsmen and a medical doctor. Now that your farm is thriving, you would like to add a bigger barn. So you find a local carpenter who has a solid track record of building large, strong structures. You hire them to help you build that new barn. You survive and continue to thrive.

In each of the three scenarios above, that most amazing tool of all – the human mind – was applied to accomplish an important goal. In all three cases, the goal was met. Shelter and survival, in varying degrees of complexity, were attained. More importantly, 'just enough' sophistication was used in each situation. The shipwreck survivor's crude shelter, the pioneer family's simple homestead, the farmer family's carpenter-designed barn – each of these solutions was appropriate and effective for the circumstances. And in each case, some level of competence – enough to do the job – was clearly present.

COMPETENCE WITHOUT FORMAL CERTIFICATION OR EXTERNAL VALIDATION

Now please turn your attention to today. For most people, the idea of building or adding to your home can be intimidating. After all, there are licensed building contractors who can provide certified craftspeople and help to ensure that your new structure will meet local building regulations and so forth. Viewed in this context, it seems that building anything for our homes is fairly complicated. So most of us avoid it.

However, you can walk into a do-it-yourself store and buy exactly the same materials and supplies that the licensed and certified builders use. In fact, you can even buy (or at least rent) most of the more powerful, sophisticated tools that help give them their professional results. What's more, there are many books, free 'how-to' articles, brief tutorials and extended classes online that can help you to learn to use all these materials, supplies and tools to get near-professional results all by yourself.

If you are like some people who have successfully completed their first do-it-yourself home improvement project, you might discover that it's really not such a big deal. In fact, you might even like it! You might enjoy the challenge and sense of accomplishment that comes from learning new skills and mastering new tools. Also, you could find that you want to tackle more projects. Better still, you may have learned that you need only three things to cross the boundary into the land of professional practice:

1. Professional-grade tools and materials.
2. Guidance from accurate information or tutoring.
3. Practice in doing what the professional does.

The more you think about that, the more you will come to realise that because it was your house you worked on, your money for materials and tools that you spent, and your own time that you invested on the project, there were three things that you did not need to succeed in that project:

1. You did not need anyone else's blessing that you had enough skill to do the job.
2. You did not need to score a pass mark on a test proving your ability to recite professional definitions and concepts.
3. You did not need a formal certification bestowed by a dues-paying group of professionals.

In short, when you acquire the same tools, information, and practice used by professionals, then you do not need external validation to get professional results. You simply set to work, evaluate your own progress, and get judge-for-yourself professional results working on your own, self-contained project. External validation is simply not needed.

FORCES CONSPIRING AGAINST DO-IT-YOURSELF COMPETENCE

By now you are probably thinking: 'All right, what if I am able to remodel my own kitchen? How am I going to get the local building inspector to approve the wiring – or approve the water and sewerage connections?'

Well, here's the deal: the local building inspector is interested in results. They usually don't care how you achieve them. So you simply find out what the local codes require for electrical installation, water and sewerage. Then you keep these in mind when you buy materials and do your construction. The codes outline the specifications; you simply follow them.

Unfortunately, it is at this point when many do-it-yourselfers might panic and give up on this part of their project. They consider that it's easier simply to hire a licensed electrician and a licensed plumber. And they may be right. It all depends on how far they want to develop their own evolving do-it-yourself skills. If they are satisfied doing everything except the electrical and the plumbing, then they can hire someone to do these things for them.

So here's the thing: external forces sometimes conspire against your acquisition of good old-fashioned do-it-yourself competence. Local building codes make things much more complicated than they were for the pioneer and his family. And local licensing requirements for electricians and plumbers mean that a cadre of specialists has evolved to do the work, so that the finished product will pass all the local inspections. As a result, many people avoid 'do-it-yourself' plumbing and electrical work.

The same is true in many other endeavours. You cannot perform surgery without a licence. And in some jurisdictions you cannot serve meals to the public without passing a health department inspection. Nor can you design and build a bridge without employing all sorts of licensed professionals and passing many safety inspections. These kinds of certifications and inspections, like the home-building electrical and plumbing guidelines, all make sense. They protect the public from harm and the community from disasters. So you would not want 'do-it-yourself' licensing and inspection to be practised in these areas. After all, public health and safety is at stake, so external standards and certifications are needed as valuable cross-checks.

But do all external certifications make sense? In particular, does it really matter if project managers are certified by one of the many external certifying bodies if they can perform the unique PM skills needed in their organisations? *I don't think so!*

I've made the case elsewhere that all good PM is 'local'. By that I mean that when good project managers apply their skills, they are using only those PM techniques that make sense for their particular organisation. Good project managers and workers in most organisations will not tolerate irrelevant PM esoterica simply because it has been recommended by some external certifying body. Effective project managers only do the PM stuff that matters locally.

Because this local emphasis is key to PM success, it follows that your unique, home-grown, do-it-yourself set of PM skills has more value to your organisation than the generic collection of skills validated in those external certifications. Those professional certifying bodies (the ones that assign those initials after your name when you pass their exams) typically do not focus on your home-grown PM skills. Still, your supervisors and HR department might want some sort of proof that you know your PM stuff. So maybe it's time you did a little formal self-validation!

How Certifications are Created and Sold

Later in this chapter I am going to recommend some specific steps you can take to self-certify your unique PM skills. But first I should like to share some behind-the-scenes insights into how certifications are created and used. These will help you make more sense of the self-certification steps I suggest later.

For the record, I know what I'm talking about here. I have participated as an external consultant in either creating from scratch, or quality-assuring, both public (essentially 'for profit') and proprietary ('in house') certification programmes. This is because I started out my professional life in the training (or more specifically 'performance improvement') business. Training and performance improvement are based on clearly identifying the skill requirements of a particular group of people. I have worked with many clients to identify missing PM skills in their organisations and then create customised PM workshops to help their people acquire those missing skills.

So I have been 'floating around' in lists of skills and competencies for most of my professional life. And this I know for certain: lists of skills inevitably seem to lead to certifications that 'officially' dub the holder of these skills as 'certified' in the eyes of someone.

TEN STEPS USED BY PROFESSIONAL ASSOCIATIONS FOR CREATING A CERTIFICATION FRAMEWORK

So how do you get from a simple skills list to a formal certification? The typical process used by professional associations for creating a certification can be summarised in 10 steps:

1. Interview and observe top-performers, experts and high-achievers who perform a particular set of skills that make up a profession or a 'want to be' profession.
2. Document and assemble these skills into a comprehensive list, often arranging them in clusters or hierarchies. If appropriate, break the clusters into such divisions as 'entry level', 'fully competent', 'senior level', 'mentor level' and so on.
3. Send a first draft of this skill list to everyone who was interviewed or observed, as well as supervisors, customers and peers who frequently work with the group to be certified. Ask them to review the list. Note their suggestions for revision.
4. Interview everyone contacted in Step 3 and get their feedback – especially their suggestions for revision.
5. Make revisions.
6. Circulate the list again, get feedback and revise. Repeat Steps 3–5 until everyone is happy with the finished product.
7. Finalise the comprehensive skill list.
8. Develop the following means of measuring and validating whether any individual has the skills listed:
   - observation checklists and guidelines;
   - supervisor interview questions;
   - objective tests of knowledge (true-false, multiple choice, essay and so on);
   - documentation of 'real world' on-the-job skills that are part of the list.
9. Establish a support infrastructure and/or designated roles for those who will be bestowing the certification. Typically, the following will be needed:
   - someone to assemble and maintain the skill list(s), measurement guidelines and other tools created in Step 8;
   - someone to conduct measurements identified in Step 8;
   - someone to create and maintain records of results of measurements;
   - someone to create and provide certificates;
   - someone to maintain a list of officially certified individuals.
10. Establish a renewal process in which certified individuals are continually re-evaluated and asked to provide:
   - recurring proof of competence or practice in the skill set;
   - proof of formal classes related to the skill set ('continuing education').

ACQUIRING CREDIBILITY AND POWER FOR THE CERTIFICATION

After the certification has been created, its creators will typically want it to be adopted as widely as possible. They want it to acquire credibility and power. Here are some things they do to attain credibility and power for a certification:

- get large, influential companies to require the certification to be held by certain classes of workers;
- get government agency buyers to require the certification of their contractors;
- get professional organisations to endorse the certification;
- get government agencies to endorse the certification for their staffs;
- get worldwide bodies to endorse the certification and link to global professions.

MARKETING THE CERTIFICATION

Now it is time for a marketing campaign to spread the word about the certification, to support its attainment, and to develop a revenue stream related to the certification. The certification creators typically do many of the following:

- establish a website;
- create a professional association to synchronise with the certification;
- sell renewable memberships to this association and establish fees for certification exams, evaluations, renewals and so forth;
- create different levels of certification to make it easier to qualify in smaller steps, whilst increasing the opportunities for testing, collecting test fees and so on;
- create publications (some free, some for sale);
- create specific training to support the certification (usually offered for a fee);
- license consultants and trainers to essentially 'teach to the test' and/or provide 'certified' training in support of the certification;
- encourage a cottage industry of teach-to-the-test companies that will market the certification themselves;
- encourage certified people to write articles, promote themselves, and, indirectly or directly, promote the value of the certification (this is often done by publishing their works through the certifying body's website, magazine and so on);
- give certified people a role in the certification process (or the certifying body's management team) to increase their loyalty and enthusiasm for the certification;
- create a lobbying group to help promote the certification in regulatory requirements, government agency contracting and so on.

As you can see from the above, there is a good chance that the number of people involved in managing the certification (or advocating it because they have worked hard to achieve it and thus feel that they have invested personally in it) will eventually reach a critical mass. When that happens, the certification develops a life of its own! It becomes 'the thing to do' if you want to get ahead in a particular field. The question of whether it has any practical, on-the-job value or is it simply pushing people to jump through a bunch of esoteric hoops – well, that question never gets asked in polite company. There's simply too much at stake for everyone involved.

Should You Certify Yourself?

To recapitulate, I have established that an enormous amount of energy has to be invested in establishing and maintaining certification programmes. And all this energy creates considerable momentum. The more popular certifications have become real juggernauts. And before you know it your individual competence – your unique collection of skills, as lean and appropriate as they might be for your work – can be made to appear trivial, simply because you lack the appropriate certification's initials after your name.

At this point, Scarecrow in the *Wizard of Oz* comes to mind. As he eventually learned for himself (but did not realise until very late in the story), he knew everything he needed to know to achieve his goals. He simply lacked a shiny badge to hang around his neck!

So how about you? Are you ready to give yourself the shiny badge of certification that you know, deep in your heart that you've earned through your own self-directed study and on-the-job effort? Are you ready for your do-it-yourself PM certification? If so, read on.

How to Create your own PM Certification

Now you are ready to create your do-it-yourself PM certification. At this point, I have some good news and some bad news.

THE GOOD NEWS

The good news is that most of the work of articulating PM skills (that is, properly wording them in terms that the HR folks and performance reviewers will like) and collecting them together in one place has already been done. In fact, that's very good news indeed, since this is the hardest and most tedious part of creating any certification. I certainly would not do it without being paid a lot of money. It would take quite a long time and much tiresome wordsmithing to pull together the giant, well-documented lists that have already been assembled by the various professional PM certifying bodies.

Better still, these lists have been peer-reviewed to death. So you will not need to engage in all those endless, how-many-PM-angels-can-fit-on-the-head-of-a-pin discussions that the original list-makers had to endure. In other words, these lists have been argued over and shaken down. And they are generally respected by most people practising PM. In short, they come pre-approved and respected!

THE BAD NEWS

The *bad news* is that you will have to spend time digging through the aforementioned lists and relating them to your own particular set of skills in order to create your own PM certification. This is not nearly as time-consuming or tedious as building the lists from scratch. Also, it will not take you as long as slogging your way through the process of getting some external certification. But you will probably still find it boring.

BENEFITS OF BUILDING YOUR OWN CUSTOMISED PM CERTIFICATION

Now we know that all this might be tedious work. But here are the benefits of building a well-documented, customised PM certification for yourself:

1. It's free. All you need to spend is your time.
2. It will allow you to show how your unique PM skills are exactly relevant to your unique industry, organisation and job.
3. It will help your managers and HR people to comprehend better your strengths and express them on your performance reviews, by giving them the specifics they need to evaluate your achievements in a fine-grained way.
4. It is likely to be a powerful networking experience, because it will involve contacting people for whom you've worked and who can vouch for your wonderful skills and abilities.

5. It's faster and it's focused on you. You will not spend years studying and taking tests on a bunch of PM esoterica that has no relevance to your particular PM practices.

If you really try, you can probably certify yourself, including pulling together all the documentation and endorsements, in a month or two. (This assumes just a few hours per week actually working on this chore, as well as calendar time circulating documents among the people who will be helping you.) It might help you identify a few new skills you need to acquire.

THE SPECIFIC STEPS FOR DO-IT-YOURSELF PM CERTIFICATION

Now I am going to list the steps you need to take if you have decided that the benefits listed above will justify your effort in the do-it-yourself process. Note that this process is not a quick-and-dirty substitute for 'real' certification. The steps outlined here are derived from my own professional work in this arena, for which I have been paid large sums of money! If you follow these steps, you will produce a solid, credible certification – one that you can defend and use to prove you have the same PM skills acquired by those people who do have PM certification initials after their names.

Step 1: Find a Comprehensive List of Generic PM Skills That Seem to Cover Most of Your Own Unique PM Skills

Here are some online sources to help you. Those prefixed ** are probably the most practical and easy for you to use. I recommend that you start with the first listed:

* ** American Society for the Advancement of Project Management (ASAPM) PM CompModel. This is a well-produced model that I reviewed and helped a little to shape in its early stages. It is quite comprehensive and probably all you need. Click the link under the heading 'Free for Visitors' at http://www.asapm.org/edu/e_compmodel3. asp
* ** GAPPS (Global Alliance for Project Performance Standards) Project Manager Standards – 'Free, open-source, competency-based standards for PM' at http://www. globalpmstandards.org/main/page_project_manager_standard.html.
* The popular certification suppliers listed below overwhelmed me with marketing and training sales pitches and are probably best ignored. They may have succinct lists of PM skills buried somewhere at their websites, but I could not find them. If you want to look for these yourself, you can start here:
* Prince2 at http://www.prince2.com/default.asp, or see the following Wikipedia article for an overview: http://en.wikipedia.org/wiki/PRINCE2
* PMI (Project Management Institute) at http://www.pmi.org/
* PMBOK (PMI's *Guide to the Project Management Body of Knowledge*). This is the PMI's main reference work. It is by definition focused on *knowledge*, as opposed to *skills*. However, if you would like to see how the various knowledge areas are organised and get a sense of their implications for your unique PM skills, you can download the 189-page 1996 edition for free. (There are a few changes in the latest versions, but you'll

have to pay a fee to acquire these). For the free option go to: http://www.unipi.gr/akad_tmhm/biom_dioik_tech/files/pmbok.pdf

- ** My own *Summary of Key Project Manager Actions and Results*. I created this easy-to-use, one-page table of 20 essential PM skills back in 1996, when I was developing my HRD-Press best-selling book, *The Project Manager's Partner*. The book has 57 tools to help you perform all the skills in this list. I created this list by 'squeezing the performance juice' out of PMI's PMBOK. My free one-page list of skills is at: http://michaelgreer.biz/?p=118

Step 2: Study Your Chosen List of Skills

Endure and unravel any 'professional speak' and jargon used by the list creators. Don't let it intimidate you. If you need some bit of PM esoterica translated, look it up. Max Wideman's glossary is a great place to start (see *Wideman's Comparative Glossary of Project Management Terms* at: http://www.maxwideman.com/pmglossary/index.htm).

Unpack the concepts that are imbedded in the skill statements and make some notes to yourself about how, despite the high-sounding terminology used, you really are competent in these skills yourself – indeed, maybe you perform them very well. Make sure you understand the PM vision and values implied in the list.

Make notes that capture any new insights you find in the meaning of your current PM skills and any new vocabulary you should be using to express the PM chores you know you are competently performing. (After all, if you get more respect as a 'sanitary engineer', why call yourself a garbage collector?)

Download PDF files, do screen captures, cut and paste, and, if necessary, try optical character recognition (OCR) conversion of relevant documents to help you more quickly assemble your skill list.

Tidy up this list and use it as the foundation for creating your own, unique, comprehensive list of PM skills.

Step 3: Sort and Edit the Skills List

Sort and cluster the list of skills so that it shows broad areas of competency and is easier for non-PM people (such as administrators and HR) to understand.

Find an ally who is a 'nit-picker' who can go over your list and challenge your language and assumptions. Then edit and revise your list accordingly.

Have someone who is a good copy-editor (someone who knows when to use a semi-colon versus a dash) edit your list.

Step 4: Get Your Comprehensive List of PM Skills Attested

Contact supervisors, respected colleagues, experts, customers or anyone who can credibly vouch for your ability to perform any of the skills on your list and ask them to do the following:

- Review the list and place a check mark and their initials beside each skill which they have observed you performing effectively (or have witnessed the results following you performing effectively).
- Sign a statement that reads: 'I have observed (or witnessed the results of) the on-the-job performance of [*insert your name here*] in the role of Project Manager or Project Team Leader. I can personally confirm that [s/he] is fully competent in completing all skills I have initialled in the previous list'.

Do not fail to thank all these people for their time. You owe it to them (perhaps you should give them a lunch?).

Step 5: Summarise and Edit the Annotated List of Skills

Following Step 4 you should now have a list of all your possible skills, with some annotated to attest to your competence. Now you must strike out those skills without such annotations. That will leave you with a single, comprehensive list of your PM skills that you can confidently say are certified (validated) by the people who have seen your work.

Step 6: Make Your Skills List Look Professional

Make your skills list pretty and easy to read by using lots of white space, appropriate unfussy fonts and so on. Give your list a name, such as 'Terry Smith's Certified Project Management Skills and Competencies' (assuming, of course that your name is Terry Smith). Then archive the list.

Step 7: Prepare Your Certificate

Create a title for your PM certification and an associated physical certificate, suitable for framing.

Suggested titles for a person called Terry Smith are:

- The Terry Smith PM Certification (TSPMC);
- Certificate of Project Management Competency (CPMC);
- Terry Smith's Professional Project Management Certification (PPMC).

Some sample certificate templates which you can edit are available online as follows:

- *MS Word versions*: http://office.microsoft.com/en-us/templates/CT010356390.aspx
- *MS PowerPoint versions*: http://www.brainybetty.com/certificates.htm

Make sure that your certificate is signed by your most well-respected senior manager(s) who signed the earlier document validating your skills. Now you can frame your certificate.

IMPLEMENTING YOUR NEW SELF-CERTIFICATION

Meet with your supervisor and the HR people and walk them through the self-certification process that you have just completed. Explain in detail how you completed the seven steps listed above. Show them your certificate and all the supporting documentation. Ask them to incorporate this certification in your future performance reviews or other formal employee records. Now you can celebrate your certification.

Conclusion

Earlier I asserted and recommended that HR and training people, as well as those individuals seeking to upgrade their PM skills should (at least, for the present) ignore the certifications put forth by the PM profession. They should focus instead on simply using the lists of competencies that underlie those certifications as inputs to their own PM performance improvement processes. Remember that you need only three things to achieve professional results:

1. professional-grade tools and materials;
2. the guidance of accurate information or tutoring;
3. practice in doing what the professional does.

In the field of PM all three of these are available to you free of charge or at very low cost. More importantly, they are available to you as an individual, regardless of your membership in any PM-related organisation or exclusive dues-paying club. You simply need to go after these things and spend time practising PM in your own, real-world projects. What you will achieve is PM competency – PM skills – completely on your own terms. You can then use the steps outlined earlier to document and certify your competency – again, on your own terms.

I have said that there are three things you do not need in order to achieve professional results:

1. You don't need anyone's blessing that you have enough skill to do the job.
2. You don't need to achieve a passing score on a test proving your ability to recite professional definitions and concepts.
3. You don't need a formal certification bestowed by a dues-paying group of professionals.

Still, you might be put under pressure to 'prove' yourself worthy of that PM-related job title or pay grade. If that should be the case, then you can save a lot of time and money by simply following the steps listed above to create your own PM certification. In this way you can document your skills and get the credibility you've earned without jumping through someone else's hoops.

SOME FINAL THOUGHTS ADDRESSED TO HR PEOPLE

Some of you have willingly handed over your authority to evaluate your organisation's project managers to external certification bodies. I can understand this. These external certification bodies have, in many cases, 'puffed up' the field of PM to make it appear so vastly complicated that no one can understand it except them and their highly-skilled members. At the same time, they have spawned extensive educate–test–certify–re-educate–retest–recertify infrastructures and cottage industries of teach-to-the-test consultants who stand ready to take over the 'highly complex' process of training and evaluating your project managers. This PM certification and training machine will be more than happy to help you, and to maintain an ongoing relationship with you (their eternally-dependent client) for years and years.

So it no doubt seems to be far easier simply to put your project managers into their PM certification pipeline than it is to create and apply your own home-grown, locally-relevant PM performance review and support. Never mind that your own, unique PM performance criteria are likely to be:

1. leaner and less complex;
2. targeted to your organisational strategies and mission;
3. free to acquire and monitor;
4. part of your own, unique, organisation-specific PM career path and training efforts.

Now, HR people – are you really going to let these PM certification organisations push you into spending bunches of money and loads of person-hours going after generic PM skills, some of which will be of no use in your organisation?

References and Further Reading

ONLINE REFERENCES CREATED BY MICHAEL GREER:

Clients served: http://michaelgreer.biz/?page_id=27
Detailed biography: http://michaelgreer.biz/?page_id=22
Greer's books and publications: http://michaelgreer.biz/?page_id=39
Testimonials: http://michaelgreer.biz/?page_id=612

Greer, Michael, 2010, *Beyond PM Certification: Achieving PM Performance Improvement*. Available at: http://michaelgreer.biz/?p=580 [Includes a discussion and summary graphic outlining a suggested relationship between PM certifying bodies and HR people]
Summary of Key Project Manager Actions and Result. Available at: http://michaelgreer.biz/?p=118 [My personal attempt to 'squeeze the performance juice' out of PMI's PMBOK and pull out 20 Key Actions & Results. This is a one-page table]
Beyond Sales Training: Designing a Learning Organization. Available at: http://www.michaelgreer.com/beyond-sales-training.pdf [A chapter from *In Action: Designing Training Programs*, American Society for Training and Development (ASTD), 1996. This details how we planned and managed a comprehensive performance analysis to create job models, career paths, curriculum architecture and corresponding training priorities]
The Project Management Minimalist: Just Enough PM to Rock Your Projects! by Michael Greer. Available at: http://michaelgreer.biz/?page_id=636 [Kindle edition: http://www.amazon.com/Project-Management-Minimalist-Projects-ebook/dp/B004J17298]

OTHER ONLINE RECOMMENDATIONS

Brad Egeland's *Project Management: Is PMP Certification Worth It?* Available at: http://pmtips.net/project-management-pmp-certification-worth/

Here is a quotation from that work:

> *I personally think that the PMP designation after your name is a nice thing to have, but is no indication of how good a project manager you are or will be. Having PMP certification means that you have the proper amount of experience and training to sit for the test, and then that you correctly answered 61% of the answers on the exam. 61%.*

Rework by 37signals. Available at: http://37signals.com/rework/ [Rrequired reading for everyone who is ready to cut the nonsense out of their business practices]

Project Management Credentials Compared – A Preliminary Analysis by Dr Paul Giammalvo. Available at: http://www.build-project-management-competency.com/download-page/

61 Stress and Project Management: Maintaining High Performance

STEPHEN FLANNES

This chapter discusses sources of stress in project management and presents techniques that can be applied to maintain high levels of individual and team performance. 'Performance' is the key word in this discussion. The ability to identify stress factors (stressors) and create compensatory mechanisms is not just an approach to assist the project manager in 'feeling better'. Rather, the emphasis is grounded in the observation that stress impacts project performance, on both individual and team levels. The chapter begins with a definition of stress, followed by a description of the impact that the stress response has on performance. A selection of stress management approaches are then presented, to provide a menu of techniques that can be applied in the project environment. Next, stress-contributing attributes of project work are identified, and specific stress management guidelines offered for each of these attributes. The chapter concludes with a discussion of best practices for making personal changes, because any personal initiative directed towards improving one's ability to modulate project stress will involve embracing personal change – abandoning less functional approaches to coping whilst simultaneously being willing to try something new.

Introduction

Many project professionals would say that project work is 'stressful'. Ironically, variable factors that make project work appealing (such as complexity, rapid work pace, solving unique problems and working with evolving groups of peers) are the same factors that can lead to individual stress and diminished performance.

Now that project management is well established and systematised, investigators are paying increasing attention to the possible negative, stress-related consequences of project work. Asquin et al. (2010) describe how project management increases pressure and stress due to the requirement for heightened levels of individual commitment, coupled with a temporary loss of professional identity. Zika-Viktorsson et al. (2006), along with Aitken and Crawford (2007), have identified stressful components of projectised work models.

Chiocchio et al. (2009) write about the impact upon team member mental health when individuals are working on a number of projects, or when team individuals are working on a project within a non-projectised organisation.

Definition of Stress

Stress is the individual's experience of cognitive, emotional or physical agitation caused by reaction to threats that exist, or are perceived to exist, in our immediate world. Whilst each person individually defines what is stressful in project work, a number of common manifestations exist, such as issues with mood (feeling unsettled or worried), interpersonal relationships (an exacerbation of conflict) and disruptive cognitions (such as negative assessments of past behaviour, or continuously 'looping' self-talk involving themes of self-criticism).

ACTIVATION OF THE STRESS RESPONSE

When a project professional makes the individualised appraisal that a project variable or situation is 'stressful', that person is now immersed in the powerful and familiar 'fight or flight' reaction. This fight or flight reaction consists first of 'appraisal', where the project professional assesses that a situation poses a threat. Following appraisal comes the 'reaction', in which the individual attempts to manage the situation by 'fighting' (engaging in goal-directed problem solving) or through 'flight' (for example by leaving a meeting early or by withdrawing from a threatening individual).

'Reappraisal' of the situation continues with the individual modifying the coping strategy based upon an assessment of its current effectiveness. This process of appraisal, action, reappraisal and the implementation of new action continues indefinitely, until the individual perceives that the threat has passed. Thus, when one has 'wound down' from the perceived stress, one is viewed as now having returned to normal homeostatic levels of baseline physical excitation, cognitive performance and emotional functioning.

Negative Performance Consequences of Acute or Chronic Stress

The optimal stress cycle of activation, stress peaking and return to homeostasis does not take place when:

1. the stress is acute and then chronic or;
2. where there are few periods of cessation or disengagement from the stressor or;
3. one's approaches to managing stress are ineffective.

The chronic stress experience is illustrated in Figure 61.1, where assorted variables (conflict, time pressure, matrix models of working, dysfunctional team leadership and so on) combine to hinder the individual from 'winding down' from a stressful event and returning to the baseline homeostatic levels described above.

When experiencing chronic stress, the individual's physiological fight or flight mechanisms get 'stuck' in the 'on' position. This 'stuck on open' process prevents

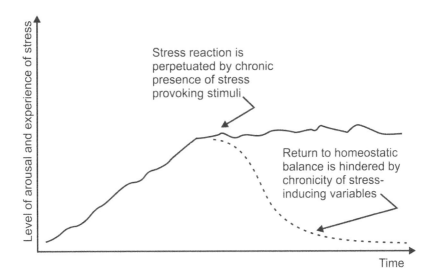

Figure 61.1 Chronic stress response is stuck in the 'on' position

the individual from returning to the homeostasis balance point. Consequently, the individual's performance suffers, as fewer cognitive resources are available.

CHRONIC STRESS: PERFORMANCE DEFICITS AND THE YERKES-DOBSON CURVE

Chronic stress and its impact upon project performance are nicely represented by the Yerkes-Dobson curve. This curve suggests that a certain amount of perceived stress is optimal towards bringing out our best performance. However, as Figure 61.2 also implies,

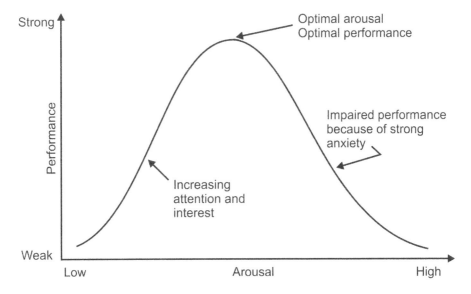

Figure 61.2 Yerkes-Dobson curve

Project variable	Performance hindrances	Investigators
Project overload (defined as a lack of time in which to recover from demanding work, inadequate routines, scarce time resources and/or simultaneous projects.	• High levels of psychological stress; • Minimal competence development; • Deviations from time schedules.	Zika-Viktorsson et al (2006).
Role ambiguity.	• Work exhaustion; • Depressed mood.	Raghavan and Sakaguchi (2008)
Requirement ambiguity.	• Increase of conflict; • Reduced final performance.	Liu et al, (2011)
Blurred lines between work and personal stress.	• Variety of stress reactions.	Aitken and Crawford (2007)
Demanding projects create chronic stress experiences.	• Poor information encoding; • Cognitive paralysis; • Decision overflow; • Task 'shedding'.	Flannes (2010)
Project work conducted in non-projectised organisations.	• Increased personal distress and decreassed sense of wellbeing.	Chiocchio et al (2009)

Figure 61.3 Sample performance defects resulting from acute or chronic stress

when arousal and stress increase the benefit of 'arousal' reaches a threshold (referred to as the point of 'eustasis'), and with increasing arousal the individual begins to experience negative subjective experiences and performance deficits.

Project managers need to be stimulated, and to be a bit 'on edge'. But, should the level of arousal get too high, or should the level remain high for too long, one becomes vulnerable to experiencing a number of cognitive, behavioural and interpersonal errors. The performance deficits emanating from acute or chronic stress are many, and a sampling of these performance deficits is presented in Figure 61.3.

How to Manage Stress and Maintain Project Performance

Clearly, we all know the things we 'should' do to reduce stress and manage its impact upon our performance. Such beliefs, within the industrialised world, have garnered the status of folk wisdom, endorsed by almost everyone. Such approaches include getting enough rest, eating well, consuming less alcohol, achieving work/life balance and regular exercise. Yet, even with such obvious stress management interventions existing in all of our knowledge bases, we often do not follow their prescriptions. Why not? I would argue that, because we have been reminded of these approaches for so long, we become numb when hearing them once again. Newer, more subtle approaches are therefore needed.

Consequently, the following section of this chapter presents an assortment of effective stress management techniques and interventions that are often not considered when facing the challenge of project stress and its impact on performance.

FUNDAMENTAL STRATEGIES FOR MANAGING STRESS AND MAINTAINING PERFORMANCE

Crafting Neutral Cognitions

The essence of using cognitive strategies to reducing stress and maintaining performance in project settings is captured in the following statement:

> *How we think, impacts how we feel, which in turn impacts how we behave.*

So, the cognitive-behavioural scientist encourages us to manage our stress by first starting with an examination of how we think. Specifically, the project manager is encouraged to monitor his/her self-talk – those often negative and repetitive messages that we play over and over in our heads during periods of agitation.

Thus Jane (a project manager experiencing negative self-talk) might find herself saying 'This project will never get completed. Mark is a disruptive team member and I'm certain he will hinder everything I suggest'. Clearly, such a cognitive message repetitively playing in her mind will create a self-perpetuating cycle of apprehension and dread. However, a project manager who desires to apply a cognitive strategy to reducing the negative self-talk might see if she can craft a more neutral self-talk message, such as:

> *Well, there's a good chance Mark will continue to be a problem. On the other hand, there is the possibility that the presence of the two new team members might moderate Mark's negativity. There are no guarantees, but I'll see what happens.*

Whilst this shift from Jane's negative cognition to a more neutral cognition may not appear to be dramatic, it can be very helpful in flavouring the stressful situation with just a bit more optimism, or at the minimum an increased sense of 'possibility'.

Involvement with 'Flow' Activities

Becoming engaged in 'flow' activities is a powerful method for reducing project stress by placing ourselves in activities that intellectually and emotionally refresh us. Csíkszentmihályi (2008) has written extensively on the concept of what he terms 'flow' activities. Flow activities are those activities which cause someone involved in the activity to lose track of time, and not to feel conscious of 'how they are doing'.

Activities individually defined as flow activities can include experiences such as listening to music, special moments with a friend (in which all distractions and an awareness of time disappear), a walk in nature or unstructured play with a child. After being immersed in a flow activity the individual is refreshed, tends to be feeling better about themselves and their world, and might come away with a new perspective that can be applied to problematic situations.

My informal research supports the idea that project managers are strongly attracted to flow activities as methods for reducing stress. During my project management seminars in recent years around the world, over 500 project managers were asked to rate their preference for a variety of stress management approaches (flow activities, journal writing, positive psychology, cognitive approaches and resilience). Impressively, the results have suggested that approximately 80 per cent of the project managers rated 'flow activities' as their first choice for managing their individual stress.

When asked during these seminars to explain why they rated flow activities so highly, project managers' answers indicated their preference for a stress management approach that allows them to: 'do something I am good at', 'not have to think analytically', and 'have the chance to finish something on my own'.

Whilst flow activities are generally most 'accessible' to a person who is not working (because of the benefit of a lengthy time immersion), one can still apply flow activities within the workplace, external variables permitting. Examples of flow activities that one might find appropriate for the workplace are:

- Having on hand reading materials such as magazines that cover topics for which the individual holds passion (like travel or a distinct hobby such as fishing). Periodically skimming through the pages as desired during the day might give one the sense of cognitive disengagement and subsequent 'refreshment' that is typical of time-intensive flow experiences.
- Looking at a selection of meaningful photos (from a holiday or a family event) during periods of emotional or intellectual exhaustion.
- Keeping a selection of favourite musical pieces on hand that one can turn to for brief listening pleasure when one feels the need to recharge and refresh.
- Should time in nature be a flow activity, one could look for a pleasant patch of green or a local park or garden close to the workplace and take breaks or lunch in those surroundings.

So, whilst being involved in flow activities during work hours is more challenging than during non-work activities, the involvement might still be worth the effort. I personally am always impressed with how giving myself such brief exposures to my flow activities has a definite positive impact of disengagement from immediate stressors, a chance for my central nervous system to return to homeostasis and a renewal of cognitive and motivational energy.

Resilience Practices: An Integrative Approach

An innovative approach to managing the negative impact of stressful situations is the concept of *resilience*. Seligman (2011) is one of the leaders in this field.

Resilience is a multifaceted approach for identifying the variables and approaches that one can use to thrive when operating under stress. Indeed, models of resilience are being presented to soldiers in the US Army so they can use these tools when under the horrific stress of military combat (Casey, 2011). Early results suggest that soldiers trained in resilience techniques are less likely to experience post traumatic stress symptoms following combat.

Writers such as Skodol (2010) describe a 'resilient personality'. This is a strong sense of self, self-knowledge, positive future orientation, the ability to moderate negative emotions and various interpersonal skills (such as the ability to engage in outgoing behaviour, the expression and modulation of personal emotions and the ability to demonstrate empathy towards others).

To manage project stress by employing the skills of the 'resilient personality', project managers need to focus on developing interpersonal skills, the ability to be self aware, and the ability to look at challenging situations and find one or two positive aspects within the negative setting. For more details, see Seligman (2011).

In addition to Seligman, key leaders in the field of research on resilience are found at the Arizona State University Resilience Solutions Group (Reich et al., 2010).

Adopt a Short-term Time Perspective

Another approach to managing project stress is the adoption of a short-term time perspective. This approach encourages one to acknowledge the immediate stress, and then focus on what can be done 'right now' or in the very near future. The time period might be two hours or two days, but it should be based on the individual's assumption of the time that is best for working on the problem. In essence, this approach says: 'Do what you can right now to deal with the problem, and then let it go for the time being'.

Here is why this approach is valuable for project managers. By nature, project managers have the ability to assess a situation, identify risks and craft plans for future initiatives. Likewise, project managers bring a pragmatic 'lessons-learned' mindset to their work, able to look back in time to different stages of the project and identify what worked and what went wrong.

Both of these abilities (the ability to conceptualise future risk and the ability to gaze retrospectively towards a lessons-learned analysis) can also cause 'anticipatory anxiety' (Nelson and Shankman, 2011).This anxiety comes from focusing temporally on events that are not immediate, rehashing the past or worrying about the future.

Such cognitive 'flights' from the immediate create anxiety because these flights focus on tasks over which one has no control. These temporal flights lead to 'what if' thinking which (when not modulated) creates an excitation of the central nervous system, coupled with anxiety.

Use Paradox or Humour

The use of paradox to manage stress helps moderate the excitation of the central nervous system and can be a playful and humorous approach. To use this approach, one must be able to look for a humorous or ironic self-statement that can be silently repeated when in the midst of a stressful experience.

Such a paradoxical statement, when repeated silently, can help extricate one from immediate worry, and can assist in gaining a broader perspective regarding the assessment of the current level of urgency.

Examples of popular applications of paradoxical intents include: 'When I'm very old and retired, will it really matter to me that this deliverable was two days late?' and 'What's the worst thing that can happen if this project is not perfect ... well, I think I can live with that'.

Develop Assertiveness Skills

Some project managers are vulnerable to stress because of their willingness to say 'yes' even when that is not the best response, both on enterprise levels (scope creep) and on personal levels (the subjective experience of being overwhelmed). Such overly agreeable project managers will benefit from the acquisition of assertive behaviour skills. Assertiveness posits that one can be firm in their position whilst also maintaining a respectful posture with their 'adversary'. In essence, being assertive is being 'very, very firm, but also very fair'.

Assertive individuals display behaviours suggestive of a willingness to stand up for themselves, their positions and their individual 'rights', plus the willingness to express beliefs openly, even when such feelings are at odds with the prevailing belief or tone (Thompson and Berenbaum, 2011). Assertive behaviours involve the willingness to set boundaries with people and draw the proverbial 'line in the sand'. To develop this skill, use paradox or 'visualisation' (thinking how one would prefer to be perceived), plus a dose of personal courage (remembering that small steps in this area create big returns).

Make Manifest What is Observed

'Making manifest' describes the process in which a project manager observes the immediate interpersonal processes among team members (on either individual or group levels) and then openly comments on such processes, if those processes should be viewed as not functional or optimal for the task in hand. For example, if the project manager observes during a team meeting (real or virtual) that the team members are unusually quiet, the project manager, making manifest his/her observation, comments on the quiet tone in the meeting. He/she then asks if any issues are contributing to the silences, and then incorporates that information into a talk with the team about how it can increase its level of discussion. Making manifest as a vehicle for reducing stress is very helpful towards removing the project manager from the stress-inducing posture of trying to be a 'mind reader', guessing why things are not working on the interpersonal or group dynamic levels.

Such willingness to 'tell it like it is' requires a confidence in one's observations, plus the assertive skills to speak to the observation. When the project manager uses the making manifest approach, personal stress levels drop whilst performance increases. This occurs because interpersonal issues are being identified and dealt with in real-time, thus increasing the likelihood of creating a solution.

Minimise Multitasking

The idea of minimising multitasking is almost an impossibility in today's world of multiproject involvement. However, if one can arrange work flow to minimise immersion in excessive multitasking, some interesting conservations of intellectual resources occur, giving one more 'horsepower' that can be applied to managing stress and maintaining performance.

The main idea here, according to Yaghootkar (2012), is that the process of multitasking requires that one expends effort to 'shut down' the involvement in one task cognitively whilst quickly expending resources to prime one for involvement in a second task. The two processes happen in milliseconds, and their existence does not rise to conscious levels of attention.

However, each time one shuts down the cognitive engagement with one task and begins to warm up the cognitive engagement with the second task, time is lost, cognitive effectiveness is diminished, and the existing cognitive thread and problem-solving progression of the first task is put on hold. One can minimise these multitasking performance hindrances by:

a) consciously assessing what the immediate mission-critical tasks are; and
b) considering how work boundaries can be established for others.

Figure 61.4 tabulates a summary of these fundamental approaches to managing project stress, plus their respective benefits for project performance.

Approach or technique	Approach or technique	Performance benefit of using this approach	Common resistances to trying this approach
Make manifest.	Observe and comment on non-productive interpersonal proecsses.	Eliminates self-imposed demand of being a 'mind reader'.	Concern about being perceived as too bold or outspoken.
Apply cognitive strategies.	Becoming aware of one's self-talk statements and repetitive cognitions.	Reduces risk of getting stuck in circular problem-solving and negative ideation.	Allowing attention to stay focused on what has worked compared to what might work.
Involvement with 'flow' strategies.	Willingness to structure flow activities into one's schedule, regardless of how busy.	Cognitive and emotional refreshment. Increase of motivation.	Believing that 'fun' or 'play' should not be engaged in until all the work is done.
Resilience practices.	Willingness to test drive a variety of techniques and approaches designed for optimal performance.	Ability to recover from stressors and maintain high levels of performance going forward.	Sticking to just one approach to handling stress that has worked well for you in the past.
Apply a short-term time perspective.	'Quieting' the mind and focusing on the present, as compared to the past or the future.	Ability to make decisions and take actions on tangible tasks: 'traction' for moving forward.	Trying to 'figure it all out' in the head, compared to taking immediate small steps.
Use paradox.	Seeing life and work from a higher and broader perspective.	Creates positive attitude and mood, plus a lightness of being.	Taking self and work too seriously.
Develop assertive skills.	Ability to speak up for what one wants or needs.	Increased opportunities for obtaining critical resources.	Desire for being liked by other stakeholders.
Proactive conflict resolution.	Comfort with seeing conflict as normal. Willingness to try different approaches.	Project tasks move forward, whilst quality remains high.	Seeing conflict as bad; giving in to personal discomfort re conflicts.
Reduce multi-tasking.	Ability to assess if a task is immediately urgent and to stay cognitively focused on priorities.	Greater efficiency in the amount of work produced, and a higher quality of work on complex tasks.	Hesitation to say 'No' to requests for involvement with additional tasks.

Figure 61.4 Fundamental approaches to managing stress and maintaining performance

Managing the Systemic Stressors of Projectised Work

The previous section presented a generic toolbox that the project professional can carry, with the goal of selecting the best stress management tool for any individual stressor. The following section examines specific attributes of project work that contribute to stress, and then offers tailored stress management approaches for these problematic, project-based situations.

MATRIX MODEL OF WORKING

Two primary attributes of matrix organisational structures are inherently stressful. The first of these two attributes is the dilemma of being responsible for the completion of a project whilst not having formal functional control over the agents (team members) who will do the work. The second attribute is the imperative of completing a task whilst the variables of the triple constraint (scheduling, specifications and resources) keep shifting, often at the behest of others not under our control.

These complicating essences of a matrix environment have been described as 'having no control but all the responsibility' and 'trying to hit a moving target'. Both factors give birth to the subjective experience of 'I have no control' and 'I'm almost powerless to be successful, when others keep changing the goals'.

There are no easily definable strategies for managing the stress-causing aspects of matrix systems. However, probably the best approach is to focus heavily on developing a variety of influencing skills, and by creating a team atmosphere of collaboration.

Influencing skills that minimise matrix-induced stress include effective communication skills, such as the use of open-ended questions, active listening and reframing (Flannes and Levin, 2005) and the general willingness to over-communicate, whilst interacting with stakeholders in a reciprocal manner.

SOLVING SINGULAR PROBLEMS AND CREATING INNOVATIVE PRODUCTS

By definition, projects are efforts at solving problems that have not been addressed previously. Such singular 'problem solving this journey into the unknown' is stressful, given the lack of precedence or technical solutions that can be adopted from previous enterprise efforts.

Too often, when project managers are developing an innovative product, they mistakenly believe that their innovative solution, because of its quality or uniqueness, will automatically be warmly embraced by all stakeholders. When such warm embraces do not occur owing to natural stakeholder resistance to change, project manager irritation and stress levels elevate, whilst the project manager 'argues' that the wisdom of the new solution speaks for itself as to why it should be adopted.

On a positive note, Denning and Dunham (2010) offer a very detailed process strategy for the acceptances of innovations that by implication can be also viewed as a method for reducing project manager stress. Denning and Dunham assert that effort needs to be devoted to getting stakeholders to 'adopt' and to 'sustain' an innovation, and that these positive results spring from the innovator's presenting a well-articulated and systemic 'offering' to the stakeholder that truly addresses stakeholder needs. At the essence of such an offering is a process of gradually laying groundwork for new product acceptance.

Applying their model to the goal of reducing individual project stress would appear to become cumulatively an effective stress management initiative through its reduction of personal frustration as a result of an increased adoption of innovations.

THE TRIPLE CONSTRAINT

Working within the triple constraint of scheduling, specifications and resources is an inherent foundation of projectised work. However, this way of working holds fundamental sources of stress for the project manager. Balancing the triple constraints causes stress because of fluidity (sponsors can change requirements at will), the implied sense of 'compromise' (a project manager can rarely get all that he/she wants), and the requirement to maintain a flexible cognitive stance and willingness to change.

Accepting the compromises and challenges inherent in the triple constraint is stressful for any project manager who has strong needs to be in control, or who has a tendency towards perfectionism. For such project managers, a plan for reducing personal stress within a projectised environment can involve:

- being realistic, accepting that the end product may not be just what the project manager wanted;
- maintaining awareness that achieving the deliverables for any project is best done through a mindset of accepting that work is a 'journey', and that the end point is elusive and will be defined as the journey progresses;
- being able to accept that every completed project does not have to be 'perfect' or 'excellent' – some projects are just fine when the deliverables are 'good' or 'satisfactory'.

OTHER KEY ATTRIBUTES CAUSING STRESS IN PROJECTISED ENVIRONMENTS

Other attributes of projectised milieux that contribute to individual stress are the proliferation of virtual teams and the experience of project conflict. These topics have been addressed in detail in other settings, and will not be pursued here. For thoughts on virtual teams, see Zofri (2011) and Lepsinger and DeRosa (2010). For current thoughts on conflict resolution, see Ramsbotham et al. (2010) and Scott (2010).

Interpersonal Variables Contributing to Stress

A number of interpersonal and cultural variables also contribute to project stress.

LEADERSHIP ATTRIBUTION ERROR

Some project managers create stress for themselves by placing too much of the burden for project success upon their own shoulders. Such extreme responsibility taking can be seen in the project manager who has difficulty saying no to team members' requests for assistance.

This process of assuming too much responsibility for the success of the project results in what Hackman and Wageman (2007) term the 'leadership attribution error'. This leadership error involves the project manager believing that too much of the success of the project rests on their shoulders, and therefore they should say yes to all requests for team member assistance.

However, Hackman and Wageman believe that when leaders create a team culture known for 'peer coaching' (team members being encouraged to seek out assistance from peers as compared to running all things through the project manager), project quality improves. And, when an atmosphere of peer coaching exists within a team, the project manager is juggling fewer problems, and the risk for leader stress is reduced.

CROSS-CULTURAL VARIABLES

Working within a project environment where a number of cultural belief systems are operating can be stressful, as the project manager attempts to interact in ways not offensive to the cultural sensitivities of other team members. Too often, the project manager's stress increases as he/she believes that somehow he/she must gain the most accurate, current information about the cultural mores represented on the team.

Whilst such cultural awareness is a desired goal, it should not be pursued in a manner in which the project manager is looking for objective absolutes, such as implied in a statement like: 'I need to remember that American project managers handle conflict by doing a, b and c …'. Rather, project managers can reduce the stress of working across cultures by asking open-ended questions of stakeholders, looking to identify how these specific individuals prefer to handle a situation. Then, using active listening to summarise what one is hearing from the other party helps secure that the message is being accurately encoded.

Also, it is very powerful, when trying to navigate the cultural differences within a team, to 'make manifest' the dilemma. Making manifest, as previously explained, is the process by which the project manager articulates to others the questions that are running through his/her mind about how to handle a certain issue with cultural sensitivity. An example of a statement in which a project manager makes manifest the dilemma of working across cultures is:

> Our team has members from different backgrounds and countries. Rather than my making guesses about how each team member prefers to handle conflict, let's spend some time in our initial meeting with each person sharing his or her preferred method of working through conflict.

Crisp and Turner (2009) offer the interesting approach of 'simulated social contact' for reducing the conflict and implied stress that can be associated when dealing with groups outside of one's own background. They found that when people mentally simulate a future positive intergroup encounter, attitudes are improved and anxiety lessens. (Their results seem to be similar to work on the benefits of visualising positive behaviours and outcomes for upcoming situations.)

WORKING WITH INDIVIDUAL DIFFERENCES

The field of individual differences suggests that even though a group may be homogenous in nature when viewed from the macro level (for example a team of software engineers working in the United Kingdom), such a team is ultimately populated by individuals holding different aptitudes, personal styles and beliefs.

The field of individual differences emerged in the twentieth century, when researchers began assessing the intellectual differences among sets of individuals. This cognitive-based path to elucidating individual's differences gradually added new dimensions, with factors of personality and personal style becoming focal points for identifying how individuals vary.

In project work, an excellent method for reducing stress is the ability to apply a model that describes individual differences, based upon one's observation of the personal style and behaviour (communication preferences, ways of getting energised and the preferred modes of decision making) of each team member. By being able to define individual differences, the project manager reduces his/her stress because he/she now has a model for effectively defining uniqueness, which leads to increased efficiency and lowered frustration.

One model of individual differences that continues to remain popular with project managers is the Myers-Briggs Type Indicator (MBTI) (Kirby and Myers, 1998). This personal style system is just one approach to identifying individual differences. It is by no means the only model. Regardless, each project manager needs to have a model for identifying individual differences; by having such a model, one can dramatically reduce the interpersonal stress component in a team. (For detailed guidelines about how a project manager can employ the MBTI model in working with team members, see Flannes and Levin (2005). This subject is also discussed in Chapter 32.)

Leveraging Individual Personality Factors

One of the most powerful determinants for the incubation of individual stress is the personal style of the individual project professional. The following section discusses two aspects of personal style that can be leveraged by the project manager towards reducing individual stress.

DISPLAY 'ADAPTIVE' TYPE A BEHAVIOUR

Periodically, most project managers display aspects of classical Type A behaviour. The cluster of behaviours and cognitions known as Type A behaviour is often described as consisting of a time urgency to get a task completed, a desire for perfectionism, and a resulting interpersonal edge or friction that surfaces in interpersonal relationships (Friedman, 1996).

Obviously, urgency and a desire for an excellent project are project-compatible values. However, when these values are employed in an unchecked manner they contribute to what has recently being described as 'maladaptive' Type A behaviour, suggestive of increased levels of personal stress and agitation, and resulting performance deficits.

Project managers can reduce the stress associated with maladaptive Type A behaviour by employing what is being termed 'adaptive' Type A behaviour. Adaptive Type A behaviour speaks to the goal of having the same high Type A standards regarding timeliness and quality, but viewing such variables as 'desired goals' as compared to 'must haves'. By maintaining such cognitive flexibility around the attributes of Type A behaviour, one can lower stress by making conscious the decision about how strident one needs to be in achieving timelines and quality levels. This modification of those variables reflects the adage of not letting the quest for 'perfect' get in the way of achieving 'excellent'.

Editorial Comment (DL)

This is also sometimes expressed as not letting the best be the enemy of the good.

USE SELF-KNOWLEDGE REGARDING PERSONAL STYLE

Self-knowledge is a key personal attribute for the effective project manager to use in managing stress. The previously mentioned MBTI is one model for identifying individual differences that can be leveraged towards reducing the performance impact of stress.

The MBTI model articulates eight different personal preferences, which then combine to determine one's individual style. The preferences include:

- extravert – one who is energised by interaction with the outside world;
- introvert – one who is energised by reflective thoughts and considerations;
- sensing – a tangible here-and-now focus;
- intuition – strategic and future oriented;
- thinking – decisions made primarily through the 'head';
- feeling – decisions made primarily through the 'heart';
- judging – desire to pursue tasks in an orderly, sequential manner;
- perceiving – desire to keep options open and be flexible.

When combined, these eight preferences offer distinct 'best practices' for handling the stress of project work. Figure 61.5 tabulates these MBTI stress management best practices.

MBTI preference	Stress management 'best practices
Extraversion:	Interact with others, but do not overload.
Introversion:	Get quiet time, but do not internalise.
Sensing:	Take action whilst also seeing the 'big picture'.
Intuition:	Define possibilities but stay practical.
Thinking:	Analyse the facts but also consider feelings.
Feeling:	Be expressive, but also attend to the facts.
Judging:	Make a plan, but do not get rigid.
Perceiving:	Be flexible, but seek some closure.

Figure 61.5 Stress management implications for each MBTI preference

How to Make Substantive Personal Changes

Managing stress with the focus of maintaining high levels of individual performance usually requires substantive changes in one's behaviour, cognitions, the regulation of affect as well as an increase of one's emotional intelligence skills (Goleman, 2011).

STEPS IN MAKING PERSONAL CHANGE

How do people really make personal changes? It is my experience that individuals are most likely to make personal changes in work life when they become acutely aware of the 'pain' (that is, the performance deficits, discomfort or physical symptoms) being experienced as a result of using stress management approaches that are not effective.

Therefore, an initial step towards making personal change (with the goal of adopting new ways of handling stress) is the willingness to take a sober and forthright assessment of one's current pain points. To identify pain points, one should examine variables such as mood, energy level, the level of internalised anger or fear, the level of interest in work and the ability to work creatively and solve complex problems. After completing this self-inventory, one may see the need to try some different stress management approaches.

Next, identify one specific new stress management technique to try – only one. By identifying just one, the project manager has a focused target, and the chance for measurable achievements is increased because of this distinct, singular goal.

Next, view making change as a process. Identify very small behavioural steps, and attempt the first step. Focus on execution of the new behaviour and not on the result. (Too much focus on the results of the new behaviour creates an anticipatory anxiety model, in which one's self-talk is focused too much on 'getting it right' and not enough on 'just trying something new'.)

After each small step, 'celebrate' your efforts. This is an iterative process. The goal is to 'keep trying', not 'doing it right'. Find others who can celebrate your efforts, and who can also avoid focusing on whether you did it 'right'. This personal process of identifying the individual pain and then moving along a path to the initiation of new approaches is summarised in Figure 61.6.

Progression 'steps' for making substantive personal change
1 Use self relfection to develp an awareness of personal 'pain' (anxiety, poor concentration, work delays, somatic discomfort and so on.
2 Identify current dysfunctional coping behaviours (denial, agressive verbal interactions, and so on.
3 Identify the resulting performance problem (poor team collaboration, loss of followership, and so on.
4 Define and employ new coping skills (*I will try using 'resilience'*).
5 Keep applying the new coping skill, focusing on the desired 'behaviour', not just the outcome.
6 Apply an ongoing iterative approach towards refining the new skills and behaviours.

Figure 61.6 Process for making substantive personal changes

Future Enterprise and Cultural Trends and the Experience of Stress

The ability to identify sources of individual project stress, coupled with the ability to craft personal initiatives that will reduce the stress, will only gain importance in the face of rapid changes in technology, societal shifts with their concomitant demands for cultural fluency, and increased project complexity emanating from multiproject assignments.

FLUID AND LESS-DEFINED WAYS OF WORKING

Dynamic enterprise forces are shaping the way that work is completed. One can see how a product, especially in technology, may become obsolete even before it is launched. Similarly, the problems for which products and solutions are designed can often change even before the solution is crafted.

Examples of attempts to respond to such fluid enterprise states and ambiguous product end-points are the various 'agile' methods found within the field of software development (Cohen, 2010). These agile ways of working, in which stakeholders craft short-term prototypes that are then refined within the context of repeated iterations, require individuals working within these models to find ways to manage individually uncertainty and ambiguity, intense interpersonal interactions with fellow stakeholders, and the commitment to a work process in which the end point (that is, the product) is not clearly defined. And as is evident, words such as 'ambiguity', 'uncertainty', 'intense interpersonal interactions', and an 'unclear end point' are words suggesting a potentially stressful way of working.

Thus, it becomes incumbent on the project manager to have a myriad of tools that can be used to manage the stress in these innovative and instructed ways of working. Many of these tools are presented within discussions of resilience (Masten and O'Dougherty Wright, 2010) and emotional intelligence (Goleman, 2011).

Summary

Stress impacts project performance on both individual and team levels. Fundamental approaches to managing stress can be applied as well as specific stress management approaches that are tailored for the unique stress-contributing attributes of projectised work systems.

In all settings, one should use an awareness of personal style, coupled with the concept of adaptive Type A behaviour, to craft personally innovative stress management approaches that are implemented in an iterative manner, remembering that small gains in new behaviour pay disproportionately big dividends towards maintaining high levels of performance. Efforts should be made towards experimenting with 'new behaviours' whilst minimising the tendency to focus on whether one is doing the new behaviour 'correctly'.

References and Further Reading

Aitken, A. and Crawford, L. (2007), 'Coping with stress: Dispositional coping strategies of project managers', *International Journal of Project Management*, 25(7), pp. 666–73.

Asquin, A., Garel, G. and Picq, T. (2010), 'When project based management causes distress at work', *International Journal of Project Management*, 28(2), pp. 158–65.

Casey, G.W. Jr (2011), 'Comprehensive soldier fitness: A vision for psychological resilience in the U.S. Army', *American Psychologist*, 66(1), pp. 1–3.

Chiocchio, F., Beaulieu, G., Boudrias, J.S., Rousseau, V., Aube, C. and Morin, E.M. (2009), 'The project involvement index, psychological distress, and psychological well being: Comparing workers from projectised and non-projectised organisations', *International Journal of Project Management*, 28(3), pp. 201–11.

Cohen, G. (2010), *Agile Excellence for Product Managers*, Cupertino, CA: Superstar Press.

Crisp, R. and Turner, R. (2009), 'Can imagined interactions produce positive perceptions? Reducing prejudice through simulated social contact', *American Psychologist*, 64(4), pp. 231–40.

Csíkszentmihályi M. (2008), *Flow: The Psychology of Optimal Experience*, New York, NY: Harper Collins.

Denning, P.J. and Dunham, R. (2010), *The Innovator's Way*, Cambridge, MA: MIT Press.

Flannes, S. (2010), 'Tangible Tips for Handling the Endless Stress in Project Management', *Proceedings of the 2010 PMI Global Congress, North America*, Dublin: Project Management Institute.

Flannes, S. and Levin, G. (2005), *Essential People Skills for Project Managers*, Vienna, VA: Management Concepts.

Friedman, M. (1996), *Type A Behavior: Its Diagnosis and Treatment*, New York, NY: Plenum Press.

Goleman, D. (2011), *The Brain and Emotional Intelligence: New Insights*, Northampton, MA: More Than Sound LLC.

Hackman, R. and Wageman, R. (2007), 'Asking the right questions about leadership: Discussion and conclusions', *American Psychologist*, 62(1), pp. 43–47.

Kirby, L. and Myers, K. (1998), *Introduction to Type: A Guide to Understanding Your Results on the Myers-Briggs Type Indicator*, Palo Alto, CA: Consulting Psychologists Press.

Lepsinger, R. and DeRosa, D. (2010), *Virtual Team Success: A Practical Guide for Working and Leading from a Distance*, San Francisco, CA: John Wiley & Sons/Jossey-Bass.

Liu, J.Y.C., Chen, H.G., Chen, C.C. and Sheu, T.S. (2011), 'Relationships among interpersonal conflict, requirements uncertainty, and software project performance', *International Journal of Project Management*, 29(5), pp. 547–56.

Masten, A.S. and O'Dougherty Wright, M. (2010), 'Resilience over the lifespan: Developmental perspectives on resistance, recovery, and transformation', in Reich, J.R. et al. (eds), *The Handbook of Adult Resilience*, New York, NY: The Guilford Press.

Nelson, B.D. and Shankman, S.A. (2011), 'Does intolerance of uncertainty predict anticipatory startle responses to uncertain threat?', *International Journal of Psychophysiology*, 81(2), pp. 107–15.

Raghavan, V.V. and Sakaguchi, T. (2008), 'Empirical investigation of stress factors in information technology professionals', *Information Resources Management Journal*, 21(2), pp. 38–62.

Ramsbotham, O., Woodhouse, T. and Miall, H. (2010), *Contemporary Conflict Resolution*, Cambridge: Polity Press.

Reich, J.W., Zautra, A.J. and Hall, J.S. (2010), *Handbook of Adult Resilience*, New York, NY: The Guilford Press.

Scott, V. (2010), *Conflict Resolution for Dummies*, Hoboken, NJ: Wiley.

Seligman, M.E.P. (2011), 'Building resilience', *Harvard Business Review*, 89(4), pp. 100–106.

Skodol, A.E. (2010), 'The resilient personality', in Reich, J.W. et al. (eds), *The Handbook of Adult Resilience*, New York, NY: The Guilford Press.

Thompson, R.J. and Berenbaum, H. (2011), 'Adaptive and aggressive assertiveness scales', *Journal of Psychopathology and Behavioral Assessment*, 33(3), pp. 323–34.

Yaghootkar, G.N. (2012), 'The effects of schedule-driven project management in multi-project environments', *International Journal of Project Management*, 30(1), pp. 127–40.

Zika-Viktorsson, A., Sundstrom, P. and Engwall, M. (2006), 'Project overload: An exploratory study of work and management in multi-project settings', *International Journal of Project Management*, 24(5), pp. 385–94.

Zofri, Y. (2011), *A Manager's Guide to Virtual Teams*, New York, NY: American Management Association.

62 *Teams and Spirituality in Project Management*[1]

JUDI NEAL and ALAN HARPHAM

All human beings are spiritual beings. We all have the potential to enhance our spiritual growth, but it takes a commitment to self-awareness and to spiritual practice. It is important as a project manager to know one's self. That means one's whole self – body, mind, emotion and spirit. In this chapter we explore the ways in which spirituality is experienced in project teams. If each individual is a spiritual being, then there is the potential for collective spiritual energy when people come together. And it is just as important for a project team to know itself – to have self-awareness about the body, mind, emotion and spirit of the team as a whole.

Introduction

There are many books about team building that focus on developing relationships and team skills. However, they tend to ignore the spiritual dimension of teams. Katzenback and Smith (2003), for instance, describe high-performance teams as having the following key characteristics:

- complementary skills;
- mutual accountability;
- common approach;
- shared goals.

These are all necessary – but not sufficient – characteristics of spirituality in project teams. High-performance teams are teams that develop a deep personal commitment among their members for one another's personal growth and well-being, whilst rising to concrete and measurable challenges.

In this chapter we go one step further, to describe teams where the project manager and team members are committed to each other's spiritual growth and to making a positive difference in the world.

Jesus said, 'Where two or three are gathered in my name, there I am' (Matthew, 18:20). Hindus gather together in Satsang, or spiritual community, as an important part of evolving in their consciousness. Native Americans gather in Wisdom Councils for

---

1   This chapter is based on extracts from our book *The Spirit of Project Management* (2012).

spiritual guidance about major decisions that affect the tribe and future generations. All of the wisdom traditions have spiritual practices that incorporate a group of people coming together for some higher purpose. Each of these traditions has something to offer to project teams that truly want to tap into the deeper dimensions of meaning, purpose and commitment to the project.

Project management provides an individual with the opportunity to find greater spirituality in his/her life through being involved in something that brings greater meaning and purpose, and through the challenges and opportunities for personal growth that come from relationships. The most effective project management teams are those that understand the balance between the discipline of process on the one hand and the valuing of relationships and spiritual connection on the other.

By taking a spiritual approach to project team development and leadership, individual team members benefit in their own spiritual development. The project stakeholders benefit too, because team members are more committed, inspired and effective in implementing the processes needed for project success.

A project manager might consider five approaches when leading a project management team in a spiritual way:

1. Alignment – aligning vision, meaning and purpose at the team level.
2. Spiritual leadership – seeing oneself as a servant leader to the team and being committed to helping each team member be a servant leader to others.
3. *Esprit de corps* – understanding and honouring the collective spirit of the team.
4. Communication – using non-traditional communication methods as a way of building trust and openness.
5. Creativity – recognising that inspiration comes from spirit, and utilising group spiritual practices from the wisdom traditions to support inspired problem solving.

We shall outline each of these approaches and offer examples of activities and processes you might use in your project team.

Alignment

In order to align vision, meaning and purpose within your project management team, you, as project manager, must first be clear about your own vision for the project, and what its meaning and purpose is for you in your own life and work. It is important to communicate your vision and to be willing to share on a personal level how this project provides meaning and purpose to you. You also need to communicate what the meaning and purpose of the project is to the stakeholders. The more you can state this in terms of values the better.

The next step is to create alignment within the team. To do this, you must be open to having your vision and meaning and purpose enhanced by what others in the team have to say. One process for creating alignment is to bring people together for an 'alignment session' and to ask each person to write a brief story about a project they have worked on in the past which provided them a strong sense of meaning and purpose. Stories are a time-honoured tradition for evoking spiritual wisdom.

Team member	Story of project, with meaning and purpose	Themes from the story	How this project can create meaning and purpose
A			
B			
C			
D			
E			

Figure 62.1 Creating alignment around meaning and purpose

Your next step is to put participants in groups of three to five people to share their stories, and ask people to listen for the themes and similarities. Have people collect these themes on flip charts or through decision software. Once each group has completed their list of themes regarding meaning and purpose, ask for two or three volunteers to tell the entire group a little bit about their story of a project where they felt a strong sense of meaning and purpose. Then list all the themes on a whiteboard or other method that is visible to the entire group. Finally, lead a discussion with full participation, to discuss what each person's vision is for the project and how this project can create a collective experience of meaning and purpose for the team. The format shown in Figure 62.1 might be useful in documenting the stories and the themes.

A very different kind of alignment process that you could use is based on the Native American process of vision questing (Neal, 2006). When you are kicking off your next new project, try to choose a retreat location where team members have access to natural features (like gardens, a forest or seashore). After sharing your personal vision, meaning and purpose, as described above, invite team members to spend time in nature, reflecting on their personal vision, meaning and purpose for the project. Ideally, you should schedule at least one hour for them to be 'in nature', and one hour for processing their experience.

In your instructions for their vision quest, ask them to look to nature for symbols and messages. Remind them that in all wisdom traditions, spiritual leaders from time immemorial have gone into nature for guidance from God. A vision quest is the process of seeking a vision and asking for guidance from the spiritual world about the purpose and meaning of what you are about to undertake. It helps if each person brings a journal, and you can suggest that if they receive a message from nature, they can bring back a symbol of that message.

When people return, assemble them into a circle for a wisdom council meeting. Each person shares something about their experience and the message they brought back, knowing that the message is not just for them, but for the community (which means in this case the project team).

The former CEO of Rockport Shoes, Angel Martinez, is a very spiritual man and took a spiritual approach to the way he ran the business. As a result of his inspired leadership, the company did a major turnaround from losing a lot of money to becoming one of the most profitable businesses in the shoe industry. The company was growing and needed a new corporate headquarters. Mr Martinez shared his vision of the company culture as being one that nurtured the artist within. At a project planning retreat for the design of the new headquarters, each of the top managers of the organisation was asked to take a camera and to go into nature for one hour to look for a symbol or message of what the new corporate headquarters should be like. When the managers returned, they loaded their photos on to a computer. Each person showed one or two photos and talked about their photo of a rock, leaf, bird or stone, provided a vision for what they would like to see in the corporate headquarters and how they would like the new design to support the organisational culture.

The vice-president of human resources pulled all their ideas together and that collective vision created the basis for the architectural plans of the new building. Thomas Merton, the famous Trappist contemplative monk of the Abbey of Gethsemane, also used photographs to capture images of the God within (De Waal, 1992).

Spiritual Leadership

Spiritual leadership means seeing oneself as a servant leader to the team, and being committed to helping each team member to be a servant leader to others.

There are many different models of spiritual leadership. One of the most popular of these is 'servant leadership', based on a framework developed by Robert Greenleaf. He was a retired executive from AT&T. Greenleaf developed this model after reading Hermann Hesse's spiritual tale *The Journey to the East* (1932). He offers the following test of whether or not someone is a servant leader:

> *Do those served grow as persons; do they while being served become healthier, wiser, freer, more autonomous, more likely themselves to become servants? (Greenleaf, 1977)*

Larry Spears, former Director of the Greenleaf Center for Servant Leadership, identified 10 characteristics of a servant leader. Several of these characteristics are quite spiritual in nature. For example, one characteristic is awareness, especially self-awareness, which is central to all the major religious traditions (Spears, 1998). Contemplative practices such as prayer, meditation and journaling are powerful tools for self-awareness.

Another characteristic is commitment to the growth of people, with a belief that people have an intrinsic value beyond their tangible contribution as workers. This is also one of the key characteristics of an effective project manager. Leaders who exhibit this characteristic are high in spiritual intelligence (Wigglesworth, 2010).

When teams climb big mountains like Everest, usually only a few members of the overall team reach the summit. But the whole team feels the sense of accomplishment. Likewise, when a racing driver wins in Formula One, it is the whole team who share in that sense of being first or winning. Alan's son, Richard, had the privilege of managing the Ghanaian Ski Team in the 2010 Winter Olympics in Whistler. The team comprised one skier, Kwame, the snow leopard, who participated in the slalom. He came 47th out of 104 entrants and achieved more than he had hoped for. His team of four (manager, ski coach, fitness coach and Internet expert) all shared in his sense of a personal victory. We were pleased that they each received a medal for their participation in helping Kwame to be there and to do as well as he did. Every backup team at the Olympics shares this real sense of lasting recognition for their achievement.

A key skill for any project leader is the ability to build relationships that work and enable alliances to form for the benefit of the project. The relationships with the key project team members are essential for building and maintaining a trusting, compact team who work well together, support each other, go the extra mile for each other and can deliver even when the going gets tough. The project manager needs to be able to inspire them to even greater levels of performance.

Fry (2003 and 2005) has done extensive research on spiritual leadership and has developed a causal model demonstrating the relationship between the following:

1. spiritual leadership values, attitudes and behaviours;
2. follower needs for spiritual survival;
3. organisational outcomes.

Fry's research shows that vision, hope/faith and altruistic love lead to organisational commitment, productivity, ethical and spiritual well-being, and corporate social responsibility. For team leaders who wonder if there is a business case for spiritual leadership, it is well worth reading Fry's work. It will inspire you to be the kind of spiritual leader your heart might be calling you to be.

One of the best ways to develop your spiritual leadership strength is to work with a spiritual business coach or a spiritual director. Many workplace chaplains have the skills to be a spiritual business coach, or you might want to contact the Tyson Center for Faith and Spirituality in the Workplace to use one of their coaches.

The coach might ask you to take a self-assessment instrument such as the Spiritual Intelligence Questionnaire (Wigglesworth, 2010), the Spiritual Leadership Survey (Fry, 2005), or the Edgewalker Assessment (Neal and Hoopes, 2011). He/she will work with you to define your vision of what spiritual leadership looks like for you and will guide you on developing your capabilities. There are also many courses and workshops on spiritual leadership development that can be helpful.

Esprit de Corps

Esprit de corps in this context means understanding and honouring the collective spirit of the team. Each of us has at one time or another been on a project team where there was an incredible sense of *esprit de corps*. Those experiences are quite memorable and are probably one of the major reasons people are interested in joining project teams. *Esprit de corps* is also defined as 'the common spirit existing in the members of a group and inspiring enthusiasm, devotion, and strong regard for the honour of the group' (Merriam-Webster). Literally it means 'spirit of the group'.

A team is a living system, and each living system has its own spirit. Just as we each have our own spirit and must consciously do things to nourish that spirit, a team must consciously do things to nourish the spirit of the team. Barry Heermann developed a

Internal customers:	Expectations of the project	Meaning and purpose of this project
Team leader		
Team member A		
Team member B		
Team member C		
Admin. assistant		
Other		
External customers: Client		
Vendor A		
Vendor B		
Gov't inspector		
Site manager		
Other		

Figure 62.2 Customer services analysis grid

programme called Team Spirit (1997) that incorporates organisational development practices, group dynamics processes and knowledge from the wisdom traditions of the world. Team Spirit has a six-phase team spirit spiral with activities at every stage, all of which centre around service. Heermann and his colleagues have learned over time that the thing which distinguishes teams with *esprit de corps* and high performance from average or low-performing teams is the focus on service to each other and to the customer or stakeholder.

You might consider conducting a 'customer service analysis' with your team (using a grid such as that shown in Figure 62.2). This approach begins with identifying your internal and external customers. Your internal customers are your fellow members on the project team. Your external customers are those who are paying for the project, your vendors and other external stakeholders. For each customer, you define what 'service' means to them. In your definition, include their expectations of the project team, and include what gives them meaning and purpose. You can adapt this grid for your particular project.

From this analysis, you can begin to see a pattern of expectations and of what provides a sense of meaning and purpose to both the internal and external customers. The team can then discuss what it means to be of service in this project. They may decide to find a way to measure customer satisfaction with their service, which can be very helpful and could be a key performance indicator for the project.

One phase of the team spirit spiral is 'celebration'. This is an important focus that is often not considered by many project managers. A unique example of celebration occurs in Pfizer's drug development project teams. Like other teams, they celebrate their successes on a regular basis. But they also celebrate their failures, when their research shows that a drug line on which they were working does not have any potential to improve medical conditions. They celebrate the closing down of that line of research because they learned important things from their experiments and because resources are now freed up to follow more promising drug compounds. As you can imagine, there is a very high sense of *esprit de corps* in these teams.

Lamont (2002) describes a similar form of celebration of failure at Happy Computers, where the CEO shows up with a bottle of champagne when someone discovers something that could fail, and then it does.

As the project team develops milestones in their project planning, we encourage you to incorporate milestone celebrations. These need not be expensive and time-consuming events, and are often most meaningful when they are designed by the project team members themselves.

Another approach to developing *esprit de corps* is to understand the different roles each project team needs in order to be effective and then to learn about the team members' natural gifts in these areas so that all the roles are fulfilled. Theories abound about team building and acceleration of the process of team members' getting to know each other and their individual strengths and weaknesses.

BELBIN

Belbin (2010) has done much on the roles team members play and how each individual has an affinity to a particular role. Most project managers are what Belbin calls 'shapers' with the drive and energy to keep the team moving forwards without losing focus or momentum. Belbin highlighted the need for the team to have a cross section of other abilities. Your team might wish to evaluate itself on these different roles. Each person can use a form like that shown in Figure 62.3 to rate themselves on the roles they play in the team, and then the information can be combined to evaluate whether or not any roles are missing or are overrepresented.

It was only after the initial research had been completed that the ninth team role, 'specialist', emerged. The simulated management exercises in Belbin's research had been deliberately set up to require no previous knowledge. In the real world, however, the value of an individual with in-depth knowledge of a key area came to be recognised as yet another essential team contribution or team role. Like the other team roles, specialists also have a weakness: a tendency to focus narrowly on their own subject of choice, and to prioritise this over the team's progress.

One role Belbin did not identify is that of the 'prima donna', a role that plays havoc with the team dynamics, as indeed can some 'specialists'. The trick is to try to not make them team members but to keep them outside the team as advisors or consultants to the team.

Team role	Definition/explanation	This role is not natural to me	I play this role sometimes	This role is natural and easy for me
Plant	Needs to be highly creative and good at solving problems in unconventional ways. This role was so-called because one such individual was planted in each team.			
Monitor/ evaluator	Needed to provide a logical eye, make impartial judgements where required and to assess the team's options in a dispassionate way.			
Coordinators	Needed to focus on the team's objectives, draw out team members and delegate work appropriately.			
Shapers	Needed to pursue objectives vigorously and even aggressively. They shape and challenge others.			
Resource investigators	Provide inside knowledge on the opposition and ensure that the team's idea would carry to the world outside the team.			
Implementers	Needed to plan a practical and workable strategy, and carry it out as efficiently as possible.			
Completer finishers	Most effectively used at the end of a task to 'polish' and scrutinise the work for errors, subjecting it to the highest standards of quality control.			
Teamworkers	Help the team to gel, using their versatility to identify the remaining work required and complete it on behalf of the team.			
Specialist	Has in-depth knowledge of a key area.			

Figure 62.3 Team role analysis

The purpose of psychometric models such as Belbin's is not to think that you can build the perfect team. Instead you need to seek a balanced team with each of these properties or characteristics being undertaken by a member of the team and not putting too many people in the team with the same characteristics (leading to dispiriting competition over leadership).

Communication

By communication here we mean using non-traditional communication methods as a way of building trust and openness.

All good project managers are very clear about traditional methods for communicating the goals of a project and the expectations about deadlines and costs. This is necessary but not sufficient for leading project management teams from a more profound spiritual place. If you really want to tap into the spiritual energy and wisdom of a team, you will need to add some non-traditional communication methods to your skill set.

One of these communication methods is Bohmian dialogue. This is a method for developing deeper self-awareness and team consciousness in a group of people, and does not have a specific agenda or task outcome. The purpose is to develop a deeper level of listening in the group's collective wisdom. David Bohm was a quantum physicist who became interested in philosophical thought and the need for a shift in consciousness to help solve the fragmentation experienced by most people. There are four principles of Bohmian dialogue, as set out below.

Bohmian Dialogue, Principle One: Freedom in Group Conversation

The group agrees that no group-level decision will be made in the conversation.

> *In the dialogue group we are not going to decide what to do about anything. This is crucial. Otherwise we are not free. We must have an empty space where we are not obliged to anything, nor to come to any conclusions, nor to say anything or not say anything. It's open and free. It's an empty space.*

Bohmian Dialogue, Principle Two: No Individual Prejudgement During Conversation

Each individual agrees to suspend judgement in the conversation. Specifically, if the individual hears an idea he/she doesn't like, he/she does not attack that idea.

> *People in any group will bring to it assumptions, and as the group continues meeting, those assumptions will come up. What is called for is to suspend those assumptions, so that you neither carry them out nor suppress them. You don't believe them, nor do you disbelieve them; you don't judge them as good or bad.*

Bohmian Dialogue, Principle Three: Honesty and Transparency

As individuals 'suspend judgement' they also simultaneously are as honest and transparent as possible. Specifically, if the individual has a 'good idea' that he/she might otherwise hold back from the group because it is too controversial, he/she will share that idea in this conversation.

Bohmian Dialogue, Principle Four: Building on the Ideas of Others

Individuals in the conversation try to build on other individuals' ideas in the conversation. The group often comes up with ideas that are far beyond what any of the individuals thought possible before the conversation began.

Read more about Bohmian dialogue in Bohm et al. (2004). The method is used when logic and analysis have run up against their limitations and a project management team needs to create something it does not know how to do. This is a form of conversation that is meant to be generative rather than problem solving. The project manager can instruct team members to use open-ended questions as much as possible, such as:

- 'Tell me more about that'; or
- 'What is it about this situation that touches you?'; or
- 'What are you sensing, even if you have no evidence?'

One of us (Judi) participated in a Bohmian dialogue session that was used for new product development in a small business. The facilitator directed the group members to listen to the soul of the group rather than to speak for themselves. More importantly, the group was advised to listen deeply and with full focus on the speaker without trying to think ahead about what to say in response. This type of listening, and letting go of ego encourages inspiration. So this group ended up coalescing with great excitement and energy around a new product that none of them had expected to create.

THE POWER OF SILENCE

Silence is one aspect of project management communication (and many other forms of communication) that is very seldom utilised. Silence is the language of God! Silence in meetings, project planning sessions and project negotiations can be a valuable way for bringing in the spiritual dimension.

Judi was on a project team at Honeywell that was working on a factory redesign. The team members agreed that anyone could ask for a moment of silence when needed. Silence was used when there was a high level of disagreement in the room, when a particular problem seemed intractable, or when a situation called for creativity.

Creativity

In this section we recognise that inspiration comes from spirit and that utilising group spiritual practices from the wisdom traditions supports inspired problem solving.

The word 'inspiration' itself comes from the Latin word *spirare*, which means spirit, and also breath. Whilst much of project management is based on linear processes and timelines, there are many opportunities for creativity, especially at the beginning of a project. But creativity is also necessary when risk and uncertainty create unexpected events.

Cleden (2009, p. 114) says that 'Creativity should be a core part of the project team's mindset ... Established wisdom – especially when confronting near-term uncertainty – can be quite limiting. Creativity offers the chance to come up with a *better* solution'.

There are many wonderful approaches to encouraging team creativity. Here we want to offer a few explicitly spiritual approaches. The Native American practice of vision quest and wisdom council, for example, can be a very powerful way to tap into inspiration and creativity.

WALKING THE LABYRINTH

One spiritual practice that supports creativity is a team experience of walking the labyrinth. The labyrinth is a meditative, creativity and problem-solving tool that is starting to be used in organisations. This has significant possibilities for providing a non-threatening, non-religious way for demonstrating the positive use of spiritual practices in the workplace.

The labyrinth is an ancient spiritual ritual common to cultures as varied as the Native Americans, Norwegians, and fourteenth-century Catholic monks. It is a form of walking meditation where one walks on a marked path, beginning on the outside of a circle and gradually working one's way into the centre. After some time for reflection in the centre, the walker returns the way he/she came, gradually working towards the outside of the labyrinth and the exit (Neal and Miguez, 1999).

Joe Miguez facilitated a three-day labyrinth strategic planning exercise for the top executives of an Italian publishing company. The leadership team used dialogue methods to develop their list of core questions about the future of the organisation and then team members were invited to participate in a reflective walk in the labyrinth whilst holding these core questions in their hearts and minds and being open to spiritual guidance. The team was able to develop a five-year plan for the organisation based on the spiritual guidance that team members received from their labyrinth walks over the three days. This process has been used for helping teams envision the future, for solving difficult challenges with a project, and for creative breakthroughs in design and implementation.

PHYSICAL ACTIVITIES

Many organisations use physical activities (often with feedback on strengths and weaknesses) as a way of helping employees to tap into their creativity. These activities can include, for example:

- the arts;
- games;
- rope courses;
- ravine crossings;
- discovery groups.

Jaworski (1996) established a leadership foundation using the wilderness to help leaders from all walks of life to learn more about themselves and in the process develop their leadership skills. It included a 24-hour session all alone in the wilderness. Judi has done similar training and vision quest experiences in her Edgewalker work.

All of these methods work to some degree, but the deepest creativity comes from having a connection to the Great Creator, the Source, God or whatever you might call the Divine. We believe that it is a great gift to individuals and teams to help them be in touch with their deeper well of creativity.

Conclusion

We have presented five different approaches to integrating spirituality into project teams, with the goal of helping teams to feel more connected to each other and to their sense of purpose, which leads to greater creativity, innovation and service to the client. These five approaches were alignment, spiritual leadership, *esprit de corps*, communication and creativity.

Approach	Programmes	Benefit to the team	Next steps
Alignment	1. Storytelling		
	2. Vision quest		
	3. Nurturing the artist within		
Spiritual leadership	1. Servant leadership		
	2. Fry's spiritual leadership survey		
	3. Spiritual intelligence assessment		
	4. Edgewalker assessment		
Esprit de corps	1. Team spirit training		
	2. Customer service analysis		
	3. Belbin's team roles		
Communication	1. Bohmian dialogue		
	2. Silence		
Creativity	1. Vision quest		
	2. Wisdom council		
	3. Labyrinth		
	4. Outdoor exercises		
	5. Edgewalker retreat		

Figure 62.4 Spiritual approaches to project management teamwork

A spiritual approach to managing project teams can be of benefit to both the organisation and to the team members. There is a long history of leaders taking spiritual approaches to projects. In more recent times project managers are being more explicit about the implementation of spiritual values and practices.

Each of these spiritual approaches has been used in project management teams, from small businesses to large organisations such as Pfizer and Xerox.

It is our hope that you will feel inspired to adopt one or more of the outlined approaches in your project management team. If you would like to find consultants who can help you adapt any of the processes to your project team, feel free to contact us for recommendations of qualified people in your geographic area or your industry. You might find the grid shown in Figure 62.4 helpful when selecting one or more specific approaches with your team.

References and Further Reading

Belbin, R. (2010), *Team Roles at Work*, 2nd edn, Oxford: Butterworth Heinemann.
Bohm, D., Nichol, L. and Senge, P. (2004), *On Dialogue*, London: Routledge.

Cleden, D. (2009), *Managing Project Uncertainty*, Aldershot: Gower.

De Waal, E. (1992), *A Seven Day Journey with Thomas Merton*, Polmont: Eagle.

Fry, L.W. (2003), 'Toward a theory of spiritual leadership', *Leadership Quarterly*, 14, 693–727.

Fry, L.W. (2005), 'Toward a theory of ethical and spiritual well-being and corporate social responsibility through spiritual leadership', in Giacalone, R.A. and Jurkiewicz, C.L. (eds), *Positive Psychology in Business Ethics and Corporate Responsibility*, Greenwich, CT: Information Age Publishing.

Greenleaf, R.K. (1977), *Servant Leadership: A Journey into the Nature of Legitimate Power and Greatness*, Mahwah, NJ: Paulist Press.

Heermann, B. (1997), *Building Team Spirit: Activities for Inspiring and Energizing Teams*, New York, NY: McGraw-Hill.

Hesse, H. (1932), *Journey to the East*, Frankfurt: Samuel Fischer.

Jaworski, J. (1997), *Synchronicity: The Inner Path of Leadership*, San Francisco, CA: Berrett-Koehler.

Katzenback, J. and Smith, D. (2003), *The Wisdom of Teams: Creating the High Performance Organization*, New York, NY: Collins Business Essentials.

Lamont, G. (2002), *The Spirited Business: Success Stories of Soul-Friendly Companies*, London: Hodder & Stoughton.

Matthew 18:20, in *The Holy Bible*, New International Version (2009), Grand Rapids, MI: Zondervan, Merriam-Webster online retrieved 8/30/10.

Neal, J. (2006), *Edgewalkers: People and Organizations that Take Risks, Build Bridges, and Break New Ground*, Westport, CT: Praeger.

Neal, J. and Harpham, A. (2012), *The Spirit of Project Management*, Farnham: Gower.

Neal, J. and Hoopes, L. (2011), 'Assessing Qualities and Skills of Edgewalkers', paper submitted to the Academy of Management, Boston, MA.

Neal, J. and Miguez, J. (1999), *The Labyrinth: A Life-Giving Tool for Organizations*, Eastern Academy of Management, Philadelphia, PA: May.

Spears, L. (ed.), (1998), *The Power of Servant-Leadership*, San Francisco, CA: Jossey-Bass.

Wigglesworth, C. (2010), 'Spiritual intelligence: Why it matters'. Available at: http://www.consciouspursuits.com/Articles/SIWhyItMatters.pdf [accessed July 19, 2010].

63 *Education and Qualifications in Project Management*

LINDSAY SCOTT and PETER SIMON

This final chapter examines a few of the ways in which people considering career development through training and education can seek education and training to achieve a project management qualification. It is clear that there are many possible paths. Notwithstanding what is written in the provocative Chapter 60, it is clear that those who have attained professional recognition through accreditation are at a distinct advantage over those who have not, particularly when seeking a new post. It is clear also from the exhibits in Chapter 45 that those with qualifications can, on balance, expect to earn more than those who do not (see for example Figures 45.6 and 45.7).

Different Types of Training and Development

Organisations and individuals can undertake training and development in a number of different ways. These can include face-to-face classes, e-learning or a combination of both (now often called blended learning). In addition an individual can self-study by reading one of many thousands of books available on all aspects of the subject of project management. Finally some organisations will undertake 'on-the-job' training (possibly through a coaching and mentoring programme). Such training can be supplemented with day-release programmes to allow training at local educational establishments. Bringing younger talent into project management has also led to apprenticeships being created – which combines 'on-the-job' training and experience alongside formal education.

KNOWLEDGE-BASED TRAINING

Most project management training and development is knowledge-based. By this we mean that individuals attend a training course (or undertake training in some other way), which they then try to apply at work. This training is often delivered out of context from the environment in which the person works and therefore it is left to the individual to apply the knowledge gained back in the work place. Typically training that leads to project management qualifications and certifications falls into this category.

Some knowledge-based training will use examples and case studies that relate to the business sector of the individual. This has both advantages and disadvantages in that

Organisation	Qualifications
Project Management Institute (PMI)	CAPM®, PMP®, PMI-ACP®, PMI-RMP®, PMI-SP®.
Association for Project Management (APM)	IC, APMP, Higher Apprenticeship, PQ, RPP, Risk Level 1, Risk Level 2.
Office of Government Commerce (OGC) which at the time of writing is part of the Cabinet Office of the UK Government.	PRINCE2® Foundation, Practitioner, Professional. Managing Successful Programmes (MSP®). Management of Portfolios (MoP®). Portfolio, Programme and Project Offices (P30®). Management of Risk (MoR®). Management of Value (MoV®).
APM Group (APMG) (also accredit OGC qualifications)	Agile PM, Earned Value Management, PMD Pro. Programme and Project Sponsorship. Change Management.
British Computer Society (BCS) Chartered Institute for IT	IS Project Management, Programme and Project Support Office Essentials.
Chartered Management Institute (CMI)	Diploma and Certificate in Programme and Project Management.
Further education establishments	NVQ (for example Diploma Level 4 in Programme and Project Management. City and Guilds Certificate in Project Control. Higher National Diploma (HND) in Project Management. Foundation Degree in Project Management.
Higher education establishments	Bachelors and Masters degrees in Project Management.

Figure 63.1 Formal project management qualification routes

having 'close to home' case studies can impair the learning process because people can be drawn into the context or detail and ignore the overarching project management process. Having 'out of context' training will allow those being trained to focus on the knowledge, tools and techniques without being distracted by day-to-day workplace details.

Examinations, Qualifications and Certifications

There is a multitude of project, programme and portfolio management training options, examinations, qualifications and certifications. Many training organisations offer courses in all aspects of project management. Some of those are accredited and others are not. Figure 63.1 concentrates more on the courses that lead to a formal accreditation or certification:

Most professional qualifications and certifications emanate from three sources:

- International Project Management Association (IPMA), the UK member of which is The Association for Project Management (APM).

- In the UK also, there is the Office of Government Commerce (OGC). This organisation has been housed in different UK government departments over the last few years and (at the time of writing) is administered by the Cabinet Office.
- Project Management Institute (PMI).

IPMA

IPMA has developed a four-level certification system to which the UK's APM and all other member associations do (or should) subscribe to. This system has four levels:

- Level A: Certified Projects Director (for management of complex project portfolios and programmes).
- Level B: Certified Senior Project Manager (for complex projects. This requires a minimum of five years' experience).
- Level C: Certified Project Manager (for managing projects of moderate complexity. Minimum three years' experience).
- Level D: Certified Project Management Associate (applies to a minimum level of project management knowledge when working on projects).

The following is taken from the IPMA's website:

IPMA's 4-L-C [four-level-certification] demonstrates a level of rigor that helps to assure knowledge, experience, competence and performance for each role. For example, our guidelines on complexity, for our Advanced, professionally assessed, competence-based certifications, Levels A, B and C, require more than experience in simple projects. Instead, we require end-to-end responsibility and authority in projects of a certain minimum size, and organisational impact. Of all the persons leading projects around the World today, many do not have the authority, or manage projects of sufficient complexity, to qualify for our advanced certifications. Still our IPMA Level D, as with other knowledge-based certifications, is an excellent starting point for advancement.

The IPMA's progressive certification framework is growing in popularity as evidenced recently by a number of major international organisations adopting its ethos and framework. We can see no reason why this popularity will not increase as the profession of project management continues to itself increase in popularity and recognition.

OGC

Most of OGC's qualifications (marketed and administered through the APM Group Limited) are tied into published methodologies such as PRINCE2 and Managing Successful Programmes (MSP). Associated training and qualifications relate to knowledge and application (under examination conditions) of the relevant methodology. A key difference between APM's qualifications and those from OGC is that in general OGC's qualifications tell the individual *what* to do whereas the PMI and APM's tell individuals *how* to do it. As such both sets of qualifications can co-exist in a true symbiotic relationship.

PMI

Unlike APM and the OGC, and with the exception of Certified Associate in Project Management (CAPM) and Project Management Professional (PMP), PMI's qualifications are lateral rather than progressive. By this we mean that there is a logical progression from CAPM to PMP but other qualifications relate to aspects of project and programme management (for example risk management and scheduling) or different approaches (such as Agile).

One key difference between PMI and the other two bodies are the prerequisites required to take the examination. Although IPMA and the OGC may assume a certain level of prior, relevant experience, PMI demand that those taking their certifications can document their experience in a prescribed manner. In addition PMI also require that those undertaking their examinations have undergone a minimum of structure training, preferably from one of their Registered Education Providers (REPs).

Assessment of Capability (Assessment Centres and Assessment-based Qualifications)

Many organisations will undertake formal assessment of their would-be or current project managers. These assessments can take the form of questionnaires, structured interviews or formal assessment centres over one or more days. The aim of any assessment is to assess the current and potential capability of an individual. Knowing this it can be used in a number of ways including as a basis for future training and development, suitability for a specific project management role or as part of a recruitment/selection process. There are a number of questionnaires available on a commercial basis that can be used as part of as an assessment itself. References to these can easily be found on the Internet.

One interesting insight to the different competencies required for project and programme management is shown in Pellegrinelli (2008). This book looks at the levels of conception required to progress from being an effective manager of a project to a large programme. One unsurprising conclusion that can be drawn from the book is that not all project managers make great programme managers (and perhaps there is no need for them to do so).

Both the IPMA and OGC qualifications include formal assessment of capability. In the case of APM (for example) these are the Practitioner Qualifications (PQ), a two-and-a-half-day assessment centre and the Registered Project Professional (RPP), a competence-based process including demonstrated relevant experience followed by self-documentation of experience against the APM's competence framework and finally a professional interview. OGC offer PRINCE2 Professional which is a two-day assessment centre.

Certificates, Diplomas and Degrees (Foundation, Undergraduate and Master's)

There are numerous certificates, diplomas and degrees available from many sources in the UK and internationally. Many are provided by higher educational establishments whilst others are available from training providers in association with an educational institution.

There are few bachelor degrees in pure, generic project management, but more combine project management with other topics (such as construction management). There are numerous higher degrees in project and programme management, including those looking at 'complex project management' and project and programme management in specific sectors. Some of these postgraduate degrees are delivered from leading business schools, which is an indication of how important and worthwhile they are seen to be by both those taking them and those delivering them.

A recent introduction from higher education has been the foundation degree in project management. Aimed at part-time study this can be extended to a full honours degree with a further one- or two-year 'top-up'.

Pathways of development that progress from a postgraduate certificate, to diploma and then culminate in a Masters degree are now becoming commonplace. The incremental nature of these pathways allows those working along them to drop off at any point. This avenue also allows individuals to participate on a part-time basis and therefore spread the development over a period that suits them.

Choosing a Training Provider

Project professionals have a choice to make when opting for development through formal project management training courses. There are a number of factors to consider:

- Is the training provider an accredited trainer? Courses through organisations like the IPMA, APMG, and PMI accredit providers to deliver courses and provide examinations on their behalf. Courses provided by these trainers tend to be at a premium but rigorously controlled.
- Word of mouth recommendations. Like most things in life, friends' and colleagues' recommendations and experiences should be heeded.
- If cost is the main deciding factor, consider the adage 'you get what you pay for' – just because it's cheaper doesn't necessarily guarantee value.
- Are the costs inclusive? Many courses require preparation work – does the course fee include materials? Does the course fee include the examination fee? Are accommodation costs included?
- Preferred supplier – if your employer is funding the training their choice may override your own. Be prepared to put your case forward to ensure you receive the training experience you want.
- Location – are there courses available near your home location? Consider the accommodation and travel costs involved.
- Pass rates (an obvious question to ask each training provider, which will indicate how successful their training was with previous delegates).
- Public courses versus bespoke. If there are a number of people within your organisation looking for the same training need it can make sense to hold the course within your organisation. This can also mean that parts of the training modules could be tailored to include details in specific areas of project management which are important to your organisation.
- Finally, how quickly will you receive news from your examinations, receive certifications and so on?

Evaluation of Training and Development

Fundamental to all learning and development is how it is evaluated. One method of evaluating training and its effectiveness was developed by Donald L. Kirkpatrick who first published his ideas in 1959, in a series of articles in the *Journal of American Society of Training Directors*. The articles were subsequently included in Kirkpatrick (2006). Kirkpatrick's four-level model is now considered an industry standard.

KIRKPATRICK'S FOUR LEVELS OF EVALUATION MODEL

The four levels of Kirkpatrick's evaluation model essentially measure the following:

1. Reaction of student – what they thought and felt about the training. This is sometimes colloquially called 'happy sheets' and is often undertaken immediately after the training course or intervention takes place. Many organisations frown upon this and refuse to partake, whilst others see it as the only means of evaluation a trainer's performance and even training effectiveness.
2. Learning – the resulting increase in knowledge or capability. This can be ascertained by some form of test; indeed the numerous examinations (leading to qualifications and certifications) that follow training courses are a prime example. Where formal qualifications and certifications are not included the resulting increase in knowledge or capability is often not identified, appreciated or assessed.
3. Behaviour – the extent of behaviour and capability improvement (and on-the-job implementation). By necessity this has to be measured in the workplace and therefore requires considerable commitment from the individual's employer. Whilst this is fundamental to any training and development, this is rarely done. But it is essential if we are to see what the 'trainee' learned and if the training has been effective.
4. Results – the effects on the business or environment resulting from the trainee's performance. All training and development is done to improve things in some way. By developing knowledge and changing behaviours the business can expect changes in performance that impact the business itself. In order to measure this, the business needs to understand how it was doing before the training took place and then be able to measure the incremental change. This is fundamental to measuring the success of the training, but this is attempted even less than assessing changes in an individual's behaviour.

All these measures are recommended for full and meaningful evaluation of learning in organisations, although their application broadly increases in complexity (and usually cost and commitment) as training progresses through the levels from A to D described above. Perhaps that is why they are not always undertaken.

Membership of Associations and Institutes

Project management professionals can also consider opting for membership of a professional association in project management. Alongside the formal training courses and accreditations on offer from these organisations, there are other resources available to assist in career development. Becoming a member gives access to further development through books and other materials on the latest developments in project management; access to local meetings with expert presenters and networking opportunities and the option to join 'communities of practices' (see Chapter 39) or 'specific interest groups' in areas of project management that are of personal interest.

ORGANISATIONS REPRESENTING THE PROFESSION OF PROJECT MANAGEMENT

IPMA

The profession of project management is represented by the IPMA. Originally known by the initials INTERNET, the Association was eventually forced to switch to the abbreviation IPMA, for very obvious reasons. The UK member of IPMA is the APM.

> IPMA,
> P.O. Box 1167,
> 3860, BD Nijkerk,
> The Netherlands
> Telephone: +31 33 247 3430
> Website: www.ipma.ch

The PMI

Founded in the US in 1969, the PMI is the world's leading not-for-profit organisation for individuals around the globe who work in, or are interested in, project management. PMI develops recognised standards, not least of which is the widely respected project management body of knowledge guide, commonly known by its abbreviated title the *PMBOK Guide*.

PMI publications include the monthly professional magazine *PM Network*, the monthly newsletter *PMI Today* and the quarterly *Project Management Journal* as well as many project management books. In addition to its research and education activities, PMI is dedicated to developing and maintaining a rigorous, examination-based professional certification programme to advance the project management profession and recognise the achievements of individual professionals. PMI's PMP certification is the world's most recognised professional credential for project management practitioners and others in the profession. For more information, contact PMI at:

> PMI Headquarters
> Four Campus Boulevard
> Newtown Square
> PA 19073-3299
> USA
> Telephone: +610-356-4600
> Email: pmihq@pmi.org
> Website: www.pmi.org

The APM

The corporate member of the IPMA in the UK is the APM and further information is available from their secretariat at:

> The Association for Project Management
> Ibis House,
> Regent Park,
> Summerleys Road,
> Princes Risborough,
> Buckinghamshire, HP27 9LE
> Telephone: 0845 458 1944
> Email: info@apm.org.uk
> Website: www.apm.org.uk

The Association arranges seminars and meetings through its network of local branches. Its numerous publications include the periodical journal *Project* and the *APM Body of Knowledge*. Personal or corporate membership of the Association enables project managers and others involved in project management to meet and to maintain current awareness of all aspects of project management. Membership starts at student level and rises through various grades to full member (MAPM) and fellow (FAPM).

The Association has a well-established certification procedure for project managers, who must already be full members. To quote from the Association's own literature, 'the certificated project manager is at the pinnacle of the profession, possessing extensive knowledge and having carried responsibility for the delivery of at least one significant project'. As evidence of competence, certification has obvious advantages for the project manager, and will increasingly be demanded as mandatory by some project purchasers. Certification provides employers with a useful measure when recruiting or assessing staff and the company that can claim to employ certificated project managers will benefit from an enhanced professional image. Certification has relevance also for project clients. It helps them to assess a project manager's competence by providing clear proof that the individual concerned has gained peer recognition of his or her ability to manage projects.

References and Further Reading

FOR COMPETENCY FRAMEWORKS

Association for Project Management (2008), *APM Competence Framework*, Princes Risborough, APM.

Australian Institute of Project Management (2008), 'The National Competency Standards for Project Management (NCSPM)'. Available at: https://www.aipm.com.au/html/2008_competency_standards.cfm

Engineering and Construction Training Board (2010), 'Project management competence framework'. Available at: http://www.ecitb.org.uk/custom/ecitb/docManager/documents/project_management_competence_framework.pdf

Global Alliance for Project Performance Standards (GAPPS). Available at: http://www.globalpmstandards.org/

Project Management Institute (2007), *Project Management Competency Development Framework (PMCDF)*, Newtown Square, PA: PMI.

GENERAL

Association for Project Management (APM) (2012), *APM Body of Knowledge*, 6th edn, Princes Risborough: APM Publications.

Kirkpatrick, D.L. (2006), *Evaluating Training Programs*, San Francisco, CA: Berrett-Koehler.

Pellegrinelli, S. (2008), *Thinking and Acting as a Great Programme Manager*, New York: Palgrave MacMillan.

PMI (2009), *A Guide to the Project Management Body of Knowledge (PMBOK® Guide)*, 4th edn, Newtown Square, PA: Project Management Institute.

Bibliography

ACAS (2003), *Disciplinary and Grievance Procedures*, London: HMSO.

Allen, D. (2001), *Getting Things Done*, London: Piatkus Books Ltd.

Amabile, T.M. and Kramer, S. (2011), *The Progress Principle: Using Small Wins to Ignite Joy, Engagement, and Creativity at Work*, Boston, MA: Harvard Business School Publishing.

Arbinger Institute (2010), *Leadership and Self-Deception: Getting out of the Box*, San Francisco, CA: Berrett-Koehler, 137–8.

Armstrong, S. (2010), *The Essential Performance Review Handbook*, Franklin Lakes, NJ: The Career Press.

Arras People (2006), *Project Management Benchmark Report*, 1st edn, Manchester: Arras People.

Arras People (2007), *Project Management Benchmark Report*, 2nd edn, Manchester: Arras People.

Arras People (2008), *Project Management Benchmark Report*, 3rd edn, Manchester: Arras People.

Arras People (2009), *Project Management Benchmark Report*, 4th edn, Manchester: Arras People.

Arras People (2010), *Project Management Benchmark Report*, 5th edn, Manchester: Arras People.

Arras People (2011), *Project Management Benchmark Report*, 6th edn, Manchester: Arras People.

Arras People (2012), *Project Management Benchmark Report*, 7th edn, Manchester: Arras People.

Arthur, D. (2007), *The First-Time Manager's Guide to Performance Appraisals*, New York: AMACOM.

Association for Project Management (APM) (2008), *APM Body of Knowledge*, 5th edn, High Wycombe: APM Publications.

Association for Project Management (APM) (2008), *APM Competence Framework*, High Wycombe: APM Publications.

Association for Project Management (APM) (2012), *APM Body of Knowledge*, 6th edn, High Wycombe: APM Publications.

Axelrod, R. (1997), *The Complexity of Cooperation: Agent-based Models of Competition and Collaboration*, Princeton, NJ: Princeton University Press.

Bakker, A.B. and Leiter, M.P. (eds) (2010), *Work Engagement: A Handbook of Essential Theory and Research*, New York: Psychology Press.

Bandler, R. and Grinder, J. (1979), *Frogs into Princes: Neuro Linguistic Programming*, Moab, UT: Real People Press.

Bartlett, J. (2000), *Managing Programmes of Business Change*, 3rd edn, Hook: Project Manager Today.

Bateson, G. (1972), *Steps to an Ecology of Mind: Collected Essays in Anthropology, Psychiatry, Evolution, and Epistemology*, Chicago, IL: University Of Chicago Press.

Beauchamp, T.L. and Bowie, N.E. (eds) (2001), *Ethical Theory and Business*, 6th edn, Upper Saddle River, NJ: Prentice Hall.

Belbin, R.M. (2003), *Management Teams: Why They Succeed or Fail*, 2nd edn, Oxford: Elsevier Butterworth-Heinemann.

Belbin, R.M. (2010), *Team Roles at Work*, 2nd edn, Oxford: Butterworth-Heinemann.

Bentley, T. (1976), *Information, Communications and the Paperwork Explosion*, Maidenhead: McGraw-Hill.

Binder, J. (2007), *Global Project Management: Communication, Collaboration and Management Across Borders*, Aldershot: Gower.

Blackshaw, P. (2008), *Satisfied Customers Tell Three Friends, Angry Customers Tell 3,000: Running a Business in Today's Consumer-Driven World*, New York: Doubleday.

Blake, R. and Mouton, J. (1964), *The Managerial Grid: The Key to Leadership Excellence*, Houston, TX: Gulf Publishing Co.

Blanchard, K. (2009), *Leading at a Higher Level, Revised and Expanded Edition*, Upper Saddle River, NJ: Pearson Education.

Blanchard, K. and Barrett, C. (2010), *Lead with LUV: A Different Way to Create Real Success*, Upper Saddle River, NJ: Pearson Education.

Blanchard, K. and Johnson, S. (1983), *The One Minute Manager*, London: HarperCollins.

Blanchard, K., Fowler, S. and Hawkins, L. (2005), *Self Leadership and the One Minute Manager: Increasing Effectiveness Through Situational Self Leadership*, New York: William Morrow and Co.

Bluckert, P. (2006), *Psychological Dimensions of Executive Coaching*, Maidenhead: McGraw-Hill.

Bohm, D., Nichol, L. and Senge, P. (2004), *On Dialogue*, London: Routledge.

Branson, R. (2007), *Screw It, Let's Do It: Lessons in Life and Business*, London: Virgin Books.

Bucero, A. (2010), *Today is a Good Day! Attitudes for Achieving Project Success*, Ontario: Multi Media Publications.

Buchanan, D. and Huczynski, A. (2010), *Organisational Behaviour*, 7th edn, Harlow: Pearson Education.

Burns, J.M. (1978), *Leadership*, New York: Harper & Row.

Cameron, K. (2008), *Positive Leadership: Strategies for Extraordinary Performance*, San Francisco, CA: Berrett-Koehler.

Cameron, K. and Quinn, R. (2006), *Diagnosing and Changing Organizational Culture*, San Francisco, CA: Jossey-Bass.

Cameron, K. and Spreitzer, G. (2011), *The Oxford Handbook of Positive Organizational Scholarship*, New York: Oxford University Press.

Cameron, K., Dutton, J.E. and Quinn, R.E. (2003), *Positive Organizational Scholarship: Foundations of a New Discipline*, San Francisco, CA: Berrett-Koehler.

Capon, C. and Didsbury, A. (2003), *Understanding Organisational Context: Inside and Outside Organisations*, 2nd edn, London: Financial Times Management.

Casey, D. and Pearce, D. (1977), *More Than Management Development: Action Learning at GEC*, Farnborough: Gower.

Centre for Business Practices (CBP) (2005), *Project Portfolio Management Maturity: A Benchmark of Current Business Practices*, Philadelphia, PA: CBP.

Chomsky, N. (1957), *Syntactic Structures*, The Hague: Mouton & Co.

Chomsky, N. (1968), *Language and Mind*, New York: Harcourt Brace & World, Inc.

Cialdini, R.B. (2009), *Influence: Science and Practice*, 5th edn, Upper Saddle River, NJ: Pearson Education.

Cirillo, R. (1978), *The Economics of Vilfredo Pareto*, Totowa, NJ: Frank Cass & Co.

Cleden, D. (2009), *Managing Project Uncertainty*, Aldershot: Gower.

Cleland, D.I. (1996), *Strategic Management of Teams*, New York: John Wiley & Sons.

Cleland, D.I. and Ireland, L.R. (2007), *Project Management, Strategic Design and Implementation*, 5th edn, New York: McGraw-Hill Professional.

Codling, S. (1998), *Benchmarking*, Aldershot: Gower.

Coens, T. and Jenkins, M. (2000), *Abolishing Performance Appraisals*, San Francisco, CA: Berrett-Koehler.

Cohen, D.S. (2005), *The Heart of Change Field Guide: Tools and Tactics for Leading Change in Your Organization*, Boston, MA: Harvard Business School Publishing.

Cohen, G. (2010), *Agile Excellence for Product Managers*, Cupertino, CA: Superstar Press.

Collison, C. and Parcell, G. (2004), *Learning to Fly: Practical Knowledge Management from Leading and Learning Organizations*, 2nd edn, Chichester: Capstone.

Connor, D. (1992), *Managing at the Speed of Change: How Resilient Managers Succeed and Prosper Where Others Fail*, New York, NY: Villard Books.

Cooper, D. (2004), *Improving People Performance in Construction*, Aldershot: Gower.

Cope, M. (2003), *The Seven C's of Consulting*, Harlow: Prentice Hall.

Cornelius, H. and Faire, S. (2006), *Everyone Can Win: Responding to Conflict*, 2nd edn, Sydney: Simon & Schuster.

Costa, P.T. Jr and McCrae, R.R. (1992), *Revised NEO Personality Inventory (NEO-PI-R) and NEO Five-Factor Inventory (NEO-FFI) Professional Manual*, Odessa, FL: Psychological Assessment Resources.

Covey, S. (1989), *The Seven Habits of Highly Effective People*, New York: Simon & Schuster.

Covey, S. (2004a), *The 7 Habits of Highly Effective People*, 2nd edn, London: Simon & Schuster.

Covey, S. (2004b), *The 8th Habit: from Effectiveness to Greatness*, London: Simon & Schuster.

Craik, K. (1943), *The Nature of Explanation*, Cambridge: Cambridge University Press.

Crawford, L., Cooke-Davies, T., Hobbs, B., Labuschagne, L., Remington, K. and Chen, P. (2008), *Situational Sponsorship of Project and Programmes: An Empirical Review*, Newtown Square, PA: Project Management Institute.

Crosby, P.B. (1979), *Quality is Free: The Art of Making Quality Certain*, New York: McGraw-Hill.

Csíkszentmihályi, M. (1997), *Finding Flow: The Psychology of Engagement with Everyday Life*, New York: Basic Books.

Csíkszentmihályi M. (2008), *Flow: The Psychology of Optimal Experience*, New York: HarperCollins.

Davis, G.A. (1986), *Creativity is Forever*, 2nd edn, Dubuque, IA: Kendall-Hunt.

Deci, E.L. and Ryan, R.M. (1985), *Intrinsic Motivation and Self-determination in Human Behavior*, New York: Plenum.

Dekker, S. (2006), *The Field Guide to Understanding Human Error*, 2nd edn, Aldershot: Ashgate.

Dekker, S. (2012), *Just Culture: Balancing Safety and Accountability*, 2nd edn, Farnham: Ashgate.

De Mascia, S. (2012), *Project Psychology*, Farnham: Gower.

Deming, W.E. (1986), *Out of the Crisis*, Cambridge, MA: MIT Press.

Deutschendorf, H. (2009), *The Other Kind of Smart: Simple Ways to Boost Your Emotional Intelligence for Greater Personal Effectiveness and Success*, New York: AMACOM.

De Waal, E. (1992), *A Seven Day Journey with Thomas Merton*, Polmont: Eagle.

Dinsmore, P.C. and Cooke-Davies, T.J. (2006), *The Right Projects Done Right!*, San Francisco, CA: Jossey-Bass.

Downey, M. (2003), *Effective Coaching: Lessons from the Coach's Coach*, London: Texere Publishing.

Drucker, P.F. (1954), *The Practice of Management*, New York: Harper & Row.

Duffy, F. (1992), *The Changing Workplace*, London: Phaidon Press.

Dutton, J.E. (2003), *Energize Your Workplace: How To Create and Sustain High-Quality Connections at Work*, San Francisco, CA: Jossey-Bass.

Edwards, M.R. and Ewen, A.J. (1996), *360 Degree Feedback: The Powerful New Model for Employee Assessment and Performance Improvement*, New York: AMACOM.

Elkington, J. (1998), *Cannibals with Forks: The Triple Bottom Line of 21st Century Business*, Oxford: Capstone.

Englund, R.L. and Bucero, A. (2006), *Project Sponsorship, Achieving Management Commitment for Project Success*, San Francisco, CA: Jossey-Bass.

Fayol, H. (1949), *General and Industrial Administration*, London: Pitman. This is an English translation of the French edition, published in 1916.

Fisher K. and Fisher M. (2001), *The Distance Manager*, New York: McGraw-Hill.

Flannes, S. and Levin, G. (2005), *Essential People Skills for Project Managers*, Vienna, VA: Management Concepts.

Follett, M.P. (1949), *Freedom and Coordination*, London: Management Publications Trust.

Fowler, A. and Lock, D. (2006), *Accelerating Business and IT Change: Transforming Project Delivery*, Aldershot: Gower.

Frame, J.D. (1995), *Managing Projects in Organizations*, San Francisco, CA: Jossey-Bass.

Friedman, M. (1996), *Type A Behavior: Its Diagnosis and Treatment*, New York: Plenum Press.

Gallwey, W.T. (2000), *The Inner Game of Work: Focus, Learning, Pleasure, and Mobility in the Workplace*, New York: Random House.

Gardner, H. (1983), *Frames of Mind*, New York: Basic Books.

Gladwell, M. (2000), *The Tipping Point: How Little Things Can Make a Big Difference*, London: Little, Brown and Company.

Goldsmith, M. and Reiter, M. (2007), *What Got You Here Won't Get You There: How Successful People Become Even More Successful*, New York: Hyperion.

Goleman, D. (1995), *Emotional Intelligence*, New York: Bantam Books.

Goleman, D. (1998), *Working with Emotional Intelligence*, New York: Bantam Books.

Goleman, D. (2011), *The Brain and Emotional Intelligence: New Insights*, Northampton, MA: More Than Sound LLC.

Goleman, D., Boyatzis. R. and McKee, A. (2002), *Primal Leadership: Realizing the Power of Emotional Intelligence*, Boston, MA: Harvard Business School.

Graham, R.J. and Englund, R.L. (1997), *Creating an Environment for Successful Projects*, San Francisco, CA: Jossey-Bass.

Greenberg, J. (1999), *Managing Behaviour in Organizations*, 2nd edn, Upper Saddle River, NJ: Prentice Hall.

Greenleaf, R.K. (1977), *Servant Leadership: A Journey into the Nature of Legitimate Power and Greatness*, Mahwah, NJ: Paulist Press.

Grote, D. (2005), *Forced Ranking: Making Performance Management Work*, Boston, MA: Harvard Business Review Press.

Gurek, B.A. (1985), *Sex and the Workplace*, San Francisco, CA: Jossey-Bass.

Hall, K. (2007), *Speed Lead*, London: Nicholas Brealey Publishing.

Handy, C. (1976), *Understanding Organizations*, Harmondsworth: Penguin.

Harrin, E. (2010), *Social Media for Project Managers*, Newtown Square, PA: Project Management Institute.

Harrin, E. and Peplow, P. (2012), *Customer Centric Project Management*, Farnham: Gower.

Hartman, F.T. (2000), *Don't Park Your Brain Outside*, Newtown Square, PA: Project Management Institute.

Heath, C. and Heath, D. (2010), Switch: How to Change Things When Change is Hard, London: Random House.

Heermann, B. (1997), *Building Team Spirit: Activities for Inspiring and Energizing Teams*, New York: McGraw-Hill.

Hersey, P.H. and Blanchard, K.H. (2007), *Management of Organizational Behaviour*, 9th edn, Englewood Cliffs, NJ: Prentice Hall.

Herzberg, F. (1959), *The Motivation to Work*, New York: John Wiley and Sons.

Hesse, H. (1932), *Journey to the East*, Frankfurt am Main: Samuel Fischer.

Hirsh, E., Hirsh, K.W. and Krebs Hirsh, S. (2003), *Introduction to Type and Teams*, 2nd edn, Mountain View, CA: CPP.

HMSO (1963), *Offices, Shops and Railway Premises Act 1963*, London: Her Majesty's Stationery Office.

HMSO (1971), *Fire Precautions Act 1971*, London: Her Majesty's Stationery Office.

HMSO (1974), *Health and Safety at Work Act 1974*, London: Her Majesty's Stationery Office.

Hofstede, G. (2001), *Culture's Consequences: Comparing Values, Behaviors, Institutions and Organizations Across Nations*, 2nd edn, London: Sage.

Hsieh, T. (2010), *Delivering Happiness*, New York: Business Plus.

Humble, J.W. (1973), *How to Manage by Objectives*, New York: AMACOM.

IBM Institute for Business Value (2010), *Capitalizing on Complexity: Insights from the Global Chief Executive Study*, New York: IBM Corporation.

IBM Institute for Business Value Human Resource Study (2010), *Working Beyond Borders*, Dublin: IBM Corporation.

Irwin, T. (2009), *Derailed: Five Lessons Learned From Catastrophic Failures of Leadership*, Nashville, TN: Thomas Nelson.

James, R.E. (2002), *The Integrity Chain: The Link to Profitability in Construction*, Raleigh, NC: FMI Corporation.

Jaworski, J. (1997), *Synchronicity: the Inner Path of Leadership*, San Francisco, CA: Berrett-Koehler.

Johnson, J. (2006), *My Life is Failure*, p. 4, Boston, MA: The Standish Group International.

Johnson, S. (1999), *Who Moved my Cheese?* London: Vermilion.

Jung, C.G. (1959), *The Basic Writings of C. G. Jung*, New York: The Modern Library.

Juran, J. and Godfrey, A.B. (eds) (1999), *Juran's Quality Handbook*, 5th edn, New York: McGraw-Hill.

Kanigel, R. (1997), *The One Best Way: Frederick Winslow Taylor and the Enigma of Efficiency*, London: Little, Brown and Co.

Kaplan, R.S. and Norton, D.P. (2006), *Alignment*, Boston, MA: Harvard Business School Press.

Katzenback, J. and Smith, D. (2003), *The Wisdom of Teams: Creating the High Performance Organization*, New York: Collins Business Essentials.

Kay, J.A. (2011), *Obliquity: Why Our Goals Are Best Achieved Indirectly*, London: Profile Books.

Kerzner, H. (2000), *Applied Project Management: Best Practices on Implementation*, New York: Wiley.

Kerzner, H. and Saladis, F.P. (2009), *What Executives Need to Know about Project Management*, Hoboken, NJ: John Wiley and Sons, Inc.

Killen, D. and Williams, G. (2009), *Introduction to Type and Innovation*, Mountain View, CA: CPP, Inc.

Kirby, L. and Myers, K. (1998), *Introduction to Type: A Guide to Understanding Your Results on the Myers-Briggs Type Indicator*, Palo Alto, CA: Consulting Psychologists Press.

Kirkpatrick, D.L. (2006), *Evaluating Training Programs*, San Francisco, CA: Berrett-Koehler.

Kliem, R.L. and Ludin, I.S. (1992), *The People Side of Project Management*, Aldershot: Gower.

Korzybski, A. (1921), *Manhood of Humanity: the Science and Art of Human Engineering*, New York: E. P. Dutton & Company.

Kotler, P. (1988), Marketing Management: Analysis, Planning, Implementation and Control, 6th edn, Englewood Cliffs, NJ: Prentice Hall.

Kotter, J.P. (1996), Leading Change, Boston, MA: Harvard Business School Press.

Kouzes, J.M. and Posner, B.Z. (2007), *The Leadership Challenge*, San Francisco, CA: Jossey-Bass.

Kübler-Ross, E. (1969), *On Death and Dying*, London: Routledge.

Lamont, G. (2002), *The Spirited Business: Success Stories of Soul-Friendly Companies*, London: Hodder & Stoughton.

Leman, K. (2009), *The Birth Order Book*, 2nd edn, Ada, MI: Revell.

Lencioni, P. (2006), *Silos, Politics and Turf Wars: A Leadership Fable About Destroying the Barriers That Turn Colleagues Into Competitors*, San Francisco, CA: Jossey-Bass.

Lennick, D., Kiel, F., Huntsman, J.M. and Parker, J.F. (2011), *Essential Lessons on Leadership* (Collection), (Kindle Locations 308–309), Pearson Education (US), Kindle Edition.

Lepsinger, R. and DeRosa, D. (2010), *Virtual Team Success: A Practical Guide for Working and Leading from a Distance*, San Francisco, CA: John Wiley & Sons/Jossey-Bass.

Linley, A.P. and Joseph, S. (2004), *Positive Psychology in Practice*, Hoboken, NJ:

John Wiley & Sons.

Linley, A., Harrington S. and Garcea N. (2009), *Oxford Handbook of Positive Psychology and Work*, New York: Oxford University Press.

Linley, A., Willars, J., Deiner, R., Garcea, N. and Stairs, M. (2010), *The Strengths Book: Be Confident, Be Successful and Enjoy Better Relationships by Realising the Best of You*, Coventry: CAPP Press.

Lipnack J. and Stamps J. (2010), *Leading Virtual Teams*, Boston, MA: Harvard Business School Publishing.

Lock, D. (ed.) (1993), *Handbook of Engineering Management*, 2nd edn, Oxford: Butterworth-Heinemann.

Lock, D. (ed.) (1998), *The Gower Handbook of Management*, 4th edn, Aldershot: Gower.

Lock, D. (2004), *Project Management in Construction*, Aldershot: Gower.

Lock, D. (2013), *Project Management*, 10th edn, Farnham: Gower.

Loehr, J.E. and Schwartz, T. (2003), *The Power of Full Engagement: Managing Energy, Not Time, is the Key to High Performance and Personal Renewal*, New York: Free Press.

Luthans, F., Youssef, C. and Avolio, B. (2007), *Psychological Capital: Developing the Human Competitive Edge*, New York: Oxford University Press.

Macchiavelli, N. (1532), *The Prince*. Modern English translation, by George Bull (1961), London: Penguin.

Marius, T.C. (2009), *The Performance of a Project Manager*, Vol. 8, University Iasi: Faculty of Economics and Business Administration.

Maslow, A.H. (1954), *Motivation and Personality*, New York: Harper & Row.

Maslow, A.H. (1970), *Motivation and Personality*, 2nd edn, New York: Harper & Row.

Maxwell, J.C. (2006), *The 360° Leader with Workbook*, Nashville, TN: Nelson Publishers.

Mayo, G.E. (1933), *The Human Problems of an Industrial Civilization*, Boston, MA: Harvard Business School.

McGrath, J.E. (1962), *Leadership Behavior: Some Requirements for Leadership Training*, Washington, DC: US Civil Service Commission.

McKenna, E. (2012), *Business Psychology and Organisational Behaviour*, 4th edn, Hove: Psychology Press.

Megginson, D. and Whitaker, V. (2007), *Continuing Professional Development*, London: The Chartered Institute of Personnel and Development.

Mehrabian, A. (1971), *Silent Messages: Implicit Communication of Emotions and Attitudes*, Belmont, CA: Wadsworth Publishing Company.

Mersino, A. (2007), *Emotional Intelligence for Project managers: The People Skills You Need to Achieve Outstanding Results*, New York: AMACOM.

Michaels, E., Handfield-Jones, H. and Axelrod, B. (2001), *The War for Talent*, Boston, MA: Harvard Business School Publishing.

Milgram, S. (1974), *Obedience to Authority: An Experimental View*, London: Harper Collins.

Minton, D. (1997), *Teaching Skills in Further & Adult Education*, 2nd edn, London: City & Guilds and Thompson learning.

Mintzberg, H. (1973), *The Nature of Managerial Work*, New York: Harper & Row.

Moore, J. (2006), *Tribal Knowledge: Business Wisdom Brewed from the Grounds of Starbucks Corporate Culture* (pp. 86–7), Kaplan, Kindle Edition.

Morris, P. (1994), *The Management of Projects*, London: Thomas Telford.

Munro Fraser, J. (1950), *A Handbook of Employment Interviewing*, London: Macdonald & Evans.

Murray, A. (2010), *The Wall Street Journal Essential Guide to Management: Lasting Lessons from the Best Leadership Minds of our Times*, New York: Harper Collins.

Myers, I.B. (1962), *Manual: The Myers-Briggs Type Indicator*, Princeton, NJ: Educational Testing Services.

Myers, I. and Briggs, K. (2000), *Introduction to Type*, 6th edn, Oxford: CPP.

Myerson, J., Bichard, J-A. and Erlich, A. (2010), *New Demographics, New Workspace*, Farnham: Gower.

Neal, J. (2006), *Edgewalkers: People and Organizations that Take Risks, Build Bridges, and Break New Ground*, Westport, CT: Praeger.

Neal, J. and Harpham, A. (2012), *The Spirit of Project Management*, Farnham: Gower.

Neal, J. and Miguez, J. (1999), *The Labyrinth: A Life-Giving Tool for Organizations*, Eastern Academy of Management, Philadelphia, PA: May.

Nettle, D. (2005), *Happiness – The Science Behind Your Smile*, Oxford: Oxford University Press.

New Word City (2010), *Nelson Mandela's Leadership Lessons* (Kindle Locations 90–92), Pearson Education (US), Kindle Edition.

Nicholson, M. (1992), *Rationality and the Analysis of International Conflict*, Cambridge: Cambridge University Press.

Noer, D.M. (1993), *Healing the Wounds – Overcoming the Trauma of Layoffs and Revitalising Downsized Organizations*, San Francisco, CA: Jossey-Bass.

Office of Government Commerce (2005), *Managing Successful Projects with PRINCE2*, 4th edn, Norwich: The Stationery Office.

Office of Government Commerce (2007), *Managing Successful Programmes*, 3rd edn, Norwich: The Stationery Office.

Olivier, R. (2001), Inspirational Leadership, London: Spiro Press.

Orridge, M. (2009), *Change Leadership*, Farnham: Gower.

O'Sullivan, A. and Sheffrin, S.M. (2003), *Economics, Principles in Action*. California: Pearson/Prentice Hall.

Park, R. (1999), *Value Engineering: a Plan for Invention*, Boca Raton, FL: St Lucie Press.

Parkinson, C. Northcote (1958), *Parkinson's Law or the Pursuit of Progress*, London: John Murray.

Pellegrinelli, S. (2008), *Thinking and Acting as a Great Programme Manager*, New York: Palgrave MacMillan.

Peter, L.J. and Hull, R. (1969), *The Peter Principle: Why Things Always Go Wrong*, New York: William Morrow and Company.

Peters, T. (1997), *The Circle of Innovation*, New York: Alfred A. Knopf.

Peters, T. and Waterman, R.H. Jnr, (1982), *In Search of Excellence*, New York: Harper & Row.

Peterson, C. and Seligman, M.E.P. (2004), *Character Strengths and Virtues: A Handbook and Classification*, New York: Oxford University Press.

Pettinger, R. (2002), *Introduction to Management*, New York: Palgrave.

Pierce, W.D. and Cheney, C.D. (2008), *Behavioural Analysis and Learning*, 4th edn, New York: Psychology Press.

Pink, D.H. (2009), Drive: The Surprising Truth About What Motivates Us, New York: Riverhead Books.

Project Management Institute (PMI) (2007), *Project Management Competency Development Framework (PMCDF)*, Newtown Square, PA: Project Management Institute.

Project Management Institute (PMI) (2009), *A Guide to the Project Management Body of Knowledge (PMBOK® Guide)*, 4th edn, Newtown Square, PA: Project Management Institute.

Project Management Institute (PMI) (2011), *Project Management Salary Survey*, 7th edn, Philadelphia, PA: Project Management Institute.

Puccio, G.J., Miller, B. and Thurber, S. (2002), *FourSight Your Thinking Profile: A Tool for Innovation*, Evanston, IL: Thinc Communications.

Quirke, B. (1996), Communicating Corporate Change, Maidenhead: McGraw-Hill.

Ramsbotham, O., Woodhouse, T. and Miall, H. (2010), *Contemporary Conflict Resolution*, Cambridge: Polity Press.

Randolph, W.A. (1991), *Getting the Job Done: Managing Project Teams and Task Forces for Success*, Hemel Hempstead: Prentice Hall.

Reich, J.W., Zautra, A.J. and Hall, J.S. (2010), *Handbook of Adult Resilience*, New York: The Guilford Press.

Revans, R. (2011), *The ABC of Action Learning*, Farnham: Gower.

Rhinehart, L. (Cockcroft, G.) (1971), *The Dice Man*, London: Talmy, Franklin Ltd.

Riggio, R.E. (2007), *Introduction to Industrial/Organizational Psychology*, 5th edn, Englewood Cliffs, NJ: Prentice Hall.

Roberts-Phelps, G. (2001), *50 Ways to Liven up your Meetings*, Aldershot: Gower.

Robinson, K. and Aronica, L. (2009), *The Element: How Finding your Passion Changes Everything*, New York: Penguin Group.

Rodger, A. (1952), *The Seven Point Plan*, London: National Institute of Industrial Psychology.

Rosen, R., Digh, P., Singer, M. and Phillips, C. (2000), *Global Literacies: Lessons on Business Leadership and Natural Cultures*, New York: Simon & Schuster.

Rothwell, W.J. (2001), *Effective Succession Planning*, New York: AMACOM.

Runco, M.A. (2007), *Creativity Theories and Themes: Research, Development and Practice*, San Diego, CA: Elsevier.

Sandler, C. and Keefe, J. (2007), *Fails to Meet Expectations*, Avon, Massachusetts: Adams Media.

Savitz, A.W. and Weber, K. (2006), *The Triple Bottom Line: How Today's Best-Run Companies Are Achieving Economic, Social, and Environmental Success: and How You Can Too*, San Francisco, CA: Jossey-Bass.

Schein, E. (1997), *Organizational Culture and Leadership*, 2nd edn, San Francisco, CA: Jossey-Bass.

Schneider, B., Macey, W., Barbera, K.M. and Young, S. (2009), *Employee Engagement: Tools for Analysis, Practice, and Competitive Advantage*, Oxford: Blackwell Publishers.

Scott, V. (2010), *Conflict Resolution for Dummies*, Hoboken, NJ: Wiley.

Seligman, M.E. (1994), *What You Can Change And What You Can't: The Complete Guide To Successful Self-Improvement*, New York: Knopf.

Seligman, M.E. (2004), *Authentic Happiness: Using the New Positive Psychology to Realize Your Potential for Lasting Fulfillment*, New York: Free Press.

Senge, P. (1990), *The Fifth Discipline: The Art & Practice of the Learning Organization*, New York: Doubleday.

Senge, P.M., Kleiner, A., Roberts, C., Ross, R.B. and Smith, B.J. (1994), *The Fifth Discipline Fieldbook*, New York: Doubleday.

Sherman Garr, S. (2011), *Performance Management Framework – Evolving Performance Management to Fit the Modern Workforce*, Oakland, CA: Bersin & Associates.

SHL and Future Foundation (2004), *Getting the Edge in the New People Economy*, London: Future Foundation.

Shone, A. and Parry, B. (2004), Successful Event Management, London: Thomson Learning.

Simmons, A. (2006), *The Story Factor: Inspiration, Influence, and Persuasion through the Art of Storytelling*, Cambridge, MA: Basic Books.

Sindell, M. and Sindell, T. (2006), *Sink or Swim*, Avon, MA: Adams Media.

Smith, E. (2008), *What Sport Tells Us about Life*, London: Penguin.

Snyder, C.R., Lopez, S.J. and Pedrotti, J.T. (2011), *Positive Psychology: The Scientific and Practical Explorations of Human Strengths*, Thousand Oaks, CA: Sage.

Spears, L. (ed.) (1998), *The Power of Servant-Leadership*, San Francisco: Jossey-Bass.

Staw, B.M. (1991), *Psychological Dimensions of Organizational Behaviour*, 2nd edn, Englewood Cliffs, NJ: Prentice Hall.

Steare, R. (2009), *Ethicability: How to Decide What's Right and Find the Courage to Do it*, 3rd edn, London: Roger Steare Consulting Limited.

Stewart, D. (ed.) (1998), *Gower Handbook of Management Skills*, 3rd edn, Aldershot: Gower.

Stewart, R. (ed.) (1999), *Gower Handbook of Teamworking*, Aldershot: Gower.

Stott, K. and Walker, A. (1995), *Teams, Teamwork and Teambuilding. The Manager's Complete Guide to Teams in Organizations*, Englewood Cliffs, NJ: Prentice Hall.

Streibel, B.J. (2007), *Plan and Conduct Effective Meetings*, New York: McGraw-Hill.

Swenson, R. (2004), *Margin: Restoring Emotional, Physical, Financial, and Time Reserves to Overloaded Lives*, Colorado Springs, CO: NavPress.

Taylor. P. (2009), *The Lazy Project Manager: How to be Twice as Productive and Still Leave the Office Early*, Oxford: Infinite Ideas.

Taylor, P. (2011), *Leading Successful PMOs: How to Build the Best Project Management Office for Your Business*, Farnham: Gower.

Thomas, K.W. and Kilmann, R.H. (2007), *Thomas-Kilmann Conflict Mode Instrument*, Mountain View, CA: Xicom (subsidiary of CPP Inc.).

Thomas, N. (2004), *The John Adair Handbook of Management and Leadership*, London: Thorogood.

Thorpe, T. and Sumner, P. (2004), *Quality Management in Construction*, Aldershot: Gower.

Trompenaars, F. and Hampden-Turner, C. (2005), *Riding the Waves of Culture: Understanding Cultural Diversity in Business*, London: Nicholas Brealey.

Trompenaars, F. and Woolliams, P. (2003), *Business across Cultures*, Oxford: Capstone Publishing Ltd.

Tucker, J. (2008), *Introduction to Type and Project Management*, Mountain View, CA: CPP.

Turner, G. and Myserson, J. (1998), *New Workspace, New Culture*, Aldershot: Gower.

Turner, J.R. (2008), *Handbook of Project Based Management*, London: McGraw-Hill Professional.

Turner, R. (2007), *Gower Handbook of Project Management*, 4th edn, Aldershot: Gower.

Verma, V.K. (1995), *The Human Aspects of project Management, vol. 1, Organizing Projects for Success*, Newtown Square, PA: Project Management Institute.

Vroom, V. (1964), *Work and Motivation*, New York: Wiley.

Wade, E. and Airitam, S. (2002), *Ethics 4 Everyone: The Handbook for Integrity-based Business Practices*, Dallas, TX: Performance Systems Corp.

Walsh, B. (2011), *VAK Self-Audit: Visual, Auditory, and Kinesthetic Communication and Learning Styles* (Kindle Locations 17–19), Victoria, Canada: Walsh Seminars Ltd.

Watzlawick, P. (1967), *Pragmatics of Human Communication*, New York: W. W. Norton & Company.

Weare, K. (2004), *Developing the Emotionally Literate School*, London: Paul Chapman (Sage).

Weisberg, R.W. (1993), *Creativity: Beyond the Myth of Genius*, New York: Freeman.

Wenger, E. (1998), *Communities of Practice: Learning, Meaning, and Identity*, New York: Cambridge University Press.

Wenger, E. (2006), *Source Communities of Practice: A Brief Introduction*, (self-published). Available at: www.ewwenger.com/pub/index.htm

Wenger, E., McDermott, R. and Snyder, W. (2002), *Cultivating Communities of Practice: a Guide to Managing Knowledge*, Cambridge, MA: Harvard Business School Press.

Whetten, D. and Cameron, K. (2011), *Developing Management Skills with MyManagementLab: Global Edition*, 8th edn, Harlow: Pearson Education.

Whitmore, J. (2007), *Coaching for Performance – GROWing People, Performance and Purpose,* London: Nicholas Brealey.

Wild, J.J., Wild, K.L. and Han, J.C.Y. (2000), *International Business: an Integrated Approach*, Harlow: Prentice Hall.

Williams, T.C. (2011), *Rescue the Problem Project: A Complete Guide to Identifying, Preventing, and Recovering from Project Failure*, New York: AMACOM.

Yates, M. (2005), *Hiring the Best*, Avon, MA: Adams Media.

Zofri, Y. (2011), *A Manager's Guide to Virtual Teams*, New York: American Management Association.

Index